THE HUMAN EPIC GLOBAL CITIZENSHIP

STORYTELLING

WHY STUDY HISTORY? EMPATHY

IDENTITY CIVILIZATION

STORIES MAKING HISTORY

EMPOWERMENT

SAVING OUR PAST

EMPATHY

HISTORY THROUGH OBJECTS

EMPOWERMENT
PRESERVING CULTURES
SAVING OUR PAST
WHY STUDY HISTORY?
GLOBAL CITIZENSHIP
IDENTITY
THE HUMAN EPIC
STORYTELLING
OUR HUMAN STORY

CIVILIZATION

PRESERVING CULTURES

GLOBAL CITIZENSHIP

PRESERVING CULTURES

EMPATHY

OUR HUMAN STORY

CIVILIZATION THE HUMAN EPIC

WHO OWNS THE PAST?

STORIES MAKING HISTORY

EMPOWERMENT

GLOBAL CITIZENSHIP

SAVING OUR PAST

EMPOWERMENT

MOMENTS IN HISTORY

IDENTITY *SAVING OUR PAST*

GLOBAL CITIZENSHIP EMPATHY

EMPOWERMENT

THE HUMAN EPIC GLOBAL CITIZENSHIP

STORYTELLING

HISTORY

OUR PAST

EMPATHY

WHY STUDY HISTORY? EMPATHY

IDENTITY CIVILIZATION

STORIES MAKING HISTORY

EMPOWERMENT

SAVING OUR PAST

EMPATHY

GLOBAL CITIZENSHIP

OUR PAST

HISTORY

THROUGH

OBJECTS

EMPOWERMENT
PRESERVING CULTURES
SAVING OUR PAST
WHY STUDY HISTORY?
GLOBAL CITIZENSHIP

IDENTITY

THE HUMAN EPIC
STORYTELLING
OUR HUMAN STORY

MOMENTS IN HISTORY

SAVING OUR PAST

EMPATHY

CIVILIZATION

PRESERVING CULTURES

GLOBAL CITIZENSHIP

PRESERVING CULTURES

SAVING OUR PAST

EMPATHY

MOMENTS

IDENTITY SAVING OUR PAST

GLOBAL CITIZENSHIP

OUR HUMAN STORY

CIVILIZATION THE HUMAN EPIC

WHO OWNS THE PAST?

STORIES MAKING HISTORY

WORLD HISTORY

ANCIENT CIVILIZATIONS

Detail of procession road
to the Ishtar Gate of
ancient Babylon

For product information and technology assistance, contact us at Customer & Sales Support, 888-915-3276

For permission to use material from this text or product, submit all requests online at **www.cengage.com/permissions**

Further permissions questions can be emailed to **permissionrequest@cengage.com**

National Geographic Learning | Cengage
1 N. State Street, Suite 900
Chicago, IL 60602

Cengage is a leading provider of customized learning solutions with office locations around the globe, including Singapore, the United Kingdom, Australia, Mexico, Brazil, and Japan. Locate your local office at **www.cengage.com/global.**

Visit National Geographic Learning online at **NGL.Cengage.com/school**

Visit our corporate website at **www.cengage.com**

ISBN: 978-13372-9194-1

Acknowledgments

Grateful acknowledgment is given to the authors, artists, photographers, museums, publishers, and agents for permission to reprint copyrighted material. Every effort has been made to secure the appropriate permission. If any omissions have been made or if corrections are required, please contact the Publisher.

LEXILE®, LEXILE® FRAMEWORK, LEXILE ANALYZER®, LEXILE ANALYZER® EDITOR ASSISTANT™, LEXILE TITLES DATABASE™, LEXILE CAREER DATABASE™, LEXILE GROWTH PLANNER™, the LEXILE® logo and POWERV™ are trademarks of MetaMetrics, Inc., and are registered in the United States and abroad. The trademarks and names of other companies and products mentioned herein are the property of their respective owners. Copyright © 2017 MetaMetrics, Inc. All rights reserved.

Pre-AP™ is a registered trademark of The College Board and used under agreement.

Photographic Credits
Front Cover: ©Peter Ptschelinzew/Alamy Stock Photo

Acknowledgments and credits continue on page R24..

Printed in the United States of America

Print Number: 05
Print Year: 2019

PROGRAM CONSULTANTS

Fredrik Hiebert

Dr. Fred Hiebert is a National Geographic Explorer and Archaeology Fellow. He has led archaeological expeditions at ancient Silk Roads sites across Asia and underwater in the Black Sea. Hiebert rediscovered the lost Bactrian gold in Afghanistan in 2004 and was curator of National Geographic's exhibition *Afghanistan: Hidden Treasures from the National Museum, Kabul*, which toured museums throughout the world. Hiebert curated National Geographic's exhibition *Peruvian Gold: Ancient Treasures Unearthed* and, most recently, the exhibition *The Greeks: Agamemnon to Alexander the Great*.

Christopher P. Thornton

Dr. Chris Thornton is the Lead Program Officer of Research, Conservation, and Exploration at the National Geographic Society, and Director of the UNESCO World Heritage Site of Bat in the Sultanate of Oman. Thornton works closely with NGS media to promote grantees and other scientists, overseeing research grants in anthropology, archaeology, astronomy, geography, geology, and paleontology. He also manages the Society's relationship with academic conferences around the world.

Jeremy McInerney

Dr. Jeremy McInerney is chairman of the Department of Classical Studies at the University of Pennsylvania. McInerney recently spent a year as Whitehead Professor in the American School of Classical Studies in Athens, Greece. He has excavated at Corinth, on Crete, and in Israel. Author of *The Cattle of the Sun: Cows and Culture in the World of the Ancient Greeks* (2010), McInerney has received top teaching awards, including the Lindback Award for Distinguished Teaching.

PROGRAM CONSULTANTS

Michael W. Smith

Dr. Michael Smith is the Associate Dean for Faculty Development and Academic Affairs in the College of Education at Temple University. He became a college teacher after 11 years of teaching high school English. His research focuses on how experienced readers read and talk about texts, as well as what motivates adolescents' reading and writing. Smith has written many books and monographs, including the award-winning *"Reading Don't Fix No Chevys": Literacy in the Lives of Young Men*.

Peggy Altoff

Peggy Altoff's long career includes teaching middle school and high school students, supervising teachers, and serving as adjunct university faculty. Peggy served as a state social studies specialist in Maryland and as a K–12 coordinator in Colorado Springs. She was president of the National Council for the Social Studies (NCSS) in 2006–2007 and was on the task force for the 2012 NCSS National Curriculum Standards.

David W. Moore

Dr. David Moore is a Professor Emeritus of Education at Arizona State University. He taught high school social studies and reading before entering college teaching. His noteworthy co-authored publications include the *Handbook of Reading Research* chapter on secondary school reading, the first International Reading Association position statement on adolescent literacy, and *Developing Readers and Writers in the Content Areas (6e)*.

PROGRAM WRITER

Special thanks to Jon Heggie for his extensive contributions to *National Geographic World History: Ancient Civilizations*. Heggie became fascinated with history as a small child, a passion nurtured by his parents and educators. He studied history at Oxford University and received his Post Graduate Certificate in Education from Bristol University. Heggie has taught English and History at a number of schools in the UK and has written for *National Geographic* magazine for the past ten years. He is currently working on a number of history projects and serving as the editor of the recently launched National Geographic *History* magazine.

REVIEWERS OF RELIGIOUS CONTENT

The following individuals reviewed the treatment of religious content in selected pages of the text.

Dr. Charles C. Haynes
Director, Religious Freedom
Center of the Newseum Institute
Washington, D.C.

Munir Shaikh
Institute on Religion and
Civic Values
Fountain Valley, California

NATIONAL GEOGRAPHIC SOCIETY

The National Geographic Society contributed significantly to *National Geographic World History: Ancient Civilizations*. Our collaboration with each of the following has been a pleasure and a privilege: National Geographic Maps, National Geographic Education and Children's Media, National Geographic Missions programs, and National Geographic Studios. We thank the Society for its guidance and support.

We BELIEVE in the power of science, exploration, and storytelling to change the world.

World History: Ancient Civilizations and the California Criteria for Evaluating Instructional Materials

World History: Ancient Civilizations aligns with the History–Social Science Content Standards for California Public Schools and the History–Social Science Framework for California Public Schools. Infused throughout the Student Edition (SE) and accompanying materials are the ideals of intellectual rigor, accuracy, and respect for our world. By presenting the history of past civilizations as a "story well told," *World History: Ancient Civilizations* draws students into the fascinating and complex narrative of our world.

As outlined in the History–Social Science Framework, the developers of *World History: Ancient Civilizations* addressed the five categories of criteria to ensure that all students receive the support they need for content comprehension. These categories are **History–Social Science Content—Alignment with Content Standards and Analysis Skills, Program Organization, Assessment, Universal Access,** and **Instructional Planning and Support**. The following is an overview of the program components and how they meet the criteria in each category.

World History: Ancient Civilizations
and the California Criteria for Evaluating Instructional Materials

World History: Ancient Civilizations meets 100 percent of the content standards and analysis skills mandated by the History–Social Science Content Standards for California Public Schools for Grade 6, as it reflects and incorporates the History–Social Science Framework. To permit easy tracking, the standards are listed both in a correlation at the beginning of the Student Edition and at point of use throughout the lessons both in the Student Edition and the Teacher's Edition (TE). To ensure factual accuracy and grammatical correctness, all student and teacher materials have been meticulously fact checked and copyedited, as well as reviewed by content-area experts and National Geographic program consultants. All maps in the program were created in consultation with National Geographic Maps.

National Geographic Learning has developed a state-of-the-art **digital correlation tool** to allow users to easily find all content associated with a particular standard. Teachers can browse to a standard to see a list of all content associated with it in both SE and TE, with links to view each page or resource. This tool will be available on MindTap, National Geographic Learning's digital platform.

The California Common Core State Standards for English Language Arts are also reflected in the SE. For example, a standards-based **Write About History** activity appears in each Chapter Review. In addition, each chapter offers a skills-based Reading Strategy that is introduced on the first page, implemented throughout the chapter, and assessed in the Chapter Review. More broadly, the **Review & Assess** questions in each lesson and the activities in the TE provide ongoing practice with many of the reading skills specified in the California Common Core State Standards for English Language Arts. The Environmental Principles & Concepts models are covered in the **Geographer's Toolbox** and throughout the SE and TE.

In addition to meeting the standards requirements, *World History: Ancient Civilizations* amply complies with the goal stated in the History–Social Science Framework of presenting history as a "story well told." Engaging, lively historical narrative forms the basis of the SE. A recurring feature, **Why Study History**, forges emotional connections to students' own lives, and helps provide continuity and a sense of narrative flow by giving students milestones for the beginning, middle, and end of the historical story.

Within each chapter, the lessons are linked through introductory paragraphs that serve the multiple purposes of engaging students and providing historical context. Most chapters include a **Moments in History** lesson, which focuses on a key place or date that had great impact on the world today. Biography lessons interspersed throughout the SE introduce students to the diverse and forceful personalities who shaped much of world history and help students view events from the perspective of the time period during which they occurred. Additional **Biographies** appear online for each chapter to help students analyze the subjects' lives and their places in the context of history.

World History: Ancient Civilizations is also animated by a wealth of primary sources. Most chapters include a **Document-Based Question** based on multiple sources—both print and visual—and the online **Primary Source Handbook** provides abundant further options. The primary sources represent the voices and perspectives of men and women from a representative variety of racial and ethnic backgrounds, highlighting the contributions of all in shaping our world.

Of course, notable individuals are not the only shapers of history. Geography, the environment, and social or religious movements all strongly influenced the development of past civilizations. The SE covers all these aspects of the narrative. World religions and ideas are discussed, when they are relevant, in an impartial, informative tone. Furthermore, all religion-related content has been reviewed by experts for accuracy and presentation. Geography features regularly throughout the book. The Geographer's Toolbox provides an overview of basic geographic concepts, and many chapters have a lesson devoted to the impact of geography on historical events. Humanity's place in the environment is covered in multiple lessons of the SE.

In line with the History–Social Science Content Standards for California Public Schools, *World History: Ancient Civilizations* is organized sequentially and regionally. Four units cover major periods from prehistoric times through the end of the Byzantine Empire in 1453. The units are divided into chronologically organized chapters, which are further divided into lessons. Each lesson builds logically on the previous ones, leading students through a clear and thoughtful presentation of world history. The Student Edition and accompanying materials provide instructional content for 180 days, with each lesson designed to be covered in a day. The relevant standards for each day of instruction are explicitly referenced in both SE and TE.

The narrative voice is engaging and detailed, drawing students into an in-depth study of people, ideas, conflicts, and achievements. As the chapters unfold, the narrative helps students link causes and effects to understand why events turned out as they did. A wealth of visuals and documents add historical perspective, and the text unifies all the elements for a coherent, powerful, and engaging presentation.

To ensure that the language is accessible to all students, Key Vocabulary and domain-specific terms are highlighted and defined within the text. In addition, these key vocabulary terms are listed at the beginning of each chapter in the SE. The TE provides suggestions for introducing and reinforcing the vocabulary. For more details about universal access in the TE and other program components, see the "Universal Access" section.

World History: Ancient Civilizations
and the California Criteria for Evaluating Instructional Materials

World History: Ancient Civilizations offers a variety of assessment options, both formal and informal, formative and summative. Students have opportunities to demonstrate their knowledge in a host of formats, including traditional tests, group discussions, essays, and creative presentations.

In the Student Edition, the **Reflect & Assess** questions at the end of each lesson provide regular opportunities for formative assessment of students' understanding of the lesson content and their progress with critical thinking skills. The **Chapter Review** that concludes each chapter is a summative assessment that evaluates students' knowledge and skills through vocabulary test items, constructed response items, and longer responses analyzing a primary source passage and illustrating a knowledge of historical events.

At the end of each unit, a test and an inquiry-based project allow for summative assessment of students' progress. The **Unit Test** reviews the content of the chapters and challenges students to make connections among the events and time periods covered within the unit and in previous units. The **Unit Inquiry** project encourages students to demonstrate their research and presentation skills, in addition to their content knowledge and analytical skills. This end-of-unit project includes an analytical rubric that teachers can share with students and use in evaluating the completed product.

In the Teacher's Edition, additional activities provide more modes for assessment. The Teach section of every TE lesson includes **Guided Discussion** and **Active Options** which function as both learning activities and formative assessments.

World History: Ancient Civilizations vigorously supports universal access for students as outlined in the History–Social Science Framework. All the strategies that are designed to address individual student populations can be implemented with little or no modification.

The Teacher's Edition offers explicit options for universal access instruction at several points. At the beginning of each chapter, a **Strategies for Differentiation** section provides ideas for teaching that chapter's content to five different student populations: Struggling Readers, Inclusion (special needs), English Language Learners, Gifted & Talented, and Pre-AP. Each lesson includes additional strategies for differentiation. These are tailored specifically for challenges or opportunities that may arise for specific populations within each lesson.

All ELL activities explicitly reference the proficiency levels (Emerging, Expanding, Bridging) outlined in the English Language Arts/English Language Development Framework. Strategies for Struggling Readers address the needs of students reading up to two grade levels below what

is specified by the English–language arts content standards. Inclusion strategies provide access to the text for students with special needs. The Pre-AP and Gifted & Talented activities challenge students to explore ideas, people, or topics in depth and to use their analytical skills at a more sophisticated level. Gifted & Talented strategies target abilities students may have outside of strictly academic disciplines—such as drawing, creative writing, and music—and encourage students to bring them to bear on the learning of history.

The digital version of *World History: Ancient Civilizations* includes a variety of universal access options for different student populations. For example, the **Modified Text** option for each lesson offers striving readers and English Language Learners a student narrative written two grade levels below that of the principal text. Accessibility issues for the Inclusion population are addressed by a variety of features such as audio, alt text for images and other visuals, and close captioning for the video components.

Teacher-support materials are available both online and in the print components to provide a general roadmap for instruction, give specific directions for teaching and assessing content and skills to students at all levels, and guide teachers in using the parts of *World History: Ancient Civilizations*. Each print and electronic component of the program includes both teacher support and answer keys for all student activities.

The Teacher's Edition is the centerpiece of this comprehensive teacher-support structure. As mandated in the History–Social Science Framework, it describes "what to teach, how to teach, and when to teach." The TE provides correlations to the History–Social Science Content Standards and Analysis Skills, among numerous other useful aids. **Chapter Planners** offer teachers a snapshot of chapter, assessment, and ancillary content.

Each TE lesson opens with an **Objective** and a specific connection to the chapter's **Essential Question**. Elements in the SE lesson are supported, enriched, and expanded upon in the TE. In addition, as mentioned above, the Teacher's Edition provides content-specific activities and instructional strategies at the unit, chapter, and lesson levels. The lesson pages also include additional background information for teachers on the people, events, and ideas covered in the SE. The TE pages for the Chapter Reviews contain answer keys.

All print and digital ancillaries are coordinated so that teachers can easily locate materials they need to augment or support a given lesson. Because not all teachers are equally conversant with all forms of instructional technology, the digital learning resources contain technical support and guidance on making the best use of electronic technology for instruction.

History–Social Science Content Standards and California Common Core State Standards

Grade 6

HSS Correlations

CA CCSS Correlations

History-Social Science Content Standards

STANDARD	STUDENT EDITION	TEACHER'S EDITION
GRADE 6 CONTENT STANDARDS		
6.1: Students describe what is known through archaeological studies of the early physical and cultural development of humankind from the Paleolithic era to the agricultural revolution.		
6.1.1 Describe the hunter-gatherer societies, including the development of tools and the use of fire.	16–17, 22–23, 24–25, 32, 46–47	10–11, 16–17, 18–19, 24–25, 50–51
6.1.2 Identify the locations of human communities that populated the major regions of the world and describe how humans adapted to a variety of environments.	12, 16–17, 18–19, 20–21, 32	10–11, 12–13, 20–21
6.1.3 Discuss the climatic changes and human modifications of the physical environment that gave rise to the domestication of plants and animals and new sources of clothing and shelter.	16–17, 26–27, 28–29, 32	10–11, 18–19, 26–27, 33C–33D
6.2: Students analyze the geographic, political, economic, religious, and social structures of the early civilizations of Mesopotamia, Egypt, and Kush.		
6.2.1 Locate and describe the major river systems and discuss the physical settings that supported permanent settlement and early civilizations.	33, 37, 40, 45, 52, 53, 66–67, 86, 90–91	28–29, 36–37, 38–39, 40–41, 44–45, 66–67, 90–91, 102–103, 104–105
6.2.2 Trace the development of agricultural techniques that permitted the production of economic surplus and the emergence of cities as centers of culture and power.	28–29, 32, 36–37, 38–39, 40–41, 42–43, 44–45, 48–49, 66–67, 68–69, 84–85, 92–93	28–29, 36–37, 38–39, 42–43, 48–49, 68–69, 92–93
6.2.3 Understand the relationship between religion and the social and political order in Mesopotamia and Egypt.	70–71, 78–79, 86, 94–95, 100–101, 102–103, 120	70–71, 76–77, 94–95, 98–99, 100–101, 102–103
6.2.4 Know the significance of Hammurabi's Code.	76–77, 86	63C–63D, 76–77
6.2.5 Discuss the main features of Egyptian art and architecture.	98–99, 118–119, 121	98–99, 118–119
6.2.6 Describe the role of Egyptian trade in the eastern Mediterranean and Nile valley.	104, 107, 120	92–93, 104–105, 106–107
6.2.7 Understand the significance of Queen Hatshepsut and Ramses the Great.	106–107, 108–109, 120, 121	106–107, 108–109
6.2.8 Identify the location of the Kush civilization and describe its political, commercial, and cultural relations with Egypt.	112–113, 120	112–113
6.2.9 Trace the evolution of language and its written forms.	48–49, 72–73, 81, 87, 114–115	72–73, 80–81, 114–115
6.3: Students analyze the geographic, political, economic, religious, and social structures of the Ancient Hebrews.		
6.3.1 Describe the origins and significance of Judaism as the first monotheistic religion based on the concept of one God who sets down moral laws for humanity.	124–125, 126–127, 140	124–125, 126–127

STANDARD	STUDENT EDITION	TEACHER'S EDITION
6.3.2 Identify the sources of the ethical teachings and central beliefs of Judaism (the Hebrew Bible, the Commentaries): belief in God, observance of law, practice of the concepts of righteousness and justice, and importance of study; and describe how the ideas of the Hebrew traditions are reflected in the moral and ethical traditions of Western civilization.	122, 128–129, 130–131, 136–137, 140, 141	122–123, 128–129
6.3.3 Explain the significance of Abraham, Moses, Naomi, Ruth, David, and Yohanan ben Zaccai in the development of the Jewish religion.	124–125, 131, 132, 136, 137	121C–121D, 124–125
6.3.4 Discuss the locations of the settlements and movements of Hebrew peoples, including the Exodus and their movement to and from Egypt, and outline the significance of the Exodus to the Jewish and other people.	124–125, 132, 134–135, 136–137, 140	132–133, 134–135, 136–137
6.3.5 Discuss how Judaism survived and developed despite the continuing dispersion of much of the Jewish population from Jerusalem and the rest of Israel after the destruction of the second Temple in A.D. 70.	134–135, 136–137	134–135, 136–137

6.4: Students analyze the geographic, political, economic, religious, and social structures of the early civilizations of Ancient Greece.

STANDARD	STUDENT EDITION	TEACHER'S EDITION
6.4.1 Discuss the connections between geography and the development of city-states in the region of the Aegean Sea, including patterns of trade and commerce among Greek city-states and within the wider Mediterranean region.	228–229, 230–231, 234–235, 236–237, 246	226–227, 228–229, 232–233, 234–235, 236–237
6.4.2 Trace the transition from tyranny and oligarchy to early democratic forms of government and back to dictatorship in ancient Greece, including the significance of the invention of the idea of citizenship (e.g., from *Pericles' Funeral Oration*).	235, 240–241, 250–251, 258–259, 260–261, 274–275, 277	234–235, 240–241, 250–251, 248–259, 260–261, 262–263
6.4.3 State the key differences between Athenian, or direct, democracy and representative democracy.	250–251, 274–275	276–277
6.4.4 Explain the significance of Greek mythology to the everyday life of people in the region and how Greek literature continues to permeate our literature and language today, drawing from Greek mythology and epics, such as Homer's *Iliad* and *Odyssey*, and from *Aesop's Fables*.	232–233, 246, 254–255, 276	226–227, 233–233, 254–255
6.4.5 Outline the founding, expansion, and political organization of the Persian Empire.	82–83, 242–243, 247	63C–63D, 82–83
6.4.6 Compare and contrast life in Athens and Sparta, with emphasis on their roles in the Persian and Peloponnesian Wars.	226, 238 239, 240 241, 242–243, 244–245, 226, 252–253, 256–257, 258–259, 260–261, 276	224–225, 238–239, 240–241, 244–245, 252–253, 256–257
6.4.7 Trace the rise of Alexander the Great and the spread of Greek culture eastward and into Egypt.	262–263, 264–265, 266–267, 276, 277	264–265, 266–267, 268–269
6.4.8 Describe the enduring contributions of important Greek figures in the arts and sciences (e.g., Hypatia, Socrates, Plato, Aristotle, Euclid, Thucydides).	232, 261, 267, 268–269, 270–271	232–233, 270–271, 272–273

History-Social Science Content Standards

STANDARD	STUDENT EDITION	TEACHER'S EDITION
6.5: Students analyze the geographic, political, economic, religious, and social structures of the early civilizations of India.		
6.5.1 Locate and describe the major river system and discuss the physical setting that supported the rise of this civilization.	144–145, 146, 162	142–143, 144–145
6.5.2 Discuss the significance of the Aryan invasions.	142, 148–149, 162	142–143, 148–149
6.5.3 Explain the major beliefs and practices of Brahmanism in India and how they evolved into early Hinduism.	148–149, 150–151, 162, 163	148–149, 150–151, 160–161
6.5.4 Outline the social structure of the caste system.	149, 150, 163	148–149
6.5.5 Know the life and moral teachings of Buddha and how Buddhism spread in India, Ceylon, and Central Asia.	154–155, 156, 160, 162	154–155, 160–161
6.5.6 Describe the growth of the Maurya empire and the political and moral achievements of the emperor Asoka.	156–157, 162	156–157
6.5.7 Discuss important aesthetic and intellectual traditions (e.g., Sanskrit literature, including the *Bhagavad Gita*; medicine; metallurgy; and mathematics, including Hindu-Arabic numerals and the zero).	150, 152–153, 159, 160–161	142–143, 152–153, 158–159, 160–161
6.6: Students analyze the geographic, political, economic, religious, and social structures of the early civilizations of China.		
6.6.1 Locate and describe the origins of Chinese civilization in the Huang-He Valley during the Shang Dynasty.	166–167, 168–169	166–167, 168–169
6.6.2 Explain the geographic features of China that made governance and the spread of ideas and goods difficult and served to isolate the country from the rest of the world.	166–167, 192	
6.6.3 Know about the life of Confucius and the fundamental teachings of Confucianism and Taoism.	164, 170–171, 172–173, 192, 193	163C–163D, 164–165, 170–171, 172–173, 180–181
6.6.4 Identify the political and cultural problems prevalent in the time of Confucius and how he sought to solve them.	170–171, 173	163C–163D, 170–171
6.6.5 List the policies and achievements of the emperor Shi Huangdi in unifying northern China under the Qin Dynasty.	174–175, 176–177, 178–179, 192	163C–163D, 174–175, 176–177, 178–179
6.6.6 Detail the political contributions of the Han Dynasty to the development of the imperial bureaucratic state and the expansion of the empire.	180–181, 192	180–181
6.6.7 Cite the significance of the trans-Eurasian "silk roads" in the period of the Han Dynasty and Roman Empire and their locations.	184–185, 186–187, 188–189, 190–191, 192, 329	184–185, 186–187, 188–189, 190–191
6.6.8 Describe the diffusion of Buddhism northward to China during the Han Dynasty.	186, 193	

STANDARD	STUDENT EDITION	TEACHER'S EDITION
6.7: Students analyze the geographic, political, economic, religious, and social structures during the development of Rome.		
6.7.1 Identify the location and describe the rise of the Roman Republic, including the importance of such mythical and historical figures as Aeneas, Romulus and Remus, Cincinnatus, Julius Caesar, and Cicero.	290–291, 292–293, 294–295, 314, 316–317, 318–319, 320–321, 322, 323	292–293, 316–317
6.7.2 Describe the government of the Roman Republic and its significance (e.g., written constitution and tripartite government, checks and balances, civic duty).	294–295, 323, 355	294–295
6.7.3 Identify the location of and the political and geographic reasons for the growth of Roman territories and expansion of the empire, including how the empire fostered economic growth through the use of currency and trade routes.	304–305, 308–309, 310–311, 312–313, 322, 328–329, 358	290–291, 306–307, 312–313, 328–329
6.7.4 Discuss the influence of Julius Caesar and Augustus in Rome's transition from republic to empire.	316–317, 318–319, 320–321, 326–327, 322, 323, 358	316–317, 326–327
6.7.5 Trace the migration of Jews around the Mediterranean region and the effects of their conflict with the Romans, including the Romans' restrictions on their right to live in Jerusalem.	136–137, 140, 338	136–137
6.7.6 Note the origins of Christianity in the Jewish Messianic prophecies, the life and teachings of Jesus of Nazareth as described in the New Testament, and the contribution of St. Paul the Apostle to the definition and spread of Christian beliefs (e.g., belief in the Trinity, resurrection, salvation).	338–339, 340–341, 342–343, 344–345	338–339, 342–343
6.7.7 Describe the circumstances that led to the spread of Christianity in Europe and other Roman territories.	340–341	340–341, 344–345
6.7.8 Discuss the legacies of Roman art and architecture, technology and science, literature, language, and law.	296–297, 302–303, 330–331, 332–333, 334–335, 352–353, 354–355, 356–357, 358	287C–287D, 330–331, 332–333, 334–335, 352–353, 354–355, 356–357

GRADE 7 CONTENT STANDARDS

STANDARD	STUDENT EDITION	TEACHER'S EDITION
7.1: Students analyze the causes and effects of the vast expansion and ultimate disintegration of the Roman Empire.		
7.1.1 Study the early strengths and lasting contributions of Rome (e.g., significance of Roman citizenship; rights under Roman law; Roman art, architecture, engineering, and philosophy; preservation and transmission of Christianity) and its ultimate internal weaknesses (e.g., rise of autonomous military powers within the empire, undermining of citizenship by the growth of corruption and slavery, lack of education, and distribution of news).	330–331, 332–333, 334–335, 344–345, 346–347, 352–353, 354–355, 356–357, 358, 359	330–331, 332–333, 334–335, 344–345, 346–347, 352–353, 354–355, 356–357
7.1.2 Discuss the geographic borders of the empire at its height and the factors that threatened its territorial cohesion.	286–287, 328–329, 346–347, 358, 359	348–349

History-Social Science Content Standards

STANDARD	STUDENT EDITION	TEACHER'S EDITION
7.1.3 Describe the establishment by Constantine of the new capital in Constantinople and the development of the Byzantine Empire, with an emphasis on the consequences of the development of two distinct European civilizations, Eastern Orthodox and Roman Catholic, and their two distinct views on church-state relations.	348–349, 362–363, 364–365, 368–369, 370–371, 374–375, 376, 377	348–349, 359C–359D, 360–361, 362–363, 364–365, 366–367, 368–369, 370–371, 372–373, 374–375
7.7: Students compare and contrast the geographic, political, economic, religious, and social structures of the Meso-American and Andean civilizations.		
7.7.1 Study the locations, landforms, and climates of Mexico, Central America, and South America and their effects on Mayan, Aztec, and Incan economies, trade, and development of urban societies.	196–197	196–197
7.7.2 Study the roles of people in each society, including class structures, family life, warfare, religious beliefs and practices, and slavery.	198–199, 200–201, 202–203, 204–205, 212, 213	198–199, 200–201, 202–203, 204–205
7.7.3 Explain how and where each empire arose and how the Aztec and Incan empires were defeated by the Spanish.	202–203	
7.7.4 Describe the artistic and oral traditions and architecture in the three civilizations.	204–205, 206–207, 210–211	204–205, 206–207, 208–209, 210–211
7.7.5 Describe the Meso-American achievements in astronomy and mathematics, including the development of the calendar and the Meso-American knowledge of seasonal changes to the civilizations' agricultural systems.	208–209, 212	206–207

HISTORICAL AND SOCIAL SCIENCES ANALYSIS SKILLS

Chronological and Spatial Thinking

	STUDENT EDITION	TEACHER'S EDITION
CST 1 Students explain how major events are related to one another in time.	7, 30, 61, 83, 105, 141, 161, 223, 285, 324, 337, 339, 351, 353, 358, 375	30–31, 112–113, 296–297, 308–309, 324–325
CST 2 Students construct various time lines of key events, people, and periods of the historical era they are studying.	30, 324, 358	9C–9D, 18–19, 30–31, 33C–33D, 63C–63D, 78–79, 82–83, 121C–121D, 132–133, 225C–225D, 242–243, 262–263, 287C–287D, 310–311, 318–319, 324–325
CST 3 Students use a variety of maps and documents to identify physical and cultural features of neighborhoods, cities, states, and countries and to explain the historical migration of people, expansion and disintegration of empires, and the growth of economic systems.	8–9, 19, 21, 28–29, 30, 33, 37, 53, 62–63, 67, 75, 80, 93, 113, 125, 137, 144, 145, 149, 157, 158, 159, 167, 181, 184–185, 193, 197, 203, 224–225, 231, 237, 265, 277, 286–287, 291, 312–313, 329, 340–341, 348–349, 363	9C–9D, 18–19, 20–21, 28–29, 30–31, 33C–33D, 66–67, 74–75, 80–81, 124–125, 136–137, 228–229, 230–231, 236–237, 264–265, 290–291, 316–317, 328–329, 340–341, 348–349, 362–363

STANDARD	STUDENT EDITION	TEACHER'S EDITION
Research, Evidence, and Point of View		
REP 1 Students frame questions that can be answered by historical study and research.	30, 31, 392	9C–9D, 16–17, 20–21, 26–27, 36–37, 38–39, 44–45, 66–67, 92–93, 94–95, 112–113, 228–229, 287C–287D, 314–315
REP 2 Students distinguish fact from opinion in historical narratives and stories.	30, 319	30–31
REP 3 Students distinguish relevant from irrelevant information, essential from incidental information, and verifiable from unverifiable information in historical narratives and stories.	30	30–31
REP 4 Students assess the credibility of primary and secondary sources and draw sound conclusions from them.	30, 31, 33, 53, 72–73, 87, 102–103, 121, 130–131, 141, 152–153, 163, 172–173, 193, 210–211, 213, 247, 260–261, 277, 318–319, 323, 342–343, 359, 377	30–31, 72–73, 76–77, 102–103, 130–131, 260–261, 322–323, 342–343
REP 5 Students detect the different historical points of view on historical events and determine the context in which the historical statements were made (the questions asked, sources used, author's perspectives).	30, 261	287C–287D, 322–323
Historical Interpretation		
HI 1 Students explain the central issues and problems from the past, placing people and events in a matrix of time and place.	31, 33, 247, 359, 377	3, 106–107, 136–137, 238–239, 292–293, 294–295, 298–299, 318–319
HI 2 Students understand and distinguish cause, effect, sequence, and correlation in historical events, including the long- and short-term causal relations.	25, 31, 32, 52, 69, 86, 91, 105, 120, 140, 142, 157, 162, 183, 192, 209, 237, 239, 253, 259, 263, 269, 275, 276, 329, 333, 347, 351, 353, 355, 360, 363, 375	16–17, 20–21, 24–25, 26–27, 46–47, 98–99, 134–135, 228–229, 236–237, 252–253, 256–257, 258–259, 264–265, 300–301, 304–305, 318–319, 320–321, 340–341, 360–361, 374–375
HI 3 Students explain the sources of historical continuity and how the combination of ideas and events explains the emergence of new patterns.	15, 29, 31, 32, 37, 77, 117, 161, 162, 271, 357, 358, 376	28–29, 33C–33D, 38–39, 130–131, 260–261, 294–295, 312–313, 330–331
HI 4 Students recognize the role of chance, oversight, and error in history.	31, 276, 315	
HI 5 Students recognize that interpretations of history are subject to change as new information is uncovered.	1, 21, 31, 97, 110, 139, 191, 207	22–23, 46–47, 96–97, 138–139, 314–315
HI 6 Students interpret basic indicators of economic performance and conduct cost-benefit analyses of economic and political issues.	109, 175, 237, 329	82–83

California Common Core State Standards

STANDARD	STUDENT EDITION	TEACHER'S EDITION
READING STANDARDS FOR LITERACY IN HISTORY/SOCIAL STUDIES		
Key Ideas and Details		
RH.6.1 Cite specific textual evidence to support analysis of primary and secondary sources.	32, 33, 52, 53, 64, 73, 86, 87, 88, 103, 120, 121, 131, 140, 141, 153, 162, 163, 173, 192, 193, 211, 212, 213, 246, 247, 261, 276, 277, 319, 322, 323, 343, 358, 359, 376, 377	
RH.6.2 Determine the central ideas or information of a primary or secondary source; provide an accurate summary of the source distinct from prior knowledge or opinions.	32, 33, 34, 52, 53, 73, 86, 87, 103, 120, 121, 122, 131, 140, 141, 153, 162, 163, 173, 192, 193, 194, 211, 212, 213, 246, 247, 261, 276, 277, 319, 322, 323, 343, 358, 359, 376, 377	9C–9D, 12–13, 14–15, 22–23, 30–31, 33C–33D, 34–35, 38–39, 42–43, 44–45, 74–75, 80–81, 87C–87D, 116–117, 124–125, 126–127, 141C–141D, 142–143, 158–159, 172–173, 174–175, 176–177, 178–179, 193C–193D, 194–195, 196–197, 202–203, 204–205, 210–211, 228–220, 240–241, 247C–247D, 262–263, 264–265, 274–275, 292–293, 304–305, 314–315, 323C–323D, 328–329, 332–333, 336–337, 338–339
RH.6.3 Identify key steps in a text's description of a process related to history/social studies (e.g., how a bill becomes law, how interest rates are raised or lowered).	46–47, 168–169, 196–197	1, 46–47
Craft and Structure		
RH.6.4 Determine the meaning of words and phrases as they are used in a text, including vocabulary specific to domains related to history/social studies.	13, 17, 32, 41, 52, 71, 86, 119, 120, 140, 149, 151, 162, 177, 192, 201, 212, 235, 246, 248, 259, 276, 299, 322, 358, 371, 376	1, 9C–9D, 10–11, 14–15, 16–17, 24–25, 33C–33D, 34–35, 38–39, 40–41, 44–45, 63C–63D, 64–65, 68–69, 80–81, 87C–87D, 88–89, 114–115, 122–123, 126–127, 134–135, 138–139, 141C–141D, 142–143, 150–151, 163C–163D, 164–165, 166–167, 180–181, 190–191, 193C–193D, 194–195, 196–197, 202–203, 206–207, 218–219, 225C–225D, 226–227, 238–239, 240–241, 247C–247D, 248–249, 254–255, 258–259, 262–263, 274–275, 287C–287D, 288–289, 290–291, 296–297, 300–301, 302–303, 310–311, 323C–323D, 324–325, 338–339, 346–347, 352–353, 382–383
RH.6.5 Describe how a text presents information (e.g., sequentially, comparatively, causally).	10, 32, 226, 246, 288, 322	10–11, 226–227, 288–289, 324–325
RH.6.6 Identify aspects of a text that reveal an author's point of view or purpose (e.g., loaded language, inclusion or avoidance of particular facts).	30, 79, 164, 171, 191, 207	164–165

STANDARD	STUDENT EDITION	TEACHER'S EDITION
Integration of Knowledge and Ideas		
RH.6.7 Integrate visual information (e.g., in charts, graphs, photographs, videos, or maps) with other information in print and digital texts.	22–23, 24–25, 26–27, 42–43, 46–47, 50–51, 68–69, 84–85, 110–111, 146–147, 168–169, 176–177, 178–179, 188–189, 204–205, 240–241, 244–245, 252–253, 272–273, 300–301, 306–307, 320–321, 356–357, 366–367, 372–373	12–13, 24–25, 50–51, 68–69, 176–177, 228–229, 230–231, 232–233, 242–243, 294–295, 320–321, 340–341
RH.6.8 Distinguish among fact, opinion, and reasoned judgment in a text.	30, 319	318–319
RH.6.9 Analyze the relationship between a primary and secondary source on the same topic.	30, 31, 319	318–319
Reading and Level of Text Complexity		
RH.6.10 By the end of grade 8, read and comprehend history/social studies texts in the grades 6-8 complexity band independently and proficiently.	The Lexile measure for the Student Edition falls within the stretch band for the California Common Core State Standards.	

WRITING STANDARDS FOR LITERACY IN HISTORY/SOCIAL STUDIES, SCIENCE, AND TECHNICAL SUBJECTS

STANDARD	STUDENT EDITION	TEACHER'S EDITION
Text Types and Purposes		

WHST.6.1 Write arguments focused on discipline-specific content.
  a. Introduce claim(s) about a topic or issue, acknowledge and distinguish the claim(s) from alternate or opposing claims, and organize the reasons and evidence logically.
  b. Support claim(s) with logical reasoning and relevant, accurate data and evidence that demonstrate an understanding of the topic or text, using credible sources.
  c. Use words, phrases, and clauses to create cohesion and clarify the relationships among claim(s), counterclaims, reasons, and evidence.
  d. Establish and maintain a formal style.
  e. Provide a concluding statement or section that follows from and supports the argument provided.
	87, 141, 193, 261, 323	68–69

California Common Core State Standards

STANDARD	STUDENT EDITION	TEACHER'S EDITION

WHST.6.2 Write informative/explanatory texts, including the narration of historical events, scientific procedures/experiments, or technical processes.
   a. Introduce a topic clearly, previewing what is to follow; organize ideas, concepts, and information into broader categories as appropriate to achieving purpose; include formatting (e.g., headings), graphics (e.g., charts, tables), and multimedia when useful to aiding comprehension.
   b. Develop the topic with relevant, well-chosen facts, definitions, concrete details, quotations, or other information and examples.
   c. Use appropriate and varied transitions to create cohesion and clarify the relationships among ideas and concepts.
   d. Use precise language and domain-specific vocabulary to inform about or explain the topic.
   e. Establish and maintain a formal style and objective tone.
   f. Provide a concluding statement or section that follows from and supports the information or explanation presented.
	33, 53, 73, 103, 121, 131, 153, 163, 173, 211, 213, 247, 277, 319, 343, 359, 377	70–71, 121C–121D

Production and Distribution of Writing

STANDARD	STUDENT EDITION	TEACHER'S EDITION
WHST.6.4 Produce clear and coherent writing in which the development, organization, and style are appropriate to task, purpose, and audience.	33, 53, 87, 121, 141, 163, 193, 213, 247, 277, 323, 359, 377	18–19, 20–21, 63C–63D, 68–69, 72–73, 76–77, 80–81, 82–83, 92–93, 96–97, 106–107, 118–119, 132–133, 136–137, 148–149, 158–159, 160–161, 168–169, 172–173, 176–177, 186–187, 198–199, 206–207, 225C–225D, 238–239, 250–251, 254–255, 268–269, 270–271, 287C–287D, 294–295, 298–299, 314–315, 316–317, 332–333, 334–335, 336–337, 338–339, 344–345
WHST.6.5 With some guidance and support from peers and adults, develop and strengthen writing as needed by planning, revising, editing, rewriting, or trying a new approach, focusing on how well purpose and audience have been addressed.	33, 53, 87, 121, 163, 213, 277	72–73, 102–103, 130–131, 152–153, 172–173, 210–211, 260–261, 318–319, 342–343
WHST.6.6 Use technology, including the Internet, to produce and publish writing and present the relationships between information and ideas clearly and efficiently.	53, 121, 213, 277	344–345

STANDARD	STUDENT EDITION	TEACHER'S EDITION
Research to Build and Present Knowledge		
WHST.6.7 Conduct short research projects to answer a question (including a self-generated question), drawing on several sources and generating additional related, focused questions that allow for multiple avenues of exploration.	392	9C–9D, 12–13, 16–17, 26–27, 33C–33D, 36–37, 42–43, 48–49, 50–51, 70–71, 90–91, 96–97, 100–101, 104–105, 112–113, 116–117, 124–125, 126–127, 130–131, 134–135, 138–139, 144–145, 146–147, 148–149, 160–161, 166–167, 184–185, 188–189, 196–197, 200–201, 202–203, 204–205, 208–209, 210–211, 228–229, 230–231, 234–235, 236–237, 240–241, 247C–247D, 250–251, 252–253, 256–257, 258–259, 260–261, 266–267, 272–273, 274–275, 287C–287D, 290–291, 296–287, 300–301, 302–303, 304–305, 306–307, 310–311, 312–313, 314–315, 318–319, 323C–323D, 326–327, 330–331, 334–335, 336–337, 340–341, 342–343, 344–345, 346–347, 354–355
WHST.6.8 Gather relevant information from multiple print and digital sources, using search terms effectively; assess the credibility and accuracy of each source; and quote or paraphrase the data and conclusions of others while avoiding plagiarism and following a standard format for citation.	392	42–43, 70–71, 124–125, 330–331
WHST.6.9 Draw evidence from informational texts to support analysis, reflection, and research.	33, 53, 87, 121, 141, 163, 193, 213, 247, 277, 323, 359, 377, 392	18–19, 346–347
Range of Writing		
WHST.6.10 Write routinely over extended time frames (time for reflection and revision) and shorter time frames (a single sitting or a day or two) for a range of discipline-specific tasks, purposes, and audiences.	33, 53, 73, 87, 103, 121, 131, 141, 153, 163, 173, 193, 211, 213, 247, 261, 277, 319, 323, 343, 359, 377	18–19, 20–21, 63C–63D, 68–69, 72–73, 76–77, 80–81, 82–83, 92–93, 96–97, 106–107, 118–119, 132–133, 136–137, 148–149, 158–159, 160–161, 168–169, 172–173, 176–177, 186–187, 198–199, 206–207, 225C–225D, 238–239, 250–251, 254–255, 268–269, 270–271, 287C–287D, 294–295, 298–299, 314–315, 316–317, 332–333, 334–335, 336–337, 338–339, 344–345

NATIONAL GEOGRAPHIC APPROACH

Most of us recognize that familiar magazine with the yellow border on newsstands in airports or on shelves in libraries. You've probably come to expect from National Geographic engaging stories on historical and global topics, with interesting photographs and graphics. But did you know that the magazine is only one part of an institution that dates back more than 128 years—and today plays an important role in world events?

OUR PURPOSE

The National Geographic Society pushes the boundaries of exploration to further our understanding of our planet and empower us all to generate solutions for a healthier and more sustainable future.

SCIENCE AND EXPLORATION

National Geographic has become one of the largest nonprofit scientific and educational institutions in the world. It supports thousands of scientists, archaeologists, marine biologists, divers, climbers, photographers, researchers, teachers, oceanographers, geologists, adventurers, physicists, artists, curators, and writers who work on projects that add to the scientific and human record.

THE NATIONAL GEOGRAPHIC LEARNING FRAMEWORK

The Learning Framework defines and shapes National Geographic's philosophy about teaching and learning. The framework is based on the Attitudes, Skills, and Knowledge that embody the explorer mindset. It covers diverse fields of knowledge and recognizes the core principles established at National Geographic, as well as the values held by families, communities, and cultures. The attributes of the Learning Framework are: **Attitudes**—Curiosity, Responsibility, and Empowerment; **Skills**—Observation, Communication, Collaboration, and Problem-solving; **Knowledge**—The Human Story, Critical Species and Places, and Our Changing Planet. You will see National Geographic Learning Framework activities in each unit of this text.

NATIONAL GEOGRAPHIC LEARNING'S SOCIAL STUDIES CREDO

National Geographic Learning (NGL) wants students to think about the impact of their own choices on themselves and others; to think critically and carefully about ideas and actions; to become lifelong learners and teachers; and to advocate for the greater good as leaders in their communities. NGL follows these guidelines:

1. Our goal is to establish relevance by connecting the physical environment and historical events to students' lives.

2. We view history as the study of Identity.

3. We foster the development of empathy, tolerance, and understanding for diverse peoples, cultures, traditions, and ideas.

4. We empower students to explore their interests and strengths, find their own voices, and speak out on their beliefs.

5. We encourage students to become active and responsible citizens on local and national levels, and to become global citizens.

6. We believe in the beauty and endurance of the human record and the need to preserve it.

7. We affirm the critical need to care for the planet and all of its inhabitants.

A Note on National Geographic Style

Throughout the text, you will see the abbreviations B.C. and A.D. As you know, a date followed by B.C. refers to the number of years the date occurred before the birth of Christ. A date preceded by A.D. refers to the number of years the date occurred after the birth of Christ. Many historians also use the abbreviations B.C.E. and C.E. for these time periods. B.C.E. stands for "Before the Common Era," and C.E. stands for "Common Era." The National Geographic Society adheres to the practice of using B.C. and A.D., and that is what is used in this text.

UNIT EXPLORERS

Each unit in this book opens and closes with a National Geographic Explorer discussing the content presented in the unit and explaining his or her own related work in the field. Within the Student eEdition, you can watch video footage of each Unit Explorer "on location" to expand and enhance your world history learning experience.

Steven Ellis
Archaeologist
National Geographic
Grantee

Fredrik Hiebert
Archaeologist
National Geographic
Fellow

Louise Leakey
Paleontologist
National Geographic
Explorer-in-Residence

William Parkinson
Archaeologist
National Geographic
Grantee

Christopher Thornton
Archaeologist
National Geographic
Lead Program Officer of Research,
Conservation, and Exploration

■ NATIONAL GEOGRAPHIC

CHAPTER EXPLORERS

In the chapters of this book, National Geographic Explorers tell the story of their work as it relates to the time in history you're learning about. Archaeologists, photographers, and writers explain their historical and cultural findings and the process involved in making the important discoveries that help us understand more about the past—and the future.

Beverly Goodman
Geo-Archaeologist
National Geographic
Emerging Explorer

Fredrik Hiebert
Archaeologist
National Geographic
Fellow

Patrick Hunt
Archaeologist
National Geographic
Grantee

Sarah Parcak
Archaeologist
National Geographic
Fellow

Jeffrey Rose
Archaeologist
National Geographic
Emerging Explorer

William Saturno
Archaeologist
National Geographic
Grantee

FEATURED EXPLORERS

Throughout the Student eEdition, National Geographic Featured Explorers take part in informal "video chat" style interviews to explain and discuss their fieldwork and explore high-interest topics covered in the book. Other Featured Explorers tell the story of important and ongoing world events in the Stories Making History section.

Salam Al Kuntar
Archaeologist
National Geographic
Emerging Explorer

Lee Berger
Paleoanthropologist
National Geographic
Explorer-in-Residence

Michael Cosmopoulos
Archaeologist, National
Geographic Grantee

Sarah Parcak
Archaeologist
National Geographic
Fellow

Thomas Parker
Archaeologist
National Geographic
Grantee

Soultana Maria Valamoti
Archaeologist, National
Geographic Grantee

WORLD HISTORY
GREAT CIVILIZATIONS

TEACHER'S EDITION

This easy-to-navigate Teacher's Edition follows a predictable pattern of units, chapters, and lessons. Easily readable Student Edition pages are included alongside the corresponding teacher material.

UNIT INTRODUCTION AND WRAP-UP

Each unit opens with six pages of introductory material, including an introduction by a National Geographic Explorer and a time line and map that relate to the historical period featured in the unit.

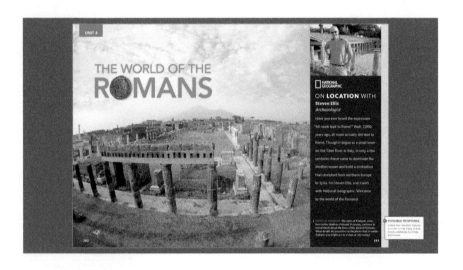

The unit wraps up with four pages of National Geographic-related content, including a feature on the Unit Explorer and his/her work, an adapted National Geographic article, and a Unit Inquiry project (with evaluation rubric).

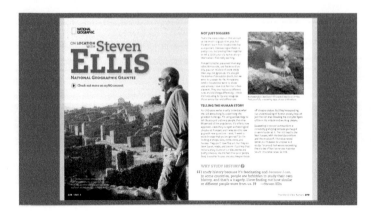

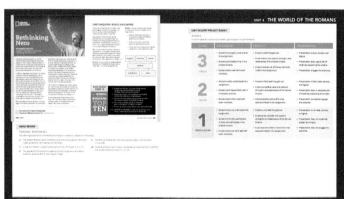

CHAPTER PLANNER

The two-page Chapter Planner outlines the instructional material that exists at the Unit, Chapter, and Lesson levels, including digital resources that are accessible at NGLSync.cengage.com.

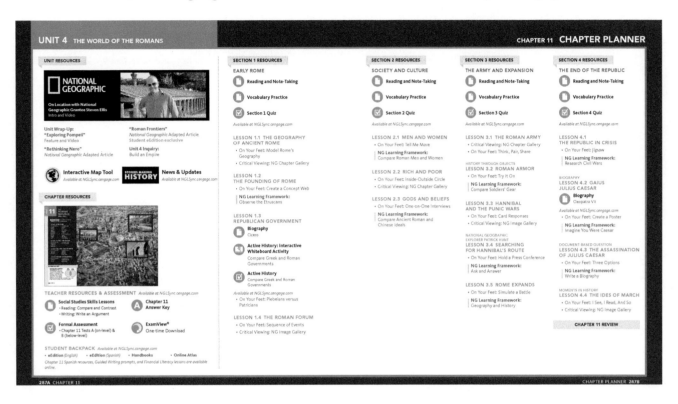

STRATEGIES FOR DIFFERENTIATION

Every student learns in his or her unique way. Five different types of Strategies for Differentiation help teachers appropriately engage every learner with the program content.

- Striving Readers
- Inclusion
- English Language Learners
- Gifted & Talented
- Pre-AP

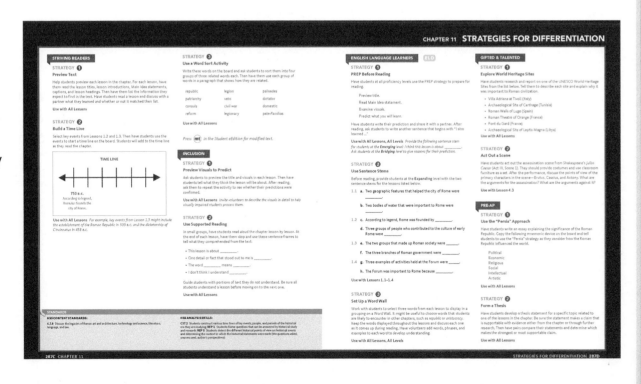

CHAPTER INTRODUCTION

The Chapter Introduction provides an entry point into the chapter, along with introductory activities and questions about the content.

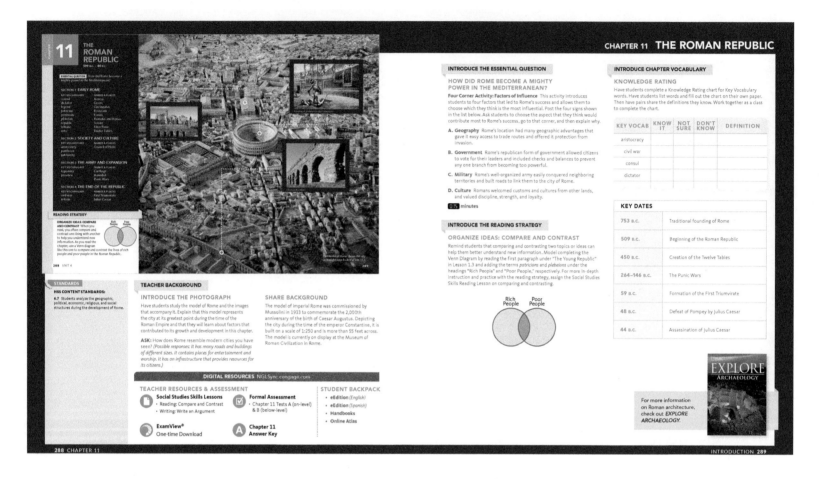

Teacher Background

- Background information helps introduce the Chapter Introduction visual.
- Supporting digital resources are available on myNGconnect.

Introduce the Essential Question

- A cooperative learning activity introduces the Essential Question and provides options for further inquiry.

Introduce the Reading Strategy

- A graphic organizer helps students focus their reading based on the chapter reading strategy.

Introduce Chapter Vocabulary

- A strategy-based activity helps introduce students to content-area vocabulary.

Key Dates

- Key dates correspond to the content in the chapter and serve as a handy chronological reference.

California Standards

- A list of HSS Content Standards and Analysis Skills is provided at point of use.

CHAPTER LESSONS

Lessons provide rich teacher material alongside Student Edition pages to make planning, teaching, and differentiating instruction easy.

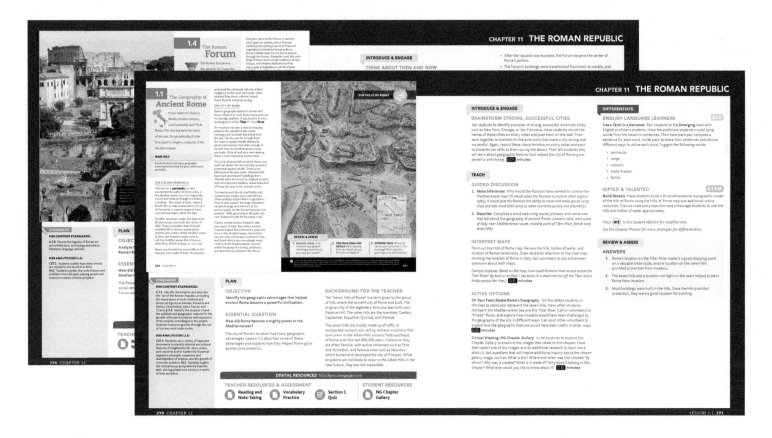

California Standards

- A list of HSS Content Standards and Analysis Skills is provided at point of use.

Plan

- Strong lessons center around a clear objective and relevant state standards.
- Consider the chapter's Essential Question as you teach each lesson.
- Valuable background information helps teachers prep for instruction.
- Supporting digital resources are available at NGLSync.cengage.com.

Introduce & Engage

- A quick activity invites student participation and serves as an entry point for lesson instruction.

Teach

- Guided Discussion questions build on lesson content.
- A lesson-based activity provides an option for students to interact with visuals or further process information.
- Active Options activities allow students to get up and move or explore the digital resources available at NGLSync.cengage.com

Differentiate

- Activities tailored to specific learning groups help all students explore the content appropriately and effectively.

Review & Assess

- Answers to Student Edition questions are provided for easy assessment of student comprehension.

CHAPTER REVIEW

The answers to Chapter Review questions along with corresponding HSS Content Standards and Analysis Skills are conveniently provided alongside the Student Edition pages so teachers can easily refer to chapter questions and answers.

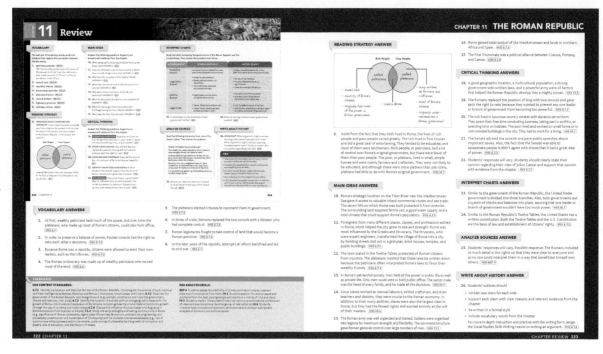

ANCILLARIES AND ASSESSMENT

In addition to the content in this Teacher's Edition, a wealth of supporting ancillaries and formal assessment options are provided at NGLSync.cengage.com.

Unit Resources
- National Geographic Explorer videos
- Additional adapted National Geographic articles
- Interactive Map Tool
- Formal Assessment Unit Tests

Chapter Resources
- Social Studies Skills Lessons (reading and writing)
- Formal Assessment Chapter Tests (two leveled versions)
- Chapter Answer Key (for ancillaries and assessment)
- ExamView® Assessment Software
- Backpack Page (containing Handbooks, the Online Atlas, and the Multilingual Glossary)

Lesson Resources
- Section Quizzes
- Reading and Note-Taking activities
- Vocabulary Practice activities
- Biographies
- Active History lessons (available as printable activity sheets or interactive whiteboard activities)

World history is filled with facts and dates—but that's only one aspect of studying history. It's equally as important for students to recognize the connections between the events of our past and their lives today. Two parts of the *National Geographic World History* program will especially help students make those connections: "Why Study History?" in the Student Edition and the separate Field Journal.

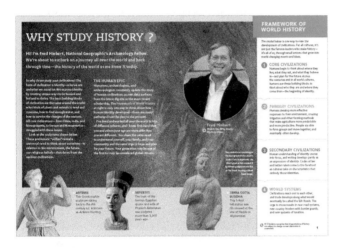

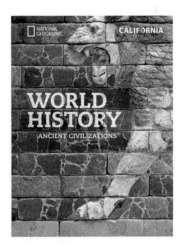

WHY STUDY HISTORY?

At the beginning of a history class, many students ask how studying the past could be relevant to them today. In *National Geographic World History*, "Why Study History?" tackles that question head-on and provides an introduction to and framework for the course right from the beginning of the text. The four-page "Why Study History" introduction sets up Dr. Fredrik Hiebert, National Geographic's Archaeologist-in-Residence and a consultant on this program, as the students' companion and guide. Fred's focus is on helping students understand the human identity as it developed over the course of various civilizations and as it plays out in their lives today.

After all, the critical questions we want students to explore are:

- What life lessons can I learn from past civilizations?

- What is my own unique identity?

- What does my identity have in common with others' experiences? How are we different, yes—but more importantly, how are we similar?

"Why Study History?" recurs roughly in the middle of the text and again at the end. Each occurrence of this feature in the print text is accompanied by a "Why Study History?" video.

FIELD JOURNAL

The Field Journal that accompanies *National Geogrpahic World History* is meant to be the student's space to comment on ideas raised in "Why Study History?" and the lessons in each chapter. Two types of lessons in the Student Edition are supported by Field Journal pages that provide intriguing questions and writing prompts. These lessons are:

- **History Through Objects lessons** featuring collections of artifacts

- **National Geographic Explorer lessons** featuring men and women doing critical research and exploration around the world

While not all students can memorize and recite the numerous dates and facts in a world history program, all students are capable of reacting to events and ideas and forming solid opinions, once they have been taught to use evidence to support those opinions—and once they have become persuaded that their opinions count. The Field Journal is their partner in that endeavor.

Students can record their thoughts about how they fit into the human story and raise questions they want to answer as they study world history. The Field Journal is key to helping students explore what it means to be a global citizen.

WHY STUDY HISTORY ?

❝ History is a living thing and students are part of it. They are stewards of the past—the protagonists of their own discoveries. ❞   —Dr. Fredrik Hiebert

WRITE ABOUT HISTORY

In order to succeed in their academic and professional lives, students must be able to write clearly and effectively in a variety of different modes—convincing arguments, meaningful informational/explanatory texts, and compelling narratives. Strong writers also need to take task, purpose, and audience into consideration and choose their words, information, organization, and format accordingly.

The "Write About History" prompts in the *National Geographic World History* Student Edition give students the opportunity to practice writing and defending claims while simultaneously showing what they have learned about events in world history. Each Chapter Review ends with a prompt that provides the support necessary to produce a well-crafted piece of academic writing.

Students are asked to produce one of three forms: a narrative, an informational/explanatory text, or an argument.

Instructions provide students with context for task, purpose, and audience.

Tips provide instruction on how to create the final product.

WRITE ABOUT HISTORY

26. **ARGUMENT** What arguments might a senator favoring Julius Caesar's assassination make? What arguments might a senator opposing his assassination make? Create an outline that lists points supporting each side.

TIPS

- Take notes from the chapter about Caesar's actions as a ruler and the manner of his death.

- Consider who benefited from Caesar's reforms and who benefited from his death.

- Consider how the Romans might have felt when Caesar declared himself dictator for life.

- Use vocabulary from the chapter in your outline.

- List the points that support assassination in the first part of your outline. List the points that support opposition to the assassination in the second part.

ASSESSMENT IN NATIONAL GEOGRAPHIC WORLD HISTORY

The California History-Social Science Framework distinguishes two types of assessment: formative and summative.

Formative assessment is assessment for learning. Its focus is to assist immediate learning, it is delivered from teacher to individual students, and it takes place during instruction or in the sequence of lessons.

Summative assessment is assessment of learning. Its focus is to measure students' progress and inform future teaching or to evaluate educational programs. Summative assessment takes place at the end of a unit, semester, or course.

Some tests or projects may serve both a formative and a summative purpose. Effective use of both formative and summative assessment enables teachers to create a positive feedback loop, in which you can use assessment results to differentiate instruction or determine which content or skills need to be retaught, and then customize future assessments to gauge learning of new and retaught material.

It is important, too, to engage in a variety of assessment modes. Some students may better demonstrate their understanding through performance assessments such as discussions, debates, or presentations. Others may be more accurately assessed using pencil-and-paper tests and writing assignments. Students should have chances to demonstrate their knowledge through both individual and cooperative assessments.

The activities and tests in *National Geographic World History* offer a generous variety of opportunities for both formative and summative assessment in numerous modes. The following assessments will enable you to support and measure learning at the lesson, chapter, and unit levels:

REVIEW & ASSESS Each lesson in the Student Edition ends with three questions that assess students' recall of the lesson's content and their ability to analyze it. You can use this quick formative assessment to help students develop their critical thinking skills and determine whether any concepts need to be reinforced or retaught.

GUIDED DISCUSSIONS AND ACTIVE OPTIONS For each lesson, this Teacher's Edition provides two Guided Discussion questions and an On Your Feet activity that requires students to either engage physically by moving in the classroom or perform collaborative activities such as fishbowl conversations, interviews, and inside-outside circles. By observing students and providing feedback, you can use these activities for formative assessment of content mastery, critical thinking skills, and discussion skills.

CHAPTER REVIEW Each chapter concludes with a Chapter Review that includes a short vocabulary test and a series of constructed-response items that require students to restate the main ideas in the chapter, engage in critical thinking, interpret a visual, analyze a primary source, and write an argument, informational/explanatory text, or narrative showing what they have learned about events in world history. This summative and formative assessment allows you to measure students' progress and determine any concepts that need to be reviewed.

UNIT TEST At the end of each unit, a summative assessment evaluates students' grasp of the main ideas and overarching themes of the unit. As in the Chapter Review, students answer historical thinking questions, interpret visuals, and analyze a primary source. In the extended response, students engage in comparative thinking as they compare two eras or themes in history.

PROJECT At the end of each unit, a Unit Inquiry can be used as a summative performance assessment. Teachers may use this project to assess students' research and presentation skills, as well as their content knowledge.

FORMAL ASSESSMENT Each section in a chapter concludes with a summative multiple-choice Section Quiz that assesses students' understanding of key concepts. Each chapter also concludes with a two-level Chapter Test that includes a mix of multiple-choice and constructed-response questions along with a document-based question. This formal summative assessment allows you to measure students' progress and give feedback in the form of a chapter grade.

The National Geographic Learning book series, *Explore* and *Global Issues,* align with much of the content of *World History: Ancient Civilizations*. Use these lists to see which *Explore* and *Global Issues* titles can be used to compliment *World History* chapters and lessons.

EXPLORE SERIES

EXPLORE ARCHAEOLOGY

aligns to these sections of **World History**

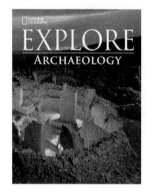

Chapter 2 Origins of Civilization

Chapter 3 Ancient Mesopotamia

Chapter 4 Ancient Egypt

Chapter 7 Ancient China

Chapter 9 Ancient Greece

Chapter 10 Classical Greece

Chapter 11 The Roman Republic

Chapter 12 The Roman Empire and Christianity

Chapter 13 The Byzantine Empire

Stories Making History Saving Cultural Heritage

Stories Making History Our Shared History

EXPLORE ANCIENT EGYPT

aligns to these sections of **World History**

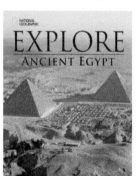

Chapter 4, Section 1
A Society on the Nile

Chapter 4, Section 2
The Old and Middle Kingdoms

Chapter 4, Section 3
The New Kingdom

Chapter 4, Section 4
The Egyptian Legacy

Stories Making History Our Shared History

EXPLORE CHINESE CIVILIZATION

aligns to these sections of **World History**

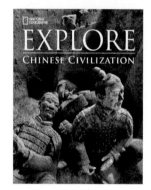

Chapter 7, Section 1
River Dynasties

Chapter 7, Section 2
China's Empires

Chapter 7, Section 3
East Meets West

EXPLORE THE MAYA

aligns to these sections of **World History**

Chapter 8, Lesson 2.1
Maya Social Structure

Chapter 8, Lesson 2.2
Maya Cities

Chapter 8, Lesson 2.3
Uncovering Maya Murals

Chapter 8, Lesson 2.4
Legacy of the Maya

Chapter 8, Lesson 2.5 Document Based Question: Creation Stories

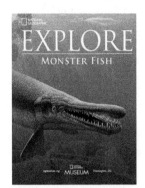

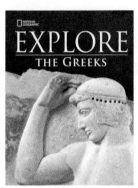

GLOBAL ISSUES SERIES

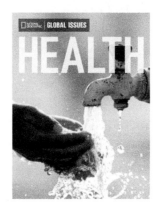

GLOBAL ISSUES: CLIMATE CHANGE

aligns to these sections of **World History**

ALL LEVELS

NG at Work: Exploring Antarctica's Ocean

Chapter 1, Lesson 1.3
Changing Environments

Chapter 1, Lesson 1.4
Moving into New Environments

GLOBAL ISSUES: WATER RESOURCES

aligns to these sections of **World History**

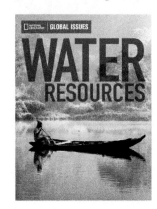

ON LEVEL

China's Powerful Rivers

Chapter 2, Lesson 1.3
China: Banpo

Chapter 7, Lesson 1.1
The Geography of Ancient China

ACTIVE LEARNING in the HISTORY CLASSROOM

Easily influenced by peers and distracted by text messaging and the lure of the latest handheld device, middle school learners can be challenging to reach. A class of middle school students is a highly diverse group of learners with myriad personalities and learning styles. Learners may be enthusiastic today and disengaged tomorrow, conversational one day and sullen the next.

Peggy Altoff

As you know from experience, a middle school teacher must be fully prepared to engage students each day and flexible enough to change plans at a moment's notice with the shifting classroom dynamic. National Geographic's *World History* program contains a wealth of teaching options that are perfect for the active teacher—and his or her active students.

VARIETY AND FLEXIBILITY

An expansive repertoire of proven strategies and appropriate activities provides the best preparation for each day's teaching. The structure of the Student Edition in this program is specifically designed to provide options that engage students in meaningful learning activities. The two-page format of each lesson in a chapter allows for several approaches, including

- selecting lessons and sections that are most appropriate for any given class of learners;

- focusing on one lesson each day to provide a depth of content knowledge;

- using cooperative learning activities that allow students to teach and learn from each other.

In a cooperative learning activity, for example, students can participate in a Jigsaw strategy in which groups of students become experts on one lesson in a chapter. Next, all expert groups switch into new groups with each new group having one "expert" on each lesson. Each expert is then responsible for teaching the others in the group about the lesson. (See *Cooperative Learning Strategies* in the Teacher's Edition for a complete explanation of the Jigsaw strategy.)

Another cooperative learning possibility involves breaking a lesson into segments by subheading. Most of the lessons in the Student Edition have two subheadings. This makes it easy for students to work in pairs, with each student reading and learning about information in one segment and then sharing and discussing with the other.

You may also consider having students work in pairs or small groups to discuss a **Review & Assess** question, a **Critical Viewing** question, or other text-based features. Experience suggests that each grouping strategy requires practice with students so that they can meet teacher expectations for appropriate conduct while acquiring knowledge of the content presented.

Student Edition activities are intended to address a variety of learning styles. The **Reading Strategy** at the beginning of each chapter provides students with a plan to organize and analyze what they are about to read. The **Review & Assess** questions at the end of each lesson provide skill practice with interpreting maps, analyzing visuals, sequencing events, and so on that can be completed individually, in small groups, or as a class. **Chapter Reviews** include a **Write About History** activity that requires students to demonstrate what they have learned through writing. A **Unit Wrap-Up** at the end of each unit offers students insight into the work of archaeologists, scientists, writers, and other experts. It also includes a **Unit Inquiry** assignment that asks students to present what they've learned using many different formats, including writing, video, and multimedia.

COMPONENTS FOR THE TEACHER

The Teacher's Edition of the *World History* program presents many possibilities for active learning and student engagement.

Cooperative Learning Strategies offers a preview of the types of strategies located throughout the Teacher's Edition with a clear explanation of how to implement each one. For the highly experienced teacher, this may offer a review of practical procedures. Those new to the profession will probably want to return to these pages frequently to plan new experiences for students.

The **Chapter Planner** in the Teacher's Edition provides an overview of the lesson support in each chapter and contains links to such tools as **Reading and Note-Taking, Vocabulary Practice, Social Studies Skills Lessons, Section Quizzes,** and **Formal Assessment Tests.** The **Strategies for Differentiation** tab offers ideas that engage striving readers, inclusion students, English language learners, gifted and talented students, and those in pre-Advanced Placement. You can decide how to apply each of these strategies to individual learners.

For daily planning, refer to each lesson's **Plan**, **Teach**, and **Differentiate** tabs. The Teach tab includes discussion questions and activities that help students summarize and analyze the lesson. It also contains an **Active Options** section that especially engages students with **Critical Viewing**, **National Geographic Learning Framework**, and (my personal favorite) **On Your Feet** activities. We know that middle school students are constantly moving and doing, and this feature provides you with ways to channel that bounding energy meaningfully.

Think carefully about how to select the options that are appropriate for your students. For me, Rule #1 in working with middle school students has always been to start simple and move toward the complex. It may not be a good idea, for example, to try to implement all of the available strategies and activities in one lesson. Start with those that make the most sense to you and gradually experiment with others. Inform students when you attempt a new strategy or activity and get their feedback on ways to improve it the next time. The activities and strategies found in this program are not meant to provide a recipe for success. Instead, they form a menu of options that support daily decision-making based on your own abilities and preferences and those of your students.

Striking images, graphics, and detailed maps engage and inform students.

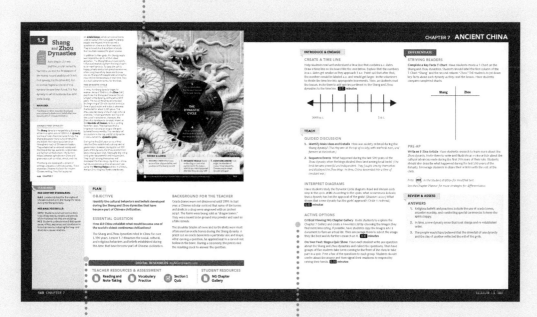

The press of a button or link opens up new activities and answers at point of use.

Teacher Notes in every lesson include extensive teacher and student resources.

SUPPORTING HISTORY
LEARNERS WITH TEXTS

As they study history, students learn how and where civilizations developed through the centuries. They learn how to think about the world and discover the ways in which cultures and civilizations are similar—and how they are unique. They come to understand that knowing why a civilization developed can help them interpret the past, analyze the present, and anticipate the future.

David W. Moore

History texts are major resources for middle school students, who are just learning to think and act like historians. Print and digital texts bring to life cultures, governments, and economic and geographic phenomena that often are too big, distant, and complex for students to experience firsthand. These texts also contribute insights and ways of thinking that deepen understandings of phenomena that can be experienced directly.

Research reviews published during the 2000s (Carnegie Council on Advancing Adolescent Literacy, 2010; Kamil et al., 2008; Torgeson et al., 2007) point to effective ways to support middle school instruction using texts. Two principles derived from these reviews underlie National Geographic's *World History* program: engage learners with considerate texts and engage learners in active processing.

ENGAGE LEARNERS WITH CONSIDERATE TEXTS

Considerate texts are reader-friendly materials that learners find understandable and memorable (Armbruster & Anderson, 1985). A key feature of such texts is the way in which they present important relationships (Armbruster, 2002). At a global level, this means helping readers see how big ideas and overarching themes unify what is presented (Goldman & Rakestraw, 2000). For example, the *World History* Teacher's Edition presents an essential question in each chapter, such as "What factors contributed to the development of civilization?" Teachers can use the questions to help students integrate concepts and bring structure to supporting details.

At a local level, considerate texts are well organized and clearly guide readers through their content (Goldman & Rakestraw, 2000).

This means providing explicit main idea statements, introductory paragraphs, and headings and subheadings and combining verbal and visual information (Mayer, 2001). For instance, a lesson in the program on ancient Egypt's daily life and religion begins with an introduction to the civilization's early religious practices. The headings that follow indicate that daily life in Egyptian society and Egyptian gods will be discussed one at a time. An image featuring ancient Egyptian gods and hieroglyphs is included to illustrate religious beliefs.

A considerate text is also appropriate for its audience: it connects with its readers' prior knowledge and interests (Armbruster, 2002). For example, a lesson in the program on changing environments during the Paleolithic Age explains how climate changes thousands of years ago altered the landscape in which Paleolithic people lived, forcing them to find new homes and adapt to new conditions. The lesson may interest students on several levels, encouraging them to reflect on the climate change many scientists believe is occurring today and recalling some of the adaptations they may have made when they moved to new places.

As digital communication technologies have emerged, definitions of texts have broadened (Coiro, Knobel, Lankshear, & Leu, 2008). Today, tools such as video screens, Web sites, and podcasts are merging with and often replacing books, paper, and pencils. Considerate digital texts offer readers the opportunity to combine information, including print and images. In line with these new digital resources, the *World History* program provides videos, a digital Student Edition, online handbooks, and interactive whiteboard materials and map tools.

ENGAGE LEARNERS IN ACTIVE PROCESSING

Considerate texts are crucial parts of instruction, but they are effective only when learners actively process them (Israel & Duffy, 2008; McNamara, 2007). For instance, learners actively process texts when they preview a lesson's contents, summarize what they have read, and synthesize what they have just learned with what they already know.

Texts can prompt learners to engage in active processing in several ways (Hartley, 2004). Interspersed questions are especially effective (Wood, Lapp, Flood, & Taylor, 2008). The *World History* program uses several types of questions. **Critical Viewing** questions regularly prompt learners to interpret images. **Review & Assess** questions at the end of each lesson encourage students to assess their understanding and think critically about what they have just read and viewed in the lesson. **Chapter Review** questions at the end of each chapter encourage active reconsideration of the chapter's main ideas, concepts, and visuals.

Text prompts that involve learners in writing and discussion also engage learners in active processing (Newell, 2008; Nystrand,

2006). *World History* provides regular opportunities for learners to write about texts through **Write About History** and **Synthesize and Write** prompts, structured reading and note-taking, and other social studies writing activities. The program also offers regular opportunities for learners to write and talk about texts through active options based on cooperative learning strategies.

Finally, differentiated text prompts generate active processing by accommodating learners with different levels of academic preparedness and approaches to learning (Tomlinson, 2005). The program's Teacher's Edition includes instructional strategies appropriate for English language learners, gifted and talented students, inclusion students, pre-Advanced Placement students, and striving readers.

The two principles underlying *World History* are complementary. Engaging learners with considerate texts goes far in promoting active processing, and engaging learners in active processing occurs best with considerate texts. As a result, the program provides middle school students with a meaningful introduction to history.

REFERENCES

Armbruster, B. B. 2002. Considerate text. In *Literacy in America: An encyclopedia of history, theory, and practice*, ed. B. J. Guzzetti, vol. 1, 97–99. Santa Barbara, Calif: ABC-CLIO.

Armbruster, B. B., and T. H. Anderson. 1985. Producing "considerate" expository text: Or, easy reading is damned hard writing. *Journal of Curriculum Studies* 17: 247–274.

Carnegie Council on Advancing Adolescent Literacy. 2010. *Time to act: An agenda for advancing adolescent literacy for college and career success*. New York: Carnegie Corporation of New York.

Coiro, J., M. Knobel, C. Lankshear, and D. J. Leu, eds. 2008. *Handbook of research on new literacies*. New York: Routledge.

Goldman, S. R., and J. A. Rakestraw, Jr. 2000. Structural aspects of constructing meaning from text. In *Handbook of reading research*, ed. M. L. Kamil, P. Mosenthal, P. D. Pearson, and R. Barr, vol. 3, 311–335. Mahwah, N.J.: Erlbaum.

Hartley, J. 2004. Designing instructional and informational text. In *Handbook of research in educational communications and technology*, ed. D. H. Jonassen, 917–947. 2d ed. Mahwah, N.J.: Erlbaum.

Hattie, J. 2009. *Visible learning: A synthesis of over 800 meta-analyses relating to achievement*. New York: Routledge.

Israel, S. E., and G. Duffy, eds. 2008. *Handbook of research on reading comprehension*. New York: Routledge.

Kamil, M. L., G. D. Borman, J. Dole, C. C. Kral, T. Salinger, and J. Torgesen. 2008. *Improving adolescent literacy: Effective classroom and intervention practices: A practice guide*. Washington, D.C.: Institute of Education Sciences, U.S. Department of Education. http://ies.ed.gov/ncee/wwc.

Mayer, R. E. 2001. *Multimedia learning*. New York: Cambridge University Press.

McNamara, D. S., ed. 2007. *Reading comprehension strategies: Theories, interventions, and technologies*. Mahwah, N.J.: Erlbaum.

Newell, G. E. 2008. Writing to learn: How alternative theories of school writing account for student performance. In *Handbook of writing* research, ed. C. A. MacArthur, S. Graham, and J. Fitzgerald, 235–247. New York: The Guilford Press.

Nystrand, M. 2006. Research on the role of discussion as it affects reading comprehension. *Research in the Teaching of English* 40: 392–412.

Tomlinson, C., ed. 2005. Differentiated instruction [special issue]. *Theory into Practice* 44(3).

Torgesen, J. K., D. D. Houston, L. M. Rissman, S. M. Decker, G. Roberts, S. Vaughn, J. Wexler, D. J. Francis, M. O. Rivera, and N. Lesaux. 2007. *Academic literacy instruction for adolescents: A guidance document from the Center on Instruction*. Portsmouth, N.H.: RMC Research Corporation, Center on Instruction. www.centeroninstruction.org.

Wood, K. D., D. Lapp, J. Flood, and D. B. Taylor. 2008. *Guiding readers through text: Strategy guides for new times*. Newark, Del: International Reading Association.

FOSTERING STUDENTS'
ABILITY TO WRITE ARGUMENTS

When the great Roman statesman, Cicero, and other supporters of the Roman Republic spoke about the role of government, they debated such questions as: What limits should be placed on the state's leaders? Who should have a say in making and passing the state's laws? What benefits should citizens in the state enjoy? What is their civic duty?

Michael W. Smith

These questions still resonate today. People have offered different answers to the questions and have provided arguments in their attempt to convince others to share their views. Arguments have always been central to public discourse. As Richard Andrews notes, "Imagine, for a moment, a world without argument. It would either be an authoritarian or tyrannical state. . . . [T]o be fully conscious, is to be ready for argumentation; for discussion 'with edge'" (2009, pp. 3–4).

Just as we want our society to be a place where intellect and differences are celebrated, so too do we want our classrooms to provide forums for vibrant intellectual exchanges. It is little wonder that schools place such an emphasis on argumentation. Turning to Andrews again: "[Argument] also refers to the most highly prized type of academic discourse: something that is deemed essential to a thesis, to an article in a research journal, to a dissertation, essay, and to many other kinds of writing within schools and the academy" (2009, p. 1).

In National Geographic's *World History* program, students do a variety of writing, but much of our instructional focus is on argument. If students are to understand why history matters, they need to engage in arguments that depend on historical knowledge. In so doing, they learn skills that prepare them not only for their future schooling but also for their lives outside of school.

THE RIGHT APPROACH

The **Social Studies Skills Writing Lessons** in the *World History* program teach students to write effective arguments by articulating the strategies experienced writers employ when they develop arguments. Students are then given extended practice in employing these strategies on their own.

The approach is in line with the recommendation of the *Writing Next* report, which found that the most powerful kind of writing instruction involves "explicitly and systematically teaching steps necessary for planning, revising, and/or editing text" (Graham & Perin, 2007, p. 15). The research of George Hillocks helps explain why this is so (cf. 1986, 1995, 2007, 2011). Throughout his writing, Hillocks draws a distinction between declarative knowledge, or knowledge that can be said, and procedural knowledge, or a kind of knowledge that has to be performed. That distinction is crucially important for, as Hillocks demonstrates again and again, declarative knowledge doesn't result in procedural knowledge. Knowing historical concepts does not mean that students can use them effectively in their writing. They have to be taught how to use them.

Unfortunately, much of the writing instruction students receive is not designed to help them develop procedural knowledge. Think back on how you were taught writing. My bet is that most of your teachers used what I call the Assign and Assess method. That is, you worked in class to develop knowledge on whatever the content of the class was and then your teachers assigned writing exercises that allowed you to display that knowledge. Finally, some weeks later, you received a grade on the assignment along with a few comments justifying the grade and providing instruction for future work.

Not only is the Assign and Assess method inadequate in helping students develop procedural knowledge, but it also may cause students to resist a teacher's efforts to help them improve. In his landmark study on childhood, psychoanalyst Erik Erikson offers an explanation for why students who need their teachers' help the most often do not seek it (1963). He identifies the central psychosocial conflict of school-age students, the stage of most students beginning middle school, as industry versus inferiority.

Middle school students are struggling to assert their competence. Pointing out where they went astray doesn't help them develop it.

My co-author Jeff Wilhelm and I repeatedly saw the importance of fostering students' competence in our study of the literate life of adolescent boys both in school and out (Smith & Wilhelm 2002). One young man provided what could have been a mantra for the whole group when we asked him why he liked playing lacrosse, his favorite outside-of-school activity: "I just like being good at it." If the young men in our study didn't feel competent in an activity, they chose not to engage in it.

Yet they did want to engage in argumentation. The young men we studied "did not want to play 'guess what the teacher already knows.' They wanted to solve problems, debate, and argue in ways through which they could stake their identity and develop both ideas and functional tools that they could share and use with others in very immediate ways. They wanted to develop the competence and capacities of real experts" (Smith & Wilhelm, p. 57).

AN ARGUMENTATION MODEL

The *World History* program helps students develop their expertise in writing effective arguments in several ways. First, Toulmin's model of argumentation, the one that informs the approach the program takes, is built on an understanding of how oral argumentation works in the real world (1958). Anyone who has spent any time with adolescents knows that they are avid and excellent arguers. The program helps them develop an articulated understanding of what they do all the time in their everyday life and then apply it to their writing. The National Commission on Writing calls for curricula to build bridges between students' in-school and out-of-school lives. This program does so.

Second, we provide lots of instruction and practice. Along with the **Social Studies Skills Writing Lessons**, the program contains **Write About History** and **Synthesize and Write** prompts that give students practice in mastering each element of Toulmin's model. We give them practice developing clear, specific, and reasonable claims. We help them understand how to provide specific evidence and how to explain the connection between the evidence and the claim. We work with them to anticipate and respond to counterarguments. We also help them master the sentence structures they will need to effectively express themselves. We then work with students to apply what they have learned to a variety of different kinds of arguments.

Third, we provide explicit instruction to help students successfully complete particular assignments. They learn to unpack the prompt, plan their paper, assess its effectiveness, and revise their argument.

A final thought experiment: Think of some complex activity you have mastered. Mastering it probably took time and instruction and practice. Writing arguments is a crucial and complex skill. *World History* provides students the time, instruction, and practice they need to become competent at it. No comparable textbook does the same.

REFERENCES

Andrews, R. 1979. *The importance of argument in education.* London: Institute of Education, University of London.

Erikson, E. 1963. *Childhood and society,* 2d ed. New York: Norton.

Hillocks, G., Jr. 1986. *Research on written composition: New directions for teaching.* Urbana, Ill: ERIC and National Conference for Research in English.

Hillocks, G., Jr. 1995. *Teaching writing as reflective practice.* New York: Teachers College Press.

Hillocks, G., Jr. 2007. *Narrative writing: Learning a new model for teaching.* Portsmouth, N.H.: Heinemann.

Hillocks, G., Jr. 2011. *Teaching argument writing: Supporting claims with relevant evidence and clear reasoning.* Portsmouth, N.H.: Heinemann.

National Commission on Writing. *Writing and school reform.* http://www.writingcommission.org.

Smith, M. W., and J. Wilhelm. 2002. *"Reading don't fix no Chevys": Literacy in the lives of young men.* Portsmouth, N.H.: Heinemann.

Smith, M. W., and J. Wilhelm. 2006. *Going with the flow: How to engage boys (and girls) in their literacy learning.* Portsmouth, N.H.: Heinemann.

Toulmin, S. 1958. *The uses of argument.* Cambridge, England: Cambridge University Press.

PROJECT-BASED LEARNING

Project-based learning is integral to successful history–social studies instruction. Well-designed projects allow students to:

- explore a topic in depth

- hone their skills in research, analysis, and critical thinking

- work collaboratively with others toward a shared goal—an ability that is highly valued in both academic circles and the professional marketplace

- become engaged and enthusiastic about a social studies topic

- exercise creative control over their final product

In addition, teachers may use projects to assess both students' grasp of content and their progress in developing collaboration and critical thinking skills.

The best projects allow students to express themselves creatively but also guide them through a rigorous, structured process of inquiry and research.

ENGAGE LEARNERS WITH CONSIDERATE TEXTS

The National Council for the Social Studies (NCSS) details the process of inquiry in the "College, Career, and Civic Life Framework for Social Studies State Standards," or C3 Framework. The document proposes an "Inquiry Arc," that enumerates four dimensions of the process:

1. **Developing Questions and Planning Inquiries.** Teachers or students generate a compelling question to guide their research and supporting questions to help them seek out specific evidence. The Essential Question at the beginning of each chapter in National Geographic World History is designed to spark inquiry-style thinking in students as they move through the text.

2. **Applying Disciplinary Concepts and Tools.** Students determine which disciplines—economics, civics, geography, or history—relate to their guiding and follow-up questions. The tools and concepts from these disciplines will enable them to seek out and analyze evidence.

3. **Evaluating Sources and Using Evidence.** Students conduct their research, determine which sources are both useful and reliable, and locate relevant evidence they can use for claims and counterclaims.

4. **Communicating Conclusions and Taking Informed Action.** Students shape and present their final projects, which may take a wide variety of forms such as traditional essays, multimedia presentations, performance pieces, virtual museum galleries, etc. When a project relates to a present-day issue, students may also follow up on their conclusions by taking constructive action within the school or in the wider community.

Of necessity, some projects during the school year will be smaller in scope and may not emphasize all four dimensions of the Arc. For example, the inquiry question may be determined in advance by the teacher, or students may be directed to use the textbook or other preselected sources for their research. Similarly, students' choices of methods for communicating their conclusions may be limited to a few options that take less time to produce.

National Geographic World History offers a variety of options for inquiry and project-based learning:

- At the end of each unit, a Unit Inquiry challenges students with open-ended questions and guides them to gather evidence from the text, synthesize a response, and present their conclusion to the class in a creative, engaging format. Teachers may choose to expand the scope of the Unit Inquiry by having students conduct independent research in other sources or explicitly apply concepts from more than one discipline in their presentations. Alternately, you might choose to limit the scope of the project by limiting students' options for presenting their projects.

- The National Geographic Learning Framework Activities that appear throughout this Teacher's Edition also offer multiple opportunities for inquiry and creative thought. Depending on students' needs, you might select an activity and explicitly guide the class through the four dimensions of the Inquiry Arc to complete it, or you might have students complete the activities independently or in small groups.

RESEARCH SKILLS

Developing good research skills benefits students both inside and outside the classroom. Learning how to locate and evaluate information helps them improve the critical thinking skills they need not only to make and support an argument within a social studies project, but also to make well-considered decisions in their everyday lives. Students can hone their research skills through instruction, guidance, and a great deal of practice.

Before launching the first inquiry project, you should make sure students understand the differences between quantitative and qualitative research:

- **quantitative research:** "hard evidence"—numbers, facts, and figures that can support an assertion

- **qualitative research:** opinions from scholars, scientists, and other experts; firsthand accounts of events; information that provides insights into reasons or motivations

You might also explain that quantitative research answers the questions *who*, *what*, *where*, and *when*. Qualitative research helps answer the questions *why* and *how*.

Social studies inquiry projects should incorporate both types of research. Often, it is qualitative research that enables students to form hypotheses or outline their arguments. Both qualitative and quantitative research can be used to support claims and counterclaims. Teachers should provide examples of sources students can use to conduct both types of research. For example, government websites, scientific articles, newspaper articles, and encyclopedia entries can be mined for quantitative information. Qualitative information can be found in firsthand accounts of historical events and analyses of those events written by scholars. Of course, many sources contain both types of information, and students might benefit from an activity in which they review an article to distinguish the qualitative and quantitative information it contains.

Similarly, at the beginning of the year, teachers should provide numerous examples of both reliable and unreliable sources and clearly explain the characteristics of each. You might also provide a list of approved sources for students to use or have students submit their sources before they proceed to gather evidence. As students gain confidence and skill, you can gradually release to them the responsibility for finding and evaluating sources.

The two principles underlying *World History* are complementary. Engaging learners with considerate texts goes far in promoting active processing, and engaging learners in active processing occurs best with considerate texts. As a result, the program provides middle school students with a meaningful introduction to history.

USING KEY INSTRUCTIONAL STRATEGIES

The California History–Social Science Framework recommends a variety of instructional strategies to support students' development of reading and thinking skills and content mastery. This Teacher's Edition provides. Many of these are cooperative learning strategies for partners, small groups, or the whole class. At right are some additional strategies you might implement across all units or in selected chapters to support and engage students.

Vocabulary

The first page of each chapter includes a list of the Key Vocabulary terms students will find as they read. Review the vocabulary terms with the class. Point out that some terms are important names, places, and events (e.g., Augustus, the Pax Romana), while others are general vocabulary words they will need to understand the chapters (e.g., *aqueduct, emperor*). The latter are Tier Two and Tier Three words for the most part. Read all the Key Vocabulary terms aloud so that students can hear the pronunciation of those unfamiliar to them. Read each general vocabulary word and have students raise their hands if they understand it. Ask students to define the words or use them in a sentence. Then encourage students to make as many connections as they can between the words and their own lives (e.g., "Dad says it's my *duty* to babysit my siblings sometimes.").

Critical Viewing

Have groups of students briefly discuss how the image at the start of each chapter is related to what they will learn. One student should be the note-taker and record the group's responses. When the class has finished reading the chapter, have the groups reconvene and examine the image again. Ask them to discuss whether they would change or expand their responses based on what they have learned. Have students share their responses with the class.

WHILE READING A CHAPTER

Reading Strategy

Assign partners to make a copy of the graphic organizer illustrated in the chapter reading strategy. At the end of each lesson, allow partners time to briefly discuss their reading and update the graphic organizer. You may wish to have partners compare their graphic organizers with other pairs before they complete the review activities at the end of the chapter. Consider varying your pairing strategy, sometimes placing more advanced learners with students who are struggling or with emerging or expanding English learners (ELs), and sometimes pairing advanced learners and challenging them to find as many entries for their graphic organizers as possible.

Collaborative Conversations

The "Teach" section that accompanies each lesson in this Teacher's Edition offers a variety of cooperative learning opportunities in the Guided Discussions and Active Options. Use these activities to introduce and practice the skills and concepts of collaborative conversations. The California History–Social Science Framework outlines some behaviors students should practice in order to have productive conversations. At the beginning of the year, explain these behaviors to students:

- Listen actively—Make eye contact and use body language to convey attentiveness.

- Use meaningful transitions—Make it clear to your classmates that you are reacting to their ideas by using transitions that indicate agreement/ disagreement, clarification, building on an idea, etc.

- Ensure that all members of the group participate.

- Take risks—Explore ideas that may be challenging and questions that have no easy answers.

- Focus on the prompt—Group members should help each other stay on topic.

- Use textual evidence—Cite specific evidence from the text to support your points.

- Keep an open mind—Consider all viewpoints presented in the conversation and be ready to change your opinion if someone presents solid evidence to support a claim.

Monitor conversations and provide feedback on students' use of these behaviors. As the year progresses, transfer responsibility for monitoring and rating their conversational skills to the students.

You may wish to provide sentence frames at the start of the year to help students use meaningful transitions and to support the participation of ELs and students who feel insecure about speaking up in a group. The California History–Social Science Framework contains an extensive list of sentence frames that you may select and customize for your class.

Analyze Author's Choices

Engage students in discussions analyzing the choices of visuals to illustrate the regular lessons and the special features such as "History Through Objects" and "Moments in History." Ask questions such as: What do these particular objects tell about the role of the legionary in the Roman Empire? What other objects could have been included in this feature? Why did the author choose to use an illustration or diagram instead of a photograph or fine art in this lesson? Questions such as these help students reach for a deeper understanding of the material and practice interrogating other texts such as primary sources.

AFTER READING A CHAPTER

Chapter Review

Use the Chapter Review to assess students' mastery of the content, and review lessons as necessary. You may wish to have students work in pairs to complete some of the items. In particular, consider pairing emerging or expanding ELs with more proficient readers for the Analyze Sources item. Encourage ELs to ask questions about words or structures they find difficult and have the partners answer to the best of their ability. This process will enable both students to gain a deeper understanding of the primary source passage.

COOPERATIVE LEARNING STRATEGIES

Cooperative learning strategies transform today's classroom diversity into a vital resource for promoting students' acquisition of both challenging academic content and language. These strategies promote active engagement and social motivation for all students.

STRUCTURE & GRAPHIC	DESCRIPTION	BENEFITS & PURPOSES
CORNERS A B A strongly agree B disagree C agree D strongly disagree C D	• Corners of the classroom are designated for focused discussion of four aspects of a topic. • Students individually think and write about the topic for a short time. • Students group into the corner of their choice and discuss the topic. • At least one student from each corner shares about the corner discussion.	• By "voting" with their feet, students literally take a position about a topic. • Focused discussion develops deeper thought about a topic. • Students experience many valid points of view about a topic.
FISHBOWL	• Part of the class sits in a close circle facing inward; the other part of the class sits in a larger circle around them. • Students on the inside discuss a topic while those outside listen for new information and/or evaluate the discussion according to pre-established criteria. • Groups reverse positions.	• Focused listening enhances knowledge acquisition and listening skills. • Peer evaluation supports development of specific discussion skills. • Identification of criteria for evaluation promotes self-monitoring.
INSIDE-OUTSIDE CIRCLE	• Students stand in concentric circles facing each other. • Students in the outside circle ask questions; those inside answer. • On a signal, students rotate to create new partnerships. • On another signal, students trade inside/outside roles.	• Talking one-on-one with a variety of partners gives risk-free practice in speaking skills. • Interactions can be structured to focus on specific speaking skills. • Students practice both speaking and active listening.
JIGSAW Expert Group 1 — A's Expert Group 2 — B's Expert Group 3 — C's Expert Group 4 — D's	• Group students evenly into "expert" groups. • Expert groups study one topic or aspect of a topic in depth. • Regroup students so that each new group has at least one member from each expert group. • Experts report on their study. Other students learn from the experts.	• Becoming an expert provides in-depth understanding in one aspect of study. • Learning from peers provides breadth of understanding of over-arching concepts.

STRUCTURE & GRAPHIC	DESCRIPTION	BENEFITS & PURPOSES
NUMBERED HEADS	• Students number off within each group. • Teacher prompts or gives a directive. • Students think individually about the topic. • Groups discuss the topic so that any member of the group can report for the group. • Teacher calls a number and the student with that number reports for the group.	• Group discussion of topics provides each student with language and concept understanding. • Random recitation provides an opportunity for evaluation of both individual and group progress.
ROUNDTABLE	• Seat students around a table in groups of four. • Teacher asks a question with many possible answers. • Each student around the table answers the question a different way.	• Encouraging elaboration creates appreciation for diversity of opinion and thought. • Eliciting multiple answers enhances language fluency.
TEAM WORD WEBBING	• Provide each team with a single large piece of paper. Give each student a different colored marker. • Teacher assigns a topic for a word web. • Each student adds to the part of the web nearest to him/her. • On a signal, students rotate the paper and each student adds to the nearest part again.	• Individual input to a group product ensures participation by all students. • Shifting point of view support both broad and in-depth understanding of concepts.
THINK, PAIR, SHARE	• Students think about a topic suggested by the teacher. • Pairs discuss the topic. • Students individually share information with the class.	• The opportunity for self-talk during the individual think time allows the student to formulate thoughts before speaking. • Discussion with a partner reduces performance anxiety and enhances understanding.
THREE-STEP INTERVIEW	• Students form pairs. • Student A interviews Student B about a topic. • Partners reverse roles. • Student A shares with the class information from Student B; then B shares information from Student A.	• Interviewing supports language acquisition by providing scripts for expression. • Responding provides opportunities for structured self-expression.

Cross-disciplinary Teaching, Building Communities of Teachers, and Connecting with Parents

CROSS-DISCIPLINARY TEACHING

The California History–Social Science Framework states, "In addition to the disciplinary understanding and content knowledge outlined in the California History–Social Science Standards, HSS teachers also bear a shared responsibility for their students' overall literacy development, as outlined by the California Common Core State Standards for English Language Arts and Literacy in History/Social Studies, Science, and Technical Subjects (CA CCSS for ELA/Literacy) and the California English Language Development Standards (CA ELD Standards)."

National Geographic World History includes numerous features to support students' reading development, including explicit vocabulary instruction, text within the Lexile band recommended by the Common Core State Standards, and differentiation notes in the Teacher's Edition to help teachers scaffold comprehension for striving readers. At the beginning of the year, you can identify striving readers in the class and provide ongoing support, such as additional vocabulary help and small-group time during which students can ask questions. Advanced readers can be offered activities from the Teacher's Edition differentiation notes for Gifted & Talented and Pre-AP students.

This Teacher's Edition also provides differentiation activities to customize instruction for emerging, expanding, and bridging English Learners (ELs). To support English language development (ELD), teachers should establish ongoing routines such as previewing the lessons to identify language that may be challenging to ELs and providing specific help with these passages, working with small groups of ELs, and occasionally pairing ELs with more proficient readers. You might also collaborate with the ELD teacher to incorporate content or language from the current *National Geographic World History* lesson. Where possible, it is valuable to encourage ELs to share the connections they can make between social studies content and their own experiences or home culture. This practice creates speaking opportunities for ELs and allows them to experience the rewards of making a unique and useful contribution to the classroom conversation.

History–social studies topics often lend themselves to cross-disciplinary lessons with concepts in science, technology, engineering, and math (STEM). Annotations throughout this Teacher's Edition highlight opportunities to connect to STEM instruction. You can also encourage students to look for such connections on their own and point them out to the class.

BUILDING COMMUNITIES OF TEACHERS AND CONNECTING TO PARENTS

Connections both within and outside of the school are essential to successful history–social studies instruction. Within the school, teachers and administrators should form a "community of practice," a concept proposed by Jean Lave and Etienne Wenger in 1991. A community of practice consists of people working in the same field collaborating to solve problems, expand the boundaries of their knowledge, and improve their practice. Working as a community, the teachers within a school can develop ways to integrate learning across disciplines and address the particular needs of their students.

Outside of school, parents can be the most helpful members of students' learning community. At the beginning of the year, teachers should reach out to parents with an invitation to support and participate in students' learning. You might use the letter on the following page to introduce *National Geographic World History*, or you may prefer to write your own letter. You can follow up with regular updates throughout the year explaining what students will be learning in the upcoming unit. The updates can encourage parents to help students read the more challenging passages in the book and act as sounding boards as students work out their own ideas. Parents can also offer invaluable learning opportunities by helping students make connections between unit topics and their own lives or family histories.

Dear Family,

Your student is about to embark on a fascinating, year-long exploration of ancient civilizations. Studying these civilizations brings students into contact with the diverse, brilliant, and brave individuals and groups of people whose actions led to the development of civilization as we know it today. Understanding our world and its past will also help your student become an informed global citizen of the 21st century. In addition, during the course of this year, your student will learn important reading, writing, and analytical skills that will support success both in and outside of school.

The textbook program your student will use, *National Geographic World History: Ancient Civilizations*, was designed and written to take advantage of the expertise of National Geographic writers, historians, archaeologists, and explorers. Woven throughout the chapters is National Geographic's mission to share knowledge about the world we live in and prepare students for their roles as active and engaged citizens.

The teaching philosophy of the *World History* program is based on the National Geographic Learning Framework (NGLF). This framework defines learning goals and core principles to equip students with the tools for successful learning. According to the NGLF, students should learn certain attitudes and skills, in addition to the knowledge found in textbooks. The attitudes are curiosity, responsibility, and empowerment. The skills are observation, communication, collaboration, and problem-solving. These attitudes and skills enable students not only to be better learners but also to navigate the world as competent consumers and decision makers.

As a parent, your support is key to your student's success in social studies class this year. Ask your student to show you *National Geographic World History: Ancient Civilizations* and spend some time familiarizing yourself with its features. The textbook is illustrated with a rich variety of photos, maps, and fine art. Each time your student begins a new chapter, look at the images together and discuss the ones you find most striking. Make yourself available to help if your student encounters reading passages that are challenging, and offer to listen when your student is working through ideas for an essay or project.

Most important, make time to simply talk about the topics, events, and people featured in *National Geographic World History: Ancient Civilizations*. Help your student find the connections between the topics in the textbook and his or her own experiences, interests, or family history. Together, you will discover your family's own global identity.

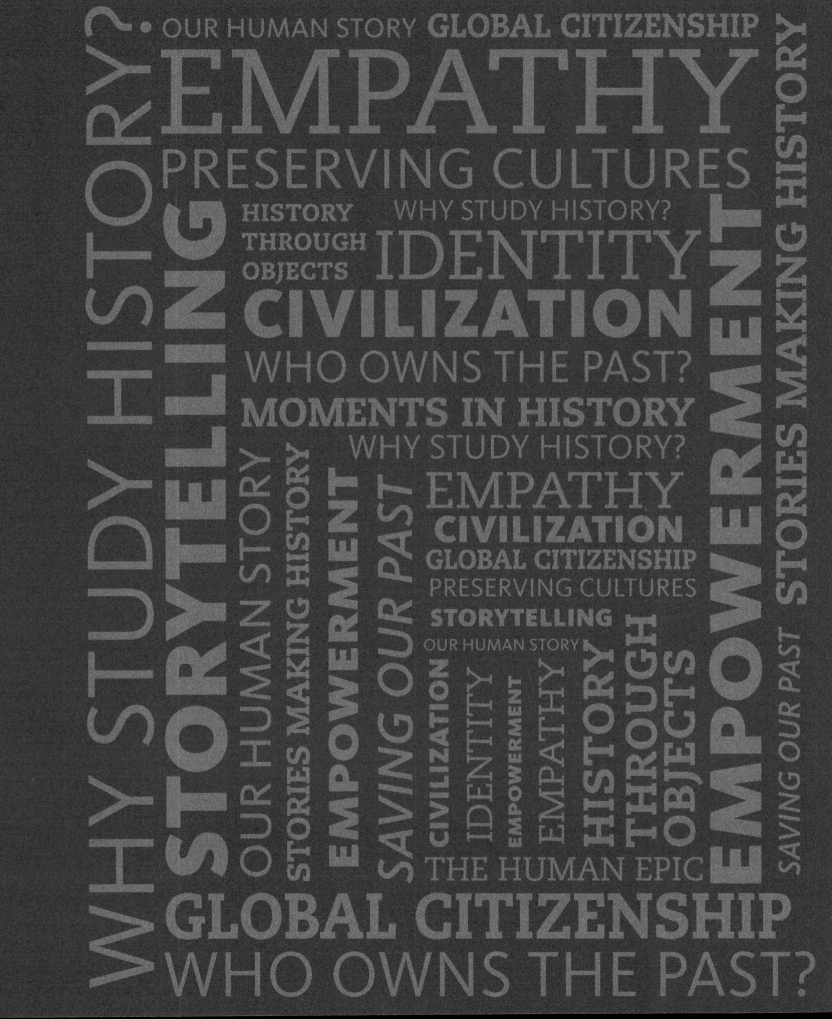

WHY STUDY HISTORY ?

☐ **Dr. Fredrik Hiebert**
Archaeology Fellow,
National Geographic Society

UNIT 1

ORIGINS OF CULTURES AND CIVILIZATIONS

(175,000 B.C.—3000 B.C.)

UNIT 2

EARLY CIVILIZATIONS

(3000 B.C.—A.D. 950)

UNIT 3

GREEK CIVILIZATION

(2000 B.C.—323 B.C.)

UNIT 4

THE WORLD OF THE
ROMANS

(509 B.C.—A.D. 1453)

The world changes on a daily basis, and National Geographic is there. Join three National Geographic voices as they tell the stories of three current global events. Learn about these newsworthy topics, discuss what might come next, and think about how these events impact you, the place you live, and the people you know—your global citizenship.

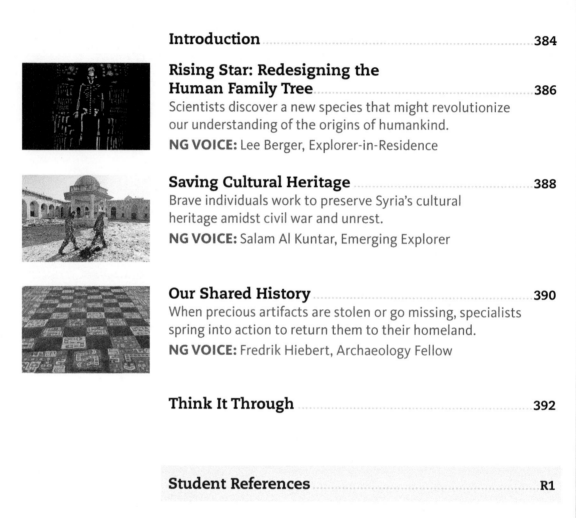

SPECIAL FEATURES

Patrick Hunt

Bronze Flying Horse

Statue of Julius Caesar

THE MAURYA EMPIRE, c. 250 B.C.

DOCUMENT-BASED QUESTIONS

TIME LINES, CHARTS, MODELS, GRAPHS, INFOGRAPHICS

MOMENTS IN HISTORY

Terra Cotta Warriors

GEOGRAPHER'S TOOLBOX

THE GEOGRAPHER'S TOOLBOX

Geographic Thinking

SPATIAL THINKING

Geography is about more than the names of places on a map. It involves spatial thinking, or thinking about the space on Earth's surface. Geographers use spatial thinking to ask questions, such as:

- **Where is a place located?**
- **Why is this location significant, or important?**
- **How does this place influence the people who live there?**
- **How do the people influence the location?**

By asking and answering these questions and many others, geographers can find patterns. Geographic patterns are similarities among places. The location of large cities near water is one example of a geographic pattern. Many geographers use computer-based Geographic Information Systems (GIS) to study patterns, such as those that affect population distribution, economic development, the spread of diseases, and water resources. They create maps and analyze their patterns using many layers of data.

The photo below shows the fertile land alongside the Nile River in Egypt. Thousands of years ago, many people settled along this river. They farmed along its shores and traveled and traded on its waters. In time, a great civilization grew in the Nile River Valley: the civilization of ancient Egypt.

Other ancient settlements and civilizations rose in river valleys in many parts of the world. Geographers note this pattern and others when they think spatially.

The Nile River is still a vital resource for present-day Egypt.

+ **GUIDED DISCUSSION**

1. **Interpret Maps** Project the Fertile Crescent and Nile River Valley maps from the Online Atlas. **ASK:** What rivers do the maps show? *(The maps show the Tigris, Euphrates, and Nile rivers.)* What geographic pattern do these rivers show? *(They all flow into larger bodies of water. The Tigris and the Euphrates flow into the Persian Gulf, and the Nile flows into the Mediterranean.)*

2. **Make Inferences** Do you think the land along the Tigris and Euphrates rivers is similar to or different from the land along the Nile (as shown in the photograph)? *(The land is probably similar-green and fertile.)* How do you know this? *(because like the Nile, a civilization also developed along the Tigris and Euphrates rivers, which implies that the land was good for farming)*

CATEGORIZE

Explain that while geographers use spatial thinking, historians use chronological thinking. Read each of the following statements aloud. Discuss whether each is an example of spatial thinking or chronological thinking.

- The agricultural revolution began in Mesoamerica around 4250 B.C. *(chronological)*

- Paleolithic people migrated from Africa to Southwest Asia. *(spatial)*

- The Carthaginian general Hannibal crossed over the Alps from Spain in order to invade the Italian peninsula. *(spatial)*

THINK LIKE A GEOGRAPHER

Summarize What are geographic patterns, and how do geographers find them?

+ **THINK LIKE A GEOGRAPHER**

ANSWER

Geographic patterns are similarities among places. Geographers find geographic patterns by using computer-based Geographic Information Systems.

Geographic Thinking THEMES AND ELEMENTS

Geographers ask questions about how people, places, and environments are arranged and connected on Earth's surface. The five themes and six elements will help you categorize, or group, information.

THE FIVE THEMES OF GEOGRAPHY

Geographers use five themes to categorize similar geographic information.

1. **Location** provides a way of locating places. Absolute location is the exact point where a place is located. Geographers use a satellite system called the Global Positioning System (GPS) to find absolute location. Relative location is where a place is in relation to other places. For example, the Great Wall of China is located near Beijing in northern China.

2. **Place** includes the characteristics of a location. A famous place in the western United States is the Grand Canyon. It has steep rock walls that were carved over centuries by the Colorado River.

3. **Human-Environment Interaction** explains how people affect the environment and how the environment affects people. For example, people throughout much of history have built dams to change the flow of rivers.

4. **Movement** explains how people, ideas, and animals move from one place to another. The spread of different religions around the world is an example of movement.

5. **Region** involves a group of places that have common characteristics. A region can be as big as a continent such as North America, which includes the United States, Canada, and Mexico. A region can also be as small as a neighborhood.

THE SIX ESSENTIAL ELEMENTS

In addition to the five themes, some geographers also identify essential elements, or key ideas, to study physical processes and human systems.

1. **The World in Spatial Terms** Geographers use tools such as maps to study places on Earth's surface.

2. **Places and Regions** Geographers study the characteristics of places and regions.

3. **Physical Systems** Geographers examine Earth's physical processes, such as earthquakes and volcanoes.

4. **Human Systems** Geographers study how humans live and what systems they create, such as economic systems.

5. **Environment and Society** Geographers explore how humans change the environment and use resources.

6. **The Uses of Geography** Geographers interpret the past, analyze the present, and plan for the future.

THINK LIKE A GEOGRAPHER

Make Inferences How do geographers use the themes and elements to better understand the world?

THINK LIKE A GEOGRAPHER
ANSWER
They use the themes and elements to categorize similar geographic information.

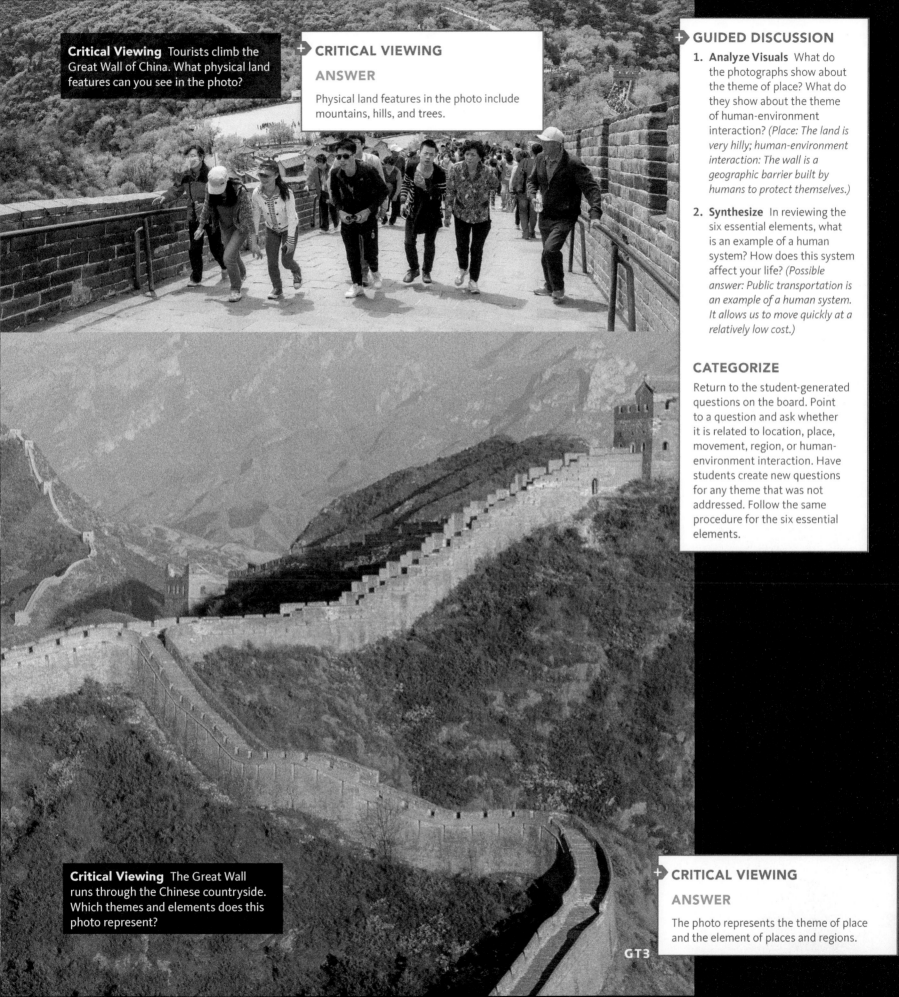

Critical Viewing Tourists climb the Great Wall of China. What physical land features can you see in the photo?

Critical Viewing The Great Wall runs through the Chinese countryside. Which themes and elements does this photo represent?

Geographic Thinking CONTINENTS

In 1413, a Chinese admiral and explorer, Zheng He, sailed from China to Arabia. When he arrived in Arabia, he saw people dressed in ways he had never seen. Yet, like him, these people wanted to trade.

Zheng He came to understand that regions of Earth have similarities and differences. The places within a region are linked by trade, culture, and other human activities. They also share similar physical processes and characteristics, such as climate.

As you've read, a region often contains an entire continent. A continent is a large landmass on Earth's surface. Geographers have identified seven continents: Africa, Asia, Australia, Europe, North America, South America, and Antarctica.

Geographers study the world's continents, but they also take a global perspective when they investigate Earth. They might, for instance, study ocean currents around the globe or how one region affects another. Both ways of looking at the world add to our understanding of it.

THINK LIKE A GEOGRAPHER

Draw Conclusions Why do geographers study the world by dividing it into continents?

THINK LIKE A GEOGRAPHER

ANSWER

Geographers divide the world into continents to learn about similarities and differences among them.

GUIDED DISCUSSION

1. **Monitor Comprehension** What characteristics do places within the same region have in common? (*They have similar human activities and physical processes.*)

2. **Interpret Maps** Have students look at the world map. **ASK:** What geographic factors separated North America and South America from Europe and Asia earlier in history? What effect do you think the separation had on the cultures of the Americas? (*The Americas were separated from Europe and Asia by long ocean distances. The separation meant that cultures in the Americas developed in different ways from those in Europe and Asia.*)

INTERPRET MAPS

Have students measure the distance in miles from western Europe to eastern Asia. Tell them that the route they measure must go around southern Africa. (*The distance is approximately 16,000 miles.*) Discuss the obstacles that traders working centuries ago would have had in trading goods between the two regions. **ASK:** How has technology increased trade between the two regions today? (*Huge cargo ships and aircraft make trade faster and more efficient.*)

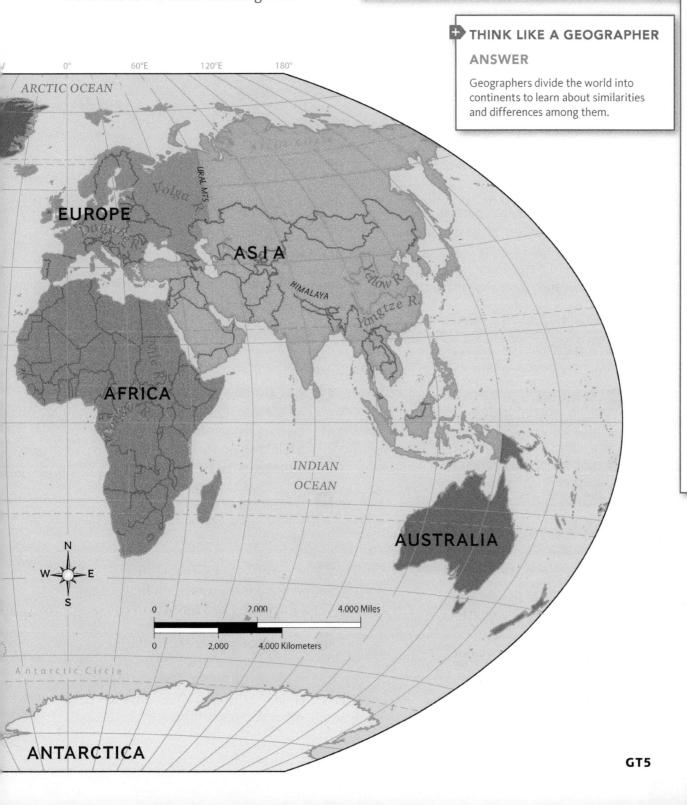

ARCTIC OCEAN

EUROPE

ASIA

URAL MTS

Volga

Danube R.

HIMALAYA

Yellow R.

Yangtze R.

AFRICA

Nile R.

Congo R.

INDIAN OCEAN

AUSTRALIA

N
W   E
S

ANTARCTICA

Antarctic Circle

0°   60°E   120°E   180°

0   2,000   4,000 Miles
0   2,000   4,000 Kilometers

GT5

Maps ELEMENTS OF A MAP

Have you ever needed to figure out how to get to a friend's house? Maybe you usually use the GPS on your phone to navigate such distances, but imagine that the only resource you had was a globe. In order to see enough detail to find your friend's house, the globe would have to be enormous—much too big to carry around in your pocket!

GLOBES AND MAPS

A three-dimensional, or spherical, representation of Earth is called a globe. It is useful when you need to see Earth as a whole, but it is not helpful if you need to see a small section of Earth.

Now imagine taking a part of the globe and flattening it out. This two-dimensional, or flat, representation of Earth is called a map. Maps and globes are different representations of Earth, but they have similar features.

MAP AND GLOBE FEATURES

Ⓐ A **title** tells the subject of the map or globe.

Ⓑ **Symbols** represent information such as natural resources and economic activities.

Ⓒ **Labels** are the names of places, such as cities, countries, rivers, and mountains.

Ⓓ **Colors** represent different kinds of information. For example, the color blue usually represents water.

Ⓔ **Lines of latitude** are imaginary horizontal lines that measure the distance north or south of the equator.

Ⓕ **Lines of longitude** are imaginary vertical lines that measure the distance east or west of the prime meridian.

Ⓖ A **scale** shows how much distance on Earth is represented by distance on the map or globe. For example, a half inch on the map above represents 100 miles on Earth.

Ⓗ A **legend,** or key, explains what the symbols and colors on the map or globe represent.

Ⓘ A **compass rose** shows the directions north (N), south (S), east (E), and west (W).

Ⓙ A **locator globe** shows the specific area of the world that is shown on a map. The locator globe on the map above shows where Germany is located.

LATITUDE

Lines of latitude are imaginary lines that run east to west, parallel to the equator. The equator is the center line of latitude. Distances north and south of the equator are measured in degrees (°). There are 90 degrees north of the equator and 90 degrees south. The equator is 0°. The latitude of Berlin, Germany, is 52° N, meaning that it is 52 degrees north of the equator.

LONGITUDE

Lines of longitude are imaginary lines that run north to south from the North Pole to the South Pole. They measure distance east or west of the prime meridian. The prime meridian runs through Greenwich, England. It is 0°. There are 180 degrees east of the prime meridian and 180 degrees west. The longitude of Berlin, Germany, is 13° E, meaning that it is 13 degrees east of the prime meridian.

Remember that absolute location is the exact point where a place is located. This point includes a place's latitude and longitude. For example, the absolute location of Berlin, Germany, is 52° N, 13° E. You say this aloud as "fifty-two degrees North, thirteen degrees East."

HEMISPHERES

A hemisphere is half of Earth. The equator divides Earth into the Northern Hemisphere and the Southern Hemisphere. North America is entirely in the Northern Hemisphere. Most of South America is in the Southern Hemisphere.

The Western Hemisphere is west of the prime meridian. The Eastern Hemisphere is east of the prime meridian. South America is in the Western Hemisphere. Most of Africa is in the Eastern Hemisphere.

THINK LIKE A GEOGRAPHER

Monitor Comprehension How are maps and globes different? How is each one used?

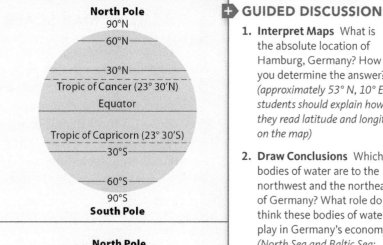
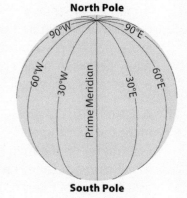
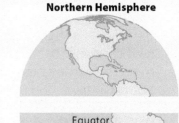
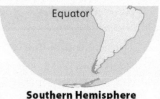

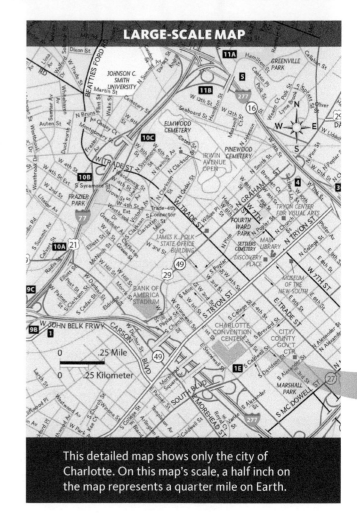
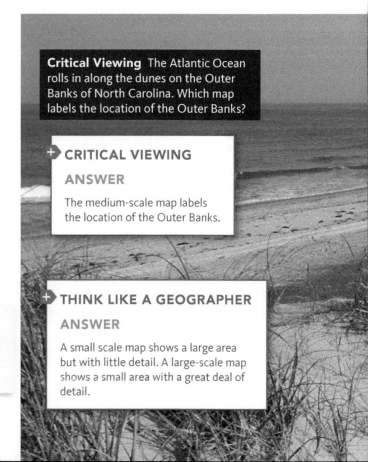

CREATE SKETCH MAPS

To introduce the idea of scale, have students create sketch maps of their classroom on letter-sized paper. Before beginning this activity, measure the dimensions of the classroom. Then ask students to sketch quickly, taking no more than five minutes. When students have finished their sketch maps, tell them the dimensions of the classroom. Ask them how many feet in the actual classroom are represented by one inch on their sketch maps. Have them write "1 inch = x feet" in one of the lower corners of their map. Explain to them that they have just created a scale for their sketch map.

Maps MAP SCALE

On a walk through a city, such as Charlotte, North Carolina, you might use a highly detailed map that shows only the downtown area. To drive up the Atlantic coast, however, you would use a map that covers a large area, including several states. These maps have different scales.

INTERPRETING A SCALE

A map's scale shows how much distance on Earth is shown on the map. A large-scale map covers a small area but shows many details. A small-scale map covers a large area but includes few details.

A scale is usually shown in both inches and centimeters. One inch or centimeter on the map represents a much larger distance on Earth, such as a number of miles or kilometers.

To use a map scale, mark off the length of the scale several times on the edge of a sheet of paper. Then hold the paper between two points to see how many times the scale falls between them. Add up the distance.

PURPOSES OF A SCALE

The scale of a map should be appropriate for its purpose. For example, a tourist map of Washington, D.C., should be large-scale, showing every street name, monument, and museum.

Maps of any scale show geographic patterns. The map of Washington, D.C., for instance, would show that many government buildings are in one area.

THINK LIKE A GEOGRAPHER

Summarize What are the purposes of a small-scale map and a large-scale map?

LARGE-SCALE MAP

This detailed map shows only the city of Charlotte. On this map's scale, a half inch on the map represents a quarter mile on Earth.

Critical Viewing The Atlantic Ocean rolls in along the dunes on the Outer Banks of North Carolina. Which map labels the location of the Outer Banks?

CRITICAL VIEWING

ANSWER

The medium-scale map labels the location of the Outer Banks.

THINK LIKE A GEOGRAPHER

ANSWER

A small scale map shows a large area but with little detail. A large-scale map shows a small area with a great deal of detail.

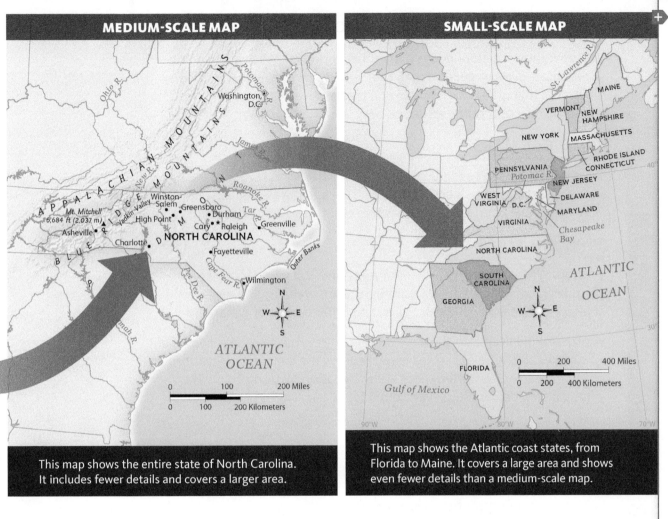

MEDIUM-SCALE MAP

This map shows the entire state of North Carolina. It includes fewer details and covers a larger area.

SMALL-SCALE MAP

This map shows the Atlantic coast states, from Florida to Maine. It covers a large area and shows even fewer details than a medium-scale map.

+ GUIDED DISCUSSION

1. **Synthesize** If an architect were designing a new subway station on one block of a city, what scale map would he or she use? What natural and human-made features would the map probably show? *(It would be a large-scale map showing details such as bedrock, underground water, pipes, and sewers.)*

2. **Interpret Maps** Which map would you use to find Raleigh, the capital of North Carolina? How far is Raleigh from the eastern boundary of the state? How far is it from the western boundary? Why is its location significant? *(medium-scale map; Raleigh is approximately 180 miles from the eastern boundary and 300 miles from the western boundary; it is in the approximate center of the state)*

CATEGORIZE

Place students into groups of three or four for this activity. Ask each group to create a three-column chart with the headings "Large-Scale Maps," "Medium-Scale Maps," and "Small-Scale Maps." Then, in each column, have students list three examples from their own experience with each type of map, including the sketch map they created earlier. Ask volunteers to present their charts to the class. Discuss why each map listed is large-scale, medium-scale, or small-scale.

Maps POLITICAL AND PHYSICAL

The governor of a state needs a map that shows counties and cities. A mountain climber needs a map that shows cliffs, canyons, and ice fields. Cartographers, or mapmakers, create different kinds of maps for these different purposes.

POLITICAL MAPS

A political map shows features that humans have created, such as countries, states, provinces, and cities. These features are labeled, and lines show boundaries, such as those between countries.

PHYSICAL MAPS

A physical map shows natural features of physical geography. It includes landforms, such as mountains, plains, valleys, and deserts. It also includes oceans, lakes, rivers, and other bodies of water.

A physical map can also show elevation and relief. Elevation is the height of a physical feature above sea level. Relief is the change in elevation from one place to another. Maps show elevation by using color. The physical map below uses seven colors for seven ranges of elevation.

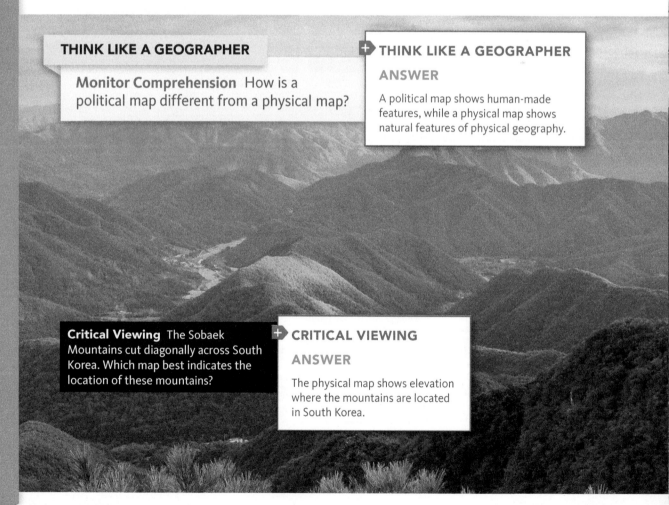

THINK LIKE A GEOGRAPHER

Monitor Comprehension How is a political map different from a physical map?

➕ THINK LIKE A GEOGRAPHER

ANSWER

A political map shows human-made features, while a physical map shows natural features of physical geography.

Critical Viewing The Sobaek Mountains cut diagonally across South Korea. Which map best indicates the location of these mountains?

➕ CRITICAL VIEWING

ANSWER

The physical map shows elevation where the mountains are located in South Korea.

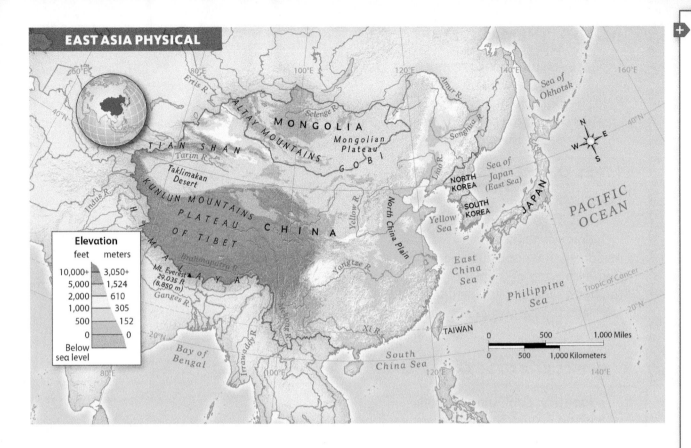

EAST ASIA PHYSICAL

Elevation

feet	meters
10,000+	3,050+
5,000	1,524
2,000	610
1,000	305
500	152
0	0
Below sea level	

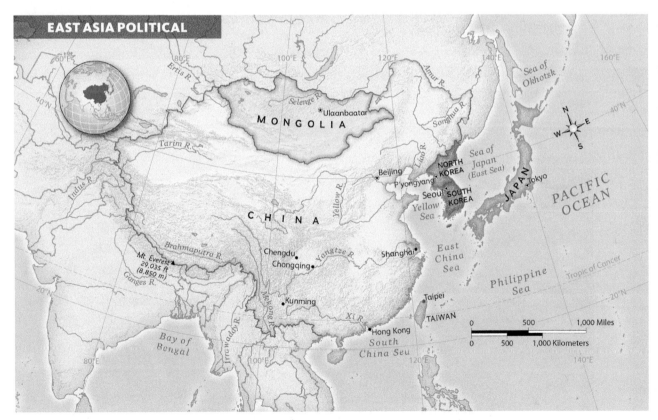

EAST ASIA POLITICAL

GUIDED DISCUSSION

1. **Interpret Maps** What information does the legend of the physical map of East Asia provide? Why doesn't the political map of East Asia need a legend? *(The legend of the physical map includes land elevation. The political map shows capitals, cities, and international boundaries. Since these are clear on the map, a legend is not necessary.)*

2. **Analyze Cause and Effect** What are the physical features of western China? How do these features help explain the absence of cities there? *(Western China is mountainous and has deserts, which could be inhospitable to building thriving communities. It is also far from the ocean.)*

COMPARE AND CONTRAST

Divide the class into two groups. Ask one group to create an itinerary, or touring plan, through East Asia, including Japan, South Korea, China, and Mongolia. Have students draw the itinerary on a large outline map. Then ask the other half of the class to create a political map showing where the tour of East Asia will go. For example, if the itinerary takes them to Beijing, they should add Beijing to the outline map of East Asia.

CREATE A THEMATIC MAP

On an interactive whiteboard, draw an outline map of the school. Ask the class to show different activities of the school on the map, such as academics and athletics. Suggest that they use symbols or colors to show the activities, and that they create a legend with symbols for the following:

- Classroom
- Offices
- Gymnasium
- Auditorium
- Cafeteria
- Library

Explain that they have just completed a thematic map, which is a map that focuses on a specific topic.

THINK LIKE A GEOGRAPHER

ANSWER

Answers will vary. Students may identify theme maps including those that show trade routes, migration patterns, or battles.

Maps THEMATIC MAPS

Suppose you wanted to create a map showing the location of sports fields in your community. You would create a thematic map, which is a map about a specific theme, or topic.

TYPES OF THEMATIC MAPS

Thematic maps are useful for showing a variety of geographic information, including economic activity, natural resources, and population density. Common types of thematic maps are the point symbol map, the dot density map, and the proportional symbol map.

THINK LIKE A GEOGRAPHER

Identify Look through your world history textbook and identify an example of a thematic map. What geographic information does the map show?

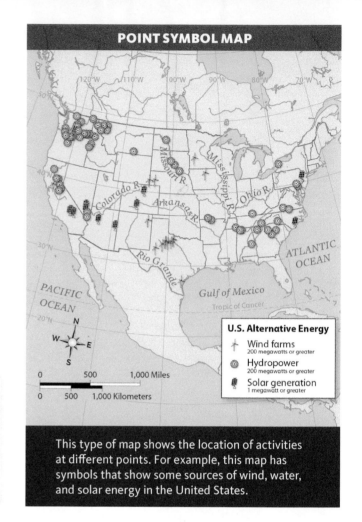

POINT SYMBOL MAP

U.S. Alternative Energy

↑ Wind farms
200 megawatts or greater

⊙ Hydropower
200 megawatts or greater

▯ Solar generation
1 megawatt or greater

This type of map shows the location of activities at different points. For example, this map has symbols that show some sources of wind, water, and solar energy in the United States.

DOT DENSITY MAP

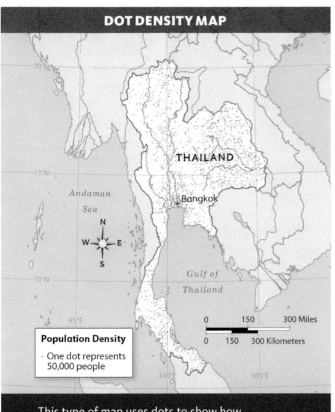

THAILAND

Bangkok

Andaman Sea

Gulf of Thailand

Population Density

· One dot represents 50,000 people

0   150   300 Miles
0   150   300 Kilometers

This type of map uses dots to show how something is distributed in a country or region. Each dot represents an amount. For example, each dot on this map represents 50,000 people living in Thailand.

PROPORTIONAL SYMBOL MAP

Earthquake Magnitude

7.3–7.6
6.8–7.2
6.3–6.7
5.5–6.2

0   150   300 Miles
0   150   300 Kilometers

Manila

Cebu

PHILIPPINES

Davao

This type of map uses symbols of different sizes to show the size of an event. For example, the size of the circles on this map shows the severity of earthquakes in the Philippines.

➕ **GUIDED DISCUSSION**

1. **Interpret Maps** In the U.S. Alternative Energy map, what are the three different kinds of energy sources? How are they represented on the map? *(wind farms—picture of a wind turbine; hydropower—picture of a turbine; solar generation— picture of a solar panel)*

2. **Interpret Maps** In the Thailand's Population Density map, what does each dot represent? What is the most heavily populated area of Thailand? *(Each dot represents 50,000 people. The most heavily populated area is Bangkok.)*

3. **Interpret Maps** In the Philippines' Earthquakes map, what do the different sizes of dots represent? Which city is most at risk for earthquakes? *(Large dot—magnitude of 7.3–7.6; second dot—6.8–7.2; third dot—6.3–6.7; fourth dot—5.5–6.2. Manila is most at risk.)*

UNDERSTAND DISTRIBUTION

Explain the term *distribution*— how something is divided up, or where things are located or how many there are. Thematic maps can show distributions with symbols or colors. Point out that charts, graphs, and databases also show distributions, using numbers or other data. Have students pose and answer a question about geographic distribution shown in the map of Thailand or the Philippines.

Solar panels in the Nevada desert absorb light from the sun and turn it into energy.

Maps MAP PROJECTIONS

The world is a sphere, but maps are flat. As a result, maps distort, or change, shapes, areas, distances, and directions found in the real world. To reduce distortion, mapmakers use projections, or ways of showing Earth's curved surface on a flat map. Five common map projections are the azimuthal, Robinson, Mercator, Winkel Tripel, and homolosine. Each projection has strengths and weaknesses—each distorts in a different way.

When cartographers make maps, they need to choose a map projection. The type of projection depends on the map's purpose. Which elements are acceptable to distort? Which are not acceptable to distort? For example, if a cartographer is creating a navigation map, it is important that direction should not be distorted. It may not matter, however, if some areas or shapes are distorted.

THINK LIKE A GEOGRAPHER

Make Inferences How do cartographers decide which projection to use?

AZIMUTHAL PROJECTION

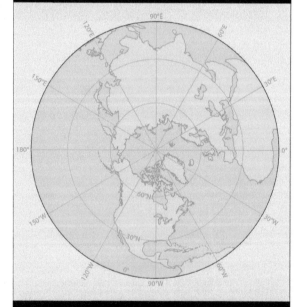

Mapmakers create the azimuthal projection by projecting part of the globe onto a flat surface. The projection shows directions accurately but distorts shapes. It is often used for the polar regions.

MERCATOR PROJECTION

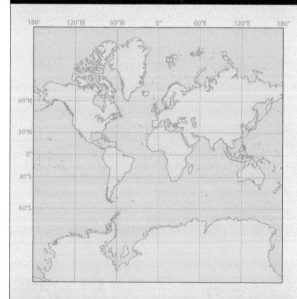

The Mercator projection shows much of Earth accurately, but it distorts the shape and area of land near the North and South poles. This projection shows direction accurately, so it is good for navigation maps.

HOMOLOSINE PROJECTION

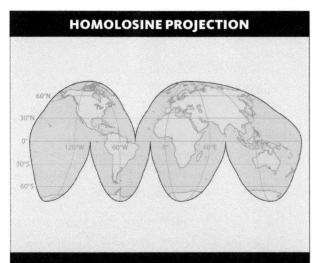

The homolosine projection resembles the flattened peel of an orange. It accurately shows the shape and area of landmasses by cutting up the oceans. However, it does not show distance accurately.

ROBINSON PROJECTION

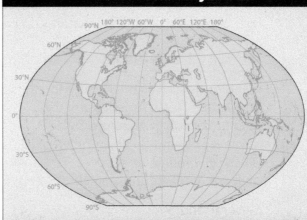

The Robinson projection combines the strengths of other projections. It shows the shape and area of the continents and oceans with reasonable accuracy. However, the North and South poles are distorted.

WINKEL TRIPEL PROJECTION

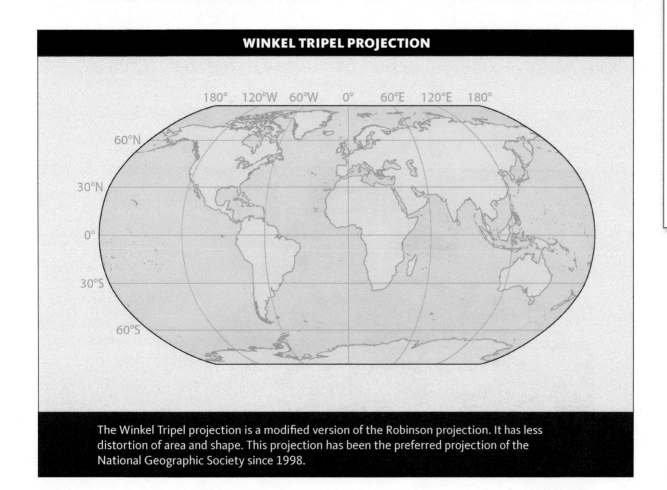

The Winkel Tripel projection is a modified version of the Robinson projection. It has less distortion of area and shape. This projection has been the preferred projection of the National Geographic Society since 1998.

➡ GUIDED DISCUSSION

1. **Compare and Contrast** Tell students that Africa has approximately 11,724,000 square miles, while Antarctica has approximately 5,500,000 square miles. **ASK:** In the Mercator projection, what is the size of Africa in relation to Antarctica? How does the map create the wrong impression about Africa? *(Even though Africa is larger, it looks much smaller than Antarctica.)*

2. **Draw Conclusions** How does Australia appear in the Mercator projection, the homolosine projection, the Robinson projection, and the Winkel Tripel projection? What does this tell you about countries near the equator on maps with these projections? *(Australia is approximately the same size on all four maps. There is less distortion of maps near the equator.)*

MORE INFORMATION

Map Distortions The four characteristics of a map that can be distorted are shape, area, distance, and direction. To remember these characteristics, use the following acronym: "Geographers are SADD (Shape, Area, Distance, Direction) because they can't make a perfect map of the world."

K-W-L CHART

Have students create a K-W-L chart for the landforms described in this lesson. Print out copies of a K-W-L chart and distribute to students. Give students the opportunity to go back to their charts to fill in information they learn during the lesson.

GEOGRAPHER'S TOOLBOX

Physical Geography EARTH'S LANDFORMS

The Rocky Mountains rise more than 14,000 feet above sea level. The Grand Canyon is more than 5,000 feet deep. Both are landforms, or physical features on Earth's surface.

SURFACE LANDFORMS

Landforms such as the Rocky Mountains in western North America and the Grand Canyon in Arizona provide a variety of physical environments. These environments support millions of plants and animals.

Several landforms are commonly found on Earth's surface. A mountain is a high, steep elevation. A hill also slopes upward but is less steep and rugged. In contrast, a plain is a level area. The Great Plains, for example, are flat landforms stretching from the Mississippi River to the Rocky Mountains. A plateau is a plain that sits high above sea level and usually has a cliff on all sides. A valley is a low-lying area that is surrounded by mountains.

OCEAN LANDFORMS

Earth's oceans also have landforms that are underwater. Mountains and valleys rise and fall along the ocean floor. Volcanoes erupt with hot magma, which hardens as it cools to form new crust.

The edge of a continent often extends out under the water. This land is called the continental shelf. Most of Earth's marine life lives at this level of the ocean. Beyond the continental shelf, the land develops a steep slope. Beyond the slope, before the ocean floor, the land slopes slightly upward. This landform is called the continental rise. It is formed by rocks and sediment carried by ocean currents. Together, these landforms are known as the continental margin.

A butte is a hill or mountain with steep sides and a flat top. These buttes in Monument Valley, Arizona, are called "the Mittens."

THE CONTINENTAL MARGINS

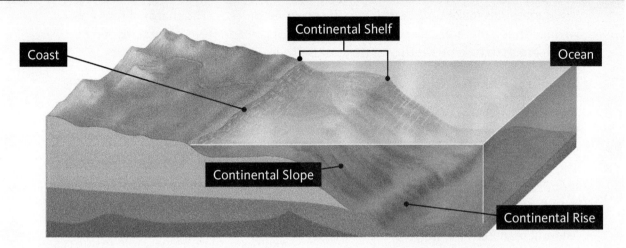

Coast

Continental Shelf

Ocean

Continental Slope

Continental Rise

THE CHANGING EARTH

Earth is always changing, and the changes affect plant and animal life. For example, a flood can cause severe erosion, which can ruin farmers' fields. Erosion is the process by which rocks and soil slowly break apart and are swept away.

THINK LIKE A GEOGRAPHER

Draw Conclusions How do physical processes reshape Earth's landforms?

GUIDED DISCUSSION

1. **Find Main Idea and Details** What is erosion, and how does it change landforms? *(Erosion is the process by which soil and rocks gradually break apart and are swept away. Erosion gradually changes all landforms. For example, it can change plains by wearing away soil.)*

2. **Synthesize** How would living in a mountainous area or living on a plain affect the ways in which people make a living? *(Responses will vary, but students may suggest that people on plains will probably farm while those in mountainous areas might work in forests or in ski resorts.)*

ANALYZE VISUALS

Project photographs from the Internet that show the natural wonders of the ancient world. Ask students to identify what kinds of landforms they see. **ASK:** How is each landform created? How might erosion change the landform? *(Possible response: Mountains such as the Himalaya were formed when tectonic plates collided against each other. Erosion might gradually wear down the mountains.)*

THINK LIKE A GEOGRAPHER

ANSWER

Weather, such as wind, rain, or sun, breaks down soil and rocks and sweeps them to other places.

GT17

Physical Geography   NATURAL RESOURCES

What materials make up a pencil? Wood comes from trees. The material that you write with is a mineral called graphite. The pencil is made from natural resources, which are materials on Earth that people use to live and to meet their needs.

EARTH'S RESOURCES

There are two kinds of resources. Biological resources are living things, such as livestock, plants, and trees. These resources are important to humans because they provide us with food, shelter, and clothing.

Mineral resources are nonliving resources buried within Earth, such as oil and coal. Some mineral resources are raw materials, or materials used to make products. Iron ore, for example, is a raw material used in making steel. The steel, in turn, is used to make skyscrapers and automobiles.

CATEGORIES OF RESOURCES

Geographers classify resources in two categories. Nonrenewable resources are resources that are limited and cannot be replaced. For example, oil comes from wells that are drilled into Earth's crust. Once a well runs dry, the oil is gone. Coal and natural gas are other examples of nonrenewable resources.

Renewable resources never run out, or a new supply develops over time. Wind, water, and solar power are all renewable. So are trees because a new supply can grow to replace those that have been cut down.

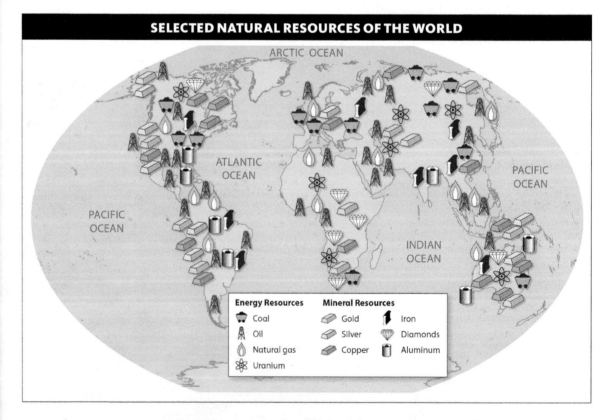

SELECTED NATURAL RESOURCES OF THE WORLD

Natural resources are an important part of everyday life, yet countries with a large supply are not always wealthy. Nigeria, for example, is a major supplier of oil, but seven out of every ten Nigerians live in poverty. Japan is one of the wealthiest countries in the world—yet it must import oil from other countries.

Pumpjacks pump oil at a field in California.

516

1. **Interpret Maps** What resources are found in the northern parts of Russia, Europe, and North America? What effect do you think latitude has on gathering these resources? *(copper, iron, oil, natural gas, silver, diamonds; it is difficult to gather resources because of cold temperatures and long winters)*

2. **Identify and Explain** Iron is used in the making of steel. In which countries are iron deposits found? How do you think the countries benefit from having iron deposits? *(China, Russia, Australia, India, the United States, Brazil; they are able to build steel mills and have the iron available to produce steel)*

COMPARE AND CONTRAST

Lead students in creating a Venn diagram to compare and contrast renewable and nonrenewable resources. **ASK:** As you think about each kind of resource, ask yourselves where the resource comes from. How is the resource used? Are new forms of the resource available? *(Possible response: Renewable resource—trees, used for lumber, new forms are constantly available; Nonrenewable resource—natural gas, used to heat buildings, may not be available for much longer)*

THINK LIKE A GEOGRAPHER

Monitor Comprehension
Why are natural resources important?

THINK LIKE A GEOGRAPHER

ANSWER

Natural resources are important because people use them to live and to meet their basic needs.

GT19

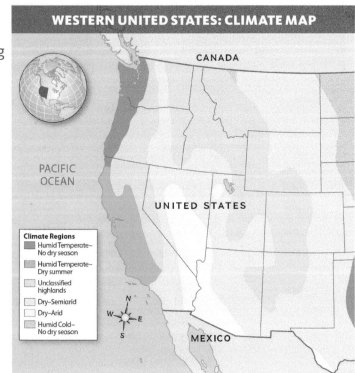

WEATHER QUICKWRITE

Have students take two minutes to write about their most memorable weather-related experience. Then ask volunteers to share what they wrote. **ASK:** How does weather affect your everyday life? How do you adapt to changes in the weather? *(Sample response: The weather affects how I dress. In the summer, I usually wear shorts, while in the winter, I have to wear a coat.)* Explain to students that in this lesson, they will learn about weather and climate. Emphasize that both help shape Earth's environments.

GEOGRAPHER'S TOOLBOX

Physical Geography CLIMATE AND WEATHER

People who live in Sacramento, California, have mild winters. When they go skiing in the nearby Sierra Nevada Mountains, they wear parkas to protect themselves from the colder temperatures. They have adapted to a different climate.

CLIMATE ELEMENTS

Climate is the average condition of the atmosphere over a long period of time. It includes average temperature, average precipitation, and the amount of change from one season to another. For example, Fairbanks, Alaska, has a cold climate. In the winter, the temperature can reach -8°F. Yet the temperature can rise to 90°F in the summer. The city goes through changes from one season to another.

Four factors that affect a region's climate are latitude, elevation, prevailing winds, and ocean currents. Places at high latitudes, such as Fairbanks, experience more change between winter and summer. Places close to the equator have nearly the same temperature throughout the year. Places at higher elevations have generally colder temperatures than places closer to sea level.

Prevailing winds are winds coming from one direction that blow most of the time. In Florida in the summer, the prevailing winds come from the south, making a warm climate even hotter.

Ocean currents also affect climate. The Gulf Stream is a current that carries warm water from the Caribbean Sea toward Europe. Air passing over the water becomes warm and helps create a mild winter climate in England and Ireland.

WEATHER CONDITIONS

Weather is the condition of the atmosphere at a particular time. It includes the temperature, precipitation, and humidity for a particular day or week. Humidity is the amount of water vapor in the air. If a weather forecaster says the humidity is at 95 percent, he or she means that the air is holding a large amount of water vapor.

Weather changes because of air masses. An air mass is a large area of air that has the same temperature and humidity. The boundary between two air masses is called a front. If a forecaster talks about a warm, humid front, he or she usually means that thunderstorms are headed toward the area.

WESTERN UNITED STATES: CLIMATE MAP

CANADA

PACIFIC OCEAN

UNITED STATES

Climate Regions
- Humid Temperate– No dry season
- Humid Temperate– Dry summer
- Unclassified highlands
- Dry–Semiarid
- Dry–Arid
- Humid Cold– No dry season

N W E S

MEXICO

CRITICAL VIEWING

ANSWER

It suggests that the weather is cold and snowy.

Critical Viewing Skiers head to the top of Clouds Rest in Yosemite National Park, California. What does the photo suggest about the weather at this location?

GUIDED DISCUSSION

1. **Describe Geographic Information** In the region where you live, how does the climate vary from one season to another? How do these variations affect animal behavior and plants in your region? *(Responses will vary, but students should discuss how seasonal changes affect both animals and plants.)*

2. **Identify Problems and Solutions** In the region where you live, what problems are caused by the weather? How do people attempt to solve those problems? *(Responses will vary, but students should discuss problems such as tornadoes, blizzards, and droughts. One problem-solving approach for blizzards is for communities to have snowplows to clear away snow.)*

COMPARE AND CONTRAST

To ensure that students understand the difference between climate and weather, read the following statements aloud and ask students to explain whether each applies to climate or weather. Have students look at the Western United States: Climate and Weather maps to help them determine the difference.

- Tomorrow, we are going to have a high temperature of 90°F with light winds from the west. *(weather)*

- Phoenix, Arizona, always has long, hot summers, when the temperature can reach 110°F. *(climate)*

- During the Little Ice Age, Europe experienced extremely cold temperatures from about 1560 to 1850. *(climate)*

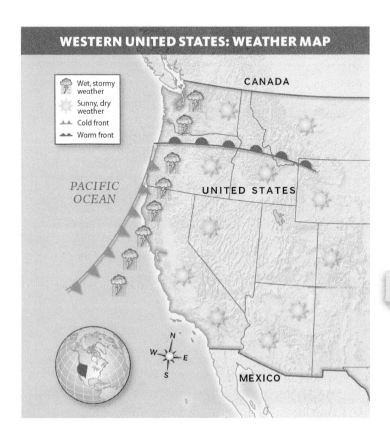

WESTERN UNITED STATES: WEATHER MAP

Wet, stormy weather
Sunny, dry weather
Cold front
Warm front

CANADA

PACIFIC OCEAN

UNITED STATES

MEXICO

N W E S

THINK LIKE A GEOGRAPHER

Make Inferences What is the difference between climate and weather?

THINK LIKE A GEOGRAPHER

ANSWER

Climate is the average condition of the atmosphere over a long period of time. Weather refers to the daily changes in atmospheric conditions.

GT21

Physical Geography   CLIMATE REGIONS AND VEGETATION

A climate region is a group of places that have similar temperatures, precipitation levels, and changes in weather. Geographers have identified 5 climate regions that are broken down into 12 subcategories. Places that are located in the same subcategory often have similar vegetation, or plant life.

Saguaro Cactus, Sonora Desert, Arizona

Mixed Forest, Great Smoky Mountains, North Carolina

B **Humid Temperate Climates** have cool winters, warm summers, and ample rainfall. Plant life includes mixed forests with evergreens and leafy trees.

A **Dry Climates** have little to no rain or snow and both hot and cold temperatures. Plant life includes shrubs and cacti.

NORTH AMERICA

PACIFIC OCEAN

ATLANTIC OCEAN

SOUTH AMERICA

Bromeliads, Amazon rain forest, Peru

C **Humid Equatorial Climates** are found near the equator. They have high temperatures and rainfall all or most of the year. Plant life includes tropical plants and rain forests or grasslands with trees.

Mosses, Disko Bay, Greenland

D **Tundra** or **Ice Climates** are north of the Arctic Circle and south of the Antarctic Circle. They have long, cold winters and short summers. Plant life includes mosses or no vegetation.

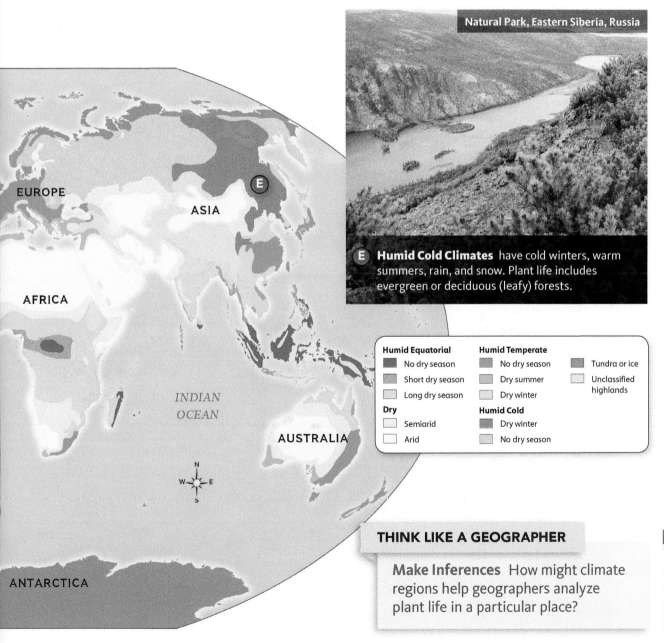
Natural Park, Eastern Siberia, Russia

E **Humid Cold Climates** have cold winters, warm summers, rain, and snow. Plant life includes evergreen or deciduous (leafy) forests.

EUROPE

ASIA

AFRICA

INDIAN OCEAN

AUSTRALIA

ANTARCTICA

N
W—E
S

Humid Equatorial
- No dry season
- Short dry season
- Long dry season

Dry
- Semiarid
- Arid

Humid Temperate
- No dry season
- Dry summer
- Dry winter

Humid Cold
- Dry winter
- No dry season

- Tundra or ice
- Unclassified highlands

THINK LIKE A GEOGRAPHER

Make Inferences How might climate regions help geographers analyze plant life in a particular place?

ANALYZE ADAPTATIONS

Divide the class into four groups. Give each group one of the following topics:

- food
- clothing
- shelter
- daily activities

Have each group discuss how the local climate affects their life with regards to their assigned topic. Then call on volunteers from each group to summarize the discussion for the class.

THINK LIKE A GEOGRAPHER

ANSWER

Answers will vary. Students may say that in cold weather, they wear coats and gloves and do indoor activities; in warmer weather, they wear light clothing and spend more time outdoors.

Human Geography ADAPTING TO THE ENVIRONMENT

Human geography explores the relationship between people and their surroundings. An important aspect of this relationship is the way in which people adapt to their environment.

Throughout history, people have had to adapt to their surroundings. Early humans did this simply to survive. They learned how to build a fire to warm themselves in cold weather and find plants and animals when food was scarce. In modern times, people have developed sophisticated technologies, including heating and cooling systems, to help them live in environments with challenging weather.

People have also learned to build structures to adapt to their environment. They build houses to protect them from the elements. They build dams to hold water back, bridges to span bodies of water, and tunnels to more easily travel over mountainous areas. In many cases, the materials people use to build these structures are obtained from the surrounding environment.

THINK LIKE A GEOGRAPHER

Make Connections What kinds of adaptations do you make in different types of weather?

China built the Three Gorges Dam on the Chang Jiang River, in part, to prevent flooding along the eastern part of the river.

In the city of Noril'sk in the Russian region of Siberia, people deal with the snow and ice that covers the ground throughout much of the city's long winter.

+ GUIDED DISCUSSION

1. **Analyze Visuals** How might people who live in Siberia need to adapt to their environment? *(Possible responses: They would need to build houses with good insulation to trap heat and keep out the cold; they would need to drive vehicles that can easily move through heavy snow.)*

2. **Make Inferences** What might be a negative consequence of building a dam such as the Three Gorges Dam to prevent flooding? *(Possible response: The dam might destroy the habitat of the animals who live along the river.)*

INTEGRATE VISUALS

Invite students to scroll through the NG Image Gallery and look at pictures of historical places with different physical characteristics. Have students choose one photo and write a paragraph about how people who lived there might have needed to adapt to their environment.

Human Geography HUMAN IMPACT ON THE ENVIRONMENT

When people adapt to their surroundings, their actions sometimes have a lasting impact on the environment. Some adaptations have a positive impact on the environment, but some can be harmful.

NEGATIVE IMPACT

As people moved to cities over the last few centuries, they needed housing and ever-increasing supplies of energy to fuel their homes, businesses, and cars. As a result, entire forests were cut down, new mines were carved into the earth, and oil and natural gas were pumped from the ground and from underwater sources.

When forests and other natural environments are cleared, an entire ecosystem can be destroyed. An ecosystem is a community of plants and animals and their natural environment. The destruction of one ecosystem can affect another. For example, many scientists believe the destruction of rain forest habitats has led to global climate change.

The use of fossil fuels—including, coal, oil, and natural gas—has had a largely negative impact on the environment. Burning these energy sources has polluted the air and contributed to global warming. Even mining and transporting the sources has affected the environment. Oil spills from tankers and underwater oil rigs have damaged our waters, shorelines, and wildlife.

POSITIVE IMPACT

As understanding of human impact on the environment has grown, people around the world have taken steps to save ecosystems, preserve natural habitats, and protect our air and water. In 1973, for example, the United States passed the Endangered Species Act, which protects the habitats of endangered species. People have also restored, or brought back, habitats such as forests by planting trees. In addition, laws and regulations have been passed to limit the amounts of pollutants released into the air, land, and bodies of water by vehicles and industrial plants.

Scientists have worked to educate the public on pollution's impact on the environment. For example, some scientists have formed Mission Blue, a program that seeks to heal and protect Earth's oceans. One of the program's goals is to establish marine-protected areas in endangered hot spots, or "hope spots." These spots are ocean habitats that can recover and grow if human impact is limited.

Critical Viewing This satellite map of the world shows the location of 17 "hope spots," places that are important to the overall health of Earth's oceans. What patterns, if any, do you notice about the location of these spots?

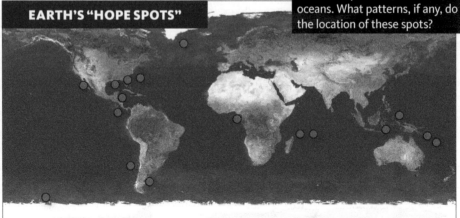

EARTH'S "HOPE SPOTS"

In 2010, the Deepwater Horizon oil rig exploded in the Gulf of Mexico. The explosion killed 11 people and dumped more than 200 million gallons of oil in the Gulf. Thousands of birds, fish, and marine mammals were injured or killed in the disaster.

Elephants roam the Samburu National Reserve in Kenya.

GUIDED DISCUSSION

1. **Make Inferences** How might the destruction of plants in an ecosystem affect animal life? (*Plants absorb energy from the sun and turn it into energy. When animals such as rabbits eat plants, they absorb that energy. If plants were no longer available, the animals would lose their source of energy and would not survive.*)

2. **Analyze Cause and Effect** How can efforts to protect rain forests around the world affect global warming? (*If rain forests can be protected from deforestation, plants can help absorb greenhouse gases. With fewer greenhouse gases warming the air, the average temperature of Earth's surface should not increase.*)

MORE INFORMATION

The *Deepwater Horizon* In April 2010, the *Deepwater Horizon* oil drilling rig in the Gulf of Mexico exploded. The explosion opened a hole in a well drilled in the seafloor. Oil gushed from that hole every day for nearly three months, leaking nearly five million barrels of oil. Before this accident, the worst U.S. oil disaster at sea was the grounding of the *Exxon Valdez* tanker in 1989. That disaster lost around 260,000 barrels of oil—a large amount, but far smaller than the amount of oil leaked after the explosion of the *Deepwater Horizon*.

THINK LIKE A GEOGRAPHER

Evaluate What can you do to have a positive impact on the environment?

THINK LIKE A GEOGRAPHER

ANSWER

Answers will vary. Students may say that they can have a positive impact on the environment by recycling and conserving resources like water and electricity.

Human Geography MOVEMENT AND SPREAD OF IDEAS

People have been on the move since early *Homo sapiens* first began moving within Africa about 100,000 years ago. The movement of people to a new location is called migration.

HUMAN MOVEMENT

Since our beginnings in Africa, we have migrated to new locations and populated the globe. Early humans moved because their survival depended on it. The climate changed, making food and water scarce. So people moved to find more hospitable homes and to follow the herds of animals they liked to hunt.

People have continued to migrate throughout history. The map on this page shows the Bantu migrations, which began about 2,000 years ago and continued for about 1,500 years. Historians say that this massive migration is the most important since our human ancestors first left Africa.

Historians don't really know why the Bantu people decided to leave their homes in West Africa and head south. Today, however, many immigrants are motivated to move by what are called push-pull factors. Push factors are those that drive people away from an area, such as war, political or religious persecution, and lack of job opportunities. Pull factors are those that attract people to a new place, such as higher wages, educational opportunities, and a more tolerant government. And of course, people are still drawn to a more favorable climate.

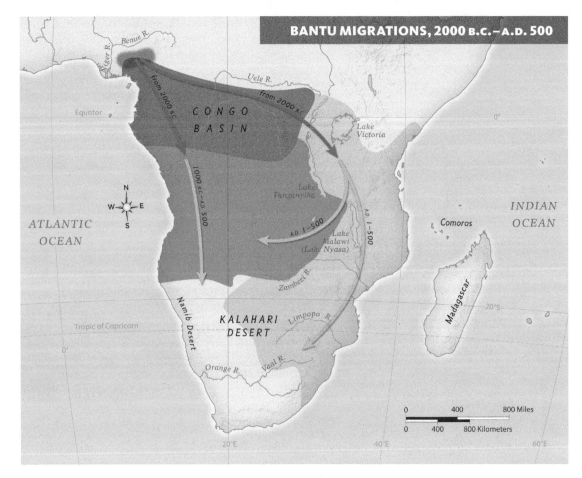

BANTU MIGRATIONS, 2000 B.C.–A.D. 500

SPREAD OF IDEAS

As people migrate, they bring their ideas, culture, skills, and language to their new homes. This spread of ideas results in great change. For example, the exchange of skills and ideas that occurred as a result of the Bantu migrations had an enormous impact on Africa's culture, economy, and government practices. You can see the impact of migration today in any large city. Restaurants, shops, and places of worship reflect the culture of the people who have moved to the city.

Trade has also spread ideas. The Silk Roads, a network of trade routes that began in China around 100 B.C., carried ideas as well as goods to Asia, Africa, and Europe. Over time, Chinese inventions and ideas reached Europe, and Indian traders brought Buddhism to China.

Movement isn't the only means by which ideas spread. Technological innovations can have the same impact. For instance, the invention of the printing press around 1450 resulted in an information explosion throughout Europe. The press produced books rapidly and cheaply and spread ideas quickly. Today, computers, the Internet, and social media carry ideas around the world at the touch of a button. These technologies—and those yet to come—are part of human geography and will continue to bring people together.

THINK LIKE A GEOGRAPHER

Evaluate What technologies and other means do you use to spread ideas?

The development of cell phones has connected people and their ideas in places where landline phone systems would be too expensive to install.

GT29

➤ **INTRODUCE THE FIELD JOURNAL**

Have each student access the Field Journal via the Student eEdition or download, print, and distribute a paper copy of the Field Journal to each student. Have students read the introduction. Explain that archaeologists like National Geographic's Fred Hiebert carefully keep track of their findings as they work in the field using a notebook, computer, or other device.

Students should use their Field Journal as they read each Why Study History? section and explore the historical record—the long story of the best and worst throughout human history. They will record their thoughts about what they've read and fit them into the larger picture of world history. They will also use the journal to record their thoughts on how they fit into that big picture and what it means to be a global citizen.

The Field Journal also contains exercises to help students process and reflect upon the information in each unit.

➤ **TURN AND TALK**

One of the headings in the Why Study History? text is "The Human Epic." Explain to students that an epic is a long, formal poem loosely based on historical themes. An epic hero or heroine displays superhuman qualities of strength and bravery. Ask students to think about someone who fits the description of an epic hero or heroine. Invite students to talk about that person with a classmate without revealing his or her name. Have students discuss whether or not they would also consider this person a role model.

The Field Journal also contains exercises to help students process and reflect upon the information in each unit.

WHY STUDY HISTORY ?

Hi! I'm Fred Hiebert, National Geographic's Archaeology Fellow. We're about to embark on a journey all over the world and back through time—the history of the world as we know it today.

So why do we study past civilizations? The basis of civilization is identity—who we are and what we stand for. We express identity by creating unique ways to be housed and fed and to thrive. The basic building blocks of civilization are the same around the world: what kinds of plants and animals to tend and consume, how to find enough water, and how to survive the changes of the seasons. All core civilizations— from China, India, and Mesopotamia, to Europe and Mesoamerica— struggled with these issues.

Look at the sculptures shown below. These prehistoric "selfies" reveal a universal need to think about ourselves—in relation to the environment, the future, our religious beliefs—that dates from the earliest civilizations.

THE HUMAN EPIC

Historians, archaeologists, and anthropologists constantly update the story of human civilizations as new data surfaces from the latest dig site or the most recent scholarship. The Framework of World History at right is only one way to think about how human identity developed—there are many pathways from the past to the present.

I've lived and worked all over the world in lots of different cultures, and I know first-hand that you and others your age are more alike than you are different. You share the same need to understand yourself, your family, and your community and the same urge to hope and plan for your future. Your generation may be one of the first to truly be considered global citizens.

◄ **ARTEMIS**
This Greek marble sculpture dating back to the 4th century B.C. is known as *Artemis Hunting*.

◄ **NEFERTITI**
The bust of this famous Egyptian queen and wife of Pharaoh Akhenaten was sculpted more than 3,300 years ago.

Fred Hiebert
▶ **Watch the Why Study History video**

The ancient cave painting in the background is located in Snake Cave in Australia. An Aboriginal artist created it by blowing pigment over his or her hand, leaving a blank hand shape.

◀ **TERRA COTTA BUDDHA**
This 5-foot tall statue was discovered at the site of Hadda in Afghanistan.

FRAMEWORK OF WORLD HISTORY

The model below is one way to view the development of civilizations. For all cultures, it's not just the famous leaders who make history—it's all of us, through small actions that grow into world-changing events and ideas.

1 ## CORE CIVILIZATIONS
Humans begin to think about where they live, what they eat, and what they believe in—and plan for the future. Across the centuries and in all world cultures, humans use these building blocks to think about who they are and where they come from—the beginning of identity.

2 ## PRIMARY CIVILIZATIONS
Humans develop more effective responses to their environment, creating irrigation and other farming methods that make agriculture more predictable and more productive. People are able to form groups and move together, and eventually cities develop.

3 ## SECONDARY CIVILIZATIONS
Human understanding of identity comes into focus, and writing develops partly as an expression of identity. Codes of law and better rulers come to the forefront as cultures take on characteristics that embody those identities.

4 ## WORLD SYSTEMS
Civilizations reach out to each other, and trade develops along what would eventually be called the Silk Roads. The urge to move results in new road systems, new country borders with border guards, and new systems of taxation.

HI 5 Students recognize that interpretations of history are subject to change as new information is uncovered.

1

WHY STUDY HISTORY ?

TO BECOME A GLOBAL CITIZEN

As you study world history, you're going to meet some National Geographic Explorers along the way—men and women who are making incredible contributions to our lives through their work. Studying world history is part of what they do because they believe they can add to our understanding of the human story. Here are just a few.

MICHAEL COSMOPOULOS ▶
Cosmopoulos directs two major excavations exploring the origins of states and social complexity in Greece.

◀ WILLIAM SATURNO
Saturno supervises excavations in the jungles of Guatemala and determines the architectural history of a site by studying the little pieces that remain.

LOUISE LEAKEY ▲
Paleontologist Louise Leakey is responsible for some of the most important hominid fossils discovered in East Africa in the past two decades.

BECOME PART OF THE GLOBAL CONVERSATION!

Think About It

1. In what ways are you a global citizen?

2. Describe a situation or problem in which you think people should strive for global citizenship. What actions do you think should be taken to solve the problem?

3. Pick one action you named above and explain how you would go about accomplishing it. Develop a detailed action plan that could be put in place to make this happen.

STEVEN ELLIS ▶
Ellis directs the excavation of a working-class district in Pompeii, focusing on the use of public and private space and the role of ordinary people in the life of the ancient city.

◀ SARAH PARCAK
Parcak combines advanced technology such as satellite archaeology with good old-fashioned digging to reveal new Egyptian sites, including temples, pyramids, and tombs.

FUTURE EXPLORER ▶
WILL THIS BE YOU?

Write About It

SYNTHESIZE What does **identity** mean to you? Answer this question in two or three paragraphs in your notebook. Be sure to include your definition of identity, explain the various parts that make up your identity, and describe how you express your identity. Then designate a spot in your notebook where you can record how your understanding of identity changes as you read each chapter.

MAKE CONNECTIONS What different types of identities do you notice in your school and community? Create a chart that represents these identities and write your description of each.

ASK AND ANSWER QUESTIONS Imagine that you are at a panel discussion that includes the Explorers shown above. Write three questions you would like to ask the panel, including specific questions for individual Explorers.

✦ PREVIEW UNITS 1 AND 2

As they read Units 1 and 2 in their textbook, have students complete pages 10–16 in their Field Journal to process the material in these units. Remind students that they will use their Field Journal as they read each Why Study History? section and explore the historical record. They will record their thoughts about what they've read and fit them into the larger picture of world history. They will also use the journal to consider how they fit into that big picture and what it means to be a global citizen.

ORIGINS OF
CULTURES AND
CIVILIZATIONS

NATIONAL GEOGRAPHIC

ON **LOCATION** WITH

Louise Leakey
Paleontologist

One of the first jobs of a paleontologist is finding a good place to dig. We look for places where fossilized bones, buried long ago by rivers and lakes, have been brought to the surface by tectonic activity and erosion. Lake Turkana in Kenya's Great Rift Valley is the world's best field laboratory for fossil discoveries going back several million years. My family has been working in this profession for three generations, uncovering the bones of human ancestors and other animals that lived in this region in the past. I'm Louise Leakey, and I help investigate and share the human story.

< **CRITICAL VIEWING** A shepherd gazes out over East Africa's Great Rift Valley. How might the geography of the valley help archaeologists carry out their work?

5

POSSIBLE RESPONSE

The valley is relatively flat and empty of vegetation, so it provides a clear site in which to dig.

The World

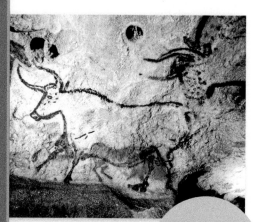

c. 10,000 B.C.
As the last Ice Age comes to an end, animals such as the woolly mammoth die out.

c. 15,000 B.C.
Lascaux Cave paintings are created.

c. 68,000 B.C.
Groups of modern humans begin to migrate out of Africa.

20,000 B.C.

175,000 B.C.

c. 9600 B.C.
Göbekli Tepe, the world's first temple, is built in present-day Turkey.
(Göbekli Tepe pillar)

What similar events took place within 1,000 years in Egypt and Mesopotamia?

POSSIBLE RESPONSE
Agriculture began in both places.

c. 5000 B.C.
Yangshao culture flourishes along the Huang and Wei rivers in China.
(Yangshao pottery)

c. 9000 B.C.
The Neolithic Age and the agricultural revolution begin. Farmers develop tools made of sharpened stone.

c. 5200 B.C.
Egypt's earliest farming community develops at Faiyum.

5000 B.C.

4500 B.C.

c. 7400 B.C.
Çatalhöyük develops in present-day Turkey.

c. 4250 B.C.
The maize revolution begins in Mesoamerica.

CST 1 Students explain how major events are related to one another in time.

7

THE LAST
ICE AGE
18,000 B.C.–10,000 B.C.

Landform: Moraine, a ridge or mound of sediment deposited by a glacier, Bylot Island, Nunavut, Canada

Landform: Glacier cave, Patagonia, Argentina

For much of history, Earth has been a cold place. It has endured long periods, called Ice Ages, during which temperatures dropped and slow-moving masses of ice called glaciers formed. The last Ice Age, which began more than two million years ago, reached its height in 18,000 B.C. Around this time, glaciers covered large areas of the world. By 12,000 B.C., the overall temperature of Earth had warmed, and much of the ice had melted. By 10,000 B.C., our world looked much the way it does now and had a climate similar to today's. As you can see in the photos, glacial movement also formed bodies of water and landforms that still make up Earth's landscape.

What continents were not affected by the last Ice Age? How can you tell?

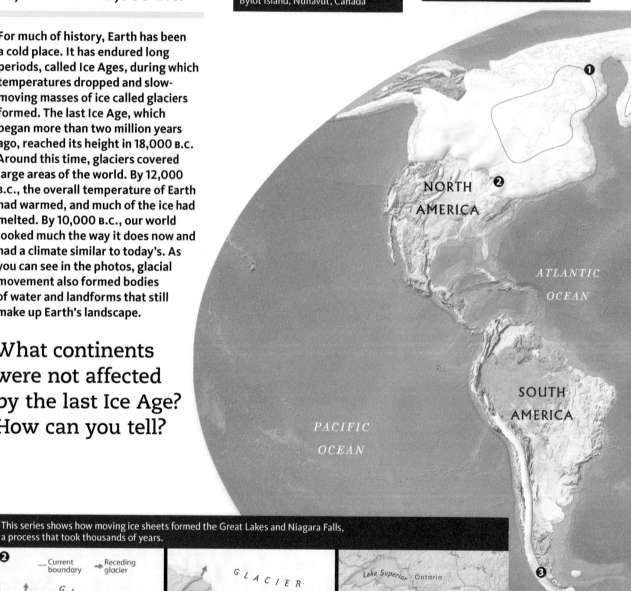

NORTH AMERICA

ATLANTIC OCEAN

PACIFIC OCEAN

SOUTH AMERICA

This series shows how moving ice sheets formed the Great Lakes and Niagara Falls, a process that took thousands of years.

— Current boundary   → Receding glacier

GLACIER

GLACIER

Lake Superior   Ontario
Wisconsin   Michigan   Lake Huron
Lake Michigan   Lake Niagara Falls   Lake Ontario   N.Y.
Illinois   Lake Erie   Finger Lakes
Indiana   Ohio   Pennsylvania

  CST 3 Students use a variety of maps and documents to identify physical and cultural features of neighborhoods, cities, states, and countries and to explain the historical migration of people, expansion and disintegration of empires, and the growth of economic systems.

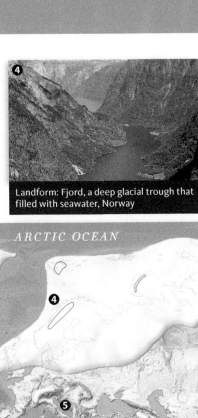

Landform: Fjord, a deep glacial trough that filled with seawater, Norway

Landform: Glacial valley, Fagaras Mountains, Romania

Landform: Sediment-filled glacier, Karakoram, Himalaya

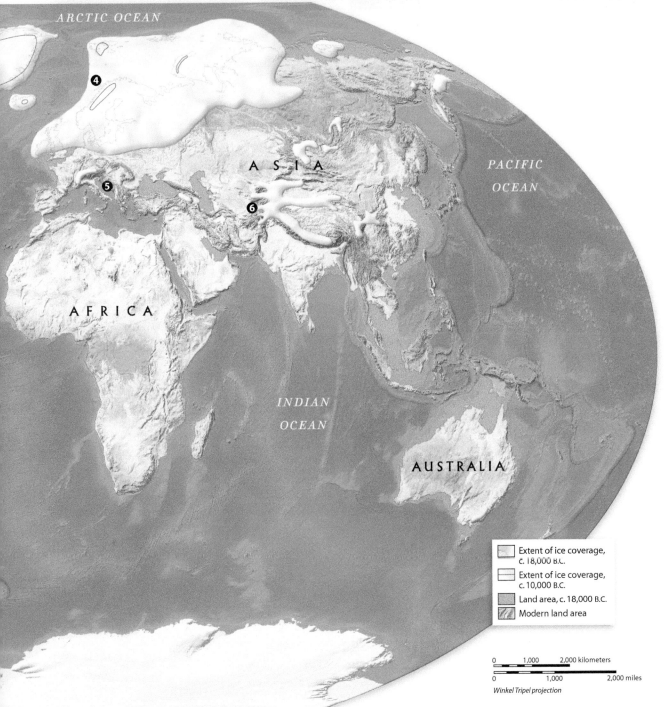

ARCTIC OCEAN

ASIA

PACIFIC OCEAN

AFRICA

INDIAN OCEAN

AUSTRALIA

Extent of ice coverage, c. 18,000 B.C.

Extent of ice coverage, c. 10,000 B.C.

Land area, c. 18,000 B.C.

Modern land area

0   1,000   2,000 kilometers

0   1,000   2,000 miles

Winkel Tripel projection

UNIT RESOURCES

On Location with National Geographic Explorer-in-Residence Louise Leakey
Intro and Video

Interactive Map Tool

News & Updates

Available at NGLSync.cengage.com

Unit Wrap-Up:
"Discovering Our Ancestors"
Feature and Video

"Scotland's Stone Age Ruins"
National Geographic Adapted Article

"First Americans"
National Geographic Adapted Article
Student eEdition exclusive

Unit 1 Inquiry:
Create a Cultural Symbol

CHAPTER RESOURCES

TEACHER RESOURCES & ASSESSMENT

Available at NGLSync.cengage.com

Social Studies Skills Lessons
• Reading: Compare and Contrast
• Writing: Write an Explanation

Formal Assessment
• Chapter 1 Tests A (on-level)
  & B (below-level)

Chapter 1 Answer Key

ExamView®
One-time Download

STUDENT BACKPACK *Available at NGLSync.cengage.com*

• **eEdition** *(English)* • **eEdition** *(Spanish)* • **Handbooks** • **Online Atlas**

Chapter 1 Spanish resources, Guided Writing prompts, and Financial Literacy lessons are available online.

SECTION 1 RESOURCES

THE PALEOLITHIC AGE

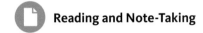 **Reading and Note-Taking**

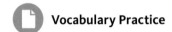 **Vocabulary Practice**

 **Section 1 Quiz**

Available at NGLSync.cengage.com

LESSON 1.1 DISCOVERING PREHISTORY

 Biography
Richard Leakey   *Available at NGLSync.cengage.com*
• On Your Feet: Inside-Outside Circle
• Critical Viewing: NG Chapter Gallery

LESSON 1.2 THE ELEMENTS OF CULTURE
• On Your Feet: Four Corners
• Critical Viewing: NG Image Gallery

LESSON 1.3 CHANGING ENVIRONMENTS
• On Your Feet: Three-Step Interview
• Critical Viewing: NG Chapter Gallery

LESSON 1.4 MOVING INTO NEW ENVIRONMENTS

 Active History: Interactive Whiteboard Activity
Compare Past and Present Land Areas

Active History
Compare Past and Present Land Areas

Available at NGLSync.cengage.com
| **NG Learning Framework:**
| Research a Critical Species

NATIONAL GEOGRAPHIC
EXPLORER JEFFREY ROSE
LESSON 1.5 TRACKING MIGRATION OUT OF AFRICA
• On Your Feet: Rotating Discussion
| **NG Learning Framework:**
| Write a Biography

LESSON 1.6 CAVE ART
• On Your Feet: Question and Answer
• Critical Viewing: NG Chapter Gallery

SECTION 2 RESOURCES

THE NEOLITHIC AGE

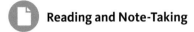 **Reading and Note-Taking**

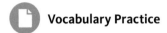 **Vocabulary Practice**

 **Section 2 Quiz**

Available at NGLSync.cengage.com

LESSON 2.1 NOMADIC HUNTER-GATHERERS
• On Your Feet: Word Chain
| **NG Learning Framework:**
| Hunting and Gathering

LESSON 2.2 THE BEGINNINGS OF DOMESTICATION
• On Your Feet: Turn and Talk on Topic
• Critical Viewing: NG Chapter Gallery

LESSON 2.3 THE AGRICULTURAL REVOLUTION

 Biography
Dame Kathleen Kenyon

Available at NGLSync.cengage.com
• On Your Feet: Numbered Heads
| **NG Learning Framework:**
| Observe, Exchange, and Discuss

LESSON 2.4 STUDYING THE PAST
• On Your Feet: Three Corners
• Critical Viewing: NG Chapter Gallery

CHAPTER 1 REVIEW

STRATEGY ❶

Turn Titles into Questions

To help students set a purpose for reading, have them read the title of each lesson in a section and then turn that title into a question they believe will be answered in the lesson. Students can record their questions and write their own answers, or they can ask each other their questions.

Use with All Lessons *For example, in Lesson 1.2 the question could be, "What are the elements of culture?"*

STRATEGY ❷

Use a TASKS Approach

Help students get information from visuals by using the following TASKS strategy:

  T Look for a **title** that may give the main idea.

  A **Ask** yourself what the visual is trying to show.

  S Determine how **symbols** are used.

  K Look for a **key** or legend.

  S **Summarize** what you learned.

Use with All Lessons

STRATEGY ❸

Play the "I Am . . ." Game

To reinforce the meanings of key terms and names, assign every student one term or name that appears in the chapter and have them write a one-sentence clue beginning with "I am." Have students take turns reading clues and calling on other students to guess answers.

Use with All Lessons

Press *in the Student eEdition for modified text.*

STRATEGY ❶

Provide Terms and Names on Audio

Decide which of the terms and names are important for mastery and have a volunteer record the pronunciations and a short sentence defining each word. Encourage students to listen to the recording as often as necessary.

Use with All Lessons *You might also use the recordings to quiz students on their mastery of the terms. Play one definition at a time from the recording and ask students to identify the term or name described.*

STRATEGY ❷

Preview Maps

Use the following suggestions to preview maps with students.

  • Explain that some maps are political maps and show country boundaries and names.

  • Remind students that physical maps highlight geographic features such as mountain ranges and bodies of land and water.

  • Discuss what thematic maps do: show resources, population movement, historical boundaries, and other specialized information.

Use with Lessons 1.4, 1.5, 2.3, and the Chapter Review *For Lessons 1.4 and 2.3, have students explain what the thematic maps are showing. Have students make connections between the maps in Lesson 1.5 and the Chapter Review.*

STRATEGY ❶

Create a Word Web

To activate prior knowledge and build vocabulary, work with students to create a Word Web for the word *culture* before beginning Section 1 and the word *agriculture* before beginning Section 2.

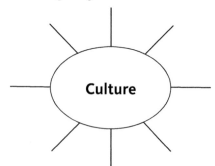

Use with Lessons 1.2 and 2.3, All Levels *Encourage students at the **Bridging** level to use each word in a sentence.*

HSS ANALYSIS SKILLS:

CST 2 Students construct various time lines of key events, people, and periods of the historical era they are studying; **CST 3** Students use a variety of maps and documents to identify physical and cultural features of neighborhoods, cities, states, and countries and to explain the historical migration of people, expansion and disintegration of empires, and the growth of economic systems; **REP 1** Students frame questions that can be answered by historical study and research.

STRATEGY ❷

Compare and Contrast

Remind students that they can use adjectives to compare and contrast Paleolithic and Neolithic people. Review with students that a comparative adjective is formed by adding -er to one-syllable adjectives and to two-syllable adjectives ending in a consonant plus y. The word *more* is added before most other two-syllable adjectives and before adjectives that have three or more syllables. Use the following strategies to help students at all proficiency levels compare and contrast.

Emerging

Ask students questions about Paleolithic and Neolithic societies and invite them to respond:

- Is Paleolithic society older than Neolithic society? (*Yes, Paleolithic society is older than Neolithic society.*)
- Are Neolithic tools more complex than Paleolithic tools? (*Yes, Neolithic tools are more complex than Paleolithic tools.*)

Expanding

Ask students what each society is like. Display adjectives and use equations to show comparative forms (*old + er = older*). Students can use the posted adjectives to complete sentence frames.

- Paleolithic society is _____.
- Neolithic tools are _____ than Paleolithic tools.

Bridging

As students compare Paleolithic and Neolithic societies, encourage them to use possessive adjectives in addition to comparative adjectives.

- Both Paleolithic and Neolithic societies used tools. **Their** tools were used to perform particular tasks. However, Neolithic tools were more complex than Paleolithic tools.

Use with Lessons 1.3–1.6 and 2.1–2.3, All Levels

STRATEGY ❸

Use Visuals to Predict Content

Before reading, ask students to read the lesson title and look at any visuals. Then ask them to write a sentence that predicts how the visual is related to the lesson title. Repeat the exercise after reading and ask volunteers to read their sentences.

Use with All Lessons, All Levels *Have students at the **Emerging** and **Expanding** levels work with a partner.*

GIFTED & TALENTED

STRATEGY ❶

Teach a Class

Before beginning the chapter, allow students to choose one of the lessons listed below and prepare to teach the content to the class. Give them a set amount of time in which to present their lesson. Suggest that students think about any visuals or activities they want to use when they teach.

Use with Lessons 1.2, 1.4, 1.6, and 2.1–2.3

STRATEGY ❷

Present a Museum Exhibit

Have groups of students prepare a museum exhibit featuring the paintings of Lascaux Cave in France. Have them photocopy images of the paintings and write museum-style captions for each one. Once students have compiled their exhibits, have them place the images on the wall and present them to the class. Encourage students to introduce the exhibit with some background information on Lascaux. Tell them that they should also be prepared to answer questions as their classmates view the exhibit.

Use with Lesson 1.6

PRE-AP

STRATEGY ❶

Consider Two Sides

Tell students that some archaeologists believe the agricultural revolution was a catastrophe for the human race. Have pairs of students research the issue and make a chart listing the positive and negative effects of the revolution. Have students share and discuss their chart with the class.

Use with Lesson 2.3

STRATEGY ❷

Create an Archaeology Time Line

Have pairs of students work together to create a time line identifying the archaeologists who have found fossils of modern humans. Tell students that the time line should begin with Richard Leakey's discovery in 1967.

Use with Lesson 1.1 *Encourage students to illustrate their time line with images of the expeditions and their findings.*

CHAPTER

1

THE
DEVELOPMENT
OF HUMAN
SOCIETIES

175,000 B.C. – 3000 B.C.

ESSENTIAL QUESTION How did people manage to survive and thrive tens of thousands of years ago?

SECTION 1 THE PALEOLITHIC AGE

KEY VOCABULARY
anthropologist
archaeologist
artifact
culture
drought
fossil
land bridge
megafauna
migration
oasis
technology

NAMES & PLACES
Beringia
Homo sapiens
Ice Age
Lascaux Cave
Paleolithic Age
Sahara

SECTION 2 THE NEOLITHIC AGE

KEY VOCABULARY
agriculture
domestication
fertile
hunter-gatherer
nomad
oral history
primary source
secondary source

NAMES & PLACES
Fertile Crescent
Neolithic Age

READING STRATEGY

ORGANIZE IDEAS: COMPARE AND CONTRAST
When you compare and contrast two or more things, you note their similarities and differences. Use a Venn diagram like this one to help you compare and contrast Paleolithic and Neolithic people as you read the chapter.

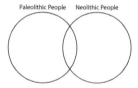

Paleolithic People   Neolithic People

This rock art found in the North African country of Algeria dates back at least 8,000 years.

11

STANDARDS

HSS CONTENT STANDARDS:

6.1.1 Describe the hunter-gatherer societies, including the development of tools and the use of fire; **6.1.2** Identify the locations of human communities that populated the major regions of the world and describe how humans adapted to a variety of environments; **6.1.3** Discuss the climatic changes and human modifications of the physical environment that gave rise to the domestication of plants and animals and new sources of clothing and shelter.

TEACHER BACKGROUND

INTRODUCE THE PHOTOGRAPH

Have students study the photograph of rock art in Algeria. Explain that people who lived in prehistoric times carved these elephants into the rock. Tell students that, in this chapter, they will learn about the development and achievements of early humans who lived in that time—our ancestors. Then have students examine the tiny human figures in the foreground of the image.

ASK: What do you think is going on between the humans and elephants? (*Possible response: The human figures are preparing to kill the elephants.*)

SHARE BACKGROUND

This rock art was carved into Algeria's Tadrart Plateau, located in the Sahara. Today, of course, the Sahara is a dry region filled with sand, rocks, and mountains, but that's because the climate changed over the last 8,000 years or so. At the time these rocks were carved, the region was a lush savanna, and elephants, giraffes, ostriches, and camels made their home there.

DIGITAL RESOURCES NGLSync.cengage.com

TEACHER RESOURCES & ASSESSMENT

 Social Studies Skills Lessons
• Reading: Compare and Contrast
• Writing: Write an Explanation

 **Formal Assessment**
• Chapter 1 Tests A (on-level) & B (below-level)

 ExamView®
One-time Download

 Chapter 1 Answer Key

STUDENT BACKPACK

• **eEdition** (*English*)
• **eEdition** (*Spanish*)
• **Handbooks**
• **Online Atlas**

HOW DID PEOPLE MANAGE TO SURVIVE AND THRIVE TENS OF THOUSANDS OF YEARS AGO?

Roundtable Activity: Factors of Influence This activity allows students to discuss four factors that helped early humans survive and thrive: adaptability, culture, technology, and intelligence. Divide the class into four groups and have each group sit at a table. Assign the following questions to the groups:

Group 1: Why might adaptability have been a key factor in early human survival?

Group 2: What role did culture play in helping early humans deal with daily life?

Group 3: How did technology help early humans improve their lives?

Group 4: Why did early humans need to possess intelligence?

Have students at each table take turns answering the question. When they have finished their discussion, ask a representative from each table to summarize that group's answers.

`0:15` minutes

ORGANIZE IDEAS: COMPARE AND CONTRAST

Remind students that comparing and contrasting two topics or ideas can help them better understand new information. Model completing the Venn Diagram. Point out the two sections of the chapter and preview the meaning of the words "Paleolithic" and "Neolithic" ("Old Stone Age" and "New Stone Age"). Model filling in the Venn Diagram with information that describes Paleolithic and Neolithic people. For more in-depth instruction and practice with the reading strategy, assign the Social Studies Skills Reading Lesson on comparing and contrasting.

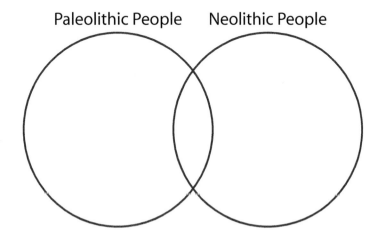

Paleolithic People   Neolithic People

WORD WALL

Have students complete a Word Wall for Key Vocabulary words as they read the chapter. Have students write each word on a piece of paper, draw a picture that helps clarify its meaning, and write its definition. At the end of the chapter, ask students what they learned about each word.

KEY DATES	
c. 2.5 million B.C.	Beginning of the Paleolithic Age
c. 200,000 B.C.	*Homo sapiens* first appear
c. 100,000 B.C.	Migration out of Africa begins
c. 10,000 B.C.	Beginning of the Neolithic Age
c. 8000 B.C.	Beginning of the agricultural revolution
c. 5000 B.C.	Agriculture established in Fertile Crescent and Indus River Valley
c. 3000 B.C.	Agriculture established in Nile River Valley and Huang He River Valley

1.1 Discovering **Prehistory**

You probably think your parents are pretty old. Well, think again. They actually belong to the newest human species on the planet—*Homo sapiens*, or "wise man"—and so do you. We'll begin our story with this species.

MAIN IDEA

The evidence uncovered by scientists helps us learn about our early human history.

GEOLOGIC AND ARCHAEOLOGICAL TIME

Earth is around 4.5 billion years old. Yet *Homo sapiens* (HOH-moh SAY-pee-uhnz) has existed for only about the last 200,000 years. Scientists know this because they have found fossils and artifacts that belonged to this species. **Fossils** are the remains, such as bones and teeth, of organisms that lived long ago. **Artifacts** are human-made objects, such as stone tools. These items provide some of the best clues to prehistory, or the time before written records existed.

Paleontologists are scientists who study fossils. Scientists called **archaeologists** interpret artifacts. These scientists piece together evidence that tells the story of what happened at a site many years ago.

Scientists sometimes use geologic techniques to find out how old fossils and artifacts are. For example, they can figure out how old an artifact is based on how deeply it is buried in layers of dirt. In a site that hasn't been disturbed over time, dirt builds up in layers, with younger layers covering the older ones. Scientists know that fossils and artifacts lying in the deepest layers are the oldest.

ORIGINS IN AFRICA

Early *Homo sapiens* looked very much like humans do today. It is now widely accepted that the species first appeared in Africa. Earlier hominins, or human-like species *(Homo hobilis* and *Homo erectus)*, are believed to have lived in Africa for millions of years before *Homo sapiens*.

In 1967, a team of scientists led by Richard Leakey found the earliest fossils of modern humans. The team discovered two *Homo sapiens* skulls near the Omo River in the Great Rift Valley of East Africa. The skulls were originally thought to be 130,000 years old, but a more recent dating has determined them to be about 195,000 years old.

Homo sapiens lived during the **Paleolithic** (pay-lee-uh-LIHTH-ihk) **Age**, a period that began around 2.5 million B.C. and ended around 8000 B.C. The period is also called the Old Stone Age because the people living then made simple tools and weapons out of stone. It was a time of dramatic changes in geography and climate. It was also a time when modern human development—and human history—began.

TIME TRAVEL

Throughout the text, you will see the abbreviations B.C. and A.D. A date followed by B.C. refers to the number of years the date occurred before the birth of Christ. A date preceded by A.D. refers to the number of years the date occurred after the birth of Christ. Many historians also use the abbreviations B.C.E. and C.E. for these time periods. However, B.C.E. stands for "Before the Common Era," and C.E. stands for "Common Era."

Homo sapiens fossils have been found in East Africa's Great Rift Valley, shown here.

REVIEW & ASSESS

1. **READING CHECK** What kinds of evidence do scientists uncover to learn about early modern humans?

2. **DETERMINE WORD MEANINGS** *Paleo* means "old." What do you suppose *lithic* means?

3. **MAKE INFERENCES** What does the fact that early *Homo sapiens* made tools suggest about this group?

6.1.2 Identify the locations of human communities that populated the major regions of the world and describe how humans adapted to a variety of environments.

STANDARDS

HSS CONTENT STANDARDS:

6.1.2 Identify the locations of human communities that populated the major regions of the world and describe how humans adapted to a variety of environments.

PLAN

OBJECTIVE

Learn what scientists have uncovered about our early history.

ESSENTIAL QUESTION

How did people manage to survive and thrive tens of thousands of years ago?

Early *Homo sapiens* lived in a time of dramatic changes in geography and climate. Lesson 1.1 discusses the origins of early modern humans and the scientific methods used to discover them.

BACKGROUND FOR THE TEACHER

According to many scientists, the earliest hominins developed around five or six million years ago in southern and eastern Africa. These human-like species were bipedal, or capable of walking upright on two legs. Over time, the brains of these species grew larger, which led to increased intelligence and the ability to make and use simple tools. They also discovered how to use fire. About one million years ago, groups of hominins began to migrate out of Africa to Europe and Asia. These groups were the ancestors of the Neanderthals, who early modern humans would encounter when they migrated out of Africa 90,000 years later.

DIGITAL RESOURCES NGLSync.cengage.com

TEACHER RESOURCES & ASSESSMENT

 Reading and Note-Taking

 Vocabulary Practice

 Section 1 Quiz

STUDENT RESOURCES

 Biography

INTRODUCE & ENGAGE

INTERPRET MODELS

Point out the photograph of East Africa's Great Rift Valley. To show students how the valley was formed, have pairs of students place two paperback books of equal thickness lengthwise between them. Then have them pull the books until they are about a half inch away from each other. Explain that the books represent plates of land that pull apart, leaving deep valleys between them. Tell students that the Great Rift Valley formed this way. **0:05** minutes

TEACH

STEM

GUIDED DISCUSSION

1. **Describe** What is one of the geologic techniques archaeologists use to find out how old artifacts are? (*Archaeologists often date artifacts based on how deeply they are buried in the dirt. Artifacts lying in the deepest layers are the oldest.*)

2. **Draw Conclusions** Why do archaeologists have to depend on finding artifacts to uncover information about early *Homo sapiens*? (*There are no written records made by early Homo sapiens, so archaeologists must depend on the physical materials these early people left behind for information.*)

MORE INFORMATION

Prehistoric Detectives Paleontologists and archaeologists rely on other specialists to help them find and analyze prehistoric evidence. Geologists tell the story of a landscape by analyzing rocks and fossils. When they investigate rock layers, they sometimes uncover prehistoric plant and animal remains that reveal what the environment was like long ago. Radiologists study x-ray images to show what the human eye cannot see, especially in bones and rusty metal. Geneticists study DNA patterns to trace human ancestry back thousands of years.

ACTIVE OPTIONS

On Your Feet: Inside-Outside Circle Use the Inside-Outside Circle strategy to check students' understanding of artifacts and fossils. Have students in the outer circle pose questions (for example, "Which of the following is not an artifact: tool, cup, bone?"), and have students in the inner circle answer them. Then have students trade inside/outside roles and rotate to create new partnerships. **0:10** minutes

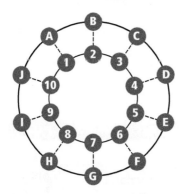

Critical Viewing: NG Chapter Gallery Invite students to explore the Chapter Gallery to examine the images that relate to Chapter 1. Have them select one of the first two images ("Skeleton of Famous Fossil Lucy" or "Peking Man Skull") and do additional research to learn more about the hominin species *Australopithecus afarensis* or *Homo erectus*. Ask questions that will inspire additional inquiry, such as: What is this? How old is it? How is it similar to modern humans? How is it different? Why does it belong in this chapter? What else would you like to know about it? As an extension to this activity, have students read the excerpt from Mary Leaky's *Disclosing the Past* in the **Primary Source Handbook** and answer the questions that follow it. **0:20** minutes

DIFFERENTIATE

ENGLISH LANGUAGE LEARNERS

ELD

Ask and Answer Questions Use the following strategies to help students at all proficiency levels participate in the Inside-Outside Circle activity.

- **Emerging** Have students work in pairs to write each question and each answer on separate strips of paper. One student asks the questions; the other student looks for and reads the answers. Then switch roles.

- **Expanding** Suggest that students turn the question into a statement for their answer. For example: What do archaeologists study? Archaeologists study artifacts.

- **Bridging** Encourage students to ask questions with answers that require an inference. For example: Why did scientists give a name that means "wise man" to early modern humans? (*because their ability to make and use tools indicates that they have intelligence*)

GIFTED & TALENTED

Perform a Play Have a group of students learn more about the discovery of early *Homo sapiens* fossils by Richard Leakey and his team in 1967. Then have the group present what they have learned to the class in a short play. Provide the following guidelines for the group:

- Assign each member of the group a role, including that of narrator.
- Compose dialogue that moves the action along.
- Heighten dramatic interest by providing a conflict.
- Convey the challenges and excitement of the dig.
- Use props, if possible, for the digging tools and fossils.
- Have the narrator or a character summarize the recent dating of the fossils.

Press **mt** *in the Student eEdition for modified text.*

See the Chapter Planner for more strategies for differentiation.

REVIEW & ASSESS

ANSWERS

1. Paleontologists study fossils and archaeologists study artifacts to understand and learn more about early modern humans.

2. *Lithic* means "stone."

3. The fact that early humans were making tools suggests that they were intelligent.

Critical Viewing Friends and neighbors in a community in China sit down to a lavish banquet. What do details in the photo tell you about the community's cultural behaviors?

+ POSSIBLE RESPONSE

The people in the community celebrate by enjoying a large meal together; they eat certain foods; they eat using chopsticks; they enjoy nature.

1.2 The Elements of Culture

Maybe you've heard the saying "You are what you eat," but did you know that you are also what you speak, what you wear, and what you believe? All of these behaviors—and many others—help identify you with your particular blend of cultures.

MAIN IDEA

Studying the culture of *Homo sapiens* in the Paleolithic Age helps reveal how people lived.

WHAT IS CULTURE?

Culture is a big part of human development. All the elements that contribute to the way of life of a particular group of people make up culture. These elements include language, clothing, music, art, law, religion, government, and family structure. Culture is passed down from parents to children and greatly affects our behaviors and beliefs. It influences people to do things in a particular way, such as eating or avoiding certain foods. It unifies a group and distinguishes that group from others.

Language, art, toolmaking, and religion are the elements that were most important in defining early cultures. Even early *Homo sapiens* communicated through speech, created cave paintings, made and used tools, and buried the dead. However, groups of people often did things slightly differently. These differences reflect each group's technical knowledge, artistic styles, and available natural resources.

WHY STUDY CULTURE?

As you've learned, cultural behaviors are passed down from generation to generation, but they can also change over time or—like the ability to make stone tools—be nearly lost altogether. In part, scientists study prehistoric cultures to learn how these cultures differ from modern cultures and discover what they all have in common. Information about modern cultures is often provided by archaeologists called **anthropologists**.

The artifacts archaeologists uncover help them piece together a picture of early humans' cultural behavior and daily life. For example, by studying tools uncovered at a prehistoric site, archaeologists learn how advanced the people who made them were and what jobs they needed to do. In addition, comparing artifacts from different sites can explain why one group was more successful than another.

Comparing artifacts from different time periods helps explain how people changed and developed. This knowledge helps us see thousands of years into the past so we can better understand the present and predict the future.

REVIEW & ASSESS

1. **READING CHECK** What do artifacts, such as stone tools, reveal about the culture of early *Homo sapiens*?

2. **SUMMARIZE** How do archaeologists and anthropologists work together?

3. **DRAW CONCLUSIONS** What might the discovery of tools used primarily as weapons suggest about a group of early humans?

HI 3 Students explain the sources of historical continuity and how the combination of ideas and events explains the emergence of new patterns.

15

STANDARDS

HSS CONTENT STANDARDS:

6.1 Students describe what is known through archaeological studies of the early physical and cultural development of humankind from the Paleolithic era to the agricultural revolution.

HSS ANALYSIS SKILLS:

HI 3 Students explain the sources of historical continuity and how the combination of ideas and events explains the emergence of new patterns.

PLAN

OBJECTIVE

Identify cultural elements of *Homo sapiens* in the Paleolithic Age.

ESSENTIAL QUESTION

How did people manage to survive and thrive tens of thousands of years ago?

Groups of early *Homo sapiens* developed cultural behaviors that helped them survive and advance. Lesson 1.2 discusses the early cultural elements that developed during the Paleolithic Age.

BACKGROUND FOR THE TEACHER

Understanding and talking about human culture is part of the job of anthropologists. Anthropology can go beyond just looking at artifacts. Margaret Mead is one of the most famous anthropologists in history. It is through Mead that many people first learned about the science of anthropology. She popularized the study of human development through a cross-cultural perspective. Mead also showed that modern societies could learn from so-called "primitive" societies. The study of past peoples helps us understand ourselves.

DIGITAL RESOURCES NGLSync.cengage.com

TEACHER RESOURCES & ASSESSMENT

 Reading and Note-Taking

 Vocabulary Practice

 Section 1 Quiz

STUDENT RESOURCES

 NG Image Gallery

MAKE A LIST

Write the following headings on the board: Food, Holidays, Clothing, Recreational Activities. Ask students to write each heading on a piece of paper and list examples from their own lives. Then have the class share and discuss their lists. Explain that what they have listed are elements of culture. Tell students that culture reflects how a group of people lives, believes, and thinks. **0:05** minutes

TEACH

GUIDED DISCUSSION

1. **Identify Main Ideas and Details** What elements were most important in defining early human cultures, and how were these elements part of people's lives? *(The most important elements were agriculture and subsistence, language, art, toolmaking, and religion. People needed to survive and feed themselves, communicated through speech, created cave paintings, made and used tools, and buried their dead.)*

2. **Make Inferences** What kinds of cultural behaviors, passed down from generation to generation, might have helped groups of early *Homo sapiens* survive? *(strategies for keeping warm, farming, irrigation, killing animals in a hunt, escaping danger)*

MAKE CONNECTIONS

Have students spend 20 minutes watching a television show or reading a magazine, a blog, or entries in a social networking site. Ask them to list five facts about culture in the United States that they observe in the media. The facts could relate to any element of culture, including customs, food, language, the arts, and religion. Once students have finished the assignment, have them share their observations and facts with the class. **0:20** minutes

ACTIVE OPTIONS

On Your Feet: Four Corners Create four signs with the following labels: Arts, Religion, Customs, Language. Tape one sign to each corner of the room. Then distribute magazines to students and ask them to cut out images that reflect these elements of culture. Have students tape each image to the appropriate corner of the room. **0:10** minutes

Critical Viewing: NG Image Gallery Have students explore the entire NG Image Gallery and choose two images that illustrate culture. Then have students compare and contrast the images, either in written form or verbally, with a partner. Ask questions that will inspire this process, such as: How are these images alike? How are they different? What aspect of culture do they represent? Why did you select these two items? How do they relate in history? **0:10** minutes

ENGLISH LANGUAGE LEARNERS ELD

Outline and Take Notes To help students develop their English comprehension skills, ask them to write an outline of this lesson. Have students at the **Emerging** and **Expanding** levels work in pairs and students at the **Bridging** level work independently. The following format can help them start writing their outlines.

I.   Culture and Cultural Elements

    A.

    B.

II. Elements of Early Cultures

    A.

    B.

III. Cultural Study

    A.

    B.

IV. What Archaeologists Learn

    A.

    B.

STRIVING READERS

Use Examples Define and review some of the words used in this lesson, using context clues or outside dictionaries if necessary: *blend, unifies, generation,* and *site.* Provide examples of each one that are recognizable and familiar to students. Then ask students to use each word in a sentence.

Press **mt** *in the Student eEdition for modified text.*

See the Chapter Planner for more strategies for differentiation.

REVIEW & ASSESS

ANSWERS

1. The artifacts reveal how technologically advanced they were, what jobs they needed to do, and what their daily life was like.

2. Anthropologists provide archaeologists with information about modern cultures. Archaeologists use this information to compare modern cultures with prehistoric ones.

3. The discovery might suggest that these early humans were accomplished hunters and that hunting was important in their culture.

Changing Environments

Today, climate change is forcing us all to make some adjustments—from switching off lights to turning off faucets. Still, we're not the first humans to be affected by shifting climate patterns. A big change in their environment drove Paleolithic people to take steps that would transform the world forever.

MAIN IDEA

A changing climate forced Paleolithic people to move to new places and develop new tools to survive.

+ POSSIBLE RESPONSE

The savannas Paleolithic people lived on would have been lush, green, and flat, with trees for shade and animals to eat.

Critical Viewing Paleolithic people first lived on savannas like this one. Savannas are areas of flat grassland where animals roam. What might have made the savanna a welcoming environment?

COMPARING TOOLS

The stone tool on the left was made about 100,000 years ago. The fishhook made from bone on the right dates back about 42,000 years. You can see that early humans' technical skill had come a long way in about 60,000 years.

FINDING NEW HOMES

About 100,000 years ago, much of Africa had a very unstable climate. Some places became warmer and wetter, while others became hot and dry. These climate changes greatly altered the landscape in which Paleolithic people lived.

Archaeologists have discovered that East Africa suffered a terrible **drought** between 100,000 and 75,000 years ago. This long period of dry, hot weather had a huge impact on the landscape. Rivers and vast lakes shrank and left people struggling for survival. The plants they ate became scarce, and the animals they hunted disappeared. At the same time, previously uninhabitable areas became livable and attractive. For example, the **Sahara**, which is one of the harshest deserts on Earth today, turned into an **oasis**, or a green area where plants can grow. These environmental changes may have encouraged some of the 10,000 Paleolithic people living in East Africa at the time to leave their homeland. They began their long **migration**, or movement, first to the Sahara in North Africa and then into the wider world.

ADAPTING TO NEW CONDITIONS

As people migrated, they responded to some of the challenges of their new environments by using technology. **Technology** is the application of knowledge, tools, and inventions to meet people's needs.

The ability to capture and control fire was a particularly valuable technology. In addition to providing much-needed warmth and light, fire helped Paleolithic people scare away enemies and drive animals into traps. Cooking meat made it easier to digest and killed bacteria.

Paleolithic people also used technology to develop tools that helped them adapt to new environments and climates. Simple tools had been used for millions of years, but *Homo sapiens* refined them to create a really effective tool kit. A hard stone called flint was especially useful, as it could be split into hard, razor-sharp flakes. Early humans learned to design a tool to perform a particular task, such as chopping wood, carving meat, or skinning animals.

Over time, tools grew increasingly advanced. Humans crafted fishhooks out of bone and sewing needles out of ivory. These specialized tools helped our ancestors survive in an amazing range of new habitats and climates—from arctic areas to deserts.

REVIEW & ASSESS

1. **READING CHECK** What led some Paleolithic people to leave their home in East Africa thousands of years ago and migrate to new places?

2. **DETERMINE WORD MEANINGS** What context clues tell you that *uninhabitable* means "unlivable"?

3. **MAKE INFERENCES** Think about the adaptations Paleolithic people made to survive in new conditions. What can you infer about their intelligence?

6.1.1 Describe the hunter-gatherer societies, including the development of tools and the use of fire; 6.1.2 Identify the locations of human communities that populated the major regions of the world and describe how humans adapted to a variety of environments; 6.1.3 Discuss the climatic changes and human modifications of the physical environment that gave rise to the domestication of plants and animals and new sources of clothing and shelter.

17

HSS CONTENT STANDARDS:

6.1.1 Describe the hunter-gatherer societies, including the development of tools and the use of fire; **6.1.2** Identify the locations of human communities that populated the major regions of the world and describe how humans adapted to a variety of environments; **6.1.3** Discuss the climatic changes and human modifications of the physical environment that gave rise to the domestication of plants and animals and new sources of clothing and shelter.

HSS ANALYSIS SKILLS:

REP 1 Students frame questions that can be answered by historical study and research; **HI 2** Students understand and distinguish cause, effect, sequence, and correlation in historical events, including the long- and short-term causal relations.

PLAN

OBJECTIVE

Discuss the impact of climate change and the challenges of new environments on Paleolithic people.

ESSENTIAL QUESTION

How did people manage to survive and thrive tens of thousands of years ago?

When climate change altered the landscape in which Paleolithic people lived, they moved and adapted to the new environments. Lesson 1.3 discusses the technology Paleolithic people developed to survive in a range of new habitats and climates.

BACKGROUND FOR THE TEACHER

The Sahara is a classic example of how environments can change over time. The Sahara, which means "great desert" in Arabic, is the third largest desert in the world and covers most of North Africa. Dry for most of its history, the Sahara undergoes a humid period every 100,000 years. Variations in Earth's tilt and orbit cause changes in how sunlight hits the planet. These humid periods last about 5,000 years, during which the desert becomes lush savanna—as it did during the Paleolithic Age. The last humid period began about 12,000 years ago. Later, the Sahara evolved back to desert over thousands of years.

DIGITAL RESOURCES NGLSync.cengage.com

TEACHER RESOURCES & ASSESSMENT

 Reading and Note-Taking

 Vocabulary Practice

 Section 1 Quiz

STUDENT RESOURCES

 NG Chapter Gallery

INTRODUCE & ENGAGE   STEM

MAKE A TOP TEN LIST

Read the following definition of *technology* aloud to students: the application of knowledge, tools, and inventions to meet people's needs. Then have students make a Top Ten list of their favorite technological inventions. Ask them to jot down how each one meets people's needs. Tell students that Paleolithic people used technology to help them survive. **0:05** minutes

TEACH

GUIDED DISCUSSION

1. **Analyze Cause and Effect** What happened to the landscape of East Africa as a result of a drought that occurred between 100,000 and 75,000 years ago? *(Rivers and vast lakes shrank, plants became scarce, and many animals disappeared.)*

2. **Draw Conclusions** Once Paleolithic people had to move to colder climates, why was it important to develop a tool for skinning animals? *(They would have needed the animal skins to help them keep warm.)*

ANALYZE VISUALS

Have students study the images of early tools. Ask them to think like archaeologists and consider the following questions: What do you think the older tool was used for? How do you think the toolmaker was able to sharpen the points on the fishhook? How do you think the tools were used? Were they thrown or thrust? Were they attached to a handle or string? How much skill was probably needed to use the tools? If possible, discuss the questions and answers in class. **0:10** minutes

ACTIVE OPTIONS

On Your Feet: Three-Step Interview Have students work in pairs to discuss the following question: *How did early humans adapt to new environments?* Instruct them to use more detailed questions to interview one another about specific aspects of the question. For example, "How did early modern humans adapt to a colder or warmer climate? "How did they deal with population growth?" "Did they compete with each other for resources?" "How did they adjust to new weather conditions, such as floods or droughts?" Remind students to listen closely to their partner so that they can report back to the class. For more in-depth coverage of this topic and to learn more about life in the Paleolithic Age, have students complete **California EEI Curriculum Unit 6.1.1**, *Paleolithic People: Tools, Tasks, and Fire.* **0:20** minutes

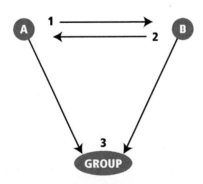

Critical Viewing: NG Chapter Gallery Have students examine the photograph of flint tools in the gallery for this chapter. Have pairs of students make a list of what the tools might have been used for. Then group pairs together to form groups of four, and have students compare their lists. Conclude with a class discussion about how the use of tools indicates that Paleolithic people were capable of advanced thought. **0:20** minutes

DIFFERENTIATE

ENGLISH LANGUAGE LEARNERS   ELD

Create Word Charts Help students at all proficiency levels understand the vocabulary words in this lesson. Display the chart below and write the four vocabulary words above it. Ask students to copy and complete the four parts of the chart for each vocabulary word.

drought	migration
oasis	technology

Definition of _____:	Draw a visual.
Tell how it relates to region.	Use it in a sentence.

PRE-AP   STEM

Compare Desert Formation Have students conduct online research on a desert area in the United States or another country that used to be green and lush. For example, fossils of rain forest plants have been found in some deserts in the United States. Encourage students to find out how scientists learned that the deserts used to be green. Once they've chosen a desert area, have them begin by finding the answers to the following questions: How does the desert today compare with the region at an earlier time? How did scientists learn what the region used to be like? Have students summarize their findings in a brief report comparing the desert today with the region in the past. Then invite them to share their reports with the class.

Press *in the Student eEdition for modified text.*

See the Chapter Planner for more strategies for differentiation.

REVIEW & ASSESS

ANSWERS

1. The changing, unstable climate, which left *Homo sapiens* struggling for survival, led them to migrate and settle in more habitable places.

2. The preceding phrase, "previously uninhabitable areas became livable and attractive" suggests that *uninhabitable* means "unlivable" or "not fit to live in."

3. Students should infer that Paleolithic people were highly intelligent and creative.

1.4 Moving into New Environments

More than 60,000 years ago, the world witnessed movement on a scale never seen before as our restless ancestors began leaving Africa in waves. They set out on a worldwide migration that would permanently populate the entire planet.

MAIN IDEA

Between 70,000 and 10,000 B.C., Paleolithic people migrated from Africa and settled throughout the world.

SPREAD OF EARLY HUMANS

As you have learned, the changing climate made Paleolithic people search for homes outside of Africa. They first migrated into Southwest Asia around 70,000 years ago. The region was warm and tropical and provided lush vegetation and abundant wildlife.

In time, people spread across the rest of the world. From Asia they reached Australia around 50,000 years ago. By about 40,000 years ago, early humans had arrived in Europe. Around 30,000 years ago, *Homo sapiens* reached Siberia on the edge of eastern Asia.

The last continents to be populated were the Americas. This final migration may have been made possible by the **Ice Age**. At its height around 20,000 years ago, the Ice Age trapped so much water as ice that the sea level was nearly 400 feet lower than it is today. This trapped ice created **land bridges** that allowed humans to walk across continents. Many scientists have proposed the theory that hunters crossed the **Beringia** (beh-RIN-gee-uh) land bridge, which connected Siberia with North America, in a series of migrations between 20,000 and 15,000 years ago.

Scientists believe that during a period of glacial melting around 12,000 years ago, more travelers pushed southward through Central America and South America. However, new evidence has emerged that challenges this timing. The genes of some South American people suggest that their ancestors arrived from Australia 35,000 years ago, and *Homo sapiens* footprints in Central America have been dated to 40,000 years ago. These findings might support the theory that the earliest Americans arrived in boats, rather than by land bridge.

IN SEARCH OF FOOD

People migrated to many of these places, possibly in hot pursuit of the animals they liked to eat. Some of these creatures were **megafauna**, which means "large animals." Megafauna included the woolly mammoth, giant ground sloth, and saber-toothed cat, which are shown below.

Megafauna

Humans hunted herds of woolly mammoths in northern Asia and parts of Europe and North America. The giant ground sloth and saber-toothed cat lived primarily in North and South America.

Woolly Mammoth   Giant Ground Sloth   Saber-Toothed Cat

18 CHAPTER 1

This map shows what Earth might have looked like many thousands of years ago. The purple shading indicates areas that were covered in ice from the Ice Age. The green shading shows land that once existed but has since eroded, or worn away.

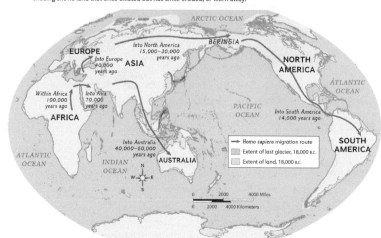

The woolly mammoth, a relative of the modern elephant, was one of the largest megafauna. It stood between 9 and 11 feet tall and weighed as much as six tons. Its curved tusks grew up to 13 feet long.

At five tons, the giant ground sloth wasn't much smaller than the woolly mammoth. However, the sloth was fairly harmless. It mostly used its long claws to tear leaves and bark, not other animals.

There was more reason to fear the saber-toothed cat with its two huge, swordlike teeth. This creature was smaller than a modern lion but much heavier, weighing more than 400 pounds.

These megafauna became extinct, or died out, about 11,000 years ago. Many scientists believe they were overhunted or wiped out by climate change as the Ice Age began to come to a close.

REVIEW & ASSESS

1. **READING CHECK** What food did Paleolithic people eat when they migrated to Asia and other parts of the world?

2. **INTERPRET MAPS** What challenges do you think people encountered as they moved into the new environments shown on the map?

3. **FORM OPINIONS** Do you think the Americas became populated by land bridge, by boat, or by a combination of the two? Explain your position.

6.1.2 Identify the locations of human communities that populated the major regions of the world and describe how humans adapted to a variety of environments; CST 3 Students use a variety of maps and documents to identify physical and cultural features of neighborhoods, cities, states, and countries and to explain the historical migration of people, expansion and disintegration of empires, and the growth of economic systems.

19

HSS CONTENT STANDARDS:

6.1.1 Describe the hunter-gatherer societies, including the development of tools and the use of fire; **6.1.2** Identify the locations of human communities that populated the major regions of the world and describe how humans adapted to a variety of environments; **6.1.3** Discuss the climatic changes and human modifications of the physical environment that gave rise to the domestication of plants and animals and new sources of clothing and shelter.

HSS ANALYSIS SKILLS:

CST 2 Students construct various time lines of key events, people, and periods of the historial era they are studying; **CST 3** Students use a variety of maps and documents to identify physical and cultural features of neighborhoods, cities, states, and countries and to explain the historical migration of people, expansion and disintegration of empires, and the growth of economic systems.

PLAN

OBJECTIVE

Identify where Paleolithic people migrated and some of the food they found there.

ESSENTIAL QUESTION

How did people manage to survive and thrive tens of thousands of years ago?

Over tens of thousands of years, many Paleolithic people left Africa and populated the world. Lesson 1.4 discusses their search for habitable environments and plentiful supplies of food.

BACKGROUND FOR THE TEACHER

In the previous lesson, students learned that climates change over time. Add to that the impact of humans, and you get additional changes. Woolly mammoths and other megafauna all died out around the same time. Most scientists offer two main reasons, which may be related, for the giant animals' extinction. Primarily, scientists point to climate change. Experts argue that woolly mammoths, with their heavy coats, could not handle the warming climate. Hotter temperatures may also have destroyed plants that the mammoths—who were herbivores—depended on for survival. After climate change decreased their numbers, humans may have dealt woolly mammoths the death blow, hunting the animals to extinction for their meat, skin, and bones.

DIGITAL RESOURCES NGLSync.cengage.com

TEACHER RESOURCES & ASSESSMENT

 Reading and Note-Taking

 Vocabulary Practice

 Section 1 Quiz

STUDENT RESOURCES

 Active History

INTRODUCE & ENGAGE

STEM

WRITE ABOUT CLIMATE

Have students take a few minutes to write about their most memorable climate-related experience. Then ask volunteers to share what they wrote. **ASK:** How does climate affect your everyday life? How do you adapt to changes in the climate? (*Sample response: The climate affects how I dress. In the summer, I usually wear shorts, while in the winter, I have to wear a coat.*) Explain to students that in this lesson, they will learn how climate-related changes affected Paleolithic people. **0:05** minutes

TEACH

GUIDED DISCUSSION

1. **Analyze Cause and Effect** What do scientists believe happened as a result of the Ice Age? (*So much water was trapped as ice that the sea level lowered significantly.*)

2. **Make Inferences** What probably allowed Paleolithic people to successfully hunt and kill woolly mammoths? (*their improved tools and weapons*)

INTERPRET MAPS

Have students study the early human migration map and trace the migrations with their finger. Point out the Beringia land bridge and the green shading that indicates land that existed about 20,000 years ago. Then have them find the areas that were covered by glaciers during this period. **ASK:** What do you think the climate was like in the northern part of North America? (*probably very cold*) Where do you think people settled in North America? (*south of the glacial area*) Why do you think South America was the last continent to be populated by humans? (*It is farthest away from Africa.*) **0:10** minutes

ACTIVE OPTIONS

Active History: Compare Past and Present Land Areas Extend the lesson by using either the PDF or Whiteboard version of the activity. These activities take a deeper look at a topic from, or related to, the lesson. Explore the activities as a class, turn them into group assignments, or even assign them individually. **0:10** minutes

NG Learning Framework: Research a Critical Species STEM

ATTITUDE: **Curiosity**
KNOWLEDGE: **Critical Species**

Have students select one of the megafauna creatures they are still curious about after learning about them in this chapter. Instruct them to write a short essay about this creature using information from the chapter and additional source material. Extend the activity by having students research a modern animal on the verge of extinction and write about why it is important to try and preserve as much biodiversity on the planet as possible. **0:15** minutes

DIFFERENTIATE

STRIVING READERS

Use a TASKS Approach Help students understand the map by using the following TASKS strategy:

T Read the **title**, which explains the subject of the map.
A **Ask** yourself what the map is trying to show.
S Determine how **symbols** are used.
K Look at the **key**, or legend.
S **Summarize** what you learned.

INCLUSION

Make a Time Line Pair each student with a proficient reader. Ask proficient readers to read aloud from the lesson and discuss the information in the map. Then have the partners work together to create a time line based on the information in the lesson and map.

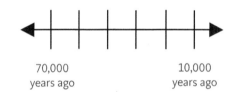

70,000
years ago

10,000
years ago

Press **mt** in the Student eEdition for modified text.

See the Chapter Planner for more strategies for differentiation.

REVIEW & ASSESS

ANSWERS

1. They fed on the vegetation and megafauna.

2. Paleolithic people must have encountered hostile climates, unfamiliar animals, and rugged landscapes in their new environments.

3. Some students will favor the land bridge theory because sailing on primitive boats for such long distances seems unlikely. Others will support the boat theory because traveling across ice on foot doesn't seem possible. Still others will support a combination of the two theories.

Tracking Migration
Out of Africa

Archaeologist Jeffrey Rose lives in a desert truck stop in the Southwest Asian country of Oman. He spends his days with his team of experts, sifting through rocks in 100-degree heat. Occasionally, he finds what he's looking for: small, sharp, egg-shaped stones. That may not sound like much, but his finds may dramatically rewrite our earliest history. Rose is looking for evidence to support his theory about who first migrated out of Africa and what route was taken. After years of exploration, he thinks he might have found the answer.

Jeffrey Rose has conducted work in many parts of Southwest Asia, including this desert outside of Dubai, United Arab Emirates.

MAIN IDEA

Jeffrey Rose has found evidence to support a new theory about which Paleolithic people first left Africa and what route they took.

LOOKING FOR EVIDENCE

National Geographic Explorer Jeffrey Rose conducted his search in Oman. Geneticists—scientists who study DNA and heredity—have suggested that the first humans to leave Africa traveled through Ethiopia to Yemen and Oman, following the coast of the Arabian Peninsula. Rose went to Oman hoping to find archaeological evidence of this migration.

He recorded the earliest traces of humans: discarded flint tools. "Our geologist constantly reads the landscape to tell us where Paleolithic humans would have found water and flint. Find those and you find early people," Rose says. However, after years of surveying, he'd found no African-style artifacts and no evidence of Paleolithic humans on the Arabian Peninsula coast.

HITTING THE JACKPOT

Then in 2010, on the final day at the last site on his list, Rose hit the jackpot. He found a stone spear point with a design unique to people of the Nubian Complex, who had lived in the Nile Valley in North Africa. "We had never considered that the link to Africa would come from the Nile Valley and that their route would be through the middle of the Arabian Peninsula rather than along the coast," says Rose. Yet it made sense that people would migrate to Arabia from the Nile Valley. As Rose points out, "It's logical that people moved from an environment they knew to another that mirrored it."

By the end of 2013, he had found more than 250 Nubian Complex sites in Oman.

When Rose dated the artifacts, he discovered they were roughly 106,000 years old, a point in time when people of the Nubian Complex flourished in Africa. The puzzle pieces fit. "Geneticists have shown that the modern human family tree began to branch out more than 60,000 years ago," says Rose. "I'm not questioning *when* it happened, but *where*. I suggest the great modern human expansion to the rest of the world was launched from Arabia rather than Africa." Rose's evidence suggests that perhaps it was a two-stage process. Paleolithic people might have left North Africa for Arabia more than 100,000 years ago. Then about 40,000 years later, they left Arabia and began to settle the rest of the world.

Now Rose wants to know why it was people of the Nubian Complex who spread from Africa. "What was it about their technology and culture that enabled them to expand so successfully," he wonders, "and what happened next?" As Rose says, "We've always looked to the beginning and wanted to understand how we got here. That's what it means to be human."

OUT OF AFRICA

(map showing EGYPT, SAUDI ARABIA / ARABIAN PENINSULA, SUDAN, SOUTH SUDAN, ETHIOPIA, SOMALIA, YEMEN, DJIBOUTI, OMAN, ASIA, AFRICA, INDIAN OCEAN, Nile Valley, Eastern Desert)
Legend: → Human migrations; Ancient land areas

REVIEW & ASSESS

1. **READING CHECK** What theory has Jeffrey Rose proposed about the migration of Paleolithic people?

2. **INTERPRET MAPS** What body of water did the Nubians cross to get to the Arabian Peninsula?

3. **MAKE INFERENCES** Why would resources of water and flint have been important to early humans?

6.1.2 Identify the locations of human communities that populated the major regions of the world and describe how humans adapted to a variety of environments; CST 3 Students use a variety of maps and documents to identify physical and cultural features of neighborhoods, cities, states, and countries and to explain the historical migration of people, expansion and disintegration of empires, and the growth of economic systems; HI 5 Students recognize that interpretations of history are subject to change as new information is uncovered.

HSS CONTENT STANDARDS:

6.1.2 Describe the hunter-gatherer societies, including the development of tools and the use of fire.

HSS ANALYSIS SKILLS:

CST 3 Students use a variety of maps and documents to identify physical and cultural features of neighborhoods, cities, states, and countries and to explain the historical migration of people, expansion and disintegration of empires, and the growth of economic systems; **REP 1** Students frame questions that can be answered by historical study and research; **HI 2** Students understand and distinguish cause, effect, sequence, and correlation in historical events, including the long- and short-term causal relations; **HI 5** Students recognize that interpretations of history are subject to change as new information is uncovered.

PLAN

OBJECTIVE

Evaluate a theory about which Paleolithic people first left Africa and what route they took.

ESSENTIAL QUESTION

How did people manage to survive and thrive tens of thousands of years ago?

Explorer Jeffrey Rose believes that the human migration out of Africa was launched from the Arabian Peninsula. Lesson 1.5 describes the evidence discovered by Rose, who believes that early humans living in the Nile Valley eventually moved to a similarly hospitable environment in Arabia.

BACKGROUND FOR THE TEACHER

Understanding the ancient environment of the Nile Valley gives Jeffrey Rose's work some context. Scientists believe that hominins first began living in the Nile Valley more than 500,000 years ago. Paleolithic humans may have lived primarily in the part of the valley that runs through present-day Sudan. During the last Ice Age, however, the changing climate had a big impact on the Nile Valley. Less rain fell, and the river became smaller. In addition, frost killed some of the vegetation in the valley. Although there were still important food resources, some of the large animals left or vanished from the region. Perhaps it was these dwindling resources that motivated the people of the Nubian Complex to leave the valley about 100,000 years ago and search for a new home in Arabia.

DIGITAL RESOURCES NGLSync.cengage.com

TEACHER RESOURCES & ASSESSMENT

 Reading and Note-Taking

 Vocabulary Practice

 Section 1 Quiz

STUDENT RESOURCES

 NG Chapter Gallery

INTRODUCE & ENGAGE

PREVIEW THE MAP

Have students examine the Out of Africa map in the lesson. Ask volunteers to use the key to identify what the red lines represent and trace them on the map. **ASK:** Where does the red line begin? (*in the Nile Valley in present-day Sudan*) On what continent is this place located? (*Africa*) Where does the line end? (*on the Arabian Peninsula*) On what continent is this place located? (*Asia*) Tell students that the map represents National Geographic Explorer Jeffrey Rose's theory about the first human migration out of Africa. `0:05` minutes

TEACH   `STEM`

GUIDED DISCUSSION

1. **Explain** Why did Jeffrey Rose first go to Oman to search for archaeological evidence of the early human migration out of Africa? (*Geneticists believed that the first humans to leave Africa traveled through Ethiopia to Yemen and Oman, following the coast of the Arabian Peninsula.*)

2. **Sequence Events** According to Jeffrey Rose, what two events launched the great modern human expansion from Africa? (*Paleolithic people left North Africa more than 100,000 years ago. Then about 40,000 years later, they left Arabia and began to settle in the rest of the world.*)

MAKE INFERENCES

Direct students to the quote from Jeffrey Rose at the end of the lesson. **ASK:** What does Rose mean by the last sentence of the quote: "That's what it means to be human."? (*Possible response: He means that it's human to be curious and want to know as much as we can about our history and where we came from.*) `0:10` minutes

ACTIVE OPTIONS

On Your Feet: Rotating Discussion Assign students to one of four corners in the room. Then have each team think of several questions about Jeffrey Rose's search and theory. Start the discussion by tossing a bean bag or other soft object to Team A and asking a question. When Team A answers the question, have them toss the bean bag to another team while asking one of their prepared questions. Continue until teams have exhausted their questions. `0:25` minutes

NG Learning Framework: Write a Biography

ATTITUDE: **Curiosity**
KNOWLEDGE: **Our Human Story**

Have students learn more about archaeologist Jeffrey Rose. Instruct them to write a short biography or profile about Rose using information from the chapter and additional source material. `0:10` minutes

DIFFERENTIATE

STRIVING READERS

Complete Sentence Starters Provide these sentence starters for students to complete after reading. You may also have students preview the starters to set a purpose for reading.

- The earliest traces of humans are _____.
- In Oman, Rose found a stone spear point with a design unique to _____.
- Rose believes that about 100,000 years ago, Paleolithic people left North Africa for _____.
- About 40,000 years later, they began to settle _____.

ENGLISH LANGUAGE LEARNERS   `ELD`

Organize Events Use the following strategies to help students at different proficiency levels organize the information they gathered for the NG Learning Framework activity.

- **Emerging** Have students draw events in Jeffrey Rose's life on index cards. Talk with students to elicit key words that describe each event on their cards. Also help them determine dates. Have students write the words and the dates on the cards. Then students can sort the events in the order in which they happened.

- **Expanding** Have students work with partners to make a list of the important events in Jeffrey Rose's life. Students can number the events in the order in which they happened. Then they can write the events in a graphic organizer such as a Sequence Chain.

- **Bridging** Have students place events in Jeffrey Rose's life in chronological order. Then have them share their work with partners to evaluate the order. Students should add dates where needed to clarify the time order. Then students can add one or two details to the events.

Press *in the Student eEdition for modified text.*

See the Chapter Planner for more strategies for differentiation.

REVIEW & ASSESS

ANSWERS

1. He suggests that Paleolithic people first migrated from Africa to Arabia and, from there, expanded to the rest of the world.

2. The Nubians crossed the Red Sea to get to the Arabian Peninsula.

3. Early humans needed water to survive, and they used flint to make tools and spark fires.

1.6 Cave Art

It wasn't all about tools in the Paleolithic Age. Early humans had an artistic side as well. Prehistoric graffiti appears on cave walls all over the world. It turns out that the urge for artistic expression is almost as old as humankind itself.

MAIN IDEA

Cave paintings reveal much about Paleolithic people and their world.

ANCIENT ARTISTS

Art is an important part of culture. It shows a capacity for creativity, which separates humans from animals. Very early humans may have collected pretty rocks, carved wood, or painted pictures of themselves and their surroundings.

However, around 35,000 years ago, an artistic explosion occurred when humans began painting detailed images on cave walls. Examples have been found across the world, but it took archaeologists a long time to accept that the cave paintings had been created during the Paleolithic Age. They found it hard to believe that prehistoric people had the ability, time, or desire to produce such beautiful works of art.

The subjects of these cave paintings vary quite a bit, which is not surprising since they were created over a span of 25,000 years. The paintings often depict side-view images of animals, including woolly mammoths and horses. Some images feature everyday scenes, such as deer being hunted by men with spears. Other images consist of lines, circles, and geometric patterns.

One type of image that appears all over the world is considered by many to be one of the most moving: handprints. An artist often created this image by blowing paint through a reed over the hands—leaving behind the imprint of people who lived thousands of years ago.

GLIMPSE INTO AN EARLY WORLD

The **Lascaux Cave** in France has some of Europe's most amazing cave paintings, which were created about 17,000 years ago. The cave contains about 600 beautifully clear paintings, mostly of animals, many in shades of red, yellow, and brown. Some of the animals, including a nearly 17-foot-long bull-like creature, are now extinct.

Spectacular cave and rock paintings in Australia's Kakadu National Park show details of daily life and also reflect the spiritual beliefs of Aborigines, the earliest people who lived in Australia. These beliefs include a strong connection to the land and nature, which is still shared by the people who live in the region today.

The Sahara is also rich in rock art. The Tassili-n-Ajjer (tuh-sill-ee-nah-JAIR) mountain range in North Africa has spectacular paintings showing the once abundant wildlife and grasslands of this now barren desert. The Cave of the Hands in Argentina contains an incredible wall of handprints, as shown on the next page.

Despite many theories, it is unclear why Paleolithic people created such beautiful images in dark and hard-to-reach caves. Some researchers believe that most early art was actually created outdoors but has long since faded away. While we are unlikely to ever fully understand the meaning of Paleolithic art, it does provide insight into the lives and culture of our ancestors.

Researchers believe that this painting from the Cave of the Hands in Argentina shows the handprints of 13-year-old boys.

REVIEW & ASSESS

1. **READING CHECK** What do cave paintings reveal about Paleolithic people?

2. **INTEGRATE VISUALS** What different purposes might cave art have served in the Paleolithic world?

3. **COMPARE AND CONTRAST** What does the rock art in North Africa reveal about how that region has changed from the Paleolithic Age to today?

6.1.1 Describe the hunter-gatherer societies, including the development of tools and the use of fire.

23

STANDARDS

HSS CONTENT STANDARDS:

6.1 Students describe what is known through archaeological studies of the early physical and cultural development of humankind from the Paleolithic era to the agricultural revolution.

HSS ANALYSIS SKILLS:

HI 5 Students recognize that interpretations of history are subject to change as new information is uncovered.

PLAN

OBJECTIVE

Learn what cave art reveals about the lives and culture of Paleolithic people.

ESSENTIAL QUESTION

How did people manage to survive and thrive tens of thousands of years ago?

Paleolithic people created beautiful works of art that have been preserved in caves throughout the world. Lesson 1.6 describes some of the Paleolithic art archaeologists have found, and suggests that the urge for artistic expression is almost as old as humankind itself. It is one of the earliest expressions of identity.

BACKGROUND FOR THE TEACHER

Archaeologists did not discover the cave paintings in Lascaux Cave. Instead, a group of French teenage boys stumbled upon them. In their village, they had heard people talk about a secret underground passage in the countryside that was supposed to contain a hidden treasure. The boys decided to look for it. After one of the boys found an opening that led to a long vertical shaft, they all went to explore. The teenagers were amazed at what they found: rooms of paintings featuring colorful animals. When scientists visited the cave, they told the teenagers that they were probably the first humans to see the paintings in 17,000 years.

DIGITAL RESOURCES NGLSync.cengage.com

TEACHER RESOURCES & ASSESSMENT

 Reading and Note-Taking

 Vocabulary Practice

 Section 1 Quiz

STUDENT RESOURCES

 NG Chapter Gallery

ANALYZE VISUALS

Have students examine the image from the Cave of the Hands in Argentina. Tell students that the artist blew paint through a reed over the hands to create a stencil, which he or she then filled in. Then ask them to outline their left or right hand. Once students have created their outlines and filled them in, use the drawings to create a collage of handprints. Discuss with students the similarities between the collage and the image from the Cave of the Hands. **ASK:** What emotions and impressions does the ancient image inspire? (*Possible responses: awe, joy, and sadness; The hands help bring the subjects and the age to life.*) `0:15` minutes

TEACH

GUIDED DISCUSSION

1. **Summarize** Why didn't archaeologists believe at first that the cave paintings they'd found all over the world had been created by Paleolithic people? (*They found it hard to believe that prehistoric people had the ability, time, or desire to produce such beautiful works of art.*)

2. **Draw Conclusions** What can archaeologists learn about Paleolithic people by studying their art? (*Possible response: They can learn about animals that are now extinct, and they can learn what the world's climate was like tens of thousands of years ago.*)

MORE INFORMATION

Australia's Aborigines The Aborigines are considered the oldest continuous human culture in the world. Their customs and beliefs are based largely on their close relationship with the land. According to their belief system, ancestral beings shaped the world during an era often referred to as *Dreamtime*. Dreamtime has a constant presence in the lives of Aborigines and is manifested in every aspect of nature. For Aborigines, Dreamtime connects the individual in the present to ancestors in the past.

ACTIVE OPTIONS

On Your Feet: Question and Answer Have half the class write true-false questions based on information in Lesson 1.6. Ask the other half to create answer cards, with "True" written on one side and "False" on the other. As each question is read aloud, students in the second group should stand and display the correct answer to the question. When discrepancies occur, review the question and discuss which answer is correct. `0:15` minutes

Critical Viewing: NG Chapter Gallery Invite students to choose one of the examples of Paleolithic cave art in the gallery for this chapter and discuss it with a partner. Ask descriptive questions that will inspire this process, such as "What colors did the artist use?" "What is shown in the painting/carving?" Then have students interpret the art based on the following questions: "What was important to Paleolithic people?" "What in the artwork supports your interpretation?" "Why do you think the artist painted this?" Have student pairs share their interpretations with the class. As an extension to this activity, have students analyze the rock art from western Australia in the **Primary Source Handbook** and answer the questions that follow it. `0:10` minutes

INCLUSION

Clarify Text Have visually impaired students work with sighted partners. As they listen to an audio recording of the text, have the visually impaired students indicate if there are words or passages they do not understand. Their partners can clarify meanings by repeating passages, emphasizing context clues, and paraphrasing.

ENGLISH LANGUAGE LEARNERS

Analyze Visuals Provide the following sentence frames to help students at different proficiency levels participate in the discussion of Paleolithic cave art in the Critical Viewing activity:

- **Emerging**
  This image makes me think/feel _____ .

- **Expanding**
  I think the artist painted/carved this because _____ .

- **Bridging**
  The artist chose this color to create a tone of _____ .

Press **mt** *in the Student eEdition for modified text.*

See the Chapter Planner for more strategies for differentiation.

ANSWERS

1. The cave paintings reveal the creativity and artistic talent of early humans. The subjects of the paintings also reveal the importance of animals and nature in their world.

2. Artists might have created the art to communicate with others, to use in religious ceremonies, or simply to express themselves.

3. Rock art in the Tassili-n-Ajjer mountain range in North Africa shows a region once abundant with wildlife and grasslands. Today, it lies in the barren Sahara.

2.1 Nomadic Hunter-Gatherers

When you're hungry, you probably raid the fridge or head for the store. When Paleolithic people were hungry, they tracked down an animal, killed it with their handmade weapons, and then cooked it over a fire they had to carefully start and keep going. That's what it took to survive every day.

MAIN IDEA

Paleolithic people were constantly on the move to find food.

MOVING WITH THE SEASONS

The Paleolithic world had no farms or stores, but it did have a rich variety of foods. People just had to search them out. During the Paleolithic Age, humans lived as hunter-gatherers. A **hunter-gatherer** hunts animals and gathers wild plants to eat. These tasks were made easier and safer by the fact that early humans worked together and shared the jobs.

Most hunter-gatherer groups were small—around 30 people. The men hunted, often herding large animals into traps or over cliffs. Meanwhile, the women and young children gathered fruits and nuts. Scientists have learned a great deal about hunter-gatherers by studying the body and belongings of a later hunter known as the Iceman, seen at right.

Because the animal herds moved with the seasons, so did the groups hunting them. People who move from place to place like this are called **nomads**. Nomadic hunter-gatherers traveled light. They carried all their possessions with them, including stone tools and clothing.

As hunter-gatherers traveled in areas outside of Africa, they learned to adapt to their new environments—especially the cold. They made needles that enabled them to sew warm clothes out of animal skins. Caves offered the best protection from the worst winter weather. However, people also made shelters of wood, bone, and animal skins, which provided temporary camps.

FOLLOWING THE HERDS

Nomadic hunter-gatherers followed herds of megafauna as the animals moved from place to place. The herds migrated with the seasons and entered new environments created by the changeable Ice Age climate. For example, the Beringia land bridge allowed herds of woolly mammoths to cross into North America, with hunter-gatherers following close behind.

It wasn't easy to kill an animal as big as a woolly mammoth. It took intelligence, teamwork, and special tools. Paleolithic people developed deadly new weapons, including barbed harpoons, spear-throwers, and bows and arrows. These weapons allowed them to kill from a distance, which made the task safer and more efficient. The rewards were also great. A woolly mammoth could feed the group for months.

As humans spread around the world, various human groups competed for resources. Conflict would have been most common during cold periods when food and shelter were scarce. It's likely that in warmer periods of plentiful food, human groups interacted more happily, sharing their technology and culture. This interaction helped spread new ideas and paved the way for a remarkable new stage in human development.

THE ICEMAN

The Iceman lived around 3300 B.C. More than 5,000 years later, hikers found his frozen body in the Alps in Europe. His clothing, his tools, and even the contents of his stomach have helped scientists understand how prehistoric people lived. The graphic here offers some clues as to how he might have died.

1 The Iceman perches on a cliff. He tests the copper blade of his ax and the flint points of his dagger with satisfaction. They're razor sharp. He searches below for his prey. With any luck, he'll bring goat meat back to his community tonight.

2 Suddenly an arrow pierces the Iceman's shoulder. Another hunter has shot him from behind. The Iceman falls off the cliff into the snowbank below.

3 Desperately the Iceman rises and struggles to fight off his attacker, but he's too weak. He falls back down but manages to crawl into a cave in the ice. As the Iceman dies, snow begins to fall. Snow and ice will hide him from view for the next 5,000 years.

REVIEW & ASSESS

1. **READING CHECK** Why were Paleolithic people constantly moving from place to place?

2. **INTEGRATE VISUALS** What words would you use to describe hunter-gatherers such as the Iceman?

3. **ANALYZE CAUSE AND EFFECT** What impact did the changing climate have on hunter-gatherers?

6.1.1 Describe the hunter-gatherer societies, including the development of tools and the use of fire; HI 2 Students understand and distinguish cause, effect, sequence, and correlation in historical events, including the long- and short-term causal relations.

25

STANDARDS

HSS CONTENT STANDARDS:

6.1.1 Describe the hunter-gatherer societies, including the development of tools and the use of fire.

HSS ANALYSIS SKILLS:

HI 2 Students understand and distinguish cause, effect, sequence, and correlation in historical events, including the long- and short-term causal relations.

PLAN

OBJECTIVE

Learn how Paleolithic people moved with the seasons and followed herds of animals to hunt and gather food.

ESSENTIAL QUESTION

How did people manage to survive and thrive tens of thousands of years ago?

Paleolithic people hunted animals and gathered wild plants for food. Lesson 2.1 describes how nomadic hunter-gatherers moved from place to place to survive.

BACKGROUND FOR THE TEACHER

The Iceman, also known as Ötzi, provided a remarkable glimpse into the lives of Neolithic hunter-gatherers. His clothing and equipment were of particular interest to archaeologists since, under normal conditions, these would have disintegrated long ago. Ötzi was wearing leggings and a coat made of goat skin. His shoes were insulated on the inside with grass and hay, while the outside was made of deerskin. Ötzi was well equipped for hunting. He carried an ax, dagger, bow, and arrows. Researchers also found a simple first-aid kit. This held two strips of hide onto each of which had been threaded a lump of tree fungus. This type of fungus was actually used for various medicinal purposes up until the 20th century.

DIGITAL RESOURCES NGLSync.cengage.com

TEACHER RESOURCES & ASSESSMENT

 Reading and Note-Taking

 Vocabulary Practice

 Section 2 Quiz

STUDENT RESOURCES

 NG Chapter Gallery

INTRODUCE & ENGAGE

PREVIEW TERMS

Introduce the concept of nomadism by asking students to imagine what their lives would be like if they were constantly on the move. Point out that nomads carry all of their belongings with them. Ask students what items they'd take with them if they were part of a nomadic family. Tell students that some people live as nomads today. For example, describe the nomads of Mongolia who carry and set up their *gers*, or portable tents, wherever they go. **0:10 minutes**

TEACH

GUIDED DISCUSSION

1. **Describe** How did nomadic hunters kill a woolly mammoth? *(They worked in groups and used weapons, such as spear-throwers and bows and arrows, to kill the animal from a distance.)*

2. **Analyze Cause and Effect** What happened when human groups enjoyed warm weather and found plentiful food? *(Groups may have interacted, sharing their culture and technology.)*

INTEGRATE VISUALS

Have students study the illustration. Then have volunteers read the introduction and captions aloud. **ASK:** Based on the drawings, what was the climate probably like for the Iceman? *(cold and snowy)* Do you think animals were plentiful or scarce while the Iceman was hunting? *(scarce)* Why do you think the other hunter killed the Iceman? *(to eliminate competition for game; to steal his equipment)* **0:10 minutes**

ACTIVE OPTIONS

On Your Feet: Word Chain Have students form three lines. Hand a piece of paper to the first person in each line with one of these words or terms from the text: *hunter-gatherer, nomad, specialized tools*. The first student in line adds a word to the list that relates to the original word. Students pass the paper from person to person, each one adding a word or phrase they associate with the previously written word. Have a volunteer from each group read off the Word Chain and ask the rest of the class to listen for any words that were used in more than one or any that may not connect correctly. **0:20 minutes**

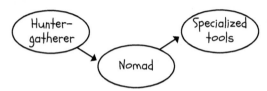

NG Learning Framework: Hunting and Gathering

ATTITUDE: Curiosity
SKILL: Problem-Solving

Have students get together in groups. Ask them to imagine they are hunter-gatherers during the Paleolithic Age and they must either hunt or gather some food. Have each group come up with a plan for finding edible plants or hunting an animal. Once the groups have devised a plan, have them share it with the class. **0:10 minutes**

DIFFERENTIATE

STRIVING READERS

Monitor Comprehension Have students work in small groups, reading aloud the text paragraph by paragraph. At the end of each paragraph, have them stop and use these sentence frames:

- This paragraph is about _____.
- One detail that stood out to me is _____.
- The word _____ means _____.
- I don't think I understand _____.

GIFTED & TALENTED

Create Graphics Have students work in groups to create a graphic illustrating another scene in the Iceman's life. Tell students to decide on the scene—for example, the Iceman on a successful hunt, the Iceman returning to his community from a hunt, or the Iceman interacting with his community. Then have students draft their ideas for the scene on a storyboard. The storyboard should include sketches of the scene as well as captions and dialogue bubbles that tell what's going on in each frame. Students should then use the storyboard to create their final graphic. Display the finished graphics in the classroom.

Press **mt** *in the Student eEdition for modified text.*

See the Chapter Planner for more strategies for differentiation.

REVIEW & ASSESS

ANSWERS

1. Paleolithic people were constantly moving in search of food. They hunted animals and gathered wild plants to eat.

2. Examples of words to describe hunter-gatherers might include *hardworking, tough, vulnerable, brave, adaptable, and intelligent.*

3. Herds of animals moved into new environments. Hunter-gatherers followed them and had to learn to adapt to the challenging conditions.

2.2

The Beginnings of Domestication

A pet poodle might lick your hand and follow you everywhere, but dogs weren't always man's best friend. All dogs are descended from wolves. Humans transformed some of these wild animals into loyal helpers, which marked a major breakthrough in learning to control their environment.

MAIN IDEA

Early humans took control of their environment by raising useful plants and taming animals.

+ POSSIBLE RESPONSE

The sheep are standing or walking peacefully around the girls, who seem to be in control of the herd.

Critical Viewing Young nomadic girls corral sheep for milking in northeastern Afghanistan. What details in the photo tell you that the animals have been domesticated?

CHANGING CLIMATE

Around 14,000 years ago, Earth grew warmer, and the ice sheets melted. These changes raised sea levels, created freshwater lakes, and increased global rainfall. Large areas of land became covered with water. As a result, land bridges disappeared, and coastal waters formed that were full of fish. Animals moved, adapted, or died as their habitats, or environments, changed.

These environmental changes also began to transform the ways that hunter-gatherers lived in some areas. The warmer, wetter climate encouraged the development of forests and grasslands and resulted in longer growing seasons. These conditions proved to be perfect for the growth of grasses. In time, people learned to raise other plants and animals, making them useful to humans. This development, called **domestication**, led to the beginning of farming.

TAMING PLANTS AND ANIMALS

Hunter-gatherers had grown plants to increase their productivity long before the ice began to melt. Now the improved climate made growing plants even easier. After scattering seeds in wet ground, hunter-gatherers knew they could return and harvest the plants the following year. Some foods, especially grains from cereals such as wheat and barley, could be stored to feed people and animals year-round.

At about the same time, humans began to tame animals. The earliest domesticated animals were dogs. All around the world, wild wolf pups were caught and bred for hunting and protection. Other animals were domesticated for food: first sheep and goats, then pigs and cattle. As well as providing meat, milk, and wool, some domesticated animals could carry heavy loads and pull carts.

Although most humans remained nomadic, the warmer climate provided certain areas with such abundant resources that some hunter-gatherer groups decided to settle down. For example, areas around estuaries made perfect places to live. An estuary is formed where a river feeds into the ocean. The combination of fresh water, salt water, and land provided people with a year-round supply of food. Settling down to live permanently in such places would bring about a great change that allowed humans to make their next big leap forward.

REVIEW & ASSESS

1. **READING CHECK** How did humans use the plants and animals they domesticated?

2. **ANALYZE CAUSE AND EFFECT** How did the warmer climate and increased rainfall in some places affect people's ability to grow plants for food?

3. **FORM OPINIONS** What do you think were some of the advantages of the settled life over the nomadic one?

6.1.3 Discuss the climatic changes and human modifications of the physical environment that gave rise to the domestication of plants and animals and new sources of clothing and shelter.

27

STANDARDS

HSS CONTENT STANDARDS:

6.1.3 Discuss the climatic changes and human modifications of the physical environment that gave rise to the domestication of plants and animals and new sources of clothing and shelter.

HSS ANALYSIS SKILLS:

HI 2 Students understand and distinguish cause, effect, sequence, and correlation in historical events, including the long- and short-term causal relations.

PLAN

OBJECTIVE

Discover how early humans took control of their environment by raising plants and taming animals.

ESSENTIAL QUESTION

How did people manage to survive and thrive tens of thousands of years ago?

Environmental changes allowed early humans to raise and grow certain plants. At the same time, they began to tame animals. Lesson 2.2 describes how learning to domesticate plants and animals began to make life easier for early humans.

BACKGROUND FOR THE TEACHER

An early example of animal domestication is under debate today. Some scientists believe that early humans didn't domesticate wolves. They claim that wolves competed with people for game, so humans would have been far more likely to kill wolves than protect them. Instead, these scientists say that wolves domesticated humans. A friendly, rather than aggressive, wolf may have approached humans while it was scavenging around a human settlement for food. Because of the animal's friendliness, humans may have begun to tolerate the wolf and adopt it. After a few generations, scientists say, these friendly wolves adopted by hunter-gatherers would have begun to look different from wild wolves. The domesticated wolves probably also learned to read human gestures—a trait that only dogs have developed.

DIGITAL RESOURCES NGLSync.cengage.com

TEACHER RESOURCES & ASSESSMENT

 Reading and Note-Taking

 Vocabulary Practice

 Section 2 Quiz

STUDENT RESOURCES

 NG Chapter Gallery

ACTIVATE PRIOR KNOWLEDGE

Have students brainstorm what they already know about domesticated animals, such as listing domesticated species and describing these animals' behavior. Then initiate a discussion about the beginnings of domestication. **ASK:** How might a hunter start to tame an animal? Why might a gatherer start planting seeds? Make a list of students' responses on the board. Tell students that in this lesson, they will investigate dramatic changes that took place when early modern humans began to domesticate plants and animals and settle in one place year round. `0:10` minutes

TEACH

GUIDED DISCUSSION

1. **Make Predictions** How did the disappearance of land bridges probably affect human migration to North America? *(Possible response: It would have made migration more difficult. Instead of being able to walk over land to reach North America from Asia, people probably had to travel across the water.)*

2. **Make Connections** How do people use domesticated animals today? *(Possible response: They still use them on the farm. Domesticated animals are also kept as pets and used to guide and help people with disabilities.)*

ANALYZE VISUALS

Preview the image in the lesson by asking volunteers to describe what they see in the photo. Then read the image caption aloud. Ask students to come up with a definition of *domesticated* based on what they see in the photo. `0:10` minutes

ACTIVE OPTIONS

On Your Feet: Turn and Talk on Topic Have students form three lines. Give each group this topic sentence: *The lives of early humans changed when they learned to domesticate plants and animals.* Tell them to build a paragraph on that topic by having each student in the line add one sentence. Allow each group to present its paragraph to the class by having each student read his or her statement. `0:15` minutes

Critical Viewing: NG Chapter Gallery Have students examine the contents of the Chapter Gallery. Then invite them to brainstorm additional images they believe would fit within the gallery to represent this lesson. Instruct them to do online research to find examples of actual images. Have students explain why these images would belong in the gallery. `0:20` minutes

INCLUSION

Work in Pairs Allow students with disabilities to work with other students who can read the lesson aloud to them. Encourage the partner without disabilities to describe the visual as well. Have students work together to determine their answers to the Critical Viewing and Review & Assess questions. You may also want to give students the option of recording their answers rather than writing them out.

ENGLISH LANGUAGE LEARNERS   ELD

Pose and Answer Questions Have students at similar proficiency levels work in pairs to read Lesson 2.2. Instruct them to pause after each paragraph and ask one another *who, what, when, where,* or *why* questions about what they have just read. Suggest students use a 5Ws Chart to help organize their questions and answers.

Who? _____

What? _____

Where? _____

When? _____

Why? _____
_____
_____

Press **mt** in the Student eEdition for modified text.

See the Chapter Planner for more strategies for differentiation.

ANSWERS

1. They domesticated and grew plants that they could store to feed them all year round. They domesticated animals for hunting and protection, to provide food and wool, and to carry heavy loads.

2. The warmer climate and increased rainfall made it easier to scatter and grow seeds in the wet ground. Later, the plants, especially certain grains, could be harvested and stored.

3. Some advantages might include greater security, stability, and comfort and the opportunity to share one's culture and knowledge with other groups.

2.3 The Agricultural Revolution

If you wanted to grow some crops, you'd probably look for a warm place with a reliable supply of water and soil full of nutrients. Thousands of years ago, a number of river valleys satisfied all of these conditions. They were at the heart of an important change in the way people lived.

MAIN IDEA

Humans settled down and farmed along river valleys and developed new farm tools and methods.

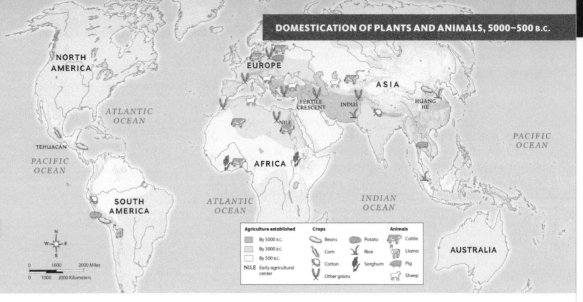

DOMESTICATION OF PLANTS AND ANIMALS, 5000–500 B.C.

Agriculture established
- By 5000 B.C.
- By 3000 B.C.
- By 500 B.C.
- NILE Early agricultural center

Crops: Beans, Corn, Cotton, Other grains, Potato, Rice, Sorghum

Animals: Cattle, Llama, Pig, Sheep

FERTILE RIVER VALLEYS

Imagine that a great change took place all over the world and transformed forever the way people lived. That is exactly what happened when farming largely replaced hunting and gathering. The slow shift to growing food began around 10,000 B.C. and ended around 8000 B.C. By then, many people had discovered that they could live year-round on what they farmed, rather than on what they found.

This shift in the way people lived is called the agricultural revolution. **Agriculture** is the practice of growing plants and rearing animals for food. The shift to agriculture also ushered in a new period known as the **Neolithic Age**, which began somewhere between 10,000 B.C. and 8000 B.C. In the early stages of this period, people began to build farming villages.

Many of the earliest farming villages were in an area called the **Fertile Crescent**. This region stretches from the Persian Gulf to the Mediterranean Sea. It includes the fertile, flat floodplains along the Tigris and Euphrates rivers in Southwest Asia. **Fertile** soil encourages the growth of crops and plants. The region provided a steady food supply. People were able to settle down and enjoy a much more comfortable lifestyle.

THE SICKLE
The sickle, which developed during the Neolithic Age, was crucial to harvesting certain grains. The tool was so important that in some places, people made sickles all the same size so that the tools could be repaired easily and quickly.

NEW FARM TOOLS AND METHODS

Even so, farming was very hard work. To make it easier, Neolithic people developed specialized tools. They fashioned hoes for digging the soil and plows for preparing the land to plant seeds. They also made curved sickles that cut through the stalks of grain and millstones that ground the grain into flour.

Farmers used domesticated animals to make their new tools more efficient. For example, they tied cattle to the plows and led the animals up and down the rows. In addition to helping turn over the soil, the cattle left behind manure that fertilized the land.

Neolithic people also developed new technology for the home. They made clay pots and hardened them in kilns, or ovens. The kilns could also be used to heat and melt the metal from rocks—a process called smelting. The liquid metal was then cast in molds to create metal tools, which eventually began to replace stone tools. The Stone Age had come to a close.

REVIEW & ASSESS

1. **READING CHECK** What new farm tools did humans develop during the agricultural revolution?

2. **INTERPRET MAPS** Along what geographic feature had most agriculture developed by 5000 B.C.?

3. **DRAW CONCLUSIONS** In what ways was the agricultural revolution an important breakthrough in human history?

6.1.3 Discuss the climatic changes and human modifications of the physical environment that gave rise to the domestication of plants and animals and new sources of clothing and shelter; 6.2.2 Trace the development of agricultural techniques that permitted the production of economic surplus and the emergence of cities as centers of culture and power; CST 3 Students use a variety of maps and documents to identify physical and cultural features of neighborhoods, cities, states, and countries and to explain the historical migration of people, expansion and disintegration of empires, and the growth of economic systems; HI 3 Students explain the sources of historical continuity and how the combination of ideas and events explains the emergence of new patterns.

HSS CONTENT STANDARDS:

6.1 Students describe what is known through archaeological studies of the early physical and cultural development of humankind from the Paleolithic era to the agricultural revolution; **6.1.3** Discuss the climatic changes and human modifications of the physical environment that gave rise to the domestication of plants and animals and new sources of clothing and shelter; **6.2.1** Locate and describe the major river systems and discuss the physical settings that supported permanent settlement and early civilizations; **6.2.2** Trace the development of agricultural techniques that permitted the production of economic surplus and the emergence of cities as centers of culture and power.

HSS ANALYSIS SKILLS:

CST 3 Students use a variety of maps and documents to identify physical and cultural features of neighborhoods, cities, states, and countries and to explain the historical migration of people, expansion and disintegration of empires, and the growth of economic systems; **HI 3** Students explain the sources of historical continuity and how the combination of ideas and events explains the emergence of new patterns.

PLAN

OBJECTIVE

Describe how humans settled down and farmed along river valleys and developed new farm tools and methods.

ESSENTIAL QUESTION

How did people manage to survive and thrive tens of thousands of years ago?

As humans moved into fertile river valleys, they began to settle down and replace hunting and gathering with farming. Lesson 2.3 describes the new tools and techniques humans developed to succeed in their new environments.

BACKGROUND FOR THE TEACHER

With the development of agriculture, the Fertile Crescent had most of the natural resources it needed to flourish. There was little wood, metal, or stone, however. What the region did have in abundance was clay. It was used for mud bricks for building and for figurines and pottery. Eventually, the soft clay was also used as a medium for writing.

DIGITAL RESOURCES NGLSync.cengage.com

TEACHER RESOURCES & ASSESSMENT

 Reading and Note-Taking

 Vocabulary Practice

 Section 2 Quiz

STUDENT RESOURCES

 Biography

INTRODUCE & ENGAGE

ANALYZE VISUALS

Bring in an image showing agriculture along the Tigris and Euphrates rivers and show it to the class. Have students discuss what they observe in the photo. **ASK:** What does this photo suggest about one benefit from the Tigris and Euphrates rivers? *(The rivers provide water for crops.)* Tell students that, in this lesson, they will learn about the role these rivers played in bringing about a fundamental change in the way people lived. **0:10** minutes

TEACH

GUIDED DISCUSSION

1. **Compare and Contrast** How does the life of a hunter-gatherer compare with that of a settled farmer? *(Possible responses: A hunter-gatherer is always on the move, while a farmer lives in one place. A hunter-gatherer searches out his food, while a farmer grows or raises most of his. A hunter-gatherer may live in a cave or other temporary home, while a farmer lives in a permanent home he built.)*

2. **Make Inferences** What new challenges might people have encountered as they built and lived together in farming villages? *(Possible responses: growing enough food for everyone, having enough building and other resources for everyone, living in close proximity and getting along)*

INTERPRET MAPS

Have students study the map and its key. Make sure students understand the symbols by asking them to identify different crops and animals on the map. Make sure, too, they understand that the early agricultural centers appear all over the world—not just along the Nile. **ASK:** In which river valleys was agriculture established by 5000 B.C.? *(Fertile Crescent and Indus)* When had agriculture been established in Huang He? *(by 3000 B.C.)* Where else had agriculture been established by this time? *(Nile)* In which river valley did agriculture develop last? *(Tehuacán)* **0:10** minutes

ACTIVE OPTIONS

On Your Feet: Numbered Heads Organize students into groups of four. Tell students to think about and discuss a response to this question: How did the agricultural revolution change people's lives? Then call a number and have the student from each group with that number report for the group. **0:15** minutes

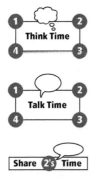

NG Learning Framework: Observe, Exchange, and Discuss

SKILLS: Observation, Collaboration
KNOWLEDGE: Our Living Planet

Have students revisit Lessons 2.2 and 2.3, specifically the information about the domestication of plants and animals and the agricultural revolution. They should work in pairs to create a list of observations about Neolithic people and how their lives changed as a result of domestication and organized agriculture. Once they have completed their list of observations, each pair should exchange lists with another pair and discuss the new list. **0:15** minutes

DIFFERENTIATE

STRIVING READERS

Create Word Squares Have students complete Word Squares for the words *agriculture* and *fertile*.

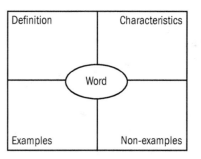

PRE-AP

Research River Valleys Divide the class into four groups and have each learn about one of the four river valleys shown on the map: Tehuacán, Fertile Crescent, Indus, and Huang He. Have them learn about the people who first settled there, what they grew, and how they lived. Tell students that they can present their findings in any form they choose, including a written report or multimedia presentation. Once they have completed their work, ask groups to present them to the class.

Press **mt** *in the Student eEdition for modified text.*

See the Chapter Planner for more strategies for differentiation.

REVIEW & ASSESS

ANSWERS

1. Humans developed new tools such as axes, hoes, plows, sickles, and millstones during the agricultural revolution.

2. Most agriculture had developed along rivers.

3. The agricultural revolution saw the shift from the nomadic life to a settled one. It also led to the development of new and specialized tools, some of which would replace stone tools. The revolution marked the end of the Old Stone Age.

Studying the Past

Historians are detectives. They ask questions about the past that begin with *Who, What, Where, When, Why,* and *How*. They then search for and examine evidence, seeking answers to their questions. As you study the past, you'll become a detective too. You'll learn to think like a historian and use the same skills. You'll develop a historian's mind-set.

MAIN IDEA

Historians—and students of history—apply distinct thinking and research skills to learn the story of human life on Earth.

THINKING ABOUT TIME AND PLACE

Historians ask questions that are rooted in a particular time and place. The most basic information that historians must establish is *when* and *where* a person lived or an event occurred.

Because time and place are so basic to the study of history, time lines and maps are crucial tools of historians. Time lines indicate how major events, people, and periods are related to one another in time. Maps show the physical and cultural features of neighborhoods, cities, states, and countries. Maps can help explain such events as the historical migration of a group of people and the growth of an empire or economic system. If you skim through this book, you'll find time lines and maps that show this kind of information.

RESEARCHING AND EVALUATING EVIDENCE

As you've learned, historians begin their research by asking questions about a particular time and place. They then conduct research by examining evidence from both primary and secondary sources. **Primary sources** are writings or recordings that were created by someone who witnessed or lived through a historical event. These sources include letters, diaries, autobiographies, photographs, and oral histories. An **oral history** is a recorded interview with a person whose experiences and memories have historical significance. **Secondary sources** are writings, recordings, or objects created after an event by someone who did not see it or live during the time when it occurred. Secondary sources are often based on primary sources. History books and many biographies are secondary sources.

As historians examine primary and secondary sources, they apply reasoning skills to evaluate information. For example, to evaluate a piece of writing, a historian asks such questions as:

- Is the author stating a fact or an opinion?
- Is this information relevant—that is, does it apply to the issue being studied?
- Is this information essential or important?
- Can the information be verified, or proven by another reliable source?
- What is the context, or setting, for this information?
- What is the author's point of view?

INTERPRETING EVIDENCE

After historians examine and evaluate evidence, they try to put together a whole picture or story. They explain the central issues, placing people and events in a particular setting. They identify causes, effects, and sequence of events. They look for patterns that continue across time and place as well as the emergence of new patterns. For example, in many eras, nations have formed armies and fought wars against other nations for political, economic, or religious reasons. Global terrorism, however, is a relatively new pattern of warfare.

All historians do not tell the same story. Different historians may interpret the same evidence in different ways. A historian may accidently overlook certain evidence or make an error in interpreting evidence. In addition, new evidence is continually being discovered. That means that interpretations of history differ and often change.

A historian's focus depends partly on the time period and the place being studied. For example, a historian examining the 1900s in Italy might choose to focus on basic indicators of economic performance—statistics that tell how strong an economy is—and analyze the costs and benefits of economic and political decisions. But a historian studying an ancient state would not choose such a focus because such statistics are not available.

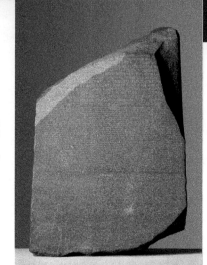

The Rosetta Stone is a primary source from ancient Egypt. Three different types of writing are carved onto the stone, which dates back to 196 B.C.

As you continue to study history, be prepared to apply the intellectual reasoning, reflection, and research skills of a historian. Like a historian, you'll analyze and evaluate primary and secondary sources. Then you'll interpret the evidence and draw some conclusions of your own.

REVIEW & ASSESS

1. **READING CHECK** Why do interpretations of history differ and often change?

2. **ASK QUESTIONS** Frame two questions that can be answered by historical study and research.

3. **COMPARE AND CONTRAST** What is the difference between a primary source and a secondary source?

CST 1 Students explain how major events are related to one another in time; CST 2 Students construct various time lines of key events, people, and periods of the historical era they are studying; CST 3 Students use a variety of maps and documents to identify physical and cultural features of neighborhoods, cities, states, and countries and to explain the historical migration of people, expansion and disintegration of empires, and the growth of economic systems; REP 1 Students frame questions that can be answered by historical study and research; REP 2 Students distinguish fact from opinion in historical narratives and stories; REP 3 Students distinguish relevant from irrelevant information, essential from incidental information, and verifiable from unverifiable information in historical narratives and stories; REP 4 Students assess the credibility of primary and secondary sources and draw sound conclusions from them; REP 5 Students detect the different historical points of view on historical events and determine the context in which the historical statements were made (the questions asked, sources used, author's perspectives); HI 1 Students explain the central issues and problems from the past, placing people and events in a matrix of time and place; HI 2 Students understand and distinguish cause, effect, sequence, and correlation in historical events, including the long- and short-term causal relations; HI 3 Students explain the sources of historical continuity and how the combination of ideas and events explains the emergence of new patterns; HI 4 Students recognize the role of chance, oversight, and error in history; HI 5 Students recognize that interpretations of history are subject to change as new information is uncovered.

HSS ANALYSIS SKILLS:

CST 1 Students explain how major events are related to one another in time; **CST 2** Students construct various time lines of key events, people, and periods of the historical era they are studying; **CST 3** Students use a variety of maps and documents to identify physical and cultural features of neighborhoods, cities, states, and countries and to explain the historical migration of people, expansion and disintegration of empires, and the growth of economic systems; **REP 1** Students frame questions that can be answered by historical study and research; **REP 2** Students distinguish fact from opinion in historical narratives and stories; **REP 3** Students distinguish relevant from irrelevant information, essential from incidental information, and verifiable from unverifiable information in historical narratives and stories; **REP 4** Students assess the credibility of primary and secondary sources and draw sound conclusions from them; **REP 5** Students detect the different historical points of view on historical events and determine the context in which the historical statements were made (the questions asked, sources used, author's perspectives); **HI 1** Students explain the central issues and problems from the past, placing people and events in a matrix of time and place; **HI 2** Students understand and distinguish cause, effect, sequence, and correlation in historical events, including the long- and short-term causal relations; **HI 3** Students explain the sources of historical continuity and how the combination of ideas and events explains the emergence of new patterns; **HI 4** Students recognize the role of chance, oversight, and error in history; **HI 5** Students recognize that interpretations of history are subject to change as new information is uncovered.

PLAN

OBJECTIVE

Describe how historians use a variety of tools and historical sources to study, evaluate, and interpret the past.

ESSENTIAL QUESTION

How did people manage to survive and thrive tens of thousands of years ago?

Historians gather and study evidence from the past to learn about and tell the human story. Lesson 2.4 describes how historians analyze and interpret evidence to find out how humans survived and thrived.

BACKGROUND FOR THE TEACHER

The scholar who cracked the code of the Rosetta Stone was a French historian named Jean-François Champollion. In 1808, at the age of 18, he began his first attempts at deciphering the hieroglyphs on the Rosetta Stone. However, his breakthrough didn't come until 1822, when Champollion concluded that the hieroglyphs were not only symbols but functioned as an alphabet and a phonetic language. Applying this strategy, he was able to successfully decipher the names of two ancient Egyptian rulers written on the stone: Ramses and Thutmose. Using what he learned, he was then able to decipher common nouns.

DIGITAL RESOURCES NGLSync.cengage.com

TEACHER RESOURCES & ASSESSMENT

 Reading and Note-Taking

 Vocabulary Practice

 Section 2 Quiz

STUDENT RESOURCES

 NG Chapter Gallery

INTRODUCE & ENGAGE

ASK QUESTIONS

Ask to borrow a student's backpack, but keep its ownership unknown to the rest of the class. Hold the backpack up so students can study it and ask them what they can learn about it by looking. **ASK:** Who do you think is the owner of this backpack? How do you know? What does the backpack tell you about its owner? Has the owner attached stickers, buttons, or other items to the backpack? How old do you think the backpack is? How can you tell? Why do you think the owner chose this type of backpack? How is this backpack similar to or different from your backpack? Then tell students that these are the types of questions historians might ask as they study evidence from the past. Tell them that they will learn more about how historians study the past in this lesson. `0:10` minutes

TEACH

GUIDED DISCUSSION

1. **Draw Conclusions** Why do historians begin their research by asking questions about a particular time and place? *(Possible response: Time and place are basic to the study of history and to establishing when and where humans lived and events took place.)*

2. **Identify Problems and Solutions** What challenges do historians face when evaluating primary and secondary sources? *(Possible response: Historians need to determine if sources are stating facts or opinions, if the information is relevant, if the information can be verified, and if the sources are reliable.)*

3. **Make Inferences** Why do historians look for patterns of events and issues when interpreting evidence? *(Possible response: By looking for patterns of events and issues, historians can identify patterns that continue across time and place and as well as identify new patterns that emerge.)*

ANALYZE VISUALS

Have students examine the image of the Rosetta Stone. Tell them that the three different types of writing carved onto the stone are hieroglyphic, demotic, and Greek. Point out that the word *hieroglyphic* comes from Greek words meaning "sacred carving." Tell students that the Rosetta Stone stands nearly four feet high and weighs about 1,700 pounds. Then ask students who they think had the writing carved on the stone and what the subject of the writing might be. After their discussion, tell students that an Egyptian ruler had the writing carved on the stone and the text describes his power and the responsibilities of Egyptian priests. `0:10` minutes

ACTIVE OPTIONS

On Your Feet: Three Corners Post these signs in three corners of the classroom: Primary Source, Secondary Source, Oral History. Organize students into groups around each sign and have them discuss that historical source and come up with examples of it. Then have students from the primary source group travel to explain their historical source to each of the other two groups. Have the secondary source and oral history groups repeat the process. `0:15` minutes

Critical Viewing: NG Chapter Gallery Invite students to explore the Chapter Gallery and choose one image that they think is a good example of a primary source. Have students provide a written explanation of what we can learn about early modern humans from this source. `0:15` minutes

DIFFERENTIATE

STRIVING READERS

Use Reciprocal Teaching Have partners take turns reading each paragraph of the lesson aloud. At the end of the paragraph, the reading student should ask the listening student questions about the paragraph. Students may ask their partners to state the main idea of the paragraph, identify important details that support the main idea, or summarize the paragraph in their own words. Then have students work together to answer the "Review & Assess" questions.

INCLUSION

Summarize Information Use a Fishbowl activity to review the lesson. Place students of mixed ability levels in each circle. Call on more advanced students to take turns summarizing the lesson content. When the first group of students has concluded its summary, switch positions and have the inclusion students review the lesson content.

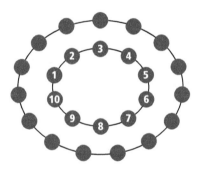

Press (**mt**) *in the Student eEdition for modified text.*

See the Chapter Planner for more strategies for differentiation.

REVIEW & ASSESS

ANSWERS

1. Interpretations of history differ and often change because different historians may interpret evidence differently or a historian may overlook evidence or make an interpretation mistake. In addition, new evidence is continually being discovered.

2. Questions will vary. Sample response: What led to the decline and fall of the Roman Empire? Which of the world's major religions is the oldest?

3. A primary source was created by someone who lived during a historical event; a secondary source was created by someone who was not alive at the time of the historical event or did not witness a historical event.

VOCABULARY

For each pair of vocabulary words, write one sentence that explains the connection between the two words.

1. fossil; artifact (HSS 6.1)
   Both fossils, the remains of living organisms, and artifacts, human-made objects, provide helpful clues to understanding our history.
2. archaeologist; anthropologist (HSS HI 3)
3. culture; oral history (HSS REP 4)
4. anthropologist; culture (HSS HI 3)
5. hunter-gatherer; nomad (HSS 6.1.1)
6. migration; land bridge (HSS CST 3)
7. agriculture; fertile (HSS 6.1.3)
8. primary source; secondary source (HSS REP 4)

READING STRATEGY

9. ORGANIZE IDEAS: COMPARE AND CONTRAST If you haven't already, complete your Venn diagram to compare and contrast the lives of Paleolithic and Neolithic people. Then answer the question.

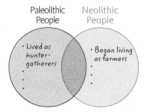

Paleolithic People — Neolithic People
- Lived as hunter-gatherers
- Began living as farmers

In what ways did the lives of Paleolithic and Neolithic people differ? In what ways were they the same? (HSS HI 1)

MAIN IDEAS

Answer the following questions. Support your answers with evidence from the chapter.

10. What do archaeologists learn about early modern humans by studying their artifacts? LESSON 1.1 (HSS HI 5)
11. What effect did a catastrophic drought in East Africa have on *Homo sapiens* thousands of years ago? LESSON 1.3 (HSS 6.1.3)
12. Why were the Paleolithic people who left Africa probably attracted to the region of Southwest Asia? LESSON 1.4 (HSS 6.1.2)
13. How did groups of hunter-gatherers work together? LESSON 2.1 (HSS 6.1.1)
14. What were some of the first plants and animals domesticated by humans? LESSON 2.2 (HSS 6.1.3)
15. Why is the development of farming called the agricultural revolution? LESSON 2.3 (HSS 6.1.3)
16. What sources do historians use to study the past? LESSON 2.4 (HSS REP 4)

CRITICAL THINKING

Answer the following questions. Support your answers with evidence from the chapter.

17. ESSENTIAL QUESTION What factors do you think were essential to the survival of humankind? (HSS HI 1)
18. COMPARE AND CONTRAST How was the culture of prehistoric *Homo sapiens* similar to our own? (HSS HI 3)
19. DRAW CONCLUSIONS What does the domestication of plants and animals suggest about the development of humans? (HSS 6.1.3)
20. YOU DECIDE Some historians think that the agricultural revolution was the most important event in human history. Others claim that the ability to control fire was the most important. Which development do you think was more important? Support your opinion. (HSS HI 3)

INTERPRET MAPS

Study the map of the Fertile Crescent. Then use the map to answer the questions that follow.

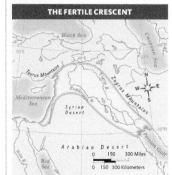

THE FERTILE CRESCENT

21. The Fertile Crescent is the area shown in green on the map. Why do you think the Fertile Crescent was so narrow? (HSS CST 3)
22. What rivers were vital to the development of early farming in the Fertile Crescent? (HSS 6.2.1)
23. What bodies of water bordering the region probably contributed to its fertility? (HSS 6.2.1)
24. MAP ACTIVITY Sketch your own physical map of the Fertile Crescent. Be sure to label all bodies of water, deserts, and mountains. Use a different color for each type of physical feature. How does your map help you visualize the Fertile Crescent and its surrounding area? (HSS CST 3)

ANALYZE SOURCES

Study this cave painting of two bison, or buffalo-like animals, from the Lascaux Cave in France. Then answer the question.

25. What details in the cave painting suggest that the Paleolithic artist who created it was highly skilled? (HSS REP 4)

WRITE ABOUT HISTORY

26. EXPLANATORY Many new developments occurred during the Neolithic Age. Write a paragraph in which you describe one important development and explain how it changed the way people lived. Use the tips below to help you plan, organize, and revise your paragraph. (HSS HI 3)

TIPS
- Take notes from the chapter on the development you chose.
- State your main idea clearly at the beginning of the paragraph.
- Support your main idea with relevant facts, definitions, specific details, and examples.
- Use vocabulary you learned from the chapter.
- Use the same formal style throughout your paragraph.
- Provide a concluding statement about the significance of the development you chose.

VOCABULARY ANSWERS

1. Both fossils, the remains of living organisms, and artifacts, human-made objects, provide helpful clues to understanding our history. (HSS 6.1)
2. An archaeologist digs up fossils and artifacts at an early settlement, and an anthropologist is an archaeologist who studies these objects to understand the culture of the people who once lived there. (HSS HI 3)
3. The songs and stories that make up the oral history of a group of people are an important part of the group's culture. (HSS REP 4)
4. An anthropologist is an archaeologist who studies culture. (HSS HI 3)
5. To survive, hunter-gatherers lived as nomads, moving with the seasons to hunt herds of animals and gather fruits, nuts, roots, and seeds to eat. (HSS 6.1.1)
6. During the Ice Age, land bridges formed that enabled the migration of *Homo sapiens* from one continent to another. (HSS CST 3)
7. The rich nutrients in the fertile soil of the river valleys in the Fertile Crescent allowed people to practice agriculture, or the practice of growing plants and rearing animals for food. (HSS 6.1.3)
8. Historians study primary sources, such as letters and tools, and secondary sources, such as biographies and history books, to understand and interpret historical events. (HSS REP 4)

STANDARDS

HSS CONTENT STANDARDS:

6.1.1 Describe the hunter-gatherer societies, including the development of tools and the use of fire; 6.1.2 Identify the locations of human communities that populated the major regions of the world and describe how humans adapted to a variety of environments; 6.1.3 Discuss the climatic changes and human modifications of the physical environment that gave rise to the domestication of plants and animals and new sources of clothing and shelter; 6.2.1 Locate and describe the major river systems and discuss the physical settings that supported permanent settlement and early civilizations; 6.2.2 Trace the development of agricultural techniques that permitted the production of economic surplus and the emergence of cities as centers of culture and power.

HSS ANALYSIS SKILLS:

CST 3 Students use a variety of maps and documents to identify physical and cultural features of neighborhoods, cities, states, and countries and to explain the historical migration of people, expansion and disintegration of empires, and the growth of economic systems; REP 4 Students assess the credibility of primary and secondary sources and draw sound conclusions about them; HI 1 Students explain the central issues and problems from the past, placing people and events in a matrix of time and place; HI 2 Students understand and distinguish cause, effect, sequence, and correlation in historical events, including the long- and short-term causal relations; HI 3 Students explain the sources of historical continuity and how the combination of ideas and events explains the emergence of new patterns; HI 5 Students recognize that interpretations of history are subject to change as new information is uncovered.

READING STRATEGY ANSWERS

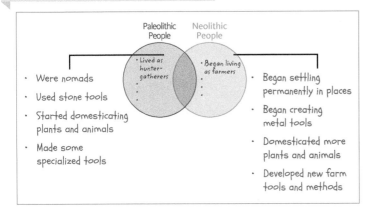

Paleolithic People — Neolithic People

- Were nomads
- Used stone tools
- Started domesticating plants and animals
- Made some specialized tools

(overlap) • Lived as hunter-gatherers • Began living as farmers

- Began settling permanently in places
- Began creating metal tools
- Domesticated more plants and animals
- Developed new farm tools and methods

9. Paleolithic and Neolithic peoples both lived in groups, used tools, and learned to adapt to new conditions by developing specialized tools. However, the way of life for Neolithic people changed when many abandoned the nomadic life of hunter-gatherers and began living as settled farmers. They also developed even more sophisticated and specialized tools and materials than Paleolithic people. (HSS HI 1)

MAIN IDEAS ANSWERS

10. Fossils and artifacts tell us when and how early modern humans lived. (HSS HI 5)

11. The drought in East Africa dried up rivers and lakes, made edible plants scarce, and left *Homo sapiens* struggling for survival. Some began migrating to more habitable locations. (HSS 6.1.3)

12. They were attracted to Southwest Asia because of its lush vegetation and abundant wildlife. (HSS 6.1.2)

13. Men in the groups went out to hunt while the women and young children gathered fruits, nuts, roots, and seeds. (HSS 6.1.1)

14. Some of the first plants were grasses and grains. Some of the first animals were dogs, sheep, goats, pigs, and cattle. (HSS 6.1.3)

15. It's called a revolution because it resulted in a major change in the way people lived. (HSS 6.1.3)

16. Historians use primary and secondary sources and oral history. (HSS REP 4)

CRITICAL THINKING ANSWERS

17. Increased intelligence and the ability to adapt to new situations and environments might have been most essential to the survival of humankind. (HSS HI 1)

18. Like early *Homo sapiens*, people today use language, create art, practice religion, and develop technology. (HSS HI 3)

19. The domestication of plants and animals suggests that humans were learning how to control their environment rather than simply reacting to it. (HSS 6.1.3)

20. Students' responses will vary. Students who believe that the agricultural revolution was more important may point out that it radically changed people's way of life and led to the settled population patterns that we still see today. Students who believe that capturing and controlling fire was more important may say that this ability allowed humans to warm themselves, conquer the dark, and cook food, thereby helping to ensure the survival of humankind. (HSS HI 3)

INTERPRET MAPS ANSWERS

21. The Fertile Crescent was narrow because it was bound by deserts and mountains. (HSS CST 3)

22. The Tigris and Euphrates rivers were vital to the development of early farming. (HSS 6.2.1)

23. The Mediterranean Sea and the Persian Gulf probably contributed to the region's fertility. (HSS 6.2.1)

24. Maps and answers will vary. Students' maps should label all bodies of water, deserts, and mountains and use a different color for each. (HSS CST 3)

ANALYZE SOURCES ANSWER

25. Students' responses will vary. Possible response: The artist's use of color, the suggestion of movement, the realistic depiction, and the use of perspective in the crossed hind legs of the two bison reveal a high level of skill. (HSS REP 4)

WRITE ABOUT HISTORY ANSWER

26. Students' paragraphs should

- provide a clear explanation of one development that changed the way people lived during the Neolithic Age
- support the explanation with evidence about the tools, methods, and materials developed during the period
- be written in a formal style
- include vocabulary words from the chapter

For more in-depth instruction and practice with the writing form, assign the Social Studies Skills Writing Lesson on writing an explanatory paragraph. (HSS HI 3)

UNIT RESOURCES

On Location with National Geographic Explorer-in-Residence Louise Leakey
Intro and Video

 Interactive Map Tool

 **News & Updates**

Available at NGLSync.cengage.com

Unit Wrap-Up:
"Discovering Our Ancestors"
Feature and Video

"Scotland's Stone Age Ruins"
National Geographic Adapted Article

"First Americans"
National Geographic Adapted Article
Student eEdition exclusive

Unit 1 Inquiry:
Create a Cultural Symbol

CHAPTER RESOURCES

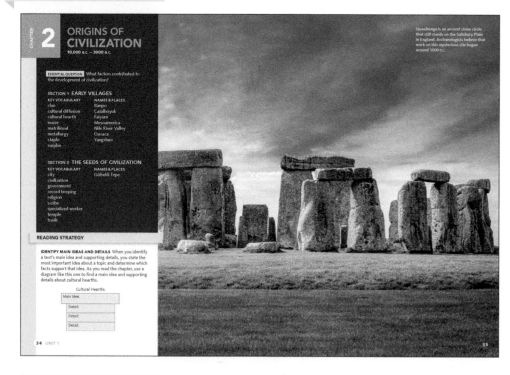

TEACHER RESOURCES & ASSESSMENT

Available at NGLSync.cengage.com

 Social Studies Skills Lessons
• Reading: Identify Main Ideas and Details
• Writing: Write an Explanatory Essay

Formal Assessment
• Chapter 2 Tests A (on-level) & B (below-level)

A **Chapter 2 Answer Key**

 ExamView®
One-time Download

STUDENT BACKPACK *Available at NGLSync.cengage.com*

• **eEdition** *(English)*   • **eEdition** *(Spanish)*   • **Handbooks**   • **Online Atlas**

Chapter 2 Spanish resources, Guided Writing prompts, and Financial Literacy lessons are available online.

SECTION 1 RESOURCES

SECTION 1 RESOURCES

EARLY VILLAGES

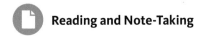 **Reading and Note-Taking**

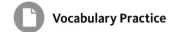 **Vocabulary Practice**

 **Section 1 Quiz**

Available at NGLSync.cengage.com

LESSON 1.1 CENTERS OF NEW IDEAS

 **Active History: Interactive Whiteboard Activity**
Analyze an Ancient Calendar

 **Active History**
Analyze an Ancient Calendar

Available at NGLSync.cengage.com

- On Your Feet: Four Corners

LESSON 1.2 SOUTHWEST ASIA: ÇATALHÖYÜK

 **Biography**
James Mellaart

Available at NGLSync.cengage.com

- On Your Feet: Inside-Outside Circle
- Critical Viewing: NG Chapter Gallery

LESSON 1.3 CHINA: BANPO

- On Your Feet: Question and Answer

NG Learning Framework:
Write About Craftsmanship

LESSON 1.4 MESOAMERICA: OAXACA

- On Your Feet: Think, Pair, Share

NG Learning Framework:
Research Uses of Corn

LESSON 1.5 NORTH AFRICA: FAIYUM

- On Your Feet: One-on-One Interviews

NG Learning Framework:
Teach Your Methods

SECTION 2 RESOURCES

THE SEEDS OF CIVILIZATION

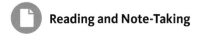 **Reading and Note-Taking**

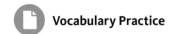 **Vocabulary Practice**

 **Section 2 Quiz**

Available at NGLSync.cengage.com

LESSON 2.1 PATHS TO CIVILIZATION: GÖBEKLI TEPE

- On Your Feet: Living Flow Chart

NG Learning Framework:
Rewrite in Your Own Words

LESSON 2.2 TRAITS OF CIVILIZATION

- On Your Feet: Build a Civilization

NG Learning Framework:
Rank the Traits

HISTORY THROUGH OBJECTS
LESSON 2.3 NEW TECHNOLOGY

- On Your Feet: Make a Tool
- Critical Viewing: NG Image Gallery

CHAPTER 2 REVIEW

STRIVING READERS

STRATEGY 1

Make Summary Statements

Before reading, have students look at the blue subheadings in each lesson. After reading, direct students to use each subheading to begin a statement that summarizes the information about the subheadings.

Use with All Lessons *For Lesson 1.1, suggest that students use these sentence starters: A cultural hearth is _____ . Four cultural hearths that developed during the Neolithic period were _____ .*

STRATEGY 2

Play Vocabulary Tic-Tac-Toe

Write nine Key Vocabulary words on a tic-tac-toe grid on the board. Position the words on the grid so that an X or O can be written below each word. Player A chooses a word. If the player correctly pronounces, defines, and uses the word in a sentence, he or she can put an X or O in the insert box in that square. Play alternates until one person has a row of Xs or Os.

Use with All Lessons *This game can also be played using teams. Divide the class into two teams, Team A and Team B, and alternate play until one team has a row of Xs or Os.*

STRATEGY 3

Use Exit Slips

For a quick, informal assessment tool, direct students to respond in writing to a single question at the end of a lesson. Preview the questions before reading each lesson. Pass out strips of paper. Have students write their responses on the paper strips. Then ask students to turn in their written responses as they exit the class.

2.1 Where was Göbekli Tepe located?
(southeast Turkey, on the edge of the Fertile Crescent)

2.2 What are two traits of civilizations?
(Students should name two of the following: cities, complex institutions, specialized workers, record keeping, improved technology.)

2.3 What development allowed people to make tools out of metal instead of just stone? *(metallurgy)*

Use with Lessons 2.1–2.3

Press *in the Student eEdition for modified text.*

INCLUSION

STRATEGY 1

Preview Content with a Map

Use the following suggestions to preview content using a map.

- Explain that this map is a topical map, meant to show the location of four cultural hearths.
- Remind students that they can identify continents and bodies of water by their labels on the map.
- Tell students to draw lines with their fingers from the four inset maps to their appropriate locations on the world map.
- Explain that these four inset maps give more information than is shown on the main map, including names of rivers, river valleys, and archaeological sites.

Use with Lesson 1.1 *Invite volunteers to describe the visuals in detail to help visually impaired students see them.*

STRATEGY 2

Modify Main Idea Statements

Have each student work with a partner to preview the chapter by reading and copying each lesson's Main Idea statement onto a sheet of paper. Then have students look at any maps, photos, and illustrations in the text and add to each lesson's Main Idea. They can write complete sentences or notes on the page.

Use with Lessons 1.1–1.5 and 2.1–2.2 *For Lesson 1.2, have students describe the illustration of Çatalhöyük. For Lesson 1.5, have students include details from the photo of Faiyum today.*

ENGLISH LANGUAGE LEARNERS   ELD

STRATEGY 1

Create Four-Square Word Charts

Give students the following list of vocabulary words and display the Word Chart model on the following page. Ask students to complete the four parts of the chart for each word on the list.

city	clan
maize	metallurgy
record keeping	scribe
temple	trade

STANDARDS

HSS CONTENT STANDARDS:

6.1.3 Discuss the climatic changes and human modfications of the physical environment that gave rise to the domestication of plants and animals and new sources of clothing and shelter.

HSS ANALYSIS SKILLS:

CST 2 Students construct various time lines of key events, people, and periods of the historical era they are studying; **CST 3** Students use a variety of maps and documents to identify physical and cultural features of neighborhoods, cities, states, and countries and to explain the historical migration of people, expansion and disintegration of empires, and the growth of economic systems; **HI 3** Students explain the sources of historical continuity and how the combination of ideas and events explains the emergence of new patterns.

Definition of *city*	Draw a visual.
A city is a political, social, and cultural center where a lot of people live.	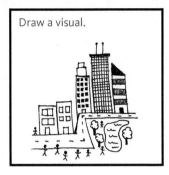

Tell how it relates to the text.	Use it in a sentence.
Cities were important in the formation of civilizations.	*Ur was a major trade center and one of the busiest cities in the ancient world.*

Use with Lessons 1.2–1.4 and 2.1–2.2, All Levels *Pair students at the Emerging level with English proficient students.*

STRATEGY ❷

Build Concept Clusters

Write the Key Vocabulary words *cultural hearth* and *civilization* on the board and ask students for words, phrases, or pictures that come to mind. Have volunteers write the words and draw simple pictures around the words *cultural hearth* and *civilization* to build two Concept Clusters. Call on students to create sentences about the words and pictures. Then have each student ask a question they would like to have answered about the Key Vocabulary words.

Use with Lessons 1.1 and 2.2, All Levels *Have students at the Bridging level assist students at the Emerging and Expanding levels with their Concept Clusters.*

STRATEGY ❸

Find Someone Who Knows

After reading, give students a time limit and tell them to find classmates who can provide the answer to each question below. Each person should write the answer and sign his or her name.

1. What jobs do specialized workers do? *(jobs other than agriculture, such as making pottery or metalworking)*

2. What is trade? *(the exchange of goods)*

3. What material were early needles made of? *(bone; some students might also guess wood)*

4. What is flint? *(a hard stone that can be shaped into a sharp point)*

Use with Lessons 2.2–2.3, All Levels *Have students at the Emerging and Expanding levels work in pairs. Have students at the Bridging level work independently.*

STRATEGY ❶

Investigate an Archaeological Site

Direct students to choose one of the archaeological sites listed below and investigate its history in more depth. Have them assemble their findings in a report that includes both visuals and text.

Çatalhöyük   Faiyum   Banpo   Oaxaca   Göbekli Tepe

Use with Lessons 1.1–1.5 and 2.1 *Encourage students to include a map showing the location of their chosen site.*

STRATEGY ❷

Identify Civilization Traits

Challenge students to identify and describe the five traits of civilization they observe in the modern world. Have students choose a country and then write one or two sentences about each trait as it applies to that country. Encourage students to locate visual examples such as photos or artifacts of the traits they describe. Have students present their modern civilization traits to the class.

Use with Lesson 2.2

STRATEGY ❶

Annotate a Time Line

Suggest that students annotate a time line that situates each location and event listed below. Have students include at least two details per location and event on their time lines.

- cultural hearths form
- climate in Sahara changes drastically
- maize revolution takes place
- Yangshao culture thrives
- Göbekli Tepe is built
- Çatalhöyük begins to develop
- Faiyum is established

Use with Lessons 1.1–1.5 and 2.1 *Some students may wish to develop a more complex time line on a specific cultural hearth. Encourage them to conduct research to identify the most significant dates.*

STRATEGY ❷

Create a Group Presentation

Have students work in small groups to discuss how the environment influenced the development of cultural hearths. Students should focus on topics such as agriculture, climate, and settlement patterns. Then have groups create a visual report to present to the class.

Use with Lessons 1.1–1.5 *Have each group assign specific roles to group members, such as researchers and presenters.*

2 ORIGINS OF CIVILIZATION

10,000 B.C. – 3000 B.C.

ESSENTIAL QUESTION What factors contributed to the development of civilization?

SECTION 1 EARLY VILLAGES

KEY VOCABULARY	NAMES & PLACES
clan	Banpo
cultural diffusion	Çatalhöyük
cultural hearth	Faiyum
maize	Mesoamerica
matrilineal	Nile River Valley
metallurgy	Oaxaca
staple	Yangshao
surplus	

SECTION 2 THE SEEDS OF CIVILIZATION

KEY VOCABULARY	NAMES & PLACES
city	Göbekli Tepe
civilization	
government	
record keeping	
religion	
scribe	
specialized worker	
temple	
trade	

READING STRATEGY

IDENTIFY MAIN IDEAS AND DETAILS When you identify a text's main idea and supporting details, you state the most important idea about a topic and determine which facts support that idea. As you read the chapter, use a diagram like this one to find a main idea and supporting details about cultural hearths.

Cultural Hearths

Main Idea:
- Detail:
- Detail:
- Detail:

Stonehenge is an ancient stone circle that still stands on the Salisbury Plain in England. Archaeologists believe that work on this mysterious site began around 3000 B.C.

HSS CONTENT STANDARDS:

6.1.2 Identify the locations of human communities that populated the major regions of the world and describe how humans adapted to a variety of environments.

TEACHER BACKGROUND

INTRODUCE THE PHOTOGRAPH

Have students study the photograph of Stonehenge. Encourage them to notice the shapes of the different parts of the structure and the shape of the structure itself.

ASK: What do you think this structure might have been used for? *(Possible responses: Perhaps the site was a meeting place, maybe for religious expression.)*

Explain that because it is round (which may not be obvious from the photograph), people may have gathered there for ceremonial purposes.

SHARE BACKGROUND

Work began on this structure around 3000 B.C., and it went through six different stages of construction, ending in 1520 B.C. Its name, Stonehenge, comes from the Saxon *sten-hangen* and means "stone hanging." It is one of the most impressive prehistoric megaliths, or stone monuments, in the world. Theories abound regarding its purpose, ranging from use for astronomy to healing to a seasonal meeting place for Neolithic and Bronze Age groups in the area.

DIGITAL RESOURCES NGLSync.cengage.com

TEACHER RESOURCES & ASSESSMENT

 Social Studies Skills Lessons
- Reading: Identify Main Ideas and Details
- Writing: Write an Explanatory Essay

 Formal Assessment
- Chapter 2 Tests A (on-level) & B (below-level)

 ExamView®
One-time Download

 Chapter 2 Answer Key

STUDENT BACKPACK

- **eEdition** *(English)*
- **eEdition** *(Spanish)*
- **Handbooks**
- **Online Atlas**

INTRODUCE THE ESSENTIAL QUESTION

WHAT FACTORS CONTRIBUTED TO THE DEVELOPMENT OF CIVILIZATION?

Brainstorming Activity: Characteristics of Civilization Introduce students to the concept of civilization by inviting them to brainstorm different characteristics of civilizations. Record student responses in a Concept Cluster. If students need help getting started, encourage them to think about these topics:

A. Food and Workers In order for a civilization to thrive, it must have a reliable way to feed its people, and it must have people who can do specific jobs.

B. Places to Live Settlements lead to villages and then to cities from which civilizations expand.

C. Institutions One characteristic of civilizations is the formation of institutions such as government and religion.

D. Writing Writing down and keeping track of information in an ordered way is important in any civilization.

E. Technology Developing new ways to do or produce things involves technology, which improves as civilizations emerge.

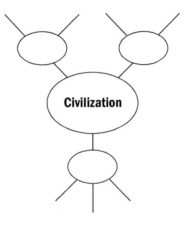

`0:15` minutes

INTRODUCE THE READING STRATEGY

IDENTIFY MAIN IDEAS AND DETAILS

Remind students that identifying a main idea and determining which facts support that idea helps them understand the text. Model finding the main idea of the first paragraph under "What is a cultural hearth?" in Lesson 1.1 and add it to the Main Idea Diagram. For more in-depth instruction and practice with the reading strategy, assign the Social Studies Skills Reading Lesson on identifying main ideas and details.

Cultural Hearths

Main Idea:
Detail:
Detail:
Detail:

INTRODUCE CHAPTER VOCABULARY

WORD SORT CHART

Have students use a Word Sort strategy for the chapter's Key Vocabulary. Tell them to sort the words into categories (see examples provided below), and then list the words under the heading with which they associate the most. Encourage students to discuss the reasoning behind their sorts.

PEOPLE	FOOD	SKILLS	SOCIETY	CONCEPTS

KEY DATES	
9500 B.C.	Temples at Göbekli Tepe first built
8000 B.C.	Cultural hearths around the world begin to take form
7400 B.C.	Çatalhöyük, a settlement in present-day Turkey, is founded
5200 B.C.	Egypt's earliest farming community, Faiyum, is established
5000–3000 B.C.	Yangshao culture in northern China thrives
4250–2000 B.C.	Domestication of maize in Mesoamerica

1.1

Centers of New Ideas

Where do new ideas come from, and how do they spread? Today's trends start with ideas that catch on all over the world. About 12,000 years ago, ideas began to spread in the same way. Groups of people living in different places invented new ways of doing things. These groups created the world's early cultural hearths.

MAIN IDEA

Cultural hearths promoted the spread of new ideas, practices, and technology in different parts of the world.

WHAT IS A CULTURAL HEARTH?

New ideas, practices, and technology began in places called **cultural hearths**. Remember that culture is a group's way of life, including the group's behaviors, beliefs, language, and customs. Ancient cultural hearths spread ideas and practices that influenced the way people did everyday things, from planting crops to burying their dead.

New practices emerged in several cultural hearths around the same time. Between 8000 and 5000 B.C., people living in different parts of the world began to develop new ways of community living. They began to practice new methods of domesticating animals and plants and living in settled communities. As settled societies thrived, they began to form organized governments. People living in settled communities also built places of worship and expressed themselves artistically.

Despite being separated by thousands of miles, ancient cultural hearths shared similar geographic features. Most were located along river systems in areas with fertile land and mild climates. The favorable conditions allowed agriculture to flourish and attracted new people. As populations grew and migrated to other places, they took the new cultural practices with them.

FOUR CULTURAL HEARTHS

Several cultural hearths developed during the Neolithic period. In this chapter, you will learn about four of them, specifically the cultural hearths that emerged in Southwest Asia, China, Mesoamerica, and North Africa.

As you can see on the map, these cultural hearths were located in widely scattered parts of the world. For example, Mesoamerica, in present-day Mexico and Central America, was thousands of miles away from Banpo, in China. Keep in mind that people living in these cultural hearths did not have the benefit of modern communication or transportation. Thousands of years ago, new ideas and practices emerged in and spread from very different places around the same time—without the benefit of the Internet or air travel.

Each of these cultural hearths made an important contribution to surrounding cultures and regions. Simultaneously, the people living in these cultural hearths accepted new ideas themselves. They learned new ways of doing things from people who traveled from other places, and they absorbed the new ideas into their own cultures. Later cultures would build upon the foundations established by these ancient cultural hearths.

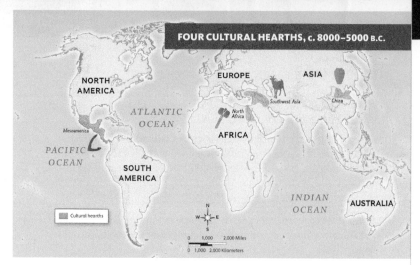

FOUR CULTURAL HEARTHS, c. 8000–5000 B.C.

Mesoamerica: Oaxaca
Farmers in Oaxaca introduced an important new crop: maize.

North Africa: Faiyum
Faiyum farmers adopted techniques from cultures across the Mediterranean.

Southwest Asia: Çatalhöyük
Builders at Çatalhöyük demonstrated advanced construction techniques.

China: Banpo
Yangshao potters at Banpo created functional, beautiful pottery.

REVIEW & ASSESS

1. **READING CHECK** What is a cultural hearth?

2. **DESCRIBE** What geographic features did ancient cultural hearths share?

3. **INTERPRET MAPS** Near what rivers did these four ancient cultural hearths emerge?

6.2.1 Locate and describe the major river systems and discuss the physical settings that supported permanent settlement and early civilizations; 6.2.2 Trace the development of agricultural techniques that permitted the production of economic surplus and the emergence of cities as centers of culture and power; CST 3 Students use a variety of maps and documents to identify physical and cultural features of neighborhoods, cities, states, and countries and to explain the historical migration of people, expansion and disintegration of empires, and the growth of economic systems; HI 3 Students explain the sources of historical continuity and how the combination of ideas and events explains the emergence of new patterns.

HSS CONTENT STANDARDS:

6.2.1 Locate and describe the major river systems and discuss the physical settings that supported permanent settlement and early civilizations; **6.2.2** Trace the development of agricultural techniques that permitted the production of economic surplus and the emergence of cities as centers of culture and power.

HSS ANALYSIS SKILLS:

CST 3 Students use a variety of maps and documents to identify physical and cultural features of neighborhoods, cities, states, and countries and to explain the historical migration of people, expansion and disintegration of empires, and the growth of economic systems; **REP 1** Students frame questions that can be answered by historical study and research; **HI 3** Students explain the sources of historical continuity and how the combination of ideas and events explains the emergence of new patterns.

PLAN

OBJECTIVE

Learn how new ideas, practices, and technology spread from cultural hearths to different parts of the world.

ESSENTIAL QUESTION

What factors contributed to the development of civilization?

Cultural hearths formed the foundation upon which later civilizations were built. Lesson 1.1 discusses four different cultural hearths that emerged at about the same time.

BACKGROUND FOR THE TEACHER

Some of the new ideas that developed were focused on tools. The sickle was an indispensable tool in the Neolithic-period domestication of plants. It was one of the most ancient tools used in the harvest of grains and other plants. Sickles usually had curved metal blades and short wooden handles, and they were hand held. This meant the person doing the harvesting had to be stooped or bent over near the plants. Longer-handled tools came later, in the form of scythes. Sickles were simple tools, but effective, and they are still used today.

DIGITAL RESOURCES NGLSync.cengage.com

TEACHER RESOURCES & ASSESSMENT

 Reading and Note-Taking

 Vocabulary Practice

 Section 1 Quiz

STUDENT RESOURCES

 Active History

INTRODUCE & ENGAGE

PREVIEW CONTENT WITH MAPS

Direct students' attention to the Four Cultural Hearths map. Ask students to locate where four cultural hearths developed. **ASK:** Which of the four cultural hearths is in North America? *(Mesoamerica, in present-day Mexico and Central America)* **ASK:** Which is in North Africa? *(Faiyum, in present-day Egypt)* Explain to students that they will learn about cultural hearths in four different parts of the world. `0:05` minutes

TEACH

GUIDED DISCUSSION

1. **Monitor Comprehension** When did the cultural hearths discussed in the text develop? *(They developed between 8000 and 5000 B.C., during the Neolithic period.)*

2. **Analyze Cause and Effect** What happened in cultural hearths when people developed a way of domesticating plants and animals? *(The domestication of plants and animals meant settled societies could thrive, which led to organized government and religion.)*

INTERPRET MAPS

Have students study the Four Cultural Hearths map. Ask for volunteers to identify river valleys on the map. *(Students should note the Tehuacán Valley, the Nile River Valley, and the Wei Huang Valley.)*

ASK: What is unique about the location of Çatalhöyük and Göbekli Tepe? *(Çatalhöyük and Göbekli Tepe were located in Southwest Asia, on the edge of the Fertile Crescent. Explain that the Fertile Crescent describes the area between and around the Tigris and Euphrates rivers because it provided fertile lands in the shape of a curve.)* `0:10` minutes

ACTIVE OPTIONS

Active History: Analyze an Ancient Calendar Extend the lesson by using either the PDF or Whiteboard version of the activity. These activities take a deeper look at a topic from, or related to, the lesson. Explore the activities as a class, turn them into group assignments, or assign them individually. `0:10` minutes

On Your Feet: Four Corners Assign students to one of four corners in the room, labeled Mesoamerica, North Africa, Southwest Asia, and China. Then have each group brainstorm four questions they have about their group's cultural hearth. Have each group of students present three of the group's questions to the other corners. Start the discussion by tossing a bean bag or other soft object to one team and asking, "What question do you have about your cultural hearth?" When the first team states its question, have them toss the bean bag to another team to hear one of their prepared questions. Continue until teams have listed all their questions. `0:15` minutes

DIFFERENTIATE

STRIVING READERS

Set a Purpose for Reading Before reading, have students use the subheadings in the lesson to create purpose-setting questions:

- What is the definition of a cultural hearth?
- What are the four cultural hearths introduced in the lesson?

After reading, have student pairs answer the questions. Then ask for student volunteers to share their answers.

GIFTED & TALENTED

Investigate Cultural Hearths Have students conduct independent research on one additional cultural hearth. Direct them to the following locations:

- Indus and Ganges river valleys
- Andean South America
- West Africa

Ask students to prepare a short presentation about the cultural hearth they researched. Explain that these cultural hearths developed at slightly different times, and that in their research, they should note similarities and differences to the cultural hearths in their textbook.

Press **mt** in the Student eEdition for modified text.

See the Chapter Planner for more strategies for differentiation.

REVIEW & ASSESS

ANSWERS

1. A cultural hearth is a place from which new ideas, practices, and technology spread.

2. Cultural hearths shared similar geographic features, including mild climates, fertile land, and access to rivers.

3. Southwest Asia: Tigris and Euphrates; North Africa: Nile; China: Huang He and Chang Jiang; Mesoamerica: Balsas

Imagine you are a traveler crossing central Turkey 9,000 years ago. Suddenly, you stumble on an amazing sight: hundreds of houses surrounded by fields of ripening wheat and barley, enclosures of cattle, and thousands of people—more people than you ever imagined existed. What is this strange place? It's Çatalhöyük.

MAIN IDEA

Çatalhöyük was an advanced settlement and an early cultural hearth in Southwest Asia.

AN AGRICULTURAL VILLAGE

By modern standards, the Neolithic village of **Çatalhöyük** (chah-tuhl-HOO-yuk) was small and simple. To Neolithic people, though, it was incredibly advanced. Çatalhöyük developed in present-day Turkey beginning around 7400 B.C. This settlement was large, both in size and population. Çatalhöyük still fascinates people thousands of years later because of the rich cultural material left behind by those who lived there.

The people who built Çatalhöyük relied on farming for food. A stable food supply contributed to population growth and Çatalhöyük's agriculture eventually supported as many as 10,000 people.

Farmers grew barley and wheat. They also raised livestock such as sheep, goats, and cattle for meat, milk, and clothing. Çatalhöyük's villagers hunted and fished, too, but farming produced more food. The **surplus**, or extra, food could be used in trading.

EARLY CULTURE

Çatalhöyük is one of the world's oldest known permanent settlements. It is also one of the largest and most advanced settlements yet discovered from this time period. Its physical structure covered more than 30 acres (or 27 football fields) and included thousands of permanent mud brick buildings. Houses were packed together so tightly that there were no streets or yards between them. Instead, the flat rooftops served as a public plaza, or an open square, reached by ladders. Because the houses were built so close together, they formed a protective wall that enclosed the settlement.

People entered their homes through doors in the roofs. Most homes had a single main room where families cooked, ate, and slept. The main room had built-in benches and a fireplace. Plastered walls were covered with murals showing scenes of hunting, daily life, and important events.

At Çatalhöyük, archaeologists found evidence of religious practices and artistic expression. Horned bulls' heads mounted on walls and symbolic clay figures suggest that the villagers worshipped gods. Villagers also buried their dead, a fact revealed by human remains discovered beneath the floors of homes. The presence of pottery, cloth, cups, and bone utensils as well as tools and jewelry shows artistic expression. Archaeologists even found lead and copper, a sign of very early **metallurgy**, or metalworking. This was an important technological advance.

Discoveries at Çatalhöyük continue even today. Each new find sheds more light on the people who lived in this ancient settlement.

IMAGINING ÇATALHÖYÜK

Çatalhöyük was unknown to modern people until its discovery in the 1950s. Since then, archaeologists have carefully excavated the site. Their discoveries have revealed details of a unique settlement and culture. This illustration shows what archaeologists think Çatalhöyük might have been like. The cutaways let you peek inside the homes.

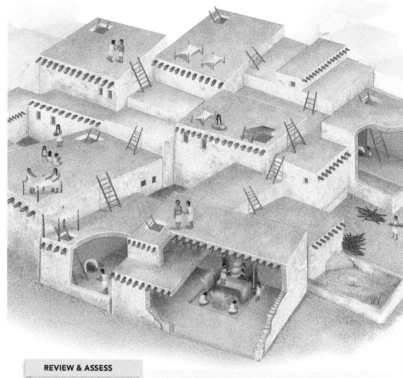

REVIEW & ASSESS

1. **READING CHECK** What archaeological evidence demonstrates that Çatalhöyük was an advanced culture?

2. **IDENTIFY MAIN IDEAS AND DETAILS** Why did the people of Çatalhöyük build their dwellings so close together?

3. **ANALYZE VISUALS** Based on the illustration, what might have been some advantages to living at Çatalhöyük?

6.2.2 Trace the development of agricultural techniques that permitted the production of economic surplus and the emergence of cities as centers of culture and power.

STANDARDS

HSS CONTENT STANDARDS:

6.2.1 Locate and describe the major river systems and discuss the physical settings that supported permanent settlement and early civilizations; **6.2.2** Trace the development of agricultural techniques that permitted the production of economic surplus and the emergence of cities as centers of culture and power.

HSS ANALYSIS SKILLS:

HI 3 Students explain the sources of historical continuity and how the combination of ideas and events explains the emergence of new patterns; **REP 1** Students frame questions that can be answered by historical study and research.

PLAN

OBJECTIVE

Explore the settlement of Çatalhöyük, an early cultural hearth in Southwest Asia.

ESSENTIAL QUESTION

What factors contributed to the development of civilization?

Different groups of people began to settle in permanent communities. Lesson 1.2 describes the settlement at Çatalhöyük, in present-day Turkey.

BACKGROUND FOR THE TEACHER

A British archaeologist named James Mellaart discovered Çatalhöyük in the late 1950s and conducted a series of excavations in the 1960s. However, his excavations were halted because Mellaart and his team realized they could not safely preserve the site. In the 1990s, another British archaeologist, Ian Hodder, restarted excavations. Today, Hodder and his team of international archaeologists protect the dig site with tents to shield it from rain and sun. They also remove artifacts, fragile parts of the buildings, and mural paintings to stabilize and conserve them.

DIGITAL RESOURCES NGLSync.cengage.com

TEACHER RESOURCES & ASSESSMENT

 Reading and Note-Taking

 Vocabulary Practice

 Section 1 Quiz

STUDENT RESOURCES

 Biography

INTRODUCE & ENGAGE

TEAM UP

Tell students to imagine that they will be building a settlement that will house several hundred people. Have them brainstorm in groups what they would build and the features they want their settlement to have. Tell them to use an Idea Web to list the structures and features of their settlement after brainstorming. Tell students to keep in mind things such as security, efficiency, and comfort. `0:05` minutes

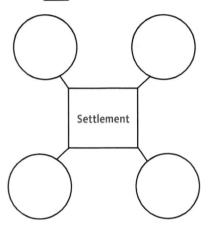

Settlement

TEACH

GUIDED DISCUSSION

1. **Draw Conclusions** How important was a stable food supply at Çatalhöyük? *(A stable food supply led to population growth. The surplus, or extra, food produced by farmers at Çatalhöyük could be stored for later use.)*

2. **Make Inferences** Why do archaeologists believe that the people at Çatalhöyük practiced some form of religion? *(Archaeologists discovered symbolic clay figures and mounted bull heads at Çatalhöyük, both of which point to the worship of gods or goddesses.)*

ANALYZE VISUALS

Ask students to study the diagram of Çatalhöyük. Elicit student descriptions of the structure depicted. **ASK:** What similarities and differences do you see between Çatalhöyük and modern apartment or condominium buildings? *(The illustration of Çatalhöyük shows a number of individual dwellings that share walls with other dwellings, like modern apartment or condominium buildings. Unlike modern dwellings, though, people entered through the roofs and used the roof space as public plazas.)* `0:10` minutes

ACTIVE OPTIONS

On Your Feet: Inside-Outside Circle Have students form concentric circles facing each other. Allow students time to write questions about the location, purpose, and construction of Çatalhöyük. Then have students in the inside circle pose questions to students in the outside circle. Have students switch roles. Students may ask for help from other students in their circle if they are unable to answer a question. `0:20` minutes

Critical Viewing: NG Chapter Gallery Invite students to examine the photograph of the necklaces from Çatalhöyük that appears in the Chapter 2 Gallery. Have students imagine that they are the archaeologists who discovered these artifacts, and ask them to analyze the necklaces to learn more about the people who lived in Çatalhöyük. Prompt students' analysis with the following questions: What are they? Where and when were they created? By whom? For whom? Why were they created? Guide students to discuss, in particular, how the necklaces might have indicated a person's social status. `0:10` minutes

DIFFERENTIATE

STRIVING READERS

Summarize Have students work in pairs and assign each student a paragraph to read aloud. The partner should summarize what he or she hears in one or two spoken sentences. Encourage students to ask each other questions as they come across complex information.

ENGLISH LANGUAGE LEARNERS `ELD`

Clarify Word Meaning Make sure students understand the word *metallurgy*. Explain that when they encounter new and confusing words, they can look for a root word. Write *metallurgy* on the board and underline the root word *metal*. Use the following strategies to help students at different proficiency levels clarify the meaning of the word.

- **Emerging** After students identify the root, have them write it on a card along with the meaning. Talk through the word.

  Metallurgy is the art of dealing with metal.

- **Expanding** To help students explain how they know the meaning of a word with an identifiable root, provide the following sentence frame:

  The root is _____ and means _____. So, _____ means _____.

- **Bridging** Encourage students to use their knowledge of affixes to determine a more exact meaning:

  The root is metal, which is a strong, shiny material used to make tools and jewelry. The suffix -urgy, means "the technique or art of working with something," so metallurgy must mean "the technique or art of working with metal."

  If needed, have students look up the affix in a dictionary.

Press **mt** *in the Student eEdition for modified text.*

See the Chapter Planner for more strategies for differentiation.

REVIEW & ASSESS

ANSWERS

1. Archaeologists have discovered evidence of worship, burial practices, creation of artistic and useful objects, and metallurgy there.

2. They built their houses close together for protection.

3. The settlement would have provided security, a stable food source, and a community for its residents.

China: Banpo

About 1,000 years after the development at Çatalhöyük, a lightbulb went off on the other side of the world. Thousands of miles from Southwest Asia, another center of new ideas developed in China's rich river valleys.

MAIN IDEA

The Yangshao culture developed as a cultural hearth in northern China.

RIVER VALLEY AGRICULTURE

Around 5000 B.C., warmer, wetter weather prompted the development of cultural hearths in the fertile river valleys of China. As in Çatalhöyük, people here domesticated pigs, chickens, and dogs. They hunted and fished, too.

In southern China, which has a relatively warm climate, people began to settle in villages. Farmers grew rice, which they had domesticated from the wild rice that grew in the Chang Jiang (chahng jyahng) Basin.

Farming villages also developed farther north in the Huang He (hwahng huh) Basin. However, the colder, drier climate in the north was less favorable for growing rice. Farmers there domesticated wild millet instead. Millet is a tiny, yellow grain. It grows fast and is a low-maintenance, or easy-to-grow, crop. As agricultural techniques improved in China, farmers produced food surpluses.

YANGSHAO CULTURE

The **Yangshao** (yahng-shou) culture was one of China's Neolithic cultural hearths. The Yangshao lived along the Huang and Wei (way) rivers from about 5000 to 3000 B.C. Archaeologists have discovered more than 1,000 Yangshao sites in northern China.

One of the best-known Yangshao sites is **Banpo**, a large farming village. This village contained many small houses that faced a community building in a central square. Archaeologists determined that Banpo houses were rebuilt many times. People may have abandoned the village when the fields were exhausted of nutrients and then later returned when the land recovered. Banpo villagers grew millet as their **staple**, or main crop. They also grew a fibrous plant called hemp and cultivated silk, which they crafted into textiles.

The Yangshao at Banpo left behind a unique style of pottery that demonstrates their artistry. Yangshao potters created bowls and vessels, or containers, that they formed by hand and baked in kilns, or ovens, just outside Banpo village. The Yangshao's painted pottery commonly features geometric designs. Other examples include shaped vessels used for food storage.

Archaeologists found many of these vessels and other useful items buried with the dead in neatly arranged graves. These "grave goods," as they are called, suggest that the Yangshao people believed in a link between the living and the dead, though their specific religious beliefs remain unknown. Because most graves contained similar grave goods, archaeologists believe that most people probably had equal status in society.

Early Yangshao graves also suggest that people were arranged into **clans**, or family groupings, when buried. These clans were **matrilineal**, which means they traced descendants through the mother rather than the father.

The Huang He in China provided fertile soil for ancient Yangshao farmers.

By about 3200 B.C. Yangshao culture had evolved into Longshan (lung-shan) culture. The Longshan crafted useful tools and beautiful objects from jade—a hard green or white stone. Longshan artists produced a distinctive black pottery using pottery wheels, and craftspeople made tools out of copper. The Longshan also established trade networks on which later Chinese cultures would build.

Yangshao Pottery

Formed in the shape of an owl, this tripod pottery vessel was used to serve food.

REVIEW & ASSESS

1. **READING CHECK** What is unique about the Yangshao culture?

2. **COMPARE AND CONTRAST** Why did farmers grow different types of crops in the southern and northern river basins of China?

3. **DETERMINE WORD MEANINGS** Based on its definition, what does the word part *matri-* mean?

6.2.1 Locate and describe the major river systems and discuss the physical settings that supported permanent settlement and early civilizations; 6.2.2 Trace the development of agricultural techniques that permitted the production of economic surplus and the emergence of cities as centers of culture and power.

HSS CONTENT STANDARDS:

6.2.1 Locate and describe the major river systems and discuss the physical settings that supported permanent settlement and early civilizations; **6.2.2** Trace the development of agricultural techniques that permitted the production of economic surplus and the emergence of cities as centers of culture and power.

PLAN

OBJECTIVE

Learn how the Yangshao culture developed as a cultural hearth in northern China.

ESSENTIAL QUESTION

What factors contributed to the development of civilization?

People in various cultural hearths developed new farming techniques, ways of organizing their societies, and forms of artistic expression. Lesson 1.3 describes the farming, societal organization, and pottery of the Yangshao culture in northern China.

BACKGROUND FOR THE TEACHER

The great river valley civilizations of East Asia developed along the Huang He. The Huang He is sometimes called the Yellow River. It is the main river in northern China, and because of a long history of settlement near it, it is believed to be the cradle of Chinese civilization. It is China's second longest river, winding more than 3,000 miles through the country. The Huang He flows east from the Plateau of Tibet into the Yellow Sea. The Huang He Basin is heavily populated today, as the river continues to support human settlement.

DIGITAL RESOURCES NGLSync.cengage.com

TEACHER RESOURCES & ASSESSMENT

 Reading and Note-Taking

 Vocabulary Practice

 Section 1 Quiz

STUDENT RESOURCES

 NG Chapter Gallery

INTRODUCE & ENGAGE

ACTIVATE PRIOR KNOWLEDGE

Write the word *domesticate* on the board. Elicit student definitions of the word. **ASK:** What does the word domesticate mean? *(In this historical context, domesticate means to tame an animal for farm produce or to cultivate a wild plant for food.)* **ASK:** What is the adjective form of the word? *(The adjective form of the word is domestic, which refers to the running of a home or existing inside a particular country. It can also mean something made at home, not abroad, and it can describe animals that are tame.)* Explain that they will encounter this word frequently when studying cultural hearths and early societies. `0:05` minutes

TEACH

GUIDED DISCUSSION

1. **Analyze Visuals** What do the shape and detail of the pottery vessel featured on the page reveal about the Yangshao culture? *(The fact that the Yangshao were making kiln-fired pottery indicates that they possessed an advanced technology and the resources and artisans to devote to pottery making. Crafting the vessel in the shape of the bird would take time and skill beyond making a basic vessel.)*

2. **Summarize** What have archaeologists learned about the Yangshao from their burial practices? *(The Yangshao buried their dead with grave goods, which indicates a belief in a link between the living and the dead. Most graves had similar grave goods, which showed equal social status among the villagers. People were also buried in family groupings.)*

ANALYZE LOCATION

Have students work in groups of four. Tell each group to review the text and images for the lesson. Then, as a class, come up with as many descriptions of the area around the Huang He in China as possible. Write groups' descriptions on the board, keeping track of the number of responses per group. *(Descriptions might include fertile, flat, green, populated with trees, perhaps in a valley. Other descriptions might focus on the width of the river and the dedicated spaces for farming.)* `0:10` minutes

ACTIVE OPTIONS

On Your Feet: Question and Answer Have half the class write True-False questions based on the information about the Yangshao culture and Banpo. Ask the other half to create answer cards, with "True" written on one side and "False" on the other. Have the question-writing students read their questions aloud. Students in the second group should display the correct answer to each question. When discrepancies occur, review the question and discuss which answer is correct. `0:15` minutes

NG Learning Framework: Write About Craftsmanship

ATTITUDE: **Curiosity**
KNOWLEDGE: **Our Human Story**

Have students select one of the forms of craftsmanship or artistic expression (such as pottery or metallurgy) that they are still curious about after reading this chapter. Instruct them to write a short description of this form of craftsmanship or artistic expression using information from the chapter and additional source material. As an extension to this activity, have students analyze the clay pot from Banpo in the **Primary Source Handbook** and answer the questions that follow it. `0:10` minutes

DIFFERENTIATE

INCLUSION

Monitor Comprehension Have students work in small groups reading aloud the text paragraph by paragraph. At the end of each paragraph, have them stop and use these sentence frames:

- This paragraph is about _____.
- One detail that stood out to me is _____.
- The word _____ means _____.
- I don't think I understand _____.

GIFTED & TALENTED

Create a Vessel Have students draw a vessel that they can then (if time permits) shape out of clay. Encourage students to create the vessel with the Yangshao culture in mind. They can conduct independent research on the designs commonly found in Yangshao pottery as inspiration for their own designs. Have the students explain their creation to the class upon completion.

Press (**mt**) *in the Student eEdition for modified text.*

See the Chapter Planner for more strategies for differentiation.

REVIEW & ASSESS

ANSWERS

1. The Yangshao culture is distinct in its domestication of millet, the textiles and pottery it created, its belief in a link between the living and the dead, and its matrilineal organization.

2. In the south, Neolithic farmers were able to domesticate and farm wild rice in the wetlands of the Chang Jiang Basin. In the north, however, the climate was cooler and drier, which were not good conditions for growing rice, so instead farmers planted millet in the Huang He Basin.

3. The word part *matri-* means *mother, woman,* or *female.*

Mesoamerica:
Oaxaca

Around the time the Yangshao were farming in China, another cultural hearth was forming across the Pacific in Mesoamerica. The people there were developing an important crop that you might recognize—corn.

MAIN IDEA

Maize domestication helped make Mesoamerica an important cultural hearth.

MESOAMERICAN NOMADS

Mesoamerica, which means "middle America," refers to the ancient geographic and cultural region that reached from central Mexico south through Central America. This region was another important Neolithic cultural hearth, similar in some ways to Çatalhöyük in Southwest Asia and Banpo in China.

For thousands of years, Mesoamericans traveled in small nomadic groups, moving from place to place with the seasons. They gathered wild plants but did little farming. For brief periods, these Mesoamericans may have tended small patches of land. However, they didn't settle in permanent sites, build permanent homes, or form villages. Eventually, though, Mesoamericans began to domesticate wild plants. In this way, they resembled people living in cultural hearths in other parts of the world.

CRADLE OF THE MAIZE REVOLUTION

One of the main plants Mesoamericans domesticated was **maize**, or what we know as corn. A cave is an unlikely place to find clues about an important development in farming, but that is where archaeologists found traces of an ancient plant. In fact, caves and rock shelters scattered across southern Mexico revealed the earliest signs of domestication in North America.

Archaeologists found prehistoric corncob fragments in the highland caves of **Oaxaca** (wah-HAH-kah) and the Tehuacán (tay-wah-KAHN) Valley. The pieces had been preserved for thousands of years by the region's hot, dry conditions. These fragments, which date to around 4250 B.C., came from an early variety of domesticated maize. Archaeologists also found stone tools for grinding the hard maize kernels into flour for baking. The first varieties of maize were probably neither juicy nor yellow, but they were easily harvested and stored, which made them a useful food source.

So where did maize come from? After decades of debate, scientists believe that maize was domesticated from a wild Mexican grass called teosinte (tay-uh-SIN-tay) that is native to the area around the Balsas River. Teosinte kernels are easily knocked off the plant, making it a difficult crop to harvest. However, hundreds of years of domestication solved this problem. Domestication also increased the number and size of kernels on the teosinte plant. Over time, it came to resemble modern corn.

As maize became a more productive crop, Mesoamericans relied on it for their annual food supply. By 2000 B.C., the maize revolution had taken place, and maize farming was widespread in Mesoamerica. Little did these farmers know they had invented a food that people would still enjoy thousands of years later.

DOMESTICATING CORN

Teosinte, the wild relative of modern corn, produced much smaller kernels. Note the size of the cobs of the teosinte plant as compared to a quarter. Now compare a quarter to the size of modern corn. In domesticating this plant, ancient farmers slowly began to encourage fewer branches on the plant. Less branching meant the plant could divert more energy into fewer cobs, which then grew larger. In addition, the hard kernel of the teosinte plant eventually gave way to the softer kernel we recognize as modern corn.

TEOSINTE

MODERN CORN

REVIEW & ASSESS

1. **READING CHECK** How did the domestication of maize help Mesoamerica become a cultural hearth?

2. **SUMMARIZE** How do archaeologists know that Mesoamericans domesticated maize?

3. **INTEGRATE VISUALS** Based on the illustration and text, what changes did domestication bring about to teosinte?

6.2.2 Trace the development of agricultural techniques that permitted the production of economic surplus and the emergence of cities as centers of culture and power.

HSS CONTENT STANDARDS:

6.2.2 Trace the development of agricultural techniques that permitted the production of economic surplus and the emergence of cities as centers of culture and power.

PLAN

OBJECTIVE

Describe how the domestication of maize helped Mesoamerica develop as a cultural hearth.

ESSENTIAL QUESTION

What factors contributed to the development of civilization?

People in cultural hearths domesticated wild plants in order to have a stable food supply. Lesson 1.4 describes how Mesoamericans domesticated maize, or corn.

BACKGROUND FOR THE TEACHER

Understanding that the achievements of ancient cultures affect us today can be difficult for students. This is not surprising considering it is also sometimes difficult to prove. Reaching the conclusion that maize came from domesticated teosinte was not easy. Geneticist George Beadle first investigated the connection between these two plants in the 1930s. Then, after a long, successful career that included winning the Nobel Prize in genetics in 1958, Dr. Beadle emerged from retirement to settle the issue once and for all. He crossbred teosinte and maize and grew 50,000 plants. Eventually, he pinpointed just four or five genes that differentiate the two plants. Later scientists went even further by determining the exact region in which maize originated: the Central Balsas River Valley in Mexico.

DIGITAL RESOURCES NGLSync.cengage.com

TEACHER RESOURCES & ASSESSMENT

 Reading and Note-Taking

 Vocabulary Practice

 Section 1 Quiz

STUDENT RESOURCES

 NG Chapter Gallery

INTRODUCE & ENGAGE

PREVIEW WITH VISUALS

Direct students' attention to the illustration of teosinte and modern corn. Call on volunteers to predict what they will learn in the lesson based on what they see in the illustration. At the end of the lesson, have students review the illustration to see how accurate their predictions were. `0:05` minutes

TEACH

GUIDED DISCUSSION

1. **Summarize** Why was teosinte a difficult plant to harvest? *(The kernels on the teosinte plant are easily knocked off if the plant is jostled, which makes collecting usable parts of the plant difficult.)*

2. **Evaluate** Why would the domestication of a single plant be important in the development of Mesoamerican civilizations? *(With the development of a hardy crop like maize, which can be used in a variety of foods, large populations would have a steady food supply. Larger populations lead to the formation of cities and, eventually, advanced civilizations.)*

SYNTHESIZE

Using the illustration and the text, have students create brief group presentations that synthesize what they have learned about Mesoamerica, Oaxaca, and maize domestication. Make sure they answer the five Ws: Who, What, Where, When, and Why it Matters. `0:25` minutes

Who? _____

What? _____

Where? _____

When? _____

Why? _____
_____
_____

ACTIVE OPTIONS

On Your Feet: Think, Pair, Share Have students think of a food that they would invent, much like the Mesoamericans "invented" maize, that could help solve a hunger problem in one part of the world. Ask them to form pairs and discuss their ideas. Then call on individuals to share their ideas for new foods. `0:15` minutes

NG Learning Framework: Research Uses of Corn

SKILL: Collaboration
KNOWLEDGE: Critical Species

Have students form groups of four. Ask each group to consider the importance of maize/corn in the modern world and research its many uses (e.g., food, animal feed, ethanol, glue). Have each group report on one use and explain how it impacts their everyday life. `0:15` minutes

DIFFERENTIATE

STRIVING READERS

Summarize Have students summarize Lesson 1.4 by creating two Word Webs with the terms *teosinte* and *maize* in the center ovals. Ask them to complete each web with relevant information from the lesson.

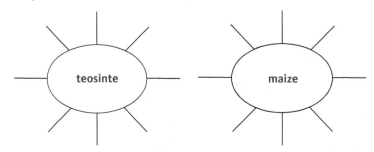

PRE-AP

Investigate Wild Grains Have students pick a grain such as wheat, barley, or oats and then research its history. Encourage them to utilize scholarly sources, such as science and university sites. Tell students they will share their findings with the class in a presentation that uses visuals to illustrate their research.

Press **mt** *in the Student eEdition for modified text.*

See the Chapter Planner for more strategies for differentiation.

REVIEW & ASSESS

ANSWERS

1. The domestication of maize made it possible for early inhabitants to stop foraging and to start farming a useful food source that could support permanent farming villages. Eventually, this led to widespread settlement throughout Mesoamerica.

2. Archaeologists discovered evidence of prehistoric corncob fragments in caves in Oaxaca. They also found stone tools for grinding maize.

3. Domestication seems to have made teosinte a taller plant with fewer branches and larger corncobs with larger kernels.

This photo of Faiyum today shows how access to a water source determines where crops can grow and people can live.

1.5

North Africa:
Faiyum

Long before building their extraordinary pyramids, the ancient Egyptians laid the building blocks of an advanced culture on the floodplains of the Nile River in North Africa. As in other cultural hearths, agriculture was at the root of cultural development in ancient Egypt, whose farmers adapted ideas from places far and wide.

MAIN IDEA

Early farmers established the Nile River Valley as an important cultural hearth.

MIGRANTS FROM THE SAHARA

As you may recall from the previous chapter, the Sahara was a tropical grassland 10,000 years ago. Then the climate changed drastically. Seasonal rains shifted south, and the grasslands dried into desert. This dramatic change forced people to migrate to more fertile lands with steadier water supplies.

The same climate shift that transformed the Sahara transformed the narrow **Nile River Valley**. Its swamps dried up, making the land usable and this fertile valley a perfect place for farming. The Nile floodplain was ideal for the agriculture that would later support a large population.

EGYPT'S EARLIEST FARMING VILLAGE

Faiyum (fy-YOOM) is an oasis about 50 miles south of present-day Cairo. Dating from around 5200 B.C., it is considered Egypt's earliest farming community. At Faiyum, archaeologists discovered storage pits for grain, postholes for building foundations, and the ruins of clay floors and fireplaces. They also stumbled upon a 7,000-year-old, Neolithic-era wood and flint sickle used for farming and left in a storage bin.

The agricultural practices used at Faiyum were not native to the Nile River Valley, though. According to archaeologists, people from neighboring cultures introduced new practices to Faiyum farmers. Grains of wheat and barley and bones of sheep and pigs found at Faiyum came from across the Mediterranean Sea or the Sinai Desert where domestication was already well established. People from these areas likely brought the domesticated grains and animals to the Nile River Valley.

The process by which cultures interact and spread from one area to another is called **cultural diffusion**. This process allowed Faiyum farmers to benefit from the skills of other cultures. It also helped establish the Nile River Valley as an important cultural hearth.

REVIEW & ASSESS

1. **READING CHECK** Why were early farmers attracted to the Nile River Valley?

2. **SUMMARIZE** How did a climate shift that took place 10,000 years ago change the Sahara and Nile River Valley?

3. **DRAW CONCLUSIONS** What impact did neighboring cultures have on the farmers at Faiyum?

6.2.1 Locate and describe the major river systems and discuss the physical settings that supported permanent settlement and early civilizations; 6.2.2 Trace the development of agricultural techniques that permitted the production of economic surplus and the emergence of cities as centers of culture and power.

45

PLAN

OBJECTIVE

Examine how early farmers along the Nile River established a cultural hearth in Egypt.

ESSENTIAL QUESTION

What factors contributed to the development of civilization?

People in cultural hearths shared ideas, practices, and skills with nearby cultures. Lesson 1.5 describes how people in Egypt's earliest farming village shared ideas with other cultures.

BACKGROUND FOR THE TEACHER

Ninety-five percent of Egypt's population lives in the Nile River Valley today, and agriculture is still an important part of the Egyptian economy. Egyptian farmers grow crops such as citrus fruits, tomatoes, sugar beets, potatoes, rice, wheat, and cotton. Construction of the Aswan High Dam in 1970 regulated the annual flooding of the Nile, making the growing season year-round instead of flood-dependent. The construction of the dam also led to the reclamation of land to use as farmland through the use of irrigation.

DIGITAL RESOURCES NGLSync.cengage.com

TEACHER RESOURCES & ASSESSMENT

 Reading and Note-Taking

 Vocabulary Practice

 Section 1 Quiz

STUDENT RESOURCES

 NG Chapter Gallery

INTRODUCE & ENGAGE

ANALYZE VISUALS

Direct students' attention to the photo of Faiyum. Ask the following questions:

- What is shown in the photo?
- Based on what you see in the photo, where do you think people live?
- What is making it possible to grow the crops?

`0:05` minutes

TEACH

GUIDED DISCUSSION

1. **Make Predictions** What type of weather event in the modern world might cause farmers to migrate to a new place to live? *(Drought commonly forces farmers to relocate, especially in parts of Saharan and sub-Saharan Africa. Another weather event that might cause farmers to relocate today would be rising sea levels that flood farmland.)*

2. **Draw Conclusions** How did archaeologists know that farming techniques were not native to Faiyum farmers? *(Archaeologists discovered evidence of domesticated wheat and barley and bones of sheep and pigs that would have originated from across the Mediterranean Sea or the Sinai Desert.)*

BUILD VOCABULARY

Explore the word *diffusion* and its other forms to help students build vocabulary skills. Review the definition of *cultural diffusion* in the reading. *(Cultural diffusion is the process by which cultures interact with each other and spread.)* Then ask if students know other forms of the word. Explain that the word *diffuse* can be a verb (meaning "to spread") or an adjective (meaning "spread out"). Tell students to come up with a sentence or question that uses either *diffusion* or *diffuse*. Then ask for student volunteers to share their sentence or question. `0:10` minutes

ACTIVE OPTIONS

On Your Feet: One-on-One Interviews Group students in pairs. Have each pair write three questions about Faiyum based on the information they learned in Lesson 1.5. Have students conduct interviews with each other as if they are on a talk news show, and then have them take questions from the "audience." Students' answers should show an understanding of Faiyum and what archaeologists learned about this early farming village. `0:20` minutes

NG Learning Framework: Teach Your Methods

ATTITUDE: **Responsibility**
SKILL: **Collaboration**

Assign students to several small groups. Ask each group to come up with a method of doing something they do everyday (such as doing homework or chores, getting to school). Then have groups share their methods with other groups. Encourage groups to use good listening skills and have them take notes on the different methods presented. To conclude the activity, ask the original groups to reconsider their methods and discuss how they might change them based on other groups' ideas. `0:15` minutes

DIFFERENTIATE

ENGLISH LANGUAGE LEARNERS `ELD`

Identify Main Ideas and Details Lesson 1.5 has two subsections. Pair students of similar proficiency levels together and assign each pair a subsection of the text to read together. Encourage students to make notes about their part of the lesson, including questions they have about vocabulary or idioms. After answering their questions, have each pair write a one- or two-sentence summary. Provide the following sentence frames to help students compose their summaries.

- **Emerging**
  The text mostly talks about _____.

- **Expanding**
  The main idea in this text is _____. I know that because _____.

- **Bridging**
  The main idea is _____, which is supported by details such as/like _____ and _____.

GIFTED & TALENTED

Make Connections Have students connect the process of cultural diffusion as it happened in history to the way cultural diffusion happens in the world today. Tell students to think of a practice, skill, or idea that started in one part of the world and then spread to another part of the world. Encourage students to identify how the practice, skill, or idea spread, and what impact it had. Have students write a paragraph about their findings. If time allows, have students present what they learn to the class.

Press (**mt**) *in the Student eEdition for modified text.*

See the Chapter Planner for more strategies for differentiation.

REVIEW & ASSESS

ANSWERS

1. The Nile River Valley provided a major water source and fertile soils on which to grow crops that could sustain a population. Farmers at Faiyum laid the groundwork for future agriculture and incorporated other cultures' practices and techniques.

2. A climate shift that took place 10,000 years ago changed the once-lush tropical grasslands of the Sahara into a dry desert. At the same time, this climate shift dried up forests and swamps, turning the Nile River Valley into an ideal place for farming.

3. People from neighboring cultures brought new practices and techniques to Faiyum that influenced the crops they grew and animals they raised.

Paths to Civilization:
Göbekli Tepe

An old riddle asks: Which came first, the chicken or the egg? Archaeologists have posed their own riddle: Which came first, organized agriculture or organized religion? Like most riddles, this one can't be easily answered.

MAIN IDEA

Throughout history, different cultures have traveled different paths to civilization.

THE WORLD'S FIRST TEMPLE

Over time, cultural hearths around the world transformed into civilizations. A **civilization** is an advanced and complex society. Two important markers of civilization are agriculture and organized **religion**, or the belief in and worship of gods and goddesses.

About 11,600 years ago in southeast Turkey on the edge of the Fertile Crescent, at least 500 people came together to create **Göbekli Tepe** (guh-bek-LEE TEH-peh), the world's first **temple**, or place of worship. Ancient builders formed massive limestone pillars into T shapes and arranged them into sets of circles.

The tallest pillars stood as high as 18 feet and weighed 16 tons. Keep in mind that Göbekli Tepe's builders did all this before the invention of the wheel. Stone workers carved ferocious animals onto the pillars after they were in place. Once completed,

the immense pillars and the frightening images of deadly animals flickering in the firelight must have been an awesome sight.

Göbekli Tepe represents an important event in the development of organized religion. As one of the first known examples of monumental architecture, or large structures built for an identified purpose, it was specifically dedicated for religious use. Its commanding views over fertile plains, evidence of ceremonies, and high levels of artistic expression all suggest a religious purpose.

Göbekli Tepe is also remarkable because archaeologists believe that hunter-gatherers, not settled farmers, built it. The structures at Göbekli Tepe were constructed miles from any Neolithic settlement, water source, or agricultural land. The absence of harvest symbols found in later farming cultures reinforces the theory that hunter-gatherers—not a settled people—built Göbekli Tepe.

THE MEANING OF GÖBEKLI TEPE

Archaeologists argue over the meaning of Göbekli Tepe. Evidence found there has changed the way some think about the human transition from hunter-gatherer to farmer. For a long time, archaeologists thought that the need to ensure good harvests led to the belief in and worship of gods and goddesses. In other words, agriculture developed before religion. However, Göbekli Tepe turns that argument around, suggesting that here, at least, humans developed organized religion before farming. In this case, perhaps the need to feed religious gatherings led to the development of agriculture.

The fact is that in some places, agriculture came before religion; in others, religion came first. Göbekli Tepe teaches us that different cultures forged different paths to civilization. Either way, by 6000 B.C., both organized religion and agriculture—two of the fundamental building blocks of civilization—had been established in the Fertile Crescent.

Göbekli Tepe's builders constructed the site without the benefit of the wheel. They relied on human muscle—and lots of it—to move the 16-ton limestone pillars from as far as a quarter mile away.

PATHS TO CIVILIZATION

HUNTER-GATHERER

A warmer climate leads to more vegetation and wildlife, allowing for . . .
→ Domestication of plants and animals
Agriculture
Permanent settlement
which led to → Religion

Curiosity about the natural world encourages the beginnings of . . .
→ Religion *which led to* →
Agriculture
Domestication of plants and animals
Permanent settlement

FARMER

REVIEW & ASSESS

1. **READING CHECK** How does Göbekli Tepe show that organized religion sometimes developed before agriculture?

2. **IDENTIFY MAIN IDEAS AND DETAILS** What features made Göbekli Tepe such an important achievement?

3. **INTEGRATE VISUALS** Based on the diagram and description of the pillars in the text, what might the hunter-gatherers who visited Göbekli Tepe have worshipped?

6.1.1 Describe the hunter-gatherer societies, including the development of tools and the use of fire.

STANDARDS

HSS CONTENT STANDARDS:

6.1.1 Describe the hunter-gatherer societies, including the development of tools and the use of fire.

HSS ANALYSIS SKILLS:

HI 2 Students understand and distinguish cause, effect, sequence, and correlation in historical events, including the long- and short-term causal relations; **HI 5** Students recognize that interpretations of history are subject to change as new information is uncovered.

PLAN

OBJECTIVE

Explore how cultures follow different paths as they develop into civilizations.

ESSENTIAL QUESTION

What factors contributed to the development of civilization?

Two important factors in the development of civilization are religion and agriculture. Lesson 2.1 explores Göbekli Tepe, an ancient temple in present-day Turkey.

BACKGROUND FOR THE TEACHER

Göbekli Tepe, which means "belly hill" in Turkish, predates Stonehenge, the site featured at the beginning of Chapter 2, by about 6,000 years. Anthropologists originally dismissed it in the 1960s, thinking it might be a medieval cemetery. In 1994, German archaeologist Klaus Schmidt was immediately transfixed when he saw the site for the first time while on a dig in the area. He keyed in on its shape: 50 feet high, with a rounded top. Schmidt knew that humans had created it. A year later, he returned with a team and has excavated the site for more than 20 years. Though he has been working there for two decades, he says only about a tenth of the 22-acre site has been explored.

DIGITAL RESOURCES NGLSync.cengage.com

TEACHER RESOURCES & ASSESSMENT

 Reading and Note-Taking

 Vocabulary Practice

 Section 2 Quiz

STUDENT RESOURCES

 NG Chapter Gallery

PREVIEW WITH VISUALS

Direct students' attention to the flow chart and photograph in Lesson 2.1. **ASK:** What do you notice in the photograph? *(Student responses will vary but should focus on the ruins of an ancient building of some sort.)* **ASK:** What is the subject of the flow chart? *(The flow chart shows two different transitions from hunter-gatherer to farmer.)* Explain that in this lesson, they will learn about different theories that explain how ancient people moved from being hunter-gatherers to farmers. **0:05** minutes

GUIDED DISCUSSION

1. **Describe** What do archaeologists think Göbekli Tepe looked like thousands of years ago? *(Massive, T-shaped limestone pillars were arranged in sets of circles. The pillars had carvings of fierce animals on them.)*

2. **Explain** Why do archaeologists believe that hunter-gatherers built Göbekli Tepe? *(Göbekli Tepe was built far from any Neolithic settlement, water source, or agricultural lands. No harvest symbols are present at the site, which would likely have meant a settled community of farmers constructed Göbekli Tepe.)*

MONITOR COMPREHENSION

The concepts presented in this lesson can be challenging to understand. After reading the lesson, devote some class time for a brief question-and-answer session. Ask students to pose questions about what they do not understand. Write questions on the board. Allow time for student volunteers to offer explanations and answers, and write their answers on the board. Clarify any outstanding questions or discrepancies before moving on. **0:10** minutes

ACTIVE OPTIONS

On Your Feet: Living Flow Chart Have students study the flow chart in Lesson 2.1. Divide the class into two groups, A and B. Assign Group A to the top part of the chart and Group B to the bottom part. Have each group meet for five minutes to review the steps in their "path to civilization." Label one side of the room "Hunter-Gatherer" and the other side "Farmer." Then have each group start at the end of the room labeled "Hunter-Gatherer" and move toward "Farmer" while narrating the steps in between. When groups reach the "Farmer" side of the room, have the class vote on which path seems more logical to them. **0:15** minutes

NG Learning Framework: Rewrite In Your Own Words

SKILL: Communication
KNOWLEDGE: Our Human Story

Have students revisit the text and the flow chart in the lesson. Explain that this flow chart is a visual summary of the text. Then have students rewrite the information in the flow chart using their own words. Encourage students to work in pairs to check each other's work and to help each other understand the two processes described. **0:10** minutes

STRIVING READERS

Complete Sequence Chains In order to reinforce comprehension of the flow chart in the lesson, have students reproduce it using the Sequence Chain graphic organizer below. Tell students to fill in two separate chains demonstrating two different paths to civilization. When students have completed their Sequence Chains, have them review each other's work and then gather as a group to check the chains for accuracy.

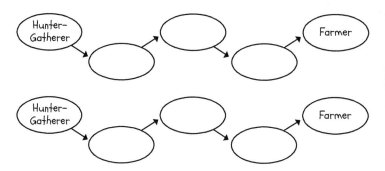

GIFTED & TALENTED

Build a Model Have students locate an illustration of Göbekli Tepe using a National Geographic resource. Tell them to use the illustration as a guide as they build a 3-D model of the site. They can use modeling clay or another material to "reconstruct" the ancient temple's sets of circles. Students might want to include human figures in their model for scale. As an extension to this activity, have students read Klaus Schmidt's description of Göbekli Tepe in the **Primary Source Handbook** and answer the questions that follow it.

Press **mt** *in the Student eEdition for modified text.*

See the Chapter Planner for more strategies for differentiation.

ANSWERS

1. Archaeologists believe that hunter-gatherers built Göbekli Tepe as a place of worship. Therefore, in this particular location, early humans developed organized religion before farming and other stepping-stones of civilization.

2. Göbekli Tepe is an enormous achievement because it was built 11,500 years ago, before large-scale social organization, before organized religion, before farming surpluses to support builders, before advanced construction techniques, before the invention of the wheel, and before writing, metal, and pottery.

3. Because they were hunter-gatherers and fierce animals were depicted on the pillars, visitors might have worshipped animals.

Traits of Civilization

You might hear the word *civilization* a lot, but do you understand what it means? All civilizations, whether past or present, have certain things in common. So, what is a civilization?

MAIN IDEA

A civilization is a complex society that is defined by five key traits.

Cultural hearths prepared the way for the next development in human history: civilization. Ancient cultures around the world transformed into complex civilizations at about the same time, and they had five traits, or characteristics, in common: cities, complex institutions, specialized workers, record keeping, and improved technology.

CITIES

The first civilizations were born in **cities**. More than just large population centers, early cities were political, economic, and cultural centers for the surrounding areas. Cities often contained monumental architecture usually dedicated to religion or government. The city's heart was its trading center, where farmers and merchants met to conduct business. **Trade**, or the exchange of goods, allowed some civilizations to grow very rich. Some merchants traveled long distances to trade goods with other groups. Over time, they established trade routes, which helped spread ideas and practices.

COMPLEX INSTITUTIONS

As cities developed, complex institutions such as government and organized religion emerged as ways to manage resources and populations. **Government**, or an organization set up to make and enforce rules in a society, provided leadership and laws. Organized religion bound communities together through shared beliefs.

SPECIALIZED WORKERS

Food surpluses made possible by the agricultural revolution led to settled communities and to another key characteristic of civilizations: **specialized workers**. Specialized workers performed jobs other than farming. Some people specialized in pottery, metalworking, weaving, or toolmaking. Others became government officials, priests, teachers, soldiers, or merchants.

RECORD KEEPING

As societies developed, they had to manage information. **Record keeping**, or organizing and storing information, became an important job. Specialized workers called **scribes** recorded business transactions, important events, customs, traditions, and laws. The first writing systems used pictographs that looked like the things they represented, such as wavy lines for water. Eventually, complex writing systems helped people record important information and abstract ideas. As writing developed, so did calendar keeping.

IMPROVED TECHNOLOGY

The fifth key characteristic civilizations have in common is improved technology. As cultures became more complex, people developed new tools and techniques to solve problems and survive. Advances in technology included metalworking methods, inventions such as the wheel and the plow, and tools to create everyday items, such as the potter's wheel.

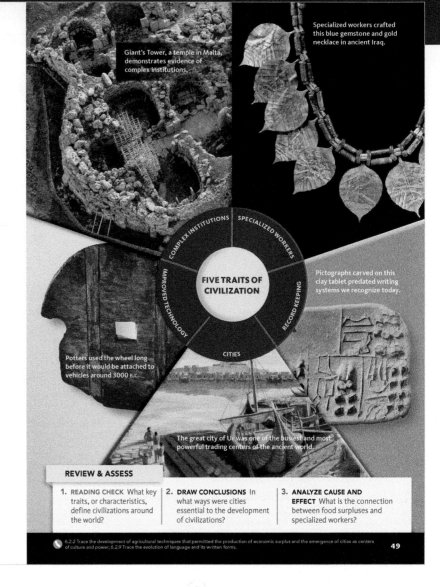

Giant's Tower, a temple in Malta, demonstrates evidence of complex institutions.

Specialized workers crafted this blue gemstone and gold necklace in ancient Iraq.

FIVE TRAITS OF CIVILIZATION

COMPLEX INSTITUTIONS · SPECIALIZED WORKERS · RECORD KEEPING · CITIES · IMPROVED TECHNOLOGY

Pictographs carved on this clay tablet predated writing systems we recognize today.

Potters used the wheel long before it would be attached to vehicles around 3000 B.C.

The great city of Ur was one of the busiest and most powerful trading centers of the ancient world.

REVIEW & ASSESS

1. **READING CHECK** What key traits, or characteristics, define civilizations around the world?

2. **DRAW CONCLUSIONS** In what ways were cities essential to the development of civilizations?

3. **ANALYZE CAUSE AND EFFECT** What is the connection between food surpluses and specialized workers?

6.2.2 Trace the development of agricultural techniques that permitted the production of economic surplus and the emergence of cities as centers of culture and power; 6.2.9 Trace the evolution of language and its written forms.

HSS CONTENT STANDARDS:

6.2.2 Trace the development of agricultural techniques that permitted the production of economic surplus and the emergence of cities as centers of culture and power;
6.2.9 Trace the evolution of language and its written forms.

PLAN

OBJECTIVE

Analyze the characteristics of civilizations.

ESSENTIAL QUESTION

What factors contributed to the development of civilization?

Civilizations are complex societies that share certain characteristics. Lesson 2.2 describes five characteristics found among civilizations.

BACKGROUND FOR THE TEACHER

Civilization is a big word and an important one in the study of human history. The root of *civilization* is *civil*, an adjective from the Latin *civilis*, meaning "relating to a citizen, relating to public life." To be "civil" or "civilized" was to have polite manners. By the 1850s, the word *civilization* began to be used to describe a "human society in a civilized condition, considered as a whole."

DIGITAL RESOURCES NGLSync.cengage.com

TEACHER RESOURCES & ASSESSMENT

 Reading and Note-Taking

 Vocabulary Practice

 Section 2 Quiz

STUDENT RESOURCES

 NG Chapter Gallery

IDENTIFY CHARACTERISTICS

Help students practice identifying common characteristics by listing common traits of mammals. Ask students to identify four characteristics of mammals. (*Mammals are vertebrates, which means they have a backbone or spine; they are endothermic, or warm-blooded; most mammals have hair on their bodies; they produce milk to feed their young.*) List the characteristics on the board. Then list different kinds of mammals and, as a class, confirm that each mammal has these characteristics. Explain that like mammals, civilizations also share common characteristics. `0:05` minutes

TEACH

GUIDED DISCUSSION

1. **Evaluate** Why might cities be considered the birthplaces of civilizations? (*In order to emerge, civilizations need people. Cities gathered lots of people together in one place. Therefore, the opportunities for other characteristics of civilizations to develop were plentiful, such as the development of specialized workers, complex institutions, record keeping, and improved technology.*)

2. **Form and Support Opinions** Which trait of civilization do you think is least important? (*Responses will vary, but students should base their opinions on information they learn from the reading.*)

ANALYZE VISUALS

Direct students' attention to the Five Traits of Civilization wheel in the lesson. For each image or illustration, ask students the following questions:

- What catches your attention first?
- What other details do you notice?
- What does the image tell you about a trait of civilization?

`0:10` minutes

ACTIVE OPTIONS

On Your Feet: Build a Civilization Divide the class into five groups and assign each group a trait of civilization covered in Lesson 2.2. Then have each group move to an assigned part of the room. Tell students to create their own form of their assigned trait. For example, the "Record-Keeping" group might come up with an original alphabet or a different way of recording information. Allow students time to brainstorm and collaborate. Encourage them to include interesting details. Then gather the five groups together and have each group present their trait to the class. As a class, come up with a name for this new civilization. `0:20` minutes

NG Learning Framework: Rank the Traits

ATTITUDE: **Empowerment**
SKILL: **Problem-Solving**

Invite students to review the text and visuals in the lesson. Ask students to consider the five traits of civilization and then rank them in order of importance. Once they have completed their list of rankings, encourage students to share their lists with the class. Write their responses on the board and have students explain how they decided to rank their traits. `0:10` minutes

INCLUSION

Match Text with Visuals Pair students with mixed ability levels. Have each pair review the text. Then have students match each section of the text with its corresponding image in the Five Traits of Civilization wheel on the opposite page. Encourage students to keep track of their matches by using this sentence frame:

The _____ section of text matches with the image of _____ .

PRE-AP

Create a Presentation Have students conduct independent research on the five characteristics of civilization as demonstrated in ancient Egypt, ancient Greece, ancient China, or another ancient civilization that they will learn about in this book. After they have completed research, have students create a presentation that demonstrates through text and visuals the five characteristics of civilization found in their chosen civilization. Encourage students to share their presentations with the class.

Press (**mt**) *in the Student eEdition for modified text.*

See the Chapter Planner for more strategies for differentiation.

ANSWERS

1. Civilizations around the world share these key characteristics: advanced cities, trade, complex institutions, specialized workers, record keeping, and improved technology.

2. With many people living in one place, cities accelerated the cultural advances of ancient civilizations. Cities were also the political, economic, cultural, and social centers for the surrounding areas.

3. Food surpluses supported growing populations and allowed people to specialize in jobs other than farming, such as toolmaking and pottery.

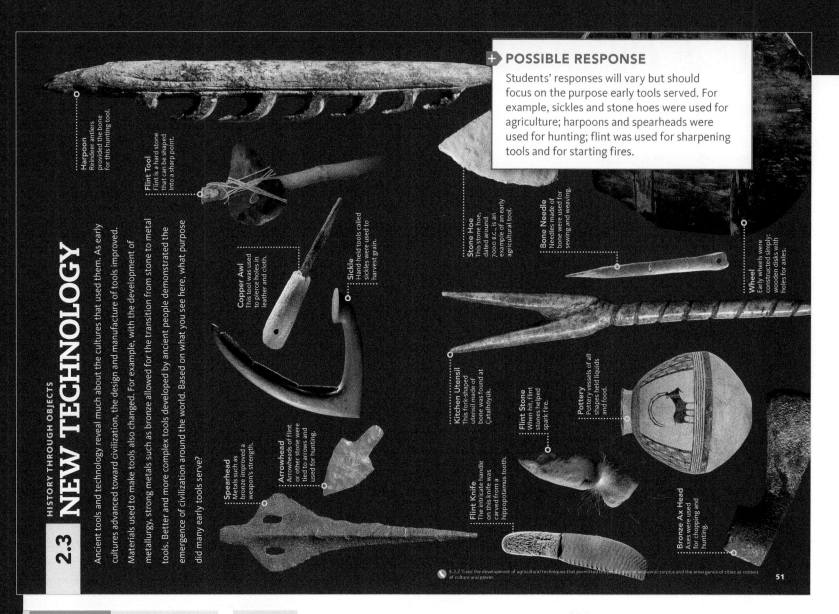

HISTORY THROUGH OBJECTS

2.3 NEW TECHNOLOGY

Ancient tools and technology reveal much about the cultures that used them. As early cultures advanced toward civilization, the design and manufacture of tools improved. Materials used to make tools also changed. For example, with the development of metallurgy, strong metals such as bronze allowed for the transition from stone to metal tools. Better and more complex tools developed by ancient people demonstrated the emergence of civilization around the world. Based on what you see here, what purpose did many early tools serve?

Harpoon
Reindeer antlers provided the bone for this hunting tool.

Flint Tool
Flint is a hard stone that can be shaped into a sharp point.

Copper Awl
This tool was used to pierce holes in leather and cloth.

Sickle
Hand-held tools called sickles were used to harvest grain.

Stone Hoe
This stone hoe, dated around 7000 B.C., is an example of an early agricultural tool.

Bone Needle
Needles made of bone were used for sewing and weaving.

Wheel
Early wheels were constructed simply: wooden disks with holes for axles.

Spearhead
Metals such as bronze improved a weapon's strength.

Arrowhead
Arrowheads of flint or other stone were tied to arrows and used for hunting.

Kitchen Utensil
This fork-shaped utensil made of bone was found at Çatalhöyük.

Flint Stone
When hit, flint stones helped spark fire.

Pottery
Pottery vessels of all shapes held liquids and food.

Flint Knife
The intricate handle on this knife was carved from a hippopotamus tooth.

Bronze Ax Head
Axes were used for chopping and hunting.

6.2.2 Trace the development of agricultural techniques that permitted the production of economic surplus and the emergence of cities as centers of culture and power.

51

PLAN

OBJECTIVE

Identify the new technology that emerged from cultural hearths.

ESSENTIAL QUESTION

What factors contributed to the development of civilization?

One characteristic of civilization is the development of new and better technology. Lesson 2.3 shows several tools used by ancient cultures.

BACKGROUND FOR THE TEACHER

One of the most prominent metals used in Neolithic tools was bronze. Bronze is an alloy, or combination of two metals, copper and another metal, usually tin. Bronze is easily melted and shaped, but the cooled metal is stronger than copper. Bronze also resists rust, unlike iron. Most tools and weapons were eventually made from iron, however, because it was more available. In addition to use in tools and weapons, bronze was used in ancient coins and, later, statues and artifacts.

DIGITAL RESOURCES NGLSync.cengage.com

TEACHER RESOURCES & ASSESSMENT

 Reading and Note-Taking

 Vocabulary Practice

 Section 2 Quiz

STUDENT RESOURCES

 NG Image Gallery

EXAMINE HISTORY THROUGH OBJECTS

Ask students to reach into their backpacks, desks, or pencil boxes and pull out an item they use every day. If personal objects are not available to them, have students select a "tool" from the classroom. **ASK:** What is your tool used for? Why is it important to you? How might you improve upon your tool? *(Responses will vary. Encourage students to hold up their tool so that others can see it.)* `0:05` **minutes**

GUIDED DISCUSSION

1. **Draw Conclusions** Many of the tools featured in the lesson have sharp points. Why might this be? *(Tools with sharp points would be used for hunting and killing animals for food, chopping wood, or planting and harvesting crops.)*

2. **Form and Support Opinions** Which two tools do you think would have been most important to have and use in a Neolithic cultural hearth? Use what you have learned in this chapter to support your opinion. *(Responses will vary, but answers should rely on information from the chapter.)*

ANALYZE VISUALS

Have students create a Venn Diagram for classifying the ancient tools into categories: *farming, cooking,* and *hunting,* based on their function. Point out that some tools may serve dual purposes. Then have students sort the artifacts into the categories, writing each item in the appropriate part of the diagram. Invite volunteers to share their categories and discuss/debate any alternative categorizing. `0:15` **minutes**

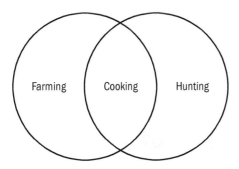

ACTIVE OPTIONS   STEM

On Your Feet: Make a Tool Divide the class into four or five groups. Have each group draw plans and create a prototype for a tool they might use in their everyday lives. Tools could range in purpose from practical to whimsical. The objective of the task is to define the use for the tool and then create the tool, or at least a mock-up of it. After groups have finished with their plans and prototyping, have each group present its tool to the rest of the class. Encourage students to notice if a particular theme emerges regarding the kinds of tools created. `0:25` **minutes**

Critical Viewing: NG Image Gallery Invite students to explore the entire NG Image Gallery and create a Favorites List by choosing the images they find most interesting. If possible, have students copy the images into a document to form an actual list. Then encourage them to select the image they like best and do further research on it. `0:10` **minutes**

INCLUSION

Analyze Visuals Pair special needs students with students at a higher proficiency level. Have them reread the lesson. Then have students identify three ancient tools that they find interesting. Have them use the three-column chart below to record each tool, its use, and a similar modern tool.

Ancient Tool	Use	Modern Tool

PRE-AP   STEM

Research and Report Have students research and prepare an oral report on the development of metallurgy, the historical transition from stone to metal tools, and where and when this shift happened. Students should explain the significance of the transition in their reports. Have them present their reports to the class and encourage them to take questions from the audience.

Press **mt** *in the Student eEdition for modified text.*

See the Chapter Planner for more strategies for differentiation.

VOCABULARY

Use each of the following vocabulary words in a sentence that shows an understanding of the term's meaning.

1. **cultural hearth** (HSS HI 3)
   A cultural hearth is a place from which new ideas and technology spread to surrounding areas.
2. **surplus** (HSS 6.2.2)
3. **metallurgy** (HSS 6.2.2)
4. **matrilineal** (HSS HI 5)
5. **maize** (HSS 6.2.2)
6. **temple** (HSS 6.1.1)
7. **cultural diffusion** (HSS HI 3)
8. **government** (HSS 6.2.2)
9. **specialized worker** (HSS 6.2.2)
10. **civilization** (HSS 6.2.1)

READING STRATEGY

11. **IDENTIFY MAIN IDEAS AND DETAILS** If you haven't already, complete your diagram to determine a main idea and supporting details about cultural hearths. Then answer the question.

Cultural Hearths

> **Main Idea:** *Cultural hearths promoted the spread of new ideas, practices, and technology around the world.*
>
> Detail:
>
> Detail:
>
> Detail:

What is a cultural hearth? What impact did the four main cultural hearths have on the ancient world? (HSS HI 3)

MAIN IDEAS

Answer the following questions. Support your answers with evidence from the chapter.

12. Why are cultural hearths referred to as centers of new ideas? LESSON 1.1 (HSS HI 3)
13. In what way was agriculture central to the people who built Çatalhöyük? LESSON 1.2 (HSS HI 1)
14. How did natural resources and climate influence the formation of cultural hearths in China? LESSON 1.3 (HSS 6.2.2)
15. In what ways did the Faiyum farmers demonstrate cultural diffusion? LESSON 1.5 (HSS HI 2)
16. What key characteristics do civilizations around the world share? LESSON 2.2 (HSS HI 3)

CRITICAL THINKING

Answer the following questions. Support your answers with evidence from the chapter.

17. **ESSENTIAL QUESTION** What are some of the factors that contribute to the development of civilization? (HSS HI 3)
18. **DRAW CONCLUSIONS** How did cultural hearths help lead to the emergence of civilization? (HSS HI 2)
19. **MAKE INFERENCES** Why do you think government became necessary as cities developed? (HSS HI 3)
20. **COMPARE AND CONTRAST** How did the lifestyles of hunter-gatherers compare with those of settlers of early agricultural communities? (HSS 6.1.1)
21. **MAKE INFERENCES** Why is it significant that hunter-gatherers built Göbekli Tepe as a place of worship? (HSS HI 2)
22. **FORM OPINIONS** Do you think agriculture or religion developed first? Support your opinion with evidence from the chapter. (HSS REP 1)
23. **YOU DECIDE** Which of the five traits of civilization do you consider the most important? Support your opinion with evidence from the chapter. (HSS REP 1)

INTERPRET MAPS

Study the map of the locations of the Yangshao and Longshan cultures that developed in China's cultural hearth. Then answer the questions that follow.

24. Which river was vital to the development of the Yangshao culture? (HSS 6.2.1)
25. Why might the Longshan culture have expanded east from the Yangshao culture? (HSS CST 3)
26. **MAP ACTIVITY** Create your own sketch maps of the other cultural hearths discussed in this chapter. Label the areas and bodies of water. Then study the maps and note the cultural hearths' physical similarities and differences. (HSS CST 3)

CHINA'S CULTURAL HEARTH

Huang He
Bonpo
Yellow Sea
Chang Jiang

0 250 500 Miles
0 250 500 Kilometers

☐ Longshan
☐ Yangshao

ANALYZE SOURCES

The dagger below is made of carved and chipped stone. Archaeologists who discovered it at Çatalhöyük believe it was made around 6000 B.C. Study the artifact. Then answer the question that follows.

27. What information might archaeologists learn about the skills of the Neolithic people who created the dagger? Use evidence from the chapter to support your answer. (HSS REP 4)

WRITE ABOUT HISTORY

28. **INFORMATIVE** Choose two cultures discussed in this chapter. Write a 3-paragraph informative essay that compares and contrasts the cultures in terms of their agricultural and technological developments. Use the tips below to help you plan, organize, and revise your essay. (HSS HI 1)

TIPS

- Take notes from the lessons about the two cultures you chose.
- State your main idea and supporting details in a clear, well-organized way.
- Use appropriate transitions to clarify the relationships among ideas.
- Use at least two vocabulary words from the chapter.
- Provide a concluding statement that wraps up the information about the two cultures.
- Use word-processing software to produce and publish your final essay.

VOCABULARY ANSWERS

1. A cultural hearth is a place from which new ideas and technology spread to surrounding areas. (HSS HI 3)
2. Farming fertile land produced a surplus of food that Neolithic people stored, traded, or used to feed non-agricultural workers. (HSS 6.2.2)
3. At the Neolithic village of Çatalhöyük, archaeologists have found lead and copper, which is evidence that these people had made advancements in metallurgy, or metalworking. (HSS 6.2.2)
4. In the Yangshao culture of China, families were grouped into matrilineal clans based on female ancestors. (HSS HI 5)
5. In Mesoamerica, the domestication of maize provided a useful and productive food source that supported permanent farming villages. (HSS 6.2.2)
6. Archaeologists believe that Göbekli Tepe is one of the world's first temples. (HSS 6.1.1)
7. Cultural diffusion is the process by which cultures spread and share ideas, practices, and techniques with surrounding cultures. (HSS HI 3)
8. Government is an organization set up to make and enforce rules for a society. (HSS 6.2.2)
9. Specialized workers such as scribes recorded important information. (HSS 6.2.2)
10. A civilization is an advanced society that has cities, complex institutions, specialized workers, record keeping, and improved technology. (HSS 6.2.1)

STANDARDS

HSS CONTENT STANDARDS:

6.1.1 Describe the hunter-gatherer societies, including the development of tools and the use of fire; **6.2.1** Locate and describe the major river systems and discuss the physical settings that supported permanent settlement and early civilizations; **6.2.2** Trace the development of agricultural techniques that permitted the production of economic surplus and the emergence of cities as centers of culture and power.

HSS ANALYSIS SKILLS:

CST 3 Students use a variety of maps and documents to identify physical and cultural features of neighborhoods, cities, states, and countries and to explain the historical migration of people, expansion and disintegration of empires, and the growth of economic systems; **REP 1** Students frame questions that can be answered by historical study and research; **REP 4** Students assess the credibility of primary and secondary sources and draw sound conclusions from them; **HI 1** Students explain the central issues and problems from the past, placing people and events in a matrix of time and place; **HI 2** Students understand and distinguish cause, effect, sequence, and correlation in historical events, including the long- and short-term causal relations; **HI 3** Students explain the sources of historical continuity and how the combination of ideas and events explains the emergence of new patterns; **HI 5** Students recognize that interpretations of history are subject to change as new information is uncovered

READING STRATEGY ANSWERS

Cultural Hearths

Main Idea: Cultural hearths promoted the spread of new ideas, practices, and technology around the world.

Detail: domesticated plants and animals

Detail: created artistic pottery

Detail: advanced building techniques

Detail: adopted new techniques from other cultures

11. A cultural hearth is place where new ideas, practices, and technology spread. The four cultural hearths of Oaxaca, Banpo, Çatalhöyük, and Faiyum made important contributions to surrounding cultures and regions. For example, farmers in Oaxaca domesticated maize, which became a staple crop for Mesoamericans. Potters at Banpo created kiln-fired, beautiful pottery. Builders at Çatalhöyük demonstrated advanced architectural techniques. Farmers at Faiyum learned new techniques from cultures across the Mediterranean Sea. (HSS HI 3)

MAIN IDEAS ANSWERS

12. Ancient cultural hearths were places where people developed new ideas and technologies that then spread to other places. These included new ways of living in communities, increasingly complex forms of artistic and religious expression, and pioneering methods of raising animals and domesticating plants. (HSS HI 3)

13. Agriculture was central to the people who built Çatalhöyük because in order to support a large population, they needed a steady food supply. They farmed barley and wheat and also raised domesticated animals such as cattle, sheep, and goats. (HSS HI 1)

14. Major rivers such as the Huang He and Wei were bountiful natural resources for water and fishing. Along these river basins fertile soils and a warmer, wetter climate also provided ideal conditions for farming and settlement, all of which enabled Neolithic cultures, such as the Yangshao and Longshan, to develop and create China's cultural hearth. (HSS 6.2.2)

15. The Neolithic farmers who settled Egypt's earliest farming community in Faiyum are a significant example of cultural diffusion because they imported domesticated crops and animals, as well as tools and farming techniques, to places where domestication was already well established. The Faiyum farmers adapted neighboring cultures' ideas to their needs, spreading these ideas from one culture and area to another. (HSS HI 2)

16. Civilizations around the world share the key characteristics of cities, complex institutions, specialized workers, record keeping, and improved technology. (HSS HI 3)

CRITICAL THINKING ANSWERS

17. Factors that contribute to the development of civilization include practices that originate in cultural hearths, the emergence of cities and complex institutions, the establishment of specialized workers and record keeping, and improved technology. (HSS HI 3)

18. They allowed people to become specialized workers; trade of agricultural products helped cities develop and become rich; technology diffused through cultural hearths led to more advanced technology. (HSS HI 2)

19. Rules and laws kept order and controlled the growing population. (HSS HI 3)

20. Hunter-gatherers lived a nomadic lifestyle, following herds of animals to hunt for food and skins and following the seasons to gather edible plants, seeds, and nuts—a difficult life of survival. While settlers of early agricultural communities continued to hunt animals and catch fish, they also domesticated plants and animals, which allowed them to farm and settle into permanent villages. (HSS 6.1.1)

21. If Göbekli Tepe was built by hunter-gatherers—before farming developed—it reverses the order in which archaeologists and historians believe that most civilizations developed: agriculture first, then religion. By building Göbekli Tepe as a temple of worship, the hunter-gatherers practiced religion before they had developed farming. (HSS HI 2)

22. Students' responses will vary. Students should clearly state their opinions about Göbekli Tepe in terms of its significance in the development of agriculture and religion and support their opinions with evidence from the chapter. (HSS REP 1)

23. Students' responses will vary. Students should clearly state their opinions regarding the most important trait of civilization and support their opinions with evidence from the chapter. (HSS REP 1)

INTERPRET MAPS ANSWERS

24. The Huang He was vital to the development of the Yangshao culture. (HSS 6.2.1)

25. It seems significant that the Longshan culture evolved from the important Huang He river basin, but expanded toward a larger water resource and outlet, suggesting a growing population and advancements in travel and trade. (HSS CST 3)

26. Students' maps will vary but should be labeled correctly. (HSS CST 3)

ANALYZE SOURCES ANSWER

27. Students' responses will vary. Sample response: The photograph of the dagger reveals a high level of technical skill in shaping the flint dagger and sharp edges. The bone handle of the dagger reveals an interest in artistic expression, as well as a high level of artistic skill in shaping it in the form of an animal's head. (HSS REP 4)

WRITE ABOUT HISTORY ANSWER

28. Students' essays should

- introduce the topic and develop it with relevant details
- contain transitions from one idea to another
- include vocabulary words from the chapter
- end with a concluding statement that supports the information presented

For more in-depth instruction and practice with the writing form, assign the Social Studies Skills Writing Lesson on writing an informative essay. (HSS HI 1)

ON **LOCATION**
WITH **Louise**

LEAKEY

NATIONAL GEOGRAPHIC EXPLORER-IN-RESIDENCE

▶ Check out more at NGLSync.Cengage.com

Meave Leakey (left) and Louise
Leakey conserve a fossil found
in Kenya. Their discoveries in
the country's Turkana Basin
have greatly contributed to our
understanding of human origins.

ALL IN THE FAMILY

I've spent quite a bit of time on my hands and knees, carefully excavating the remains of our ancestors and other animals. I have been fortunate to have done this work alongside my mother, Meave Leakey. She is also a highly acclaimed paleontologist, so there's a lot to live up to! This is what happens when you're born into a family famous for finding prehuman fossils. My grandfather, Louis Leakey, made important discoveries in Tanzania, at Olduvai Gorge, that helped explain the human fossil record. I remember when my father, Richard Leakey, discovered a well-preserved 1.6-million-year-old skeleton of *Homo erectus*, one of our ancestors that left Africa for the first time 1.8 million years ago. I was twelve years old at the time, and they compared my teeth with the teeth of this skeleton, the Nariokotome Boy, to determine that it was about the same age as I was.

EARLY HUMAN FOSSILS

My mother and I continue with our field work, on the east side of Lake Turkana in Kenya's Rift Valley. We organize and coordinate the search for fossil remains in extensive fossil deposits in northern Kenya. During every expedition, we discover and collect exciting new fossils that help us answer important questions about the past. These fossils are kept at the Turkana Basin Institute or in the National Museums of Kenya. In 1999, we

Louise Leakey uses GPS to locate fossils in Kenya. You can explore many of her family's fossil discoveries at www.africanfossils.org.

organized a National Geographic-sponsored expedition to the Turkana Basin. It was there that my mother and I uncovered a 3.3-million-year-old human skull and part of a jaw. The skull is very flat, and that makes it different from anything else ever found. In fact, it is so different that we believe it belongs to an entirely new branch of early human that we named *Kenyanthropus platyops*. To prove this beyond doubt, we still need to find more remains, ideally another intact skull! From this same site, the earliest stone tools known to the world have recently been announced, which strongly suggests that this species was also the earliest tool maker.

WHY STUDY HISTORY ?

“ When you look at the state of the world today, with its many conflicts and ethnic divisions, it's hard to believe that we are a single species with a common ancestor. We have to understand our past to contemplate our future. The fossils in east Africa are our *global heritage.* ”   —Louise Leakey

Scotland's Stone Age Ruins

BY ROFF SMITH
Adapted from "Scotland's Stone Age Ruins,"
by Roff Smith, in *National Geographic*, August 2014

Orkney is a fertile, green archipelago off the northern tip of Scotland. Five thousand years ago, people there built something unlike anything they had ever attempted before. They had Stone Age technology, but their vision was millennia ahead of their time.

The ancient people of Orkney quarried thousands of tons of sandstone and transported it several miles to a grassy hill. There they constructed a complex of buildings and surrounded them with imposing walls. The complex featured paved walkways, carved stonework, colored facades, and slate roofs. Many people gathered here for seasonal rituals, feasts, and trade.

Archaeologist Nick Card says the recent discovery of these stunning ruins is turning British prehistory on its head. "This is almost on the scale of some of the great classical sites in the Mediterranean, like the Acropolis in Greece, except these structures are 2,500 years older." Only a small part of the site has been excavated, but this sample has opened a window into the past. It has also yielded thousands of artifacts, including ceremonial mace heads, polished stone axes, flint knives, stone spatulas, and colored pottery. Archaeologists have also discovered more than 650 pieces of Neolithic art at the site.

"Nowhere else in all Britain or Ireland have such well-preserved stone houses from the Neolithic survived," says archaeologist Antonia Thomas. "To be able to link these structures with art, to see in such a direct and personal way how people embellished their surroundings, is really something."

Sometime around the year 2300 B.C., it all came to an end. Climate change may have played a role. Or perhaps it was the disruptive influence of a new toolmaking material: bronze.

Whatever the reason, the ancient temple was deliberately destroyed and buried under stone and trash. Card surmises, "It seems that they were attempting to erase the site and its importance from memory, perhaps to mark the introduction of new belief systems."

For more from National Geographic
Check out "First Americans" at NGLSync.Cengage.com

UNIT INQUIRY: CREATE A CULTURAL SYMBOL

In this unit, you learned about the origins of early human cultures and civilizations. Based on your understanding of the text, what elements of culture developed in early human societies? How did those elements help make each society unique?

ASSIGNMENT Create a symbol that represents the culture of an early human society you studied in this unit. The symbol should reflect one or more cultural characteristics that made that early society unique. Be prepared to present your cultural symbol and explain its significance to the class.

Plan As you create your symbol, think about specific characteristics that were unique to the society you have selected. For example, what elements of culture defined and unified early Stone Age humans? What customs, social structure, arts, tools, and major achievements distinguished them from other groups of early humans? You might want to use a graphic organizer to help organize your thoughts. Identify the early society and at least one specific detail about different characteristics of its culture. ▶

Produce Use your notes to produce detailed descriptions of the elements of culture that defined the early human society you

selected. You might want to draw or write descriptions of visual icons for each element.

Present Choose a creative way to present your cultural symbol to the class. Consider one of the following options:

- Write an introduction to the cultural symbol that describes the early human society it represents.

- Create a multimedia presentation showing different elements of the society's culture and what made it unique.

- Paint a flag of your symbol using colors that also express significance or meaning to the culture.

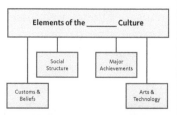

Elements of the _____ Culture

- Social Structure
- Major Achievements
- Customs & Beliefs
- Arts & Technology

RAPID REVIEW
UNIT 1

ORIGINS OF CULTURES AND CIVILIZATIONS

TOP TEN

1. Humans originated from a common ancestor who lived in Africa 60,000 years ago.

2. For thousands of years, humans lived in small, nomadic groups, hunted wild animals, and gathered edible plants.

3. Farming produced food surpluses that allowed rapid population growth and job specialization.

4. Agriculture encouraged people to group together in villages that grew into more complex cities.

5. Cultural hearths emerged around the world during the Neolithic period.

6-10. **NOW IT'S YOUR TURN** Complete the list with five more things to remember about the origins of cultures and civilizations.

POSSIBLE RESPONSES

Possible responses for the remaining five things to remember:

6. Societies grew more complex and developed into civilizations.

7. Humans migrated out of Africa and populated most of the world by about 10,000 B.C.

8. Early humans domesticated plants and animals, which led to the agricultural revolution.

9. Domestication and a more temperate climate encouraged settlement in fertile river valleys.

10. Early humans developed new technology, including harnessing fire and inventing specialized tools.

UNIT INQUIRY PROJECT RUBRIC

ASSESS

Use the rubric to assess each student's participation and performance.

SCORE	ASSIGNMENT	PRODUCT	PRESENTATION
3 GREAT	• Student thoroughly understands the assignment. • Student engages fully with the project process. • Student works well independently.	• Cultural symbol is well thought out. • Cultural symbol reflects characteristics of the selected society. • Descriptions of the society's elements of culture are detailed.	• Presentation is clear, concise, and logical. • Presentation does a good job of creatively explaining the cultural symbol and elements of the selected society's culture. • Presentation engages the audience.
2 GOOD	• Student mostly understands the assignment. • Student engages fairly well with the project process. • Student works fairly well independently.	• Cultural symbol is fairly well thought out. • Cultural symbol somewhat reflects characteristics of the selected society. • Descriptions of the society's elements of culture are somewhat detailed.	• Presentation is fairly clear, concise, and logical. • Presentation does an adequate job of creatively explaining the cultural symbol and elements of the selected society's culture. • Presentation somewhat engages the audience.
1 NEEDS WORK	• Student does not understand the assignment. • Student minimally engages or does not engage with the project process. • Student does not work well independently.	• Cultural symbol is not well thought out. • Cultural symbol does not reflect characteristics of the selected society. • Descriptions of the society's elements of culture are few or nonexistent.	• Presentation is not clear, concise, or logical. • Presentation does an inadequate job of creatively explaining the cultural symbol and elements of the selected society's culture. • Presentation does not engage the audience.

EARLY
CIVILIZATIONS

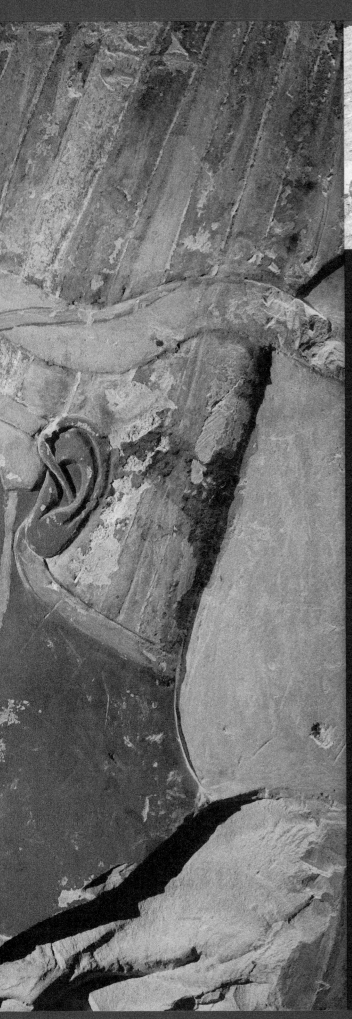

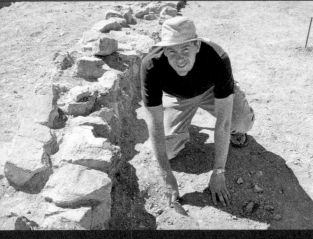

ON **LOCATION** WITH

Christopher Thornton
Archaeologist
Lead Program Officer, Research,
Conservation, and Exploration,
National Geographic

The past is a window to the future. Early civilizations differ in many ways from those today, but there are also many similarities between then and now. Studying early civilizations is exciting because of what we can learn from the ancients, and also because what we know—or think we know— is always changing. I'm Christopher Thornton, and I time travel between the past and present. Join me on my journey!

< **CRITICAL VIEWING** This painted bas-relief shows ancient Egyptian king Thutmose III wearing the Atef crown, which was worn during religious rituals. What details in the artwork convey the king's strength and power?

POSSIBLE RESPONSE

Details that convey the king's strength and power include the figure's confident expression, his elaborate headdress and clothing, and his broad shoulders.

Early
Civilizations

Mesopotamia, Egypt, Israel, India, China, and Mesoamerica

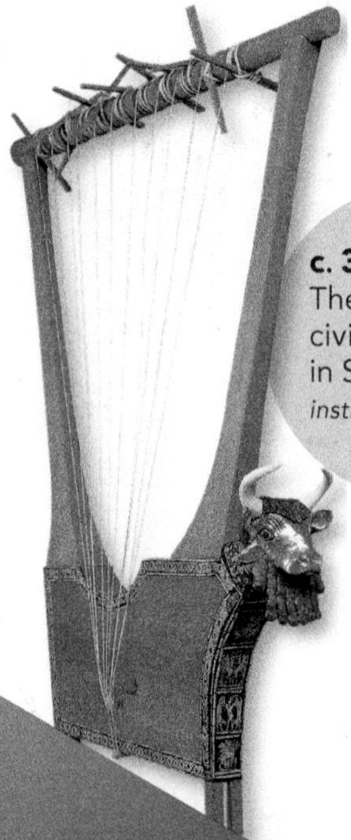

c. 3500 B.C.
The world's first civilization arises in Sumer. *(stringed instrument from Ur)*

c. 1600 B.C.
The Shang dynasty emerges along the Huang He in China.

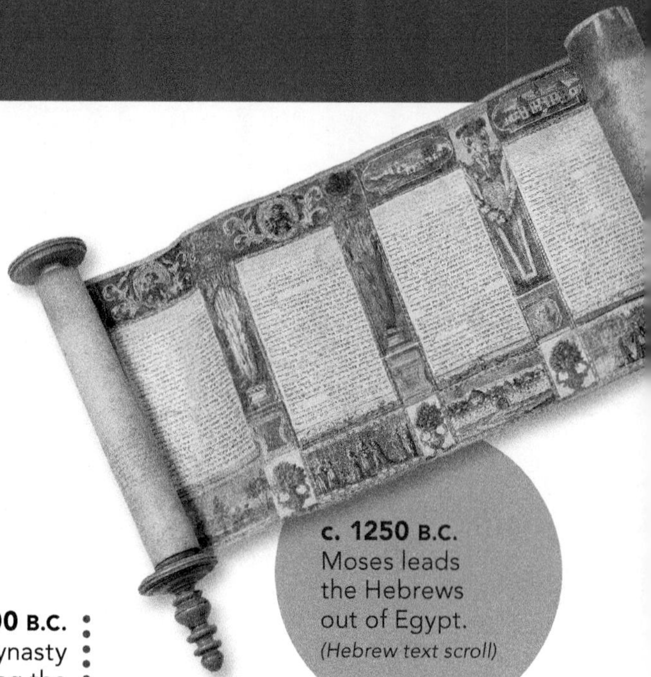

c. 1250 B.C.
Moses leads the Hebrews out of Egypt.
(Hebrew text scroll)

2334 B.C.
Sargon the Great conquers Sumer and creates the world's first empire.

1500 B.C.

c. 1790 B.C.
Hammurabi issues his Code of Laws at Babylon.

c. 2500 B.C.
Harappan civilization develops in the Indus Valley.

3500 B.C.

c. 1470 B.C.
Hatshepsut becomes Egypt's first female pharaoh.

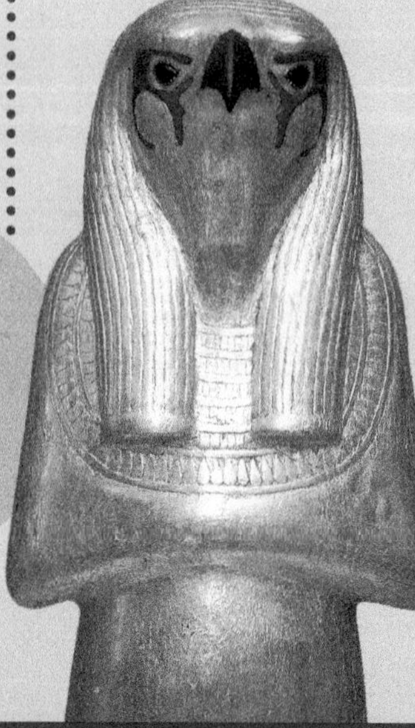

c. 3100 B.C.
Upper and Lower Egypt are united under a single ruler.
(Horus, Egyptian sky god)

c. 1000 B.C.
Aryan civilization spreads through the northern Indian subcontinent.

What can you infer about the Qin dynasty in China based on this time line?

+ POSSIBLE RESPONSE
The dynasty did not last very long.

A.D. 320
Chandra Gupta I establishes the Gupta Empire, which oversees India's golden age.
(Gupta gold coin)

c. 269 B.C.
Asoka becomes ruler of the Maurya Empire and eventually rules by Buddhist principles.

A.D. 105
The Chinese invent paper.

200 B.C.

A.D. 100

563 B.C.
Siddhartha Gautama, the Buddha, is born.

202 B.C.
The Han dynasty comes to power.
(Han bronze dragon)

500 B.C.
The Zapotec build Monte Albán.

600 B.C.

c. 221 B.C.
The Qin dynasty begins with the reign of Shi Huangdi.

587 B.C.
Jerusalem falls to the Babylonians, beginning the Babylonian Exile.

CST 1 Students explain how major events are related to one another in time.

61

FIRST CIVILIZATIONS

(Southwest Asia and North Africa)
3500 B.C.–1800 B.C.

Most of the world's earliest civilizations, including Mesopotamia, Egypt, India, and China, developed in fertile river valleys. The good soil made the river valleys ideal for growing crops. By contrast, the Hebrews established their civilization along the Mediterranean, and, across the Atlantic Ocean, the Olmec, Zapotec, and Maya civilizations developed in the highlands and lowlands of Mesoamerica.

What landforms separated the civilizations?

POSSIBLE RESPONSE
Mountains and bodies of water separated the civilizations.

ANCIENT MESOPOTAMIA

Water sources:	Tigris and Euphrates rivers, Mediterranean Sea
Civilizations and empires:	Sumer, Akkadia, Babylon, Assyria, Chaldea, Phoenicia, Persia
Significant leaders:	Sargon, Hammurabi, Nebuchadnezzar II, Cyrus
Legacy:	farming, writing, government, law, shipbuilding, math

E U R O P E

Black Sea

Caucasus Mts.

Caspian Sea

Mediterranean Sea

Tigris

Mesopotamia

Euphrates

Persian Gulf

Egypt

Nile

Red Sea

A F R I C A

ANCIENT EGYPT

Water sources:	Nile River
Civilizations and empires:	Egypt, Kush
Significant leaders:	Khufu, Ahmose, Hatshepsut, Ramses II, Piankhi
Legacy:	writing, math, science, medicine, art, architecture

JUDAISM & ISRAELITE KINGDOMS

Water sources:	Mediterranean Sea
Civilizations and empires:	Israel, Judah
Significant leaders:	Abraham, Moses, Saul, David, Solomon
Legacy:	education, religion, philosophy

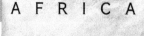

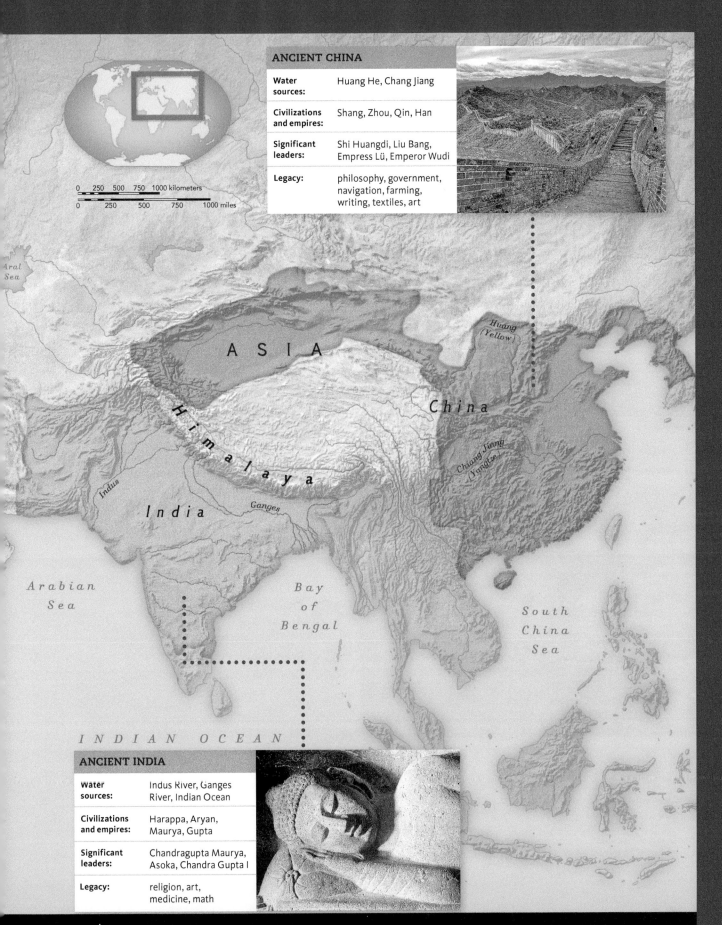

ANCIENT CHINA

Water sources:	Huang He, Chang Jiang
Civilizations and empires:	Shang, Zhou, Qin, Han
Significant leaders:	Shi Huangdi, Liu Bang, Empress Lü, Emperor Wudi
Legacy:	philosophy, government, navigation, farming, writing, textiles, art

0   250   500   750   1000 kilometers
0   250   500   750   1000 miles

Aral Sea

ASIA

Himalaya

Indus

India

Ganges

Huang (Yellow)

China

Chiang Jiang (Yangtze)

Arabian Sea

Bay of Bengal

South China Sea

INDIAN OCEAN

ANCIENT INDIA

Water sources:	Indus River, Ganges River, Indian Ocean
Civilizations and empires:	Harappa, Aryan, Maurya, Gupta
Significant leaders:	Chandragupta Maurya, Asoka, Chandra Gupta I
Legacy:	religion, art, medicine, math

CST 3 Students use a variety of maps and documents to identify physical and cultural features of neighborhoods, cities, states, and countries and to explain the historical migration of people, expansion and disintegration of empires, and the growth of economic systems.

63

UNIT RESOURCES

On Location with National Geographic Lead Program Officer Christopher Thornton
Intro and Video

Interactive Map Tool

STORIES MAKING HISTORY **News & Updates**

Available at NGLSync.cengage.com

Unit Wrap-Up:
"Encounters with History"
Feature and Video

"China's Ancient Lifeline"
National Geographic Adapted Article

"Faces of the Divine"
National Geographic Adapted Article
Student eEdition exclusive

Unit 2 Inquiry:
Write a Creation Myth

CHAPTER RESOURCES

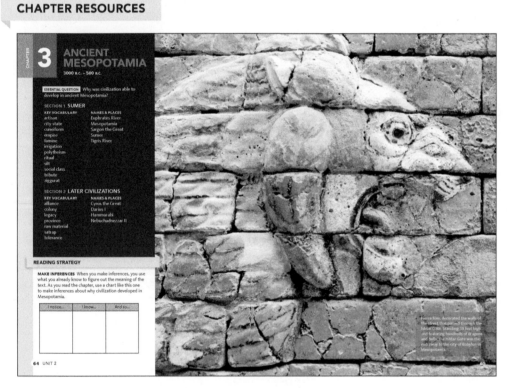

TEACHER RESOURCES & ASSESSMENT

Available at NGLSync.cengage.com

Social Studies Skills Lessons
• Reading: Make Inferences
• Writing: Write an Argument

Formal Assessment
• Chapter 3 Tests A (on-level) & B (below-level)

A **Chapter 3 Answer Key**

ExamView®
One-time Download

STUDENT BACKPACK *Available at NGLSync.cengage.com*

• **eEdition** *(English)*   • **eEdition** *(Spanish)*   • **Handbooks**   • **Online Atlas**

Chapter 3 Spanish resources, Guided Writing prompts, and Financial Literacy lessons are available online.

SECTION 1 RESOURCES

SUMER

 **Reading and Note-Taking**

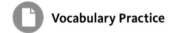 **Vocabulary Practice**

 **Section 1 Quiz**

Available at NGLSync.cengage.com

LESSON 1.1 THE GEOGRAPHY OF ANCIENT MESOPOTAMIA

NG Learning Framework:
Create a Map

• On Your Feet: Inside-Outside Circle

LESSON 1.2 CITY-STATES DEVELOP

NG Learning Framework:
Redesign the City of Ur

• On Your Feet: Create Trade Networks

LESSON 1.3 RELIGION IN SUMER

• Critical Viewing: NG Chapter Gallery

• On Your Feet: Three-Step Interview

DOCUMENT-BASED QUESTION
LESSON 1.4 SUMERIAN WRITING

NG Learning Framework:
Compare Two Writing Systems

• On Your Feet: Telephone

LESSON 1.5 SARGON CONQUERS MESOPOTAMIA

• Critical Viewing: NG Chapter Gallery

• On Your Feet: Fishbowl

SECTION 2 RESOURCES

LATER CIVILIZATIONS

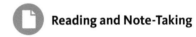 **Reading and Note-Taking**

 **Vocabulary Practice**

 **Section 2 Quiz**

Available at NGLSync.cengage.com

LESSON 2.1 HAMMURABI'S CODE OF LAWS

 **Active History: Interactive Whiteboard Activity**
Analyze Primary Sources:
Hammurabi's Code

 **Active History**
Analyze Primary Sources: Hammurabi's Code

Available at NGLSync.cengage.com

• On Your Feet: Code of Laws Roundtable

LESSON 2.2 THE ASSYRIANS AND THE CHALDEANS

• Critical Viewing: NG Chapter Gallery

• On Your Feet: Create a Time Line

LESSON 2.3 THE PHOENICIANS

NG Learning Framework:
Create Your Own Figurehead

• On Your Feet: Three-Step Interview

LESSON 2.4 PERSIAN LEADERS

 Biography
Darius I

Available at NGLSync.cengage.com

NG Learning Framework:
Learn More About Persian Leaders

• On Your Feet: Create a Living Time Line

LESSON 2.5 THE LEGACY OF MESOPOTAMIA

• Critical Viewing: NG Chapter Gallery

• On Your Feet: Hold a Debate

CHAPTER 3 REVIEW

STRIVING READERS

STRATEGY ❶

Record and Compare Facts

After reading, ask each student to write at least three facts they can recall from the lesson. Allow pairs of students to compare and check their facts and then combine their facts into one longer list. Challenge students to become the pair with the longest list of accurate facts.

Use with All Lessons

STRATEGY ❷

Turn Headings into Outlines

Model how headings can be made into an outline. Direct students to copy the outline and then read the lesson to record details to complete the outline.

I. New Empire in Mesopotamia

    A.

    B.

    C.

II. Hammurabi's Code

    A.

    B.

    C.

Use with Lesson 2.1

STRATEGY ❸

Identify Chronological Order

Help students track historical events. Explain that dates in the text can be a helpful guide. As students read, they can create a time line to show events in the order in which they happened.

Use with All Lessons

Press (**mt**) *in the Student eEdition for modified text.*

INCLUSION

STRATEGY ❶

Modify Main Idea Statements

Provide these modifications of the Main Idea statements at the beginning of each lesson:

1.1 The rivers, location, and good land helped bring people together as groups and encouraged human social development.

1.2 The group of cities in Sumer, and land surrounding those cities, formed an extended group that allowed for enhanced social development.

Use with Lessons 1.1–1.2

STRATEGY ❷

Use Supported Reading

In small groups, have students read the chapter aloud, lesson by lesson. At the end of each lesson, have them stop and use these sentence frames to tell what they understood from their reading:

This lesson is about _____ .

One detail that stood out to me is _____ .

The vocabulary word _____ means _____ .

I don't think I understand _____ .

Guide students through portions of text they do not understand. Be sure all students understand a lesson before moving on to the next one.

Use with All Lessons

ENGLISH LANGUAGE LEARNERS ELD

STRATEGY ❶

Use Context Clues

Remind students that they can use context clues to figure out the meaning of an unknown word. Review the following types of context clues and their signal words: Definition or restatement (*called, which is, or, in other words*); examples (*for example, like, such as, including*). Model using context to determine the meaning of the word *silt* in Lesson 1.1. Then have students choose a different word from the chapter to identify on their own. Provide the strategies on the next page to help students explain their thinking.

STANDARDS

HSS CONTENT STANDARDS:

6.2.4 Know the significance of Hammurabi's Code; **6.4.5** Outline the founding, expansion, and political organization of the Persian Empire.

HSS ANALYSIS STANDARDS:

CST 2 Students construct various time lines of key events, people, and periods of the historical era they are studying.

Emerging

Use these prompts to help students explain the meaning of the word they chose:

- What is the topic of the passage?
- What is the unfamiliar word?
- Which signal words were used?
- Which words or phrases helped you figure out the meaning?

Expanding

To help students explain how they determined the meaning of the word, display the following sentence frames:

- The signal word(s) _____ point to _____.
- This tells me _____.
- The sentences around the word tell me _____.
- I think the word means _____.

Bridging

Encourage students to explain their thinking with elaborated language, and provide the following sentence frames as necessary:

- The signal word is _____, which means that the clue is _____.
- When I read the phrase _____, I know that _____ means _____.

Use with All Lessons, All Levels

 STRATEGY 2

Pair Partners for Dictation

After students read each lesson in the chapter, ask them to write a sentence summarizing its main idea. Have students get together in pairs and dictate their sentences to each other. Then have them work together to check the sentences for accuracy and spelling.

Use with All Lessons, All Levels

STRATEGY 3

PREP Before Reading

Have students at all proficiency levels use the PREP strategy to prepare for reading. Write this acrostic on the board:

PREP	**P**review title.
	Read Main Idea statement.
	Examine visuals.
	Predict what you will learn.

Have students write their prediction and share it with a partner. After reading, ask students to write another sentence that begins with "I also learned . . .

Use with All Lessons, All Levels *Provide the following sentence stem for students at the **Emerging** level: I think this lesson is about _____. Ask students at the **Bridging** level to give reasons for their prediction.*

 GIFTED & TALENTED

 STRATEGY 1

Write a Dialogue

Tell students to review Lesson 2.4 under the heading "Darius Expands the Empire." Then have them use facts from the text to write a dialogue that might have taken place between Darius I and a satrap in one of the provinces. Encourage students to cover topics that might have been discussed between two officials who governed the people.

Use with Lesson 2.4

STRATEGY 2

Interview a King

Allow students to work in teams of two to plan, write, and perform a simulated television interview with King Hammurabi of Babylon. Tell students the purpose of the interview is to focus on the achievements of the king during his reign.

Use with Lesson 2.1 *Invite students to use the Internet or library resources to learn more about Hammurabi.*

 PRE-AP

STRATEGY 1

Brainstorm Solutions

Have students reread Lesson 2.4 to understand how Cyrus the Great and Darius I united their empires. Then allow students to work in pairs to brainstorm a list of other ways they could have solved the problem of uniting the people of a large empire. Allow the pairs to share their solutions with the class.

Use with Lesson 2.4

STRATEGY 2

Create a Travel Brochure

Tell students to create a travel brochure for visitors to the historical Phoenician trading settlement called Carthage. Instruct students to create the brochure as though they are living in 1000 B.C. and trying to attract travelers or traders from around the region. Allow students to create their brochure in a medium of their choosing.

Use with Lesson 2.3

3 ANCIENT MESOPOTAMIA

3000 B.C. – 500 B.C.

ESSENTIAL QUESTION Why was civilization able to develop in ancient Mesopotamia?

SECTION 1 SUMER

KEY VOCABULARY	NAMES & PLACES
artisan	Euphrates River
city-state	Mesopotamia
cuneiform	Sargon the Great
empire	Sumer
famine	Tigris River
irrigation	
polytheism	
ritual	
silt	
social class	
tribute	
ziggurat	

SECTION 2 LATER CIVILIZATIONS

KEY VOCABULARY	NAMES & PLACES
alliance	Cyrus the Great
colony	Darius I
legacy	Hammurabi
province	Nebuchadnezzar II
raw material	
satrap	
tolerance	

READING STRATEGY

MAKE INFERENCES When you make inferences, you use what you already know to figure out the meaning of the text. As you read the chapter, use a chart like this one to make inferences about why civilization developed in Mesopotamia.

I notice...	I know...	And so...

Fierce lions decorated the walls of the street that passed through the Ishtar Gate. Standing 38 feet high and featuring hundreds of dragons and bulls, the Ishtar Gate was the entryway to the city of Babylon in Mesopotamia.

65

STANDARDS

HSS CONTENT STANDARDS:

6.2 Students analyze the geographic, political, economic, religious, and social structures of the early civilizations of Mesopotamia, Egypt, and Kush.

TEACHER BACKGROUND

INTRODUCE THE PHOTOGRAPH

Have students study the photograph of the lion's head from the walls leading to the Ishtar Gate. The lions here are nearly life-sized on a background of blue- and yellow-glazed bricks. The walls also feature dragons and bulls. Tell students that animals often represent different things in different cultures.

ASK: Using what you know and what you can observe, what do you infer the lion might represent? *(Possible response: The lion looks fierce and like it is about to attack.*

Lions are known to be protective of their territory and pride, so maybe the lion is supposed to represent the leader of the city.)

SHARE BACKGROUND

The Ishtar Gate is one of the most famous structures from the ancient world. In the 20th century, archaeologists actually found the walls of the ancient city of Babylon. Archaeologists believe that the lions represent Ishtar, the Babylonian goddess of love and war.

DIGITAL RESOURCES NGLSync.cengage.com

TEACHER RESOURCES & ASSESSMENT

 Social Studies Skills Lessons
- Reading: Make Inferences
- Writing: Write an Argument

 ExamView®
One-time Download

 Formal Assessment
- Chapter 3 Tests A (on-level) & B (below-level)

 Chapter 3
Answer Key

STUDENT BACKPACK
- eEdition *(English)*
- eEdition *(Spanish)*
- Handbooks
- Online Atlas

INTRODUCE THE ESSENTIAL QUESTION

WHY WAS CIVILIZATION ABLE TO DEVELOP IN ANCIENT MESOPOTAMIA?

Roundtable Activity: Factors of Influence This activity allows students to discuss four factors that allowed civilization to develop in Mesopotamia: geography of the region, aspects of culture, development of empires, and technology. Divide the class into four groups and have each group sit at a table. Assign the following questions to the groups:

Group 1: Why might geography have been a key factor in early civilizations?

Group 2: What role did culture play in helping to build early civilizations?

Group 3: Why did building empires play a key role in developing civilizations?

Group 4: How did technology help spread early civilizations?

Have students at each table take turns answering the question. When they have finished their discussion, ask a representative from each table to summarize that group's answers. **0:15** minutes

INTRODUCE THE READING STRATEGY

MAKE INFERENCES

Remind students that when you make inferences, you use what you already know to figure out the meaning of the text. Use a chart like this one to make inferences about why civilization developed in Mesopotamia by organizing topics or ideas to help students better understand new information. Model completing the chart by reading the paragraphs under "Farming in the Fertile Crescent" in Lesson 1.1 and continue the exercise for each lesson of the chapter. For more in-depth instruction and practice with the reading strategy, assign the Social Studies Skills Reading Lesson on making inferences.

I notice...	I know...	And so...
farming spread	irrigation was the answer	food surplus

INTRODUCE CHAPTER VOCABULARY

WORD WEB

Have students complete a Word Web for Key Vocabulary words as they read the chapter. Ask them to write each word in the center of an oval. Have them look through the chapter to find examples, characteristics, and descriptive words that may be associated with the vocabulary word. At the end of the chapter, ask students what they learned about each word.

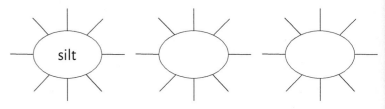

KEY DATES	
c. 8000 B.C.	Beginning of farming in the Fertile Crescent
c. 3500 B.C.	Mesopotamia's first civilization, Sumer, rises
2334 B.C.	Sumer is conquered and becomes part of the Akkadian Empire
1792 B.C.	Hammurabi becomes king of Babylon
c. 650 B.C.	Assyrian army conquers all of Mesopotamia, parts of Asia Minor, and Egypt
539 B.C.	Cyrus the Great captures the Babylonian Empire

The Geography of Ancient Mesopotamia

Long after Çatalhöyük was settled, Southwest Asia was home to another group of people. They lived between two flowing rivers in a fertile land. Because of the advances in government, culture, and technology that took place there, the region is often called a "cradle of civilization."

MAIN IDEA

The geography of Mesopotamia helped create the conditions for civilization.

THE LAND BETWEEN THE RIVERS

As you have learned, the Fertile Crescent sweeps its way across Southwest Asia. In the west it bends down the coast of the Mediterranean. In the east it follows the course of the **Tigris** (TY-gruhs) **River** and the **Euphrates** (yu-FRAY-teez) **River** until they merge and empty into the warm waters of the Persian Gulf. Today this river valley lies mostly in the country of Iraq. Historians call this flat, fertile area **Mesopotamia** (meh-suh-puh-TAY-mee-uh), which means "land between the rivers." The people who once lived there are known as Mesopotamians.

The people of Mesopotamia called the Tigris "swift river" because it flowed fast. The Euphrates flowed more slowly. It frequently changed course, leaving riverside

settlements without water. Both rivers flooded unpredictably. Mesopotamians never knew when or how much water would come. Too much, too little, or too late spelled disaster for crops.

On the plus side, the often-destructive floodwaters deposited **silt**, an especially fine and fertile soil, that was excellent for agriculture. In this way, the rivers brought life to the otherwise dry land of Mesopotamia and supported the early civilization that was developing there. As farming thrived in this river valley, populations grew and cities developed.

FARMING IN THE FERTILE CRESCENT

Farming began as early as 9800 B.C. in the Fertile Crescent. It eventually spread throughout Mesopotamia. However, Mesopotamia was far from perfect for agriculture. In addition to flooding, farmers had to deal with hot summers and unreliable rainfall. However, the region's fertile soils promised plentiful crops, such as wheat, barley, and figs—if the people could come up with a way to control the water supply.

Irrigation, or watering fields using human-made systems, was the answer. Farmers in Mesopotamian villages cooperated to dig and maintain irrigation canals that carried water from the rivers to the fields. Farmers also stored rainwater for later use and built walls from mounds of earth to hold back floodwaters. The people developed important new technology, such as the ox-driven plow, a tool that broke up the hard-baked summer soil and prepared large areas for planting. These creative methods enabled farmers to use the rich soil to their advantage.

The result was a reliable and abundant agricultural surplus. The ample food fed the area's growing population. Because food was plentiful, the people of Mesopotamia could afford to develop art, architecture, and technology. The agricultural surpluses allowed a great civilization to develop.

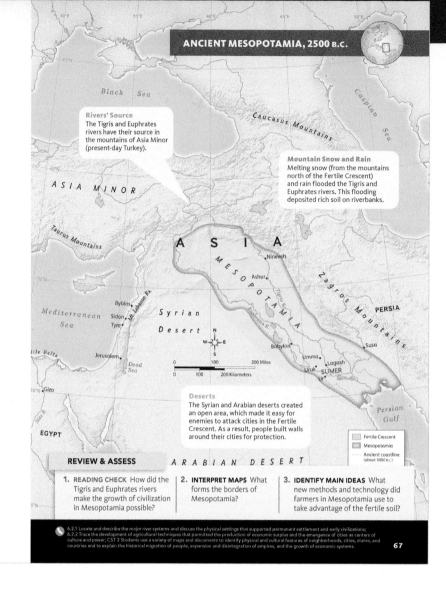

ANCIENT MESOPOTAMIA, 2500 B.C.

Rivers' Source
The Tigris and Euphrates rivers have their source in the mountains of Asia Minor (present-day Turkey).

Mountain Snow and Rain
Melting snow (from the mountains north of the Fertile Crescent) and rain flooded the Tigris and Euphrates rivers. This flooding deposited rich soil on riverbanks.

Deserts
The Syrian and Arabian deserts created an open area, which made it easy for enemies to attack cities in the Fertile Crescent. As a result, people built walls around their cities for protection.

Legend: Fertile Crescent / Mesopotamia / Ancient coastline (about 5000 B.C.)

REVIEW & ASSESS

1. **READING CHECK** How did the Tigris and Euphrates rivers make the growth of civilization in Mesopotamia possible?

2. **INTERPRET MAPS** What forms the borders of Mesopotamia?

3. **IDENTIFY MAIN IDEAS** What new methods and technology did farmers in Mesopotamia use to take advantage of the fertile soil?

6.2.1 Locate and describe the major river systems and discuss the physical settings that supported permanent settlement and early civilizations; 6.2.2 Trace the development of agricultural techniques that permitted the production of economic surplus and the emergence of cities as centers of culture and power; CST 3 Students use a variety of maps and documents to identify physical and cultural features of neighborhoods, cities, states, and countries and to explain the historical migration of people, expansion and disintegration of empires, and the growth of economic systems.

STANDARDS

HSS CONTENT STANDARDS:

6.2.1 Locate and describe the major river systems and discuss the physical settings that supported permanent settlement and early civilizations; **6.2.2** Trace the development of agricultural techniques that permitted the production of economic surplus and the emergence of cities as centers of culture and power.

HSS ANALYSIS SKILLS:

CST 3 Students use a variety of maps and documents to identify physical and cultural features of neighborhoods, cities, states, and countries and to explain the historical migration of people, expansion and disintegration of empires, and the growth of economic systems; **REP 1** Students frame questions that can be answered by historical study and research.

PLAN

OBJECTIVE

Analyze how the geography of Mesopotamia helped create the conditions for civilization to emerge.

ESSENTIAL QUESTION

Why was civilization able to develop in ancient Mesopotamia?

The geography of Mesopotamia helped create favorable conditions for developing civilizations. Lesson 1.1 discusses the Fertile Crescent and how its physical geography allowed for a food surplus.

BACKGROUND FOR THE TEACHER

The Tigris and Euphrates rivers are among the most important features of the physical geography in Southwest Asia. The sources of both of these rivers are in the Taurus Mountains of modern-day Turkey and are only about 50 miles apart. As they flow southeast through modern-day Iraq, toward the Persian Gulf, these rivers are never more than about 250 miles apart. The land between the rivers was historically very fertile because yearly floods deposited silt in the floodplain area.

DIGITAL RESOURCES NGLSync.cengage.com

TEACHER RESOURCES & ASSESSMENT

 Reading and Note-Taking

 Vocabulary Practice

 Section 1 Quiz

STUDENT RESOURCES

 NG Chapter Gallery

INTRODUCE & ENGAGE

INTERPRET MAPS

Have students look at the Ancient Mesopotamia map in Lesson 1.1. Explain that the map shows the physical geography of Mesopotamia in 2500 B.C. Remind students that the map legend shows what the green area and red outlines mean. Point out that the ancient coastline was farther inland in 5000 B.C. than it was in 2500 B.C. **ASK:** What role did silt play in changing the coastline of the rivers? *(The rivers deposited so much silt at the mouth of the river that, over time, more land built up on the coast.)* `0:05` minutes

TEACH

GUIDED DISCUSSION

1. **Make Inferences** Review the map of Mesopotamia showing the Tigris and Euphrates rivers. How might the location of the rivers explain why the area is known as the Fertile Crescent? *(Students should notice that the Fertile Crescent is mostly between the rivers. They should make the inference that water played a role in why the region is so fertile.)*

2. **Compare and Contrast** What are the benefits of the Tigris and Euphrates rivers' flooding? What are the drawbacks? *(The benefits are that the floods bring fertile silt to areas that may have poor soil. The drawbacks are that the floods were unpredictable and could lead to destroyed crops.)*

INTERPRET MAPS

Help students interpret the map. **ASK:** What can you infer about the location of the cities in ancient Mesopotamia? *(They were located on or near the rivers, and people probably relied on the rivers for fresh water, food, and transportation.)* To learn more about the role of rivers in the development of ancient cities, have students complete **California EEI Curriculum Unit 6.2.1**, *River Systems and Ancient Peoples.* `0:10` minutes

ACTIVE OPTIONS

NG Learning Framework: Create a Map

SKILL: Observation
KNOWLEDGE: Our Living Planet

Have students work in pairs. Instruct students to observe the map of ancient Mesopotamia for two minutes. Then instruct them to take five minutes to work with their partner to draw their own map of ancient Mesopotamia. They should include as many landforms, cities, and labels as possible. After the five minutes are up, have students compare their map to the original and make any additions to their map in a different color. Ask students to make observations on the details they now notice compared with their observation at the beginning of this activity. `0:10` minutes

On Your Feet: Inside-Outside Circle Have students form concentric circles facing each other. Allow them time to write questions about the geographic and historical conditions leading to the civilization of ancient Mesopotamia. Then have students in the inside circle pose questions to students in the outside circle. Have students switch roles. Students may ask for help from other students in their circle if they are unable to answer a question. `0:15` minutes

DIFFERENTIATE

ENGLISH LANGUAGE LEARNERS `ELD`

Identify Facts Have students form groups of mixed proficiency levels and conduct a Round Robin activity to review what they have learned in the lesson. Ask groups to generate facts for about 3–5 minutes. Provide the following sentence frames to help students at the **Emerging** and **Expanding** levels contribute to the discussion.

- **Emerging**
  Two rivers in Mesopotamia are _____.

  Farmers used _____ to _____.

- **Expanding**
  Mesopotamia is located between _____.

  The technology of _____ helped farmers _____.

Finally, invite one student from each group to share his or her group's responses. Write all the facts on the board and correct any misconceptions.

GIFTED & TALENTED

Host a Talk Show Have students assume the roles of a talk show host, a historian, and an economics expert in Southwest Asia. Have students conduct research to learn more about the Tigris and Euphrates rivers. Suggest that they gather information on historical uses of the Fertile Crescent and the types of crops produced in ancient times. Then have them gather statistics on how the Tigris and Euphrates are used today. Include statistics on the types of agricultural products and goods produced and what the modern exports are for the region. Then have students explain how the way people use the land has changed over time.

Press **mt** *in the Student eEdition for modified text.*

See the Chapter Planner for more strategies for differentiation.

REVIEW & ASSESS

ANSWERS

1. The rivers were the primary source of fresh water in the region. Using irrigation methods to bring that water to fields allowed farmers to grow an abundance of crops. A better food supply made it possible for people to focus on other aspects of culture, such as art, architecture, and technology.

2. The Zagros Mountains to the north and east, the Euphrates River to the west, and the Persian Gulf to the south form the borders of Mesopotamia.

3. The farmers created irrigation methods and built canals to bring water to fields. They also developed an ox-driven plow to work the soil.

1.2 City-States Develop

The present-day location that was once Mesopotamia is made up of windswept deserts. It's hard to imagine that 5,500 years ago this dusty land was filled with people living their busy city lives. The city streets were not just filled with people—there were also buildings and temples so tall they seemed to rise up to the heavens.

MAIN IDEA

The city-states of Sumer formed Southwest Asia's first civilization.

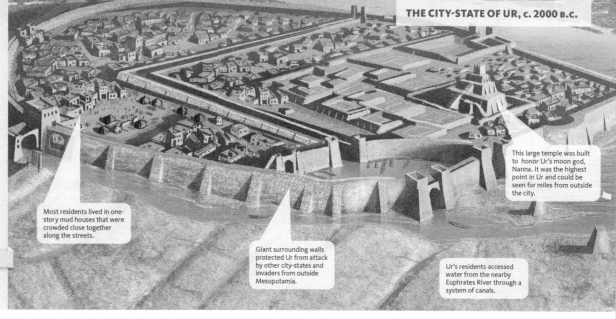

THE CITY-STATE OF UR, c. 2000 B.C.

This large temple was built to honor Ur's moon god, Nanna. It was the highest point in Ur and could be seen for miles from outside the city.

Most residents lived in one-story mud houses that were crowded close together along the streets.

Giant surrounding walls protected Ur from attack by other city-states and invaders from outside Mesopotamia.

Ur's residents accessed water from the nearby Euphrates River through a system of canals.

SUMER

Around 3500 B.C., Mesopotamia's first civilization arose in **Sumer** (SOO-mur), an area in the southern part of the region. (See the map in Lesson 1.1.) Sumer was not controlled by a single, unified government. Instead, the area was made up of a dozen advanced, self-governing city-states. A **city-state** included the city and its surrounding lands and settlements. These units developed when villages united to build major irrigation projects.

Most of Sumer's 12 city-states, including Ur, were built on the Tigris or Euphrates rivers. City-states also clustered close to the coast of the Persian Gulf, where the people developed fishing and trade. Frequent wars were fought between city-states to protect fertile land, limited natural resources, and profitable trade routes.

CENTERS OF CIVILIZATION

Surplus food gave Sumerians time to learn new skills and encouraged trade. Though Sumer had productive farmland, the area lacked important natural resources, such as tin and copper. These resources had to be acquired through trade. When combined, tin and copper produce bronze, a strong metal used by Sumerians to create tools and weapons. Because of the importance of bronze, the period around 3000 B.C. is called the Bronze Age.

Surplus food also led to a growth in population. New government systems had to be established to meet the challenge of managing so many people. Kings arose to provide strong leadership, and administrators supervised taxes and kept order. Because of the wealth created by agricultural surpluses, Sumerians could afford to support these government administrators.

Sumerian society was organized by **social class**, an order based on power and wealth. Kings ruled at the top, with priests just beneath them. Next came administrators, scribes, merchants, and **artisans**, or people who are skilled at making things by hand. These groups in turn looked down on farmers and less-skilled workers. However, even people at the bottom of this system ranked higher than Sumerian slaves.

REVIEW & ASSESS

1. **READING CHECK** How did the organization of Sumerian society affect the way different roles were viewed by others?

2. **INTEGRATE VISUALS** In what ways did the rivers support agriculture and the city-states?

3. **ANALYZE CAUSE AND EFFECT** How did food surpluses encourage local and long-distance trade?

6.2.2 Trace the development of agricultural techniques that permitted the production of economic surplus and the emergence of cities as centers of culture and power; HI 2 Students understand and distinguish cause, effect, sequence, and correlation in historical events, including the long- and short-term causal relations.

HSS CONTENT STANDARDS:

6.2.2 Trace the development of agricultural techniques that permitted the production of economic surplus and the emergence of cities as centers of culture and power.

HSS ANALYSIS SKILLS:

HI 2 Students understand and distinguish cause, effect, sequence, and correlation in historical events, including the long- and short-term causal relations.

PLAN

OBJECTIVE

Describe how the city-states of Sumer formed Southwest Asia's first civilization.

ESSENTIAL QUESTION

Why was civilization able to develop in ancient Mesopotamia?

The geography and location of Mesopotamia helped create the conditions that allowed civilization to develop in the region. Lesson 1.2 discusses how the city-states of Sumer formed the first civilization in Southwest Asia.

BACKGROUND FOR THE TEACHER

Human beings have existed for thousands of years with the social structure of small groups. The small groups of people survived for ages as hunter-gatherers when they eventually started cultivating crops. The "land between the rivers," known as Mesopotamia, is one of the earliest areas where large numbers of people settled to farm. There is archaeological evidence of early village settlements by 5000 B.C. By 3000 B.C., a strong urban culture existed with social structures and communities, which was possible because of the agricultural surpluses.

DIGITAL RESOURCES NGLSync.cengage.com

TEACHER RESOURCES & ASSESSMENT

 Reading and Note-Taking

 Vocabulary Practice

 Section 1 Quiz

STUDENT RESOURCES

 NG Chapter Gallery

MAKE A WORD MAP

Have students discuss the meaning of the word *civilization*. Begin by adding the word to the center of a Word Map. Fill in the map during classroom discussion. Have students consider the root of the word and use a dictionary, if necessary. Revisit this activity at the end of the lesson to fill in any missing details. `0:05` minutes

TEACH

GUIDED DISCUSSION

1. **Integrate Visuals** What new information can you observe about the illustration of the city-state of Ur that you did not read about in the text? *(Ur has walls surrounding it. It also appears to have been planned with canals going through it that would allow crops to be moved easily from the fields to the people.)*

2. **Make Inferences** Why might city-states that work together to build canals end up fighting wars? *(They are competing against each other for scarce resources and the best land, and each city-state wanted the best for themselves.)*

3. **Draw Conclusions** What reasons would there be for thick walls around the city? *(The walls are for protection. They may protect against their enemies, or possibly also from flood waters.)*

MORE INFORMATION

Women in Mesopotamian Society The social classes that developed in Sumer included both men and women, but all Mesopotamian city-states were patriarchal in that power was held primarily by older adult men. However, women, especially those in the upper classes, did have some influence. Those who served as high priestesses ruled over their temples; others received a formal education and worked as scribes. Women in the lower classes also served as midwives, shopkeepers, and tavern keepers.

For more insight into Mesopotamian society, have students read "Sumerian School Days" in the **Primary Source Handbook** and answer the questions that follow.

ACTIVE OPTIONS

NG Learning Framework: Redesign the City of Ur

SKILL: Problem-Solving
KNOWLEDGE: Our Human Story

Have students examine the illustration of the city-state of Ur and point out that the captions show that the city was crowded and surrounded by walls. Additionally, food surpluses meant that the population kept growing. **ASK:** How would you have done things differently if you were running the city? Have students work in groups to draw their design for the city, or give a description on how they would handle the crowding situation in a walled city in 2000 B.C. `0:10` minutes

On Your Feet: Create Trade Networks On pieces of paper, write the names of commonly traded goods, and indicate if they are goods that are found locally or if they are goods from far away that require trading from a long-distance. *(Examples: figs—local; wheat—local; timber—long distance; tin—long distance; fish—local; flour—local.)* Hand each student the name of a good to trade, and instruct all students to trade among themselves. Upon completion, lead a discussion about what each student was willing to trade and why students traded their items. `0:15` minutes

STRIVING READERS

Complete Sentence Starters Provide these sentence starters for students to complete after reading. You may also have students preview to set a purpose for reading.

- A city and its surrounding lands and settlements were called a
  _____ .

- Ur is among the 12 city-states of _____ .

- The order based on wealth by which Sumerian society was organized is called _____ .

- People who are skilled at making things by hand are called
  _____ .

PRE-AP

Write an Argument Have students individually research and analyze the roles of ancient merchants. Then have them write an argument about whether they would rather be a local merchant or a long distance merchant.

Press **mt** *in the Student eEdition for modified text.*

See the Chapter Planner for more strategies for differentiation.

ANSWERS

1. The organization by social class meant that some people looked down on others who held a lesser status.

2. The water supply from the two rivers was crucial to agriculture in Sumer.

3. Sumerians used their food surpluses to trade for natural resources that they lacked, such as building materials of timber and stone.

Religion in Sumer

In the blazing sun, Sumerian priests carry food offerings step by step to the top of the great temple. The purpose of this feast is to secure the gods' favor for another day. In the dangerous and unpredictable world of Sumer, it's important to keep the gods on your side.

MAIN IDEA

Sumerians took religion seriously and built monumental structures to please their gods.

VOTIVE STATUES

To demonstrate their devotion to the gods, Sumerians placed small statues called votives in temples. Sumerians believed that while they worked on earthly activities like farming or fishing, the statues would pray on their behalf.

LAND OF MANY GODS

Sumerian lives depended on natural forces they could not control, including rivers that flooded and changed course. The people worshipped hundreds of gods, who they believed could control these forces. A belief in many gods is called **polytheism**.

Sumerians believed that their gods ruled the earth and had created humans to serve them. They also believed that the gods possessed superhuman powers. Unfortunately, the gods could use these powers to cause droughts, floods, and disease. For example, Ishkur was a storm god who was believed to have the power to cause destructive rains and floods whenever he liked.

To keep the gods happy, Sumerian priests tried to please them. Everyone paid a temple tax, which was offered to the gods in elaborate public **rituals**, or formal series of acts always performed in the same way. By observing natural events, including the movement of the sun, moon, and stars, priests tried to predict what the gods were planning. These observations helped the Sumerians develop a calendar, astronomy, and mathematics.

OFFERINGS AT THE TEMPLES

City-states were important religious, political, and social centers. The most important building within a city-state was a huge pyramid-shaped temple called a **ziggurat** (ZIH-guh-rat). *Ziggurat* means "mountaintop." Every city was dedicated to a major deity, a god or goddess, who was its guardian. Sumerians believed that the deity lived in a shrine, or sacred place, on top of the ziggurat.

Priests were powerful leaders in Sumerian society. They were responsible for conducting religious practices at the ziggurat. These practices included various rituals, such as offering food to the city god or goddess. A statue representing the deity was placed in a space called the adytum (A-duh-tuhm), or holy place. A meal was set on a table before the statue. Sumerians believed that the god or goddess would eat the meal.

Priests also performed purification, or cleansing, rituals using holy water. This purification process was often used on kings before they entered shrines.

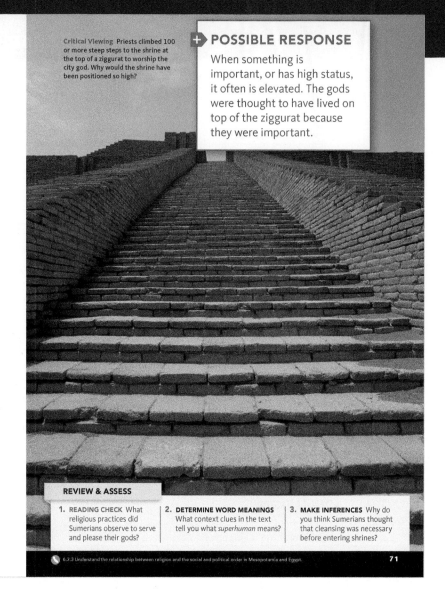

Critical Viewing Priests climbed 100 or more steep steps to the shrine at the top of a ziggurat to worship the city god. Why would the shrine have been positioned so high?

REVIEW & ASSESS

1. **READING CHECK** What religious practices did Sumerians observe to serve and please their gods?

2. **DETERMINE WORD MEANINGS** What context clues in the text tell you what *superhuman* means?

3. **MAKE INFERENCES** Why do you think Sumerians thought that cleansing was necessary before entering shrines?

6.2.3 Understand the relationship between religion and the social and political order in Mesopotamia and Egypt.

71

STANDARDS

HSS CONTENT STANDARDS:

6.2.3 Understand the relationship between religion and the social and political order in Mesopotamia and Egypt.

PLAN

OBJECTIVE

Summarize how important religion was to Sumerians and describe the monumental structures they built to please their gods.

ESSENTIAL QUESTION

Why was civilization able to develop in ancient Mesopotamia?

Religion is a part of culture and key to the development of civilization in the Mesopotamian region. Lesson 1.3 discusses how the Sumerians built monuments and carried out rituals to honor their gods.

BACKGROUND FOR THE TEACHER

Religion is defined as an organized system of beliefs, ceremonies, and rules used to worship a god or group of gods. The Sumerians were among the first to engage in an organized system of spiritual practices, which included belief in several gods and goddesses. Sumerians believed in the idea that each of these gods controlled different aspects of everyday life. They also chose to build large and impressive structures to honor the gods. In these structures, they performed rituals to honor and please the gods, hoping to win their favor.

DIGITAL RESOURCES NGLSync.cengage.com

TEACHER RESOURCES & ASSESSMENT

 Reading and Note-Taking

 Vocabulary Practice

 Section 1 Quiz

STUDENT RESOURCES

 NG Chapter Gallery

MAKE A K-W-L CHART

Provide each student with a K-W-L chart like the one below.

K What Do I Know?	W What Do I Want To Learn?	L What Did I Learn?

Have students brainstorm what they know about religions around the world. Then ask them to write questions that they would like to answer as they study the lesson. Allow time at the end of the lesson for students to fill in what they learned. `0:05` minutes

TEACH

GUIDED DISCUSSION

1. **Make Inferences** What might Sumerians have considered a benefit to developing a calendar? (*The Sumerians observed the movements of the sun, moon, and stars and noticed patterns. They thought that by tracking the movements, they might be able to predict what natural events their gods were planning next.*)

2. **Draw Conclusions** What reason might there have been for the Sumerians to worship so many gods? (*The Sumerians believed that these multiple gods governed the many aspects of their lives.*)

ASK AND ANSWER QUESTIONS

Review the text under the heading "Offerings at the Temple." Ask volunteers to summarize the content by asking the following questions:

1. What is a ziggurat?

2. What is a ritual offering?

3. Why did Sumerians make offerings at the top of ziggurats?

`0:05` minutes

ACTIVE OPTIONS

Critical Viewing: NG Chapter Gallery Invite students to explore the Chapter Gallery to examine the images that relate to this chapter. Have them select one of the images and do additional research to learn more about it. Ask questions that will inspire additional inquiry about the chosen gallery image, such as: What is this? Where and when was this created? By whom? Why was it created? What is it made of? Why does it belong in this chapter? What else would you like to know about it? `0:10` minutes

On Your Feet: Three-Step Interview Have students choose a partner. One student should interview the other on the question: Why do you think Sumerians paid a temple tax as part of some rituals? Then have students reverse roles. Finally, each student should share the results of his or her interview with the class `0:10` minutes

ENGLISH LANGUAGE LEARNERS   ELD

Complete Sentence Frames Use sentence frames such as those below to help students at the **Emerging** and **Expanding** levels demonstrate their understanding of the main ideas in Lesson 1.3. You may wish to allow students to choose the correct word to fill in the blanks from a list on the board.

- In ancient Sumer, _____ was the practice of worshipping many gods. (*polytheism*)

- A _____ is a small statue of a god that was placed in a temple. (*votive*)

- A series of acts called _____ were performed to honor the gods. (*rituals*)

- Sumerians believed a god, also called a _____, lived on top of the ziggurat. (*deity*)

PRE-AP

Write a Research Paper Have students individually research a deity of a city in Sumer. Tell students that they should use the map in Lesson 1.1 to choose a city before starting their research. To help organize their paper, students can take notes and complete an outline. Have students use the information in the outline to write an informative paper in which they develop the topic with relevant details. Ask students to close with a concluding statement summarizing the information presented.

Press (**mt**) in the Student eEdition for modified text.

See the Chapter Planner for more strategies for differentiation.

ANSWERS

1. The Sumerians performed rituals to please the gods.

2. The text indicates that the gods could use powers to do things that are outside of the control of a human being—that they could cause big things, good or bad, to happen.

3. Cleansing would be a way of showing respect to something. Rituals were important, and performing ritual cleansing would be an important display of respect to honor the gods.

Sumerian Writing

Sumerians invented the earliest form of writing, known as pictographs, or images of objects. Detailed pictographs evolved into symbols called **cuneiform** (kyoo-NEE-uh-fawrm), which, over time, represented sounds rather than objects. Scribes began forming words and combining them into sentences in religious and scientific works and in stories. This change marked the beginning of written history and a major step forward in the development of civilization.

This 20th-century illustration depicts Gilgamesh arriving at the palace of the goddess Siduri-Sabitu in his search for immortality.

DOCUMENT ONE

Primary Source: Artifact

Cuneiform Tablet, Northern Iraq, c. 600s B.C.

Scribes used reeds, or sharpened blades of grass, to carve the wedge-shaped cuneiform symbols—600 in all—into wet clay tablets that were then dried. This tablet describes a flood scene from *The Epic of Gilgamesh*, explained in more detail below.

CONSTRUCTED RESPONSE Why did the Sumerians dry the clay cuneiform tablets?

DOCUMENT TWO

Primary Source: Epic

from *Gilgamesh*, translated by Stephen Mitchell
The Epic of Gilgamesh is the world's oldest recorded story. The author is unknown. Gilgamesh was probably a real king of Uruk. In the story, he sets off on a fantastic adventure with his loyal friend Enkidu. This passage describes their encounter with a monster.

CONSTRUCTED RESPONSE Why would the Sumerians record a story about their king encountering a monster?

> They came within sight of the monster's den.
> He was waiting inside it. Their blood ran cold.
> He saw the two friends, he grimaced, he bared his teeth, he let out a deafening roar.
> He glared at Gilgamesh. "Young man," he said, "you will never go home. Prepare to die."

DOCUMENT THREE

Primary Source: Creation Story

from *The Epic of Creation*,
translated by Stephanie Dalley
This Babylonian creation story by an unknown author explains how the world was formed. In this passage, the chief god, Marduk, creates the stars and a 12-month calendar.

CONSTRUCTED RESPONSE Why might Babylonians want to tell and record their story of the creation of the world?

> He [Marduk] fashioned stands for the great gods.
> As for the stars, he set up constellations corresponding to them.
> He designated the year and marked out its divisions,
> Apportioned three stars each to the twelve months.

SYNTHESIZE & WRITE

1. **REVIEW** Review what you have learned about Sumerian writing and the world's oldest stories.
2. **RECALL** On your own paper, write down the main idea expressed in each document.
3. **CONSTRUCT** Construct a topic sentence that answers this question: What did the Sumerians' cuneiform writing system make possible?
4. **WRITE** Using evidence from the documents, write a paragraph that supports your topic sentence from Step 3.

6.2.9 Trace the evolution of language and its written forms; REP 4 Students assess the credibility of primary and secondary sources and draw sound conclusions from them.

HSS CONTENT STANDARDS:

6.2.9 Trace the evolution of language and its written forms.

HSS ANALYSIS SKILLS:

REP 4 Students assess the credibility of primary and secondary sources and draw sound conclusions from them.

PLAN

OBJECTIVE

Synthesize information about how the evolution from pictograph symbols to cuneiform marked the beginning of the written word and a major step forward in developing civilizations.

ESSENTIAL QUESTION

Why was civilization able to develop in ancient Mesopotamia?

Cultural advances in the form of writing help spread culture and develop civilizations. Lesson 1.4 discusses how the evolution from pictograph symbols to cuneiform shaped Mesopotamian civilization and eventually world civilizations.

BACKGROUND FOR THE TEACHER

One of the most widely known epic tales ever written stars the character Gilgamesh. This character is believed to be based upon the 5th king of Uruk (a city in the southern region of Sumer), who had such notoriety that the stories of his greatness made him appear divine to the masses. In some tales, he appears alongside Mesopotamian deities. In one poem, he comes to the rescue of the goddess of love and war. His appearance alongside deities shows how highly he was regarded, and explains why, even though he was a human, he was viewed as a god himself.

DIGITAL RESOURCES NGLSync.cengage.com

TEACHER RESOURCES & ASSESSMENT

 Reading and Note-Taking

 Vocabulary Practice

 Section 1 Quiz

STUDENT RESOURCES

 NG Chapter Gallery

PREPARE FOR THE DOCUMENT-BASED QUESTION

Before students start on the activity, briefly preview the three documents and the illustration. Remind students that a constructed response requires full explanations in complete sentences. Emphasize that students should use their knowledge of Mesopotamia and the Mesopotamians' contributions to civilization in addition to the information in the documents. **0:05** minutes

TEACH

GUIDED DISCUSSION

1. **Make Inferences** Why do you think scribes used reeds and clay to record the cuneiform symbols? *(probably because these materials were common)*

2. **Draw Conclusions** Why would it be useful to have cultural tales written down? *(When a story is written, it is more likely that the story will not change much, whereas a story told verbally may be forgotten or the details may change significantly.)*

3. **Form and Support Opinions** Do you think that Gilgamesh really existed? Why or why not? *(Responses will vary. Accept answers that are supported by reasoning.)*

EVALUATE

After students have completed the "Synthesize & Write" activity, allow time for them to exchange paragraphs and read and comment on the work of their peers. Guidelines for comments should be established prior to this activity so that feedback is constructive and encouraging. **0:15** minutes

ACTIVE OPTIONS

NG Learning Framework: Compare Two Writing Systems

ATTITUDE: **Curiosity**
KNOWLEDGE: **Our Human Story**

Have students explore characters and symbols of past and present writing systems. Instruct them to compare and contrast two or three characters and symbols of a writing system from the past, such as cuneiform, with two or three characters and symbols of a writing system from the present, such as Cyrillic, Chinese, or Arabic. Encourage students to share visuals and observations about their comparisons with the class. **0:10** minutes

On Your Feet: Telephone Play a game of telephone to demonstrate the importance of written documents. Divide the class in half and have each group stand in a line. Then write a sentence on a piece of paper and hand it to the first student in each line. Instruct these two students to read the sentence silently. Then have each student whisper the sentence to the student next to her or him. Continue to do so until the last student in line has the message. Ask the last student to repeat out loud what they were told. Compare that sentence with the piece of paper that the first student is holding. Discuss the results with the class. Point out that people tend to write down information when we need to remember the details, and that while the gist of a story may be remembered, written information is valuable for remembering details. **0:10** minutes

INCLUSION

Analyze Primary Sources You may choose to have students work in pairs to analyze the primary source excerpts. Provide the steps below to help them with their analysis.

1. Find definitions of words that are unfamiliar and write them down on a piece of paper.

2. Summarize each sentence in your own words and write your summaries on a piece of paper.

PRE-AP

Write Epic Tales Ask students to research what epic tales are and what purpose they served. They can use an epic tale, such as *Gilgamesh*, as an example of how to structure their tale. Then have students write their own epic tale. Instruct them to write a narrative that is based on either a real or imagined experience. Have them develop their characters and organize a sequence of events. Then they should use their research to establish what other details to include in their tale. Encourage them to share their tale with the class.

Press **mt** *in the Student eEdition for modified text.*

See the Chapter Planner for more strategies for differentiation.

CONSTRUCTED RESPONSE

ANSWERS
DOCUMENT 1
The cuneiform symbols pressed into the clay would have been smudged or smeared if the clay tablets were not dried.

DOCUMENT 2
Cultures like to portray their leaders as strong and brave. Encountering a monster shows that the king is worthy of leading people because he is brave, and able to face a monster, which could represent the king facing enemies.

DOCUMENT 3
Babylonians most likely wanted to tell and record their story of the creation of the world in order to understand their place in the world and in order to pass the story on to future generations.

SYNTHESIZE & WRITE

ANSWERS
1. Responses will vary.

2. Responses will vary.

3. Possible response: The writing system marked the beginning of the written word, affecting nearly every aspect of civilization.

4. Students' paragraphs should include their topic sentence from Step 3 and provide several details from the documents to support the sentence.

Sargon Conquers Mesopotamia

Have you heard the expression, "Uneasy lies the head that wears a crown"? It applied well to Sargon the Great. He conquered many peoples, lands and cities, including Sumer. As ruler, Sargon was expected to keep his people safe, peaceful, happy, and fed. His role involved much responsibility. It was not easy being in charge of what was, at that time, the world's largest civilization.

MAIN IDEA

Sargon conquered Sumer and other lands in Mesopotamia to create the world's first empire.

AN OUTSIDER TAKES OVER

Sargon the Great was an ancient Mesopotamian ruler who has inspired stories for nearly 4,500 years. It is difficult to separate fact from fiction about his life. According to one story about his childhood, Sargon's mother was a royal priestess who abandoned him as a baby. A humble gardener from Kish raised him after finding him in a basket floating in a river.

Kish was a city-state in Akkad (AH-kahd), an area in central Mesopotamia. Akkadians and Sumerians shared a similar culture but had different ethnic origins and spoke different languages. Before becoming a ruler, Sargon was a servant to the king of Kish. After serving in the royal court, Sargon became a powerful official in Kish and eventually overthrew the king.

While Sargon gained power, Sumer was weakened by internal wars and invasions. In 2334 B.C., Sargon's armies swept through Sumer, conquering it completely. They also took control of northern Mesopotamia. These conquests created the world's first **empire**, a group of different lands and people governed by one ruler. Sargon's empire stretched from the Mediterranean Sea to the Persian Gulf. He ruled the Akkadian Empire from Akkad, his now long-lost capital city.

EMPIRE AND EXPANSION

The Akkadian Empire lasted 150 years, and Sargon ruled for 56 of them. He personally led the fight to expand the empire and claimed to have won 34 battles and taken 50 rulers prisoner. Sargon was an effective warrior and skilled at managing people and projects.

In the lands he conquered, Sargon allowed the people to keep their local rulers and customs. However, they had to obey him and pay a protection tax called a **tribute**. Sargon's policy helped keep peace and win the loyalty of people throughout his empire. He also introduced standard weights and measures and made Akkadian the official language of the government.

Sargon's powerful empire brought prosperity to his people and encouraged trade. Akkad's farmers managed agriculture so well that 100 years went by without **famine**, or widespread hunger. Sargon's wars were spread over large areas. As a result, Akkad traded with distant suppliers for timber, metal, and other raw materials Mesopotamia lacked. His wars concentrated on controlling trade centers and protecting natural resources, such as cedar forests.

Despite Sargon's abilities, the empire became too big to control. After he died, his sons took over but were unable to maintain order. City-states rebelled, and a great deal of time and effort went into trying to keep the peace. Enemies from the northeast raided the empire's unprotected borders. Famine returned, spreading suffering and unrest among the people. By 2200 B.C., the Akkadian Empire had come to an end.

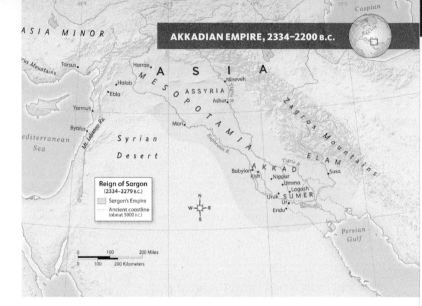

AKKADIAN EMPIRE, 2334–2200 B.C.

Reign of Sargon (2334–2279 B.C.)
☐ Sargon's Empire
---- Ancient coastline (about 5000 B.C.)

SARGON THE GREAT

To guarantee loyalty from the governors who ruled parts of his empire, Sargon gave trusted relatives powerful positions. To keep control of his army, he created a group of professional soldiers whose sole purpose was to fight for him.

‹ This sculptured head is believed to depict Sargon with his crown and long beard.

REVIEW & ASSESS

1. **READING CHECK** What measures did Sargon take to unite his empire?

2. **INTERPRET MAPS** Where were most of the cities of the empire located? Why do you think that was so?

3. **DRAW CONCLUSIONS** What conclusions can you draw about Sargon's abilities as a ruler?

CST 3 Students use a variety of maps and documents to identify physical and cultural features of neighborhoods, cities, states, and countries and to explain the historical migration of people, expansion and disintegration of empires, and the growth of economic systems.

STANDARDS

HSS CONTENT STANDARDS:

6.2 Students analyze the geographic, political, economic, religious, and social structures of the early civilizations of Mesopotamia, Egypt, and Kush.

HSS ANALYSIS SKILLS:

CST 3 Students use a variety of maps and documents to identify physical and cultural features of neighborhoods, cities, states, and countries and to explain the historical migration of people, expansion and disintegration of empires, and the growth of economic systems.

PLAN

OBJECTIVE

Identify how Sargon conquered Sumer and other lands in Mesopotamia to create the world's first empire.

ESSENTIAL QUESTION

Why was civilization able to develop in ancient Mesopotamia?

Great leaders play important roles in developing civilizations. Lesson 1.5 discusses how Sargon conquered lands in Mesopotamia to create an empire.

BACKGROUND FOR THE TEACHER

Sargon the Great was a man of legend. His military prowess and strong leadership abilities brought him great fame and power. He was the first person in recorded history to have created an empire. Though stories of his later years are prevalent, very little is really known about his early life. A manuscript describing his early life and rise to power exists. However, there are many gaps in the written version of his story, and it appears to have been written well after his lifetime. Many of the tales of the early years appear to actually be legends.

DIGITAL RESOURCES NGLSync.cengage.com

TEACHER RESOURCES & ASSESSMENT

 Reading and Note-Taking

 Vocabulary Practice

 Section 1 Quiz

STUDENT RESOURCES

 NG Chapter Gallery

DISCUSS GOVERNMENT POWER

Ask students whether they think the government should have the authority to control activities that affect their daily life. Have them discuss what they would think if government legislated the following:

- what language they speak at home
- how much they pay to keep their communities safe
- how to measure the amount of foods they buy

Encourage students to explain why some governments might want to control such activities. Then, at the end of the discussion, tell students that Sargon the Great implemented a protection tax that had to be paid. He also declared an official language and established standard weights and measures. **0:05** minutes

TEACH

GUIDED DISCUSSION

1. **Analyze Cause and Effect** How did Sargon come to conquer Sumer? *(Sargon was able to invade and conquer Sumer because Sumer had become weak from civil wars between city-states, and other invasions.)*

2. **Make Predictions** Do you think another ruler or empire will take over the land and people of the Akkadian Empire, knowing that this empire ended in 2200 B.C.? *(Students should indicate that it is very likely that another empire will take over where the Akkadian Empire ended. That is generally what happens over the course of time.)*

INTERPRET MAPS

Have students analyze the map of the Akkadian Empire in Lesson 1.5. Then have them compare it to the Ancient Mesopotamia map in Lesson 1.1. Direct them to use the mountains, grid lines, and rivers to compare the size and shape of the Akkadian Empire against the red borders of Mesopotamia in Lesson 1.1. Discuss how much of the Fertile Crescent Sargon had within his empire. **0:10** minutes

ACTIVE OPTIONS

Critical Viewing: NG Chapter Gallery Have students examine the contents of the Chapter Gallery for this lesson. Then invite them to brainstorm additional images they believe would fit for this lesson. Have them write a description of these additional images and provide an explanation of why they would fit within the Chapter Gallery. Then instruct them to do online research to find examples of actual images they would like to add to the gallery. If no images are available, ask why they think the images are not available and what illustrations they would like to see added for this lesson. **0:10** minutes

On Your Feet: Fishbowl Have one half of the class sit in a close circle, facing inward. The other half of the class sits in a larger circle around them. Post the question: What advantages do you think Mesopotamia had when it was an empire united under Sargon? Students in the inner circle should discuss the question for five minutes while those in the outer circle listen to the discussion and evaluate the points made. Then have the groups reverse roles and continue the discussion. **0:10** minutes

INCLUSION

Complete a 5Ws Chart Guide students in completing a 5Ws Chart to help them understand the text. Review vocabulary words that students might have difficulty comprehending, such as *tribute* and *famine*. Review each "W" of the chart as students work through the lesson.

Who? _____

What? _____

Where? _____

When? _____

Why? _____

_____

_____

STRIVING READERS

Summarize Read the lesson aloud while students follow along in the text. At the end of each paragraph, ask students to write a sentence on their own paper to summarize what they read.

Press **(mt)** *in the Student eEdition for modified text.*

See the Chapter Planner for more strategies for differentiation.

ANSWERS

1. He allowed people to keep their local rulers and customs. He also standardized weights and measures, making it easier to trade goods and make payments for goods. He also had policies to keep peace in the kingdom.

2. Most of the cities of the empire were located near rivers and near where the coast of the Persian Gulf was at that time. They were located there because of the need for water for farming and trade.

3. Sargon's abilities were effective enough to keep him in power for 56 years. He must have been organized, a fierce warrior, and a leader who commanded respect or instilled fear.

Hammurabi's
Code of Laws

Would you know how to play a game if you didn't know its rules? Probably not. This is how people from Mesopotamia must have felt when it came to following laws enforced by rulers. Though they did exist, laws were not laid out in a clear fashion. This changed when a king decided it was time to literally spell out the laws for his people.

MAIN IDEA

Hammurabi changed civilization by organizing laws and displaying them.

NEW EMPIRE IN MESOPOTAMIA

After the fall of Sargon's Akkadian Empire, a tribe called the Amorites invaded western Mesopotamia around 2000 B.C. They established their capital at Babylon (BA-buh-lahn), a city-state overshadowed by powerful neighbors. (See the map in Lesson 1.5.) Then in 1792 B.C., **Hammurabi** (ha-muh-RAH-bee) became the sixth king of Babylon. Hammurabi was Babylon's most influential and powerful ruler. He expanded the kingdom and established his Babylonian Empire across Mesopotamia and other parts of the Fertile Crescent.

Hammurabi spent the first 29 years of his rule working on domestic improvements.

These included directing large projects, such as creating straight streets, strong city walls, magnificent temples, and efficient irrigation canals. Hammurabi also skillfully built up a network of **alliances**, or partnerships. This helped him conquer all of Mesopotamia in just eight years and claim the title "King of Sumer and Akkad."

HAMMURABI'S CODE

Hammurabi was a skillful ruler, but he is best remembered for his Code of Laws. His vast empire contained many different peoples who all followed different laws. To help unite his empire, Hammurabi took the best existing laws, added new rules, and then organized them into a clear, written system. The Code of Laws marked a major step forward for civilization. The code helped bring justice to everyday life. It also serves as an important primary source for historians because it offers insight into Babylonian society, including its structures, priorities, problems, and attitudes.

The Code of Laws was often applied based on a person's social class. For example, landowners could be fined more heavily than slaves. Hammurabi also laid down detailed laws about agriculture and the buying and selling of goods, highlighting the importance of these activities.

Three experienced judges heard cases. They listened to statements, examined evidence, and heard from witnesses. The judges even assumed the defendant's innocence. Guilt had to be proven. (Courts in the United States today also assume that people are innocent until proven guilty.) Hammurabi's Code of Laws influenced later legal systems, including those of ancient Greece and Rome.

After Hammurabi's death in 1750 B.C., the first Babylonian Empire declined rapidly and disappeared about 150 years later. However, Hammurabi's achievements ensured that Babylon remained a center of political, cultural, and religious importance for centuries to come.

CODE OF HAMMURABI

Hammurabi's Code of Laws was carved into an eight-foot-high stone slab, called a stela (STEE-luh), for everyone to see and read. An introduction announced its purpose: "To prevent the strong from oppressing the weak and to see that justice is done to widows and orphans."

The code's 282 laws covered all aspects of life and dictated specific penalties for specific crimes. Punishments were often as brutal as the crime. For example, a son's hand would be cut off for striking his father, and those who robbed burning houses were burned alive. Additional examples of the numbered laws include the following:

196 If a man put out the eye of another man, his eye shall be put out.

197 If he [a man] break another man's bone, his bone shall be broken.

ˇ This top portion of the stela shows King Hammurabi receiving the Babylonian laws from Shamash, the god of justice.

REVIEW & ASSESS

1. **READING CHECK** How was Hammurabi's court system similar to the one we have today?

2. **IDENTIFY MAIN IDEAS AND DETAILS** What details illustrate the improvements Hammurabi made as Babylon's king?

3. **MAKE INFERENCES** Why was Hammurabi's Code of Laws displayed in public for everyone to see?

6.2.4 Know the significance of Hammurabi's Code; HI 3 Students explain the sources of historical continuity and how the combination of ideas and events explains the emergence of new patterns.

HSS CONTENT STANDARDS:

6.2.3 Understand the relationship between religion and the social and political order in Mesopotamia and Egypt; **6.2.4** Know the significance of Hammurabi's Code.

HSS ANALYSIS SKILLS:

REP 4 Students assess the credibility of primary and secondary sources and draw sound conclusions from them; **HI 3** Students explain the sources of historical continuity and how the combination of ideas and events explains the emergence of new patterns.

PLAN

OBJECTIVE

Summarize how Hammurabi changed civilization by organizing and displaying laws.

ESSENTIAL QUESTION

Why was civilization able to develop in ancient Mesopotamia?

Having a code of conduct is considered a necessary part of a developing civilization. Lesson 2.1 discusses how Hammurabi developed and enforced the first laws for a civilization.

BACKGROUND FOR THE TEACHER

The familiar phrase "an eye for an eye" is frequently used to describe what justice means to some people. This idea was first put into writing by Hammurabi. While this famous phrase is the takeaway from his ideas, his intent was to create rules in society that he deemed to be fair and just. Hammurabi determined justice by using a system based on social and economic status. He created a system to protect the weak and people of lesser status from suffering and having their status further decreased through wrongdoings by someone else.

DIGITAL RESOURCES NGLSync.cengage.com

TEACHER RESOURCES & ASSESSMENT

 Reading and Note-Taking

 Vocabulary Practice

 Section 2 Quiz

STUDENT RESOURCES

 Active History

INTRODUCE & ENGAGE

MAKE A K-W-L CHART

Provide each student with a K-W-L Chart like the one below.

K What Do I Know?	W What Do I Want To Learn?	L What Did I Learn?

Have students brainstorm what they know about justice and law from their knowledge of the United States justice system. Then ask them if they know anything about the justice systems in other countries. Ask them to write questions that they would like to have answered as they study the lesson. Allow time at the end of the lesson for students to complete the chart with information they learn in Lesson 2.1. **0:05** minutes

TEACH

GUIDED DISCUSSION

1. **Analyze Cause and Effect** How did the Code of Laws that Hammurabi displayed help to unite the empire? *(The many different peoples and cultures in Hammurabi's empire were following different rules. When Hammurabi displayed the same rules for all to see, they learned how they were expected to behave. The goal of displaying the new rules was to ensure fair treatment for all people.)*

2. **Ask and Answer Questions** What was Hammurabi's Code of Laws? *(Hammurabi's Code of Laws was a system of 282 laws that covered all aspects of life in the Babylonian Empire.)*

ANALYZE PRIMARY SOURCES

Have students form small groups and read the excerpt from Hammurabi's Code of Laws in the **Primary Source Handbook**. Have groups make a list of the crimes and their related punishments. **ASK:** What do you notice about the punishments for crimes against people in different social groups? Have students discuss this question in their groups, and then continue the discussion with the class as a whole. **0:15** minutes

ACTIVE OPTIONS

Active History: Analyze Primary Sources: Hammurabi's Code Have students individually complete the activity by analyzing Hammurabi's code. After they have completed the activity, ask them to form opinions on which of the six laws presented seem the least fair to them. Have students support their opinions with evidence. **0:15** minutes

On Your Feet: Code of Laws Roundtable Divide the class into groups of four. Have students create a "Code of Laws" for their classroom that will provide guidelines for good behavior and the consequences for bad

behavior. Tell the first student in each group to write a law on a piece of paper, read it aloud, and pass the paper clockwise to the next student. When the groups have finished writing their laws, invite each group to decide which two laws they think are the most necessary. Then have the class vote on five laws they believe to be the most fair. Post these rules on a bulletin board. **0:10** minutes

DIFFERENTIATE

ENGLISH LANGUAGE LEARNERS

Understand Main Ideas Monitor the comprehension of students at the **Emerging** level by asking them to correctly complete either/or statements such as the following:

- Hammurabi spent [much or little] time making improvements in the empire.
- Hammurabi is best remembered for [uniting or dividing] his empire by using his Code of Laws.
- The Code of Laws punished a landowner [more or less] harshly than a slave for the same offense.
- The panel of judges assumes you are [innocent or guilty].

PRE-AP

Write Hammurabi's Profile Ask an interested group of students to do online research to learn more about Hammurabi. Then tell them to write a social networking profile for Hammurabi, providing a brief summary and "photos" of the king. Have the group share the profile with the rest of the class. Then invite students to "friend" Hammurabi and send him messages about his life and society.

Press **mt** *in the Student eEdition for modified text.*

See the Chapter Planner for more strategies for differentiation.

REVIEW & ASSESS

ANSWERS

1. Hammurabi's court system had judges hearing cases from witnesses and examining evidence. It assumed the defendant was innocent until proven guilty.

2. Hammurabi's many domestic improvements included establishing a centralized government and administration, building straight streets and strong city walls, building magnificent temples, and building irrigation canals that boosted Babylon's agriculture and economy.

3. A public display of the Code of Laws made the rules of Babylonian society very clear to everyone—the poor and wealthy, the weak and strong. A public display of the laws also reminded everyone of the purpose of the Code of Laws: "To prevent the strong from oppressing the weak and to see that justice is done to widows and orphans."

For 1,000 years after Hammurabi, Mesopotamia came under the rule of empire after empire. Then around 1000 B.C., the region shook with the sounds of an approaching army: marching feet, pounding hooves, frightening war cries. The Assyrian army had arrived.

MAIN IDEA

The Assyrians and then the Chaldeans conquered Mesopotamia.

THE ASSYRIAN EMPIRE

The Assyrians (uh-SIHR-ee-uhnz) were a people of northern Mesopotamia who developed a different culture. They were united by their worship of the god Ashur, for whom the Assyrian capital was named. (See the map in Lesson 1.5.) A strong agricultural economy and a large professional army helped the Assyrians conquer all of Mesopotamia, parts of Asia Minor, and even the rich state of Egypt by 650 B.C.

Destructive iron weapons gave Assyrian armies an advantage over their enemies, whose weapons were made of a weaker bronze. The armies also had horse-drawn chariots and soldiers who used bows and arrows while riding horses. Assyrian soldiers were experts at capturing cities.

It was not uncommon for soldiers to kill or enslave captured people and then burn their cities to the ground.

Villages, towns, and cities answered to the unforgiving Assyrian king, who held absolute power. Even the highest officials were closely watched. The government sometimes forced rebellious people to move to faraway lands. In time, however, the Assyrian Empire grew too big, and its subjects became tired of being treated so unfairly and violently. By about 626 B.C., the Assyrians were weakened by internal power struggles. This made it possible for a people known as the Chaldeans (kal-DEE-unz) to eventually defeat them.

CHALDEANS OVERTAKE THE ASSYRIANS

The Chaldeans were a seminomadic people who originally came from southern Babylonia. After overthrowing the Assyrians in 612 B.C., the Chaldeans became the ruling power of Babylon and extended their rule over all of Mesopotamia. **Nebuchadnezzar II** (ne-byuh-kuhd-NE-zuhr) was the most famous Chaldean king. Under his rule, which lasted for 43 years, the New Babylonian Empire included Mesopotamia and all of the Fertile Crescent.

Though he was often cruel, Nebuchadnezzar also made improvements to Babylon by rebuilding the city and adding incredible beauty to it. From miles away, the Tower of Babel, a soaring seven-story multicolored ziggurat, inspired awe. Visitors entered the inner city through the colorful Ishtar Gate with its gleaming blue-glazed bricks and images of dragons and bulls.

The king's most famous accomplishment was the Hanging Gardens of Babylon. Pumps operated by slaves irrigated a large, leveled terrace of trees and plants. The terrace formed a green mountain that seemed to float in the city. Although his empire outlasted him by fewer than 25 years, Nebuchadnezzar had built a monumental city fitting its name: Babylon, Gate of God.

+ POSSIBLE RESPONSE

If this is how the Hanging Gardens might have looked, visitors would have been amazed at its spectacular size and beauty. They may have wondered how it was even possible to build, and how the gardens could grow in a building without much ground for roots to spread out.

from *Wonders of the Past*, J. A. Hammerton, ed., 1923

Critical Viewing This painting shows what the Hanging Gardens of Babylon might have looked like. What reaction might the gardens have inspired in visitors?

REVIEW & ASSESS

1. **READING CHECK** In what ways were the rule of the Assyrians and the Chaldeans similar and different?

2. **MAKE INFERENCES** Why do you think the two empires did not last very long?

3. **ANALYZE LANGUAGE USE** What does "the terrace formed a green mountain that seemed to float in the city" mean?

6.2.3 Understand the relationship between religion and the social and political order in Mesopotamia and Egypt.

79

STANDARDS

HSS CONTENT STANDARDS:

6.2 Students analyze the geographic, political, economic, religious, and social structures of the early civilizations of Mesopotamia, Egypt, and Kush.

HSS ANALYSIS SKILLS:

CST 2 Students construct various time lines of key events, people, and periods of the historical era they are studying.

PLAN

OBJECTIVE

Identify how the Assyrians and then the Chaldeans conquered Mesopotamia.

ESSENTIAL QUESTION

Why was civilization able to develop in ancient Mesopotamia?

For about 1,000 years after Hammurabi's empire was conquered, Mesopotamia was controlled by a series of empires. Lesson 2.2 discusses how the Assyrians and the Chaldeans each conquered Mesopotamia.

BACKGROUND FOR THE TEACHER

Nebuchadnezzar II was the most famous Babylonian king, but some of his accomplishments are more famous than others. He was the first Babylonian king to rule Egypt. His empire was vast. It included Egypt and Mesopotamia and stretched to the Persian Gulf.

However, Nebuchadnezzar is best known for adding beauty to the city of Babylon, while adding fortification to the city. One of his most famous accomplishments was his palace and the massive walls around Babylon. The Ishtar Gate is one of his greatest feats. It was found by archaeologists and a reconstruction of it can be viewed in a museum.

DIGITAL RESOURCES NGLSync.cengage.com

TEACHER RESOURCES & ASSESSMENT

 Reading and Note-Taking

 Vocabulary Practice

 Section 2 Quiz

STUDENT RESOURCES

 NG Chapter Gallery

INTRODUCE & ENGAGE

ANALYZE CHARACTERISTICS OF CIVILIZATIONS

Provide a list of characteristics of powerful, successful civilizations. Some examples are: *a strong army, stable government, meaningful traditions, scientific advances, arts and culture, peace among citizens.* Ask students if they have anything to add. Tell them they will use this list as they compare the Assyrians and Chaldeans. `0:05` minutes

TEACH

GUIDED DISCUSSION

1. **Evaluate** What are some of the advantages that the Assyrians had by having a professional army? *(By having a professional army, the Assyrians were organized and could efficiently plan and execute attacks. The professional army knew what role each person played and they were able to attack an unprepared city and conquer it.)*

2. **Make Inferences** What might have caused the Assyrians to have internal power struggles that led to their defeat? *(The power struggles could have been caused by poor treatment of the people, or the lack of any unifying aspects of culture, such as language or religion. It could have been that the people just didn't like the king. It could have been a combination of these factors.)*

ANALYZE VISUALS

Have students examine the illustration of the Hanging Gardens of Babylon in Lesson 2.2. Explain that historians are not sure what this extraordinary structure looked like, so any illustration is a guess, based on historical texts. **ASK:** Why might people be fascinated with the Hanging Gardens of Babylon, centuries after it existed? *(It was so technologically advanced, so large, and so reportedly beautiful that people many years later remain curious about how it might have looked.)* `0:05` minutes

ACTIVE OPTIONS

Critical Viewing: NG Chapter Gallery Ask students to investigate one of the images in the Chapter Gallery and become an expert on it. They should do additional research to learn about it. Then, students should share their findings with a partner, a small group, or the entire class. `0:10` minutes

On Your Feet: Create a Time Line Have students work in small groups to create a time line of the events from when the Assyrians came to power to after Nebuchadnezzar II's empire ended. Encourage students to copy the graphic organizer below and use it to fill out their time lines. When students have completed them, call on volunteers from different groups to explain how each event on the time line led to the eventual fall of the empire. `0:10` minutes

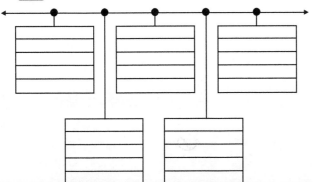

DIFFERENTIATE

STRIVING READERS

Pose and Answer Questions Have students work in pairs to read Lesson 2.2. Instruct them to pause after each paragraph and ask one another *who, what, when, where,* or *why* questions about what they have just read. Advise students to read more slowly and focus on specific details if they have difficulty answering the questions or to reread a paragraph to find the answers.

GIFTED & TALENTED

Build Models Have students review the text description of the Tower of Babel. Then ask them to do research to find more information about what it may have looked like. Students may create a 3-D model, use computer software, draw, or paint their own representation of how they believe the Tower of Babel may have looked. Invite students to share their models with the class.

Press (**mt**) *in the Student eEdition for modified text.*

See the Chapter Planner for more strategies for differentiation.

REVIEW & ASSESS

ANSWERS

1. The Assyrians had a professional army to keep expanding the empire. Their soldiers had iron weapons, horse-drawn chariots, and mounted archers. They also knew how to capture cities. They often killed or enslaved people. The king had absolute power. The Chaldeans were semi-nomadic and not as organized as the Assyrians in warfare. Nebuchadnezzar II was the most famous ruler. He was also known to be cruel and enslaved people. He built grand structures, whereas the Assyrians were destructive.

2. The Assyrian kings held absolute power and ruled with brutal efficiency. Nebuchadnezzar II was also known to be cruel. Cruel rulers usually do not win loyalty from the people they try to control, and the people tend to rebel.

3. The language describes how the Hanging Gardens of Babylon must have looked to a viewer from outside the walls of the city. It was described as an enormous, tiered, terrace of plants and trees. It must have appeared as a lush green wonder in the middle of a desert landscape.

PHOENICIAN SHIP

The Phoenicians sailed their ships in the Mediterranean and beyond. Through trade, the Phoenicians also had contact with Mesopotamia. They established **colonies**, or outposts of people from one land who live in another land, in places as far away as Spain. Phoenicia's most famous colony was Carthage in North Africa.

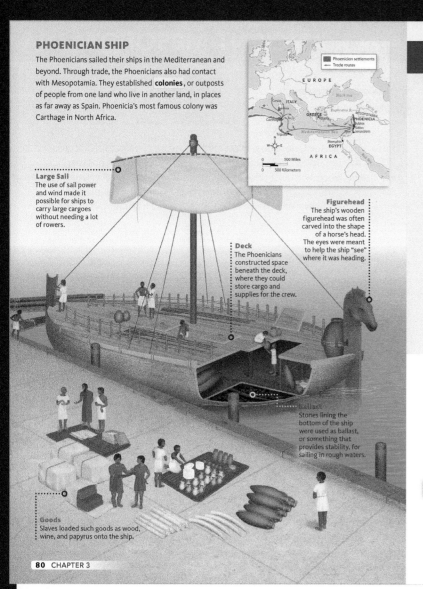

Large Sail
The use of sail power and wind made it possible for ships to carry large cargoes without needing a lot of rowers.

Deck
The Phoenicians constructed space beneath the deck, where they could store cargo and supplies for the crew.

Figurehead
The ship's wooden figurehead was often carved into the shape of a horse's head. The eyes were meant to help the ship "see" where it was heading.

Stones lining the bottom of the ship were used as ballast, or something that provides stability, for sailing in rough waters.

Goods
Slaves loaded such goods as wood, wine, and papyrus onto the ship.

2.3
The Phoenicians

Do you have a well-traveled friend who always has interesting information about places you've never been? You can think of the Phoenicians as this worldly friend. While conducting trade throughout the Mediterranean and Mesopotamia, the Phoenicians spread cultural practices from one stop on their trade route to the next.

MAIN IDEA

Through their extensive trade network, the Phoenicians spread different cultures throughout the Mediterranean and beyond.

A TRADING PEOPLE

The narrow strip of coast along the eastern Mediterranean (present-day Lebanon) contained many natural resources and had good harbors. This combination was perfect for the development of industry and trade. About 1000 B.C., independent city-states emerged in the area. They shared cultural similarities, including language and a trading economy. The Greeks called the people from these city-states Phoenicians (fih-NEE-shuhnz), which means "purple dye people." The Phoenicians processed local shellfish into a purple dye used to color fabric. This dye was their most famous trade good. They exported wood from their highly desired cedar trees to Egypt and Mesopotamia. From other lands, they imported **raw materials**, or substances from which other things are made. Phoenician artisans crafted these materials into luxury goods for trade.

Phoenicia's most important export was its culture. To record trade transactions, the Phoenicians used their own 22-letter alphabet, which was adapted from Sumerian cuneiform. Each symbol from the Phoenician alphabet stood for a sound. First the ancient Greeks adopted the Phoenician alphabet, then the ancient Romans modified it to form the basis of our modern Western alphabet.

SHIPBUILDERS AND SEAFARERS

The Phoenicians were also skilled shipbuilders and sailors. They built strong, wide ships. Powered mainly by wind and a large, square sail, these ships carried huge cargoes thousands of miles. The Phoenicians became one of the first Mediterranean peoples to sail on the Atlantic Ocean. They sailed north to Britain, west to the Azores (nine volcanic islands located in the mid-Atlantic), and possibly even around Africa.

Despite their talents and enormous wealth, the Phoenicians were militarily weak and were eventually absorbed into the New Babylonian Empire. However, they performed a valuable service by spreading different cultures from one area to another. Their accomplishments show the importance of trade in building civilizations.

REVIEW & ASSESS

1. **READING CHECK** What goods and ideas did the Phoenicians spread through their sea trade network?

2. **ANALYZE VISUALS** Why might ballast have been important to the condition of goods transported by ship?

3. **MAKE INFERENCES** Why would the Phoenicians have established trading colonies in faraway places?

6.2.9 Trace the evolution of language and its written forms; CST 3 Students use a variety of maps and documents to identify physical and cultural features of neighborhoods, cities, states, and countries and to explain the historical migration of people, expansion and disintegration of empires, and the growth of economic systems.

PLAN

OBJECTIVE

Describe how the Phoenicians spread different cultures throughout the Mediterranean and beyond.

ESSENTIAL QUESTION

Why was civilization able to develop in ancient Mesopotamia?

Spreading culture through trade interactions is an effective way to develop a civilization. Lesson 2.3 discusses how the Phoenicians spread different cultures throughout the Mediterranean region and beyond.

BACKGROUND FOR THE TEACHER

The Phoenicians lived in a small area of land on the coast of the Mediterranean Sea. The geography of the area dictated their lives and professions. Other than their much sought-after cedar trees, Phoenician land offered little in terms of agriculture. Playing to their geographical strengths, the Phoenicians used the sea extensively. They obtained numerous resources, such as snails used for dye, from the sea. They built boats and traveled for trade.

DIGITAL RESOURCES NGLSync.cengage.com

TEACHER RESOURCES & ASSESSMENT

 Reading and Note-Taking

 Vocabulary Practice

 Section 2 Quiz

STUDENT RESOURCES

 NG Chapter Gallery

INTRODUCE & ENGAGE

MAP THE SPREAD OF CULTURE

Examine the map of the Mediterranean region in Lesson 2.3. Ask students to observe where the trade routes and the Phoenician settlements were. Invite students to think about reasons why the settlements were located where they were, and how these settlements could have helped a culture that had much land along a coast and small amounts of land for agriculture. **0:05** minutes

TEACH

GUIDED DISCUSSION

1. **Make Inferences** Why might the Phoenicians have been militarily weak? *(They had good harbors, but only a small amount of land. They spent much time building ships, trading and developing their culture and less time developing a military.)*

2. **Make Connections** How is the alphabet we use today in the Western world related to the Phoenician alphabet? *(The Western alphabet is the result of other alphabets that started with the Phoenician alphabet. The Phoenician alphabet was adapted from the Sumerian cuneiform. Then the Greeks adopted this writing form, then the Romans, and later the Western world.)*

ANALYZE VISUALS

Have students study the illustration of the Phoenician ship in Lesson 2.3. **ASK:** Why do you think it would have been important to use sails instead of many rowers on a cargo ship? *(Possible answer: Cargo ships would have been larger and heavier.)* **0:05** minutes

ACTIVE OPTIONS

NG Learning Framework: Create Your Own Figurehead

ATTITUDE: **Empowerment**
KNOWLEDGE: **Our Human Story**

Review the illustration of the Phoenician ship with students. Discuss the presence and purpose of figureheads. Figureheads were decorative, but they were also symbolic. Have students imagine they are sailors who are empowered to create their own figureheads. They can shape clay, draw, or use a computer to create a figurehead on their own ship. Have students share their figureheads with the class and describe what their figurehead symbolizes. **0:15** minutes

On Your Feet: Three-Step Interview Have students work in pairs. One student should interview the other using this question: *How do you think the Phoenicians became skilled artisans?* Then students should reverse roles. Finally, each student should share the results of his or her interview with the class. **0:10** minutes

DIFFERENTIATE

STRIVING READERS

Summarize Have students read Lesson 2.3 in pairs and write a sentence that restates the main idea of each paragraph as they read. Then have students review those sentences and write a four- or five-sentence paragraph that summarizes the whole lesson. Remind students that they should use their own words in their summary and include only the most important ideas and details. Call on volunteers to share their paragraphs with the class.

GIFTED & TALENTED

Write Travel Blogs Explain that a blog is an online journal. Students may want to read some examples of travel blogs to see how they combine facts and personal experiences. Invite students to imagine that they have traveled back in time and are Phoenician sailors traveling to different outposts in the Mediterranean region. Encourage students to refer to the map in Lesson 2.3 and to use the cities as starting points as they do an Internet search to find out more about these places. Then have them tell their story. Remind them to include the basics of a good news story—the 5Ws—as well as vivid sensory details to make the historical trip come alive for readers. Allow students to share their writing with the class. An example follows.

> November 15: As daylight broke through the clouds, the porters started loading the ship with cedar trees, wine, gold and fine textiles dyed purple. Around noon, we set sail from Byblos, heading west toward Carthage. This is my first trip as a deck hand, and I'm still learning how to unfurl the sail and navigate the sea. This will be an exciting journey and I'll get to see the world!

Press **mt** *in the Student eEdition for modified text.*

See the Chapter Planner for more strategies for differentiation.

REVIEW & ASSESS

ANSWERS

1. The exported goods included purple dye and wood. They imported raw materials, and artisans created luxury goods out of the raw materials to trade. They also exported their alphabet and culture.

2. Ballast would have been useful to keep the ships upright and keep water from getting in and damaging the goods. It would also keep the ship steady and minimize rocking, keeping the cargo from breaking.

3. Faraway places would have different goods and materials to trade and different raw materials. This would allow the Phoenicians to gain access to more goods that they didn't have access to locally.

Persian Leaders

Palaces in the Persian Empire were built with diverse materials: bricks from Mesopotamia, timber from Phoenicia, ebony and silver from Egypt. This mix of materials was a deliberate celebration of the Persian Empire's rich ethnic diversity—a diversity that was encouraged by the wise leadership of two men.

MAIN IDEA

Under the rule of Cyrus and Darius I, the Persian Empire united different peoples and cultures.

CYRUS THE GREAT

The region of Persia was located in what is present-day southwestern Iran, just east of Mesopotamia. Around 700 B.C., the Persians were ruled by a people called the Medes (meedz). Then in 550 B.C., a Persian king known as **Cyrus the Great** led a successful uprising against the Medes. In 539 B.C., he captured the Babylonian Empire. Cyrus continued to add to his empire until it stretched from Afghanistan to the Aegean Sea, including Mesopotamia. Under Persian rule, these lands enjoyed 200 years of peace and economic well-being.

The secret of Cyrus's success was **tolerance**, or sympathy for the beliefs and practices of others. After winning a war, he showed mercy to conquered kings by allowing them to keep their thrones. Cyrus demanded only tribute that defeated people could afford, sparing them great hardships. He also honored local customs, religions, and institutions. His tolerance won him widespread respect and acceptance from conquered subjects.

DARIUS EXPANDS THE EMPIRE

After Cyrus's death around 529 B.C., his son Cambyses (kam-BY-seez) became king and added Egypt and Libya to the empire. The next king, **Darius I** (duh-RY-uhs), ruled Persia at its height. Darius expanded the empire until it grew to about 2,800 miles, stretching from India in the east to southeastern Europe in the west, with the Fertile Crescent in the middle.

Like Cyrus, Darius was a wise ruler. He avoided problems that had weakened other empires. For example, he divided his empire into 20 smaller **provinces**, or administrative districts, that were ruled by governors called **satraps** (SAY-traps). They helped him maintain control of his huge empire. Darius introduced regular taxation and fixed each province's tribute at only half of what the people could afford to pay. He also introduced a form of currency, which made it easier to pay taxes and buy goods.

Understanding that communications were essential to good government, Darius built the 1,500-mile-long Royal Road, running from Susa in Persia to Sardis in Anatolia (present-day Turkey). Other roads connected all 20 provinces so that messengers could carry his orders anywhere in under 15 days. The roads helped unify the blend of people and cultures that made up the Persian Empire.

Darius also built a new capital, called Persepolis, for his empire. Decorated with palaces and jeweled statues, Persepolis was meant to symbolize the magnificence of the Persian Empire—the largest, most stable, and most powerful empire of ancient Mesopotamia.

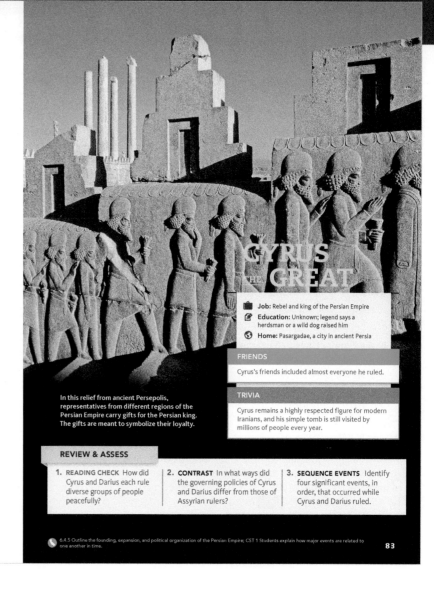

In this relief from ancient Persepolis, representatives from different regions of the Persian Empire carry gifts for the Persian king. The gifts are meant to symbolize their loyalty.

CYRUS THE GREAT

Job: Rebel and king of the Persian Empire

Education: Unknown; legend says a herdsman or a wild dog raised him

Home: Pasargadae, a city in ancient Persia

FRIENDS

Cyrus's friends included almost everyone he ruled.

TRIVIA

Cyrus remains a highly respected figure for modern Iranians, and his simple tomb is still visited by millions of people every year.

REVIEW & ASSESS

1. **READING CHECK** How did Cyrus and Darius each rule diverse groups of people peacefully?

2. **CONTRAST** In what ways did the governing policies of Cyrus and Darius differ from those of Assyrian rulers?

3. **SEQUENCE EVENTS** Identify four significant events, in order, that occurred while Cyrus and Darius ruled.

6.4.5 Outline the founding, expansion, and political organization of the Persian Empire; CST 1 Students explain how major events are related to one another in time.

STANDARDS

HSS CONTENT STANDARDS:

6.4.5 Outline the founding, expansion, and political organization of the Persian Empire.

HSS ANALYSIS SKILLS:

CST 2 Students construct various time lines of key events, people, and periods of the historical era they are studying;
HI 6 Students interpret basic indicators of economic performance and conduct cost-benefit analyses of economic and political issues.

PLAN

OBJECTIVE

Analyze how Cyrus and Darius I unified different peoples and cultures of the Persian Empire.

ESSENTIAL QUESTION

Why was civilization able to develop in ancient Mesopotamia?

The unification of people and cultures encouraged the development of civilization. Lesson 2.4 discusses how Cyrus the Great and Darius I practiced tolerance to unite the Persian Empire.

BACKGROUND FOR THE TEACHER

The mighty Persian Empire was the primary political and cultural power in southwestern Asia from 500 B.C. to A.D. 630. It was ruled by several dynasties—the Achaemenids from 550–330 B.C.; the Seleucids from 323–64 B.C.; the Parthians from 247 B.C.–A.D. 224; and the Sasanians from A.D. 224–651. Much of what we know about this empire comes from the writings of the Greek historian Herodotus, who covered its rise in *The Histories*. The Persian Empire is known for its policy of tolerance, its efficient government, and Zoroastrianism—one of the world's oldest monotheistic religions.

DIGITAL RESOURCES NGLSync.cengage.com

TEACHER RESOURCES & ASSESSMENT

 Reading and Note-Taking

 Vocabulary Practice

 Section 2 Quiz

STUDENT RESOURCES

 Biography

THINK, PAIR, SHARE

Have students use a Think, Pair, Share strategy to discuss what they know about the differences between rulers with absolute power and rulers who practice tolerance. Tell students they will explore the reactions of the subject people and levels of success for uniting an empire. `0:05` minutes

TEACH

GUIDED DISCUSSION

1. **Make Inferences** Why would it be important to communicate orders from one province to another in fewer than 15 days? *(In order to keep the empire united, the people in the empire had to have clear, efficient, and consistent communications. All of the satraps had to be aware of what was happening and have clear direction about how to maintain control in their province.)*

2. **Draw Conclusions** How would having one currency be beneficial to an empire? *(It would mean that all the people paid their tribute or taxes with a currency of a consistent value so it ensured that people paid taxes in a fair way.)*

FORM AND SUPPORT OPINIONS

Have students discuss whether they think Cyrus's policy of tolerance while conquering other lands made him a fair ruler. **ASK:** Do you think that Cyrus's tolerance of other cultures won him loyalty? *(Responses will vary, but students may suggest that Cyrus's tolerant approach made him more favored among conquered people.)* `0:10` minutes

ACTIVE OPTIONS

NG Learning Framework: Learn More About Persian Leaders

ATTITUDE: **Curiosity**
SKILL: **Collaboration**

Have students select the leader they are still curious about after learning about the Persian leaders in this lesson. Have students work in pairs and collaborate to write a short biography about this person using information from the chapter and additional source material. `0:10` minutes

On Your Feet: Create a Living Time Line Ask volunteers to create a living time line of the events associated with the unification of the Persian Empire starting with when the Medes ruled the region. Write each of the dates from the time line in Lesson 2.4 on an index card and distribute the cards randomly to volunteers. Have students arrange themselves in a line in correct chronological order. Then have each student in turn explain to the class the significance of the date he or she is holding. `0:10` minutes

STRIVING READERS

Use Reciprocal Teaching Have students read Lesson 2.4 in pairs. Instruct students to take turns reading each paragraph aloud. At the end of the paragraph, the reading student should ask the listening student a question or two about what they have just heard. For example, students may ask their partners to summarize the paragraph in their own words.

ENGLISH LANGUAGE LEARNERS

Make Word Cards Help students at all proficiency levels make word cards for these three different ideas that helped to unite the Persian Empire: *tolerance*, *provinces*, and *satraps*. For each one, students should list words or phrases related to that word, such as the following:

- tolerance: sympathy for others, accepting beliefs, allowing people to keep their normal lives
- provinces: small parts of the whole empire, administrative parts
- satraps: governors who maintained control of provinces and helped the ruler maintain control

Encourage students at the **Bridging** level to use each word in a sentence that illustrates an understanding of the word's meaning.

Press **mt** *in the Student eEdition for modified text.*

See the Chapter Planner for more strategies for differentiation.

ANSWERS

1. Cyrus the Great was a tolerant king who won the respect of his conquered subjects. He allowed local rulers to remain in power, he spared defeated people from great hardship, and perhaps most importantly, he honored local customs and religions. Darius was also wise and divided his empire into provinces for more efficient administration, set regular taxes, and built a network of roads.

2. The governing policies of Cyrus and Darius were fair. The Assyrian rulers' governing policies were cruel. For example, Cyrus only asked for tribute that defeated people could afford. People under Darius's rule only had to pay half of what they could afford. Under the Assyrian rulers, failure to pay tribute resulted in severe punishment or death.

3. First: Cyrus demands tribute from defeated people, but only what they could afford. Second: Darius I expands his empire to reach from India to southwestern Europe. Third: Darius I divides his empire into 20 provinces. Fourth: Darius I builds the Royal Road.

2.5

The Legacy of Mesopotamia

As you check your calendar, text a friend, or ride your bike, you probably aren't thinking about the people who walked the earth more than 3,000 years ago. But if it weren't for the people of ancient Mesopotamian civilizations, you might not be able to do any of these things.

MAIN IDEA

Mesopotamian civilizations were responsible for major cultural and technological developments.

CULTURAL DEVELOPMENTS

The advances developed in ancient Mesopotamia form the region's **legacy**—or the things, both cultural and technological, left to us from the past. Mesopotamia's cultural legacy touches our lives every day. For example, the written word took important leaps forward with Sumer's development of pictograph and cuneiform writing and then with the spread of the Phoenician alphabet.

Mesopotamia also left us a legacy in forms of government. The city-state unit that developed in Sumer, Babylon, and Phoenicia became an important governmental form in the ancient world. Equally important were the styles of government that emerged. Hammurabi highlighted the importance of law. His Code of Laws influenced later legal systems. Cyrus the Great demonstrated the power of tolerance to future leaders. Finally, the use of provinces, governors, and good communications are still essential to modern governments.

TECHNOLOGICAL ADVANCES

It is easy to take Mesopotamia's technological advances for granted because they seem so commonplace to us today. Yet at the time, Mesopotamian technology clearly furthered the development of human civilization. During the Bronze Age, tools and weapons became more effective than ever before. Strong axes, swords, and daggers were crafted from bronze.

Mesopotamian technology also had an impact on agriculture and on land and sea travel. The ox-drawn plow made it easier to cultivate large areas of land. Irrigation techniques pioneered by the Sumerians are still used around the world. The wheel revolutionized transportation and trade on land. Phoenician shipbuilding and navigation did the same at sea by spreading Phoenicia's Mesopotamian-influenced culture.

With advances like the abacus, people from Mesopotamia laid the foundations of mathematics and science. The abacus is a device that uses sliding beads for counting. The Mesopotamians were also among the first to perform complex calculations and develop a calendar. Additionally, they devised number systems based on 60, which is what we use today to keep track of time.

The application of mathematics made it possible for Mesopotamians to build larger and more complex buildings, including Mesopotamia's cultural and technological masterpiece, the ziggurat. So the next time you ride in a car, use a tool, or see a skyscraper, thank ancient Mesopotamia.

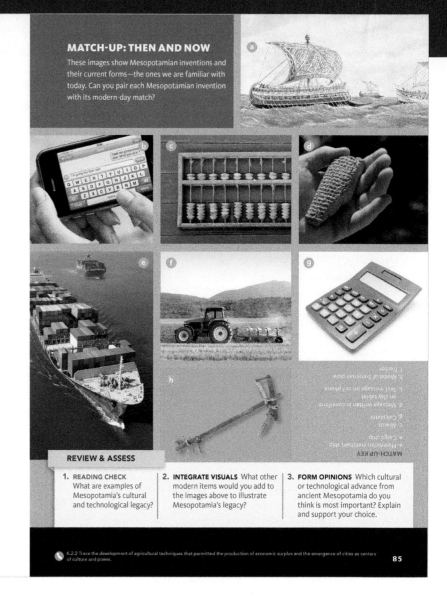

MATCH-UP: THEN AND NOW

These images show Mesopotamian inventions and their current forms—the ones we are familiar with today. Can you pair each Mesopotamian invention with its modern-day match?

MATCH-UP KEY
a. Phoenician merchant ship
e. Cargo ship
c. Abacus
g. Calculator
d. Message written in cuneiform on clay tablet
b. Text message on cell phone
f. Model of Sumerian plow
h. Tractor

REVIEW & ASSESS

1. **READING CHECK** What are examples of Mesopotamia's cultural and technological legacy?

2. **INTEGRATE VISUALS** What other modern items would you add to the images above to illustrate Mesopotamia's legacy?

3. **FORM OPINIONS** Which cultural or technological advance from ancient Mesopotamia do you think is most important? Explain and support your choice.

6.2.2 Trace the development of agricultural techniques that permitted the production of economic surplus and the emergence of cities as centers of culture and power.

HSS CONTENT STANDARDS:

6.2 Students analyze the geographic, political, economic, religious, and social structures of the early civilizations of Mesopotamia, Egypt, and Kush.

PLAN

OBJECTIVE

Identify how Mesopotamian civilizations were responsible for major cultural and technological developments.

ESSENTIAL QUESTION

Why was civilization able to develop in ancient Mesopotamia?

Technological advances help spread culture and develop civilization. Lesson 2.5 discusses Mesopotamian civilizations that brought about major cultural and technological advancements.

BACKGROUND FOR THE TEACHER

The Mesopotamians needed to be able to track time in order for their civilization to thrive. Tracking seasons and weather patterns helped them determine when the rivers may have been prone to flooding, or when they could expect crops to be ready. The Mesopotamians used a fairly complicated time tracking system with the number 60 as the base. Historians do not know the exact reason Mesopotamians chose 60 as the base for time. However, the number 60 is divisible by several numbers, including 1, 2, 3, 4, 5, 6, 10, 12, 15, and 30. Given that about half of the day is dark and half of the day is light because of Earth's rotation, they likely chose 60 to allow for a flexible system of tracking time.

DIGITAL RESOURCES NGLSync.cengage.com

TEACHER RESOURCES & ASSESSMENT

 Reading and Note-Taking

 Vocabulary Practice

 Section 2 Quiz

STUDENT RESOURCES

 NG Chapter Gallery

STEM

INTRODUCE & ENGAGE

ANALYZE MESOPOTAMIAN INNOVATION

Show students an analog clock and a calendar showing all 12 months. Ask them what they observe. Do they notice that there are 12 months in a year and there are 12 numbers on the clock? **ASK:** How many minutes are in an hour? Point out to students that the Sumerians had a number system based on 60. Point out that 60 is divisible by several numbers, including 2, 4, and 15, among others. Ask students to discuss why the number 60 would have been a solution to tracking time. Some other topics to discuss may include: How are the numbers on the clock divided? How many seasons are there? How many degrees are there in a circle? How long does it take for Earth to revolve around the Sun? `0:10` minutes

TEACH

GUIDED DISCUSSION

1. **Make Inferences** Why would it be useful to have a written alphabet of symbols representing sounds? (*Having specific symbols to represent sounds would be faster and more efficient than drawing a picture of something when a person is trying to communicate. Letters would also be a clear way to communicate an idea.*)

2. **Draw Conclusions** Why would developing a system to keep track of time be important to people? (*Tracking time can be important to everything from knowing when to expect the mountain snows to melt and cause the rivers to flood; when it is time to harvest the crops; when a captain should leave the port with the ship, or how long a journey at sea may take so people can decide how much water and what types of supplies to take on the ship.*)

SYNTHESIZE

Discuss the many ways the advances of Mesopotamian civilizations transformed civilization and how these developments now impact our lives today. Include advances in communication and technology. Then have students imagine they have a time-traveling visitor from Mesopotamia in the classroom to interview. **ASK:** What modern technology do you think a time-traveling Mesopotamian would be most fascinated by? (*Responses will vary, but students should support their opinions with details from the chapter.*) `0:05` minutes

ACTIVE OPTIONS

Critical Viewing: NG Chapter Gallery Invite students to explore the Chapter Gallery and choose one image they feel best represents their understanding of Mesopotamian civilization. Have them provide a written explanation of why they selected their particular image. `0:10` minutes

On Your Feet: Hold a Debate Divide the class into two teams and explain that they will be debating cultural legacies of Mesopotamia, and discussing which one has more impact on our culture today. One side will argue that Hammurabi's Code of Laws is more important to today's society. The other side will argue that Cyrus the Great's legacy of the power of tolerance is more important in today's society. `0:10` minutes

DIFFERENTIATE

STRIVING READERS

Create Charts Help students better understand the legacy of Mesopotamian society by creating a chart of technological and cultural inventions. As they read Lesson 2.5 have them complete the chart below. Tell students to use the chart to help them evaluate the positive and negative effects of each invention and to decide which invention they think had the greatest impact on society.

Invention	Effect on Civilization

GIFTED & TALENTED   STEM

Describe Inventions Have students think of an idea for an invention of their own. They might come up with a new electronic device, a vehicle, or an item that simply makes everyday life easier. Ask students to write a description of their invention and share it with the class.

Press **mt** in the Student eEdition for modified text.

See the Chapter Planner for more strategies for differentiation.

REVIEW & ASSESS

ANSWERS

1. Some examples include the city-state, the legal system, writing, calendars, ox-drawn plows, and other math and science foundations.

2. Possibilities might include photos of a calendar, a clock, an irrigation system, and a courthouse.

3. Students' opinions will vary. Accept reasonable responses that are supported by logical reasoning and relevant evidence.

3 Review

VOCABULARY

Match each word in the first column with its definition in the second column.

WORD	DEFINITION
1. city-state HSS 6.2	a. a pyramid-shaped temple with a shrine at the top
2. artisan HSS 6.2	b. the governor of a district
3. polytheism HSS 6.2.3	c. an order based on power and wealth
4. ziggurat HSS 6.2.3	d. a person skilled at making things by hand
5. social class HSS 6.2.3	e. an administrative district
6. province HSS 6.4.5	f. a self-governing city that controlled the surrounding land
7. satrap HSS 6.4.5	g. things left to us from the past
8. legacy HSS 6.2	h. the belief in many gods

READING STRATEGY

9. MAKE INFERENCES If you haven't already, complete your chart to make inferences about why civilization developed in Mesopotamia. Then answer the question.

I notice ...	I know ...	And so ...
Two rivers flowed through Mesopotamia	Rivers provide water to sustain agriculture.	

Consider the traits of civilization that you learned about in Chapter 2. How did they develop in the region? HSS 6.2.1

MAIN IDEAS

Answer the following questions. Support your answers with evidence from the chapter.

10. How did the geography of Mesopotamia contribute to the development of civilization? LESSON 1.1 HSS 6.2.1

11. What caused city-states to develop in Sumer and form the world's first civilization? LESSON 1.2 HSS 6.2.2

12. What purpose did the ziggurat serve in each Sumerian city-state? LESSON 1.3 HSS 6.2.3

13. What is important about the empire Sargon created in Mesopotamia? LESSON 1.5 HSS HI 1

14. What did Hammurabi establish to help unite his vast empire? LESSON 2.1 HSS 6.2.4

15. What factors helped the Assyrians of northern Mesopotamia conquer all of Mesopotamia? LESSON 2.2 HSS HI 2

16. How did Phoenician sea traders affect Mesopotamian culture? LESSON 2.3 HSS 6.2.9

17. In what ways were Cyrus and Darius wise rulers? LESSON 2.4 HSS HI 1

CRITICAL THINKING

Answer the following questions. Support your answers with evidence from the chapter.

18. ESSENTIAL QUESTION Based on what you've learned, why was civilization able to develop in Mesopotamia? HSS REP 1

19. DRAW CONCLUSIONS How might unpredictable natural forces, such as floods, have influenced the development of polytheism in Sumer? HSS HI 2

20. ANALYZE CAUSE AND EFFECT What led to Hammurabi's Code of Laws? HSS HI 2

21. SUMMARIZE What were the important achievements of Mesopotamian civilizations? HSS HI 1

22. YOU DECIDE Were the punishments in Hammurabi's Code of Laws appropriate? Support your opinion with evidence from the text. HSS REP 1

INTERPRET CHARTS

Study the chart comparing letters in the Phoenician, early Greek, early Latin, and modern English alphabets. Then answer the questions that follow.

Phoenician	Early Greek	Early Latin	Modern English

23. Which letter is most similar in all four alphabets? HSS 6.2.9

24. What conclusions can you draw about language in the ancient world? HSS HI 3

ANALYZE SOURCES

Read the following translation of an Assyrian king's description of one of his raids. Then answer the question.

> I carried off his silver, gold, possessions, property, bronze, iron, tin, . . . captives of the guilty soldiers together with their property, his gods together with their property, precious stone of the mountain, his harnessed chariot, his teams of horses, the equipment of the troops, garments with multi-colored trim, linen garments, fine oil, cedar, fine aromatic plants, cedar shavings, purple wool, red-purple wool, his wagons, his oxen, his sheep—his valuable tribute which, like the stars of heaven, had no number.

25. Based on this passage, what can you conclude about the nature of Assyrian attacks on city-states in Mesopotamia? HSS REP 4

WRITE ABOUT HISTORY

26. ARGUMENT Of all the achievements of Mesopotamian civilizations, which one do you think has had the most significant and lasting impact on the modern world? Write a persuasive essay outlining your argument. HSS REP 1

TIPS

- Take notes about the many important achievements of Mesopotamian civilizations discussed in the chapter.
- State your argument in a clear, persuasive way.
- Present strong evidence to support your argument.
- Use vocabulary words from the chapter as appropriate.
- Provide a concluding statement that wraps up the argument presented.
- Ask a teacher or a classmate to read your essay and make revisions based on their feedback.

VOCABULARY ANSWERS

WORD	DEFINITION
1. city-state f. HSS 6.2	a. a pyramid-shaped temple with a shrine at the top
2. artisan d. HSS 6.2	b. the governor of a district
3. polytheism h. HSS 6.2.3	c. an order based on power and wealth
4. ziggurat a. HSS 6.2.3	d. a person skilled at making things by hand
5. social class c. HSS 6.2.3	e. an administrative district
6. province e. HSS 6.4.5	f. a self-governing city that controlled the surrounding land
7. satrap b. HSS 6.4.5	g. things left to us from the past
8. legacy g. HSS 6.2	h. the belief in many gods

STANDARDS

HSS CONTENT STANDARDS:

6.2.1 Locate and describe the major river systems and discuss the physical settings that supported permanent settlement and early civilizations; 6.2.2 Trace the development of agricultural techniques that permitted the production of economic surplus and the emergence of cities as centers of culture and power; 6.2.3 Understand the relationship between religion and the social and political order in Mesopotamia and Egypt; 6.2.4 Know the significance of Hammurabi's Code; 6.2.9 Trace the evolution of language and its written forms; 6.4.5 Outline the founding, expansion, and political organization of the Persian Empire.

HSS ANALYSIS SKILLS:

REP 1 Students frame questions that can be answered by historical study and research; REP 4 Students assess the credibility of primary and secondary sources and draw sound conclusions from them; HI 2 Students understand and distinguish cause, effect, sequence, and correlation in historical events, including the long- and short-term causal relations; HI 3 Students explain the sources of historical continuity and how the combination of ideas and events explains the emergence of new patterns.

READING STRATEGY ANSWERS

I notice...	I know...	And so...
Two rivers flowed through Mesopotamia.	Rivers provide water to sustain agriculture.	The physical geography of having two rivers helped civilization to develop.

9. The Tigris and Euphrates rivers flowed through Mesopotamia, and the yearly floods brought fertile soil to the land. The river also provided the water needed to sustain agriculture in the region. People settled here because they could grow food. Eventually, groups of people joined together, forming villages. Successful food crops led to larger populations and allowed those people to have free time to develop arts, culture, and technology, including weapons. A succession of rulers used their power to spread culture and unite peoples of different races and religions. These peoples exchanged goods, cultures, and technologies. (HSS 6.2.1)

MAIN IDEAS ANSWERS

10. Mesopotamia, located between the Tigris and Euphrates rivers, was a flat, fertile river valley that was excellent for agriculture. As farming flourished, populations grew, cities were built, and civilization developed. (HSS 6.2.1)

11. City-states developed in Sumer when the people in farming villages worked together on major irrigation projects; their collaboration led to united villages that formed city-states. (HSS 6.2.2)

12. The ziggurat was the heart of each Sumerian city-state. It was a monumental temple, where priests performed rituals to ensure the city-state's well-being. (HSS 6.2.3)

13. The Akkadian Empire that Sargon created in Mesopotamia was the world's first empire, as well as the world's largest empire. (HSS HI 1)

14. Hammurabi's Code of Laws helped to unite his vast empire. (HSS 6.2.4)

15. The Assyrians had a strong agricultural economy, which afforded them a large professional army. Armed with iron weapons and skilled at archery, Assyrian armies had the power and force to conquer all of Mesopotamia. (HSS HI 2)

16. As the Phoenicians traveled to different harbors in the Mediterranean for trade, they not only exported goods but they exported their alphabet and other aspects of culture as well. (HSS 6.2.9)

17. Cyrus and Darius practiced tolerance toward their conquered subjects, allowed conquered kings to keep their thrones, and only charged small tributes. This allowed their conquered kingdoms to be united. (HSS HI 1)

CRITICAL THINKING ANSWERS

18. Civilization was able to develop in Mesopotamia because of its location between the Tigris and Euphrates river systems that included fertile land for farming, which supported permanent settlement and population growth. (HSS REP 1)

19. Unpredictable natural forces, such as destructive floods, might have led to the development of polytheism because this belief helped Sumerians feel more in control in an unpredictable world. With multiple gods governing every aspect of life, Sumerians believed that if they pleased their gods with gifts and ceremonies, they would be protected and spared from such disasters of flooding, drought, and disease. (HSS HI 2)

20. Hammurabi had a vast empire that contained many different peoples who all followed different laws. To help bring justice to everyday life, Hammurabi took the best laws of the land, added a few more, and organized the rules. Then he had them written in stone and posted for everyone to see so that everyone had rules to follow. (HSS HI 2)

21. Important achievements of Mesopotamian civilizations include the development of improved agriculture, Sumerian cuneiform writing, the Phoenician alphabet, the city-state, codified laws, metal tools, innovative irrigation techniques, foundations of mathematics and science, and complex building structures. (HSS HI 1)

22. Students' responses will vary. Students should support their opinions with evidence from the chapter. (HSS REP 1)

INTERPRET CHARTS ANSWERS

23. The letter "E" is the most similar in all four alphabets. (HSS 6.2.9)

24. Languages evolve over time, developing further as people come in contact, communicating and sharing elements of different languages. (HSS HI 3)

ANALYZE SOURCES ANSWER

25. Students' responses will vary. Sample response: The excerpt reveals a remarkably detailed list of items taken by the Assyrians. This list includes mention of the highly valued "purple" dyed cloth, so it suggests that the city-state that was raided had traded with the Phoenicians, or were in contact with others who had. This list also reveals how ruthlessly thorough the Assyrians were when raiding city-states; basically, they took absolutely everything of value, leaving nothing for those they had conquered. (HSS REP 4)

WRITE ABOUT HISTORY ANSWER

26. Students' essays will vary, but students should construct a persuasive argument and support it with evidence from the chapter.

    Students' essays should

    - contain one claim that they will argue
    - support each claim with clear reasons and relevant evidence from the chapter
    - be written in a formal style
    - include vocabulary words from the chapter

    For more in-depth instruction and practice with the writing form, assign the Social Studies Skills Writing Lesson on writing a persuasive essay. (HSS REP 1)

UNIT 2 EARLY CIVILIZATIONS

On Location with National Geographic Lead Program Officer Christopher Thornton
Intro and Video

Unit Wrap-Up:
"Encounters with History"
Feature and Video

"China's Ancient Lifeline"
National Geographic Adapted Article

"Faces of the Divine"
National Geographic Adapted Article
Student eEdition exclusive

Unit 2 Inquiry:
Write a Creation Myth

 Interactive Map Tool
Available at NGLSync.cengage.com

 **News & Updates**
Available at NGLSync.cengage.com

CHAPTER RESOURCES

TEACHER RESOURCES & ASSESSMENT *Available at NGLSync.cengage.com*

 Social Studies Skills Lessons
• Reading: Draw Conclusions
• Writing: Write a Narrative

 Chapter 4
Answer Key

 Formal Assessment
• Chapter 4 Tests A (on-level)
  & B (below-level)

 ExamView®
One-time Download

STUDENT BACKPACK *Available at NGLSync.cengage.com*

• **eEdition** *(English)* • **eEdition** *(Spanish)* • **Handbooks** • **Online Atlas**

Chapter 4 Spanish resources, Guided Writing prompts, and Financial Literacy lessons are available online.

SECTION 1 RESOURCES

A SOCIETY ON THE NILE

 Reading and Note-Taking

 Vocabulary Practice

 Section 1 Quiz

Available at NGLSync.cengage.com

LESSON 1.1 THE GEOGRAPHY OF ANCIENT EGYPT

• Critical Viewing: NG Chapter Gallery
• On Your Feet: Think, Pair, Share

LESSON 1.2 AGRICULTURE DEVELOPS

NG Learning Framework:
Observe Upper and Lower Egypt

• On Your Feet: Card Responses

LESSON 1.3 EGYPT UNITES

• Critical Viewing: NG Image Gallery
• On Your Feet: Inside-Outside Circle

NATIONAL GEOGRAPHIC
EXPLORER SARAH PARCAK
LESSON 1.4 SENSING UNDER THE SURFACE

NG Learning Framework:
Learn More About Tanis

• On Your Feet: Create a Quiz

SECTION 2 RESOURCES

THE OLD AND MIDDLE KINGDOMS

 Reading and Note-Taking

 Vocabulary Practice

 Section 2 Quiz

Available at NGLSync.cengage.com

LESSON 2.1 THE OLD KINGDOM

NG Learning Framework:
Discuss the Importance of Pyramids

• On Your Feet: Fishbowl

LESSON 2.2
DAILY LIFE AND RELIGION

• Critical Viewing: NG Chapter Gallery
• On Your Feet: Compare and Contrast Two Civilizations

DOCUMENT-BASED QUESTION
LESSON 2.3 LIFE, DEATH, AND RELIGION

NG Learning Framework:
Review Information About the Nile

• On Your Feet: Three Options

LESSON 2.4
THE MIDDLE KINGDOM

NG Learning Framework:
Review Information About the Middle Kingdom

• On Your Feet: Turn and Talk on Topic

SECTION 3 RESOURCES

THE NEW KINGDOM

 Reading and Note-Taking

 Vocabulary Practice

 Section 3 Quiz

Available at NGLSync.cengage.com

LESSON 3.1 HATSHEPSUT EXPANDS TRADE

 Biography
Hatshepsut

Available at NGLSync.cengage.com

NG Learning Framework:
Map Ancient Trade Routes

• On Your Feet: Present a Period of Egyptian History

BIOGRAPHY
LESSON 3.2 RAMSES II

NG Learning Framework:
Compare the Reigns of Ramses II and Hatshepsut

• On Your Feet: Hold a Panel Discussion

HISTORY THROUGH OBJECTS
LESSON 3.3 TUT'S TREASURES

• Critical Viewing: NG Chapter Gallery
• On Your Feet: Three-Step Interview

LESSON 3.4 THE RISE OF KUSH

NG Learning Framework:
Research Cultural Influences

• On Your Feet: Create a Concept Web

SECTION 4 RESOURCES

THE EGYPTIAN LEGACY

 Reading and Note-Taking

 Vocabulary Practice

 Section 4 Quiz

Available at NGLSync.cengage.com

LESSON 4.1
HIEROGLYPHS AND PAPYRUS

 Active History: Interactive Whiteboard Activity
Decipher Egyptian Hieroglyphics

 Active History
Decipher Egyptian Hieroglyphics

Available at NGLSync.cengage.com

• On Your Feet: Compare Two Forms of Writing

LESSON 4.2 MEDICINE, SCIENCE, AND MATHEMATICS

NG Learning Framework:
Learn More About Medicine in Ancient Egypt

• On Your Feet: Create a Quiz

LESSON 4.3
ART AND ARCHITECTURE

• Critical Viewing: NG Image Gallery
• On Your Feet: Fishbowl

CHAPTER 4 REVIEW

STRATEGY
Focus on Main Idea

Help students locate the Main Idea statements at the beginning of Lessons 1.1, 1.2, 1.3, and 1.4. Explain that these statements summarize the important ideas of the reading and will be useful for helping them pay attention to what matters most in the text.

Use with Lessons 1.1, 1.2, 1.3, and 1.4 *Help students get in the habit of using the Main Idea statements to set a purpose for reading.*

STRATEGY
Play Vocabulary Tic-Tac-Toe

Write nine Key Vocabulary words on a tic-tac-toe grid. Have Player A choose a word. If the player correctly pronounces, defines, and uses the word in a sentence, he or she can put an X in the box. Then have Player B do the same using O. Keep playing until there is a winner.

Use with All Lessons *This activity works well on the Interactive Whiteboard. It can be used to review Key Vocabulary for a single section or the entire chapter.*

STRATEGY
Read and Recall

Allow students to work in groups of two to four. First have each student read the same lesson independently. After reading, students should meet without the book and share ideas they recall. One person should take notes. As a group, students should look at the lesson and decide what should be added or changed in the notes.

Use with All Lessons *For an extension of this strategy, have different groups compare their notes.*

Press *in the Student eEdition for modified text.*

STRATEGY
Preview Visuals to Predict

Ask students to preview the title and visuals in each lesson. Then have students tell what they think the lesson will be about. After reading, ask them to repeat the activity to see whether their predictions were confirmed.

Use with All Lessons *Invite volunteers to describe the visuals in detail to help visually impaired students see them.*

STRATEGY ❷
Complete Cloze Statements

Provide copies of these cloze statements for students to complete during or after reading.

Ancient Egypt had abundant _____ to _____, or exchange, for things the land couldn't produce, especially _____ and exotic luxuries. These goods traveled along _____ routes and pathways established by traders over land and _____. The _____ generated through these expeditions stimulated Egypt's economy and funded great _____ projects.

Use with Lesson 3.1

STRATEGY ❶
Draw Conclusions

The reading strategy for this chapter focuses on drawing conclusions. After introducing the strategy to the class, provide the following sentence frames to help students draw conclusions about the importance of geography to the development of civilization in ancient Egypt.

- Two details from the text are _____ and _____.
- I know that _____.
- When I combine the details with what I know about geography, I understand _____.

Use with Lessons 1.1 and 1.2, All Levels

STANDARDS

HSS CONTENT STANDARDS:

6.2 Students analyze the geographic, political, economic, relkgious, and social structures of the early civilizations of Mesopotamia, Egypt, and Kush.

STRATEGY ②
Pair Partners for Dictation

After students read each lesson in the chapter, have them write a sentence summarizing its main idea. Pair students at the **Emerging** level with students at a higher proficiency level and have partners dictate their sentences to each other. Then have them work together to check the sentences for accuracy and spelling.

Use with All Lessons, All Levels *Provide the following sentence stem for students at the **Emerging** level: I think the main idea of the lesson is _____. For Lessons 4.1, 4.2, and 4.3, monitor students at all proficiency levels for their comprehension of the advances ancient Egyptians made in writing, medicine, science, mathematics, art, and architecture.*

STRATEGY ③
Set Up a Word Wall

Work with students to choose three words from each section to display in a grouping on a Word Wall. Keep the words displayed throughout the lessons and discuss each one as it comes up during reading. Have volunteers add words, phrases, and examples to each word to develop understanding.

Use with All Lessons, All Levels

GIFTED & TALENTED

STRATEGY ①
Host an Interview

Allow students to work in teams of two to plan, write, and perform a simulated television interview with a person in ancient Egypt. Tell students that they may choose to interview a farmer, trader, builder, scribe, or any other person that was part of ancient Egyptian society.

Use with Lessons 1.2, 1.3, 2.1, 2.2, 4.1, 4.2, and 4.3

STRATEGY ②
Teach a Class

Before beginning the chapter, allow students to choose one of the lessons listed below and prepare to teach the contents to the class. Give them a set amount of time in which to present their lesson. Suggest that students think about any visuals or activities they want to use when they teach their lesson.

Use with Lessons 1.2, 1.3, 2.1, 2.2, 4.1, 4.2, and 4.3

PRE-AP

STRATEGY ①
Create a Group Presentation

Have students work in small groups to discuss how living near the Nile River influenced the development of the ancient Egyptian culture. Students should include information about climate, accessibility to trade routes, and the lives of the Egyptians who lived in the area. Then have groups create a report to present to the class.

Use with Lessons 1.1 and 1.2

STRATEGY ②
Debate Contributions

Have students research the many contributions of ancient Egypt to civilization. Tell each student to decide which contribution he or she believes had the greatest impact and make a list of the reasons that support his or her choice. Suggest that students hold a panel discussion to share and debate their decisions.

Use with Lessons 2.1, 2.2, 3.3, 4.1, 4.2, and 4.3 *For Lessons 2.1 and 2.2, suggest that students consider how the pyramids and their contents have influenced what people today know about ancient Egypt.*

4 ANCIENT EGYPT
3000 B.C. – 500 B.C.

ESSENTIAL QUESTION How did ancient Egypt's rulers use the land's resources and geography to found a civilization?

SECTION 1 A SOCIETY ON THE NILE

KEY VOCABULARY	NAMES & PLACES
cataract	Lower Egypt
delta	Menes
dynasty	Nile River
pharaoh	Upper Egypt
vizier	

SECTION 2 THE OLD AND MIDDLE KINGDOMS

KEY VOCABULARY	NAMES & PLACES
hierarchy	Ahmose
mummy	Hyksos
pyramid	Khufu
	Middle Kingdom
	Old Kingdom
	Re

SECTION 3 THE NEW KINGDOM

KEY VOCABULARY	NAMES & PLACES
barter	Hatshepsut
	Kush
	New Kingdom
	Nubia
	Ramses II

SECTION 4 THE EGYPTIAN LEGACY

KEY VOCABULARY
hieroglyph
papyrus
scribe

READING STRATEGY

DRAW CONCLUSIONS
When you draw conclusions, you use the facts in a text to make educated guesses. As you read the chapter, use an organizer like this one to draw conclusions about the importance of ancient Egypt's geographic features.

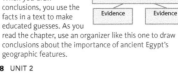

Conclusion

Evidence   Evidence

Egyptian ruler Ramses II built this massive temple at Abu Simbel to honor Egypt's gods—and himself. Each of the four 66-foot statues is an image of Ramses.

HSS CONTENT STANDARDS:

6.2 Students analyze the geographic, political, economic, religious, and social structures of the early civilizations of Mesopotamia, Egypt, and Kush.

TEACHER BACKGROUND

INTRODUCE THE PHOTOGRAPH

Have students study the photograph that shows the four figures of King Ramses II. Point out that two of the figures are located on either side of the entrance to the temple. Tell students that Ramses II had this huge temple carved out of a sandstone cliff on the west bank of the Nile. Explain to students that, in this chapter, they will learn about ancient Egypt—its culture, its religion, and its leaders.

ASK: What do the number and size of the figures of Ramses II indicate about his importance in ancient Egyptian society? (*Possible responses: The number and size of the statues indicate that Ramses II was most likely very important and powerful in ancient Egyptian society.*)

SHARE BACKGROUND

The four statues of King Ramses II at this temple provide an example of ancient Egyptian art. Small figures of Ramses' children, his queen, and his mother are carved around his feet. Dedicated to the sun gods, the temple was built in such a way that, on two days of the year, the first rays of the morning sun shine through the building and light up the entire temple.

DIGITAL RESOURCES NGLSync.cengage.com

TEACHER RESOURCES & ASSESSMENT

 Social Studies Skills Lessons
- Reading: Draw Conclusions
- Writing: Write a Narrative

 ExamView®
One-time Download

 Formal Assessment
- Chapter 4 Tests A (on-level) & B (below-level)

 Chapter 4 Answer Key

STUDENT BACKPACK

- **eEdition** (*English*)
- **eEdition** (*Spanish*)
- **Handbooks**
- **Online Atlas**

INTRODUCE THE ESSENTIAL QUESTION

HOW DID ANCIENT EGYPT'S RULERS USE THE LAND'S RESOURCES AND GEOGRAPHY TO FOUND A CIVILIZATION?

Four Corners Activity: Factors of Influence This activity introduces students to four factors that led to ancient Egypt's success and allows them to choose which factor they think is the most influential. Post the four signs shown in the list below. Ask students to choose the factor that they think contributed most to Egypt's success, go to that corner, and then explain why.

A. Geography The Nile River in Egypt was central to the development of Egyptian civilization, providing water, fertile soil for planting crops, and easy access to trade routes.

B. Government Ancient Egypt was governed by a long series of strong rulers who had complete authority over all religious, civil, and military matters.

C. Military During the New Kingdom, Egypt grew powerful and its army expanded the empire. Egypt became rich from war and taxes from conquered lands.

D. Knowledge of Medicine, Science, and Mathematics Ancient Egyptian advances in medicine, science, and mathematics helped the Egyptians understand human anatomy, treat illnesses, develop a calendar, design buildings, and become successful in trade.

`0:15` minutes

INTRODUCE THE READING STRATEGY

DRAW CONCLUSIONS

Explain to students that when you draw conclusions, you use the facts in a text to make educated guesses. Model filling out the graphic organizer by reading aloud the section "The Gift of the Nile" in Lesson 1.1. Add a fact about the Nile from the text to the first "Evidence" box of the organizer. Tell students that they can add more evidence about the Nile as they read the chapter. Then they can use the evidence to help them draw a conclusion about the importance of the Nile River to the civilization of ancient Egypt. For more in-depth instruction and practice with the reading strategy, assign the Social Studies Reading Lesson on drawing conclusions.

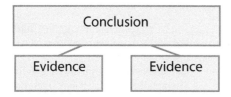

INTRODUCE CHAPTER VOCABULARY

KNOWLEDGE RATING

Have students complete a Knowledge-Rating Chart for Key Vocabulary words. Have students list words and fill out the chart. Work together as a class to complete the chart.

KEY VOCAB	KNOW IT	NOT SURE	DON'T KNOW	DEFINITION
barter				
cataract				
delta				
dynasty				

KEY DATES	
3200 B.C.	Separate kingdoms of Upper Egypt and Lower Egypt
3100 B.C.	Unification of Upper Egypt and Lower Egypt
2700 B.C.–2200 B.C.	The Old Kingdom
2040 B.C.	The Middle Kingdom
1550 B.C.–1070 B.C.	The New Kingdom
728 B.C.	Egypt under Kushite rule
30 B.C.	Conquest of Egypt by Rome

1.1
The Geography of
Ancient Egypt

"Hail to thee, O Nile! Who manifests thyself over this land and comes to give life to Egypt!" These words written 4,000 years ago emphasize the importance of the Nile River to Egyptians: No Nile, no life, no Egypt. It was that simple.

MAIN IDEA

The Nile was the source of life in Egypt's dry, barren deserts.

+ POSSIBLE RESPONSE

The photo shows that the soil alongside the Nile River is rich enough to support the growth of plants.

Critical Viewing This photo shows the fertile land alongside the Nile River. How does it illustrate the way Egyptians depended on the Nile?

THE GIFT OF THE NILE

The **Nile River** was central to the civilization that developed in Egypt. At around 4,132 miles in length, it is the world's longest river. It flows northward from sources deep in Africa to the Mediterranean Sea. Six **cataracts**, rock formations that create churning rapids, break the river's smooth course. The 550 miles from the most northerly cataract to the Mediterranean Sea formed ancient Egypt's heartland, which was divided into two distinct regions: the Upper (southern) Nile and the Lower (northern) Nile. The Lower Nile region included the Nile Delta, next to the Mediterranean. A **delta** is an area where a river fans out into various branches as it flows into a body of water.

The Nile was generally a peaceful river. Its current carried ships gently downstream, while the winds above it usually blew upstream, making it easy for ships to row downstream or sail upstream.

Water was the Nile's greatest gift. Without it there could be no agriculture in Egypt's desert. Every year faraway rains sent a surge of water downstream to Egypt, swelling the river with the annual flood.

Unlike the rivers of Mesopotamia, the Nile's flood was predictable, occurring every summer. The waters spilled over the riverbanks, depositing another great gift: silt, or very fine particles carried from upriver. The silt-enriched soil was fertile, or full of nutrients to support abundant crops. This soil made agriculture extremely productive—a key to the development of Egyptian civilization. With good management and a little luck, the soil delivered huge harvests.

THE BLACK LAND AND THE RED LAND

Egypt's climate was consistently dry, and sunshine was plentiful. Seven months of hot, sunny weather were followed by a winter of mild, sunny weather. The lack of rainfall created a landscape of striking contrast, made up of regions called the "black land" and the "red land."

The black land was the narrow stretch that ran along both sides of the Nile. There, the river's waters and nourishing dark silt allowed plants to grow and people to live.

The red land was a vast, scorching desert that surrounded the Nile. This desert formed a powerful barrier against invasion and helped separate Egypt from the world beyond. The seemingly empty desert also held a treasure trove of raw materials, including stone for building and gold. The only major resource Egypt lacked was timber.

Egypt's geography, its climate, and—above all—the Nile River all played parts in the kind of civilization that Egypt would become. The land was rich in resources, produced a huge food surplus, and had well-protected borders. In addition, Egypt was a crossroads for trade, lying along important trade routes connecting Africa, the Mediterranean, the Red Sea, and the Middle East. The scene was set for Africa's most famous civilization of ancient times.

REVIEW & ASSESS

1. **READING CHECK** Why was the Nile River essential to life in ancient Egypt?

2. **ANALYZE CAUSE AND EFFECT** What effect did the annual flooding of the Nile River have on the development of agriculture in Egypt?

3. **COMPARE AND CONTRAST** What did the black and red lands have in common? How were they different?

6.2.1 Locate and describe the major river systems and discuss the physical settings that supported permanent settlement and early civilizations; HI 2 Students understand and distinguish cause, effect, sequence, and correlation in historical events, including the long- and short-term causal relations.

PLAN

OBJECTIVE

Identify the Nile River as the source of life in Egypt's dry deserts.

ESSENTIAL QUESTION

How did ancient Egypt's rulers use the land's resources and geography to found a civilization?

The Nile River provided fresh water that sustained plant and animal life. Lesson 1.1 discusses how the Nile was a source of life in Egypt's deserts.

BACKGROUND FOR THE TEACHER

Nearly 10,000 years ago, the Sahara was a tropical grassland. Around 5300 B.C., seasonal rains that watered the Sahara began shifting southward. Over time, the Sahara became a desert. People living in the Sahara left and settled in the Nile River Valley where they had a reliable water source.

The Nile's main sources are the Blue Nile River and the White Nile River. The Blue Nile River originates from Lake Tana in the Ethiopian highlands. The White Nile River originates from Lake Victoria, which lies in Tanzania, Uganda, and part of Kenya. The Nile River flows north because the southern sources of the river are higher in elevation than the mouth of the river on the Mediterranean Sea.

DIGITAL RESOURCES NGLSync.cengage.com

TEACHER RESOURCES & ASSESSMENT

 Reading and Note-Taking

 Vocabulary Practice

 Section 1 Quiz

STUDENT RESOURCES

 NG Chapter Gallery

INTRODUCE & ENGAGE

ACTIVATE PRIOR KNOWLEDGE

Have students work in teams to brainstorm ways in which the climate in which they live affects their school, family, and community. Ask them to consider the effect of physical features such as mountains and deserts, as well as proximity to bodies of water. Invite students to share their ideas with the class. Tell students they will learn about climate and physical features of ancient Egypt in this lesson. `0:05` minutes

TEACH

GUIDED DISCUSSION

1. **Make Inferences** In what way did the Sahara protect Egypt from invasion? *(It would have been difficult to travel across such a hot dry place. Invading enemies would also have to bring food, water, and animals for themselves to survive because there was no water source and crops could not grow in the desert.)*

2. **Draw Conclusions** How do you think the development of civilization in Egypt would have been different without the Nile River? *(The land would not have supported settled farming without the Nile. Without the wealth from farming and the trade made possible by transportation on the Nile, civilization would probably not have developed in the same way.)*

ANALYZE VISUALS

Have students examine the photo of the land alongside the Nile River. Ask them to write sentences to describe what they see in the photo. `0:10` minutes

ACTIVE OPTIONS

Critical Viewing: NG Chapter Gallery Invite students to explore the Chapter Gallery to examine the images that relate to this chapter. Have them select one of the images and do additional research to learn more about it. Ask questions that will inspire additional inquiry about the chosen gallery image, such as: What is this? Where and when was it created? By whom? Why was it created? Why does it belong in this chapter? What else would you like to know about it? `0:10` minutes

On Your Feet: Think, Pair, Share Have students work in pairs to discuss the Reading Check question. Then have each pair meet with another pair to compare answers. Call on volunteers to share and compare their answers with the class. `0:10` minutes

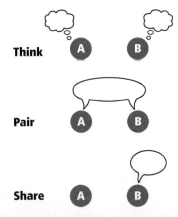

Think A B

Pair A B

Share A B

DIFFERENTIATE

STRIVING READERS

Use an Anticipation Guide Write the following statements on the board:

1. The Nile River was important to the development of civilization in ancient Egypt.

2. Egypt's geography made trade with other countries very difficult.

3. Fertile soil that resulted from the flooding of the Nile led to productive agriculture.

4. The desert that surrounded the Nile helped separate Egypt from the world and helped protect it from invasion.

5. Flooding of the Nile River occurred rarely.

Before reading the lesson, ask students to copy each statement and put an A (agree) or D (disagree) before it. After students read Lesson 1.1, allow volunteers to explain why each statement is correct or incorrect.

PRE-AP

Present a Skit Have students work in small groups to create a skit in which they take the roles of ancient Egyptians who lived in the black land and those who lived in the red land. Ask students to highlight ways in which life in the two areas would have been alike and different. Have students present their skits to the class.

Press **(mt)** *in the Student eEdition for modified text.*

See the Chapter Planner for more strategies for differentiation.

REVIEW & ASSESS

ANSWERS

1. The Nile River provided the water necessary for life in Egypt's arid desert.

2. The annual flooding of the Nile River deposited silt on the riverbanks. This fertile soil made agriculture along the Nile River very productive.

3. Both lands received very little rainfall. The black land, however, was very fertile because it straddled the Nile River. The location of the black land meant it benefited from the floodwaters and silt, creating a fertile landscape for plants to grow and people to live. In contrast, the red land was located in the desert area surrounding the Nile, far from access to water.

1.2 Agriculture
Develops

It's August, and all that can be seen of the flooded fields is water lapping at the stones marking each farmer's boundary. In the dark of night, a farmer paddles nervously out and shifts the stones to steal a few feet from his neighbor. It's a profitable but serious crime—the penalty is death. Farmland in Egypt is so valuable that some are willing to risk it.

MAIN IDEA

Agriculture encouraged the development of communities and kingdoms in Egypt.

THE FERTILE NILE DELTA

Five thousand years ago, the lives of most Egyptians revolved around farming. Along with raising livestock, Egyptians grew a wide variety of crops such as wheat, barley, beans, lentils, peas, onions, and leeks. Fruits included grapes, dates, figs, and watermelons. Farmers grew flax to make cloth. Fish and birds were plentiful, and even poor Egyptians could eat well.

The cycles of the river dictated the farming year. From July to October, the fields were flooded, so farmers did other work. When the floods receded, farmers plowed the soft ground, scattered seeds, and used animals to trample the seeds into the soil. The growing crops were carefully watered through

irrigation. Farmers captured floodwater in artificial lakes and channeled it to the fields. Later, the shaduf (shuh-DOOF) made irrigation easier. This tool was a long pole with a bucket on one end and a weight on the other. Farmers could use a shaduf to effortlessly lift water to their fields. The grain harvest started in mid-March. During the hot summer that followed, farmers prepared their fields before the next flood.

Irrigation and the Nile's fertile soil allowed for extremely productive farming. As in Mesopotamia, successful farming generated surpluses, which led to population growth, trade, and specialized jobs. Building and maintaining irrigation networks took a lot of labor, so farmers grouped together to create larger communities. Leadership was needed to coordinate and manage these increasingly complex societies. As villages grew into towns, village chiefs became kings.

TWO KINGDOMS ARISE

Some historians believe that by around 3200 B.C., two kings ruled over two separate kingdoms—**Upper Egypt** and **Lower Egypt**. Lower Egypt was the Nile Delta region with its wide expanse of fertile land and access to the Mediterranean Sea. Upper Egypt was the long, narrow stretch of the Nile south of modern Cairo and hemmed in by desert.

The Nile served as a superhighway, encouraging contact between Upper and Lower Egypt. Movement along the Nile was easy, and all the villages and towns were located near the great river. Goods and ideas were traded freely between the kingdoms, unifying Egyptians economically and culturally. Unlike Mesopotamia, Egypt would come to be a strong, unified state rather than a group of city-states.

However, Upper Egypt and Lower Egypt remained proudly distinct. Even after Egypt was united, it was represented by a double crown. Every time Egypt descended into disorder, the two kingdoms were usually on opposite sides of the power struggle.

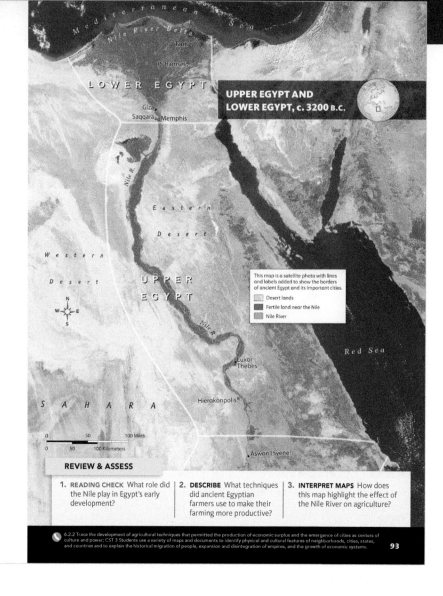

UPPER EGYPT AND LOWER EGYPT, c. 3200 B.C.

This map is a satellite photo with lines and labels added to show the borders of ancient Egypt and its important cities.

- Desert lands
- Fertile land near the Nile
- Nile River

REVIEW & ASSESS

1. **READING CHECK** What role did the Nile play in Egypt's early development?

2. **DESCRIBE** What techniques did ancient Egyptian farmers use to make their farming more productive?

3. **INTERPRET MAPS** How does this map highlight the effect of the Nile River on agriculture?

6.2.2 Trace the development of agricultural techniques that permitted the production of economic surplus and the emergence of cities as centers of culture and power; CST 3 Students use a variety of maps and documents to identify physical and cultural features of neighborhoods, cities, states, and countries and to explain the historical migration of people, expansion and disintegration of empires, and the growth of economic systems.

HSS CONTENT STANDARDS:

6.2.2 Trace the development of agricultural techniques that permitted the production of economic surplus and the emergence of cities as centers of culture and power; **6.2.6** Describe the role of Egyptian trade in the eastern Mediterranean and Nile valley.

HSS ANALYSIS SKILLS:

CST 3 Students use a variety of maps and documents to identify physical and cultural features of neighborhoods, cities, states, and countries and to explain the historical migration of people, expansion and disintegration of empires, and the growth of economic systems; **REP 1** Students frame questions that can be answered by historical study and research.

PLAN

OBJECTIVE

Explain how agriculture encouraged the development of communities and kingdoms in Egypt.

ESSENTIAL QUESTION

How did ancient Egypt's rulers use the land's resources and geography to found a civilization?

Egypt was rich in natural resources. Lesson 1.2 discusses how the resources and geography influenced the development of the Egyptian civilization in ancient times.

BACKGROUND FOR THE TEACHER

One of the crops Egyptians grew in the fertile Nile Valley was flax. They used the fibers from the stems of the plants. These fibers were split length-wise and spun into thread. The Egyptians wove the thread into sheets of linen they used for clothing. Another plant, papyrus, grew in marshy areas around the Nile River. Ancient Egyptians used papyrus to make paper, rope, sandals, and baskets.

DIGITAL RESOURCES NGLSync.cengage.com

TEACHER RESOURCES & ASSESSMENT

 Reading and Note-Taking

 Vocabulary Practice

 Section 1 Quiz

STUDENT RESOURCES

 NG Chapter Gallery

INTRODUCE & ENGAGE

COMPARE AND CONTRAST

Have students begin a Venn Diagram to compare and contrast the farming methods used in ancient Egypt with farming methods used today. Have them write about farming methods today in the left circle. Then, as they read the lesson, ask them to write details about the methods used in ancient Egypt in the right circle. They should write details about how the methods are alike where the circles overlap. `0:10` minutes

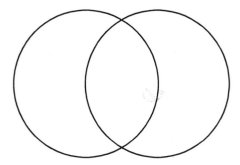

TEACH

GUIDED DISCUSSION

1. **Summarize** What types of crops did the ancient Egyptians grow? *(They grew wheat, barley, beans, lentils, peas, onions, leeks, grapes, dates, figs, and watermelon.)*

2. **Draw Conclusions** How did the Nile River encourage contact between Upper Egypt and Lower Egypt? *(It was easy to travel along the Nile. People traded goods and ideas.)*

INTERPRET MAPS

Point out the map of Upper Egypt and Lower Egypt. Explain that the map is based on a satellite photo of the region. Have students identify desert lands, fertile lands near the Nile River, and the Nile itself. Remind students that the Nile flows from south to north. `0:10` minutes

ACTIVE OPTIONS

NG Learning Framework: Observe Upper and Lower Egypt

ATTITUDE: Curiosity
KNOWLEDGE: Our Human Story

Have students observe the map showing Lower Egypt and Upper Egypt. Ask students to think of questions they might have about the two kingdoms of ancient Egypt. Then have them use information from the chapter and additional source material to write sentences comparing and contrasting ways of life in the two kingdoms. To learn more about the relationship between agriculture and the development of political, economic, religious, and social structures in early civilizations, have students complete **California EEI Curriculum Unit 6.2.2,** *Agricultural Advances in Ancient Civilizations.* `0:10` minutes

On Your Feet: Card Responses Have half the class write six true-false questions based on the lesson. Have the other half create answer cards, writing "True" on one side and "False" on the other. Students from the first group should take turns asking their questions. Students from the second group should hold up their cards, showing either "True" or "False" in response to the questions. Have students keep track of their correct answers. `0:10` minutes

DIFFERENTIATE

INCLUSION

Use Echo Reading Pair students so that there is a proficient reader in each pair. Have the proficient reader read aloud the Main Idea statement at the beginning of the lesson. Have the other student "echo" the same statement in their own words.

GIFTED & TALENTED

Create a Travel Brochure Have students work in small groups to create a travel brochure encouraging people to visit Lower Egypt. Have students describe the kinds of work Egyptians were doing, tell what kind of food to expect, and include information about travel and trade at the time. Ask students to illustrate their brochures. Have each group present its travel brochure to the class.

Press **mt** *in the Student eEdition for modified text.*

See the Chapter Planner for more strategies for differentiation.

REVIEW & ASSESS

ANSWERS

1. As agriculture became more productive because of the Nile and farmers began to accumulate surpluses of food, populations grew and farmers grouped together to create larger communities. These growing villages and towns eventually became two kingdoms—Upper Egypt and Lower Egypt.

2. Ancient Egyptian farmers used irrigation to water their crops with floodwater saved in reservoirs and channeled through canals. They also used a tool called a *shaduf*, which made irrigation easier.

3. The land along the Nile is green on the map. It is green because of the vegetation that grows in the fertile black soil.

1.3 Egypt
Unites

Egypt's ancient civilization was unified for close to 3,000 years—twelve times as long as the United States has been a country. Of course, ancient Egypt witnessed its share of good rulers and good times and bad rulers and bad times. Still, ancient Egypt will be long remembered for its wealth and power.

MAIN IDEA

Strong kings united Egypt and ruled with the authority of gods.

DYNASTIES BEGIN

Egypt was governed by a long series of strong rulers. Exactly how Egypt united under a single ruler is uncertain. Tradition says that around 3100 B.C., the king of Upper Egypt conquered Lower Egypt and became ruler of all Egypt. Historians believe this king was called **Menes** (MEH-nehz). The complete unification of Egypt was probably a process that took place over the reigns of the kings who followed Menes. A double crown that combined the white crown of Upper Egypt with the red crown of Lower Egypt symbolized the newly unified country.

During this early period, the Egyptians built a magnificent new capital city at Memphis (MEHM-fihs). They also established the foundations of Egypt's political, economic, technological, artistic, and religious practices. The first kings

founded a ruling **dynasty** (DY-nuh-stee)—a series of rulers from the same family. Egypt had 31 dynasties and was ruled by a total of more than 330 kings.

PHARAOHS RULE

Even though Egyptians did not call their kings **pharaoh** (FEHR-oh) until after 1000 B.C., the title is generally used for all Egyptian kings. The people used the term because they were afraid to speak the king's name. Why did the pharaoh inspire such fear in his subjects? He had complete authority over all religious, civil, and military matters. He exercised absolute power of life and death over everyone. A pharaoh was more than a man; he was worshipped as the son of Egypt's gods and a living god himself.

In Egypt, religion and government strongly overlapped. The pharaoh's main religious role was to keep harmony by maintaining communication between Egypt's people and their gods. He was high priest of every temple and led the most important ceremonies, especially the New Year rituals to ensure bountiful harvests. With this godly role came risk. Success reinforced the pharaoh's power. Defeat, disease, or famine threatened his authority.

On the government side, the pharaoh dictated all the important decisions. He also led his armies into battle as commander-in-chief. However, much of his day-to-day work was actually done by his **viziers** (vuh-ZEERZ), or chief officials. At first each pharaoh had one vizier. Later pharaohs had two viziers—one ran Upper Egypt and the other ran Lower Egypt. Thousands of lesser officials supported the viziers.

Most pharaohs were men and had many wives. Commonly, the eldest son of the pharaoh's principal wife inherited the throne. He often ruled alongside his father, learning on the job and ensuring a smooth succession (the passing of the throne to the next ruler) when the pharaoh died.

+ POSSIBLE RESPONSE
The double crown symbolized the uniting of Upper Egypt and Lower Egypt into one country.

Critical Viewing This carving shows a pharaoh wearing the double crown of Egypt. Why was it important for the pharaohs to wear the double crown?

REVIEW & ASSESS

1. **READING CHECK** What made the pharaohs of ancient Egypt so strong and powerful?

2. **DRAW CONCLUSIONS** Why would disease or famine threaten the pharaoh's authority over the people?

3. **ANALYZE LANGUAGE USE** Why does the text refer to Egypt's rulers as *strong*?

6.2.3 Understand the relationship between religion and the social and political order in Mesopotamia and Egypt.

95

STANDARDS

HSS CONTENT STANDARDS:

6.2.3 Understand the relationship between religion and the social and political order in Mesopotamia and Egypt.

HSS ANALYSIS SKILLS:

REP 1 Students frame questions that can be answered by historical study and research.

PLAN

OBJECTIVE

Explain how strong kings united Egypt and ruled with the authority of gods.

ESSENTIAL QUESTION

How did ancient Egypt's rulers use the land's resources and geography to found a civilization?

Egypt had strong kings. Lesson 1.3 explains how the kings had complete authority over all religious, civil, and military matters.

BACKGROUND FOR THE TEACHER

In addition to crediting Menes with the unification of Egypt, he is also considered the founder of the capital, Memphis, near present-day Cairo. Memphis was an important center during much of Egyptian history. It is located south of the Nile River delta, on the west bank of the river, about 24 kilometers (15 miles) south of modern Cairo. As a series of dynasties ruled Egypt for nearly three millennia, Egyptian culture flourished and remained distinctively Egyptian in its religion, arts, language, and customs.

DIGITAL RESOURCES NGLSync.cengage.com

TEACHER RESOURCES & ASSESSMENT

 Reading and Note-Taking

 Vocabulary Practice

 Section 1 Quiz

STUDENT RESOURCES

 NG Image Gallery

INTRODUCE & ENGAGE

THINK, TALK, AND SHARE

Have students work in small groups. Ask each group to think about an elected government position in the United States. Then have students briefly tell about the kinds and amounts of authority an elected official in the United States has. Have them compare the authority of that elected official with the authority a pharaoh had. Ask one student from each group to present their ideas to the class. Tell students they will learn more about the rulers of Egypt in this lesson. **0:05** minutes

TEACH

GUIDED DISCUSSION

1. **Analyze Cause and Effect** For what reasons did ancient Egyptians respect the pharaoh's authority in the area of religion? *(A pharaoh was worshipped as the son of Egypt's gods and a living god himself. His main religious role was to maintain communication between Egypt's people and their gods.)*

2. **Make Inferences** Why might some of Egypt's pharaohs have been very capable and others less capable? *(The pharaohs were not chosen because of their intelligence or abilities. They inherited the throne regardless of their strengths and weaknesses.)*

ANALYZE VISUALS

Have students examine the photo of the carving showing a pharaoh wearing the double crown of Egypt. Invite volunteers to describe the crown. Make sure students understand that the crown represents the unification of Egypt. **0:10** minutes

ACTIVE OPTIONS

Critical Viewing: NG Image Gallery Invite students to explore the entire NG Image Gallery and create a Favorites List by choosing the images they find most interesting. If possible, have students copy the images into a document to form an actual list. Then encourage them to select the image they like best and do further research on it. **0:10** minutes

On Your Feet: Inside-Outside Circle Have students form concentric circles facing each other. Allow students time to write questions about the power and responsibilities of the pharaoh. Then have students in the inside circle pose questions to students in the outside circle. Have students switch roles. Students may ask for help from other students in their circle if they are unable to answer a question. **0:10** minutes

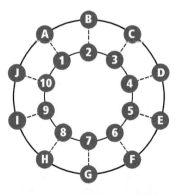

DIFFERENTIATE

INCLUSION

Expand the Main Idea Statement Pair each student with a proficient reader. Provide students with the expanded Main Idea statement below. Have students ask any clarifying questions before reading the lesson. To expand the Main Idea even further, ask students to add a sentence to the expanded statement after reading the lesson.

Historians believe the king of Upper Egypt conquered Lower Egypt and became ruler of all Egypt. This king and the rulers that followed had complete power over all matters in Egypt and were worshipped like gods.

ENGLISH LANGUAGE LEARNERS `ELD`

Monitor Comprehension Monitor the comprehension of students at the **Emerging** level by asking them to answer either/or questions about the lesson.

- Did the double crown represent Upper Egypt, Lower Egypt, or both Upper and Lower Egypt? *(both Upper and Lower Egypt)*
- Is a dynasty a series of rulers from different families or from the same family? *(the same family)*
- Did the pharaoh share power over religious matters or did he hold all the power? *(He held all the power.)*
- Did the pharaoh make important military decisions alone or with help from his lesser officials? *(alone)*
- Did the viziers assist with day-to-day work or did the pharaohs handle the day-to-day work themselves? *(The viziers assisted.)*

Press **mt** *in the Student eEdition for modified text.*

See the Chapter Planner for more strategies for differentiation.

REVIEW & ASSESS

ANSWERS

1. Pharaohs had complete authority over all aspects of government and the power of life and death over all Egyptians. Egyptians believed pharaohs were living gods.

2. The pharaoh was supposed to control natural events, such as disease and crops. If he failed, that might mean he was not keeping the other gods happy.

3. In this sense of the word, *strong* means "powerful." Because the pharaoh had complete power in Egypt, he must be considered "strong."

Sensing Under the Surface

"Indiana Jones is so old school," laughs National Geographic Explorer Sarah Parcak. "I'm sorry, Indy, but things have moved on!" Parcak should know—she's a leading specialist in satellite archaeology. She is pioneering technology that archaeologists never would have dreamed of decades ago.

After identifying the likely location of an ancient city, Sarah Parcak and her team head for the site to begin the hands-on excavation. Together, technology and muscle power are revealing ancient Egypt.

MAIN IDEA

Sarah Parcak uses satellite imagery to guide her archaeological excavations in Egypt.

SATELLITE TECHNOLOGY

Sarah Parcak prepares for another tough day of searching beneath Egypt's desert for evidence of ancient Egyptian civilization and its people's daily lives. However, instead of digging, she boots up her laptop.

Parcak relies on remote sensing, using powerful infrared cameras mounted on satellites. These cameras use invisible rays of light to pinpoint even small objects buried beneath sand, soil, vegetation, or new buildings. "The Egyptians built with mud-bricks, which are denser than the surrounding soil," explains Parcak. "The infrared picks out this denser material. Computer programs refine the detail until we start to see recognizable shapes—houses, streets, temples, tombs, and pyramids. It's a real 'wow' moment."

Yet these revelations only happen after painstaking processing and analysis. "We don't just grab an image, flip it into the computer, and press a button. I've spent more than 10,000 hours of my life staring at satellite imagery to understand what I'm seeing," says Parcak. This effort pays off, saving enormous amounts of time and money. Before leading an expedition to Egypt, Parcak analyzed satellite imagery to figure out exactly where to dig. Within three weeks, she found about 70 sites. With traditional methods, this research would have taken around three and a half years.

A satellite image of the Great Pyramid of Giza

MAPPING TANIS

Parcak's hard work has uncovered the main settlement area of Tanis, an important city in the eastern part of the Nile Delta. Over the centuries, Tanis was flooded and buried beneath Nile silt. Until recently only a tiny area had been excavated, but archaeologists, with the help of remote sensing, are changing that. Parcak turned the cameras onto Tanis with startling results. "We've created a map of this ancient city that's so clear it looks like something you'd use to navigate a town today," she says.

Excavations on the ground are proving the value of remote sensing. Scientists found an 80 percent match between the satellite image and the houses they unearthed. "This isn't just another 'gee whiz' toy," Parcak claims. "Less than one percent of ancient Egypt has been discovered and excavated, and, with the pressures of urbanization [the growth of cities], we're in a race against time. We need to use the most advanced tools to explore, map, and protect our past." Right now, satellites are just the tools for the job.

REVIEW & ASSESS

1. **READING CHECK** How does satellite imagery help guide Sarah Parcak's archaeological excavations in Egypt?

2. **COMPARE AND CONTRAST** What advantages does satellite archaeology have compared to more traditional methods of archaeology?

3. **MAKE INFERENCES** Why do you think urbanization creates a problem for the discovery and exploration of ancient Egyptian sites?

HI 5 Students recognize that interpretations of history are subject to change as new information is uncovered.

HSS ANALYSIS SKILLS:

HI 5 Students recognize that interpretations of history are subject to change as new information is uncovered.

PLAN

OBJECTIVE

Explain how National Geographic Explorer Sarah Parcak uses satellite imagery to guide her archaeological excavations in Egypt.

ESSENTIAL QUESTION

How did ancient Egypt's rulers use the land's resources and geography to found a civilization?

Egypt's geography and its resources affected the development of its civilization. Lesson 1.4 explains how National Geographic Explorer Sarah Parcak uses satellite imagery to get information about the land, geography, and civilization in ancient Egypt.

BACKGROUND FOR THE TEACHER

Sarah Parcak received her Bachelor's degree in Egyptology and Archaeological Studies from Yale University and her Ph.D. from Cambridge University. Parcak is an American archaeologist, space archaeologist, and Egyptologist who uses satellite imaging to identify potential archaeological sites in Egypt and Rome. Parcak believes that one of her most important contributions, however, is writing the first methodology book on satellite archaeology, which will allow the next generation of students to learn and advance the new field. She has pointed out that people need deep knowledge of historical events, the geology of how materials degrade over time, the landscapes, weather conditions, and culture before they can use satellites to make discoveries.

DIGITAL RESOURCES NGLSync.cengage.com

TEACHER RESOURCES & ASSESSMENT

 Reading and Note-Taking

 Vocabulary Practice

 Section 1 Quiz

STUDENT RESOURCES

 NG Chapter Gallery

INTRODUCE & ENGAGE

PREVIEW AND DISCUSS

Organize students into groups of four and assign each student a number: one, two, three, or four. Tell students to think about and discuss a response to this question: *What would you like to learn about an ancient city in Egypt and the people who lived there?* Then call a number and have the student from each group with that number explain their group's response to the question. If time permits, repeat the process with an additional question: *What types of ancient artifacts from a region might give information about an ancient city and the people who lived there?* Tell students they will learn about the work of National Geographic Explorer Sarah Parcak in this lesson. **0:10** minutes

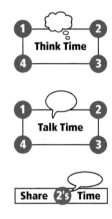

TEACH   STEM

GUIDED DISCUSSION

1. **Evaluate** How might the use of satellite imagery affect scientists' abilities to learn details about ancient civilizations? *(Satellite imagery can pinpoint even very small objects under the surface of the earth. This imagery can give accurate information to scientists about where to dig and what they might expect to find. It helps scientists explore and map things from the past in a way that saves much time and money.)*

2. **Draw Conclusions** Why might uncovering a city such as Tanis provide a wealth of information about ancient Egyptian society? *(The satellite imagery helped scientists map the ancient city of Tanis in great detail. It led to excavations that included unearthing many houses, which helped scientists understand more about how ancient Egyptians lived.)*

ANALYZE VISUALS

Have students examine the satellite image of the Great Pyramid of Giza. Ask students to describe what they see in the image. Then initiate a class discussion on the benefits of using satellite images in archaeology. **0:10** minutes

ACTIVE OPTIONS

NG Learning Framework: Learn More About Tanis

ATTITUDE: **Curiosity**
KNOWLEDGE: **Our Human Story**

Have students review the information about National Geographic Explorer Sarah Parcak. Then have them do research about the ancient city of Tanis and the tombs and treasures archaeologists have found there. **ASK:** What can scientists learn about ancient Egypt and its people from the burial chambers and the objects found at Tanis? **0:10** minutes

---

On Your Feet: Create a Quiz Organize students into two teams and have each team write ten True-False questions about using satellite imagery to guide archaeological excavations in Egypt. Then have each team answer the questions the other team created. Review the student answers as a class and have teams keep track of their number of correct answers. **0:15** minutes

DIFFERENTIATE

STRIVING READERS

Pose and Answer Questions Have students work in pairs to read the lesson. Instruct them to pause after each paragraph and ask one another a *who, what, when, where,* or *why* question about what they have just read. Suggest students use a 5Ws Chart to help organize their questions and answers.

What?
Who?
Where?
When?
Why?

GIFTED & TALENTED

Write a Documentary Script Have students conduct research about the work of Sarah Parcak. Tell them to write a five-minute documentary about Sarah that focuses on her use of satellite imagery to guide her archaeological excavations. Students should include information about the value of satellite imagery as well as the importance of doing hands-on excavations. Have students present their documentary scripts to the class.

Press **mt** *in the Student eEdition for modified text.*

See the Chapter Planner for more strategies for differentiation.

REVIEW & ASSESS

ANSWERS

1. Satellite imagery helps Sarah Parcak figure out where to dig by revealing details of objects, houses, streets, temples, tombs, and pyramids buried beneath sand, soil, vegetation, or new buildings.

2. Because of the accuracy of the satellite imagery captured by powerful infrared cameras, space archaeology can save archaeologists enormous amounts of time and money in locating excavation sites.

3. With urbanization, large populations of people need more land and resources and more buildings in which to live. That means people are always building new structures over ancient Egyptian sites that have not yet been excavated. Urbanization could literally pave over the past of ancient Egypt.

2.1 The Old Kingdom

It is taller than the Statue of Liberty, twice the area of the U.S. Capitol building, double the volume of the Rose Bowl Stadium, and 4,500 years older than all of them. For thousands of years, the Great Pyramid of Khufu was the largest structure on the planet.

MAIN IDEA

Old Kingdom pharaohs demonstrated their power by building monumental pyramids.

The great pyramids of Giza dwarf the human figures nearby. These imposing structures would have awed the average Egyptian in ancient times, just as they amaze visitors today.

PYRAMIDS ALONG THE NILE

The **Old Kingdom** was Egypt's first great period of unity and prosperity, lasting from around 2700 B.C. to 2200 B.C. During these centuries, Egypt prospered under effective pharaohs, a strong central government, and an efficient administration. As Egyptian power grew, trade, technology, building, writing, and art also flourished. The pharaohs used their enormous wealth and power to build the **pyramids** (PEER-uh-mihdz), massive monumental tombs to house their dead bodies. The pyramids represented the Egyptian belief that life is a passageway to the afterlife, an existence believed to follow death. As a result, people made careful preparations for death.

Egyptian kings were originally buried beneath low mud-brick buildings. Around 2650 B.C., King Djoser (JOH-sur) took this idea to the next level—literally. Djoser's talented vizier, Imhotep (ihm-HOH-tehp), designed a 200-foot-high tomb made of giant steps. Beneath this step pyramid was a maze of chambers packed with items for the pharaoh's spirit to use in the afterlife. A huge complex of buildings and temples surrounded the step pyramid, creating a palace where the king's spirit could live in luxury for eternity.

THE GREAT PYRAMID

In Giza (GEE-zuh), near Cairo, the Great Pyramid of **Khufu** (KOO-foo) dominates the skyline. It is so extraordinarily huge that historians once assumed Khufu had been a cruel tyrant who used brutal methods to build it. In fact, he probably employed farmers unable to farm during the annual floods. Even so, Khufu must have commanded exceptional power and wealth to build his Great Pyramid.

The pyramids were an impressive achievement for a civilization with limited technology. Using copper tools, ropes, sleds, and ramps, some 18,000 workers quarried, cut, and precisely placed 2.3 million two-and-a-half-ton limestone and granite blocks. It took 20 years. The pyramid they built was symmetrical—all sides were the same. It covered 571,158 square feet and stood 481 feet high. Deep inside were Khufu's tomb and treasure. Two other large pyramids were built in Giza by Khufu's successors, Menkaure (mehn-KO-ray) and Khafre (KAH-fray). Khafre also built the Great Sphinx (sfihnks), a symbol of divine power with a lion's body and Khafre's head. The sphinx was carved out of a huge piece of limestone.

The Great Pyramid was a powerful symbol of the pharaoh's status as a living god and the unity of religion and government in Egypt. A proper burial within the great tomb would ensure the pharaoh's smooth passage to life after death. Until then, a vast city of pyramid builders surrounded Giza. Here, too, were palaces and government buildings that allowed the pharaoh to run the country while building his home for the afterlife.

REVIEW & ASSESS

1. **READING CHECK** Why did Old Kingdom pharaohs build pyramids?

2. **DESCRIBE** What was new and different about the design of King Djoser's burial building?

3. **DRAW CONCLUSIONS** What do the pyramids reveal about Egyptian society?

6.2.5 Discuss the main features of Egyptian art and architecture.

HSS CONTENT STANDARDS:

6.2.3 Understand the relationship between religion and the social and political order in Mesopotamia and Egypt; **6.2.5** Discuss the main features of Egyptian art and architecture.

HSS ANALYSIS SKILLS:

HI 2 Students understand and distinguish cause, effect, sequence, and correlation in historical events, including the long- and short-term causal relations.

PLAN

OBJECTIVE

Explain how Old Kingdom pharaohs demonstrated their power by building monumental pyramids.

ESSENTIAL QUESTION

How did ancient Egypt's rulers use the land's resources and geography to found a civilization?

The Egyptian pyramids remain today as evidence of an advanced civilization that prospered along the Nile River. Lesson 2.1 discusses the purpose of the pyramids, explains how they were built, and describes the largest of them.

BACKGROUND FOR THE TEACHER

Initially, the Great Pyramid of Khufu stood 481 feet high. Over time, erosion has worn away the limestone and granite surface that once covered the outside of the pyramid. As a result, today the Great Pyramid is only 449 feet tall.

The interior of the Great Pyramid has three separate burial chambers. Ancient Egyptians believed that the dead could enjoy earthly possessions, so they filled burial chambers with clothes, food, and furniture for that purpose. Pyramid builders tried to guard against robberies by building heavy walls around the entrance. However, many pyramids were looted and many treasures disappeared.

DIGITAL RESOURCES NGLSync.cengage.com

TEACHER RESOURCES & ASSESSMENT

 Reading and Note-Taking

 Vocabulary Practice

 Section 2 Quiz

STUDENT RESOURCES

 NG Chapter Gallery

INTRODUCE & ENGAGE

MAKE A TEAM WORD WEB

Organize students into teams of four and give each team a large sheet of paper, like the one shown, with the word *pyramids* in the center. Give each student a different colored marker. Encourage students to write what they already know about the pyramids. Prompt students to rotate the paper clockwise every 60 seconds. After students have written on all four sides of the paper, have a spokesperson from each team summarize what the team knows about the pyramids. Tell students they will learn more about Egyptian pyramids in this lesson. At the conclusion of the lesson, you may want to return to this activity to verify accuracy of the information students offered. `0:05` **minutes**

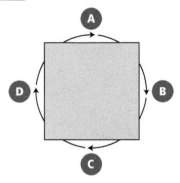

TEACH

GUIDED DISCUSSION

1. **Summarize** How did Egyptian workers build monumental pyramids with limited technology? *(Approximately 18,000 workers used copper tools, ropes, sleds, and ramps to quarry, cut, move, and place the heavy stone blocks that were used to build the pyramids.)*

2. **Make Inferences** Why did cities arise near Giza? *(Many workers were needed to build the pyramids at Giza. They needed places to live, leaders, and government services located close to the place at which they were working.)*

ANALYZE VISUALS

Have students examine the photo of the great pyramids of Giza. Ask small groups of students to brainstorm a list of adjectives that describe the pyramids. Have students share their adjectives with the class. `0:10` **minutes**

ACTIVE OPTIONS

NG Learning Framework: Discuss the Importance of Pyramids

ATTITUDE: **Responsibility**
SKILL: **Collaboration**

Invite small groups of students to discuss the importance of the pyramids in ancient Egypt. **ASK:** What do the pyramids tell us about the respect the ancient Egyptians had for their pharaohs? What do the pyramids tell us about the importance of religion in Egyptian society? Ask each person in every group to contribute his or her ideas. Encourage students to listen quietly and politely when another person is talking. `0:10` **minutes**

On Your Feet: Fishbowl Use a Fishbowl strategy to have students discuss the pyramids in ancient Egypt. Instruct students in the inside circle to discuss the significance of the pyramids while the outside circle listens. Then call on volunteers in the outside circle to summarize what they heard. Have students switch places and ask those now on the inside to discuss how the pyramids were built and how the building of the pyramids affected the growth of communities. The outside circle should listen and then summarize what they heard. `0:10` **minutes**

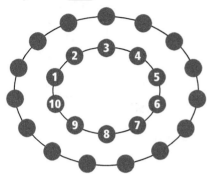

DIFFERENTIATE

GIFTED & TALENTED   STEM

Build Models Work with students to build three-dimensional paper models of the pyramids. Pair students up and give each pair a large sheet of paper and a template for a six-inch square and a six-inch equilateral triangle. Instruct them to trace the square in the middle of the paper. Next, have them trace an equilateral triangle off of each side of the square, so that the base of each triangle is one of the sides of the square. Now tell them to cut out the diagram and then fold each triangle along the edge attached to the square. They will see how the points come together to form the pyramid. Students may use tape to hold the sides in place.

PRE-AP

Create Photo Displays Have students do research to learn more about famous pieces of art, artifacts, and buildings inspired by the religion of the ancient Egyptians. Instruct them to create a display of pictures and information based on their research. Invite students to share their displays with the class.

Press (**mt**) *in the Student eEdition for modified text.*

See the Chapter Planner for more strategies for differentiation.

REVIEW & ASSESS

ANSWERS

1. Old Kingdom pharaohs used their wealth and power to build the pyramids as monumental tombs where their dead bodies could be guarded and their immortal spirits could live in luxury for eternity.

2. King Djoser's pyramid was the first completely stone building. Its design looked like a series of giant steps.

3. The pyramids reveal much about ancient Egyptian culture and religion. They also demonstrate the engineering skills of ancient Egyptians.

2.2 Daily Life and Religion

There's a saying that "you can't take it with you" when you die. But Egyptians did! In fact, they were buried with everything they might need in the afterlife. The graves of wealthy Egyptians contained food, furniture, and jewelry. The Egyptians were ready for anything.

MAIN IDEA

The Egyptians had strong beliefs about religion and burial that affected all social classes.

Eight Gods of Ancient Egypt

Horus Sky god

Hathor Goddess of love, birth, and death

Re God of the sun (sometimes called Ra)

Nut Sky goddess

Anubis God of the dead

Osiris God of agriculture and judge of the dead

Isis Wife of Osiris and mother of Horus

Thoth God of writing, counting, and wisdom

EGYPTIAN SOCIETY

Ancient Egypt's society was a **hierarchy** (HY-rar-kee), meaning that people belonged to different social classes and each class had a rank in society. The social structure resembled Egypt's pyramids. At the top was the pharaoh, the all-powerful ruler and living god.

Beneath the pharaoh came the priests and nobles who ran the country and army. At the next step in the pyramid were all the officials and scribes who kept the government running smoothly by collecting taxes, organizing building projects, and keeping records. Beneath the officials and scribes were craftsmen and merchants. Farmers formed the next layer, and at the bottom came unskilled laborers and slaves who did all the hardest work.

Unlike in Mesopotamia, Egyptian women shared some rights with men. They could own property, conduct business, and take part in court cases. Poorer women often worked alongside their husbands, but they could do almost any job. Still, a woman's main role was to be a wife and raise children.

EGYPTIAN GODS

Like the people of Mesopotamia, the Egyptians believed in multiple gods. Modern scholars know 1,500 of them by name. The Egyptians believed that the gods controlled every aspect of life and death. The most important god was **Re** (RAY), the sun god, who created the world. The Egyptians also worshipped Osiris (oh-SY-rihs), the god of the underworld. The god Anubis (uh-NOO-bihs) weighed each dead person's heart against the weight of an ostrich feather. If the person was good, his or her heart would weigh the same as the feather, and the person would be admitted to the afterlife.

These beliefs encouraged Egyptians to lead good lives and take burial seriously. They believed a dead person's spirit needed food and a body to live in. The spirit would need to recognize the body after death. That is why the bodies of pharaohs and other powerful people were preserved as **mummies**. Specialized workers removed and preserved the internal organs (except for the heart, which Anubis had to weigh). Then the workers dried out the body and wrapped it in linen. Last, the body was placed in a coffin, and priests performed special rituals that were intended to give life to the mummy.

+ POSSIBLE RESPONSE

Egyptians painted the god Anubis on their tombs because Anubis was the god who weighed each dead person's heart against the weight of an ostrich feather. If the person had been good, his or her heart would weigh the same as the feather, and the person would be admitted to the afterlife.

Critical Viewing The jackal-headed god Anubis often appears on tomb walls. Why did Egyptians paint this god on their tombs?

REVIEW & ASSESS

1. **READING CHECK** How was Egyptian society organized?

2. **COMPARE** How were the ancient Egyptians' religious beliefs similar to those of the people of Mesopotamia?

3. **DRAW CONCLUSIONS** How did religion affect daily life in ancient Egypt?

6.2.3 Understand the relationship between religion and the social and political order in Mesopotamia and Egypt.

PLAN

OBJECTIVE

Explain how the strong beliefs the Egyptians had about religion and burial affected all social classes.

ESSENTIAL QUESTION

How did ancient Egypt's rulers use the land's resources and geography to found a civilization?

The Egyptians' strong beliefs about religion and burial affected all parts of their society. Lesson 2.2 discusses the hierarchy in Egyptian society and the importance of religion and burial in Egyptian civilization.

BACKGROUND FOR THE TEACHER

When they preserved mummies, the Egyptians began by covering the body with a salty substance to dry it out. Once the body was dry, they used lotions on the skin to preserve it. They then wrapped the entire body in layers of linen and glued the layers together. The total process could take up to 40 days. Once the body was all wrapped, it was covered in a sheet and placed in a stone coffin called a sarcophagus.

The heart was left in the body of the mummy because it was considered to be the center of intelligence. The brain was thrown away because it was thought to be useless. Sometimes the mummy's mouth would be opened to symbolize breathing in the afterlife.

DIGITAL RESOURCES NGLSync.cengage.com

TEACHER RESOURCES & ASSESSMENT

 Reading and Note-Taking

 Vocabulary Practice

 Section 2 Quiz

STUDENT RESOURCES

 NG Chapter Gallery

INTRODUCE & ENGAGE

CHOOSE A CORNER

Divide the class into four groups. Then give each group one of the following topics:

- Lives of pharaohs
- Lives of everyday people
- Religion
- Building of pyramids

Have each group of students create a list of questions about their topic. Then have at least one student from each group share the group's questions with the class. Tell students they will learn about daily life and religion in ancient Egypt. After students read the lesson, have them answer their questions. **0:10 minutes**

 1's   3's

 2's   4's

TEACH

GUIDED DISCUSSION

1. **Describe** What was the role of women in ancient Egyptian society? *(Women shared some rights with men. They could own property and do almost any job. However, their main role was to be a wife and mother.)*

2. **Summarize** For what reason were bodies of pharaohs and other important people preserved as mummies? *(The Egyptians believed that a dead person's spirit needed a body in which to live. They also believed that the spirit would need to recognize the body after death.)*

ANALYZE VISUALS

Have students examine the picture of the tomb wall. Ask them to discuss the images that relate to nature and make inferences about the significance of these images. **0:10 minutes**

ACTIVE OPTIONS

Critical Viewing: NG Chapter Gallery Ask students to choose one image from the Chapter Gallery and become an expert on it. They should do additional research to learn all about it. Then, students should share their findings with a partner, small group, or the class. **0:10 minutes**

On Your Feet: Compare and Contrast Two Civilizations Tape the following signs to the wall in different parts of the classroom: Mesopotamia; Egypt; Both. Read aloud the following characteristics of Mesopotamian and Egyptian society. For each characteristic, instruct students to stand near the sign of the society that displays it. If there are differences of opinion, stop to discuss the correct choice.

- Society was organized according to a strict hierarchy. *(Both)*
- Women shared some rights with men. *(Egypt)*
- The ruler was worshipped as a god. *(Egypt)*
- Religion involved the worship of many gods. *(Both)*
- Government was controlled by individual city-states. *(Mesopotamia)*

0:15 minutes

DIFFERENTIATE

STRIVING READERS

Use Exit Slips Preview the following questions before reading the lesson.

- What does it mean when we say that ancient Egypt's society was a hierarchy?
- Who was at the top of the Egyptian hierarchy?
- What do you know about whether the Egyptians believed in gods?

After reading the lesson, direct students to provide a written response to each question. Pass out strips of paper. Have students write their responses on the paper strips. Then ask students to turn in their written responses as they exit the class.

PRE-AP

Research an Egyptian God Have students do research to learn more about one of the eight gods of ancient Egypt. Then have them write and illustrate a book about the god. Have them include ideas about how the god may have influenced Egyptian life.

Press **mt** *in the Student eEdition for modified text.*

See the Chapter Planner for more strategies for differentiation.

REVIEW & ASSESS

ANSWERS

1. Ancient Egypt's society was a hierarchy. People belonged to different social classes and each class had a rank in society. The social structure resembled a pyramid. At the top was the pharaoh, then priests and nobles, then the officials and scribes, then the craftsmen and merchants, then farmers. At the bottom were unskilled laborers and slaves who did the hardest work.

2. Similar to the Mesopotamians, ancient Egyptians practiced polytheism. They believed in many different gods and goddesses who controlled every aspect of life and death.

3. Religious beliefs encouraged Egyptians to lead good lives and take burial seriously.

DOCUMENT-BASED QUESTION

Life, Death, and Religion

The majority of ancient Egyptians could not read or write. Still, a vast amount of writing has survived in the form of official records, business transactions, religious texts, technical manuals, and stories. These documents tell us a lot about life in ancient Egypt.

The ancient Egyptian *Book of the Dead* helped archaeologists learn much about the civilization's religious beliefs. Here, a section of the book illustrates a vision of the afterlife that closely resembles the living world.

DOCUMENT ONE
Primary Source: Poem

from *Hymn to the Nile*, c. 2100 B.C., translated by Paul Guieysse
Hymn to the Nile is a religious poem. It may have been read aloud at festivals celebrating the annual Nile flood. It has about 200 lines divided into 14 verses, although historians are not sure how the verses should be read. The hymn praises the Nile as the source of all life in Egypt. It expresses the people's joy when the flood brings water and silt and their misery when the flood fails. The author is unknown.

CONSTRUCTED RESPONSE Why might ancient Egyptians have wanted to praise the Nile River each year by reciting this religious poem?

> Hail to thee, O Nile!
> Who manifests [reveals] thyself over this land, and comes to give life to Egypt!
> Mysterious is thy issuing forth from the darkness, on this day whereon it is celebrated!
> Watering the orchards created by Re, to cause all the cattle to live, you give the earth to drink, inexhaustible one!

DOCUMENT TWO
Primary Source: Sacred Text

from the *Book of the Dead*, 1240 B.C., translated by E.A. Wallis Budge
The *Book of the Dead* was a series of texts that contained around 200 spells for helping the dead reach the afterlife. The texts were usually placed in the coffin or in the mummy's wrappings. This passage describes the sun god's journey as he rises and sets each day.

CONSTRUCTED RESPONSE What does this passage suggest about Re's role in ancient Egyptian beliefs?

> The gods are glad [when] they see Re in his rising; his beams flood the world with light. The majesty of the god, who is to be feared, sets forth and comes unto the land of Manu [a sacred place]; he makes bright the earth at his birth each day; he comes unto the place where he was yesterday.

DOCUMENT THREE
Primary Source: Artifact

Sun God Re in Falcon Form, Ancient Egypt
This statue depicts Re, god of the sun and creator of Earth.

CONSTRUCTED RESPONSE What can you infer about Re's connection to nature from his representation in this statue?

SYNTHESIZE & WRITE

1. **REVIEW** Review what you have learned about ancient Egyptian religious beliefs from the text and these documents.

2. **RECALL** On your own paper, write down the main idea expressed in the artifact and in each document.

3. **CONSTRUCT** Construct a topic sentence that answers this question: What did the Egyptians believe about their gods' control of their world?

4. **WRITE** Using the evidence from the artifact and documents, write an informative paragraph that supports your topic sentence in Step 3.

6.2.3 Understand the relationship between religion and the social and political order in Mesopotamia and Egypt; REP 4 Students assess the credibility of primary and secondary sources and draw sound conclusions from them.

STANDARDS

HSS CONTENT STANDARDS:

6.2.1 Locate and describe the major river systems and discuss the physical settings that supported permanent settlement and early civilizations; **6.2.3** Understand the relationship between religion and the social and political order in Mesopotamia and Egypt.

HSS ANALYSIS SKILLS:

REP 4 Students assess the credibility of primary and secondary sources and draw sound conclusions from them.

PLAN

OBJECTIVE

Synthesize information about life, death, and religion in ancient Egypt from primary source documents.

ESSENTIAL QUESTION

How did ancient Egypt's rulers use the land's resources and geography to found a civilization?

The Egyptians had very strong religious beliefs. Lesson 2.3 provides several examples from primary sources of the importance of religion in Egyptian society.

BACKGROUND FOR THE TEACHER

The *Book of the Dead* was an ancient Egyptian funerary text. It contained spells and illustrations that, according to Egyptian belief, gave a dead person the knowledge and power he or she needed to journey safely through the dangers of the netherworld (a place the dead went immediately after death). The spells also spoke of the ultimate goal of every ancient Egyptian—eternal life. Written by many priests over about 1,000 years, the *Book of the Dead* was put into use at the beginning of the New Kingdom.

DIGITAL RESOURCES NGLSync.cengage.com

TEACHER RESOURCES & ASSESSMENT

 Reading and Note-Taking

 Vocabulary Practice

 Section 2 Quiz

STUDENT RESOURCES

 NG Chapter Gallery

INTRODUCE & ENGAGE

PREPARE FOR THE DOCUMENT-BASED QUESTION

Before students start on the activity, briefly preview the three documents. Remind students that a constructed response requires full explanations in complete sentences. Emphasize that students should use their knowledge of ancient Egyptian society and religious beliefs as well as information in the documents. **0:05** minutes

TEACH

GUIDED DISCUSSION

1. **Identify** What does the hymn say about the Egyptian people's responses to the annual Nile flood? (*The hymn says that people are joyful about the annual Nile flood.*)

2. **Draw Conclusions** What does the text from the *Book of the Dead* tell us about the role of religion in the lives of the ancient Egyptians? (*The text indicates that Egyptians had a strong religious belief that life on Earth was a passageway to the afterlife.*)

3. **Describe** Which words or phrases would you use to describe this artifact of Sun God Re? (*Responses will vary. Possible responses: looks like a falcon; has a model of the earth on his head; model or sculpture*)

EVALUATE

After students have completed the "Synthesize & Write" activity, allow time for them to exchange paragraphs and read and comment on the work of their peers. Guidelines for comments should be established prior to this activity so that feedback is constructive and encouraging in nature. **0:15** minutes

ACTIVE OPTIONS

NG Learning Framework: Review Information About the Nile

SKILL: Collaboration
KNOWLEDGE: Our Living Planet

Have pairs of students revisit Lessons 1.1 and 1.2 to review information about the Nile River. **ASK**: How was the Nile River important to the development of Egyptian civilization? What does the poem *Hymn to the Nile* tell you about how the Egyptians felt about the Nile? **0:10** minutes

On Your Feet: Three Options Label three locations in the room with the name of one of the documents featured in the lesson. Have students reread the lesson and walk to the corner of the room with the document that best helped support their understanding or further their interest in life, death, and religion in ancient Egypt. Have students who chose the same document discuss why they made their selection. Then have volunteers from each group explain what their document is and offer some of the group's reasons for choosing that one. **0:20** minutes

DIFFERENTIATE

INCLUSION

Work in Pairs Consider pairing students with disabilities with students able to read the documents aloud to them. You may also want to give students the option of recording their responses.

GIFTED & TALENTED

Present a Report Have students work in small groups to do research about famous pieces of art, artifacts, and buildings inspired by the religion of the ancient Egyptians. Instruct them to prepare a report based on their research. Encourage students to include visuals such as photographs or drawings to illustrate the report. Have each group present its report to the class.

Press **mt** in the Student eEdition for modified text.

See the Chapter Planner for more strategies for differentiation.

CONSTRUCTED RESPONSE

ANSWERS
DOCUMENT 1
By reciting this religious poem in praise of the Nile River each year, ancient Egyptians probably hoped to ensure another successful flooding of the Nile, which brought them much needed water and fertile soil.

DOCUMENT 2
It suggests that Re is responsible for causing the sun to rise and for keeping the world running.

DOCUMENT 3
It can be inferred that Egyptians associated Re with other forms of nature in addition to the sun. It shows that Re was connected with all parts of the natural world.

SYNTHESIZE & WRITE

ANSWERS
1. Responses will vary but should show a comprehension of the materials.

2. Responses will vary but should specifically reference the sources.

3. Possible response: The Egyptians believed that the gods controlled every aspect of life and death.

4. Students' paragraphs should include their topic sentence from Step 3 and provide several details from the documents to support the sentence.

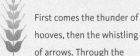

2.4 The Middle Kingdom

First comes the thunder of hooves, then the whistling of arrows. Through the dust of battle bursts a line of horse-drawn chariots. From these wheeled wooden platforms, enemy archers rain arrows into your ranks before crashing through them, scattering your Egyptian army. These foreign war machines are effective; it's time to adopt, adapt, and fight back.

MAIN IDEA

The Middle Kingdom was strong and peaceful between periods of weakness and foreign rule.

CONFLICT AND STABILITY

The peace and prosperity of the Old Kingdom gave way to chaos and war between rival Egyptian groups around 2200 B.C. Building monumental tombs had drained the royal treasury. Water shortages and famines made the people doubt the pharaoh's power as a living god. The kingdom descended into a long period of conflict within its borders.

Then, around 2040 B.C., a king named Mentuhotep II (mehn-too-HOH-tehp) reunited the kingdom and launched a new era of peace and prosperity known as the **Middle Kingdom**. This period

lasted until about 1650 B.C. During the Middle Kingdom, the pharaohs restored the power of the centralized government. Farmers expanded agriculture into new regions, and the building of great monuments, including pyramids, resumed.

The pharaohs also pursued an active foreign policy to increase Egypt's wealth. Trade expanded greatly. Egypt's trade network reached to several nearby lands and possibly as far as East Africa. To support and expand the prosperity of the Middle Kingdom, the pharaohs increased Egypt's military power. In the northeast, they conquered lands along the eastern Mediterranean. They also extended Egypt's southern border further up the Nile by leading successful military campaigns against the kingdoms of Nubia (NOO-bee-uh).

INVADERS

Egypt's wealth made a tempting target. One group of foreigners, the **Hyksos** (HIHK-sohs), came to live in Egypt and rose to power in Lower Egypt. The Hyksos brought an end to the Middle Kingdom.

Hyksos means "rulers of foreign lands," and, from their capital Avaris (AH-var-ihs) in the Nile Delta, they controlled much of Egypt for more than 100 years. The Hyksos probably ruled pretty much as the pharaohs had, adopting native ways and practices. Even so, native Egyptians resented being under foreign rule. Finally, in Upper Egypt, King **Ahmose** (AH-mohz) rebelled. The Hyksos brought to the battlefield deadly new tools including horse-drawn chariots, powerful new bows, curved swords, and body armor. Ahmose adopted these deadly weapons and threw the invaders out of Egypt.

Although Ahmose reunited Egypt under native Egyptian rule, he faced new challenges. Egypt had been largely on its own for centuries, but now the pharaohs had to deal with the wider world. Armed with their new military might, the pharaohs set out to forge an empire.

+ POSSIBLE RESPONSE

The depiction shows that the Egyptians considered the pharaoh to be the son of Egypt's gods and a living god himself.

Critical Viewing This pendant depicts the pharaoh Ahmose being purified by the gods Re and Amun. Why is the pharaoh shown with the gods?

REVIEW & ASSESS

1. **READING CHECK** Who were the Hyksos?

2. **ANALYZE CAUSE AND EFFECT** Why did the pharaohs lose control of the Old Kingdom?

3. **SEQUENCE EVENTS** What events marked Egypt's movements back and forth between disorder and order?

6.2.6 Describe the role of Egyptian trade in the eastern Mediterranean and Nile valley; CST 1 Students explain how major events are related to one another in time; HI 2 Students understand and distinguish cause, effect, sequence, and correlation in historical events, including the long- and short-term causal relations.

STANDARDS

HSS CONTENT STANDARDS:

6.2.1 Locate and describe the major river systems and discuss the physical settings that supported permanent settlement and early civilizations; **6.2.6** Describe the role of Egyptian trade in the eastern Mediterranean and Nile valley.

HSS ANALYSIS SKILLS:

CST 1 Students explain how major events are related to one another in time; **HI 2** Students understand and distinguish cause, effect, sequence, and correlation in historical events, including the long- and short-term causal relations.

PLAN

OBJECTIVE

Describe the Middle Kingdom as strong and peaceful between periods of weakness and foreign rule.

ESSENTIAL QUESTION

How did ancient Egypt's rulers use the land's resources and geography to found a civilization?

The Middle Kingdom had strong and successful periods in which its civilization advanced. It also had periods of weakness and foreign invasion. Lesson 2.4 discusses some of the changes and events that occurred during the Middle Kingdom.

BACKGROUND FOR THE TEACHER

The Egyptians achieved much during the Middle Kingdom. New styles and techniques in art developed, including art that was produced using large blocks of stone. New irrigation projects were also developed on the west bank of the Nile in Lower Egypt, which increased harvests. Writing changed, too. Before the Middle Kingdom, Egyptians used writing for record-keeping and for honoring the gods and goddesses. In the Middle Kingdom, Egyptians began to use writing to tell stories.

DIGITAL RESOURCES NGLSync.cengage.com

TEACHER RESOURCES & ASSESSMENT

 Reading and Note-Taking

 Vocabulary Practice

 Section 2 Quiz

STUDENT RESOURCES

 NG Chapter Gallery

HOLD A ROUNDTABLE DISCUSSION

Have students sit in groups of four. Prompt them to talk about the importance of the Nile River to the development of civilization in Egypt. **ASK:** How might changes in the annual Nile flooding cycle have affected Egypt? Encourage each student to contribute ideas about the effect on Egypt. Tell students they will learn about how changes in the Nile affected the Middle Kingdom in this lesson. **0:05** minutes

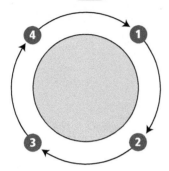

GUIDED DISCUSSION

1. **Describe** What was Egypt's trade policy during the Middle Kingdom? *(Trade expanded greatly. The trade network reached to several nearby lands and possibly as far as East Africa.)*

2. **Summarize** How did the pharaoh's increased military power help expand the Middle Kingdom? *(In the northeast, the pharaohs conquered lands along the eastern Mediterranean. They extended Egypt's southern border farther up the Nile by leading successful military campaigns against the kingdoms of Nubia.)*

ANALYZE VISUALS

Have students examine the depiction of Ahmose being purified by the gods. Ask them to discuss the influence and power of the pharaohs in the daily lives of Egyptians. **0:15** minutes

ACTIVE OPTIONS

NG Learning Framework: Review Information About the Middle Kingdom

ATTITUDE: **Empowerment**
SKILL: **Problem-Solving**

Invite students to review the information in Lesson 2.4 about the Middle Kingdom. **ASK:** How might you have done things differently from King Mentuhotep and other kings of the Middle Kingdom? How would your actions have affected the successes in the Middle Kingdom? How would your actions have affected how long the Middle Kingdom controlled Egypt? **0:10** minutes

On Your Feet: Turn and Talk on Topic Have students form three to five groups. Give each group this topic sentence: *When the Hyksos rose to power in Egypt, many changes followed.* Tell students to build a paragraph on that topic by having each student in the group contribute one sentence. Allow each group to present its paragraph to the class by having each student read her or his statement. **0:10** minutes

ENGLISH LANGUAGE LEARNERS   ELD

Complete Sentence Starters Have students form groups of mixed proficiency levels to discuss the main ideas of what they read. Provide the following sentence starters to help students at the **Emerging** level engage in academic discussion.

- At the end of the Old Kingdom, a great deal of money was spent on building monumental tombs called _____.
- Mentuhotep II started an era of peace and prosperity known as the _____.
- A group of outsiders who brought an end to the Middle Kingdom was called the _____.

PRE-AP

Debate Contributions Ask students to research the many contributions of ancient Egypt to civilization. Tell each student to choose a contribution they believe had the greatest impact and make a list of the reasons that explain why. Suggest that students hold a panel discussion to share and debate their contribution choice.

Press **mt** *in the Student eEdition for modified text.*

See the Chapter Planner for more strategies for differentiation.

ANSWERS

1. The Hyksos were foreign invaders who seized control of Lower Egypt, made Upper Egypt dependent on them, and controlled much of Egypt for more than 100 years.

2. They had spent too many resources on royal tombs, and the nobility no longer followed them.

3. There was a war between rival groups after the pharaohs lost control of the Old Kingdom. Mentuhotep reunited Egypt and initiated the Middle Kingdom. The next period of disorder was brought about by the invasion of the Hyksos, a group of foreign invaders. Then Egypt returned to a time of order when Ahmose reunited the country again.

This statue shows Hatshepsut wearing the false beard traditionally worn by the male pharaohs.

3.1 Hatshepsut Expands Trade

 At any grocery store, you can find exotic fruits from distant lands right alongside the crunchy apples from a nearby orchard. Like you, the ancient Egyptians had access to food and other goods from near and far.

MAIN IDEA

Under a great female pharaoh, Egypt grew wealthy through conquest and trade.

EGYPT'S GREAT FEMALE RULER

On the heels of the defeat of the Hyksos came the **New Kingdom**, which spanned nearly 500 years from 1550 B.C. to 1070 B.C. This period of prosperity saw Egypt grow more powerful than ever as it built a mighty empire. Its large professional army expanded the empire northeast into Palestine and south into Nubia. Plunder from war and taxes from conquered lands made Egypt rich, but so did trade. Under the rule of **Hatshepsut** (haht-SHEHP-soot), history's earliest well-known female ruler, trade flourished.

Hatshepsut came to power sometime around 1470 B.C. After her husband the pharaoh died, she ruled with her stepson, Thutmose III (thoot-MOH-suh), who was very young. Hatshepsut played a smart political game and won enough support to be crowned sole king. She performed all the religious, military, and political functions of the pharaoh, and she even dressed as a king.

TRADE AND EXPANSION

Like other pharaohs, Hatshepsut fought wars to expand the empire, but she also promoted trade. Egypt had abundant resources to **barter**, or exchange, for things the land couldn't produce—especially timber and exotic luxuries. These goods traveled on trade routes and pathways along the Nile valley and in the eastern Mediterranean. Egyptian merchants and traders bartered Egyptian beer, wine, food, and manufactured goods for myrrh trees, incense, ebony, ivory, leopard skins, and monkeys. The wealth generated through these expeditions stimulated Egypt's economy and funded great building projects.

Back in Egypt, Hatshepsut moved the capital city to Thebes and ordered many great monuments constructed to celebrate her rule. After 15 years in power, she disappeared suspiciously, possibly murdered by her stepson. Thutmose III became a mighty pharaoh in his own right and tried to erase Hatshepsut's name from all monuments and records. Luckily for future generations, he did not entirely succeed. Instead, a solid trail of clues has allowed historians to reconstruct Hatshepsut's remarkable reign.

REVIEW & ASSESS

1. **READING CHECK** In what ways did Egypt prosper during the reign of Hatshepsut?

2. **DRAW CONCLUSIONS** Why did the pharaohs engage in trade with other countries?

3. **FORM AND SUPPORT OPINIONS** What details support the opinion that Hatshepsut was an ambitious leader?

 6.2.6 Describe the role of Egyptian trade in the eastern Mediterranean and Nile valley; 6.2.7 Understand the significance of Queen Hatshepsut and Ramses the Great.

HSS CONTENT STANDARDS:

6.2.6 Describe the role of Egyptian trade in the eastern Mediterranean and Nile valley; **6.2.7** Understand the significance of Queen Hatshepsut and Ramses the Great.

HSS ANALYSIS SKILLS:

HI 1 Students explain the central issues and problems from the past, placing people and events in a matrix of time and place.

PLAN

OBJECTIVE

Explain how Egypt grew wealthy through conquest and trade under a female pharaoh.

ESSENTIAL QUESTION

How did ancient Egypt's rulers use the land's resources and geography to found a civilization?

Egyptians continued to use their vast resources to further develop their civilization. Lesson 3.1 discusses how Egypt grew wealthy under the leadership of a female pharaoh.

BACKGROUND FOR THE TEACHER

Hatshepsut was the widowed queen of the pharaoh Thutmose II. She had been given power after his death to rule for her young stepson, Thutmose III, until he came of age. At first, Hatshepsut acted on her stepson's behalf. But before long, she proclaimed herself pharaoh, the supreme power in Egypt. Her formal portraits began to show Hatshepsut dressing in the traditional male style with a crown and a false beard. By giving the outward appearance of a male king, it appears that Hatshepsut wanted to guarantee she would indeed be recognized as a ruler in the same way a male ruler would. Hatshepsut ruled for 21 years.

DIGITAL RESOURCES NGLSync.cengage.com

TEACHER RESOURCES & ASSESSMENT

 Reading and Note-Taking

 Vocabulary Practice

 Section 3 Quiz

STUDENT RESOURCES

 Biography

INTRODUCE & ENGAGE

ACTIVATE PRIOR KNOWLEDGE

Have students brainstorm ways in which the trading of goods is part of today's society. Have students think about various foods, clothing items, and building materials that come from other parts of the country or from other countries. **ASK:** How did trading food and other goods affect Egyptian society during the New Kingdom? Tell students that, in this lesson, they will learn about trade under the reign of Hatshepsut. **0:05** minutes

TEACH   STEM

GUIDED DISCUSSION

1. **Summarize** How did Egypt's army contribute toward making Egypt rich? *(The army expanded the empire northeast into Palestine and south into Nubia. Plunder from war and taxes from conquered lands made Egypt rich.)*

2. **Describe** What were some of the resources that Egyptian traders bartered? *(Egyptians bartered Egyptian beer, wine, food, and manufactured goods for myrrh trees, incense, ebony, ivory, leopard skins, and monkeys.)*

MORE INFORMATION

Egypt's Female Rulers Hatshepsut was not the only woman to hold power in ancient Egypt. Several other women ruled either directly as pharaoh or as a regent for a young son. Along with Hatshepsut, the two most famous Egyptian women are probably Nefertiti and Cleopatra VII. Nefertiti co-ruled with her husband, Akhenaten, and is best known for establishing a religion based on the worship of the sun god, Aten. Cleopatra VII was Egypt's last pharaoh and is best known for her relationships with Julius Caesar and Mark Antony.

For more about Hatshepsut's reign, have students view the image of Hatshepsut's obelisk in the **Primary Source Handbook** and answer the questions that follow.

ACTIVE OPTIONS

NG Learning Framework: Map Ancient Trade Routes

ATTITUDE: **Curiosity**
KNOWLEDGE: **Our Human Story**

Find and make copies of an outline map showing northern Africa and southwest Asia. Have students form pairs and give each pair a copy of the map. Have pairs use the textbook and reliable online sources to research key trading cities during the time of the New Kingdom and the goods that came from each city. Students should plot the cities on their map, connect them via likely trade routes, and label which goods traveled from place to place. **0:25** minutes

On Your Feet: Present a Period of Egyptian History Organize students into four groups and assign each group a period of Egyptian history on which they will prepare a short presentation. In every group some students should represent farmers, traders, and pharaohs from each period shown below.

- The early period of dynasties that began under the rule of Menes
- The Old Kingdom
- The Middle Kingdom
- The New Kingdom

0:15 minutes

DIFFERENTIATE

ENGLISH LANGUAGE LEARNERS   ELD

Summarize Lesson 3.1 has four paragraphs. Have students work in pairs or small groups, and assign each pair or group one paragraph to read. Then each group should write a one to two sentence summary of their paragraph. Provide the following sentence frames to help students at each proficiency level write an effective summary.

- **Emerging**

  This paragraph is about _____.

  First, _____. Then, _____. At the end _____.

- **Expanding**

  This paragraph is about _____ and _____.

  First, _____ and then _____. Finally, _____.

- **Bridging**

  The paragraph begins by _____. It then _____, and concludes by _____.

  To summarize, the paragraph provides information about _____.

Press **mt** *in the Student eEdition for modified text.*

See the Chapter Planner for more strategies for differentiation.

REVIEW & ASSESS

ANSWERS

1. Hatshepsut traded items Egypt had in abundance, such as beer, food, and wine, for goods from other lands. She forced Nubia to make trades favorable to the Egyptians, and she gained riches from a trading trip to the land of Punt.

2. They engaged in trade with other countries to obtain things their land couldn't produce—and, thereby, strengthened Egypt.

3. Hatshepsut ruled with her stepson, but she won enough political support from high officials and priests to be crowned pharaoh and perform all of the pharaoh's functions. The expeditions to Punt were difficult and dangerous; the fact that Hatshepsut was willing to take those risks to bring more wealth to Egypt also suggests that she was an ambitious leader.

RAMSES II

Ruled 1279 B.C. – 1213 B.C.

The women and children wail, and the men look up to the sun god in desperation. After ruling for 66 years, the pharaoh is dead. Most Egyptians have known no other king, and the dead pharaoh wasn't just any ruler. He was **Ramses II**—also known as Ramses the Great, a man who earned his title. Egypt was never more powerful than during Ramses' long reign.

Job: Pharaoh of Egypt
Education: Ruled alongside his father, Seti I
Home: Pi-Ramses

FINEST HOUR

He led Egypt's army against the Hittites at the Battle of Kadesh around 1274 B.C.

WORST MOMENT

He saw 12 of his sons die before he did.

FRIENDS

The people loved him, affectionately calling him Sese (SEH-say), a nickname for "Ramses." He had about 200 wives and more than 100 children.

TRIVIA

His mummified nose was stuffed with peppercorns to keep its distinctive shape. When his mummy was exhibited in Paris, it received the Presidential Guard of Honor reserved for visiting royalty.

Critical Viewing Visitors at a museum in Memphis, Egypt, marvel at a statue of Ramses II. What does the size of this statue say about how Ramses was viewed in his day?

+ POSSIBLE RESPONSE

The huge size of the statue indicates that Ramses was viewed as very powerful and important to his people.

A LONG AND POWERFUL REIGN

Lasting 66 years, Ramses' (RAM-zeez) reign was one of the longest in Egyptian history. Ramses expanded Egypt's empire south into Nubia, west into Libya, and into the eastern Mediterranean. There he clashed with another ancient people, the Hittites (HIH-tyts).

The Hittites had a powerful empire centered around present-day Turkey, and they also sought to control the eastern Mediterranean. In his fifth year as pharaoh, Ramses fought a huge battle against the Hittites at Kadesh (kay-DEHSH). The battle stopped the Hittites' advance, but war with the Hittites dragged on for more than 15 years. At last, Ramses wrote letters to the Hittite king and negotiated a peace treaty. Peace with the Hittites and Egypt's territorial expansion helped Ramses create a strong economy.

Ramses went on to carve his legacy in stone and make himself unforgettable. First he built a new capital city, which he called Pi-Ramses (puh-RAM-zeez). Then he commissioned an awesome number of temples, monuments, and statues. At Abu Simbel (ah-boo SIHM-buhl) in Egyptian-controlled Nubia, Ramses had two cavernous temples carved out of the rock cliff face. His massive tomb at Thebes had a long wait for him—Ramses outlived 12 sons, dying in 1213 B.C. at more than 90 years of age.

THE NEW KINGDOM ENDS

Egypt's power was at its peak under Ramses the Great. After his death, several challenges emerged. Members of the ruling dynasty clashed with each other. In addition, Egypt was repeatedly invaded by a group known as the Sea Peoples.

Although they never conquered Egypt, the Sea Peoples waged a lengthy war that left Egypt's civilization weak and unstable.

In the years following the New Kingdom, Egypt was conquered and controlled by various foreign powers. First the Libyans and then the Nubians seized large areas of land. Later, another people from Southwest Asia, the Persians, conquered Egypt. After 332 B.C., Egypt came under the control of the Macedonians, a people from the Greek peninsula. The final pharaohs were all Macedonians, right down to the last one, the famous Cleopatra VII. When Rome conquered Egypt in 30 B.C., Cleopatra committed suicide. It was a suitably dramatic end to 3,000 years of pharaohs.

REVIEW & ASSESS

1. **READING CHECK** What weakened Egypt's power after the death of Ramses II?

2. **MAKE INFERENCES** Why did peace with the Hittites help strengthen Egypt's economy?

3. **COMPARE AND CONTRAST** Think about Ramses II and Hatshepsut. What did these two strong pharaohs have in common?

6.2.7 Understand the significance of Queen Hatshepsut and Ramses the Great; HI 6 Students interpret basic indicators of economic performance and conduct cost-benefit analyses of economic and political issues.

HSS CONTENT STANDARDS:

6.2.7 Understand the significance of Queen Hatshepsut and Ramses the Great.

HSS ANALYSIS SKILLS:

HI 6 Students interpret basic indicators of economic performances and conduct cost-benefit analyses of economic and political issues.

PLAN

OBJECTIVE

Explain how Ramses II was one of the most powerful pharaohs in Egypt.

ESSENTIAL QUESTION

How did ancient Egypt's rulers use the land's resources and geography to found a civilization?

Ramses II had a long reign as pharaoh. Lesson 3.2 discusses how Ramses II influenced the Egyptian civilization.

BACKGROUND FOR THE TEACHER

Ramses II was the third king of the 19th dynasty of Egypt. He is known for the many temples he built throughout Egypt. The most famous of these are the temple at Abu Simbel, and his mortuary temple at Thebes, the Ramesseum. The tomb of his principal wife, Nefertari, at Thebes is one of the best-preserved royal tombs. The tomb of many of his sons has also recently been found in the Valley of the Kings. Ramses II is known for the many huge statues of him all over Egypt.

DIGITAL RESOURCES NGLSync.cengage.com

TEACHER RESOURCES & ASSESSMENT

 Reading and Note-Taking

 Vocabulary Practice

 Section 3 Quiz

STUDENT RESOURCES

 NG Chapter Gallery

PREVIEW THE LESSON

Call students' attention to the information in the chart about Ramses II. Ask volunteers to predict what they will learn in the lesson based on the information in the chart. Then tell students they will learn about Ramses II and his reign as pharaoh. At the end of the lesson, have students review how accurate their predictions were. `0:05` minutes

TEACH

STEM

GUIDED DISCUSSION

1. **Summarize** How did Ramses expand Egypt's empire? *(He expanded Egypt's empire south into Nubia, west into Libya, and into the eastern Mediterranean.)*

2. **Describe** How did Ramses carve his legacy in stone? *(Ramses built a new capital city, Pi-Ramses. He commissioned many temples, monuments, and statues. He had a massive tomb built for himself.)*

ANALYZE VISUALS

Have students look at the artistic representations of the pharaohs Ahmose (Lesson 2.4), Hatshepsut (Lesson 3.1), and Ramses II (Chapter 4 Introduction and Lesson 3.2). **ASK:** Based on your analysis of these images, how did ancient Egyptian artists represent the power of the pharaoh? *(Possible response: Egyptian artists represented the power of the pharaoh by showing him as an equal to the gods, creating enormous statues, and, in the case of Hatshepsut, adding the false beard that was usually worn by male pharaohs.)* `0:10` minutes

ACTIVE OPTIONS

NG Learning Framework: Compare the Reigns of Ramses II and Hatshepsut

SKILLS: Communication, Collaboration
KNOWLEDGE: **Our Human Story**

Invite students to revisit Lessons 3.1 and 3.2. Ask them to work in small groups to discuss how the reigns of Ramses II and Hatshepsut were alike and different. Ask each group to present three of their ideas to the class. `0:10` minutes

On Your Feet: Hold a Panel Discussion Have students work in groups of five to conduct a panel discussion. One group member is the moderator, posing the question, "For what reasons did many people consider Ramses II a great pharaoh?" Other group members will contribute ideas about how Ramses earned the title "Ramses the Great." `0:15` minutes

STRIVING READERS

Complete Sentence Starters Provide these sentence starters for students to complete after reading. You may also have students preview to set a purpose for reading.

• Ramses' reign as Egyptian pharaoh lasted _____.

• Ramses fought a huge battle at Kadesh against the _____.

• Egypt's power was at its peak under _____.

• When Rome conquered Egypt, it was the end to 3,000 years of _____.

PRE-AP

Interview a Pharaoh Have students work in teams of two to plan, write, and perform a simulated television interview with Pharaoh Ramses II. Tell students that the purpose of the interview is to focus on the many achievements of the pharaoh during his reign. For more insight into the life of Ramses II, have students read the excerpt from "Pen-ta-ur: The Victory of Ramses II Over the Khita" in the **Primary Source Handbook** and answer the questions that follow.

Press **mt** in the Student eEdition for modified text.

See the Chapter Planner for more strategies for differentiation.

ANSWERS

1. After the death of Ramses II, several factors contributed to the decline of Egypt, including weak pharaohs, invasions by the Sea Peoples, and conquests by foreign powers.

2. Peace with the Hittites allowed for Egypt's territorial expansion, which helped Ramses create a strong economy.

3. They both had the ability to form and maintain good trade relationships with neighboring countries, military strength, personal ambition, and an urge to build cities and monuments to themselves.

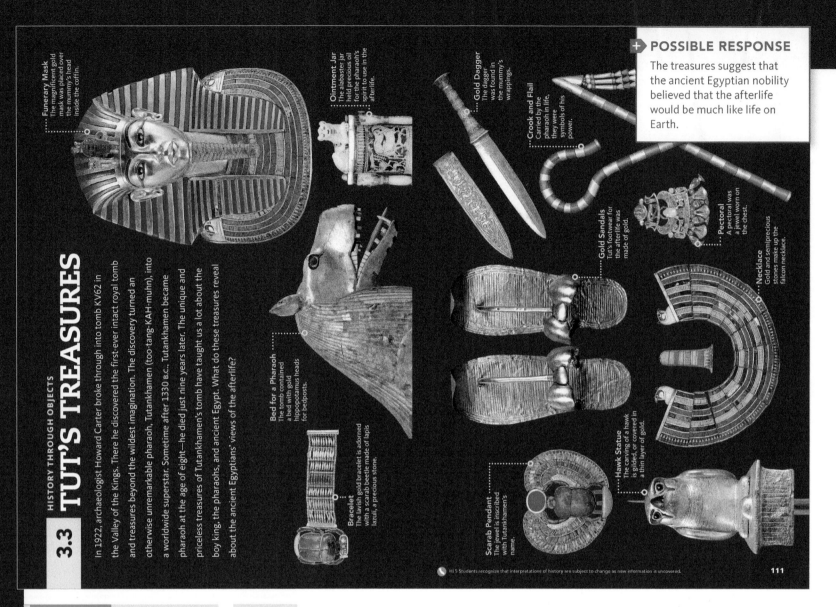

POSSIBLE RESPONSE

The treasures suggest that the ancient Egyptian nobility believed that the afterlife would be much like life on Earth.

HISTORY THROUGH OBJECTS

3.3 TUT'S TREASURES

In 1922, archaeologist Howard Carter broke through into tomb KV62 in the Valley of the Kings. There he discovered the first-ever intact royal tomb and treasures beyond the wildest imagination. The discovery turned an otherwise unremarkable pharaoh, Tutankhamen (too-tang-KAH-muhn), into a worldwide superstar. Sometime after 1330 B.C., Tutankhamen became pharaoh at the age of eight—he died just nine years later. The unique and priceless treasures of Tutankhamen's tomb have taught us a lot about the boy king, the pharaohs, and ancient Egypt. What do these treasures reveal about the ancient Egyptians' views of the afterlife?

Funerary Mask The magnificent gold mask was placed over the mummy's head inside the coffin.

Ointment Jar The alabaster jar held precious oil for the pharaoh's spirit to use in the afterlife.

Gold Dagger The dagger was found in the mummy's wrappings.

Crook and Flail Carried by the pharaoh in life, they were symbols of his power.

Bed for a Pharaoh The tomb contained a bed with gold hippopotamus heads for bedposts.

Gold Sandals Tut's footwear for the afterlife was made of gold.

Pectoral A pectoral was a jewel worn on the chest.

Necklace Gold and semiprecious stones make up the falcon necklace.

Bracelet The lavish gold bracelet is adorned with a scarab beetle made of lapis lazuli, a precious stone.

Scarab Pendant The jewel is inscribed with Tutankhamen's name.

Hawk Statue The carving of a hawk is gilded, or covered in a thin layer of gold.

HI 5 Students recognize that interpretations of history are subject to change as new information is uncovered.

111

STANDARDS

HSS CONTENT STANDARDS:

6.2 Students analyze the geographic, political, economic, religious, and social structures of the early civilizations of Mesopotamia, Egypt, and Kush.

HSS ANALYSIS SKILLS:

HI 5 Students recognize that interpretations of history are subject to change as new information is uncovered.

PLAN

OBJECTIVE

Identify some of the treasures found in the tomb of the pharaoh Tutankhamen.

ESSENTIAL QUESTION

How did ancient Egypt's rulers use the land's resources and geography to found a civilization?

In ancient Egyptian civilization, pharaohs were honored as gods. Their tombs contained items it was believed the pharaohs' spirits would need in the afterlife. Lesson 3.3 shows some of the items that were found in the tomb of the pharaoh Tutankhamen.

BACKGROUND FOR THE TEACHER

Tutankhamen was an Egyptian pharaoh during the New Kingdom. He is often referred to as King Tut. Press coverage of the 1922 discovery of Tutankhamen's tomb by archaeologist Howard Carter went worldwide. The discovery led to much public interest in ancient Egypt. Tutankhamen is a well-known pharaoh largely because his tomb is among the best preserved and his image and the artifacts in his tomb are the most exhibited, having been displayed all over the world. Probably the best-known exhibition tour ran from 1972 to 1979. More than 1.6 million visitors saw the exhibition.

DIGITAL RESOURCES NGLSync.cengage.com

TEACHER RESOURCES & ASSESSMENT

 Reading and Note-Taking

 Vocabulary Practice

 Section 3 Quiz

STUDENT RESOURCES

 NG Chapter Gallery

INTRODUCE & ENGAGE

EXAMINE HISTORY THROUGH OBJECTS

Ask students to form small groups and brainstorm a list of items that they think Egyptians would consider important to include in a pharaoh's tomb. Reconvene as a class and ask each group to share their list. Use the group lists to create a master list on the whiteboard. Then tell students that, in this lesson, they will learn about some of the items that were found in the tomb of the pharaoh Tutankhamen, or King Tut. `0:05` minutes

TEACH

STEM

GUIDED DISCUSSION

1. **Make Inferences** Why do you think Egyptians might have included items such as the crook and flail in the tomb? (*Possible response: Egyptians believed that the pharaoh's spirit may have needed these symbols of power in the afterlife.*)

2. **Draw Conclusions** What do the treasures from the tomb of Tutankhamen tell you about the status of the pharaoh in Egyptian society? (*The tomb contained gold and other riches, indicating that the pharaoh was considered to have a very high status in Egyptian society.*)

ANALYZE VISUALS

Have students reform their small groups from the Introduce & Engage activity. Have each group of students revisit their list and examine the artifacts shown here from the tomb of King Tut. Then they should discuss why each of these items may have been included in the tomb. Then have each group share its ideas with the class. `0:10` minutes

ACTIVE OPTIONS

Critical Viewing: NG Chapter Gallery Have students examine the contents of the Chapter Gallery for this chapter. Then invite them to brainstorm additional images they believe would fit within the Chapter Gallery. Have them write a description of these additional images and provide an explanation of why they would fit within the Chapter Gallery. Then instruct them to do online research to find examples of actual images they would like to add to the gallery. `0:15` minutes

On Your Feet: Three-Step Interview Have students choose a partner from the opposite side of the classroom. One student should interview the other on the topic of King Tut and the treasures found in his tomb. Then have students reverse roles. Finally, invite each student to share the results of his or her interview with the class. `0:15` minutes

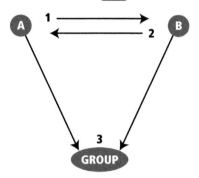

DIFFERENTIATE

GIFTED & TALENTED

Host a Talk Show Have students assume the roles of a talk show host and an expert on the reign of King Tut. Have students do research to determine the appropriate questions for the host to ask and the appropriate responses from the expert. Have students present their talk show to the class.

PRE-AP

Create a Magazine Ad Have students create an ad for a magazine inviting people to come to an exhibit of some of the treasures found in King Tut's tomb. Students may want to illustrate their written ads with drawings or other images.

Press (**mt**) *in the Student eEdition for modified text.*

See the Chapter Planner for more strategies for differentiation.

The Rise of Kush

How well do you know your neighbors? How do their lives affect yours? From annoyingly loud parties to borrowing tools or exchanging gifts, neighbors interact. Egypt couldn't ignore its closest neighbor, Nubia.

MAIN IDEA

The Nubian kingdom of Kush followed Egypt as a center of power, culture, and trade.

KUSH CONTROLS EGYPT

Just south of Egypt, across the first cataract of the Nile, lay the land of **Nubia**. Rich in gold, copper, and other important resources needed by Egypt, Nubia also provided a critical trade route for exotic goods from central Africa. This helps explain why the histories of Egypt and Nubia are so deeply connected. Early Nubia was a collection of chiefdoms dominated by Egypt. Later, when stronger Nubian kingdoms emerged, Egypt took more active control of its southern neighbor. It conquered and colonized large areas of Nubia, and Nubia's people adopted many Egyptian practices and customs during a thousand years of direct rule. Eventually, however, the tables were turned.

In the generations following the reign of Ramses II, the Nubian kingdom of **Kush** asserted its independence. It grew strong and ambitious. The Kushite king, Piankhi, invaded Egypt, sweeping north to take control of Thebes, Memphis, and Upper and Lower Egypt. In 728 B.C., Piankhi united the kingdoms of Egypt and Kush under a new line of Kushite kings.

Piankhi did not think of himself as a foreign conqueror but as a traditional pharaoh reviving Egyptian traditions. The Kushite kings styled themselves as pharaohs and continued classic Egyptian religious, social, and political practices. They built pyramids, mummified their dead, and worshipped Egyptian gods.

Eventually, the Kushite kings came into conflict with the iron-weapon wielding superpower of Assyria to the northeast of Egypt. In the course of the war, Kush lost control of Egypt to the Assyrians. Some of the fighting was fierce; the city of Thebes was destroyed before the Kushite kings abandoned Egypt.

TRADE IN IRON AND GOLD

After being pushed out of Egypt, Kush continued to flourish as an independent power. Its capital, Napata (nah-PAH-tuh), had a palace and a temple to the Egyptian god Amun (AH-muhn), one of the creator gods. The city's strategic location across two major trade routes ensured that Kush remained an important center of international trade. The Kushites had stores of gold, and they began to mine and produce iron as well.

Around 590 B.C., the Kushite capital moved south to another important trading city called Meroë (MAIR-oh-ee). Here the Egyptian influence continued with royal pyramids and temples to Amun and the goddess Isis. The Nubians expanded their kingdom and opened up many new trading routes, especially for iron.

Iron was increasingly important in the ancient world because it was used to make strong tools, and Meroë had abundant supplies of iron ore. Because of its resources, the city remained an important economic and political center for several centuries.

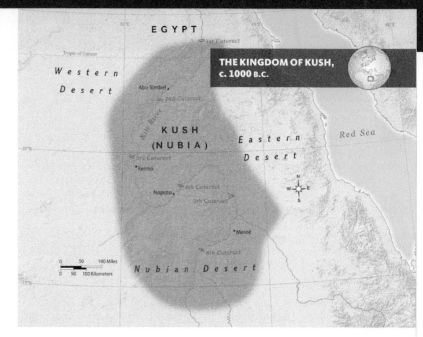

THE KINGDOM OF KUSH, c. 1000 B.C.

GOLD

The importance of gold to Nubia is clear from its name. *Nub* was the Egyptian word for gold, and Nubia was rich with it. Skilled goldsmiths turned gold ore into intricate jewelry, such as this pendant of the goddess Isis.

REVIEW & ASSESS

1. **READING CHECK** In what ways did Kush follow Egypt as a center of power, culture, and trade in Africa?

2. **MAKE INFERENCES** Would life have changed a great deal for Egyptians living under the rule of the Kushite kings? Why or why not?

3. **INTERPRET MAPS** Why do you think Kushite kings established the kingdom's two capital cities—Napata and later Meroë—along the Nile River?

6.2.8 Identify the location of the Kush civilization and describe its political, commercial, and cultural relations with Egypt; CST 3 Students use a variety of maps and documents to identify physical and cultural features of neighborhoods, cities, states, and countries and to explain the historical migration of people, expansion and disintegration of empires, and the growth of economic systems.

113

HSS CONTENT STANDARDS:

6.2.8 Identify the location of the Kush civilization and describe its political, commercial, and cultural relations with Egypt.

HSS ANALYSIS SKILLS:

CST 1 Students explain how major events are related to one another in time; **CST 3** Students use a variety of maps and documents to identify physical and cultural features of neighborhoods, cities, states, and countries and to explain the historical migration of people, expansion and disintegration of empires, and the growth of economic systems; **REP 1** Students frame questions that can be answered by historical study and research.

PLAN

OBJECTIVE

Explain how the Nubian kingdom of Kush followed Egypt as a center of power, culture, and trade.

ESSENTIAL QUESTION

How did ancient Egypt's rulers use the land's resources and geography to found a civilization?

The Nubian kingdom of Kush was a neighbor of Egypt. Lesson 3.4 discusses how Kush used the land's resources to become a center of power.

BACKGROUND FOR THE TEACHER

The Nubian kingdom of Kush was the empire to the south of Egypt. Kush was built at the base of the mountains near the beginning of the Nile River. The location along the Nile River was important for communication and trade routes both within the kingdom and throughout northeastern Africa. The people of Kush enjoyed plenty of rainfall throughout the year, so their crops grew well. Kush also had gold mines, iron ore, and ivory.

DIGITAL RESOURCES NGLSync.cengage.com

TEACHER RESOURCES & ASSESSMENT

 Reading and Note-Taking

 Vocabulary Practice

 Section 3 Quiz

STUDENT RESOURCES

 NG Chapter Gallery

INTRODUCE & ENGAGE

ASK QUESTIONS

Have students form groups of four and come up with a list of three questions about the Nubian kingdom of Kush. After the lesson, review the questions and have students from each group answer the questions they listed or give them the opportunity to research answers if their particular question was not addressed in the text. Have each group share its questions and answers with the class. **0:05 minutes**

TEACH

GUIDED DISCUSSION

1. **Summarize** How did the Nubian kingdom of Kush assert its independence? *(The Kushite king, Piankhi, invaded and took control of Egypt.)*

2. **Draw Conclusions** How was the abundance of iron ore important to the economic development of Nubia? *(Iron was increasingly important in the ancient world because it was used to make strong tools. Nubia opened up trading routes, especially for iron.)*

CREATE GRAPHIC ORGANIZERS

As a class, complete the following graphic organizer to help students understand the sequence of events that led to the rise and fall of Kush. **0:10 minutes**

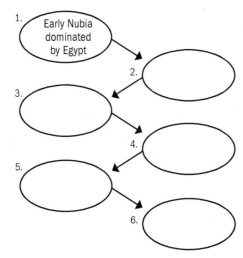

1. Early Nubia dominated by Egypt
2.
3.
4.
5.
6.

ACTIVE OPTIONS

NG Learning Framework: Research Cultural Influences

SKILL: Observation
KNOWLEDGE: Our Human Story

Review with students the concept of cultural diffusion. Then have groups of students use information from the chapter and additional source material to research the cultural influences of Egypt on the kingdom of Kush. Suggest that they research the following topics: architecture; social order; government; and religion. Have groups record their information in a graphic organizer, such as a chart or a concept web, and compare their information with each other. As a class, discuss reasons why Egypt might have had such an influence on Kush. As an extension and to learn more about the relationship between Egypt and Kush, have students complete **California EEI Curriculum Units 6.2.6/8,** *Egypt and Kush: A Tale of Two Kingdoms.* **0:20 minutes**

On Your Feet: Create a Concept Web Have students form groups of four around a section of a bulletin board or a table. Provide each group with a large sheet of paper. Have group members take turns contributing a concept or phrase to a Concept Web with the words *The Nubian kingdom of Kush* at the center. When time for the activity has elapsed, call on volunteers from each group to share their webs. **0:10 minutes**

DIFFERENTIATE

INCLUSION

Preview Maps Have students identify the location of the Nile River in the kingdom of Nubia. Divide the class into three groups of mixed ability levels. Ask each group to brainstorm two explanations for how the location of Nubia affected the growth of crops and the growth of trade in the kingdom of Nubia. Have one member from each group share their explanations with the class.

PRE-AP

Create a Group Presentation Have students work in small groups to discuss life in the Nubian kingdom of Kush. Students should include information about its rulers, religious beliefs, and use of resources. Have each group give a presentation to the class.

Press **mt** *in the Student eEdition for modified text.*

See the Chapter Planner for more strategies for differentiation.

REVIEW & ASSESS

ANSWERS

1. Kush invaded and conquered Egypt, continued Egyptian religious, social, and political practices, and became an important center of international trade.

2. No, because the Kushite kings came from a culture that was very Egyptianized, and the first Kushite king saw himself as a pharaoh in the Egyptian tradition.

3. It was important for the kingdom to have access to the Nile River for transportation. Trade routes to other countries probably went along the Nile.

4.1 Hieroglyphs and Papyrus

You might be able to guess the meaning of some foreign words. But try reading a store bar code. The seemingly random arrangement of lines is actually a unique writing system telling you the product and price. To read it, you need to crack the code. Egyptian writing was just as baffling until archaeologists discovered the key—a slab of rock called the Rosetta Stone.

MAIN IDEA

The Egyptians valued writing and wrote for many purposes.

Critical Viewing This carving shows a pair of scribes at work during the Old Kingdom. What does the image tell you about a scribe's job?

➕ POSSIBLE RESPONSE

The image shows that a scribe's job involved writing and sharing information.

COMMON HIEROGLYPHS

Sun
(or day)

R
(a mouth symbol)

S
(a folded cloth symbol)

N
(water ripple)

WRITING AND WRITERS

Egyptian writing developed sometime before 3000 B.C., and it used **hieroglyphs** (HY-ruh-glihfs) instead of letters. A hieroglyph could be a picture representing an object, or it could represent a sound or an idea. By combining hieroglyphs, the Egyptians formed words and sentences.

The hieroglyphic writing system was very complex. There were nearly 800 hieroglyphs, no vowels, and very complicated rules. Few people mastered the skill of writing in hieroglyphs.

These special people were known as **scribes**, or professional writers, and they were among the most highly respected people in Egypt. It took five years of intense training to become a scribe, but the benefits made up for the hard work. Scribes were powerful, well paid, and had many privileges.

Reading and writing were just part of a scribe's job. Scribes were also skilled in art, mathematics, bookkeeping, law, engineering, and architecture. All scribes were important, but a really talented scribe could move up in Egypt's social hierarchy. One royal scribe eventually became the pharaoh Horemheb.

PAPER AND THE ROSETTA STONE

Hieroglyphs were painted and carved on tombs, temples, and monuments. For important documents, the Egyptians used sheets of a paperlike material called **papyrus** (puh-PY-ruhs), made from reeds that grew along the banks of the Nile. Sheets of papyrus could be glued together to make scrolls—some scrolls were several yards long. Papyrus was light and easy for a scribe to carry.

Eventually, the Egyptians abandoned the old forms of writing. For many years, scholars tried to crack the code of the hieroglyphs. Then, in A.D. 1799, a slab of rock was discovered near Rosetta, Egypt. On it was carved the same text in hieroglyphs, another form of writing, and Greek. Because scholars understood Greek, they were able to figure out what the hieroglyphs meant. Thanks to the Rosetta Stone, historians can read hieroglyphs and learn about the lives of the people who produced them.

REVIEW & ASSESS

1. **READING CHECK** How much time did it take to become a scribe in ancient Egypt?

2. **IDENTIFY MAIN IDEAS AND DETAILS** What details support the idea that scribes were among the most highly respected people in Egypt?

3. **MAKE INFERENCES** What does the complexity of the hieroglyphic writing system tell us about the role of scribes?

6.2.9 Trace the evolution of language and its written forms.

STANDARDS

HSS CONTENT STANDARDS:

6.2.9 Trace the evolution of language and its written forms.

PLAN

OBJECTIVE

Explain that the Egyptians valued writing and wrote for many purposes.

ESSENTIAL QUESTION

How did ancient Egypt's rulers use the land's resources and geography to found a civilization?

Writing was an important part of Egyptian civilization. Lesson 4.1 discusses hieroglyphs, the use of papyrus, and the importance of the Rosetta Stone.

BACKGROUND FOR THE TEACHER

Art from ancient Egypt often depicts scribes carrying the tools of their craft, such as pigments, water pots, and pens. Scribes handled such things as personal letters, government communications and proclamations, legal documents, and religious documents. The closing phrase of many ancient letters, "May you be well when you hear this," implies that the scribes not only wrote but also read communications between people. The training of the scribes was rigorous and the harsh treatment of apprentices is recorded both in texts and representations.

DIGITAL RESOURCES NGLSync.cengage.com

TEACHER RESOURCES & ASSESSMENT

 Reading and Note-Taking

 Vocabulary Practice

 Section 4 Quiz

STUDENT RESOURCES

 Active History

HOLD A ROUNDTABLE DISCUSSION

Have students sit in groups of four. Ask the groups to brainstorm and then list different forms of communication. Have each group share its ideas with the class. Tell students they will learn more about written communication in ancient Egypt in this lesson. **0:05** minutes

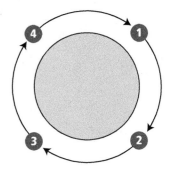

GUIDED DISCUSSION

1. **Describe** What is a hieroglyph? *(A hieroglyph could be a picture representing an object, or it could represent a sound or an idea.)*

2. **Summarize** What is the importance of the Rosetta Stone? *(On the Rosetta Stone, the same text was carved in hieroglyphs and in Greek. Because scholars understood Greek, they were able to figure out what the hieroglyphs meant.)*

MORE INFORMATION

The Rosetta Stone The scholar who cracked the code of the Rosetta Stone was a French historian named Jean-François Champollion. In 1808, at the age of 18, he began his first attempts at deciphering the hieroglyphs on the Rosetta Stone. However, his breakthrough didn't come until 1822, when Champollion concluded that the hieroglyphs were not only symbols but functioned as an alphabet and a phonetic language. Applying this strategy, he was able to successfully decipher the names of two ancient Egyptian rulers written on the stone: Ramses and Thutmos. Using what he learned, he was then able to decipher common nouns.

ACTIVE OPTIONS

Active History: Decipher Egyptian Hieroglyphics Extend the lesson by using either the PDF or Whiteboard version of Decipher Egyptian Hieroglyphics. These activities take a deeper look at a topic from, or related to, the lesson. Explore the activities as a class, turn them into group assignments, or even assign them individually. **0:10** minutes

On Your Feet: Compare Two Forms of Writing Ask students to work in small groups. Ask each group to review Lesson 1.4 in Chapter 3 and compare Egyptian writing with Mesopotamian cuneiform. Have groups create a list of similarities and differences to share with the class. **0:10** minutes

STRIVING READERS

Use a Word Splash Present the words below on the board in a random arrangement (splash) as shown, and ask students to choose four pairs of words that are related to each other. Have students write a sentence telling how each pair of words is related.

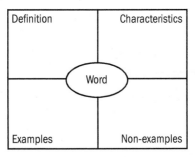

ENGLISH LANGUAGE LEARNERS ELD

Create Four-Square Word Charts Give students the following list of words and display the chart below. Ask students to copy and complete the four parts of the chart for each word on the list. Have students at the **Emerging** level work in pairs. Have students at the **Expanding** and **Bridging** levels work independently.

- hieroglyph
- scribe
- papyrus

Definition	Characteristics
	Word
Examples	Non-examples

Press (**mt**) *in the Student eEdition for modified text.*

See the Chapter Planner for more strategies for differentiation.

ANSWERS

1. It took five years of training to become a scribe.

2. The scribes were powerful, well paid, and earned many privileges that other Egyptians did not have. Scribes could rise to high office.

3. Scribes were important and powerful people in society. They were probably among the best and brightest people in the society.

4.2 Medicine, Science, and Mathematics

The priest chants magic spells while the doctor applies a fragrant lotion to your wound. He carefully bandages it and gives you a foul-smelling medicine sweetened with honey. You gag on it, but the chances are you'll live. The ancient Egyptians were advanced medical practitioners for their time.

MAIN IDEA

Egyptians put their advanced knowledge of medicine, science, and mathematics to practical use.

CANOPIC JARS
Canopic (kuh-NOH-pihk) jars contained the internal organs of a mummified body. The head-shaped lids on the jars represent the sons of the god Horus.

MEDICINE

Egypt had the most advanced medical practices in the ancient world. Some ancient Egyptian science was so accurate that it formed the foundation of later medical practices in Europe. The Egyptians had developed a detailed understanding of anatomy through mummifying bodies. They identified the heart as the most important organ and the pulse as its "voice."

Doctors provided medicines made from plants and minerals, set broken bones, and even performed surgery. Researchers have found medical texts written on papyrus that give doctors instructions and advice for treating a variety of illnesses. Texts and carvings also show some of the surgical tools that doctors used to treat their patients. Magical spells to heal different illnesses were also considered part of medical treatment.

SCIENCE AND MATHEMATICS

Ancient Egyptians were gifted astronomers as well as talented doctors. Astronomy is the branch of science that studies the sun, moon, stars, planets, and space. By making observations of the moon, ancient Egyptian astronomers developed a 365-day calendar. It had 24-hour days, 10-day weeks, 3-week months, and 12-month years. The extra five days were added as birthdays for five gods and were considered unlucky.

The Egyptians were also excellent mathematicians. Like us, they used a decimal counting system that included fractions. However, they did not use zero. Egyptian mathematicians established several key principles of geometry, accurately calculating angles and areas. They could calculate the area of a circle and the volume of a pyramid or cylinder. These skills made it possible to design big buildings like the pyramids.

Less visible but equally impressive was their mastery of the mathematics needed to run an empire. Scribes accurately calculated how many workers would be needed for building projects and how much food they would eat. Similar assessments estimated trade profits, crop yields, and taxes. Along with trade and military might, math and science were foundations of ancient Egypt's civilization.

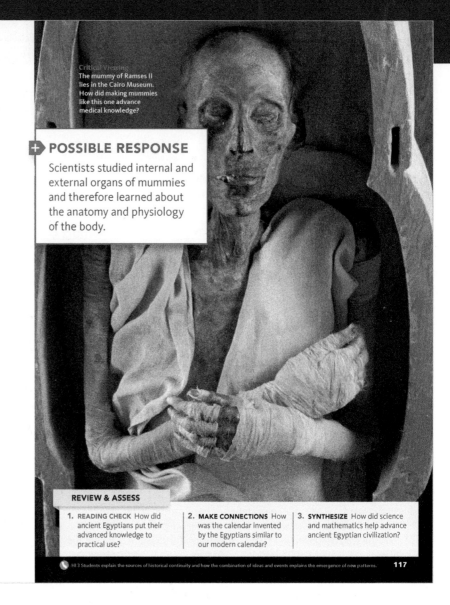

Critical Viewing
The mummy of Ramses II lies in the Cairo Museum. How did making mummies like this one advance medical knowledge?

＋ POSSIBLE RESPONSE
Scientists studied internal and external organs of mummies and therefore learned about the anatomy and physiology of the body.

REVIEW & ASSESS

1. **READING CHECK** How did ancient Egyptians put their advanced knowledge to practical use?

2. **MAKE CONNECTIONS** How was the calendar invented by the Egyptians similar to our modern calendar?

3. **SYNTHESIZE** How did science and mathematics help advance ancient Egyptian civilization?

HI 3 Students explain the sources of historical continuity and how the combination of ideas and events explains the emergence of new patterns. **117**

STANDARDS

HSS CONTENT STANDARDS:

6.2 Students analyze the geographic, political, economic, religious, and social structures of the early civilizations of Mesopotamia, Egypt, and Kush.

HSS ANALYSIS SKILLS:

HI 3 Students explain the sources of historical continuity and how the combination of ideas and events explains the emergence of new patterns.

PLAN

OBJECTIVE

Explain how Egyptians put their advanced knowledge of medicine, science, and mathematics to practical use.

ESSENTIAL QUESTION

How did ancient Egypt's rulers use the land's resources and geography to found a civilization?

Egyptian rulers worked to advance knowledge in their society. Lesson 4.2 discusses how important knowledge of medicine, science, and mathematics was to the Egyptian civilization.

BACKGROUND FOR THE TEACHER

The ancient Egyptians have provided modern historians with a great deal of information about the medical knowledge that they had. Some of the information comes from writings found in papyruses discovered during archaeological searches. Historians have determined that some Egyptian beliefs about medicine were based on myths. However, ancient writings indicate that Egyptians had discovered many things about how the human body worked. For example, evidence shows that Egyptian physicians were aware of the connection between a person's pulse and heart.

DIGITAL RESOURCES NGLSync.cengage.com

TEACHER RESOURCES & ASSESSMENT

 Reading and Note-Taking

 Vocabulary Practice

 Section 4 Quiz

STUDENT RESOURCES

 NG Chapter Gallery

INTRODUCE & ENGAGE

USE A K-W-L CHART

Provide each student with a K-W-L Chart like the one shown. Have students use their prior knowledge to brainstorm ideas about how ancient Egyptians might have learned about medicine, science, and mathematics. Ask students to write questions that they would like to have answered as they study the lesson. Allow time at the end of the lesson for students to fill in what they have learned. `0:05` minutes

K	W	L
What Do I Know?	What Do I Want To Learn?	What Did I Learn?

TEACH

STEM

GUIDED DISCUSSION

1. **Describe** How did the ancient Egyptians develop a detailed understanding of anatomy? *(They learned about anatomy through mummifying bodies.)*

2. **Summarize** How did mastery of mathematics help scribes contribute to the advancement of the Egyptian empire? *(Ancient Egyptians were able to calculate how many workers would be needed for building projects and how much food they would eat. They estimated trade profits, crop yields, and taxes.)*

CREATE GRAPHIC ORGANIZERS

Have students form groups of four around a section of a bulletin board or a table. Provide each group with a large sheet of paper. Have group members take turns contributing a concept or phrase to a Concept Web with the words *Medicine, Science, and Mathematics* at the center. When time for the activity has elapsed, call on volunteers from each group to share their webs. `0:10` minutes

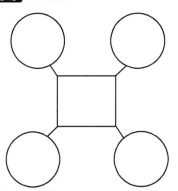

ACTIVE OPTIONS

NG Learning Framework: Learn More About Medicine in Ancient Egypt

ATTITUDE: **Curiosity**
KNOWLEDGE: **Our Human Story**

Ask students to select one or more medical practices used in ancient Egypt about which they would like to learn more. Then have students do research about the practices and present their findings to the class. `0:10` minutes

On Your Feet: Create a Quiz Organize students into two teams and have each team write ten True-False questions about ancient Egypt's contributions to the fields of medicine, science, and mathematics. Then have each team answer the questions created by the other team. Review student answers as a class and have teams keep track of their number of correct answers. `0:10` minutes

DIFFERENTIATE

STRIVING READERS

Make Summary Statements Have students look at the subheadings in the lesson. After reading the lesson, direct students to use each subheading to begin a statement that summarizes the information about the subheading.

GIFTED & TALENTED

Research Issues Have students work in small groups to learn more about how ancient Egyptians understood and practiced medicine. Have each group present its findings to the class.

Press **mt** *in the Student eEdition for modified text.*

See the Chapter Planner for more strategies for differentiation.

REVIEW & ASSESS

ANSWERS

1. The ancient Egyptian doctors provided medicines, set broken bones, and performed surgery. They treated a variety of illnesses. They gained a detailed understanding of human anatomy. They studied astronomy and used information they learned to develop a calendar. They used math to calculate geometry and to help them efficiently handle large building projects.

2. Like our modern calendar, the Egyptian calendar had 365 days. It had 24-hour days, and 12-month years.

3. In order to build the pyramids, Egyptians needed to solve difficult problems, including calculating angles, areas, and volumes for various shapes and forms. Solving these mathematical problems led to some of the first developments of geometry. The study of medicine in ancient Egypt helped them understand human anatomy and physiology.

Egyptian architects used their knowledge of proportion and shapes to create these impressive columns in the temple of Amun Re at Karnak. The columns were decorated with hieroglyphs and carved figures.

4.3 Art and Architecture

The figures in ancient Egyptian paintings look awkward with their bodies facing the viewer, heads and feet facing right. Surely the artist didn't believe people really look like this!

MAIN IDEA

The ancient Egyptians created distinctive art and architecture.

A DISTINCTIVE ART STYLE

Ancient Egyptian art is easily recognizable. That is because artists used a distinctive style called frontalism. According to this style, the head and legs were drawn in profile, but the shoulders, chest, and arms were drawn as if they were facing front. The result looked pretty unnatural, but realism wasn't the goal. Most portraits were painted for religious purposes, which made it important to show as much of the body as possible. Frontalism achieved this goal.

Artists arranged each figure in a painting precisely to achieve balance and order. To get the sizes and proportions right, they followed a strict formula. Typically the human body was divided into three equal parts: from foot to knee, from knee to elbow, and from elbow to hairline. A figure's waist appeared exactly halfway up the body.

Most paintings showed scenes from everyday life. These included pharaohs performing religious rituals, fighting battles, or feasting, and ordinary people at work or play. Artists painted and carved figures and scenes like these in great temples, monuments, and tombs. This ancient art has revealed much about Egyptian life and beliefs.

ARCHITECTURE AND SACRED SHAPES

Egyptian architects also used clever techniques to make their soaring temples and other buildings look impressive. The architects used grid lines to create precise designs. They also applied mathematics to their designs using the "golden ratio." This mathematical formula helped architects achieve the most pleasing proportions—what looks good, in other words. The Greeks borrowed and developed the formula, and the golden ratio is still used today.

Certain geometric shapes, such as squares and triangles, were considered sacred, so architects included these in their designs. The most important shape, though, was the pyramid, which dominated Egyptian architecture throughout the civilization's 3,000-year history. In addition to the Great Pyramid of Khufu, architects built many other pyramids all over Egypt. Small pyramids even topped the tombs of the skilled craftspeople who built Egypt's great monuments.

REVIEW & ASSESS

1. **READING CHECK** What makes ancient Egyptian art and architecture stand out?

2. **DRAW CONCLUSIONS** What do Egyptian art and architecture reveal about the place of religion in ancient Egyptian society?

3. **DETERMINE WORD MEANINGS** How does the base word *front* clarify the meaning of the *frontalism* style of art?

6.2.5 Discuss the main features of Egyptian art and architecture.

HSS CONTENT STANDARDS:

6.2 Discuss the main features of Egyptian art and architecture.

PLAN

OBJECTIVE

Explain how ancient Egyptians created distinctive art and architecture.

ESSENTIAL QUESTION

How did ancient Egypt's rulers use the land's resources and geography to found a civilization?

Art and architecture were important in Egyptian civilization. Lesson 4.3 discusses these important elements of Egyptian culture.

BACKGROUND FOR THE TEACHER

Egyptian artwork included drawings on walls and pillars. Some of this art was intended to help the dead live forever by giving them instructions they would need as they met up with gods on their way to eternal life. The good deeds of the deceased were often celebrated through artwork. Many artists used colors such as blue, red, orange, and white to create pictures that told about the life of the dead. Sculptors were important artists in Egypt. Artists made statues of kings, queens, scribes, animals, gods, and goddesses.

DIGITAL RESOURCES NGLSync.cengage.com

TEACHER RESOURCES & ASSESSMENT

 Reading and Note-Taking

 Vocabulary Practice

 Section 4 Quiz

STUDENT RESOURCES

 NG Image Gallery

INTRODUCE & ENGAGE

CREATE A WORD WEB

Have students use a Word Web like the one shown, with the word *Architecture* in the center. Encourage students to write what they already know about designing and constructing buildings and structures in ancient Egypt. Tell students they will learn more about Egyptian art and architecture in this lesson. **0:05** minutes

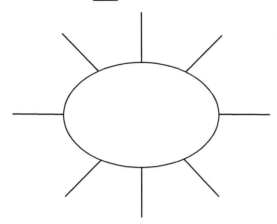

TEACH

STEM

GUIDED DISCUSSION

1. **Summarize** How did ancient Egyptian artists determine sizes and proportions of art of the human body when they drew, painted, or sculpted it? *(They followed a mathematical formula that divided the human body into three equal parts: from foot to knee, from knee to elbow, and from elbow to hairline. A figure's waist appeared exactly halfway up the body.)*

2. **Analyze Cause and Effect** How was mathematics used to make temples and other buildings look impressive? *(Architects used grid lines to create precise designs. They used the "golden ratio" mathematical formula to achieve pleasing proportions. This formula is still used today.)*

ANALYZE VISUALS

Have students look at the image of the scribes in Lesson 4.1 and point out the characteristics of frontalism that they read about in the current lesson. Then have students take a few minutes to look back through the chapter and identify other examples of frontalism in chapter photographs. **0:10** minutes

ACTIVE OPTIONS

Critical Viewing: NG Image Gallery Invite students to explore the entire NG Image Gallery and choose one image from the gallery they feel best represents their understanding of each chapter or unit. Have students provide a written explanation of why they selected each of the images they chose. **0:15** minutes

On Your Feet: Fishbowl Have one group of students sit in a close circle facing inward. Have another group sit in a larger circle around them. Have students on the inside discuss ancient Egyptian art. Then have students on the outside summarize the information they heard. Have groups reverse positions and repeat the same activity. **0:10** minutes

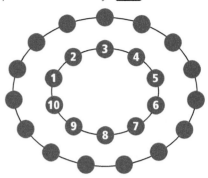

DIFFERENTIATE

STRIVING READERS

Set a Purpose for Reading Direct students to read and find at least three details about ancient Egyptian art and at least three details about ancient Egyptian architecture. After reading, have students record the details on note cards. Encourage partners to compare cards and discuss the details they chose.

PRE-AP

Write Feature Articles Assign students the role of a journalist reporting on ancient Egyptian art and architecture. Show students examples of feature articles from newspapers or magazines, and ask students to focus on specific examples of art and architecture and write their own feature article. Then have students share their articles with the class.

Press (mt) *in the Student eEdition for modified text.*

See the Chapter Planner for more strategies for differentiation.

REVIEW & ASSESS

ANSWERS

1. The use of frontalism makes ancient Egyptian art distinctive, with its profile view of the head and legs and frontal view of the shoulders, chest, and arms.

2. In their buildings, ancient Egyptians incorporated shapes such as squares and triangles that they considered sacred. Religious images appear in ancient Egyptian art, even in depictions of everyday life. The art and architecture reveal that religion was very important in ancient Egyptian life.

3. From the base word *front*, one can infer that most of the image of a person was facing toward the front.

VOCABULARY

Use each of the following vocabulary words in a sentence that shows an understanding of the word's meaning.

1. **cataract** (HSS 6.2.1)
   Cataracts make river travel difficult because boats must navigate around these rapids.
2. **dynasty** (HSS 6.2)
3. **pharaoh** (HSS 6.2.3)
4. **hierarchy** (HSS 6.2)
5. **mummy** (HSS 6.2)
6. **hieroglyph** (HSS 6.2.9)
7. **scribe** (HSS 6.2.9)
8. **papyrus** (HSS 6.2.9)

READING SKILL

9. **DRAW CONCLUSIONS** If you haven't already, complete your organizer to draw conclusions about the importance of ancient Egypt's geographic features. Then answer the question.

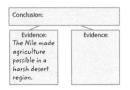

Conclusion:

Evidence:
The Nile made agriculture possible in a harsh desert region.

Evidence:

How did the Nile River affect civilization in ancient Egypt? Explain. (HSS 6.2.1)

MAIN IDEAS

Answer the following questions. Support your answers with evidence from the chapter.

10. Why was Egyptian agriculture dependent on the Nile? **LESSON 1.1** (HSS 6.2.1)
11. What was the relationship between Upper Egypt and Lower Egypt? **LESSON 1.2** (HSS HI 1)
12. What was the role of the pharaoh in Egyptian life? **LESSON 1.3** (HSS 6.2.3)
13. How did the Great Pyramid of Khufu demonstrate the pharaoh's power? **LESSON 2.1** (HSS 6.2.3)
14. How were the classes of Egyptian society organized? **LESSON 2.2** (HSS 6.2.3)
15. What contributions did Hatshepsut make to Egypt during her reign? **LESSON 3.1** (HSS 6.2.7)
16. In what ways were Kush and Egypt connected? **LESSON 3.4** (HSS 6.2.8)
17. Why was it desirable to be a scribe in ancient Egypt? **LESSON 4.1** (HSS HI 1)

CRITICAL THINKING

Answer the following questions. Support your answers with evidence from the chapter.

18. **ESSENTIAL QUESTION** How did the pharaohs use Egypt's resources to increase the country's wealth and power? (HSS 6.2.2)
19. **DRAW CONCLUSIONS** What impact did the Nile have on Egypt's trade industry? (HSS 6.2.6)
20. **ANALYZE CAUSE AND EFFECT** How did the absolute power of the pharaohs contribute to Egypt's cycles of order and disorder? (HSS HI 2)
21. **MAKE GENERALIZATIONS** What position did women have in Egyptian society? (HSS HI 1)
22. **YOU DECIDE** The Egyptians had many important achievements in math, science, art, and architecture. Which achievement do you think left the greatest legacy, and why? (HSS 6.2.5)

INTERPRET DIAGRAMS

Study the cross-section diagram of the interior of King Khufu's Great Pyramid at Giza. Then answer the questions that follow.

GREAT PYRAMID AT GIZA

Ⓐ **King's Chamber,** where Khufu was buried
Ⓑ **Queen's Chamber,** which was found empty
Ⓒ **Grand Gallery,** leading to the King's Chamber
Ⓓ **Entrance,** which was sealed off by a heavy wall
Ⓔ **Unfinished Chamber,** built underground, beneath the pyramid
Ⓕ **Air Vents**

23. What features of the pyramid might help discourage tomb robbers? (HSS CST 3)
24. What features of the pyramid were created to help the workers who built it? (HSS CST 3)

ANALYZE SOURCES

Read the following translation of advice from an ancient Egyptian father to his son, who is training to be a scribe. Then answer the question.

> I have compared the people who are artisans and handicraftsmen [with the scribe], and indeed I am convinced that there is nothing superior to letters. Plunge into the study of Egyptian Learning, as you would plunge into the river, and you will find that this is so. . . . I wish I were able to make you see how beautiful Learning is. It is more important than any trade in the world.

25. What conclusions can you draw about the role of scribes in ancient Egyptian society? (HSS REP 4)

WRITE ABOUT HISTORY

26. **NARRATIVE** Suppose you were a scribe when Ramses II was pharaoh of Egypt. Write an eyewitness account that tells about his greatest achievements. Use the tips below to help you plan, organize, and revise your narrative. (HSS HI 1)

TIPS
- Take notes from the chapter about the reign of Ramses II and his achievements.
- Make an outline of the achievements and events you will include.
- Be sure to include details and examples.
- Use at least two vocabulary words from the chapter.
- Provide a concluding statement that summarizes why Ramses II was an effective pharaoh.
- Use word-processing software to produce and publish your final narrative.

VOCABULARY ANSWERS

1. Cataracts make river travel difficult because boats must navigate around these rapids. (HSS 6.2.1)
2. In an Egyptian dynasty, the throne passed from the pharaoh to his son. (HSS 6.2)
3. Egyptians believed that their king, or pharaoh, was a living god who had absolute power over everyone. (HSS 6.2.3)
4. In a hierarchy, such as that in ancient Egypt, people belong to different social classes and each class has a rank in society. (HSS 6.2)
5. After death, the body of an Egyptian pharaoh was preserved as a mummy in a royal tomb. (HSS 6.2)
6. Each hieroglyph in the Egyptian writing system represented a sound, an object, or an idea. (HSS 6.2.9)
7. To become a scribe, an Egyptian trained for five years to acquire the skill of writing. (HSS 6.2.9)
8. Egyptian scribes wrote on sheets of paper-like material called papyrus. (HSS 6.2.9)

STANDARDS

HSS CONTENT STANDARDS:

6.2.1 Locate and describe the major river systems and discuss the physical settings that supported permanent settlement and early civilizations; **6.2.2** Trace the development of agricultural techniques that permitted the production of economic surplus and the emergence of cities as centers of culture and power; **6.2.3** Understand the relationship between religion and the social and political order in Mesopotamia and Egypt; **6.2.5** Discuss the main features of Egyptian art and architecture; **6.2.6** Describe the role of Egyptian trade in the eastern Mediterranean and Nile valley; **6.2.7** Understand the significance of Queen Hatshepsut and Ramses the Great; **6.2.8** Identify the location of the Kush civilization and describe its political, commercial, and cultural relations with Egypt; **6.2.9** Trace the evolution of language and its written forms.

HSS ANALYSIS SKILLS:

CST 3 Students use a variety of maps and documents to identify physical and cultural features of neighborhoods, cities, states, and countries and to explain the historical migration of people, expansion and disintegration of empires, and the growth of economic systems; **REP 4** Students assess the credibility of primary and secondary sources and draw sound conclusions from them; **HI 1** Students explain the central issues and problems from the past, placing people and events in a matrix of time and place; **HI 2** Students understand and distinguish cause, effect, sequence, and correlation in historical events, including the long- and short-term causal relations.

READING STRATEGY ANSWER

Conclusion: The Nile was important to the success of Egyptian civilization.

Evidence: The Nile made agriculture possible in a harsh desert region.

Evidence: The Nile was easy to navigate, making it a good trade route.

9. The Nile River flooded every year, depositing fertile soil along its banks. For this reason, the Nile made agriculture possible in a harsh desert region. The large harvests and food surpluses were key to the development of Egyptian civilization. The Nile also provided important trade routes for Egypt. Trade was important to the development of Egyptian civilization. (HSS 6.2.1)

MAIN IDEAS ANSWERS

10. The floods brought water to the crops, as well as silt, which was rich in nutrients. A year with low floodwaters could mean famine. (HSS 6.2.1)

11. The two kingdoms were next to each other, and goods and ideas were easily traded between them. They probably already shared a culture before being united under the pharaohs. Even so, they maintained their own identities and stood on opposite sides when there were power struggles in Egypt. (HSS HI 1)

12. He went between the people and the gods of ancient Egypt. He was also the absolute ruler of all aspects of government. (HSS 6.2.3)

13. The Great Pyramid took tremendous resources to build, both in terms of materials and manpower. The pharaoh would have to be very wealthy and powerful to cause such a monumental work to be done. (HSS 6.2.3)

14. After the pharaoh, the nobles and priests held the most power. Then came the officials and scribes, then the craftsmen and merchants, and then the farmers. At the bottom, came unskilled laborers and slaves. (HSS 6.2.3)

15. Hatshepsut expanded the Egyptian empire, but her most important contributions were in the promotion and expansion of trade, which greatly increased Egypt's wealth. She risked difficult and dangerous trade expeditions to the coast of East Africa, which further boosted Egypt's wealth and stimulated its economy. (HSS 6.2.7)

16. Egypt dominated Nubia and Kush for centuries and exploited its resources. During that time, the people of Nubia and Kush adopted Egyptian culture. When Egypt became weak, the Kushites moved in to conquer their former masters. (HSS 6.2.8)

17. Scribes were important people in society. A scribe could become very powerful, and possibly even a king. (HSS HI 1)

CRITICAL THINKING ANSWERS

18. The pharaohs pursued an active foreign policy to increase Egypt's wealth. They increased trade and military power. (HSS 6.2.2)

19. Because the Nile River was easily navigable, it became a "superhighway" that encouraged contact and the trade of goods and ideas among different communities along the river. (HSS 6.2.6)

20. Every aspect of government depended on the pharaoh. That meant that when there was a strong pharaoh, he could maintain order and support trade and expansion. When the pharaoh was weak, there was nobody to impose order on the country. (HSS HI 2)

21. Even though women were first and foremost wives and mothers, they enjoyed many individual rights, including the right to own property, conduct business, participate in legal proceedings, and pursue a great variety of professions. (HSS HI 1)

22. Students' responses will vary. Students should clearly state their opinion regarding their view of which achievement made by the Egyptian civilization left the greatest legacy and support that opinion with evidence from the chapter. (HSS 6.2.5)

INTERPRET CHARTS ANSWERS

23. The entrance was sealed off by a heavy wall. (HSS CST 3)

24. The air vents helped the workers who built the pyramid. (HSS CST 3)

ANALYZE SOURCES ANSWER

25. Students' responses will vary. Sample response: The advice from the father to his son indicates that learning is valued and that scribes are well-respected in ancient Egyptian society. (HSS REP 4)

WRITE ABOUT HISTORY ANSWER

26. Students' narratives will vary, but should

- include details and examples
- use vocabulary words
- summarize why Ramses II was an effective pharaoh

For more in-depth instruction and practice with the writing form, assign the Social Studies Skills Writing Lesson on writing a narrative. (HSS HI 1)

UNIT RESOURCES

On Location with National Geographic Lead Program Officer Christopher Thornton Intro and Video

 Interactive Map Tool

 **News & Updates**

Available at NGLSync.cengage.com

Unit Wrap-Up:
"Encounters with History"
Feature and Video

"China's Ancient Lifeline"
National Geographic Adapted Article

"Faces of the Divine"
National Geographic Adapted Article
Student eEdition exclusive

Unit 2 Inquiry:
Write a Creation Myth

CHAPTER RESOURCES

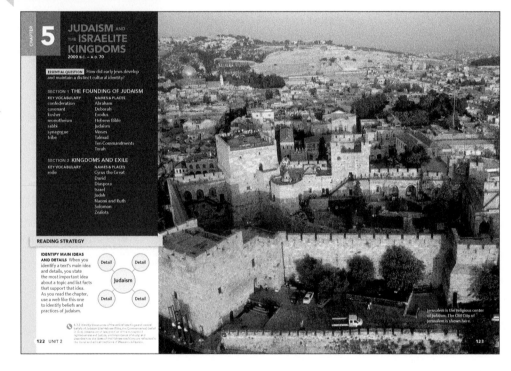

Jerusalem is the religious center of Judaism. The Old City of Jerusalem is shown here.

122 UNIT 2   123

TEACHER RESOURCES & ASSESSMENT

Available at NGLSync.cengage.com

Social Studies Skills Lessons
• Reading: Identify Main Ideas and Details
• Writing: Write an Argument

Formal Assessment
• Chapter 5 Tests A (on-level) & B (below-level)

Chapter 5 Answer Key

ExamView®
One-time Download

STUDENT BACKPACK *Available at NGLSync.cengage.com*
• **eEdition** *(English)*   • **eEdition** *(Spanish)*   • **Handbooks**   • **Online Atlas**
Chapter 5 Spanish resources, Guided Writing prompts, and Financial Literacy lessons are available online.

SECTION 1 RESOURCES

THE FOUNDING OF JUDAISM

 Reading and Note-Taking

 Vocabulary Practice

 Section 1 Quiz

Available at NGLSync.cengage.com

LESSON 1.1 ABRAHAM AND MOSES

- Critical Viewing: NG Chapter Gallery

NG Learning Framework:
A Man Called Moses

LESSON 1.2 A DISTINCT CULTURE

 **Active History: Interactive Whiteboard Activity**
Investigate Major Religious Holidays

 Active History
Investigate Major Religious Holidays

Available at NGLSync.cengage.com

- On Your Feet: Create a Concept Web

LESSON 1.3 BELIEFS AND TEXTS OF JUDAISM

- Critical Viewing: NG Chapter Gallery
- On Your Feet: Inside-Outside Circle

DOCUMENT-BASED QUESTION
LESSON 1.4 WRITINGS FROM THE HEBREW BIBLE

- Critical Viewing: NG Chapter Gallery
- On Your Feet: Two Options

SECTION 2 RESOURCES

KINGDOMS AND EXILE

 Reading and Note-Taking

 Vocabulary Practice

 Section 2 Quiz

Available at NGLSync.cengage.com

LESSON 2.1 ISRAEL AND JUDAH

 Biography
Solomon

Available at NGLSync.cengage.com

NG Learning Framework:
Write a Biography

- On Your Feet: Tell Me More

LESSON 2.2 EXILE AND RETURN

- Critical Viewing: NG Chapter Gallery
- On Your Feet: Card Responses

LESSON 2.3 THE DIASPORA

- Critical Viewing: NG Chapter Gallery
- On Your Feet: One-on-One Interviews

NG EXPLORER BEVERLY GOODMAN
LESSON 2.4 UNCOVERING THE STORY OF CAESAREA'S PORT

NG Learning Framework:
Learn More About Tsunamis

- On Your Feet: Three-Step Interview

CHAPTER 5 REVIEW

STRATEGY ❶

Preview Text

Help students preview each lesson in the chapter. For each lesson, have them read the lesson titles, lesson introductions, Main Idea statements, captions, and headings. Then have them list the information they expect to find in the text. Have students read a lesson and discuss with a partner what they learned and whether or not it matched their list.

Use with All Lessons

STRATEGY ❷

Use Pair-Share Reading

Allow students to work in pairs and divide each two-page lesson into two parts. Have students decide which part each one will handle. Both students will read the first part. The student responsible for it will sum up orally the important information in that part. The second student will make notes and ask a question about the information. The students will switch roles and repeat the procedure with the second part.

Use with Lessons 1.1–1.3 and 2.1–2.3

STRATEGY ❸

Turn Lesson Titles into Questions

Before reading each lesson, display the appropriate question based on the lesson title. After reading, have students write the answers to the questions and compare their answers.

1.1	Who were Abraham and Moses?
1.2	How did the Israelites develop a distinct culture?
1.3	What are the beliefs and texts of Judaism?

Use with Lessons 1.1–1.3 *Use the same strategy for the titles in Section 2. Tell students to pay careful attention to words in the titles so that their questions are relevant. For Lessons 2.1–2.3, have students share their questions and answers with classmates.*

Press *in the Student eEdition for modified text.*

STRATEGY ❶

Use Supported Reading

In small groups, have students read aloud the chapter lesson by lesson. At the end of each lesson, have them stop and use these frames to tell what they comprehended from the text:

This lesson is about _____ .

One detail that stood out to me is _____ .

The vocabulary word _____ means _____ .

I don't think I understand _____ .

Guide students with portions of text they do not understand. Be sure all students understand a lesson before moving on to the next one.

Use with All Lessons

STRATEGY ❷

Sequence Events

Write events from Section 2 on index cards. Read the events aloud and then have students put the cards in chronological order.

Use with Lessons 2.1–2.3

STRATEGY ❶

Identify Main Ideas and Details

Each lesson in the chapter has two subsections. Pair students of similar proficiency levels together and assign each pair a subsection of the text to read together. Encourage students to make notes about their part of the lesson, including questions they have about vocabulary or idioms. After answering their questions, have each pair write a one- or two-sentence summary. Provide the following sentence frames to help students compose their summaries.

Emerging

The text mostly talks about _____ .

Expanding

The main idea in this text is _____ . I know that because _____ .

Bridging

The main idea is _____ , which is supported by the details such as/like _____ and _____ .

Use with All Lessons, All Levels

STANDARDS

HSS CONTENT STANDARDS:

6.3.3 Explain the significance of Abraham, Moses, Naomi, Ruth, David, and Yohanan ben Zaccai in the development of the Jewish religion.

HSS ANALYSIS STANDARDS:

CST 2 Students construct various time lines of key events, people, and periods of the historical era they are studying.

STRATEGY ❷

Review Vocabulary

After reading, write the following words on the board and ask students to write a phrase to describe each word. Then have volunteers use each word in an oral sentence.

confederation   covenant   monotheism

Use with Lessons 1.1–1.4, All Levels

STRATEGY ❸

Use Sentence Stems

Before reading, provide students with the two sentence stems for the lessons listed below. Call on volunteers to read the stems orally and explain any unclear vocabulary. After reading, have students complete the stems in writing and compare completed sentences with a partner.

1.1 **a.** The worship of a single God is _____.

 b. Abraham's descendants had a special religious agreement, called a _____.

1.2 **a.** The Israelites consisted of 12 extended family units, or _____.

 b. The tribes of Israel lived separately but acted as a loose _____.

1.3 **a.** According to religious codes, Jews could eat only _____.

 b. In the Hebrew Bible, the five books of Moses make up the _____.

Use with Lessons 1.1–1.3, All Levels *Pair students at the **Emerging** level with students at a higher proficiency level to complete the stems in writing.*

GIFTED & TALENTED

STRATEGY ❶

Teach a Class

Before beginning the chapter, allow students to choose one of the two-page lessons listed below and prepare to teach the contents to the class. Give them a set amount of time in which to present their lesson. Suggest that students think about any visuals or activities they want to use when they teach.

Use with Lessons 1.1–1.3 and 2.1–2.3

STRATEGY ❷

Read Historical Biographies

Work with the school librarian to find biographical information about the kings of the Israelites, such as David and Solomon. Allow students to choose one of the kings and read a book or story about the individual and design a way to report on the book or story to the class.

Use with Lessons 2.1–2.4

PRE-AP

STRATEGY ❶

Explain the Significance

Allow students to choose one name below to investigate and design a presentation that explains the significance of the person to the history of the Israelites.

Saul

David

Solomon

Cyrus the Great

Yohannan Ben Zakai

Use with Lessons 2.1–2.3

STRATEGY ❷

Form a Thesis

Have students develop a thesis statement for a specific topic related to one of the lessons in the chapter. Be sure the statement makes a claim that is supportable with evidence either from the chapter or through further research. Then have pairs compare their statements and determine which makes the strongest or most supportable claim.

Use with All Lessons

5 JUDAISM AND THE ISRAELITE KINGDOMS

2000 B.C. – A.D. 70

ESSENTIAL QUESTION How did early Jews develop and maintain a distinct cultural identity?

SECTION 1 THE FOUNDING OF JUDAISM

KEY VOCABULARY	NAMES & PLACES
confederation	Abraham
covenant	Deborah
kosher	Exodus
monotheism	Hebrew Bible
rabbi	Judaism
synagogue	Moses
tribe	Talmud
	Ten Commandments
	Torah

SECTION 2 KINGDOMS AND EXILE

KEY VOCABULARY	NAMES & PLACES
exile	Cyrus the Great
	David
	Diaspora
	Israel
	Judah
	Naomi and Ruth
	Solomon
	Zealots

READING STRATEGY

IDENTIFY MAIN IDEAS AND DETAILS When you identify a text's main idea and details, you state the most important idea about a topic and list facts that support that idea. As you read the chapter, use a web like this one to identify beliefs and practices of Judaism.

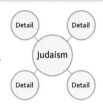

6.3.2 Identify the sources of the ethical teachings and central beliefs of Judaism (the Hebrew Bible, the Commentaries): belief in God, observance of law, practice of the concepts of righteousness and justice, and importance of study; and describe how the ideas of the Hebrew traditions are reflected in the moral and ethical traditions of Western civilization.

122 UNIT 2

Jerusalem is the religious center of Judaism. The Old City of Jerusalem is shown here.

123

HSS CONTENT STANDARDS:

6.3.2 Identify the sources of the ethical teachings and central beliefs of Judaism (the Hebrew Bible, the Commentaries): belief in God, observance of law, practice of the concepts of righteousness and justice, and importance of study; and describe how the ideas of the Hebrew traditions are reflected in the moral and ethical traditions of Western civilization.

TEACHER BACKGROUND

INTRODUCE THE PHOTOGRAPH

Have students study the photograph of the Old City of Jerusalem. Explain that Jerusalem has held significance for Judaism, Christianity, and Islam for many centuries. While rulers and governments have come and gone, adherents of each religion have maintained a presence in the city because it is holy for Jews, Christians, and Muslims alike. Explain that in this chapter students will learn about the development of Judaism and the significance of Jerusalem in that development.

ASK: Why might people from all over the world travel to Jerusalem? (Possible responses: They travel to Jerusalem to visit its holy sites and to learn about the city's rich history.)

SHARE BACKGROUND

The Old City of Jerusalem is a walled area within the modern city of Jerusalem. The Old City has been continuously inhabited for nearly 5,000 years. It includes important sites of religious significance for three religions: the Dome of the Rock and al-Aqsa Mosque for Muslims, the Church of the Holy Sepulchre for Christians, and the Temple Mount and Western Wall for Jews.

DIGITAL RESOURCES NGLSync.cengage.com

TEACHER RESOURCES & ASSESSMENT

 Social Studies Skills Lessons
- Reading: Identify Main Ideas and Details
- Writing: Write an Argument

 ExamView®
One-time Download

 Formal Assessment
- Chapter 5 Tests A (on-level) & B (below-level)

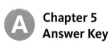 **Chapter 5 Answer Key**

STUDENT BACKPACK
- **eEdition** (English)
- **eEdition** (Spanish)
- **Handbooks**
- **Online Atlas**

INTRODUCE THE ESSENTIAL QUESTION

HOW DID EARLY JEWS DEVELOP AND MAINTAIN A DISTINCT CULTURAL IDENTITY?

Roundtable Activity: Elements of Culture This activity will allow students to explore the Essential Question by discussing what elements make up a culture. Divide the class into groups of four. Have group members position their desks in a circle. Hand each group a sheet of paper with these questions at the top: What elements make up a culture? What are some ways that cultures are different from one another? The first student in each group should write an answer, read it aloud, and then pass the paper clockwise to the next student who may add a new answer. The paper should be circulated around the group until the time is up. After ten minutes, ask for volunteers to read their group's answers to the class. Write groups' responses on the board. (*Possible responses: Culture includes a group's way of life; cultures differ in their foods, customs, and beliefs.*)

`0:20` minutes

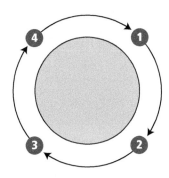

INTRODUCE THE READING STRATEGY

IDENTIFY MAIN IDEAS AND DETAILS

Remind students that the main idea tells what a selection or paragraph is about. Supporting details are facts that support the main idea. Model completing the Main Idea Cluster by reading aloud the first paragraph under "The Promised Land" in Lesson 1.1 and adding the phrase "believed in one God" as one of the details. For more in-depth instruction and practice with the reading strategy, assign the Social Studies Skills Reading Lesson on identifying main ideas and details.

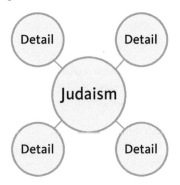

INTRODUCE CHAPTER VOCABULARY

KNOWLEDGE RATING

Have students complete a Knowledge-Rating Chart for Key Vocabulary words. Have students list words and fill out the chart. Then have pairs share the definitions they know. Work together as a class to complete the chart.

KEY VOCAB	KNOW IT	NOT SURE	DON'T KNOW	DEFINITION
confederation				
covenant				
exile				
kosher				

KEY DATES	
c. 1290 B.C.	The Exodus: Moses leads the Israelites in their escape from slavery in Egypt
970 B.C.	King Solomon builds his temple in Jerusalem
922 B.C.	Israel is divided into two separate kingdoms: Israel and Judah
722 B.C.	Assyrians conquer the kingdom of Israel
586 B.C.	King Nebuchadnezzar destroys Jerusalem and Solomon's Temple and exiles many Jews
538 B.C.	Cyrus the Great allows thousands of Jews to return to Judah

1.1
Abraham
and Moses

While mighty empires rose and fell, a group of shepherds grew into a small nation. These people never ruled a powerful empire. But they were bound together by a strong religious faith, and their influence has been greater than that of many empires. These people are known by various names, including Hebrews, Israelites, and Jews.

MAIN IDEA

Abraham and Moses were important leaders of **Judaism**, the first religion based on the worship of a single God.

THE PROMISED LAND

The Hebrews were a people who settled in Canaan (KAY-nuhn) around 1800 B.C. Canaan was on the eastern coast of the Mediterranean Sea. This region was later called Israel and also Palestine. The Hebrews differed from all other ancient people in an important way: they practiced **monotheism**, the worship of a single God. All other ancient people practiced polytheism, which you may recall is the worship of many gods. Monotheism was a significant development in religion and has had a great impact on cultures around the world.

Most of what we know about the Hebrews comes from the **Hebrew Bible**, a collection of ancient religious writings. According to these writings, God told **Abraham**, a Mesopotamian shepherd, to take his family and settle in Canaan. The region would be their Promised Land—a land that would belong to Abraham and his family forever. Abraham's descendants would have a special **covenant** (KUHV-uh-nuhnt), or religious agreement, with God. According to the covenant, God would protect the Hebrews if they accepted no other god and did what God asked.

The early Hebrews led a quiet, seminomadic life in Canaan. Seminomadic people move frequently with their flocks, but they often return to one place where they grow crops.

THE EXODUS

The land of Canaan sometimes became too dry for growing crops. According to the Hebrew Bible, a devastating drought, or dry period, caused such a severe shortage of food that the Hebrews left Canaan and settled in northern Egypt, perhaps around 1650 B.C. Here, the pharaoh enslaved them to work on his building projects. Around this time, the Hebrews became known as the Israelites.

The Hebrew Bible relates that the Israelites endured centuries of suffering before God chose a man named **Moses** to help them escape from Egypt. The Israelites returned to Canaan in a journey from slavery to freedom called the **Exodus**, possibly in the 1200s B.C. According to the Bible, the Israelites traveled through the desert for 40 years before finally returning to Canaan. Along the way Moses climbed Mount Sinai (SY-ny), where God gave him the **Ten Commandments** and other laws. This religious, moral, and civil code reaffirmed and expanded the Israelites' covenant with God. Today, the Ten Commandments form the basis of many modern laws, such as the law against stealing another person's property.

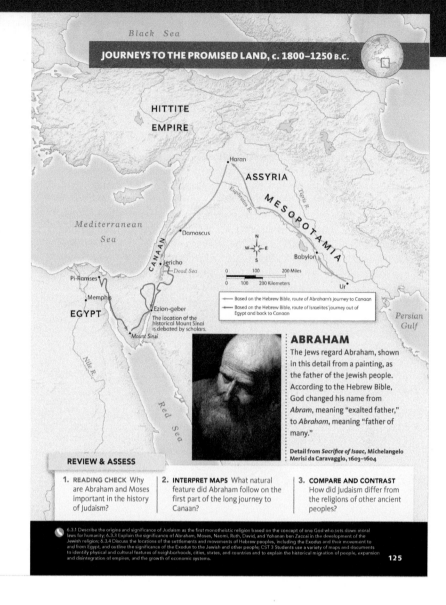

JOURNEYS TO THE PROMISED LAND, c. 1800–1250 B.C.

Based on the Hebrew Bible, route of Abraham's journey to Canaan
Based on the Hebrew Bible, route of Israelites' journey out of Egypt and back to Canaan

The location of the historical Mount Sinai is debated by scholars.

ABRAHAM

The Jews regard Abraham, shown in this detail from a painting, as the father of the Jewish people. According to the Hebrew Bible, God changed his name from *Abram*, meaning "exalted father," to *Abraham*, meaning "father of many."

Detail from *Sacrifice of Isaac*, Michelangelo Merisi da Caravaggio, 1603–1604

REVIEW & ASSESS

1. **READING CHECK** Why are Abraham and Moses important in the history of Judaism?

2. **INTERPRET MAPS** What natural feature did Abraham follow on the first part of the long journey to Canaan?

3. **COMPARE AND CONTRAST** How did Judaism differ from the religions of other ancient peoples?

6.3.1 Describe the origins and significance of Judaism as the first monotheistic religion based on the concept of one God who sets down moral laws for humanity; 6.3.3 Explain the significance of Abraham, Moses, Naomi, Ruth, David, and Yohanan ben Zaccai in the development of the Jewish religion; 6.3.4 Discuss the locations of the settlements and movements of Hebrew peoples, including the Exodus and their movement to and from Egypt, and outline the significance of the Exodus to the Jewish and other people; CST 3 Students use a variety of maps and documents to identify physical and cultural features of neighborhoods, cities, states, and countries and to explain the historical migration of people, expansion and disintegration of empires, and the growth of economic systems.

HSS CONTENT STANDARDS:

6.3.1 Describe the origins and significance of Judaism as the first monotheistic religion based on the concept of one God who sets down moral laws for humanity; **6.3.3** Explain the significance of Abraham, Moses, Naomi, Ruth, David, and Yohanan ben Zaccai in the development of the Jewish religion; **6.3.4** Discuss the locations of the settlements and movements of Hebrew peoples, including the Exodus and their movement to and from Egypt, and outline the significance of the Exodus to the Jewish and other peoples.

HSS ANALYSIS SKILLS:

CST 3 Students use a variety of maps and documents to identify physical and cultural features of neighborhoods, cities, states, and countries and to explain the historical migration of people, expansion and disintegration of empires, and the growth of economic systems.

PLAN

OBJECTIVE

Explain why Abraham and Moses were important leaders of Judaism.

ESSENTIAL QUESTION

How did early Jews develop and maintain a distinct cultural identity?

Judaism differed from other ancient religions in that it was the first religion based on the worship of a single God. Lesson 1.1 describes the roles of Abraham and Moses in the development of Judaism.

BACKGROUND FOR THE TEACHER

Early Jewish history can be challenging because the Hebrews did not occupy and control a defined territory as many of their contemporaries did. Remind students that what united Hebrews was their belief system. Point out that this can be a much more powerful bond than a common geography. A common belief system can maintain cultural ties across geographic boundaries. Foreshadow the later history of the Jews, including the Diaspora, and point out that the strength of this belief system will become evident.

DIGITAL RESOURCES NGLSync.cengage.com

TEACHER RESOURCES & ASSESSMENT

 Reading and Note-Taking

 Vocabulary Practice

 Section 1 Quiz

STUDENT RESOURCES

 NG Chapter Gallery

INTRODUCE & ENGAGE

BRAINSTORM STRONG LEADERS

Ask students to identify people in history who are considered strong leaders. Students' lists might include George Washington, Abraham Lincoln, or Martin Luther King, Jr. Have students record the names of these leaders on sticky notes and post them on the wall. Then work together to brainstorm characteristics that strong leaders possess. Again, record these characteristics on sticky notes and post. Tell students that in this lesson they will learn about the importance of two strong leaders to Judaism. **0:05** minutes

TEACH

GUIDED DISCUSSION

1. **Draw Conclusions** What development by the Hebrew people had a great impact on other cultures? *(the development of monotheism)*

2. **Make Inferences** Why was it important for the Israelites to return to Canaan? *(God promised that Canaan would be their Promised Land and would be theirs forever.)*

INTERPRET MAPS

Draw students' attention to the legend and the distance scale on the Journeys to the Promised Land map. Ask students to calculate the distance that Abraham traveled to Canaan and the distance the Israelites traveled out of Egypt and back to Canaan. Have students work with partners to calculate the distances. It might be helpful to use string to follow the lines on the map against the distance scale. *(Abraham's journey is approximately 900 miles. The Israelites' journey is approximately 850 miles.)* **0:15** minutes

ACTIVE OPTIONS

Critical Viewing: NG Chapter Gallery Have students explore the NG Chapter Gallery and choose two of the items to compare and contrast, either in written form or verbally with a partner. Ask questions that will inspire this process, such as "How are these images alike? How are they different? Why did you select these two items? How do they relate in history?" **0:10** minutes

NG Learning Framework: A Man Called Moses

ATTITUDE: Curiosity
SKILLS: Communication, Collaboration

Invite students to reread the information about Moses in Lesson 1.1. Invite them to work in pairs to make a fact sheet about Moses based on the information in the text. Then have each pair pose one additional question about Moses they would like to answer. Have student pairs conduct responsible online research in an attempt to find the answer to their question. Encourage students to add to their Moses fact sheets as they do their research and uncover more information. Have student pairs share their fact sheets with the rest of the class. **0:10** minutes

DIFFERENTIATE

STRIVING READERS

Summarize Read the lesson aloud while students follow along in their print or digital text. At the end of each paragraph, ask students to summarize what you read in a sentence. Allow them time to write the summary on their own paper.

ENGLISH LANGUAGE LEARNERS ELD

Find Main Ideas and Details Have students form two groups with mixed proficiency levels. Give each group a piece of construction paper or a flip chart with the main idea of the lesson written on it: *Abraham and Moses were important leaders of Judaism, the first religion based on the worship of a single God.* Ask each group to list as many details from the lesson as they can to support the main idea. They should write their details on the flip chart or construction paper. Then have the two groups compare their lists.

Press **mt** *in the Student eEdition for modified text.*

See the Chapter Planner for more strategies for differentiation.

REVIEW & ASSESS

ANSWERS

1. Abraham and Moses are important to Judaism because they guided their people in significant ways. Abraham followed God's directive and moved his family to Canaan, which would be their Promised Land. Abraham's descendants would have a covenant with God in which God would protect the Hebrews if they accepted no other god and did what God asked. Moses helped the Israelites escape from Egypt and return to Canaan. Moses also received the Ten Commandments and other laws from God, which expanded the Israelites' covenant with God.

2. Abraham followed the Euphrates River on the first part of his long journey to Canaan.

3. Judaism focused on the worship of only one God, which is called monotheism. In contrast, the religions of other ancient peoples focused on the worship of multiple gods, which is called polytheism.

1.2

A Distinct
Culture

You need a lot of nerve to go against a common belief. Abraham had this courage. But his strong belief ended up leading his people down a path filled with intolerance and harsh treatment, which continue in some places today. As you will see, acting out of strong belief became an important part of the distinct culture of the Israelites.

MAIN IDEA

As the Israelites fought to win control of their Promised Land, their religious beliefs and practices set them apart from the Canaanites.

POSSIBLE RESPONSE

The terrain is hilly, with level land that appears to be good for agriculture.

Critical Viewing At Mount Tabor, the Israelites battled the Canaanites. This view shows the town of Dabburiya at the foot of Mount Tabor today. Based on this view, how would you describe the terrain of the Promised Land?

BELIEF IN ONE GOD

The belief in one God is central to Judaism. This idea may seem normal to many people today, but it was a radical idea in the ancient world. The Israelites were the first people to reject polytheism, making Judaism the world's oldest monotheistic religion.

DEBORAH

Deborah was the Israelites' only female judge. At the Battle of Mount Tabor around 1125 B.C., she led the Israelites to victory against a Canaanite king.

Belief in one God helped unify the Israelites, but their beliefs and practices also set them apart from other ancient cultures. According to the Hebrew Bible, God gave Moses a code of religious practices that governed most aspects of life. The Israelites did not worship idols, or false gods. They ate only certain foods. They did not work on the Sabbath, a weekly day of rest. While they traded with other peoples, they tried to keep a distinct cultural identity. Most Israelites did not marry outside their faith, and they were careful not to adopt foreign customs. They generally avoided the cultural diffusion, or mixing, that was a major part of many other civilizations.

THE TWELVE TRIBES

According to the Hebrew Bible, when the Israelites returned to Canaan from Egypt, they consisted of 12 **tribes**, or extended family units. Each tribe was descended from a son of Jacob, Abraham's grandson. Since Jacob was also called Israel, the tribes were called the Twelve Tribes of Israel, and Jacob's descendants were called Israelites. They referred to Canaan as the Promised Land.

Moses had died before the Israelites returned to Canaan. The Bible describes how a new leader named Joshua brought the Israelites into the Promised Land around 1250 B.C. Joshua went to war against local people known as the Canaanites, who practiced polytheism. After battling for about 200 years, the Israelites conquered most of Canaan. The tribes then divided up the conquered lands among themselves. They lived separately but acted together as a loose **confederation**, or group of allies. Powerful leaders called judges came to head the confederation of tribes. The judges directed battles, made decisions on policy, and helped keep the tribes united.

REVIEW & ASSESS

1. **READING CHECK** What was a major difference between the Israelites and the Canaanites?

2. **IDENTIFY MAIN IDEAS AND DETAILS** According to the text, how was Israelite society organized?

3. **MAKE INFERENCES** How did the Israelites maintain a distinct cultural identity?

6.3.1 Describe the origins and significance of Judaism as the first monotheistic religion based on the concept of one God who sets down moral laws for humanity.

HSS CONTENT STANDARDS:

6.3.1 Describe the origins and significance of Judaism as the first monotheistic religion based on the concept of one God who sets down moral laws for humanity.

PLAN

OBJECTIVE

Identify how the religious beliefs and practices of the Israelites set them apart from the Canaanites.

ESSENTIAL QUESTION

How did early Jews develop and maintain a distinct cultural identity?

The belief in one God helped unify the Israelites. Lesson 1.2 discusses how the Israelites won control of the Promised Land and how their religious beliefs and practices set them apart from the Canaanites.

BACKGROUND FOR THE TEACHER

The land of Canaan covered an area that today includes Israel, Lebanon, Palestinian territories, and western Jordan. According to the book of Genesis in the Bible, the land was named after a man called Canaan, who was the grandson of Noah. Archaeologists' findings of ancient writings show that the Canaanites were ancestors of later Phoenicians. The name *Phoenician* likely comes from the Greek word *phoenix,* a red-purple color. The color refers to the red-purple dye that Phoenicians produced and exported. The name *Canaan* likely comes from the word *kinahhu,* a word for the same color from the language of a Mesopotamian group of people called the Hurrians.

DIGITAL RESOURCES NGLSync.cengage.com

TEACHER RESOURCES & ASSESSMENT

 Reading and Note-Taking

 Vocabulary Practice

 Section 1 Quiz

STUDENT RESOURCES

 Active History

INTRODUCE & ENGAGE

ACTIVATE PRIOR KNOWLEDGE

Write the term *tribe* on the board. Ask students to indicate what comes to mind when they hear the term. List students' responses on the board. Students might indicate Native American groups. Discuss the characteristics of a tribe. Students' responses might indicate that a tribe has a leader, shared values, and unique cultural characteristics. Tell students that in this lesson they will learn about the 12 tribes of Israel. `0:05` minutes

TEACH

GUIDED DISCUSSION

1. **Summarize** How did a code of religious practices given to Moses from God govern most aspects of life for the Israelites? (*Under the code, the Israelites did not worship idols, did not work on the Sabbath, did not marry outside their faith, and were careful not to adopt foreign customs.*)

2. **Draw Conclusions** How did Joshua bring the Israelites into the Promised Land? (*Joshua and the Israelites fought the Canaanites; after about 200 years, the Israelites conquered most of Canaan and divided the territory among the tribes.*)

ANALYZE VISUALS

Have students examine the photo of Mount Tabor and the town of Dabburly. Have them read the caption and answer the question. Discuss with students how the Israelites might have reacted when they viewed the Promised Land. Make a list of the reactions as students provide them. `0:10` minutes

ACTIVE OPTIONS

Active History: Investigate Major Religious Holidays Extend the lesson by using either the PDF or Whiteboard version of the activity. These activities take a deeper look at a topic from, or related to, the lesson. Explore the activities as a class, turn them into group assignments, or even assign them individually. `0:10` minutes

On Your Feet: Create a Concept Web Have students form groups of four around a section of a bulletin board or a table. Provide each group with a large sheet of paper. Have group members take turns contributing a concept or phrase to a Concept Web with the words *Distinct Culture* at the center. When time for the activity has elapsed, call on volunteers from each group to share their webs. `0:10` minutes

DIFFERENTIATE

ENGLISH LANGUAGE LEARNERS `ELD`

Summarize Lesson 1.2 has four paragraphs. Have students work in pairs or small groups, and assign each pair or group one paragraph to read. Then each group should write a one to two sentence summary of their paragraph. Provide the following sentence frames to help students at each proficiency level write an effective summary.

- **Emerging**

  This paragraph is about _____.

  First, _____. Then, _____. At the end _____.

- **Expanding**

  This paragraph is about _____ and _____.

  First, _____ and then _____. Finally, _____.

- **Bridging**

  The paragraph begins by _____. It then _____, and concludes by _____.

  To summarize, the paragraph provides information about _____.

PRE-AP

Extend Knowledge Have students conduct Internet research to find out more about the Twelve Tribes of Israel. Their findings should include the names of the tribes, whom each tribe was named after, and where each tribe settled. Ask students to present their findings in an oral report to the class

Press **mt** *in the Student eEdition for modified text.*

See the Chapter Planner for more strategies for differentiation.

REVIEW & ASSESS

ANSWERS

1. The Israelites practiced monotheism and the Canaanites practiced polytheism.

2. Israelite society was made up of 12 tribes, or family units, which formed a confederation led by judges who decided on collective policy and kept the tribes organized.

3. The strict code of religious practices reinforced Judaism among Hebrews and set the Israelites apart from everyone else.

Beliefs and Texts of **Judaism**

Your teachers probably have high expectations of you. At the very least, they'd like you to act responsibly and follow the class rules. Likewise, the Israelites believed that God had high expectations of them and wanted them to follow his rules. These rules were written down and covered almost every aspect of their lives.

MAIN IDEA

The Israelites followed religious teachings written down in their holy books.

JEWISH BELIEFS AND PRACTICES

The Hebrew Bible describes how Moses transmitted a religious code that governed the lives of the Israelites. It addressed all aspects of life, including how to worship God, how to treat all members of society well, and what to eat. For example, they could eat only **kosher** foods, foods that were specially prepared according to Jewish dietary laws. According to these laws, animals had to be killed humanely, dairy and meat could not be eaten together, and pork and shellfish were not allowed.

Judaism stressed the importance of treating others well. It promoted social justice, equality, and the holiness of human life. The Israelites also highly valued

education, charity, and hospitality, or the kind treatment of guests. In addition, Israelite women were treated well for the time. Religious teachings told husbands to love and respect their wives, who were considered to be the heart of the family.

In time, Jews began gathering to worship in buildings called **synagogues** (SIHN-uh-gahgs), meaning "places of assembly." A spiritual leader called a **rabbi**, or "teacher," usually conducted services. Rabbis upheld Jewish customs and provided guidance for living a Jewish life.

An important practice of Judaism is the observance of a weekly day of rest known as the Sabbath. It begins at sunset on Friday and ends on Saturday night. On the Sabbath, the Jewish community gathers for prayer and to read from sacred texts. Families enjoy festive meals, and people leave behind weekday work and concerns.

SACRED TEXTS

The Hebrew Bible consists of 24 books in three sections: the **Torah**, Prophets, and Writings. The Torah consists of the five books of Moses. The name *Torah* means "the teachings." Jews believe that the Torah contains the word of God as revealed to Moses on Mount Sinai. The Torah includes religious and moral guidance covering most areas of life. In fact, it forms the basis of all Jewish law. Every synagogue has a Torah scroll, handwritten on parchment, which is treated with enormous respect and read from beginning to end over the course of a year. The Torah and other Jewish laws are discussed and explained in the **Talmud**, a collection of writings by early rabbis.

The books in the Hebrew Bible also make up the Old Testament of the Christian Bible, though the books are ordered, divided, and sometimes named differently. Many stories related in the Hebrew Bible and in the Christian Bible also appear in the Qur'an, the holy book of Islam. For example, stories about Abraham appear in all three texts.

This page from a Hebrew Bible dated A.D. 1299 is written in Hebrew script.

REVIEW & ASSESS

1. **READING CHECK** What are some important beliefs and texts of Judaism?

2. **MAKE GENERALIZATIONS** What were important values in Judaism, and why might they have stood out in the ancient world?

3. **DRAW CONCLUSIONS** Why do you think the Torah is treated with great respect by Jews?

6.3.2 Identify the sources of the ethical teachings and central beliefs of Judaism (the Hebrew Bible, the Commentaries): belief in God, observance of law, practice of the concepts of righteousness and justice, and importance of study; and describe how the ideas of the Hebrew traditions are reflected in the moral and ethical traditions of Western civilization.

HSS CONTENT STANDARDS:

6.3.2 Identify the sources of the ethical teachings and central beliefs of Judaism (the Hebrew Bible, the Commentaries): belief in God, observance of law, practice of the concepts of righteousness and justice, and importance of study; and describe how the ideas of the Hebrew traditions are reflected in the moral and ethical traditions of Western civilization.

PLAN

OBJECTIVE

Describe the religious teachings written down in the religious books of the Israelites.

ESSENTIAL QUESTION

How did early Jews develop and maintain a distinct cultural identity?

The beliefs and teachings of the Jews led to the development of a distinct cultural identity. Lesson 1.3 describes the beliefs and practices and the sacred texts of the Jews.

BACKGROUND FOR THE TEACHER

According to Jewish law, keeping kosher involves three elements. The first is to avoid any non-kosher animals. These include animals that do not chew their cud and have cleft hooves and fish that don't have fins and scales. Cud is the plant material that cows and some other animals regurgitate and chew again. A second element in keeping kosher is to avoid eating meat and dairy together. The third element involves only eating meat that was slaughtered in a certain way and drained of blood. For Jews, keeping kosher was a way to obey God's laws and to preserve a distinct identity. Today the observance of keeping kosher often depends on the denomination of Judaism that one belongs to.

DIGITAL RESOURCES NGLSync.cengage.com

TEACHER RESOURCES & ASSESSMENT

 **Reading and Note-Taking**

 Vocabulary Practice

 Section 1 Quiz

STUDENT RESOURCES

 **NG Chapter Gallery**

INTRODUCE & ENGAGE

EXPLORE A CONCEPT

Display the Concept Web shown here. Discuss the concept of values with the class. Then divide the class into small groups. Have each group discuss what values they think people in their school and community have. Then call on a member from each group to share the values the group elicited. Record the responses in one of the circles of the Concept Web. Tell students that in this lesson they will learn about the values that were important to Judaism. **0:10** minutes

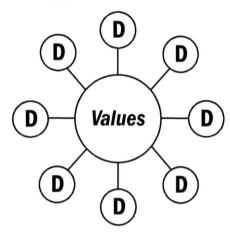

TEACH

GUIDED DISCUSSION

1. **Form Opinions** Judaism included important values and practices that Jews were to follow. Which of the practices and values do you consider to be most important? (*Responses will vary, but students should provide reasons for their opinion.*)

2. **Explain** Why is the Torah important in Judaism? (*Jews believe that the Torah contains the word of God as revealed to Moses on Mount Sinai. It includes religious and moral guidance covering most areas of life and forms the basis of all Jewish law.*)

MORE INFORMATION

Illuminated Manuscript The picture in the lesson is a page from a rare Hebrew manuscript known as the Cervera Bible. The Bible is a manuscript on parchment in Hebrew characters, written and illustrated in Cervera, Spain, between 1299 and 1300. By 1300, Jews had lived in parts of Spain for hundreds of years. The pages in the Bible include ornamental frames and intricate patterns, as well as pictures of mythological creatures such as the unicorn and centaur. The Cervera Bible is richly illustrated, making it one of the most beautiful manuscripts of Medieval Europe. **0:15** minutes

ACTIVE OPTIONS

Critical Viewing: NG Chapter Gallery Invite students to explore the Chapter Gallery to examine the images that relate to this chapter. Have them select one of the images and do additional research to learn more about it. Ask questions that will inspire additional inquiry about the chosen gallery image, such as: What is this? Where and when was this created? By whom? Why was it created? What is it made of? Why does it belong in this chapter? What else would you like to know about it? **0:10** minutes

On Your Feet: Inside-Outside Circle Arrange students in concentric circles facing each other. Have students in the outside circle ask the students in the inside circle a question about the lesson. Then have the outside circle rotate one position to the right to create new pairings. After five questions, have students switch roles and continue. **0:15** minutes

DIFFERENTIATE

INCLUSION

Use Supported Reading Have students work in pairs and assign each pair one paragraph to read aloud together. At the end of each paragraph, have them use the following sentence frames to tell what they do and do not understand:

This paragraph is about _____.

One fact that stood out to me is _____.

_____ is a word I had trouble understanding, so I

figured it out by _____.

Be sure students understand the content before moving on to the next paragraph.

GIFTED & TALENTED

Create Illuminated Manuscripts Direct students to study the page from a Hebrew Bible that appears in the lesson and ask them to describe what they see. Have students research illuminated manuscripts, particularly those from medieval times. Provide students with several examples of these types of manuscripts. Then ask students to choose a page from a favorite book and create their own illuminated pages. Share students' pages in a bulletin-board display.

Press (mt) *in the Student eEdition for modified text.*

See the Chapter Planner for more strategies for differentiation.

REVIEW & ASSESS

ANSWERS

1. Some important beliefs of Judaism include how to worship, live, and even what to wear and eat. Important texts include the 24 books of the Hebrew Bible, consisting of the Torah, Prophets, and Writings, and the Talmud, a collection of writings by early rabbis.

2. Social justice, equality, the holiness of human life, education, charity, and hospitality were important values in Judaism. These values are comparatively modern and would have been unusual in the ancient world.

3. The Torah is treated with great respect by the Jews because the Jews believe that the Torah contains the word of God as revealed to Moses, and it forms the basis of all Jewish laws.

DOCUMENT-BASED QUESTION
Writings from the Hebrew Bible

Judaism was originally based on an oral tradition, in which stories are passed down by word of mouth. After the Israelites developed writing, they wrote down their religious texts. In 1947, a shepherd discovered a set of texts near the Dead Sea. Later known as the Dead Sea Scrolls, these texts included portions of the Hebrew Bible dating from around 150 B.C.

In this part of a painting by Italian artist Guido Reni, Moses is shown with one of the two tablets containing the Ten Commandments.

Moses with the Tablets of the Law, Guido Reni, 17th century

130

DOCUMENT ONE
Primary Source: Sacred Text

from the Book of Genesis
Genesis is the first book of the Hebrew Bible. In this excerpt, God speaks to Abraham and tells him to bring his family to the land of Canaan.

CONSTRUCTED RESPONSE What does God promise Abraham?

> Go forth from your native land and from your father's house to the land that I will show you. I will make of you a great nation, and I will bless you.
>
> *Genesis 12:1–2*

DOCUMENT TWO
Primary Source: Sacred Text

from the Book of Exodus
Exodus is the second book of the Hebrew Bible. It describes the oppression of the Israelites in Egypt and their escape from slavery to freedom during the Exodus. It also depicts Moses' experience on Mount Sinai, where God gave Moses the Ten Commandments. According to the Bible, these laws were written on two stone tablets. This excerpt details the Ten Commandments.

CONSTRUCTED RESPONSE What do the first four commandments have in common? What do the last six have in common?

The Great Isaiah Scroll, one of the Dead Sea Scrolls

> *Ten Commandments*
>
> 1. I the Lord am your God. . . . You shall have no other gods besides Me.
> 2. You shall not make for yourself a sculptured image [idol].
> 3. You shall not swear falsely by the name of the Lord your God.
> 4. Remember the Sabbath day and keep it holy.
> 5. Honor your father and your mother.
> 6. You shall not murder.
> 7. You shall not commit adultery.
> 8. You shall not steal.
> 9. You shall not bear false witness against your neighbor.
> 10. You shall not covet [desire] . . . anything that is your neighbor's.
>
> *Exodus 20:2–14*

SYNTHESIZE & WRITE

1. **REVIEW** Review what you have learned about the covenant made between God and the Israelites.

2. **RECALL** On your own paper, write down the main idea expressed in each document above.

3. **CONSTRUCT** Construct a topic sentence that answers this question: What did God promise the Israelites?

4. **WRITE** Using evidence from the documents, write an explanatory paragraph that supports your topic sentence from Step 3.

6.3.2 Identify the sources of the ethical teachings and central beliefs of Judaism (the Hebrew Bible, the Commentaries): belief in God, observance of law, practice of the concepts of righteousness and justice, and importance of study; and describe how the ideas of the Hebrew traditions are reflected in the moral and ethical traditions of Western civilization; 6.3.3 Explain the significance of Abraham, Moses, Naomi, Ruth, David, and Yohanan ben Zaccai in the development of the Jewish religion; REP 4 Students assess the credibility of primary and secondary sources and draw sound conclusions from them.

131

HSS CONTENT STANDARDS:

6.3.2 Identify the sources of the ethical teachings and central beliefs of Judaism (the Hebrew Bible, the Commentaries): belief in God, observance of law, practice of the concepts of righteousness and justice, and importance of study; and describe how the ideas of the Hebrew traditions are reflected in the moral and ethical traditions of Western civilization; **6.3.3** Explain the significance of Abraham, Moses, Naomi, Ruth, David, and Yohanan ben Zaccai in the development of the Jewish religion.

HSS ANALYSIS SKILLS:

REP 4 Students assess the credibility of primary and secondary sources and draw sound conclusions from them; **HI 3** Students explain the sources of historical continuity and how the combination of ideas and events explains the emergence of new patterns.

PLAN

OBJECTIVE

Synthesize information about the Hebrew Bible from primary source documents.

ESSENTIAL QUESTION

How did early Jews develop and maintain a distinct cultural identity?

The Hebrew Bible forms the basis of all Jewish law. Lesson 1.4 includes excerpts of writings from two books of the Hebrew Bible.

BACKGROUND FOR THE TEACHER

The Dead Sea Scrolls are one of the greatest archaeological finds in modern times. They include about 800 to 900 ancient manuscripts in roughly 15,000 fragments. The fragments were discovered in 11 caves along the northwest shore of the Dead Sea. The scrolls include fragments from almost all the books of the Hebrew Bible. The first seven scrolls were found in 1947 when a shepherd followed a runaway goat into a cave. The decomposed scrolls, made of leather and wrapped in linen cloth, were found inside several large pottery jars. The scrolls show the variety of Jewish thought and practice at the time. For a long time, only a small number of scholars had access to the scrolls. Finally, in the early 1990s, copies of the scrolls were published.

DIGITAL RESOURCES NGLSync.cengage.com

TEACHER RESOURCES & ASSESSMENT

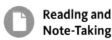 **Reading and Note-Taking**

 Vocabulary Practice

 Section 1 Quiz

STUDENT RESOURCES

 **NG Chapter Gallery**

INTRODUCE & ENGAGE

PREPARE FOR THE DOCUMENT-BASED QUESTION

Before students start on the activity, briefly preview the two documents. Remind students that a constructed response requires full explanations in complete sentences. Emphasize that students should use their knowledge of the beliefs and practices of Judaism in addition to the information in the documents. **0:05** minutes

TEACH

GUIDED DISCUSSION

1. **Identify** Which of the Ten Commandments reflect the Hebrew belief in a single God? *(the first and second commandments)*

2. **Make Generalizations** Have students review the Ten Commandments in Document 2. **ASK:** What modern-day laws are reflected in the Ten Commandments? *(Student responses will vary but might point to the sixth, eighth, and ninth commandments.)*

EVALUATE

After students have completed the "Synthesize & Write" activity, allow time for them to exchange paragraphs and read and comment on the work of their peers. Guidelines for comments should be established prior to this activity so that feedback is constructive and encouraging in nature. **0:15** minutes

ACTIVE OPTIONS

Critical Viewing: NG Chapter Gallery Ask students to choose one image from the Chapter Gallery and become an expert on it. They should do additional research to learn all about it. Then students should share their findings with a partner, small group, or the class. **0:10** minutes

On Your Feet: Two Options Label two locations in the room with the name of one of the documents featured in the lesson. Have students reread the lesson and walk to the corner of the room with the document that best helped support their understanding of the importance of the Hebrew Bible to the beliefs and practices of the Israelites. Have students who chose the same document discuss why they made their selection. Then have volunteers from each group explain what their document is and offer some of the group's reasons for choosing that one. As an extension, have students read additional excerpts from the books of Genesis and Exodus in the **Primary Source Handbook** and answer the questions that follow. **0:20** minutes

DIFFERENTIATE

INCLUSION

Work in Pairs If some students have disabilities, consider pairing them with other students who can read the documents aloud to them. You may also want to give students the option of recording their responses.

PRE-AP

Research Have students conduct Internet research to find out more about the Dead Sea Scrolls. Have them report to the rest of the class about the information that the Dead Sea Scrolls provided archaeologists and historians. Suggest that students include a map showing the location of the findings with their report.

Press **(mt)** *in the Student eEdition for modified text.*

See the Chapter Planner for more strategies for differentiation.

CONSTRUCTED RESPONSE

ANSWERS
DOCUMENT 1
God promises to make Canaan a great nation and to bless Abraham.

DOCUMENT 2
The first four commandments focus on how to worship and show respect to God. The last six commandments tell people how to conduct themselves and interact with others.

SYNTHESIZE & WRITE

ANSWERS

1. Responses will vary.

2. Responses will vary.

3. Possible response: God promised the Israelites that they would have a great nation and be blessed if they did what he told them.

4. Students' paragraphs should include their topic sentence from Step 3 and provide several details from the documents to support the sentence.

Israel and Judah

Twelve friends decide to go to a movie, but everyone has different ideas about what to see. Finally, they agree to put one person in charge—a natural-born leader. His decision is quick and readily accepted. For a similar reason, the Israelites swapped decision-making by judges for rule by a single strong king.

MAIN IDEA

The Israelites united under a line of kings, but they later became divided and were defeated by external powers.

DAVID

David, a simple shepherd, attracted attention when he killed a gigantic warrior called Goliath using only his shepherd's sling and stones. David became one of the Israelites' greatest kings. His emblem, the six-pointed star called the Star of David or Shield of David, became a symbol of Judaism and modern Israel.

A LINE OF KINGS

The Israelites realized they needed greater unity and stronger leadership when they were attacked by another people called the Philistines (FIH-luh-steens), who lived in the area. The Israelites appointed a king named Saul to rule. In 1020 B.C., Saul defended Israel against the Philistines and other enemies.

When Saul died, **David** was crowned king. David united the tribes and continued the fight against the Philistines and other enemies. He captured Jerusalem and made it his capital, starting its transformation into one of history's most important cities.

David's son **Solomon** inherited a peaceful kingdom. He built a great stone temple in Jerusalem. Solomon's Temple became the focus of religious life. Solomon used trade and taxes to fund other huge building projects. However, most of the tax burden fell on the northern tribes, who came to resent Solomon's rule. Once again, trouble began.

Soon war broke out between the northern and southern tribes. Around 922 B.C., Israel was divided into two kingdoms: **Israel** in the north and **Judah** in the south. The northern kingdom consisted of ten of the original tribes, while the southern kingdom consisted of the remaining two. The kingdoms sometimes fought each other and sometimes formed alliances against common enemies. Eventually, Judaism and the Jewish people would be named after Judah.

INVADED AND CONQUERED

In 722 B.C., the Assyrian Empire conquered Israel. The ten tribes of Israel were scattered to other lands and disappeared from history. Judah, though, survived and was able to fight off Assyria.

However, Judah soon found itself the battleground between two warring groups: the Egyptians and the New Babylonians. Egypt conquered Judah first. Then the New Babylonian army, led by King Nebuchadnezzar, overran Judah.

Judah rebelled. In 597 B.C., the king responded by invading Jerusalem. He moved the elite members of society to Babylon, leaving the poor behind. In 586 B.C., Nebuchadnezzar's army destroyed Jerusalem, including Solomon's Temple. For the Jews, the age of kings was over.

SOLOMON'S TEMPLE

According to the Hebrew Bible, King Solomon built a magnificent temple in Jerusalem with walls and a floor of cedarwood overlaid in gold. The Bible indicates that Solomon's Temple housed the Ark of the Covenant, a container holding the stone tablets with the Ten Commandments. This reconstruction is based on descriptions of the Temple in the Hebrew Bible.

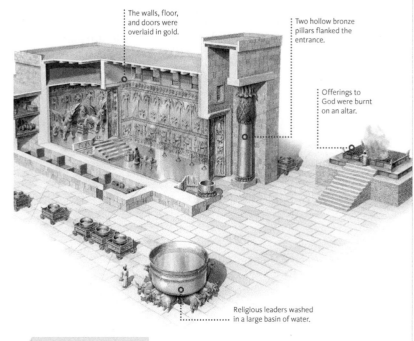

The walls, floor, and doors were overlaid in gold.

Two hollow bronze pillars flanked the entrance.

Offerings to God were burnt on an altar.

Religious leaders washed in a large basin of water.

REVIEW & ASSESS

1. **READING CHECK** What events mark the rise and fall of the Jews' age of kings?

2. **IDENTIFY PROBLEMS** What was one source of conflict between the northern and southern tribes of the Israelites?

3. **MAKE INFERENCES** What do you think the destruction of Solomon's Temple meant to the Israelites?

6.3.3 Explain the significance of Abraham, Moses, Naomi, Ruth, David, and Yohanan ben Zaccai in the development of the Jewish religion; 6.3.4 Discuss the locations of the settlements and movements of Hebrew peoples, including the Exodus and their movement to and from Egypt, and outline the significance of the Exodus to the Jewish and other people.

HSS CONTENT STANDARDS:

6.3.3 Explain the significance of Abraham, Moses, Naomi, Ruth, David, and Yohanan ben Zaccai in the development of the Jewish religion; **6.3.4** Discuss the locations of the settlements and movements of Hebrew peoples, including the Exodus and their movement to and from Egypt, and outline the significance of the Exodus to the Jewish and other people.

HSS ANALYSIS SKILLS:

CST 2 Students construct various time lines of key events, people, and periods of the historical era they are studying.

PLAN

OBJECTIVE

Explain why the Israelites, at first united under a line of kings, later became divided and defeated by external powers.

ESSENTIAL QUESTION

How did early Jews develop and maintain a distinct cultural identity?

The need for greater unity and strong leadership to defend against attacks by another people led the Israelites to appoint a king to rule. Lesson 2.1 discusses the rise of a line of kings of the Israelites, the division of Israel into two kingdoms, and the defeat of the kingdoms by external powers.

BACKGROUND FOR THE TEACHER

Most of what is known about King Solomon comes from the Hebrew Bible. He is known for accumulating enormous wealth while ruling a kingdom that extended from the Euphrates River in the north to Egypt in the south. He is also known for his wisdom. One famous story illustrating his wisdom was about two women coming to Solomon's court with a baby each claimed as her own. Solomon threatened to solve the claim by splitting the baby in half. One woman accepted that decision while the second woman begged Solomon to give the baby to the other woman. Solomon immediately knew that the second woman was the mother. People from long distances came to hear Solomon's wisdom. Solomon is said to have composed thousands of proverbs and hundreds of songs.

DIGITAL RESOURCES NGLSync.cengage.com

TEACHER RESOURCES & ASSESSMENT

 Reading and Note-Taking

 Vocabulary Practice

 Section 2 Quiz

STUDENT RESOURCES

 Biography

INTRODUCE & ENGAGE

PREVIEW VISUALS

Direct students' attention to the illustration of Solomon's Temple in the lesson. Ask them to read the captions describing the elements of the temple. **ASK:** What was the purpose of the temple? (*It was a place of worship.*) How do you think King Solomon was able to pay for such an elaborate structure? (*Students might indicate that money from trade and taxes collected from his subjects might have been used to pay for building the structure.*) Tell students that in this lesson they will learn about King Solomon and the effect that taxing his subjects had on the Israelite tribes. **0:05** minutes

TEACH

GUIDED DISCUSSION

1. **Draw Conclusions** Why did war break out between the northern and southern tribes? (*People in the northern tribes resented having the greater tax burden placed on them to fund Solomon's huge building project.*)

2. **Analyze Effects** What was the effect of the Assyrian Empire conquering Israel? (*The ten tribes of Israel were scattered to other lands and disappeared from history. Judah survived and fought off Assyria.*)

CREATE TIME LINES

Have students work in pairs to create a time line of events in this lesson. Instruct students to include the dates as discussed in the text and a key event for each date. Work with students to space their dates appropriately on the time line. **0:15** minutes

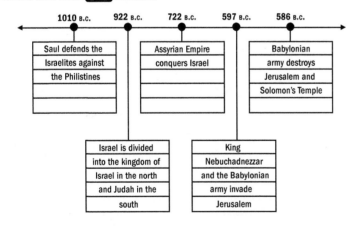

ACTIVE OPTIONS

NG Learning Framework: Write a Biography

ATTITUDE: **Curiosity**
KNOWLEDGE: **Our Human Story**

Have students select one of the people they are still curious about after learning about this individual in this chapter. Instruct them to write a short biography about this person using information from the chapter and additional source material. **0:10** minutes

On Your Feet: Tell Me More Have students form four teams and assign each team one of the following topics:

- King David
- King Solomon
- Israel
- Judah

Each group should write down as many facts about its topic as it can. Have the class reconvene and have each group stand up, one at a time. The rest of the class calls out "Tell me more about [the topic]." The group recites one fact. The class again requests a fact until the group runs out of facts to share. Then the next group presents its facts. **0:10** minutes

DIFFERENTIATE

ENGLISH LANGUAGE LEARNERS `ELD`

Use Sentence Strips Choose a paragraph from the lesson and make sentence strips out of it. Read the paragraph aloud, having students at the **Emerging** and **Expanding** levels follow along in their books. Have students close their books and give them the set of sentence strips. Students should put the strips in order and then read the paragraph aloud.

GIFTED & TALENTED `STEM`

Create Models Have pairs of students work on creating a model of Solomon's Temple. Suggest building materials such as paper, cardboard, or clay. Direct students to use the illustration of the temple in the lesson as well as other sources to make the model. Encourage students to display their models once they have completed them.

Press (mt) *in the Student eEdition for modified text.*

See the Chapter Planner for more strategies for differentiation.

REVIEW & ASSESS

ANSWERS

1. The rise of the Jews' age of kings came when the Israelites, realizing that they needed strong leadership to defend against the Philistines, appointed a king named Saul. The fall of the age of kings came when the Babylonian army invaded and destroyed Jerusalem and Solomon's Temple.

2. One source of conflict between the northern and southern tribes was Solomon's taxes, especially on the northern tribes, to pay for his huge building projects. This tax burden caused them to resent Solomon's rule.

3. For the Israelites, the destruction of Solomon's Temple might have meant the end of their religious life and their distinct identity.

Jews come to pray at Jerusalem's Western Wall, a remnant of the Second Temple. Many visitors leave written prayers in cracks in the wall.

2.2 Exile and Return

Psalm 137, from a book in the Hebrew Bible, captures the terrible upheaval the Jews suffered when they were forced to leave Judah and live in Babylon: "By the rivers of Babylon, there we sat, sat and wept, as we thought of Zion [Israel]. How can we sing of the Lord on alien [foreign] soil?" But the Jews found a way, and they grew stronger as a result of the experience.

MAIN IDEA

While in Babylon, the Jews maintained, developed, and strengthened their identity and religion.

BABYLONIAN CAPTIVITY

The removal of some of the Jewish people from their homeland to faraway Babylonia was a deeply distressing experience. Their captivity, called the Babylonian Exile, lasted about 50 years. **Exile** is the forced removal from one's native country. During the exile, Jews built their first synagogues.

Any remaining tribal divisions disappeared, to be replaced by a sense of religious and social unity among the Jewish people. Scribes started writing down the holy texts in a new script that is still used today. Most importantly, the Jews found that it actually was possible to "sing of the Lord on alien soil." Although they had lost control of the Promised Land, the Jews held on to their cultural identity and their religious faith.

CYRUS THE GREAT OF PERSIA

The Jews' efforts to maintain their faith were aided when **Cyrus the Great**, king of the Persian Empire, conquered Babylon in 539 B.C. As you may remember, Cyrus became known as "the Great" because of his impressive military conquests and wise rule. He adopted a policy of tolerance, allowing conquered people to keep their own customs and beliefs.

While Judah remained under Persian control, Cyrus freed the Jewish people in Babylon and encouraged them to return to their homeland and rebuild the Jewish state. Because of his policy of tolerance, Cyrus became a hero to the Jews.

Many of the Jewish people decided to stay in Babylonia. They formed a large Jewish community that thrived for centuries and remains in small numbers in present-day Iran and Iraq. However, in 538 B.C., about 42,000 Jews returned to Judah. There, they began rebuilding the temple in Jerusalem, called the Second Temple. Religious leaders began to refine Judaism into something like its modern form. In particular, they finalized the Hebrew Bible, which became the central document of the Jewish faith, and began public readings of the Torah.

REVIEW & ASSESS

1. **READING CHECK** Why did Cyrus the Great become a hero to the Jews?

2. **IDENTIFY DETAILS** While in exile, how did the Jews maintain their identity?

3. **MAKE INFERENCES** Why did a large number of Jews return to Judah in 538 B.C.?

6.3.4 Discuss the locations of the settlements and movements of Hebrew peoples, including the Exodus and their movement to and from Egypt, and outline the significance of the Exodus to the Jewish and other people; 6.3.5 Discuss how Judaism survived and developed despite the continuing dispersion of much of the Jewish population from Jerusalem and the rest of Israel after the destruction of the second Temple in A.D. 70.

134   135

PLAN

OBJECTIVE

Explain how the Jews maintained, developed, and strengthened their identity and religion while in Babylon.

ESSENTIAL QUESTION

How did early Jews develop and maintain a distinct cultural identity?

The Jewish people were held in captivity in Babylon for about 50 years. Lesson 2.2 explains how the Jews maintained and strengthened their identity and religion.

BACKGROUND FOR THE TEACHER

Cyrus the Great is known for more than just being a great Persian emperor. He is also known as being the epitome of what a great ruler should be. Though he was an impressive military conqueror, Cyrus considered himself a liberator of people and not a conqueror. He treated his subjects equally regardless of religion or ethnicity, allowing them to keep their religion and customs. His rule differed greatly from that of other rulers, such as those of the Assyrians.

DIGITAL RESOURCES NGLSync.cengage.com

TEACHER RESOURCES & ASSESSMENT

 Reading and Note-Taking

 Vocabulary Practice

 Section 2 Quiz

STUDENT RESOURCES

 NG Chapter Gallery

INTRODUCE & ENGAGE

BUILD WORD KNOWLEDGE

Ask students if they know what the word *exile* means. Write students' responses on the board. Explain that *exile* is the forced removal from one's native country. Then direct students' attention to the lesson title. Tell students that the title applies to the Jewish people. Ask students what they think the lesson will be about based on the title. `0:10` minutes

TEACH

GUIDED DISCUSSION

1. **Explain** What was the Babylonian captivity? *(The Babylonian captivity refers to the removal of the Jewish people from Judah to Babylon, where they were held captive for about 50 years.)*

2. **Analyze Cause and Effect** How did the Babylonian Exile affect the Jewish faith? *(It caused the faith to grow stronger as Jews put aside any tribal divisions and wrote down the holy texts.)*

MORE INFORMATION

The Western Wall The Western Wall, sacred to the Jewish people, is a place of prayer in the Old City of Jerusalem. The wall is all that remains of the Second Temple of Jerusalem. Its authenticity has been confirmed by history and archaeological research. What remains of the Western Wall today measures about 160 feet long and about 60 feet high. Jews who visit the wall express sadness over the temple's destruction and pray that it will be restored. Visitors to the Western Wall (pictured in the lesson) often wedge small slips of paper, on which they write prayers and petitions, into the cracks between the stones.

ACTIVE OPTIONS

Critical Viewing: NG Chapter Gallery Have students examine the contents of the Chapter Gallery for this chapter. Then invite them to brainstorm additional images they believe would fit within the Chapter Gallery. Have them write a description of these additional images and provide an explanation of why they would fit within the Chapter Gallery. Then instruct them to do online research to find examples of actual images they would like to add to the gallery. `0:10` minutes

On Your Feet: Card Responses Have half the class create ten true-false questions based on information in the lesson. Ask the other half to create answer cards, with "True" written on one side and "False" on the other. As each question is read aloud, students in the second group should display the correct answer to the question. `0:10` minutes

DIFFERENTIATE

STRIVING READERS

Preview Text Help students preview the lesson. Point out the text features, such as the lesson title, Main Idea, and headings. **ASK:** Based on the subheadings, what do you expect this lesson to be about? As students begin reading, help them confirm their understanding of each paragraph before moving on to the next one.

PRE-AP

Research and Present Have students use the Internet to research the life of Cyrus the Great. Students should find out about his early life, his conquests and achievements, and his legacy. Then ask them to write a short biography and share it with the class.

Press (**mt**) *in the Student eEdition for modified text.*

See the Chapter Planner for more strategies for differentiation.

REVIEW & ASSESS

ANSWERS

1. Cyrus the Great became a hero to the Jews because he freed the Jewish people and encouraged them to return to Judah and rebuild the Jewish state.

2. While living in exile, old tribal divisions disappeared and a sense of unity developed as Jews practiced their religious faith and held onto their cultural identity.

3. A large number of Jews likely returned to Judah in 538 B.C. to reestablish their community and strengthen their identity.

2.3

The Diaspora

If you moved to another country to live, you might adopt its language and customs to get along. But when Jews settled abroad, most tried hard to keep practicing their own religion and customs. The ability of the Jewish people to preserve their religion and heritage has been one of the most remarkable achievements in world history.

MAIN IDEA

The Syrians and then the Romans tried to destroy Judaism but ultimately failed.

YOHANNAN BEN ZAKAI

When the Romans destroyed the Second Temple, a Jewish teacher named Yohannai Ben Zakai asked permission to establish a school to teach Jewish scholars. The school was important in preserving Jewish traditions. Today, Jews regard Zakai as a great hero.

SYRIAN CONTROL

After the Persians, competing foreign powers controlled Judah. By about 300 B.C., Egypt took over the Jewish homeland. The Egyptian rulers tolerated Judaism and largely left Judah alone.

In 198 B.C., a Syrian empire, the Seleucids, conquered Judah. The Seleucids treated the Jews well until 168 B.C., when the Seleucid king tried to force the Jews to worship Greek gods. He dedicated the Second Temple to the Greek god Zeus. Outraged Jews rebelled, led by a family called the Maccabees. Their small army fought hard, defeated the Seleucids, and rededicated the Second Temple to Judaism.

ROMAN RULE

Judah's freedom from foreign rule did not last long. In 63 B.C., Rome seized control of the region. At first the Romans allowed the Jews to rule themselves. In time, however, Rome took direct control of Judah and insisted that Jews worship the Roman gods. Many Jews, including revolutionaries called **Zealots**, favored armed rebellion.

War finally broke out in A.D. 66. Unfortunately, Jewish resistance was no match for the powerful Roman army. Rome's soldiers destroyed much of Jerusalem, including the Second Temple. By A.D. 70, the war was almost over. The Zealots fought on from the mountaintop fortress of Masada, but the Roman army eventually crushed the revolt.

After the rebellion, many Jews were forced to leave Jerusalem and settle in new places. The migration of Jews to places around the world, which began with the Babylonian Exile, is called the **Diaspora** (dy-AS-puh-ruh). Yet even after leaving their homeland, Jews kept their religion alive and maintained a strong connection to the land of Israel. The rabbis transformed Judaism into a home- and synagogue-based religion that could be practiced anywhere. By holding on to their religion and customs, the dispersed Jews ensured Judaism would become a worldwide religion.

The legacy of the Jewish people is important in world history. Judaism was the first monotheistic religion. Its emphasis on justice and morality influenced later religions, including Christianity. Judaism also had a great influence on other aspects of Western civilization, such as law.

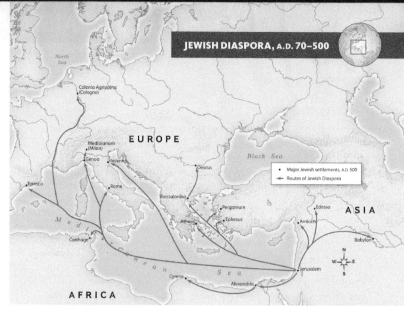

JEWISH DIASPORA, A.D. 70–500

Major Jewish settlements, A.D. 500
Routes of Jewish Diaspora

NAOMI AND RUTH

A strong connection to Israel is a major theme in the story of **Naomi and Ruth** in the Hebrew Bible. Naomi is an Israelite woman who moves with her family to the country of Moab to escape a famine in Israel. Her two sons marry Moabite women named Ruth and Orpah. After her husband and two sons die, Naomi decides to return to her homeland. Her daughter-in-law Ruth insists upon going with her. Ruth says to Naomi, "Where you go, I will go; where you lodge, I will lodge; your people shall be my people, and your God my God." (Ruth 1:16) After moving with Naomi, Ruth remarries and has a son. She becomes the great-grandmother of the Israelite king David. Ruth stands out in the Bible as a model of devoted love and loyalty.

REVIEW & ASSESS

1. **READING CHECK** How were Syrian rule and Roman rule of Judah similar?

2. **INTERPRET MAPS** In what direction did most Jews travel during the Diaspora?

3. **DRAW CONCLUSIONS** Why did Judaism become a worldwide religion?

6.3.2 Identify the sources of the ethical teachings and central beliefs of Judaism (the Hebrew Bible, the Commentaries): belief in God, observance of law, practice of the concepts of righteousness and justice, and importance of study; and describe how the ideas of the Hebrew traditions are reflected in the moral and ethical traditions of Western civilization; 6.3.3 Explain the significance of Abraham, Moses, Naomi, Ruth, David, and Yohanan ben Zaccai in the development of the Jewish religion; 6.3.5 Discuss how Judaism survived and developed despite the continuing dispersion of much of the Jewish population from Jerusalem and the rest of Israel after the destruction of the second Temple in A.D. 70; 6.7.5 Trace the migration of Jews around the Mediterranean region and the effects of their conflict with the Romans, including the Romans' restrictions on their right to live in Jerusalem; CST 3 Students use a variety of maps and documents to identify physical and cultural features of neighborhoods, cities, states, and countries and to explain the historical migration of people, expansion and disintegration of empires, and the growth of economic systems.

137

HSS CONTENT STANDARDS:

6.3.2 Identify the sources of the ethical teachings and central beliefs of Judaism (the Hebrew Bible, the Commentaries): belief in God, observance of law, practice of the concepts of righteousness and justice, and importance of study; and describe how the ideas of the Hebrew traditions are reflected in the moral and ethical traditions of Western civilization; **6.3.3** Explain the significance of Abraham, Moses, Naomi, Ruth, David, and Yohanan ben Zaccai in the development of the Jewish religion; **6.3.4** Discuss the locations of the settlements and movements of Hebrew peoples, including the Exodus and their movement to and from Egypt, and outline the significance of the Exodus to the Jewish and other people; **6.3.5** Discuss how Judaism survived and developed despite the continuing dispersion of much of the Jewish population from Jerusalem and the rest of Israel after the destruction of the second Temple in A.D. 70; **6.7.5** Trace the migration of Jews around the Mediterranean region and the effects of their conflict with the Romans, including the Romans' restrictions on their right to live in Jerusalem.

HSS ANALYSIS SKILLS:

CST 3 Students use a variety of maps and documents to identify physical and cultural features of neighborhoods, cities, states, and countries and to explain the historical migration of people, expansion and disintegration of empires, and the growth of economic systems; **HI 1** Students explain the central issues and problems from the past, placing people and events in a matrix of time and place.

PLAN

OBJECTIVE

Explain why the Syrians and the Romans failed in their attempts to destroy Judaism.

ESSENTIAL QUESTION

How did early Jews develop and maintain a distinct cultural identity?

Syrians and Romans both controlled Judah. Lesson 2.3 examines why their attempts to destroy Judah failed.

BACKGROUND FOR THE TEACHER

Zealots were members of a Jewish sect and an aggressive political party who opposed Roman rule and the Romans' polytheism. Zealots also opposed those Jews who sought improved relations with the Roman authorities. Extremist groups of Zealots turned to terrorism. They would even attack Jews who were friendly to Rome. In A.D. 66–70, Zealots played a leading role in the first revolt against Rome.

DIGITAL RESOURCES NGLSync.cengage.com

TEACHER RESOURCES & ASSESSMENT

 Reading and Note-Taking

 Vocabulary Practice

 Section 2 Quiz

STUDENT RESOURCES

 NG Chapter Gallery

MAKE CONNECTIONS

Present a situation to students in which people have to move from their homes and settle in an unfamiliar place. Discuss with students what issues people might face in making such a move. Students' responses might include issues such as figuring out what to take with them, setting up a new home, getting to know people in the new area, or anxiety about living in an unfamiliar place. Point out to students that in this lesson they will learn why many Jews were forced to move from Jerusalem and where they settled. `0:10` minutes

TEACH

GUIDED DISCUSSION

1. **Draw Conclusions** How were the Jews able to maintain their identity even after being forced to leave their homeland? *(The Jews kept their religion alive and maintained a strong connection to the land of Israel. The rabbis transformed Judaism into a home-based and synagogue-based religion that Jews could practice anywhere.)*

2. **Form Opinions** The legacy of the Jewish people is important in world history. What do you think is their most important legacy? Why do you think so? *(Responses will vary, but students should provide reasons for their opinions. Students might indicate that monotheism was the biggest legacy. Others might indicate Judaism's influence on other religions, particularly Christianity, or its influence on law.)*

INTERPRET MAPS

Draw students' attention to the map of the Jewish Diaspora. Have students review the map legend. **ASK:** What Jewish settlements were located in Africa? *(Alexandria and Cyrene)* What was the main water route for the Diaspora? *(the Mediterranean Sea)* `0:15` minutes

ACTIVE OPTIONS

Critical Viewing: NG Chapter Gallery Invite students to explore the NG Chapter Gallery and choose one image from the gallery they feel best represents their understanding of the chapter. Have students provide a written explanation of why they selected the images they chose. `0:10` minutes

On Your Feet: One-on-One Interviews Group students into pairs. Have both students in each pair write three questions about Syrian and Roman rule of Judah. Start with one student using his or her questions to interview the other student "expert" about Judah under Syrian and Roman rule. Students' answers should show an understanding of the material from the lesson. Once the interview is complete, students should reverse roles. `0:15` minutes

INCLUSION

Clarify Text Have visually-impaired students work with sighted partners. As they listen to an audio recording of the text, have the visually-impaired students indicate if there are words or passages they do not understand. Their partners can clarify meaning by repeating passages, emphasizing context clues, and paraphrasing.

GIFTED & TALENTED

Write Journal Entries Have students imagine that they are reporters covering the story of the Diaspora. Ask them to create a set of four or five journal entries that tell why the Jews are moving, Jewish thoughts about the move, and what the Jews hope their life will be like in their new home. Encourage students to use descriptive words and include their personal reactions to the move. Students can then take turns sharing their entries.

Press **mt** *in the Student eEdition for modified text.*

See the Chapter Planner for more strategies for differentiation.

ANSWERS

1. They were similar in that they both insisted that the Jews worship their gods.

2. Most Jews traveled westward from Jerusalem, spreading throughout the Roman Empire.

3. The Roman destruction of the Second Temple contributed to the dispersal of Jews throughout the world, known as the Diaspora, which spread the Jewish religion worldwide.

Uncovering the Story of
Caesarea's Port

In the first century B.C., Judea was a province of Rome and was ruled by a Roman-appointed king named Herod. He founded the city of Caesarea on the coast of what is now Israel. Sometime in the A.D. 100s, the city's port was mysteriously destroyed. That's where National Geographic Explorer Beverly Goodman comes in. Goodman is a geo-archaeologist, a scientist who investigates ancient cultures by applying the tools of earth science. By studying broken seashells, she concluded that a natural disaster destroyed Caesarea's port.

^
Beverly Goodman, shown above, studies archaeological sites along the Mediterranean coast.

MAIN IDEA

Geo-archaeologist Beverly Goodman has shown that a natural disaster likely destroyed the ancient port of Caesarea.

ISRAEL'S ANCIENT COASTLINE

Goodman's research focuses on the complex interaction between nature and humans along coastlines. "No place is more vulnerable than our coasts," she explains. Her findings from the port of Caesarea prove this thesis while ringing alarm bells that echo across 2,000 years.

At the end of the first century B.C., King Herod built a huge harbor at Caesarea to tap into the valuable trade between the East and ancient Rome. Caesarea had no geographic features useful for a harbor, so Herod relied on "modern" technology.

Herod's builders used waterproof concrete to build huge breakwaters, or walls extending out from the coast. These breakwaters created a deepwater harbor where sailing ships could shelter from great storms. Nevertheless, the harbor could not escape the sea's deadliest force. That force came in the form of a tsunami (su-NAH-mee), a giant ocean wave caused by an underwater earthquake, a volcanic eruption, or a landslide. Tsunamis have threatened humans for as long as people have lived on the world's coastlines.

A 2,000-YEAR-OLD DISASTER

Before Goodman began her investigation, no researchers had ever found physical evidence of a major disaster. Scholars had always thought that the harbor had disappeared because of the builders' poor workmanship and inferior materials.

An aerial view of the ruins of Caesarea

However, when Goodman began exploring the coastline, she uncovered an unusual concentration of shell fragments. "Instead of the normal half-inch layer, this band of shells was more than three feet deep!" she said.

To gather more evidence, she developed a new way of taking deep-sea core samples, sinking hollow tubes into the seabed and then pulling them out to show the layers of deposits. The layers can be read like tree rings. Analysis and dating suggested that a single, sudden, and violent event caused the shell concentrations. Goodman concluded that a major tsunami had destroyed Herod's great harbor.

Goodman is now putting her findings to the test. She's examining other archaeological sites around the Mediterranean region, looking for signs of tsunami damage. Goodman's research could help save lives in the future. "Analyzing the causes and effects of ancient environmental events like tsunamis can help tell us which types of coast are at greatest risk, and what kind of damage to expect in the future," Goodman explains. "I hope I'm collecting clues that will help us avoid catastrophic consequences down the line."

REVIEW & ASSESS

1. **READING CHECK** What natural disaster likely destroyed the ancient port of Caesarea?

2. **IDENTIFY MAIN IDEAS AND DETAILS** What findings support Goodman's conclusion about the cause of the port's destruction?

3. **MAKE CONNECTIONS** Why does Goodman's discovery have important implications for other sites on the Mediterranean?

HSS CONTENT STANDARDS:

HI 5 Students recognize that interpretations of history are subject to change as new information is uncovered.

PLAN

OBJECTIVE

Explain how geo-archaeologist Beverly Goodman has shown that a natural disaster likely destroyed the ancient port of Caesarea.

ESSENTIAL QUESTION

How did early Jews develop and maintain a distinct cultural identity?

Rome seized control of Judah in the first century B.C. and appointed a Roman king, Herod, as its ruler. Herod built a huge harbor at Caesarea, along the Mediterranean coast. Lesson 2.4 introduces National Geographic geo-archaeologist Beverly Goodman and describes her investigations into the effects of environmental events on ancient cultures, particularly on Caesarea's port.

BACKGROUND FOR THE TEACHER

The harbor at Caesarea built by King Herod was probably the first harbor ever built entirely in the open sea. It did not have the benefit of a protective bay or peninsula. Instead, huge breakwaters of concrete blocks filled with stone rubble protected the harbor, which was one of the technological marvels of the ancient world. The harbor served as a major port for trade between the Roman Empire and Asia.

DIGITAL RESOURCES NGLSync.cengage.com

TEACHER RESOURCES & ASSESSMENT

 Reading and Note-Taking

 Vocabulary Practice

 Section 2 Quiz

STUDENT RESOURCES

 NG Chapter Gallery

INTRODUCE & ENGAGE

ACTIVATE PRIOR KNOWLEDGE

Write the term *tsunami* on the board. Discuss what students know about tsunamis. Students might indicate hearing about tsunamis in Japan and Indonesia on television broadcasts. They might also indicate that they heard about tsunami warnings for places that have experienced earthquakes. Tell students that a tsunami is a giant ocean wave caused by an underwater earthquake, a volcanic eruption, or a landslide. Tell students that in this lesson they will learn how a tsunami affected an ancient port along Israel's Mediterranean coast. **0:05 minutes**

TEACH   STEM

GUIDED DISCUSSION

1. **Synthesize** How did Beverly Goodman's conclusions differ from previous conclusions about what destroyed the ancient port of Caesarea? *(Previous findings suggested the port disappeared because of the builders' poor workmanship and inferior materials. Goodman's findings pointed to a tsunami as the reason for the port's disappearance.)*

2. **Describe** What evidence led to Beverly Goodman's conclusions about what happened to the ancient port of Caesarea? *(Goodman uncovered a concentration of shells more than three feet deep instead of the usual half inch. She developed a new way of taking deep-sea core samples, sinking hollow tubes into the seabed and then pulling them out to show the layers of deposits. Analysis and dating suggested that a single, sudden, and violent event caused the shell concentrations, leading Goodman to conclude that a tsunami destroyed the ancient port.)*

ANALYZE VISUALS

Have students study the photograph of Beverly Goodman. **ASK:** Where was this photograph apparently taken? *(along the Mediterranean coast)* Does the photograph of this area remind you of anywhere you have been or have seen? *(Students' responses will vary.)* Have students offer locations and discuss the similarities and differences between the location shown in the photograph and the location they are thinking about. Students might also offer activities they participated in while at the location. **0:15 minutes**

ACTIVE OPTIONS

NG Learning Framework: Learn More About Tsunamis

SKILL: Collaboration
KNOWLEDGE: Our Living Planet

Have students find out more about tsunamis. Have them work in pairs and use the Internet to find out more about what causes tsunamis, where they have occurred, and how they affect the environment after they occur. Call on student pairs to present their findings to the class. Encourage them to include visuals with their oral reports. **0:15 minutes**

On Your Feet: Three-Step Interview Have students choose a partner. One student should interview the other on the following question: *Why is the work of geo-archaeologists like Beverly Goodman important to the understanding of past events?* Then they should reverse roles. Finally, each student should share the results of his or her interview with the class. **0:20 minutes**

DIFFERENTIATE

ENGLISH LANGUAGE LEARNERS   ELD

Teach Compound Words Remind students that two words can be put together to make a new word. Write these words and have students copy them.

deepwater   underwater   earthquake

Ask students to circle the two words within each word. Then help them define each of the two smaller words and the resulting compound word. Challenge students at the **Bridging** level to identify at least two additional compound words in the lesson.

PRE-AP

Prepare an Interview Have students prepare a mock interview with Beverly Goodman about her work and about the work of geo-archaeologists in general. Direct students to use the Internet to research the work of geo-archaeologists. After taking notes and gathering information, have pairs of students develop a list of questions to ask Beverly Goodman about her work in the field of geo-archaeology and her work in particular on the interaction between nature and humans along coastlines. Ask pairs of students to act out their interviews for the class.

Press *in the Student eEdition for modified text.*

See the Chapter Planner for more strategies for differentiation.

REVIEW & ASSESS

ANSWERS

1. A tsunami struck Israel's coast, destroying the ancient port of Caesarea around A.D. 200.

2. Goodman's conclusion is supported by an unusual concentration of shell fragments more than three feet deep, which suggested that a single, sudden, and violent event, like a tsunami, caused the shell concentration.

3. By analyzing the causes and effects of ancient tsunamis, she hopes to find clues about which types of coastlines are at the greatest risk, what kind of damage to expect, and how to avoid catastrophic consequences in the future.

VOCABULARY

Match each word in the first column with its definition in the second column.

WORD	DEFINITION
1. exile (HSS 6.3.4)	a. a Jewish spiritual leader and teacher
2. tribe (HSS 6.3)	b. the belief in only one God
3. monotheism (HSS 6.3.1)	c. a place where Jews assemble to worship
4. covenant (HSS 6.3.1)	d. an extended family unit
5. rabbi (HSS 6.3.2)	e. a period of forced absence from one's homeland or native country
6. synagogue (HSS 6.3.2)	f. a religious agreement with God

READING STRATEGY

7. **IDENTIFY MAIN IDEAS AND DETAILS** Complete your web of beliefs and practices of Judaism. Then answer the question.

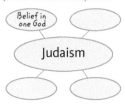

What are some of the beliefs and practices of Judaism? What is one way in which Judaism differs from other ancient religions? (HSS 6.3.2)

MAIN IDEAS

Answer the following questions. Support your answers with evidence from the chapter.

8. What did the Israelites believe God wanted them to do to fulfill their covenant? **LESSON 1.1** (HSS 6.3.1)

9. What important religious belief set the Israelites apart from other ancient cultures? **LESSON 1.2** (HSS 6.3.1)

10. Why is the Torah the most important holy book in Judaism? **LESSON 1.3** (HSS 6.3.2)

11. What did Saul achieve as the first king of the Israelites? **LESSON 2.1** (HSS 6.3.1)

12. Who was David, and what were his major accomplishments? **LESSON 2.1** (HSS 6.3.3)

13. How did Cyrus the Great's policy of tolerance affect Jews during their exile in Babylon? **LESSON 2.2** (HSS HI 2)

14. What was the Diaspora? **LESSON 2.3** (HSS HI 1)

15. What natural disaster likely destroyed King Herod's harbor at Caesarea 2,000 years ago? **LESSON 2.4** (HSS HI 1)

CRITICAL THINKING

Answer the following questions. Support your answers with evidence from the chapter.

16. **ESSENTIAL QUESTION** How did the Jews develop and maintain their cultural identity? (HSS HI 3)

17. **DRAW CONCLUSIONS** Why did the Israelites believe that the Ten Commandments reaffirmed their covenant with God? (HSS 6.3.1)

18. **EVALUATE** Why was the Exodus such an important event in Jewish history? (HSS 6.3.4)

19. **ANALYZE CAUSE AND EFFECT** What effect did the Diaspora have on the religion of Judaism? (HSS 6.3.5)

20. **YOU DECIDE** Who do you think was the most important person in the history of the Jewish people? Why? (HSS 6.3.3)

INTERPRET TIME LINES

Study the time line of selected events in Jewish history. Then answer the questions that follow.

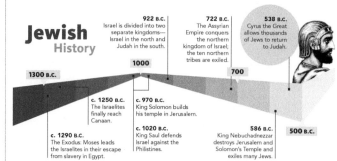

Jewish History

1300 B.C.

1000

700

500 B.C.

c. 1290 B.C. The Exodus: Moses leads the Israelites in their escape from slavery in Egypt.

c. 1250 B.C. The Israelites finally reach Canaan.

c. 1020 B.C. King Saul defends Israel against the Philistines.

c. 970 B.C. King Solomon builds his temple in Jerusalem.

922 B.C. Israel is divided into two separate kingdoms—Israel in the north and Judah in the south.

722 B.C. The Assyrian Empire conquers the northern kingdom of Israel; the ten northern tribes are exiled.

586 B.C. King Nebuchadnezzar destroys Jerusalem and Solomon's Temple and exiles many Jews.

538 B.C. Cyrus the Great allows thousands of Jews to return to Judah.

21. Who destroyed the First Temple and exiled the two tribes of Judah to Babylon? (HSS CST 2)

22. Which empire destroyed the northern kingdom of Israel? (HSS CST 2)

ANALYZE SOURCES

Read the following psalm, or sacred song, from the Hebrew Bible. Then answer the question.

The Lord is my shepherd; I lack nothing. He makes me lie down in green pastures; he leads me to water in places of repose [calm]; he renews my life; he guides me in right paths as befits his name. Though I walk through a valley of deepest darkness, I will fear no harm, for you are with me; your rod and your staff—they comfort me. You spread a table for me in full view of my enemies; you anoint [rub] my head with oil; my drink is abundant. Only goodness and steadfast love shall pursue me all the days of my life, and I shall dwell in the house of the Lord for many long years.

Psalms 23:1–6

23. What qualities are attributed to God? (HSS REP 4)

WRITE ABOUT HISTORY

24. **ARGUMENT** Which one of the Ten Commandments do you think has had the greatest impact on society? Make a list of some of its important effects on society. (HSS REP 1)

TIPS

- Reread the Ten Commandments in Lesson 1.4. Choose the one that you think has had the greatest impact on society.
- Write down the commandment. Under it, list at least three effects of this commandment on society.
- Use vocabulary from the chapter as appropriate.
- If you have difficulty identifying three effects, you might draw evidence from informational texts. For example, you might look up the Ten Commandments in an encyclopedia or another reference book.

VOCABULARY ANSWERS

WORD	DEFINITION
1. exile — e (HSS 6.3.4)	a. a Jewish spiritual leader and teacher
2. tribe — d (HSS 6.3)	b. the belief in only one God
3. monotheism — b (HSS 6.3.1)	c. a place where Jews assemble to worship
4. covenant — f (HSS 6.3.1)	d. an extended family unit
5. rabbi — a (HSS 6.3.2)	e. a period of forced absence from one's homeland or native country
6. synagogue — c (HSS 6.3.2)	f. a religious agreement with God

STANDARDS

HSS CONTENT STANDARDS:

6.3.1 Describe the origins and significance of Judaism as the first monotheistic religion based on the concept of one God who sets down moral laws for humanity; **6.3.2** Identify the sources of the ethical teachings and central beliefs of Judaism (the Hebrew Bible, the Commentaries): belief in God, observance of law, practice of the concepts of righteousness and justice, and importance of study; and describe how the ideas of the Hebrew traditions are reflected in the moral and ethical traditions of Western civilization; **6.3.3** Explain the significance of Abraham, Moses, Naomi, Ruth, David, and Yohana ben Zaccai in the development of the Jewish religion; **6.3.4** Discuss the locations of the settlements and movements of Hebrew peoples, including the Exodus and their movement to and from Egypt, and outline the significance of the Exodus to the Jewish and other people; **6.3.5** Discuss how Judaism survivied and developed despite the continuing dispersion of much of the Jewish population from Jerusalem and the rest of Israel after the destruction of the second Temple in A.D. 70; **6.7.5** Trace the migration of Jews around the Mediterranean region and the effects of their conflict with the Romans, including the Romans' restrictions on their right to live in Jerusalem.

HSS ANALYSIS SKILLS:

CST 2 Students construct various time lines of key events, people, and periods of the historical era they are studying; **REP 1** Students frame questions that can be answered by historical study and research; **REP 4** Students assess the credibility of primary and secondary sources and draw sound conclusions from them; **HI 1** Students explain the central issues and problems from the psat, placing people and events in a matrix of time and place; **HI 2** Students understand and distinguish cause, effect, sequence, and correlation in historical events, including the long- and short-term causal relations.

READING STRATEGY ANSWER

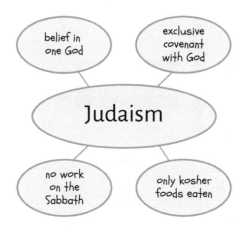

7. Jews practiced monotheism, the worship of a single God. They believed that they had a special covenant with God. They believed that God would protect the Hebrews if they accepted no other god and did what God asked. They did not work on the Sabbath, a weekly holy day. They ate only kosher foods, which were specially prepared according to Jewish dietary laws. Judaism differed from other ancient religions in that it included the worship of a single God. (HSS 6.3.2)

MAIN IDEAS ANSWERS

8. The Israelites believed they had to obey strict rules in order to keep God's goodwill and the covenant as God's "chosen people." (HSS 6.3.1)

9. The practice of monotheism—the belief in only one God—set the Israelites apart from other ancient cultures. (HSS 6.3.1)

10. The Torah is Judaism's most important holy book because Jews believe it contains the word of God as revealed to Moses on Mount Sinai. (HSS 6.3.2)

11. As the first appointed king of the Israelites, Saul united the Twelve Tribes and successfully defended the Israelites against the Philistines and other enemies. (HSS 6.3.1)

12. David was crowned the Hebrew king after the death of Saul. As king, David brought peace to Canaan and captured Jerusalem and made it the capital. (HSS 6.3.3)

13. Cyrus the Great's policy of tolerance helped the Jews maintain their identity and religion. Furthermore, Cyrus encouraged Jews to return to Judah and rebuild their Jewish state. (HSS HI 2)

14. The Diaspora was the dispersal of Jews from their homeland to locations around the world. (HSS HI 1)

15. A tsunami most likely destroyed King Herod's harbor at Caesarea. (HSS HI 1)

CRITICAL THINKING ANSWERS

16. The belief in one God helped unify the Jews, and their beliefs and practices also set them apart from other ancient cultures. They followed a code of religious practices that governed most aspects of life. They did not marry outside their faith and were careful not to adopt foreign customs. The Jews also generally avoided cultural diffusion, which was a major part of many other civilizations. (HSS HI 3)

17. The Israelites believed that the Ten Commandments reaffirmed their covenant with God because the commandments outlined a religious, moral, and civil code that needed to be obeyed in order to stay in God's favor. (HSS 6.3.1)

18. The Exodus was an important event in Jewish history because it was a journey from slavery in Egypt to freedom in Canaan, the Israelites' Promised Land. According to the Hebrew Bible, in this journey God gave Moses the Ten Commandments and other laws, which reaffirmed the Israelites' covenant with God. (HSS 6.3.4)

19. During the Diaspora, Jews dispersed to locations around the world, taking with them their religious beliefs and practices, which led to the emergence of Judaism as a world religion. (HSS 6.3.5)

20. Students' responses will vary. Students should clearly state their opinion regarding their view of which person was most important in the history of the Jewish people and support that opinion with evidence from the chapter. (HSS 6.3.3)

INTERPRET TIME LINES ANSWERS

21. King Nebuchadnezzar destroyed the first temple and exiled the two tribes of Judah to Babylon. (HSS CST 2)

22. The Assyrian Empire destroyed the northern kingdom of Israel. (HSS CST 2)

ANALYZE SOURCES ANSWER

23. Students' responses will vary. Sample response:
In Psalm 23, the author describes God as generous and benevolent—a shepherd who cares for all the physical and spiritual needs of his followers. (HSS REP 4)

WRITE ABOUT HISTORY ANSWER

24. Students' lists will vary but should include valid effects that had an impact on society. For more in-depth instruction and practice with the writing form, assign the Social Studies Skills Writing Lesson on writing an argument. (HSS REP 1)

UNIT RESOURCES

On Location with National Geographic Lead Program Officer Christopher Thornton Intro and Video

Interactive Map Tool

STORIES MAKING HISTORY **News & Updates**

Available at NGLSync.cengage.com

Unit Wrap-Up:
"Encounters with History"
Feature and Video

"China's Ancient Lifeline"
National Geographic Adapted Article

"Faces of the Divine"
National Geographic Adapted Article
Student eEdition exclusive

Unit 2 Inquiry:
Write a Creation Myth

CHAPTER RESOURCES

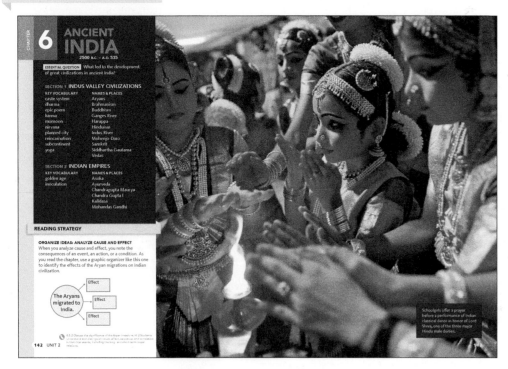

CHAPTER 6 ANCIENT INDIA
2500 B.C. – A.D. 535

ESSENTIAL QUESTION What led to the development of great civilizations in ancient India?

SECTION 1 INDUS VALLEY CIVILIZATIONS

KEY VOCABULARY: caste system, dharma, epic poem, karma, monsoon, nirvana, planned city, reincarnation, subcontinent, yoga

NAMES & PLACES: Aryans, Brahmanism, Buddhism, Ganges River, Harappa, Hinduism, Indus River, Mohenjo-Daro, Sanskrit, Siddhartha Gautama, Vedas

SECTION 2 INDIAN EMPIRES

KEY VOCABULARY: golden age, inoculation

NAMES & PLACES: Asoka, Ayurveda, Chandragupta Maurya, Chandra Gupta I, Kalidasa, Mohandas Gandhi

READING STRATEGY

ORGANIZE IDEAS: ANALYZE CAUSE AND EFFECT
When you analyze cause and effect, you note the consequences of an event, an action, or a condition. As you read the chapter, use a graphic organizer like this one to identify the effects of the Aryan migrations on Indian civilization.

The Aryans migrated to India. → Effect / Effect / Effect

142 UNIT 2

Schoolgirls offer a prayer before a performance of Indian classical dance in honor of Lord Shiva, one of the three major Hindu male deities.

TEACHER RESOURCES & ASSESSMENT

Available at NGLSync.cengage.com

Social Studies Skills Lessons
• Reading: Analyze Cause and Effect
• Writing: Write an Informative Text

Formal Assessment
• Chapter 6 Tests A (on-level) & B (below-level)

Chapter 6 Answer Key

ExamView®
One-time Download

STUDENT BACKPACK *Available at NGLSync.cengage.com*

• **eEdition** *(English)*   • **eEdition** *(Spanish)*   • **Handbooks**   • **Online Atlas**

Chapter 6 Spanish resources, Guided Writing prompts, and Financial Literacy lessons are available online.

SECTION 1 RESOURCES

INDUS VALLEY CIVILIZATIONS

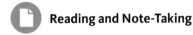 **Reading and Note-Taking**

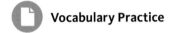 **Vocabulary Practice**

 **Section 1 Quiz**

Available at NGLSync.cengage.com

LESSON 1.1 THE GEOGRAPHY OF ANCIENT INDIA
- On Your Feet: Fishbowl
- Critical Viewing: NG Chapter Gallery

LESSON 1.2 HARAPPAN CIVILIZATION
- On Your Feet: Card Responses
- Critical Viewing: NG Chapter Gallery

LESSON 1.3 ARYAN MIGRATIONS
- On Your Feet: Create a Quiz

  NG Learning Framework:
  Research Brahmanism

LESSON 1.4 HINDU BELIEFS AND PRACTICES
- On Your Feet: Numbered Heads
- Critical Viewing: NG Image Gallery

DOCUMENT-BASED QUESTION
LESSON 1.5 HINDU SACRED TEXTS
- On Your Feet: Talk and Share

  NG Learning Framework:
  Study Primary Sources

LESSON 1.6 SIDDHARTHA AND BUDDHISM

 Active History: Interactive Whiteboard Activity
Map the Spread of Buddhism

 Active History
Map the Spread of Buddhism

Available at NGLSync.cengage.com

  NG Learning Framework:
  Research and Compare Religions

SECTION 2 RESOURCES

INDIAN EMPIRES

 Reading and Note-Taking

 Vocabulary Practice

 Section 2 Quiz

Available at NGLSync.cengage.com

LESSON 2.1 THE MAURYA EMPIRE

 Biography
Asoka

Available at NGLSync.cengage.com
- On Your Feet: Build a Paragraph
- Critical Viewing: NG Image Gallery

LESSON 2.2 THE GUPTA EMPIRE
- On Your Feet: Present an Empire

  NG Learning Framework:
  Write a Biography

LESSON 2.3 THE LEGACY OF ANCIENT INDIA
- On Your Feet: Inside-Outside Circle

  NG Learning Framework:
  Compare Approaches to Nonviolence

CHAPTER 6 REVIEW

STRATEGY ①

Use a Word Sort Activity

Write these words on the board and ask students to sort them into four groups of four related words each. Then have them use each group of words in a paragraph that shows how they are related.

subcontinent	medicine	reincarnation	Ganges River
dharma	Hinduism	mathematics	science
yoga	Buddhism	karma	nirvana
moral conduct	Indus River	Himalaya	Asoka

Use with Lessons 1.1, 1.4, 1.6, and 2.3

STRATEGY ②

Summarize Information

Help students summarize information using Idea Webs. Provide the phrase in the middle and have students complete the web using information from the lesson.

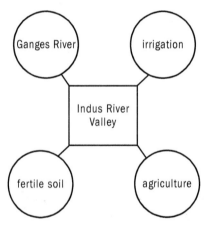

Use with Lessons 1.1, 1.2, 1.3, 1.4, 2.1, 2.2, and 2.3 *For Lesson 1.1, use the phrase "Indus River Valley" and have students fill in related information.*

STRATEGY ③

Ask Questions

Have students follow the strategy below to increase comprehension of lesson content.

1. Pairs of students read each lesson in the chapter and formulate one question that will help them understand it.

2. Pair One begins by asking Pair Two their question about the first lesson. Pair Two answers the question.

3. Pair One confirms the answer.

4. Pair Two asks Pair Three their question, and so on.

Use with All Lessons *For Lesson 1.1, have students ask questions about the Indus River Valley. For Lesson 2.3, have students ask questions about achievements of ancient India.*

Press **mt** *in the Student eEdition for modified text.*

STRATEGY ①

Modify Vocabulary Lists

Limit the number of vocabulary words, terms, and names students will be required to master. Have students write each word from your modified list on a colored sticky note and put it on the page next to where it appears in context.

Use with Lessons 1.1, 1.2, 1.3, 1.4, 1.6, 2.2, and 2.3

STRATEGY ②

Use Supported Reading

In small groups, have students read aloud the chapter lesson by lesson. At the end of each lesson, have them stop and use these sentence frames to tell what they comprehended from the text:

This lesson is about _____.

One detail that stood out to me is _____.

The vocabulary word _____ means _____.

I don't think I understand _____.

Guide students with portions of text they do not understand. Be sure all students understand a lesson before moving on to the next one.

Use with Lessons 1.1, 1.2, 1.3, 1.4, 2.2, and 2.3

STANDARDS

HSS CONTENT STANDARDS:

6.5 Students analyze the geographic, political, economic, religious, and social structures of the early civilizations of India.

STRATEGY 1

Pronounce Words

Provide students at all proficiency levels with pronunciations for proper nouns prior to reading. Say and write each word and have students repeat. Then read the passage aloud as a class, assisting as needed.

Use with Lesson 1.1, All Levels *Say and write the following words, with students repeating:*

South Asia (south A-zhuh)

Himalaya (HIH-muh-LAY-uh)

Everest (EHV-ruhst)

Nepal (nuh-PAWL)

Ganges (GAN-jeez)

Indus (IN-dus)

Bangladesh (BAHNG-gluh-DEHSH)

STRATEGY 2

Use Paired Reading

Pair students at the **Emerging** level with students at a higher proficiency level. Have student pairs read a passage from the text aloud. Then:

1. Partner 1 reads another passage; Partner 2 retells the passage in his or her own words.

2. Partner 2 reads a different passage; Partner 1 retells it.

3. Pairs repeat the whole exercise, switching roles.

Use with Lessons 1.2, 1.3, 1.4, 1.6, 2.1, 2.2, and 2.3 *For Lesson 1.2, have Partner 1 read the text under the heading "Well-Planned Cities" and have Partner 2 retell the passage. Have partners switch places for the text under the heading "An Advanced Culture."*

STRATEGY 3

Find Someone Who Knows

Give students copies of some or all of the questions below and have them find three different classmates to answer them.

1. What are strong seasonal winds that are important elements of the climate in South Asia? *(monsoons)*

2. What civilization was among the first in the world to have planned cities? *(the Harappan civilization)*

3. Where were Brahmanism's rituals and hymns recorded? *(in sacred texts called the Vedas)*

4. What is the Hindu belief that the soul is reborn in different bodies over different life cycles? *(reincarnation)*

5. What is the oldest of the Hindu sacred texts? *(the Rig Veda)*

6. What is the religion based on the teachings of Siddhartha Gautama? *(Buddhism)*

7. What king in ancient India converted to Buddhism and actively encouraged its spread by sending missionaries to preach abroad? *(Asoka)*

8. What empire brought 200 years of peace and prosperity to India? *(the Gupta Empire)*

9. What Indian leader in the twentieth century led nonviolent protests against British rule in India? *(Mohandas Gandhi)*

Use with All Lessons, All Levels *Give students a time limit for the activity. When time is up, discuss the questions and their answers in class.*

STRATEGY 1

Develop a Model

Have students investigate a process of physical geography related to South Asia. Students can create a diagram that illustrates the concept.

Use with Lesson 1.1 *Have students do research about tectonic shifts in the Himalaya. Then have them create a diagram that shows the plate movement. Have students write answers to the following questions: How much are the Himalaya rising each year? What other risks are associated with tectonic shifting?*

STRATEGY 2

Research a Celebration

Explain to students that it is part of Indian culture to celebrate by having festivals such as Holi, the Festival of Colors, and Diwali, the Festival of Lights. Ask students to write a report including information about the history and traditions of these two festivals.

Use with Lesson 2.3

STRATEGY 1

Form a Thesis

Have students develop a thesis statement for a specific topic related to one of the lessons in the chapter. Be sure the statement makes a claim that is supportable with evidence either from the chapter or through further research. Then have pairs compare their statements and determine which makes the strongest or most supportable claim.

Use with All Lessons

STRATEGY 2

Support an Opinion

Present a challenge to students to decide which two contributions from ancient India made the greatest impact on history. Have them develop a statement that explains their decision.

Use with All Lessons

6 ANCIENT INDIA

2500 B.C. – A.D. 535

ESSENTIAL QUESTION What led to the development of great civilizations in ancient India?

SECTION 1 INDUS VALLEY CIVILIZATIONS

KEY VOCABULARY	NAMES & PLACES
caste system	Aryans
dharma	Buddhism
epic poem	Ganges River
karma	Harappa
monsoon	Hinduism
nirvana	Indus River
planned city	Mohenjo-Daro
reincarnation	Sanskrit
subcontinent	Siddhartha Gautama
yoga	Vedas
	Vedic civilization

SECTION 2 INDIAN EMPIRES

KEY VOCABULARY	NAMES & PLACES
golden age	Asoka
inoculation	Ayurveda
	Chandragupta Maurya
	Chandra Gupta I
	Kalidasa
	Mohandas Gandhi

READING STRATEGY

ORGANIZE IDEAS: ANALYZE CAUSE AND EFFECT
When you analyze cause and effect, you note the consequences of an event, an action, or a condition. As you read the chapter, use a graphic organizer like this one to identify the effects of the Vedic people on Indian civilization.

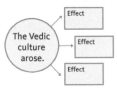

The Vedic culture arose. → Effect / Effect / Effect

6.5.2 Discuss the significance of the Aryan invasions; HI 2 Students understand and distinguish cause, effect, sequence, and correlation in historical events, including the long- and short-term causal relations.

142 UNIT 2

Schoolgirls offer a prayer before a performance of Indian classical dance in honor of Lord Shiva, one of the three major male Hindu Deities.

143

STANDARDS

HSS CONTENT STANDARDS:

6.5.1 Locate and describe the major river system and discuss the physical setting that supported the rise of this civilization; **6.5.2** Discuss the significance of the Aryan invasions; **6.5.7** Discuss important aesthetic and intellectual traditions (e.g., Sanskrit literature, including the Bhagavad Gita; medicine; metallurgy; and mathematics, including Hindu-Arabic numerals and the zero).

HSS ANALYSIS SKILLS:

HI 2 Students understand and distinguish cause, effect, sequence, and correlation in historical events, including the long- and short-term causal relations.

TEACHER BACKGROUND

INTRODUCE THE PHOTOGRAPH

Have students study the photo of the Hindu schoolgirls offering a prayer. Point out that honoring Lord Shiva and the other Deities is an important part of the Hindu religion and culture.

ASK: What are some ways people today give honor to their religion in their everyday life? *(Possible response: People say prayers and sing hymns before meals, before sports activities, and before, during, and after many activities of daily life.)*

SHARE BACKGROUND

Hindus show reverence to their Deities through rituals, songs, and prayers. Hindus pray in order to make a spiritual connection to their Gods. Hindu worship can occur in a variety of settings and on a variety of occasions. Festivals to the Gods are held during the year, but prayer may happen whenever an individual wishes. Hindus commonly pray at shrines in temples, in homes, and in outdoor public places.

DIGITAL RESOURCES NGLSync.cengage.com

TEACHER RESOURCES & ASSESSMENT

 Social Studies Skills Lessons
- Reading: Analyze Cause and Effect
- Writing: Write an Informative Text

 Formal Assessment
- Chapter 6 Tests A (on-level) & B (below-level)

 ExamView®
One-time Download

 Chapter 6 Answer Key

STUDENT BACKPACK
- eEdition *(English)*
- eEdition *(Spanish)*
- Handbooks
- Online Atlas

INTRODUCE THE ESSENTIAL QUESTION

WHAT LED TO THE DEVELOPMENT OF GREAT CIVILIZATIONS IN ANCIENT INDIA?

Think, Pair, Share Have students use the Think, Pair, Share strategy to discuss the Essential Question. Allow students to look through the chapter for clues in photos, maps, titles, and subheadings. Have them focus on each of the following aspects of the question:

A. How mountain ranges and major river systems can influence and restrict settlement

B. How religion can play a role in unifying a people and a nation

C. How traditions can linger after an empire has faded

`0:15` minutes

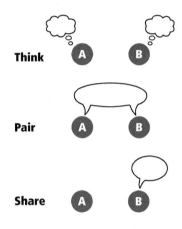

INTRODUCE THE READING STRATEGY

ORGANIZE IDEAS: ANALYZE CAUSE AND EFFECT

Remind students that analyzing cause and effect can help them better understand new information. Model completing the Cause and Effect Web by reading the first paragraph under "Impact on Indian Society" in Lesson 1.3 and adding the phrase *introduced the Sanskrit language* in the first box labeled "Effect." For more in-depth instruction and practice with the reading strategy, assign the Social Studies Skills Reading Lesson on analyzing cause and effect.

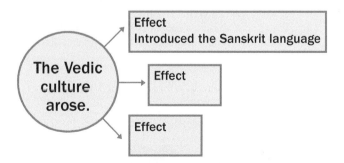

INTRODUCE CHAPTER VOCABULARY

VOCABULARY STUDY CARDS

Have students perform the six steps shown for each Key Vocabulary word in this chapter. It might be helpful to model this strategy for the first vocabulary word. Encourage students to work in pairs as they complete the six steps for the remaining words. Call on volunteers to share examples of their work with the rest of the class.

Vocabulary Word:

1. Write the sentence in which the word appears in your text.

2. Study how the word is used in the sentence. What do you think it means?

3. Now look up the word in a dictionary or use the glossary in your text.

4. Use the word in a sentence of your own.

5. To help you remember the meaning, draw a quick sketch that relates to the word. You might think of an action the word suggests or connect the word to a story or news report.

6. Tell why you chose this way of representing the meaning.

KEY DATES	
3300 B.C.	Development of civilization in the Indus River Valley
1500 B.C.	Immigration of Aryans to India
563 B.C.	Birth of Siddhartha Gautama, the Buddha
325 B.C.	Establishment of the Maurya Empire
A.D. **320**	Establishment of the Gupta Empire
A.D. **1947**	Independence of India

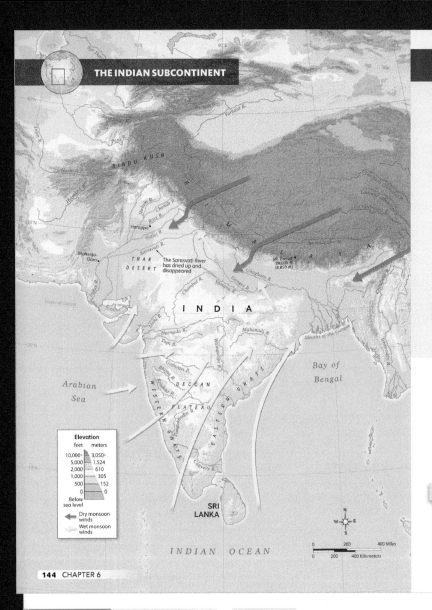

1.1

The Geography of Ancient India

Geographically, India has it all. If you were to travel around India, you could climb snowcapped mountains, cross wide grassy plains, hack through dense tropical forests, sail down mighty rivers, and skirt around sun-scorched deserts. You might travel under a bright blue sky or get soaked by seasonal rains.

MAIN IDEA

South Asia's physical geography affected the development of Indus Valley civilizations.

MOUNTAINS, RIVERS, AND MONSOONS

Present-day India, Bangladesh, Bhutan, Nepal, and Pakistan make up the large landmass, or **subcontinent**, of South Asia. This diamond-shaped landmass was originally an island. However, 40 million years ago, the large moving plates on which the continents lie drove the subcontinent into Asia. As the lands collided, they pushed Earth's crust upward to form the Himalaya, a 1,500-mile mountain range.

The Himalaya are the world's highest mountains. Many Himalayan peaks rise about 24,000 feet. Thirty peaks, including Mount Everest—Earth's highest point—are over 25,000 feet high.

On either side of the Himalaya lie lower mountain ranges, including the Hindu Kush, which separates what was once northwest India from present-day Afghanistan. These northern mountains form a natural barrier against invaders. The Arabian Sea, Indian Ocean, and Bay of Bengal have provided further protection. The Deccan Plateau, which contains smaller mountain systems, makes up much of southern India.

The two major rivers of northern India, the **Indus** and the **Ganges**, both start in the Himalaya. Like the Tigris and the Euphrates in Mesopotamia, these rivers provide water for irrigation and deposit fertile soil for farming.

Strong seasonal winds called **monsoons** have long been an important element of the subcontinent's climate. These winds bring a dry season in winter. In summer, they bring a wet season with heavy rainfall.

INDUS RIVER VALLEY

Physical characteristics of the Indus River Valley offered nearly ideal conditions for agriculture. The valley's fertile soil and plentiful water supply most likely encouraged nomadic herdsmen to settle there and farm. Villages emerged. Then some villages grew into cities and a civilization developed, reaching its peak between 2600 and 1900 B.C.

REVIEW & ASSESS

1. **READING CHECK** How did physical geography affect the development of Indus Valley civilizations?

2. **INTERPRET MAPS** What physical feature separates India from the continent of Asia?

3. **MAKE INFERENCES** What positive and negative effects might the summer monsoons have had on farmers?

6.5.1 Locate and describe the major river system and discuss the physical setting that supported the rise of this civilization; CST 3 Students use a variety of maps and documents to identify physical and cultural features of neighborhoods, cities, states, and countries and to explain the historical migration of people, expansion and disintegration of empires, and the growth of economic systems.

HSS CONTENT STANDARDS:

6.5.1 Locate and describe the major river system and discuss the physical setting that supported the rise of this civilization.

HSS ANALYSIS SKILLS:

CST 3 Students use a variety of maps and documents to identify physical and cultural features of neighborhoods, cities, states, and countries and to explain the historical migration of people, expansion and disintegration of empires, and the growth of economic systems.

PLAN

OBJECTIVE

Explain how South Asia's physical geography affected the development of Indus Valley civilizations.

ESSENTIAL QUESTION

What led to the development of great civilizations in ancient India?

The physical characteristics of the Indus River Valley included fertile soil and a plentiful water supply. Lesson 1.1 discusses how these physical characteristics led people to settle in the area and led to the growth of villages and cities.

BACKGROUND FOR THE TEACHER

South Asia has some of the most dramatic topography in the world, including the majestic Mount Everest of the Himalaya in Nepal. The plate on which the subcontinent of South Asia is located is still moving northward. As a result, the Himalaya are growing about 5 centimeters (2 inches) higher every year. Sir Edmund Hillary and his Sherpa guide were the first to reach the summit of Mount Everest in 1953. Since then, thousands have made the attempt.

DIGITAL RESOURCES NGLSync.cengage.com

TEACHER RESOURCES & ASSESSMENT

 Reading and Note-Taking

 Vocabulary Practice

 Section 1 Quiz

STUDENT RESOURCES

 **NG Chapter Gallery**

INTRODUCE & ENGAGE

INTERPRET MODELS

To show students how the Himalaya were formed, have pairs of students place two sheets of paper lengthwise between them, and then push the papers toward each other. Explain that the papers represent plates of land that are forced upward when pushed together, similar to the colliding plates that formed the Himalaya. Tell students they will be learning more about the Himalaya. **0:05** minutes

TEACH

GUIDED DISCUSSION

1. **Identify** What present-day countries make up the subcontinent of South Asia? *(Present-day India, Bangladesh, Bhutan, Nepal, and Pakistan make up the large subcontinent of South Asia.)*

2. **Analyze Cause and Effect** What caused the formation of the Himalaya? *(Large moving plates on which the continents lie drove the subcontinent of South Asia into Asia. As the lands collided, they pushed Earth's crust upward to form the Himalaya mountain range.)*

INTERPRET MAPS

Project the Indian Subcontinent map on a whiteboard or screen. Have volunteers read the lesson aloud while other volunteers point out the geographic features on the map as they are referenced in the text. **0:15** minutes

ACTIVE OPTIONS

On Your Feet: Fishbowl Have students form an inner and outer circle, both facing the center. Use a Fishbowl strategy to have them pose questions and take notes about South Asia's physical features. Then have students switch places to pose questions and take notes about South Asia's climate. **0:10** minutes

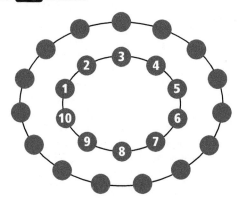

Critical Viewing: NG Chapter Gallery Have students examine the contents of the Chapter Gallery for this chapter. Then invite them to brainstorm additional images they think would fit within the Chapter Gallery. Have them write a description of these additional images and provide an explanation of why they would fit within the Chapter Gallery. Then instruct them to do online research to find examples of actual images they would like to add to the gallery. **0:10** minutes

DIFFERENTIATE

STRIVING READERS

Preview Text Have students preview the lesson. Have them read the title, the Main Idea, subheadings in blue type, map, and questions. Then have them list information about ancient India's geography and climate that they expect to find in the text. Have students read the lesson and discuss with a partner what they learned and whether or not it matched their list.

GIFTED & TALENTED

Create a Presentation Have small groups of students do research to learn more about summer monsoons and winter monsoons in India. Ask students to prepare a presentation explaining the monsoons' effects on farmers, the economy, cities, and coastal communities. Have students share what they learned with the class.

Press *in the Student eEdition for modified text.*

See the Chapter Planner for more strategies for differentiation.

REVIEW & ASSESS

ANSWERS

1. The Indus and Ganges rivers provided fertile soils and a plentiful water supply, essential natural resources that encouraged human settlement and the development of agriculture in ancient India.

2. The Himalaya separates India from the continent of Asia.

3. They bring much needed rain, but they also cause flooding.

Harappan Civilization

Historians have studied ancient Egyptian civilization for many centuries. But evidence of ancient India's great civilization was not discovered until the early 20th century. Then, in 1921, archaeologists unearthed an Indian culture every bit as vast and sophisticated as that of ancient Egypt: the Harappan civilization.

MAIN IDEA

One of the world's earliest and most advanced civilizations emerged in ancient India's Indus River Valley.

WELL-PLANNED CITIES

Around 3300 B.C., civilization developed in the Indus Valley. Fertile soil and irrigation delivered food surpluses that generated wealth. As populations boomed, villages grew into large cities. **Mohenjo-Daro** (moh-HEHN-joh DAHR-oh), one of the civilization's major cities, covered over 250 acres. Another important city, **Harappa** (huh-RA-puh), gave the Harappan civilization its name. These cities were the largest of their time. Their influence spread across a 500,000-square-mile area, which was greater than that of either ancient Egypt or Mesopotamia.

Indus Valley cities were among the world's first **planned cities**. Many were built with the same layout and the same features. Such cities had an eastern housing and business area guarded by defensive walls. To the west were public buildings, as well as structures that may have been used to store grain. Main roads as straight as rulers intersected at right angles with streets exactly half their width. Wells were another common feature. People used bricks that were all the same size to build houses. Homes had indoor plumbing with a bathroom and a toilet that emptied into excellent underground sewers.

Archaeologists have found similarly styled pottery, jewelry, toys, and tools at more than 1,000 Harappan sites. These similar goods demonstrate strong cultural ties among people living hundreds of miles apart. The similarities also suggest that the Harappan civilization was a single state with a strong central government. However, historians have no idea how it was ruled.

AN ADVANCED CULTURE

In fact, there is a lot historians do not know about Harappan civilization because archaeologists have not figured out its writing system. It seems to be based, at least in part, on pictograms, like Sumerian cuneiform. The only writing found is on small items such as pottery, tools, and tiny square stone seals. Traders probably pressed these seals into soft clay to leave their mark on trading goods. Traders also used stone cubes as standard weights and measures.

The Harappans were long-distance traders, using boats and possibly the world's first wheeled vehicles. Their enormous trade network stretched over the mountains into what are now Afghanistan, Iran, and Iraq. There, archaeologists have found records of Harappan copper, gold, and ivory.

Some of the images on Harappan seals show features that are all present in modern Hinduism, such as a male figure that resembles the Hindu God Shiva.

POSSIBLE RESPONSE
The elevation of the mound and its accessibility to a stairway and roads indicate that the mound had a specific purpose.

Critical Viewing This photo shows the ruins of Mohenjo-Daro. What detail indicates that the high mound had a specific purpose?

REVIEW & ASSESS

1. **READING CHECK** What is one characteristic of the advanced culture of Harappan civilization?

2. **INTEGRATE VISUALS** What details in the photo support the conclusion that Harappa was an advanced civilization?

3. **MAKE INFERENCES** Why do you think it is important to use standard weights and measures in trade?

6.5.1 Locate and describe the major river system and discuss the physical setting that supported the rise of this civilization.

HSS CONTENT STANDARDS:

6.5 Students analyze the geographic, political, economic, religious, and social structures of the early civilizations of India.

HSS ANALYSIS SKILLS:

HI 3 Students explain the sources of historical continuity and how the combination of ideas and events explains the emergence of new patterns.

PLAN

OBJECTIVE

Explain how one of the world's earliest and most advanced civilizations emerged in ancient India's Indus River Valley.

ESSENTIAL QUESTION

What led to the development of great civilizations in ancient India?

The fertile farmland led to food surpluses and wealth. Lesson 1.2 discusses how the productive agriculture led to the growth of cities and the development of civilization in ancient India.

BACKGROUND FOR THE TEACHER

The physical geography of a region often influences its history. The good farmland and geographic isolation of South Asia made the Indus and Ganges river valleys cultural hearths, or centers of civilization from which ideas spread. The first urban civilization in South Asia was the Harappan. It developed along the Indus River in what is now Pakistan. The early cities of Mohenjo-Daro and Harappa provide early examples of organized city planning. Architects built heavy walls around the cities for protection. Some buildings in Harappa were partly built on platforms made of mud and brick to keep them from flooding.

DIGITAL RESOURCES NGLSync.cengage.com

TEACHER RESOURCES & ASSESSMENT

 Reading and Note-Taking

 Vocabulary Practice

 Section 1 Quiz

STUDENT RESOURCES

 NG Chapter Gallery

INTRODUCE & ENGAGE

PREVIEW AND PREDICT

Have students read the lesson title, the main idea, and any text in large blue type. Have students use that information to write a sentence that predicts what the lesson is about. Allow pairs of students to compare sentences. **0:05** minutes

TEACH

GUIDED DISCUSSION

1. **Identify** What were the two largest cities at the time of the Harappan civilization? *(Mohenjo-Daro and Harappa)*

2. **Draw Conclusions** What might discoveries of Harappan copper, gold, and ivory in what is now Afghanistan, Iran, and Iraq indicate? *(Harappan people were long-distance traders.)*

ANALYZE VISUALS

Have students study the photograph of Mohenjo-Daro. As a class, fill in a T-Chart to make comparisons between this ancient city and modern cities. **0:10** minutes

Mohenjo-Daro	Modern Cities

ACTIVE OPTIONS

On Your Feet: Card Responses Have half the class write 10 true-false questions based on the lesson. Have the other half create answer cards, writing "True" on one side and "False" on the other side. Students from the first group take turns asking their questions. Students from the second group hold up their cards, showing either "True" or "False." Have students keep track of their correct answers. **0:10** minutes

Critical Viewing: NG Chapter Gallery Invite students to explore the Chapter Gallery to examine the images that relate to this chapter. Have them select one of the images and do additional research to learn more about it. Ask questions that will inspire additional inquiry about the chosen gallery image: What is this? Where and when was this created? By whom? Why was it created? What is it made of? Why does it belong in this chapter? What else would you like to know about it? **0:10** minutes

DIFFERENTIATE

STRIVING READERS

Make a Concept Cluster Organize students into teams of four. Invite each team to fill out a concept web. Have students write the words *Harappan Civilization* in the center. Have them write the words *Cities*, *Culture*, and *Trade* in the other ovals. Then encourage students to write words or phrases they know about the cities, the culture, and the trading practices of the Harappans.

ENGLISH LANGUAGE LEARNERS `ELD`

Ask Questions Remind students that they can ask themselves *Who, What, When, Where, Why,* and *How* questions while reading and look for answers by rereading the text. Use the following question starters to help students ask questions about the text.

- **Emerging**

  Who is _____ ?

  Who are _____ ?

  What is _____ ?

  What are _____ ?

- **Expanding**

  Where was the _____ ?

  Where did _____ ?

  When did _____ ?

  Why did _____ ?

- **Bridging**

  Have students form questions without any prompts.

Press (**mt**) *in the Student eEdition for modified text.*

See the Chapter Planner for more strategies for differentiation.

REVIEW & ASSESS

ANSWERS

1. The immense size of the Harappan civilization, its strong cultural influence, its large planned cities, an enormous commercial network, and the use of standard weights and measures all reveal an advanced culture.

2. Straight roads that intersected with other streets, bricks that were the same size, the appearance of a planned city, and defensive walls support the conclusion that Harappa was an advanced civilization.

3. Standard weights and measures help ensure fair and honest trade.

The
Vedic People

Historians believe the Indus Valley suffered a series of earthquakes from which the Harappan civilization never recovered.

Other forces were also in play. Eventually, a people referred to as Aryans are said to have forged a new Indian civilization.

MAIN IDEA

After the Harappan civilization declined, a people referred to as Aryans are said to have forged a new Indian civilization.

END OF HARAPPA

A combination of natural forces probably contributed to the Harappan civilization's downfall. First agriculture declined when rainfall diminished. Then earthquakes caused flooding and drastically changed the course of rivers. One river, the Sarasvati, no longer flowed near Harappan cities. With reduced access to river water for irrigation, agriculture became more difficult.

As food supplies declined, people abandoned the cities. By 1900 B.C., a simple village way of life had largely replaced the Harappans' advanced urban civilization.

According to many historians, around 1500 B.C., waves of

HARAPPAN SEAL

Found at Mohenjo-Daro, this soft stone seal was probably used to mark trade goods. The marks at the top are an example of the Harappan language, which archaeologists have not yet learned to read.

new people began crossing the Hindu Kush into India. The migrants were a collection of tribes called **Aryans**, meaning "noble ones." They belonged to the Indo-European people who had populated central Asia. (Some scholars have begun to dispute this theory, however. They believe that the Aryans were descendants of earlier Indus civilizations and there was no invasion or migration at all.)

The Aryans were seminomadic herders of horses and cattle and were also fierce warriors. They built only basic houses but rode horses and used wheeled chariots.

Around 1000 B.C., what became known as **Vedic civilization** expanded south and east. There the people adopted agriculture, cleared the forests to cultivate crops, and settled down in villages. The villages grouped together into chiefdoms and then into kingdoms. Over time, the people referred to as Aryans had a huge impact on religion, class, and language. The culture that arose is called the Vedic culture and its people the Vedic people.

IMPACT ON INDIAN SOCIETY

The Vedic people worshipped many gods from nature. They also had gods for friendship and for moral authority. To honor their gods, priests known as Brahmins performed rituals in the ancient language of **Sanskrit**. Their religion came to be called Brahmanism, or early Hinduism.

In time Brahmanism's rituals and hymns were recorded in sacred texts called the **Vedas**. The oldest text is the Rig Veda, which contains 1,028 melodic hymns. Hindus later developed the Upanishads, which contain many spiritual

SANSKRIT AND TAMIL LITERATURE

The Vedas (shown above) were probably composed between 1500 and 1200 B.C. For a thousand years, people passed the Vedas down orally, along with other religious and secular texts.

Texts in Tamil began to appear around 300 B.C. These works were also transmitted orally for many centuries before being written down.

ideas. These texts discuss the Hindu belief in the oneness of all living beings.

As in all early civilizations, a social class system developed in ancient India. Society formed into groups, or jatis, that were determined by birth. The Vedas also describe four main social categories, known as varnas: Brahmins (priests), Kshatriyas (warriors), Vaishyas (merchants), and Sudras (laborers). People belonged to these classes primarily by birth but also by professional achievement and good

ARYAN MIGRATIONS, c. 1500 B.C.

conduct. For example, two of Hinduism's most revered sages, Valmiki and Vyasa, were not born Brahmins. Many centuries later, another group, the Dalits, developed outside of this system. People belonging to this class did the most unclean work.

This system, called the **caste system** by Europeans, provided each group with its own culture. People's castes impacted the kind of work they did and also whom they could marry. Such definitions applied to people's children as well.

REVIEW & ASSESS

1. **READING CHECK** Who were the Aryans?

2. **INTERPRET MAPS** What physical features did the Aryan migrations pass through?

3. **DETERMINE WORD MEANINGS** What does *waves* mean in the sentence, "Around 1500 B.C. waves of new people began crossing the Hindu Kush into India"?

6.5.2 Discuss the significance of the Aryan invasions; 6.5.3 Explain the major beliefs and practices of Brahmanism in India and how they evolved into early Hinduism; 6.5.4 Outline the social structure of the caste system; CST 3 Students use a variety of maps and documents to identify physical and cultural features of neighborhoods, cities, states, and countries and to explain the historical migration of people, expansion and disintegration of empires, and the growth of economic systems.

HSS CONTENT STANDARDS:

6.5.2 Discuss the significance of the Aryan invasions; **6.5.3** Explain the major beliefs and practices of Brahmanism in India and how they evolved into early Hinduism; **6.5.4** Outline the social structure of the caste system.

HSS ANALYSIS SKILLS:

CST 3 Students use a variety of maps and documents to identify physical and cultural features of neighborhoods, cities, states, and countries and to explain the historical migration of people, expansion and disintegration of empires, and the growth of economic systems; **REP 1** Students frame questions that can be answered by historical study and research; **HI 2** Students understand and distinguish cause, effect, sequence, and correlation in historical events, including the long- and short-term causal relations.

PLAN

OBJECTIVE

Analyze the emergence of Vedic culture and its lasting impact on Indian civilization.

ESSENTIAL QUESTION

What led to the development of great civilizations in ancient India?

After the decline of Harappan civilization, a group called the Aryans migrated to the Indian subcontinent. Lesson 1.3 discusses their culture and its impact on Indian civilization.

BACKGROUND FOR THE TEACHER

Scholars believe that there are 7,097 languages spoken in the world today. These languages are classified into major and minor family groups. The Sanskrit language belongs to the Indo-Aryan family, which has a sister branch known as the Iranian family. These branches belong to the larger Indo-European family, which also encompasses many of the languages spoken in Europe today, including Greek, German, Spanish, Italian, and French. Many linguists believe that the ancestor of all of these languages originated in the Eurasian steppes north and east of the Black Sea.

DIGITAL RESOURCES NGLSync.cengage.com

TEACHER RESOURCES & ASSESSMENT

 Reading and Note-Taking

 Vocabulary Practice

 Section 1 Quiz

STUDENT RESOURCES

 NG Chapter Gallery

TEAM UP

Have students work in groups of four to brainstorm a list of factors that contribute toward the development of civilization in a particular region. Have students share their lists with the class. Tell students they will learn more about how factors in a region can affect the civilization that lives there. `0:05` minutes

TEACH

GUIDED DISCUSSION

1. **Analyze Cause and Effect** What natural forces contributed to the Harappan civilization's downfall? (*Rainfall diminished causing agriculture to decline. Earthquakes caused flooding and changed the course of rivers. For these reasons, food supplies declined.*)

2. **Describe** What are two theories about the Aryans? (*One theory is that the Aryans migrated from central Asia. Another theory is that the Aryans were descendants of earlier Indus civilizations.*)

CREATE GRAPHIC ORGANIZERS

To help students understand the structure of India's ancient caste system, have them work in groups of four to create a graphic that accurately represents each caste. For instance, students might create a chart with priests at the top, freemen, farmers, and traders at the next level, and so on. Discuss with students the social hierarchies of other ancient civilizations, such as ancient Mesopotamia and ancient Egypt, and how they compare and contrast with the caste system. `0:15` minutes

ACTIVE OPTIONS

On Your Feet: Create a Quiz Based on what they learned in the lesson, have students work in groups to create a fill-in-the-blank quiz about the Aryan migrations and civilization. Encourage students to use the text to confirm their answers. Then have each group ask another group their questions. Have students keep track of the number of correct answers for their group scores. `0:10` minutes

NG Learning Framework: Research Brahmanism

ATTITUDE: **Curiosity**
KNOWLEDGE: **Our Human Story**

Have students work in small groups. Ask members of each group to think about questions they would like to ask about Brahmanism. Then have them do research to learn more about the religion. Ask students to write short sentences describing what they learned. `0:10` minutes

INCLUSION

Use Echo Reading Pair each proficient reader with a student with special needs. Have the proficient reader read aloud the Main Idea statement about the Aryans at the beginning of the lesson. Have his or her partner "echo" by reading the same statement. Repeat for each of the blue subheadings in the lesson.

PRE-AP

Write a Report Have small groups of students do research about the caste system at the time of the Aryans. Have students write a report about how a person's caste affected his or her life in ancient India. Encourage students to share their reports with the class.

Press (**mt**) *in the Student eEdition for modified text.*

See the Chapter Planner for more strategies for differentiation.

ANSWERS

1. The Aryans were a collection of Indo-European tribes who began crossing the Hindu Kush into India in 1500 B.C.

2. The Aryans passed through the Hindu Kush mountains to reach the Indus Valley.

3. In the quoted sentence, *waves* means great numbers of people arriving all at once.

Hindu Beliefs and Practices

If you are into computer games, you might have an online avatar, a character that represents you. The concept of avatars is nothing new. The Hindu god Vishnu had many avatars, including a godlike hero called Krishna. Unlike your avatar, Vishnu's avatars were versions of himself in various forms.

MAIN IDEA

Over 5,000 years, Hinduism absorbed and integrated many beliefs found throughout South Asia.

GODS AND SACRED TEXTS

The religion that grew out of the diverse ideas and practices of Vedic culture is known as **Hinduism**, the world's third largest religion. Hinduism evolved over many centuries. Brahman, or the universal spirit, appears in many forms, including many Gods and Goddesses. Three important Hindu Deities are Brahma, Vishnu, and Shiva. Female Deities include Saraswati, Goddess of knowledge, science, and the arts, and Parvati, who is both a Goddess and the beautiful wife of Shiva. She is considered a mother Goddess and nurturer. Lakshmi, wife of Vishnu, is often worshipped to bring about success and prosperity. Hinduism is the only major religion in which the divine is worshipped in both female and male forms.

The Vedas are Hinduism's holiest books, but two **epic poems**, or long narrative poems, are also important. One, called *Mahabharata* (MAH-ha-BHAR-ah-tah), teaches the importance of living and acting righteously. The other poem, the *Ramayana* (rah-MAH-yah-nah), tells the story of Rama, the perfect king, who fought evil forces in the world.

Within the *Mahabharata* is a spiritual poem called Bhagavad Gita (BAH-gah-vuhd GEET-ah), or "Song of the Lord." In this poem Krishna praises duty. He also encourages action over inaction, knowledge over ignorance, belief over disbelief, and good over evil. This poem remains popular as a source of spiritual guidance and inspiration.

BELIEFS AND PRACTICES

While Hindus occasionally worship in temples, the home is the center of religious activity. Many homes have a temple room where family members worship. Some Hindus still observe certain cultural practices related to the caste system. They also believe the soul is eternal and is reborn in different bodies over different life cycles. This is known as **reincarnation**.

According to Hindu beliefs, people's thoughts and actions create **karma**, which determines the kind of life into which they will be reborn. The karma of someone who leads a good and moral life leads to a better life. A life filled with misdeeds leads to a life of greater hardship and suffering. Good thoughts and actions are said to be in accordance with **dharma**, or the way of righteous conduct. Hindu scripture also places importance on artha (wealth) and kama (love). The ultimate goal of a Hindu is to end the cycle of rebirth by living selflessly and eliminating material desires.

There are many paths to a spiritual life. One path involves the practice of **yoga**—a series of practices intended to help a person achieve spiritual insight, which involves the desire to seek and know the truth.

These women in northern India are throwing flowers in the air to celebrate the Hindu festival of Holi, which marks the coming of spring.

HINDU DEITIES

Brahma, *the Creator:* Brahma created the universe, the world, and the human race. His four heads represent the four Vedas.

Vishnu, *the Preserver:* Vishnu contains and balances good and evil. It is his job to maintain the divine order of the universe. If evil is winning, Vishnu comes to Earth in human form to restore the balance.

Shiva, *the Destroyer:* Shiva is responsible for all forms of change, from giving up bad habits to death. He is closely associated with yoga.

REVIEW & ASSESS

1. **READING CHECK** Who are the three most important Gods in Hinduism, and what is the role of each?

2. **MAKE INFERENCES** How might the concept of karma guide a Hindu during his or her lifetime?

3. **ANALYZE LANGUAGE USE** How does knowing that *carne* refers to "flesh" help you understand the word *reincarnation*?

6.5.3 Explain the major beliefs and practices of Brahmanism in India and how they evolved into early Hinduism; 6.5.4 Outline the social structure of the caste system; 6.5.7 Discuss important aesthetic and intellectual traditions (e.g., Sanskrit literature, including the *Bhagavad Gita*; medicine; metallurgy; and mathematics, including Hindu-Arabic numerals and the zero).

STANDARDS

HSS CONTENT STANDARDS:

6.5.3 Explain the major beliefs and practices of Brahmanism in India and how they evolved into early Hinduism; **6.5.4** Outline the social structure of the caste system; **6.5.7** Discuss important aesthetic and intellectual traditions (e.g., Sanskrit literature, including the *Bhagavad Gita*; medicine; metallurgy; and mathematics, including Hindu-Arabic numerals and the zero).

HSS ANALYSIS SKILLS:

REP 1 Students frame questions that can be answered by historical study and research.

PLAN

OBJECTIVE

Explain how, over 5,000 years, Hinduism absorbed and integrated many beliefs found throughout South Asia.

ESSENTIAL QUESTION

What led to the development of great civilizations in ancient India?

Hinduism developed over many centuries. Lesson 1.4 discusses how Hinduism integrated and absorbed many beliefs found throughout South Asia.

BACKGROUND FOR THE TEACHER

Over many years, the ideas in the Vedas, the sacred texts of Brahmanism, began to blend with ideas from other cultures. For example, people from kingdoms in Central Asia, such as Persia, brought their ideas to India. This mix of ideas, customs, and beliefs eventually led to the religion of Hinduism. Hinduism is one of the oldest religions in the world. Hindus believe that eventually their souls will join the Deity Brahma, the creator and universal spirit.

DIGITAL RESOURCES NGLSync.cengage.com

TEACHER RESOURCES & ASSESSMENT

 Reading and Note-Taking

 Vocabulary Practice

 Section 1 Quiz

STUDENT RESOURCES

 NG Image Gallery

INTRODUCE & ENGAGE

ASK QUESTIONS

Have students work in groups of four. Have each group come up with a list of three questions about Hinduism. Tell students that they will learn about some beliefs and practices associated with Hinduism. After the lesson, review the questions and have students from each group answer the questions they listed. Have each group share its questions and answers with the class. **0:05** minutes

TEACH

GUIDED DISCUSSION

1. **Identify** Where do Hindus worship? *(They occasionally worship in temples, but the home is the center of religious activity. Many homes have a temple room in which family members worship.)*

2. **Summarize** What is the ultimate goal of a Hindu? *(The ultimate goal is to end the cycle of reincarnation by living selflessly and eliminating material desires.)*

MORE INFORMATION

Hindu Rituals Rituals are an important part of Hinduism. *Pujas*—a type of blessing—and traditional decorations such as henna are two important rituals. Others include ritual bathing, participation in festivals, fasting, and prayer and meditation. Pujas can be performed by priests or by individual worshippers. One common type is *arati*, or the use of a lighted lamp in front of the object Deity, or person to be blessed. Pujas are used under specific circumstances and also as a practice of devotion.

ACTIVE OPTIONS

On Your Feet: Numbered Heads Organize students into groups of four and assign each group member a number (1-4). Tell students to think about and discuss a response to this question: *How are the religious beliefs of the Hindus and the Aryans similar?* Then call a number and have the student from each group with that number report for the group. If time permits, repeat the process with an additional question: *How might a caste system have affected the lives of Aryans and many Hindus?* **0:10** minutes

Critical Viewing: NG Image Gallery Invite students to explore the entire NG Image Gallery, including the images for this chapter. Ask students to choose two images they think represent Hindu values or customs and do further research on each of them using this text and using other sources. Then have students present their findings to the class. Prompt students to explain why they chose their two images. **0:10** minutes

DIFFERENTIATE

STRIVING READERS

Make Lists Have students work in groups of four. Post the title "Four Things I Learned About Hindu Practices and Beliefs." Ask each group to copy the title. Then ask each person in the group to write or say a sentence about the title. Encourage students to share their lists with the class.

ENGLISH LANGUAGE LEARNERS   ELD

Create Webs for Key Words Display the word *Hinduism* and draw a circle around it. Have students at the **Expanding** and **Bridging** levels volunteer words they have learned that are related to Hinduism. Draw spokes for the circle and write the words suggested at the ends of the spokes. Have students write or say sentences that use any of the words in the web.

Press **mt** *in the Student eEdition for modified text.*

See the Chapter Planner for more strategies for differentiation.

REVIEW & ASSESS

ANSWERS

1. In Hinduism, the three most important Gods are Brahma the creator, Vishnu the preserver, and Shiva the destroyer and re-creator.

2. The concept of karma determines the kind of life into which Hindus will be reborn. The karma of someone who leads a good and moral life leads to rebirth into a better life.

3. Possible response: Knowing that *carne* means "flesh" helps me understand that reincarnation is related to the body.

Hindu Sacred Texts

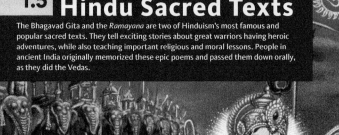

The *Bhagavad Gita* and the *Ramayana* are two of Hinduism's most famous and popular sacred texts. They tell exciting stories about great warriors having heroic adventures, while also teaching important religious and moral lessons. People in ancient India originally memorized these epic poems and passed them down orally, as they did the Vedas.

This painting shows the Lord Krishna, an avatar of Vishnu, and Prince Arjuna as they head into battle.

DOCUMENT ONE

Primary Source: Sacred Text

from the Bhagavad Gita,
translated by Stephen Mitchell
The Bhagavad Gita is a 700-verse poem describing a conversation between Vishnu's avatar Krishna and the hero Arjuna. In this excerpt, Krishna speaks to Arjuna before a great battle. Krishna tells the warrior about the soul—the "it" in the poem.

CONSTRUCTED RESPONSE According to Krishna, what is special about a soul?

> The sharpest sword will not pierce it;
> the hottest flame will not singe [burn] it;
> water will not make it moist;
> wind will not cause it to wither [die].
>
> It cannot be pierced or singed,
> moistened or withered; it is vast,
> perfect and all-pervading [everywhere],
> calm, immovable, timeless.

DOCUMENT TWO

Primary Source: Epic Poem

from the *Ramayana*,
a retelling by William Buck
The *Ramayana* is a story of a heroic journey in which the good king Rama, an avatar of Vishnu, rescues his kidnapped wife Sita from Ravana, the evil ruler of an island off India's southeastern coast. In this passage, Rama speaks to his brother after they learn that their father has died.

CONSTRUCTED RESPONSE What comfort might his brother take from Rama's words?

> Life is passing as a river ever flowing away, never still, never returning. Life is changeable as the flashing lightning, a pattern of as little meaning, and impermanent. . . . Life is bright and colored for a passing moment like the sunset. Then it is gone and who can prevent it going?

DOCUMENT THREE

Primary Source: Sacred Text

from the Rig Veda,
translated by Wendy Doniger
The Rig Veda is a series of 1,028 hymns grouped into 10 books. It is also the oldest of the Hindu sacred texts. This excerpt from a poem in Book 10 addresses a person who has just died.

CONSTRUCTED RESPONSE According to the passage, what happens to a person after death?

> May your eye go to the sun, your life's breath to the wind. Go to the sky or to earth, as is your nature; or go to the waters, if that is your fate. Take root in the plants with your limbs.

SYNTHESIZE & WRITE

1. **REVIEW** Review what you have learned about Hinduism, the Bhagavad Gita, the *Ramayana*, and the Rig Veda.

2. **RECALL** On your own paper, write down the main idea expressed in each document.

3. **CONSTRUCT** Construct a topic sentence that answers this question: What do the passages from the Bhagavad Gita, the *Ramayana*, and the Rig Veda suggest about Hinduism's attitude toward life and death?

4. **WRITE** Using evidence from the documents, write an explanatory paragraph that answers the question in Step 3.

6.5.7 Discuss important aesthetic and intellectual traditions (e.g., Sanskrit literature, including the *Bhagavad Gita*; medicine; metallurgy; and mathematics, including Hindu-Arabic numerals and the zero); REP 4 Students assess the credibility of primary and secondary sources and draw sound conclusions from them.

PLAN

OBJECTIVE

Synthesize information about Hindu sacred texts from primary and secondary source documents.

ESSENTIAL QUESTION

What led to the development of great civilizations in ancient India?

The Hindu sacred texts include the Hindu philosophy, verse, and hymns. These texts provided spiritual guidance for Hindus as their civilization developed. Lesson 1.5 provides excerpts from these sacred texts.

BACKGROUND FOR THE TEACHER

The Bhagavad Gita comprises chapters 23 to 40 of Book 6 of the *Mahabharata*. It includes a long conversation between the deity Vishnu and Prince Arjuna. On the eve of a great battle, Arjuna expresses doubts about killing. Vishnu tells Arjuna that because he is a warrior, he must go into battle. However, after death, the soul is released from the body and is transferred to another body. If the soul attains true wisdom, it achieves *moksha*, or release from the cycles of rebirth.

DIGITAL RESOURCES NGLSync.cengage.com

TEACHER RESOURCES & ASSESSMENT

 Reading and Note-Taking

 Vocabulary Practice

 Section 1 Quiz

STUDENT RESOURCES

 NG Chapter Gallery

INTRODUCE & ENGAGE

PREPARE FOR THE DOCUMENT-BASED QUESTION

Before students start on the activity, briefly preview the three documents. Remind students that a constructed response requires full explanations in complete sentences. Emphasize that students should use their knowledge of Hindu beliefs in addition to the information in the documents.
0:05 minutes

TEACH

GUIDED DISCUSSION

1. **Identify** What is the role of Krishna in the Bhagavad Gita? *(Krishna is the avatar of the god Vishnu.)*

2. **Make Inferences** What does the excerpt from the Rig Veda indicate about the importance of nature in the Hindu religion? *(The excerpt includes the words* sun, wind, sky, earth, nature, waters, root, *and* plant. *The use of these words would indicate that nature is very important to the Hindu religion.)*

3. **Summarize** In the *Ramayana*, what does Rama do that makes him a hero? *(He rescues his kidnapped wife, Sita, from Ravana, an evil ruler.)*

EVALUATE

After students have completed the "Synthesize & Write" activity, allow time for them to exchange paragraphs and read and comment on the work of their peers. Guidelines for comments should be established prior to this activity so that feedback is constructive and encouraging in nature.
0:15 minutes

ACTIVE OPTIONS

On Your Feet: Talk and Share Ask students to work in small groups. Ask each group to list things they have learned about the importance of the Hindu sacred texts in the lives of Hindus. Have each group share its list with the class. **0:10** minutes

NG Learning Framework: Study Primary Sources

SKILL: Communication
KNOWLEDGE: Our Human Story

Invite students to review the text of the primary sources in the lesson. **ASK:** What do these documents reveal about the Hindu attitude toward life, death, and beliefs about a person's soul? Have students write a short paragraph to explain their answer. **0:10** minutes

DIFFERENTIATE

STRIVING READERS

Write a Tweet Divide students into three groups. Assign one of the documents to each group. Have each group write a tweet that describes the document. Have each group read their tweets to the class.

PRE-AP

Present an Oral Report Ask small groups of students to research and prepare an oral report on the Hindu view of nature, including information about Hindus' respect for animals, plants, and the environment as a whole. Have groups present their findings to the class. Encourage each person in the group to take part in the oral presentation.

Press (**mt**) *in the Student eEdition for modified text.*

See the Chapter Planner for more strategies for differentiation.

CONSTRUCTED RESPONSE

ANSWERS
DOCUMENT 1
Krishna's words reassure Arjuna that even if he was injured or killed in battle, his soul would live on.

DOCUMENT 2
Rama's brother might be comforted by the idea that life is short and that everyone dies.

DOCUMENT 3
After death, a person becomes one with nature.

SYNTHESIZE & WRITE

ANSWERS
1. Responses will vary.

2. Students should convey and support the main idea with appropriate evidence from the primary sources.

3. Students should construct a clearly written topic sentence that answers the question.

4. Students' paragraphs should include their topic sentence from Step 3 and provide several details from the documents to support the sentence. Students should organize the information in a logical, clearly written paragraph.

Siddhartha and Buddhism

Like many people, you might very much want to own the latest cell phone or tablet. But what if someone told you that your desire for such material possessions would only bring you suffering? That's exactly what a man who lived about 2,500 years ago said.

MAIN IDEA

Buddhism emerged in India around 500 B.C.

Buddhist monks pray before a statue that represents the Buddha.

SIDDHARTHA GAUTAMA

EIGHTFOLD PATH

Right View: See and understand things as they really are

Right Intention: Commit to ethical self-improvement

Right Speech: Tell the truth and speak gently

Right Action: Act kindly, honestly, and respectfully

Right Livelihood: Earn a living in a moral, legal, and peaceful way

Right Effort: Focus your will onto achieving good things

Right Mindfulness: Value a good mind

Right Concentration: Single-mindedness

THE LIFE OF BUDDHA

Earlier in this chapter, you learned about the development of Hinduism in India. Another major religion, called **Buddhism**, also began there. Buddhism is based on the teachings of **Siddhartha Gautama** (sih-DAR-tuh GOW-tuh-muh). According to tradition, Siddhartha was born in 563 B.C. He was a prince who lived a life of luxury in what is now Nepal.

Siddhartha enjoyed his life until, at the age of 29, he came across an old man, a sick man, a dead man, and a holy man who was poor but very happy. These men made Siddhartha think about suffering brought on by old age, disease, and death and wonder what had made the holy man so happy. Siddhartha

gave up his wealth, his wife, and his child to search for the answer to this question. Then, after six years of wandering, he meditated beneath a tree and finally understood how to be free from suffering. Because of this revelation, or understanding of truth, Siddhartha came to be known as the Buddha, or "Enlightened One."

BUDDHIST BELIEFS

The Buddha spent the rest of his life teaching what he had learned. Much of what he taught is contained in a set of guidelines called the Four Noble Truths. The first truth teaches that all life is suffering. The second truth is that the cause of suffering is desire. The third truth teaches that the end of desire means the end of suffering; the fourth, that following the Eightfold Path can end suffering. The Eightfold Path is also called the Middle Way because it

promotes a life balanced between happiness and self-denial. Like Hindus, the Buddha believed in rebirth. He taught that following the Eightfold Path would lead to **nirvana** (nihr-VAH-nuh), a state of bliss or the end of suffering caused by the cycle of rebirth.

The totality of the Buddha's teachings are known as the **dharma** (DUHR-muh), or divine law. The Buddha taught that a person of any caste could attain nirvana, and he also promoted nonviolence. Buddhism spread throughout Asia and beyond. After the Buddha died, his remains were buried under eight mound-like structures called stupas.

Job: Prince, poor man, Enlightened One, and founder of Buddhism

Education: Princely pursuits followed by soul searching

Home: Northeast India

FINEST HOUR

He finally achieved enlightenment after 49 days of intense meditation.

WORST MOMENT

He struggled to find the answers he sought, despite putting himself through much suffering and hardship.

MILESTONE

The Buddha is said to have received enlightenment at the age of 35.

REVIEW & ASSESS

1. **READING CHECK** Who is Siddhartha Gautama and what did he seek to learn?

2. **DRAW CONCLUSIONS** What is the purpose of the Four Noble Truths and the Eightfold Path?

3. **MAKE INFERENCES** Why do you think Buddhism became popular in ancient India?

6.5.5 Know the life and moral teachings of Buddha and how Buddhism spread in India, Ceylon, and Central Asia.

STANDARDS

HSS CONTENT STANDARDS:

6.5.5 Know the life and moral teachings of Buddha and how Buddhism spread in India, Ceylon, and Central Asia.

HSS ANALYSIS SKILLS:

CST 3 Students use a variety of maps and documents to identify physical and cultural features of neighborhoods, cities, states, and countries and to explain the historical migration of people, expansion and disintegration of empires, and the growth of economic systems; **REP 1** Students frame questions that can be answered by historical study and research.

PLAN

OBJECTIVE

Explain how Buddhism emerged in India around 500 B.C.

ESSENTIAL QUESTION

What led to the development of great civilizations in ancient India?

Buddhism was founded in ancient India. Lesson 1.6 discusses how Buddhism influenced the development of Indian civilization.

BACKGROUND FOR THE TEACHER

The Buddha did not leave written records of his teachings. His early disciples preserved the teachings by transmitting them orally from one generation to the next. Around 80 B.C., followers of the Buddha recorded his teachings in a set of books called the *Tripitaka*, or "Three Baskets." Over a period of centuries, Buddhism spread throughout Asia and other parts of the world. In South Asia today, Buddhism is the main religion of Bhutan and Sri Lanka.

Buddhism focuses on helping people end their physical and mental suffering by teaching them to give up worldly possessions. According to Buddhist teachings, one way to alleviate suffering in life is through meditation. Meditation is the practice of using concentration to quiet and control one's thoughts.

DIGITAL RESOURCES NGLSync.cengage.com

TEACHER RESOURCES & ASSESSMENT

 Reading and Note-Taking

 Vocabulary Practice

 Section 1 Quiz

STUDENT RESOURCES

 Active History

INTRODUCE & ENGAGE

K-W-L CHART

Provide each student with a K-W-L Chart like the one shown below. Have students brainstorm what they know about religions in ancient India. Then ask them to write questions that they would like to have answered as they learn about Buddhism. Allow time at the end of the lesson for students to fill in what they have learned. **0:05** minutes

K What Do I Know?	W What Do I Want To Learn?	L What Did I Learn?

TEACH

STEM

GUIDED DISCUSSION

1. **Identify** For what reason was the Buddha considered the "Enlightened One?" *(After wandering and then meditating, he finally understood the truth about how to be free from suffering.)*

2. **Describe** What are three teachings of the Buddha? *(Responses can include: the Four Noble Truths, guidelines for ending suffering, the Eightfold Path that leads to nirvana; the attainment of nirvana by a person of any caste; nonviolence; reincarnation.)*

ANALYZE VISUALS

Have students examine the photo of the Buddhist monks. Direct students to write a sentence about how the appearance and dress of the monks might give a clue about their religious beliefs and practices. *(Possible response: The monks are wearing simple robes with no jewelry or other accessories. This indicates that the monks probably lead a simple life with few material possessions.)* **0:10** minutes

ACTIVE OPTIONS

Active History: Map the Spread of Buddhism Extend the lesson by using either the PDF or Whiteboard version of the activity. These activities take a deeper look at a topic from, or related to, the lesson. Explore the activities as a class, turn them into group assignments, or even assign them individually. **0:10** minutes

---

NG Learning Framework: Research and Compare Religions

SKILL: Observation
KNOWLEDGE: Our Human Story

Around the sixth century B.C., the religion of Jainism emerged through the teachings of Mahavira, who gave up his wealth and property and renounced family life to become an ascetic. Jainism emphasizes and promotes the shared Hindu idea of ahimsa, or nonviolence. Have groups of students research Jainism. Then have each group create a chart that illustrates similarities and differences among Jainism, Buddhism, and Hinduism. Guide students in their comparisons according to the following categories: founder, basic beliefs, and sacred texts. After groups have completed their charts, review the information as a class and discuss the similarities and differences among the three religions. **0:15** minutes

DIFFERENTIATE

INCLUSION

Use Supported Reading In small groups, have students read the lesson aloud. At the end of the lesson, have them stop and use these sentence frames to tell what they understood from the text.

- This lesson is about _____.
- One detail that stood out to me is _____.
- The vocabulary word _____ means _____.
- One thing I would like to understand more clearly is _____

Guide students through portions of the text they do not understand. Make sure all students understand this lesson before moving on to the next lesson.

GIFTED & TALENTED

Host a Talk Show Have pairs of students assume the roles of a talk show host and an expert on Buddhism. Ask students to plan, write, and perform a simulated television talk show in which the expert is the guest. Tell students to focus the talk show on the life of Siddhartha Gautama and his teachings, including the Four Noble Truths and the Eightfold Path.

Press **mt** *in the Student eEdition for modified text.*

See the Chapter Planner for more strategies for differentiation.

REVIEW & ASSESS

ANSWERS

1. Siddhartha was a prince who gave up everything to learn how to be truly happy.

2. Buddhists believe that following the Four Noble Truths and the Eightfold Path will lead to the end of suffering.

3. Buddhism rejects the rigid caste system and favors equality, which most likely appealed to many people, especially those belonging to the lowest social classes in India's caste system.

The Maurya Empire

Bite into oven-hot food and you'll burn your tongue. But nibble away at the cooler edges and you can eventually eat the whole meal. That's the principle one king applied to defeat some weaker kingdoms until he was strong enough to conquer them all.

MAIN IDEA

The Maurya Empire united much of India under a single ruler.

A UNITED INDIA

Earlier in this chapter, you read about the Aryans who migrated to India. Some historians believe that many kingdoms were established during the Vedic period in the subcontinent. For hundreds of years, no major power arose. Then, around 550 B.C., a kingdom called Magadha in northeast India grew powerful.

Chandragupta Maurya (chuhn-druh-GUP-tuh MOWR-yuh) became king of Magadha around 325 B.C. Believed to have been a soldier, Chandragupta gained power with the help of Kautilya, a teacher who strategized Chandragupta's rise. Once Chandragupta became king, he conquered many of the other kingdoms and established an empire. His Maurya Empire united most of northern India and was the first great Indian empire.

Chandragupta established a strong central government. He used taxes to pay for a network of spies and a large army to crush troublemakers. Then, somewhat surprisingly, Chandragupta gave up the throne in 297 B.C. Instead of continuing to rule his empire, he chose to become a monk committed to nonviolence.

THE BUDDHIST KING

Around 269 B.C., **Asoka** (uh-SHOH-kuh), Chandragupta's grandson, became king. At first he earned a reputation for cruelty. His unprovoked attack on another Indian kingdom caused the deaths of hundreds of thousands of people. In the aftermath of so much violence, Asoka underwent a dramatic change. He converted to Buddhism and began to rule using Buddhist principles about peace.

Asoka made a pilgrimage to Buddhist holy places in northern India, preaching to his subjects as he traveled. He encouraged the spread of Buddhism by sending missionaries to preach abroad. This helped Buddhism reach other countries, such as Ceylon (present-day Sri Lanka) and China. Traders also brought Buddhism to Central Asia.

Asoka had his Buddhist policies inscribed on rocks and tall pillars across his empire. The inscriptions were written in the appropriate regional languages. These policies encouraged everyone to live good lives. State officials monitored moral conduct.

Asoka built more than 1,000 stupas in honor of the Buddha. He donated to charity and built hospitals for animals as well as for humans. To govern his vast empire effectively, Asoka built good roads with plenty of shade and water. These roads were useful for trade and allowed his instructions, inspectors, and armies to travel quickly.

Although Asoka may have been India's greatest king, his well-run empire did not last long. After his death, the Maurya Empire collapsed into many warring kingdoms.

THE MAURYA EMPIRE, c. 250 B.C.

Arabian Sea · Bay of Bengal · Pataliputra · MAGADHA · HINDU KUSH · HIMALAYA · Indus R. · Ganges R.

Maurya Empire

0   300   600 Miles
0   300   600 Kilometers

This pillar is one of many that Asoka had erected during his reign.

REVIEW & ASSESS

1. **READING CHECK** How did Chandragupta Maurya unite much of India into the first great Indian empire?

2. **INTERPRET MAPS** Where was Magadha located?

3. **ANALYZE CAUSE AND EFFECT** What caused Asoka to renounce violence? What was the effect?

6.5.5 Know the life and moral teachings of Buddha and how Buddhism spread in India, Ceylon, and Central Asia; 6.5.6 Describe the growth of the Maurya empire and the political and moral achievements of the emperor Asoka; CST 3 Students use a variety of maps and documents to identify physical and cultural features of neighborhoods, cities, states, and countries and to explain the historical migration of people, expansion and disintegration of empires, and the growth of economic systems; HI 2 Students understand and distinguish cause, effect, sequence, and correlation in historical events, including the long- and short-term causal relations.

157

HSS CONTENT STANDARDS:

6.5.5 Know the life and moral teachings of Buddha and how Buddhism spread in India, Ceylon, and Central Asia; **6.5.6** Describe the growth of the Maurya empire and the political and moral achievements of the emperor Asoka.

HSS ANALYSIS SKILLS:

CST 3 Students use a variety of maps and documents to identify physical and cultural features of neighborhoods, cities, states, and countries and to explain the historical migration of people, expansion and disintegration of empires, and the growth of economic systems; **HI 2** Students understand and distinguish cause, effect, sequence, and correlation in historical events, including the long- and short-term causal relations.

PLAN

OBJECTIVE

Describe how the Maurya Empire united much of India under a single ruler.

ESSENTIAL QUESTION

What led to the development of great civilizations in ancient India?

The Maurya Empire united much of India under Chandragupta Maurya and then his grandson, Asoka. Lesson 2.1 discusses the development and then the decline of the Maurya Empire.

BACKGROUND FOR THE TEACHER

Chandragupta Maurya was an Indian prince who conquered almost all of northern India and united it into one empire. The Maurya Empire had a complex government. In addition to having spies and an army of around 600,000 soldiers, the government had thousands of chariots and war elephants. Chandragupta also set up a postal system to facilitate communications within the empire.

Asoka was a very strong ruler who made the empire powerful and rich. After he died, the kings who followed him were weak. They turned the people against them. After the Maurya Empire declined, India broke up into several kingdoms and endured several invasions until the rise of the Gupta Empire.

DIGITAL RESOURCES NGLSync.cengage.com

TEACHER RESOURCES & ASSESSMENT

 Reading and Note-Taking

 Vocabulary Practice

 Section 2 Quiz

STUDENT RESOURCES

 Biography

INTRODUCE & ENGAGE

MAKE A TEAM WORD WEB

Have students sit around a large piece of paper. Give each team member a different colored marker. Give students the following topic for their Word Web: *What are some characteristics of a successful civilization?* Ask students to write words or phrases that answer the topic question. Have each student add to the part of the web nearest to her or him. On a signal, have students rotate the paper and have each student add to the nearest part again. Tell students they will learn about how the Maurya Empire was successful. `0:05` minutes

TEACH

GUIDED DISCUSSION

1. **Describe** What was the government like under Chandragupta? *(It was a strong central government. Taxes paid for a network of spies and a large army.)*

2. **Summarize** What were some ways in which Asoka governed his empire? *(He ruled using Buddhist principles about peace. He had policies to encourage people to lead good lives. He donated to charity and built hospitals for animals and humans. He built good roads that were used for trade and that allowed armies to travel quickly.)*

CREATE GRAPHIC ORGANIZERS

Have students copy and fill in the following chart to help them remember the achievements and accomplishments of the two Maurya rulers mentioned in the lesson. `0:10` minutes

	Political Achievements	Religious Achievements
Chandragupta		
Asoka		

ACTIVE OPTIONS

On Your Feet: Build a Paragraph Direct students to form four lines. Provide each line of students with the same topic sentence: *Asoka may have been India's greatest king.* Each line, or group of students, should build a paragraph about the topic, with each person in line adding one sentence. Then have the groups record and share their paragraphs with the class. As an extension, have students read the excerpt from Asoka's Edicts in the **Primary Source Handbook** and answer the questions that follow. `0:10` minutes

Critical Viewing: NG Image Gallery Have students explore the NG Chapter Gallery and then the complete NG Image Gallery. Invite students to choose two images: one from this chapter and one from another chapter. Have students create a T-Chart with the column headings "Similar" and "Different." Students should complete their T-Chart by listing ways the two images are similar and ways they are different. Encourage students to move beyond physical comparison statements such as "one image shows a sculpture and the other shows a painting" by asking students to consider what the item in each gallery image represents, when it was made, and how it reflects the time or location in which it was made. `0:10` minutes

DIFFERENTIATE

ENGLISH LANGUAGE LEARNERS

Ask Yes/No Questions Ask the questions below and have students at the **Emerging** level say or write *yes* or *no* in response. Then reread the questions and ask students to correct the information in any sentence that has *no* as an answer. *(numbers 2, 3, 6, 7)*

1. Did Chandragupta's empire have a strong government?

2. Did Chandragupta rule until the end of his life?

3. Did Chandragupta divide his empire?

4. Did Asoka's government encourage people to lead good lives?

5. Did Asoka help Buddhism reach other countries?

6. Did Asoka convert to Hinduism?

7. Was Asoka a weak ruler?

8. Did Asoka build roads and hospitals?

PRE-AP

Create a Travel Brochure Have pairs of students prepare a travel brochure for India during the rule of Asoka. The brochure should illustrate and describe places or structures that visitors should be sure to see. It also should describe activities or policies that they will notice on their visit to India.

Press **(mt)** *in the Student eEdition for modified text.*

See the Chapter Planner for more strategies for differentiation.

REVIEW & ASSESS

ANSWERS

1. First Chandragupta Maurya became king of Magadha, a powerful kingdom in northeast India. From there, he conquered other kingdoms and united them into an empire.

2. Magadha was located in the most northeastern part of the subcontinent.

3. A particularly bloody war caused Asoka to renounce violence. Asoka became a Buddhist and decided to rule India through the peaceful principles of Buddhism, which spread throughout India and other regions.

Dedicated to the God Vishnu, the Dashavatar Temple in northern India is an example of Gupta architecture.

2.2

The Gupta Empire

History has some weird coincidences.

Two of India's greatest empires began in Magadha with a king called Chandragupta. But the kings weren't related. And both empires began around 320, although the Maurya Empire began in 320 B.C. and the Gupta in A.D. 320.

MAIN IDEA

The Gupta Empire brought 200 years of peace and prosperity to India.

A WISE RULER

The collapse of the Maurya Empire led to 500 years of anarchy in India in which smaller kingdoms ruled. Despite this disorder, the period brought continued economic, social, and cultural progress. Then around A.D. 320 a new unifying power arose. A leader in Magadha called **Chandra Gupta I** began gaining new land and established the Gupta

Empire. A dynasty of strong Gupta kings continued to expand the empire until it covered most of northern India. Instead of establishing a strong central government like the Mauryas did, the Guptas allowed the defeated kings to continue to rule. In exchange the Guptas required obedience and tribute, or payment, from the defeated kings.

A series of strong, wise, and long-lived Gupta rulers brought India 200 years of political stability, peace, and prosperity. The expanding empire and its extensive trade routes spread Indian cultural influences around Asia and beyond. Hinduism was reestablished and eventually became India's main religion.

A GOLDEN AGE

Chandra Gupta II, grandson of Chandra Gupta I, ruled during India's **golden age**, a period of great cultural achievement. **Kalidasa** (kah-lih-DAH-suh), the greatest poet in Chandra Gupta II's court and one of India's greatest writers, composed poems and plays in Sanskrit. Scribes, or writers, wrote down the spoken stories, including the *Mahabharata* and the *Ramayana*.

Indian artists painted and sculpted statues of Hindu Deities. Architects designed and built elegant new temples. Metalworking, improved dramatically. A 24-foot iron pillar weighing more than 6 tons still stands in Delhi some 1,500 years after being installed.

Medical understanding also increased. **Ayurveda** (y-uhr-VAY-duh), a traditional guide to medicine, diet, exercise, and disease, developed and remains an alternative form of healing. In medicine, as in many other areas, ancient Indian knowledge and culture reached far around the world.

REVIEW & ASSESS

1. **READING CHECK** How did the Gupta kings bring peace to their empire?

2. **INTERPRET MAPS** In which directions did the Gupta Empire spread out from Magadha?

3. **FORM AND SUPPORT OPINIONS** Which achievement during India's golden age do you think was most significant? Explain your answer.

6.5.7 Discuss important aesthetic and intellectual traditions (e.g., Sanskrit literature, including the *Bhagavad Gita*; medicine; metallurgy; and mathematics, including Hindu-Arabic numerals and the zero; CST 3 Students use a variety of maps and documents to identify physical and cultural features of neighborhoods, cities, states, and countries and to explain the historical migration of people, expansion and disintegration of empires, and the growth of economic systems.

HSS CONTENT STANDARDS:

6.5.7 Discuss important aesthetic and intellectual traditions (e.g., Sanskrit literature, including the *Bhagavad Gita*; medicine; metallurgy; and mathematics, including Hindu-Arabic numerals and the zero).

HSS ANALYSIS SKILLS:

CST 3 Students use a variety of maps and documents to identify physical and cultural features of neighborhoods, cities, states, and countries and to explain the historical migration of people, expansion and disintegration of empires, and the growth of economic systems.

PLAN

OBJECTIVE

Describe how the Gupta Empire brought 200 years of peace and prosperity to India.

ESSENTIAL QUESTION

What led to the development of great civilizations in ancient India?

The Gupta Empire brought prosperity to India. Lesson 2.2 discusses the development and contributions of the Gupta Empire.

BACKGROUND FOR THE TEACHER

The Gupta Empire began in the fertile Ganges River Valley. Gupta artists and scientists created lasting cultural contributions. Advances in metalworking, literature, mathematics (including the development of the decimal), and astronomy were part of this legacy. Trade helped make the Gupta Empire wealthy. Cloth, salt, and iron were among the goods the Guptas traded. Cities grew along trade routes. People in the kingdom prospered. Eventually, invasions weakened the Guptas, and by A.D. 540 their reign was over.

DIGITAL RESOURCES NGLSync.cengage.com

TEACHER RESOURCES & ASSESSMENT

 Reading and Note-Taking

 Vocabulary Practice

 Section 2 Quiz

STUDENT RESOURCES

 NG Chapter Gallery

ACTIVATE PRIOR KNOWLEDGE

Have students work in small groups. Ask students to think about how trading goods and sharing ideas with other countries can influence a country's prosperity, religions, and advances in arts and sciences. Have each group present three ideas to the class. Tell students they will learn about some of the factors that influenced the success of the Gupta civilization. `0:05` minutes

TEACH

GUIDED DISCUSSION

1. **Compare and Contrast** How was the Gupta government similar to and different from the Maurya government? *(Both governments had strong kings who expanded the empires. The Guptas did not establish a strong central government like the Mauryas. They allowed defeated kings to rule. In return, the Guptas required obedience and tribute, or payment, from the defeated kings.)*

2. **Identify** What was India's main religion during the Gupta Empire? *(Hinduism was the main religion in India during the Gupta Empire.)*

ANALYZE VISUALS

Have students examine the photo of part of the Dashavatar Temple in India. Ask them to list adjectives that describe what they see. Ask students what the style of the art and architecture might suggest about the art and architecture of the time. *(Students may respond that the art and architecture are quite elaborate and might indicate that art and architecture were important in the Gupta civilization.)*

As an extension, have students read Kalidasa's poem "Look to This Day" in the **Primary Source Handbook** and answer the questions that follow it. Discuss with students traits of the literature at that time. `0:10` minutes

ACTIVE OPTIONS

On Your Feet: Present an Empire Divide the class into two groups. Assign one group to the Maurya Empire and the other group to the Gupta Empire. Have each group prepare a presentation of "their" empire. The Maurya Empire should include government officials, members of the military, and the leader Asoka. The Gupta Empire should include Hindus, artists, and people who studied medicine. `0:10` minutes

NG Learning Framework: Write a Biography

ATTITUDE: **Curiosity**
KNOWLEDGE: **Our Human Story**

Have students select one of the leaders they are curious about after reading Lessons 2.1 and 2.2. Instruct them to write a short biography about this person using information from the chapter and additional source material. `0:20` minutes

STRIVING READERS

Find Main Ideas and Details Remind students that a main idea is a statement that summarizes the key idea of an article, speech, or paragraph. Details are facts, dates, events, and descriptions that support a main idea. Ask students to write one main idea and four details for the Gupta Empire. They should use their own words. Have students share their ideas when they have finished. The Maurya Empire is shown as an example.

The Maurya Empire united much of India under a single ruler.

The king, Chandragupta, conquered many other kingdoms and established an empire.

Chandragupta established a strong central government.

Asoka ruled using Buddhist principles about peace.

Asoka built hospitals and roads.

INCLUSION

Complete Cloze Statements Provide copies of these cloze statements for students to complete during or after reading.

A _____ of strong Gupta kings expanded the empire until it covered most of northern _____. They did not establish a strong central _____. Instead, the Guptas allowed the defeated _____ to continue to _____. The Guptas required _____ and tribute, or _____ from the defeated kings.

Press (**mt**) *in the Student eEdition for modified text.*

See the Chapter Planner for more strategies for differentiation.

ANSWERS

1. The Gupta kings brought peace by allowing rulers of conquered kingdoms to continue to rule.

2. The Gupta Empire spread out to the north and the west of Magadha.

3. Responses will vary. Students may choose achievements in literature, art, metalworking, design and building of structures, or medicine.

2.3

The
Legacy of
Ancient India

Martin Luther King, Jr., championed nonviolent protest to win rights for African Americans. His methods were inspired by the nonviolent protests of Mohandas Gandhi, who helped India gain its independence in 1947. And Gandhi took his nonviolent principles from Hinduism and Buddhism. In that way alone, Indian thinking has had an immense impact on the modern world.

MAIN IDEA

The achievements of ancient India have influenced much of the world.

RELIGION

Four major religions had their origins in India: Hinduism, Buddhism, Jainism, and Sikhism. These religions remain important and influential in much of the modern world. Today four out of five Indians are Hindu, which greatly affects the country's culture. Although caste-based discrimination is now officially illegal, some people still observe certain cultural practices according to caste. The ideas of reincarnation and karma are widespread. Ancient Sanskrit texts continue to teach ethics through stories. Millions of people in many countries practice Hinduism, including more than two million people in the United States alone.

A number of great leaders, including **Mohandas Gandhi**, have encouraged the Hindu, Buddhist, and Jain principle of nonviolence. People throughout the world engage in nonviolence to protest injustice. Many vegetarians, people who do not eat meat, follow the Hindu, Buddhist, and Jain principle of nonviolence toward animals. Today around one percent of India's population is Buddhist. However, Buddhism thrives in countries such as Sri Lanka, Thailand, Vietnam, Japan, Korea, and China. Buddhism also has a following in Europe and in the United States.

ARTS AND SCIENCE

You've learned that religion influenced Indian writing. The *Mahabharata* and the Bhagavad Gita are popular around the world. Religion also influenced Indian architecture, an influence that spread to other parts of the world. The temple of Angkor Wat in Cambodia, a country in Asia, is considered one of the world's greatest architectural achievements. The building's elaborate style evolved from ancient Indian architecture. Similar examples can be found in Myanmar (Burma), Vietnam, and Thailand.

Ancient India also contributed much to the fields of science and mathematics. Indians were among the first to practice **inoculation**, which stimulates mild forms of disease in people so that they do not develop more serious forms. Inoculation has greatly reduced the threat of smallpox.

Indian mathematicians created the decimal system and numerals (the number symbols we use today). They also developed the concept of zero, which is crucial to mathematics and computing. Indian astronomers, scientists who study the sun, moon, stars, and planets, accurately calculated the length of the solar year. They also asserted that Earth traveled around the sun and proved that the world was round 1,000 years before Columbus's voyage to America.

LEGACIES OF ANCIENT INDIA

Moral Conduct

Mohandas Gandhi's understanding of the Bhagavad Gita inspired his nonviolent protests in the mid-twentieth century against the British rule of India.

Science

Ancient astronomers determined that Earth is round. They also correctly calculated the length of the solar year.

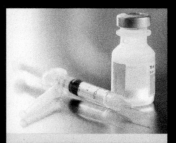

Medicine

Inoculation protects people's health by increasing one's resistance to disease. It has virtually eliminated smallpox.

Mathematics

Mathematicians of ancient India devised both the decimal system and numerals. They were the first to use zero.

REVIEW & ASSESS

1. **READING CHECK** How did ancient India influence religion in other parts of the world?

2. **SEQUENCE EVENTS** How did mathematicians in ancient India contribute to the age of computers?

3. **MAKE CONNECTIONS** What is the legacy of India's ancient Sanskrit texts?

6.5.5 Know the life and moral teachings of Buddha and how Buddhism spread in India, Ceylon, and Central Asia; 6.5.7 Discuss important aesthetic and intellectual traditions (e.g., Sanskrit literature, including the *Bhagavad Gita*; medicine; metallurgy; and mathematics, including Hindu-Arabic numerals and the zero); CST 1 Students explain how major events are related to one another in time; HI 3 Students explain the sources of historical continuity and how the combination of ideas and events explains the emergence of new patterns.

PLAN

OBJECTIVE

Describe how the achievements of ancient India have influenced much of the world.

ESSENTIAL QUESTION

What led to the development of great civilizations in ancient India?

Achievements in ancient India had a great influence on the rest of the world. Lesson 2.3 discusses some of these achievements in the areas of religion, the arts, and science.

BACKGROUND FOR THE TEACHER

Doctors in ancient India made many advances in medicine. They could perform operations such as removing infected tonsils, removing tumors, and rebuilding broken noses. They treated and stitched wounds and set broken bones. Doctors put much of their medical knowledge in writing. Some of these writings describe ways to make medicines from herbs and minerals. Doctors in ancient India invented a variety of medical tools. At times, they also would cast magic spells to try to cure diseases.

DIGITAL RESOURCES NGLSync.cengage.com

TEACHER RESOURCES & ASSESSMENT

 Reading and Note-Taking

 Vocabulary Practice

 Section 2 Quiz

STUDENT RESOURCES

 NG Chapter Gallery

FORM A ROUNDTABLE

Have students sit in groups of four. Ask students to talk about what they know about Hinduism and Buddhism and, if time allows, the effect these religions had on ancient Indian civilization. Encourage each student to contribute ideas about the religions. Tell students they will learn more about the influence of Hinduism and Buddhism on society. They also will learn about Indian contributions to the arts and sciences. `0:05` minutes

TEACH

STEM

GUIDED DISCUSSION

1. **Cause and Effect** How does innoculation reduce the occurrence of disease? *(Innoculation stimulates mild forms of a disease in people so they do not develop more serious forms of the disease.)*

2. **Identify** What were some achievements of astronomers in ancient India? *(Astronomers accurately calculated the length of the solar year. They asserted that Earth traveled around the sun. They determined that Earth is round.)*

MORE INFORMATION

Gandhi Mohandas Gandhi is considered to be the father of modern India. His understanding of Hinduism inspired his nonviolent protests against the British rule of India in the first half of the 20th century. One such protest was the Salt March of 1930 in response to Britain's heavy tax on salt. Thousands of Indians followed Gandhi for a distance of some 240 miles. The result of the march was the arrest of nearly 60,000 people, including Gandhi, but his actions won him admiration around the world. After the end of World War II, Britain worked with Gandhi and other leaders to grant India's independence, which was finally achieved in 1947. Sadly, Gandhi did not get to enjoy it for long. In 1948, he was assassinated by a young Hindu extremist who resented Gandhi's work with Muslim leaders.

ACTIVE OPTIONS

On Your Feet: Inside-Outside Circle Arrange students in concentric circles facing each other. Have students in the outside circle ask the students in the inside circle a question about the lesson. Then have the outside circle rotate one position to the right to create new pairings. After five questions, have students switch roles and continue. `0:10` minutes

NG Learning Framework: Compare Approaches to Nonviolence

ATTITUDE: **Empowerment**
KNOWLEDGE: **Our Human Story**

Explain that Mohandas Gandhi's use of nonviolent protest influenced other people who fought for what they believed in—most notably Dr. Martin Luther King, Jr., in his fight for civil rights for African Americans. Provide students with copies of Gandhi's March 2, 1930 letter to the Viceroy and King's April 13, 1960 essay "Pilgrimage to Nonviolence." (Both are available at multiple online sources.) Have students read both texts and take notes on each man's approach to nonviolent protest. Then have students form small groups and discuss similarities and differences between their approaches. Continue the discussion as a class and, as a homework assignment, have students write a brief essay on the philosophy of nonviolence and how it might still be used today. `0:20` minutes

ENGLISH LANGUAGE LEARNERS   ELD

Use Sentence Stems Before reading, provide the sentence stems listed below to students at all proficiency levels. Call on volunteers to read the stems orally and explain any unclear vocabulary. After reading, have students complete the stems in writing and compare completed sentences with a partner.

1. Two major religions that originated in India are _____ and _____.

2. To protest injustice, Gandhi and other leaders encouraged the principle of _____.

3. Ancient astronomers determined that Earth is _____.

4. The medical practice practiced in ancient India that greatly reduced the threat of smallpox is _____.

5. Ancient mathematicians in India created the concept of the numeral _____.

PRE-AP

Write a Feature Article Have students do research about the temple of Angkor Wat. Have them find information about its religious significance. Ask them to look for interesting details about its history and architecture. Then have them write a feature article describing what they learned.

Press (mt) *in the Student eEdition for modified text.*

See the Chapter Planner for more strategies for differentiation.

ANSWERS

1. Ancient India developed two of the world's great religions, Hinduism and Buddhism. These religions spread to many other countries, where they are still practiced today.

2. Mathematicians in ancient India developed the concept of zero, the decimal system, and numerals, all of which we continue to use today in the age of computers.

3. Religion influenced Indian writing. The ancient texts the *Mahabharata* and the Bhagavad Gita are still popular around the world.

VOCABULARY

On your paper, write the vocabulary word that completes each of the following sentences.

1. Today, five countries make up the Indian _____, which is separated from the rest of Asia by the Himalaya. [HSS 6.5.1]
2. Strong seasonal winds called _____ shape India's climate. [HSS 6.5.1]
3. The *Ramayana* is an example of an _____. [HSS 6.5.3]
4. Ancient Indians had a social hierarchy that developed into a rigid _____. [HSS 6.5.4]
5. Hindus believe in _____, which means that when a person dies, his or her soul is reborn in another body. [HSS 6.5.3]
6. In Hindu teachings, _____ is the practice of postures, breathing exercises, and meditation as a path to spiritual insight. [HSS 6.5.3]
7. The totality of the Buddha's teachings are known as the _____, or divine law. [HSS 6.5.5]
8. Buddhists believe that the Eightfold Path leads to the end of suffering, or _____. [HSS 6.5.5]

READING STRATEGY

9. **ORGANIZE IDEAS: ANALYZE CAUSE AND EFFECT** Complete your organizer to identify the effects of the Aryan migrations on ancient Indian civilization. Then answer the question.

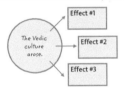

The Vedic culture arose.

Effect #1

Effect #2

Effect #3

How did the Vedic people change civilization in ancient India? [HSS HI 2]

MAIN IDEAS

Answer the following questions. Support your answers with evidence from the chapter.

10. How did geographic features contribute to the development of the Harappan civilization? **LESSON 1.1** [HSS 6.5.1]
11. In what way were the cities of Mohenjo-Daro and Harappa signs of an advanced civilization? **LESSON 1.2** [HSS HI 1]
12. Who were the Vedic people? **LESSON 1.3** [HSS 6.5.2]
13. How did Hinduism develop in India? **LESSON 1.4** [HSS 6.5.3]
14. What did Siddhartha Gautama achieve? **LESSON 1.6** [HSS 6.5.5]
15. How did Asoka spread Buddhism? **LESSON 2.1** [HSS 6.5.5]
16. In what ways was the reign of Chandra Gupta II a golden age? **LESSON 2.2** [HSS HI 1]
17. What Hindu beliefs and values still deeply influence people's behavior in India today? **LESSON 2.3** [HSS HI 3]

CRITICAL THINKING

Answer the following questions. Support your answers with evidence from the chapter.

18. **ESSENTIAL QUESTION** What geographic factors led to the development of great civilizations in ancient India? [HSS 6.5.1]
19. **MAKE CONNECTIONS** What did early Indus River Valley civilizations have in common with other ancient river valley civilizations? [HSS HI 2]
20. **EVALUATE** How important were the contributions of ancient India to the fields of science and mathematics? Support your evaluation with evidence from the chapter. [HSS 6.5.7]
21. **COMPARE AND CONTRAST** How are Hindu and Buddhist beliefs similar? How are they different? [HSS HI 2]
22. **YOU DECIDE** What do you think were Asoka's two greatest leadership qualities? Support your opinion with evidence from the chapter. [HSS 6.5.6]

INTERPRET CHARTS

Study the chart of the caste system that developed in ancient Indian society. Then answer the questions that follow.

THE CASTE SYSTEM

BRAHMINS	Priests
KSHATRIYAS	Kings and warriors
VAISHYAS	Merchants, artisans, and farmers
SUDRAS	Peasants and laborers
DALITS	Workers in sanitation, disposal of dead animals, cremation

23. To which caste do you think most ancient Indians belonged? [HSS 6.5.4]
24. Which caste do you think was the smallest? Why do you think this was so? [HSS 6.5.4]

ANALYZE SOURCES

Read the following words spoken by the Buddha. Then answer the question.

Hold fast to the truth as a lamp. Hold fast as a refuge [place of safety] to the truth. Look not for refuge to any one besides yourselves. . . .

And whosoever, . . . either now or after I am dead, shall be a lamp unto themselves, . . . shall look not for refuge to any one besides themselves—it is they . . . who shall reach the very topmost Height!—but they must be anxious to learn.

from *The Last Days of Buddha,* trans. T.W. Rhys David

25. In the passage, the Buddha is telling his followers how to act. What is his message? [REP 4]

WRITE ABOUT HISTORY

26. **INFORMATIVE** Suppose you are writing a pamphlet for a museum exhibit about India. Write a short essay that explains the lasting influence of ancient India on religion. Use the following tips to help you plan, write, and revise your essay. [HSS HI 3]

TIPS

- Develop an outline that shows how ancient India's influence on religion continues to this day.
- Write the introductory paragraph of your essay using your outline as a guide.
- Develop the topic with relevant, well-chosen facts, concrete details, and examples.
- Use vocabulary from the chapter to explain your ideas.
- Provide a concluding statement that summarizes the information presented.

VOCABULARY ANSWERS

1. subcontinent [HSS 6.5.1]
2. monsoons [HSS 6.5.1]
3. epic poem [HSS 6.5.3]
4. caste system [HSS 6.5.4]
5. reincarnation [HSS 6.5.3]
6. yoga [HSS 6.5.3]
7. dharma [HSS 6.5.5]
8. nirvana [HSS 6.5.5]

READING STRATEGY ANSWER

The Vedic culture arose.

Effect #1: The Aryans imported their religion to India.

Effect #2: The Aryans imported their social hierarchy, which developed into a rigid caste system.

Effect #3: The Aryans also brought their language, Sanskrit, which became dominant in India.

STANDARDS

HSS CONTENT STANDARDS:

6.5.1 Locate and describe the major river system and discuss the physical setting that supported the rise of this civilization; **6.5.2** Discuss the significance of the Aryan invasions; **6.5.3** Explain the major beliefs and practices of Brahmanism in India and how they evolved into early Hinduism; **6.5.4** Outline the social structure of the caste system; **6.5.5** Know the life and moral teachings of Buddha and how Buddhism spread in India, Ceylon, and Central Asia; **6.5.6** Describe the growth of the Maurya empire and the political and moral achievements of the emperor Asoka; **6.5.7** Discuss important aesthetic and intellectual traditions (e.g., Sanskrit literature, including the *Bhagavad Gita*; medicine; metallurgy; and mathematics, including Hindu-Arabic numerals and the zero).

HSS ANALYSIS SKILLS:

REP 4 Students assess the credibility of primary and secondary sources and draw sound conclusions from them; **HI 1** Students explain the central issues and problems from the past, placing people and events in a matrix of time and place; **HI 2** Students understand and distinguish cause, effect, sequence, and correlation in historical events, including the long- and short-term causal relations; **HI 3** Students explain the sources of historical continuity and how the combination of ideas and events explains the emergence of new patterns.

9. The Aryans brought to India their religion, their social hierarchy, and their Sanskrit language, all of which had a great impact on the civilization of ancient India. (HSS HI 2)

MAIN IDEAS ANSWERS

10. Rivers provided water for irrigation and enriched the soil by depositing silt, which led to settlement and farming. Mountain ranges to the north and surrounding oceans helped protect India from invaders. (HSS 6.5.1)

11. Mohenjo-Daro and Harappa were not only the largest cities of their time, but they were the world's first planned cities, with standardized layouts, buildings, advanced sanitation, and grid-pattern roads. (HSS HI 1)

12. The Vedic people were a collection of Indo-European tribes who migrated into India beginning in 1500 B.C. They had a tremendous impact on India's culture, specifically religion, social hierarchy, and language. (HSS 6.5.2)

13. Over many centuries, Aryan Brahmanism fused with native Indian religions to form Hinduism. (HSS 6.5.3)

14. Siddhartha Gautama was the founder of Buddhism. He sought to learn the secret of happiness. (HSS 6.5.5)

15. Asoka helped spread Buddhism by making it the state religion and sending missionaries to other countries to preach and spread Buddhist ideas. (HSS 6.5.5)

16. Two hundred years of political stability, peace, and prosperity, plus a long line of wise, strong kings greatly stimulated culture and learning during the reign of Chandra Gupta II. (HSS HI 1)

17. The Hindu beliefs in reincarnation and the importance of ethics are still effective influences on people's behavior. (HSS HI 3)

CRITICAL THINKING ANSWERS

18. The Indus and Ganges rivers were geographic factors crucial to the development of great civilizations in ancient India. These major river systems provided a plentiful water supply and fertile soil that encouraged human settlement and the growth of villages and cities. (HSS 6.5.1)

19. Like other ancient river valley civilizations, the Indus Valley civilizations enjoyed fertile soil, plentiful water from river sources, and good climate, all of which encouraged settlement and farming. (HSS HI 2)

20. Ancient Indian civilization made many important achievements and contributions in the fields of science and mathematics. In science, these achievements and contributions included proving the world was round and that Earth revolved around the sun. In mathematics, achievements and contributions included the decimal system, numerals, and the concept of zero. (HSS 6.5.7)

21. Hindus and Buddhists both believe in reincarnation. Buddhists reject the caste system and believe in equality, promoting a nonviolent way of life toward all living things. Hindus believe in a complex array of deities. Buddhists follow a moral way of life based on the Four Noble Truths and the Eightfold Path. (HSS HI 2)

22. Students' responses will vary. Students should cite two of Asoka's leadership qualities and explain their importance with evidence from the chapter. (HSS 6.5.6)

INTERPRET CHARTS ANSWERS

23. Most people probably belonged to the Sudra caste. (HSS 6.5.4)

24. The Brahmin caste was probably the smallest. The brahmins seemed to have the most power in early Vedic society, and the group with the most power is often the smallest in number. (HSS 6.5.4)

ANALYZE SOURCES ANSWER

25. Students' responses will vary. Sample response:
A lamp creates light, illuminating the dark to guide one's way. In comparing truth to a lamp, the Buddha suggests that like a lamp, the truth will illuminate one's thoughts and lead the way to nirvana, the end of suffering. (HSS REP 4)

WRITE ABOUT HISTORY ANSWER

26. Students' essays will vary but should be clear and well organized. Students should use relevant details and examples to support the main points of their essay. For more in-depth instruction and practice with the writing form, assign the Social Studies Skills Writing Lesson on writing an informative essay. (HSS HI 3)

UNIT RESOURCES

On Location with National Geographic Lead Program Officer Christopher Thornton
Intro and Video

Interactive Map Tool

News & Updates

Available at NGLSync.cengage.com

Unit Wrap-Up:
"Encounters with History"
Feature and Video

"China's Ancient Lifeline"
National Geographic Adapted Article

"Faces of the Divine"
National Geographic Adapted Article
Student eEdition exclusive

Unit 2 Inquiry:
Write a Creation Myth

CHAPTER RESOURCES

The lion's dance, a Chinese tradition for more than 1,000 years, is performed during a New Year's celebration in Beijing, China's capital.

TEACHER RESOURCES & ASSESSMENT

Available at NGLSync.cengage.com

Social Studies Skills Lessons
• Reading: Analyze Language Use
• Writing: Write an Argument

Formal Assessment
• Chapter 7 Tests A (on-level) & B (below-level)

A **Chapter 7 Answer Key**

ExamView®
One-time Download

STUDENT BACKPACK *Available at NGLSync.cengage.com*
• **eEdition** *(English)*   • **eEdition** *(Spanish)*   • **Handbooks**   • **Online Atlas**
Chapter 7 Spanish resources, Guided Writing prompts, and Financial Literacy lessons are available online.

SECTION 1 RESOURCES

RIVER DYNASTIES

 Reading and Note-Taking

 Vocabulary Practice

 Section 1 Quiz

Available at NGLSync.cengage.com

LESSON 1.1 THE GEOGRAPHY OF ANCIENT CHINA

- Critical Viewing: NG Chapter Gallery
- On Your Feet: Fishbowl

LESSON 1.2 SHANG AND ZHOU DYNASTIES

- Critical Viewing: NG Chapter Gallery
- On Your Feet: Stage a Quiz Show

LESSON 1.3 CHINESE PHILOSOPHIES

 Biography
Confucius

Available at NGLSync.cengage.com

- Critical Viewing: NG Chapter Gallery
- On Your Feet: Code of Conduct Roundtable

DOCUMENT-BASED QUESTION
LESSON 1.4 CONTRASTING BELIEF SYSTEMS

NG Learning Framework:
Learn About Different Chinese Philosophies

- On Your Feet: Use a Jigsaw Strategy

SECTION 2 RESOURCES

CHINA'S EMPIRES

 Reading and Note-Taking

 Vocabulary Practice

 Section 2 Quiz

Available at NGLSync.cengage.com

BIOGRAPHY
LESSON 2.1 SHI HUANGDI

NG Learning Framework:
Learn About Shi Huangdi

- On Your Feet: Hold a Panel Discussion

LESSON 2.2 THE GREAT WALL

NG Learning Framework:
Learn About the Great Wall

- On Your Feet: Build a Wall

MOMENTS IN HISTORY
LESSON 2.3 TERRA COTTA WARRIORS

NG Learning Framework:
Learn About Shi Huangdi's Army

- On Your Feet: I See, I Read, And So

LESSON 2.4 THE HAN DYNASTY

- Critical Viewing: NG Chapter Gallery
- On Your Feet: Stage a Quiz Show

LESSON 2.5 THE LEGACY OF ANCIENT CHINA

- Critical Viewing: NG Chapter Gallery
- On Your Feet: Inventions and Ideas

SECTION 3 RESOURCES

EAST MEETS WEST

 Reading and Note-Taking

 Vocabulary Practice

 Section 3 Quiz

Available at NGLSync.cengage.com

LESSON 3.1 THE SILK ROADS

NG Learning Framework:
Learn About the Silk Roads

- On Your Feet: Team Word Webbing

LESSON 3.2 TRADE ON THE SILK ROADS

 Active History: Interactive Whiteboard Activity
Barter on the Silk Roads

 Active History
Barter on the Silk Roads

Available at NGLSync.cengage.com

- On Your Feet: Inside-Outside Circle

HISTORY THROUGH OBJECTS
LESSON 3.3 GOODS FROM THE SILK ROADS

- Critical Viewing: NG Chapter Gallery
- On Your Feet: Set Up a Market

NG EXPLORER FREDRIK HIEBERT
LESSON 3.4 EXCAVATING ALONG THE SILK ROADS

NG Learning Framework:
Learn About Fredrik Hiebert

- On Your Feet: Tell Me More

CHAPTER 7 REVIEW

STRATEGY ①

Make Predictions About Content

Before students read the lessons listed below, have them examine the headings and visuals in each one and write their predictions on what the lesson will be about. After students read the lessons, have them check to see whether their predictions were accurate.

Use with Lessons 1.3, 2.5, and 3.4 *You might want to pair students whose predictions were inaccurate with students who correctly predicted the content of the lessons and have them compare the conclusions they drew from viewing the subheadings and visuals in each one.*

STRATEGY ②

Use a Word Sort

Display these words and tell students to sort them into groupings and label each group by category. Then have students write a sentence that explains how each group of words is connected.

Shi Huangdi	Confucianism
caravan	filial piety
Han	barter
cultural diffusion	Great Wall
Qin	

Use with Lessons 1.3, 2.1, 2.4, 3.1, and 3.2

STRATEGY ③

Complete a Key Facts T-Chart

Have students create a T-Chart on the early Chinese dynasties. In one column of the T-Chart, students should list the Shang, Zhou, Qin, and Han dynasties. In the other column, students should jot down key facts about each dynasty as they read the lesson. Have students compare completed charts.

Use with Lessons 1.2 and 2.1–2.4 *You might have students use this strategy in other lessons in the chapter.*

Press *in the Student eEdition for modified text.*

STRATEGY ①

Describe Lesson Visuals

Pair visually challenged students with students who are not visually challenged. Ask the latter to help their partners "see" the visuals in the chapter by describing the images and answering any questions the visually impaired student might have.

Use with All Lessons *For example, for the dynastic cycle diagram in Lesson 1.2, students might describe the dragon around the diagram: its expression, teeth, claws, long, curving tail. Students might also read aloud the captions on the diagram in order.*

STRATEGY ②

Expand Main Idea Statements

After reading, direct students to copy each of the following Main Idea statements and write a paragraph that expands on the statement. Use these starters as examples if needed:

1.1 China's deserts, mountains, and rivers helped shape its civilization. The deserts include _____.

1.2 The Shang and Zhou dynasties developed many cultural behaviors and beliefs that have become part of Chinese civilization. For example, _____.

1.3 Chinese philosophies developed important ideas on how society should be organized. One of these philosophies is called _____.

Use with Lessons 1.1–1.3

STRATEGY ①

Analyze Word Choice

Explain that similar-meaning words have different connotations. They suggest different feelings or ideas, and one word might have a stronger effect than another. As an example, ask students to consider the words *bad*, *awful*, and *horrible*. Explain that they have increasingly negative connotations. Have students read or reread the lessons that contain information about Confucianism, Daoism, and Legalism and try to find descriptive words or phrases with strong connotations. Provide the sentence frames on the next page to support students at each proficiency level as they analyze the effects of word choices.

HSS CONTENT STANDARDS:

6.6.3 Know about the life of Confucius and the fundamental teachings of Confucianism and Taoism; **6.6.4** Identify the political and cultural problems prevalent in the time of Confucius and how he sought to solve them; **6.6.5** List the policies and achievements of the emperor Shi Huangdi in unifying northern China under the Qin Dynasty.

Emerging

The word/phrase _____ connotes _____. It makes me feel _____.

Expanding

The word/phrase _____ connotes _____. The effect is that _____.

Bridging

The word/phrase _____ has the connotation _____, and the effect is that _____.

Use with Lessons 1.3 and 1.4, All Levels

STRATEGY ❷
Make Predictions with Visuals

Before reading, have students examine all the visuals in Section 2 and write down what they think each lesson will be about based on the visuals. Ask students to write their predictions on a sheet of paper. After reading and discussing the lessons, have students determine if their predictions were correct. Provide the following sentence frames to help students at each proficiency level make and confirm predictions.

Emerging

I saw _____. I thought the lesson was about _____.

I read _____. I thought the lesson was about _____.

Expanding

When I saw _____, I thought the lesson was about _____.

But/And when I read _____, I thought the lesson was about _____.

Bridging

When I saw _____, I predicted that the lesson was about _____.

After reading the lesson, I confirmed/learned that the lesson was about _____.

Use with Lessons 2.1–2.5, All Levels

STRATEGY ❸
Find Someone Who Knows

Read aloud the questions below. Then give students copies of the questions and have them find five different classmates to answer them. Students at the **Emerging** and **Expanding** levels might benefit by working in pairs.

1. Between what two rivers did China's civilization develop? *(Huang He and Chang Jiang)*

2. What was China's first dynasty? *(Shang)*

3. Whose teachings have influenced China for centuries? *(Confucius)*

4. Who was China's first emperor? *(Shi Huangdi)*

5. What is the name of the trade routes that connected China and other countries? *(Silk Roads)*

Use with Lessons 1.1–1.3, 2.1, and 3.1

STRATEGY
Create a Multimedia Presentation

Have students choose a research topic for ancient China and create a presentation. Students can use photos, maps, and other visuals that they find online or photocopy from written material to support their presentation.

Use with Lessons 2.1–2.3 and 3.1–3.3 *For a presentation on the Silk Roads, students might want to research and include the history of the trade routes during the time of Genghis Khan.*

STRATEGY
Interview a Historical Figure

Allow students to work in teams of two to plan, write, and perform a simulated television interview with Shi Huangdi or Confucius. Tell students that the purpose of the interview is to focus on the achievements, actions, and goals of the historical figure.

Use with Lessons 1.3 and 2.1 *Invite students to do research to learn more about the historical figure they have chosen. Encourage them to elicit in-depth answers by asking the historical figures why and how they did the things they did.*

STRATEGY ❶
Form a Thesis

Have students develop a thesis statement for a specific topic related to one of the lessons. Be sure the statement makes a claim that is supportable with evidence either from the lesson or through further research. Then have pairs compare their statements and determine which makes the strongest or most supportable claims.

Use with All Lessons

STRATEGY
Explain the Significance

Allow students to choose one term below to investigate and design a presentation that explains the significance of the term to the history of China.

Mandate of Heaven	Great Wall
Confucianism	Han
Legalism	Silk Roads

Use with Lessons 1.2, 1.3, 2.1, 2.2, 2.4, and 3.1

7 ANCIENT CHINA

2000 B.C. – A.D. 220

ESSENTIAL QUESTION How did China establish what would become one of the world's oldest continuous civilizations?

SECTION 1 RIVER DYNASTIES

KEY VOCABULARY	NAMES & PLACES
dynastic cycle	Chang Jiang
dynasty	Confucianism
filial piety	Daoism
isolate	Huang He
oracle bone	Legalism
	Mandate of Heaven
	Shang
	Warring States
	Zhou

SECTION 2 CHINA'S EMPIRES

KEY VOCABULARY	NAMES & PLACES
bureaucracy	Great Wall
emperor	Han
peasant	Qin
silk	Shi Huangdi
terra cotta	

SECTION 3 EAST MEETS WEST

KEY VOCABULARY	NAMES & PLACES
barter	Silk Roads
caravan	
cultural diffusion	
maritime	

READING STRATEGY

ANALYZE LANGUAGE USE
When you analyze language use, you note how specific word choices indicate the author's point of view and purpose. As you read the chapter, use concept clusters like this one to analyze the language used to describe the philosophies of Confucianism, Daoism, and Legalism.

164 UNIT 2 6.6.3 Know about the life of Confucius and the fundamental teachings of Confucianism and Taoism.

The lion's dance, a Chinese tradition for more than 1,000 years, is performed during a New Year's celebration in Beijing, China's capital.

165

HSS CONTENT STANDARDS:

6.6.3 Know about the life of Confucius and the fundamental teachings of Confucianism and Taoism.

TEACHER BACKGROUND

INTRODUCE THE PHOTOGRAPH

Have students study the photograph of the lion's dance in Beijing. Explain that in Chinese culture, the lion represents power, strength, and stability. The lion's dance, with its firecrackers and banging drums, is believed to chase away evil spirits. Tell students that, in this chapter, they will learn about the culture and civilization of ancient China. Then have students examine the faces of the lions in the photo.

ASK: What details in the lions' faces convey power and strength? (*Possible response: large, fierce eyes; teeth and fangs; menacing expression*)

SHARE BACKGROUND

The lion's dance starts at a temple and proceeds through the streets of the town or city. Performers of the dance often stop at a shop or home during the procession. These visits are thought to bring good luck in the year to come for the owners. The owners will enjoy even greater luck if they are allowed to stick their heads in the lions' mouths. The dance ends at another temple.

DIGITAL RESOURCES NGLSync.cengage.com

TEACHER RESOURCES & ASSESSMENT

 Social Studies Skills Lessons
• Reading: Analyze Language Use
• Writing: Write an Argument

 ExamView®
One-time Download

 Formal Assessment
• Chapter 7 Tests A (on-level) & B (below-level)

 **Chapter 7 Answer Key**

STUDENT BACKPACK

• eEdition (*English*)
• eEdition (*Spanish*)
• Handbooks
• Online Atlas

INTRODUCE THE ESSENTIAL QUESTION

HOW DID CHINA ESTABLISH WHAT WOULD BECOME ONE OF THE WORLD'S OLDEST CONTINUOUS CIVILIZATIONS?

Roundtable Activity: Leaders, Beliefs, Encounters Seat students around tables in groups of four. Ask groups to discuss what they have learned about other ancient civilizations, such as those of Mesopotamia, Egypt, and India. Encourage them to consider the factors that helped these civilizations thrive. If students need help coming up with ideas, have them consider the questions below. After students have finished the activity, tell them that, in this chapter, they will learn about the factors that helped China establish and develop a thriving civilization.

1. **What role did strong leaders play in the ancient civilizations you have learned about?**

2. **What beliefs unified the people of these civilizations?**

3. **How did the civilizations benefit from trade and other encounters with different cultures?** `0:15` minutes

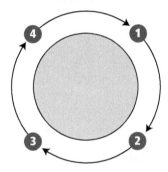

INTRODUCE THE READING STRATEGY

ANALYZE LANGUAGE USE

Tell students that analyzing language use can help them understand an author's meaning, tone, and purpose. Model completing the Concept Cluster by reading the second and third paragraphs under "A Ruthless Ruler" in Lesson 2.1 and writing "punishing anyone who disagreed with him" in the central oval. Then have students discuss the meaning, tone, and purpose of this phrase. For more in-depth instruction and practice with the reading strategy, assign the Social Studies Skills Reading Lesson on analyzing language use.

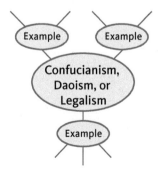

INTRODUCE CHAPTER VOCABULARY

KNOWLEDGE RATING

Have students complete a Knowledge-Rating Chart for Key Vocabulary words. Have students list words and fill out the chart. Then have pairs share the definitions they know. Work together as a class to complete the chart.

KEY VOCAB	KNOW IT	NOT SURE	DON'T KNOW	DEFINITION
barter				
bureaucracy				
caravan				
cultural diffusion				

KEY DATES

c. 1600 B.C.	Shang dynasty, China's first, develops
c. 1045 B.C.	Zhou dynasty overthrows Shang
551 B.C.	Birth of Confucius
221 B.C.	Shi Huangdi becomes first emperor
202 B.C.	Han dynasty begins
100 B.C.	Silk Roads are well established
A.D. **105**	Paper is invented by the Chinese
A.D. **220**	Han dynasty ends

The Geography of
Ancient China

At about 240 years of age, the United States may seem like an old civilization, but it's young compared to China. The Chinese civilization has continued for more than 5,000 years. China's geography helped set the stage for the early development of its civilization.

MAIN IDEA

China's deserts, mountains, and rivers helped shape its civilization.

NATURAL BARRIERS

In the beginning of its growth, natural barriers somewhat **isolated**, or cut off, China's civilization from much of the rest of the world. As a result, ancient China developed differently from other early civilizations, with relatively little outside cultural influence. This early isolation helped unify Chinese culture and allowed China to establish a firm foundation for its civilization.

Some of China's natural barriers included vast deserts. The Gobi to the north and the Taklimakan (tah-kluh-muh-KAHN) to the west discouraged invaders and peaceful immigrants alike. The Himalaya, Tian Shan, and Pamir mountain ranges formed a significant obstacle in the west. The waters of the Pacific Ocean, Yellow Sea, and East China Sea on China's east coast separated the region from its nearest neighbors, Japan and Korea.

MAJOR RIVERS

Like the ancient civilizations of Mesopotamia, Egypt, and India, China's civilization arose along fertile river valleys. It developed on the land between China's two great rivers: the **Huang He** (hwahng huh) and the **Chang Jiang** (chahng jyahng).

The 3,395-mile-long Huang He lies in northern China. It is also called the Yellow River because of its high concentration of yellow silt, or fine, fertile soil. The river deposits this silt along its floodplains, creating good farmland. However, the Huang He is unpredictable. Its course, or the direction in which a river flows, has changed many times. Throughout China's history, heavy rains have also caused the river to flood—with deadly results.

At about 4,000 miles long, the Chang Jiang, or Yangtze, in central China is the third longest river in the world. Like the Huang He, the Chang Jiang carries fertile yellow silt. Unlike the Huang He, the Chang Jiang maintains a relatively predictable course. For thousands of years, the river helped unify China by serving as a useful transportation and trade network within its borders.

The area between the two rivers, called the North China Plain, is the birthplace of Chinese civilization. In Chapter 2, you read about the Yangshao culture, which developed along the Huang He. Another important culture in the area was the Longshan, which developed around 3200 B.C. Other advanced Chinese cultures arose in other river valleys. These cultures include the Liangzhu (lyahng-jew) and the Hongshan. Archaeologists have uncovered beautifully carved jade objects from these cultures in other parts of China. All of these ancient cultures contributed to the development of China's unique civilization and to the rise of its earliest rulers: the Shang and the Zhou.

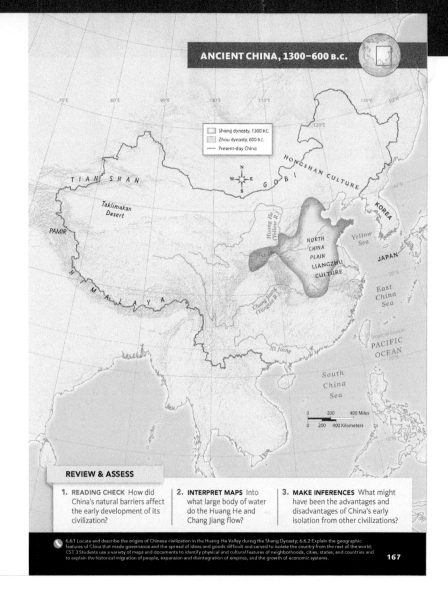

ANCIENT CHINA, 1300–600 B.C.

Shang dynasty, 1300 B.C.
Zhou dynasty, 600 B.C.
Present-day China

REVIEW & ASSESS

1. **READING CHECK** How did China's natural barriers affect the early development of its civilization?

2. **INTERPRET MAPS** Into what large body of water do the Huang He and Chang Jiang flow?

3. **MAKE INFERENCES** What might have been the advantages and disadvantages of China's early isolation from other civilizations?

6.6.1 Locate and describe the origins of Chinese civilization in the Huang-He Valley during the Shang Dynasty; 6.6.2 Explain the geographic features of China that made governance and the spread of ideas and goods difficult and served to isolate the country from the rest of the world; CST 3 Students use a variety of maps and documents to identify physical and cultural features of neighborhoods, cities, states, and countries and to explain the historical migration of people, expansion and disintegration of empires, and the growth of economic systems.

PLAN

OBJECTIVE

Analyze how China's deserts, mountains, and rivers helped shape its civilization.

ESSENTIAL QUESTION

How did China establish what would become one of the world's oldest continuous civilizations?

Natural barriers somewhat isolated China's early civilization from much of the rest of the world. Lesson 1.1 discusses the deserts, mountains, and bodies of water that helped unify Chinese culture and allowed China to establish a firm foundation for its civilization.

BACKGROUND FOR THE TEACHER

Gobi means "place without water." The extreme dryness and strong winds that sometimes blow through the desert result in blinding dust storms. At most, only about seven inches of rain fall in the Gobi every year. Some parts receive no rain at all. Temperatures in the desert can reach 113°F in the summer and –40°F in the winter. The temperatures in the Gobi can rise and fall by as much as 60 degrees within the same day.

Parts of the Gobi have been turned into nature reserves and national parks. One of the parks in the southern part of the desert is one of the richest sources for dinosaur fossils in the world. The Gobi's harsh climate and remote location have helped protect and preserve the fossils for millions of centuries.

DIGITAL RESOURCES NGLSync.cengage.com

TEACHER RESOURCES & ASSESSMENT

 Reading and Note-Taking

 Vocabulary Practice

 Section 1 Quiz

STUDENT RESOURCES

 NG Chapter Gallery

DEMONSTRATE LANDFORMS

Use a sheet of unlined paper to help students differentiate among the landforms discussed in the lesson. Tell students that a *plain* is flat like a sheet of paper. Then fold the paper lengthwise and open it as a V. Explain that the sides of the paper are mountains, and the river *valley* is at the bottom. **0:05** minutes

GUIDED DISCUSSION

1. **Compare and Contrast** How are the Huang He and Chang Jiang similar? How do they differ? *(Both are long and carry fertile yellow silt. However, while the Chang Jiang maintains a relatively predictable course, the course of the Huang He has changed many times.)*

2. **Make Inferences** Why do you think Chinese civilization developed on the North China Plain? *(The plain lies between the fertile river valleys of the Huang He and Chang Jiang and would have been excellent for growing crops.)*

INTERPRET MAPS

Have students study the map of ancient China. Point out the North China Plain and the two major rivers that flow through it. Have students trace the Huang He on the map. **ASK:** What is the name of the river's tributary that flows through the North China Plain? *(Wei He)* Then point out the general area where the Liangzhu and Hongshan cultures developed. **ASK:** What is unusual about the area where the Hongshan culture developed? *(The Hongshan culture didn't develop around a major river. Instead, it developed in a desert area.)* **0:10** minutes

ACTIVE OPTIONS

Critical Viewing: NG Chapter Gallery Invite students to explore the Chapter Gallery to examine the images that relate to Chapter 7. Have them select one of the images and do additional research to learn more about it. Ask questions that will inspire additional inquiry about the chosen gallery image, such as: What is this? Where and when was this created? By whom? Why was it created? What is it made of? Why does it belong in this chapter? What else would you like to know about it? **0:10** minutes

On Your Feet: Fishbowl Have half the class sit in a close circle, facing inward. Have the other half of the class sit in a larger circle around them. Instruct students in the inside circle to discuss what they know about the Huang He while the outside circle listens. The discussion should include details about the river's location, size, and importance. Then call on volunteers in the outside circle to summarize what they heard. Have students switch places and ask those now on the inside circle to discuss what they know about the Chang Jiang. The outside circle should listen and then summarize what they heard. Have students learn more about the influence of the Huang He in the development of Chinese civilization by completing Lesson 5 of the **California EEI Curriculum Unit** *The Rivers and Ancient Empires of China and India.* **0:20** minutes

STRIVING READERS

Take Notes Have students take notes on China's landforms as they read the lesson, using a Concept Cluster like the one shown below. Tell them to add more clusters as needed. Allow students to compare their completed clusters in small groups and make any necessary corrections. Then call on volunteers to use their diagrams to summarize what they know about the landforms.

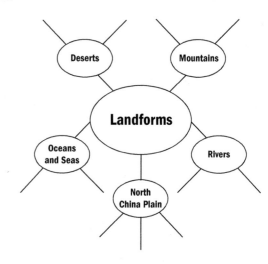

ENGLISH LANGUAGE LEARNERS ELD

Use Geographic Terms Write the following words on the board: *mountain, desert, plain, river, ocean.* Say each word and have students at all proficiency levels repeat it after you. Then have students copy the words on individual sticky notes. Monitor students as they work and clarify understanding as needed. Finally, invite students at the **Expanding** and **Bridging** levels to use the words in sentences.

Press **mt** *in the Student eEdition for modified text.*

See the Chapter Planner for more strategies for differentiation.

ANSWERS

1. The deserts, mountain ranges, and water were natural barriers that isolated China physically from other civilizations. As a result, early China developed with relatively little cultural influence from other civilizations.

2. The Huang He and the Chang Jiang flow into the Pacific Ocean.

3. The advantages include protection from invaders and the development of a homogeneous culture. The disadvantages include insulation and the inability to benefit from the ideas of other early cultures.

Shang and Zhou Dynasties

According to Chinese tradition, a ruler named Yu learned to control the floodwaters of the Huang He and established China's first dynasty, the Xia (shee-AH). But no archaeological evidence of this dynasty has ever been found. The first dynasty for which evidence does exist is the Shang.

MAIN IDEA

The Shang and Zhou dynasties developed many cultural behaviors and beliefs that have become part of Chinese civilization.

CHINA'S FIRST DYNASTY

The **Shang** dynasty emerged along the banks of the Huang He around 1600 B.C. A **dynasty** is a line of rulers from the same family. The Shang developed many cultural behaviors and beliefs that rulers would continue throughout much of Chinese civilization. They established an ordered society with the king at the top, warlords coming next, and farmers at the bottom. The farmers helped advance agriculture in China and grew crops such as millet, wheat, and rice.

The Shang also developed a system of writing using about 3,000 characters. These characters became the basis for modern Chinese writing. They first appeared

on **oracle bones**, which are animal bones used to consult the many gods the Shang people worshipped. Priests carved a question on a bone and then heated it. They believed that the pattern of cracks that resulted revealed the gods' answer.

In addition to their gods, the Shang people worshipped the spirits of their dead ancestors. The Shang believed these spirits influenced everything from the king's health to farmers' harvests. To keep the spirits happy, priests conducted special ceremonies, often using beautifully decorated bronze vessels. Shang craftspeople were among the most skilled metalworkers at that time. They also built elaborate tombs for the dead.

THE DYNASTIC CYCLE

In time, the Shang dynasty began to weaken. Around 1045 B.C., the **Zhou** (joh) overthrew the Shang and became China's longest ruling dynasty, lasting about 800 years. The rise of the Zhou also marked the beginning of China's classical period, a time of great social and cultural advances that lasted for about 2,000 years. The Zhou adopted many of the Shang's cultural practices, including ancestor worship and the use of oracle bones. However, the Zhou also developed a concept, known as the **Mandate of Heaven**, to be a guiding force for rulers. They believed that a king could rule only as long as the gods believed he was worthy. The mandate led to a pattern in the rise and fall of dynasties in China called the **dynastic cycle**.

During the first 200 years or so of their rule, the Zhou established a strong central government. However, during the last 500 years of the dynasty, the Zhou divided their lands among local lords. Eventually the ruling lords grew too powerful and independent. They fought among themselves and disobeyed the Zhou kings. By 475 B.C., China had descended into a time of constant war called the **Warring States** period. In 256 B.C., the last Zhou king was finally overthrown.

THE DYNASTIC CYCLE

1. The people believe that the gods approve of the new dynasty.
2. The dynasty weakens.
3. Disasters occur.
4. The people believe that the gods no longer approve of the dynasty.
5. The dynasty is overthrown.
6. A new dynasty re-establishes order.

REVIEW & ASSESS

1. **READING CHECK** What were some of the religious beliefs and practices of the Shang people?

2. **INTEGRATE VISUALS** Based on the diagram and what you've read in the lesson, what do you think happened after the Zhou dynasty fell?

3. **DRAW CONCLUSIONS** How might the Mandate of Heaven have helped the Chinese people accept dynastic changes?

6.6.1 Locate and describe the origins of Chinese civilization in the Huang-He Valley during the Shang Dynasty.

STANDARDS

HSS CONTENT STANDARDS:

6.6.1 Locate and describe the origins of Chinese civilization in the Huang-He Valley during the Shang Dynasty.

HSS ANALYSIS SKILLS:

CST 2 Students construct various time lines of key events, people, and periods of the historical era they are studying; **HI 2** Students understand and distinguish cause, effect, sequence, and correlation in historical events, including the long- and short-term causal relations.

PLAN

OBJECTIVE

Identify the cultural behaviors and beliefs developed during the Shang and Zhou dynasties that have become part of Chinese civilization.

ESSENTIAL QUESTION

How did China establish what would become one of the world's oldest continuous civilizations?

The Shang and Zhou dynasties ruled in China for over 1,300 years. Lesson 1.2 discusses the social, cultural, and religious behaviors and beliefs established during this time that have become part of Chinese civilization.

BACKGROUND FOR THE TEACHER

Oracle bones were not discovered until 1899. In that year, a Chinese scholar noticed that some of the bones and shells in a shop were engraved with an ancient script. The items were being sold as "dragon bones." They were meant to be ground into powder and used as a folk remedy.

The shoulder blades of oxen and turtle shells were most often used as oracle bones during the Shang dynasty. A priest cut an oracle bone into a particular size and shape. After carving a question, he applied heat to a carved-out hollow in the bone. During a ceremony, the priest read the resulting crack to answer the question.

DIGITAL RESOURCES NGLSync.cengage.com

TEACHER RESOURCES & ASSESSMENT

 Reading and Note-Taking

 Vocabulary Practice

 Section 1 Quiz

STUDENT RESOURCES

 NG Chapter Gallery

CREATE A TIME LINE

Help students read and understand a time line that contains B.C. dates. Draw a time line on the board like the one below. Explain that the numbers in B.C. dates get smaller as they approach 1 B.C. Point out that after that, the numbers would be labeled A.D. and would get larger. Invite volunteers to divide the time line into appropriate increments. Then, as students read the lesson, invite them to add entries pertinent to the Shang and Zhou dynasties to the time line. **0:15** minutes

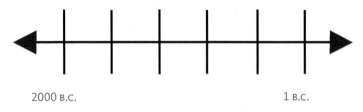

2000 B.C.   1 B.C.

GUIDED DISCUSSION

1. **Identify Main Ideas and Details** How was society ordered during the Shang dynasty? *(The king was at the top of society, with warlords next, and farmers at the bottom.)*

2. **Sequence Events** What happened during the last 500 years of the Zhou dynasty when the kings divided their land among local lords? *(The lords became powerful and independent. They fought among themselves and disobeyed the Zhou kings. In time, China descended into a time of constant war.)*

INTERPRET DIAGRAMS

Have students study the Dynastic Cycle diagram. Read and discuss each step in the cycle. **ASK:** According to the cycle, what occurrences indicate that a dynasty has lost the approval of the gods? *(Disasters occur.)* What shows that a new dynasty has the gods' approval? *(Order is restored.)* **0:10** minutes

ACTIVE OPTIONS

Critical Viewing: NG Chapter Gallery Invite students to explore the Chapter 7 Gallery and create a Favorites List by choosing the images they find most interesting. If possible, have students copy the images into a document to form an actual list. Then encourage them to select the image they like best and do further research on it. **0:10** minutes

On Your Feet: Stage a Quiz Show Have each student write one question about the Shang and Zhou dynasties and collect the questions. Then have groups of five students take turns coming to the front of the class to take part in a quiz. Pose a few of the questions to each group. Students should confer about the answer and then signal their readiness to respond by raising their hands. **0:20** minutes

STRIVING READERS

Complete a Key Facts T-Chart Have students create a T-Chart on the Shang and Zhou dynasties. Students should label the first column of the T-Chart "Shang" and the second column "Zhou." Tell students to jot down key facts about each dynasty as they read the lesson. Have students compare completed charts.

Shang	Zhou

PRE-AP

Write an E-Zine Article Have students research to learn more about the Zhou dynasty. Invite them to write and illustrate an e-zine article about the cultural advances made during the first 200 years of their rule. Students should also describe what happened during the last 500 years of the dynasty. Encourage students to share their articles with the rest of the class.

Press (**mt**) *in the Student eEdition for modified text.*

See the Chapter Planner for more strategies for differentiation.

ANSWERS

1. Religious beliefs and practices include the use of oracle bones, ancestor worship, and conducting special ceremonies to keep the spirits happy.

2. In time, a new dynasty arose that took charge and re-established order.

3. The people would have believed that the downfall of one dynasty and the rise of another reflected the will of the gods.

1.3 Chinese Philosophies

"What you do not wish for yourself, do not do to others." Sound familiar? You may have heard this saying before—or another version of it. It's a simple but powerful guide for moral behavior, and it was written 2,500 years ago by a man called Confucius.

MAIN IDEA

Chinese philosophers developed important ideas on how society should be organized.

CONFUCIANISM

As you've read, China began to fall into disorder during the Zhou dynasty. By the time Confucius was born in 551 B.C., China was already experiencing unrest. A teacher and government official, Confucius believed that Chinese society was breaking down as a result of the constant conflict. In an effort to restore order, he taught that people should respect authority and one another.

Confucius' teachings formed the basis of a belief system known as **Confucianism**. His teachings focused on the duties and responsibilities in the following five relationships: father and son, older brother and younger brother, husband and wife, friend and friend, and ruler and subject. Confucius also promoted education, family unity, and **filial piety**, or the respect children owe their parents and ancestors.

Confucius died believing he had failed to restore order to society. Yet after his death, his students collected his teachings in a book called the *Analects*, and Confucian ideas spread. In time Confucius' teachings became required reading for all government officials. Today Confucianism influences millions of people. The philosophy has been a unifying force in Chinese culture and civilization.

DAOISM AND LEGALISM

Another thinker called Laozi (low-dzuh) is believed to have lived around the same time as Confucius. He founded a belief system called **Daoism**, which emphasizes living in harmony with nature and the Dao. *Dao* means "the Way" and is believed to be the driving force behind everything that exists. Daoists seek order and balance in their lives by merging, or blending, with nature "like drops of water in a stream."

In contrast with both Confucianism and Daoism, **Legalism** emphasizes order through strong government and strictly enforced laws. Legalism developed after 400 B.C. This philosophy does not have a founder, but Han Feizi (fay-zee) set down its ideas around 260 B.C. He maintained that people were naturally bad and needed to be controlled through the threat of harsh punishment. As you will see, a Chinese dynasty would arise that would govern according to this philosophy.

DAOIST YIN-AND-YANG SYMBOL

This symbol is often used in Daoism to show how seemingly opposite forces form a whole. Daoists believe that everything contains aspects of both yin and yang. The symbol shows some of the aspects of each force.

REVIEW & ASSESS

1. **READING CHECK** What are the basic beliefs of Confucianism?

2. **ANALYZE LANGUAGE USE** What Daoist idea does the phrase "blending with nature like drops of water in a stream" help convey?

3. **COMPARE AND CONTRAST** How does Legalism's attitude toward people's nature differ from that of both Confucianism and Daoism?

6.6.3 Know about the life of Confucius and the fundamental teachings of Confucianism and Taoism; 6.6.4 Identify the political and cultural problems prevalent in the time of Confucius and how he sought to solve them.

+ POSSIBLE RESPONSE

The notes indicate that people today still respect and try to follow his teachings.

Critical Viewing Followers write comments and questions to Confucius on notes that bear his image. What do the notes suggest about the lasting influence of Confucius?

STANDARDS

HSS CONTENT STANDARDS:

6.6.3 Know about the life of Confucius and the fundamental teachings of Confucianism and Taoism; **6.6.4** Identify the political and cultural problems prevalent in the time of Confucius and how he sought to solve them.

PLAN

OBJECTIVE

Examine the beliefs and philosophies that developed in Chinese civilization.

ESSENTIAL QUESTION

How did China establish what would become one of the world's oldest continuous civilizations?

Three different philosophies arose in China around the Warring States period. Lesson 1.3 describes the unifying force of Confucianism in Chinese culture and civilization.

BACKGROUND FOR THE TEACHER

Confucius was born Kong Qiu and often called Kongfuzi (Master Kong) in Chinese. Confucius is the name used by Europeans. He saw teaching as a calling and a way of life. He wanted education to be available to all, not just to rich families who could hire professional tutors for their sons.

Confucianism continued to influence Chinese society until the Communist Party seized power in 1949. The Communists outlawed Confucianism because they considered it a religion. The government ended its ban in 1977. Since then, Confucianism has regained much of its influence. It is taught in schools, and many leaders have rediscovered Confucius' wisdom.

DIGITAL RESOURCES NGLSync.cengage.com

TEACHER RESOURCES & ASSESSMENT

 Reading and Note-Taking

 Vocabulary Practice

 Section 1 Quiz

STUDENT RESOURCES

 Biography

INTRODUCE & ENGAGE

ANALYZE MORAL CODES

Write this saying of Confucius on the board: "What you do not wish for yourself, do not do to others." Ask students what they think the saying means and if they know of similar sayings from other sources. Explain that this saying is similar to the Golden Rule—"Do unto others as you would have them do unto you"—a guideline for human behavior from Christian scripture. Discuss as a class how students think Confucius' saying applies to their own lives. Then ask students to brainstorm as many sources for rules for good behavior as they can. *(parents or family, teachers, government, religion, philosophy, community organizations)* Write students' responses on the board. Explain that they will learn about an ethical system in China that provided many rules for good behavior. **0:10** minutes

TEACH

GUIDED DISCUSSION

1. **Make Generalizations** How did the society in which Confucius lived influence his teachings? *(Society during the Zhou dynasty was already experiencing unrest. Confucius wanted to use his teachings to restore harmony.)*

2. **Draw Conclusions** What was the guiding principle behind all three Chinese philosophies? *(They all sought to bring order to society.)*

MORE INFORMATION

Yin and Yang The forces of yin and yang do not influence only Chinese philosophy. The duality of yin and yang also guides traditional Chinese medicine. The upper body is considered part of yang because it is closer to heaven. The lower body is considered part of yin because it is closer to Earth. Internal organs are also divided into yin and yang aspects. Doctors who practice traditional Chinese medicine try to keep their patients' yin and yang in balance. Yin and yang imbalance within the body is believed to result in disease.

ACTIVE OPTIONS

Critical Viewing: NG Chapter Gallery Have students explore the Chapter 7 Gallery and choose two items that illustrate religion or belief systems in China. Have students compare and contrast the images, either in written form or verbally with a partner. Ask questions that will inspire this process, such as: How are these images alike? How are they different? Why did you select these two items? How do they relate in history? As an extension, you might also have students read and discuss the poem "The Slanderers" by Confucius and the excerpt from the *Dao de Jing* in the **Primary Source Handbook.** **0:10** minutes

On Your Feet: Code of Conduct Roundtable Divide the class into groups of four. Have the groups move desks together to form a table where they can all sit. Hand each group a sheet of paper with the title *Code of Conduct*. Tell students that they will create a list of rules for their classroom that will provide guidelines for good behavior. Then have the first student in each group write a rule, read it aloud, and pass the paper clockwise to the next student. Each student in each group should write two rules. When the groups have finished writing their codes, invite each group to share their rules. After all groups have shared, have the class vote on the five rules they like best. Post these rules on a bulletin board. **0:20** minutes

DIFFERENTIATE

ENGLISH LANGUAGE LEARNERS (ELD)

Find Someone Who Knows Give students copies of the questions below and have them find five different classmates to answer them. Have students at the **Emerging** and **Expanding** levels work in pairs. Have students at the **Bridging** level work independently. Encourage students to answer in complete sentences by inverting the questions into statements.

1. Whose teachings have influenced China for centuries? (*Confucius*)

2. What does Dao mean? (*the way*)

3. Which Chinese philosophy emphasizes order through strong government and strict laws? (*Legalism*)

4. Who is the founder of Daoism? (*Laozi*)

5. What book contains the teachings of Confucius? (*the* Analects)

STRIVING READERS

Monitor Comprehension Have students work in pairs to read the lesson, pausing after each paragraph to ask and answer questions about words or passages they did not understand.

Press **mt** *in the Student eEdition for modified text.*

See the Chapter Planner for more strategies for differentiation.

REVIEW & ASSESS

ANSWERS

1. Confucianism provides ideas on promoting proper conduct through respect. The belief system also promotes filial piety.

2. The phrase helps convey the idea of achieving harmony with nature.

3. Legalism takes the attitude that people are naturally bad, while Confucianism and Daoism take the attitude that people are generally good.

Contrasting
Belief Systems

You've seen that the suffering caused by weak government and conflict in China led many to think about the best ways to ensure an orderly and peaceful society. As a result, China produced some of the world's greatest philosophical thinkers and writers. Their ideas were so powerful that they not only shaped the future of China for 2,000 years but also continue to influence world thinking today.

Children dressed in traditional clothing perform in China during a celebration of Confucius' birthday.

172

DOCUMENT ONE

Primary Source: Philosophical Teaching

from *Analects of Confucius*,
translated by Simon Leys
The *Analects*, a collection of Confucius' ideas, sayings, and stories, was probably recorded by many people over many years. In this passage from the *Analects*, a lord asks Confucius (often referred to as "the Master") how to govern his people.

CONSTRUCTED RESPONSE What details in the passage support the idea that Confucius believed rulers had to set a good example for their people?

> Lord Ji Kang asked: "What should I do in order to make the people respectful, loyal, and zealous [enthusiastic]?" The Master said: "Approach them with dignity and they will be respectful. Be yourself a good son and a kind father, and they will be loyal. Raise the good and train the incompetent [those unable to do a good job], and they will be zealous."

DOCUMENT TWO

Primary Source: Philosophical Teaching

from *Dao de Jing*,
translated by Stephen Mitchell
The *Dao de Jing* is a key text of Daoism. In general, it stresses inaction over action and silence over words. This passage explains the power of the Dao.

CONSTRUCTED RESPONSE According to the passage, how can powerful people live peaceful, happy lives?

> The Dao never does anything, yet through it all things are done. If powerful men and women could center themselves in it, the whole world would be transformed by itself, in its natural rhythms. People would be content with their simple, everyday lives, in harmony, and free of desire.

DOCUMENT THREE

Primary Source: Philosophical Teaching

from *Han Feizi: Basic Writings*,
translated by Burton Watson
Han Feizi lived from 280 to 233 B.C. He did not believe Confucianism was the answer to the chaos brought about in China during the Warring States period. In this passage from a collection of his writings, Han Feizi describes the role of rulers.

CONSTRUCTED RESPONSE What does the passage suggest about the kind of ruler and government Legalism supported?

> Discard wisdom, forswear [reject] ability, so that your subordinates [those beneath you] cannot guess what you are about. Stick to your objectives and examine the results to see how they match; take hold of the handles of government carefully and grip them tightly. Destroy all hope, smash all intention of wresting [taking] them [the handles of government] from you; allow no man to covet [desire] them.

SYNTHESIZE & WRITE

1. **REVIEW** Review what you have learned about Confucianism, Daoism, and Legalism.

2. **RECALL** On your own paper, write down the main idea expressed in each document.

3. **CONSTRUCT** Write a topic sentence that answers this question: What ideas about leadership do each of the ancient Chinese philosophies convey?

4. **WRITE** Using evidence from the documents, write a paragraph to support your answer from Step 3.

6.6.3 Know about the life of Confucius and the fundamental teachings of Confucianism and Taoism; 6.6.4 Identify the political and cultural problems prevalent in the time of Confucius and how he sought to solve them; REP 4 Students assess the credibility of primary and secondary sources and draw sound conclusions from them.

173

PLAN

OBJECTIVE

Synthesize the different ideas presented by three Chinese philosophies.

ESSENTIAL QUESTION

How did China establish what would become one of the world's oldest continuous civilizations?

Confucianism, Daoism, and Legalism have guided the people and rulers of China for centuries. Lesson 1.4 provides primary source excerpts, conveying core ideas of each philosophy.

BACKGROUND FOR THE TEACHER

Many legends have been told about Laozi. One of the most famous tells the story of a meeting—which likely never took place—between Laozi and Confucius. According to the tale, Laozi chastised the other philosopher for his pride and ambition. Confucius is said to have been so impressed with Laozi's insight that he likened him to a dragon riding on the wind and clouds. This was high praise since, in Chinese culture, the dragon symbolizes power, strength, and good luck.

DIGITAL RESOURCES NGLSync.cengage.com

TEACHER RESOURCES & ASSESSMENT

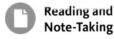 **Reading and Note-Taking**

 Vocabulary Practice

 Section 1 Quiz

STUDENT RESOURCES

 NG Chapter Gallery

INTRODUCE & ENGAGE

PREPARE FOR THE DOCUMENT-BASED QUESTION

Before students start on the activity, briefly preview the three documents. Remind students that a constructed response requires full explanations in complete sentences. Emphasize that students should use what they have learned about ancient Chinese philosophies in addition to the information in the documents. `0:05` minutes

TEACH

GUIDED DISCUSSION

1. **Form and Support Opinions** Do you support Confucius' ideas about how to make people respectful, loyal, and zealous? (*Responses will vary. Possible responses: Yes, I believe that treating people with respect, setting a good example, and adapting to the needs of individuals will make people respectful, loyal, and zealous; No, I think that some people would take advantage of this kind of leadership and would require more forceful treatment.*)

2. **Draw Conclusions** What does the writer of the Dao de Jing suggest about powerful men and women? (*The writer suggests that powerful men and women do not live simple, harmonious lives and are not free of desire.*)

3. **Make Inferences** What emotions would a ruler who lived by the philosophy supported by Han Feizi probably inspire in his people? (*Responses will vary. Possible responses: fear, hatred, distrust*)

EVALUATE

After students have completed the "Synthesize & Write" activity, allow time for them to exchange paragraphs and read and comment on the work of their peers. Guidelines for comments should be established prior to this activity so that feedback is constructive and encouraging in nature. `0:15` minutes

ACTIVE OPTIONS

NG Learning Framework: Learn About Different Chinese Philosophies

SKILLS: Observation; Collaboration
KNOWLEDGE: Our Human Story

Have students revisit Lessons 1.3 and 1.4 and review the information about Confucianism, Daoism, and Legalism. Then ask students to work in pairs to create a list of what they consider the best aspects of each philosophy. Once they have completed their list of observations, each pair should exchange lists with another pair and discuss the new list. `0:10` minutes

On Your Feet: Use a Jigsaw Strategy Organize students into three "expert" groups and have students from each group analyze one of the documents and summarize the main ideas of the teaching in their own words. Then have the members of each group count off using the letters A, B, C, and so on. Regroup students into three new groups so that each new group has at least one member from each expert group. Have students in the new groups take turns sharing the simplified summaries they came up with in their expert groups. `0:10` minutes

DIFFERENTIATE

STRIVING READERS

Summarize Read each document aloud to students. Have one group of students work together to reread each document and summarize it for the larger group. After each document is summarized, read the constructed response question with the larger group and make sure all students understand it. Then have volunteers suggest responses.

GIFTED & TALENTED

Write a Profile Ask groups of students to learn more about Confucius, Laozi, and Han Feizi. Then have each group select a philosopher and write a social-networking profile on him, providing a brief summary and "photos." Have the groups share their profiles with the rest of the class. Then invite students to "friend" the philosophers and send them messages about their lives and teachings.

Press (mt) *in the Student eEdition for modified text.*

See the Chapter Planner for more strategies for differentiation.

CONSTRUCTED RESPONSE

ANSWERS
DOCUMENT 1
Confucius tells Lord Ji Kang that in order for the people to be loyal, the ruler himself must set a good example by being a good son and father.

DOCUMENT 2
Powerful people can live peaceful, happy lives by centering themselves in the Dao, becoming content with their simple, everyday lives, and freeing themselves from desire.

DOCUMENT 3
The passage suggests that Legalism supported strong, even ruthless rulers who had no concern for those beneath them.

SYNTHESIZE & WRITE

ANSWERS
1. Responses will vary.
2. Responses will vary.
3. Possible response: Confucianism, Daoism, and Legalism have very different ideas about how a leader should rule.
4. Students' paragraphs should include their topic sentence from Step 3 and provide several details from the documents to support the sentence.

SHI HUANGDI

259 B.C. – 210 B.C.

The flames rise higher as officials toss more books onto the fire. Their emperor, Shi Huangdi, has ordered them to burn any writing that contains ideas he doesn't like. High on the list is anything to do with Confucianism. Shi Huangdi is a cruel but skilled ruler—and he intends his dynasty to last for 10,000 generations.

This digital re-creation shows how Shi Huangdi's army of terra cotta warriors might have been painted and posed around the emperor's tomb.

Job: First emperor of China
Home: Kingdom of Qin

FINEST HOUR

After unifying and expanding China, he became its first emperor.

WORST MOMENT

He supposedly died after taking pills he thought would keep him alive forever.

HOBBIES

He built a huge tomb for himself filled with life-size statues of warriors and horses.

GREATEST FEAR

Convinced that his enemies wanted to kill him, he slept in a different apartment in his palace every night.

A RUTHLESS RULER

China's Warring States period finally ended when the leader of the **Qin** (chin) kingdom defeated all other kingdoms around 221 B.C. The leader's name was Ying Zheng, and he united the kingdoms to form an empire. He would come to call himself **Shi Huangdi** (shee hwahng-dee), meaning "first emperor." An **emperor** is the ruler of an empire.

Shi Huangdi established his government based on Legalist ideas. He set up his capital in Xianyang (shee-ahn-yang) and built magnificent palaces in the city to demonstrate his power. The emperor then forced thousands of China's most powerful families to relocate to the capital so he could keep an eye on them.

In addition, Shi Huangdi divided his empire into 36 areas governed by officials he himself had selected. He also followed Legalist ideas by punishing anyone who disagreed with or criticized him. Shi Huangdi is said to have put to death hundreds of Confucian scholars.

A UNIFIED EMPIRE

Although his methods were cruel, Shi Huangdi brought order to China. He made sure units used to weigh and measure items throughout the empire were standardized, or the same, to ensure that buyers were not being cheated. He also brought a single writing system and currency, or form of money, to China.

As Shi Huangdi conquered new lands and expanded his empire, he made further improvements that united his territory. He had thousands of miles of roads built to link different parts of the empire. These roads were all constructed at the same width. He also built canals and irrigation systems. Shi Huangdi's most famous construction project was the **Great Wall** of China, which you will learn more about in the next lesson. Many historians believe these structures were built by forced labor and funded by high taxes.

Shi Huangdi's rule came to an end when he died in 210 B.C. Throughout his reign, the emperor had feared being murdered by assassins. It seems he believed evil spirits could also attack him in the afterlife. As a result, Shi Huangdi had an army of **terra cotta**, or baked clay, warriors buried beside his tomb to protect him. The burial site probably forms his greatest legacy—an odd twist of fate for a man who spent much of his life trying to cheat death.

REVIEW & ASSESS

1. **READING CHECK** How did Shi Huangdi link the new lands of his empire?

2. **DRAW CONCLUSIONS** What are the benefits of using a single currency within a country?

3. **FORM OPINIONS** What do you think was Shi Huangdi's greatest achievement? Why?

6.6.5 List the policies and achievements of the emperor Shi Huangdi in unifying northern China under the Qin Dynasty; HI 6 Students interpret basic indicators of economic performance and conduct cost-benefit analyses of economic and political issues.

STANDARDS

HSS CONTENT STANDARDS:

6.6.5 List the policies and achievements of the emperor Shi Huangdi in unifying northern China under the Qin Dynasty.

HSS ANALYSIS SKILLS:

HI 6 Students interpret basic indicators of economic performance and conduct cost-benefit analyses of economic and political issues.

PLAN

OBJECTIVE

Explain how Shi Huangdi ruled his people and united his empire.

ESSENTIAL QUESTION

How did China establish what would become one of the world's oldest continuous civilizations?

Shi Huangdi united the kingdoms of China to form an empire. Lesson 2.1 discusses the steps Shi Huangdi took to establish and unify his empire and bring order to China.

BACKGROUND FOR THE TEACHER

Shi Huangdi had good reason to fear for his life. Between 227 and 218 B.C., three attempts were made to murder him. The emperor wanted his dynasty to last for 10,000 generations, but he also wanted his life to continue as long as possible. To that end, Shi Huangdi had his servants search out pills and potions that would prolong his life. He even sent them on missions to find herbs that supposedly had magical properties. Unfortunately, these herbs were said to grow on the mythical islands of the gods, so the servants were not successful in their quest. Ironically, Shi Huangdi died at the age of 49 after ingesting pills made by his doctors to keep him alive. The pills contained mercury.

DIGITAL RESOURCES NGLSync.cengage.com

TEACHER RESOURCES & ASSESSMENT

 Reading and Note-Taking

 Vocabulary Practice

 Section 2 Quiz

STUDENT RESOURCES

 NG Chapter Gallery

INTRODUCE & ENGAGE

PREVIEW A PROFILE

Before students read the lesson, go over Shi Huangdi's profile with the class. Ask them to share their impressions of the emperor based on the profile entries. `0:05` minutes

TEACH

GUIDED DISCUSSION

1. **Make Predictions** How might Shi Huangdi's rule have been different if he had established his government based on Confucian or Daoist ideas? *(Possible response: His rule wouldn't have been as ruthless, and he might have been more tolerant of those who disagreed with his ideas.)*

2. **Draw Conclusions** Why did Shi Huangdi have all roads constructed at the same width? *(so that vehicles could travel on all the roads throughout the empire)*

ANALYZE VISUALS

Have students compare the photograph of the digital re-creation of the soldiers with the photograph in Lesson 2.3. Have them use the photograph in the other lesson to study the soldiers' faces, clothing, and poses. **ASK:** What do you find most striking about the digital re-creation? *(Possible response: the number of soldiers, the colors, the weapons)* What does the army shown suggest about Shi Huangdi? *(Possible response: He was afraid of death and wanted a huge army to protect him; he was proud and arrogant and believed that he deserved a full army to protect him, even in death.)* `0:10` minutes

ACTIVE OPTIONS

NG Learning Framework: Learn About Shi Huangdi

ATTITUDE: **Empowerment**
SKILL: **Decision-Making**

Invite students to revisit the biography of Shi Huangdi in Lesson 2.1 and imagine they were in the emperor's place. **ASK:** How would you have done things differently from Shi Huangdi? How do you feel these changes would have affected China and the world? `0:10` minutes

On Your Feet: Hold a Panel Discussion Build on the third question in "Review & Assess" by asking volunteers to stage a panel discussion before the rest of the class about Shi Huangdi's greatest achievements. Students can choose any achievement they learned about in the lesson to discuss. `0:20` minutes

DIFFERENTIATE

STRIVING READERS

Use Reciprocal Teaching Have partners take turns reading each paragraph of the lesson aloud. At the end of the paragraph, the reading student should ask the listening student questions about the paragraph. Students may ask their partners to state the main idea of the paragraph, identify important details that support the main idea, or summarize the paragraph in their own words. Then have students work together to answer the Review & Assess questions.

INCLUSION

Summarize Have students complete a Concept Cluster like the one shown to keep track of important details about Shi Huangdi as they read the lesson. Then have students form pairs and use their completed charts to summarize what they learned about Shi Huangdi.

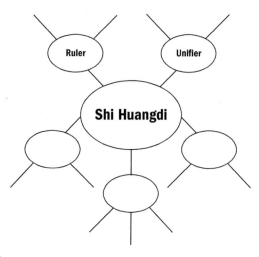

Ruler

Unifier

Shi Huangdi

Press **mt** in the Student eEdition for modified text.

See the Chapter Planner for more strategies for differentiation.

REVIEW & ASSESS

ANSWERS

1. He linked the empire by building roads, canals, and irrigation systems throughout the empire.

2. People within a country do not have to change money into another currency. Prices are easier to compare.

3. Responses will vary, but students may say that bringing a single writing system and currency to China was his greatest achievement.

The
Great Wall

Groaning under the weight of another brick, you set it in place on the wall. You didn't volunteer for this work, and you won't be paid very much for it either. It's possible you'll even die working on the wall. But under Shi Huangdi's rule, you do as you're told.

MAIN IDEA

Shi Huangdi began building the Great Wall to keep invaders out of China.

KEEPING OUT INVADERS

While mountains, deserts, and seas protected most of China, part of its northern border was vulnerable, or open to attack. Riding on horseback, nomadic tribes from Central Asia often swept over the border, destroying farms, villages, and towns. Small walls had been built along the border during the Warring States period, but Shi Huangdi decided to join them into one long wall that would stretch over 2,500 miles.

The emperor forced hundreds of thousands of **peasants**, or poor farmers, to build his wall. He also conscripted soldiers and prisoners to perform the backbreaking labor, often in extreme conditions. Many of the laborers died from exhaustion, hunger, and disease. After Shi Huangdi's death, the wall fell into disrepair. However, later rulers built and extended it. In fact, work on the wall continued into the 1600s.

176 CHAPTER 7

+ POSSIBLE RESPONSE

Details include the fortified walls and the rugged mountains that extend for miles.

Critical Viewing This photo of the Great Wall shows the structure as it appears today. Little of the original wall built under Shi Huangdi remains. What details in the photo show how the wall would have discouraged invaders?

REVIEW & ASSESS

1. **READING CHECK** What methods did Shi Huangdi use to get his wall built?

2. **INTEGRATE VISUALS** Based on the text and the photo, what "extreme conditions" do you think workers on the wall had to endure?

3. **DETERMINE WORD MEANINGS** What does the word *conscripted* mean as used in the sentence, "He also conscripted soldiers and prisoners to perform the backbreaking labor"?

6.6.5 List the policies and achievements of the emperor Shi Huangdi in unifying northern China under the Qin Dynasty.

177

HSS CONTENT STANDARDS:

6.6.5 List the policies and achievements of the emperor Shi Huangdi in unifying northern China under the Qin Dynasty.

HSS ANALYSIS SKILLS:

REP 1 Students frame questions that can be answered by historical study and research.

PLAN

OBJECTIVE

Describe and explain the purpose of the Great Wall.

ESSENTIAL QUESTION

How did China establish what would become one of the world's oldest continuous civilizations?

Shi Huangdi undertook a project to join and expand small walls along China's border that had been built during the Warring States period. Lesson 2.2 describes the beginnings of the Great Wall, which would protect China for hundreds of years.

BACKGROUND FOR THE TEACHER

As Chinese rulers after Shi Huangdi extended the Great Wall, they had watchtowers built every 200 or 300 yards along its length. Soldiers manned the towers. When an enemy was sighted, one of these soldiers lit a fire as a signal. The soldier at the next tower saw the smoke and lit a fire in turn. The signal continued along the wall. The smoke alerted troops to the danger.

In times of peace, the soldiers on the towers kept watch but also stored animal dung and firewood. Other soldiers raised sheep and cattle for food and brought the dung to the towers. Some of the dung they brought came from wolves. In fact, the smoke created by a fire set at a tower was often called "Langyan," which means "wolves' smoke" in Chinese.

DIGITAL RESOURCES NGLSync.cengage.com

TEACHER RESOURCES & ASSESSMENT

 Reading and Note-Taking

 Vocabulary Practice

 Section 2 Quiz

STUDENT RESOURCES

 NG Chapter Gallery

INTRODUCE & ENGAGE

COMPLETE A K-W-L CHART

Have students use a K-W-L Chart to record what they already know about the Great Wall. Encourage students to draw on what they have learned in school or what they have seen on television or online. Then have students jot down what they would like to learn about the Great Wall. After they have read the lesson, ask them to record what they learned.
`0:10` minutes

K What Do I Know?	W What Do I Want To Learn?	L What Did I Learn?

TEACH

GUIDED DISCUSSION

1. **Identify Main Ideas and Details** Who built the wall and under what conditions did they labor? *(Peasants, soldiers, and prisoners worked on the wall, often in extreme conditions. Many died from exhaustion, hunger, and disease.)*

2. **Form Opinions** Do you think the Great Wall was worth the human price it exacted to build? Why or why not? *(Some students may say the wall was worth the toll in human lives because it helped to safeguard China for centuries. Others may say that the construction of the wall could have been carried out in a more humane manner.)*

INTEGRATE VISUALS

Have students study the photograph of the Great Wall as it appears today. Initiate a discussion about the length of the wall, its building materials, and its setting in the photograph. **ASK:** Why do you think the passageway is so wide? *(Possible response: to allow troops of soldiers and vehicles to travel along the wall)* What purpose might the shelter have served? *(Possible response: It might have served as a shelter for soldiers who stopped there for the night. It might have provided a post from which to watch for or fire at the enemy.)*
`0:10` minutes

ACTIVE OPTIONS

NG Learning Framework: Learn About the Great Wall

SKILL: Communication
KNOWLEDGE: Our Living Planet

Have students imagine they have been conscripted to work on the Great Wall of China. Ask students to write a letter home telling their family about their experiences and the geographic challenges they encounter as they try to build the wall. `0:10` minutes

On Your Feet: Build a Wall Have students use chairs or blocks to build a wall across the classroom. Remind them that the Great Wall began as a series of small walls that were later joined together. After the wall is complete, **ASK:** How does a wall help a country defend itself? *(A wall forms a barrier that makes it easier for a country's soldiers to guard. Enemies cannot get horses or equipment over a wall easily.)* Invite students to evaluate how effective they think a wall would be today compared to periods in the past.
`0:20` minutes

DIFFERENTIATE

INCLUSION

Practice Summarizing Have partners work together to understand the lesson. Ask the pairs to read the first paragraph together. Then have them close the book and write down all the facts they can remember. When students have finished, tell them to open the book and check their facts. Have them repeat the exercise with the second paragraph in the lesson.

GIFTED & TALENTED

Draw the Great Wall Have students research to learn more about the features of the Great Wall: the height and materials of the walls; the battlements, the passageways, and the watchtowers. Then ask them to use what they learned to draw a portion of the Great Wall and label each of the features. Invite students to share their drawings and compare them with the photo in this lesson.

Press (**mt**) *in the Student eEdition for modified text.*

See the Chapter Planner for more strategies for differentiation.

REVIEW & ASSESS

ANSWERS

1. He forced hundreds of thousands of workers to labor on the wall.

2. They had to endure hauling materials up mountains, laboring in cold, snowy weather, doing everything by hand, and getting little to eat and little rest.

3. It means "to force someone to serve or work."

209 B.C.

+ **POSSIBLE RESPONSE**

The warriors' eyes, expressions, hair, clothing, and positions help make them look lifelike.

On the morning of March 29, 1974, farmers digging a well in a village near Xi'an (shee-ahn), China, made an incredible discovery. They found a body—but one made of baked clay. It was one of an estimated 8,000 life-size terra cotta warriors that had been created to protect Shi Huangdi more than 2,000 years ago. The army of warriors—and their chariots and horses—stood in battle formation, ready to fight Shi Huangdi's battles in the afterlife. Historians estimate that more than 700,000 laborers worked for 38 years to complete the project around 209 B.C. As wonderful as the warriors are, archaeologists believe even greater treasures lie in the emperor's tomb itself, which remains unexplored. What details in the statues help make the warriors look lifelike?

178

6.6.5 List the policies and achievements of the emperor Shi Huangdi in unifying northern China under the Qin Dynasty.

179

HSS CONTENT STANDARDS:

6.6.5 List the policies and achievements of the emperor Shi Huangdi in unifying northern China under the Qin Dynasty.

PLAN

OBJECTIVE

Describe the terra cotta warriors Shi Huangdi had created and placed around his tomb.

ESSENTIAL QUESTION

How did China establish what would become one of the world's oldest continuous civilizations?

Shi Huangdi was China's first and one of its greatest emperors. Lesson 2.3 provides a glimpse of some of the clay warriors the emperor had buried beside his tomb.

BACKGROUND FOR THE TEACHER

When archaeologists first excavated the site in Xi'an, they found the terra cotta warriors armed with real weapons. These included bronze swords and about 40,000 arrowheads. About 100 of these were tied together to fit in a single quiver. Archaeologists also found life-size clay horses standing four abreast with wooden chariots behind them. Interestingly, Shi Huangdi's body has not yet been found.

DIGITAL RESOURCES NGLSync.cengage.com

TEACHER RESOURCES & ASSESSMENT

 Reading and Note-Taking

 Vocabulary Practice

 Section 2 Quiz

STUDENT RESOURCES

 NG Chapter Gallery

INTRODUCE & ENGAGE

ACCESS PRIOR KNOWLEDGE

Invite students to share what they already know or have heard about the terra cotta warriors. Record student responses in a Concept Cluster on the board. Then call on volunteers to use the completed cluster to summarize the class discussion. `0:15` minutes

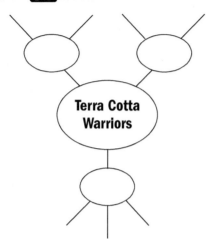

Terra Cotta
Warriors

TEACH

GUIDED DISCUSSION

1. **Describe** How would you describe the look on the face of the warrior shown on the right page? *(Responses will vary. Possible response: He looks alert, watchful, confident, ready to do battle.)*

2. **Make Inferences** Why do you think the two warriors shown on the left page are holding their hands up? *(Responses will vary. Possible responses: When they were made, they were probably holding something in their hands, such as a weapon or the reins of a chariot.)*

MORE INFORMATION

Variety of Terra Cotta Figures In the two largest pits, archaeologists uncovered infantry soldiers. The soldiers include archers armed with bows and arrows, armed warriors, and horses ready to pull chariots. Warriors holding long poles were found in the smallest pit. Archaeologists believe this pit was meant to be a command post. Other pits contain non-military figures. Some of these terra cotta figures are civil servants holding knives and tablets to write on. Others appear to be acrobats, probably meant to entertain the emperor in the afterlife. `0:10` minutes

ACTIVE OPTIONS

NG Learning Framework: Learn About Shi Huangdi's Army

ATTITUDE: **Curiosity**
KNOWLEDGE: **Our Human Story**

Have students research to learn more about Shi Huangdi's actual military force. Encourage students to find images of what the real soldiers, weapons, and war machinery would have looked like and compare them with the terra cotta versions. `0:10` minutes

On Your Feet: I See, I Read, And So On a large sheet of chart paper or a whiteboard, create a chart like the one pictured below. As a group, reexamine the photograph of the terra cotta warriors. Have volunteers describe something they observe in the photo and something they have read to draw conclusions about Shi Huangdi and the terra cotta warriors. Record their observations on the chart. `0:15` minutes

I See	I Read	And So

DIFFERENTIATE

ENGLISH LANGUAGE LEARNERS ELD

Develop Vocabulary Spanish-speaking students may recognize the term *terra cotta* because it is similar to the Spanish word for baked clay: *terracota*. Invite students to teach the Spanish term to the class and explain that the parts of the word translate literally as "baked earth."

PRE-AP

Create a Top Ten List Have groups of students research to learn more about the terra cotta warriors. Then have them create a list of ten interesting facts about the warriors and their discovery. Tell groups to list the facts beginning with number ten, the least important, and ending with number one, the most important. Then have the groups take turns reading the lists to the class.

Press (mt) *in the Student eEdition for modified text.*

See the Chapter Planner for more strategies for differentiation.

The Han Dynasty

Maybe you've gotten in trouble for coming to class late, but that predicament would be nothing next to this: In 209 B.C., some farmers arrived late to sign up for their required military service, and they were sentenced to death. The farmers got away and spurred thousands of others to rebel against the Qin dynasty.

MAIN IDEA

Han dynasty rulers reformed the government, expanded the empire, and brought prosperity to China.

GOVERNMENT

After Shi Huangdi died, his son became emperor but proved to be a weak ruler. The farmers who escaped their death sentence fueled a bloody rebellion that brought about the collapse of the Qin dynasty. Rebels struggled for power until Liu Bang (lee-oo bahng), a peasant from the Han kingdom, seized control and began the **Han** dynasty in 202 B.C.

Han emperors introduced practices that were less cruel than those of Shi Huangdi. They lowered taxes and put an end to laws that were especially harsh. They also required lighter punishments for crimes.

You may recall that Shi Huangdi had forced workers to labor for years on his building projects. The Han, on the other hand, had peasants work for only one month per year to build roads, canals, and irrigation systems.

The Han rulers also replaced Legalism with Confucianism and used Confucius' teachings as a guide. Furthermore, they valued the well-educated and obedient officials Confucianism produced. As a result, the officials they appointed had to pass an examination that tested their knowledge of Confucianism. The rulers established their government based on a **bureaucracy**, in which these appointed officials ran the bureaus, or offices.

Later Han rulers included Liu Bang's wife, who came to be known as Empress Lü. Women were not allowed to rule as emperor in ancient China, but Lü found a way around that restriction. After her husband died in 195 B.C., Lü placed their young son on the throne and ruled in his name. When she outlived her son, she held on to power by crowning a couple of infants emperor and ruling in their place. After Lü died in 180 B.C., all of her relatives were executed by a group of rival court officials. They made sure that no other member of her family could rule again.

Emperor Wudi (woo-dee), who ruled from 141 to 87 B.C., was another notable emperor. He used military conquests to expand the empire's boundaries—nearly to the size of present-day China. His reign lasted 54 years, which set a record that would not be broken for more than 1,800 years.

DAILY LIFE

China prospered under the Han dynasty. Many merchants, government workers, and craftspeople lived in large houses in the cities. Like modern cities, these were crowded places filled with restaurants, businesses, and places of entertainment. Some cities had populations of up to 500,000 people.

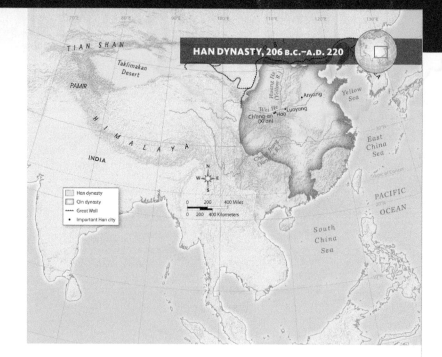

HAN DYNASTY, 206 B.C.–A.D. 220

Most of the Chinese people, however, were peasants. They lived in small mud houses in villages close to their farms. Some peasants could not afford farm animals and so pulled their plows themselves. They had few possessions and barely produced enough to feed their own families. For the most part, peasants lived on the rice, wheat, and vegetables they grew on their farms.

Perhaps because the Han leaders ruled more wisely than Shi Huangdi had, their dynasty lasted about 400 years—until A.D. 220. Most Chinese people today are proud of their ancient civilization and of the contributions made during the Han dynasty in particular. As a result, many Chinese call themselves "people of the Han" in recognition of the dynasty's great achievements.

REVIEW & ASSESS

1. **READING CHECK** What government reforms did the Han rulers put in place?

2. **INTERPRET MAPS** How does the size of the Qin dynasty compare to that of the Han?

3. **COMPARE AND CONTRAST** How did the lives of poor peasants and rich merchants differ?

6.6.6 Detail the political contributions of the Han Dynasty to the development of the imperial bureaucratic state and the expansion of the empire; CST 3 Students use a variety of maps and documents to identify physical and cultural features of neighborhoods, cities, states, and countries and to explain the historical migration of people, expansion and disintegration of empires, and the growth of economic systems.

---

180 CHAPTER 7

STANDARDS

HSS CONTENT STANDARDS:

6.6.3 Know about the life of Confucius and the fundamental teachings of Confucianism and Taoism; **6.6.6** Detail the political contributions of the Han Dynasty to the development of the imperial bureaucratic state and the expansion of the empire.

HSS ANALYSIS SKILLS:

CST 3 Students use a variety of maps and documents to identify physical and cultural features of neighborhoods, cities, states, and countries and to explain the historical migration of people, expansion and disintegration of empires, and the growth of economic systems.

PLAN

OBJECTIVE

Discuss the ways in which Han dynasty rulers reformed the government, expanded the empire, and brought prosperity to China.

ESSENTIAL QUESTION

How did China establish what would become one of the world's oldest continuous civilizations?

Han rulers established a dynasty that brought reform and prosperity to China that lasted for about 400 years. Lesson 2.4 describes the achievements of Han dynasty rulers, which continue to instill pride in Chinese people today.

BACKGROUND FOR THE TEACHER

When Liu Bang died, his 15-year-old son became emperor, but the boy's mother dominated him from the beginning. Empress Lü, as his mother came to be called, had many challengers to her authority murdered, including several of her stepsons. Her actions so frightened the boy emperor that he never dared challenge her himself.

After her son died, Lü placed her grandson on the throne and adopted another child as her grandson. Both became puppet emperors while Lü ruled in their names. Lü received a marriage proposal from a nomad ruler, which was designed to join their empires and, thus, weaken her power. The empress declined the proposal but sent a Han princess to be his bride in her place.

DIGITAL RESOURCES NGLSync.cengage.com

TEACHER RESOURCES & ASSESSMENT

 Reading and Note-Taking

 Vocabulary Practice

 Section 2 Quiz

STUDENT RESOURCES

 NG Chapter Gallery

INTRODUCE & ENGAGE

THINK, PAIR, SHARE

Have students use a Think, Pair, Share strategy to discuss what they have already learned about Confucianism. Tell students that they will learn how Confucianism was implemented into Chinese government in this lesson. `0:10` minutes

TEACH

GUIDED DISCUSSION

1. **Explain** How did Han rulers integrate Confucianism into government? *(They used Confucius' teachings as a guide for their own rule and appointed only government officials who passed an examination that tested their knowledge of Confucianism.)*

2. **Summarize** Who benefited most from the prosperity brought about by the Han dynasty? *(Merchants, government workers, and craftspeople mostly benefited from the prosperity.)*

INTERPRET MAPS

Have students examine the map showing the extent of the Han and Qin dynasties and the Great Wall. Invite students to trace the dynasty boundaries and Great Wall on the map. **ASK:** In which directions did Han rulers extend the empire? *(to the south and west)* Why do you think the Great Wall did not fully extend around the borders of the Han Empire? *(Possible response: because desert and mountains provided a natural obstacle to invaders)* `0:10` minutes

ACTIVE OPTIONS

Critical Viewing: NG Chapter Gallery Invite students to explore the Chapter Gallery and choose one image they feel best represents their understanding of Section 2. Have students provide a written explanation of why they selected that particular image. `0:10` minutes

On Your Feet: Stage a Quiz Show Have each student write one question about the Han dynasty. Then have groups of five students take turns coming to the front of the class to take part in a quiz. Pose a few of the questions to each group. Students should signal their readiness to answer by raising their hands. `0:20` minutes

DIFFERENTIATE

STRIVING READERS

Understand Main Ideas Check students' understanding of the main ideas in Lesson 2.4 by asking them to correctly complete either/or statements such as the following:

1. Han rulers introduced practices that were [less cruel or more cruel] than those of Shi Huangdi.

2. Under Han rulers, Legalism was [replaced or kept] as a guide for government.

3. [Most or a small number] of the Chinese people lived in large houses in the cities during the Han dynasty.

4. The Han dynasty [lasted longer or for a briefer amount of time] than the Qin dynasty.

ENGLISH LANGUAGE LEARNERS

Use a Word Square Model for students of all proficiency levels how to use context clues to complete a Word Square, using another word in the lesson, such as *dynasty*. Then have students use context clues to complete their own Word Square for *bureaucracy*. Have students at the **Emerging** and **Expanding** levels work in pairs. Have students at the **Bridging** level work independently.

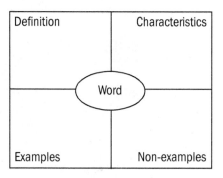

Press **mt** *in the Student eEdition for modified text.*

See the Chapter Planner for more strategies for differentiation.

REVIEW & ASSESS

ANSWERS

1. They lowered taxes, enforced lighter punishments, required shorter periods of labor on building projects, and established their government based on a bureaucracy.

2. The Han dynasty was almost twice as big as the Qin dynasty.

3. Poor farmers lived in small mud houses, had little to eat, and often had to pull their own plows. Rich merchants lived in large houses in the city, where they could eat in restaurants and enjoy entertainment.

THE LEGACY OF CHINA'S EARLY COMPASS

Over the centuries, people have used the technology behind ancient Chinese inventions to develop their own inventions. For example, this Chinese compass from the Han dynasty paved the way for the development of the items shown below. The compass wasn't used for navigation, but it did show direction. The spoon is a special type of magnet that aligns with Earth's poles and can point in the eight main directions marked on the plate.

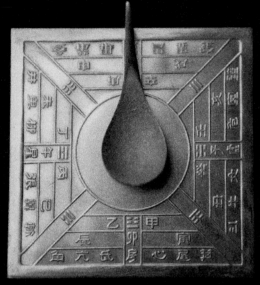

Sextant from the 1700s
Developed in the 1730s, the sextant measured the angle between a star and the horizon, enabling navigators to determine latitude.

World War II Radio Receiver
This navigational device was used on ships and planes during World War II. The device determines the direction of incoming radio signals.

Present-Day GPS Receiver
A global positioning system, or GPS, device uses satellite information to determine the location of almost any place on or near Earth.

2.5

The Legacy of
Ancient China

Ancient China's contributions to world civilization are so many and so varied that it's difficult to know where to begin. But consider that whenever you read a book, you're looking at one of China's most important inventions: paper.

MAIN IDEA

Early Chinese achievements, including inventions, cultural contributions, and ideas, left the world a lasting legacy.

INVENTIONS

Although historians believe the use of paper in China goes back even further, China is officially said to have invented paper in A.D. 105. The invention transformed writing. The ancient Chinese made paper from tree bark, plant fibers, and old rags. It was cheap to produce and easy to write on. The availability of paper allowed ideas to spread farther and faster than ever.

During the Han dynasty, the ancient Chinese also invented the first compass (shown opposite). The Chinese sometimes used the instrument to determine the best location for burials. However, this early compass would eventually lead to the development of the navigational compass, which made exploration of distant lands possible.

As you have learned, most Chinese worked as farmers. Many benefited from early agricultural inventions, such as an improved plow, a wheelbarrow, and a harness that fitted around a horse's neck.

CULTURE AND IDEAS

Not all of ancient China's contributions were strictly practical. One of its most valued inventions is the beautiful textile, or cloth, called **silk**. The Chinese developed the technique for making silk and kept it secret for thousands of years. (Hint: It had something to do with worms.) Demand for silk grew until it became China's most traded good. It is still a prized textile today.

Chinese craftspeople worked in metals as well. Remember reading about the advanced bronze sculptures developed during the Shang dynasty? Hundreds of years later, the Chinese would also teach the world to cast iron. This process involves heating iron until it becomes liquid and then pouring it into a mold to solidify into different shapes.

Finally, Chinese philosophies remain one of ancient China's greatest legacies. One of these philosophies—Confucianism—got a boost from the invention of paper. Confucian ideas were among the first spread by China's new writing material. Today, Confucianism continues to influence thinking, just as Chinese inventions make our lives easier.

REVIEW & ASSESS

1. **READING CHECK** What were a few of the inventions that ancient China contributed to world civilization?

2. **ANALYZE CAUSE AND EFFECT** What impact did agricultural advancements probably have on ancient China's food production and economy?

3. **FORM OPINIONS** Which ancient Chinese invention, cultural development, or idea do you think is the most significant? Explain your reasons.

HI 2 Students understand and distinguish cause, effect, sequence, and correlation in historical events, including the long- and short-term causal relations.

HSS ANALYSIS SKILLS:

HI 2 Students understand and distinguish cause, effect, sequence, and correlation in historical events, including the long- and short-term causal relations; **HI 3** Students explain the sources of historical continuity and how the combination of ideas and events explains the emergence of new patterns.

PLAN

OBJECTIVE

Discuss the lasting legacy of early Chinese achievements.

ESSENTIAL QUESTION

How did China establish what would become one of the world's oldest continuous civilizations?

The ancient Chinese developed important inventions and cultural ideas that continue to influence thinking today. Lesson 2.5 describes ancient China's legacy, which helped advance and strengthen Chinese civilization.

BACKGROUND FOR THE TEACHER

China's early compass was considered a divining board rather than a compass. The oval bowl that the compass rested on symbolized heaven, while the square plate represented Earth. Its primary use in ancient times was to determine the best location and time for burials. This was an important tool for a society that practiced ancestor worship. In fact, the compass was used for this purpose well into the 1800s.

The compass had other uses. For example, it was used to position buildings and furniture in ways believed to bring good luck. It was also used to predict the future. According to legend, Shi Huangdi used the compass to affirm his right to the throne.

DIGITAL RESOURCES NGLSync.cengage.com

TEACHER RESOURCES & ASSESSMENT

 Reading and Note-Taking

 Vocabulary Practice

 Section 2 Quiz

STUDENT RESOURCES

 NG Chapter Gallery

INTRODUCE & ENGAGE

DISCUSS INVENTIONS

Initiate a class discussion about inventions. Ask students to name some inventions that have had an important impact on people. Then have them discuss inventions that are important in their lives. Finally, open a book and point to a page in it. Tell students that in ancient times, paper was an important development and that the Chinese invented it. **0:10** minutes

TEACH

GUIDED DISCUSSION

1. **Summarize** What did the ancient Chinese use to make paper? *(tree bark, plant fibers, and old rags)*

2. **Make Inferences** Why do you think the Chinese kept the technique for making silk a secret? *(They kept the technique secret so that they could remain the exclusive manufacturers of silk, charge high prices for it, and use it in trade.)*

ANALYZE VISUALS STEM

Help students understand the visual in this lesson. First, read aloud the introduction. Then discuss the central image of the compass. Ask students to identify the eight directions marked on the plate. Emphasize that the magnetized spoon could point in these directions. Finally, read the labels for the smaller images and discuss the items' use. **ASK:** What do all of the items have in common with the early compass? *(They all indicate direction.)* **0:10** minutes

ACTIVE OPTIONS

Critical Viewing: NG Chapter Gallery Ask students to choose one image from the Chapter Gallery and become an expert on it. They should do additional research to learn all about it. Then, students should share their findings with a partner, small group, or the class. **0:10** minutes

On Your Feet: Inventions and Ideas Post these signs in the four corners of the classroom: paper, compass, silk, Confucianism. Have students vote for the invention or idea they think is most significant by going to the appropriate corner. Once students have made their decisions, ask each group to defend their choice. **0:20** minutes

DIFFERENTIATE

STRIVING READERS

Make an Invention Chart Help students answer the third question in "Review & Assess" by completing a chart like the one shown here as they read the lesson. Have students work in pairs to read the lesson and take notes in the chart. Then instruct them to use the chart to help them evaluate the impact of each invention and decide which invention they think was most significant.

Invention	Date	Impact

GIFTED & TALENTED

Describe Inventions Have students think of their own inventions. They might come up with a new electronic device, vehicle, or concept or an item that simply makes everyday life easier. Ask students to write a description of their invention and share it with the class.

Press **mt** *in the Student eEdition for modified text.*

See the Chapter Planner for more strategies for differentiation.

REVIEW & ASSESS

ANSWERS

1. Some inventions include paper, the compass, the plow, the wheelbarrow, and silk.

2. Agricultural advancements, such as the plow and wheelbarrow, probably made work easier for farmers and improved agricultural productivity in ancient China.

3. Responses will vary.

The Silk Roads

The desert sun beats down on your back as you trudge wearily across the sand. Peering ahead, all you see is a long line of camels, each loaded with bundles of silk. Still, you know that the profit you'll make from trading these goods will make your journey worthwhile.

MAIN IDEA

The Silk Roads were some of the world's most important international trade routes.

SILK ROADS MAIN ROUTE, 150 B.C.–A.D. 500

While crossing the deserts, camels could close their nostrils against the blowing sand.

Traders had to deal with dangerous animals along the routes, including poisonous snakes.

In time, market towns developed along the Silk Roads in places like Samarqand. Some of these, in turn, grew into great cities.

CAMELS

Camels sometimes bite and spit, but they're terrific on a long journey—like one along the Silk Roads. They can store fat in their humps and survive without eating or drinking for days. When they get a chance to drink, however, they can take in as much as 25 gallons of water at one time.

ROUTES ACROSS ASIA

You have learned about ancient China's legacy of inventions, culture, and ideas. However, a series of international trade routes called the **Silk Roads** is also one of China's great legacies. The Silk Roads had been well established by 100 B.C., but the name for the routes was coined many centuries later. A German geographer came up with the name because silk was the main good China traded on the routes. The Silk Roads brought great wealth to China and its trading partners.

The Silk Roads began as a network of local overland routes. These eventually joined to form a huge network that connected China with the rest of Asia, Europe, and Africa. The main route stretched more than 4,000 miles and ran from China through Central Asia and Mesopotamia. Other land routes branched off the main road. Some of these routes brought traders to northern India.

The Silk Roads also included **maritime**, or sea, routes. Traders could sail along these routes to the Mediterranean Sea and to Europe. Other maritime routes led across the Indian Ocean to East Africa and across the Pacific Ocean to Korea, Japan, and Southeast Asia.

A DEMANDING JOURNEY

Chinese goods might have traveled thousands of miles, but Chinese traders did not. They traded their goods somewhere around Kashgar, near China's western border. They may have passed their goods along to Central Asian nomads. The nomads, in turn, may have gone on to trade the goods with other merchants from Asia, Africa, and Europe. The goods probably changed hands so many times that no one knew where they originated.

Actually, few traders made the entire journey from one end of the main Silk Roads route to the other. The trip over the rugged terrain would have taken at least six months. At best, traders followed rough paths or tracks. At worst, they scaled ice-covered mountain passes or encountered sandstorms as they crossed scorching-hot deserts.

These difficult conditions made camels the ideal pack animals because they were strong, sure-footed, and tough. They could carry huge loads—about 400 to 500 pounds of goods—for long distances in the driest, hottest weather.

The traders on the Silk Roads usually walked alongside the camels and traveled in groups called **caravans**. They found safety in numbers. The valuable caravans created a tempting target for the bandits and thieves who often lay in wait along the routes. After all, a single camel carried more wealth than most people could possibly imagine.

REVIEW & ASSESS

1. **READING CHECK** What continents were connected by the Silk Roads?

2. **INTERPRET MAPS** Why do you think the main route of the Silk Roads divided in two between the cities of Dunhuang and Kashgar?

3. **MAKE INFERENCES** What impact do you think the Silk Roads had on China's economy?

6.6.7 Cite the significance of the trans-Eurasian "silk roads" in the period of the Han Dynasty and Roman Empire and their locations; CST 3 Students use a variety of maps and documents to identify physical and cultural features of neighborhoods, cities, states, and countries and to explain the historical migration of people, expansion and disintegration of empires, and the growth of economic systems.

HSS CONTENT STANDARDS:

6.6.7 Cite the significance of the trans-Eurasian "silk roads" in the period of the Han Dynasty and Roman Empire and their locations.

HSS ANALYSIS SKILLS:

CST 3 Students use a variety of maps and documents to identify physical and cultural features of neighborhoods, cities, states, and countries and to explain the historical migration of people, expansion and disintegration of empires, and the growth of economic systems.

PLAN

OBJECTIVE

Describe the routes and the journey involved on the Silk Roads.

ESSENTIAL QUESTION

How did China establish what would become one of the world's oldest continuous civilizations?

By 100 B.C., China had established the Silk Roads, trade routes that eventually connected China with the rest of Asia, Europe, and Africa. Lesson 3.1 describes the Silk Roads, which became some of the world's most important international trade routes.

BACKGROUND FOR THE TEACHER

The Silk Roads depended on strong governments to protect travelers and allow trade to flourish. Beyond China, empires in Persia and Rome protected the routes. When the Han dynasty declined after A.D. 204, trade fell off until the time of the Tang dynasty in the 600s to 900s.

After another period of decline, the Mongol empire of Genghis Khan in the 1200s allowed the routes to prosper. The land routes were little used after the mid-1400s. Sea trade, which was safer and faster for large cargo, then became more important.

DIGITAL RESOURCES NGLSync.cengage.com

TEACHER RESOURCES & ASSESSMENT

 Reading and Note-Taking

 Vocabulary Practice

 Section 3 Quiz

STUDENT RESOURCES

 NG Chapter Gallery

INTRODUCE & ENGAGE

ACTIVATE PRIOR KNOWLEDGE

Invite students to share what they know about camels from what they have read or seen on television or at the zoo. Ask these questions and write students' responses on the board:

- What region of the world do camels come from?
- What do camels look like?
- What do camels eat?
- What are camels used for?

Then tell students they will learn more about camels and their role on the trade routes known as the Silk Roads in this lesson. **0:10** minutes

TEACH

GUIDED DISCUSSION

1. **Make Connections** In what way were the Silk Roads a form of global economy? *(Traders from many parts of the world conducted business there.)*

2. **Make Inferences** In addition to being good businesspeople, what skills or qualities did traders on the Silk Roads probably need? *(They would have had to be tough, brave, persuasive, patient, and able to ride a camel.)*

INTERPRET MAPS

Discuss the map of the Silk Roads with students. Have students trace the route on the map and emphasize that the map shows only the main overland route of the Silk Roads. Ask students to use the distance scale to determine the length of the route. Then read aloud and discuss the captions on the map. **ASK:** What physical obstacles did the traders encounter on the main route? *(mountains and deserts)* Over what body of water might goods have traveled from Antioch? *(the Mediterranean Sea)* **0:10** minutes

ACTIVE OPTIONS

NG Learning Framework: Learn About the Silk Roads

SKILLS: Collaboration; Communication
KNOWLEDGE: Our Human Story

Have groups of students work together to create a storyboard about a caravan on the Silk Roads. For example, students might illustrate and tell the story of traders scaling a mountain, taking care of their camels, or encountering thieves. Tell students to include captions and dialogue in their storyboards. **0:10** minutes

On Your Feet: Team Word Webbing Organize students into teams of four and have them record what they know about the Silk Roads on a piece of paper. Encourage students to build on their teammates' entries as they rotate the paper from one member to the next. Then call on volunteers from each group to make statements about the Silk Roads based on their webs. **0:15** minutes

DIFFERENTIATE

STRIVING READERS

Ask and Answer Questions Have students work in pairs to understand the lesson by turning the subheadings in the lesson into questions and then reading to find the answers. Instruct students to use the words *who, what, when, where, why,* and *how* to begin their questions. For example, students might turn the subheading "Routes Across Asia" into questions such as the following:

- What were the routes across Asia called?
- How far did the routes extend?
- What were the routes used for?

PRE-AP

Map Trade Routes Have groups of students use reliable online sources to learn more about the maritime routes of the Silk Roads and other trade routes in Europe and in northern Africa. Groups should find a map of the routes to photocopy or trace. They should also learn what cities along the routes were important trading centers and what civilizations were connected by these routes. Ask students to prepare a brief report on the routes that they will deliver to the class.

Press **(mt)** in the Student eEdition for modified text.

See the Chapter Planner for more strategies for differentiation.

REVIEW & ASSESS

ANSWERS

1. Asia, Africa, and Europe were connected by the Silk Roads.

2. It divided to bypass the most difficult area of the Taklimakan Desert.

3. The Silk Roads probably greatly improved China's economy and wealth.

Trade
on the
Silk Roads

In the late 1930s, archaeologists discovered two sealed rooms in Begram, Afghanistan, an ancient city on the Silk Roads. Inside they found decorative bowls from China, ivory statues from India, and glassware from Europe. Stored away about 2,000 years ago, the objects illustrate the worldwide trade that flowed along the Silk Roads.

MAIN IDEA

Many different goods and ideas from three continents were traded on the Silk Roads.

GOODS

As you have learned, silk was China's chief trade good. Production of the fabric was not easy, though. Silk is made from the cocoons, or protective coverings, of silkworms, which live only on mulberry trees. Chinese workers had to remove strands of silk from the cocoons by hand and spin them into thread. Even so, the process was worth the trouble. Demand for the rare fabric allowed Chinese merchants to charge high prices for it. In fact, silk was so valuable that the Chinese government sometimes used it to pay its soldiers.

In addition to silk, China traded paper, highly polished decorative items called lacquerware, and objects made of iron or bronze. In return for these goods, Chinese merchants often sought gold, silver, and olive oil. One of the items the Chinese especially valued was Central Asian horses.

Market towns sprang up all along the Silk Roads. Major market towns in China included Chang'an, where the main route began, and Kashgar. A dazzling variety of items, including Central Asian rugs, Indian spices, and European wool, landed in the stalls in these towns. Traders from these and many other places used different currencies. Many had no money at all. As a result, the traders often **bartered**, or exchanged, items for other goods.

INVENTIONS AND IDEAS

Goods were not all that passed along the Silk Roads. With so many traders from so many parts of the world, the routes served as a network for the exchange of inventions and ideas as well. You have already learned that the process by which ideas spread from one culture to another is called **cultural diffusion**. By this process, Chinese ideas about papermaking, metalwork, and farming techniques began to spread beyond China's borders. In time, these ideas and inventions reached as far as Western Europe.

China also absorbed new ideas. Chief among these was Buddhism. You might remember that Buddhism began in India around 500 B.C. Indian merchants introduced Buddhist ideas to Chinese traders and even established Buddhist shrines along the Silk Roads.

Buddhism's ideas about ending suffering appealed to the Chinese, and eventually the religion became an important part of Chinese life. Many Chinese blended its practices with Confucianism. From China, Buddhism would spread throughout East Asia. Other ideas also reached China, including Greek and Indian styles in sculpture, painting, and temple building. All of these ideas enriched Chinese culture and civilization.

Critical Viewing It took artists more than 90 years to carve this Giant Buddha in southwest China, the largest carved stone Buddha in the world. What qualities does the Buddha's face convey?

➕ POSSIBLE RESPONSE

The Buddha's face seems still, peaceful, contemplative, patient, and solemn.

REVIEW & ASSESS

1. **READING CHECK** What were some of the goods and ideas exchanged on the Silk Roads?

2. **DRAW CONCLUSIONS** Why do you think Buddhism's ideas about ending suffering might have appealed to the ancient Chinese?

3. **MAKE INFERENCES** Why were Chinese traders able to demand high prices for their silk?

6.5.5 Know the life and moral teachings of Buddha and how Buddhism spread in India, Ceylon, and Central Asia; 6.6.7 Cite the significance of the trans-Eurasian "silk roads" in the period of the Han Dynasty and Roman Empire and their locations; 6.6.8 Describe the diffusion of Buddhism northward to China during the Han Dynasty.

HSS CONTENT STANDARDS:

6.6.5 Know the life and moral teachings of Buddha and how Buddhism spread in India, Ceylon, and Central Asia; **6.6.7** Cite the significance of the trans-Eurasian "silk roads" in the period of the Han Dynasty and Roman Empire and their locations; **6.6.8** Describe the diffusion of Buddhism northward to China during the Han Dynasty.

HSS ANALYSIS SKILLS:

REP 1 Students frame questions that can be answered by historical study and research.

PLAN

OBJECTIVE

Describe the goods and ideas that were traded on the Silk Roads.

ESSENTIAL QUESTION

How did China establish what would become one of the world's oldest continuous civilizations?

Many different goods and ideas were traded on the Silk Roads. Lesson 3.2 discusses the goods and ideas traded on the Silk Roads, all of which enriched Chinese culture and civilization.

BACKGROUND FOR THE TEACHER

According to legend, a Chinese queen first got the idea for making silk in the 2000s B.C. The empress was drinking tea when a silkworm cocoon from a mulberry tree fell into her cup. She picked up the cocoon and discovered that it was made of a strong, soft thread. Intrigued by the thread, the empress is said to have figured out how to extract it and invented a loom to weave it into cloth.

When production of silk first began in ancient China, only the king and his family could wear clothes made of the fabric. Eventually, members of the nobility were allowed to wear silk. However, people of the merchant and peasant class could not wear silk clothing.

DIGITAL RESOURCES NGLSync.cengage.com

TEACHER RESOURCES & ASSESSMENT

 Reading and Note-Taking

 Vocabulary Practice

 Section 3 Quiz

STUDENT RESOURCES

 Active History

INTRODUCE & ENGAGE

POSE QUESTIONS

Have students use an Idea Web like the one shown here to jot down questions about trade on the Silk Roads that they think the lesson will answer. If needed, start them off with an example, such as *What items were traded on the Silk Roads?* `0:15` minutes

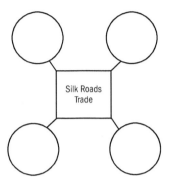

Silk Roads Trade

TEACH

STEM

GUIDED DISCUSSION

1. **Analyze Cause and Effect** Why did many traders on the Silk Roads engage in bartering? *(because traders were from different places and used different currencies and because some traders had no money at all)*

2. **Make Inferences** Why do you think market towns such as Kashgar developed into thriving cities? *(Trade brought people and wealth to the towns. In time, the towns would have grown larger and developed into cities as trade increased.)*

MORE INFORMATION

Buddhism in East Asia The branch of Buddhism mainly practiced in East Asia is Mahayana Buddhism, which teaches that ordinary people can be released from suffering without having to become monks or nuns. Buddhists in East Asia created many large sculptures of the Buddha and other wise beings called bodhisattvas (boh-duh-SUHT-vuhz). Buddhist temples are similar to Confucian and Daoist temples, and many temples contain deities from both Buddhist and Daoist traditions. Many Chinese Buddhist temples feature pagodas.

ACTIVE OPTIONS

Active History: Barter on the Silk Roads Extend the lesson by using either the PDF or Whiteboard version of the activity. These activities take a deeper look at a topic from, or related to, the lesson. Explore the activities as a class, turn them into group assignments, or even assign them individually. `0:10` minutes

On Your Feet: Inside-Outside Circle Have students stand in concentric circles facing each other. Have students in the outside circle ask students in the inside circle a question about the lesson. Then have the outside circle rotate one position to the right to create new pairings. After five questions, have students switch roles and continue. `0:15` minutes

DIFFERENTIATE

STRIVING READERS

Understand Bartering Help students understand the concept of bartering. Give students index cards or pieces of paper with names and drawings of some of the goods traded on the Silk Roads, such as silk, spices, wool, horses, gold, and olive oil. Have pairs of students trade their goods by bartering. Explain that they will decide the value of their goods and what they should receive in exchange for them. For example, in exchange for gold, students might insist on receiving silk and wool. At the conclusion of the activity, have students discuss any difficulties they encountered.

GIFTED & TALENTED

Analyze Silk Road Art Have artistically inclined students access the UNESCO World Heritage Centre website to view photos of the Buddhist carvings and paintings at the Mogao Caves and Yungang Grottoes in China. Based on their observations of ancient Indian and Chinese art in this and the previous chapter, ask students to create a brief presentation on how the Buddhist cave art illustrates a blending of South and East Asian cultures. Encourage students to include visuals in their presentation.

Press **mt** *in the Student eEdition for modified text.*

See the Chapter Planner for more strategies for differentiation.

REVIEW & ASSESS

ANSWERS

1. Goods and ideas exchanged on the Silk Roads included silk, paper, lacquerware, iron and bronze objects, papermaking, metalwork, and farming techniques from China; rugs from Central Asia; ivory, spices, and Buddhism from India; and glassware and wool from Europe.

2. Buddhism's ideas about ending suffering might have appealed to the ancient Chinese because their lives were very hard.

3. Chinese traders were able to demand high prices for their silk because China held the secret for silk production.

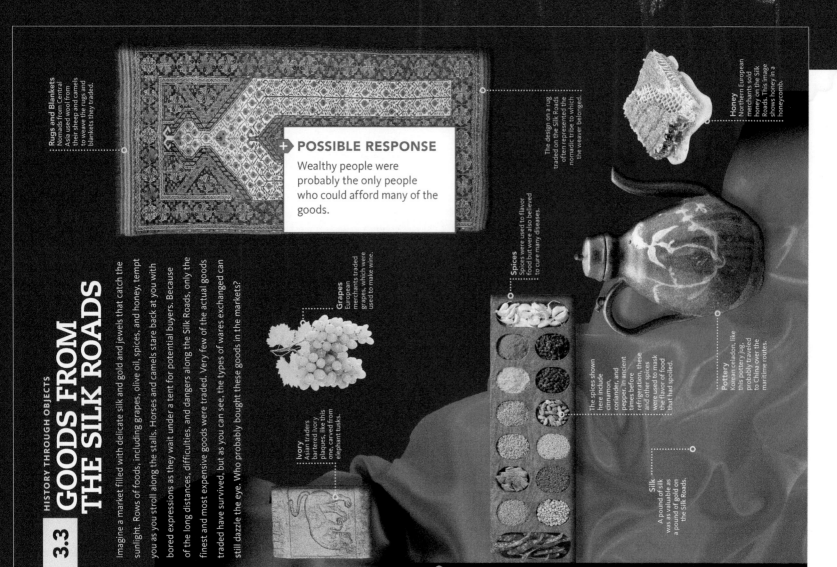

GOODS FROM THE SILK ROADS

Imagine a market filled with delicate silk and gold and jewels that catch the sunlight. Rows of foods, including grapes, olive oil, spices, and honey, tempt you as you stroll along the stalls. Horses and camels stare back at you with bored expressions as they wait under a tent for potential buyers. Because of the long distances, difficulties, and dangers along the Silk Roads, only the finest and most expensive goods were traded. Very few of the actual goods traded have survived, but as you can see, the types of wares exchanged can still dazzle the eye. Who probably bought these goods in the markets?

Rugs and Blankets
Nomads from Central Asia used wool from their sheep and camels to weave the rugs and blankets they traded.

+ **POSSIBLE RESPONSE**
Wealthy people were probably the only people who could afford many of the goods.

The design on a rug traded on the Silk Roads often represented the nomadic tribe to which the weaver belonged.

Honey
Northern European merchants sold honey on the Silk Roads. This image shows honey in a honeycomb.

Grapes
European merchants traded grapes, which were used to make wine.

Ivory
Asian traders bartered ivory plaques, like this one, carved from elephant tusks.

Spices
Spices were used to flavor food but were also believed to cure many diseases.

The spices shown here include cinnamon, coriander, and pepper. In ancient times before refrigeration, these and other spices were used to mask the flavor of food that had spoiled.

Pottery
Korean celadon, like this pottery jug, probably traveled to China over the maritime routes.

Silk
A pound of silk was as valuable as a pound of gold on the Silk Roads.

6.6.7 Cite the significance of the trans-Eurasian "silk roads" in the period of the Han Dynasty and Roman Empire and their locations.

189

STANDARDS

HSS CONTENT STANDARDS:

6.6.7 Cite the significance of the trans-Eurasian "silk roads" in the period of the Han Dynasty and Roman Empire and their locations.

HSS ANALYSIS SKILLS:

HI 6 Students interpret basic indicators of economic performance and conduct cost-benefit analyses of economic and political issues.

PLAN

OBJECTIVE

Identify some of the goods traded on the Silk Roads.

ESSENTIAL QUESTION

How did China establish what would become one of the world's oldest continuous civilizations?

Many different goods from three continents were traded on the Silk Roads. Lesson 3.3 shows some of the trade goods that enriched and influenced Chinese civilization and culture.

BACKGROUND FOR THE TEACHER

Ivory is still greatly in demand on the international market. The good is obtained mainly from elephant tusks, as it was when traders bartered it on the Silk Roads. However, in modern times, there has been an outcry against this harvesting, which results in the death of thousands of elephants every year. In 2012, more than 25,000 elephants were killed in Africa alone. In 1989, a ban on ivory trade put a halt to the killing and resulted in a rebound in the elephant population. The ban was somewhat lifted, though, in 1999 and 2008. Bowing to pressure from countries in Asia and southern Africa, sales of ivory in limited markets were allowed once again.

DIGITAL RESOURCES NGLSync.cengage.com

TEACHER RESOURCES & ASSESSMENT

 Reading and Note-Taking

 Vocabulary Practice

 Section 3 Quiz

STUDENT RESOURCES

 NG Chapter Gallery

INTRODUCE & ENGAGE

EXAMINE HISTORY THROUGH OBJECTS

Initiate a discussion about international trade today. Tell students that the goods that one country receives from another for sale or distribution are called *imports*, while those that one country sends to another for sale or distribution are called *exports*. For example, the United States imports many cars and other vehicles from other countries and exports computers around the world. Ask students if they can name other goods the United States—or another country they are familiar with—imports and exports. Point out that most of these goods arrive at their destinations on ships. Then tell students that, in this lesson, they will see some of the goods that were traded on the Silk Roads—carried on foot, on camels, or on ships. `0:05` minutes

TEACH

GUIDED DISCUSSION

1. **Form Opinions** Which item would you have been interested in buying? Explain why. *(Responses will vary. Possible response: I would have bought the rug because it is both beautiful and useful.)*

2. **Make Inferences** Which item could probably have been bartered to purchase all the other items combined? Why? *(Possible response: Silk could probably have been used to buy all the other items because it was literally worth its weight in gold.)*

ANALYZE VISUALS

Have students create a three-column chart for classifying the Silk Roads goods into the following categories: *food or drink, useful items, luxury items*. (Or, as a class, brainstorm different headings that could be used to categorize the goods.) Then have students sort the goods into the categories, writing each item in the appropriate column. Point out that some goods could belong in more than one category. End the activity by inviting volunteers to share their categories and discuss/debate any alternative categorizing. `0:15` minutes

Food or Drink	Useful Items	Luxury Items

ACTIVE OPTIONS

Critical Viewing: NG Chapter Gallery Have students examine the contents of the Chapter Gallery for this chapter. Then invite them to brainstorm additional images they believe would fit within the Chapter Gallery. Have them write a description of these additional images and provide an explanation of why they would fit within the Chapter Gallery. Then instruct them to do online research to find examples of actual images they would like to add to the gallery. `0:10` minutes

On Your Feet: Set Up a Market Photocopy full-page images of the types of goods shown in this lesson. Distribute several copies of the goods to four small groups of students. Have these groups set up a market in each corner of the classroom. Then have the remaining students act as buyers. Encourage the sellers to try to attract the buyers' interest by "pitching" their goods—extolling their value, usefulness, beauty, or flavor. The buyers should make their choices and "buy" each good with a pen, pencil, or paper clip. At the end of the activity, tally up the money to see which market sold the most goods. `0:15` minutes

DIFFERENTIATE

INCLUSION

Help Students See This lesson might pose a challenge to the visually impaired. Have students who are not visually challenged help their classmates see the goods shown in the lesson by describing them in detail—their colors, shapes, patterns, and designs. You might also bring some of the items to class so the visually impaired can feel, smell, and taste the goods, too.

PRE-AP

Research Silk Roads Goods Have students research to find out more about goods traded on the Silk Roads and where they came from. Ask students to sketch a map showing the items and their place of origin. They should also prepare a poster or digital presentation, featuring images of the goods.

Press (**mt**) *in the Student eEdition for modified text.*

See the Chapter Planner for more strategies for differentiation.

Excavating Along the Silk Roads

Fredrik Hiebert likes to challenge accepted ideas. "As an archaeologist," he says, "my main job is to try to make the textbooks go out of date. History is a living thing, and we're always rewriting it." Some of Hiebert's major excavations, or archaeological digs, have been in Turkmenistan, a country in Central Asia. Based on his discoveries there, Hiebert has concluded that traders began traveling along the Silk Roads about 4,000 or 5,000 years ago—much earlier than historians had once thought.

^ Fredrik Hiebert's study of the ancient trade routes led him to Afghanistan, where he uncovered a golden treasure. Here he examines some of the artifacts.

MAIN IDEA

Archaeologist Fredrik Hiebert's explorations have uncovered lost gold and challenged ideas about when trading began on the Silk Roads.

CONNECTED CULTURES

National Geographic Explorer Fredrik Hiebert has been conducting excavations at Silk Roads sites—like cities in Turkmenistan—for more than 20 years. "Historians thought the Silk Roads had emerged about 100 B.C.," says Hiebert. "But when we dug deeper into Silk Roads cities, we found they'd been built on much older Bronze Age settlements, which contained artifacts from as far away as India and Mesopotamia. This means that long-distance trade along the Silk Roads took place 2,000 years before we'd thought it had started."

The realization didn't surprise Hiebert. He believes that ancient cultures were always connected. "It's easy to argue that ancient cultures were isolated by geography and the lack of transport," he claims, "but that really didn't stop people from traveling and trading. They just did it more slowly."

LOST GOLD

Hiebert's explorations of the Silk Roads have also taken him to Afghanistan, which borders Turkmenistan in the south. In 1988, a Russian archaeologist told him about 21,000 pieces of ancient gold that he'd excavated ten years earlier near the Afghan region of Bactria. He later showed Hiebert photos of the collection, which came to be known as the Bactrian Hoard. The gold had belonged to nomads who herded and traded along the Silk Roads around the first century B.C. The collection

Necklace from the Bactrian Hoard

was placed in a museum in Afghanistan. However, after war erupted in the country in 1978, the gold disappeared. The Russian archaeologist believed it was lost forever.

"Fast-forward to 2003 when I heard rumors of ancient gold hidden in the Afghan presidential palace," Hiebert continues the story. "I thought: Could it be the Bactrian Hoard?" Working with the National Geographic Society, Hiebert persuaded the Afghan authorities to let him open the safes where he thought the treasure might be found. Inside were all 21,000 pieces of gold, including a necklace, shown here, that Hiebert recognized from the photos he had seen of the hoard.

"Against all odds it had survived intact, thanks to a few dedicated museum workers who had kept it secret for so many years," Hiebert says. His study of the gold revealed more evidence of cultural connections. The items were imitations of Chinese, Greek, and Indian artifacts traded on the Silk Roads. The gold is beautiful and valuable beyond measure, but that's not what most interests Hiebert. As he says, "We don't actually search for treasure. We search for knowledge—that's our real gold."

REVIEW & ASSESS

1. **READING CHECK** When does Hiebert believe trade along the Silk Roads first took place?

2. **IDENTIFY MAIN IDEAS AND DETAILS** What evidence did Hiebert find to support his ideas about cultural connections on the Silk Roads?

3. **ANALYZE LANGUAGE USE** What does Hiebert suggest about knowledge when he compares it to gold?

6.6.7 Cite the significance of the trans-Eurasian "silk roads" in the period of the Han Dynasty and Roman Empire and their locations; HI 5 Students recognize that interpretations of history are subject to change as new information is uncovered.

HSS CONTENT STANDARDS:

6.6.7 Cite the significance of the trans-Eurasian "silk roads" in the period of the Han Dynasty and Roman Empire and their locations.

HSS ANALYSIS SKILLS:

HI 5 Students recognize that interpretations of history are subject to change as new information is uncovered.

PLAN

OBJECTIVE

Describe the findings and explorations of archaeologist Fredrik Hiebert on the Silk Roads.

ESSENTIAL QUESTION

How did China establish what would become one of the world's oldest continuous civilizations?

Explorer Fred Hiebert has excavated the Silk Roads for more than 20 years. Lesson 3.4 describes the evidence he has uncovered, suggesting that trade along the Silk Roads began about 2,000 years earlier than formerly believed. This evidence indicates that China began to influence other cultures around 2000 B.C.

BACKGROUND FOR THE TEACHER

Much of the Bactrian hoard was secreted in trunks in the Central Bank treasury vault in the presidential palace. In 2001, the Taliban, which had taken control of the Afghan government, destroyed thousands of priceless items—but they didn't find everything.

In 2003, after the Taliban had been overthrown, the Central Bank announced that the trunks in the vault had not been broken into. Dr. Fredrik Hiebert and Russian archaeologist Viktor Sarianidi were both present at the opening of the vault. Sarianidi was among those who had discovered the hoard. When the vault was opened, he immediately recognized an artifact that he had repaired himself.

DIGITAL RESOURCES NGLSync.cengage.com

TEACHER RESOURCES & ASSESSMENT

 Reading and Note-Taking

 Vocabulary Practice

 Section 3 Quiz

STUDENT RESOURCES

 NG Chapter Gallery

HIDING AND FINDING A TREASURE

Ask students where they would hide a prized possession for safekeeping. Would they hide it under a bed or in a drawer? Would they bury it? Then ask students if they have ever gone on a treasure hunt. If so, how did they feel when they discovered the treasure? Tell students that, in this lesson, they will learn how a priceless golden treasure traded on the Silk Roads was hidden for years and then found. `0:05` **minutes**

TEACH   `STEM`

GUIDED DISCUSSION

1. **Explain** What evidence did Fredrik Hiebert find that suggested long-distance trade on the Silk Roads had begun 2,000 years earlier than archaeologists had thought? *(He found that Silk Roads cities in present-day Turkmenistan had been built on settlements from the later Bronze Age.)*

2. **Sequence Events** What happened shortly after a Russian archaeologist had excavated the Bactrian Hoard? *(War broke out in Afghanistan, and the hoard disappeared.)*

MAKE INFERENCES

Direct students to the quote from Fredrik Hiebert on the first page of the lesson. **ASK:** What does Hiebert mean when he says, "As an archaeologist, my main job is to try to make the textbooks go out of date"? *(Possible response: He means that he wants to find new evidence and information that challenge and overturn accepted ideas.)*
`0:10` **minutes**

ACTIVE OPTIONS

NG Learning Framework: Learn About Fredrik Hiebert

ATTITUDE: Curiosity
KNOWLEDGE: Our Human Story

Have students learn more about archaeologist Fredrik Hiebert. Instruct them to write a short biography or profile about this person using information from the chapter and additional source material.
`0:10` **minutes**

On Your Feet: Tell Me More Have students form two teams and assign each team one of the following topics: *Trade on the Silk Roads* and *Finding Hidden Gold*. Each group should write down as many facts about their topic as they can. Have the class reconvene and have each group stand up, one at a time. The sitting group calls out, "Tell me more about [Trade on the Silk Roads or Finding Hidden Gold]!" The standing group recites one fact. The sitting group should keep calling, "Tell me more!" until the standing group runs out of facts to share. Then have the groups switch places.
`0:15` **minutes**

STRIVING READERS

Use a Five-Ws Chart Students may have trouble understanding that the lesson describes the results of two different archaeological expeditions. To help students clarify and organize their reading, have them take notes for the text under each subheading using a 5Ws Chart.

What?
Who?
Where?
When?
Why?

ENGLISH LANGUAGE LEARNERS   `ELD`

Give a Thumbs Up or Thumbs Down Write a set of true-false statements about the lesson, such as "Trade along the Silk Roads began about 2,000 years before archaeologists thought it had started." Read the lesson aloud with students at all proficiency levels following along in their books. Then have them close the books and listen as you read the true-false statements. Students should give a thumbs up if a statement is true and a thumbs down if a statement is false.

Press *in the Student eEdition for modified text.*

See the Chapter Planner for more strategies for differentiation.

ANSWERS

1. He believes trade along the Silk Roads first took place about 2,000 years before originally believed.

2. In Turkmenistan, he found very early artifacts that had been made in India and Mesopotamia. In Afghanistan he found that the Bactrian gold items were local imitations of Chinese, Greek, and Indian artifacts.

3. He suggests that knowledge is as valuable as gold.

VOCABULARY

Complete each of the following sentences using one of the vocabulary words from the chapter.

1. During China's early development, physical features such as mountains and deserts helped _isolate_ China. (HSS 6.6.2)
2. The Han dynasty's government was based on a _____ run by appointed officials. (HSS 6.6.6)
3. Rather than sell silk for money, Chinese merchants would _____ it for gold. (HSS 6.6.7)
4. According to the _____, a dynasty is overthrown once it has lost the approval of the gods. (HSS 6.6)
5. Many historians believe that hundreds of thousands of _____ were forced to build the Great Wall. (HSS 6.6.5)
6. Confucius taught that children should show their parents _____. (HSS 6.6.3)
7. Traders on the Silk Roads often traveled in groups called _____. (HSS 6.6.7)

READING STRATEGY

8. **ANALYZE LANGUAGE USE** Complete your concept clusters to analyze language used to describe Confucianism, Daoism, and Legalism. Then answer the question.

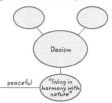

Based on the author's choice of words, how would you describe the overall theme of each philosophy? (HSS 6.6.3)

MAIN IDEAS

Answer the following questions. Support your answers with evidence from the chapter.

9. Why did civilization in ancient China first develop with relatively little cultural influence from the outside world? **LESSON 1.1** (HSS 6.6.2)
10. What was the Mandate of Heaven? **LESSON 1.2** (HSS HI 1)
11. How did Shi Huangdi organize his empire? **LESSON 2.1** (HSS 6.6.5)
12. Why did Shi Huangdi begin building the Great Wall? **LESSON 2.2** (HSS 6.6.5)
13. How did Han rulers bring Confucianism into their government? **LESSON 2.4** (HSS 6.6.6)
14. What were the benefits of traveling on the Silk Roads in camel caravans? **LESSON 3.1** (HSS 6.6.7)
15. How did trade on the Silk Roads encourage the process of cultural diffusion? **LESSON 3.2** (HSS 6.6.7)

CRITICAL THINKING

Answer the following questions. Support your answers with evidence from the chapter.

16. **ESSENTIAL QUESTION** How did China establish one of the world's oldest continuous civilizations? (HSS HI 3)
17. **DRAW CONCLUSIONS** How did the dynastic cycle help ensure the rise of new dynasties throughout China's early history? (HSS HI 2)
18. **MAKE INFERENCES** Why do you think Shi Huangdi was drawn to Legalist ideas rather than Confucian ideas? (HSS 6.6.5)
19. **COMPARE AND CONTRAST** What did the governments under the Qin and Han dynasties have in common? How did they differ? (HSS HI 2)
20. **MAKE INFERENCES** What role do you think the Silk Roads played in the Han dynasty's prosperity? (HSS 6.6.7)
21. **YOU DECIDE** Do you think Shi Huangdi was an effective emperor? Why or why not? Support your opinion with evidence from the chapter. (HSS 6.6.5)

INTERPRET MAPS

Study the map showing the spread of Buddhism. Then answer the questions that follow.

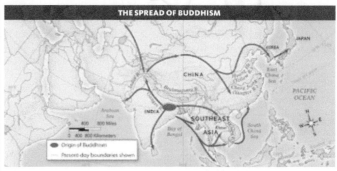

THE SPREAD OF BUDDHISM

22. Why do you think Buddhism spread to China before Korea and Japan? (HSS 6.6.8)
23. What other region shown on the map was influenced by Buddhism? (HSS CST 3)

ANALYZE SOURCES

Study this bronze statue of a flying horse, one of the finest examples of art from the Han dynasty. Then answer the question.

24. What details in the statue make it appear as if the horse is actually flying? (HSS REP 4)

WRITE ABOUT HISTORY

25. **ARGUMENT** Which Chinese philosophy might be most effective as the basis for a governing policy? Choose one of the philosophies—Confucianism, Daoism, or Legalism—and create a bulleted list of arguments you might use in a debate on the subject. (HSS REP 1)

TIPS

- Take notes from the lessons about each philosophy and its application in ancient Chinese government.
- Study the excerpt from each philosophy's teachings in Lesson 1.4.
- Consider what each philosophy offers governments and the people they rule.
- Use vocabulary terms from the chapter.
- Organize your ideas into a bulleted list of arguments. Include points that might counter, or answer, arguments proposed by the opposing side.

VOCABULARY ANSWERS

1. isolate (HSS 6.6.2)
2. bureaucracy (HSS 6.6.6)
3. barter (HSS 6.6.7)
4. dynastic cycle (HSS 6.6)
5. peasants (HSS 6.6.5)
6. filial piety (HSS 6.6.3)
7. caravans (HSS 6.6.7)

READING STRATEGY ANSWER

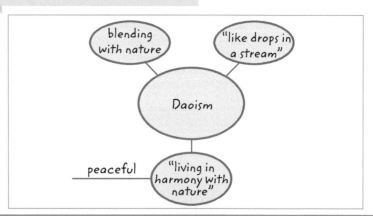

STANDARDS

HSS CONTENT STANDARDS:

6.6.2 Explain the geographic features of China that made governance and the spread of ideas and goods difficult and served to isolate the country from the rest of the world; **6.6.3** Know about the life of confucius and the fundamental teachings of Confucianism and Taoism; **6.6.5** List the policies and achievements of the emperor Shi Huangdi in unifying northern China under the Qin Dynasty; **6.6.6** Detail the political contributions of the Han Dynasty to the development of the imperial bureaucratic state and the expansion of the empire; **6.6.7** Cite the significance of the trans-Eurasian "silk roads" in the period of the Han Dynasty and Roman Empire and their locations'; **6.6.8** Describe the diffusion of Buddhism northward to China during the Han Dynasty.

HSS ANALYSIS SKILLS:

CST 3 Students use a variety of maps and documents to identify physical and cultural features of neighborhoods, cities, states, and countries and to explain the historical migration of people, expansion and disintegration of empires, and the growth of economic systems; **REP 1** Students frame questions that can be answered by historical study and research; **REP 4** Students assess the credibility of primary and secondary sources and draw sound conclusions from them, placing people and events in a matrix of time and place; **HI 2** Students understand and distinguish cause, effect, sequence, and correlation in historical events, including the long- and short-term causal relations; **HI 3** Students explain the sources of historical continuity and how the combination of ideas and events explains the emergence of new patterns.

8. Daoism: People should blend with nature; Confucianism: People should respect authority and one another; Legalism: Order comes from strong government and law enforcement. (HSS 6.6.3)

MAIN IDEAS ANSWERS

9. Civilization in ancient China developed with relatively little cultural influence from the outside world because of formidable geographical barriers that isolated much of China. (HSS 6.6.2)

10. The Mandate of Heaven was the idea that a king could rule only as long as the gods believed he was worthy. If he ruled badly, the gods would withdraw their approval, and a good ruler would overthrow him. (HSS HI 1)

11. He divided his empire into 36 areas governed by officials he had selected. (HSS 6.6.5)

12. Shi Huangdi built the Great Wall to protect China's weak northern border from attack by nomadic tribes from Central Asia. (HSS 6.6.5)

13. They only appointed government officials who had passed an exam that tested their knowledge of Confucianism. (HSS 6.6.6)

14. The camels could endure the rough conditions of the routes, and the caravans helped protect the traders from bandits and thieves. (HSS 6.6.7)

15. As people from different parts of the world came in contact with one another on the Silk Roads, they exchanged ideas, which greatly encouraged cultural diffusion. (HSS 6.6.7)

CRITICAL THINKING ANSWERS

16. In its early history, mountains and deserts protected China from invaders and isolated its people from other cultures. Strong rulers unified and expanded China's empire and established effective governments. The philosophical ideas of Confucianism, Daoism, and Legalism and the religious ideas of Buddhism strengthened government and helped stabilize society. Inventions improved all aspects of life in China and influenced other civilizations. The Silk Roads brought wealth and new ideas to China. (HSS HI 3)

17. According to the dynastic cycle, the rise and fall of dynasties was natural and the will of the gods. (HSS HI 2)

18. Shi Huangdi probably didn't believe that he needed to respect his people or lead them by his good example. He wanted to remain in control, punish those who disobeyed his laws or were opposed to him, and keep a tight rein on those beneath him. (HSS 6.6.5)

19. Governments under both dynasties were strong and expected peasants to work on building projects for the state. However, the Han emperors based their government on Confucianism rather than Legalism and were less harsh in their dealings with the Chinese people. (HSS HI 2)

20. The trade of goods it promoted—particularly China's expensive silk—must have brought in a good deal of wealth and greatly bolstered the empire's economy. (HSS 6.6.7)

21. Students' responses will vary. Students should clearly state their opinion of Shi Huangdi's effectiveness and support it with evidence from the chapter. (HSS 6.6.5)

INTERPRET MAPS ANSWERS

22. China was geographically closer to India, and Buddhism was carried along China's Silk Roads. (HSS 6.6.8)

23. Southeast Asia was also influenced by Buddhism. (HSS CST 3)

ANALYZE SOURCES ANSWER

24. Students' responses will vary. Possible response: The horse is balanced on one hoof; its other hooves are raised above the ground; the horse's tail is lifted in the air. (HSS REP 4)

WRITE ABOUT HISTORY ANSWER

25. Students' bulleted arguments should

- explain why one of the philosophies would be effective as the basis for a governing policy
- present the information clearly and logically
- include points that might counter opposing arguments
- include vocabulary words from the chapter

For more in-depth instruction and practice with the writing form, assign the Social Studies Skills Writing Lesson on writing an argument. (HSS REP 1)

UNIT RESOURCES

On Location with National Geographic Lead Program Officer Christopher Thornton
Intro and Video

Interactive Map Tool

News & Updates

Available at NGLSync.cengage.com

Unit Wrap-Up:
"Encounters with History"
Feature and Video

"China's Ancient Lifeline"
National Geographic Adapted Article

"Faces of the Divine"
National Geographic Adapted Article
Student eEdition exclusive

Unit 2 Inquiry:
Write a Creation Myth

CHAPTER RESOURCES

TEACHER RESOURCES & ASSESSMENT
Available at NGLSync.cengage.com

Social Studies Skills Lessons
• Reading: Identify Main Ideas and Details
• Writing: Write an Explanation

Formal Assessment
• Chapter 8 Tests A (on-level) & B (below-level)

Chapter 8 Answer Key

ExamView®
One-time Download

STUDENT BACKPACK *Available at NGLSync.cengage.com*
• **eEdition** *(English)*   • **eEdition** *(Spanish)*   • **Handbooks**   • **Online Atlas**
Chapter 8 Spanish resources, Guided Writing prompts, and Financial Literacy lessons are available online.

CHAPTER 8 CHAPTER PLANNER

SECTION 1 RESOURCES

THE OLMEC AND THE ZAPOTEC

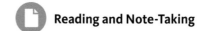 **Reading and Note-Taking**

Vocabulary Practice

Section 1 Quiz

Available at NGLSync.cengage.com

LESSON 1.1 THE GEOGRAPHY OF MESOAMERICA

- Critical Viewing: NG Chapter Gallery
- On Your Feet: Team Word Webbing

LESSON 1.2 OLMEC CULTURE

- On Your Feet: Inside-Outside Circle

NG Learning Framework:
Learn About Olmec Artists

LESSON 1.3 THE ZAPOTEC AND MONTE ALBÁN

- Critical Viewing: NG Chapter Gallery
- On Your Feet: Question and Answer

SECTION 2 RESOURCES

THE MAYA

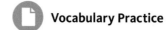 **Reading and Note-Taking**

 **Vocabulary Practice**

Section 2 Quiz

Available at NGLSync.cengage.com

LESSON 2.1 MAYA SOCIAL STRUCTURE

- On Your Feet: Model Maya Society

NG Learning Framework:
Learn About Maya Gods

LESSON 2.2 MAYA CITIES

- On Your Feet: Numbered Heads

NG Learning Framework:
Learn About Maya Daily Life

NG EXPLORER WILLIAM SATURNO
LESSON 2.3 UNCOVERING MAYA MURALS

- On Your Feet: Three-Step Interview

NG Learning Framework:
Learn About William Saturno

LESSON 2.4 LEGACY OF THE MAYA

- Critical Viewing: NG Chapter Gallery
- On Your Feet: Turn and Talk on Topic

DOCUMENT-BASED QUESTION
LESSON 2.5 CREATION STORIES

- Critical Viewing: NG Chapter Gallery
- On Your Feet: Jigsaw Strategy

CHAPTER 8 REVIEW

STRATEGY 1

Use a Word Splash

Present the words on the board in a random arrangement (splash) as shown, and ask students to choose three pairs of words that are related to each other. Have students use this sentence starter to write how each pair of words is related.

_____ and _____ are related because . . . .

cacao
maize
mother culture
Mesoamerica
terrace
Yucatan Peninsula
highland
Zapotec
lowland
slash-and-burn agriculture
Olmec

Use with Lessons 1.1–1.3

STRATEGY 2

Build an ABC Summary

For a review of the reading, suggest that students write important words from the lessons that begin with each letter of the alphabet starting with A and working through to Z, filling in as many letters as they can. Students can compare summaries.

ABC SUMMARY CHART MESOAMERICA	
A	C
B	D

Use with All Lessons *Encourage students to look beyond Key Vocabulary words and proper nouns. For example, the word* influenced *in Lesson 1.1 might help students think about how the Mesoamerican cultures developed.*

STRATEGY 3

Make a "Top Five Facts" List

Assign a lesson to be read. After reading, have students write in their own words five important facts that they have learned. Let them meet with a partner to compare lists and consolidate the two lists into one final list. Call on students to offer facts from their lists.

Use with All Lessons

Press *in the Student eEdition for modified text.*

STRATEGY 1

Provide Terms and Names on Audio

Decide which of the terms and names are important for mastery and have a volunteer record the pronunciations and a short sentence defining each word. Encourage students to listen to the recording as often as necessary.

Use with All Lessons *You might also use the recordings to quiz students on their mastery of the terms. Play one definition at a time from the recording and ask students to identify the term or name described.*

STRATEGY 2

Modify Main Idea Statements

Provide these modifications of the Main Idea statements at the beginning of each lesson:

1.1 Geography had a big impact on Mesoamerican civilizations.

1.2 The Olmec civilization was one of Mesoamerica's earliest civilizations. It influenced cultures that came later.

1.3 The Zapotec started their civilization in the Oaxaca Valley. They controlled the area for more than 1,000 years.

Use with Lessons 1.1–1.3

STANDARDS

HSS CONTENT STANDARDS:

7.7 Students compare and contrast the geographic, political, economic, religious, and social structures of the Meso-American and Andean civilizations.

ENGLISH LANGUAGE LEARNERS

STRATEGY ❶
Set Up a Word Wall

Work with students at all proficiency levels to choose three words from each lesson to display in a grouping on a Word Wall. It might be useful to choose words that students are likely to encounter in other contexts, such as *terrace* or *noble*. Keep the words displayed throughout the lessons and discuss each one as it comes up during reading. Have volunteers add words, phrases, and examples to each word to develop understanding.

Use with All Lessons, All Levels

STRATEGY ❷
PREP Before Reading

Have students at all proficiency levels use the PREP strategy to prepare for reading. Write this acrostic on the board:

PREP　　　　**P**review title.

　　　　　　　Read Main Idea statement.

　　　　　　　Examine visuals.

　　　　　　　Predict what you will learn.

Have students write their prediction and share it with a partner. After reading, ask students to write another sentence that begins, "I also learned . . ."

Use with All Lessons, All Levels *Provide the following sentence stem for students at the* **Emerging** *level: I think this lesson is about _____. Ask students at the* **Bridging** *level to give reasons for their prediction.*

STRATEGY ❸
Illustrate a Word Tree

Write the following word tree on the board to help students at all proficiency levels understand the relationship among the groups. Then ask them to copy and draw pictures to illustrate each branch of the tree.

king

priests warriors

merchants merchants craftspeople craftspeople

farmers farmers farmers slaves slaves slaves

Use with Lesson 2.1 *You might also have students at the* **Bridging** *level write sentences explaining the relationships.*

GIFTED & TALENTED

STRATEGY ❶
Teach a Class

Before beginning the chapter, allow students to choose one of the lessons listed below and prepare to teach the content to the class. Give them a set amount of time in which to present their lesson. Suggest that students think about any visuals or activities they may want to use when they teach.

Use with Lessons 1.3 and 2.2–2.4

STRATEGY ❷
Create an Early Mesoamerican Art Gallery

Have students research and find a picture of a piece of art created by each of the civilizations covered in this chapter: the Olmec, the Zapotec, and the Maya. They should find several examples and choose the piece that they like best from each civilization. Encourage them to reproduce the picture, label it, and learn as much as they can about that piece. They can create an art gallery to display as the class reads the chapter.

Use with All Lessons

PRE-AP

STRATEGY ❶
Profile a King

Have students work in groups to learn about Maya king Pacal. Have them create a profile of Pacal and illustrate it with images they find on reliable online sites.

Use with Lessons 2.1–2.5 *Encourage students to discuss Pacal's long reign, his building projects, and his tomb.*

STRATEGY ❷
Form a Thesis

Have students develop a thesis statement for a specific topic related to each of the lessons in the chapter. Be sure the statements make a claim that is supportable with evidence either from the lesson or through further research. Then have students get together in pairs to compare their statements and determine which make the strongest or most supportable claims.

Use with All Lessons

ESSENTIAL QUESTION How did the Maya adopt and adapt the cultures of earlier Mesoamerican civilizations?

SECTION 1 THE OLMEC AND THE ZAPOTEC

KEY VOCABULARY	NAMES & PLACES
cacao	Mesoamerica
highland	Monte Albán
lowland	Olmec
maize	Yucatán Peninsula
mother culture	Zapotec
slash-and-burn agriculture	
terrace	

SECTION 2 THE MAYA

KEY VOCABULARY	NAMES & PLACES
codex	El Mirador
creation story	Maya
glyph	*Popol Vuh*

READING STRATEGY

IDENTIFY MAIN IDEAS AND DETAILS
When you identify key topics in a text, you need to support them with details from the text. As you read the chapter, use diagrams like this one to identify details about each Mesoamerican civilization.

Main-Idea Diagram

Main Idea: Olmec Civilization

Detail:
Detail:
Detail:
Detail:
Detail:

The Temple of the Great Jaguar at Tikal, Guatemala, served as a tomb for a Maya ruler. Its steep staircase is divided into nine levels and may represent the nine levels of the underworld in Maya religious belief.

STANDARDS

HSS CONTENT STANDARDS:

7.7 Students compare and contrast the geographic, political, economic, religious, and social structures of the Meso-American and Andean civilizations.

TEACHER BACKGROUND

INTRODUCE THE PHOTOGRAPH

Have students study the photograph of the Maya temple in Tikal, Guatemala. Explain that the Maya and other cultures developed advanced civilizations in a region called Mesoamerica. Tell students that, in this chapter, they will learn about the rise and fall of these civilizations and their lasting legacies. Then read aloud the image caption to the class.

ASK: What feelings might this temple have inspired in Maya worshippers? (*Possible responses: awe, fear, devotion, calm*)

SHARE BACKGROUND

The Temple of the Great Jaguar was built around A.D. 700. The very steep staircase in the center of the pyramid leads to a shrine at the top of the temple. After the decline of the Maya civilization around 900, this temple and many others were hidden by dense jungle growth for centuries. The Temple of the Great Jaguar was finally uncovered by European archaeologists in the 1800s.

DIGITAL RESOURCES NGLSync.cengage.com

TEACHER RESOURCES & ASSESSMENT

 Social Studies Skills Lessons
- Reading: Identify Main Ideas and Details
- Writing: Write an Explanation

 ExamView®
One-time Download

 Formal Assessment
- Chapter 8 Tests A (on-level) & B (below-level)

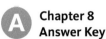 **Chapter 8 Answer Key**

STUDENT BACKPACK

- **eEdition** (*English*)
- **eEdition** (*Spanish*)
- **Handbooks**
- **Online Atlas**

INTRODUCE THE ESSENTIAL QUESTION

HOW DID THE MAYA ADOPT AND ADAPT THE CULTURES OF EARLIER MESOAMERICAN CIVILIZATIONS?

Four Corner Activity: Spread of Culture This activity allows students to discuss the ways in which culture spreads. Post the following four signs in the corners of the classroom: Immigration, Trade, Technology, War. Divide the class into four groups and have each group meet at one of the corners. Assign the following questions to the groups:

1. **Immigration:** How do immigrants spread their culture?

2. **Trade:** What types of goods and ideas can be spread by trade?

3. **Technology:** How has technology made culture spread faster?

4. **War:** How might war introduce new cultures?

Have students in each corner discuss their question. When they have finished their discussion, ask a representative from each group to summarize that group's answers. `0:15` minutes

INTRODUCE THE READING STRATEGY

IDENTIFY MAIN IDEAS AND DETAILS

Remind students that identifying main ideas and details will help them get more out of a text. Model completing the Main Idea and Details List by reading the second paragraph under "Agriculture" in Lesson 1.1 and writing "Agricultural Practices" under Main Idea, and "irrigation in drier areas" under the first Detail. Then have students identify the other details in the paragraph. For more in-depth instruction and practice with the reading strategy, assign the Social Studies Skills Reading Lesson on identifying main ideas and details.

Main Idea: Agricultural Practices
Detail: *irrigation in drier areas*
Detail:
Detail:
Detail:
Detail:

INTRODUCE CHAPTER VOCABULARY

KNOWLEDGE RATING

Have students complete a Knowledge-Rating Chart for Key Vocabulary words. Have students list words and fill out the chart. Then have pairs share the definitions they know. Work together as a class to complete the chart.

KEY VOCAB	KNOW IT	NOT SURE	DON'T KNOW	DEFINITION
cacao				
mother culture				
codex				
glyph				

KEY DATES	
c. 1300 B.C.	San José Mogote emerges as the Zapotec center of power
c. 1200 B.C.	Olmec culture begins to develop
c. 500 B.C.	The Zapotec build Monte Albán
c. 400 B.C.	Olmec civilization disappears
c. A.D. 250	The Maya Classic Period begins
c. 900	The Maya abandon many of their cities

1.1 The Geography of
Mesoamerica

You walk among the ruins, gazing at the remains of temple complexes, carved stone sculptures, and towering pyramids. Are you visiting a city that thrived during the time of ancient Egypt? No. You're in the middle of a jungle in a region of North America known as Mesoamerica.

MAIN IDEA

Geographic factors greatly influenced the development of civilizations in Mesoamerica.

HIGHLANDS AND LOWLANDS

Thousands of years ago, advanced civilizations arose in **Mesoamerica**, which stretches from southern Mexico into part of Central America. The region's climate and fertile land helped the civilizations thrive.

Mesoamerica's landscape is divided into two main geographic areas: **highlands**, or land high above the sea, and **lowlands**, or land that is low and level. The highlands lie between the mountains of the Sierra Madre, a mountain system in Mexico, and consist of fairly flat and fertile land. This land was good for agriculture, but it also posed some challenges for its early residents. They were rocked from time to time by volcanic eruptions and powerful earthquakes. The lowlands are less active. They lie along the coast of the

Gulf of Mexico. They are also found in the jungles of the **Yucatán** (you-kuh-TAN) **Peninsula**, which is located between the Gulf of Mexico and the Caribbean Sea.

If you hiked from the lowlands to the highlands, you would experience a wide variety of climates, from tropical rain forests to very cold, dry zones in the higher mountains. In general, the climate in the highlands is cooler and drier than that in the lowlands, where it can rain more than 100 inches a year. The lowlands are also crisscrossed by many rivers. Some of these rivers flood during heavy seasonal rains and wash fertile silt onto their floodplains.

AGRICULTURE

Early Mesoamerican farmers learned what crops would grow well in the different climates of the highlands and lowlands. In the drier highland areas, the main crops included **maize** (also known as corn), squash, and beans. These three crops are often called the Three Sisters because they benefit from being planted close together. The beans grow up the maize stalks, while the squash spreads over the ground, preventing the growth of weeds. Farmers in the lowlands grew these three crops as well as palm, avocado, and **cacao** (kuh-COW) trees. Cacao beans were used to make chocolate. Sometimes the beans were even used as money.

Mesoamerica's farmers developed different agricultural practices in the region's varied landscapes. In drier areas, farmers redirected the course of streams to irrigate their fields. In the dense lowland jungles, farmers cleared fields through a technique known as **slash-and-burn agriculture**, shown on the opposite page. These agricultural techniques helped ancient cultures produce food surpluses and allowed people to do jobs other than farming. As a result, civilizations began to arise in Mesoamerica more than 3,000 years ago—first the Olmec and later the Zapotec.

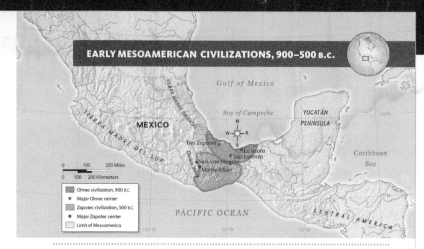

EARLY MESOAMERICAN CIVILIZATIONS, 900–500 B.C.

Olmec civilization, 900 B.C.
Major Olmec center
Zapotec civilization, 500 B.C.
Major Zapotec center
Limit of Mesoamerica

SLASH-AND-BURN AGRICULTURE

1 Slash
Wooded areas and jungles are too thick to plant crops. Farmers slash, or cut down, trees.

2 Burn
Fallen trees and leaves are burned to clear the land. Ash produced by the fires is used as fertilizer.

3 Fertilize and Plant
Cleared land is fertilized with ash. Farmers plant crops such as maize and squash.

4 Migrate
Farmers move on to new locations after soil on cleared land becomes less productive.

REVIEW & ASSESS

1. **READING CHECK** What geographic factors influenced the development of civilizations in Mesoamerica?

2. **INTERPRET MAPS** Why do you think the Olmec and Zapotec civilizations developed along coastal areas?

3. **ASK QUESTIONS** Frame a question about early farming practices in Mesoamerica that could be answered by historical research.

7.7.1 Study the locations, landforms, and climates of Mexico, Central America, and South America and their effects on Mayan, Aztec, and Incan economies, trade, and development of urban societies; CST 3 Students use a variety of maps and documents to identify physical and cultural features of neighborhoods, cities, states, and countries and to explain the historical migration of people, expansion and disintegration of empires, and the growth of economic systems; REP 1 Students frame questions that can be answered by historical study and research.

HSS CONTENT STANDARDS:

7.7.1 Study the locations, landforms, and climates of Mexico, Central America, and South America and their effects on Mayan, Aztec, and Incan economies, trade, and development of urban societies.

HSS ANALYSIS SKILLS:

CST 3 Students use a variety of maps and documents to identify physical and cultural features of neighborhoods, cities, states, and countries and to explain the historical migration of people, expansion and disintegration of empires, and the growth of economic systems; **REP 1** Students frame questions that can be answered by historical study and research.

PLAN

OBJECTIVE

Discuss how geographic factors influenced the development of civilizations in Mesoamerica.

ESSENTIAL QUESTION

How did the Maya adopt and adapt the cultures of earlier Mesoamerican civilizations?

Mesoamerica has a varied landscape, with some areas experiencing occasional volcanic eruptions and earthquakes. Lesson 1.1 describes how early Mesoamerican farmers developed different agricultural practices that were adopted and adapted by later civilizations.

BACKGROUND FOR THE TEACHER

Corn, often eaten as a vegetable, is actually a grain related to other cereal plants such as wheat and rice. Originating in the Americas, it has spread around the world and become a food staple. In addition to its many uses as human food, corn is often used as an animal feed. The United States is the world's leading producer of corn. Mexico is fourth.

The maize that was first domesticated in Mesoamerica did not look exactly like the corn we eat today. Early maize plants produced many branches on the stalks and ears that were quite small. Over time, Mesoamerican farmers learned to suppress the growth of branches, which resulted in a lower number of larger ears. Today, maize plants produce just a few ears of corn growing on a single stalk.

DIGITAL RESOURCES NGLSync.cengage.com

TEACHER RESOURCES & ASSESSMENT

 **Reading and Note-Taking**

 Vocabulary Practice

 Section 1 Quiz

STUDENT RESOURCES

 NG Chapter Gallery

INTRODUCE & ENGAGE

ANALYZE VISUALS

Have students study the illustrations of slash-and-burn agriculture. Read aloud each caption in the illustrations. **ASK:**

- How are the people using the tools in the first illustration? *(They are chopping down trees.)*
- What tasks are they doing in the second and third illustrations? *(They are burning trees and plants. They are planting crops.)*
- Why are the farmers walking away in the fourth illustration? *(The soil is not productive anymore.)*

Tell students that, in this lesson, they will learn how Mesoamerican farmers used this technique to grow abundant food. `0:05` minutes

TEACH

GUIDED DISCUSSION

1. **Compare and Contrast** How does the climate of Mesoamerica's highlands and lowlands differ? *(The climate in the highlands is generally cooler and drier than that in the lowlands, where it can rain more than 100 inches a year.)*

2. **Summarize** How did Mesoamerican farmers adapt to their environment? *(They learned what crops would grow well in the different climates. They planted crops that benefited from being planted close together. They learned how to irrigate their crops and clear their fields.)*

INTERPRET MAPS

Have students study the map of early Mesoamerican civilizations. Point out the yellow coloring that indicates the limit of Mesoamerica. Have students trace the area with a finger on the map. Tell them that the Sierra Madre del Sur, on the southwestern edge of Mexico, and the Sierra Madre Oriental, on the eastern edge, are mountain ranges. Then point out the areas where the Olmec and Zapotec civilizations arose. **ASK:** How would you describe their location in relation to each other? *(The civilizations developed very close to each other.)* Why do you think that is so? *(They both developed in advantageous areas: near the coast and in mountain valleys.)* `0:10` minutes

ACTIVE OPTIONS

Critical Viewing: NG Chapter Gallery Invite students to explore the Chapter Gallery to examine the images that relate to Chapter 8. Have them select one of the images and do additional research to learn more about it. Ask questions that will inspire additional inquiry about the chosen gallery image, such as: What is this? Where and when was this created? By whom? Why was it created? What is it made of? Why does it belong in this chapter? What else would you like to know about it? `0:10` minutes

On Your Feet: Team Word Webbing Divide the class into four groups and have them gather at desks in the four corners of the room. Give each group a large sheet of paper and different colored markers. Assign each group one of these topics: highlands, lowlands, climates, slash-and-burn agriculture. Then have the groups create a Word Web for their topic. Have them write words for their topic, adding as many circles as they need. Tell them to pass the paper to each group member and rotate it as they add to the Word Web. `0:20` minutes

DIFFERENTIATE

STRIVING READERS

Identify Main Ideas and Details Allow students to form two groups and give each group a copy of a Main Ideas and Details List. Assign each group one of the two subsections of the lesson. Have them work together to identify the main idea in their assigned section and the details that support that idea. Then guide groups in constructing a one- or two-sentence statement that unites the two main ideas. *(Sample statements: Mesoamerica is divided into highlands and lowlands, which have a variety of climates and geographic features. Mesoamerican farmers learned to adapt to their environment and lay the foundation for thriving civilizations.)*

Main Idea:
Detail:
Detail:
Detail:
Detail:
Detail:

ENGLISH LANGUAGE LEARNERS   `ELD`

Make Vocabulary Cards Have students use flash cards to learn and practice unfamiliar words they encounter in this lesson. On one side of each card, they should write the target word. On the other, they should write related words they are familiar with, draw or paste images that will help them recall the meaning of the target word, or write out other mnemonic devices. Have students at the **Emerging** and **Expanding** levels work in pairs and students at the **Bridging** level work independently. Encourage students to use their flash cards for review.

Press (**mt**) *in the Student eEdition for modified text.*

See the Chapter Planner for more strategies for differentiation.

REVIEW & ASSESS

ANSWERS

1. Geographic factors that influenced the development of civilizations in Mesoamerica include the flat, fertile land in the highlands, the rainy climate of the lowlands, and the fertile floodplains of the lowlands.

2. The Olmec and Zapotec civilizations developed along coastal areas in order to be close to water sources.

3. Students' answers will vary. Example response: What caused early Mesoamerican farmers to develop the technique of slash-and-burn agriculture?

Olmec Culture

After a long search, the foreman has finally found the right rock. It's huge and heavy. He directs his men to begin their work. Their task: to haul the rock 50 miles through the jungle to the city where an artist will carve it into a sculpture. Their challenge: to move the rock without using a wheeled cart or animals. Welcome to the world of the Olmec.

MAIN IDEA

The Olmec civilization that arose in Mesoamerica was one of the region's earliest civilizations and influenced later cultures.

JAGUAR GOD

The Olmec worshipped many gods, but one of the most important was the jaguar god. When Olmec priests visited the spirit world, the priests believed they transformed into powerful jaguars.

OLMEC CITIES

The **Olmec** (AHL-mehk) culture began along Mexico's Gulf Coast around 1200 B.C. The development of this culture led to the birth of Mesoamerica's first civilization.

Like the ancient civilizations of Mesopotamia, Egypt, India, and China, the Olmec emerged on the floodplains of rivers. Heavy rains caused these rivers to flood and deposit fertile silt on their plains. The rich soil allowed farmers to grow abundant crops. In time, the culture's economy expanded and cities, including San Lorenzo, La Venta, and Tres Zapotes, began to develop. (See the map in Lesson 1.1.)

Olmec cities contained pyramids and temples built on earthen mounds. The Olmec also built courts where athletes played a game that was a sort of combination of modern soccer and basketball. You will learn more about this game later in the chapter.

Archaeologists have also found extraordinary works of art in Olmec cities. Chief among these are the huge stone heads the Olmec carved out of rock. The heads stand as tall as 10 feet and can weigh up to 20 tons. They are believed to represent different Olmec rulers.

DAILY LIFE AND LEGACY

Workers, including those who hauled the rocks for the stone sculptures, and farmers made up most of Olmec society. They were at the bottom of the civilization's class structure. Rulers were at the top, followed by priests, merchants, and artists. The farmers and workers lived in simple houses made of wood or mud. The upper classes lived in more elaborate stone structures and wore fine clothes and precious jewelry.

Archaeologists are not sure why, but around 400 B.C., the Olmec civilization disappeared. However, elements of the civilization's legacy can be seen in later civilizations. The Olmec had established an extensive trade network. In addition to the exchange of goods, the trade routes carried Olmec culture throughout Mesoamerica. As new civilizations arose, their people were influenced by Olmec art and religious practices. As a result, many archaeologists consider the Olmec to be the **mother culture** of Mesoamerica.

Critical Viewing The rock this head was carved out of may have been rolled onto a log raft and floated downriver. Why might Olmec laborers have chosen to use this method to move the head?

+ POSSIBLE RESPONSE

It would have been much easier to transport the huge block of stone on a raft rather than push and haul it by hand.

REVIEW & ASSESS

1. **READING CHECK** What geographic features played a key role in the development of Olmec civilization?

2. **INTERPRET VISUALS** What does the stone head suggest about the power and authority of Olmec rulers?

3. **DRAW CONCLUSIONS** What conclusions can you draw about daily life for most of the Olmec people?

7.7.2 Study the roles of people in each society, including class structures, family life, warfare, religious beliefs and practices, and slavery. **199**

PLAN

OBJECTIVE

Discuss the Olmec civilization and explain how it influenced later cultures.

ESSENTIAL QUESTION

How did the Maya adopt and adapt the cultures of earlier Mesoamerican civilizations?

The Olmec developed Mesoamerica's first civilization and built elaborate cities and created great works of art. Lesson 1.2 explains how the Olmec, with their extensive trade network, spread their culture to later Mesoamerican civilizations and became the mother culture of Mesoamerica.

BACKGROUND FOR THE TEACHER

Only 17 stone Olmec heads have been uncovered, 10 of which were found in San Lorenzo and La Venta. Archaeologists have determined that each head was carved from a single basalt boulder. Experts theorize that sculptors only depicted the head because, according to Mesoamerican culture, the head was believed to be where the soul resided.

Artists carved the heads using hard stones. They used reeds and wet sand to form the eyes, nose, mouth, and ears. Originally, the heads were probably painted in bright colors, but these have long since worn off.

DIGITAL RESOURCES NGLSync.cengage.com

TEACHER RESOURCES & ASSESSMENT

 Reading and Note-Taking

 Vocabulary Practice

 Section 1 Quiz

STUDENT RESOURCES

 NG Chapter Gallery

INTRODUCE & ENGAGE

DISCUSS TERMS

Draw an Idea Web on the board and write *culture* in the center square. Ask students to volunteer what comes to mind when they hear the word *culture* and add their ideas to the web. Then tell them that the Olmec civilization became a mother culture to later Mesoamerican civilizations. Discuss the term and encourage students to identify other civilizations that have been so influential that they might be considered mother cultures. `0:10` minutes

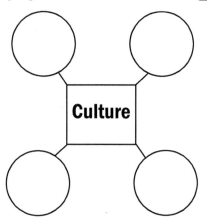

TEACH

GUIDED DISCUSSION

1. **Compare and Contrast** How was the emergence of the Olmec similar to the rise of the ancient civilizations of Mesopotamia, Egypt, India, and China? *(Like these civilizations, the Olmec emerged on the floodplains of rivers.)*

2. **Make Inferences** Which classes of Olmec society probably lived in the cities? *(probably only the upper classes, including rulers, priests, merchants, and artists)*

INTERPRET VISUALS

Have students examine the image of the Olmec head. Discuss the size, facial features, and head covering of the head. **ASK:** How would you describe the expression carved on the head? *(Possible responses: stern, serious, angry)* What might have been the purpose of the heads? *(Possible responses: to celebrate Olmec rulers, to frighten enemies, to inspire awe and respect for the rulers)* `0:10` minutes

ACTIVE OPTIONS

On Your Feet: Inside-Outside Circle Have students form concentric circles facing each other. Allow students time to write questions about the geography, cities, culture, and society of the Olmec. Ask students in the inside circle to pose questions to students in the outside circle. Then have students switch roles. Students may ask for help from other students in their circle if they are unable to answer a question. `0:20` minutes

NG Learning Framework: Learn About Olmec Artists

SKILL: Communication
KNOWLEDGE: Our Human Story

Have students imagine they are workers hauling rocks to the city so that Olmec artists can create stone heads. Ask students to write journal entries about the difficulties and challenges they encounter as they drag the rocks through the jungle. Suggest, too, that they record their experiences and conversations with the other workers. `0:10` minutes

DIFFERENTIATE

STRIVING READERS

Pose and Answer Questions Have students work in pairs to read the lesson. Instruct them to pause after each paragraph and ask each other *who, what, where, when,* or *why* questions about what they have just read.

GIFTED & TALENTED

Prepare an Interview Have pairs of students use online sources to learn more about the Olmec civilization. Then ask them to imagine that they could interview an Olmec man or woman living in an Olmec city or on a farm. Have them come up with ten questions to ask about Olmec culture and prepare the answers. Pairs should then take turns sharing several of their questions and answers with the class.

Press (**mt**) *in the Student eEdition for modified text.*

See the Chapter Planner for more strategies for differentiation.

REVIEW & ASSESS

ANSWERS

1. A geographic feature that played a key role in the development of Olmec civilization includes the floodplains of rivers, where heavy rains caused rivers to flood and deposit fertile silt along the plains.

2. The head suggests that Olmec rulers were powerful and revered.

3. Since most of the Olmec people were farmers and workers, their daily lives were probably filled with hard work and deprivation.

The Zapotec and Mixtec Civilizations

Rivera 1945

POSSIBLE RESPONSE

Members of the upper class are being served by those of the lower class and wear fancy clothes, elaborate headdresses, and shoes. Members of the lower classes kneel before those of the upper class, wear simple and minimal clothing, and are barefoot. The artists, who rank above the workers, wear more clothing as well as some pieces of jewelry.

Critical Viewing This mural by Mexican artist Diego Rivera shows Zapotec artists at work. What details in the mural convey class differences in the society?

1.3 The **Zapotec** and **Monte Albán**

As the Olmec declined, the Zapotec people were developing an advanced society to the southwest. Although their culture reflected Olmec influence, the Zapotec developed their own distinct and powerful civilization. They became a leading player in Mesoamerica.

MAIN IDEA

The Zapotec established a civilization and controlled the Oaxaca Valley for more than 1,000 years.

PEOPLE OF THE VALLEY

The **Zapotec** people would build one of the first major cities in Mesoamerica, but their beginnings were humble. They developed their society in the Oaxaca (wuh-HAH-kah) Valley, a large, open area where three smaller valleys meet. (See the map in Lesson 1.1.) This fertile area, with its river, mild climate, and abundant rainfall, proved excellent for growing crops, especially maize.

For centuries, the Zapotec lived in farming villages located throughout the Oaxaca Valley. Then, around 1300 B.C., a settlement called San José Mogote (san ho-ZAY moh-GOH-tay) emerged as the Zapotec center of power. Leaders built temples there and had artists decorate them with huge sculptures. In time, nearly half of the Zapotec people lived in San José Mogote.

URBAN CENTER

Around 500 B.C., the center of power shifted when the Zapotec built a city known now as **Monte Albán** (MAHN-tay ahl-BAHN) high atop a mountain. The site overlooked the Oaxaca Valley. Its location helped the Zapotec defend themselves against their enemies. Monte Albán must have been a spectacular sight. The city's rulers flattened the top of the mountain and built great plazas on it filled with pyramids, palaces, and even an astronomical observatory.

Monte Albán became the center of the Zapotec civilization. There, the Zapotec built magnificent tombs in which they buried the bodies of wealthy people wearing their gold jewelry. The Zapotec believed the deceased would carry the jewelry into the afterlife. Artificial **terraces**, or stepped platforms built into the mountainside, provided additional area for building and agriculture.

Around A.D. 750, Monte Albán's power began to weaken. By 900, the city had disappeared. Economic difficulties may have caused the decline, but no one knows for sure. Like the fall of the Olmec, the decline of the Zapotec civilization remains a mystery.

REVIEW & ASSESS

1. **READING CHECK** What geographic features of the Oaxaca Valley encouraged the development of the Zapotec civilization?

2. **MAKE INFERENCES** How do you think the location of Monte Albán helped the Zapotec defend themselves from their enemies?

3. **DETERMINE WORD MEANINGS** What does *deceased* mean in the phrase, "the deceased would carry the jewelry into the afterlife"?

 7.7.2 Study the roles of people in each society, including class structures, family life, warfare, religious beliefs and practices, and slavery.

201

STANDARDS

HSS CONTENT STANDARDS:

7.7.2 Study the roles of people in each society, including class structures, family life, warfare, religious beliefs and practices, and slavery.

HSS ANALYSIS SKILLS:

HI 3 Students explain the sources of historical continuity and how the combination of ideas and events explains the emergence of new patterns.

PLAN

OBJECTIVE

Explain how the Zapotec established a civilization and controlled the Oaxaca Valley for more than 1,000 years.

ESSENTIAL QUESTION

How did the Maya adopt and adapt the cultures of earlier Mesoamerican civilizations?

The Zapotec developed a powerful civilization in the Oaxaca Valley. Lesson 1.3 explains how the Zapotec lived in a fertile river valley, where they successfully grew maize, an agricultural crop that was also important to the Maya civilization that emerged around the same time in Mesoamerica.

BACKGROUND FOR THE TEACHER

Monte Albán was the first true urban center in the Americas. In 200 B.C., it was home to 15,000 people. At its peak, about 25,000 people lived in the city. Remains of the city of Monte Albán still stand. Archaeologists have studied what's left of its magnificent temples, ball courts, tombs, and works of art.

Experts have also admired Monte Albán's advanced plan and design. The city was laid out in a sophisticated grid pattern, with buildings following a strict and harmonious design. Zapotec architects even earthquake-proofed the buildings by making them solid and dense. In addition to the terraces built into the mountainside, the Zapotec developed a system of dams and conduits that carried water to agricultural areas.

DIGITAL RESOURCES NGLSync.cengage.com

TEACHER RESOURCES & ASSESSMENT

 Reading and Note-Taking

 Vocabulary Practice

 Section 1 Quiz

STUDENT RESOURCES

 NG Chapter Gallery

BUILD A CITY

Ask students to imagine that they are rulers of a developing civilization and want to build a great city to demonstrate their power. Have them discuss the following questions:

- Where would you want to build the city? Encourage students to think about the need for water sources, a good climate, and natural defenses.

- What types of buildings would your city contain? Remind students that the buildings should include those used for government, work, recreation, and residence.

- What infrastructure would the city have? Tell students that infrastructure includes roads, transportation and communication services, energy sources, and schools.

When the discussion has concluded, tell students that, in this lesson, they will learn about the Zapotec civilization, whose rulers built a city on a mountaintop that became the first urban center in Mesoamerica. `0:10` minutes

TEACH

GUIDED DISCUSSION

1. **Make Inferences** Why was Monte Albán probably a good place to build an astronomical observatory? *(The city was built on top of a mountain, so astronomers would have had a good, clear view of the stars and other heavenly bodies.)*

2. **Draw Conclusions** What aspects of Olmec culture did the Zapotec adopt? *(Like the Olmec, the Zapotec grew maize, built temples, pyramids, and ball courts, and created huge sculptures.)*

ANALYZE VISUALS

Have students examine the mural. Make sure students understand which members of society the different figures represent. **ASK:** Who are the artists? *(The artists are the modestly clothed figures who mostly appear seated in the foreground of the mural.)* What are the artists creating? *(headdresses and, possibly, paintings)* Which figures probably belong to a class beneath the artists? How can you tell? *(the figures helping the artists and kneeling in front of the figures in the background; They appear to be more subservient and are dressed only in a type of loincloth.)* What level of society do the figures trying on the headdresses probably belong to? How can you tell? *(the upper classes; They are elegantly dressed and are being waited on.)* `0:10` minutes

ACTIVE OPTIONS

Critical Viewing: NG Chapter Gallery Ask students to choose one image from the Chapter Gallery for Section 1 and become an expert on it. They should do additional research to learn all about it. Then have students share their findings with a partner, a small group, or the class. `0:10` minutes

On Your Feet: Question and Answer Have half the class write true-false questions based on information in the lesson. Ask the other half to create answer cards, with "True" written on one side and "False" on the other. As each question is read aloud, students in the second group should stand and hold up the correct answer to the question. When discrepancies occur, review the question and discuss which answer is correct. `0:15` minutes

DIFFERENTIATE

INCLUSION

Discuss Key Events Have students conduct roundtables in groups of four. Students should take turns identifying key events that shaped the rise, dominance, and fall of the Zapotec civilization. **ASK:** How would you summarize the course of the Zapotec civilization?

> The Zapotec civilization developed in the Oaxaca Valley and grew to become a leading player in Mesoamerica until it mysteriously began to decline around A.D. 750.

PRE-AP

Compare and Contrast Have students conduct online research to learn more about the Olmec and Zapotec and compare the two cultures. Have them address the following questions:

- What were some of the two cultures' religious beliefs?

- What, if any, writing system did they have?

- What artwork did they produce?

- What scientific studies did they pursue?

Ask students to present their findings to the class.

Press (**mt**) *in the Student eEdition for modified text.*

See the Chapter Planner for more strategies for differentiation.

REVIEW & ASSESS

ANSWERS

1. The Oaxaca Valley had fertile soil, a mild climate, adequate rainfall, and access to water provided by a river running through the valley.

2. From their position high atop the mountain, the Zapotec could see the enemy advancing and had time to prepare their defense.

3. The word *deceased* means "dead people."

2.1 Maya Social Structure

Can people be made of corn? According to Maya tradition, they can. But it took the Maya gods a while to figure out how to do it. At first, they made people out of things like mud and wood, but these creatures couldn't speak. Finally, the gods mixed their blood with maize flour. The result? Walking, talking human beings. No wonder the early Maya called themselves "the people of the maize."

MAIN IDEA

Maya society was structured according to a class system, and religion shaped daily life.

CLASS SYSTEM

The **Maya** emerged around the same time as the Zapotec. Their culture began to develop to the east of the Zapotec in areas of present-day southern Mexico and Central America around 1500 B.C. These areas included lowlands in the north, highlands in the south, the forests of the Yucatán Peninsula, and the tropical jungles of Mexico and Guatemala.

Like Olmec farmers, Maya farmers developed successful agricultural practices. They produced surpluses of crops, including beans, chili peppers, cacao beans, and, of course, maize, which the Maya considered sacred. These surpluses allowed some people to become priests, merchants, and craftspeople and some villages to gain great wealth. Wealthier villages with religious ceremonial centers arose around 500 B.C. In time, these villages grew into cities.

The development of Maya cities produced a class system with four main classes. At the top was the king, who performed religious ceremonies and was believed to have descended from the gods. Next came priests and warriors. The priests decided when farmers could plant and when people could marry. They also conducted important religious rituals and ceremonies. Warriors were well respected and well trained.

Merchants and craftspeople followed these upper classes. Craftspeople made articles out of pottery and designed buildings and temples. The merchants sold and traded goods—often with buyers in other Maya cities. Finally, farmers—who made up the majority of the population—and slaves were at the bottom of the heap. Most of the slaves were prisoners of war. They were given the worst jobs and were often killed when their masters died.

DAILY LIFE

Class determined where people lived and how they dressed. People who belonged to the upper classes lived in stone buildings and wore colorfully decorated clothes and jewelry. Farmers wore plain clothes and lived in mud huts.

While the wealthy enjoyed a comfortable lifestyle, farmers worked hard in the heat to grow their crops. On hillsides they carved out terraces on which to grow their maize, cacao beans, and chili peppers. In drier areas they dug channels that carried river water to their fields. In addition to doing their own work, sometimes farmers had to tend the king's fields and build monuments and temples in his cities.

MAYA MAIZE GOD
The maize god was one of the most important Maya gods. The god often appeared as a handsome young man with hair made of maize silk. The god represented the cycle of life (birth, death, rebirth) as well as the cycle of maize (planting, harvesting, replanting).

Eventually the Maya learned how to track seasonal changes. This knowledge helped them predict the best time to plant and harvest their crops. You will learn more about how the Maya measured time later in the chapter.

Above all, however, the farmers looked to their gods to control the weather and increase their harvests. Religion was central to everyone's lives, and the Maya worshipped many gods, including the gods of fire, sun, war, rain, and maize. (You can learn more about the importance of the maize god in the feature above.) All of these gods were thought to influence every aspect of the people's lives—in both good and bad ways.

To please the gods, the Maya made frequent offerings of food, animals, plants, and precious objects. As you have already learned, the Maya believed that the gods had given their blood to create people. In return, the Maya sometimes offered their own blood or made human sacrifices to honor the gods. Just as maize nourished people, the Maya believed that blood nourished the gods. Rather than sacrifice one of their own, however, the Maya often sacrificed a member of the lowest class in their society: a slave.

MAYA CIVILIZATION, A.D. 250–900

REVIEW & ASSESS

1. **READING CHECK** What were the four main classes of early Maya society?

2. **INTERPRET MAPS** On what geographic landform were many of the major Maya cities located?

3. **COMPARE AND CONTRAST** How did the daily life of farmers differ from that of people belonging to the wealthier classes?

7.7.2 Study the roles of people in each society, including class structures, family life, warfare, religious beliefs and practices, and slavery; 7.7.3 Explain how and where each empire arose and how the Aztec and Incan empires were defeated by the Spanish; CST 3 Students use a variety of maps and documents to identify physical and cultural features of neighborhoods, cities, states, and countries and to explain the historical migration of people, expansion and disintegration of empires, and the growth of economic systems.

HSS CONTENT STANDARDS:

7.7.2 Study the roles of people in each society, including class structures, family life, warfare, religious beliefs and practices, and slavery; **7.7.3** Explain how and where each empire arose and how the Aztec and Incan empires were defeated by the Spanish.

HSS ANALYSIS SKILLS:

CST 3 Students use a variety of maps and documents to identify physical and cultural features of neighborhoods, cities, states, and countries and to explain the historical migration of people expansion and disintegration of empires, and the growth of economic systems.

PLAN

OBJECTIVE

Describe the class system in Maya society and the importance of religion in daily life.

ESSENTIAL QUESTION

How did the Maya adopt and adapt the cultures of earlier Mesoamerican civilizations?

The Maya developed a social structure and worshipped many different gods. Lesson 2.1 describes the development of Maya civilization, which was similar to that of the Olmec and Zapotec.

BACKGROUND FOR THE TEACHER

Chac, the Maya god of rain and lightning, was especially revered in the Yucatán Peninsula, where rain tended to be unpredictable. However, the Maya also somewhat feared Chac, who was believed to live in the underworld. Because the Maya thought caves provided a doorway to the underworld, they often made offerings to Chac in caves. Some of these offerings were in the form of human sacrifices.

Modern Maya still sometimes appeal to Chac, particularly in times of drought. Of course, they no longer offer sacrifices to the god. Instead, they often mix water with ground corn and drink it. In some ceremonies, they also burn incense to create rain. The smoke rising from the incense is meant to symbolize rain clouds.

DIGITAL RESOURCES NGLSync.cengage.com

TEACHER RESOURCES & ASSESSMENT

 Reading and Note-Taking

 Vocabulary Practice

 Section 2 Quiz

STUDENT RESOURCES

 NG Chapter Gallery

INTRODUCE & ENGAGE

PREVIEW WITH THE VISUAL

Have students study the photograph of the Maya maize god. Read the caption aloud to the class. Explain that maize silk refers to the soft, glossy strands that surround and cling to a fresh ear of corn. Encourage students to discuss and describe the maize god. Then ask students why they think the Maya worshipped a maize god. Point out that, in this lesson, students will learn about Maya gods and religious practices. **0:05** minutes

TEACH

GUIDED DISCUSSION

1. **Make Inferences** Why do you think priests occupied such a high place in the Maya class system? *(because the Maya gods were central to Maya life and priests conducted the rituals and ceremonies honoring the gods)*

2. **Draw Conclusions** Why was it important to the Maya to please their gods? *(because the gods could influence every aspect of people's lives in both good and bad ways)*

INTERPRET MAPS

Have students study the Maya Civilization map. Point out the Yucatán Peninsula and remind students that a peninsula is a body of land that is bordered by water on three sides. Point out the major cities and archaeological sites shown on the map. Explain that dots represent the cities and small squares represent the sites. **ASK:** Which major city is located far away from most of the other cities? *(Chichén Itzá)* Between which two cities are the two archaeological sites located? *(between El Mirador and Tikal)* Tell students that they will learn about these Maya cities and archaeological sites in the next few lessons. **0:15** minutes

ACTIVE OPTIONS

On Your Feet: Model Maya Society Have students model Maya society. Have one student stand at the front of the class to represent the king. Place two students representing the priests and two students representing warriors behind the king. Next, place six students representing merchants and craftspeople after the priests and warriors. Finally, have all remaining students stand at the back of the classroom. Tell these students that they represent the farmers and slaves in Maya society.

While standing in this pyramid formation, students should describe their places in Maya society. Ask the student who holds the highest position in the society to raise his or her hand. *(the king)* Ask students who hold the lowest position to raise their hands. *(farmers and slaves)* **ASK:** What inequalities in the society do you see? *(Most of the people belong in the bottom class and have no power.)* **0:20** minutes

NG Learning Framework: Learn About Maya Gods

ATTITUDE: **Curiosity**
SKILLS: **Communication, Collaboration**

Have groups of five students research to learn about five important Maya gods. Each student in a group should then pick one of the gods and take turns presenting him or her to the class. Students should provide the god's name, explain what the god represented, and tell how the god was worshipped. **0:10** minutes

DIFFERENTIATE

STRIVING READERS

Take Notes Have students take notes as they read the lesson by completing a chart like the one shown below. Allow students to compare their completed charts in small groups and make any necessary corrections. Then call on volunteers to use their charts to summarize what they know about Maya society and daily life.

	Class and Role	Daily Life
King		
Priests and Warriors		
Merchants and Craftspeople		
Farmers and Slaves		

ENGLISH LANGUAGE LEARNERS `ELD`

Read in Pairs Pair students at the **Emerging** and **Expanding** levels with native English speakers and have them read the lesson together. Instruct the native speakers to pause whenever they encounter a word or sentence construction that is confusing to their partners. Suggest that the native speakers point out context clues to help their partners understand the meanings of unfamiliar terms. Encourage English language learners to restate sentences in their own words.

Press **mt** *in the Student eEdition for modified text.*

See the Chapter Planner for more strategies for differentiation.

REVIEW & ASSESS

ANSWERS

1. The four main classes included the king, priests and warriors, merchants and craftspeople, and farmers and slaves.

2. Many were located on the Yucatán Peninsula.

3. Wealthy people lived in stone buildings and wore colorfully decorated clothes and jewelry. Farmers wore plain clothes and lived in mud huts. While the wealthy enjoyed a comfortable lifestyle, farmers worked hard to grow their crops.

Maya Cities

In the 1800s, explorers battled mosquitoes, illness, and thick jungle growth in their search for the ruined remains of the Maya civilization. Their efforts paid off. When they came upon the half-buried monuments in the ancient Maya city of Copán, one of the explorers—John Lloyd Stephens—was so fascinated by what he saw that he purchased the site on the spot.

MAIN IDEA

The Maya built sophisticated cities that contained impressive structures and artwork.

CLASSIC PERIOD

Many of the great Maya cities lay hidden beneath the jungle growth for centuries. One of the earliest of these cities was **El Mirador**, which has been called the "cradle of the Maya civilization." (See the map in Lesson 2.1.) The city flourished from about 300 B.C. to A.D. 150 and was home to as many as 200,000 people. Most Maya cities, however, developed during the Classic Period, which lasted between A.D. 250 and 900. These cities included Copán (koh-PAHN), Tikal (tee-KAHL), Chichén Itzá (chee-CHEHN ee-TSAH), and Palenque (pah-LEHNG-keh). Although

each was an independent city-state ruled by a king, trade linked the city-states. Merchants from the cities exchanged goods such as salt and jade jewelry and often paid for them with cacao beans.

Most Maya cities followed a similar layout. A large plaza in the center of the city served as both a public gathering place and market. Each city also contained a palace for the king, administrative buildings, temples, and stepped pyramids. The pyramids rose hundreds of feet in the air and were lined with steep staircases. Many of the pyramids featured platforms at the top. Priests conducted ceremonies on the platforms so that the entire population could witness them.

The Maya built temples on the top of some of the pyramids. A huge ball court was constructed at the foot of at least one of these pyramids in each city to allow athletes to play the sacred Mesoamerican ball game. The Maya played this game, which began with the Olmec, to honor their gods. The illustration on the opposite page shows Maya athletes in action on the court.

CULTURE AND ART

Like the ball game, many other aspects of Maya culture and art were linked to religion. Artists made sculptures that honored and brought to life the various Maya gods. They also carved stone slabs called stelae to honor their kings. Artists carved a king's likeness on the slab and recorded his actions on it as well—actually setting his story in stone.

All of these stories were probably passed down orally from generation to generation. This oral tradition continued long after the great Maya civilization had come to an end. It may have been weakened by war, food shortages, or overcrowding. For whatever reason, by A.D. 900, the Maya had abandoned many of their cities. When Spanish conquerors arrived in the 1500s, only weakened city-states had been left behind—a shadow of their former glory.

MESOAMERICAN BALL GAME

The game the Maya and other Mesoamerican peoples played on a court like this one was much more than a game. It was often a matter of life and death. The captain of the losing Maya team probably climbed the temple steps to be sacrificed to the gods.

Players weren't allowed to touch the ball with their hands. They could only bounce the ball off their knees, hips, and elbows.

The solid ball was hard enough to break bones, so the players wore some heavy padding.

The goal of the game was to launch the ball through a stone ring. Since this wasn't easy, a game could go on for days.

REVIEW & ASSESS

1. **READING CHECK** What was the layout of most of the great Maya cities?

2. **INTEGRATE VISUALS** Based on the illustration and what you have learned about the Mesoamerican ball game, what qualities were probably necessary to play the game?

3. **MAKE INFERENCES** How do you think the Maya reacted as they witnessed a religious ceremony performed at the top of a towering pyramid?

7.7.2 Study the roles of people in each society, including class structures, family life, warfare, religious beliefs and practices, and slavery; 7.7.4 Describe the artistic and oral traditions and architecture in the three civilizations.

STANDARDS

HSS CONTENT STANDARDS:

7.7.2 Study the roles of people in each society, including class structures, family life, warfare, religious beliefs and practices, and slavery; **7.7.4** Describe the artistic and oral traditions and architecture in the three civilizations.

PLAN

OBJECTIVE

Describe the cities, structures, and art of the Maya in the Classic Period.

ESSENTIAL QUESTION

How did the Maya adopt and adapt the cultures of earlier Mesoamerican civilizations?

The Maya built sophisticated cities and created impressive artwork. Lesson 2.2 describes the influence of the Olmec on Maya structures and culture.

BACKGROUND FOR THE TEACHER

The Mesoamerican ballgame, sometimes called *pok-a-tok*, may have been the first team sport in human history. The game was played on an I-shaped court painted in bright colors. When the ball players made their ceremonial entrance onto the court, they wore elaborate headdresses, animal skins, and jewelry. To play the game, however, they wore minimal clothing.

The life-and-death game was surrounded by religious ritual and symbolism. The Maya and other Mesoamerican peoples believed that sacrificing a member of the losing team would help ensure plentiful crops or rain. Human sacrifice wasn't always performed, but it occurred often enough to have been recorded and celebrated in the paintings and stelae of various cultures.

DIGITAL RESOURCES NGLSync.cengage.com

TEACHER RESOURCES & ASSESSMENT

 Reading and Note-Taking

 Vocabulary Practice

 Section 2 Quiz

STUDENT RESOURCES

 NG Chapter Gallery

ACTIVATE PRIOR KNOWLEDGE

Invite students to share what they know about the pyramids of ancient Egypt from their knowledge of world history. Ask these questions and write students' responses on the board:

- What did the pyramids in ancient Egypt look like?
- Where were they located?
- What were the pyramids used for?
- What happened to the pyramids after the power of ancient Egypt declined?

Then ask students if they know about pyramids located in other places. Tell them that they will learn about the pyramids built by the Maya in this lesson. **0:10** minutes

TEACH

GUIDED DISCUSSION

1. **Draw Conclusions** Why do you think the market occupied a central place in most Maya cities? *(because trade was so important to the Maya)*

2. **Sequence Events** What happened around A.D. 900? *(The Maya abandoned many of their cities.)*

INTERPRET VISUALS

Review the illustration of the Mesoamerican ball game with students in class. Read aloud the introduction and captions. Have students study the stone ring in the illustration and invite students to imagine how difficult it must have been to launch a ball through it. Then point out the athlete in the illustration bouncing the hard rubber ball off of his hip. Remind students that, in an earlier lesson, they learned that the Mesoamerican ball game has some aspects in common with basketball and soccer. **ASK:** In what ways is the Mesoamerican game similar to basketball and soccer? *(In basketball, players try to throw a ball through a hoop. In soccer, most players are not allowed to touch the ball with their hands.)* **0:10** minutes

ACTIVE OPTIONS

On Your Feet: Numbered Heads Organize students into groups of four. Tell students to think about and discuss a response to this question: *What were important elements of Maya civilization?* Then call a number and have the student from each group with that number report for the group. **0:15** minutes

NG Learning Framework: Learn About Maya Daily Life

SKILLS: Observation, Collaboration
KNOWLEDGE: Our Human Story, Our Living Planet

Have students revisit Lessons 2.1 and 2.2 to put together a complete picture of the Maya. Ask students to focus on the following topics: geographic challenges, agriculture, class system, daily life, cities, religion, and art. Students should work in groups, with each member choosing a topic. Have students become an expert in their chosen topic and then take turns presenting what they've learned to the class. **0:10** minutes

STRIVING READERS

Summarize Have students complete a graphic organizer like the one shown to keep track of important details about Maya cities as they read the lesson. Then have students form pairs and use their completed charts to summarize what they learned about Maya cities.

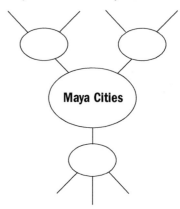

Maya Cities

PRE-AP

Create a Multimedia Presentation Have students research to find information about some aspect of the Maya, such as religion, architecture, the writing system, or the Mesoamerican ball game. Tell students to create a multimedia display that uses text and images to describe their findings. Allow them to draw the images if they wish. Encourage students to share their presentations with the class.

Press **mt** *in the Student eEdition for modified text.*

See the Chapter Planner for more strategies for differentiation.

ANSWERS

1. Most Maya cities included a palace for the king, administrative buildings, temples, and stepped pyramids.

2. Qualities such as exceptional athletic skill, endurance, strength, bravery, intense religious feeling, and self-sacrifice were probably necessary.

3. The people were probably awestruck, deeply inspired, and made more devout by the spectacle.

Uncovering Maya Murals

Sometimes you're just lucky. Ask William Saturno. He had spent three days—instead of the three hours he thought the trip would take—trudging through the jungles of Guatemala looking for carved Maya monuments. During the search, he and his team had been lost and near death. When a pyramid appeared in the midst of the dense undergrowth, Saturno ducked inside it to escape the terrible heat. He turned around to find a stunning Maya mural of the maize god right back at him. Now Saturno's lucky find is rewriting Maya history.

^ William Saturno is dedicated to preserving and interpreting the remains of the early Maya. In this photo, he removes debris from a mural he uncovered at the Maya site of Xultún.

MAIN IDEA

Archaeologist William Saturno's discoveries have challenged ideas about the early Maya and provided insight into their way of thinking.

A LUCKY FIND

National Geographic Explorer William Saturno has spent his life studying the Maya and searching out the civilization's secrets. His greatest discovery occurred in 2001, when he found the mural at a site he later named San Bartolo.

Saturno spent several years excavating the wall painting, which represented the Maya creation story in graceful and sophisticated detail. However, when Saturno dated the work of art, he found that it had been created around 100 B.C.—more than 300 years before the Maya Classic Period had even begun. As Saturno says, "Clearly Maya painting had achieved glory centuries before the great works of the Classic Maya."

The far end of the mural revealed another surprise—the portrait of a king. "Some scholars thought that at this early stage in Maya history, the Preclassic, city-states had not yet evolved into full-fledged monarchies, with all the trappings seen later," explains Saturno. "But here was a king, named and titled, receiving his crown. In short, this one chamber upended much of what we thought we knew about the early Maya."

ROOM OF WONDER

About ten years later and just five miles from San Bartolo, Saturno got lucky again. He was digging under a mound in the Maya site of Xultún (shool-tuhn) when a

student assistant claimed he'd found traces of paint on a wall. "I was curious," Saturno says. "So I excavated to the back wall, and I saw a beautiful portrait of a king. There he was in Technicolor, with blue feathers."

After more painstaking work, Saturno uncovered an entire room with paintings of other figures and a wall covered with columns of numbers. He thinks that mathematicians had been using the walls like a whiteboard to see whether the movements of the moon and planets matched the dates they had calculated. The mural and numbers dated back to about A.D. 750, around the time Xultún was beginning to decline.

Portrait of a scholar in the San Bartolo mural

According to Saturno, the Maya knew the collapse of their city had begun. Still, as he says, "They wanted to tie events in their king's life to larger cosmic cycles. They wanted to show that the king would be okay and that nothing would change. We keep looking for endings. It's an entirely different mind-set. I would never have identified this nondescript [uninteresting] mound as special. But this discovery implies that special things are everywhere."

REVIEW & ASSESS

1. **READING CHECK** Why are William Saturno's discoveries so remarkable?

2. **DRAW CONCLUSIONS** Saturno emphasizes the luck he's had in his explorations, but what other qualities must he possess to carry out his work?

3. **ANALYZE LANGUAGE USE** Saturno says that the Maya had "an entirely different mind-set." What do you think he is suggesting about how the Maya viewed the world?

7.7.4 Describe the artistic and oral traditions and architecture in the three civilizations; HI 5 Students recognize that interpretations of history are subject to change as new information is uncovered.

HSS CONTENT STANDARDS:

7.7.4 Describe the artistic and oral traditions and architecture in the three civilizations; **7.7.5** Describe the Meso-American achievements in astronomy and mathematics, including the development of the calendar and the Meso-American knowledge of seasonal changes to the civilizations' agricultural systems.

HSS ANALYSIS SKILLS:

HI 5 Students recognize that interpretations of history are subject to change as new information is uncovered.

PLAN

OBJECTIVE

Discuss how archaeologist William Saturno's discoveries are challenging ideas about the early Maya.

ESSENTIAL QUESTION

How did the Maya adopt and adapt the cultures of earlier Mesoamerican civilizations?

William Saturno discovered early Maya murals that had been hidden for many centuries. Lesson 2.3 describes the ways in which Saturno's findings have provided insight into Maya culture and their view of the world.

BACKGROUND FOR THE TEACHER

William Saturno believes that the Maya artists who painted the murals at San Bartolo began their artistic training when they were young. Saturno believes that the artists probably worked day and night on the masterpiece, both by the light of torches and by morning sunshine.

When the artists finished, their murals covered at least two walls of a room at the pyramid's base. Saturno says, "The masterpiece had two purposes: to honor the gods and to illustrate that the king derived his power from those gods." In time, however, a new king came to power, and a new pyramid was built on top of the older one. That's how the murals came to be hidden until Saturno found them more than 2,000 years later.

DIGITAL RESOURCES NGLSync.cengage.com

TEACHER RESOURCES & ASSESSMENT

 Reading and Note-Taking

 Vocabulary Practice

 Section 2 Quiz

STUDENT RESOURCES

 NG Chapter Gallery

DISCUSS IMPORTANT FINDINGS

Initiate a class discussion about findings—their own and those in history. Ask students to think of a time when they found something that had been missing or lost or that had meaning for them. Invite them to share how they felt when they made their discovery. Then see if students can identify some important findings in history, such as the discovery of King Tut's tomb in Egypt or Columbus' voyage to the Americas. Tell students that, in this lesson, they will learn about an archaeologist who uncovered Maya murals that had been hidden for centuries. `0:05` minutes

TEACH

`STEM`

GUIDED DISCUSSION

1. **Summarize** What did Saturno's findings at the archaeological site of San Bartolo reveal about the Maya? *(They had been creating great works of art and were under the rule of monarchs before the Maya Classic Period.)*

2. **Draw Conclusions** What do the columns of numbers Saturno uncovered at Xultún suggest about Maya mathematicians? *(They were very advanced.)*

SYNTHESIZE

Divide the class into groups of four students. Each group should analyze Saturno's explorations in San Bartolo and Xultún, synthesizing information in Lesson 2.3. Have students record their findings in a chart like the one shown and use the information to answer the "Reading Check" question in Review & Assess. `0:10` minutes

SAN BARTOLO	XULTÚN

ACTIVE OPTIONS

On Your Feet: Three-Step Interview Have students work in pairs to discuss the third question in Review & Assess. Ask students what they think William Saturno means when he says that the Maya had "an entirely different mind-set." As pairs conduct their interviews, tell them to use more detailed questions about the quotation. For example: "What do you think *mind-set* means?" "What is our modern mind-set?" "What was the Maya mind-set?" Remind students to listen closely as their partner answers so that they can report what they hear to the rest of the class. `0:20` minutes

NG Learning Framework: Learn About William Saturno

ATTITUDE: **Curiosity**
KNOWLEDGE: **Our Human Story**

Have students learn more about William Saturno. Instruct them to write a short biography about the archaeologist using information from the chapter and additional source material. `0:10` minutes

INCLUSION

Clarify Text Have visually impaired students work with sighted partners. As they listen to an audio recording of the text, have the visually impaired students indicate if there are words or passages they do not understand. Their partners can clarify meaning by repeating passages, emphasizing context clues, and paraphrasing.

GIFTED & TALENTED

Write an Explorer Blog Ask students to imagine that they are archaeologists exploring Maya archaeological sites where they make a great discovery. Ask them to write a brief blog about their experiences at the site, the challenges they face searching for it, and their thoughts and emotions when they make their discovery.

> Just made the discovery of a lifetime!

Press **mt** in the Student eEdition for modified text.

See the Chapter Planner for more strategies for differentiation.

REVIEW & ASSESS

ANSWERS

1. Before the discovery at San Bartolo, archaeologists had thought that great works of Maya art had only been produced during the Classic Period. Archaeologists also didn't believe that city-states had evolved into monarchies before the Classic Period.

2. Possible responses include intelligence, a deep interest and love of the past, perseverance, skill, patience, enthusiasm, tenacity, empathy, and optimism.

3. He is suggesting that the Maya believed the world would continue, that there would be cycles—new beginnings, but never endings.

Legacy of the Maya

In 2012, the prediction went viral: On December 21, the world was going to end. The prediction was based on the Maya calendar, which some people claimed would end on that day. But the date simply marked the completion of a 5,125-year cycle. The Maya had calculated that a new cycle would begin on the 22nd.

MAIN IDEA

Important advances in mathematics, astronomy, and writing allowed the Maya to create their calendar.

The Maya calendar is actually a system of several calendars used together to track days and cycles. Glyphs, like those you see here, represent days and months in the complex calendar.

MAYA NUMBERS

The Maya represented numbers using only three symbols: a shell for zero, a dot for one, and a bar for five. A few of the numbers are shown above. Try using the symbols to create some simple subtraction problems.

0	1
2	5
6	10

MATH AND ASTRONOMY

The Maya were superb mathematicians. Like the people of ancient India, they developed the concept of zero. They also developed a sophisticated number system using positions to show place value and to calculate sums up to the hundreds of millions.

Such calculations were used to record astronomical observations as well. Maya astronomers observed the sun, moon, planets, and stars and were able to predict their movements with great accuracy—all without the aid of any instruments. Instead, they studied the sky from temples and observatories. Astronomers used their observations to calculate the best times for planting and harvesting crops and for religious celebrations.

These astronomical observations and calculations were used to develop an elaborate 365-day calendar that was nearly as accurate as our own. Remember the room that William Saturno uncovered in Xultún? The mathematical calculations on its walls were probably used to work out dates in the calendar.

WRITING SYSTEM AND BOOKS

Archaeologists gained a better understanding of the Maya people's scientific achievements and culture once they began to crack the code of their writing system. The Maya used symbolic pictures called **glyphs** (glihfs) to represent words, syllables, and sounds that could be combined into complex sentences.

The Maya carved glyphs into their monuments, stelae, and tombs. Maya writers, called scribes, also used them to record their people's history in a folded book made of tree-bark paper called a **codex**. The Spanish conquerors destroyed most of the codices in the 1500s. However, after the Spanish arrived, the Maya wrote other books in which they recorded Maya history and culture. The most famous of these books is called the **Popol Vuh**, which recounts the Maya creation story.

As you've already learned, the Maya civilization had greatly declined by A.D. 900. However, Maya people today still keep their culture alive. Many of them speak the Maya languages and tell their ancestors' stories. They are a living legacy of the Maya civilization.

REVIEW & ASSESS

1. **READING CHECK** What important mathematical ideas did the Maya develop?

2. **IDENTIFY MAIN IDEAS AND DETAILS** According to the text, why did Maya astronomers study the sun, moon, planets, and stars?

3. **ANALYZE CAUSE AND EFFECT** What breakthrough helped archaeologists gain a better understanding of Maya history and culture?

7.7.5 Describe the Meso-American achievements in astronomy and mathematics, including the development of the calendar and the Meso-American knowledge of seasonal changes to the civilizations' agricultural systems; HI 2 Students understand and distinguish cause, effect, sequence, and correlation in historical events, including the long- and short-term causal relations.

HSS CONTENT STANDARDS:

7.7.4 Describe the artistic and oral traditions and architecture in the three civilizations;
7.7.5 Describe the Meso-American achievements in astronomy and mathematics, including the development of the calendar and the Meso-American knowledge of seasonal changes to the civilizations' agricultural systems.

HSS ANALYSIS SKILLS:

REP 1 Students frame questions that can be answered by historical study and research;
HI 2 Students understand and distinguish cause, effect, sequence, and correlation in historical events, including the long- and short-term causal relations.

PLAN

OBJECTIVE

Describe the important advances the Maya made in mathematics, astronomy, and writing.

ESSENTIAL QUESTION

How did the Maya adopt and adapt the cultures of earlier Mesoamerican civilizations?

Earlier Mesoamerican civilizations left many cultural legacies, and the Maya left a great legacy in mathematics and science. Lesson 2.4 describes the Maya number system and the accuracy of the observations made by Maya astronomers.

BACKGROUND FOR THE TEACHER

Before archaeologists cracked the code of the Maya writing system, many researchers believed the ancient civilization was a peaceful one. They believed the Maya were farmers who were ruled by wise astronomer-priests. Once archaeologists learned to read the glyphs, however, they discovered that the Maya were as warlike and political as any civilization. New technologies are helping them learn even more. For example, using electron microscopes and satellites, archaeologists have made images of raised highways built by the Maya. In time, they hope that all their questions about the Maya will be answered.

DIGITAL RESOURCES NGLSync.cengage.com

TEACHER RESOURCES & ASSESSMENT

 Reading and Note-Taking

 Vocabulary Practice

 Section 2 Quiz

STUDENT RESOURCES

 NG Chapter Gallery

INTRODUCE & ENGAGE

CALCULATE LIKE THE MAYA

Copy the Maya numbers from the lesson on the board and explain them to the class. Then jot down a couple of simple addition and subtraction problems using the numbers and challenge students to solve them. Finally, ask volunteers to write their own math problems on the board using the Maya numbers. Invite other students to come up and write the answers. **0:10** minutes

TEACH

GUIDED DISCUSSION

1. **Make Inferences** Why do you think the Maya recorded their history and culture after the Spanish conquered them? *(They didn't want their culture to disappear without a trace.)* As an extension, have students read the Maya account of the Spanish Conquest in the **Primary Source Handbook** and answer the questions.

2. **Summarize** Where have archaeologists found Maya glyphs? *(on Maya calendars, monuments, stelae, tombs, and in codices)*

MORE INFORMATION

December 21, 2012 The world didn't come to an end on this date, but it was still a very important one for the Maya. They believed that, on that day, the gods who created the world would return. The gods would conduct certain rites and set space and time in order. In other words, the Maya believed the world would be renewed on December 21, 2012, not destroyed.

ACTIVE OPTIONS

Critical Viewing: NG Chapter Gallery Invite students to explore the Chapter 8 Gallery to examine the images that relate to this section. Have them select one of the images and do additional research to learn more about it. Ask questions that will inspire additional inquiry about the chosen gallery image, such as: What is this? Where and when was this created? By whom? Why was it created? What is it made of? Why does it belong in this chapter? What else would you like to know about it? **0:10** minutes

On Your Feet: Turn and Talk on Topic Have students form four lines. Give each line the same topic sentence: *The Maya civilization left a great legacy.* Tell groups to build a paragraph on that topic by having each student in each line add one sentence about a different achievement of the Maya civilization. Finally, have groups present their paragraphs to the class, with each student reading his or her sentence. **0:15** minutes

DIFFERENTIATE

STRIVING READERS

Create Charts Provide students with a three-column chart with the heads *Math, Astronomy,* and *Writing,* similar to the one shown below. Have them work in pairs to fill out the chart with information from the lesson on Maya achievements in these areas.

MATH	ASTRONOMY	WRITING

ENGLISH LANGUAGE LEARNERS

Use Sentence Strips Choose a paragraph from the lesson and make sentence strips out of it. Read the paragraph aloud, having students follow along in their books. Then have students close their books and give them the set of sentence strips. Students should put the strips in order and then read the paragraph aloud. Have students at the **Emerging** and **Expanding** levels work in pairs and students at the **Bridging** level work independently.

Press **(mt)** *in the Student eEdition for modified text.*

See the Chapter Planner for more strategies for differentiation.

REVIEW & ASSESS

ANSWERS

1. They developed the concept of zero and a sophisticated number system using positions to show place values.

2. They studied the sun, moon, planets, and stars to calculate the best times for planting and harvesting crops and for religious celebrations. They used this information to develop their elaborate calendar.

3. Cracking the code of the Maya writing system helped them gain a better understanding of Maya history and culture.

Creation Stories

Every culture has a **creation story**: an account that explains how the world began and how people came to exist. Creation stories are often considered sacred and are usually passed down by oral tradition before they are written down. Like the excerpts you are about to read, creation stories often begin by describing how a god or gods brought order to the universe.

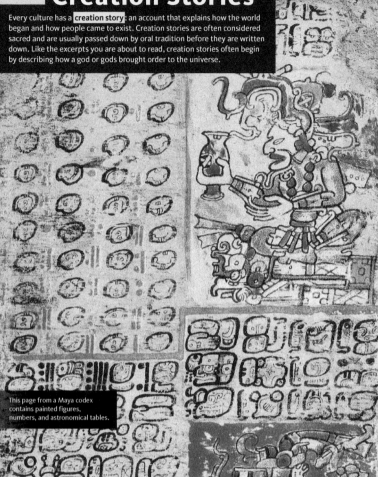

This page from a Maya codex contains painted figures, numbers, and astronomical tables.

DOCUMENT ONE
Primary Source: Sacred Text

from the *Popol Vuh*,
translated by Dennis Tedlock
Spanish conquerors destroyed much of Maya culture in the 1500s. To preserve their sacred stories for future generations, Maya scribes wrote them down in the *Popol Vuh*. In this passage, two Maya gods form Earth from a world that contains only the sea.

CONSTRUCTED RESPONSE According to this passage, how did the Maya gods form Earth?

"Let it be this way, think about it: this water should be removed, emptied out for the formation of the earth's own plate and platform . . ." they said. And then the earth arose because of them, it was simply their word that brought it forth. For the forming of the earth they said, "Earth." It arose suddenly, just like a cloud, like a mist, now forming, unfolding.

DOCUMENT TWO
Primary Source: Sacred Text

from the Book of Genesis
Genesis is the first book of the Hebrew Bible, a collection of sacred Jewish texts. It is also the first book of the Old Testament in the Christian Bible. Followers of both religions believe in a single God. In this passage from Genesis, which means "the origin, or beginning," God creates night and day.

CONSTRUCTED RESPONSE In this excerpt, what was the world like before God brought light to the earth?

When God began to create heaven and earth—the earth being unformed and void [empty] . . .—God said, "Let there be light"; and there was light. God saw that the light was good, and God separated the light from the darkness. God called the light Day, and the darkness He called Night. And there was evening and there was morning, a first day.

DOCUMENT THREE
Primary Source: Myth

from *Pan Gu Creates Heaven and Earth*,
translated by Jan and Yvonne Walls
Pan Gu is a god in an ancient Chinese creation story that has been told and passed down for more than 2,000 years. According to the story, Pan Gu created heaven and earth. In this passage, Pan Gu bursts from a disordered universe that is shaped like an egg.

CONSTRUCTED RESPONSE In this myth, what elements formed heaven and what elements formed the earth?

Pan Gu, an enormous giant, was being nurtured [cared for] in the dark chaos of that egg. . . . Then one day he woke and stretched himself, shattering the egg-shaped chaos into pieces. The pure lighter elements gradually rose up to become heaven and the impure heavier parts slowly sank down to form the earth.

SYNTHESIZE & WRITE

1. **REVIEW** Review what you have learned about the creation stories and religious beliefs of early civilizations.

2. **RECALL** On your own paper, write down the main idea expressed in each document.

3. **CONSTRUCT** Write a topic sentence that answers this question: What are some common characteristics of creation stories?

4. **WRITE** Using evidence from the documents, write a paragraph to support your answer in Step 3.

7.7.4 Describe the artistic and oral traditions and architecture in the three civilizations; REP 4 Students assess the credibility of primary and secondary sources and draw sound conclusions from them.

211

HSS CONTENT STANDARDS

7.7.4 Describe the artistic and oral traditions and architecture in the three civilizations.

HSS ANALYSIS SKILLS:

REP 4 Students assess the credibility of primary and secondary sources and draw sound conclusions from them.

PLAN

OBJECTIVE

Synthesize information about creation stories from three sacred texts.

ESSENTIAL QUESTION

How did the Maya adopt and adapt the cultures of earlier Mesoamerican civilizations?

Every culture has a creation story that explains how the world began and people came to exist. Lesson 2.5 provides creation stories from three different cultures, including the Maya.

BACKGROUND FOR THE TEACHER

According to the *Popol Vuh*, the first four humans who could speak were given godlike powers. The people could speak the language of the gods. They could also see beyond Earth to the heavens and knew what had happened at the beginning of time and would occur at its end. Soon, however, the gods decided that they didn't want humans to be their equals. As a result, the gods limited human speech, sight, and knowledge.

DIGITAL RESOURCES NGLSync.cengage.com

TEACHER RESOURCES & ASSESSMENT

 Reading and Note-Taking

 Vocabulary Practice

 Section 2 Quiz

STUDENT RESOURCES

 NG Chapter Gallery

INTRODUCE & ENGAGE

PREPARE FOR THE DOCUMENT-BASED QUESTION

Before students start on the activity, briefly preview the three documents. Remind students that a constructed response requires full explanations in complete sentences. Emphasize that students should use what they have learned about the Maya in addition to the information in the documents. As an extension, have students read the additional excerpt from the *Popol Vuh* in the **Primary Source Handbook** and answer the questions.
`0:05` minutes

TEACH

GUIDED DISCUSSION

1. **Identify** According to the excerpt from the *Popol Vuh*, what did Earth look like as it arose? *(like a mist or cloud unfolding)*

2. **Compare and Contrast** How is God's formation of light in the Bible excerpt similar to how the Maya gods form Earth in the *Popol Vuh*? *(Both light and Earth are formed when the words are spoken.)*

3. **Make Connections** What does the description in the Chinese creation story of Pan Gu's bursting from an egg remind you of? *(Possible response: of a chick being hatched from an egg; of birth; of life)*

EVALUATE

After students have completed the "Synthesize & Write" activity, allow time for them to exchange paragraphs and read and comment on the work of their peers. Guidelines for comments should be established prior to this activity so that feedback is constructive and encouraging in nature.
`0:15` minutes

ACTIVE OPTIONS

Critical Viewing: NG Chapter Gallery Have students examine the contents of the Chapter Gallery for this chapter. Then invite them to brainstorm additional images they believe would fit within the Chapter Gallery. Have them write a description of these additional images and provide an explanation of why they would fit within the Chapter Gallery. Then instruct them to do online research to find examples of actual images they would like to add to the gallery. `0:10` minutes

On Your Feet: Jigsaw Strategy Organize students into three "expert" groups and have students from each group analyze one of the documents and summarize the main ideas of the teaching in their own words. Then have the members of each group count off using the letters A, B, C, and so on. Regroup students into three new groups so that each new group has at least one member from each expert group. Have students in the new groups take turns sharing the simplified summaries they came up with in their expert groups. `0:10` minutes

DIFFERENTIATE

INCLUSION

Put It Together Help students minimize distractions by typing the three excerpts on one sheet of paper. Give photocopies of these to students along with highlighters. Tell students to highlight important words that appear in all three documents. Then have them write a summary sentence using several of the words.

PRE-AP

Research Creation Stories Ask students to research the creation stories of other cultures. For example, students might study the creation stories of Native American tribes, including the Hopi and Cherokee. They might also read creation stories from Japan and India. Encourage students to find similarities between the creation stories they find and those in this lesson. Students should share the results of their research with the class.

Press (mt) in the Student eEdition for modified text.

See the Chapter Planner for more strategies for differentiation.

CONSTRUCTED RESPONSE

ANSWERS
DOCUMENT 1
They formed Earth by removing and emptying out the water and calling forth the earth.

DOCUMENT 2
It was formless, empty, and dark.

DOCUMENT 3
Pure lighter elements rose up to become heaven. Impure heavier parts sank down to form the earth.

SYNTHESIZE & WRITE

ANSWERS
1. Responses will vary.

2. Responses will vary.

3. Possible response: In many creation stories, gods form Earth out of emptiness, darkness, or chaos.

4. Students' paragraphs should include their topic sentence from Step 3 and provide several details from the documents to support the sentence.

8 Review

VOCABULARY

On your paper, match the vocabulary word in the first column with its definition in the second column.

WORD	DEFINITION
1. terrace (HSS 7.7.1)	a. a civilization that greatly influences other civilizations
2. mother culture (HSS HI 3)	b. a stepped platform built into a mountainside
3. codex (HSS 7.7.4)	c. a symbolic picture used to represent a word, syllable, or sound
4. glyph (HSS 7.7.4)	d. land high above the sea
5. maize (HSS 7.7.1)	e. a folded book made from tree-bark paper
6. highland (HSS 7.7.1)	f. corn

READING STRATEGY

7. IDENTIFY MAIN IDEAS AND DETAILS If you haven't already, complete your diagram for each early Mesoamerican civilization. Then answer the question.

Main-Idea Diagram

Main Idea: Olmec Civilization
Detail: Developed along a floodplain
Detail:
Detail:
Detail:
Detail:

What feature do you think was the greatest legacy of each civilization? Explain. (HSS 7.7.5)

MAIN IDEAS

Answer the following questions. Support your answers with evidence from the chapter.

8. What agricultural techniques helped early Mesoamericans produce food surpluses? **LESSON 1.1** (HSS HI 1)

9. Why is the Olmec civilization considered to be Mesoamerica's mother culture? **LESSON 1.2** (HSS HI 3)

10. Why is Monte Albán considered one of the first major cities in Mesoamerica? **LESSON 1.3** (HSS 6.2.2)

11. Which groups of people made up the largest social class in the Maya civilization? **LESSON 2.1** (HSS 7.7.2)

12. During what time period did most of the great Maya cities develop? **LESSON 2.2** (HSS CST 2)

13. What ideas about the early Maya did William Saturno's discoveries change? **LESSON 2.3** (HSS HI 5)

14. What did the Maya use to develop their elaborate 365-day calendar? **LESSON 2.4** (HSS 7.7.5)

CRITICAL THINKING

Answer the following questions. Support your answers with evidence from the chapter.

15. **ESSENTIAL QUESTION** How did the Olmec civilization influence the Maya civilization? (HSS HI 3)

16. **ANALYZE CAUSE AND EFFECT** What happened as a result of the Olmec's trade network? (HSS 7.7.1)

17. **DRAW CONCLUSIONS** What conclusions can you draw about cacao beans based on the fact that the Maya often used them to pay for goods? (HSS 7.7.2)

18. **COMPARE AND CONTRAST** What are some of the similarities surrounding the decline of the Zapotec and Maya civilizations? (HSS HI 2)

19. **MAKE CONNECTIONS** How did the Mesoamerican ball game differ from today's game of soccer? (HSS HI 2)

20. **YOU DECIDE** What do you think is the Maya civilization's greatest legacy? Support your opinion with evidence from the chapter. (HSS 7.7.5)

INTERPRET VISUALS

Study the images of a Maya pyramid and an ancient Egyptian pyramid. Then answer the questions that follow.

Maya pyramid

Egyptian pyramid

21. How are the pyramids alike, and how do they differ? (HSS HI 2)

22. What challenges did both pyramid styles present to the people who built them? (HSS HI 2)

ANALYZE SOURCES

This jade mask was placed over the face of King Pacal, a great ruler of Palenque, when he died. The mask shows the king's own features.

23. The Maya highly valued jade and often used it to represent the maize god. Study the mask. Why do you think the Maya associated jade with the maize god? (HSS 7.7.4)

WRITE ABOUT HISTORY

24. EXPLANATORY How were the Olmec, Zapotec, and Maya civilizations similar? How did they differ? Write an essay comparing and contrasting the civilizations for tourists who are planning to visit some of the civilizations' archaeological and historic sites. Use the tips below to help you plan, organize, and revise your essay. (HSS HI 2)

TIPS

- Take notes from the lessons about the three civilizations. You might jot down your comparisons in a chart.
- State your main idea clearly at the beginning of the essay. Support your main idea with relevant facts, details, and examples.
- Use vocabulary from the chapter in your essay.
- Provide a concluding statement about the similarities and differences among the Olmec, Zapotec, and Maya civilizations.
- Use word-processing software to produce and publish your final essay.

213

VOCABULARY ANSWERS

WORD	DEFINITION
1. terrace — b (HSS 7.7.1)	a. a civilization that greatly influences other civilizations
2. mother culture — a (HSS HI 3)	b. a stepped platform built into a mountainside
3. codex — e (HSS 7.7.4)	c. a symbolic picture used to represent a word, syllable, or sound
4. glyph — c (HSS 7.7.4)	d. land high above the sea
5. maize — f (HSS 7.7.1)	e. a folded book made from tree-bark paper
6. highland — d (HSS 7.7.1)	f. corn

STANDARDS

HSS CONTENT STANDARDS:

6.2.2 Trace the development of agricultural techniques that permitted the production of economic surplus and the emergence of cities as centers of culture and power; **7.7.1** Study the locations, landforms, and climates of Mexico, Central America, and South America and their effects on Mayan, Aztec, and Incan economies, trade, and development of urban societies; **7.7.2** Study the roles of people in each society, including class structures, family life, warfare, religious beliefs and practices, and slavery; **7.7.4** Describe the artistic and oral traditions and architecture in the three civilizations; **7.7.5** Describe the Meso-American achievements in astronomy and mathematics, including the development of the calendar and the Meso-American knowledge of seasonal changes to the civilizations' agricultural systems.

HSS ANALYSIS SKILLS:

CST 2 Students construct various time lines of key events, people, and periods of the historical era they are studying; **REP 4** Students assess the credibility of primary and secondary sources and draw sound conclusions from them; **HI 1** Students explain the central issues and problems from the past, placing people and events in a matrix of time and place; **HI 2** Students understand and distinguish cause, effect, sequence, and correlation in historical events, including the long- and short-term causal relations; **HI 3** Students explain the sources of historical continuity and how the combination of ideas and events explains the emergence of new patterns; **HI 5** Students recognize that interpretations of history are subject to change as new information is uncovered.

READING STRATEGY ANSWER

Main-Idea Diagram

Main Idea: Olmec Civilization

| Detail: Developed along a floodplain |
| Detail: Became Mesoamerica's first civilization |
| Detail: Built cities with pyramids, temples, and ball courts |
| Detail: Civilization mysteriously disappeared |
| Detail: Considered mother culture of Mesoamerica |

7. Students' responses will vary. Possible response: The Olmec left their greatest legacy in religion and art. The greatest legacy of the Zapotec was Monte Alban. The Maya left their greatest legacy in mathematics and science. (HSS 7.7.5)

MAIN IDEAS ANSWERS

8. Agricultural techniques such as irrigation and slash-and-burn agriculture helped early Mesoamericans produce food surpluses. (HSS HI 1)

9. It is considered to be Mesoamerica's mother culture because later Mesoamerican civilizations adopted and adapted many aspects of Olmec civilization, including religion and art. (HSS HI 3)

10. It is considered one of the first major cities because it was a major center of power, because it contained many monumental structures, and because it had such a big population. (HSS 6.2.2)

11. Farmers and slaves made up the largest social class. (HSS 7.7.2)

12. Most of the great Maya cities developed during the Classic Period, which lasted from about A.D. 250 to 900. (HSS CST 2)

13. William Saturno's discoveries changed many ideas about the early Maya, including that they created great works of art hundreds of years before the Classic Period. His discoveries also revealed that city-states had evolved into monarchies before the Classic Period. (HSS HI 5)

14. They used astronomical observations and mathematical calculations. (HSS 7.7.5)

CRITICAL THINKING ANSWERS

15. Considered to be the mother culture of Mesoamerica, the Olmec civilization influenced the Maya civilization in many ways, including the development of successful agricultural practices and crop surpluses, which led to the growth of cities, class structure, religion, and art and architecture, including the building of pyramids and temples. (HSS HI 3)

16. The trade routes spread Olmec civilization throughout Mesoamerica. As later civilizations arose, their people adopted aspects of Olmec culture. (HSS 7.7.1)

17. Possibly because the trees were hard to grow or produced few beans, cacao beans were considered as valuable as money. (HSS 7.7.2)

18. The causes for the declines are not known, and both civilizations fell at around the same time. (HSS HI 2)

19. The Mesoamerican ball game had one distinctive difference from today's soccer game: it was often a matter of life and death, with the losing team's captain often sacrificed to the gods. Similar to today's soccer game, the Mesoamerican ball game was played with a solid ball and players weren't allowed to touch the ball with their hands. (HSS HI 2)

20. Students' responses will vary. Some students may say that introducing the concept of zero to the Americas is the Maya's greatest legacy. (HSS 7.7.5)

INTERPRET MAPS ANSWERS

21. The pyramids have the same shape, with outer surfaces forming triangles. The Egyptian pyramid has smooth sides and comes to a point at the top. The Maya pyramid has steep outer steps on each side, and its top is flat. (HSS HI 2)

22. Complex mathematical calculations had to be made to get the proportions right. Both pyramid styles were built without the use of machines. People had to haul and raise the building materials by hand and using ropes. (HSS HI 2)

ANALYZE SOURCES ANSWER

23. Students' responses will vary. Possible response: The green color of the jade may have reminded them of young, growing corn. (HSS 7.7.4)

WRITE ABOUT HISTORY ANSWER

24. Students' essays should do the following:

- compare and contrast aspects of the Olmec, Zapotec, and Maya civilizations
- support the comparison with relevant facts, details, and examples
- be written in a formal style
- include vocabulary words from the chapter
- provide a concluding statement about the similarities and differences among the civilizations

For more in-depth instruction and practice with the writing form, assign the Social Studies Skills Writing Lesson on writing an essay. (HSS HI 2)

ON **LOCATION** WITH

Christopher
THORNTON

**NATIONAL GEOGRAPHIC LEAD PROGRAM OFFICER,
RESEARCH, CONSERVATION, AND EXPLORATION**

▶ Check out more at NGLSync.Cengage.com

Christopher Thornton directs
excavations at the archaeological
site of Bat in Oman. He has
uncovered information that is
providing new insights into the
social history of the region.

EARLY PASSION

I'd always planned to major in chemistry in college, but in my freshman year, I took a seminar on archaeological chemistry and got hooked! From that moment on, archaeology became my passion and my career.

Today I specialize in late prehistory in Southwest Asia, from the beginning of agriculture to the rise of empires. I love working in this region because, while people's lives have been modernized, their cultures remain fairly traditional. You get a sense of "the old ways" while still enjoying hot showers!

Chris Thornton works near a 4,500-year-old Bronze Age monument in northwestern Oman at the site of Bat.

DIGGING FOR CLUES

Because this region had very limited literacy during the late prehistoric and early historic periods, it needs an archaeologist's eye to investigate and figure out what was going on then. One of the key questions I'm trying to answer is how and why people living in harsh regions like present-day Oman managed to create relatively large settlements 4,000 years ago but, 1,000 or so years later, were content to live in much smaller areas. A clue lies in copper.

Mesopotamian texts from the Bronze Age refer to modern Oman as "Magan," noting that it was then a major producer of copper for the entire region. Most archaeologists believed that the people of Magan were being exploited by traders from Mesopotamia and the Indus Valley. However, for nine years, my team and I have been excavating a site called Bat in northwestern Oman. In the course of our digs, we've discovered not only evidence of copper production, but also indications of the local use of copper in tools, weapons, and jewelry. This suggests that despite the harsh geography of the region, the people of Magan were a very important part of the Bronze Age economic trade networks that led to the rise of cities. This puts a whole new slant on the history of the region.

Now we hope to find clues that will help us understand how the adoption of farming led to early settled villages in Magan, and how these eventually grew into the large centers we find by 2200 B.C. These are the kind of answers we keep digging for.

WHY STUDY HISTORY ❓

❝ History helps us *to understand the similarities* between apparently different nations, peoples, and cultures. Studying history lets us look back on all that we have accomplished and to consider where we are going now! ❞ —Christopher Thornton

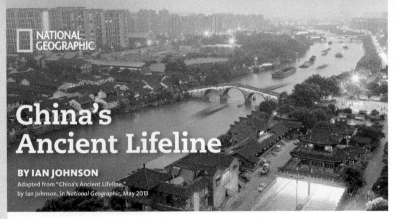

NATIONAL GEOGRAPHIC

China's Ancient Lifeline

BY IAN JOHNSON

Adapted from "China's Ancient Lifeline,"
by Ian Johnson, in *National Geographic*, May 2013

Barges sailing the Grand Canal have knit China together for 14 centuries. They carried grain, soldiers, and ideas between the economic heartland in the south and the political capitals in the north.

Old Zhu, as everyone calls him, is a modern barge captain. Barge captains live by tough calculations that determine whether they get rich or are ruined. One captain said, "The product owners set the price, the moneylenders set the interest, and the government officials set the fees. All we can do is nod and continue working."

On paper, the Grand Canal runs 1,100 miles between Beijing and the southern city of Hangzhou. But for nearly forty years, part of its course has been too dry for shipping. Today, the waterway's main commercial section is the 325 miles from Jining to the Yangtze.

Emperor Yang of the Sui dynasty built the original canal system. Ancient China's main rivers ran west to east, and he needed a way to move rice from south to north to feed his armies. The emperor forced one million workers to build the canal. It took six years to complete and many workers died, but goods began to flow. The Grand Canal also moved culture. Emperors inspecting the canal took some local customs back to the capital.

Along one section, Old Zhu pointed and said, "That's the old Grand Canal, or what's left of it," pointing to a channel about 15 feet wide curving between a small island and the bank. Today, local governments aim to boost tourism and development by beautifying the canal. But beautification can also destroy. In Yangzhou, the makeover required leveling nearly every canal-side building.

In 2005, a small group of citizens campaigned for the Grand Canal to become a UNESCO World Heritage site. "Every generation wants the next generation to look at its monuments," said Zhu Bingren, who co-wrote the proposal. "But if we wipe out the previous generations' work, what will following generations think of us?"

For more from National Geographic
Check out "Faces of the Divine" at NGLSync.Cengage.com

UNIT INQUIRY: WRITE A CREATION MYTH

In this unit, you learned about the development of early civilizations in Mesopotamia, Egypt, India, China, and Mesoamerica. Based on your understanding of the text, what crucial roles did geography and natural resources play in the development of early civilizations? What other factors were important to their growth and longevity?

ASSIGNMENT Write a creation myth for one of the civilizations you learned about in this unit. The narrator of your creation myth should be a geographic feature or a natural resource—such as a river—that was vital to the civilization's development. Be prepared to present your creation myth to the class and explain your choice of narrator.

Plan As you write your creation myth, think about the essential roles geography and natural resources played in that civilization's development. To describe the civilization, answer from the narrator's point of view the questions *Who? What? Where? When? Why?* and *How?* Try to incorporate these descriptions in your myth. You might want to use a graphic organizer to help organize your thoughts. ▶

Produce Use your notes to produce detailed descriptions of the factors that were important in the development of the civilization you selected. Begin your creation myth with an engaging introduction to capture your audience's attention.

Present Choose a creative way to present your myth to the class. Consider one of these options:

- Create a multimedia presentation using illustrations or photographs of the civilization's geography to produce a sense of place.

- Dress in costume and play the role of an ancient storyteller for an oral presentation of the myth.

- Illustrate cover art featuring the narrator of the creation myth.

Who?	_____
What?	_____
Where?	_____
When?	_____
Why?	_____
How?	_____

RAPID REVIEW UNIT 2

EARLY CIVILIZATIONS

TOP TEN

1. Farming in the fertile lands of Mesopotamia led to the emergence of city-states such as Sumer and Ur.

2. The fertile farmland along the Nile River enabled the development of ancient Egyptian civilization.

3. Judaism was the first monotheistic religion.

4. Several important religions developed in India, including Hinduism and Buddhism.

5. Ancient China spread innovative forms of government, philosophy, technology, writing, and art via trade routes.

6-10. **NOW IT'S YOUR TURN** Complete the list with five more things to remember about early civilizations.

POSSIBLE RESPONSES

Possible responses for the remaining five things to remember:

6. Rulers in ancient China believed they had divine authority but that the people had the right to rise up and replace them.

7. Mesopotamia's city-states were centers of learning, commerce, religion, and culture.

8. Pharaohs ruled with absolute authority and were believed to be intermediaries with ancient Egyptian gods.

9. Because their homeland was repeatedly conquered, Jews dispersed around the world.

10. Nomadic Aryans who brought their language, religious beliefs, and class system, replaced the Harappan civilization in India's Indus Valley.

UNIT INQUIRY PROJECT RUBRIC

ASSESS

Use the rubric to assess each student's participation and performance.

SCORE	ASSIGNMENT	PRODUCT	PRESENTATION
3 GREAT	• Student thoroughly understands the assignment. • Student engages fully with the project process. • Student works well independently.	• Creation myth is well thought out. • Creation myth reflects the essential roles played by geography and natural resources in the selected civilization's development. • Creation myth contains all of the key elements listed in the assignment.	• Presentation is clear, concise, and logical. • Presentation does a good job of creatively presenting the creation myth. • Presentation engages the audience.
2 GOOD	• Student mostly understands the assignment. • Student engages fairly well with the project process. • Student works fairly independently.	• Creation myth is fairly well thought out. • Creation myth somewhat reflects the essential roles played by geography and natural resources in the selected civilization's development. • Creation myth contains some of the key elements listed in the assignment.	• Presentation is fairly clear, concise, and logical. • Presentation does an adequate job of creatively presenting the creation myth. • Presentation somewhat engages the audience.
1 NEEDS WORK	• Student does not understand the assignment. • Student minimally engages or does not engage with the project process. • Student does not work independently.	• Creation myth is not well thought out. • Creation myth does not reflect the essential roles played by geography and natural resources in the selected civilization's development. • Creation myth contains few or none of the key elements listed in the assignment.	• Presentation is not clear, concise, or logical. • Presentation does not creatively present the creation myth. • Presentation does not engage the audience.

TURN AND TALK

One of the themes in this Why Study History? text is "establishing identity." Write the word *identity* in the center of a Concept Cluster circle and draw lines coming out from the circle. Ask volunteers to add words that relate to and help define the concept of identity. Then place students in small groups and have them discuss what their own personal identity means to them and how they make their identity known to others.

WHY STUDY HISTORY ?

TO LEARN ABOUT THE BUILDING BLOCKS OF CIVILIZATION

In Units 1 and 2, you've learned about the origins of culture and how the building blocks of civilization allowed humans to move from individuals struggling to survive to groups creating a life together. All early civilizations faced the same challenges—and the urge to establish an identity was key to their survival.

The record of human occupation involves the study of stones, bones, and artifacts that go back hundreds of thousands of years. Archaeologists rely on that record to learn about the way we've lived on this earth. Artifacts represent people's identity. When an artifact is looted, or excavated illegally, we lose the context for that artifact—where it was found and who created it. It becomes lost to history. The human record is a non-renewable resource that can never be replaced.

Fred Hiebert
▶ Watch the Why Study History video

PREVIEW
UPCOMING UNITS

Have students examine the images at the bottom of the Why Study History? spread, and read the labels on each photograph. Invite volunteers to make observations and predictions about what the upcoming units (3–4) will bring.

WHAT COMES NEXT? PREVIEW UNITS 3–4

3

ACROPOLIS

4

POMPEII

GREEK CIVILIZATION

Learn how the Greeks left a legacy in government, art, and architecture that would have an impact on all civilizations.

THE WORLD OF THE ROMANS

See how the Roman developments in government, engineering, and religion continue to affect your life today.

KEY TAKEAWAYS UNITS 1 AND 2

PATTERNS IN HISTORY: SIMILAR DEVELOPMENTS ACROSS LOCATIONS

All centers of civilization develop the same basic structures:

- the beginnings of social organization that lead to governments
- origins of religion as a way to make sense of the world
- the development of crafts that lead to technology
- basic economies that lead to today's economy

GOVERNMENT

Advancements include the rise of dynasties, such as those in Egypt and China; the creation of laws, including Hammurabi's Code; and the building of cities.

MOVEMENT OF PEOPLE AND IDEAS

People adapt to new places, environments, and climates, from the earliest exodus from Africa to migrations in India.

TRADE

Peoples and cultures gradually intermingle, a first step toward global citizenship.

ARTISTIC EXPRESSION

Cave art, including the handprints shown here, become early expressions of identity.

TECHNOLOGY & INNOVATION

Tools, settlements, and the development of agriculture increase chances of survival.

AS YOU READ ON

History is more than just one fact after another. Keep in mind the key takeaways from Units 1 and 2. Be sure to ask "how" and "why," and not just "what." Watch as the human story continues with the civilizations that may be most familiar to you: the Greek, Roman, and Byzantine civilizations.

+ GUIDED DISCUSSION

In Units 1 and 2, students learned about the origins of culture and the earliest civilizations. All early civilizations faced the same challenges—and the urge to establish an identity was key to their survival.

1. **Time Out for a Definition!**
   The word *looting* is sadly one students will come across frequently as they study world history. What it refers to in a historical context is the stealing of cultural artifacts, typically during a time of unrest. As you teach each unit, ask students to assess and discuss the effects of looting on a civilization or culture. If time permits, invite them to conduct a responsible Internet search for news stories relating to looting in the present-day. Discuss why groups or individuals might be motivated to steal artifacts from a culture—either their own or someone else's.

2. **Technologies and Innovations**
   Invite students to consider the different types of tools and innovations, including agricultural advances, that increased the chances of survival and shaped the earliest civilizations. Have students choose one of these innovations and create a one-page explanation of it, including an illustration or other visual and one or two paragraphs of explanatory text.

+ REFLECT ON UNITS 3–4

As they read Units 3 and 4 in their textbook, have studnents complete pages 19–24 in their Field Journal to process the material in these units. Remind students that they will use their Field Journal as they read each Why Study History? section and explore the historical record. They will record their thoughts about what they've read and fit them into the larger picture of world history. They will also use the journal to consider how they fit into that big picture and what it means to be a global citizen.

GREEK
CIVILIZATION

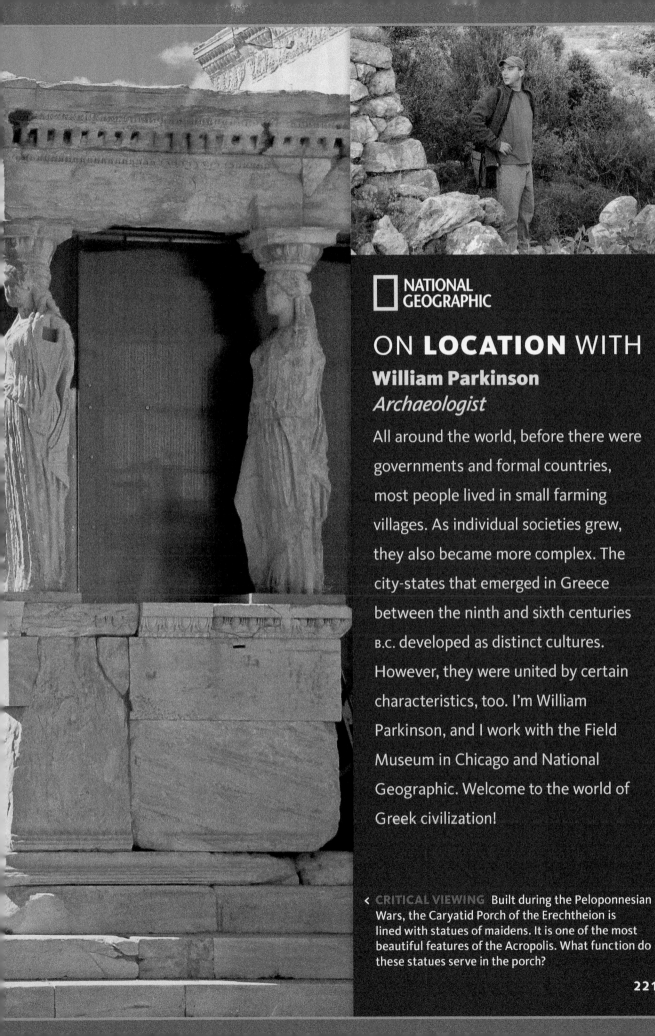

NATIONAL GEOGRAPHIC

ON **LOCATION** WITH

William Parkinson
Archaeologist

All around the world, before there were governments and formal countries, most people lived in small farming villages. As individual societies grew, they also became more complex. The city-states that emerged in Greece between the ninth and sixth centuries B.C. developed as distinct cultures. However, they were united by certain characteristics, too. I'm William Parkinson, and I work with the Field Museum in Chicago and National Geographic. Welcome to the world of Greek civilization!

< **CRITICAL VIEWING** Built during the Peloponnesian Wars, the Caryatid Porch of the Erechtheion is lined with statues of maidens. It is one of the most beautiful features of the Acropolis. What function do these statues serve in the porch?

▶ **POSSIBLE RESPONSE**

The statues are holding up the top of that portion of the Erechtheion.

Greek Civilization

c. 2000 B.C.
Minoan civilization
flourishes on the
island of Crete.
*(a lady of the
Minoan court)*

c. 1450 B.C.
Mycenaean civilization
thrives on the Greek
mainland and takes
control of Crete, ending
Minoan civilization.
(Lion Gate of Mycenae)

1500 B.C.

2000 B.C.

The World

c. 2000 B.C.
EUROPE
Stonehenge is
built in England.

1790 B.C.
ASIA
Hammurabi's Code
is issued in the
Babylonian Empire.

1300 B.C.
ASIA
The kingdom of
Israel is established
by the Hebrews.

1279 B.C.
AFRICA
Ramses II
begins 66-year
reign in Egypt.

1200 B.C.
AMERICAS
Olmec culture
rises in the
Americas.
*(Olmec stone
head)*

STANDARDS

HSS ANALYSIS SKILLS:

CST 1 Students explain how major events
are related to one another in time.

222

What happened in the world just before democracy was established in Athens?

➕ **POSSIBLE RESPONSE**

The Roman Republic was established just before democracy was established in Athens.

334 B.C.
Alexander the Great enters Asia Minor in order to conquer Persia. He dies in 323 B.C., marking the end of the Classic Age. *(gold coin with Alexander's profile)*

800 B.C.
Greeks begin using an alphabet. Literature is written down, including the *Iliad* and *Odyssey*.

431 B.C.
The Peloponnesian War between Athens and Sparta begins. *(Greek pot with scene from Peloponnesian War)*

1000 B.C.

c. 750 B.C.
Phoenicia develops into wealthy city-states, including the colony of Carthage.

c. 500 B.C.
The first democracy is established in Athens.

1100s B.C.
ASIA
The Zhou dynasty rules China. *(Zhou vessel)*

500 B.C.

509 B.C.
EUROPE
The Roman Republic is established.

551 B.C.
Confucius is born in China.

🕐 CST 1 Students explain how major events are related to one another in time.

223

ANCIENT GREECE c. 500 B.C.

The area colored orange on the map may look like a small and fragmented collection of peninsulas and islands, but these areas of land formed one of the most sophisticated cultures and civilizations the world has ever known: the civilization of ancient Greece. Not even its geography stood in Greece's way. Greek traders used the waters of the Mediterranean to secure and control trade routes. Mountains made travel and communication difficult, but independent city-states formed around them. The city-states are labeled with dots on the map. In the city-state called Athens, a form of government developed that would change the world: democracy.

What empire might have challenged Greek power in the region?

+ POSSIBLE RESPONSE
The Persian Empire might have challenged Greek power in the region.

Bosporus

Sea of Marmara

Mount Olympus

G R E E C E

P E R S I A N   E M P I R E

Dardanelles

Aegean Sea

Delphi
Thebes
Megara
Corinth
Athens
Mycenae
Argos
Olympia
Ephesus
Miletus

Ionian Sea

Sparta

Delos

| 0 | 25 | 50 | 75 | 100 kilometers |
| 0 | 25 | 50 | 75 | 100 miles |

Sea of Crete

Knossos
Crete

Mediterranean Sea

STANDARDS

HSS ANALYSIS SKILLS:

CST 3 Students use a variety of maps and documents to identify physical and cultural features of neighborhoods, cities, states, and countries and to explain the historical migration of people, expansion and disintegration of empires, and the growth of economic systems.

THE OLYMPICS

The first Olympic Games took place in 775 B.C. and lasted one day. Today's games include 28 different sports in summer and 7 in winter and last a couple of weeks. The early games had just a few events, not all of which are played today. You can read about the original events in the early Greek Olympics below. Emperor Theodosius banned the games in A.D. 393, calling them a "pagan cult." The first modern Olympics took place in 1896.

 Running   Contestants ran the 200-meter dash, 400-meter dash, and long distance events.

 Jumping   Athletes carried stone weights that they threw at the end of their jump to increase their distance.

 Discus   Athletes tossed a heavy disk made of stone, or later, of heavy metal.

 Boxing   Athletes fought one another using wrapped straps around their hands to strengthen their punches.

 Equestrian   Horse races and chariot-driven races took place in the Hippodrome, an ancient Greek stadium.

 Pentathlon   The pentathlon included five events: long jump, javelin throw, discus throw, foot race, and wrestling.

 Pankration   This event was a blend of wrestling and boxing and had few rules.

CST 3 Students use a variety of maps and documents to identify physical and cultural features of neighborhoods, cities, states, and countries and to explain the historical migration of people, expansion and disintegration of empires, and the growth of economic systems.

225

UNIT RESOURCES

NATIONAL GEOGRAPHIC

On Location with National Geographic Grantee William Parkinson
Intro and Video

Interactive Map Tool

STORIES MAKING HISTORY **News & Updates**

Available at NGLSync.cengage.com

Unit Wrap-Up:
"The Emergence of Cities"
Feature and Video

"Greek Statues Sparkle Once Again"
National Geographic Adapted Article

"Behind the Tomb"
National Geographic Adapted Article
Student eEdition exclusive

Unit 3 Inquiry:
Define Good Citizenship

CHAPTER RESOURCES

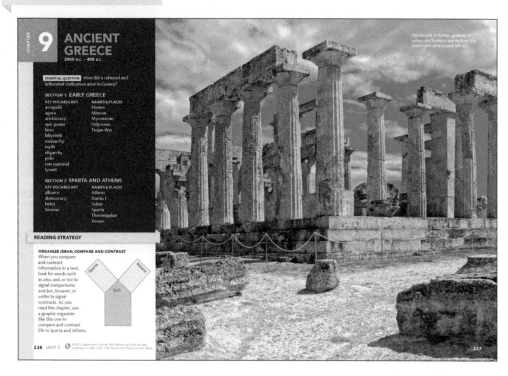

TEACHER RESOURCES & ASSESSMENT

Available at NGLSync.cengage.com

Social Studies Skills Lessons
• Reading: Compare and Contrast
• Writing: Write an Informative Paragraph

Formal Assessment
• Chapter 9 Tests A (on-level) & B (below-level)

Chapter 9 Answer Key

ExamView®
One-time Download

STUDENT BACKPACK *Available at NGLSync.cengage.com*

• **eEdition** *(English)*   • **eEdition** *(Spanish)*   • **Handbooks**   • **Online Atlas**

Chapter 9 Spanish resources, Guided Writing prompts, and Financial Literacy lessons are available online.

EARLY GREECE

 Reading and Note-Taking

 Vocabulary Practice

 Section 1 Quiz

Available at NGLSync.cengage.com

LESSON 1.1 MYSTERIOUS MINOANS

- Critical Viewing: NG Chapter Gallery
- On Your Feet: Card Responses

LESSON 1.2 MYCENAEAN CIVILIZATION

NG Learning Framework:
Learn More About Greek Origins

- On Your Feet: Chart Relay

LESSON 1.3 THE AGE OF HEROES

 Biography
Homer

Available at NGLSync.cengage.com

NG Learning Framework:
Write an Epic Poem

- On Your Feet: Conduct Talk Show Interviews

LESSON 1.4 CITY-STATES

- Critical Viewing: NG Chapter Gallery
- On Your Feet: Tell Me More

LESSON 1.5 COLONIZATION AND TRADE

NG Learning Framework:
Advertise a New Colony

- On Your Feet: Create Trade Networks

SPARTA AND ATHENS

 Reading and Note-Taking

 Vocabulary Practice

 Section 2 Quiz

Available at NGLSync.cengage.com

LESSON 2.1 SPARTA'S MILITARY SOCIETY

NG Learning Framework:
Create a Government

- On Your Feet: In This Corner

LESSON 2.2 ATHENS'S DEMOCRATIC SOCIETY

 Active History: Interactive Whiteboard Activity
Analyze Primary Sources: Democracy

 Active History
Analyze Primary Sources: Democracy

Available at NGLSync.cengage.com

- On Your Feet: Create a Concept Web

LESSON 2.3 UNITING AGAINST THE PERSIANS

NG Learning Framework:
Learn More About Triremes

- On Your Feet: Inside-Outside Circle

MOMENTS IN HISTORY
LESSON 2.4 THE BATTLE OF THERMOPYLAE

- Critical Viewing: NG Image Gallery

NG Learning Framework:
Analyze Historical Perspective

CHAPTER 9 REVIEW

STRATEGY ❶

Set a Purpose for Reading

Before students read a lesson, help them set a purpose for reading by turning the Main Idea statement into a question. Tell students to answer the question in writing after they read. Below are sample questions for Section 1.

1.1 Who established the earliest civilization in ancient Greece?

1.2 Why did the Mycenaeans copy and then conquer the Minoans?

1.3 What strong tradition did the ancient Greeks create?

1.4 How did city-states establish different ways of governing?

1.5 How did the ancient Greeks spread their culture throughout the region?

Use with All Lessons

STRATEGY ❷

Make Predictions About Content

Before students read the lessons listed below, have them examine the headings and visuals in each one and write their prediction on what the lesson will be about. After students read the lessons, have them check to see whether their predictions were accurate.

Use with Lessons 2.1–2.4 *Pair students whose predictions were inaccurate with students who correctly predicted the content of the lessons and have them compare the conclusions they drew from viewing the subheadings and visuals in each one.*

STRATEGY ❸

Make a "Top Five Facts" List

Assign a lesson to be read. After reading, have students write in their own words five important facts that they have learned. Let them meet with a partner to compare lists and consolidate the two lists into one final list. Call on students to offer facts from their lists.

Use with All Lessons

Press *in the Student eEdition for modified text.*

STRATEGY ❶

Modify Vocabulary Lists

Using your standards as a guide, limit the number of vocabulary words that students will be required to master. As they read, have students create a vocabulary card for each word in the modified list. Students may create a picture to illustrate each word or write definitions, synonyms, or examples. Encourage students to refer to their vocabulary cards often as they read.

Use with All Lessons *You may want to focus on the content-specific words that may be the most unfamiliar with students, including acropolis, agora, polis, helot, and trireme, and possibly others.*

STRATEGY ❷

Build a Time Line

Select key events from Lessons 1.1, 1.2, 2.2, and 2.3. Then have students use the events to start a time line on the board. Students will add to the time line as they read the chapter.

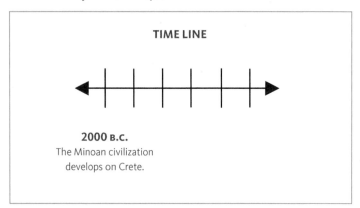

TIME LINE

2000 B.C.
The Minoan civilization develops on Crete.

Use with All Lessons *A key event from each lesson could be included on the time line. For example, in Lesson 1.4, students might add 750 B.C. Greek city-states emerge. Explain that some dates may carry multiple events.*

STRATEGY ❶

Activate Prior Knowledge

Display the following words in a random "splash" arrangement: *citizens, city-state, civilization, colonies, courage, epic poem, hero, myth, raw materials.* Ask students to talk about what the words bring to mind. Then have them work in pairs and write sentences using two of the words in each sentence.

Use with Lessons 1.1–1.5, All Levels *Challenge students at the **Bridging** level to create their own word splash for words they encounter in Lessons 2.1–2.4.*

STANDARDS

HSS CONTENT STANDARDS:

6.4 Students analyze the geographic, political, economic, religious, and social structures of the early civilizations of Ancient Greece.

HSS ANALYSIS SKILLS:

CST 2 Students construct various time lines of key events, people, and periods of the historical era they are studying.

STRATEGY ❷

Provide Sentence Frames

Have students read the lessons and complete the sentences below. Have students at the **Emerging** and **Expanding** levels work in pairs and students at the **Bridging** level work independently.

1.1 The Minoans were expert _____.

1.2 The _____ conquered the Minoans.

1.3 The Odyssey is an _____ _____.

1.4 The highest point in a Greek city was called the _____.

1.5 The ancient Greeks established _____ all over the Mediterranean region.

Use with All Lessons, All Levels *For Lessons 2.1–2.4, have students work in pairs to write their own sentence frames for each lesson. Pairs can then trade sentence frames with another pair and complete them together.*

STRATEGY ❸

Compare and Contrast

Use the following strategies to help students at each proficiency level make comparisons as they complete the graphic organizer for the chapter Reading Strategy.

Emerging

Ask "or" questions, and tell students to use the answers in their graphic organizer. For example:

- Were the Athenians or the Spartans fierce warriors?
- Was Athens or Sparta governed by a democracy?
- Where could women own property—in Athens or in Sparta?

Expanding

Tell students to complete sentence frames to use in their graphic organizer:

- _____ was governed by a(n) _____, but _____ was governed by a(n) _____.
- Women in both Athens and Sparta _____.
- _____ was more _____ than _____.

Bridging

Provide the following three categories and tell students to talk about details for each before adding to their graphic organizer: type of government; role of women; and culture.

Use with Lessons 2.1, 2.2, and 2.3, All Levels

STRATEGY ❶

Act Out a Scene

Have students act out the Trojan Horse scene from the *Odyssey*. They should provide costumes and use classroom furniture as a set. After the performance, discuss the points of view of the primary characters in the scene—Odysseus, the Greeks, the Trojans, and Helen. Encourage students to read the relevant passages from the epic poem to create their dialogue and stage directions. Have the group appoint a Director and a Stage Manager. Reinforce the importance of leadership and teamwork as students rehearse their scene.

Use with Lesson 1.3

STRATEGY ❷

Write a Historic Dialogue

Tell students to use the facts they have learned to write a dialogue that might have taken place between Xerxes, emperor of Persia, and King Leonidas of Sparta. Encourage students to convey Xerxes' outrage at the rebelling Greeks and Leonidas' commanding direction as he marched into battle. Students may want to augment their dialogues with additional research. Remind them to use academic sources in their research.

Use with Lessons 2.3 and 2.4

STRATEGY ❶

Use the "Persia" Approach

Have students write an essay explaining the significance of the ancient Greeks from 2000 B.C. to 480 B.C. Copy the following mnemonic on the board and tell students to use the "Persia" strategy:

Political

Economic

Religious

Social

Intellectual

Artistic

Use with All Lessons *Offer bonus points to those students who integrate the name of this exercise into their essays.*

STRATEGY ❷

Create an Exhibit

Challenge students to create an exhibit of ancient Greek culture from 2000 B.C. to 480 B.C. Direct them to research art museum sites online to select representative artifacts from early Greece as well as Spartan and Athenian artifacts. Then have students work together to write labels for their artifacts, no longer than 100 words each. Tell students that their labels should situate the artifacts in their historical and cultural contexts, and they should explain the significance of that particular artifact.

Use with All Lessons *Tell students to use Lesson 2.2 as a model for discussing artifacts in cultural context.*

ESSENTIAL QUESTION How did a cultured and influential civilization arise in Greece?

SECTION 1 EARLY GREECE

KEY VOCABULARY	NAMES & PLACES
acropolis	Homer
agora	Minoan
aristocracy	Mycenaean
epic poem	Odysseus
hero	Trojan War
labyrinth	
monarchy	
myth	
oligarchy	
polis	
raw material	
tyrant	

SECTION 2 SPARTA AND ATHENS

KEY VOCABULARY	NAMES & PLACES
alliance	Athens
democracy	Darius I
helot	Solon
trireme	Sparta
	Thermopylae
	Xerxes

READING STRATEGY

ORGANIZE IDEAS: COMPARE AND CONTRAST
When you compare and contrast information in a text, look for words such as *also*, *and*, or *too* to signal comparisons and *but*, *however*, or *unlike* to signal contrasts. As you read the chapter, use a graphic organizer like this one to compare and contrast life in Sparta and Athens.

Sparta / Athens / Both

The Temple of Aphaia, goddess of sailors and hunters, was built on the island of Aegina around 500 B.C.

6.4.6 Compare and contrast life in Athens and Sparta, with emphasis on their roles in the Persian and Peloponnesian Wars.

STANDARDS

HSS CONTENT STANDARDS:

6.4.6 Compare and contrast life in Athens and Sparta, with emphasis on their roles in the Persian and Peloponnesian Wars.

TEACHER BACKGROUND

INTRODUCE THE PHOTOGRAPH

Have students study the photograph of the Temple of Aphaia. Explain that in the study of ancient Greece, they will encounter a number of temples. **ASK:** What is a temple? *(A temple is a building used for worship.)* What does the presence of temples tell us about a civilization? *(Temples are evidence of the practice of religious beliefs.)*

SHARE BACKGROUND

The Temple of Aphaia shown in the photograph was built on the Greek island of Aegina around 500 B.C. Aphaia was a local goddess whose worship eventually became blended with that of the more recognizable Athena, the Greek goddess of wisdom and war. The temple is an example of Doric architecture and a precursor to the more famous Parthenon of Athens.

DIGITAL RESOURCES NGLSync.cengage.com

TEACHER RESOURCES & ASSESSMENT

 Social Studies Skills Lessons
- Reading: Compare and Contrast
- Writing: Write an Informative Paragraph

 ExamView®
One-time Download

 Formal Assessment
- Chapter 9 Tests A (on-level) & B (below-level)

 Chapter 9 Answer Key

STUDENT BACKPACK

- **eEdition** *(English)*
- **eEdition** *(Spanish)*
- **Handbooks**
- **Online Atlas**

INTRODUCE THE ESSENTIAL QUESTION

HOW DID A CULTURED AND INFLUENTIAL CIVILIZATION ARISE IN GREECE?

Four Corner Activity: Civilization Traits This activity introduces students to the culture and influence of ancient Greek civilization. Tell students that in this chapter, they will learn about the formation of early Greece, which led to the development of a civilization that continues to influence the world today. Remind students that civilizations have particular traits in common. **ASK:** What are some common traits among civilizations? Historians and archaeologists study these traits to learn about a civilization as a whole. Designate a section of the room to each of the traits below and have students move to the area that interests them most. Once students are organized into their groups, have them discuss the questions below. Then call on volunteers from each group to summarize their thoughts for the class.

A. Government What is government? Why is it important? What kind of government does the United States have?

B. Art What can we learn about a culture or civilization through its art? What kinds of art do you enjoy?

C. Trade What is trade? What kinds of goods are traded? What do you use to trade for goods?

D. Cities Do you like to visit cities? What are some important cities in the world? What can you find in cities?

 minutes

INTRODUCE THE READING STRATEGY

ORGANIZE IDEAS: COMPARE AND CONTRAST

Remind students when they compare and contrast information in a text, they should look for words such as *also, and,* or *too* to signal comparisons and *but, however,* or *unlike* to signal contrasts. Model finding signal words in the introductory paragraph in Lesson 2.1. Show students how to fill out a Y-Notes Chart. For more in-depth instruction and practice with the reading strategy, assign the Social Studies Skills Reading Lesson on comparing and contrasting.

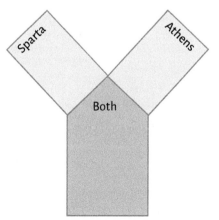

INTRODUCE CHAPTER VOCABULARY

KNOWLEDGE RATING

Have students complete a Knowledge-Rating Chart for Key Vocabulary words. Have students list words and fill out the chart. Then have pairs share the definitions they know. Work together as a class to complete the chart.

KEY VOCAB	KNOW IT	NOT SURE	DON'T KNOW	DEFINITION
acropolis				
agora				
aristocracy				
epic poem				

KEY DATES	
2000 B.C.	Minoan civilization emerges
1450 B.C.	Mycenaeans conquer Minoans
750 B.C.	Greek bard Homer creates epic poems
750 B.C.	Greek city-states form
508 B.C.	Athenians establish democracy
480 B.C.	Battle of Thermopylae
479 B.C.	Greeks defeat Persians

Mysterious
Minoans

You step forward and grasp the horns of the huge panting bull. Its head twitches; your muscles tighten in anticipation. Blocking out the cheers of the crowd, you spring over the bull's back and land behind the enormous animal. In ancient Crete such deadly games as bull-leaping are your way of worship.

MAIN IDEA

The Minoans established the earliest civilization in ancient Greece.

ANCIENT DISASTER

Around 1600 B.C., a volcano called Thira (THIH-ruh) erupted on an island 70 miles north of Crete. The eruption destroyed most of the island and caused death and destruction across the Mediterranean.

Scholars disagree about whether this eruption caused the decline of Minoan civilization, but this is one possibility.

MINOAN CIVILIZATION

Historians trace the origins of Greek civilization to Crete, a mountainous island about 150 miles off the coast of mainland Greece. Neolithic farmers settled there around 7000 B.C. and agriculture flourished. By 2000 B.C., a sophisticated **Minoan** (mih-NOH-uhn) civilization had emerged, centered on cities governed from magnificent royal palaces.

Though the Minoans left behind written records, historians cannot read their language. Their knowledge of Minoan civilization is pieced together through archaeology and the writings of ancient Greek historians. There are also many myths about this civilization. **Myths** are very old stories told to explain events or to justify beliefs and actions. The word *Minoan* comes from a mythical Cretan king named Minos (MY-nuhs). According to the myth, Minos built a **labyrinth** (LAB-uh-rinth), or maze, beneath his palace. A monstrous Minotaur (MIHN-uh-tawr)—half man, half bull—lived in this labyrinth and was offered regular sacrifices of unlucky humans. Unlikely? Perhaps, but archaeological evidence confirms that a powerful Minoan king built a labyrinth-like palace, and Minoans did in fact worship bulls and perform sacrifices.

CITIES AND CULTURE

The Minoans grew wealthy through trade across the Mediterranean. One of the Minoans' strengths was that they were expert sailors. Their well-built ships carried olive oil, wine, cloth, pottery, and metalwork to Greece, Egypt, Cyprus, and Spain. The Minoans returned from trading voyages with important **raw materials**, or substances from which other products are made, such as tin, gold, pearls, and ivory. Minoans spread their culture throughout Greece and along the coasts of the Aegean (ee-JEE-uhn) Sea. Their strong navy controlled the seas, making the Minoans feel so safe they did not build city walls.

The great palace at Knossos (NAW-suhss) dominated Crete. The size and complexity of the palace may have encouraged some people to believe it was Minos's labyrinth. Home to almost 20,000 people, Knossos was more like a city than a palace. It was the center of Minoan culture, religion, and economy. The palace included a central courtyard for ceremonies, hundreds of rooms,

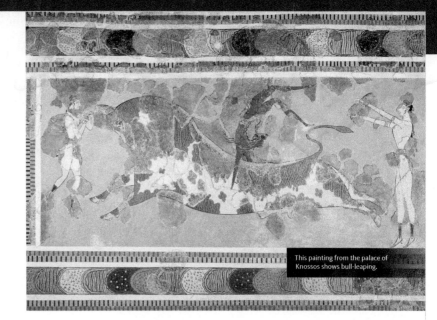

This painting from the palace of Knossos shows bull-leaping.

and even advanced plumbing. It also provided workshops for Minoan artisans and storerooms for surplus crops, such as grains. Minoans worked to support the palace and enjoyed a relatively prosperous life.

Minoan religion was polytheistic, which means that people believed in many gods and goddesses. Lifelike Minoan wall paintings suggest forms of worship involving bull-leaping, boxing, wrestling, and dancing as well as sacrifices to pacify the gods.

Mysteries surround the end of the Minoans. Around 1500 B.C., Minoan civilization declined sharply and its palaces fell into ruins. Possible causes for their collapse include natural disasters such as earthquakes, tidal waves, or volcanic eruptions. Some historians think all three factors—as well as an invasion by people from mainland Greece—contributed to the Minoans' decline. By 1450 B.C., a new civilization would overtake the Minoans.

REVIEW & ASSESS

1. **READING CHECK** What were some of the traits of the earliest civilization in ancient Greece?

2. **DRAW CONCLUSIONS** What does the great palace at Knossos reveal about the Minoan civilization?

3. **ANALYZE CAUSE AND EFFECT** How did trade help the Minoans develop wealth?

6.4.1 Discuss the connections between geography and the development of city-states in the region of the Aegean Sea, including patterns of trade and commerce among Greek city-states and within the wider Mediterranean region.

STANDARDS

HSS CONTENT STANDARDS:

6.4.1 Discuss the connections between geography and the development of city-states in the region of the Aegean Sea, including patterns of trade and commerce among Greek city-states and within the wider Mediterranean region; **6.4.4** Explain the significance of Greek mythology to the everyday life of people in the region and how Greek literature continues to permeate our literature and language today, drawing from Greek mythology and epics, such as Homer's *Iliad* and *Odyssey*, and from *Aesop's Fables*.

HSS ANALYSIS SKILLS:

CST 3 Students use a variety of maps and documents to identify physical and cultural features of neighborhoods, cities, states, and countries and to explain the historical migration of people, expansion and disintegration of empires, and the growth of economic systems; **REP 1** Students frame questions that can be answered by historical study and research; **HI 2** Students understand and distinguish cause, effect, sequence, and correlation in historical events, including the long- and short-term causal relations.

PLAN

OBJECTIVE

Identify the origins of ancient Greek civilization.

ESSENTIAL QUESTION

How did a cultured and influential civilization arise in Greece?

Historians and archaeologists trace the origins of different civilizations. Lesson 1.1 discusses the earliest civilization in ancient Greece, the Minoans.

BACKGROUND FOR THE TEACHER

A British archaeologist named Sir Arthur Evans first excavated the ruins of Knossos at the turn of the 20th century. Evans had earlier theorized that Mycenaean civilization originated on the island of Crete. He began a formal archaeological dig at Knossos, revealing an ancient cultural capital. Because he believed King Minos once ruled the palace at Knossos, he named this civilization *Minoan*. Evans tried to decipher the hieroglyphic-like symbols and the writing system, called Linear A, used by the Minoans, but he was unsuccessful. To date, later archaeologists and historians have not been able to, either.

DIGITAL RESOURCES NGLSync.cengage.com

TEACHER RESOURCES & ASSESSMENT

 Reading and Note-Taking

 Vocabulary Practice

 Section 1 Quiz

STUDENT RESOURCES

 NG Chapter Gallery

INTRODUCE & ENGAGE

ACTIVATE PRIOR KNOWLEDGE

Direct students' attention to a present-day map of the Mediterranean region. Ask a volunteer to point out Greece, another to point out Crete, and another to identify the Mediterranean Sea and the Aegean Sea. **ASK:** What types of geographic features can you identify in Greece? *(islands, mountains, coastlines, cities)* Where is Crete in relation to the mainland? *(It is located in the Mediterranean off the southern coast of the mainland of Greece.)* What kind of skills might ancient people who lived in this part of the Mediterranean have to have had to thrive? *(Because of their location on the Mediterranean Sea, they would have had to be good sailors and good fishermen.)* **0:05** minutes

TEACH

GUIDED DISCUSSION

1. **Describe** Who was King Minos and why is he important in understanding Minoan civilization? *(Minos was a mythological king of Crete. According to myth, he built a labyrinth under a great palace where he kept a Minotaur. His name is also the base of the word Minoan.)*

2. **Evaluate** What factors do you think led to the decline of Minoan civilization, natural disasters or invasions? Support your answer with evidence from the text. *(Minoan civilization was centered on Crete, an island in the Mediterranean, which might make it vulnerable to natural disasters such as volcanic eruptions, earthquakes, and tidal waves. Or, invasions by outside groups may have led to collapse. The Minoans did not build walls around their city and may have not expected outsiders could overpower their navy.)*

ANALYZE VISUALS

Have students examine the painting from the palace of Knossos. Tell the class that analyzing details about a piece of art can help us understand a past culture. Ask students to describe the details they see in the painting of bull-leaping. Have a volunteer record students' observations on the board. Then, as a class, create a description of Minoans based on details students mention. Compare that description to the text and point out similarities or discrepancies between them. **0:10** minutes

ACTIVE OPTIONS

Critical Viewing: NG Chapter Gallery Have students explore the NG Chapter Gallery and choose two of the items to compare and contrast, either in written form or verbally with a partner. Ask questions that will inspire this process, such as: How are these images alike? How are they different? Why did you select these two items? How do they relate in history? **0:10** minutes

On Your Feet: Card Responses Have half the class create ten true-false questions based on information in the lesson. Ask the other half to create answer cards, with "True" written on one side and "False" on the other. As each question is read aloud, students in the second group should display the correct answer to the question. **0:20** minutes

DIFFERENTIATE

ENGLISH LANGUAGE LEARNERS ELD

Summarize This lesson has two sections. Pair students at different proficiency levels and assign each pair a section of the text to read together. Encourage students to use a graphic organizer such as the one below to make notes about their part of the lesson, including questions they have about vocabulary or idioms. After answering their questions, have each pair write a one- to two-sentence summary.

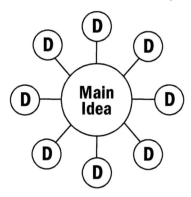

PRE-AP

Explore Mythology Have students conduct research on the myth of the labyrinth of Minos and the Minotaur. Direct them to investigate the basic questions of *who, what, where,* and *when,* but also to explore *why* bulls play such a prominent role in the myths of this civilization. Encourage students to research and integrate visuals, such as the mosaic in the lesson, in a short oral presentation for the class.

Press **mt** *in the Student eEdition for modified text.*

See the Chapter Planner for more strategies for differentiation.

REVIEW & ASSESS

ANSWERS

1. The Minoans established city-states, built great palaces, engaged in agriculture and extensive trade, and practiced religion.

2. The great palace at Knossos reveals a highly skilled and wealthy civilization that enjoyed cultural advancements of religion, architecture, and art, as well as a stable, central government and a prosperous economy.

3. Trade helped the Minoans develop wealth because they returned from voyages with raw materials with which they produced goods.

1.2 Mycenaean Civilization

The fascinating thing about history is often what we *don't* know.

Though we know the Mycenaeans overtook the Minoans, we don't know for sure what caused their own violent end. Along with the Minoans, the Mycenaeans helped lay the foundation of Greek civilization.

MAIN IDEA

After copying Minoan culture, the Mycenaeans conquered the Minoan people.

CONQUERORS

Around 2000 B.C., a new group of people from farther east settled in mainland Greece. They became known as **Mycenaeans** (my-SEE-nee-uhnz) based on the name of their main city, Mycenae (my-SEE-nee). The early Mycenaeans established villages throughout Greece, picked up influences from Minoan culture which had spread there, and spoke an early version of the Greek language.

After invading Crete in 1500 B.C., the Mycenaeans adopted Minoan culture. The Mycenaeans copied Minoan art, architecture, religion, writing, trade, metalworking, and shipbuilding. Elements of Minoan and Mycenaean culture became part of the foundation of Greek civilization.

The Mycenaeans had an aggressive streak, though, and they eventually turned against the Minoans. The Mycenaeans seized and conquered lands across the eastern Mediterranean and Greece. Around 1450 B.C., they conquered the Minoans, taking their treasure, land, people, and palaces.

RICH KINGS

The city of Mycenae was the center of Mycenaean civilization. Built high on a hill, the city was surrounded by thick walls that protected houses, storerooms, and a grand palace. The Mycenaeans protected Mycenae and other cities with great stone walls—so huge that later Greeks believed they were built by mythical giants called Cyclopes (SY-klohps). A network of good roads connected Mycenae to other important cities.

While most Mycenaean farmers lived in simple mud-brick houses in the countryside, important officials, artisans, and traders lived in three-story stone houses in cities. Warriors had it even better. Mycenaean kings gave elite warriors fine houses and lands to rule. Everyone else worked to support the warriors.

Extensive trade and wars made Mycenaean kings rich. The fierce Mycenaean military, wearing metal armor and driving fast-moving chariots, raided and conquered surrounding people. Yet at the height of its power, around 1200 B.C., the Mycenaean civilization came to a violent end. Suddenly most Mycenaean cities and towns were mysteriously destroyed.

Historians have several theories about why Mycenaean civilization declined. One theory suggests that natural disasters caused shortages that turned cities against one another or led to peasant uprisings. Another theory suggests that Mycenaean cities were invaded by the mysterious Sea Peoples. The Sea Peoples were seaborne and land raiders who had also attacked the ancient Egyptians and fought the Hittites of Mesopotamia.

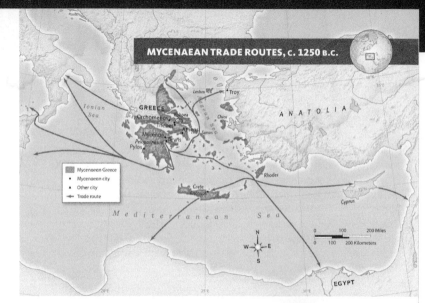

MYCENAEAN TRADE ROUTES, c. 1250 B.C.

Whatever the cause of the collapse, the end of Mycenaean civilization meant that ancient Greece entered a period of decline that lasted until about 950 B.C. The people abandoned cities, trade halted, and the economy floundered. During this time, the ancient Greeks also stopped keeping written records.

Without written records, historians know little about this 400-year period of Greek history. Luckily, though, the Greeks would learn to write again and record some of the greatest stories ever told.

MASK OF AGAMEMNON

This gold funeral mask discovered at Mycenae in 1876 is called the Mask of Agamemnon, named after the mythical Greek king. The mask most likely covered the face of a Mycenaean leader, though archaeologists are unsure which leader it was.

REVIEW & ASSESS

1. **READING CHECK** How did the Mycenaeans become so powerful?

2. **COMPARE AND CONTRAST** In what ways were the Mycenaeans similar to and different from the Minoans?

3. **INTERPRET MAPS** Describe the route Mycenaean traders used to reach Egypt from Tiryns.

6.4.1 Discuss the connections between geography and the development of city-states in the region of the Aegean Sea, including patterns of trade and commerce among Greek city-states and within the wider Mediterranean region; CST 3 Students use a variety of maps and documents to identify physical and cultural features of neighborhoods, cities, states, and countries and to explain the historical migration of people, expansion and disintegration of empires, and the growth of economic systems.

HSS CONTENT STANDARDS:

6.4.1 Discuss the connections between geography and the development of city-states in the region of the Aegean Sea, including patterns of trade and commerce among Greek city-states and within the wider Mediterranean region.

HSS ANALYSIS SKILLS:

CST 3 Students use a variety of maps and documents to identify physical and cultural features of neighborhoods, cities, states, and countries and to explain the historical migration of people, expansion and disintegration of empires, and the growth of economic systems; **REP 1** Students frame questions that can be answered by historical study and research.

PLAN

OBJECTIVE

Determine the influence of the Mycenaeans in ancient Greek civilization.

ESSENTIAL QUESTION

How did a cultured and influential civilization arise in Greece?

Civilizations develop by adopting practices and culture from other civilizations. Lesson 1.2 explores the Mycenaeans, who adopted Minoan culture and then conquered them.

BACKGROUND FOR THE TEACHER

As the photo of the Mask of Agamemnon shows, the Mycenaeans were wonderful metalworkers. They shaped gold, silver, and bronze into fine gold jewelry, intricate drinking cups and ritual vessels, and strong armor and weapons, such as daggers made of bronze. They also pounded sheets of gold into thin and detailed funeral masks like the one in Lesson 1.2. Metalworkers used metals from Greek rivers and mines as well as from trade with surrounding civilizations.

DIGITAL RESOURCES NGLSync.cengage.com

TEACHER RESOURCES & ASSESSMENT

 Reading and Note-Taking

 Vocabulary Practice

 Section 1 Quiz

STUDENT RESOURCES

 NG Chapter Gallery

INTRODUCE & ENGAGE

TEAM UP

Tell students to imagine they will be building a powerful civilization in a prime location in a region with seas, extensive and accessible coastlines, and inhabited by many different cultures. Have them brainstorm in groups. Tell them to use an Idea Web to list what they would build and the features they want their civilization to have. Tell students that the Mycenaeans had created a powerful maritime civilization in the Mediterranean region by around 1450 B.C. **0:05** minutes

TEACH

GUIDED DISCUSSION

1. **Explain** Why might the Mycenaeans have been interested in conquering Crete? (*As an island in the Mediterranean, Crete's location would have been strategic and advantageous for Mycenaeans to control.*)

2. **Make Inferences** In what ways can trade and warfare make a civilization strong? (*Trade and warfare can make civilizations strong by building wealth through the exchange of goods and through conquering people and taking their treasures and land.*)

INTERPRET MAPS

Help students interpret the map of Mycenaean trade routes. **ASK:** Based on the map and information in the text, what can you infer about the location of Mycenae, the main city of Mycenaeans? (*Mycenae was located slightly inland and on a high hill. This location would keep the city safe from invaders. Also, the city was protected with high walls.*) **ASK:** If you lived in Mycenae and wanted to trade with someone in Troy, how would you get there? (*You could leave from the port of Tiryns, sail north and east between various islands, and cross the Aegean Sea to land on the Anatolian coast.*) **0:10** minutes

ACTIVE OPTIONS

NG Learning Framework: Learn More About Greek Origins

ATTITUDE: **Curiosity**
SKILL: **Collaboration**

Have pairs or small groups of students review Lessons 1.1 and 1.2. Ask them to consider a group or event from those lessons that they are still curious about. Instruct them to collaborate in writing five questions about their group or event that they would like to answer. If time allows, encourage students to pursue answers to their questions through research at the library or online. **0:15** minutes

On Your Feet: Chart Relay Tape large pieces of paper to the wall in different locations of the classroom. Have students work in teams of four. Provide each team with a bold marker. Tell them to make four columns on their paper: City, Trade, War, and Invasions. Allow teams time to come up with three facts about each topic. Individual team members are each responsible for one topic. Then, on your signal, have teams write their facts on the charts. The first team that finishes wins. **0:25** minutes

DIFFERENTIATE

STRIVING READERS

Complete Sentence Starters Provide these sentence starters for students to complete after reading. You may also have students preview to set a purpose for reading.

- The Mycenaeans conquered the _____ in 1450 B.C.
- The city of _____ was the center of Mycenaean civilization.
- Later Greeks believed that _____ had built the great stone walls around Mycenaean cities.
- The Mycenaean civilization came to a violent end around _____ B.C.

GIFTED & TALENTED

Research the Sea Peoples Have students conduct research on the Sea Peoples, a group of ancient raiders. Some historians believe an invasion of the Sea Peoples led to the decline of Mycenaean civilization. Students can represent their research using a map, or by illustrating and annotating a time line. Encourage students to share their findings with the class.

Press **mt** *in the Student eEdition for modified text.*

See the Chapter Planner for more strategies for differentiation.

REVIEW & ASSESS

ANSWERS

1. The Mycenaeans settled in mainland Greece, copied Minoan culture, conquered the Minoans and surrounding cultures, and grew wealthy through trade and wars.

2. The Minoan and Mycenaean cultures were similar in many ways because after the Mycenaeans settled in mainland Greece, they adopted and copied virtually every aspect of Minoan culture, including art, architecture, government, religion, writing, shipbuilding, and trade. The Mycenaeans were different from the Minoans in that they seemed to be more focused on conquering other people.

3. Mycenaean traders set sail from Tiryns on the shores of the Aegean Sea and then sailed southeast across the Mediterranean Sea to Egypt.

1.3 The Age of Heroes

A good story needs an exciting plot, a little suspense, fascinating characters, and an exotic location. The ancient Greeks knew this and invented stories filled with adventure, romance, revenge, and intense action. This was the age of heroes.

MAIN IDEA

The ancient Greeks created a strong storytelling tradition.

HOMER'S EPIC POEMS

The ancient Greeks believed in many gods, goddesses, monsters, and heroes. Stories about these characters were told and retold. About 750 B.C., a man named **Homer** emerged. Historians do not know much about Homer, but tradition says he was a blind bard who lived in ancient Greece. A bard is a poet who tells stories as a rhythmic chant accompanied by music.

Homer composed two of the world's greatest stories, the *Iliad* and the *Odyssey*. Both are **epic poems**, or long poetic stories. Every epic poem has a **hero**, or a character who faces a challenge that demands courage, strength, and intelligence. Homer's epic poems dramatized how gods and goddesses influenced the lives of humans. They also helped establish the characteristics of Greek gods and goddesses.

The *Iliad* and the *Odyssey* followed a strong Greek storytelling tradition that mixed history, religion, and fantasy. These epic poems also united the Greeks through pride in their shared past and set the stage for future Western literature.

HEROIC DEEDS

The setting for Homer's epic poems was the **Trojan War**, which historians believe was fought between the Greeks and the Anatolian city of Troy around 1200 B.C. The *Iliad* tells of events in the final weeks of the war. According to the story, the Trojan War started because Paris, the prince of Troy, ran away with Helen, the wife of Menelaus (mehn-uh-LAY-uhs), the king of Sparta.

The *Odyssey* tells the story of the Greek hero **Odysseus** (oh-DIH-see-uhs). After ten years of fighting the Trojan War, Odysseus suggests that the Greeks play a trick on the Trojans. The Greeks leave a huge wooden horse as a gift and pretend to sail away from Troy. The Trojans drag the horse into the city, not knowing that Odysseus and his men are hiding inside. That night, Odysseus and his men sneak out of the horse. They open the city gates to Greek soldiers waiting outside. The Greeks take the city and recover Helen.

The *Odyssey* also tells the story of Odysseus's journey home after the war. He has many adventures involving creatures such as a one-eyed Cyclops and the Sirens—women whose singing lures sailors to crash their ships onto rocks.

FACT OR FICTION?

For thousands of years Troy and the Trojan War were considered nothing more than myths. However, Homer's stories inspired archaeologists to explore Greece. In the 1820s, they discovered the remains of a great city in Turkey. It matched Homer's description of Troy and had been violently destroyed about the same time, so Homer's war may have actually happened.

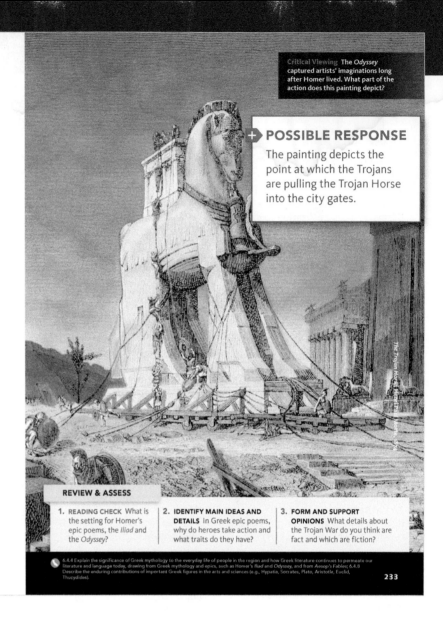

Critical Viewing The *Odyssey* captured artists' imaginations long after Homer lived. What part of the action does this painting depict?

+ **POSSIBLE RESPONSE**
The painting depicts the point at which the Trojans are pulling the Trojan Horse into the city gates.

REVIEW & ASSESS

1. **READING CHECK** What is the setting for Homer's epic poems, the *Iliad* and the *Odyssey*?

2. **IDENTIFY MAIN IDEAS AND DETAILS** In Greek epic poems, why do heroes take action and what traits do they have?

3. **FORM AND SUPPORT OPINIONS** What details about the Trojan War do you think are fact and which are fiction?

6.4.4 Explain the significance of Greek mythology to the everyday life of people in the region and how Greek literature continues to permeate our literature and language today, drawing from Greek mythology and epics, such as Homer's *Iliad* and *Odyssey*, and from *Aesop's Fables*; 6.4.8 Describe the enduring contributions of important Greek figures in the arts and sciences (e.g., Hypatia, Socrates, Plato, Aristotle, Euclid, Thucydides).

---

232 CHAPTER 9

STANDARDS

HSS CONTENT STANDARDS:

6.4.4 Explain the significance of Greek mythology to the everyday life of people in the region and how Greek literature continues to permeate our literature and language today, drawing from Greek mythology and epics, such as Homer's *Iliad* and *Odyssey*, and from *Aesop's Fables*; **6.4.8** Describe the enduring contributions of important Greek figures in the arts and sciences (e.g., Hypatia, Socrates, Plato, Aristotle, Euclid, Thucydides).

PLAN

OBJECTIVE

Understand the role of the epic hero in ancient Greek culture.

ESSENTIAL QUESTION

How did a cultured and influential civilization arise in Greece?

Myths and storytelling are key elements of cultural development in a civilization. Lesson 1.3 discusses the importance of the epic poem and Homer in ancient Greek culture.

BACKGROUND FOR THE TEACHER

Though historians attribute the *Iliad* and *Odyssey* to Homer, he did not write his epic poems down. Instead, he composed and told or "sang" his epics. In fact, Homer's word for poet—*aoidos*—means "singer." Homer's style differed from other poetic singers because his stories took longer to tell than simply a performance at a festival, feast, or other gathering. Homer's poems were longer and more expansive. Perhaps that characteristic is why they have endured through the centuries.

DIGITAL RESOURCES NGLSync.cengage.com

TEACHER RESOURCES & ASSESSMENT

 Reading and Note-Taking

 Vocabulary Practice

 Section 1 Quiz

STUDENT RESOURCES

 Biography

INTRODUCE & ENGAGE

PREVIEW USING VISUALS

Call students' attention to the art in the lesson. Ask students to come up with one or two words that describe what they see in the painting. Write their responses on the board. Then ask for a volunteer to read the Critical Viewing caption and question on the page. Tell students that they will be able to answer the question after they read. **0:05** minutes

TEACH

GUIDED DISCUSSION

1. **Compare and Contrast** What are some similarities and differences between oral and written stories? *(Stories told orally have to be passed down directly from one person to another. Written stories can be read at any time. Oral stories may change in details as they move through a culture. Written stories might tend to stay mostly the same.)*

2. **Make Inferences** Why might war be a good topic for an epic poem? *(A topic of war would provide an author like Homer many opportunities to describe actions of a hero up against difficult challenges. It would also be a topic an audience would recognize as part of their own experience.)*

MAKE CONNECTIONS

Explain to students that Homer's idea of the Trojan Horse has fascinated people for centuries. Today, in the world of modern computing and connectivity, a "Trojan horse virus" refers to malware, or destructive software, which once downloaded onto a computer or computer system, can do great damage. Trojan horse viruses can attack millions of computers at the same time and can completely disable entire systems. The virus is disguised as something helpful, entertaining, or otherwise innocent, much like the Greeks' gift to the Trojans. However, once opened, the virus attacks computer hardware and can destroy its components. **0:10** minutes

ACTIVE OPTIONS

NG Learning Framework: Write an Epic Poem

ATTITUDE: **Curiosity**
SKILLS: **Communication, Problem-Solving**

Invite students to think of an adventure they have experienced that could be the subject of a modern epic poem. Have them sketch out an outline of the events, heroes and heroines, and problems that they encountered in their adventures. Encourage students to tell their stories with a partner or in small groups. **0:25** minutes

On Your Feet: Conduct Talk Show Interviews Have teams of three students conduct talk show interviews on Homer and epic poems. Student 1, the interviewer, develops a question to ask the show's "guest." Student 2, an "expert" on Homer and epic poems, answers the question, citing information from Lesson 1.3. Student 3, a member of the studio audience, asks a spin-off question that the whole class can answer. Have participants ask and answer several questions to ensure a solid review of the topic. As an extension, have students read the excerpt from Homer's *Odyssey* in the **Primary Source Handbook** and answer the questions. **0:15** minutes

DIFFERENTIATE

INCLUSION

Analyze Visuals Provide concrete questions to help students describe the painting of the Trojan Horse. **ASK:** How big is the Trojan Horse compared to a real horse? What are the warriors in the painting doing? Does this painting look like it represents the Trojan Horse story before or after the Greek warriors inside escape and fight the Trojans? Encourage students to point to details that they don't understand and help them frame questions about these details.

GIFTED & TALENTED

Storyboard an Epic Poem Have artistically inclined students storyboard an epic poem of their own creation. Students might base their storyboards on a current news story, a tall tale, or even on an event in their own community or school. Encourage students to identify a hero or heroine, a challenge, and a set of gods, goddesses, or otherworldly beings with which the hero or heroine must interact. Then tell the students to create a storyboard of their epics. Have them include sketches of characters and a clear direction for the storyline.

Press **mt** *in the Student eEdition for modified text.*

See the Chapter Planner for more strategies for differentiation.

REVIEW & ASSESS

ANSWERS

1. The *Iliad* and the *Odyssey* are set during the Trojan War.

2. Heroes in Greek epic poems are characters who take action to meet challenges relying on the traits of extraordinary courage, strength, and intelligence.

3. Details about the Trojan War that may be factual are when and where it was fought. The idea that a horse filled with men was key to the victory of the Greeks is fiction. Students should support their answers with evidence from the text.

1.4 City-States

Though ancient Greek cities seemed to lie quiet for 400 years, around 800 B.C. they began to thrive again. Eventually they would extend their influence across the Mediterranean.

MAIN IDEA

Ancient Greek city-states established different ways of governing as they gained power.

Critical Viewing The ruins of a temple called the Parthenon still stand atop the Acropolis in Athens. What details in this photo convey the advantages of the Acropolis's location?

➕ POSSIBLE RESPONSE

The Acropolis's location is advantageous because it seems one could see for miles around, especially to be alerted to invading enemies.

CITIES AND CITY-STATES

As population, trade, and wealth grew, the ancient Greeks began to build cities near coastlines for trade and on hilltops for defense. Greek cities were distinct from one another, each with its own personality. However, these ancient cities shared certain similarities, too.

The highest point in an ancient Greek city was the **acropolis** (uh-KRAHP-uh-lihs), or upper city. This stone-walled fortress was the city's last line of defense against invasion. From the acropolis one could see houses and narrow streets and easily spot the open space of the **agora**, the city's marketplace and social center for sports, festivals, and meetings.

A powerful city grew into an even more powerful city-state, also called a **polis** (POH-luhs). As you may recall, a city-state is an independent political unit in which a dominant city rules the surrounding

area. A number of Greek city-states emerged after 750 B.C. Some city-states grew larger than others. Smaller towns and villages supplied food, trade goods, labor, and soldiers for the city-states.

Geographic isolation influenced how city-states developed in ancient Greece. High mountains surrounded plains and valleys, separating cities from one another. The mountains made it more challenging for some city-states to communicate and engage in trade with other city-states.

City-states developed at the same time all over ancient Greece, but they did so in different ways. Although they shared a common language, religion, heritage, and culture, city-states remained independent from one another. Each city-state had its own sets of customs and laws. Even more, citizens identified themselves as Athenians or Spartans—not as Greeks.

EARLY GOVERNMENT

Greek city-states were as different as they were independent. Each city-state established its own way of governing its citizens. One form of governing was a **monarchy**, a government ruled by a single person, such as a king. Another form was an **aristocracy**, a government ruled by a small group of elite, landowning families.

Aristocratic rule was soon challenged by a growing merchant class. As trade expanded, the merchants became more powerful. The 600s saw increasing tensions involving aristocratic landowners and an uneven

distribution of wealth. These tensions led to fighting and civil strife. Sometimes powerful men took advantage of the situation and seized power as **tyrants**. Some tyrants were ruthless, but others made positive changes, including giving farms to the landless and work to the unemployed. Not everyone favored their rule, though. In order to take power from tyrants, merchants formed an **oligarchy**, or a government ruled by a few powerful citizens.

Eventually, some city-states, such as Athens, wanted to give citizens a greater voice and began to experiment with a new type of government. You will read more about this government later in the chapter.

REVIEW & ASSESS

1. **READING CHECK** How were ancient Greek city-states alike and different?

2. **DETERMINE WORD MEANING** Based on what you have read, from what ancient Greek word do you think the word *politics* originates?

3. **ANALYZE CAUSE AND EFFECT** How did the geography of Greece influence the development of city-states?

6.4.1 Discuss the connections between geography and the development of city-states in the region of the Aegean Sea, including patterns of trade and commerce among Greek city-states and within the wider Mediterranean region; 6.4.2 Trace the transition from tyranny and oligarchy to early democratic forms of government and back to dictatorship in ancient Greece, including the significance of the invention of the idea of citizenship (e.g., from Pericles' Funeral Oration).

235

HSS CONTENT STANDARDS:

6.4.1 Discuss the connections between geography and the development of city-states in the region of the Aegean Sea, including patterns of trade and commerce among Greek city-states and within the wider Mediterranean region; **6.4.2** Trace the transition from tyranny and oligarchy to early democratic forms of government and back to dictatorship in ancient Greece, including the significance of the invention of the idea of citizenship (e.g., from Pericles' Funeral Oration).

PLAN

OBJECTIVE

Learn about the formation and importance of city-states.

ESSENTIAL QUESTION

How did a cultured and influential civilization arise in Greece?

An important component of civilization is organized government. Lesson 1.4 discusses the development of city-states and different forms of governing in ancient Greece.

BACKGROUND FOR THE TEACHER

The word *acropolis* means "city at the top" in Greek. The ancient Greeks founded their cities on the highest points for military and religious reasons. Militarily, having a city located up high would allow citizens to spot and prepare for invaders. Cities were also built in high places because for the Greeks, establishing a city involved invoking their gods for protection, and the city was to provide an earthly home for the gods.

DIGITAL RESOURCES NGLSync.cengage.com

TEACHER RESOURCES & ASSESSMENT

 Reading and Note-Taking

 Vocabulary Practice

 Section 1 Quiz

STUDENT RESOURCES

 NG Chapter Gallery

INTRODUCE & ENGAGE

ACTIVATE PRIOR KNOWLEDGE

Explain that in this lesson, students will learn about the development of Greek city-states and early government in ancient Greece. Ask students to draw on what they already know about cities and states to discuss these questions.

- What is a city? (*A city is a place where a number of people live and interact.*)
- What is a state? (*A state is a formal political unit.*)
- Based on your understanding of cities and states and on what you have read in previous chapters, what do you think a city-state is? (*A city-state is an independent political unit in which a dominant city rules the surrounding area.*) **0:05** minutes

TEACH

GUIDED DISCUSSION

1. **Make Inferences** Why do you think citizens of city-states identified with their city-states more than as Greeks? (*The city-state, not a larger, more inclusive country, was the central political unit. As such, ancient Greeks identified as Athenians or Spartans instead of as Greeks. Explain that this identity might be like citizens of the United States identifying as Texans or Californians rather than as Americans.*)

2. **Compare and Contrast** What are similarities and differences between aristocracies and oligarchies? (*Both aristocracies and oligarchies are forms of government in which small groups of people make decisions. Aristocracies are based on heredity, elite status, and land ownership; oligarchies are formed from small groups of powerful people, but not necessarily based on wealth or land ownership.*)

MORE INFORMATION

Geography of Greece Three particular physical features—specifically the mountains, the lowlands, and the coastline—impacted the development of independent city-states in ancient Greece. About 80 percent of the land is mountainous; the remaining 20 percent is lowlands. Several mountain chains run through the mainland, creating steep valleys. These mountains and valleys separated some parts of ancient Greece from one another, which some historians theorize led to more independent development. Greece also has many miles of coastline and no interior land is more than 50 miles from the coast. City-states' proximity to the Mediterranean, Ionian, and Aegean seas helped shape ancient Greece as a maritime power in the region.

ACTIVE OPTIONS

Critical Viewing: NG Chapter Gallery Ask students to choose one image from the Chapter Gallery and become an expert on it. They should do additional research to learn all about it. Then, students should share their findings with a partner, small group, or the class. **0:15** minutes

On Your Feet: Tell Me More Have students form three teams and assign each team one of the following topics:

- Geography of Greece
- City-States of Ancient Greece
- Forms of Government in Early Greece

Each group should write down as many facts about their topic as they can. Have the class reconvene, and have each group stand up, one at a time. The rest of the class calls out, "Tell me more about [the topic]!" A spokesperson for the group recites one fact. The class again calls, "Tell me more!" until the group runs out of facts to share. Then the next group presents its facts. Keep track of which group has shared the most facts on its topic. **0:15** minutes

DIFFERENTIATE

STRIVING READERS

Chart Forms of Government Have students record the different governments that ruled in ancient Greece using a chart such as the one shown below. In the rows, they should write a short description of the way each form of government shaped ancient Greece. Allow students to work in pairs to read the lesson. Have them read the text once and fill in their charts. Then have them read the text a second time and check their work. Have students share their charts with the rest of the group and add any information they might have missed to their own charts.

Monarchy	Aristocracy	Tyranny	Oligarchy

PRE-AP

Research a City-State Have students select a city-state that emerged around 750 B.C. and research its history. Students should explore their city-state's location, geographic features, form(s) of government, famous rulers, and economy. Have students prepare a presentation about their city-state and encourage them to include visuals. Groups of students could present together in a panel discussion with a question-and-answer session with their audience.

Press **mt** *in the Student eEdition for modified text.*

See the Chapter Planner for more strategies for differentiation.

REVIEW & ASSESS

ANSWERS

1. Ancient Greek city-states were alike because many were organized around an acropolis above an agora, and they shared a common language, religion, and culture. City-states were different because of the way each governed.

2. The word *politics* is based on the ancient Greek word, *polis*.

3. High mountains and surrounding plains and valleys separated cities from one another, which encouraged tightly knit communities and distinct identities as city-states.

1.5 Colonization and Trade

The ancient Greeks were always on the look out for fertile land and materials such as timber, metals, and luxury goods. Together these prompted the Greeks to trade and settle around parts of the Mediterranean where they could control the land.

MAIN IDEA

Ancient Greeks spread their culture around the Mediterranean and Black seas.

NEW SETTLEMENTS

Growing city-states meant growing populations and new problems. The hot, dry, and mountainous Greek countryside did not have enough usable farmland to feed everyone. As hunger fueled unrest, the leaders of city-states had two choices. They could fight other city-states for space or they could reduce their own populations.

Most did both. Between 750 and 550 B.C., the city-states waged wars with one another for control over limited natural resources. They also sent people overseas to establish new colonies in places with better farmland and valuable raw materials. Remember, a colony is an area controlled by a distant ruler. City-states selected their colonists by lottery and often prevented them from returning to Greece. The rulers wanted to make sure the new colonies would stay populated.

Greek city-states established hundreds of colonies in the Mediterranean region. Most colonies were situated on or near the coastlines of the Black and Mediterranean seas. They were located in present-day Spain, France, and Italy, in North Africa, and on the islands of Sardinia, Corsica, and Cyprus.

The new colonies were self-governing, but they maintained close political and economic links with their parent city-states. Although colonists adopted some local ways, they remained proudly Greek in their culture and outlook. They shared a common language, worshipped the same gods, and took part in Greek festivals such as the Olympic Games.

WATER HIGHWAYS

Colonies served many purposes for the ancient Greeks. Overall, they allowed access to land and resources not available in Greece. Some colonies were specifically set up to secure and control trade routes.

The Mediterranean and Black seas were relatively easy to navigate. Because most colonies were positioned near good harbors, sea trade flourished throughout the region. Expert sailors on well-built merchant ships carried raw materials such as silver and tin from present-day Spain and France back to Greece.

The flow of new resources to and from these colonies stimulated the production of goods. These goods were then traded at home and abroad. Trade boosted Greece's growing economy, as did the introduction of coins after 600 B.C.

Wide-ranging sea trade also encouraged cultural diffusion, or the spread of ideas from one culture to another. This dual exchange of goods and ideas was important in shaping civilizations in the ancient world. For example, the ancient Egyptians welcomed learning about Greek military skills. Ancient Greece had a strong cultural influence on early Rome and carried Mediterranean culture as far away as

GREEK TRADE, c. 500 B.C.

Region of Greek influence
Major trade route
Greek trade goods found

+ ANSWER

This cup represents ancient Greek trade because it was made in a Greek colony and shows fish, a commonly traded product.

present-day France. The ancient Greeks also incorporated ideas from other cultures. Elements of Egyptian culture influenced Greek art and architecture. Some historians think that ancient Greeks may have gotten their ideas of city-states, colonization, and sea trade from the Phoenicians.

One of the major effects of cultural diffusion in the ancient Mediterranean was the Greek adoption of the Phoenician alphabet. The Greeks made changes to the Phoenician alphabet, which then became the foundation of the modern alphabet we use today.

GREEK POTTERY IN ITALY

Tuna fish decorate this pottery cup found in the Apulia region, in the heel of Italy's boot. The cup may have been produced there by Greek colonists, or it may have been a trade good. Archaeologists believe the cup dates to about 500 B.C. In what ways does this cup represent Greek colonization and trade?

REVIEW & ASSESS

1. **READING CHECK** Why did the ancient Greeks establish colonies in the Mediterranean region?

2. **ANALYZE CAUSE AND EFFECT** In what ways did trade and cultural diffusion shape the ancient Greek world?

3. **INTERPRET MAPS** How far north did Greek influence reach as a result of trade?

6.4.1 Discuss the connections between geography and the development of city-states in the region of the Aegean Sea, including patterns of trade and commerce among Greek city-states and within the wider Mediterranean region; CST 3 Students use a variety of maps and documents to identify physical and cultural features of neighborhoods, cities, states, and countries to explain the historical migration of people, expansion and disintegration of empires, and the growth of economic systems; HI 2 Students understand and distinguish cause, effect, sequence, and correlation in historical events, including the long- and short-term causal relations; HI 6 Students interpret basic indicators of economic performance and conduct cost-benefit analyses of economic and political issues.

STANDARDS

HSS CONTENT STANDARDS:

6.4.1 Discuss the connections between geography and the development of city-states in the region of the Aegean Sea, including patterns of trade and commerce among Greek city-states and within the wider Mediterranean region.

HSS ANALYSIS SKILLS:

CST 3 Students use a variety of maps and documents to identify physical and cultural features of neighborhoods, cities, states, and countries and to explain the historical migration of people, expansion and disintegration of empires, and the growth of economic systems; **HI 2** Students understand and distinguish cause, effect, sequence, and correlation in historical events, including the long- and short-term causal relations; **HI 6** Students interpret basic indicator of economic performance and conduct cost-benefit analyses of economic and political issues.

PLAN

OBJECTIVE

Explore the impact of colonization and trade in ancient Greece.

ESSENTIAL QUESTION

How did a cultured and influential civilization arise in Greece?

The creation of colonies and the exchange of goods in the Mediterranean region transformed ancient Greece into a regional power. Lesson 1.5 explores colonization and trade routes in ancient Greece.

BACKGROUND FOR THE TEACHER

Colonization and trade were intensely competitive in the ancient Mediterranean. Greek city-states competed with each other, sometimes to the point of war, over access to resources and for claims to new locations that would help relieve population pressures. At the same time, the Greeks competed with the Phoenicians and the Carthaginians over resources and power in the seas. Despite the competition, the ancient Greeks greatly expanded their power and influence in the region between 750 and 500 B.C. through colonization and trade.

DIGITAL RESOURCES NGLSync.cengage.com

TEACHER RESOURCES & ASSESSMENT

 Reading and Note-Taking

 Vocabulary Practice

 Section 1 Quiz

STUDENT RESOURCES

 NG Chapter Gallery

INTRODUCE & ENGAGE

PREVIEW CONTENT WITH MAPS

Direct students' attention to the map of Greek trade. Have them scan the title, legend, and other map features to determine the upcoming content. **ASK:** What do you think this map shows? *(The map shows trade routes of ancient Greeks.)* What three features on the map do you notice right away? *(Students may say the parts of land colored green, the green lines, and the purple squares.)* Ask for volunteers to identify what each map feature represents. `0:05` **minutes**

TEACH

GUIDED DISCUSSION

1. **Identify** What stresses did increased populations put on ancient Greek city-states by 750 B.C.? *(Growing populations meant that more people needed food, which was hard to produce on hot, dry lands in Greece. Hunger began to fuel unrest and city-states began to fight with one another over resources and space.)*

2. **Evaluate** In what ways did Greek colonization and trade foster cultural diffusion in the Mediterranean region? *(Colonization introduced people from different cultures to each other, and trade brought merchants, seamen, and travelers into contact with one another.)*

INTERPRET MAPS

Have students study the map of Greek trade. **ASK:** What does the presence of Greek trade goods in places far away from Greece indicate about the extent and strength of ancient Greek trade? *(Greek trade goods found in Egypt and the city of Cyrene make sense, because these places were located on major trade routes. However, trade goods found in places much farther away, and off major trade routes, as in parts of present-day France and even Russia, could indicate that the goods traded were valuable and had a long trade life, or it could indicate that traders involved in ancient Greek networks traded with many different groups.)* `0:10` **minutes**

ACTIVE OPTIONS

NG Learning Framework: Advertise a New Colony

SKILL: Collaboration
KNOWLEDGE: Our Human Story

Invite students to imagine that they are in charge of an ad campaign announcing a new colony in ancient Greece. Have them work in small groups to collaborate on a poster that could advertise the new colony and that might persuade citizens of the mainland to move there. Encourage groups to share their posters with the class. `0:15` **minutes**

On Your Feet: Create Trade Networks Have students work with two or three partners and create a description of a product or good they could trade with other groups. When each group is ready, replicate the Mediterranean region by assigning groups to separate parts of the room, leaving the middle of the room fairly empty. Then have groups trade their goods with each other. Allow students to explore different methods of trade. Some groups may grow wealthy; others may run out of products to trade. Come back together as a class to discuss the experience of trading. Ask students if they preferred one exchange system over another, or if their group formed an alliance with another group to benefit as trade partners. `0:25` **minutes**

DIFFERENTIATE

ENGLISH LANGUAGE LEARNERS

Ask Questions Remind students that they can ask themselves *Who, What, When, Where, Why,* and *How* questions while reading and look for answers by rereading the text. Use the following question starters to help students at different proficiency levels ask questions about the text.

Emerging

- Who is _____?
- Who are _____?
- What is _____?
- What are _____?

Expanding and Bridging

- Where was the _____?
- Where did _____?
- When did _____?
- Why did _____?

GIFTED & TALENTED

Explore Greek Trade Have students research five products or goods exchanged along ancient Greek trade routes. They might focus on raw materials the Greeks wanted and could not produce in Greece, such as metals, grains, or wood. Or they might concentrate on goods produced in Greece that other places in the Mediterranean wanted, such as pottery or olive oil. Encourage students to use a visual such as a map or flow chart to show the origin and movement of the traded products and goods. Have students show their maps or flow charts to the class and describe their findings.

Press (**mt**) *in the Student eEdition for modified text.*

See the Chapter Planner for more strategies for differentiation.

REVIEW & ASSESS

ANSWERS

1. Ancient Greeks established colonies in the Mediterranean region to relieve overcrowding and find places with better farmland and resources.

2. The colonies stimulated sea trade as well as the production of manufactured goods that were traded at home and abroad—all of which boosted Greece's growing economy. Trade stimulated the production of manufactured goods that were traded at home and abroad. This trade boosted Greece's growing economy. Cultural diffusion meant that ideas and practices from Greece spread to other civilizations in the ancient world, and vice versa.

3. Greek influence reached as far north as Olbia, on the northern shore of the Black Sea.

Sparta's
Military Society

One of the greatest rivalries in the ancient world was between the city-states of Athens and Sparta. The Athenians, whom you'll learn about in the next lesson, emphasized culture and learning. The Spartans, though, were the fierce warriors of ancient Greece. They fought hard and could handle more pain than anyone. They were almost unbeatable, thanks to tough military training.

MAIN IDEA

Sparta was a powerful ancient Greek city-state devoted to war.

STRONG WOMEN

This bronze sculpture from Sparta reflects the expectation that Spartan girls and women be tough. Girls' education focused on physical strength and athletic skills, and Spartan girls learned how to defend themselves.

SPARTAN SOCIETY

The Spartans lived in one of the most fertile areas of southern Greece. The city-state of **Sparta** was located in the Eurotas river valley, protected by mountains that made attacking this city-state difficult. This physical separation may have led to an outlook and values in sharp contrast with those of other ancient Greek city-states.

Spartan government was an unusual blend of rule by kings, elected officials, and the ruling class. Two kings who shared power ruled Sparta. Together, they led Sparta's armies into battle. Real power rested with the five officials who were elected each year by an assembly of Spartan citizens. In addition, the two kings and a council of elders, made up of 28 men over 60 years of age, proposed laws. The Spartans' unique government helped maintain a balance of power and prevent revolts.

Spartan society was a rigid hierarchy. Groups of citizens were ranked by importance based on wealth and power. Elite, landowning families of Sparta formed the upper class. A second class included free noncitizens from the villages around Sparta. They were farmers and traders and sometimes served in the army.

The lowest social class was made up of the **helots**, or state-owned slaves captured from conquered lands. Helots farmed the Spartans' land and were only allowed to keep a tiny portion of their harvest. The helots outnumbered the Spartans, and fear of helot uprisings was a main reason for Sparta's military society. The army was at the center of everything in Sparta—and everything in Sparta was centered on the army.

DAILY LIFE

Spartan soldiers considered it an honor to die in battle for Sparta, but they did not die easily. At seven years of age, all boys were taken from their families and raised by the state to be soldiers. Their training was brutal. They wore thin tunics and no shoes, even in winter. Their meals were purposely small and nasty so that they had to steal food to survive but were punished if caught.

Such intense physical training and endless military drills created strong and obedient

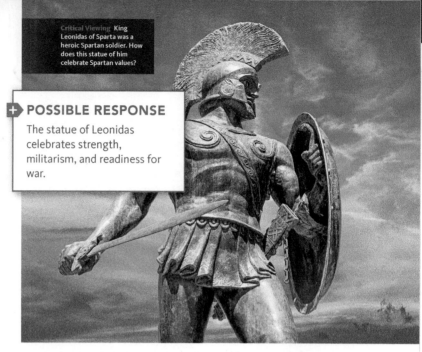

Critical Viewing King Leonidas of Sparta was a heroic Spartan soldier. How does this statue of him celebrate Spartan values?

➕ POSSIBLE RESPONSE

The statue of Leonidas celebrates strength, militarism, and readiness for war.

soldiers. At age 20, they joined a military mess, or regiment, a commitment that dominated the rest of their lives.

Family life supported Sparta's military values. Women's primary role was to produce future soldiers for the state, and husbands and wives spent much time apart. One result of this separation was that Spartan women lived their daily lives independent of men. Spartan women could also own property.

Sparta's extraordinary commitment to war transformed this city-state into an ancient power, but this success came at a price. Although Sparta boasted the best soldiers, it claimed few artists, philosophers, or scientists, unlike its rival Athens.

REVIEW & ASSESS

1. **READING CHECK** What was one reason Sparta developed a military society?

2. **SUMMARIZE** In what ways was Sparta's government unique?

3. **ANALYZE CAUSE AND EFFECT** What effect did Sparta's commitment to the military have on other aspects of its society and culture?

6.4.6 Compare and contrast life in Athens and Sparta, with emphasis on their roles in the Persian and Peloponnesian Wars; HI.2 Students understand and distinguish cause, effect, sequence, and correlation in historical events, including the long- and short-term causal relations.

239

HSS CONTENT STANDARDS:

6.4.6 Compare and contrast life in Athens and Sparta, with emphasis on their roles in the Persian and Peloponnesian Wars.

HSS ANALYSIS SKILLS:

HI 1 Students explain the central issues and problems from the past, placing people and events in a matrix of time and place;
HI 2 Students understand and distinguish cause, effect, sequence, and correlation in histtorical events, including the long- and short-term causal relations.

PLAN

OBJECTIVE

Learn about Spartan society in ancient Greece.

ESSENTIAL QUESTION

How did a cultured and influential civilization arise in Greece?

Many different groups contributed to the development of civilization in ancient Greece. Lesson 2.1 discusses the Spartans and their military society.

BACKGROUND FOR THE TEACHER

The rigorous military training Spartan boys endured was called *agoge*. One reason for the training was to maintain control over the helots, or state-owned slaves. This dynamic led to a self-perpetuating cycle: training Spartan warriors to control slaves working to provide food (and time) for Spartan warriors to train. This training and approach set Sparta quite apart from other ancient Greek city-states. As they became more committed to this approach, Spartans turned away from any artistic expression or development to focus solely on the development of the military and its warriors. To give students more insight into the life of Spartan boys, have them read "Treatment of Spartan Boys" in the **Primary Source Handbook** and answer the questions that follow it.

DIGITAL RESOURCES NGLSync.cengage.com

TEACHER RESOURCES & ASSESSMENT

 Reading and Note-Taking

 Vocabulary Practice

 Section 2 Quiz

STUDENT RESOURCES

 NG Chapter Gallery

INTRODUCE & ENGAGE

IDENTIFY WORD RECOGNITION

Ask students if they're familiar with the word *spartan* and ask them to volunteer guesses about its meaning. Write student guesses on the board. Explain that the word means, "showing or characterized by a lack of comfort or luxury." The word comes from the name of a group of ancient Greeks called Spartans who were known for their indifference to comfort and luxury. The word is used today to describe things that are bare and without frills, or things that are stern or rigorous. Encourage students to look for uses of the word *spartan*. `0:05` minutes

TEACH

GUIDED DISCUSSION

1. **Describe** What different social classes existed in Sparta? *(Elite, landowning families formed the upper class; a second class included free noncitizens; the lowest social class was made up of helots.)*

2. **Make Inferences** How might the rigid hierarchy of Spartan society have been mirrored in its military? *(Any military is characterized by rank, so a Spartan citizen would understand the hierarchy in the Spartan military.)*

COMPARE AND CONTRAST

Have students compare the photo of Leonidas to photos of modern soldiers in battle uniform. **ASK:** What are some similarities between Spartan soldier uniforms and modern soldier uniforms? *(Spartan soldiers and modern soldiers wear helmets and armor, have a standardized uniform, and carry weapons.)* What are some differences between Spartan and military uniforms? *(In the photo in Lesson 2.1, Leonidas is depicted in a short tunic; modern soldiers wear long pants to protect their legs. Modern soldiers also don't carry metal shields or wear heavy adornments on their helmets.)* `0:10` minutes

ACTIVE OPTIONS

NG Learning Framework: Create a Government

ATTITUDE: **Responsibility**
SKILL: **Decision-Making**

Invite students to imagine that they are responsible for leading a new society. Have them select one of the groups discussed in this chapter and use it as a model or example for how they might structure their society's government and societal roles. **ASK:** Why did you decide to use this group as your model? What characteristics do you want your government to have? How are leaders chosen? What kinds of responsibilities do citizens in your society have? `0:10` minutes

On Your Feet: In This Corner Place cards in two corners of the room, one labeled "Spartan Warrior" and the other labeled "Helot." Call on individual students, giving each a word or phrase—such as *farmer, soldier, slave, battle, uprising, war, majority, minority*. Students are to go to one of the two labeled areas and explain why their word or phrase fits the label. As a class, discuss any differences in opinion about how students have categorized terms. `0:10` minutes

DIFFERENTIATE

INCLUSION

Identify Main Ideas and Details Have pairs of students use the graphic organizer shown to identify the main idea and supporting details in the lesson. First, they should write the lesson's Main Idea statement in the Main Idea box. Then have students work together to identify and write supporting details.

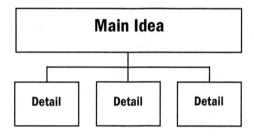

GIFTED & TALENTED

Write Journal Entries Have students conduct research to learn about the life of a helot, a Spartan man, or a young Spartan girl. Then have them write a series of journal entries from the perspective of their chosen person. Students should include factual information from their research in their journal entries. Ask for volunteers to read some entries aloud.

Press **mt** *in the Student eEdition for modified text.*

See the Chapter Planner for more strategies for differentiation.

REVIEW & ASSESS

ANSWERS

1. They developed a military society in order to control the helots—slaves captured from conquered countries—and to prevent uprisings.

2. Sparta's government was made up of a unique combination of monarchy, democracy, and oligarchy that helped to maintain a balance of power and suppress radical politics.

3. Sparta's commitment to its military strength meant that other aspects of society and culture—such as the arts and sciences—were not developed. Therefore, Sparta produced the strongest and most obedient soldiers, but very few artists, poets, musicians, philosophers, or scientists.

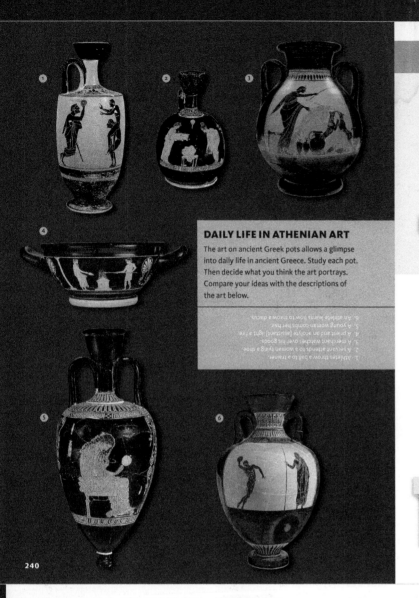

①

②

③

④

⑤

⑥

DAILY LIFE IN ATHENIAN ART

The art on ancient Greek pots allows a glimpse into daily life in ancient Greece. Study each pot. Then decide what you think the art portrays. Compare your ideas with the descriptions of the art below.

1. Athletes throw a ball to a trainer.
2. A servant attends to a woman tying a shoe.
3. A merchant watches over his goods.
4. A priest and an acolyte [assistant] light a fire.
5. A young woman combs her hair.
6. An athlete learns how to throw a discus.

2.2 Athens's Democratic Society

The city-state of Athens was named for its devotion to Athena, the Greek goddess of wisdom. Ancient Athenians developed one of the world's great forms of government.

MAIN IDEA

The culturally rich city-state of Athens developed democracy.

DAILY LIFE

The daily lives of people in ancient **Athens** helped shape their approach to governing. Citizenship was open to adult men who had been born in Athens. Foreign-born residents could live in Athens. However, they did not generally become citizens, vote, or own property—even though they paid taxes and fought in the army. Slaves were at the bottom of society.

Athenian women were firmly controlled by their husbands. Wealthy women ran the household and raised children, but they could not go out alone. Poorer women had more freedom but had to work for wages.

Children were raised much differently in Athens than in Sparta. Athenians valued education, and boys attended school if their families could afford it. After a well-rounded education, Athenian boys went through two years of military training in preparation for citizenship. Athenian girls did not attend school, but they learned household skills at home. Poor children worked from an early age.

BEGINNINGS OF DEMOCRACY

Even as the city-state of Athens thrived, many Athenians felt they had little voice in their government. Unlike Sparta, Athens replaced its monarchy with an aristocracy. Trouble arose when aristocratic families began to fight with each other and farmers started to protest decreasing wealth and land. A time of increasing strife and, on occasion, violence in Athens followed. A harsh code of laws made things worse.

In 594 B.C., the aristocrats responded to the crisis by granting special powers to a trusted man named **Solon**. He improved conditions for the poor by limiting the power of the aristocracy and allowing an assembly of free citizens to pass laws. In 508 B.C., Athens established **democracy**, a form of government in which citizens have a direct role in governing.

Athenians were less devoted to war than were Spartans. Although their citizen-soldiers were capable, they did not form a professional army. To defend itself, Athens joined forces with other city-states, including Sparta. In 490 B.C., the Persians attacked Greece from the east. The resulting war would test Spartans and Athenians alike.

REVIEW & ASSESS

1. **READING CHECK** What role do citizens play in a democracy?

2. **ANALYZE CAUSE AND EFFECT** What steps did Solon take to reform Athens's government?

3. **INTEGRATE VISUALS** How do the depictions of ancient Greek women on the pots fit with the text's description of them?

6.4.2 Trace the transition from tyranny and oligarchy to early democratic forms of government and back to dictatorship in ancient Greece, including the significance of the invention of the idea of citizenship (e.g., from *Pericles' Funeral Oration*); 6.4.6 Compare and contrast life in Athens and Sparta, with emphasis on their roles in the Persian and Peloponnesian Wars.

PLAN

OBJECTIVE

Explore the culture and society of ancient Athens.

ESSENTIAL QUESTION

How did a cultured and influential civilization arise in Greece?

Ancient Athens provided a fertile environment for cultural and artistic expression to thrive. Lesson 2.2 describes Athens's democratic society.

BACKGROUND FOR THE TEACHER

Black-and-red pottery is an iconic ancient Greek art form. First, potters shaped and fired, or baked, the vessels in a kiln. Some pots had handles on one or both sides. Sometimes vessels were tall vases and sometimes they were bowls. Plain, undecorated vessels were used for everyday tasks, such as food service and preparation, beverages, or washing. Finely painted pots such as the ones shown in Lesson 2.2 were reserved for more important occasions. Illustrations on the pots depicted myths and stories, seemingly unimportant tasks such as combing hair, as well as athletic training and contests, musical performances, historical events, and students listening to teachers.

DIGITAL RESOURCES NGLSync.cengage.com

TEACHER RESOURCES & ASSESSMENT

📄 **Reading and Note-Taking**

📄 **Vocabulary Practice**

☑️ **Section 2 Quiz**

STUDENT RESOURCES

📄 **Active History**

INTRODUCE & ENGAGE

COMPLETE A K-W-L CHART

Provide each student with a K-W-L Chart like the one shown. Have students brainstorm what they know about ancient Athens and the development of democracy. Then ask them to write questions that they would like to have answered as they study the lesson. Allow time at the end of the lesson for students to fill in what they have learned. `0:10` minutes

K What Do I Know?	W What Do I Want To Learn?	L What Did I Learn?

TEACH

GUIDED DISCUSSION

1. **Identify** To whom was citizenship available in ancient Athens? *(Citizenship was open to adult men who had been born in Athens.)* **ASK:** Could Athenian women be citizens? *(No)*

2. **Compare and Contrast** How did life differ between young Spartan and young Athenian boys? *(Spartan boys went into military training and then became soldiers. Athenian boys had some military training but they also received well-rounded educations.)*

ANALYZE VISUALS

Have students examine the ancient Greek pots shown in the lesson. As a class, work through their responses to the prompt asking them to describe what they think the art on the pots portrays. If students offer different answers than those listed, ask them to explain what they think the art depicts. Ask students to think of objects that they own or use that depict ordinary events. Allow time for students to make a connection between modern and ancient expressions of the everyday. `0:10` minutes

ACTIVE OPTIONS

Analyze Primary Sources: Democracy Extend Lesson 2.2 on the beginnings of democracy in ancient Greece by using either the PDF or Whiteboard version of the activity. These activities take a deeper look at a topic from, or related to, the lesson. Explore the activities as a class, turn them into group assignments, or even assign them individually. `0:10` minutes

On Your Feet: Create a Concept Web Have students form groups of four around a section of a bulletin board or a table. Provide each group with a large sheet of paper. Have group members take turns contributing a concept or phrase to a Concept Web with the words *Early Greeks* at the center. When time for the activity has elapsed, call on volunteers from each group to share their webs. `0:10` minutes

DIFFERENTIATE

ENGLISH LANGUAGE LEARNERS `ELD`

Teach and Learn Pair students at the **Emerging** level with English-proficient students. Have English-proficient students teach words from the lesson that appear in various forms throughout Lesson 2.2. Have pairs compose a sentence for each word and then share their sentences with the class. Suggest the following words:

- aristocracy, aristocratic
- wealth, wealthy
- citizen, citizenship
- governing, government

PRE-AP

Create an Exhibit Have students research a type of ancient Greek art and create a virtual exhibit of the artifacts they bring together. Students should create a theme and title for their exhibit, write accurate labels for each artifact, and represent each object through a photograph. Encourage students to put their exhibits on display, perhaps sharing them on a school- or classroom-owned Web site.

Press **mt** *in the Student eEdition for modified text.*

See the Chapter Planner for more strategies for differentiation.

REVIEW & ASSESS

ANSWERS

1. In a democracy, citizens have a direct role in governing themselves or elect representatives to lead them.

2. Solon established a limited democracy by reducing the power of the aristocracy and empowering an assembly made up of free citizens, which led to a growing equality among the people of Athens (excluding women, children, foreigners, and slaves).

3. The art on the pots idealizes Athenian women as focused on the home and children and on personal beauty. This depiction matches with the text, which asserts that women were centered on the home and childrearing and that girls had little education.

2.3 Uniting Against the Persians

When the Persians attacked Greece, they triggered the Persian Wars. We know much about these wars from the ancient Greek historian Herodotus. Modern historians consider him to be reliable even though it's likely that he exaggerated the size of the Persian threat. Whatever the numbers, these wars changed the course of Greek history.

MAIN IDEA

City-states in ancient Greece united to drive back invasions by the Persian Empire.

26.2

The modern marathon has its roots in the Persian Wars. According to one legend, upon defeating the Persians at Marathon, Miltiades sent his best runner to Athens to announce the victory. After he reported the news, the runner collapsed and died.

The distance from Marathon to Athens was just over 24 miles. Today's race measures 26.2 miles.

IONIAN REVOLT

In 546 B.C., the Persian Empire conquered Ionia, an area of Greek colonies on the west coast of present-day Turkey. Life under Persian rule was not especially harsh, but the Ionians wanted to regain their independence. They rebelled in 499 B.C. with the support of Athens. Despite Athenian help, Persia crushed the Ionian revolt in 494 B.C. The Persian emperor **Darius I** vowed to punish Athens as revenge for helping Ionia.

In 490 B.C., the Persian army landed at Marathon, just over 24 miles east of Athens. Knowing they were outnumbered by at least two to one, the Athenians knew their strategy would have to be clever—and bold. As the Persian foot soldiers stood in formation, the Greek general Miltiades (mihl-TY-ah-deez) ordered his troops to lock shields and advance at a full run. The Greeks charged into the surprised Persians, forced them back to their ships, and claimed victory over them.

DEFEAT OF THE PERSIAN EMPIRE

Ten years after the Battle at Marathon, **Xerxes** (ZURK-seez), Darius's successor, invaded Athens. In 480 B.C., hundreds of Persian ships and more than 150,000 soldiers went on the attack. Athens was ready this time—and it did not have to face the Persians alone. Athens had forged strong **alliances**, or partnerships, with other Greek city-states, including Sparta. Because the Athenians needed more time to prepare for battle, King Leonidas of Sparta occupied the important mountain pass of **Thermopylae** (thur-MAHP-uh-lee). Leonidas's small army fought off the Persians, giving the Greeks time to assemble further south.

The Athenians fought on. At the Battle of Salamis (SAL-uh-mihs) a small fleet of Greek warships called **triremes** (try-REEMZ) faced the Persian navy. The Greeks lured the Persians into a trap in the strait at Salamis and destroyed nearly a third of the Persian fleet. In 479 B.C., a large and united Greek army finally defeated the Persians at the Battle of Plataea. After this, the Persians left Greece and never invaded again. Although the war flared on and off for a few more decades, Greece was safe. Athens and Sparta emerged triumphant as the most powerful city-states in Greece.

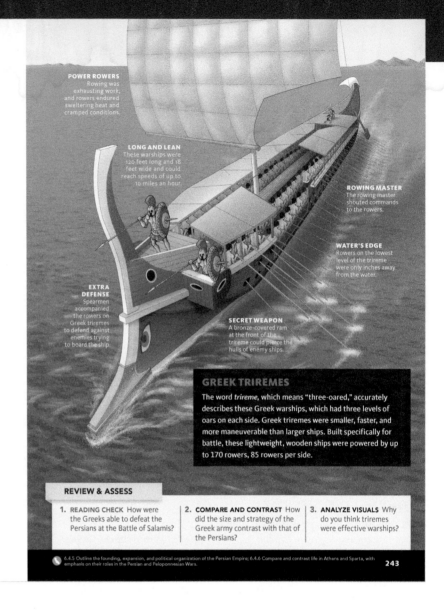

POWER ROWERS Rowing was exhausting work, and rowers endured sweltering heat and cramped conditions.

LONG AND LEAN These warships were 120 feet long and 18 feet wide and could reach speeds of up to 10 miles an hour.

ROWING MASTER The rowing master shouted commands to the rowers.

WATER'S EDGE Rowers on the lowest level of the trireme were only inches away from the water.

EXTRA DEFENSE Spearmen accompanied the rowers on Greek triremes to defend against enemies trying to board the ship.

SECRET WEAPON A bronze-covered ram at the front of the trireme could pierce the hulls of enemy ships.

GREEK TRIREMES

The word *trireme*, which means "three-oared," accurately describes these Greek warships, which had three levels of oars on each side. Greek triremes were smaller, faster, and more maneuverable than larger ships. Built specifically for battle, these lightweight, wooden ships were powered by up to 170 rowers, 85 rowers per side.

REVIEW & ASSESS

1. **READING CHECK** How were the Greeks able to defeat the Persians at the Battle of Salamis?

2. **COMPARE AND CONTRAST** How did the size and strategy of the Greek army contrast with that of the Persians?

3. **ANALYZE VISUALS** Why do you think triremes were effective warships?

6.4.5 Outline the founding, expansion, and political organization of the Persian Empire; 6.4.6 Compare and contrast life in Athens and Sparta, with emphasis on their roles in the Persian and Peloponnesian Wars.

STANDARDS

HSS CONTENT STANDARDS:

6.4.5 Outline the founding, expansion, and political organization of the Persian Empire; **6.4.6** Compare and contrast life in Athens and Sparta, with emphasis on their roles in the Persian and Peloponnesian Wars.

HSS ANALYSIS SKILLS:

CST 2 Students construct various time lines of key events, people, and periods of the historical era they are studying.

PLAN

OBJECTIVE

Learn about military victories by the ancient Greeks.

ESSENTIAL QUESTION

How did a cultured and influential civilization arise in Greece?

As the ancient Greeks became more powerful, they clashed with powers in the region. Lesson 2.3 describes the events of the Persian Wars.

BACKGROUND FOR THE TEACHER

The defeat of the Persian Empire at the hands of the ancient Greeks was the underdog story of its day. The Persian Empire dwarfed the Greek armies in size and power. After his embarrassing defeat at Thermopylae, the Persian emperor Xerxes wanted to totally destroy the Greeks. At the Battle of Salamis, the size of the Persian military and its ships became a detriment rather than a guarantee of victory. Persian ships were large and difficult to maneuver. The Greeks were able to navigate between the Persian ships, setting them on fire. Spartans waiting at water's edge killed the Persians who abandoned ship and made it to shore.

DIGITAL RESOURCES NGLSync.cengage.com

TEACHER RESOURCES & ASSESSMENT

 Reading and Note-Taking

 Vocabulary Practice

 Section 2 Quiz

STUDENT RESOURCES

 NG Chapter Gallery

INTRODUCE & ENGAGE

PREVIEW WITH VISUALS

Direct students' attention to the illustration of the Greek trireme. Ask volunteers to read the main caption and the smaller captions. **ASK:** Based on what you see and what you've heard, what do you think Lesson 2.3 will be about? *(Students' responses will vary, but should focus on Greek warships and soldiers.)* Encourage students to refer to the illustration as they read the last paragraph of the text. **0:05** minutes

TEACH

GUIDED DISCUSSION

1. **Summarize** Why did the Persians attack the Greeks at the Battle of Marathon? *(The Persian emperor wanted to punish Athens for helping Ionia revolt against Persian rule.)*

2. **Form and Support Opinions** What do you think helped the Greeks more as they defended themselves against the Persians: their size or their alliances? Use details in the reading to support your opinion. *(Students' responses will vary, but should be supported by details in the reading.)*

ANALYZE VISUALS

As a class, review the illustration of the Greek trireme. **ASK:** Based on the illustration's captions, what do you think it might have been like to be a rower on a Greek trireme? *(Students responses will vary, but may note that the ships were probably very hot, that it was hard to hear, that rowers probably couldn't see what was going on, and that it was probably quite frightening to engage in battle with much larger ships.)* **0:10** minutes

ACTIVE OPTIONS

NG Learning Framework: Learn More About Triremes **STEM**

ATTITUDE: Curiosity
SKILL: Problem-Solving

Invite students to review the text and illustration in the lesson. Encourage them to share their observations about how the triremes were constructed, how rowers had to work together, and how wind and water conditions might affect a battle. **ASK:** What might be one of the problems a rower on a trireme would have had to solve? **0:10** minutes

On Your Feet: Inside-Outside Circle Have students form concentric circles facing each other. Allow students time to write questions about the events of the Persian Wars. Then have students in the inside circle pose questions to students in the outside circle. Have students switch roles. Students may ask for help from other students in their circle if they are unable to answer a question. **0:20** minutes

DIFFERENTIATE

STRIVING READERS

Set a Purpose for Reading Before reading, have students use the lesson subheadings and the illustration to create purpose-setting questions:

- Who were the Ionians? Why did they revolt?
- Who defeated the Persian Empire? How did they do it?
- What is a trireme?

After reading, have student pairs answer the questions. Then ask for student volunteers to share their answers.

PRE-AP

Annotate a Time Line Have students annotate a time line of the Persian Wars. They should conduct independent research to support the reading in the lesson and to include more details and dates. Their time lines should extend from 546 B.C. to 479 B.C. Encourage students to include visuals on their time lines that might help illustrate events. Have students post their time lines on the wall in the classroom.

The Persian Wars

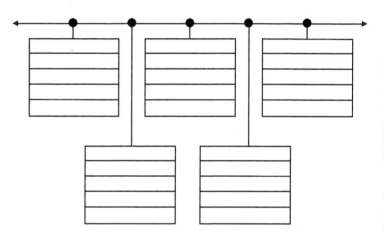

Press **mt** *in the Student eEdition for modified text.*

See the Chapter Planner for more strategies for differentiation.

REVIEW & ASSESS

ANSWERS

1. Greek city-states had formed alliances with each other so were better prepared for battle. The use of the triremes was a strategic advantage for the Greeks because of their small size and speed.

2. The Greek army was vastly smaller than the Persian army. The Greeks relied on surprise attacks and clever maneuvers, while the Persians relied on size and might.

3. Greek triremes were effective warships probably because they were maneuverable, fast, and lightweight. The rams could also pierce enemy ships' hulls.

+ POSSIBLE RESPONSE

The actions of Leonidas and the 300 reflect the culture of Sparta because the soldiers fought to the death to protect against the invading Persians and they sacrificed themselves for the good of the Greek city-states.

480 B.C.

Heroic events inspire exciting movies. Here, outnumbered Spartan soldiers force Persians over a cliff in a scene from the 2007 film *300*. At the Battle of Thermopylae in 480 B.C., 6,000 Greek soldiers led by Spartans fought off more than 100,000 Persian soldiers. Exhausted, the soldiers battled bravely, but their strength was running out. King Leonidas of Sparta realized the battle was lost and ordered most of the soldiers to withdraw. He and his 300 elite Spartans stayed behind to protect the retreating army and delay the Persians. It meant certain death. The ensuing battle was fierce. When swords broke, the Spartans fought with bare hands. None escaped alive. Thanks to the sacrifice of the 300, the Greeks were able to regroup and eventually defeat the Persians. How do the actions of Leonidas and the 300 reflect the culture of Sparta?

6.4.6 Compare and contrast life in Athens and Sparta, with emphasis on their roles in the Persian and Peloponnesian Wars.

245

HSS CONTENT STANDARDS:

6.4.6 Compare and contrast life in Athens and Sparta, with emphasis on their roles in the Persian and Peloponnesian Wars.

HSS ANALYSIS SKILLS:

REP 5 Students detect the different historical points of view on historical events and determine the context in which the historical statements were made (the questions asked, sources used, author's perspectives).

PLAN

OBJECTIVE

Explore the drama of the Battle of Thermopylae.

ESSENTIAL QUESTION

How did a cultured and influential civilization arise in Greece?

As they grew from small city-states into an advanced civilization, the ancient Greeks often clashed with regional powers. Lesson 2.4 provides a modern, cinematic interpretation of the events of the Battle of Thermopylae in 480 B.C. between the Persians and the Greeks.

BACKGROUND FOR THE TEACHER

The Persian Empire was mighty. When the ancient Greeks defeated this military giant, a definite shift in power took place in the region. The epic battle at Thermopylae has captured the attention of historians and military buffs alike for centuries. The notion of a tiny, scrappy army defeating one of the most powerful empires in the region strikes a chord with audiences, even today. The actual pass at Thermopylae is about four miles long, and 480 B.C. was not the last time the location would see battle. The Greeks fought off the Celts there in 279 B.C. and the Seleucids defended against the Romans in 191 B.C.

DIGITAL RESOURCES NGLSync.cengage.com

TEACHER RESOURCES & ASSESSMENT

 Reading and Note-Taking

 Vocabulary Practice

 Section 2 Quiz

STUDENT RESOURCES

 NG Image Gallery

MAKE PREDICTIONS USING VISUALS

Ask students to look at the photograph in the lesson. Then ask for volunteers to describe what is happening in the photograph and what mood the photo strikes. **ASK:** Which group of soldiers has the upper hand in this scene? *(the Spartans, who are pushing the Persians over a cliff)*
`0:05` minutes

GUIDED DISCUSSION

1. **Analyze Visuals** What details in the photo help the viewer know who the Spartans are? *(The Spartans are identifiable by their characteristic helmets.)*

2. **Make Connections** The Battle of Thermopylae has come to represent courage in battle and victory in the face of overwhelming odds. Can you think of another instance, not necessarily based on war, in which the underdog emerged victorious against seemingly insurmountable odds? *(Responses will vary. Possible responses: The American colonies defeat of the British Empire in the American Revolution; the victory of the English navy over the Spanish Armada; the victory of the U.S. Olympic hockey team over the Soviets in 1980; Billy Mills' come-from-behind win in the 10,000-meter race in the 1964 Olympics in Tokyo.)*

MORE INFORMATION

King Leonidas As leader of the Spartans, King Leonidas took charge of the strategy at Thermopylae. In order to protect retreating Greeks, he and his elite team of 300 stayed behind to fight off the Persians. The Greek historian Herodotus wrote that Leonidas handpicked his soldiers for the mission at Thermopylae. All the soldiers he selected were fathers, perhaps because they were considered reliable and battle-tested. When Leonidas first understood the huge size of the army that awaited him and his Spartans, he had second thoughts, according to Herodotus. In the end, all the Spartans died, including Leonidas, but not without first demonstrating courage, sacrifice, and heroism.

ACTIVE OPTIONS

Critical Viewing: NG Image Gallery Invite students to explore the entire NG Image Gallery and choose one image from the gallery they feel best represents their understanding of each chapter or the unit. Have students provide a written explanation of why they selected each of the images.
`0:15` minutes

NG Learning Framework: Analyze Historical Perspective

ATTITUDE: **Responsibility**
KNOWLEDGE: **Our Human Story**

Explain to students that much of what historians know about the Persian Empire comes from the writings of Herodotus and other Greek sources. Have students study the image from the movie *300* and discuss how the film portrays the Spartans and Persians. Then have students turn to Lesson 2.4 in Chapter 3 and study the relief from ancient Persepolis. Have volunteers point out differences in the way the Greeks represented the Persians and the way the Persians represented themselves. `0:15` minutes

STRIVING READERS

Analyze Visuals Provide concrete questions to help students of different ability levels process the photograph. Make sure students understand that the photo is a movie still and not a representation of the actual battle. **ASK:** Which soldiers in the photo represent the Persians? Which represent the Spartans? Encourage students to point to things they don't understand about the photo and help them frame questions about these details.

GIFTED & TALENTED

Offer an Alternative Ending Have students offer an alternate outcome for the Battle of Thermopylae. Encourage them to imagine what might have happened if the Spartans had somehow pushed the Persians back and, ultimately, out of Greece? Have students discuss different outcomes with each other and then select one to present to the class. Then have the class ask questions and offer suggestions about other outcomes.

Press (**mt**) *in the Student eEdition for modified text.*

See the Chapter Planner for more strategies for differentiation.

VOCABULARY

Complete each of the following sentences using one of the vocabulary words from the chapter.

1. According to an ancient myth, King Minos of Crete built a large maze, or _____, beneath his palace. HSS 6.4.4

2. The *Odyssey* is a(n) _____ that was written by Homer and tells the many adventures of Odysseus. HSS 6.4.4

3. _____ is the Greek word for city-state. HSS 6.4.2

4. In ancient Greek city-states, the _____ was the city's marketplace and social center. HSS 6.4

5. Typically built on a hilltop, the _____ was a city's last line of defense. HSS 6.4

6. During the Persian Wars, Athens formed _____ with other Greek city-states. HSS 6.4.6

7. In Spartan society, _____ were slaves from conquered regions. HSS 6.4.6

8. Gold and tin are examples of _____. HSS 6.4.1

READING STRATEGY

9. ORGANIZE IDEAS: COMPARE AND CONTRAST If you haven't already, complete your graphic organizer to compare and contrast life in Sparta and Athens. Then answer the question.

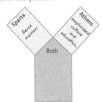

Sparta — fierce warriors
Athens — emphasized culture and education
Both

How was life in Sparta and Athens similar? How was it different? HSS 6.4.6

MAIN IDEAS

Answer the following questions. Support your answers with evidence from the chapter.

10. Where did the Minoan civilization settle and flourish? LESSON 1.1 HSS 6.4.1

11. How did the Mycenaeans gain wealth and power in the Mediterranean? LESSON 1.2 HSS 6.4.1

12. What are epic poems and what kinds of stories do they tell? LESSON 1.3 HSS 6.4.4

13. What was the function of the polis as it developed in Greek civilization? LESSON 1.4 HSS HI 1

14. How did sea trade affect ancient Greek civilization? LESSON 1.5 HSS 6.4.1

15. What were the advantages and disadvantages of Sparta's military society? LESSON 2.1 HSS 6.4.6

16. How did the roles of Athenian men and women differ? LESSON 2.2 HSS HI 1

17. What caused the Persian Wars? LESSON 2.3 HSS 6.4.5

CRITICAL THINKING

Answer the following questions. Support your answers with evidence from the chapter.

18. ESSENTIAL QUESTION What were some of the developments that led to the establishment of a cultured and influential civilization in ancient Greece? HSS REP 1

19. COMPARE AND CONTRAST How were the Minoan and Mycenaean civilizations alike? How were they different? HSS HI 3

20. DRAW CONCLUSIONS Why were epic poems and their heroes important to the ancient Greeks? HSS 6.4.4

21. EVALUATE Why was the Greek adoption of the Phoenician alphabet an important development? HSS HI 3

22. YOU DECIDE Which city-state—Athens or Sparta—had the most effective system of government? Support your opinion with evidence from the chapter. HSS 6.4.6

INTERPRET MAPS

Study the map of the Persian Wars. Then answer the questions that follow.

PERSIAN WARS, 499–497 B.C.

1. Athenian army defeats Persian army.
2. Greek force, led by Spartans, falls to Persian army.
3. Greek fleet defeats Persian navy.
4. Greeks defeat Persians, ending the war.

Thermopylae 480 B.C. · Marathon 490 B.C. · Plataea 479 B.C. · Salamis 480 B.C. · Sardis · Miletus · Sparta · Crete

Persian Wars, 499–479 B.C.
- Greek states
- Persian Empire
- 1st Persian invasion, 490 B.C.
- 2nd Persian invasion, 480 B.C.
- Major battle

23. How did the routes of the first and second Persian invasions differ? HSS 6.4.5

24. Which of the major battles shown was a naval battle? HSS CST 3

ANALYZE SOURCES

Read the following description of Darius I, the emperor of Persia, written by Herodotus after the Ionian revolt.

Darius did, however, ask who the Athenians were, and after receiving the answer, he called for his bow. This he took and, placing an arrow on it, shot it into the sky, praying as he sent it aloft, "O Zeus, grant me vengeance on the Athenians."

Then he ordered one of his servants to say to him three times whenever dinner was set before him, "Master, remember the Athenians."

25. What does this description of Darius I reveal about him? HSS REP 4

WRITE ABOUT HISTORY

26. INFORMATIVE Suppose you have been asked to participate in a radio program that examines important topics from history. Write a paragraph to inform your audience about the beginnings of democracy in ancient Greece between 600 and 500 B.C. HSS 6.4.2

TIPS

- Take notes from the lesson about Athens's democratic society.
- Introduce the topic clearly.
- Develop the topic with relevant, well-chosen facts, concrete details, and examples.
- Use vocabulary from the chapter to explain democratic ideas.
- Provide a concluding statement that summarizes the information presented.

VOCABULARY ANSWERS

1. labyrinth HSS 6.4.4
2. epic poem HSS 6.4.4
3. Polis HSS 6.4.2
4. agora HSS 6.4
5. acropolis HSS 6.4
6. alliances HSS 6.4.6
7. helots HSS 6.4.6
8. raw materials HSS 6.4.1

STANDARDS

HSS CONTENT STANDARDS:

6.4.1 Discuss the connections between geography and the development of city-states in the region of the Aegean Sea, including patterns of trade and commerce among Greek city-states and within the wider Mediterranean region; **6.4.2** Trace the transition from tyranny and oligarchy to early democratic forms of government and back to dictatorship in ancient Greece, including the significance of the invention of the idea of citizenship (e.g., from Pericles' Funeral Oration); **6.4.4** Explain the significance of Greek mythology to the everyday life of people in the region and how Greek literature continues to permeate our literature and language today, drawing from Greek mythology and epics, such as Homer's Illad and Odyssey, and from Aesop's Fables; **6.4.5** Outline the founding, expansion, and political organization of the Persian Empire; **6.4.6** Compare and contrast life in Athens and Sparta, with emphasis on their roles in the Persian and Peloponnesian Wars.

HSS ANALYSIS SKILLS:

CST 3 Students use a variety of maps and documents to identify physical and cultural features of neighborhoods, cities, states, and countries and to explain the historical migration of people, expansion and disintegration of empires, and the growth of economic systems; **REP 1** Students frame questions that can be answered by historical study and research; **REP 4** Students assess the credibility of primary and secondary sources and draw sound conclusions from them; **HI 1** Students explain the central issues and problems from the past, placing people and events in a matrix of time and place; **HI 3** Students explain the sources of historical continuity and how the combination of ideas and events explains the emergence of new patterns.

READING STRATEGY ANSWER

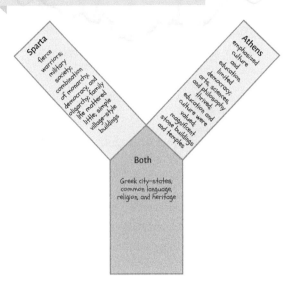

Sparta
fierce warriors, military society, combination of monarchy, democracy, and oligarchy, family life mattered little, simple village-style buildings

Athens
emphasized culture and education, limited democracy, arts, sciences, and philosophy thrived, education and culture were valued, magnificent stone buildings and temples

Both
Greek city-states; common language, religion, and heritage

9. Both Sparta and Athens were Greek city-states that shared a common language, religion, and heritage, but that is where their similarities ended. Each Greek city-state developed differently due to their relative isolation. Sparta developed a military society with a rigid hierarchy—every element of Sparta's society was devoted to war and maintaining firm control over the helots. Athens, on the other hand, valued arts, sciences, and education in their more liberal society, where a limited democracy developed. Athens was a beautiful city-state with many magnificent stone buildings and temples. (HSS 6.4.6)

MAIN IDEAS ANSWERS

10. Minoan civilization settled and flourished on the island of Crete in the Mediterranean. (HSS 6.4.1)

11. The Mycenaeans gained wealth and power by waging war and conquering lands across the Mediterranean and through trade. (HSS 6.4.1)

12. Epic poems are long, poetic stories that tell of a hero's adventures with humans and with gods and goddesses. (HSS 6.4.4)

13. The polis, or city-state, was a small, independent unit in which a dominant city—such as Athens, Sparta, or Thebes—ruled the surrounding area from a centralized location. (HSS HI 1)

14. Sea trade helped early Greeks spread their culture throughout the Mediterranean by establishing hundreds of new colonies and by their wide-ranging trade in the region. (HSS 6.4.1)

15. The advantages of a military society included being able to control the helots and the general population and to wage effective wars. The disadvantages included harsh living conditions and childhoods. (HSS 6.4.6)

16. Athenian men could be citizens and received educations; Athenian women were not considered citizens and were not educated. Men's roles centered on the city-state; women's roles centered on the home. (HSS HI 1)

17. The Persian Wars were caused by Athens, who encouraged the Ionians to rebel against the Persians. To punish Athens, the Persians invaded Greece. (HSS 6.4.5)

CRITICAL THINKING ANSWERS

18. The Minoans and Mycenaeans established the foundation for ancient Greek civilization. Later, ancient Greek city-states developed unique cultures, various types of government, and established a complex and rich trade network in the Mediterranean. The ancient Greeks also developed strong militaries that enabled them to defend themselves against huge empires such as the Persians. (HSS REP 1)

19. The Minoan and Mycenaean civilizations were alike in terms of culture. After they settled in mainland Greece, the Mycenaeans copied nearly all aspects of Minoan culture, including government, religion, architecture, shipbuilding, and trade. The Minoans focused on building ships and trading, while the Mycenaeans were a warring people who used their military power to seize other lands and expand their power in the region. (HSS HI 3)

20. Epic poems united the Greeks through pride in their shared past. (HSS 6.4.4)

21. The Greek adoption of the Phoenician alphabet was important because after the Greeks adopted the Phoenician alphabet, they improved it, eventually making it the Greek alphabet. This alphabet was in turn adopted and became the basis of the modern alphabet used today. (HSS HI 3)

22. Students' responses will vary. Students should clearly state their opinion regarding their view of government in Sparta and Athens and support that opinion with evidence from the chapter. (HSS 6.4.6)

INTERPRET MAPS ANSWERS

23. In the first invasion the Persians attacked Greece from the south, by sea. In the second invasion, the Persians attacked from the north, by both land and sea. (HSS 6.4.5)

24. The Battle of Salamis was a naval battle. (HSS CST 3)

ANALYZE SOURCES ANSWER

25. Students' responses will vary. Sample response:
The description reveals how fiercely angry Darius I is toward the Athenians for their role in the Ionian revolt. Details such as Darius shooting an arrow, swearing to God, and wanting to be reminded of the Athenians all show the extent of his anger and determination to punish the Athenians. (HSS REP 4)

WRITE ABOUT HISTORY ANSWER

26. Students' informative paragraphs will vary, but students should present the information in a clear, logical manner that explains how democracy began to form in ancient Greece between 600 and 500 B.C.

For more in-depth instruction and practice with the writing form, assign the Social Studies Skills Writing Lesson on writing an informative paragraph. (HSS 6.4.2)

UNIT RESOURCES

On Location with National Geographic Grantee William Parkinson Intro and Video

Unit Wrap-Up:
"The Emergence of Cities"
Feature and Video

"Greek Statues Sparkle Once Again"
National Geographic Adapted Article

"Behind the Tomb"
National Geographic Adapted Article
Student eEdition exclusive

Unit 3 Inquiry:
Define Good Citizenship

 Interactive Map Tool
Available at NGLSync.cengage.com

 **News & Updates**
Available at NGLSync.cengage.com

CHAPTER RESOURCES

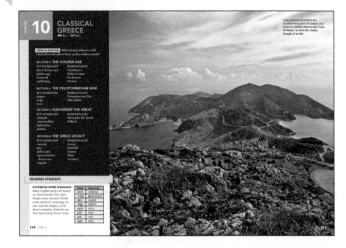

TEACHER RESOURCES & ASSESSMENT *Available at NGLSync.cengage.com*

 Social Studies Skills Lessons
• Reading: Determine Word Meanings
• Writing: Write an Informative Text

 Chapter 10 Answer Key

 Formal Assessment
• Chapter 10 Tests A (on-level) & B (below-level)

 ExamView®
One-time Download

STUDENT BACKPACK *Available at NGLSync.cengage.com*

• **eEdition** *(English)*   • **eEdition** *(Spanish)*   • **Handbooks**   • **Online Atlas**

Chapter 10 Spanish resources, Guided Writing prompts, and Financial Literacy lessons are available online.

SECTION 1 RESOURCES

THE GOLDEN AGE

 Reading and Note-Taking

 Vocabulary Practice

 Section 1 Quiz

Available at NGLSync.cengage.com

LESSON 1.1 PERICLES AND DEMOCRACY

 Biography
Cleisthenes

Available at NGLSync.cengage.com

• On Your Feet: Small Groups

| **NG Learning Framework:**
Democracy in Action

LESSON 1.2 THE ATHENIAN EMPIRE

• On Your Feet: Debate

| **NG Learning Framework:**
Research the Acropolis

LESSON 1.3 RELIGION AND THE GODS

• On Your Feet: Play a Game of Telephone

| **NG Learning Framework:**
Retell a Myth

SECTION 2 RESOURCES

THE PELOPONNESIAN WAR

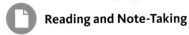 **Reading and Note-Taking**

Vocabulary Practice

Section 2 Quiz

Available at NGLSync.cengage.com

LESSON 2.1 WAR BREAKS OUT
- On Your Feet: Inside-Outside Circle
- Critical Viewing: NG Chapter Gallery

LESSON 2.2 THE DEFEAT OF ATHENS
- On Your Feet: Identifying Issues
- Critical Viewing: NG Image Gallery

DOCUMENT-BASED QUESTION
LESSON 2.3 ATHENIAN DEMOCRACY
- On Your Feet: Jigsaw

| **NG Learning Framework:**
Attitudes Toward Democracy

SECTION 3 RESOURCES

ALEXANDER THE GREAT

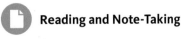 **Reading and Note-Taking**

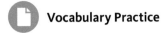 **Vocabulary Practice**

 **Section 3 Quiz**

Available at NGLSync.cengage.com

LESSON 3.1 PHILIP OF MACEDONIA
- On Your Feet: Tell Me More

| **NG Learning Framework:**
Role-Play

BIOGRAPHY
LESSON 3.2 ALEXANDER THE GREAT
- On Your Feet: Make Inferences About Character
- Critical Viewing: NG Image Gallery

LESSON 3.3 THE SPREAD OF HELLENISTIC CULTURE
- On Your Feet: Culture Roundtable
- Critical Viewing: NG Chapter Gallery

SECTION 4 RESOURCES

THE GREEK LEGACY

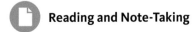 **Reading and Note-Taking**

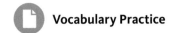 **Vocabulary Practice**

 **Section 4 Quiz**

Available at NGLSync.cengage.com

LESSON 4.1 PHILOSOPHY AND LITERATURE

 Biography
Aristotle

Available at NGLSync.cengage.com

| **NG Learning Framework:**
Write a Fable

- On Your Feet: Understand Multiple Perspectives

LESSON 4.2 ARTS AND ARCHITECTURE
- On Your Feet: Small Groups

| **NG Learning Framework:**
Write a Play

MOMENTS IN HISTORY
LESSON 4.3 THE PARTHENON
- On Your Feet: Debate
- Critical Viewing: NG Chapter Gallery

LESSON 4.4 DEMOCRACY AND LAW

 Active History: Interactive Whiteboard Activity
Research Ancient Greek Contributions

 Active History
Research Ancient Greek Contributions

Available at NGLSync.cengage.com
- On Your Feet: Democracy from Scratch

CHAPTER 10 REVIEW

STRATEGY ❶

Use a TASKS Approach

Help students get information from visuals by using the following TASKS strategy:

T Look for a **title** that may give the main idea.

A **Ask** yourself what the visual is trying to show.

S Determine how **symbols** are used.

K Look for a **key** or legend.

S **Summarize** what you learned.

Use with All Lessons

STRATEGY ❷

Make Summary Statements

Before reading, have students look at the blue subheadings within the lessons. After reading, direct students to use each subheading to begin a statement that summarizes the information about the subheading.

Use with Lesson 1.2 *Suggest that students use these sentence starters: Athens and other states banded together to form the _____, to defend themselves from Persia. Athens used money from the Delian League to _____.*

STRATEGY ❸

Play the "I Am . . ." Game

To reinforce the meanings of key terms and names, assign every student one term or name that appears in the chapter and have them write a one-sentence clue beginning with "I am." Have students take turns reading clues and calling on other students to guess answers.

Use with All Lessons

Press *in the Student eEdition for modified text.*

STRATEGY ❶

Provide Terms and Names on Audio

Decide which of the terms and names are important for mastery and have a volunteer record the pronunciations and a short sentence defining each word. Encourage students to listen to the recording as often as necessary.

Use with All Lessons *You might also use the recordings to quiz students on their mastery of the terms. Play one definition at a time from the recording and ask students to identify the term or name described.*

STRATEGY ❷

Preview Visuals to Predict

Ask students to preview the title and visuals in each lesson. Then have students tell what they think the lesson will be about. After reading, ask them to repeat the activity to see whether their predictions were confirmed.

Use with All Lessons *Invite volunteers to describe the visuals in detail to help visually impaired students see them.*

STRATEGY ❶

PREP Before Reading

Have students at all proficiency levels use the PREP strategy to prepare for reading. Write this acrostic on the board:

PREP   **P**review title.

                Read Main Idea statement.

                Examine visuals.

                Predict what you will learn.

Have students write their prediction and share it with a partner. After reading, ask students to write another sentence that begins "I also learned . . ."

Use with All Lessons, All Levels *Provide the following sentence stem for students at the **Emerging** level: I think this lesson is about _____. Ask students at the **Bridging** level to give reasons for their prediction.*

HSS CONTENT STANDARDS:

6.4 Students analyze the geographic, political, economic, religious, and social structures of the early civilizations of Ancient Greece.

STRATEGY ②

Visualize Vocabulary

Ask students to look at the visuals in the chapter and see if they help clarify the meaning of important vocabulary words. In Lesson 1.3 have them work out the meaning of the word *mythology*, while in Lesson 2.2 see if the visual helps them understand the word *siege*. Provide the following sentence frames to help students at each proficiency level explain their reasoning.

Emerging

The image helps me understand the word _____ because _____ .

Expanding and Bridging

This picture is useful because _____ . It helps me see that _____ means _____ .

Use with Lessons 1.3 and 2.2, All Levels

STRATEGY ③

Speak, Listen, and Learn

After students have read several lessons, divide the class into small groups of mixed proficiency levels and conduct a round-robin activity. Write the topic of the lesson on the board and have groups generate facts for about three to five minutes, with all students contributing. Then have one student from each group share the group's responses without repeating any fact already stated by another group. Have the volunteer write the fact on the board.

Use with Lessons 3.1, 3.3, and 4.4, All Levels

GIFTED & TALENTED

STRATEGY ①

Teach a Class

Before beginning the chapter, allow students to choose one of the lessons listed below and prepare to teach the content to the class. Give them a set amount of time in which to present their lesson. Suggest that students think about any visuals or activities they want to use when they teach.

Use with Lessons 1.2, 1.4, 1.6, and 2.1–2.3

STRATEGY ②

Create a Fan Zine for a Classical Greek Author or Philosopher

Using any author or philosopher mentioned in the text, suggest that students create a comic or zine to celebrate and teach about the person. Tell students to use both visuals and text, quotations from the thinker, and examples illustrating his ideas.

Use with Lessons 2.3, 4.1, and 4.2

PRE-AP

STRATEGY ①

Consider Two Sides

Tell students that some people believe that direct democracy is superior to representative democracy, or the type of democracy that is practiced in the United States. Have pairs of students research the issue and make a chart listing the positive and negative aspects of the two types of democracy. Have students share and discuss their chart with the class.

Use with Lessons 1.1 and 4.4

STRATEGY ②

Read Literature

Work with the school librarian to find and display a variety of titles from the period of classical Greece or historical fiction about that period. Allow students to choose a book (or part of a book) to read and design a way to report on the book to the class.

Use with All Lessons

Cape Tainaron, located at the southernmost point of Greece, was known in ancient times as the "Gate to Hades," or what the Greeks thought of as hell.

ESSENTIAL QUESTION What lasting influences did classical Greek culture have on the modern world?

SECTION 1 THE GOLDEN AGE

KEY VOCABULARY	NAMES & PLACES
direct democracy	Cleisthenes
golden age	Delian League
immortal	Parthenon
mythology	Pericles

SECTION 2 THE PELOPONNESIAN WAR

KEY VOCABULARY	NAMES & PLACES
plague	Peloponnesian War
siege	Thucydides
truce	

SECTION 3 ALEXANDER THE GREAT

KEY VOCABULARY	NAMES & PLACES
catapult	Alexander the Great
cosmopolitan	Philip II
Hellenistic	
phalanx	

SECTION 4 THE GREEK LEGACY

KEY VOCABULARY	NAMES & PLACES
comedy	Aesop
jury	Aristotle
philosophy	Homer
representative	Plato
democracy	Socrates
tragedy	

READING STRATEGY

DETERMINE WORD MEANINGS
Many English words are based on Greek words. This chart shows some common Greek roots and their meanings. As you read the chapter, write down examples of words you find that include these roots.

Root	Meaning
cosm-	universe
-cracy	government
dem-	people
-logy	speech
myth-	story
phil-	love
poli-	city
soph-	wise

249

HSS CONTENT STANDARDS:

6.4 Students analyze the geographic, political, economic, religious, and social structures of the early civilizations of Ancient Greece.

TEACHER BACKGROUND

INTRODUCE THE PHOTOGRAPH

Have students study the photograph of Cape Tainaron. Explain that a cape is a large extension of land that sticks out into a body of water. Explain that the geography of Greece influenced its history and culture and that students will learn more about these characteristics in the chapter.

ASK: What can you tell about the geography of Greece from this picture? *(Possible response: It is hilly, rocky, and near water.)*

SHARE BACKGROUND

Hades was the name of both the Greek underworld—the place where souls went after death—and its god. After death, a soul journeyed to the underworld through a cave thought to be on Cape Tainaron. There the soul was greeted by Charon, the ferryman who took souls across the river Styx to the gates of Hades. Each soul then appeared before a panel of judges who passed sentence according to deeds performed during the previous life. Good souls went to the Elysian Fields, a type of paradise, while bad souls remained in Hades and were punished for eternity.

DIGITAL RESOURCES NGLSync.cengage.com

TEACHER RESOURCES & ASSESSMENT

 Social Studies Skills Lessons
- Reading: Determine Word Meanings
- Writing: Write an Informative Text

 Formal Assessment
- Chapter 10 Tests A (on-level) & B (below-level)

 ExamView®
One-time Download

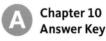 **Chapter 10 Answer Key**

STUDENT BACKPACK

- **eEdition** *(English)*
- **eEdition** *(Spanish)*
- **Handbooks**
- **Online Atlas**

INTRODUCE THE ESSENTIAL QUESTION

WHAT LASTING INFLUENCES DID ANCIENT GREEK CULTURE HAVE ON THE MODERN WORLD?

Jigsaw: Cultural Influence This activity introduces students to four factors of culture in order to differentiate the various influences that classical Greek civilization has had on modern society. Have students form four expert groups and then tell them to research and brainstorm one aspect of Greek culture and how it has influenced a modern culture. Students may focus on religion, government, customs and traditions, arts and recreation, or some other aspect. Then have students regroup so that one member from each expert group is in the new group. Each expert should then report on his or her topic of study to the members of the new group. **0:15** minutes

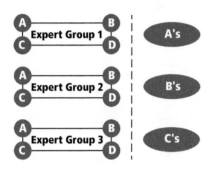

INTRODUCE THE READING STRATEGY

DETERMINE WORD MEANINGS

Read through the chart of Greek roots and their meanings with students. Model the strategy by using knowledge of the roots *dem-* and *-cracy* to determine the meaning of the word *democracy*, or government of the people. For more in-depth instruction and practice with the reading strategy, assign the Social Studies Skills Reading Lesson on determining word meanings.

Root	Meaning
cosm-	universe
-cracy	government
dem-	people
-logy	speech
myth-	story
phil-	love
poli-	city
soph-	wise

INTRODUCE CHAPTER VOCABULARY

KNOWLEDGE RATING

Have students complete a Knowledge-Rating Chart for Key Vocabulary words. Have students list words and fill out the chart. Then have pairs share the definitions they know. Work together as a class to complete the chart.

KEY VOCAB	KNOW IT	NOT SURE	DON'T KNOW	DEFINITION
catapult				
comedy				
cosmopolitan				
direct democracy				

KEY DATES	
c. 500 b.c.	Development of democracy in Athens
478 b.c.	Creation of the Delian League
431 b.c.	Beginning of the Peloponnesian War; Pericles' funeral oration
414 b.c.	Athens's siege of Syracuse
404 b.c.	End of the Peloponnesian War; the defeat of Athens
338 b.c.	Unification of Greece under Philip of Macedonia
331 b.c.	Conquest of the Persian Empire by Alexander the Great

Pericles and Democracy

When you go out with your friends after school, how does your group decide what to do? Does one friend make this decision? Do two or three take charge? Or do you all have a say? If you all weigh in, that's democracy, a concept that began in Athens more than 2,500 years ago.

MAIN IDEA

Athens established the world's first democracy.

ELECTED BY LOTTERY

Athenians used this machine, known as a *kleroterion*, to elect officials. Each eligible male placed a token with his name on it in one of the slots. A series of balls were then released from a tube to determine whose tokens would be chosen.

SEEDS OF DEMOCRACY

As you may recall from the previous chapter, the leader Solon made life better for the poor. He canceled their debts, freed enslaved farmers, and abolished unfair payments to greedy landowners.

Solon also reduced the power of the aristocracy. He organized citizens into four classes based on wealth. Rich men still had more power, but all male citizens, rich and poor, were allowed to join the assembly and help elect leaders. Solon also created a council chosen by lottery, or chance, from the assembly. Solon made Athenian government fairer, but it was not yet a true democracy.

Around 500 B.C., a leader named **Cleisthenes** (KLYS-thuh-neez) took things further. Under his rule, the assembly members debated openly and heard court cases. Citizens were organized into groups based on where they lived. Each group sent 50 representatives a year to the Council of 500. The council proposed laws and debated policies, and the assembly voted on them. The citizens were now fully engaged in government. This was democracy—but a limited one. Only male property owners born in Athens could participate. Women, foreigners, and slaves had no political rights.

ATHENS'S GREATEST LEADER

Pericles (PEHR-uh-kleez), one of Athens's greatest leaders, expanded this limited democracy into one that would allow all male citizens to participate in government. He transferred the remaining powers of the aristocrats to the assembly. He paid jurors, which allowed poor citizens to take time off to serve the state. This idea was later extended to all public officials, who previously were unpaid. Pericles also opened up powerful political positions to the middle classes. Neither social class nor poverty was a barrier to political power anymore. Athens now had a **direct democracy**, in which citizens gathered together to vote on laws and policies.

Pericles was also determined to glorify Athens by transforming it from a city ravaged by the Persian Wars to a center of learning, creativity, and beauty. By encouraging the work of great thinkers and artists, Pericles guided Athens through a **golden age**—a period of great cultural achievement.

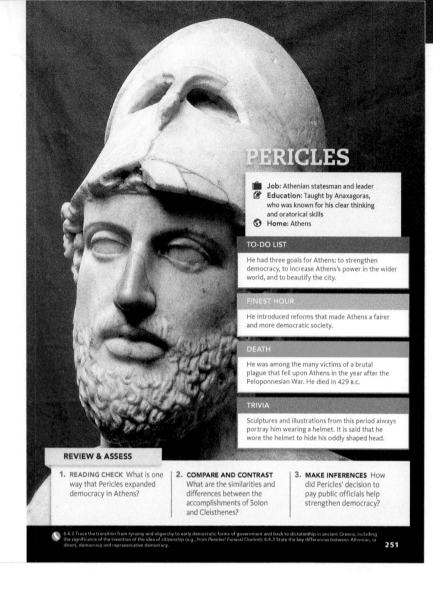

PERICLES

- **Job:** Athenian statesman and leader
- **Education:** Taught by Anaxagoras, who was known for his clear thinking and oratorical skills
- **Home:** Athens

TO-DO LIST

He had three goals for Athens: to strengthen democracy, to increase Athens's power in the wider world, and to beautify the city.

FINEST HOUR

He introduced reforms that made Athens a fairer and more democratic society.

DEATH

He was among the many victims of a brutal plague that fell upon Athens in the year after the Peloponnesian War. He died in 429 B.C.

TRIVIA

Sculptures and illustrations from this period always portray him wearing a helmet. It is said that he wore the helmet to hide his oddly shaped head.

REVIEW & ASSESS

1. **READING CHECK** What is one way that Pericles expanded democracy in Athens?

2. **COMPARE AND CONTRAST** What are the similarities and differences between the accomplishments of Solon and Cleisthenes?

3. **MAKE INFERENCES** How did Pericles' decision to pay public officials help strengthen democracy?

6.4.2 Trace the transition from tyranny and oligarchy to early democratic forms of government and back to dictatorship in ancient Greece, including the significance of the invention of the idea of citizenship (e.g., from *Pericles' Funeral Oration*); 6.4.3 State the key differences between Athenian, or direct, democracy and representative democracy.

HSS CONTENT STANDARDS:

6.4.2 Trace the transition from tyranny and oligarchy to early democratic forms of government and back to dictatorship in ancient Greece, including the significance of the invention of the idea of citizenship (e.g., from *Pericles' Funeral Oration*);
6.4.3 State the key differences between Athenian, or direct, democracy and representative democracy.

PLAN

OBJECTIVE

Identify the process by which Athens became a democracy.

ESSENTIAL QUESTION

What lasting influences did ancient Greek culture have on the modern world?

Greece introduced the world to the concept of democracy. Lesson 1.1 describes the evolution of Greece's democratic government.

BACKGROUND FOR THE TEACHER

Athens is credited with having the first direct democracy in history. Democracy comes from two Greek words—*kratos*, meaning "rule" and *demos*, meaning "village or people." The idea that not just the rich and powerful should have a say in government gave rise to the idea of the assembly. The assembly gave ordinary people more say in government and made it harder for corrupt individuals to use power for personal gain. It was used to check the power of the council, the full-time government of Athens that ran the daily affairs of the city. The council was elected by lottery and changed every year, but it contained eligible citizens from the top three classes of society only. The council debated on matters and voted, and anything it passed then went on to the assembly for a vote.

DIGITAL RESOURCES NGLSync.cengage.com

TEACHER RESOURCES & ASSESSMENT

 Reading and Note-Taking

 Vocabulary Practice

 Section 1 Quiz

STUDENT RESOURCES

 Biography

INTRODUCE & ENGAGE

COMPLETE A K-W-L CHART

Provide each student with a K-W-L Chart like the one shown. Have students brainstorm what they know about Pericles and democracy. Then ask them to write questions that they would like to have answered as they study Lesson 1.1. Allow time at the end of the lesson for students to fill in what they have learned. `0:05` minutes

K What Do I Know?	W What Do I Want To Learn?	L What Did I Learn?

TEACH

GUIDED DISCUSSION

1. **Make Inferences** Why might a leader like Solon have wanted to reduce the power of the aristocracy and improve the lives of the poor? *(because he wanted to improve the lives of the poor, gaining their approval and reducing discontent, as well as strengthening his own position)*

2. **Analyze Causes** What was the motivation to pay jurors under Pericles' leadership? *(Paying jurors allowed poor citizens to serve on juries. Otherwise they could not afford to take time off from their jobs.)*

ANALYZE VISUALS

Direct students' attention to the photo of the statue of Pericles. **ASK:** What can you tell about the style of Greek sculpture? How does it compare to figures created by the ancient Egyptians? *(Greek sculpture is very realistic with lots of attention to detail. Egyptian figures were less detailed and more symbolic in appearance.)* `0:10` minutes

ACTIVE OPTIONS

On Your Feet: Small Groups Have students form small groups. Have each group find a different country that has some form of democracy today and report to the class some details about the country's system, including whether it is a limited or unlimited democracy, a mix, a republic, or perhaps, a democracy with a monarch. `0:10` minutes

NG Learning Framework: Democracy in Action

ATTITUDES: Empowerment, Responsibility
SKILLS: Collaboration, Problem-Solving

Have students observe Athenian direct democracy in action by letting them vote on some aspect of the day's instruction or the classroom layout. For example, they might vote on whether or not to answer lesson questions in groups or on whether or not to arrange desks in a circle for the day. Students should give a yes or no vote on the aspect and a simple majority should determine whether the measure passes. After the vote, discuss the strengths and weaknesses of this form of government. `0:10` minutes

DIFFERENTIATE

STRIVING READERS

Chart Athenian Leaders Have students use the chart to keep track of reforms made by the three leaders in Lesson 1.1.

	Solon	Cleisthenes	Pericles
Let only male property owners participate in government	✓	✓	
Made life better for the poor	✓		
Allowed women to participate in government			
Organized citizens into classes	✓		
Paid jurors and public officials			✓
Created a council by lottery	✓		
Guided Athens to a golden age			✓
Created a limited democracy		✓	

PRE-AP

Write Reports Use Lesson 1.1 as a starting point to have students explore the concept of democracy further. Tell students to research the characteristics of limited and unlimited democracies, finding historical and contemporary examples for each. Then direct students to write a short report about the advantages and disadvantages of both types of democracy. Encourage volunteers to share their reports with the class.

Press **mt** in the Student eEdition for modified text.

See the Chapter Planner for more strategies for differentiation.

REVIEW & ASSESS

ANSWERS

1. Pericles expanded democracy by transferring the remaining powers of the aristocrats to the assembly, opening up powerful political positions to the middle classes, and establishing a direct democracy.

2. Both Solon and Cleisthenes made life fairer for the poor. But under Solon's rule, wealthy men still had more power. Cleisthenes reduced wealthy men's power by reorganizing citizens into classes based on location, not wealth.

3. Paying public officials strengthened democracy by allowing all men, not just wealthy ones, to have the opportunity to hold government positions.

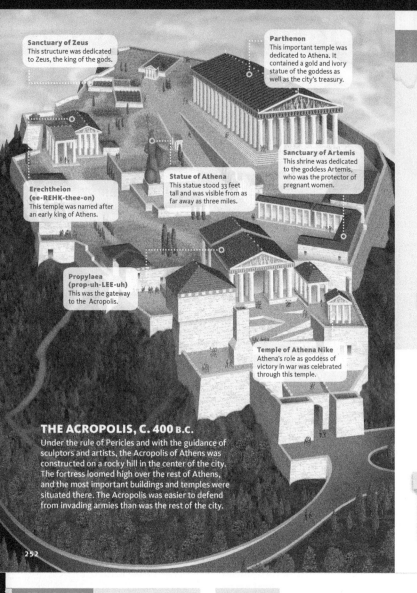

Sanctuary of Zeus
This structure was dedicated to Zeus, the king of the gods.

Parthenon
This important temple was dedicated to Athena. It contained a gold and ivory statue of the goddess as well as the city's treasury.

Sanctuary of Artemis
This shrine was dedicated to the goddess Artemis, who was the protector of pregnant women.

Statue of Athena
This statue stood 33 feet tall and was visible from as far away as three miles.

Erechtheion
(ee-REHK-thee-on)
This temple was named after an early king of Athens.

Propylaea
(prop-uh-LEE-uh)
This was the gateway to the Acropolis.

Temple of Athena Nike
Athena's role as goddess of victory in war was celebrated through this temple.

THE ACROPOLIS, C. 400 B.C.
Under the rule of Pericles and with the guidance of sculptors and artists, the Acropolis of Athens was constructed on a rocky hill in the center of the city. The fortress loomed high over the rest of Athens, and the most important buildings and temples were situated there. The Acropolis was easier to defend from invading armies than was the rest of the city.

1.2

The Athenian Empire

The war with Persia made the Greeks realize that there really is strength in numbers. So Athens and numerous other city-states joined forces to protect themselves against enemies. But Athens was always the strongest of the city-states, and it soon became apparent that Athenians had their own interests in mind.

MAIN IDEA

Athens grew into a powerful empire and was rebuilt to reflect its important status.

THE DELIAN LEAGUE

To defend themselves from Persia, which still posed a possible threat, Athens and the other city-states formed an anti-Persian alliance. The **Delian** (DEE-lee-uhn) **League**, formed in 478 B.C., was based on the island of Delos, where funds were kept to fight future wars with Persia.

Each city-state contributed cash, ships, or soldiers and had equal votes in the league's council. However, Athens was always the league's leader and took control over the other city-states in the alliance.

Pericles used the league's money to build Athens's powerful navy. This naval force allowed Athens to rule the Mediterranean region and the Delian League. In 454 B.C., the league's treasury was moved from the island of Delos to Athens. The other city-states in the alliance were now powerless against Athens.

The Spartans were not happy that the Athenians were gaining so much power. Although distracted by regular slave revolts, Sparta remained a major power. It established its own network of alliances called the Peloponnesian League. Resentment built between the two leagues, causing tension to run dangerously high.

REBUILDING THE CITY

Meanwhile, Athens was still in ruins from the Persian Wars. The Delian League began funding the rebuilding of Athens, which would be grander than ever.

The city walls were rebuilt. Then Pericles rebuilt the Acropolis with richly decorated temples and monuments. One structure on the Acropolis was the **Parthenon** (PAHR-thuh-nahn), the awe-inspiring temple that was dedicated to Athens's goddess, Athena. The city's leaders poured money into beautifying the city with the finest architecture, art, and sculpture. Pericles transformed Athens into one of the most magnificent cities in the ancient world. It was a fitting capital for a powerful empire.

REVIEW & ASSESS

1. **READING CHECK** How did the Delian League make Athens more powerful?

2. **ANALYZE CAUSE AND EFFECT** How did the Spartans respond to the creation of the Delian League?

3. **INTEGRATE VISUALS** Why do you think the Parthenon was located on the Acropolis?

6.4.6 Compare and contrast life in Athens and Sparta, with emphasis on their roles in the Persian and Peloponnesian Wars; HI 2 Students understand and distinguish cause, effect, sequence, and correlation in historical events, including the long- and short-term causal relations.

PLAN

OBJECTIVE

Understand Athens's transformation into a powerful empire.

ESSENTIAL QUESTION

What lasting influences did ancient Greek culture have on the modern world?

The Acropolis of Athens and its buildings and temples, especially the Parthenon, continue to attract visitors today. The Athenian city on a hill is known for its architectural beauty. Lesson 1.2 explains how the rebuilding of the Acropolis became a symbol of Athens's power and glory.

BACKGROUND FOR THE TEACHER

The word *acropolis* means "high city" in Greek. Most city-states had an acropolis at their center—a rocky mound or hill that housed important temples and served as a fortress during an attack. Undoubtedly, the most famous acropolis is the one in Athens. Most of its early temples were destroyed by the Persians in 480 B.C., which paved the way for its rebuilding under the leadership of Pericles. While temples were built to honor a variety of gods and goddesses, the largest one, the Parthenon, was dedicated to Athena, the patron goddess of Athens. At one time the Parthenon was decorated with elaborate sculpture. Today, these friezes reside in the British Museum.

DIGITAL RESOURCES NGLSync.cengage.com

TEACHER RESOURCES & ASSESSMENT

 Reading and Note-Taking

 Vocabulary Practice

 Section 1 Quiz

STUDENT RESOURCES

 NG Chapter Gallery

INTRODUCE & ENGAGE

PREVIEW WITH PROBLEM-SOLVING

Describe the following scenario to students: Imagine that you and a group of friends decided to pool your money together to order pizza. One friend volunteers to hold all the money until it is time to order, but then you find out that this friend used the money to buy a new video game for him- or herself instead. Have students discuss how this action would make them feel toward their friend. Explain that in Lesson 1.2 they will learn how Athens behaved in a similar way toward its fellow city-states. **0:05** minutes

TEACH

GUIDED DISCUSSION

1. **Analyze Cause and Effect** When Athens began using its power to control the Delian League, what was the effect on the other city-states? *(They felt powerless against Athens, and Sparta established its own Peloponnesian League.)*

2. **Form and Support Opinions** Was Athens right to use Delian League money to build a navy and rebuild the city? *(yes, because a strong Athens would help protect all the city-states; no, because the money was not distributed fairly to help the defenses of all the city-states who contributed to it)*

INTEGRATE VISUALS

Direct students' attention to the illustration of the Acropolis. Ask them to consider how the physical characteristics of the land influenced how people lived and constructed their buildings. As a class, make a list of the challenges the Athenians must have faced as they built structures on the hill. **0:10** minutes

ACTIVE OPTIONS

On Your Feet: Debate Divide the class into two groups. Have one side represent Athens and the other Sparta. Offer the issue of Athens's growing power under the Delian League as a topic of debate. Alternatively, come up with a different topic as a class. Then, have the groups use the information from Lesson 1.2 to organize the strongest arguments in favor of their group's position. Each group should also generate some suggestions to address the concerns of the other group. Then give the two groups a chance to debate the topic by taking turns presenting their arguments and offering their suggestions. Encourage the class to reach consensus on one or two suggestions. **0:10** minutes

NG Learning Framework: Research the Acropolis

ATTITUDES: **Curiosity, Empowerment**
KNOWLEDGE: **Our Human Story**

Have pairs of students research a building at the Acropolis other than the Parthenon. They should determine what the building looked like, what it was used for, and what it tells us about ancient Greek society. Then have pairs share their information by giving a brief presentation with visuals. **0:20** minutes

DIFFERENTIATE

STRIVING READERS

Complete Sentence Starters Provide these sentence starters for students to complete after reading. You may also have students preview to set a purpose for reading.

- The Delian League was formed because _____ .
- Pericles used the league's money to _____ .
- The _____ were not happy about Athens's rising power.
- Sparta established its own network of alliances, called the _____ .
- The _____ funded the rebuilding of the Acropolis.

GIFTED & TALENTED   STEM

Build a Model Have students work in groups to create a three-dimensional model of the Acropolis for the classroom. Encourage them to explore different materials to use for their model and to draft plans for the model before trying to build it. Some groups may want to select a particular feature to highlight. Other groups might want to situate the Acropolis by building it on a hill as part of their model.

Press **mt** *in the Student eEdition for modified text.*

See the Chapter Planner for more strategies for differentiation.

REVIEW & ASSESS

ANSWERS

1. Pericles used money from the Delian League to build a powerful navy. This gave Athens enough power to become an empire. Pericles also used money from the league to rebuild, strengthen, and beautify Athens.

2. The Spartans formed a rival alliance called the Peloponnesian League, which increased tensions between the two leagues in the Mediterranean.

3. The Parthenon was sacred to Athenians because it was dedicated to their goddess, Athena. By locating the Parthenon high up on the Acropolis, it would be easier for Athenians to defend the temple from enemies.

Religion and the Gods

Greek gods and goddesses may seem more like cartoon superheroes than divine deities. According to Greek belief, the gods looked and acted like humans: They married, had children, got jealous, and started wars. But they did it all with fantastic superpowers! Ordinary people had to either keep them happy or face their wrath.

MAIN IDEA

The Greeks believed that the many gods they worshipped could strongly influence daily life.

BELIEFS

Greek gods played an important role in ancient Greece. The gods were considered **immortal**, or able to live forever. Like the Mesopotamians and Egyptians, the Greeks believed that

The 12 Olympians

Zeus King of the gods	Athena Goddess of wisdom and war
Hera Queen of the gods	Demeter Goddess of the harvest
Aphrodite Goddess of love and beauty	Dionysus God of wine
Apollo God of the sun and music	Hephaestus God of fire and metalworking
Ares God of war	Hermes Messenger of the gods
Artemis Goddess of the moon and hunting	Poseidon God of the sea

unhappy gods showed their displeasure by causing problems in people's lives. Greeks obtained the gods' help by leaving offerings outside temples—the gods' earthly homes. Temples were usually impressive stone buildings housing a statue of the god. A city's biggest temple was dedicated to its patron god, who protected it.

There were hundreds of Greek gods. According to Greek belief, the top 12 gods were the Olympians, or the ones who lived in luxury on Mount Olympus, the highest mountain in Greece. A holy day, celebrated with colorful and noisy public festivals, was dedicated to each god and goddess. These special days involved great processions, offerings, poetry recitals, and competitive sports, including the original Olympic Games. For private worship, most Greek homes had small altars where people would pray to the gods.

MYTHS

The Greeks had a close relationship with their gods, who often got involved in human affairs. This is how Greek religion blended with **mythology**—a collection of stories that explained events, beliefs, or actions. In Greek myths, the gods, kings, heroes, and ordinary people had amazing adventures together. The gods often rewarded or punished humans for their deeds. These stories were written down to form a group of exciting tales that are still popular today. One of these myths appears on the next page.

THE MYTH OF DAEDALUS AND ICARUS

On the island of Crete, there lived a skilled craftsman named Daedalus. Daedalus wanted to leave the island with his son, Icarus, but the king would not let him go. So he came up with a plan to escape. He took feathers and wax and constructed two pairs of wings that would allow him and Icarus to fly like the birds.

As Daedalus attached the wings to his son's arms, he told Icarus to follow him closely. "If you fly too low, the sea will soak the wings. If you fly too high, the sun will burn them," he warned.

The father and son were soon flying through the air. Icarus grew excited and began to fly higher and higher in spite of his father's warning. Apollo, the god of the sun, decided to teach the boy a lesson, and soon the wax holding Icarus's wings together was melting away. Icarus tumbled down to the water below. Daedalus could only watch helplessly as his beloved son was claimed by the sea.

When he safely reached land, Daedalus built a shrine to Apollo and hung his wings on it. He never tried to fly again.

REVIEW & ASSESS

1. **READING CHECK** What role did gods and goddesses play in the lives of the ancient Greeks?

2. **MAKE INFERENCES** What lesson do you think Apollo was trying to teach Icarus?

3. **DRAW CONCLUSIONS** Why were myths important to ancient Greek culture?

6.4.4 Explain the significance of Greek mythology to the everyday life of people in the region and how Greek literature continues to permeate our literature and language today, drawing from Greek mythology and epics, such as Homer's *Iliad* and *Odyssey*, and from *Aesop's Fables*.

HSS CONTENT STANDARDS:

6.4.4 Explain the significance of Greek mythology to the everyday life of people in the region and how Greek literature continues to permeate our literature and language today, drawing from Greek mythology and epics, such as Homer's *Iliad* and *Odyssey*, and from *Aesop's Fables*.

PLAN

OBJECTIVE

Understand religious beliefs of the ancient Greeks.

ESSENTIAL QUESTION

What lasting influences did ancient Greek culture have on the modern world?

The ancient Greeks believed that their gods and goddesses played an active role in their daily life. Lesson 1.3 introduces important Greek deities and describes how ancient beliefs have carried over to the present day.

BACKGROUND FOR THE TEACHER

Religion was central to culture in ancient Greece. All Greeks worshipped the same gods and goddesses, who looked and behaved like humans, but had superpowers. Each god controlled a particular area of life. Some Greeks visited an oracle, or a priest or priestess who was believed to speak on behalf of a god or goddess. People visited oracles in shrines located deep below temples and would ask questions about their future. The oracle was believed to be a connection between the god and the person receiving the answer. Often, answers from oracles were in the form of riddles.

DIGITAL RESOURCES NGLSync.cengage.com

TEACHER RESOURCES & ASSESSMENT

 Reading and Note-Taking

 Vocabulary Practice

 Section 1 Quiz

STUDENT RESOURCES

 NG Chapter Gallery

INTRODUCE & ENGAGE

ACTIVATE PRIOR KNOWLEDGE

Greek heroes, gods, and goddesses have been portrayed in comics, electronic games, films, and novels. Ask students if they are familiar with any Greek myths. Discuss why the dramatic stories of the Greeks continue to fire our imaginations many centuries later. `0:05` minutes

TEACH

GUIDED DISCUSSION

1. **Explain** How did the gods interact with ordinary mortals, both positively and negatively, in Greek myths? *(Humans left offerings to the gods to win their favor and assistance. Gods showed their displeasure by causing problems for humans.)*

2. **Make Inferences** What was the lesson of the myth of Daedalus and Icarus retold in the lesson? *(Possible response: Don't try to reach too high, too soon, especially if you are in unfamiliar circumstances. Stay humble, or you might start to think you can go higher than you can.)*

MORE INFORMATION

Greek vs. Roman Mythology The Romans took much of Greek mythology and made it their own. Every major Greek god has a Roman counterpart: Zeus is Jupiter; Hera is Juno; Aphrodite is Venus; and Ares is Mars. Notice that many of these Latin names were used to name both the planets in our solar system and days of the week (such as Saturday).

ACTIVE OPTIONS

On Your Feet: Play a Game of Telephone Ask students to retell a myth. First tell one student the myth, and then have that student tell another student, and so on. The last student should tell the myth out loud. Have students discuss how the story changed from one person to the next. Explain that this is an example of how stories can change through multiple tellings. `0:15` minutes

NG Learning Framework: Retell a Myth

ATTITUDES: **Curiosity, Empowment**
KNOWLEDGE: **Our Human Story**

Have students research and read a Greek myth other than the one that appears in the lesson. Some ideas include "Pygmalion," "King Midas," "Arachne," or "Echo and Narcissus." Ask volunteers to narrate their particular myth for the rest of the class. Some students may want to work in groups and act out a particular myth. After each student or group presents their myth, discuss what event, belief, or action the myth was created to explain. `0:25` minutes

DIFFERENTIATE

ENGLISH LANGUAGE LEARNERS   ELD

Use Word Parts Explain to students that when they encounter new and confusing words, they can look for roots and affxes. Write *immortal* on the board and underline the root word *mort* and the prefix *im-*. Use the following strategies to help students at different proficiency levels clarify the meaning of the word.

- **Emerging** After students identify the root and prefix, have them write them on a card along with the meaning. Talk through the word. (Example: Im- *means "not."* Mort *means "death."* Immortal *means "never dies."*)

- **Expanding** To help students explain how they know the meaning of a word with an identifiable root, provide the following sentence frame: The root is _____ and means _____. So, _____ means _____.

- **Bridging** Encourage students to determine a more exact meaning: *The root is* mort, *which means "death." The prefix* im- *means "not." The suffix* -al *means "characterized by," so immortal* must mean "not capable of dying." Repeat the process with the word *mythology.*

GIFTED & TALENTED

Rewrite an Ancient Myth Have students research ancient Greek myths. Have each student choose a different myth and rewrite it for the present day. Students may want to illustrate their myths or present them as short plays or videos. Make sure students include the usual mythical figures: humans, heroes, gods, and demi-gods. Encourage students to share their present-day myths with the class.

Press **mt** *in the Student eEdition for modified text.*

See the Chapter Planner for more strategies for differentiation.

REVIEW & ASSESS

ANSWERS

1. Greeks believed that if they didn't keep their gods happy, bad things would happen. They kept the gods happy by leaving them offerings, celebrating them during public festivals, and worshipping them privately.

2. Apollo was trying to teach Icarus to listen to his father and not fly too high for his own good.

3. Greek myths about gods, kings, and heroes helped the people of ancient Greece understand their world and gave explanations for how things came to be the way they were.

2.1

War Breaks Out

As Athens became wealthier and more powerful, other city-states, especially Sparta, became suspicious and fearful of Athens's future plans. Athens and Sparta had created very different societies. Athens championed a democratic government, while Sparta focused on military strength. These differences contributed to a growing distrust that exploded into war.

MAIN IDEA

Rivalry between Sparta and Athens plunged Greece into war.

TENSIONS RISE

In addition to societal differences, Sparta resented Athens's use of money from the Delian League. Remember, Athens had used this money, intended to protect all of the city-states, for its own benefit. When the city-states protested this inequality and attempted to free themselves from Athenian rule, Pericles punished them. By 431 B.C., Sparta had had enough of Athenian aggression and declared war on Athens. The **Peloponnesian War** had begun.

Sparta had a strong army and Athens had a strong navy. This contrast in military strength forced the two sides to develop very different plans for winning the war. Athens, under Pericles, avoided fighting Sparta and its allies on land and planned to attack from the sea. Athens withdrew behind its strong city walls. Its ships kept the city stocked with supplies and were also used to raid its enemies' land.

Meanwhile, Sparta marched its army into Athenian lands expecting a big battle, but the Athenian army stayed protected behind the city walls. The frustrated Spartans attempted to weaken the Athenian economy by burning its crops. Though the walls protected Athenians from the Spartans, they could not prevent a devastating attack from an unexpected enemy.

A PLAGUE STRIKES ATHENS

In 430 B.C., Athenians began suffering from rashes, headaches, vomiting, and fever. This was probably an outbreak of typhoid fever, a highly infectious disease. In the narrow streets of Athens, overcrowded with refugees from the countryside, the fever quickly became a deadly **plague**, or a disease that causes many deaths. In four years the plague killed one in three Athenians—about 60,000 people—including Pericles. Disease was doing more damage than Sparta's soldiers.

Elsewhere the war raged on with brutal acts committed by both sides. It was typical for a captured city to have all its male citizens executed and its women and children enslaved. Despite all the deaths, the war seemed unwinnable. Athens was dominant at sea and Sparta ruled on land, but neither was able to overpower the other. In 421 B.C., Athens signed a **truce**, or an agreement to stop fighting. Sparta and Athens entered a period of peace, but it would not last for long.

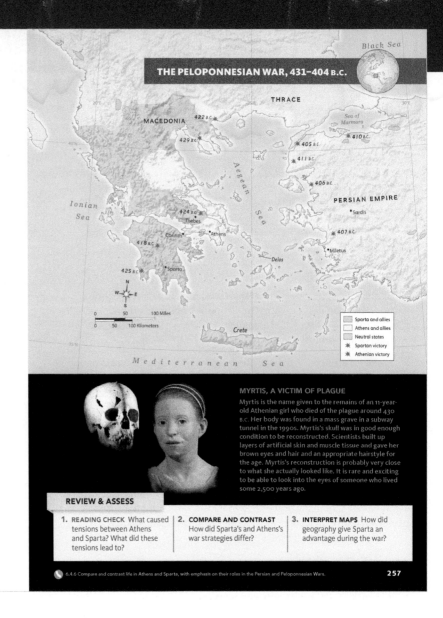

THE PELOPONNESIAN WAR, 431–404 B.C.

Black Sea

THRACE

MACEDONIA

Ionian Sea

Aegean Sea

PERSIAN EMPIRE
• Sardis

Thebes
Corinth • Athens
• Miletus
Delos
• Sparta

Crete

Mediterranean Sea

- Sparta and allies
- Athens and allies
- Neutral states
- ★ Spartan victory
- ★ Athenian victory

MYRTIS, A VICTIM OF PLAGUE

Myrtis is the name given to the remains of an 11-year-old Athenian girl who died of the plague around 430 B.C. Her body was found in a mass grave in a subway tunnel in the 1990s. Myrtis's skull was in good enough condition to be reconstructed. Scientists built up layers of artificial skin and muscle tissue and gave her brown eyes and hair and an appropriate hairstyle for the age. Myrtis's reconstruction is probably very close to what she actually looked like. It is rare and exciting to be able to look into the eyes of someone who lived some 2,500 years ago.

REVIEW & ASSESS

1. **READING CHECK** What caused tensions between Athens and Sparta? What did these tensions lead to?

2. **COMPARE AND CONTRAST** How did Sparta's and Athens's war strategies differ?

3. **INTERPRET MAPS** How did geography give Sparta an advantage during the war?

6.4.6 Compare and contrast life in Athens and Sparta, with emphasis on their roles in the Persian and Peloponnesian Wars.

257

HSS CONTENT STANDARDS:

6.4.6 Compare and contrast life in Athens and Sparta, with emphasis on their roles in the Persian and Peloponnesian Wars.

HSS ANALYSIS SKILLS:

HI 2 Students understand and distinguish cause, effect, sequence, and correlation in historical events, including the long- and short-term causal relations.

PLAN

OBJECTIVE

Understand the factors that led to war between Athens and Sparta.

ESSENTIAL QUESTION

What lasting influences did ancient Greek culture have on the modern world?

The war between Sparta and Athens was a turning point in the classical period, when Athens's power began to wane. Lesson 2.1 explains the events that led up to the war.

BACKGROUND FOR THE TEACHER

The Peloponnesian War is remembered and its details so well known because of one main account, Thucydides' *History of the Peloponnesian War*. Thucydides was a historian and an Athenian general during the war, and he wrote a chronological account containing the speeches of leaders and generals. The most famous of these is Pericles' funeral oration for Athenian soldiers who died during the war. An excerpt from Thucydides' work is included later in this chapter.

DIGITAL RESOURCES NGLSync.cengage.com

TEACHER RESOURCES & ASSESSMENT

 Reading and Note-Taking

 Vocabulary Practice

 Section 2 Quiz

STUDENT RESOURCES

 NG Chapter Gallery

INTRODUCE & ENGAGE

ACTIVATE PRIOR KNOWLEDGE

The differences between Sparta and Athens were both military and cultural. Remind students of the development of the city-states, discussed in Chapter 9, and what they learned about Sparta's military society. **ASK:** How might Sparta's military society have caused the city-state to conflict with Athens and its democratic society? **0:05** minutes

TEACH

GUIDED DISCUSSION

1. **Sequence Events** Complete the Sequence Chain with four events that occurred after the Peloponnesian War began. *(Athens has a strong navy, and Sparta has a strong army. Athens withdraws behind the city walls to avoid a land war. Sparta ruins Athens's food source. Athenians begin to be affected by the plague.)*

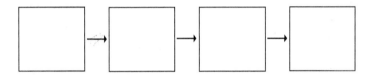

2. **Draw Conclusions** What were the reasons for the truce that ended the Peloponnesian War? *(The deaths caused by plague and war became so great, and both sides were equally matched, so both sides decided to stop fighting and declare a truce.)*

INTERPRET MAPS

Have students study the map of the Peloponnesian War. **ASK:** Would you rather have land or sea power (army or navy) in this particular geographic area? Have students give reasons to support their opinion. **0:10** minutes

ACTIVE OPTIONS

On Your Feet: Inside-Outside Circle Have students stand in concentric circles facing each other. Have students in the outside circle ask students in the inside circle a question about the lesson. Then have the outside circle rotate one position to the right to create new pairings. After five questions, have students switch roles and continue. **0:15** minutes

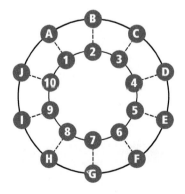

Critical Viewing: NG Chapter Gallery Invite students to explore the Chapter Gallery to examine the images that relate to this chapter. Have them select one of the images and do additional inquiry about the chosen gallery image, such as: What is this? Where and when was this created? By whom? Why was it created? What is it made of? Why does it belong in this chapter? What else would you like to know about it? **0:10** minutes

DIFFERENTIATE

INCLUSION

Work in Pairs Pair students who have visual or learning disabilities with partners who are proficient readers. Have the proficient student read the section titled "Tensions Rise" aloud. After reading each paragraph, the reader should stop and his or her partner should retell the same information in his or her own words to check comprehension.

PRE-AP

Hold a Panel Discussion Have groups of students do research and find out different ways that the plague affected Greek society. Ask them to present a panel discussion about the disease. Encourage students to cover the following points in their discussion:

- the plague's physical effects
- the percent of the total population that was afflicted
- the effect of the plague on the war for Athens

As an extension, have students read the excerpt about the plague from Thucydides' *History of the Peloponnesian War* in the **Primary Source Handbook** and answer the questions.

Press **mt** *in the Student eEdition for modified text.*

See the Chapter Planner for more strategies for differentiation.

REVIEW & ASSESS

ANSWERS

1. Tensions rose between Athens and Sparta because of societal differences, Sparta's mistrust of Athens's increase in wealth and power, and Sparta's resentment toward Athens's use of Delian League money.

2. Sparta relied on its strong army to march into Athenian lands. Athens avoided a land battle by staying behind strong city walls. Athens used its powerful navy to raid enemy land.

3. Because of Sparta's location farther inland, Sparta was probably less vulnerable to an attack from Athens's powerful navy.

The **Defeat** of **Athens**

Both Sparta and Athens wanted to control all of Greece. Sparta thought its soldiers, with their strict military training, would crush any opponent. Athens attempted to dominate the region by building a powerful navy. But Sparta and Athens failed to notice that their constant warring was causing Greece to slowly fall apart.

MAIN IDEA

After many years of fighting, Greece found itself in a weakened and vulnerable state.

THE WAR DRAGS ON

The truce was supposed to last 50 years. Instead it ended in only two. Sparta and Athens were drawn back into war over the rich lands of Sicily, a fertile island near Italy that the Greeks had colonized. A dispute between a pro-Athenian colony and a pro-Spartan colony prompted Athens to invade.

In 414 B.C., Athens laid **siege** to Syracuse, Sicily's strongest and richest city. In a siege, soldiers surround a city in an attempt to take control of it. The invasion of Syracuse was disorganized, and Athens made many mistakes. Spartan reinforcements arrived and attacked the Athenians on land and sea. The Spartans sank all 200 of Athens's ships, and killed or enslaved 40,000 soldiers.

Meanwhile, Sparta seized control of the land around Athens, cutting off the Athenians' agricultural and economic resources. With Athens weakened, its allies revolted. Athens's situation just kept getting worse. The city-state had no good leaders left, and its naval fleet had been completely destroyed by Sparta.

In 412 B.C., Sparta strengthened its forces by allying with its old enemy Persia. The Spartan army steadily advanced on Athens, deliberately causing refugees to flee to the already overcrowded city. Blocked by Spartans on land and sea, a desperate Athens had only two choices: surrender or starve. In 404 B.C., Athens surrendered and the Peloponnesian War was finally over.

SPARTA IS VICTORIOUS

Sparta's fellow members in the Peloponnesian League wanted Athens to be completely destroyed and its people enslaved, but Sparta rejected these calls for revenge. Still, surrendering to Sparta was humiliating to the proud Athenians. The long walls linking Athens to the sea were torn down, and the Athenian navy was reduced to just 12 ships. As a final insult, Sparta replaced Athenian democracy with an oligarchy, a government made up of a small group of people. It was run by tyrants who ruled in a ruthless and controlling way. This form of leadership caused further conflicts within democracy-loving Athens.

The once powerful city of Athens was reduced to a second-rate state. However, Athens was not alone in its suffering. The long war had been costly in men, money, and resources to all the city-states involved. Greece as a whole was left weakened and vulnerable. To repair the damage, the city-states needed to cooperate with one another. Unfortunately, the end of the war did not stop conflicts from erupting. The city-states were soon warring among themselves again. In its weakened condition, Greece was a prime target for attack.

+ POSSIBLE RESPONSE

Spartan soldiers were well-prepared with battle gear and ordered themselves into organized lines when they attacked.

Critical Viewing Spartan soldiers raise their weapons for battle. What does the illustration suggest about how Spartan soldiers fought?

Spartan Warriors, Howard David Johnson, 2013

REVIEW & ASSESS

1. **READING CHECK** What finally caused Athens to surrender to Sparta, ending the Peloponnesian War?

2. **DETERMINE WORD MEANINGS** How does knowing that *olig-* means "few" and *arch-* means "ruler" clarify the meaning of *oligarchy*?

3. **ANALYZE CAUSE AND EFFECT** What were the effects of the Peloponnesian War on the Greek city-states?

6.4.2 Trace the transition from tyranny and oligarchy to early democratic forms of government and back to dictatorship in ancient Greece, including the significance of the invention of the idea of citizenship (e.g., from *Pericles' Funeral Oration*); 6.4.6 Compare and contrast life in Athens and Sparta, with emphasis on their roles in the Persian and Peloponnesian Wars; HI 2 Students understand and distinguish cause, effect, sequence, and correlation in historical events, including the long- and short-term causal relations.

PLAN

OBJECTIVE

Examine the consequences of the Peloponnesian War and their effect on ancient Greece.

ESSENTIAL QUESTION

What lasting influences did ancient Greek culture have on the modern world?

The Peloponnesian War and its contemporary historians have influenced how we write history and wage war today. Lesson 2.2 examines the effects of the war on the cultural center of Athens.

BACKGROUND FOR THE TEACHER

The Athenian siege of Syracuse was the brainchild of the military commander Alcibiades. Athens spent all the money in its treasury to build a large fleet and army for the endeavor. If the siege had succeeded, it would have been a huge victory for Athens. However, it failed. Alcibiades escaped to Sparta, where he betrayed Athens's plans to the Spartans. Athenians looked to their leaders to figure out what had gone wrong. Aristocrats blamed democracy, which they had always opposed, for the failure of the campaign. Oligarchs known as the Thirty Tyrants took over. It was the beginning of the end of Athens's power.

DIGITAL RESOURCES NGLSync.cengage.com

TEACHER RESOURCES & ASSESSMENT

 Reading and Note-Taking

 Vocabulary Practice

 Section 2 Quiz

STUDENT RESOURCES

 NG Image Gallery

INTRODUCE & ENGAGE

IDENTIFY POINTS OF VIEW

Organize the class into small groups. Invite them to discuss two different strategies that military and government leaders use, defensive and offensive. Explain that in ancient Greece, Pericles' strategy against the Spartans was a defensive one. After his death, some government leaders wanted to use a more offensive strategy. Assign half the groups to represent those who support a defensive strategy and assign the other half to represent those who think an offensive strategy is better. Have groups use a chart like the one below to list their group's views. In the "Viewpoint" column, groups should list their positions. In the "Support" column, they should list their reasons why. Have groups representing both sides of the argument discuss their viewpoints. Tell groups to complete the "Opposing Viewpoint" column during their discussion. Tell students that they will read about Athens's strategies in its campaign in Sicily in Lesson 2.2. **0:15** minutes

Viewpoint	Support	Opposing Viewpoint

TEACH

GUIDED DISCUSSION

1. **Make Predictions** After reading the lesson, ask students to predict what might happen next among the city-states. *(They might keep fighting each other in small conflicts. Another enemy might target them because they are so disorganized and divided among themselves.)*

2. **Identify Main Ideas and Details** Ask students to pair up and work together. Have them write down the main idea of the first paragraph. Then they should add details that support that main idea. Have them repeat this for two more paragraphs in the lesson.

MORE INFORMATION

Athens's New War Strategy Most historians blame Athens's loss of its dominance in the region on its own decision to enter into war too rashly. Overturning Pericles' policy of staying out of the war and behind their strong city walls, Athenian leaders wanted action—and they plunged ahead despite the superior strength of their opponents. One leader, Nicias, trying to stop the momentum toward war, thought of a plan. He would ask the treasury for such a huge amount of money for the ships and soldiers needed that they would not agree to it. His plan backfired. Nicias was granted his request, and Athens spent all of its money on the plan to attack Syracuse. Most historians think that Athens might have held onto its power in the region if it had just kept going with Pericles' strategy. But in his *History of the Peloponnesian War,* Thucydides makes the case that the war was inevitable, along with the loss of democracy and Athenian power in the region.

ACTIVE OPTIONS

On Your Feet: Identifying Issues Divide students into four groups and have them move to different corners of the classroom. Ask each group to address the following question: *What might be a challenge to upholding a democracy when your country is surrounded by oligarchies?* Encourage students to consider the question individually and then discuss their responses as a group. Suggest that one person in the group act as the recorder. Then invite recorders to take turns stating their group's conclusions. **0:15** minutes

Critical Viewing: NG Image Gallery Have students explore the entire NG Image Gallery and choose two of the items to compare and contrast, either in written form or verbally with a partner. Ask questions that will inspire this process, such as: How are these images alike? How are they different? Why did you select these two items? How do they relate in history? **0:10** minutes

DIFFERENTIATE

STRIVING READERS

Sequence Events Have students summarize the events of the section in chronological order, using a chart like this:

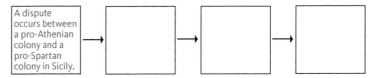

PRE-AP

Research Sieges in History Have students research other sieges in history and compare their findings to the events of the Athenian siege of Syracuse. Then have students write about their findings in a short report. Encourage them to answer three questions: Why did the military leaders attempt a siege? What challenges emerged? How do the outcomes compare?

Press **mt** *in the Student eEdition for modified text.*

See the Chapter Planner for more strategies for differentiation.

REVIEW & ASSESS

ANSWERS

1. Sparta had effectively blocked Athens on land and sea, forcing Athens into choosing between surrendering and starving.

2. The word parts make up a word that means rule by the few.

3. The Peloponnesian War weakened the economies and resources of all the Greek city-states, which left Greece as a whole very vulnerable and open to attack.

2.3 DOCUMENT-BASED QUESTION
Athenian Democracy

In 431 B.C., Pericles delivered an oration, a kind of formal speech, at a large public funeral held in honor of Athenian soldiers who had died fighting in the Peloponnesian War. Pericles used the opportunity to inspire the living to keep fighting for Athens. He talked about the many reasons that Athenians could be proud of their great city, including all of the advantages that came with living in a democratic society.

POSSIBLE RESPONSE
The Athenians in the picture have differing reactions, but many seem upset, worried, or expectant.

Critical Viewing An artist imagines what the scene might have looked like as Pericles delivered his oration. How do the Athenians appear to react to Pericles' words?

DOCUMENT ONE
Primary Source: Speech

from *History of the Peloponnesian War* by Thucydides (translated by Rex Warner)
Thucydides (thoo-SIH-duh-deez) was a Greek historian and general best known for his historical account of the events of the Peloponnesian War. As an Athenian military commander, he failed to prevent the capture of an important city from Sparta and was exiled for 20 years. During this time, he was able to witness events firsthand and interview participants much as a modern journalist would. His account provides a detailed record of Pericles' funeral oration. In this excerpt, Pericles reminds Athenians of the power they have as members of a democratic society.

CONSTRUCTED RESPONSE According to Pericles, what was special about the Athenian system of government? Would a Spartan citizen feel the same way? Explain.

Our constitution is called a democracy because power is in the hands not of a minority but of the whole people. When it is a question of settling private disputes, everyone is equal before the law; when it is a question of putting one person before another in positions of public responsibility, what counts is not membership of a particular class, but the actual ability that the man possesses. No one, so long as he has it in him to be of service to the state, is kept in political obscurity because of poverty.

DOCUMENT TWO
Primary Source: Artifact

Ostracon, Greece, c. 400s B.C.
Ostracism was an enforced banishment. Athenians used it to prevent an individual from gaining too much power. Each citizen carved the name of someone he believed to be dangerous on a piece of pottery called an ostracon, seen at right. If the same name appeared often enough, the named person had to leave Athens. He did not lose citizenship, property, or wealth, but he was forbidden to return for ten years.

CONSTRUCTED RESPONSE What does the practice of ostracism tell you about Athenian values?

SYNTHESIZE & WRITE
1. **REVIEW** Review what you have learned about democracy in Athens from the text and the sources above.
2. **RECALL** On your own paper, write down the main idea expressed in the speech and artifact.
3. **CONSTRUCT** Write a topic sentence that answers this question: What was most important in Athenian democracy—the individual or the community?
4. **WRITE** Using evidence from the speech and artifact, write an argument to support your answer to the question in Step 3.

261

260 CHAPTER 10

STANDARDS
HSS CONTENT STANDARDS:
6.4.2 Trace the transition from tyranny and oligarchy to early democratic forms of government and back to dictatorship in ancient Greece, including the significance of the invention of the idea of citizenship (e.g., from *Pericles' Funeral Oration*);
6.4.6 Compare and contrast life in Athens and Sparta, with emphasis on their roles in the Persian and Peloponnesian Wars;
6.4.8 Describe the enduring contributions of important Greek figures in the arts and sciences (e.g., Hypatia, Socrates, Plator, aristotle, Euclid, Thucydides).

HSS ANALYSIS SKILLS:
REP 4 Students assess the credibility of primary and secondary sources and draw sound conclusions from them;
REP 5 Students detect the different historical points of view on historical events and determine the context in which the historical statements were made (the questions asked, sources used, author's perspectives);
HI 3 Students explain the sources of historical continuity and how the combination of ideas and events explains the emergence of new patterns.

PLAN
OBJECTIVE
Synthesize information about Athenian democracy from two primary sources.

ESSENTIAL QUESTION
What lasting influences did ancient Greek culture have on the modern world?

Democracy is one of the most widely spread forms of government in the modern world. Lesson 2.3 provides insight into Athenian democracy through the analysis of primary sources.

BACKGROUND FOR THE TEACHER
The practice of ostracism began under Cleisthenes when the democratic-minded leader took power after the last of the Greek tyrants. Ostracism was practiced in the Athenian democracy as a way to check the power of individuals or to punish them for failed policies. Other city-states, such as Argos, Miletus, Syracuse, and Megara, also used the practice at times. Ostracism was used only rarely, and the practice fell into disuse after it was found that some politicians attempted to manipulate the process to their own ends. The similar practice of exile was used in ancient Rome, but it was more of a punishment, involving loss of property and status, and usually lasting for the rest of the person's life.

DIGITAL RESOURCES NGLSync.cengage.com
TEACHER RESOURCES & ASSESSMENT
 Reading and Note-Taking
 Vocabulary Practice
 Section 2 Quiz
STUDENT RESOURCES
 NG Chapter Gallery

INTRODUCE & ENGAGE

PREPARE FOR THE DOCUMENT-BASED QUESTION

Before students start on the activity, briefly preview the document and artifact. Remind students that a constructed response requires full explanations in complete sentences. Emphasize that students should use their knowledge of Greek history in addition to the information in the documents. **0:05** minutes

TEACH

GUIDED DISCUSSION

1. **Make Inferences** Why might Pericles have felt the need to make this speech to his people? *(The people might have doubted the validity of democracy or Pericles' leadership after some very hard years of war and plague. They may have been disillusioned that the new system failed to fix anything. Pericles is trying to inspire them again by emphasizing democracy's greater aims and truths.)*

2. **Make Connections** Explain to students that an ostracon is a small clay piece with a name written on it. It was used by Athenians to vote to ostracize a citizen. **ASK:** Can you think of any similar practice in today's world? *(Possible response: Certain clubs and corporate organizations might use a similar process to vote a member out of the group.)*

EVALUATE

After students have completed the "Synthesize & Write" activity, allow time for them to exchange paragraphs and read and comment on the work of their peers. Guidelines for comments should be established prior to this activity so that feedback is constructive and encouraging in nature. **0:15** minutes

ACTIVE OPTIONS

On Your Feet: Jigsaw Divide students into four "expert" groups. Offer each group one of these features of democracy: assembly, checks and balances, paid legislators, or courts. Have groups research their feature using the following steps: 1. Define what their feature is. 2. Find out what problem their feature solved. 3. Identify how their feaure reflected democratic ideals. 4. Describe what problems, if any, the feature created. Use the Jigsaw strategy to have experts report their findings to different groups. **0:25** minutes

NG Learning Framework: Attitudes Toward Democracy

SKILL: Collaboration
KNOWLEDGE: **Our Human Story**

Have students read an excerpt from another speech about democracy, such as John F. Kennedy's inaugural address in 1961 or Ronald Reagan's address for the Goldwater presidential campaign in 1964. Discuss how the democratic principles mentioned in the speech are similar to or different from those in Pericles' funeral oration. **0:15** minutes

DIFFERENTIATE

INCLUSION

Check Understanding Have students write the letters A, B, and C on three separate index cards. Then check students' understanding of the lesson by asking them questions that have three possible answer choices, labeled A, B, and C. Instruct students to hold up the card with the letter that corresponds to the correct answer. Help students find the answers in Lesson 2.3 for any questions that cause them difficulty.

PRE-AP

Research Ostracism Tell students to research the practice of ostracism and some of the men who were ostracized in ancient Greece. Give them the name of Aristides—who was ostracized for being too popular—as a starting point in their research. Tell students to research other men who were ostracized, as well as the rationale behind the practice of ostracism. Encourage students to share their findings with the class.

Press **mt** *in the Student eEdition for modified text.*

See the Chapter Planner for more strategies for differentiation.

CONSTRUCTED RESPONSE

ANSWERS
DOCUMENT 1
Athenian democracy was special because power was in the hands of the majority of people, not just the rich, creating a more equal society. A Spartan citizen, led by a militaristic oligarchy, would most likely not feel the same way.

DOCUMENT 2
The principles of fairness and democracy were more important than one person's power.

SYNTHESIZE & WRITE

ANSWERS
1. Responses will vary.
2. Responses will vary but will reflect upon the meaning of democracy.
3. Possible Response: In Athenian democracy, the needs of individuals were less important than what was good for the community. Selfishness was less important than service.
4. Students' arguments should include their topic sentence from Step 3 and provide several details from the documents to support the sentence.

Philip of Macedonia

Your king wants to conquer Greece, located just south of your homeland. Weakened from internal fighting, Greece has become a prime target for attack. You and your fellow soldiers grip your 18-foot-long spears tighter as Greek soldiers approach. You are terrified, but you trust King Philip II. His military skills are extensive. In his capable hands, the act of war is turned into an art.

MAIN IDEA

Greece became unified under the military influence of Philip II.

CONQUEROR OF GREECE

The Greeks didn't think much of the kingdom of Macedonia (ma-suh-DOH-nee-uh), located just north of Greece. They dismissed its residents as uncultured foreigners. However, in 359 B.C., **Philip II** seized the Macedonian throne. He was an intelligent general and a clever politician—skills he combined with ambition, determination, and ruthlessness. An inspiring king, Philip completely controlled all political, military, legal, and religious matters.

Philip admired many things about Greece, including its ideas and art. He set his sights on uniting the Greek city-states with his own kingdom to create a combined kingdom strong enough to conquer the Persian Empire—his ultimate goal.

Philip built a powerful professional army and used new warfare methods. For example, he placed large groups of soldiers close together, forming an almost unstoppable battle formation called a **phalanx** (FAY-langks). Each soldier carried a spear that was much longer than the enemy's. The soldiers stood close to one another so that their shields overlapped, making it difficult for the enemy to attack them. Another new method of waging war was the use of war machines like the **catapult**, which hurled huge stones to shatter city walls.

Philip conquered the lands around Macedonia and seized Greek colonies that were rich in natural resources like gold mines, increasing his wealth. Greek city-states were still weak from the Peloponnesian War and were constantly quarrelling among themselves.

They were no match for Philip's strong army, great wealth, and political skill. By 348 B.C., Philip had won control of much of Greece. Any remaining Greek resistance crumbled when Athens and the strong city-state of Thebes fell to Philip at the Battle of Chaeronea (kair-uh-NEE-uh) in 338 B.C. Philip had united Greece for the first time ever. However, his son, **Alexander the Great**, would soon surpass his achievements.

YOUNG ALEXANDER

Born in 356 B.C., Alexander demonstrated his courage at a young age. One story tells how 12-year-old Alexander bravely stepped up to a nervous wild horse named Bucephalus (byoo-SEHF-uh-luhs), spoke gently to calm him down, and then rode him. Philip proudly announced that Macedonia would never be big enough for such a brave boy—and he was right.

Alexander trained for war with "the companions," a group of aristocratic sons

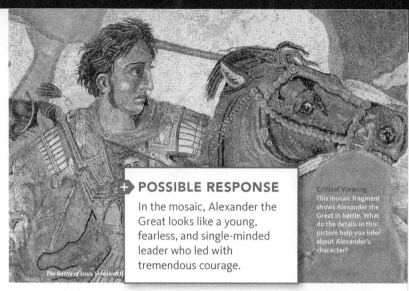

+ POSSIBLE RESPONSE

In the mosaic, Alexander the Great looks like a young, fearless, and single-minded leader who led with tremendous courage.

The Battle of Issus, House of t...

Critical Viewing
This mosaic fragment shows Alexander the Great in battle. What do the details in this picture help you infer about Alexander's character?

who became his loyal lifelong friends. His most important training came from his father, who took Alexander into battle with him. This gave his son firsthand experience in planning and carrying out a war.

The Greek scientist and great thinker Aristotle (A-ruh-stah-tuhl) was Alexander's tutor. He taught him geography, science, and literature. Alexander was greatly influenced by Homer's *Iliad* and kept a copy of it under his pillow. He wanted to be like the *Iliad*'s courageous hero, Achilles (uh-KIH-leez). According to myth, Achilles was one of the greatest warriors Greece had ever known.

Alexander soon became a warrior himself. At the age of 16, he was fighting off invasions and founding cities. In 336 B.C., Philip was assassinated, and 20-year-old Alexander became king.

The people of Thebes rebelled after Philip's death. They thought Macedonia would become weak without him. They could not have been more mistaken. Alexander marched into Greece to assert his leadership. He destroyed Thebes, terrifying all of Greece into submission. Alexander was well on his way to becoming "the Great."

REVIEW & ASSESS

1. **READING CHECK** What was Philip II's key achievement in Greece?

2. **ANALYZE CAUSE AND EFFECT** Why were the Greek city-states unprepared for an attack by Philip II?

3. **IDENTIFY MAIN IDEAS AND DETAILS** What evidence from the text demonstrates that Philip II was an intelligent general?

262 CHAPTER 10

6.4.7 Trace the rise of Alexander the Great and the spread of Greek culture eastward and into Egypt; HI 2 Students understand and distinguish cause, effect, sequence, and correlation in historical events, including the long- and short-term causal relations.

263

STANDARDS

HSS CONTENT STANDARDS:

6.4.7 Trace the rise of Alexander the Great and the spread of Greek culture eastward and into Egypt.

HSS ANALYSIS SKILLS:

CST 2 Students construct various time lines of key events, people, and periods of the historical era they are studying; **HI 2** Students understand and distinguish cause, effect, sequence, and correlation in historical events, including the long-and short-term causal relations.

PLAN

OBJECTIVE

Learn about the fate of Greek city-states after they were conquered by Macedonia.

ESSENTIAL QUESTION

What lasting influences did ancient Greek culture have on the modern world?

Philip of Macedonia and his son, Alexander the Great, united Greece and helped spread Greek culture throughout the known world. Lesson 3.1 explains how Greece was unified under Macedonian rule.

BACKGROUND FOR THE TEACHER

While the Greek city-states were embroiled in fighting each other during the 27-year-long Peloponnesian War, the kingdom just north of Greece, Macedonia, grew stronger under King Philip II. After seizing the throne and uniting the tribes of Macedonia, Philip turned his attention to Greece. He wanted to bring the Greek city-states under his control in order to build an empire to rival that of the Persians. By 338 B.C., he had succeeded. He allowed the city-states to maintain many freedoms, but for the first time they were unified under one leader.

DIGITAL RESOURCES NGLSync.cengage.com

TEACHER RESOURCES & ASSESSMENT

 Reading and Note-Taking

 Vocabulary Practice

 Section 3 Quiz

STUDENT RESOURCES

 NG Chapter Gallery

ACTIVATE PRIOR KNOWLEDGE

Explain to students that Lesson 3.1 will discuss Philip of Macedonia and his son, Alexander the Great. Ask students if they have ever heard of either man. Discuss any popular culture references they might know. **0:05** minutes

TEACH

GUIDED DISCUSSION

1. **Identify Main Ideas and Details** Ask students to pair up and work together. Have them write down the main idea of the third paragraph. Then they should add details that support that main idea. Have them repeat this for two more paragraphs in the lesson.

2. **Make Predictions** After reading the lesson, ask students to predict what might happen as a result of Alexander's destruction of Thebes. *(Possible response: The rest of the city-states would not dare to oppose Alexander, and he would keep his campaign going to conquer even more territory.)*

BUILD A TIME LINE

Have students build a time line of Philip II's reign. Tell students to record the major events of Philip's reign on a time line that they make themselves. Time lines can be organized horizontally or vertically. Students should include dates and descriptions of events at hash marks in chronological order on their time lines. Encourage students to include pictures or drawings on their time lines. **0:15** minutes

ACTIVE OPTIONS

On Your Feet: Tell Me More Have students form two teams and assign each team one of the following topics: Philip II of Macedonia or Alexander the Great. Each group should write down as many facts about their topic as they can. Have the class reconvene and have each group stand up, one at a time. The sitting group calls out, "Tell me more about [Philip II of Macedonia or Alexander the Great]!" The standing group recites one fact. The sitting group again calls, "Tell me more!" until the standing group runs out of facts to share. Then the groups switch places. **0:15** minutes

NG Learning Framework: Role-Play

ATTITUDE: **Curiosity**
SKILLS: **Observation, Problem-Solving**

Invite students to revisit the information on Alexander the Great in Lesson 3.1 and to imagine that they were in Alexander's place. **ASK:** What made Alexander so successful in expanding his empire? How would you have done things differently from Alexander? What modern aspects of life might change how Alexander behaved if he lived today? **0:10** minutes

STRIVING READERS

Venn Diagram Have students use a Venn Diagram to take notes on Philip and Alexander. Explain that facts unique to either man should be entered in the outer circles with common characteristics placed in the overlapping area. When students have finished, have them make a generalization about the two men.

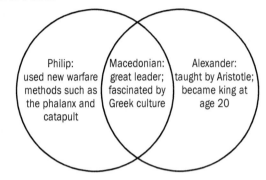

Philip: used new warfare methods such as the phalanx and catapult

Macedonian: great leader; fascinated by Greek culture

Alexander: taught by Aristotle; became king at age 20

ENGLISH LANGUAGE LEARNERS ELD

Word Squares Pair students at the **Emerging** level with English proficient students. Have students create separate Word Squares for the vocabulary words in the text and for at least three other words that are confusing or interesting. Encourage students to write the meaning of the words and to include examples and related words. For example, a Word Square for *phalanx* might include the words and phrases such as those shown below:

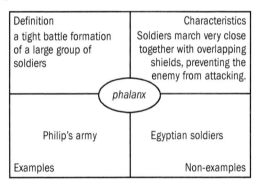

Definition	Characteristics
a tight battle formation of a large group of soldiers	Soldiers march very close together with overlapping shields, preventing the enemy from attacking.
	phalanx
Philip's army	Egyptian soldiers
Examples	Non-examples

Press **mt** *in the Student eEdition for modified text.*

See the Chapter Planner for more strategies for differentiation.

ANSWERS

1. Philip II conquered all of Greece and unified it for the first time.

2. The Greek city-states were open to attack by Philip II because they were still weak from the Peloponnesian War and constant infighting; they could not unify against an attack by Philip II.

3. Philip II combined military force and wealth to win control of Greece. He built a powerful army using methods such as the phalanx battle formation and catapults. He seized Greek colonies rich in natural resources, which funded his army.

ALEXANDER
THE GREAT
356 B.C. – 323 B.C.

According to legend, the city of Gordium in Asia Minor contained a knot so complex that it was impossible to untie. Whoever could unravel the Gordian knot would conquer Asia. When Alexander saw the knot, he drew his sword and asked, "What does it matter how I untie it?" He then sliced the knot in two.

Job: King of Macedonia and general of the army

Education: Taught by Aristotle, the great Greek thinker and scientist

Home: Born in Pella, Macedonia

FINEST HOUR

He led his unbeaten army to conquer lands as far east as India.

WORST MOMENT

In a drunken rage, he murdered his friend Cleitus.

FRIENDS

- Ptolemy (boyhood friend and general in the army)
- Hephaestion (lifelong friend and second-in-command)
- His soldiers

ENEMIES

- Thebans (Greek warriors)
- Darius (Persian king)
- Porus (Indian king)

TRIVIA

To honor his beloved horse, Alexander named a city in present-day India after him: Bucephala.

ALEXANDER'S EMPIRE, C. 323 B.C.

ALEXANDER'S TRIUMPHS

In 334 B.C., Alexander set out to fulfill his father's plans to conquer Persia. Philip was a skilled politician and general, but Alexander was even more gifted. He was a military genius who never once lost a battle. Alexander invaded and freed Persian-controlled Anatolia (present-day Turkey). Then he marched his army south toward Egypt, taking control of Persia's Mediterranean naval bases along the way. Persia responded with an attack from its huge army. However, Alexander cleverly forced the battle to occur on a narrow coastline, which destroyed Persia's advantage of having more soldiers.

When Alexander arrived in Egypt, the people, who had been living under Persian rule, greeted him as a liberator and crowned him pharaoh. Here, as elsewhere, Alexander won the support of conquered people by honoring local traditions. While in Egypt, he founded Alexandria, the first of many cities to bear his name. As a center of education, culture, and trade, Alexandria was one of the most important cities in the ancient world.

In 331 B.C., Alexander defeated the Persians near Babylon and soon controlled the rest of the Persian Empire. Instead of returning home to celebrate, Alexander and his soldiers continued east. They conquered present-day Afghanistan and Uzbekistan before turning toward what is now India, which was then thought to be the edge of the world. In 326 B.C., Alexander crossed the Indus River and won a number of bloody battles, but his soldiers had had enough. Deeply homesick after 11 years away, they wanted to return home. Alexander reluctantly agreed. Over the course of 13 years, Alexander had carved out an empire stretching 3,000 miles from Europe to India. Legend says that he wept because he had no more worlds to conquer.

ALEXANDER'S DEATH

Thousands of soldiers died during the long trip home. Alexander himself did not survive the return journey. In 323 B.C., he became sick with a fever while in Babylon and died a few days later at the age of 32. His generals fought each other for control of the empire, which eventually fell apart. Alexander's empire was replaced with four kingdoms: the Egyptian, Macedonian, Pergamum (PUR-guh-muhm), and Seleucid (suh-LOO-suhd) kingdoms.

REVIEW & ASSESS

1. **READING CHECK** How did Alexander the Great win the support of the people he conquered?

2. **COMPARE AND CONTRAST** How were Philip II and Alexander similar and different as leaders?

3. **INTERPRET MAPS** What physical feature marks the eastern extent of Alexander's empire?

6.4.7 Trace the rise of Alexander the Great and the spread of Greek culture eastward and into Egypt; CST 3 Students use a variety of maps and documents to identify physical and cultural features of neighborhoods, cities, states, and countries and to explain the historical migration of people, expansion and disintegration of empires, and the growth of economic systems.

STANDARDS

HSS CONTENT STANDARDS:

6.4.7 Trace the rise of Alexander the Great and the spread of Greek culture eastward and into Egypt.

HSS ANALYSIS SKILLS:

CST 3 Students use a variety of maps and documents to identify physical and cultural features of neighborhoods, cities, states, and countries and to explain the historical migration of people, expansion and disintegration of empires, and the growth of economic systems; **HI 2** Students understand and distinguish cause, effect, sequence, and correlation in historical events, including the long- and short-term causal relations.

PLAN

OBJECTIVE

Examine the growth of the Macedonian empire under the reign of Alexander the Great.

ESSENTIAL QUESTION

What lasting influences did ancient Greek culture have on the modern world?

The growth of Alexander's empire, detailed in Lesson 3.2, brought Greek culture into new parts of the world.

BACKGROUND FOR THE TEACHER

By the time Alexander inherited the kingdom of Macedonia, his father had unified the city-state and grown it into a powerful force in the region. Macedonia was mountainous in the west and flatter in the east with gentle hills and plains for farming. It also had warm summers and very cold winters. Though Macedonians spoke Greek, their language had many words that were hard for others to understand, and so they were considered foreign by other Greeks.

DIGITAL RESOURCES NGLSync.cengage.com

TEACHER RESOURCES & ASSESSMENT

 Reading and Note-Taking

 Vocabulary Practice

 Section 3 Quiz

STUDENT RESOURCES

 NG Image Gallery

INTERPRET MAPS

Have students preview the lesson by studying the map of Alexander's empire. Use the distance scale to estimate how wide the empire was at its greatest extent. *(over 2,400 miles)* **ASK:** How might the growth of Alexander's empire have affected the influence of Greek culture? *(It would have allowed Greek culture to spread south and east.)* `0:05` **minutes**

TEACH

GUIDED DISCUSSION

1. **Sequence Events** What sequence of events led Alexander to conquer the Persian Empire? *(First Alexander freed Anatolia from Persian control. Then he marched south to take control of Persia's Mediterranean naval bases. After this, he arrived in Egypt, where the people greeted him as a liberator. Finally, Alexander defeated the Persians near Babylon and gained control of the rest of the Persian Empire.)*

2. **Form and Support Opinions** Based on what you read in the lesson, why do you think Alexander was so driven to conquer Persia? Point out ideas or details in the text that support your response. *(Responses will vary but should be supported by examples from the text. Possible responses: He wanted to carry out his father's plans. He had great military genius and a drive to conquer other lands. He wanted to spread Greek culture and trade.)*

MORE INFORMATION

Aristotle and Alexander Aristotle was already a respected Greek philosopher when he was chosen by Philip to tutor Alexander. At the time, Alexander was 13 years old. Aristotle already had a connection with Macedonia, as his father was court physician to a king there. Today, the tutor is as well known as his famous pupil. He taught Alexander literary studies, as well as political theory and history, and possibly natural science, a subject that would fascinate Alexander throughout his life and travels. But later, Aristotle and Alexander were not close. Alexander became a king and conqueror, while Aristotle believed that the only case where a monarchy would be acceptable was if the person was far superior to others in character and quality of mind. Aristotle never mentioned that Alexander or anyone else he had known was so exceptional.

ACTIVE OPTIONS

On Your Feet: Make Inferences About Character Have students work in pairs to conduct Three-Step Interviews. One student should interview the other using this question: *What might Alexander's actions tell us about his character?* Then students should reverse roles. Finally, each student should share the results of his or her interview with the class. `0:25` **minutes**

Critical Viewing: NG Image Gallery Invite students to explore the entire NG Image Gallery and choose one image from the gallery they feel best represents their understanding of the unit. Have students provide a written explanation of why they selected the image they chose. `0:10` **minutes**

STRIVING READERS

Summarize Have students read Lesson 3.2 in pairs. Tell them to write a sentence that restates the main idea of each paragraph as they read. Then have students review those sentences and write a four- or five-sentence paragraph that summarizes the whole lesson. Remind students that they should use their own words in their summary and include only the most important ideas and details. Call on volunteers to share their paragraphs with the class.

ENGLISH LANGUAGE LEARNERS

Read a Map Direct students' attention to the map in Lesson 3.2 and ask them questions to ensure they comprehend what the map shows . **ASK:** Did Alexander's empire extend to the Caucasus Mountains? *(No)* Did Alexander conquer Egypt or Babylon first? *(Egypt)* What is one major battle site? *(Chaeronea, Granicus, Issus, Gaugamela)*

Press **mt** *in the Student eEdition for modified text.*

See the Chapter Planner for more strategies for differentiation.

ANSWERS

1. He honored their local traditions.

2. Both Philip II and Alexander were excellent leaders and skilled conquerors. However, as a military genius who never lost a battle, Alexander was even more successful than his father, and he conquered many more lands than Philip II did.

3. Physical features that mark the eastern extent of Alexander's empire include the Arabian Sea, Bucephala, and a river system including the Indus River.

This statue, known as *Winged Victory of Samothrace*, is an example of Hellenistic sculpture from the second century B.C. It depicts Nike, the Greek goddess of victory. The head and arms of the statue have been lost.

3.3

The Spread of
Hellenistic Culture

People enjoy going to museums to check out new exhibits. The library is the perfect quiet spot for research and reading. Sports fans gather in stadiums to be entertained by sporting events. Theaters showcase the latest dramatic play for an eager audience. Thousands of years ago, ancient Greeks enjoyed these very same activities.

MAIN IDEA

Alexander's conquests spread Greek culture across Asia.

CULTURAL BLEND

Hellas is Greek for "Greece," and the three centuries after Alexander's death are called the **Hellenistic** era because the known world was dominated by Greek culture. Alexander founded Greek colonies wherever he went, and Greek culture spread from these centers through cultural diffusion. Thousands of Greek colonists carried Greek practices and ideas to the plains of Persia, deserts of Egypt, mountains of Afghanistan, and river valleys of northern India. Each area adopted and adapted Greek culture differently, blending it with its own culture.

Alexander founded more than 70 cities, each with Greek designs and features such as temples, gymnasiums, and theaters. These cities flourished, cementing Greek influence in faraway places for centuries. The ultimate Hellenistic city was Alexandria, Egypt's new capital.

WORLDLY ALEXANDRIA

Alexandria became one of the largest, wealthiest, and most cultured cities in the ancient world. Many parks and open spaces created a pleasant environment, and the main streets were lined with colonnades, a series of columns that support a roof to provide shade. Alexandria's multiethnic mix of Greeks, Egyptians, Jews, and others created a **cosmopolitan**, or worldly, atmosphere.

Alexandria had a museum used as a research center and the Great Library, which boasted a copy of every book written in Greek—some 500,000 scrolls. The library drew scientists from around the world, including the Greek scholar Euclid and the Egyptian scholar Hypatia, both of whom worked to advance the field of mathematics. Alexandria also attracted the best artists, sculptors, writers, and musicians. The city was the cultural and trade center of the Hellenistic world.

REVIEW & ASSESS

1. **READING CHECK** How did Alexander spread Greek culture across Asia?

2. **DRAW CONCLUSIONS** What made Hellenistic culture unique?

3. **IDENTIFY MAIN IDEAS AND DETAILS** In what ways was Alexandria the cultural center of the Hellenistic world?

6.4.7 Trace the rise of Alexander the Great and the spread of Greek culture eastward and into Egypt; 6.4.8 Describe the enduring contributions of important Greek figures in the arts and sciences (e.g., Hypatia, Socrates, Plato, Aristotle, Euclid, Thucydides).

HSS CONTENT STANDARDS:

6.4.7 Trace the rise of Alexander the Great and the spread of Greek culture eastward and into Egypt; **6.4.8** Describe the enduring contributions of important Greek figures in the arts and sciences (e.g., Hypatia, Socrates, Plato, Aristotle, Euclid, Thucydides)

PLAN

OBJECTIVE

Identify traits of Hellenistic culture.

ESSENTIAL QUESTION

What lasting influences did ancient Greek culture have on the modern world?

Alexander the Great helped spread Greek culture through his conquests of the ancient world. Lesson 3.3 describes the Hellenistic world and its grandest city—Alexandria.

BACKGROUND FOR THE TEACHER

The Great Library of Alexandria attracted a variety of scholars whose work influenced the modern world: Euclid, the father of geometry; Ptolemy, author of the geocentric theory of the universe; Hypatia, a female mathematician and philosopher who expanded upon the works of Plato; and Eratosthenes, who first calculated the circumference of Earth.

DIGITAL RESOURCES NGLSync.cengage.com

TEACHER RESOURCES & ASSESSMENT

 Reading and Note-Taking

 Vocabulary Practice

 Section 3 Quiz

STUDENT RESOURCES

 NG Chapter Gallery

UNDERSTAND CULTURE

Remind students that a culture region is an area unified by language, religion, or other traits. Alexandria had a mix of cultures, which contributed to a cosmopolitan atmosphere. Divide the class into four groups and have each group discuss how one of the following topics might influence cultures in close contact to change.

1. Seeing and learning about other lands, their people, and cultures

2. Creating new styles in art and architecture

3. Adopting and applying ideas to design new inventions

4. Challenging one's assumptions and being open to new explanations

`0:05` minutes

TEACH

GUIDED DISCUSSION

1. **Analyze Cause and Effect** As Greek culture began to spread through the city centers, how did it affect the further spread of Greek culture? (*More people in different places adopted Greek culture, making it even more influential and cross-cultural.*)

2. **Form and Support Opinions** What was the most influential aspect of Greek culture? Use examples from the text to support your opinion.

ANALYZE VISUALS

Direct students' attention to the photo of the *Winged Victory of Samothrace* in Lesson 3.3. As a class, consider how Nike's figure represents Greek culture and its diffusion by exploring the following questions:

- What do you notice most?
- What details do you see?
- What do you see that demonstrates Greek culture?

`0:10` minutes

ACTIVE OPTIONS

On Your Feet: Culture Roundtable Divide the class into groups of four or five. Hand each group a sheet of paper with the question *What does culture mean to you?* on it. The first student in each group should sit at the desk and write an answer, read it aloud, and pass the paper clockwise to the next student. Each student should add at least one answer. The paper should circulate around the table until students run out of answers or time is up. `0:15` minutes

Critical Viewing: NG Chapter Gallery Ask students to choose one image from the Chapter Gallery and become an expert on it. They should do additional research to learn all about it. Then, students should share their findings with a partner, small group, or the class. `0:15` minutes

GIFTED & TALENTED

Locate Greek References Encourage students to explore their everyday worlds and locate references to Greek culture that surround them in our modern world. Offer as an example the Nike brand of shoes. Ask students to locate at least three items or ideas that reflect ancient Greek culture. Tell them to bring in examples to share with the class. As students share their examples, list their findings on the board under broad categories, such as *Politics, Sports, Literature, Architecture,* and *Art.*

PRE-AP

Research Alexandrias Point out to students the different cities named after Alexander in the text in Lessons 3.2 and 3.3 and on the map in Lesson 3.2. Have students work in four groups to research one of these ancient cities: Alexandria, Egypt; Alexandria Areion; Alexandria Arachoton; Alexandria Eschate. Encourage students to present their findings to the class. After each group presents, determine as a class the similarities and differences among the Alexandrias.

Press (**mt**) *in the Student eEdition for modified text.*

See the Chapter Planner for more strategies for differentiation.

ANSWERS

1. Alexander founded Greek colonies in the lands he conquered. Greek culture spread from these colonies through cultural diffusion across Asia.

2. Hellenistic culture was unique in that it influenced arts, sports, architecture, and cities all over the world.

3. Alexandria had a multiethnic population that enjoyed parks, temples, a museum, and a library. This library drew scholars and scientists from all over the world. In this way, the best minds came to Alexandria, making it the cultural center of the Hellenistic world.

4.1 Philosophy and Literature

What is right? What is wrong? What is good? What is bad? We all think we know the answers, but do we really? These are some of the questions posed by Greek thinkers over 2,000 years ago. Today we are still searching for the answers.

MAIN IDEA

Greek ideas and writings remain influential today. They are the foundation of Western thought.

SOCRATES, PLATO, AND ARISTOTLE

Philosophy comes from a Greek word meaning "love of wisdom." Philosophers try to understand the universe and our place in it. Instead of explaining the world through gods and myths, they use logic and reason. Greek city-states provided an open environment where philosophers excelled. They also studied and taught other subjects, such as science, math, and biology.

Socrates (SAH-kruh-teez) was an Athenian philosopher interested in ethics, or the study of right and wrong. He challenged people to think more deeply, asking probing questions like, "What is justice?" His question-and-answer teaching style became known as the Socratic method. Socrates' methods made him unpopular among the leaders of Athens. He was accused of not believing in the official gods and of encouraging young

Athenians to rebel. He was put on trial, found guilty, and sentenced to death.

Socrates taught **Plato** (PLAY-toh), one of the most influential philosophers in history. Plato believed that this world was a shadow of a superior world. He disliked democracy, believing instead that philosopher-kings should rule. Plato founded an elite academy, where he taught **Aristotle**, the tutor of Alexander the Great.

Aristotle searched for understanding by examining the world closely. He categorized everything, laying the foundations for the study of biology, law, physics, and politics. Aristotle opened an academy, the Lyceum, where anyone could study a wide range of subjects. Together these three Greek philosophers formed the basis of modern Western philosophy, mathematics, and science and continue to influence our thinking.

EPICS AND HISTORIES

Homer was the most famous writer of epic poetry, a form of poetry that combines elements of drama and narrative. With their mythical beasts, interfering gods, and adventurous heroes, Homer's epics about the Trojan War—the *Iliad* and the *Odyssey*—continue to entertain modern readers. Another Greek writer still popular today was a slave called **Aesop** (EE-sahp). He wrote a series of fables, or short stories with animals as the central characters. Each fable taught a moral lesson.

The Greeks were among the first people to research their past and write it down accurately. When the Greek historian Herodotus (hih-RAH-duh-tuhs) wrote a history of the Persian Wars, he made sure to check his sources and to understand the significance of the events he described. He is considered the father of history. Similarly, Thucydides wrote an accurate account of the Peloponnesian War, while Xenophon (ZEH-nuh-fuhn) described life in Greece. They provided useful insights into ancient Greece and created a model for the future study of history.

THE SCHOOL OF ATHENS (Detail)

The Renaissance artist Raphael worked on this fresco over a three-year period. It was painted on a wall in the pope's palace in Rome. The painting shows the greatest thinkers of classical Greek society. There are mathematicians, natural philosophers, artists, and scientists. They all lived at different times, but Raphael painted them under one roof. The two central figures are Plato and Aristotle, who have had a lasting effect on Western thought.

Detail from *The School of Athens*, Raphael, A.D. 1511

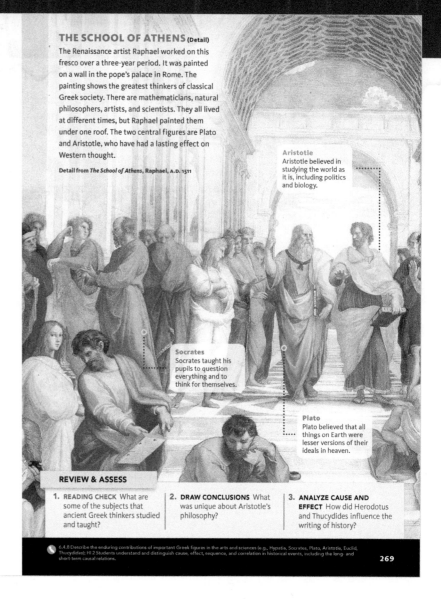

Aristotle
Aristotle believed in studying the world as it is, including politics and biology.

Socrates
Socrates taught his pupils to question everything and to think for themselves.

Plato
Plato believed that all things on Earth were lesser versions of their ideals in heaven.

REVIEW & ASSESS

1. **READING CHECK** What are some of the subjects that ancient Greek thinkers studied and taught?

2. **DRAW CONCLUSIONS** What was unique about Aristotle's philosophy?

3. **ANALYZE CAUSE AND EFFECT** How did Herodotus and Thucydides influence the writing of history?

6.4.8 Describe the enduring contributions of important Greek figures in the arts and sciences (e.g., Hypatia, Socrates, Plato, Aristotle, Euclid, Thucydides); HI 2 Students understand and distinguish cause, effect, sequence, and correlation in historical events, including the long- and short-term causal relations.

HSS CONTENT STANDARDS:

6.4.8 Describe the enduring contributions of important Greek figures in the arts and sciences (e.g., Hypatia, Socrates, Plato, Aristotle, Euclid, Thucydides).

HSS ANALYSIS SKILLS:

HI 2 Students understand and distinguish cause, effect, sequence, and correlation in historical events, including the long- and short-term causal relations.

PLAN

OBJECTIVE

Understand how ancient Greek achievements in philosophy and literature influenced the ancient and modern worlds.

ESSENTIAL QUESTION

What lasting influences did ancient Greek culture have on the modern world?

The sophisticated thinkers and writers detailed in Lesson 4.1 brought to the study of the world, both metaphysical and scientific, a curiosity, transparency, and logic still valued today.

BACKGROUND FOR THE TEACHER

The Greek philosophical tradition began with the Agora, which means "gathering place" or "assembly." It was a location in the open air where men gathered to discuss the world of politics, nature, and more abstract subjects such as the meaning of life and justice. The first man to be called a philosopher was not Socrates, who is possibly the most famous of the Greek philosophers today, but Pythagoras. A religious cult sprang up around Pythagoras's beliefs. Little is known about these beliefs, as his writings have not survived. We do know that the Pythagoreans believed in the magic of numbers. They also were vegetarians and believed in reincarnation. The Pythagoreans were only one of several "mystery cults" that augmented the official Greek religion at the time.

DIGITAL RESOURCES NGLSync.cengage.com

TEACHER RESOURCES & ASSESSMENT

 Reading and Note-Taking

 Vocabulary Practice

 Section 4 Quiz

STUDENT RESOURCES

 Biography

PLAY "THUMBS UP, THUMBS DOWN"

Ask students whether they've heard of the philosophers and writers mentioned in the chapter. Have students give each one a thumbs up if they've heard of the person or a thumbs down if they have not. For each figure, ask students who put their thumb up to share any details that they know about the person. Tell students they will learn about the famous philosophers who defined rational thought. **0:05** minutes

GUIDED DISCUSSION

1. **Explain** How did Socrates' teaching methods work? *(He asked probing questions to get people to think more deeply.)*

2. **Compare and Contrast** How were the three philosophers mentioned in the lesson alike, and how were they different? *(Possible response: Socrates, Plato, and Aristotle were all deep thinkers and were interested in the reasons behind the way things are in the world. Socrates emphasized thinking for one's self, Plato was more interested in an ideal world, and Aristotle wanted to understand the way in which the world actually worked.)*

ANALYZE VISUALS

Have students examine *The School of Athens*. Tell them that the people depicted did not all live during the same time period. Instead, they reflect the most important minds in Greek philosophy, art, and science throughout ancient Greek history. Ask students to describe the figures and what they are doing. Have them look at the figures of Aristotle and Plato and read the captions to make educated guesses at what they might be talking about. **0:10** minutes

ACTIVE OPTIONS

NG Learning Framework: Write a Fable

SKILL: Communication
KNOWLEDGE: Our Human Story

Have students familiarize themselves with the concept of a fable by reading the examples of Aesop's fables in the **Primary Source Handbook**. Then, have students work in small groups to create a fable of their own. Point out that fables usually have the following characteristics:

- They teach a moral lesson.
- They are short.
- The main characters are usually animals that are given human qualities.
- One character displays the action that is being critiqued.

When groups have finished composing their fables, have representatives read them aloud to the class. Discuss how well each fable displays the characteristics of the genre. **0:20** minutes

On Your Feet: Understand Multiple Perspectives Divide the class to form two groups, and have them stand on either side of the room. Have one side represent philosophy and the other, science or natural law. Give them some topic ideas and have them decide whether philosophical or scientific perspective is more relevant and helpful to discuss the topic. Start with a term mentioned in the reading, such as "What is justice?" or "What is perfection?" and have students argue whether the philosophers or the scientists can discuss this, or both, and whether they can debate each other on the topic. If not, ask them why not? Then give the two groups a chance to debate the topic by taking turns offering their suggestions. Encourage the class to reach consensus on at least one topic. **0:25** minutes

STRIVING READERS

Chart Athenian Thought Leaders Have students complete the following chart to keep track of the ideas of the three philosophers mentioned in the lesson.

	Socrates	Plato	Aristotle
Known for			
Famous Pupil			
Main Interest			

PRE-AP

Write About It Use the lesson as a starting point to research one of the figures shown in *The School of Athens* but not mentioned in the lesson. Have them write a short narrative paragraph about this person. Then have volunteers share their paragraph with the class.

Press **mt** *in the Student eEdition for modified text.*

See the Chapter Planner for more strategies for differentiation.

ANSWERS

1. Some of the subjects include philosophy, science, math, and biology.

2. Aristotle used logic to systematically examine, categorize, and understand the world.

3. Herodotus and Thucydides were among the first to apply careful research and accurate written accounts of past events in order to understand the significance of those events from which insights could be gained.

Arts and Architecture

GREEK MASKS
Greek actors hid their faces with masks that represented the faces of a play's characters. Since three actors played multiple roles, the masks helped the audience recognize character changes.

A well-known ancient Greek tyrant cruelly enjoyed burying his enemies alive. Surprisingly, actors performing a Greek play were able to make him cry during sad scenes. The tyrant would weep for the suffering the actors mimicked onstage. Greek drama was powerful.

MAIN IDEA

The Greeks developed forms of art and architecture that are still appreciated today.

Critical Viewing This theater in Taormina, Sicily, is one of the best-preserved examples of a Greek amphitheater. What modern structure does this theater resemble?

POSSIBLE RESPONSE
The amphitheater resembles a sports stadium.

DRAMA AND SCULPTURE

The Greeks loved the theater. Plays sometimes lasting entire days were performed in huge semicircular theaters, or amphitheaters. Greek drama evolved from plays honoring the god Dionysus (dy-uh-NY-suhs) into two main forms. **Comedy** was humorous and often mocked famous people. **Tragedy** was serious, with characters suffering before an unhappy ending.

Only three male actors performed each play, which required each actor to play many parts. The chorus, a group of actors who spoke, sang, and danced together, narrated the story. Costumes, props, and music brought the action to life.

The greatest Greek playwrights were Sophocles (SAH-fuh-kleez), Aeschylus (EHS-kuh-luhs), and Euripides (yu-RIH-puh-deez), who all wrote tragedies, and Aristophanes (a-ruh-STAH-fuh-neez), who wrote comedy.

Greek sculptors were dedicated to capturing the human form in their art. They carved sculptures from marble, wood, and bronze. The sculptures were painted to look amazingly alive. The Colossus of Rhodes was a 100-foot-tall bronze statue of the sun god Helios, similar in style to the Statue of Liberty. It was once considered one of the Seven Wonders of the Ancient World, but the original no longer stands. In fact, many of the best examples of Greek sculpture are actually newer Roman copies of Greek originals.

COLUMNS AND TEMPLES

Ancient Greek architecture was a democratic art. It expressed beauty and harmony for everyone to enjoy. Temples were designed to be admired from outside, and all followed a similar plan. The temple usually faced east, toward the sunrise. The main room was rectangular and contained a statue of the temple god. Columns supported the roof. The features of Greek architecture continue to influence the style of buildings today. The Supreme Court Building in Washington, D.C., is a good example of this influence.

THREE COLUMN TYPES

Doric
Mainland, western colonies

Corinthian
More rarely found

Ionic
Eastern Greece and the islands

REVIEW & ASSESS

1. **READING CHECK** What art forms did the Greeks develop that we still appreciate today?

2. **COMPARE AND CONTRAST** What is the difference between the two main forms of Greek drama—comedy and tragedy?

3. **IDENTIFY MAIN IDEAS AND DETAILS** The text states that Greek architecture was a democratic art form. What evidence supports this claim?

HI 3 Students explain the sources of historical continuity and how the combination of ideas and events explains the emergence of new patterns. **271**

STANDARDS

HSS CONTENT STANDARDS:

6.4.8 Describe the enduring contributions of important Greek figures in the arts and sciences (e.g., Hypatia, Socrates, Plato, Aristotle, Euclid, Thucydides).

HSS ANALYSIS SKILLS:

HI 3 Students explain the sources of historical continuity and how the combination of ideas and events explains the emergence of new patterns.

PLAN

OBJECTIVE

Explain how classical Greek achievements in the arts and architecture influenced the ancient and modern worlds.

ESSENTIAL QUESTION

What lasting influences did ancient Greek culture have on the modern world?

Lesson 4.2 shows the influence of Greece's dramatic and architectural legacy and how these forms are still used in the world today.

BACKGROUND FOR THE TEACHER

One of the major legacies of the classical Greeks is architecture. Modern theaters and sports arenas are based on the design of the Greek amphitheater, and Greek columns are used to support the roofs of buildings around the world. Three styles of columns are attributed to the Greeks: Doric, which are simple and sturdy with a plain top; Ionic, which are thinner and carved with narrow lines and a scroll style top; and Corinthian, which have tops elaborately decorated with leaves. Other common aspects of Greek architecture still seen today include the colonnade, which is a long row of columns, and the pediment, which is a triangular area below the roof of a building. The U.S. Supreme Court Building is a good example of the influence of ancient Greek architecture.

DIGITAL RESOURCES NGLSync.cengage.com

TEACHER RESOURCES & ASSESSMENT

 Reading and Note-Taking

 Vocabulary Practice

 Section 4 Quiz

STUDENT RESOURCES

 NG Chapter Gallery

INTRODUCE & ENGAGE

UNDERSTAND CULTURE

Tell students that they probably know a lot of art and architecture that is based on the forms that the classical Greeks invented. Athenian culture emphasized the importance of human experience, the pursuit of knowledge, and harmony and balance in architecture. It was also a religious society, and stories of Greek gods and goddesses occupied a featured place in Greek literature, theater, and architecture, and continue to influence Western literature and film today. In the early fourth century, the philosopher named Aristotle was the most important critic of Greek drama. He analyzed plays, classified types of plays, and defined rules for tragic drama. **0:05** minutes

TEACH

GUIDED DISCUSSION

1. **Describe** Have students look at the columns depicted in the lesson and write a sentence to describe each column's features. *(Doric columns have a simple top; Corinthian columns have an ornate top; and Ionic columns have a scroll-like top.)*

2. **Form and Support Opinions** Ask students whether they like stories that are tragedies or comedies, and have them give some examples or reasons to back up their responses. *(Responses will vary.)*

ANALYZE VISUALS

Direct students' attention to the photograph of the amphitheater in Lesson 4.2. Ask them to consider how the physical characteristics of the land influenced how people lived and constructed such buildings. Make a list of the challenges the Greeks might have faced as they built structures on the mountainous terrain. **0:10** minutes

ACTIVE OPTIONS

On Your Feet: Small Groups Organize students into small groups and have each group read a passage from a play by one of the playwrights mentioned in Lesson 4.2 and discuss its meaning. Then have a volunteer from each group read the passage aloud to the class and give a short summary of the passage. **0:25** minutes

NG Learning Framework: Write a Play

ATTITUDE: **Empowerment**
KNOWLEDGE: **Storytelling**

Have students revisit earlier lessons in the chapter and have them work in small groups to write a short scene (comic or tragic) based on some dramatic event in the chapter. Examples include the plague of Athens, the funeral oration of Pericles, the Peloponnesian War, or Alexander's conquest of Greece. Students should use information from the chapter and their own creativity to build their scenes. Then have them perform the scenes for the class. **0:20** minutes

DIFFERENTIATE

INCLUSION

Describe a Photograph Have students look at the photograph of the amphitheater in Lesson 4.2. Ask them to describe it and then talk about why the shape and features of the building might be good for a performance space.

GIFTED & TALENTED

Write a Short Play Have students research and read a Greek comedy or tragedy, or part of one, and then create their own new play, either wholly invented or partially based on the source play. Have students cast the different parts and act out the play for the class.

Press **mt** *in the Student eEdition for modified text.*

See the Chapter Planner for more strategies for differentiation.

REVIEW & ASSESS

ANSWERS

1. The Greeks developed many art forms that we still appreciate today, including drama, sculpture, and architecture.

2. A comedy is funny and often makes fun of famous people; in contrast, a tragedy is serious and includes characters who suffer terribly before an unhappy ending.

3. According to the text, Greek architecture was designed and built for everyone to enjoy.

432 B.C.

+ POSSIBLE RESPONSE

The columns are sturdy and thick, and the building is beautiful, tall, and intimidating.

The Parthenon, one of the world's most recognizable buildings, was completed in 432 B.C. It took workers almost 15 years to build this magnificent marble temple, which honored Athena, goddess and protector of Athens. Like much Greek architecture, the Parthenon was made to be looked at from the outside. Its elegant proportions communicated a sense of harmony and balance. Inside, towering from floor to ceiling, was a 33-foot gold and ivory statue of Athena. The Parthenon was both an expression of Athens's wealth and a symbol of its cultural, political, and military superiority. What details in the Parthenon's design help convey these ideas?

STANDARDS

HSS CONTENT STANDARDS:

6.4 Students analyze the geographic, political, economic, religious, and social structures of the early civilizations of Ancient Greece.

PLAN

OBJECTIVE

Identify the cultural ideas that found expression in Greek architecture's most stunning example: the Parthenon.

ESSENTIAL QUESTION

What lasting influences did ancient Greek culture have on the modern world?

Lesson 4.3 discusses the Parthenon, one of Athens's most magnificent buildings.

BACKGROUND FOR THE TEACHER

Building with stone has it origins in the seventh century B.C., when Greece began to first have knowledge of Egypt and its workers' method of quarrying and constructing stone. By the time the Parthenon was built, the basics of the different styles, or orders, of Greek architecture were well in place. The Parthenon is in the Doric style, which is plain but conveys an essence of power for those gazing upon it. It is one of the most famous—and most studied—buildings on Earth. It was built after the completion of the Persian War to celebrate the war's end and represent Athens's authority in the region.

DIGITAL RESOURCES NGLSync.cengage.com

TEACHER RESOURCES & ASSESSMENT

 Reading and Note-Taking

 Vocabulary Practice

 Section 4 Quiz

STUDENT RESOURCES

 NG Chapter Gallery

INTRODUCE & ENGAGE

EXPLORE RENEWAL

Engage students in a discussion about ways that people recover a sense of normalcy and peaceful living after years of long and grueling warfare. Fixing or replacing buildings that were destroyed, having feasts or contests, attending performances, and getting back to normal, everyday routines are some ways societies renew after traumatic events. Then tell students they will learn about a building that was vital to the restoration of Athens's spirit. **0:10** minutes

TEACH

GUIDED DISCUSSION

1. **Describe** How do the details in the Parthenon's design convey power? What other qualities do you think it conveys? *(The columns are sturdy and thick, without many curves or unnecessary designs. The building itself looks very tall, so it would make an observer feel tiny. The building is also slightly raised, with stairs on every side, making it inviting and open, allowing people to approach it freely and without fear.)*

2. **Make Connections** Have you seen other buildings that have a similar look or design style as the Parthenon? *(Responses will vary, but students may cite specific buildings or more general buildings such as government buildings, libraries, colleges, and museums.)*

ANALYZE VISUALS

Give students some background on the Parthenon. Remind them how Athens was burned to the ground during the Persian Wars. Even the olive tree, which according to legend had been a gift to the city from Athena, was dead. But someone saw a tiny leaf growing from the burned tree, and from this sign the Athenians decided to rebuild the city. Ask students why the construction of the Parthenon was such an important moment in Greek history. Encourage students to volunteer their ideas as you add them to the board. Responses will vary, but students should make the connection between the building of the Parthenon and Athens becoming a strong force in the region again. **0:15** minutes

ACTIVE OPTIONS

On Your Feet: Debate Divide the class into two groups and have one side discuss reasons why they might support rebuilding Athens, while the other side finds reasons to argue against it. Have students from each group take turns debating the topic, and make sure that they also try to address the concerns of the other group. See if either group can persuade opposing students to change sides. At the end, reward the side with the most remaining students as the winner of the debate. **0:20** minutes

Critical Viewing: NG Chapter Gallery Have students examine the contents of the Chapter Gallery for this chapter. Then invite them to brainstorm additional images they believe would fit within the Chapter Gallery. Have them write a description of these additional images and provide an explanation of why they would fit within the Chapter Gallery. Then instruct them to do online research to find examples of actual images they would like to add to the gallery. **0:10** minutes

DIFFERENTIATE

GIFTED & TALENTED

Draw the Parthenon Have students work in pairs on a drawing of the Parthenon based on the photograph in the lesson. Then have them discuss how they would have built the building, starting from the ground up. Remind them that the building took about 15 years to build, and that it had a statue of Athena inside it. They also may try to draw the statue based on their imagination and what they have read or seen of Athena in books or pictures.

PRE-AP

Research Symbols Have students research online to find visual depictions of abstract concepts such as justice, harmony, balance, strength, and mercy, and report on the characteristics usually associated with each one.

Press **mt** *in the Student eEdition for modified text.*

See the Chapter Planner for more strategies for differentiation.

Democracy and Law

Sometimes we might take our system of government for granted. However, our democracy is a legacy that has been passed down to us from thousands of years ago. Our modern ideas of democracy, justice, and citizenship all have their roots in ancient Greece.

MAIN IDEA

The Constitution of the United States was influenced by ancient Greek ideas.

GOVERNMENT OF THE PEOPLE

Ancient Greece was the birthplace of democracy and citizenship. Thousands of Greek citizens met regularly to vote on policies and laws. Greek colonies in Italy spread democracy to the ancient Romans, who carried it around the ancient world. They firmly established Greek political ideas in Europe. From these ideas evolved our modern ideas about government and civic life.

Ancient Greece also laid the foundations of American constitutional democracy. The cornerstone of Greek democratic ideas was that political power should rest with the people. The Greeks established the concept of citizenship with its rights and responsibilities toward the state and a duty to participate in politics and civic life.

The Greeks also embraced the principle of political equality, in which one citizen has one vote and where officials are paid, allowing the poor to serve as well as the rich. The Greeks put checks and balances into place. They limited terms of office and separated the three key branches of government—lawmaking, executive, and judicial—to prevent any one branch from becoming too powerful.

The **representative democracy** of the United States is based on the Greek system. Because the U.S. population is so large, its millions of citizens cannot vote directly on policies. Instead, citizens exercise their political power by electing representatives to vote on their behalf.

RULE OF LAW

Greek democracy was built on the rule of law. Greek citizens proposed and voted on laws that were enforced in courts. These courts established innocence or guilt through trials by **jury**. A jury is a group of people chosen to decide guilt or innocence in a trial. Greek jurors were selected randomly so that the results would be impartial. They also were paid so that even poor citizens could take part.

In Greek trials, the accuser and the accused represented themselves. There were no lawyers. Both parties had the same amount of time to speak, and both relied on witnesses. Under oath, witnesses sometimes testified to events but usually provided character statements.

Both sides presented their case, but they did not sum up the evidence, as lawyers do in court cases today. Nor was the jury allowed to discuss the case. Instead, jurors voted immediately by placing metal discs called ballots into a pot. The jury also passed sentence. Some penalties were automatic, such as death for murder, but more involved fines. Few people were actually imprisoned. There were no appeals, and the entire process was completed in a day.

+ POSSIBLE RESPONSE

The people in the photograph demonstrate citizenship by standing up for their beliefs and gathering together to discuss or debate public matters.

Critical Viewing
Supporters of immigration rights march through downtown Los Angeles. How are these people demonstrating citizenship?

REVIEW & ASSESS

1. **READING CHECK** Why were jury members chosen randomly and why were they paid?

2. **ANALYZE CAUSE AND EFFECT** What ancient Greek ideas laid the foundation for the U.S. system of government?

3. **COMPARE AND CONTRAST** What are the differences between ancient Greek trials and modern trials in the United States?

6.4.2 Trace the transition from tyranny and oligarchy to early democratic forms of government and back to dictatorship in ancient Greece, including the significance of the invention of the idea of citizenship (e.g., from *Pericles' Funeral Oration*); 6.4.3 State the key differences between Athenian, or direct, democracy and representative democracy; 6.4.8 Describe the enduring contributions of important Greek figures in the arts and sciences (e.g., Hypatia, Socrates, Plato, Aristotle, Euclid, Thucydides); HI 2 Students understand and distinguish cause, effect, sequence, and correlation in historical events, including the long- and short-term causal relations; HI 3 Students explain the sources of historical continuity and how the combination of ideas and events explains the emergence of new patterns.

HSS CONTENT STANDARDS:

6.4.2 Trace the transition from tyranny and oligarchy to early democratic forms of government and back to dictatorship in ancient Greece, including the significance of the invention of the idea of citizenship (e.g., from Pericles' Funeral Oration); **6.4.3** State the key differences between Athenian, or direct, democracy and representative democracy; **6.4.8** Describe the enduring contributions of important Greek figures in the arts and sciences (e.g., Hypatia, Socrates, Plato, Aristotle, Euclid, Thucydides).

HSS ANALYSIS SKILLS:

HI 2 Students understand and distinguish cause, effect, sequence, and correlation in historical events, including the long- and short-term causal relations; **HI 3** Students explain the sources of historical continuity and how the combination of ideas and events explains the emergence of new patterns.

PLAN

OBJECTIVE

Learn about the influence of Greek ideas on the government of the United States.

ESSENTIAL QUESTION

What lasting influences did ancient Greek culture have on the modern world?

Lesson 4.4 shows the influence of Greek government, particularly democracy, on the world today.

BACKGROUND FOR THE TEACHER

At first glance, the city-state of Athens had a more democratic government than that of the United States because its government was a direct democracy in which all citizens could vote on laws. Citizenship in Athens was strictly limited to men, however, and women, foreigners, and slaves were excluded. Some scholars estimate that citizens made up only 10 to 15 percent of the population. Nevertheless, the concept of rule by many (*citizens/democracy*), rather than rule by few (*noblemen/oligarchy*) or one (*king/monarchy*), was put into practice.

DIGITAL RESOURCES NGLSync.cengage.com

TEACHER RESOURCES & ASSESSMENT

 Reading and Note-Taking

 Vocabulary Practice

 Section 4 Quiz

STUDENT RESOURCES

 Active History

INTRODUCE & ENGAGE

COMPARE DEMOCRACIES

Tell students that they will be reading about Greek democracy. Explain that Lesson 4.4 explores the differences between classical Greek laws and practices and the laws and practices of the United States today. Draw a large Venn diagram on the board and write *democracy* where the circles overlap. Label one side of the diagram *Classical Greece* and the other *United States*. Model filling out the diagram by pointing out the difference between Greece's direct democracy and the United States' representative democracy. Have students make their own Venn diagrams that they will complete as they read the lesson. Once they have finished reading, review their responses as a class and add items to the large diagram on the board. `0:15` minutes

TEACH

GUIDED DISCUSSION

1. **Analyze Causes** Why do you think the United States is a representative democracy instead of a direct democracy? *(Possible response: There are too many people in the country—for everyone to cast a vote directly on every policy would be unworkable.)*

2. **Draw Conclusions** What are some of the benefits and drawbacks of the classical Greek system of law? *(Possible responses: Having trials last only one day would be good because people would not have to wait to stand trial very long. Automatic penalties could be bad because there are different motivations for crimes, and motivations are important.)*

ANALYZE VISUALS

Direct students' attention to the photograph of activists in Los Angeles in Lesson 4.4. Ask the class to describe what they see in the photo and write students' descriptions on the board. Ask students to consider why the flag is an important symbol and why people are holding it up. **ASK:** In what way does the flag symbolize citizenship? What else can a flag symbolize? *(Possible responses: commonality, strength, fairness, justice, idealism, nationalism)* `0:10` minutes

ACTIVE OPTIONS

Active History: Research Ancient Greek Contributions Extend the lesson by using either the PDF or Whiteboard version of the Research Ancient Greek Contributions activity. These activities take a deeper look at a topic from, or related to, the lesson. Explore the activities as a class, turn them into group assignments, or even assign them individually. `0:10` minutes

On Your Feet: Democracy from Scratch Have students gather into small groups to think of what rights and responsibilities they would include in a democracy. Encourage them to be creative and to draw on what they already know about democracy. Have them share with the class three of their main ideas, and have them explain why each would be important and useful to the people in their nation or state. Encourage other students to ask questions and offer constructive criticism of each other's plans. `0:20` minutes

DIFFERENTIATE

INCLUSION

Work in Pairs Pair students who have visual or learning disabilities with partners who are proficient readers. Have the proficient student read the subsection titled "Government of the People" aloud. After reading each paragraph, the reader should stop and their partner should retell the same information in their own words to check comprehension.

ENGLISH LANGUAGE LEARNERS

Build Vocabulary Help students understand words used in Lesson 4.4 that may be unfamiliar to them. Begin with the Key Vocabulary words for this lesson: *representative democracy* and *jury*. Have students at the **Emerging** and **Expanding** levels work in pairs. Have students at the **Bridging** level work independently. Provide students with index cards or small pieces of paper. Have students write each word and its definition based on context clues in the text on separate index cards. Then have them compare their definitions with definitions in the Glossary. Once students have established solid definitions, encourage them to write sentences using the Key Vocabulary. Other words in Lesson 4.4 that students may need extra practice with include *civic, constitutional, citizenship, equality, trial, innocence,* and *appeal*. Challenge students at the **Bridging** level to analyze word parts to help understand word definitions and expand their vocabulary. Have students refer to a dictionary in the classroom or online to gather definitions for these or other words and then write sentences using the words.

Press **mt** *in the Student eEdition for modified text.*

See the Chapter Planner for more strategies for differentiation.

REVIEW & ASSESS

ANSWERS

1. Jury members were chosen randomly so that they would be impartial. They were paid so that poor citizens could also take part.

2. Ancient Greek ideas of citizenship, justice, political equality, rule of law, and the right to vote are among the many ideas that laid the foundation for democracy in the United States.

3. Both sides presented their cases at court, but did not sum up the evidence like lawyers today do. Greek juries did not discuss their vote, as they do today, but simply voted after the evidence was presented. Also the jury passed sentences in Greek democracy, unlike today.

VOCABULARY

Use each of the following vocabulary words in a sentence that shows an understanding of the meaning of the word.

1. **direct democracy** (HSS 6.4.3)
   Athens's government was a direct democracy, in which citizens voted for or against laws.
2. **immortal** (HSS 6.4.4)
3. **plague** (HSS HI 4)
4. **siege** (HSS 6.4.6)
5. **philosophy** (HSS 6.4.8)
6. **comedy** (HSS 6.4.8)
7. **tragedy** (HSS 6.4.8)
8. **jury** (HSS 6.4.2)

READING STRATEGY

9. **DETERMINE WORD MEANINGS** Copy the chart below and add your examples of words that include each Greek root. Then write a paragraph about Greek culture that includes each word. (HSS HI 3)

Root	Meaning	Example(s)
cosm-	universe	
-cracy	government	democracy
dem-	people	democracy
-logy	speech	
myth-	story	
phil-	love	
poli-	city	
soph-	wise	

MAIN IDEAS

Answer the following questions. Support your answers with evidence from the chapter.

10. How did Athens become a powerful empire after the Persian Wars? LESSON 1.2 (HSS 6.4.6)
11. Why did the Greeks make offerings to the gods and goddesses they worshipped? LESSON 1.3 (HSS 6.4.4)
12. What caused the outbreak of the Peloponnesian War between Athens and Sparta? LESSON 2.1 (HSS 6.4.6)
13. How did Sparta defeat Athens and end the Peloponnesian War? LESSON 2.2 (HSS 6.4.6)
14. What was Phillip II's most important achievement in Greece? LESSON 3.1 (HSS HI 1)
15. Why did Alexander's conquests end? LESSON 3.2 (HSS 6.4.7)
16. How is Hellenistic culture an example of cultural diffusion? LESSON 3.3 (HSS 6.4.7)
17. What evidence is there that the ideas of the Greek philosophers and writers are still important today? LESSON 4.1 (HSS 6.4.8)

CRITICAL THINKING

Answer the following questions. Support your answers with evidence from the chapter.

18. **ESSENTIAL QUESTION** What are three ways in which Greek influences are felt today? (HSS HI 3)
19. **ANALYZE CAUSE AND EFFECT** How did the plague contribute to the failure of Pericles' war strategy against the Spartans? (HSS HI 2)
20. **EVALUATE** What factors contributed to Philip II's success in conquering and unifying Greece? (HSS 6.4.7)
21. **YOU DECIDE** Where would you rather have lived—Athens or Sparta? Why? Support your opinion with details from the chapter. (HSS 6.4.6)

INTERPRET MAPS

Study the map of the Hellenistic world after Alexander's death, when his empire broke apart. Then answer the questions that follow.

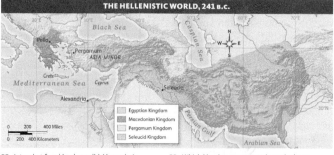

THE HELLENISTIC WORLD, 241 B.C.

Egyptian Kingdom
Macedonian Kingdom
Pergamum Kingdom
Seleucid Kingdom

22. Into what four kingdoms did Alexander's empire separate? (HSS CST 3)
23. Which kingdom appears to have the least territory? (HSS CST 3)

ANALYZE SOURCES

Read the following excerpt from the American Declaration of Independence. Then answer the question.

> We hold these truths to be self-evident, that all men are created equal, that they are endowed by their Creator with certain unalienable Rights, that among these are Life, Liberty, and the pursuit of Happiness.

24. How are the thoughts on democracy expressed by the authors of the Declaration of Independence similar to those of the Athenians? (HSS HI 3)

WRITE ABOUT HISTORY

25. **INFORMATIVE** Write a speech for new American citizens explaining how Greek democratic concepts laid the foundation for democracy in the United States. Use the tips below to plan, organize, and revise your speech. (HSS HI 3)

TIPS

- Take notes from the lessons about Pericles and democracy and the legacy of ancient Greece.
- Introduce the topic clearly.
- Develop the topic with details and examples.
- Use vocabulary from the chapter as appropriate.
- Use appropriate transitions to clarify the relationships among concepts.
- Provide a concluding statement that summarizes the information presented.
- Use word-processing software to produce and publish your final speech.

VOCABULARY ANSWERS

1. Athens's government was a direct democracy, in which citizens voted for or against laws. (HSS 6.4.3)
2. The Greeks believed that their gods and goddesses were immortal, or lived forever. (HSS 6.4.4)
3. A deadly plague killed thousands of Athenians, including Pericles. (HSS HI 4)
4. Athens ended the truce with Sparta when it laid siege to Syracuse in Sicily. (HSS 6.4.6)
5. The study of philosophy has been greatly influenced by the ideas of Socrates, Plato, and Aristotle. (HSS 6.4.8)
6. One form of Greek drama was comedy, which was funny and often made fun of famous people. (HSS 6.4.8)
7. Another form of Greek drama was tragedy, in which characters suffered terrible events and tragic endings. (HSS 6.4.8)
8. At trials, Greeks used a jury, or a group of people chosen to determine whether an accused person is innocent or guilty. (HSS 6.4.2)

STANDARDS

HSS CONTENT STANDARDS:

6.4.2 Trace the transition from tyranny and oligarchy to early democratic forms of government and back to dictatorship in ancient Greece, including the significance of the invention of the idea of citizenship (e.g., from *Pericles' Funeral Oration*); **6.4.3** State the key differences between Athenian, or direct, democracy and representative democracy; **6.4.4** Explain the significance of Greek mythology to the everyday life of people in the region and how Greek literature continues to permeate our literature and language today, drawing from Greek mythology and epics, such as Homer's *Iliad* and *Odyssey*, and from *Aesop's Fables*; **6.4.6** Compare and contrast life in Athens and Sparta, with emphasis on their roles in the Persian and Peloponnesian Wars; **6.4.7** Trace the rise of Alexander the Great and the spread of Greek culture eastward and into Egypt; **6.4.8** Describe the enduring contributions of important Greek figures in the arts and sciences (e.g., Hypatia, Socrates, Plato, Aristotle, Euclid, Thucydides).

HSS ANALYSIS SKILLS:

CST 3 Students use a variety of maps and documents to identify physical and cultural features of neighborhoods, cities, states, and countries and to explain the historical migration of people, expansion and disintegration of empires, and the growth of economic systems; **HI 1** Students explain the central issues and problems from the past, placing people and events in a matrix of time and place; **HI 2** Students understand and ditinguish cause, effect, sequence, and correlation in historical events, including the long- and short-term causal relations; **HI 3** Students explaIn the sources of historical continuity and how the combination of ideas and events explains the emergence of new patterns; **HI 4** Students recognize the role of chance, oversight, and error in history.

READING STRATEGY ANSWER

Root	Meaning	Example(s)
cosm-	universe	cosmopolitan
-cracy	government	democracy
dem-	people	democracy
-logy	speech	mythology
myth-	story	mythology
phil-	love	philosophy
poli-	city	cosmopolitan
soph-	wise	philosophy

9. Students' paragraphs should include each word and accurately describe Greek culture. (HSS HI 3)

MAIN IDEAS ANSWERS

10. After the Persian Wars, Athens and other Greek city-states formed an alliance called the Delian League, which Athens led. Pericles used funds from the league to build and expand Athens's navy and dominate the Mediterranean. Eventually, the other city-states became part of the Athenian empire. (HSS 6.4.6)

11. The Greeks believed that they must keep the gods and goddesses happy, otherwise they would become angry and interfere with their lives. (HSS 6.4.4)

12. The outbreak of war between Athens and Sparta was sparked by an argument between two minor rival states, Corinth and Corfu. Confrontations between Athens and Sparta escalated, and Sparta declared war on Athens in 432 B.C. (HSS 6.4.6)

13. Sparta effectively blockaded Athens on land and sea, cutting off resources and forcing Athens to make a desperate choice—surrender or starve. Athens surrendered, and the war ended. (HSS 6.4.6)

14. Philip II conquered all of Greece and unified it for the first time ever. (HSS HI 1)

15. Alexander's conquests ended in India because Alexander's army was homesick and weary of battle after eleven years; they mutinied against Alexander, who reluctantly ordered the men to leave India and return home. (HSS 6.4.7)

16. Hellenistic culture is an example of cultural diffusion because thousands of Greek colonists spread Greek ideas and practices throughout Asia, with each area adopting and adapting Greek culture differently and blending it with their own cultures. (HSS 6.4.7)

17. The ideas and writings of Socrates, Plato, and Aristotle formed the basis of modern western philosophy, which continues to influence our way of thinking and examining the world and all areas of study—from law and politics to math and science. (HSS 6.4.8)

CRITICAL THINKING ANSWERS

18. The legacy of ancient Greek culture is important to the modern world because Greek culture has influenced many different aspects of present-day life around the world. For example, in the United States, the influence of Greek culture is demonstrated in its government, in the architecture of many buildings, in its philosophers and writers, and in its artists and the work they produce. (HSS HI 3)

19. During the Peloponnesian War, a key part of Pericles' war strategy was to take a defensive position on land with Athenians and refugees staying together behind the city's strong walls. The outbreak of the plague quickly spread throughout the overcrowded city, killing thousands of people, including Pericles. (HSS HI 2)

20. After the Peloponnesian War, Greek cities were weak and open to attack by Philip II and his army. In addition, Philip II and his army used new weapons of warfare, such as the phalanx battle formation and catapults to conquer Greek colonies and cities. (HSS 6.4.7)

21. Students' responses will vary. Students should clearly state their opinion regarding where they would rather live and support that opinion with evidence from the chapter. (HSS 6.4.6)

INTERPRET MAPS ANSWERS

22. After Alexander's death, his empire separated into the Egyptian Kingdom, Macedonian Kingdom, Pergamum Kingdom, and Seleucid Kingdom. (HSS CST 3)

23. The Macedonian Kingdom has the least amount of territory. (HSS CST 3)

ANALYZE SOURCES ANSWER

24. Students' responses will vary. Sample response: The thoughts on democracy expressed in the U.S. Declaration of Independence shares with Athenian democracy the ideals of rights and an equal voice for all people. (HSS HI 1)

WRITE ABOUT HISTORY ANSWER

25. Students' speeches should

- introduce the topic clearly
- contain relevant, well-chosen facts, concrete details, and examples
- incorporate chapter vocabulary
- include a concluding statement

  For more in-depth instruction and practice with the writing form, assign the Social Studies Skills Writing Lesson on writing a speech. (HSS HI 3)

ON **LOCATION** WITH William
PARKINSON

NATIONAL GEOGRAPHIC GRANTEE

▶ Check out more at NGLSync.Cengage.com

In the field, Parkinson uses hi-tech equipment like this Real-Time-Kinetic GPS. It makes accurate maps by communicating with multiple satellites at one time.

FROM VILLAGE TO CITY

Like many kids who grew up in the Midwest, I loved searching for arrowheads in the fields and woods. Finding them made me want to learn more about people who lived long ago. Lucky for me, I had excellent college professors who encouraged me to study archaeology, and now I'm living my dream!

Today, I study how small farming villages turned into big cities. From an archaeological perspective, cities are weird. Until about 8,000 years ago humans lived in small groups and moved around as hunter-gatherers. Today, more than half of all humans live in cities. This has dramatic implications for our future. Archaeologists have done a good job explaining human development from hunter-gatherers to settled farmers. However, we still don't really understand how those early villages turned into massive cities.

Bill Parkinson explores a coastline while conducting an archaeological survey in Diros Bay, Greece.

A TEAM SPORT

In Europe and the Near East, the turning point came during the Neolithic and the Bronze Ages. My team has been excavating an ancient farming village in Greece, just outside a big cave called Fox Hole Cave. This cave was used for rituals and habitation during the Neolithic period, when the first farmers emerged in southeastern Europe. Greek archaeologists have explored this cave for 40 years, and we wanted to build on their great work. Archaeology is a team sport that relies on the collaboration of many different specialists, so we brought together an international crew to study the cave.

Our excavations show that people built an agricultural settlement at the site about 6,000 years ago. This settlement gives us greater insight into how early agricultural villages developed. I'm studying a similar site from the same time period in Hungary, so we're able to compare and contrast how societies changed over time in different parts of the world. Now we are publishing the results of our research, another crucial part of archaeology. Soon we'll be back in the field, hunting for the next clues about how ancient villages transformed into cities.

WHY STUDY HISTORY ❓

❝ Nothing can describe how exciting it is to put your trowel in the ground and uncover something nobody has seen for several thousand years. *It never gets old.* ❞ —William Parkinson

NATIONAL GEOGRAPHIC

Greek Statues Sparkle Once Again

BY A. R. WILLIAMS

Adapted from "2,500-Year-Old Greek Statues Sparkle After Facelift," by A. R. Williams, news.nationalgeographic.com, June 19, 2014

Four marble maidens from ancient Greece have gotten a makeover. Using a specially designed laser, conservators have stripped away the black grime that covered the statues. Sculpted in the late fifth century B.C., the figures served as columns for the Erechtheion, one of the temples that stood on the Acropolis. The maidens, known as the Caryatids, stand more than seven and a half feet tall and hold the roof of the Erechtheion's south porch on their heads.

As Athens rapidly industrialized over the past century, the Caryatids suffered from the effects of air pollution. Their golden hue turned dark, and their features began to dissolve under the constant assault of acid rain. In 1979 the figures were moved to protect them from further damage. Cement replicas were installed in their place on the Erechtheion's porch.

The Caryatids got their makeover in the public gallery of the Acropolis Museum. Conservators focused on one figure at a time in a makeshift room whose walls were sheets of heavy fabric hung from a frame. A video

monitor outside allowed visitors to see the statues slowly changing color. The curtain walls protected museumgoers' eyes from the laser system that conservators, wearing protective goggles, used to clean the statues. This system uses two pulsed beams of radiation—one infrared and the other ultraviolet—to zap away dust, soot, minerals, and metals.

Conservators and technicians considered several different kinds of cleaning, including chemicals and micro-sandblasting. The dual-wavelength laser system was the best option. It allows for safe, controlled cleaning that leaves the marble's ancient patina intact.

A future project may reveal even more of the maidens' original beauty. Their clothing was once brightly painted. However, centuries of winter rain have washed away all visible traces of pigment. Modern imaging techniques can peer into the invisible parts of the light spectrum and find long-faded hues. The result may be even more dazzling than the maidens' current makeover.

For more from National Geographic
Check out "Behind the Tomb" at NGLSync.Cengage.com

UNIT INQUIRY: DEFINE GOOD CITIZENSHIP

In this unit, you learned about ancient Greek civilization and its influence on our modern world. Based on your understanding of the text, what new form of government was central to Greek civilization? What role did citizenship play in Greek civilization and government?

ASSIGNMENT Create your own definition for good citizenship. Your definition should include a clear statement of what constitutes good citizenship and why it is important today. Be prepared to present your definition to the class and explain your reasoning.

Plan As you write your definition, think about the active role citizens played in ancient Greek civilization and government. Also think about the rights and responsibilities ancient Greek citizens had and how those ideas have influenced our ideas about citizenship today. You might want to use a graphic organizer to help organize your thoughts. ▶

Produce Use your notes to produce descriptions of the elements that make up your definition of good citizenship.

Present Choose a creative way to present your definition to the class. Consider one of these options:

- Create a video presentation using examples from everyday life showing good citizens "in action" in their community.

- Design a good citizenship medal to present to someone who exemplifies what it means to be a good citizen.

- Design a good citizenship brochure that outlines citizens' rights and responsibilities.

Good Citizenship

RAPID REVIEW UNIT 3

GREEK CIVILIZATION

TOP TEN

1. The Minoans and the Mycenaeans were the first advanced Greek civilizations.

2. Ancient Greek city-states established colonies and trade networks throughout the Mediterranean.

3. The city-state of Athens developed the world's first democracy.

4. Alexander the Great conquered Persia, Egypt, Afghanistan, and India, building a vast empire that spread Greek culture.

5. The ancient Greeks influenced Western art, architecture, literature, philosophy, science, medicine, government, and law.

6-10. **NOW IT'S YOUR TURN** Complete the list with five more things to remember about Greek civilization.

RAPID REVIEW

POSSIBLE RESPONSES

Possible responses for the remaining five things to remember:

6. Two rival factions of Greek city-states—the Delian League led by Athens and the Peloponnesian League led by Sparta—fought the Peloponnesian War.

7. City-states governed through many forms of government, including monarchies, aristocracies, oligarchies, and tyrannies.

8. Independent city-states in ancient Greece shared a common language and culture but established their own governments, laws, and customs.

9. Athens and Sparta formed an alliance to defeat the Persian Empire in the Persian Wars.

10. The Macedonian general, King Philip II, conquered the Greek city-states and united Greece under his sole control.

UNIT INQUIRY PROJECT RUBRIC

ASSESS

Use the rubric to assess each student's participation and performance.

SCORE	ASSIGNMENT	PRODUCT	PRESENTATION
3 GREAT	• Student thoroughly understands the assignment. • Student engages with the project topic. • Student works well independently.	• Definition is well thought out. • Definition clearly states what constitutes good citizenship and why it is important today. • Definition clearly reflects Greek ideals about citizenship.	• Presentation is clear, concise, and logical. • Presentation does a good job demonstrating good citizenship. • Presentation engages the audience.
2 GOOD	• Student mostly understands the assignment. • Student engages fairly well with the project topic. • Student works fairly independently.	• Definition is fairly well thought out. • Definition somewhat clearly states what constitutes good citizenship and why it is important today. • Definition somewhat clearly reflects Greek ideals about citizenship.	• Presentation is fairly clear, concise, and logical. • Presentation does a fairly good job demonstrating good citizenship. • Presentation somewhat engages the audience.
1 NEEDS WORK	• Student does not understand the assignment. • Student minimally engages or does not engage with the project topic. • Student struggles to work independently.	• Definition is not well thought out. • Definition does not clearly state what constitutes good citizenship and why it is important today. • Definition does not reflect Greek ideals about citizenship.	• Presentation is not clear, concise, or logical. • Presentation does not demonstrate good citizenship. • Presentation does not engage the audience.

THE WORLD OF THE ROMANS

NATIONAL GEOGRAPHIC

ON **LOCATION** WITH

Steven Ellis
Archaeologist

Have you ever heard the expression "All roads lead to Rome?" Well, 2,000 years ago, all roads actually did lead to Rome. Though it began as a small town on the Tiber River in Italy, in only a few centuries Rome came to dominate the Mediterranean and build a civilization that stretched from northern Europe to Syria. I'm Steven Ellis, and I work with National Geographic. Welcome to the world of the Romans!

< **CRITICAL VIEWING** The ruins of Pompeii, seen here in the shadow of Mount Vesuvius, continue to reveal much about the lives of the ancient Romans. What details do you notice in the photo that resemble features you might see in a town or city today?

+ POSSIBLE RESPONSE

Details that resemble features in a town or city today include streets, walkways, buildings, and houses.

Ancient Rome

44 B.C.
Julius Caesar is assassinated by a group of Roman senators.

753 B.C.
According to legend, Romulus founds the city of Rome. *(illustration of Romulus on a coin)*

509 B.C.
Rome becomes a republic.

100 B.C.

800 B.C.

The World

750 B.C.
EUROPE
Greek city-states flourish with shared Greek identity but individual loyalties, customs, and governments.

334 B.C.
EUROPE
Alexander the Great begins to build his massive empire.
(detail from statue of Alexander)

STANDARDS

HSS ANALYSIS SKILLS:

CST 1 Students explain how major events are related to one another in time.

What other world event happened around the time Rome became an empire?

A.D. 26–29
Jesus preaches religious ideas that will form the basis of Christianity.

A.D. 476
Invasions bring about the fall of the Western Roman Empire.
(painting of the sack of Rome)

A.D. 177
The Roman Empire reaches its greatest extent, stretching over parts of Europe, Asia, and Africa.

A.D. 395
The Roman Empire is divided into the Eastern and Western empires.

27 B.C.
Rome becomes an empire, and Augustus becomes its first emperor.

A.D. 300

A.D. 500

A.D. 100

A.D. 250
AMERICAS
The Maya build great cities and make significant advances in learning.
(Maya pyramid)

A.D. 300s
AFRICA
The kingdom of Aksum in East Africa reaches its height under Ezana.

10 B.C.
ASIA
The Silk Roads connect China to the Mediterranean.

FROM REPUBLIC TO EMPIRE

146 B.C.–A.D. 117

Hadrian's Wall

Find Rome on the map. That's how it began: as a small dot in a land once known as Italia. Actually, Rome was even smaller, since it began as a village of farmers. But the Romans developed a civilization that grew to become one of the greatest empires the world has ever seen.

At its full extent, the Roman Empire stretched over three continents. It was held together by taxes, the powerful Roman army, and an amazing network of roads. Through periods of peace and war, Rome remained the center of the Western world for hundreds of years.

What body of water probably helped link the Roman Empire?

STANDARDS

HSS CONTENT STANDARDS:

7.1.2 Discuss the geographic borders of the empire at its height and the factors that threatened its territorial cohesion.

HSS ANALYSIS SKILLS:

CST 3 Students use a variety of maps and documents to identify physical and cultural features of neighborhoods, cities, states, and countries and to explain the historical migration of people, expansion and disintegration of empires, and the growth of economic systems.

Time Line of Good and Bad Emperors

"Bad" emperor
Historians traditionally call the first three emperors below "bad" because they abused their power.

"Good" emperor
The other five emperors are considered "good" because, like Augustus, they presided over a period of peace and ruled wisely.

 Caligula
A.D. 37–41

- Reigned as a cruel tyrant
- Insisted on being treated as a god

 Nero
A.D. 54–68

- Committed many murders
- Did nothing while much of Rome burned

 Domitian
A.D. 81–96

- Ruled as a dictator
- Murdered many of his enemies

 Nerva
A.D. 96–98

- First emperor chosen for the job
- Tried to end tryannical rule

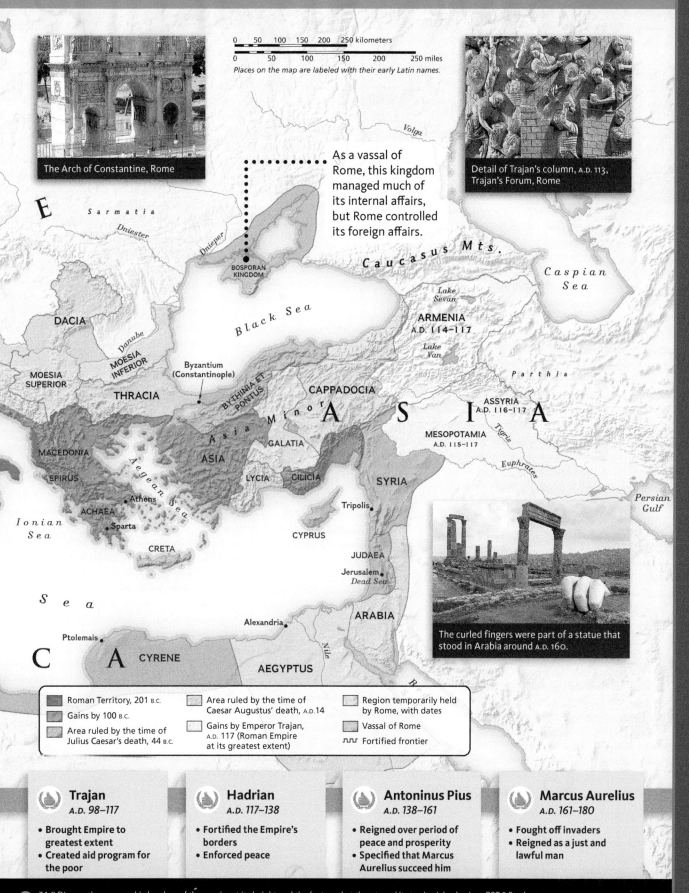

The Arch of Constantine, Rome

0 50 100 150 200 250 kilometers

0   50   100   150   200   250 miles

Places on the map are labeled with their early Latin names.

Detail of Trajan's column, A.D. 113, Trajan's Forum, Rome

As a vassal of Rome, this kingdom managed much of its internal affairs, but Rome controlled its foreign affairs.

Volga

E

Sarmatia

Dniester

Dnieper

BOSPORAN KINGDOM

Caucasus Mts.

Caspian Sea

DACIA

Black Sea

Lake Sevan

ARMENIA
A.D. 114–117

Lake Van

Danube

MOESIA INFERIOR

Byzantium (Constantinople)

Parthia

MOESIA SUPERIOR

THRACIA

BYTHINIA ET PONTUS

CAPPADOCIA

ASSYRIA
A.D. 116–117

Asia Minor

A S I A

MESOPOTAMIA
A.D. 115–117

Tigris

MACEDONIA

Aegean Sea

ASIA

GALATIA

Euphrates

EPIRUS

LYCIA

CILICIA

SYRIA

Persian Gulf

Ionian Sea

ACHAEA

•Athens

Tripolis•

•Sparta

CYPRUS

CRETA

JUDAEA

Jerusalem•
Dead Sea

Sea

Alexandria•

ARABIA

The curled fingers were part of a statue that stood in Arabia around A.D. 160.

Ptolemais•

C

A

CYRENE

Nile

AEGYPTUS

	Roman Territory, 201 B.C.		Area ruled by the time of Caesar Augustus' death, A.D.14		Region temporarily held by Rome, with dates
	Gains by 100 B.C.		Gains by Emperor Trajan, A.D. 117 (Roman Empire at its greatest extent)		Vassal of Rome
	Area ruled by the time of Julius Caesar's death, 44 B.C.				Fortified frontier

Trajan
A.D. 98–117
- Brought Empire to greatest extent
- Created aid program for the poor

Hadrian
A.D. 117–138
- Fortified the Empire's borders
- Enforced peace

Antoninus Pius
A.D. 138–161
- Reigned over period of peace and prosperity
- Specified that Marcus Aurelius succeed him

Marcus Aurelius
A.D. 161–180
- Fought off invaders
- Reigned as a just and lawful man

7.1.2 Discuss the geographic borders of the empire at its height and the factors that threatened its territorial cohesion; CST 3 Students use a variety of maps and documents to identify physical and cultural features of neighborhoods, cities, states, and countries and to explain the historical migration of people, expansion and disintegration of empires, and the growth of economic systems.

UNIT RESOURCES

On Location with National Geographic Grantee Steven Ellis
Intro and Video

Unit Wrap-Up:
"Exploring Pompeii"
Feature and Video

"Rethinking Nero"
National Geographic Adapted Article

"Roman Frontiers"
National Geographic Adapted Article
Student eEdition exclusive

Unit 4 Inquiry:
Build an Empire

 Interactive Map Tool
Available at NGLSync.cengage.com

 **News & Updates**
Available at NGLSync.cengage.com

CHAPTER RESOURCES

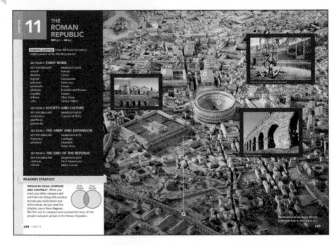

TEACHER RESOURCES & ASSESSMENT *Available at NGLSync.cengage.com*

 Social Studies Skills Lessons
• Reading: Compare and Contrast
• Writing: Write an Argument

 Chapter 11
Answer Key

 Formal Assessment
• Chapter 11 Tests A (on-level) &
  B (below-level)

 ExamView®
One-time Download

STUDENT BACKPACK *Available at NGLSync.cengage.com*

• **eEdition** *(English)*   • **eEdition** *(Spanish)*   • **Handbooks**   • **Online Atlas**

Chapter 11 Spanish resources, Guided Writing prompts, and Financial Literacy lessons are available online.

SECTION 1 RESOURCES

EARLY ROME

 Reading and Note-Taking

 Vocabulary Practice

 Section 1 Quiz

Available at NGLSync.cengage.com

LESSON 1.1 THE GEOGRAPHY OF ANCIENT ROME

• On Your Feet: Model Rome's Geography
• Critical Viewing: NG Chapter Gallery

LESSON 1.2 THE FOUNDING OF ROME

• On Your Feet: Create a Concept Web

| **NG Learning Framework:** Observe the Etruscans

LESSON 1.3 REPUBLICAN GOVERNMENT

 Biography
Cicero

 Active History: Interactive Whiteboard Activity
Compare Greek and Roman Governments

 Active History
Compare Greek and Roman Governments

Available at NGLSync.cengage.com
• On Your Feet: Plebeians versus Patricians

LESSON 1.4 THE ROMAN FORUM

• On Your Feet: Sequence of Events
• Critical Viewing: NG Image Gallery

SECTION 2 RESOURCES

SOCIETY AND CULTURE

 Reading and Note-Taking

 Vocabulary Practice

 Section 2 Quiz

Available at NGLSync.cengage.com

LESSON 2.1 MEN AND WOMEN

• On Your Feet: Tell Me More

NG Learning Framework:
Compare Roman Men and Women

LESSON 2.2 RICH AND POOR

• On Your Feet: Inside-Outside Circle
• Critical Viewing: NG Chapter Gallery

LESSON 2.3 GODS AND BELIEFS

• On Your Feet: One-on-One Interviews

NG Learning Framework:
Compare Ancient Roman and
Chinese Ideals

SECTION 3 RESOURCES

THE ARMY AND EXPANSION

 Reading and Note-Taking

 Vocabulary Practice

 Section 3 Quiz

Available at NGLSync.cengage.com

LESSON 3.1 THE ROMAN ARMY

• Critical Viewing: NG Chapter Gallery
• On Your Feet: Think, Pair, Share

HISTORY THROUGH OBJECTS
LESSON 3.2 ROMAN ARMOR

• On Your Feet: Try It On

NG Learning Framework:
Compare Soldiers' Gear

LESSON 3.3 HANNIBAL AND THE PUNIC WARS

• On Your Feet: Card Responses
• Critical Viewing: NG Image Gallery

NATIONAL GEOGRAPHIC
EXPLORER PATRICK HUNT
LESSON 3.4 SEARCHING FOR HANNIBAL'S ROUTE

• On Your Feet: Hold a Press Conference

NG Learning Framework:
Ask and Answer

LESSON 3.5 ROME EXPANDS

• On Your Feet: Simulate a Battle

NG Learning Framework:
Geography and History

SECTION 4 RESOURCES

THE END OF THE REPUBLIC

 Reading and Note-Taking

 Vocabulary Practice

 Section 4 Quiz

Available at NGLSync.cengage.com

LESSON 4.1
THE REPUBLIC IN CRISIS

• On Your Feet: Jigsaw

NG Learning Framework:
Research Civil Wars

BIOGRAPHY
LESSON 4.2 GAIUS JULIUS CAESAR

 Biography
Cleopatra VII

Available at NGLSync.cengage.com

• On Your Feet: Create a Poster

NG Learning Framework:
Imagine You Were Caesar

DOCUMENT-BASED QUESTION
LESSON 4.3 THE ASSASSINATION OF JULIUS CAESAR

• On Your Feet: Three Options

NG Learning Framework:
Write a Biography

MOMENTS IN HISTORY
LESSON 4.4 THE IDES OF MARCH

• On Your Feet: I See, I Read, And So
• Critical Viewing: NG Image Gallery

CHAPTER 11 REVIEW

STRIVING READERS

STRATEGY 1

Preview Text

Help students preview each lesson in the chapter. For each lesson, have them read the lesson titles, lesson introductions, Main Idea statements, captions, and lesson headings. Then have them list the information they expect to find in the text. Have students read a lesson and discuss with a partner what they learned and whether or not it matched their list.

Use with All Lessons

STRATEGY 2

Build a Time Line

Select key events from Lessons 1.2 and 1.3. Then have students use the events to start a time line on the board. Students will add to the time line as they read the chapter.

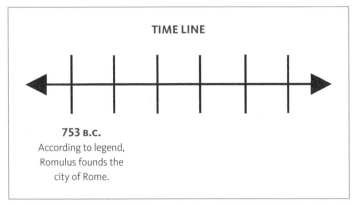

TIME LINE

753 B.C.
According to legend,
Romulus founds the
city of Rome.

Use with All Lessons *For example, key events from Lesson 1.3 might include the establishment of the Roman Republic in 509 B.C. and the dictatorship of Cincinnatus in 458 B.C.*

STRATEGY 3

Use a Word Sort Activity

Write these words on the board and ask students to sort them into four groups of three related words each. Then have them use each group of words in a paragraph that shows how they are related.

republic	legion	palisades
patriarchy	veto	dictator
consuls	civil war	domestic
reform	legionary	paterfamilias

Use with All Lessons

Press **mt** *in the Student eEdition for modified text.*

INCLUSION

STRATEGY 1

Preview Visuals to Predict

Ask students to preview the title and visuals in each lesson. Then have students tell what they think the lesson will be about. After reading, ask them to repeat the activity to see whether their predictions were confirmed.

Use with All Lessons *Invite volunteers to describe the visuals in detail to help visually impaired students process them.*

STRATEGY 2

Use Supported Reading

In small groups, have students read aloud the chapter lesson by lesson. At the end of each lesson, have them stop and use these sentence frames to tell what they comprehended from the text:

- This lesson is about _____.
- One detail or fact that stood out to me is _____.
- The word _____ means _____.
- I don't think I understand _____.

Guide students with portions of text they do not understand. Be sure all students understand a lesson before moving on to the next one.

Use with All Lessons

STANDARDS

HSS CONTENT STANDARDS:

6.7.8 Discuss the legacies of Roman art and architecture, technology and science, literature, language, and law.

HSS ANALYSIS SKILLS:

CST 2 Students construct various time lines of key events, people, and periods of the historical era they are studying; **REP 1** Students frame questions that can be answered by historical study and research; **REP 5** Students detect the different historical points of view on historical events and determining the context in which the historical statements were made (the questions asked, sources used, author's perspectives).

ENGLISH LANGUAGE LEARNERS

STRATEGY ❶
PREP Before Reading

Have students at all proficiency levels use the PREP strategy to prepare for reading.

    Preview title.

    Read Main Idea statement.

    Examine visuals.

    Predict what you will learn.

Have students write their prediction and share it with a partner. After reading, ask students to write another sentence that begins with "I also learned ..."

Use with All Lessons, All Levels *Provide the following sentence stem for students at the **Emerging** level: I think this lesson is about _____. Ask students at the **Bridging** level to give reasons for their prediction.*

STRATEGY ❷
Use Sentence Stems

Before reading, provide students at the **Expanding** level with the two sentence stems for the lessons listed below.

1.1   **a.** Two geographic features that helped the city of Rome were _____.

      b. Two bodies of water that were important to Rome were _____.

1.2   **c.** According to legend, Rome was founded by _____.

      d. Three groups of people who contributed to the culture of early Rome were _____.

1.3   **e.** The two groups that made up Roman society were _____.

      f. The three branches of Roman government were _____.

1.4   **g.** Three examples of activities held at the Forum were _____.

      h. The Forum was important to Rome because _____.

Use with Lessons 1.1–1.4

STRATEGY ❸
Set Up a Word Wall

Work with students to select three words from each lesson to display in a grouping on a Word Wall. It might be useful to choose words that students are likely to encounter in other chapters, such as *republic* or *aristocracy*. Keep the words displayed throughout the lessons and discuss each one as it comes up during reading. Have volunteers add words, phrases, and examples to each word to develop understanding.

Use with All Lessons, All Levels

GIFTED & TALENTED

STRATEGY ❶
Explore World Heritage Sites

Have students research and report on one of the UNESCO World Heritage Sites from the list below. Tell them to describe each site and explain why it was important to Roman civilization.

- Villa Adriana at Tivoli (Italy)
- Archaeological Site of Carthage (Tunisia)
- Roman Walls of Lugo (Spain)
- Roman Theatre of Orange (France)
- Pont du Gard (France)
- Archaeological Site of Leptis Magna (Libya)

Use with All Lessons

STRATEGY ❷
Act Out a Scene

Have students act out the assassination scene from Shakespeare's *Julius Caesar* (Act III, Scene 1). They should provide costumes and use classroom furniture as a set. After the performance, discuss the points of view of the primary characters in the scene—Brutus, Cassius, and Antony. What are the arguments for the assassination? What are the arguments against it?

Use with Lesson 4.3

PRE-AP

STRATEGY ❶
Use the "Persia" Approach

Have students write an essay explaining the significance of the Roman Republic. Copy the following mnemonic device on the board and tell students to use the "Persia" strategy as they consider how the Roman Republic influenced the world.

    Political

    Economic

    Religious

    Social

    Intellectual

    Artistic

Use with All Lessons

STRATEGY ❷
Form a Thesis

Have students develop a thesis statement for a specific topic related to one of the lessons in the chapter. Be sure the statement makes a claim that is supportable with evidence either from the chapter or through further research. Then have pairs compare their statements and determine which makes the strongest or most supportable claim.

Use with All Lessons

11

THE ROMAN REPUBLIC

509 B.C. – 44 B.C.

ESSENTIAL QUESTION How did Rome become a mighty power in the Mediterranean?

SECTION 1 EARLY ROME

KEY VOCABULARY	NAMES & PLACES
consul	Aeneas
dictator	Cicero
legend	Cincinnatus
patrician	Etruscans
peninsula	Forum
plebeian	Romulus and Remus
republic	Senate
tribune	Tiber River
veto	Twelve Tables

SECTION 2 SOCIETY AND CULTURE

KEY VOCABULARY	NAMES & PLACES
aristocracy	Council of Plebs
pantheon	
patriarchy	

SECTION 3 THE ARMY AND EXPANSION

KEY VOCABULARY	NAMES & PLACES
legionary	Carthage
province	Hannibal
	Punic Wars

SECTION 4 THE END OF THE REPUBLIC

KEY VOCABULARY	NAMES & PLACES
civil war	First Triumvirate
reform	Julius Caesar

READING STRATEGY

ORGANIZE IDEAS: COMPARE AND CONTRAST When you read, you often compare and contrast one thing with another to help you understand new information. As you read the chapter, use a Venn diagram like this one to compare and contrast the lives of rich people and poor people in the Roman Republic.

Rich People / Poor People

Temple of Venus and Rome

Painting of gladiators in the Colosseum

Claudian Aqueduct

This model of Rome shows the city as it might have looked in A.D. 312.

HSS CONTENT STANDARDS:

6.7 Students analyze the geographic, political, economic, religious, and social structures during the development of Rome.

TEACHER BACKGROUND

INTRODUCE THE PHOTOGRAPH

Have students study the model of Rome and the images that accompany it. Explain that this model represents the city at its greatest point during the time of the Roman Empire and that they will learn about factors that contributed to its growth and development in this chapter.

ASK: How does Rome resemble modern cities you have seen? *(Possible responses: It has many roads and buildings of different sizes. It contains places for entertainment and worship. It has an infrastructure that provides resources for its citizens.)*

SHARE BACKGROUND

The model of imperial Rome was commissioned by Mussolini in 1933 to commemorate the 2,000th anniversary of the birth of Caesar Augustus. Depicting the city during the time of the emperor Constantine, it is built on a scale of 1:250 and is more than 55 feet across. The model is currently on display at the Museum of Roman Civilization in Rome.

DIGITAL RESOURCES NGLSync.cengage.com

TEACHER RESOURCES & ASSESSMENT

 Social Studies Skills Lessons
- Reading: Compare and Contrast
- Writing: Write an Argument

 Formal Assessment
- Chapter 11 Tests A (on-level) & B (below-level)

 ExamView®
One-time Download

 **Chapter 11 Answer Key**

STUDENT BACKPACK

- **eEdition** (*English*)
- **eEdition** (*Spanish*)
- **Handbooks**
- **Online Atlas**

HOW DID ROME BECOME A MIGHTY POWER IN THE MEDITERRANEAN?

Four Corner Activity: Factors of Influence This activity introduces students to four factors that led to Rome's success and allows them to choose which they think is the most influential. Post the four signs shown in the list below. Ask students to choose the aspect that they think would contribute most to Rome's success, go to that corner, and then explain why.

A. Geography Rome's location had many geographic advantages that gave it easy access to trade routes and offered it protection from invasion.

B. Government Rome's republican form of government allowed citizens to vote for their leaders and included checks and balances to prevent any one branch from becoming too powerful.

C. Military Rome's well-organized army easily conquered neighboring territories and built roads to link them to the city of Rome.

D. Culture Romans welcomed customs and cultures from other lands, and valued discipline, strength, and loyalty.

0:15 minutes

ORGANIZE IDEAS: COMPARE AND CONTRAST

Remind students that comparing and contrasting two topics or ideas can help them better understand new information. Model completing the Venn Diagram by reading the first paragraph under "The Young Republic" in Lesson 1.3 and adding the terms *patricians* and *plebeians* under the headings "Rich People" and "Poor People," respectively. For more in-depth instruction and practice with the reading strategy, assign the Social Studies Skills Reading Lesson on comparing and contrasting.

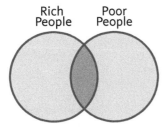

Rich People   Poor People

KNOWLEDGE RATING

Have students complete a Knowledge Rating chart for Key Vocabulary words. Have students list words and fill out the chart on their own paper. Then have pairs share the definitions they know. Work together as a class to complete the chart.

KEY VOCAB	KNOW IT	NOT SURE	DON'T KNOW	DEFINITION
aristocracy				
civil war				
consul				
dictator				

KEY DATES

753 B.C.	Traditional founding of Rome
509 B.C.	Beginning of the Roman Republic
450 B.C.	Creation of the Twelve Tables
264–146 B.C.	The Punic Wars
59 B.C.	Formation of the First Triumvirate
48 B.C.	Defeat of Pompey by Julius Caesar
44 B.C.	Assassination of Julius Caesar

1.1 The Geography of
Ancient Rome

If you wanted to build a Mediterranean empire, you'd probably start from Rome. The city lies near the heart of the sea. Geographically, it's the best place to begin a conquest of the Mediterranean.

MAIN IDEA

Rome's location had many geographic advantages that helped it grow and become powerful.

THE ITALIAN PENINSULA

Italy lies on a **peninsula**, or land surrounded by water on three sides, in the Mediterranean Sea. It is shaped like a boot and looks as though it is kicking a football—the island of Sicily—toward North Africa. Italy is attached to the rest of Europe by a massive range of snow-covered mountains called the Alps.

Another mountain range, the Apennines (A-puh-nynz), runs down the center of Italy. These mountains slope through wooded hills to sunny coastal plains and the blue waters of the Mediterranean. In time, the Romans would come to call the Mediterranean *Mare Nostrum* (MAHR-ay NOHS-truhm), or "Our Sea."

Rome was founded on seven hills on the volcanic west coast of Italy. The Romans embraced the advanced cultures of their neighbors to the north and south. Ideas adopted from these cultures helped Rome flourish and grow strong.

THE CITY OF ROME

Rome's geography helped it survive and thrive. What first made Rome important was its strategic position. It was located at a key crossing point of the **Tiber** (TY-bur) **River**.

The location was also a natural stopping point on the valuable trade routes running north to south and inland from the sea. The city was far enough from the coast to escape deadly attacks by pirates and enemies but close enough to benefit from the Mediterranean's busy sea trade. Olive oil and wine were among Rome's most commonly traded items.

The circle of seven hills on which Rome was built rose above the river and also provided protection against attack. These seven hills became Rome's center. Romans built important government buildings there. The hills were also home to religious temples and entertainment facilities. Roads branched off from this area to the outside world.

The land around the city had fertile soil, a good water supply, and a mild climate. These qualities helped Rome's agriculture flourish and support the large population needed to wage and win wars in the ancient world. As the Roman historian Livy boasted, "With good reason did gods and men choose this site for founding a city."

Rome's central location helped it take over much of Italy. Then Italy's central location helped Rome become a powerful force in the Mediterranean. Around the sea, the riches of Europe, Southwest Asia, and North Africa were temptingly close. Control of the Mediterranean seemed within the grasp of a strong, ambitious, and determined civilization like Rome.

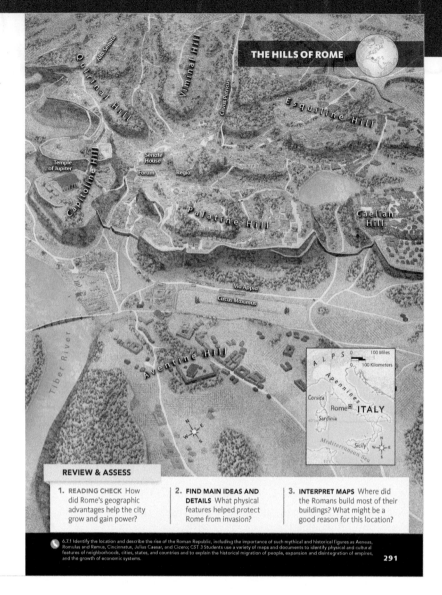

THE HILLS OF ROME

REVIEW & ASSESS

1. **READING CHECK** How did Rome's geographic advantages help the city grow and gain power?

2. **FIND MAIN IDEAS AND DETAILS** What physical features helped protect Rome from invasion?

3. **INTERPRET MAPS** Where did the Romans build most of their buildings? What might be a good reason for this location?

6.7.1 Identify the location and describe the rise of the Roman Republic, including the importance of such mythical and historical figures as Aeneas, Romulus and Remus, Cincinnatus, Julius Caesar, and Cicero; CST 3 Students use a variety of maps and documents to identify physical and cultural features of neighborhoods, cities, states, and countries and to explain the historical migration of people, expansion and disintegration of empires, and the growth of economic systems.

HSS CONTENT STANDARDS:

6.7.1 Identify the location and describe the rise of the Roman Republic, including the importance of such mythical and historical figures as Aeneas, Romulus and Remus, Cincinnatus, Julius Caesar, and Cicero; **6.7.3** Identify the location of and the political and geographic reasons for the growth of Roman territories and expansion of the empire, including how the empire fostered economic growth through the use of currency and trade routes.

HSS ANALYSIS SKILLS:

CST 3 Students use a variety of maps and documents to identify physical and cultural features of neighborhoods, cities, states, and countries and to explain the historical migration of people, expansion and disintegration of empires, and the growth of economic systems; **HI 1** Students explain the central issues and problems from the past, placing people and events in a matrix of time and place.

PLAN

OBJECTIVE

Identify the geographic advantages that helped ancient Rome become a powerful civilization.

ESSENTIAL QUESTION

How did Rome become a mighty power in the Mediterranean?

The city of Rome's location had many geographic advantages. Lesson 1.1 describes some of these advantages and explains how they helped Rome grow and become powerful.

BACKGROUND FOR THE TEACHER

The "seven hills of Rome" is a term given to the group of hills where the ancient city of Rome was built. The original city of the legendary Romulus was built upon Palatine Hill. The other hills are the Aventine, Caelian, Capitoline, Esquiline, Quirinal, and Viminal.

The seven hills are mostly made up of tuffs, or compacted volcanic ash, left by volcanic eruptions that took place in the Alban Hills volcanic field southeast of Rome over the last 600,000 years. Visitors to Italy are often familiar with active volcanoes such as Etna and Stromboli, and famous ones such as Vesuvius, which buried and destroyed the city of Pompeii. While eruptions are not likely to occur in the Alban Hills in the near future, they are not impossible.

DIGITAL RESOURCES NGLSync.cengage.com

TEACHER RESOURCES & ASSESSMENT

 Reading and Note-Taking

 Vocabulary Practice

 Section 1 Quiz

STUDENT RESOURCES

 NG Chapter Gallery

INTRODUCE & ENGAGE

BRAINSTORM STRONG, SUCCESSFUL CITIES

Ask students to identify examples of strong, successful American cities, such as New York, Chicago, or San Francisco. Have students record the names of these cities on sticky notes and post them on the wall. Then work together to brainstorm characteristics that make a city strong and successful. Again, record these characteristics on sticky notes and post so students can refer to them during the lesson. Then tell students they will learn about geographic features that helped the city of Rome grow powerful and strong. **0:05** minutes

TEACH

GUIDED DISCUSSION

1. **Make Inferences** Why would the Romans have wanted to control the Mediterranean Sea? *(It would allow the Romans to explore other regions safely. It would give the Romans the ability to move and trade goods using ships and also move their army to other countries quickly and discreetly.)*

2. **Describe** Complete a word web using words, phrases, and sentences that tell about the geography of ancient Rome. *(volcanic land, west coast of Italy, near Mediterranean coast, crossing point of Tiber River, fertile land, seven hills)*

INTERPRET MAPS

Point out the Hills of Rome map. Review the hills, bodies of water, and location of Roman landmarks. Draw students' attention to the inset map showing the location of Rome in Italy. Ask volunteers to ask and answer questions about both maps.

(Sample response: Based on the map, how could Romans have moved across the Tiber River? By boat or on foot. I see boats in a small marina off the Tiber and a bridge across the river.) **0:15** minutes

ACTIVE OPTIONS

On Your Feet: Model Rome's Geography Tell the tallest students in the class to stand and represent the seven hills. Have other students represent the Mediterranean Sea and the Tiber River. Call on volunteers to "invade" Rome, and explore how invaders would have been challenged by the geography of the city in different ways. Call upon other volunteers to explain how the geographic features would have been useful in other ways. **0:05** minutes

Critical Viewing: NG Chapter Gallery Invite students to explore the Chapter Gallery to examine the images that relate to this chapter. Have them select one of the images and do additional research to learn more about it. Ask questions that will inspire additional inquiry about the chosen gallery image, such as: What is this? Where and when was this created? By whom? Why was it created? What is it made of? Why does it belong in this chapter? What else would you like to know about it? **0:10** minutes

DIFFERENTIATE

ENGLISH LANGUAGE LEARNERS

Use a Term in a Sentence Pair students at the **Emerging** level with English proficient students. Have the proficient students model using words from the lesson in sentences. Then have each pair compose a sentence for each word. Invite pairs to share their sentences and discuss different ways to utilize each word. Suggest the following words:

- peninsula
- range
- volcanic
- trade/traded
- fertile

GIFTED & TALENTED

Build Models Have students build a three-dimensional topographic model of the hills of Rome using the Hills of Rome map and additional online resources. Discuss scale and proportion and encourage students to size the hills and bodies of water appropriately.

Press **mt** *in the Student eEdition for modified text.*

See the Chapter Planner for more strategies for differentiation.

REVIEW & ASSESS

ANSWERS

1. Rome's location on the Tiber River made it a good stopping point on a valuable trade route, and its location on the seven hills provided protection from invaders.

2. The seven hills and a location not right on the coast helped protect Rome from invasion.

3. Most buildings were built in the hills. Since the hills provided protection, they were a good location for building.

The Founding of Rome

Three thousand years ago, a few small huts stood scattered across the hills that overlooked the Tiber River's swampy floodplain. Within just 250 years, this humble landscape was transformed into the heart of a mighty empire.

MAIN IDEA

Rome grew from a tiny village to a city between 753 and 509 B.C.

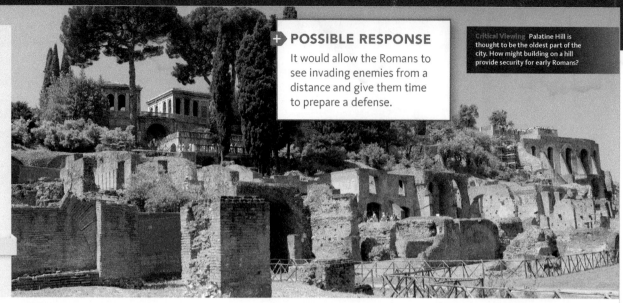

+ POSSIBLE RESPONSE

It would allow the Romans to see invading enemies from a distance and give them time to prepare a defense.

Critical Viewing Palatine Hill is thought to be the oldest part of the city. How might building on a hill provide security for early Romans?

MYTHICAL BEGINNINGS

The Romans loved stories, especially bloody ones with great heroes. One of the most popular **legends**, or stories about famous people and events in the past, was about the founding of Rome. Not only did the story contain a hero and plenty of blood, but it also linked Rome to the great civilization of ancient Greece.

According to the legend, a Trojan hero named **Aeneas** (ih-NEE-uhs) was the ancestor of Rome's founders—the twin brothers **Romulus** (RAHM-yuh-luhs) and **Remus** (REE-muhs). As babies, the brothers were abandoned. They were rescued by a wolf and raised by a shepherd. When they grew up, the brothers founded their own city. In 753 B.C., Romulus became the first king of the city, which he named Rome, after himself.

Research actually supports a part of the story of Romulus and Remus. Archaeologists have uncovered ruins suggesting that the hills around Rome contained many small villages in 1000 B.C. Some of these villages merged with villages in the valleys to create a larger settlement around 750 B.C. This was early Rome.

EARLY ROMANS

At this time, Italy was a patchwork of different peoples with their own rulers, customs, and languages. Most of Rome's original residents were Latins, who came from an area around the Tiber River called Latium. The Latins were not united, and their many cities were often at war with one another as well as with neighboring peoples. In its early days, Rome was a small village in a violently competitive world.

What helped make Rome strong was that it welcomed people from many different lands. Foreigners of different classes and professions settled in the city and helped it grow in size and strength. The people who most influenced early Rome were the Greeks to the south and the **Etruscans** (ih-TRUHS-kuhnz) to the north.

The Greeks dominated the Mediterranean and had many colonies in southern Italy. Through travel and trade, they introduced the Romans to important advances in agriculture, architecture, and learning.

The Romans learned to grow olives and modified the Greek alphabet for writing. Roman poets copied the Greek style of the long epic poem.

The Etruscans were expert traders, metalworkers, and engineers. Three Etruscan kings who came to rule Rome brought these professional skills with them. They laid out the city's streets in a grid plan around a central square. The Etruscans replaced mud huts with stone houses and built Rome's first temples and public buildings. By 509 B.C., Rome was becoming the city we still see traces of today.

REVIEW & ASSESS

1. **READING CHECK** How did people from different cultures help Rome develop into a city?

2. **IDENTIFY MAIN IDEAS AND DETAILS** According to legend, how was Rome founded?

3. **MAKE INFERENCES** What does the willingness to adopt other peoples' ideas suggest about Roman values?

6.7.1 Identify the location and describe the rise of the Roman Republic, including the importance of such mythical and historical figures as Aeneas, Romulus and Remus, Cincinnatus, Julius Caesar, and Cicero.

HSS CONTENT STANDARDS:

6.7.1 Identify the location and describe the rise of the Roman Republic, including the importance of such mythical and historical figures as Aeneas, Romulus and Remus, Cincinnatus, Julius Caesar, and Cicero.

HSS ANALYSIS SKILLS:

HI 1 Students explain the central issues and problems from the past, placing people and events in a matrix of time and place.

PLAN

OBJECTIVE

Identify how Rome grew from a village to a large city.

ESSENTIAL QUESTION

How did Rome become a mighty power in the Mediterranean?

Rome welcomed people from other lands and adopted aspects of their culture. Lesson 1.2 discusses how this cultural influence helped Rome grow from a tiny village to a city.

BACKGROUND FOR THE TEACHER

The Etruscans, as expert builders and metalworkers, had a great influence over the layout and construction of the city of Rome. It is thought that the tiled roofs of Rome were first introduced by the Etruscans. The Etruscans are also believed to have influenced religious rituals, Roman numerals, and even the Latin alphabet. Etruscan ruling families such as the Tarquins were eventually replaced by Roman rulers, but their legacy lived on through Roman customs, culture, and architecture.

DIGITAL RESOURCES NGLSync.cengage.com

TEACHER RESOURCES & ASSESSMENT

 Reading and Note-Taking

 Vocabulary Practice

 Section 1 Quiz

STUDENT RESOURCES

 NG Chapter Gallery

GIVE A THUMBS UP, THUMBS DOWN

Ask students to volunteer the names of legends that they've read, heard, or seen a movie about, such as Hercules, Odysseus, or Achilles. Make a list of these legends, then read the list aloud and have students give each one a thumbs up or a thumbs down, depending on whether they know it or like it. Explain that a legend is a story that has been passed on for many generations. A legend usually has important meaning or symbolism, is based somewhat on facts, and contains a hero or heroes. Tell students they will learn about one famous legend that explains how Rome was founded. **0:05** minutes

TEACH

GUIDED DISCUSSION

1. **Explain** Which two peoples had the most influence on early Rome, and what did they contribute to Roman civilization? *(Rome was most influenced by the Greeks to the south and the Etruscans to the north. The Greeks introduced the Romans to important advances in agriculture, architecture, and learning. The Etruscans helped structure Rome's city and built the first stone houses, temples, and public buildings.)*

2. **Make Inferences** What might be the negative effects of a city such as Rome welcoming people from many different lands? *(It could make communication difficult and could lead to overcrowding and cultural clashes.)*

ANALYZE VISUALS

Have students examine the photo of Palatine Hill. Direct them to consider how the physical characteristics of the land influenced how people lived and constructed their buildings. Make a list of the challenges the Romans must have faced as they built structures on the hill. **0:10** minutes

ACTIVE OPTIONS

On Your Feet: Create a Concept Web Have students form groups of four around a section of a bulletin board or a table. Provide each group with a large sheet of paper. Have group members take turns contributing a concept or phrase to a concept web with the words *Early Romans* at the center. When time for the activity has elapsed, call on volunteers from each group to share their webs. **0:10** minutes

NG Learning Framework: Observe the Etruscans

SKILLS: Observation, Collaboration
KNOWLEDGE: **Our Living Planet**

Have students revisit Lesson 1.2, specifically the information about the Etruscans. They should work in pairs to create a list of observations about the Etruscan people and how their lives were impacted by their environment and nature. Once they have completed their list of observations, each pair should exchange lists with another pair and discuss the new list. **0:10** minutes

STRIVING READERS

Chart Early Roman Influences Have students record the different peoples who influenced early Rome using a chart such as the one shown below. In the rows, they should write a short description of the people and the way they influenced early Rome. Allow students to work in pairs to read the lesson. Have them read the text once and fill in their charts. Then have them read the text a second time and check their work. Have students share their charts with the rest of the group and add any information they might have missed.

Latins	Greeks	Etruscans

PRE-AP

Read a Legend Have students read three different versions of the legend of Romulus and Remus and write about or discuss the following:

- similarities and differences between the different versions of the legend
- facts that support the legend
- mythical elements, locations, and characters within the legend
- heroes or heroism within the legend
- a summary of how the legend explains the founding of Rome

Press (**mt**) *in the Student eEdition for modified text.*

See the Chapter Planner for more strategies for differentiation.

ANSWERS

1. They each brought elements of their own culture, which the Romans adopted as their own.

2. It was founded by the brothers Romulus and Remus.

3. It suggests that the Romans were tolerant of other cultures and open to new ideas.

1.3 Republican Government

You wouldn't have wanted to meet the Etruscan king Tarquin the Proud in a dark alley. He ruled as a tyrant—a cruel ruler—and had many of his opponents killed. In 509 B.C., the people of Rome overthrew Tarquin and established a new form of government.

MAIN IDEA

Rome developed a republican form of government that protected the rights of ordinary citizens.

THE YOUNG REPUBLIC

In a **republic**, citizens vote for their leaders. Only free adult men were citizens in Rome, but not all citizens were equal. Roman society was divided into two groups: the patricians and the plebeians. The **patricians** (puh-TRIH-shuhnz) were wealthy landowners. The **plebeians** (plih-BEE-uhnz), who included poorer farmers and craftsmen, made up the majority of Rome's citizens but were under-represented in the government.

The plebeians wanted a say in how Rome was run. As a result, in 494 B.C., they went on strike. The plebeians left the city, shutting down Roman shops and businesses, and set up their own government. Economic activity came to a halt. Once the patricians started losing money, they became frightened and agreed to share their power. In time, the plebeians were allowed to elect their own representatives, called **tribunes**, who fought to protect the rights of ordinary citizens.

The plebeians had one more demand. Because Rome's laws were not written down, the patricians often interpreted them to favor their rich friends. The plebeians fought back. They insisted that the laws be not only written down but carved into bronze tablets and displayed for all to see. These laws became known as the **Twelve Tables**. They protected all Roman citizens from injustice. Some of these laws are the basis of our own laws today.

ROMAN GOVERNMENT

Rome's new, more representative government contained three branches. An executive branch led the government and the army, a legislative branch made the laws, and a judicial branch applied the laws.

The Romans put checks and balances in place to prevent any one branch from becoming too powerful. They also replaced the position of king with two leaders called **consuls**. The consuls had the authority of a king but for only one year. They shared power so equally that the consuls had the right to **veto**, or reject, each other's decisions.

The legislative branch was made up of the **Senate**, elected judicial officers, and two assemblies. The Senate advised the consuls. The assemblies represented the plebeians. In the beginning, most of the 300 members of the Senate were patricians. Over time, however, plebeians were also allowed to participate.

Senators often spoke out about issues in the Senate House and in public squares. Delivering such speeches was a highly valued skill in Rome. One of Rome's most brilliant speakers was **Cicero** (SIH-suh-roh), who often used his speeches to attack those who he believed were a threat to the republic.

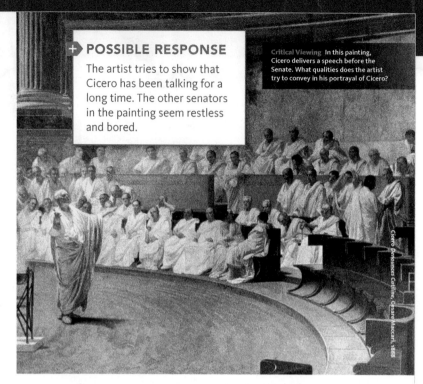

+ POSSIBLE RESPONSE

The artist tries to show that Cicero has been talking for a long time. The other senators in the painting seem restless and bored.

Critical Viewing In this painting, Cicero delivers a speech before the Senate. What qualities does the artist try to convey in his portrayal of Cicero?

Cicero Denounces Catiline, Cesare Maccari, 1888

In times of crisis, the Romans appointed **dictators** who had complete control but were expected to give up power after danger had passed. One such Roman dictator was **Cincinnatus** (sihn-suh-NA-tuhs). In 458 B.C., Rome's army was facing defeat by a fierce enemy, and the Senate wanted Cincinnatus to take charge. He accepted the dictatorship, defeated the enemy, and then surrendered his power and returned to his farm. The example set by Cincinnatus was celebrated by the Romans, who valued the idea of civic duty—putting service to the community ahead of personal interest.

REVIEW & ASSESS

1. **READING CHECK** How did the Roman government come to protect the rights of the citizens?

2. **COMPARE AND CONTRAST** In what ways are the governments of the Roman Republic and the United States similar?

3. **DRAW CONCLUSIONS** Why was it important to the plebeians to have Roman laws written down?

6.7.1 Identify the location and describe the rise of the Roman Republic, including the importance of such mythical and historical figures as Aeneas, Romulus and Remus, Cincinnatus, Julius Caesar, and Cicero; 6.7.2 Describe the government of the Roman Republic and its significance (e.g., written constitution and tripartite government, checks and balances, civic duty); HI 3 Students explain the sources of historical continuity and how the combination of ideas and events explains the emergence of new patterns.

HSS CONTENT STANDARDS:

6.7.1 Identify the location and describe the rise of the Roman Republic, including the importance of such mythical and historical figures as Aeneas, Romulus and Remus, Cincinnatus, Julius Caesar, and Cicero; **6.7.2** Describe the government of the Roman Republic and its significance (e.g., written constitution and tripartite government, checks and balances, civic duty).

HSS ANALYSIS SKILLS:

HI 1 Students explain the central issues and problems from the past, placing people and events in a matrix of time and place; **HI 3** Students explain the sources of historical continuity and how the combination of ideas and events explains the emergence of new patterns.

PLAN

OBJECTIVE

Describe the government of the Roman Republic and explain how it protected citizens' rights.

ESSENTIAL QUESTION

How did Rome become a mighty power in the Mediterranean?

The Romans created a republic with three branches of government and written laws. Lesson 1.3 discusses how the republic protected the rights of ordinary citizens and prevented any one group from becoming too powerful.

BACKGROUND FOR THE TEACHER

Marcus Tullius Cicero was born in 106 B.C. in Latium. He was a famous Roman lawyer, scholar, writer, and orator who devoted himself to upholding the principles of the Roman Republic during the civil wars that ultimately destroyed it. Appointed as consul in 63 B.C., Cicero gave many famous speeches designed to preserve the republic and expose what he viewed to be dangerous civil uprisings. His efforts to achieve equality among Rome's social classes earned him the title of "father of his country" by some. He died in 43 B.C., leaving behind numerous writings including hundreds of letters, speeches, books, and works of philosophy and politics.

DIGITAL RESOURCES NGLSync.cengage.com

TEACHER RESOURCES & ASSESSMENT

 Reading and Note-Taking

 Vocabulary Practice

 Section 1 Quiz

STUDENT RESOURCES

 Biography

INTRODUCE & ENGAGE

TOSS AND TELL

Provide students with a soft ball or small beanbag that can be safely tossed. Ask students to think of the branches of the U.S. government. Toss the ball or beanbag to a student and ask him or her to name one of the branches. If the student cannot, he or she can toss the ball or beanbag to someone else. Repeat the tossing and telling throughout the classroom until all three branches have been named. Then tell students they will learn how the Romans developed these three branches of government. **0:05** minutes

TEACH

GUIDED DISCUSSION

1. **Make Generalizations** Were the demands of the Roman plebeians and the way they went about having their demands met reasonable and/ or successful? (*Possible response: Yes, their demands were reasonable and successful. The plebeians just wanted to have equal rights to the patricians, and they proved they had a powerful voice in society. There were more plebeians than patricians, and the plebeians provided most of the goods and services to the patricians. When the plebeians closed their shops and businesses, the patricians were forced to listen to their demands.*) How did the plebeian demand for written laws benefit all Romans? (*Having permanent, public laws protected Roman citizens from having laws be interpreted in different ways that benefitted only the friends of powerful people.*)

2. **Draw Conclusions** As shown through Cincinnatus's actions, the Romans valued setting aside personal interests to benefit the community. Do you believe politicians and leaders today are willing to set aside their personal goals, wealth, or interests to benefit their country or community? Why or why not? (*Responses will vary. Students should be encouraged to defend their views using examples.*)

COMPARE AND CONTRAST

ASK: How does the structure of the U.S. government compare to the structure of the representative government of Rome? As a group, work to make two diagrams on large sheets of paper or a whiteboard. One diagram should show the structure of Rome's representative government, and the other should show the structure of the U.S. government. Include the three branches in both, but be sure to acknowledge and draw students' attention to distinguishing features, such as having two Roman consuls versus having one American president. As an extension, have students read examples of laws from the Twelve Tables in the **Primary Source Handbook** and compare and contrast them to present-day national, state, or local laws. **0:20** minutes

ACTIVE OPTIONS

Active History: Compare Greek and Roman Governments Extend the lesson by using either the PDF or Whiteboard version of the Compare Greek and Roman Governments Active History activity. These activities take a deeper look at a topic from or related to the lesson. Explore the Active History activities as a class, turn them into group assignments, or even assign them individually. **0:15** minutes

On Your Feet: Plebeians versus Patricians Divide the class into two groups: plebeians and patricians. Provide each group with a large sheet of paper, and ask them to imagine it is 495 B.C. Have the groups create a list of their sentiments about the current state of Roman society, including what they like, dislike, fear, and would like to change or keep the same. After ten minutes, ask each group to share their concerns. You may wish to facilitate a debate or dialogue between the groups by asking questions such as, "Patricians, how do you feel about the fact that Rome's laws are not currently written down?" "Plebeians, there are more of you in Rome than patricians, but you are under-represented in the government. Are you satisfied with this arrangement?" **0:20** minutes

DIFFERENTIATE

STRIVING READERS

Analyze Visuals Have students study the painting of Cicero giving a speech before the Roman Senate. In pairs, have students make a list of observations about the Roman Senate based on what they see in the painting. Encourage students to compare the layout of the Roman Senate to the United States Senate, providing photographs of the latter, if needed.

GIFTED & TALENTED

Become an Orator Many consider Cicero to be the greatest speaker that ever lived. Even Julius Caesar acknowledged that Cicero's achievements in learning and sharing knowledge were greater than his own expansion of the Roman Republic. Provide students with topics to speak about, or invite them to select their own. Brainstorm qualities that make a good speech and a successful orator. Remind students that speeches should have a clear theme and details that support the main idea. Guide students to write a short speech of 3–5 minutes and present it to their peers. As an added extension, consider studying one of Cicero's famous speeches.

Press **(mt)** *in the Student eEdition for modified text.*

See the Chapter Planner for more strategies for differentiation.

REVIEW & ASSESS

ANSWERS

1. It wrote all laws down on bronze tablets so everyone could see them and not misinterpret them.

2. Both governments have three branches—legislative, executive, and judicial; both have written laws.

3. It was important because the plebeians wanted the laws to be applied equally. They didn't want the patricians to get away with interpreting the laws in different ways that favored themselves.

The ruins of the Roman Forum represent different periods of Rome's ancient history. Here older ruins of buildings surround the Arch of Titus. The Colosseum stands in the background.

1.4

The Roman
Forum

The Roman Forum was the place to be. It was the place to meet, shop, do business, worship, celebrate, and be entertained. This public square was one of the liveliest and most important places in all of Rome.

MAIN IDEA

The Roman Forum was the political, religious, economic, and social center of the Roman Republic.

BURIAL GROUND TO PUBLIC SQUARE

The **Forum** developed over several centuries in a valley between the Palatine and Capitoline hills. In heavy rain, the banks of the Tiber River would burst, flooding the marshy valley. Long before Rome was founded, this scrap of swamp had been used as a burial ground. However, once Rome began to grow and its population spilled down the hills, the swamp became a piece of desirable real estate. Around 600 B.C., an Etruscan king built a sewer to drain the area and created an open public square paved with pebbles. The Roman Forum was born.

Everyone came to the Forum. It was the city's open-air market, where Romans could buy everything from local fruit and vegetables to imported Greek pottery. Rome's oldest road, the Via Sacra, looped through the Forum. Along the road, the early kings of Rome built a royal residence, shops, houses, and temples dedicated to their many gods and goddesses. At first these buildings were little more than mud huts or raised-earth platforms. Over time, these were replaced with permanent structures, and the Forum became the center of Rome's religious, economic, and social activity.

THE CENTER OF ROME

After the republic was founded, the Forum also became the center of Roman politics. Although the Forum's open space remained small, huge public and government buildings sprang up around it. The Temple of Saturn, dedicated to one of Rome's most important gods, became the treasury, holding the growing riches of the republic. The Curia was the meeting place of the Roman Senate. Political activity, ranging from public speeches to rioting mobs, took place at the Forum. Because it was where ordinary Romans gathered, the Forum was the perfect place to display the Twelve Tables.

The Forum also provided a setting for public spectacles. Crowds came to watch theatrical performances and athletic games. Even the funerals of important men were held at the Forum.

In later centuries, the Forum's buildings were transformed from brick to marble, and great bronze statues were added. Later rulers built other public places, but none ever rivaled the importance of the great Roman Forum.

REVIEW & ASSESS

1. **READING CHECK** Why did the ancient Romans gather in the Forum?

2. **IDENTIFY MAIN IDEAS AND DETAILS** How did the Forum change over time?

3. **MAKE INFERENCES** How did the Roman Forum reflect the democratic values of the Roman Republic?

 6.7.8 Discuss the legacies of Roman art and architecture, technology and science, literature, language, and law.

STANDARDS

HSS CONTENT STANDARDS:

6.7.8 Discuss the legacies of Roman art and architecture, technology and science, literature, language, and law.

HSS ANALYSIS SKILLS:

CST 1 Students explain how major events are related to one another in time;
HI 1 Students explain the central issues and problems from the past, placing people and events in a matrix of time and place.

PLAN

OBJECTIVE

Analyze the purpose of the Roman Forum in the Roman Republic.

ESSENTIAL QUESTION

How did Rome become a mighty power in the Mediterranean?

The Roman Forum was the political, economic, and social center of the republic. Lesson 1.4 describes the Forum and explains its place in Roman society.

BACKGROUND FOR THE TEACHER

One of the most famous forms of entertainment offered in the Forum was fighting. The large open space of the rectangular Forum was the perfect place for hand-to-hand combat between trained fighters known as gladiators. Spectators would flock to the Forum to watch the fights from rows of seats that stretched up the Capitoline Hill. One of the most famous early gladiator battles took place in 216 B.C. as part of a series of "funeral games" put on by the sons of the consul Marcus Aemilius Lepidus to honor their late father. Eventually, the Colosseum was constructed just east of the Forum, offering spectators a better view of gladiator fights from higher seats and enclosing the gladiators within an arena to prevent them from leaving.

DIGITAL RESOURCES NGLSync.cengage.com

TEACHER RESOURCES & ASSESSMENT

 Reading and Note-Taking

 Vocabulary Practice

 Section 1 Quiz

STUDENT RESOURCES

 NG Image Gallery

INTRODUCE & ENGAGE

THINK ABOUT THEN AND NOW

Ask students to think about "the" place to hang out in their town, community, or neighborhood—a busy, lively place where they know they'll meet up with friends or family members. Is it a park? A restaurant? A gymnasium? Perhaps it's a community center or a church or temple. Write a list on the whiteboard of the locations students consider to be the important places in their community or neighborhood, and have volunteers describe what happens in these places. `0:05` minutes

TEACH

GUIDED DISCUSSION

1. **Describe** Tell how the Forum was used by the people of Rome. *(It was used as a market and as a religious center. It also became a center for politics and government after the republic was formed. The Senate met in a building in the Forum, the city's riches were housed in another building, and people met in the open spaces to give speeches and express their opinions. Many people also gathered in the Forum to watch performances and games.)*

2. **Draw Conclusions** The Forum served many purposes, but one of its chief roles was as a gathering place. Why is it important for a community to have such a place? *(Possible responses: People in a community feel more connected to each other and the place they live if they have a central place to spend their free time and get important things done. Also, a central gathering place can be a good location to gather, share information, and find safety.)*

MORE INFORMATION

The Arch of Titus Among the surviving structures in the Roman Forum is the Arch of Titus (visible in the photograph in the lesson). This arch is located at the highest point of Rome's oldest road, the Via Sacra. It is one of the most famous monuments in the Forum and the oldest surviving arch in Rome. The Arch of Titus was built to honor the popular Roman emperor Titus, who died in A.D. 81. The carvings on the arch celebrate Titus's famous suppression of a rebellion in Jerusalem.

ACTIVE OPTIONS

On Your Feet: Sequence of Events Provide pairs of students with large sheets of paper with events written on them specific to the development of the Forum over time. Use the following events (but provide them in a scrambled order):

- Heavy rains caused the Tiber River to overflow, making the valley between the Palatine and Capitoline Hills a marshy swamp.
- The swampy land in the valley was used as a burial ground.
- An Etruscan king drained the swampy land in the valley by building a sewer.
- The drained swampland was paved and turned into an open public square.
- Romans came to the open public square known as the Forum to do their shopping out of mud huts and raised-earth platforms.
- Permanent structures were built and the Forum became the center of Rome's religious, economic, and social activity.

- After the republic was founded, the Forum became the center of Rome's politics.
- The Forum's buildings were transformed from brick to marble, and great bronze statues were added.

Have students move around the classroom and read other students' events. Then have students work as a group to place their events in order, consulting their book if desired. Review the events as a class to determine if they are properly arranged. `0:15` minutes

Critical Viewing: NG Image Gallery Have students explore the entire NG Image Gallery and choose two of the items to compare and contrast, either in written form or verbally with a partner. Ask questions that will inspire this process, such as: How are these images alike? How are they different? Why did you select these two items? How do they relate in history? `0:10` minutes

DIFFERENTIATE

INCLUSION

Review Concepts Provide definitions of this key concept from the lesson:

The **Forum** was a public square for shopping, gathering, and working. People came to the **market** at the Forum to buy and sell things like food and pottery. A road called the Via Sacra passed through the Forum, and shops, houses, and **religious temples** were built there. The Forum also had buildings for **government** meetings and storing riches. People came to the Forum to watch actors put on shows and athletes compete in games. **Funerals** were also held there.

Then examine the photo of the Forum and point out some of the features and buildings that are shown.

PRE-AP   STEM

Describe Have students do research to find out more about the buildings and structures from the Forum that still exist. Have each student choose a building or structure (or assign one) and find out how and when it was built, where in the Forum it exists, and what its purpose and design were. Then have students present their findings to the class. As a class, create a diagram or model of the Forum that shows each of the buildings/structures students researched.

Press **mt** *in the Student eEdition for modified text.*

See the Chapter Planner for more strategies for differentiation.

REVIEW & ASSESS

ANSWERS

1. They gathered in the Forum for religious, economic, political, and social activities.

2. It went from being a swamp and a burial ground to an open-air market. When more permanent structures were built, it became a center for Roman politics and culture. Eventually, the buildings were transformed into marble masterpieces.

3. Everyone had a right to congregate there. Also, the Twelve Tables were on display there.

2.1 Men and Women

Growing up in Rome wasn't easy. There were no laws to protect children. Boys were expected to head their own families one day, but most girls never had any real control over their futures.

MAIN IDEA

Men and women had different roles in Roman society.

MEN IN ANCIENT ROME

If you were born a boy in Rome, you already had a head start in life. Rome was a **patriarchy** (PAY-tree-ahr-kee), or a society in which men have all the power. Only men could vote or hold public office, fight in wars, and perform important ceremonies. In Rome's patriarchy, men were in charge of everything—especially the family.

The family was at the core of Roman society. At the head of every family was the senior male, the *paterfamilias* (pa-tur-fuh-MIH-lee-uhs). He made all decisions. He could put family members on trial and punish them—even execute them. The Twelve Tables eventually limited the power of the paterfamilias, but he still had a lot of control over his family.

Boys from poorer families received little education and often could not read or write. Instead they went out to work beginning at an early age. Wealthier families sent their sons to school. Classes started at dawn, and teachers, who were often Greek slaves, taught reading, writing, and arithmetic. Public speaking was another important lesson. Long poems had to be memorized, and mistakes were often punished with a beating.

After the age of 14, boys destined for government jobs continued their education with private tutors at home. At the age of 17, boys were considered to be men and registered as Roman citizens in the Forum.

WOMEN IN ANCIENT ROME

Roman women had more rights than women in ancient Greece, but those still didn't amount to much by modern standards. Roman women were subject to the authority of men—their husbands, fathers, or brothers. They could not vote or hold public office, though they could eventually own property and manage their own businesses and finances. A wife could also manage her husband's business, and women with powerful husbands had some political influence.

In Rome, a woman's main role was to be a good wife and mother. For many, this meant doing the daily domestic chores of spinning yarn, making clothes, cooking, cleaning, and looking after the children. Sometimes women would have paying jobs as well. In wealthier families, the wife managed the household and its finances, but slaves did all the physical labor.

If they were lucky, some girls from wealthy families learned basic reading, writing, and arithmetic at home. However, they mostly learned household skills to prepare them for married life, which could begin when girls were as young as 12. Most marriages had little to do with love but were arranged to benefit the family. However, divorce was easy and acceptable, and ambitious politicians might remarry many times to gain support from increasingly important families.

Critical Viewing This fresco, a style of painting on fresh plaster, shows a Roman woman and man holding writing tools. Based on the details you can see in the fresco, what conclusions can you draw about these people?

+ POSSIBLE RESPONSE

The man and woman must be from a wealthy family because usually only wealthy people learned to read and write. Also, it is more likely that a woman from a wealthy family would have been educated.

REVIEW & ASSESS

1. **READING CHECK** What was a woman's role in Roman society?

2. **DETERMINE WORD MEANINGS** How does knowing that *pater* is Latin for "father" help clarify what *patriarchy* and *paterfamilias* mean?

3. **COMPARE AND CONTRAST** How did roles differ for boys and girls in Rome?

HSS CONTENT STANDARDS:

6.7 Students analyze the geographic, political, economic, religious, and social structures during the development of Rome.

HSS ANALYSIS SKILLS:

HI 1 Students explain the central issues and problems from the past, placing people and events in a matrix of time and place.

PLAN

OBJECTIVE

Explain the different roles of men and women in Roman society.

ESSENTIAL QUESTION

How did Rome become a mighty power in the Mediterranean?

Men and women in ancient Rome had different rights and responsibilities. Lesson 2.1 describes these differences and explains how men and women each contributed to Roman society.

BACKGROUND FOR THE TEACHER

Roman *patresfamilias* had a surprising amount of power and were the only people who could own property. Even successful married adult sons continued to receive an allowance until their father died. They could not own any property. Still, sons were valued because of the fact that they carried forth the family's name. Roman fathers without sons might adopt a son just to ensure the family's name and legacy would carry on after their death.

Roman women did not have many rights and were not given the educational opportunities that men were given. But they were rewarded for bearing many children. Many babies and children died at a young age during the first century A.D., so if a woman gave birth to three or four children who survived, she was given legal freedom. This allowed her to become independent from men if she wanted to be.

DIGITAL RESOURCES NGLSync.cengage.com

TEACHER RESOURCES & ASSESSMENT

 Reading and Note-Taking

 Vocabulary Practice

 Section 2 Quiz

STUDENT RESOURCES

 NG Chapter Gallery

INTRODUCE & ENGAGE

THINK ABOUT GENDER IN THE WORKPLACE

Ask students to think about the roles of men and women in American culture today. **ASK:** Are there certain jobs that are usually done only by men or only by women? Why? Make a list of such jobs on the whiteboard and discuss possible reasons why one gender might be suited to doing particular jobs or why certain jobs typically attract males or females. Then tell students that in this lesson, they will learn about how men and women were treated differently in Roman society. `0:05` minutes

TEACH

GUIDED DISCUSSION

1. **Make Inferences** How does the ability to get an education affect someone? *(Students might discuss how an education affects job opportunities, social and economic advancement, financial independence, or power.)*

2. **Form and Support Opinions** In your opinion, did women or men have a harder life in the culture of ancient Rome? Support your opinion using facts from the text. *(Responses will vary. Possible responses: Men had a harder life because they had to go through more schooling, and the punishments for making mistakes during their lessons were very harsh. Also, men were responsible for stressful tasks like voting, fighting in wars, and leading their families. Women had a harder life because they were usually not as educated as men, and had very few rights. They had to stay home, do household chores, and care for the children, which is very hard work. Also, some girls had to get married by the age of 12, which is very young.)*

CREATE GRAPHIC ORGANIZERS

To help students understand important concepts, have them work in small groups and create a graphic organizer. They can use a Concept Cluster to explain a term such as *patriarchy*, or a T-Chart to compare the lifestyle and rights of a wealthy Roman man or woman to the life of a poor one. `0:15` minutes

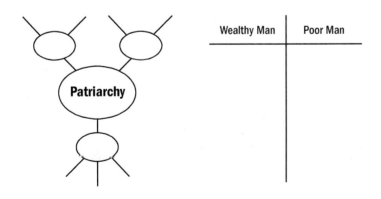

Wealthy Man	Poor Man

ACTIVE OPTIONS

On Your Feet: Tell Me More Have students form three teams and assign each team one of the following topics:

- paterfamilias
- education of young people in ancient Rome
- women's rights in ancient Rome

Each group should write down as many facts about their topic as they can. Have the class reconvene and have each group stand up, one at a time. The rest of the class calls out "Tell me more about [the topic]." The group recites one fact. The class again requests a fact until the group runs out of facts to share. Then the next group presents its facts. `0:10` minutes

NG Learning Framework: Compare Roman Men and Women

ATTITUDES: **Responsibility, Empowerment**
SKILLS: **Collaboration, Problem-Solving**
KNOWLEDGE: **Our Human Story**

In small groups, have students review the different roles of men and women in Roman society. Ask each group to create a T-Chart to compare the roles. Then have each student write a paragraph to assess how the roles benefitted Roman society as a whole. Empower students to return to their small groups to discuss how expanding gender roles might have been even more beneficial to Roman society. `0:10` minutes

DIFFERENTIATE

STRIVING READERS

Compare and Contrast Provide students with slips of paper. Ask them to write a sentence that tells about some facet of how women lived in Roman times on one side of the paper. On the other side, have them write a comparison statement showing how women live today. Invite students to share their contrasting statements with the group.

GIFTED & TALENTED

Make Predictions Have students imagine what daily life would have been like for a 14-year-old girl and a 14-year-old boy living in ancient Rome. Have them work in pairs to write a short narrative, possibly in the form of a diary entry, from the perspective of a Roman girl or boy, telling about a typical day.

Press **mt** *in the Student eEdition for modified text.*

See the Chapter Planner for more strategies for differentiation.

REVIEW & ASSESS

ANSWERS

1. A woman's role in Roman society was to be a good wife and mother.

2. It hints that both words have to do with the head male of a family.

3. They differed extremely. Boys were educated and became citizens who could vote or hold public office. Girls were not usually educated and focused primarily on the home.

Rich and Poor

If you were rich in Rome, life was good, but if you were poor, life was miserable. The huge gap between rich and poor was reinforced by a rigid class structure that kept all Romans firmly in their places.

MAIN IDEA

Roman society was divided among different classes of people.

CLASS DIVISIONS

At the top of society was the **aristocracy**, the small group of wealthy patricians who owned most of the land and dominated the government. The majority of citizens were plebeians. Some were well-off and owned farms or businesses, but many were very poor. At the bottom was Rome's huge population of slaves.

The wealthiest families lived in luxurious country estates. These were built around elegant courtyards and decorated with works of fine art. Slaves did the hard work, leaving the homeowners free to conduct business, take part in politics, or spend time on their hobbies.

Most poor Romans lived and worked on small farms. Often, the wealthy used their money to buy up land and create huge farms worked entirely by slaves. This practice forced many farmers off their farms and into the city to look for work. There they lived in overcrowded buildings and worked at manual labor for very low wages.

Romans' diets also differed greatly. The poor used cheap pottery bowls to eat porridge or bread with vegetables. Meat was a luxury. Only the largest houses had kitchens, so even wealthier plebeians relied on restaurants for hot food. There they could eat fish, cooked meat, and vegetables and perhaps a dessert of sweet pastries. The very rich enjoyed lavish banquets with dozens of courses, including exotic foods.

Around 287 B.C., the plebeians finally achieved political equality when their representative assembly, the **Council of Plebs**, was allowed to make laws for all citizens. However, the patricians continued to dominate society.

SLAVES IN THE REPUBLIC

Slaves were the largest class in Rome, but they had the fewest rights. They were considered property to be bought and sold. Some slaves were prisoners from Rome's conquests. However, most were bought from foreign traders.

Slaves were very useful in Rome's economy. Most worked at manual labor, from household chores to construction work or agriculture. Skilled slaves might be craftspeople, while educated slaves might be teachers, doctors, or managers of their master's business. The worst slave jobs were in the mines or factories, where the work was tough, and the life expectancy was short.

Some slaves were treated well, but others suffered very badly. Excessive punishments could spark rebellion. A slave named Spartacus led the most famous rebellion in 73 B.C. For about two years, his slave army fought the Roman soldiers and controlled large areas of the countryside. When Spartacus was finally defeated, 6,000 of his followers were executed as a warning to other slaves.

A WEALTHY ROMAN FAMILY'S HOME

The diagram below shows four key areas in a house belonging to a wealthy family. While the house contained rooms for the family's private use, much of the space was designed for business and social gatherings.

① ENTRANCE HALL
The front door opened up on a large entrance hall. Most mornings clients seeking favors waited here for the chance to pay their respects to their patron, or financial supporter.

③ OFFICE
This room was located behind the reception area and functioned as the patron's office. The room could also be used for family gatherings.

② RECEPTION ROOM
In this large, airy space, the patron showed off his wealth and received visitors. The rectangular space beneath the opening in the roof served to collect rainwater.

④ COURTYARD
A roofed porch enclosed the courtyard garden. The space often included fountains, benches, and sculptures. In the richest homes, the porch's inner walls were often decorated with frescoes.

REVIEW & ASSESS

1. **READING CHECK** How did the lives of the Roman classes differ?

2. **INTEGRATE VISUALS** In what ways might plebeian or slave homes have differed from the home illustrated above?

3. **MAKE INFERENCES** How do you think the patricians reacted at first to the plebeians' political equality?

STANDARDS

HSS CONTENT STANDARDS:

6.7 Students analyze the geographic, political, economic, religious, and social structures during the development of Rome.

HSS ANALYSIS SKILLS:

HI 1 Students explain the central issues and problems from the past, placing people and events in a matrix of time and place;
HI 2 Students understand and distinguish cause, effect, sequence, and correlation in historical events, including the long- and short-term causal relations.

PLAN

OBJECTIVE

Compare life in the Roman Republic for people of different social classes.

ESSENTIAL QUESTION

How did Rome become a mighty power in the Mediterranean?

Roman society was divided among different classes of people. Lesson 2.2 describes these classes and their role in Roman society.

BACKGROUND FOR THE TEACHER

One of the most famous slaves of all time, Spartacus, has served as an inspiration to revolutionary groups throughout history because of his successful, albeit temporary, organized slave revolt. Once a soldier in the Roman army, Spartacus was later sold into slavery and trained as a gladiator. He escaped from slavery in 73 B.C. and assembled a large army of escaped slaves, leading this army to defeat the Romans in a series of attacks. As 72 B.C. drew to a close, Spartacus's rebel forces were finally subdued by the Roman army, and Spartacus was killed.

DIGITAL RESOURCES NGLSync.cengage.com

TEACHER RESOURCES & ASSESSMENT

 Reading and Note-Taking

 Vocabulary Practice

 Section 2 Quiz

STUDENT RESOURCES

 NG Chapter Gallery

INTRODUCE & ENGAGE

ACTIVATE PRIOR KNOWLEDGE ABOUT SLAVERY

Most students will have some understanding of the history of slavery in the United States. Ask volunteers to offer what they know about American slavery. Have other students record facts from their prior knowledge using a chart or bullet points on the whiteboard. If appropriate, guide students to discuss topics such as the jobs American slaves did, where they worked, how they lived and were treated, and how they were acquired, so that this activity serves as a precursor to the information students will learn about Roman slaves. `0:10` minutes

TEACH

GUIDED DISCUSSION

1. **Analyze Cause and Effect** How did slaves affect the jobs of farmers? *(When the wealthy used their money to buy up land and create large farms, they oftentimes brought in slaves to work and run the farms. That meant many farmers were forced off their farms and had to move into the city to find work. Many were forced to live in overcrowded buildings and work manual labor jobs for poor wages.)*

2. **Compare** What types of different jobs did Roman slaves have? *(Most slaves worked in manual labor, doing household chores, construction work, or farm work. Unlucky slaves worked in mines or factories, doing very difficult or unsafe work. Skilled slaves might have been craftspeople. Educated slaves might have been teachers, doctors, or managers of their master's business.)*

CREATE GRAPHIC ORGANIZERS

Place students in small groups and ask each group to create a graphic organizer to show and describe the social classes into which Roman society was divided. Then have students review the social structure of societies in Mesopotamia, ancient Egypt, ancient India, ancient China, and ancient Greece (both Sparta and Athens). Discuss with students similarities and differences of these social hierarchies. `0:10` minutes

ACTIVE OPTIONS

On Your Feet: Inside-Outside Circle Arrange students in concentric circles facing each other. Have each student in the outside circle ask a question about Roman social classes. Then have each student in the inside circle answer their partner's question. On a signal, have students on the inside circle rotate counterclockwise to meet a new partner and begin again. On a different signal, have students trade roles so those in the inside circle ask the questions and those in the outside circle answer the questions. `0:10` minutes

Critical Viewing: NG Chapter Gallery Ask students to choose one image from the Chapter Gallery and become an expert on it. They should do additional research to learn all about it. Then, students should share their findings with a partner, small group, or the class. `0:10` minutes

DIFFERENTIATE

STRIVING READERS

Use Context Clues Model how to use textual definitions and context to understand key words in this lesson: *aristocracy, Council of Plebs*. Then guide students in using the text to understand other unfamiliar academic vocabulary words such as *exotic, conquests, craftspeople,* and *rebellion*. Students can use a chart like the one below to record their ideas.

Key Vocabulary	Definition From Context

GIFTED & TALENTED

Research and Present Have students research Roman homes. Then have them create a presentation that includes descriptions of the homes of people in different Roman social classes as well as photographs, diagrams, or possibly models.

Press **mt** *in the Student eEdition for modified text.*

See the Chapter Planner for more strategies for differentiation.

REVIEW & ASSESS

ANSWERS

1. Patricians owned most of the land and dominated government; some plebeians owned farms or businesses, but most were very poor; slaves had few rights and could be bought and sold.

2. Plebeian or slave homes were probably not as large or fancy. They probably had fewer, simpler rooms and homes that were more practical.

3. They probably reacted harshly because they were used to having all of the power and now had to share it with the plebeians.

2.3

Gods and Beliefs

To Romans, the wrath of their gods was always present. They felt that honoring the gods—or at least not upsetting them—was a matter of life and death.

MAIN IDEA

Religious worship was an important part of Roman life.

Ten Gods of Ancient Rome

Jupiter King of the gods

Saturn God of agriculture

Mercury Messenger of the gods

Apollo God of poetry and music

Mars God of war

Neptune God of the sea and earthquakes

Ceres Goddess of the harvest

Juno Goddess of women; wife of Jupiter

Diana Goddess of the moon and the hunt

Venus Goddess of love and beauty

ROMAN WORSHIP

Roman religion was based on a **pantheon** (PAN-thee-ahn), or group of many gods, most adopted from the ancient Greeks. These gods had Roman names and were believed to have human traits and to control areas of Roman life. For example, Jupiter was the king of the gods. Juno was the goddess of women, marriage, childbirth, and children. Mars was the god of war, and Venus was the beautiful goddess of love.

The pantheon constantly grew to include the gods of people Rome conquered. Later, the Romans worshipped their rulers as gods after their death. Some rulers claimed to be living gods, but this claim made them very unpopular.

Romans worshipped their gods almost anywhere. Nearly every home had a shrine where the paterfamilias would make daily offerings to the gods that protected his family and his house. Priests managed temples for the most important gods. The priests conducted the rituals that Romans believed would secure the gods' favor.

The Roman calendar had many religious festivals that attracted huge audiences. The government funded many of them to ensure that the gods granted Rome good harvests or victories in war. These festivals included colorful processions, feasts, music, dance, theater, and sports.

THE ROMAN WAY

Roman gods had human traits that often highlighted the qualities most prized by the Romans. The Romans were a very practical and ambitious people, so they valued qualities that would help them achieve success. They considered the Greek virtues of beauty, grace, and elegance as nice but not essential. Instead, they preferred qualities like discipline, strength, and loyalty. Discipline and strength helped Romans endure hardship and overcome problems. Loyalty bound strong individuals together into even more powerful groups.

These valued qualities emphasize an important aspect of the Roman personality—*gravitas* (GRA-vuh-tahs). Having gravitas means being solemn and serious. Romans respected people who acted with great consideration, determination, and energy. These characteristics helped the people of the Roman Republic accomplish remarkable achievements in war, politics, law, commerce, and engineering. These qualities came to be known as "the Roman Way."

Critical Viewing A statue of Neptune, god of the sea, stands above the flowing water of Rome's Trevi Fountain. What details in the statue convey the qualities that the ancient Romans admired?

Trevi Fountain, Nicola Salvi and Giuseppe Pannini, 1762.

➕ POSSIBLE RESPONSE

The statue's face looks solemn and serious, and the body is muscular, illustrating strength.

REVIEW & ASSESS

1. **READING CHECK** Why was the worship of gods an important part of Roman life?

2. **SUMMARIZE** In what ways did the Romans expect the gods to affect daily life?

3. **DRAW CONCLUSIONS** What qualities did the Romans value? Why did they value these qualities more than others?

6.7.8 Discuss the legacies of Roman art and architecture, technology and science, literature, language, and law.

PLAN

OBJECTIVE

Explain the roles of religion and values in Roman culture.

ESSENTIAL QUESTION

How did Rome become a mighty power in the Mediterranean?

Religion and values were an important part of Roman culture. Lesson 2.3 examines how these aspects contributed to ancient Rome's success.

BACKGROUND FOR THE TEACHER

King of all Roman gods, Jupiter was a god of the sky. His original temple was built in Rome on the Capitoline Hill. For Romans, Jupiter, or Jove as he was also called, symbolized keeping one's promises or oaths to other people and to the Roman state. He was associated with keeping heroes focused on their duties and was considered the protector of the Roman Republic and people.

DIGITAL RESOURCES NGLSync.cengage.com

TEACHER RESOURCES & ASSESSMENT

 Reading and Note-Taking

 Vocabulary Practice

 Section 2 Quiz

STUDENT RESOURCES

 NG Chapter Gallery

INTRODUCE & ENGAGE

MAKE CONNECTIONS

Post descriptions of two different people for students to read. Describe Person A as practical, strong, disciplined, and loyal. Describe Person B as beautiful or handsome, graceful, and elegant. Ask students to predict which individual would be more valued by the Romans, and which would be more valued by the Greeks. Tally students' predictions and post them on the whiteboard. Then have students brainstorm people from today's society who might fit each description, record their names on sticky notes, and post them under the appropriate descriptions. **0:10** minutes

TEACH

GUIDED DISCUSSION

1. **Compare and Contrast** How is Roman worship similar to and different from the modern religions that you are familiar with today? *(Responses will vary, but may focus on the following points, which may be contrasted or compared to present-day religions: the Romans worshipped many gods and goddesses, not one; the gods had human names and traits and had control over specific facets of daily life, such as music or farming; the Romans added more gods to the pantheon as they conquered different peoples; Roman gods had shrines and temples where people worshipped them; the Romans held festivals in honor of their gods and goddesses.)*

2. **Make Inferences** Given what you know about the Romans' religious beliefs, how might a Roman farmer have gone about ensuring a successful growing season and a good harvest? *(A farmer might have visited the temple for Saturn, the god of agriculture, or Ceres, the goddess of the harvest, and made an offering or said a prayer for a successful growing season. The farmer also might have attended a religious festival funded by the Roman government to honor Ceres or Saturn.)*

SYNTHESIZE

This lesson introduces students to the concept of *gravitas*. Put students into small groups and ask them to create a Concept Web with the term *gravitas* in the center. Students should discuss what they have learned about gravitas in terms of Rome, and then add phrases, words, and examples to the web to explain the term and relate it to Roman culture and values. *(Students' webs will vary but should reflect the word's meaning: solemn and serious.)* **0:15** minutes

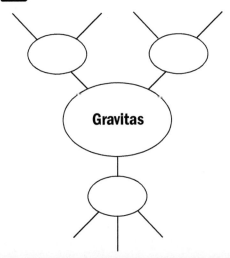

ACTIVE OPTIONS

On Your Feet: One-on-One Interviews Group students into pairs. Have both students in the pair write three questions about Roman religious practices and "the Roman Way." Start with one student using his or her questions to interview the other student "expert" about Roman religion and culture. Students' answers should show an understanding of the material from the lesson. Once the interview is complete, students should reverse roles. **0:15** minutes

NG Learning Framework: Compare Ancient Roman and Chinese Ideals

SKILL: Collaboration
KNOWLEDGE: Our Human Story

Have small groups of students review the principles of Confucianism and the ways in which the philosophy influenced Chinese government under the Han dynasty (Chapter 7). Then have groups make comparisons between Confucian principles and the Roman Way. Ask them to consider how each set of ideals strengthened the government and society of their respective civilization. **0:10** minutes

DIFFERENTIATE

STRIVING READERS

Who's Who? Assign pairs of students one of the ten gods of ancient Rome listed in the lesson. Have the students discuss what the god is known for (doing additional research, if desired) and work together to create a flag, crest, or trading card that represents the deity and his or her role in Roman religion.

GIFTED & TALENTED

Research a Roman God Allow students (or student pairs) to select a Roman god or goddess and conduct further research on him or her in order to create a short presentation for their classmates. Presentations should include information about the following:

*   the name of the assigned god or goddess and his or her role in Roman religion
*   any relevant connections to Greek gods and goddesses
*   festivals or events planned in honor of the god or goddess
*   positive and negative qualities of the selected deity
*   photographs of artwork, sculptures, architecture, or other representations of the deity

Press **mt** *in the Student eEdition for modified text.*

See the Chapter Planner for more strategies for differentiation.

REVIEW & ASSESS

ANSWERS

1. The worship of gods was important because they controlled areas of Roman life.

2. Romans expected the gods to affect daily life, the harvest, and performance in war.

3. The Romans valued discipline, strength, and loyalty because they felt these qualities would help them endure hardship, overcome problems, and accomplish remarkable achievements.

3.1

The Roman Army

War in the ancient world was extremely physical, and the Romans were good at it. The republic developed a formidable fighting force of well-trained professional soldiers called the legion. It was the ultimate weapon of ancient warfare.

MAIN IDEA

Organization and training brought Rome's army military success.

+ POSSIBLE RESPONSE

It might have been effective because it turned all the individuals in the unit into a solid formation that could easily ram into the enemy. The formation also probably offered additional protection to the soldiers.

Roman Legionaries

Roman soldiers kept fit by running, marching, and practice fighting. They could march 20 miles a day wearing armor, swim or cross rivers in boats, and build bridges.

This photo shows a reenactment of a Roman army battle formation. As you can see, Roman legionaries usually fought in tight lines with their shields held before the attacking enemy. Why might this battle tactic, or strategy, have been effective?

< A Roman legionary stands guard in a reenactment of ancient warfare.

THE ROMAN LEGION

It was a privilege to serve in Rome's legions. At first only property-owning citizens could join, and they had to supply their own weapons. A legion contained around 4,200 men, and each consul led an army of two legions. When the battle season finished in October, everybody went home.

Yet as the republic fought longer wars farther from Rome, citizens who owned property became reluctant to serve. In 107 B.C., the consul Marius (MAIR-ee-uhs) found himself short of recruits, so he allowed poor, landless citizens to volunteer. The government supplied their equipment, which included a bronze helmet, mail armor, a short sword, a javelin, and an oval shield. These men became professional soldiers known as **legionaries**.

Marius also reorganized the legions for maximum strength and flexibility. He often grouped squads of men into 100-man centuries, or units. These units, in turn, were grouped into 600-man cohorts, or divisions. Ten cohorts made up a legion, now 6,000 strong. This command structure gave Roman generals control over large numbers of men, and it continues to be a model for modern military organization.

The legions became an efficient military machine that Rome used to conquer its enemies and expand its territory. Rome recruited additional soldiers from the regions it defeated, which led to more military might and manpower. If a Roman army was defeated, Rome would send an even bigger army the next time. This stubborn determination made Rome unstoppable.

LIFE OF A LEGIONARY

Legionaries joined young and served for a maximum of 16 years. A recruit had to pass a physical inspection. Then in front of the legion's revered flag, the eagle, he swore an oath to serve the republic. This oath inspired a powerful sense of duty to comrades, to commanders, and to Rome itself.

Daily life revolved around a squad that trained, marched, and fought together. Soldiers built strong bonds of friendship and loyalty through sharing a tent, duties, and meals. When off duty, a legionary might play games or visit the public baths. However, duty always came first. While bravery led to rewards, failure led to severe punishment.

Training was key to the legions' success. Legionaries learned to carry out complicated instructions in the chaos of battle. At the end of each day, they built a fortified camp with deep ditches and high walls called palisades. Over time, they also built the straight roads and strong bridges that connected the republic and carried its men into battle.

REVIEW & ASSESS

1. **READING CHECK** How did the Roman army's organization and training lead to success?

2. **IDENTIFY MAIN IDEAS AND DETAILS** What were the duties of a legionary?

3. **SUMMARIZE** What changes did Marius make to the Roman army?

6.7.3 Identify the location of and the political and geographic reasons for the growth of Roman territories and expansion of the empire, including how the empire fostered economic growth through the use of currency and trade routes.

HSS CONTENT STANDARDS:

6.7.3 Identify the location of and the political and geographic reasons for the growth of Roman territories and expansion of the empire, including how the empire fostered economic growth through the use of currency and trade routes.

HSS ANALYSIS SKILLS:

HI 1 Students explain the central issues and problems from the past, placing people and events in a matrix of time and place.

PLAN

OBJECTIVE

Explain how the organization and training of Roman soldiers led to Rome's military success.

ESSENTIAL QUESTION

How did Rome become a mighty power in the Mediterranean?

The organization of Rome's army is still used as a model for modern military units. Lesson 3.1 describes the Roman legion and explains how it contributed to Rome's success.

BACKGROUND FOR THE TEACHER

Professional soldiers, or legionaries, supplied the Roman army with the strength it needed in battle to defend and expand the republic. However, legionaries were not the only type of soldiers in the army, and fighting was not the only thing that Roman soldiers did. Roman auxiliaries were soldiers who weren't Roman citizens, but who were paid a small wage to guard forts and sometimes fight in battles. Artillery soldiers used weapons such as catapults and crossbows against enemies, and cavalry battled on horseback. Other soldiers gathered supplies, constructed buildings and roads, made and repaired weapons and shields, and cared for the wounded.

DIGITAL RESOURCES NGLSync.cengage.com

TEACHER RESOURCES & ASSESSMENT

 Reading and Note-Taking

 Vocabulary Practice

 Section 3 Quiz

STUDENT RESOURCES

 NG Chapter Gallery

INTRODUCE & ENGAGE

JOIN THE RANKS

March students drill-style, through the school, ask them to stand at attention, or spend a few minutes barking orders at them as a drill sergeant might. Ask students to reflect about and share how they might feel about serving their country as a member of the military. What would they like about it? *(travel, education, room and board, pride in serving their country)* What would they dislike? *(being away from family and friends, danger, difficult living conditions, having to take orders)* Record these likes and dislikes on the whiteboard. Then tell students they are going to learn what life was like for soldiers in the Roman army. `0:10` minutes

TEACH

GUIDED DISCUSSION

1. **Draw Conclusions** What were the short-term and long-term impacts of the legionaries on Rome? *(On a daily basis, legionaries protected the city of Rome, conquered enemies, and expanded Rome's territory. They also had a lasting impact on the Roman Republic because they were responsible for building the straight roads and strong bridges that connected the republic and carried soldiers into battle. Many other civilizations modeled their infrastructure after Rome's.)*

2. **Make Inferences** What might have been the advantages and disadvantages of joining the Roman legions as a volunteer? *(For people who were poor and landless, joining the legions provided an opportunity to serve the republic, which instilled in them a deep sense of loyalty and pride. The legionaries were kept very busy and made many friends. Joining the legions also provided volunteers with shelter, food, and military instruction. The disadvantages of joining the legions included the risk of death or injury during battle, hard work under difficult conditions, and severe punishments for failing to perform one's duties.)*

CREATE GRAPHIC ORGANIZERS

To help students understand how the consul Marius organized the Roman legions for maximum effectiveness, have them work together (or as a class) to create a graphic organizer or visual to show how the soldiers were organized. (Organizers may vary but should be organized in a similar fashion.) `0:15` minutes

ACTIVE OPTIONS

Critical Viewing: NG Chapter Gallery Have students examine the contents of the Chapter Gallery for this chapter. Then invite them to brainstorm additional images they believe would fit within the Chapter Gallery. Have them write a description of these additional images and provide an explanation of why they would fit within the Chapter Gallery. Then instruct them to do online research to find examples of actual images. `0:10` minutes

On Your Feet: Think, Pair, Share Have students consider the following questions:

- Originally, only property-owning citizens who supplied their own weapons were permitted to join Roman legions as soldiers. By 107 B.C., Marius was forced to allow poor, landless citizens to volunteer as legionaries. What changed in Roman society to require this dramatic shift in how the legions were staffed?

- Do you think legions made up largely of poor volunteers would be any different from legions made up of privileged property-owning citizens? Why or why not? What advantages or disadvantages might each social group bring to their legion?

After students have time to consider the topics individually, place them in pairs to discuss them together. Then invite a volunteer from each pair to share the results of their discussion with the rest of the class. `0:10` minutes

DIFFERENTIATE

ENGLISH LANGUAGE LEARNERS

Summarize Lesson 3.1 has seven paragraphs. Have students work in pairs or small groups, and assign each pair or group one paragraph to read. Then each pair or group should write a one to two sentence summary of their paragraph. Provide the following sentence frames to help students at each proficiency level write an effective summary.

- **Emerging** This paragraph is about _____.

  First, _____. Then, _____. At the end _____.

- **Expanding** This paragraph is about _____ and _____.

  First, _____ and then _____. Finally, _____.

- **Bridging** The paragraph begins by _____. It then _____,

  and concludes by _____.

  To summarize, the paragraph provides information about _____.

PRE-AP

Comparing Armies Have students do Internet research and create a chart that compares today's U.S. Army and the duties and obligations of the enlisted to those of the Roman legion and its legionaries. Have them consider the following:

- the minimum recruitment age and length of service
- the organization of each army
- the duties and daily lives of the soldiers

ASK: What generalizations can you make about how the two armies compare? Why might some of the differences and similarities exist?

Press **mt** *in the Student eEdition for modified text.*

See the Chapter Planner for more strategies for differentiation.

REVIEW & ASSESS

ANSWERS

1. The army's organization made it easy for generals to control large numbers of men, and the soldiers' training prepared them for the chaos of battle.

2. A legionary served the republic in battle and through various construction projects.

3. Marius allowed poor, landless citizens to volunteer for the army, and he reorganized the structure of the legion.

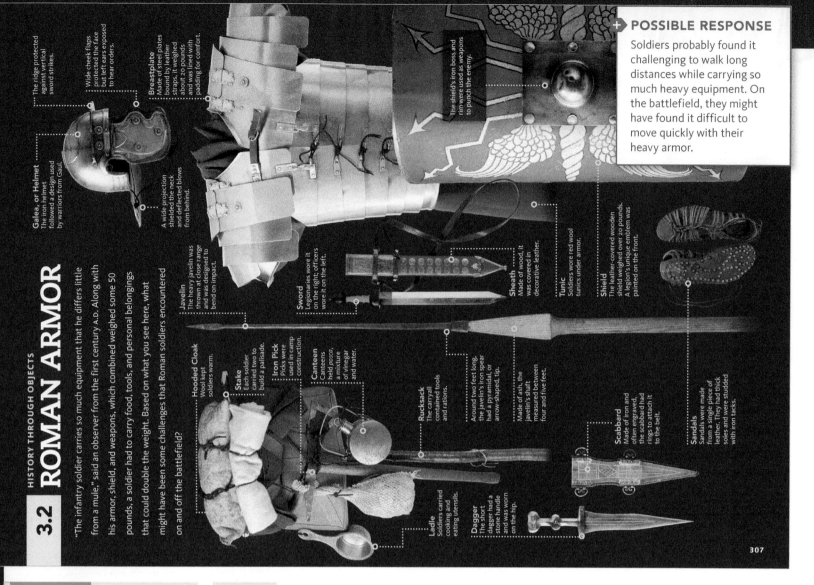

STANDARDS

HSS CONTENT STANDARDS:

6.7.3 Identify the location of and the political and geographic reasons for the growth of Roman territories and expansion of the empire, including how the empire fostered economic growth through the use of currency and trade routes.

HSS ANALYSIS SKILLS:

HI 1 Students explain the central issues and problems from the past, placing people and events in a matrix of time and place.

PLAN

OBJECTIVE

Identify the equipment used to keep Roman soldiers safe and successful on and off the battlefield.

ESSENTIAL QUESTION

How did Rome become a mighty power in the Mediterranean?

Roman legionaries carried everything they needed to survive on and off the battlefield. Lesson 3.2 shows what Roman soldiers wore and carried, and explains the importance of these items to a soldier's survival.

BACKGROUND FOR THE TEACHER

Not all Roman soldiers were equally well equipped with gear and weaponry. Legionaries posted on the edges of the expanding Roman Republic often found themselves without the supplies they needed as they dealt with dangerous local peoples who were most likely unhappy about the presence of the legions. Like the soldiers of today, Roman legionaries spent their free time writing letters home, sharing details about their work and living conditions, and asking for care packages to be sent to them. Warm clothing and news from home were at the top of their lists.

DIGITAL RESOURCES NGLSync.cengage.com

TEACHER RESOURCES & ASSESSMENT

 Reading and Note-Taking

 Vocabulary Practice

 Section 3 Quiz

STUDENT RESOURCES

 NG Chapter Gallery

LEARN ABOUT HISTORY THROUGH OBJECTS

Ask students to form small groups and brainstorm a list of equipment and items a soldier, explorer, or survivalist would be likely to carry with them to travel on foot over rough terrain and to live outdoors. Reconvene as a class and ask each group to share their list. Use the group lists to create a master list on the whiteboard. Discuss the best way to transport the gear and the challenges this would pose. Then tell students they will learn about equipment that was vital to the survival of Roman soldiers. `0:05` **minutes**

TEACH

GUIDED DISCUSSION

1. **Describe** How were Roman helmets designed to protect a soldier's head? *(They were made of iron and designed to be similar to helmets worn by successful warriors from Gaul. They had a ridge along the forehead to protect the soldier from vertical sword slashes. They had a wide piece at the back to protect the soldier's neck. Wide flaps on the sides of the helmet protected the soldier's face, but allowed him to hear his superiors.)*
   ASK: What types of problems might Roman soldiers have had with their helmets? *(They were heavy because they were made of iron, which means they were probably uncomfortable. They may have made it hard to see.)*

2. **Draw Conclusions** What do the armor, weapons, and tools used by the Romans tell you about the success of their army? *(Responses will vary. Possible responses: The Roman soldiers had a wide variety of weapons, so they were probably able to adapt to many different challenges in battle. The details on the weapons, such as the engraving on the scabbard and dagger, make me think they took pride in creating well-made weapons. Pieces of heavy armor like the breastplate, shield, and helmet show that soldiers were well-protected as they went into dangerous combat, and that the Romans were fine crafters of armor.)*

ANALYZE VISUALS

Have students create a three-column chart for classifying the Roman artifacts into the following categories: staying warm, staying safe, and daily living, based on their function. (Or, as a class, brainstorm different headings that could be used to categorize the items.) Then have students sort the artifacts into the categories, writing each item in the appropriate column. End the activity by inviting volunteers to share their categories and discuss/debate any alternative categorizing. `0:15` **minutes**

Staying Warm	Staying Safe	Daily Living

ACTIVE OPTIONS

On Your Feet: Try It On Gather items similar to the armor and gear that Roman soldiers wore and carried, so students can experience how it would feel to wear and carry it. Here are some modern equivalents to traditional Roman gear:

- Steel breastplate = weighted vest, lifejacket, or backpack filled with 20 lbs. of weight, worn on the chest rather than on the back
- Helmet = catcher's helmet, football helmet, or motorcycle helmet
- Shield = 20-pound piece of plywood or flat stone
- Tunic = long t-shirt or short dress
- Javelin = long pole or dowel rod
- Sword = shorter pole or dowel rod
- Rucksack = backpack
- Hooded cloak = poncho or blanket
- Canteen = water bottle

Ask volunteers to wear and carry the equipment around and share their experience. Challenge them to crouch, hop, run, walk, and climb onto a chair carrying all of that gear to simulate what Roman soldiers would have done while they were on the move. `0:20` **minutes**

NG Learning Framework: Compare Soldiers' Gear

ATTITUDE: **Responsibility**
SKILLS: **Collaboration, Communication**

Pair students up to use a Venn Diagram to compare a Roman soldier's gear to a modern soldier's gear and explore the similarities and differences. Have each group present their similarity findings. `0:20` **minutes**

DIFFERENTIATE

INCLUSION

Identify New Words Pair special needs students with students at a higher proficiency level. Have them reread the lesson. Then have students identify three pieces of Roman equipment that were unfamiliar to them before they read the lesson. Have them use the two-column chart below to record each piece of equipment and its purpose.

Equipment	Purpose

PRE-AP

Research a Roman Weapon Have students research and report on one of the Roman weapons featured in the lesson. Possible concepts to research: how, when, and why the weapon was used, what it was made of, and what it was designed to do.

Press (mt) *in the Student eEdition for modified text.*

See the Chapter Planner for more strategies for differentiation.

3.3 Hannibal and the Punic Wars

To win in the big leagues, you've got to take on the champion. In 264 B.C., Rome turned its might against the Mediterranean superpower of Carthage. The two enemies fought a series of wars, called the **Punic** (PYOO-nihk) **Wars**, that lasted, off and on, for about 100 years.

MAIN IDEA

Rome and Carthage fought the Punic Wars for control of the Mediterranean Sea.

In the early battles, many of the Roman soldiers, who had never seen an elephant before, fled in terror.

War Elephants

Hannibal's war elephants were the "battle tanks" of the ancient world. Their size and power made them a terrifying and innovative battle weapon. Normally gentle creatures, however, the elephants had to be provoked and prodded to attack.

THE FIRST PUNIC WAR

The North African city of **Carthage** was immensely rich. It had grown from a Phoenician colony (*Punic* is Latin for "Phoenician") into a trading empire. Carthage had established colonies and trading ports around the western Mediterranean, and the city controlled valuable mineral resources in North Africa and present-day Spain. In time, Rome began to compete with Carthage for control of the sea.

The First Punic War broke out in 264 B.C. over the strategic island of Sicily (see the map in Section 3.5). The war was fought mainly at sea, but Carthage's navy was vastly superior to Rome's. After suffering a key defeat, Rome quickly built a fleet of 120 powerful warships that beat the Carthaginian navy in almost every battle. These victories allowed Rome to occupy the important islands of Sicily, Sardinia, and Corsica. In 241 B.C., Carthage surrendered to Rome. Its defeated general was Hamilcar Barca, the father of a young boy named **Hannibal**.

THE SECOND PUNIC WAR

When Hannibal was a child, he promised his father that he would always hate Rome. When he became a Carthaginian general, he made good on that promise. After Hannibal attacked one of Rome's allies in southern Spain, the Second Punic War began in 218 B.C. While the Romans planned a counterattack, Hannibal outsmarted them. He led about 60,000 soldiers and a herd of war elephants out of Spain and across the Alps to invade the Italian Peninsula by land. This astonishing action caught the Romans by surprise. Hannibal swiftly defeated the Roman army in battle after battle as he swept south toward Rome itself.

By 216 B.C., Hannibal was in southeast Italy, facing a huge Roman army at Cannae (KA-nee). Although outnumbered, Hannibal defeated the legions. His brilliant tactics are still studied at military academies today.

Rome fought on, however, and steadily wore down Hannibal's army. In 205 B.C., the Roman general Scipio (SIHP-ee-oh) was elected consul. He invaded North Africa in a plan devised to draw Hannibal out of Italy. It worked. Hannibal left Italy to defend his homeland. At the Battle of Zama (ZAY-muh) in 202 B.C., Hannibal and Scipio faced each other in a desperate fight. They were both brilliant generals, but after a long, bloody battle, Hannibal was defeated and later fled abroad to Asia Minor in present-day Turkey. In 201 B.C., the Second Punic War ended, and Rome once again ruled the western Mediterranean.

REVIEW & ASSESS

1. **READING CHECK** What events led Rome to fight two wars with Carthage?

2. **COMPARE AND CONTRAST** How were the two Punic Wars alike and how were they different?

3. **DRAW CONCLUSIONS** Why was Hannibal's trek through the Alps such an astonishing accomplishment?

6.7.3 Identify the location of and the political and geographic reasons for the growth of Roman territories and expansion of the empire, including how the empire fostered economic growth through the use of currency and trade routes.

HSS CONTENT STANDARDS:

6.7.3 Identify the location of and the political and geographic reasons for the growth of Roman territories and expansion of the empire, including how the empire fostered economic growth through the use of currency and trade routes.

HSS ANALYSIS SKILLS:

CST 1 Students explain how major events are related to one another in time;
CST 2 Students construct various time lines of key events, people, and periods of the historical era they are studying;
HI 1 Students explain the central issues and problems from the past, placing people and events in a matrix of time and place;
HI 3 Students explain the sources of historical continuity and how the combination of ideas and events explains the emergence of new patterns.

PLAN

OBJECTIVE

Explain the causes and impact of the First and Second Punic Wars on the Roman Republic.

ESSENTIAL QUESTION

How did Rome become a mighty power in the Mediterranean?

In 264 B.C., Rome challenged the mighty Mediterranean city of Carthage. Lesson 3.3 explains how the First and Second Punic Wars helped Rome expand its territory along the Mediterranean.

BACKGROUND FOR THE TEACHER

Many wonder how Hannibal was able to bring more than 30 elephants to Spain as he prepared to attack the Roman army in 218 B.C., and where those elephants came from. The only evidence that exists is a Carthaginian coin made around the time of the invasion. The coin shows one of Hannibal's elephants with large, flat, fan-shaped ears, a concave back, and a flattened forehead. These physical features indicate that Hannibal's elephants were probably small African elephants, not Asian elephants. There is evidence that this smaller African elephant subspecies lived in the Atlas Mountains of present-day Morocco and Algeria, which could be where Hannibal got them.

DIGITAL RESOURCES NGLSync.cengage.com

TEACHER RESOURCES & ASSESSMENT

 Reading and Note-Taking

 Vocabulary Practice

 Section 3 Quiz

STUDENT RESOURCES

 NG Image Gallery

POSE AND ANSWER QUESTIONS

Ask students if they think a parent's views and opinions are passed down to their children. Split students into small groups and invite them to discuss this question. Help guide groups to consider how it is possible for a parent's feelings about religion, politics, race, even sports teams to be passed down to a child, and why that happens. Tell them to consider this topic as they read about Hannibal and his father, the Carthaginian general Hamilcar Barca. As an extension, have interested students read the excerpt from Polybius's Histories in the **Primary Source Handbook** to learn more about Hannibal's character. `0:05` minutes

GUIDED DISCUSSION

1. **Identify** How did the Romans respond to their original defeat during the First Punic War? *(They strengthened their navy by building 120 powerful warships. This allowed them to beat the Carthaginian navy in almost every subsequent battle, and occupy the islands of Sicily, Sardinia, and Corsica.)*

2. **Draw Conclusions** Why might modern military academies study the strategies of Hannibal, a general who fought over 2,000 years ago? *(Hannibal led the Carthaginian army to defeat the strong and disciplined Roman army multiple times. He used creative battle tactics, including war elephants and surprise attacks, to outsmart and outfight the Romans. His strategies could be valuable and useful to the military forces of today.)*

SEQUENCE EVENTS

Work as a class to create a time line on chart paper or a whiteboard to document the main events involved during the wars between the Carthaginians and Romans. Be sure to include the following dates and events:

- 264 B.C. First Punic War breaks out over control of Sicily.
- 241 B.C. Carthage surrenders to Rome, who occupied the islands of Sicily, Sardinia, and Corsica.
- 218 B.C. Hannibal attacks Rome's ally in Spain—Second Punic War breaks out. Hannibal surprises the Romans by invading the Italian Peninsula by land using elephants. Romans are defeated.
- 216 B.C. Hannibal defeats Roman legions in Southeast Italy even though he was outnumbered.
- 205 B.C. Roman general Scipio invades North Africa to draw Hannibal back to his homeland.
- 202 B.C. Hannibal is defeated by Scipio in the battle of Zama and flees to present-day Turkey.
- 201 B.C. Second Punic War ends.

`0:15` minutes

On Your Feet: Card Responses Have half the class write 15 true-false or yes-no questions based on the lesson. Have the other half create answer cards, writing "True" or "Yes" on one side of the cards and "False" or "No" on the other side. Students from the question group should take turns asking their questions. Students from the answer group should hold up their cards, showing the correct answer. Have students keep track of their correct answers. `0:15` minutes

Critical Viewing: NG Image Gallery Invite students to explore the entire NG Image Gallery and create a Top Ten List by choosing the images they think are most representative of the Roman Empire. If possible, have students copy the images into a document to form an actual list. Then encourage them to select the image they like best and do further research on it. `0:10` minutes

STRIVING READERS

Write About It Tell students to imagine they are Roman soldiers seeing elephants for the first time in their lives during a battle against Hannibal's army. Have them write short narrative paragraphs explaining this experience. Then have volunteers share their paragraphs with the class.

PRE-AP

Sequence Events Have students complete the Sequence Events activity individually or in pairs, without any prompts or suggestions about identifying important events and creating a graphic organizer.

Press (mt) *in the Student eEdition for modified text.*

See the Chapter Planner for more strategies for differentiation.

ANSWERS

1. The events included an argument over possession of the island of Sicily and an attack by Hannibal on one of Rome's allies.

2. Rome won both wars. The first war was fought mainly at sea, and the second was fought primarily on land.

3. It was astonishing because he accomplished it in a cold winter with a large amount of men and elephants.

3.4 NATIONAL GEOGRAPHIC EXPLORER **PATRICK HUNT**

Searching for
Hannibal's Route

Patrick Hunt is a man on a mission to solve one of history's mysteries: Where did Hannibal cross the Alps? One of the most daring military maneuvers of all time, Hannibal's invasion of Italy in 218 B.C. required marching about 40,000 men and 37 elephants across these rugged mountains in winter. Hannibal didn't leave a map behind though. "For the last decade plus, we've been trying to pinpoint Hannibal's route," says Hunt. Because of his research, now he's close to an answer.

Patrick Hunt theorizes that Hannibal used the Col du Clapier-Savine Coche mountain pass, shown above, to cross the Alps into Italy.

MAIN IDEA

Geo-archaeologist Patrick Hunt is rediscovering the route of Hannibal's army.

HANNIBAL'S FOOTSTEPS

Patrick Hunt is a National Geographic grantee and the director of the Hannibal Expedition. Since 1994, he has used everything from ancient literature to satellite imaging to find the mountain pass Hannibal traveled. "It's like looking for a needle in a haystack," Hunt says, "but it's not just for the sake of mystery." The Alps were considered impassable in winter. Historians know Hannibal crossed them, but they don't know how because they don't know where. If someone were to find the route, historians might begin to understand how Hannibal achieved this amazing military feat.

The Roman historians Polybius (puh-LIH-bee-uhs) and Livy (LIH-vee) wrote accounts of Hannibal's campaign. Although they use few place-names, they describe the geographic features Hannibal saw and the distances he traveled each day. Hunt uses these clues to work out probable routes. "It's a bit like sleuthing," he admits. "We've been over close to 30 Alpine passes, mostly on foot, constantly comparing how they fit the descriptions."

A SCIENTIFIC APPROACH

Geo-archaeology applies earth sciences such as geography and geology to archaeology. These sciences are vital to Hunt's search because he has to factor in 2,000 years of change. Mountains may look different because of erosion; climate changes may have moved the snow line. "The first thing we do on-site is to examine the basic rock

types to check how stable the geology is," he says. "The more stable it is, the less likely it is to have changed much." It's a scientific approach and a physically challenging one, too. Several team members have suffered broken bones because of the treacherous working conditions.

Through a process of elimination, Hunt is now confident he knows most of Hannibal's route. The view from the summit of the Col du Clapier-Savine Coche fits perfectly with the descriptions in the ancient texts. "Now we're looking for physical evidence, and we are focused on the campsites," he explains. "Ash has a chemical signature that lasts over 2,000 years. We think we've found the ash of Hannibal's camps and have pinpointed a major summit campground. Now we're looking at stone deposits that may mark graves. An elephant burial would be fantastic!"

"Hannibal is very close to my heart," asserts Hunt. "He lost close to 40 percent of his men crossing the Alps. That would be unacceptable today, but Hannibal went on to defeat the Romans multiple times. This is a man who wins battle after battle but ultimately doesn't win the war."

HANNIBAL'S ROUTE

REVIEW & ASSESS

1. **READING CHECK** What tools is Patrick Hunt using to determine Hannibal's route through the Alps?

2. **INTERPRET MAPS** In what ways did the Alps both protect Rome and help Hannibal attempt a sneak attack?

3. **MAKE INFERENCES** What knowledge of geography and maps might Hannibal have had in order to believe his campaign over the Alps could be successful?

6.7.3 Identify the location of and the political and geographic reasons for the growth of Roman territories and expansion of the empire, including how the empire fostered economic growth through the use of currency and trade routes; HI 5 Students recognize that interpretations of history are subject to change as new information is uncovered.

HSS CONTENT STANDARDS:

6.7.3 Identify the location of and the political and geographic reasons for the growth of Roman territories and expansion of the empire, including how the empire fostered economic growth through the use of currency and trade routes.

HSS ANALYSIS SKILLS:

REP 1 Students frame questions that can be answered by historical study and research; **HI 1** Students explain the central issues and problems from the past, placing people and events in a matrix of time and place; **HI 5** Students recognize that interpretations of history are subject to change as new information is uncovered.

PLAN

OBJECTIVE

Describe how and why geo-archaeologist Patrick Hunt is tracing the route of Hannibal's army, and how geo-archaeology can help historians make sense of past events and individuals.

ESSENTIAL QUESTION

How did Rome become a mighty power in the Mediterranean?

Rome's defeat of Carthage and its brilliant general, Hannibal, were key to the success of the growing republic. Lesson 3.4 introduces National Geographic Grantee, Patrick Hunt, and describes his search for Hannibal's historic route through the Alps.

BACKGROUND FOR THE TEACHER

It's not easy to hike for miles over snowy mountains leading a herd of elephants, and National Geographic Grantee, Patrick Hunt, is determined to figure out how Hannibal did it. As a Stanford University professor and director of the Stanford Alpine Archaeology Project, Hunt has been exploring and excavating the Alps since 1994. His high-altitude archaeology explorations are done mostly on foot over treacherous Alpine terrain that often reaches elevations of 10,000 feet. Hunt's team searches for confirmation of Hannibal's route as well as signs of human modifications to the Alpine passes, both of which would aid in our understanding of this legendary military leader.

DIGITAL RESOURCES NGLSync.cengage.com

TEACHER RESOURCES & ASSESSMENT

 Reading and Note-Taking

 Vocabulary Practice

 Section 3 Quiz

STUDENT RESOURCES

 NG Chapter Gallery

ACTIVATE PRIOR KNOWLEDGE

Discuss what students know about the meaning of the prefix *geo-* and the job of an archaeologist. Invite student volunteers to use a dictionary or other resources as needed. Write the following questions on the whiteboard: What might a geo-archaeologist do that is different from a regular archaeologist? What might be the challenges of this field? Have students brainstorm and discuss answers, and record them on the whiteboard. Tell students that in this lesson they will learn about a geo-archaeologist's search to uncover Hannibal's route across the Alps. **0:05 minutes**

TEACH

STEM

GUIDED DISCUSSION

1. **Synthesize** Why is it important to historians to determine Hannibal's route through the Alps? *(Determining where Hannibal crossed through the Alps would help historians understand how Hannibal completed a journey considered to be impossible during the winter, and shed new light on this famous general's knowledge of geography and impressive military tactics.)*

2. **Describe** What types of physical evidence would confirm for Hunt and his team that Hannibal and his troops had passed through a specific region? *(Finding ash from campfires dating back to the time of Hannibal's crossing of the Alps would confirm where he and his army camped during their journey. Gravesites of people or animals, such as elephants, would also confirm the route.)*

ANALYZE VISUALS

Have students study the photograph of Patrick Hunt. Ask them the following questions about the photograph:

- Where was this photograph of Hunt taken? *(the Col du Clapier-Savine Coche in the Alps)*

- How would you describe the terrain shown in this photograph? *(rocky, uneven, grassy, mountainous)*

- How might the terrain have been different when Hannibal crossed through this region to surprise the Romans? *(It was winter when he crossed, so it would have been snowy and icy, hard to see, and hard to climb. Also, years of erosion have probably changed the landscape, altering the shape of the land and the mountains.)*

ASK: Does the photograph of this region remind you of anywhere you have been or seen? Have students offer locations with similar terrain or geography, and discuss the similarities and differences between the location shown in the photograph (the Col du Clapier-Savine Coche in the Alps) and the location they are thinking about. **0:15 minutes**

ACTIVE OPTIONS

On Your Feet: Hold a Press Conference Assign one third of the class the role of geo-archaeologist from Patrick Hunt's team and tell them they have just returned from an expedition through the Alps in search of evidence of Hannibal's path. Assign the remaining students the role of "reporters,"

and challenge them to write down three questions they'd like to ask the geo-archaeologist. The questions should primarily be based on information from the lesson, but may also include questions they have about Hannibal's route, geo-archaeology, or other related topics. Each reporter should then ask the geo-archaeologists a question, and the geo-archaeologists should respond. Encourage students to draw upon their knowledge from this lesson and the other lessons in the section. **0:15 minutes**

NG Learning Framework: Ask and Answer

ATTITUDES: Curiosity, Responsibility
SKILL: Communication
KNOWLEDGE: Our Human Story

Patrick Hunt is uncovering a centuries-old mystery. After reading the lesson, have students write down one question they would like to have answered about Hunt's work. Tell students to research their question and see if they can find an answer. If not, have them keep their question in a log that they can come back to later and see if they can find an answer then. **0:10 minutes**

INCLUSION

Watch a Movie If appropriate, show students the National Geographic documentary *Hannibal v. Rome* (or clips of it) to help students experience and understand the content in this lesson and subsequent lessons.

GIFTED & TALENTED

Investigate High-Altitude Archaeology and Geo-Archaeology Have students use the Internet to research the fields of high-altitude archaeology and geo-archaeology. (Or refer to the National Geographic book *Explore Archaeology*, which also includes material on high-altitude archaeology.) After taking notes and gathering information, have them create a Two-Column Chart to compare the two types of archaeology, noting their similarities, differences, objectives, tools, and challenges.

Press (**mt**) in the Student eEdition for modified text.

See the Chapter Planner for more strategies for differentiation.

ANSWERS

1. He is using everything from satellite imaging to ancient literature.

2. The Alps were high and hard to cross, which helped protect Rome. However, they also provided places for Hannibal and his men to hide before their attack.

3. He must have known that there were some passes through the mountains. He also must have known about weather conditions there to adapt to them.

3.5 Rome Expands

The geographic location of Rome made it the perfect place to begin building a Mediterranean empire. By 146 B.C., Rome had proved this point at the expense of its conquered neighbors. Its navy ruled the seas, its army dominated the land, and many once-great countries were now run by a Roman governor.

MAIN IDEA

Between 264 and 146 B.C., Rome's armies conquered a vast amount of land stretching from the Iberian Peninsula to Greece.

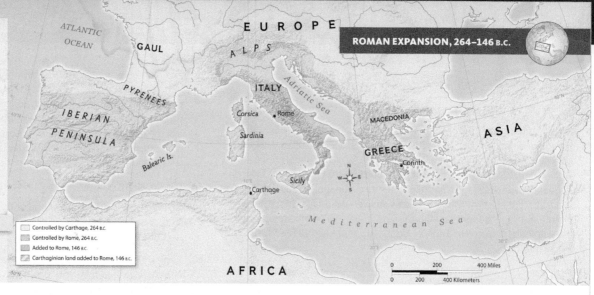

ROMAN EXPANSION, 264–146 B.C.

Legend:
- Controlled by Carthage, 264 B.C.
- Controlled by Rome, 264 B.C.
- Added to Rome, 146 B.C.
- Carthaginian land added to Rome, 146 B.C.

THE THIRD PUNIC WAR

The Catapult

The catapult was one of the Roman army's most effective weapons. It was capable of launching 60-pound rocks, long wooden beams, and even vats of fire. This powerful war machine relied on a system of tension and release to hurl missiles 500 to 1,000 feet across battlefields.

After the Second Punic War, Carthage focused on trade and began to grow very rich. This worried the Romans, who were still suspicious of their old enemy. The famous Roman statesman Cato the Elder visited Carthage and was alarmed by its wealth, which he believed would be used to fight Rome. Cato shared his fears with the Senate in a unique way. Whenever he spoke, whatever the subject, he always ended with the dramatic exclamation *"Carthago delenda est"* ("Carthage must be destroyed").

Roman leaders eventually ordered the city of Carthage to be abandoned. Bullied into a corner, Carthage declared war. After decades of conflict, Rome decided that only the total destruction of its old enemy would do.

In 149 B.C., Rome laid siege to Carthage, surrounding it and stopping its food supply. Roman soldiers battered the city with huge rocks hurled from catapults and then stormed its shattered walls. The starving defenders fought bravely, but the Romans' victory was inevitable—and their revenge was merciless. The Romans sold Carthaginian survivors as slaves and destroyed every building. Carthage ceased to exist. Carthage and its adjoining lands were renamed the Roman **province** of Africa. The Iberian Peninsula, which Carthage had controlled, eventually became the Roman province of Hispania.

THE MACEDONIAN WARS

While Hannibal was rampaging through Italy in the Second Punic War, Philip V of Macedonia launched the First Macedonian War against Rome. Because Rome's army was focused on Hannibal, Rome could not fight against Macedonia and was forced to make peace. However, after Hannibal's defeat, two legions of battle-hardened Roman warriors invaded Macedonia, starting the Second Macedonian War.

The legions were pitched against the Macedonian phalanx, a solid body of troops bristling with long spears. The phalanx was strong, but it lacked the flexibility of the legion—and this flaw proved decisive. Once past the spears, fresh Roman reserves would fight ferociously until they destroyed the enemy army. These tactics defeated Philip's army in 197 B.C., ending the war. Macedonia later became a Roman province. Rome also destroyed the city of Corinth and conquered Greece, turning it into a Roman province in 146 B.C.

Roman power now extended from the Iberian Peninsula to the islands of Greece. Control of this vast area made Rome the new superpower of the ancient world.

REVIEW & ASSESS

1. **READING CHECK** In what order did the events of the Punic and Macedonian wars occur?

2. **INTERPRET MAPS** How did the defeat of Philip of Macedonia help Rome dominate the Mediterranean?

3. **ANALYZE LANGUAGE USE** How does Cato's exclamation about Carthage convey the Romans' fear of their enemy?

6.7.3 Identify the location of and the political and geographic reasons for the growth of Roman territories and expansion of the empire, including how the empire fostered economic growth through the use of currency and trade routes; CST 3 Students use a variety of maps and documents to identify physical and cultural features of neighborhoods, cities, states, and countries and to explain the historical migration of people, expansion and disintegration of empires, and the growth of economic systems.

STANDARDS

HSS CONTENT STANDARDS:

6.7.3 Identify the location of and the political and geographic reasons for the growth of Roman territories and expansion of the empire, including how the empire fostered economic growth through the use of currency and trade routes.

HSS ANALYSIS SKILLS:

CST 3 Students use a variety of maps and documents to identify physical and cultural features of neighborhoods, cities, states, and countries and to explain the historical migration of people, expansion and disintegration of empires, and the growth of economic systems; **HI 1** Students explain the central issues and problems from the past, placing people and events in a matrix of time and place.

PLAN

OBJECTIVE

Explain the causes and impact of the Third Punic War and the Macedonian Wars on the Roman Republic.

ESSENTIAL QUESTION

How did Rome become a mighty power in the Mediterranean?

Through victories over Carthage and Macedonia, the Roman Republic tripled in size. Lesson 3.5 describes the events of the Third Punic War and the First and Second Macedonian Wars.

BACKGROUND FOR THE TEACHER

Beginning around 700 B.C., early Macedonia was populated by a group with unknown ethnic origins who called themselves Macedonians. Between 500 and 400 B.C., the Macedonians formed a unified empire and began speaking Greek. Under the rule of Alexander III, or Alexander the Great, Macedonia expanded its empire into Asia and up to the Nile and Indus rivers, conquering the Persian Empire. This made Macedonia the world's largest empire—even larger than the Roman Republic—spanning lands from Europe to North Africa and India.

DIGITAL RESOURCES NGLSync.cengage.com

TEACHER RESOURCES & ASSESSMENT

 Reading and Note-Taking

 Vocabulary Practice

 Section 3 Quiz

STUDENT RESOURCES

 NG Chapter Gallery

INTRODUCE & ENGAGE

COMPARE MAPS

Show students a current map of the Mediterranean region. Ask them to review the countries that border the Mediterranean Sea and nearby Atlantic Ocean. Remind them that while the physical features of this region have remained largely the same, the region has been organized into empires, republics, territories, and countries and controlled by many different groups in different ways throughout history. Next, preview the map in Lesson 3.5. Invite students to share observations about the names of the different regions during the time of Roman expansion. Finally, study the map key and draw students' attention to how the land changed hands during the period of Roman expansion. `0:10` minutes

TEACH

GUIDED DISCUSSION

1. **Sequence** How did Rome manage to destroy Carthage completely? (*First, Roman soldiers surrounded Carthage and stopped its food supply. Then the soldiers used catapults to batter the city and shatter its walls. The Romans fought the Carthaginians and sold any survivors as slaves. Finally, the Romans tore down all of the Carthaginian buildings and renamed Carthage the Roman province of Africa.*)

2. **Synthesize** How was the defeat of the Macedonians during the Second Macedonian War a victory for the Romans in many different ways? (*Defeating the Macedonians was a military victory for the Romans because they were able to overpower the Macedonian phalanx by recognizing its lack of flexibility. It was a geographic victory for the Romans because they gained Macedonia and Greece as Roman provinces and destroyed the city of Corinth. And it was a victory for the Roman Republic because it was transformed into the new superpower of the world.*)

INTERPRET MAPS

Have students examine the Roman Expansion, 264–146 B.C. map. Help students interpret the map. Explain and discuss the color-coded map legend. **ASK:** Which land was controlled by Rome originally, and where was this land located? (*Students should point to Italy.*) What does the purple color represent on the map? (*land that was added to Rome in 146 B.C.*) Who held most of the islands in this region prior to 146 B.C.? (*Carthage*) What were the largest areas of land that the Romans acquired in 146 B.C.? (*most of the Iberian Peninsula, Greece, Macedonia, and north into the Alps*) `0:15` minutes

ACTIVE OPTIONS

On Your Feet: Simulate a Battle Guide students to use plastic figures (such as army men) to simulate the invasion of Macedonia by Roman warriors at the beginning of the Second Macedonian War. Use one type or color of figures to represent the Roman legions and another type or color to represent the Macedonian phalanx. Help students simulate the strategic positioning and movement of each army, demonstrating how the phalanx was strong but less flexible than the legion. Once past the phalanx, simulate the defeat of the Macedonian army by the Roman legion. `0:10` minutes

NG Learning Framework: Geography and History

ATTITUDES: Curiosity, Responsibility
SKILLS: Collaboration, Problem-Solving
KNOWLEDGE: Our Living Planet

Have students review Lessons 3.3, 3.4, and 3.5 and examine the relationships between geography and history. Then ask them to work in groups of five to select a topic, research, and produce a visual representation of the relationship between geography and history. Examples might be: a diorama of Hannibal crossing the Alps, a drawing of soldiers using rivers for transport, or a map positioning catapults around Carthage. `0:10` minutes

DIFFERENTIATE

ENGLISH LANGUAGE LEARNERS `ELD`

Use a Term in a Sentence To demonstrate their understanding of the terms *province*, *phalanx*, and *catapult*, have students write two sentences using each word appropriately, and draw a picture to go with each word. If needed, show students photographs or illustrations to help them visualize the phalanx and the catapult. Have students at the **Emerging** and **Expanding** levels work in pairs. Have students at the **Bridging** level work independently.

PRE-AP `STEM`

Build a Catapult Have students do research to learn more about catapults, namely how they are designed, built, and used. Then place students in groups and tell them they will be designing and building a simple catapult. First, have each group sketch how their catapult will look. Then discuss the simple supplies needed to build classroom catapults, such as popsicle sticks or wooden dowels, paper cups, and string. After obtaining those supplies, allow students time to build their catapults and test them. Finally, organize a contest to see whose catapult can throw an object the farthest.

Press (**mt**) in the Student eEdition for modified text.

See the Chapter Planner for more strategies for differentiation.

REVIEW & ASSESS

ANSWERS

1. Hannibal invaded Italy. Meanwhile, Macedonia launched a war against Rome. Rome was forced to make peace with Macedonia. After Hannibal's defeat, Rome invaded Macedonia and defeated Philip's army. Rome ordered Carthage to be abandoned. Carthage declared war on Rome. Rome laid siege to Carthage and destroyed it. Rome destroyed Corinth and conquered Greece.

2. The defeat gave Rome control over more land along the Mediterranean.

3. It shows that the Romans still viewed Carthage as a serious threat to their republic.

The Republic in Crisis

Politics in Rome had often been crooked, selfish, and occasionally even violent. But after 133 B.C., the corruption and greed spiraled out of control and threatened the survival of the republic.

MAIN IDEA

The Roman Republic collapsed into civil war following a series of major events.

ATTEMPTS AT REFORM

Expansion following the Punic Wars brought great wealth to the Roman Republic, but this wealth was not evenly distributed among the people. Roman generals returned with great riches from the conquered territories. They used their new wealth to buy large areas of farmland, which drove many small farmers out of business. Unemployment and poverty became common in the republic, but the rich ignored the problems of the poor.

In 133 B.C., the tribune Tiberius Gracchus (ty-BIHR-ee-uhs GRA-kuhs) proposed a bill to take land from the rich and give it to the poor for farming. He knew the senators would reject his bill, so he had it approved by the plebeian assembly instead.

The Senate was furious at being bypassed. In response, members of the Senate arranged to assassinate, or murder, Tiberius. Ten years later his brother, Gaius (GAY-uhs) Gracchus, tried to introduce **reforms**, or changes to make things better, in the Senate. He, too, was assassinated.

In 107 B.C., the people elected the army general Marius as consul. As you have learned, he allowed landless citizens to join the army. When these soldiers retired, they relied on the generosity of their generals to support them, which made them more loyal to their commanders than to the state.

BATTLES FOR CONTROL

Marius's reforms did not help him when a general named Sulla rose up against him. Sulla was a brilliant general with political ambitions of his own. He marched his army into Rome, starting a **civil war**, or war between groups in the same country, and took control of the Senate. Marius fled, and Sulla set himself up as dictator of Rome. He created a list of his enemies and had many of them killed.

When Sulla left Rome to fight in the east, Marius led his army into Rome and attacked Sulla's supporters. Sulla invaded Rome a second time and regained control. By 81 B.C., he was declared dictator once again.

In the following decades, crises arose that forced the Senate to give extraordinary powers to two generals named Pompey (PAHM-pee) and Crassus. You have read about the slave rebellion that spread throughout the republic in 73 B.C. Pompey and Crassus combined their two large armies to put down the rebellion.

By 63 B.C., the republic was in chaos, and the consul Cicero argued strongly for reducing the powers of the army and restoring the government's system of checks and balances. However, his words failed to persuade Rome's leaders.

FACTORS THAT WEAKENED THE REPUBLIC
- Greed of the rich
- Inequality between rich and poor
- Failed reforms
- Ambitious generals and powerful armies
- Soldiers' shifting loyalty to their generals
- Civil war

Critical Viewing Sulla, shown here on horseback, never lost a battle. What qualities of a successful general are conveyed in this painting?

+ POSSIBLE RESPONSE

His men are gathered around him, which shows that they like and respect him. It also appears that he and his horse are unharmed, which indicates that he is a successful warrior.

REVIEW & ASSESS

1. **READING CHECK** What happened when Marius and Sulla fought over Rome?

2. **IDENTIFY MAIN IDEAS AND DETAILS** What problems led to civil war in Rome?

3. **FORM OPINIONS** Could Roman leaders have helped the republic survive? Why or why not?

6.7.1 Identify the location and describe the rise of the Roman Republic, including the importance of such mythical and historical figures as Aeneas, Romulus and Remus, Cincinnatus, Julius Caesar, and Cicero; HI 4 Students recognize the role of chance, oversight, and error in history.

315

PLAN

OBJECTIVE

Explain the factors that weakened the Roman Republic during the transition from republic to empire.

ESSENTIAL QUESTION

How did Rome become a mighty power in the Mediterranean?

A series of major events led to civil war as the republic began to fall apart. Lesson 4.1 describes these events and explains how they set the stage for the emergence of a strong leader.

BACKGROUND FOR THE TEACHER

Historically, dictators don't have a great reputation, and the verdict is still out among historians on whether Sulla helped or hurt the Roman Republic. As dictator of Rome from 81 to 79 B.C., Sulla held complete power over the Roman military, people, judiciary, and legislature. However, Sulla did use his considerable power to reform and reorganize the republic, restore power to the Senate, and increase the number of courts for criminal trials. He also instituted new laws against treason and for the protection of citizens.

DIGITAL RESOURCES NGLSync.cengage.com

TEACHER RESOURCES & ASSESSMENT

 Reading and Note-Taking

 Vocabulary Practice

 Section 4 Quiz

STUDENT RESOURCES

 NG Chapter Gallery

INTRODUCE & ENGAGE

USE A K-W-L CHART

Have students brainstorm the names of famous dictators and write them on the whiteboard. (Adolf Hitler, Josef Stalin, Saddam Hussein, and Kim Jung Un are possible examples.) Provide students with a K-W-L Chart. Have students think about what they know about dictators. Then ask them to write questions that they would like to have answered as they study the lesson. Allow time at the end of the lesson for students to fill in what they have learned. `0:10` minutes

TEACH

GUIDED DISCUSSION

1. **Identify Problems and Solutions** Which problem did Tiberius Gracchus try to address through his bill in 133 B.C.? *(Unemployment and poverty became common in the Roman Republic as wealthy Roman generals used their money to buy large areas of farmland, driving small farmers out of business.)* What was the problem with Tiberius's bill, and how did he solve it? *(The problem was that he knew the senators would reject the bill. Tiberius solved this by having it approved by the plebeian assembly instead. However, this solution led to his assassination, which was arranged for by the Senate.)*

2. **Make Inferences** While the Roman Republic was in crisis, it was controlled by powerful generals such as Sulla, Pompey, and Crassus. How might having military leaders in control of the republic have benefited Rome? How might it have been damaging? *(Having powerful military leaders would have been helpful during battles and conflicts against other civilizations. Generals like Sulla knew how to lead a large group of people and command their respect. However, having generals with so much control also weakened the republic because power was unbalanced and the army was too strong. Also, retired soldiers were loyal to their own generals rather than to the state, so the loyalty of the Romans was divided, which led to civil war.)*

ANALYZE CAUSE AND EFFECT

This lesson presents opportunities to discuss numerous cause and effect relationships that played a role in the crisis in the Roman Republic. Have students copy the chart below and work in pairs to identify and write effects. Ask for volunteers to share their results. `0:15` minutes

Cause	Effect
Rich generals bought up farmland.	Many small farmers were driven out of business.
Tiberius and Gaius Gracchus tried to introduce reform in the Senate.	They angered the senators and were assassinated.
Retired soldiers had to rely on the generosity of their generals after they retired.	They were loyal to their generals instead of to the state.
Sulla marched his army into Rome.	Civil war began between followers of Marius and followers of Sulla.
Pompey and Crassus were given extraordinary powers.	The slave rebellion was put down. The balance of power was tipped toward the army.

ACTIVE OPTIONS

On Your Feet: Jigsaw Divide the class into six groups. Assign each group one of the factors that weakened the Roman Republic:

- Greed of the rich and inequality of the poor
- Failed reforms
- Ambitious generals and powerful armies
- Soldiers' shifting loyalty to their generals
- Civil war

Have each group study their assigned factor and become "experts" on it. Then regroup students so that each new group contains at least one expert from the original groups. As a whole, each new group should discuss the six factors with each group member reporting on their area of expertise. `0:15` minutes

NG Learning Framework: Research Civil Wars

ATTITUDES: Curiosity, Responsibility
SKILLS: Collaboration, Communication

Have students work in groups to research the term *civil war* and do research on another example of a civil war, its causes, timeframe, and outcomes. Have the groups present their findings to the rest of the class. After the presentations, ask the class what similarities they noticed between the civil wars that were discussed. `0:30` minutes

DIFFERENTIATE

INCLUSION

Match Key Dates and Events Write the key dates and events presented in this lesson on separate note cards. Pair special-needs students with students of a higher proficiency level or with a teacher's aide to reread the passage aloud. Then have students match dates and events and arrange them in chronological order.

PRE-AP

Analyze Cause and Effect Have students complete the Analyze Cause and Effect activity, but do not provide them with the chart. Instead, have students work independently or in pairs to identify key conditions or events and determine their effects.

Press **mt** *in the Student eEdition for modified text.*

See the Chapter Planner for more strategies for differentiation.

REVIEW & ASSESS

ANSWERS

1. A civil war broke out.

2. Problems that led to civil war include an unequal distribution of wealth and the ambition of the generals Marius and Sulla.

3. Possible response: Yes, a strong leader who put the interests of the republic and the people ahead of his own ambition might have been able to provide the leadership necessary to reunite the republic.

BIOGRAPHY
GAIUS JULIUS CAESAR
100 B.C. – 44 B.C.

Julius Caesar is by far the most famous Roman. He overcame obstacles to success with his military brilliance, political cunning, and amazing speeches. When his power-sharing triumvirate collapsed, he led his army into Rome and was voted dictator for life by the frightened Senate. Caesar's rule marked the end of the republic.

- **Job:** Dictator for life
- **Education:** Taught by Greek tutors
- **Home:** Rome

FINEST HOUR
His conquest of Gaul was his most impressive military achievement.

WORST MOMENT
His enemies finally won when dozens of them joined in stabbing him to death.

FRIENDS

‹ Cleopatra VII, Queen of Egypt
- Commoners of Rome
- Veteran soldiers

TRIVIA
His most noted connection was with Egypt's last queen, Cleopatra VII. Both a love affair and a political alliance, their relationship was short lived. It began in 48 B.C. and ended with Caesar's assassination in 44 B.C.

Many movies and television series have focused on the life of Julius Caesar. Here, actor Ciarán Hinds portrays Caesar in the 2005 television series *Rome*.

THE FIRST TRIUMVIRATE

Generals Crassus and Pompey were elected consuls in 70 B.C. However, they soon made themselves unpopular with the Senate by seizing much of its power for themselves. As a result, the Senate turned to a rising political star, **Julius Caesar**.

Caesar had already proved himself as a politician and general. Pompey and Crassus used their influence to have him elected consul. In return, Caesar persuaded the Senate to pass Pompey and Crassus' legislation. This political alliance became known as the **First Triumvirate** (try-UHM-vuh-ruht)—a sharing of power between three people. The triumvirate lasted for about seven years but was always an uneasy alliance full of suspicions and jealousies.

The triumvirate granted Caesar a huge army, which he used to conquer Gaul (present-day France). This conquest extended Roman territory north and made Caesar very popular with the people. He also won immense wealth and the fierce loyalty of his soldiers.

END OF THE REPUBLIC

In 53 B.C., Crassus died, and the triumvirate collapsed. Law and order in Rome broke down. To end the chaos, the Senate appointed Pompey sole consul. This, however, resulted in a power struggle between Caesar in Gaul and Pompey in Rome. To regain control, Caesar led his army into Rome, sparking a bloody civil war. In August 48 B.C., Caesar defeated Pompey and declared victory.

Many Romans expected Caesar to restore the republic, but he had other ideas. Backed by his army, he ruled alone. Caesar declared himself dictator for life and introduced reforms that were popular with the people, such as creating jobs for the poor. But the Senate hated his reforms. On March 15, 44 B.C., a group of senators assassinated Caesar.

Another civil war followed Caesar's death. Fourteen years later, the Roman Republic transformed into a monarchy and, ultimately, an empire.

Et tu, and tu, and tu, and tu, and tu?

Julius Caesar was assassinated by about 60 senators under a statue of his old enemy Pompey. According to legend, as Caesar died, he cried out to a man who he had thought was his friend, *"Et tu, Brute?"* ("And you, Brutus?")

REVIEW & ASSESS

1. **READING CHECK** What were Caesar's major successes and failures?
2. **SUMMARIZE** Why was Caesar assassinated, and what happened after he was killed?
3. **COMPARE AND CONTRAST** How does Caesar's career as a general compare with his role as a leader?

6.7.1 Identify the location and describe the rise of the Roman Republic, including the importance of such mythical and historical figures as Aeneas, Romulus and Remus, Cincinnatus, Julius Caesar, and Cicero; 6.7.4 Discuss the influence of Julius Caesar and Augustus in Rome's transition from republic to empire.

HSS CONTENT STANDARDS:

6.7.1 Identify the location and describe the rise of the Roman Republic, including the importance of such mythical and historical figures as Aeneas, Romulus and Remus, Cincinnatus, Julius Caesar, and Cicero;
6.7.4 Discuss the influence of Julius Caesar and Augustus in Rome's transition from republic to empire.

HSS ANALYSIS SKILLS:

HI 1 Students explain the central issues and problems from the past, placing people and events in a matrix of time and place;
HI 2 Students understand and distinguish cause, effect, sequence, and correlation in historical events, including the long- and short-term causal relations.

PLAN

OBJECTIVE

Analyze the impact that Julius Caesar had on the Roman Republic and summarize his key achievements.

ESSENTIAL QUESTION

How did Rome become a mighty power in the Mediterranean?

The rise of Julius Caesar transformed Rome forever. Lesson 4.2 provides an overview of Caesar's accomplishments and explains how his assassination affected the republic.

BACKGROUND FOR THE TEACHER

Caesar's military victories and legislative reforms gained him admiration from his soldiers and appreciation from the Roman people, but he was not necessarily a beloved ruler. In spite of the surprising generosity Caesar showed toward the opponents he defeated in war, they still disliked him. In fact, his own Senate may have killed him in part because of his generosity toward the people he conquered. Caesar successfully instituted many reforms to benefit his people, at the risk of angering the Senate. He oftentimes made decisions without consulting the senators or asking for their support. During his rule, he made it easier for veterans and the poor to gain land, developed a police force, revised the calendar, eliminated the tax system, and demanded that the city of Carthage be rebuilt.

DIGITAL RESOURCES NGLSync.cengage.com

TEACHER RESOURCES & ASSESSMENT

 Reading and Note-Taking

 Vocabulary Practice

 Section 4 Quiz

STUDENT RESOURCES

 Biography

IDENTIFY CHARACTERISTICS

As a class, work to brainstorm a list of characteristics of powerful, successful leaders. Have students record their characteristics on sticky notes and post them on the classroom wall. Some examples may include: *respectable, intelligent, experienced, sympathetic, fair.* Tell students they will add to and/or modify this list as they read about Julius Caesar, one of the world's most famous leaders. **0:10 minutes**

TEACH

GUIDED DISCUSSION

1. **Analyze Cause and Effect** What were the effects of Caesar's conquest of Gaul? *(Rome's territory was extended north. Caesar became very popular with the people, and very wealthy. Caesar also secured the loyalty of his soldiers because of this victory.)*

2. **Compare and Contrast** Compare the Roman leaders Sulla and Caesar. How were they alike? How were they different? *(Sulla and Caesar were both self-appointed Roman dictators and legendary military leaders. They both came into power due to civil wars in Rome. They are different because Sulla rose up against the current consul, Marius, and Caesar instead formed a political alliance with the consuls, creating the First Triumvirate. Sulla had many of his enemies killed, but Caesar befriended the Roman people.)*

FORM AND SUPPORT OPINIONS

Pose the following question to students: There's no doubt that Caesar was one of the world's most famous leaders, but was he a great leader? Give students a few minutes to think about this question and jot down notes to support their opinion. Then form small groups and invite students to present and support their opinions. You may wish to form groups that contain students who have different views on Caesar's greatness. **0:15 minutes**

ACTIVE OPTIONS

On Your Feet: Create a Poster Encourage students to use their knowledge from the lesson to create a poster featuring Julius Caesar. They should focus on what they have learned about the ruler and his accomplishments, and should include a drawing of, or related to, Caesar. Before starting on the poster, students should plan out the content and do a rough sketch, asking themselves: what are the most important things to know about Julius Caesar? **0:20 minutes**

NG Learning Framework: Imagine You Were Caesar

ATTITUDE: **Empowerment**
SKILL: **Problem-Solving**

Invite students to revisit the biography of Julius Caesar in Lesson 4.2 and imagine they were in Caesar's place. **ASK:** How would you have done things differently from Caesar? How do you feel these changes would have affected both Rome and your life? **0:10 minutes**

DIFFERENTIATE

STRIVING READERS

Identify Main Ideas and Details Remind students that a main idea is a statement that summarizes the key idea of an article, speech, or paragraph. Details are facts, dates, events, and descriptions that support a main idea. Ask students to write one main idea and three or four details for the segment "The First Triumvirate."

Main Idea: The First Triumvirate was a sharing of power between three people: Caesar, Pompey, and Crassus.

Detail: The triumvirate lasted 7 years.

Detail: The three rulers were always suspicious of each other.

Detail: The triumvirate gave Caesar a huge army that he used to conquer Gaul.

Detail: The triumvirate ended when Crassus died.

GIFTED & TALENTED

Write a Biography Have students review the information about Julius Caesar presented in the text. Then instruct them to work in pairs to write a short biography of Caesar. Finally, have them do online research to find additional visuals to pair with their biography.

Press **mt** *in the Student eEdition for modified text.*

See the Chapter Planner for more strategies for differentiation.

REVIEW & ASSESS

ANSWERS

1. Major successes include conquering Gaul, beating Pompey in civil war, and introducing popular reforms. Major failures include angering the Senate, not restoring the republic, and getting assassinated.

2. He was assassinated because the Senate hated the reforms he introduced as dictator. After he was killed, civil war broke out.

3. He was a better general in that he was victorious and popular in that role; the same could not be said of him as a leader.

4.3 DOCUMENT-BASED QUESTION
The Assassination of
Julius Caesar

Caesar's assassination commanded much attention right after his death—and for many centuries after that. The ancient Romans commemorated, or remembered, the date with special coins. Historians who lived in later years tried to describe Caesar's death, and playwrights dramatized the event. We may never know all the details of his death, but the story and fate of a leader who became too hungry for power still fascinates us.

Critical Viewing The woman fainting in the painting is a soothsayer, or a fortune-teller, warning Caesar not to go to the Senate. What elements of this painting forewarn of a terrible event?

➕ **POSSIBLE RESPONSE**

The ominous sky and the fainting woman hanging onto Caesar's clothing are details that forewarn of a terrible event.

318 CHAPTER 11

DOCUMENT ONE
Primary Source: Artifact

Silver Denarius of Marcus Junius Brutus, Macedonia, 43–42 B.C.
This commemorative coin, called a denarius, shows the profile of Marcus Brutus, Caesar's former friend and assassin. The reverse features two daggers and a "cap of liberty." Underneath are the words EID MAR, or Ides of March. In the Roman calendar, the ides referred to the day that fell in the middle of the month.

CONSTRUCTED RESPONSE What did Roman leaders want people to remember about Caesar when they saw the commemorative coin?

DOCUMENT TWO
Secondary Source: Biography

from *The Lives of the Twelve Caesars*, by Gaius Suetonius Tranquillus, translated by J.C. Rolfe
In Volume 1 of his biography, written in the second century A.D., Suetonius describes Caesar's assassination by a group of senators who called themselves "the liberators."

CONSTRUCTED RESPONSE What does the violence of Caesar's death tell about the liberators' view of Caesar?

> When he saw that he was beset [surrounded] on every side by drawn daggers, he muffled his head in his robe . . . with the lower part of his body also covered . . . [H]e was stabbed with three and twenty wounds, uttering not a word . . . All the conspirators made off, and he lay there lifeless.

DOCUMENT THREE
Secondary Source: Drama

from William Shakespeare's *Julius Caesar*
In this excerpt from Act 3, Scene 2 of Shakespeare's play *Julius Caesar*, written in 1599, Mark Antony, a Roman politician and general, speaks at Caesar's funeral.

CONSTRUCTED RESPONSE According to Mark Antony, why was Caesar assassinated?

> Friends, Romans, countrymen, lend me your ears;
> I come to bury Caesar, not to praise him.
> The evil that men do lives after them;
> The good is oft interred [buried] with their bones;
> So let it be with Caesar. The noble Brutus
> Hath told you Caesar was ambitious:
> If it were so, it was a grievous [serious] fault,
> And grievously hath Caesar answer'd it.

SYNTHESIZE & WRITE

1. **REVIEW** Review what you have learned about the Roman Republic, Julius Caesar, and Caesar's assassination.

2. **RECALL** On your own paper, write down the main idea expressed in each document and in the photograph of the coin.

3. **CONSTRUCT** Construct a topic sentence that answers this question: What do the Roman leaders' actions and words tell about their opinion of Caesar?

4. **WRITE** Using evidence from the documents, write a paragraph that supports your answer to the question in Step 3.

🔖 6.7.1 Identify the location and describe the rise of the Roman Republic, including the importance of such mythical and historical figures as Aeneas, Romulus and Remus, Cincinnatus, Julius Caesar, and Cicero; 6.7.4 Discuss the influence of Julius Caesar and Augustus in Rome's transition from republic to empire; REP 2 Students distinguish fact from opinion in historical narratives and stories; REP 4 Students assess the credibility of primary and secondary sources and draw sound conclusions from them.

319

HSS CONTENT STANDARDS:

6.7.1 Identify the location and describe the rise of the Roman Republic, including the importance of such mythical and historical figures as Aeneas, Romulus and Remus, Cincinnatus, Julius Caesar, and Cicero;
6.7.4 Discuss the influence of Julius Caesar and Augustus in Rome's transition from republic to empire.

HSS ANALYSIS SKILLS:

REP 2 Students distinguish fact from opinion in historical narratives and stories;
REP 4 Students assess the credibility of primary and secondary sources and draw sound conclusions from them;
REP 5 Students detect the different historical points of view on historical events and determing the context in which the historical statements were made (the questions asked, sources used, author's perspectives); **HI 1** Students explain the central issues and problems from the past, placing people and events in a matrix of time and place.

PLAN

OBJECTIVE

Synthesize information about the assassination of Julius Caesar from primary and secondary source documents.

ESSENTIAL QUESTION

How did Rome become a mighty power in the Mediterranean?

The assassination of Julius Caesar was a turning point in the history of ancient Rome as it moved from a republic to an empire. Lesson 4.3 provides several interpretations of this event from primary and secondary sources.

BACKGROUND FOR THE TEACHER

Shakespeare's play *Julius Caesar* was most likely written in 1599 and is one of the famous playwright's three "Roman plays," all of which take place in ancient Rome. *Julius Caesar* tells the story of the conspiracy against Caesar, the dictator's dramatic assassination, and the defeat of his murderers at the Battle of Philippi. Like many of Shakespeare's plays, *Julius Caesar* was written and performed many years before it was published.

DIGITAL RESOURCES NGLSync.cengage.com

TEACHER RESOURCES & ASSESSMENT

 **Reading and Note-Taking**

 Vocabulary Practice

 Section 4 Quiz

STUDENT RESOURCES

 **NG Chapter Gallery**

PREPARE FOR THE DOCUMENT-BASED QUESTION

Before students start on the activity, briefly preview the three documents. Remind students that a constructed response requires full explanations in complete sentences. Emphasize that students should use their knowledge of Julius Caesar and ancient Roman history in addition to the information in the documents. `0:05` minutes

TEACH

GUIDED DISCUSSION

1. **Identify** What is shown on the silver denarius of Marcus Junius Brutus? *(A denarius is a commemorative coin. This one shows the profile of Caesar's friend and murderer, Marcus Brutus on one side, and two daggers, a hat called a "cap of liberty," and the words EID MAR, which means "Ides of March.")*

2. **Draw Conclusions** Can Shakespeare's play be considered a reliable source of historical information about Caesar's assassination? *(A play is a work of fiction, and fiction contains made-up characters, events, and information. Although Shakespeare's play may be about real people and real events, it is still fiction and cannot be considered a reliable source about an event in history. It is still useful, however, to read the play to see how Shakespeare and others interpreted Caesar's assassination.)*

3. **Describe** Which words would you use to describe Suetonius' retelling of Caesar's death? *(Responses will vary. Possible responses: dramatic, violent, scary, sad.)* **ASK:** Based on this excerpt from Suetonius' biography, who do you believe Suetonius sympathized with more: Caesar's assassins or Caesar himself? *(Responses will vary. Possible response: I believe Suetonius sympathized with Caesar more than the assassins. He draws attention to the brutality of the killing and makes you feel sorry for Caesar. At the end of the excerpt, he makes the conspirators sound very mean, sneaking off to let Caesar die alone.)*

PEER REVIEW

After students have completed the Synthesize & Write activity, allow time for them to exchange paragraphs and read and comment on the work of their peers. Guidelines for comments should be established prior to this activity so that feedback is constructive and encouraging in nature. `0:15` minutes

ACTIVE OPTIONS

On Your Feet: Three Options Label three locations in the room with the name of one of the documents featured in the lesson. Have students reread the lesson and walk to the corner of the room with the document that best helped support their understanding or further their interest in Julius Caesar's assassination. Have students who chose the same document discuss why they made their selection. Then have volunteers from each group explain what their document is, and offer some of the group's reasons for choosing that one. `0:20` minutes

NG Learning Framework: Write a Biography

ATTITUDE: Curiosity
KNOWLEDGE: Our Human Story

Have students select one of the people they are still curious about after learning about this individual in this chapter. Instruct them to write a short biography about this person using information from the chapter and additional source material. `0:10` minutes

INCLUSION

Work in Pairs Consider pairing students with disabilities with other students who can read the documents aloud to them. You may also want to give students the option of recording their responses.

PRE-AP

Research "Et tu, Brute" Ask students to research the famous phrase "Et tu, Brute" from Shakespeare's *Julius Caesar*. Encourage them to report on its meaning, context, and Shakespeare's controversial use of Latin, although it is likely that Caesar primarily spoke in Greek. Encourage students to consider and give examples of modern uses of this antiquated phrase.

Press **mt** *in the Student eEdition for modified text.*

See the Chapter Planner for more strategies for differentiation.

CONSTRUCTED RESPONSE

ANSWERS

DOCUMENT 1
Roman leaders wanted people to remember the fate of Julius Caesar when they saw the commemorative coin.

DOCUMENT 2
The violence of Caesar's death shows that the liberators heartily disliked Caesar.

DOCUMENT 3
According to Mark Antony, Caesar was assassinated because of his ambition.

SYNTHESIZE & WRITE

ANSWERS

1. Responses will vary.

2. Responses will vary.

3. Possible response: The actions and words of Roman leaders show that they did not have a good opinion of Julius Caesar.

4. Students' paragraphs should include their topic sentence from Step 3 and provide several details from the documents to support the sentence.

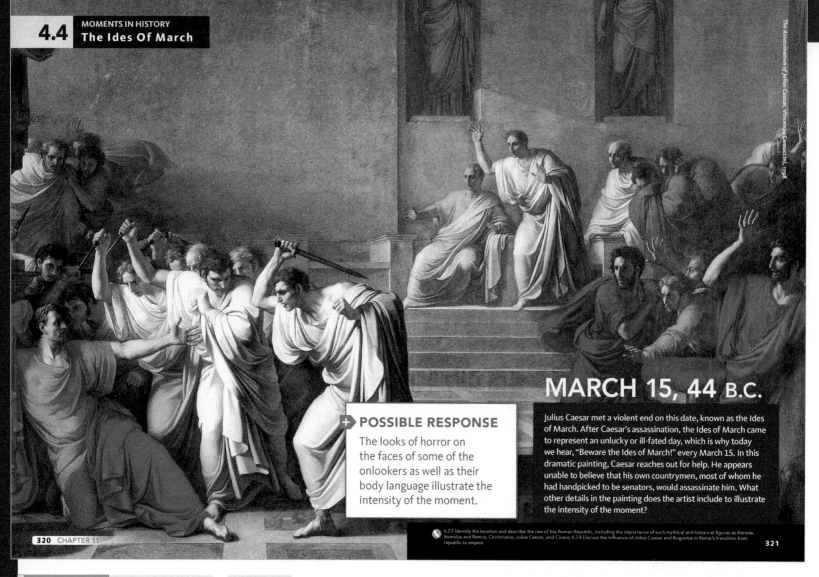

The Assassination of Julius Caesar, Vincenzo Camuccini, 1798

MARCH 15, 44 B.C.

Julius Caesar met a violent end on this date, known as the Ides of March. After Caesar's assassination, the Ides of March came to represent an unlucky or ill-fated day, which is why today we hear, "Beware the Ides of March!" every March 15. In this dramatic painting, Caesar reaches out for help. He appears unable to believe that his own countrymen, most of whom he had handpicked to be senators, would assassinate him. What other details in the painting does the artist include to illustrate the intensity of the moment?

➕ POSSIBLE RESPONSE

The looks of horror on the faces of some of the onlookers as well as their body language illustrate the intensity of the moment.

6.7.1 Identify the location and describe the rise of the Roman Republic, including the importance of such mythical and historical figures as Aeneas, Romulus and Remus, Cincinnatus, Julius Caesar, and Cicero; 6.7.4 Discuss the influence of Julius Caesar and Augustus in Rome's transition from republic to empire.

320 CHAPTER 11   321

PLAN

OBJECTIVE

Determine the impact of Julius Caesar's assassination on the Roman Republic.

ESSENTIAL QUESTION

How did Rome become a mighty power in the Mediterranean?

While Julius Caesar was assassinated because he held too much power, his death ironically paved the way for the end of the republic and the beginning of imperial rule. Lesson 4.4 provides one artist's interpretation of the events of March 15, 44 B.C.

BACKGROUND FOR THE TEACHER

Before the murder of Julius Caesar on March 15, 44 B.C., the word *ides* was simply a term used to mark the full moon on the Roman calendar and not anything to be concerned about. After Caesar's assassination, however, the Ides of March took on a new meaning. It became a reference to a day that brings with it drastic change. For the Romans, that Ides of March completely reshaped their civilization.

DIGITAL RESOURCES NGLSync.cengage.com

TEACHER RESOURCES & ASSESSMENT

 Reading and Note-Taking

 Vocabulary Practice

 Section 4 Quiz

STUDENT RESOURCES

 NG Image Gallery

INTRODUCE & ENGAGE

ANALYZE DATES

Briefly explain the concept of the Ides of March and its relationship to the anniversary of the assassination of Julius Caesar. Discuss how March 15 still represents an unlucky or ill-fated day, or a day associated with great change. Ask student volunteers to identify other dates that have a negative or a positive connotation or special significance attached to them. Post these dates on the whiteboard. Examples may include being born on a Friday the 13th or a good luck day such as March 17th (Saint Patrick's Day). You may even wish to talk about lucky or unlucky numbers, and why people perceive them that way. **0:05** minutes

TEACH

GUIDED DISCUSSION

1. **Analyze Visuals** Examine Camuccini's painting of Caesar's assassination. What do the onlookers' reactions indicate about the conspiracy to assassinate Caesar? *(Responses will vary. Possible response: Some onlookers seem to be supportive of what is taking place. Some seem shocked and horrified, like they didn't know the murder was going to happen. One onlooker even has his head covered, which might suggest that he is either terrified or feels guilty about what is happening, and therefore doesn't want to watch.)*

2. **Make Connections** Caesar's assassination on the Ides of March in 44 B.C. marked the start of the transition from the Roman Republic to the Roman Empire. What other examples of events can you think of that led to a new era or other type of significant change or reform? *(Responses will vary. Possible responses: The attacks on the World Trade Center on September 11, 2001, led to an era of heightened security and an escalated war on terrorism. Columbus's discovery of the New World began an era of conquest and exploration that led to the creation of the United States of America.)* **0:10** minutes

MORE INFORMATION   `STEM`

The Roman Calendar The first Roman calendar was based on the Greek lunar calendar. It had only 10 months and a year of 304 days and included terms like *Kalends* (new moon), *Nones* (first quarter moon), and *Ides* (full moon). This calendar was revised to add two months: January and February. In 46 B.C., Caesar again revised the calendar, creating a new system of dates called the Julian calendar. The Julian calendar had a 365-day year divided into 12 months of 30 or 31 days, with the exception of the shorter month of February. Interestingly, the Julian calendar wasn't completely adopted until A.D. 8, long after Caesar's assassination. The Ides of March remained the same as on the Roman calendar.

ACTIVE OPTIONS

On Your Feet: I See, I Read, And So On a large sheet of chart paper or a whiteboard, create a chart like the one pictured below. As a group, reexamine the painting of Caesar's assassination. Have volunteers describe something they observe in the painting and something they have read to draw conclusions about the assassination of Julius Caesar. Record their observations on the chart. **0:15** minutes

I See	I Read	And So

Critical Viewing: NG Image Gallery Invite students to explore the entire NG Image Gallery and look for other images of historical events. Have them choose one and write a paragraph that compares and contrasts it with Camuccini's depiction of the Ides of March. **0:10** minutes

DIFFERENTIATE

STRIVING READERS

Analyze Visuals Provide concrete questions to help students of different ability levels process and interpret the painting.

ASK: Which figure represents Julius Caesar in the painting? Do all of the senators shown in the painting appear to be part of the plot to assassinate him? If no, which ones do and which ones do not? How can you tell? Pick one of the men in the painting and describe how you believe he is reacting to the attack on Caesar. Encourage students to point to things they don't understand about the painting and help them frame questions about these details.

GIFTED & TALENTED

Act Out a Scene As a group, read Act 1, Scene 2 of William Shakespeare's play *Julius Caesar*, which contains the famous soothsayer's line about the Ides of March. Discuss the characters, setting, and any unfamiliar words or phrases. Then have volunteers do a dramatic reading of the scene.

Press **mt** in the Student eEdition for modified text.

See the Chapter Planner for more strategies for differentiation.

VOCABULARY

For each pair of vocabulary words, write one sentence that explains the connection between the two words.

1. patrician; plebeian (HSS 6.7)
   At first wealthy patricians held much of the power, but over time the plebeians, who made up most of Rome's citizens, could also hold office.

2. consul; veto (HSS 6.7.2)

3. republic; tribune (HSS 6.7.2)

4. aristocracy; patrician (HSS 6.6)

5. plebeian; tribune (HSS 6.7.2)

6. consul; dictator (HSS 6.7.2)

7. legionary; province (HSS 6.7.3)

8. civil war; reform (HSS 6.7)

READING STRATEGY

9. **ORGANIZE IDEAS: COMPARE AND CONTRAST** If you haven't already, complete your Venn diagram to compare and contrast the lives of rich people and poor people in the Roman Republic. Then answer the question.

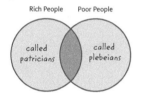

Rich People   Poor People

called patricians | called plebeians

How did the lives of the rich and poor differ in the Roman Republic? Did they share any similarities? (HI 1)

MAIN IDEAS

Answer the following questions. Support your answers with evidence from the chapter.

10. What geographic advantages helped Rome grow into a city? LESSON 1.1 (6.7.3)

11. How did different cultures help transform Rome from a small village into a city? LESSON 1.2 (6.7.1)

12. What was the purpose of the Twelve Tables? LESSON 1.3 (6.7.2)

13. What was the role of men in Rome's patriarchal society? LESSON 2.1 (HI 1)

14. Why were slaves important to the Roman economy? LESSON 2.2 (HI 6)

15. What factors made the Roman army successful? LESSON 3.1 (7.1.1)

16. What did Rome gain from its battles with Carthage during the Punic Wars? LESSON 3.3 (6.7.3)

17. What was the First Triumvirate? LESSON 4.2 (6.7.4)

CRITICAL THINKING

Answer the following questions. Support your answers with evidence from the chapter.

18. **ESSENTIAL QUESTION** Based on what you've learned about ancient Rome, what factors helped the republic develop into a mighty power? (7.1.1)

19. **DRAW CONCLUSIONS** Why did the Romans replace the position of king with two consuls and give each the right to veto? (6.7.2)

20. **COMPARE AND CONTRAST** How did the lives of the rich and poor differ in the Roman Republic? (HI 1)

21. **IDENTIFY MAIN IDEAS AND DETAILS** What details in the chapter support the idea that the Roman Senate had a great deal of power? (6.7.2)

22. **YOU DECIDE** Was Julius Caesar a great leader? Was he a dictator who abused his power? Did he fall somewhere in between? Support your opinion with evidence from the chapter. (6.7.1)

INTERPRET CHARTS

Study the chart comparing the governments of the Roman Republic and the United States. Then answer the questions that follow.

GOVERNMENT	ROMAN REPUBLIC	UNITED STATES
Executive Branch	Led by two consuls elected for a one-year term; led government and army	Led by a president elected for a four-year term; heads government and military
Legislative Branch	• Senate of 300 members • Senate advised consuls and set policies • Two assemblies made laws and selected officials	• Senate of 100 members • House of Representatives of 435 members • Laws approved by both groups
Judicial Branch	• Eight judges oversaw courts and governed provinces	• Supreme Court of nine justices • Supreme Court interprets the Constitution and federal law
Legal Code	• Twelve Tables basis of Roman law • Twelve Tables established laws protecting citizens' rights	• U.S. Constitution basis of U.S. law • Constitution established individual rights of citizens and powers of government

23. In what ways are the branches of each government similar? (HI 3)

24. What do the legal codes of each government protect? (6.7.2)

ANALYZE SOURCES

Read the following translation from one of the Twelve Tables. Then answer the question.

> TABLE VII: Rights Concerning Land
>
> The width of a road extends to 8 feet where it runs straight ahead, 16 round a bend . . .
>
> Persons shall mend roadways. If they do not keep them laid with stone, a person may drive his beasts where he wishes . . .
>
> Should a tree on a neighbor's farm be bent crooked by a wind and lean over your farm, action may be taken for removal of that tree.
>
> It is permitted to gather up fruit falling down on another man's farm.

25. Why do you think the Romans included so much detail in the laws of the Twelve Tables? (REP 4)

WRITE ABOUT HISTORY

26. **ARGUMENT** What arguments might a senator favoring Julius Caesar's assassination make? What arguments might a senator opposing his assassination make? Create an outline that lists points supporting each side. (6.7.4)

TIPS

- Take notes from the chapter about Caesar's actions as a ruler and the manner of his death.
- Consider who benefited from Caesar's reforms and who benefited from his death.
- Consider how the Romans might have felt when Caesar declared himself dictator for life.
- Use vocabulary from the chapter in your outline.
- List the points that support assassination in the first part of your outline. List the points that support opposition to the assassination in the second part.

VOCABULARY ANSWERS

1. At first, wealthy patricians held much of the power, but over time the plebeians, who made up most of Rome's citizens, could also hold office. (HSS 6.7)

2. In order to preserve a balance of power, Roman consuls had the right to veto each other's decisions. (HSS 6.7.2)

3. Because Rome was a republic, citizens were allowed to elect their own leaders, such as the tribunes. (HSS 6.7.2)

4. The Roman aristocracy was made up of wealthy patricians who owned most of the land. (HSS 6.6)

5. The plebeians elected tribunes to represent them in government. (HSS 6.7.2)

6. In times of crisis, Romans replaced the two consuls with a dictator who had complete control. (HSS 6.7.2)

7. Roman legionaries fought to take control of land that would become a Roman province. (HSS 6.7.3)

8. In the later years of the republic, attempts at reform backfired and led to civil war. (HSS 6.7)

STANDARDS

HSS CONTENT STANDARDS:

6.7.1 Identify the location and describe the rise of the Roman Republic, including the importance of such mythical and historical figures as Aeneas, Romulus and Remus, Cincinnatus, Julius Caesar, and Cicero; **6.7.2** Describe the government of the Roman Republic and its significance (e.g., written constitution and tripartite government, checks and balances, civic duty); **6.7.3** Identify the location of and the political and geographic reasons for the growth of Roman territories and expansion of the empire, includin=g how the empire fostered economic growth through the use of currency and trade routes; **6.7.4** Discuss the influence of Julius Caesar and Augustus in Rome's transition from republic to empire; **7.1.1** Study the early strengths and lasting contributions of Rome (e.g., significance of Roman citizenship; rights under Roman law; Roman art, architecture, engineering, and philosophy; preservation and transmission of Christianity) and its ultimate internal weaknesses (e.g., rise of autonomous military powers within the empire, undermining of citizenship by the growth of corruption and slavery, lack of education, and distribution of news).

HSS ANALYSIS SKILLS:

REP 4 Students assess the credibility of primary and secondary sources and draw sound conclusions from them; **HI 1** Students explain the central issues and problems from the past, placing people and events in a matrix of time and place; **HI 3** Students explain the sources of historical continuity and how the combination of ideas and events explains the emergence of new patterns; **HI 6** Students interpret basic indicators of economic performance and conduct cost-benefit analyses of economic and political issues.

READING STRATEGY ANSWER

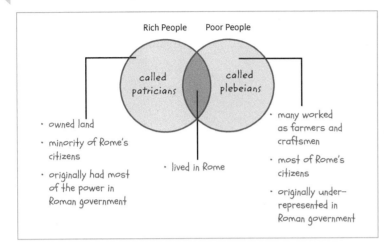

Rich People   Poor People

called patricians | called plebeians

- owned land
- minority of Rome's citizens
- originally had most of the power in Roman government

- lived in Rome

- many worked as farmers and craftsmen
- most of Rome's citizens
- originally under-represented in Roman government

9. Aside from the fact that they both lived in Rome, the lives of rich people and poor people varied greatly. The rich lived in fine houses and did a great deal of entertaining. They tended to be educated, and most of them were landowners. Rich people, or patricians, had a lot of control over Rome's original government, but there were fewer of them than poor people. The poor, or plebians, lived in small, simple homes and were mainly farmers and craftsmen. They were not likely to be educated, and although there were more plebians than patricians, plebians had little to do with Rome's original government. (HSS HI 1)

MAIN IDEAS ANSWERS

10. Rome's strategic location on the Tiber River near the Mediterranean Sea gave it access to valuable inland commercial routes and sea trade. The seven hills on which Rome was built protected it from enemies. The surrounding land supplied fertile soil, a good water supply, and a mild climate that could support Rome's population. (HSS 6.7.3)

11. Foreigners from many different places, classes, and professions settled in Rome, which helped the city grow in size and strength. Rome was most influenced by the Greeks and Etruscans. The Etruscans, who were expert engineers, transformed the village of Rome into a city by building streets laid out in a grid plan, brick houses, temples, and public buildings. (HSS 6.7.1)

12. The laws stated in the Twelve Tables protected all Roman citizens from injustice. The plebeians insisted that these laws be written down because the patricians often interpreted Rome's laws to favor their wealthy friends. (HSS 6.7.2)

13. In Rome's patriarchal society, men held all the power in public life as well as private life. Only men could vote or hold public office. The senior male was the head of every family, and he made all the decisions. (HSS HI 1)

14. Since slaves worked as manual laborers, skilled craftsmen, and even teachers and doctors, they were crucial to the Roman economy. In addition to their many abilities, slaves were also the largest class in Rome, but they had the fewest rights and worked entirely at the will of their masters. (HSS HI 6)

15. The Roman army was well organized and trained. Soldiers were organized into legions for maximum strength and flexibility. The command structure gave Roman generals control over large numbers of men. (HSS 7.1.1)

16. Rome gained total control of the Mediterranean and lands in northern Africa and Spain. (HSS 6.7.3)

17. The First Triumvirate was a political alliance between Crassus, Pompey, and Caesar. (HSS 6.7.4)

CRITICAL THINKING ANSWERS

18. A good geographic location, a multicultural population, a strong government with written laws, and a powerful army were all factors that helped the Roman Republic develop into a mighty power. (HSS 7.1.1)

19. The Romans replaced the position of king with two consuls and gave each the right to veto because they wanted to prevent any one leader or branch of government from becoming too powerful. (HSS 6.7.2)

20. The rich lived in luxurious country estates with slaves to serve them. They spent their free time conducting business, taking part in politics, or spending time on hobbies. The poor lived and worked on small farms or in overcrowded buildings in the city. They had to work for a living. (HSS HI 1)

21. The Senate advised the consuls and gave public speeches about important issues. Also, the fact that the Senate was able to assassinate people it didn't agree with shows that it had a great deal of power. (HSS 6.7.2)

22. Students' responses will vary. Students should clearly state their opinion regarding their view of Julius Caesar and support that opinion with evidence from the chapter. (HSS 6.7.1)

INTERPRET CHARTS ANSWERS

23. Similar to the government of the Roman Republic, the United States government is divided into three branches. Also, both governments put a system of checks and balances into place, assuring that one leader or branch of government wouldn't have too much power. (HSS HI 3)

24. Similar to the Roman Republic's Twelve Tables, the United States has a written constitution. Both the Twelve Tables and the U.S. Constitution are the basis of law and establishment of citizens' rights. (HSS 6.7.2)

ANALYZE SOURCES ANSWER

25. Students' responses will vary. Possible response: The Romans included so much detail in the rights so that they were clear to everyone and so no one could interpret them in a way that benefitted himself over others. (HSS REP 4)

WRITE ABOUT HISTORY ANSWER

26. Students' outlines should

- contain one claim for each side
- support each claim with clear reasons and relevant evidence from the chapter
- be written in a formal style
- include vocabulary words from the chapter

For more in-depth instruction and practice with the writing form, assign the Social Studies Skills Writing Lesson on writing an argument. (HSS 6.7.4)

UNIT RESOURCES

On Location with National Geographic Grantee Steven Ellis
Intro and Video

Unit Wrap-Up:
"Exploring Pompeii"
Feature and Video

"Rethinking Nero"
National Geographic Adapted Article

"Roman Frontiers"
National Geographic Adapted Article
Student eEdition exclusive

Unit 4 Inquiry:
Build an Empire

 Interactive Map Tool
Available at NGLSync.cengage.com

 **News & Updates**
Available at NGLSync.cengage.com

CHAPTER RESOURCES

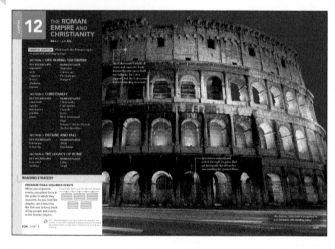

TEACHER RESOURCES & ASSESSMENT *Available at NGLSync.cengage.com*

 Social Studies Skills Lessons
• Reading: Sequence Events
• Writing: Write an Explanation

 Chapter 12 Answer Key

 Formal Assessment
• Chapter 12 Tests A (on-level) &
B (below-level)

 ExamView®
One-time Download

STUDENT BACKPACK *Available at NGLSync.cengage.com*

• **eEdition** (*English*)   • **eEdition** (*Spanish*)   • **Handbooks**   • **Online Atlas**

Chapter 12 Spanish resources, Guided Writing prompts, and Financial Literacy lessons are available online.

SECTION 1 RESOURCES

LIFE DURING THE EMPIRE

 Reading and Note-Taking

 Vocabulary Practice

 Section 1 Quiz

Available at NGLSync.cengage.com

LESSON 1.1 AUGUSTUS AND THE PAX ROMANA

• On Your Feet: Numbered Heads

NG Learning Framework:
Evaluate Augustus' Reforms

LESSON 1.2 GROWTH AND TRADE

• On Your Feet: Fishbowl
• Critical Viewing: NG Chapter Gallery

LESSON 1.3 ROMAN ENGINEERING

• On Your Feet: Three Corners

NG Learning Framework:
Research and Compare

LESSON 1.4 THE COLOSSEUM

• On Your Feet: Three-Step Interview

NG Learning Framework:
Write a Brochure

LESSON 1.5 VILLAS AND FRESCOES

• On Your Feet: Build a Mosaic

NG Learning Framework:
Write a Travel Guide

LESSON 1.6 POMPEII

• On Your Feet: Card Responses
• Critical Viewing: NG Chapter Gallery

SECTION 2 RESOURCES

CHRISTIANITY

 Reading and Note-Taking

 Vocabulary Practice

 Section 2 Quiz

Available at NGLSync.cengage.com

LESSON 2.1 THE ORIGINS OF CHRISTIANITY

- On Your Feet: Roundtable

| **NG Learning Framework:**
Write a Biography

LESSON 2.2 CHRISTIANITY SPREADS

 Biography
Paul

Available at NGLSync.cengage.com

- On Your Feet: Numbered Heads
- Critical Viewing: NG Chapter Gallery

DOCUMENT-BASED QUESTION
LESSON 2.3 NEW TESTAMENT LITERATURE

- On Your Feet: Think, Pair, Share

| **NG Learning Framework:**
Ask and Answer

LESSON 2.4 THE EARLY CHRISTIAN CHURCH

- On Your Feet: Research and Present

| **NG Learning Framework:**
Multimedia Presentation

SECTION 3 RESOURCES

DECLINE AND FALL

 Reading and Note-Taking

 Vocabulary Practice

 Section 3 Quiz

Available at NGLSync.cengage.com

LESSON 3.1 THE THIRD CENTURY CRISIS

- On Your Feet: Four Corners

| **NG Learning Framework:**
Support an Argument

LESSON 3.2 EASTERN AND WESTERN ROMAN EMPIRES

- On Your Feet: Team Word Webbing
- Critical Viewing: NG Chapter Gallery

LESSON 3.3 END OF THE WESTERN ROMAN EMPIRE

 Biography
Attila

Available at NGLSync.cengage.com

- On Your Feet: Fishbowl

| **NG Learning Framework:**
Write a Speech

SECTION 4 RESOURCES

THE LEGACY OF ROME

 Reading and Note-Taking

 Vocabulary Practice

 Section 4 Quiz

Available at NGLSync.cengage.com

**LESSON 4.1
LATIN AND LITERATURE**

 Active History: Interactive Whiteboard Activity
Analyze the Roots of Modern Languages

 Active History
Analyze the Roots of Modern Languages

Available at NGLSync.cengage.com

- On Your Feet: Word Race

LESSON 4.2 ART, ARCHITECTURE, AND LAW

- On Your Feet: Legacy Debate

| **NG Learning Framework:**
Compare Observations

MOMENTS IN HISTORY
LESSON 4.3 THE ROMAN AQUEDUCT

- On Your Feet: True-False
- Critical Viewing: NG Chapter Gallery

CHAPTER 12 REVIEW

STRATEGY 1

Turn Titles into Questions

To help students set a purpose for reading, have them read the title of each lesson in a section and then turn that title into a question they believe will be answered in the lesson. Students can record their questions and write their own answers, or they can ask each other their questions.

Use with All Lessons *For example, in Lesson 1.1, the question could be, "Who was Augustus and what was the Pax Romana?"*

STRATEGY 2

Play Vocabulary Tic-Tac-Toe

Write nine Key Vocabulary words on a tic-tac-toe grid on the board. Position the words on the grid so that an X or O can be written below each word. Player A chooses a word. If the player correctly pronounces, defines, and uses the word in a sentence, he or she can put an X or O in that square. Play alternates until one person has a row of Xs or Os.

Use with All Lessons *This game can also be played using teams. Divide the class into two teams, Team A and Team B, and alternate play until one team has a row of Xs or Os.*

STRATEGY 3

Play the "I Am . . ." Game

To reinforce the meanings of key terms and names, assign every student one term or name that appears in the chapter and have them write a one-sentence clue beginning with "I am . . ." Have students take turns reading clues and calling on other students to guess answers.

Use with All Lessons

Press *in the Student eEdition for modified text.*

STRATEGY 1

Provide Terms and Names on Audio

Decide which of the terms and names are important for mastery and have a volunteer record the pronunciations and a short sentence defining each word. Encourage students to listen to the recording as often as necessary.

Use with All Lessons *You might also use the recordings to quiz students on their mastery of the terms. Play one definition at a time from the recording and ask students to identify the term or name described.*

STRATEGY 2

Preview Content Using a Map

Use the following suggestions to preview content using a map:

- Point to the map key and discuss the ways it helps to explain the content shown on a map. Discuss that the different colors on the map represent different things.
- Remind students that they can identify continents and bodies of water by their labels on the map.
- Call out specific map features, such as rivers, mountain ranges, oceans, and countries, and ask students to point to them.

Use with Lessons 1.2, 2.2, and 3.2 *Invite volunteers to describe the visuals in detail to help visually impaired students see them.*

STRATEGY 1

Sequence Events

Remind students that they can look at dates and other signal words in a lesson to help them determine the order of events. Have students form groups after reading each lesson to discuss the organization of historical events and complete their time lines for the Reading Strategy. Provide the following sentence frames to help students at all proficiency levels participate in the discussion.

Emerging

First _____ happened. Then/Next _____ happened. Last _____ happened.

Expanding and Bridging

_____ happened first and then _____ occurred. The last thing to happen was _____ .

Use with All Lessons, All Levels

STANDARDS

HSS CONTENT STANDARDS:

7.1 Students analyze the causes and effects of the vast expansion and ultimate disintegration of the Roman Empire.

323C CHAPTER 12

STRATEGY ②

Pair Partners for Dictation

After students read each lesson in the chapter, have them write a sentence summarizing its main idea. Have students get together in pairs and dictate their sentences to each other. Then have them work together to check the sentences for accuracy and spelling.

Use with All Lessons, All Levels

STRATEGY ③

Use Visuals to Predict Content

Before reading, ask students to read the lesson title and look at any visuals. Then ask them to write a sentence that predicts how the visual is related to the lesson title. Repeat the exercise after reading and ask volunteers to read their sentences.

Use with All Lessons, All Levels *Provide the following sentence stem for students at the **Emerging** level: I think the visual is related to the lesson title because _____.*

GIFTED & TALENTED

STRATEGY ①

Teach a Class

Before beginning the chapter, allow students to choose one of the lessons listed below and prepare to teach the content to the class. Give them a set amount of time in which to present their lesson. Suggest that students think about any visuals or activities they want to use when they teach.

Use with Lessons 1.1, 1.2, 1.4, and 1.6

STRATEGY ②

Present a Museum Exhibit

Have groups of students prepare a museum exhibit featuring the ruins of Pompeii. Have them photocopy images of the ruins and write museum-style captions for each one. Once students have compiled their exhibits, have them place the images on the wall and present them to the class. Encourage students to introduce the exhibit with some background information about Pompeii. Tell them that they should also be prepared to answer any questions as their classmates view the exhibit.

Use with Lesson 1.6

PRE-AP

STRATEGY ①

Consider Multiple Sides

Tell students that historians have different opinions about why the Roman Empire came to an end. Have pairs of students research the issue and make a chart listing the different perspectives about the causes of the fall of the Roman Empire. Have students share and discuss their chart with the class.

Use with Lessons 3.1–3.3

STRATEGY ②

Debate Contributions

Have students research the many contributions of Rome to civilization. Tell each student to decide which contribution he or she believes had the greatest impact and make a list of the reasons why. Suggest that students hold a panel discussion to share and debate their decisions.

Use with Lessons 1.3, 1.4, 1.6, 2.4, and 4.1–4.3

12

THE ROMAN EMPIRE AND CHRISTIANITY

44 B.C. – A.D. 476

ESSENTIAL QUESTION What made the Roman Empire so powerful and long lasting?

SECTION 1 LIFE DURING THE EMPIRE

KEY VOCABULARY	NAMES & PLACES
aqueduct	Augustus
arch	Colosseum
emperor	Pax Romana
fresco	Pompeii
gladiator	
mosaic	

SECTION 2 CHRISTIANITY

KEY VOCABULARY	NAMES & PLACES
catacomb	Christianity
epistle	Constantine
missionary	Gospels
parable	Jesus
pope	New Testament
	Paul
	Roman Catholic Church
	Twelve Apostles

SECTION 3 DECLINE AND FALL

KEY VOCABULARY	NAMES & PLACES
barbarian	Attila
tetrarchy	Diocletian

SECTION 4 THE LEGACY OF ROME

KEY VOCABULARY	NAMES & PLACES
bas-relief	Latin
oratory	Virgil

READING STRATEGY

ORGANIZE IDEAS: SEQUENCE EVENTS
When you sequence events, you place them in the order in which they occurred. As you read the chapter, use a time line like this one to keep track of key people and events in the Roman Empire.

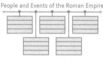
People and Events of the Roman Empire

 CST 1 Students explain how major events are related to one another in time; CST 2 Students construct various time lines of key events, people, and periods of the historical era they are studying.

The Colosseum is made of stone and concrete. Early Roman theaters were built into hillsides for extra support, but the Colosseum is a freestanding structure.

Spectators entered and exited through 76 gates that sat just inside the 80 arches surrounding the ground floor.

The Roman Colosseum was opened in A.D. 80 and is still standing today.

HSS ANALYSIS SKILLS:

CST 1 Students explain how major events are related to one another in time;
CST 2 Students construct various time lines of key events, people, and periods of the historical era they are studying.

TEACHER BACKGROUND

INTRODUCE THE PHOTOGRAPH

Have students study the photograph of the Colosseum in Rome. Explain that this is a modern photo of a structure built nearly 2,000 years ago. Point out that the very existence of these ruins is a testament to the lasting influence of the Roman Empire.

ASK: What type of modern structure does the 2,000-year-old Colosseum resemble? *(Possible response: a sports stadium)*

SHARE BACKGROUND

The Colosseum is one example of Rome's enduring legacy. Romans made significant contributions to art, engineering, and philosophy, and spread Christianity across the ancient world. All of these achievements shaped, and continue to shape, the world today. Ultimately, however, Rome's greatest lesson may not be in its achievements, but rather in its demise—arguably the greatest empire in history did ultimately come to an end.

DIGITAL RESOURCES NGLSync.cengage.com

TEACHER RESOURCES & ASSESSMENT

 Social Studies Skills Lessons
- Reading: Sequence Events
- Writing: Write an Explanation

 Formal Assessment
- Chapter 12 Tests A (on-level) & B (below-level)

 ExamView®
One-time Download

 Chapter 12 Answer Key

STUDENT BACKPACK

- **eEdition** *(English)*
- **eEdition** *(Spanish)*
- **Handbooks**
- **Online Atlas**

WHAT MADE THE ROMAN EMPIRE SO POWERFUL AND LONG LASTING?

Roundtable Activity: International Influence This activity will allow students to explore the question by categorizing types of power and types of lasting influence. Divide the class into groups of four or five students and assign each group a number. Hand the odd numbered groups a sheet of paper with this question at the top: What types of power can one country have over another? Hand the even numbered groups a sheet of paper with this question at the top: What types of lasting influence can countries have? The first student in each group should write an answer and then pass the paper clockwise to the next student, who may add a new answer. The paper should be circulated around the group until the time is up. Students may pass at any time. After ten minutes, ask for volunteers to read their group's answers to the class. **0:15** minutes

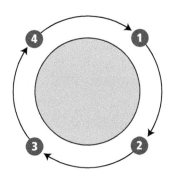

ORGANIZE IDEAS: SEQUENCE EVENTS

Remind students that sequencing events can help them keep track of new information. Model sequencing events by using the first three dates listed in the Key Dates table. Take the opportunity to explain the change between "B.C." and "A.D." For more in-depth instruction and practice with the reading strategy, assign the Social Studies Skills Reading Lesson on sequencing events.

People and Events of the Roman Empire

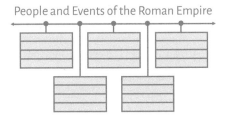

WORD SORT CHART

Divide the class into groups and have them copy each word from the list on a separate note card or slip of paper. Then have the groups discuss what they think the words might mean and sort them into the following categories: art, architecture, people, reading/speaking, government. Groups may also choose their own categories if they prefer. When groups have finished, ask them to explain their categories to the class.

aqueduct	emperor	mosaic
arch	epistle	oratory
barbarian	fresco	parable
bas-relief	gladiator	pope
catacomb	missionary	tetrarchy

KEY DATES	
31 B.C.	Augustus becomes emperor of Rome
c. 6 B.C.	Birth of Jesus
A.D. 79	Vesuvius erupts, destroying Pompeii
A.D. 80	Colosseum opens
A.D. 285	Diocletian divides Roman Empire into East and West
A.D. 312	Constantine converts to Christianity
A.D. 476	Last emperor of the Western Roman Empire leaves the throne

Augustus and the Pax Romana

When Julius Caesar was assassinated, Romans rolled their eyes and thought, "Here we go again." After decades of dictatorships and civil wars, they hoped for stability in the empire. They got it, but the republic was dead. A new type of leader was about to rule Rome for the next 500 years.

MAIN IDEA

Augustus transformed Rome from a violent republic into a peaceful empire.

A NEW EMPIRE

After Caesar's death, his heir, Octavian, found himself at the center of a deadly power struggle. At 18 years old, he had to kill or be killed. He survived and thrived. Octavian defeated his rivals, killed Caesar's assassins, and crushed revolts. He emerged victorious, immensely rich, and all-powerful. In 31 B.C., he became Rome's sole ruler. Four years later, the Senate gave him the name **Augustus**, or "exalted one."

Augustus was smarter than Caesar had been. He used his wealth and political skill to take control of the army and secure the people's support. He also won over the Senate, which awarded him dictator-like powers. He did all this while working within the law and appearing to uphold republican

ideals. The Senate, among other institutions, continued, but Augustus controlled its decisions. He was the supreme ruler in Rome, or its **emperor**. His powers were granted for life and could be passed to a successor, which was something that made the Romans uneasy. They didn't want to return to the harsh rule of kings. However, the people accepted Augustus because he moved slowly, carefully, and legally. Above all, he finally brought peace to Rome.

PEACE UNDER AUGUSTUS

Augustus' reign began the **Pax Romana**, or "Roman Peace"—200 years of peace and prosperity enjoyed across the empire. The Pax Romana was possible because Augustus tackled some long-standing problems. The poor thanked Augustus for guaranteeing free handouts of grain. Most of the people might not have noticed that Augustus' newly paid officials were improving government. However, everyone took immense pride in his transformation of Rome into an impressive capital with magnificent marble monuments. Meanwhile, Augustus' new laws were restoring order, and he actively encouraged art, literature, and education.

Augustus also cleverly prevented any threat that might have been posed by the army. He cut its size in half but kept out-of-work veterans happy with grants of land. Soldiers still serving were kept constantly busy defending and expanding the empire's frontiers. The army also now had standardized pay and conditions and a new oath of loyalty to the emperor himself.

The elite Praetorian (pree-TAWR-ee-uhn) Guard were the only soldiers stationed in Rome, and they were committed to upholding the emperor's authority. In addition, to protect the empire's coasts and shipping trade, Augustus created Rome's first permanent navy. All of these changes helped ensure long-term stability for the empire and for many Roman emperors to come.

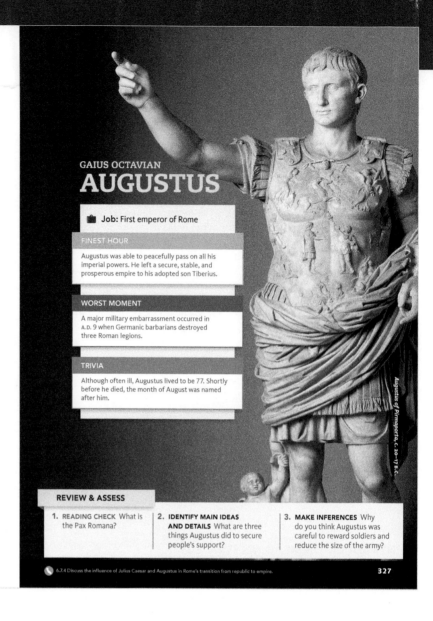

GAIUS OCTAVIAN
AUGUSTUS

💼 **Job:** First emperor of Rome

FINEST HOUR

Augustus was able to peacefully pass on all his imperial powers. He left a secure, stable, and prosperous empire to his adopted son Tiberius.

WORST MOMENT

A major military embarrassment occurred in A.D. 9 when Germanic barbarians destroyed three Roman legions.

TRIVIA

Although often ill, Augustus lived to be 77. Shortly before he died, the month of August was named after him.

Augustus of Primaporta, c. 20–17 B.C.

REVIEW & ASSESS

1. **READING CHECK** What is the Pax Romana?

2. **IDENTIFY MAIN IDEAS AND DETAILS** What are three things Augustus did to secure people's support?

3. **MAKE INFERENCES** Why do you think Augustus was careful to reward soldiers and reduce the size of the army?

6.7.4 Discuss the influence of Julius Caesar and Augustus in Rome's transition from republic to empire.

327

HSS CONTENT STANDARDS:

7.1 Students analyze the causes and effects of the vast expansion and ultimate disintegration of the Roman Empire.

PLAN

OBJECTIVE

Identify how Augustus secured and solidified his leadership of the Roman Empire and Rome's lasting legacy.

ESSENTIAL QUESTION

What was the power and enduring legacy of the Roman Empire?

Augustus was a smart and strong leader whose name is almost synonymous with the power and legacy of Rome. Lesson 1.1 discusses how he used his skills to transform Rome and Roman society.

BACKGROUND FOR THE TEACHER

During his reign, Augustus reorganized the government, reforming the administrative structures and beginning the first Roman civil service. These improvements fostered communication and trade and thus helped hold the empire together. He also embarked on a massive public works project of improving Rome. According to the historian Suetonius, Augustus boasted that he found the city built of brick and left it built of marble.

DIGITAL RESOURCES NGLSync.cengage.com

TEACHER RESOURCES & ASSESSMENT

 Reading and Note-Taking

 Vocabulary Practice

 Section 1 Quiz

STUDENT RESOURCES

 NG Chapter Gallery

CONDUCT A THREE-STEP INTERVIEW

Ask the class to think about how living in peace-time conditions for 200 years might affect the government. What are possible advantages and disadvantages? Have pairs of students take turns asking each other those questions. Then ask pairs to share their interview results with the class. **0:10** minutes

TEACH

GUIDED DISCUSSION

1. **Explain** What personal qualities did Augustus have that helped him secure power? (*Augustus was smart, decisive, and understood that happy people were much easier to manage than dissatisfied ones. His intelligence allowed him to understand and exploit the nuances of Roman government. By taking quick action against his enemies, Augustus was able to stop opposition before it ever got started. Finally, Augustus made the most powerful Romans—the senate and the soldiers—feel that he had their interests at heart. At the same time, Augustus brought peace to the empire, which made Romans from all ranks happy.*)

2. **Make Inferences** How might Augustus' support of art, literature, and education have helped to stabilize Roman society? (*By giving people outlets in other areas, they might be less likely to use their leisure time to cause unrest. Additionally, an educated population might better realize that a strong leader and a stable society brought many practical benefits, such as a reliable food supply and better overall infrastructure.*)

COMPARE AND CONTRAST

Ask students to compare and contrast the leadership of Julius Caesar versus that of Augustus. Suggest they use a Venn Diagram to list the similarities and differences. After students have finished their diagram, **ASK:** Why do you think the Romans, who had been living in a republic, allowed Julius Caesar and then Augustus to take over control of Rome? (*Possible response: Both were popular and successful generals who commanded the loyalty of the military and who delivered peace after years of civil war.*) **0:10** minutes

ACTIVE OPTIONS

On Your Feet: Numbered Heads Count students off in groups of four. Have the groups discuss how Augustus contributed to the longevity and lasting influence of the Roman Empire. Choose a number and have the student with that number from each group summarize their discussion for the class. **0:10** minutes

NG Learning Framework: Evaluate Augustus' Reforms

ATTITUDE: Responsibility
SKILLS: Communication, Collaboration

Invite students to revisit the biography of Augustus in Lesson 1.1 and his reforms once he was in power. **ASK:** Which reform had the most immediate effect? Which had the longest legacy? Pair up students and have them collaborate on answers to these two questions. Then combine two pairs of students into groups of four and have the small groups discuss their answers respectfully. **0:10** minutes

ENGLISH LANGUAGE LEARNERS ELD

Use Sentence Strips Choose a paragraph from the lesson and make sentence strips out of it. Read the paragraph aloud, having students follow along in their books. Have students close their books and give them the set of sentence strips. Students should put the strips in order and then read the paragraph aloud. Have students at the **Emerging** and **Expanding** levels work in pairs. Have students at the **Bridging** level work independently.

GIFTED & TALENTED

Research Roman Emperors Have students research an emperor who came after Augustus. Suggest they create a T-Chart to compare the two leaders as they did with Julius Caesar. Then suggest they develop a table or chart that effectively compares and contrasts the traits of all three leaders.

Press **mt** *in the Student eEdition for modified text.*

See the Chapter Planner for more strategies for differentiation.

ANSWERS

1. The Pax Romana refers to the 200 years of peace and prosperity enjoyed across the Roman Empire.

2. Augustus gave free grain to the poor and land and cash to veteran soldiers. He built monuments that turned Rome into an impressive capital of the empire.

3. An organized army has great power. By rewarding soldiers and reducing the size of the standing army, Augustus made sure this powerful group was happy and less of a threat to his leadership.

1.2 Growth and Trade

During the Pax Romana, you could travel easily and safely across the entire Roman Empire. By A.D. 117, that meant you could cross most of the known western world. It was a merchant's dream, and the economy boomed as Romans enjoyed goods imported from almost everywhere.

MAIN IDEA

As the Roman Empire expanded, trade became easier and the economy boomed.

IMPERIAL EXPANSION

Under Augustus, the Roman army became the mightiest in the world. Its relentless march expanded the empire's frontiers and cultural influence farther than ever before. Soldiers in forts on three continents—Europe, Asia, and Africa—protected the empire's frontiers from attacks by numerous enemies. The soldiers could be soaking in the rains of northern Britain, sweltering in the deserts of southern Egypt, battered by Atlantic winds in western Spain, or swimming in the waters of the Red Sea.

Some of the frontier military camps became permanent settlements. Soldiers stationed at these settlements often stayed in the community when they retired. This practice helped expand Roman culture and influence in the region.

The Roman Empire did not always rely on military conquest to expand its borders. If an area looked like it would be difficult or costly to conquer outright, Augustus would support a local ruler. In return, the territory would be required to provide the empire with military aid if needed. In this way, Augustus was able to expand the empire while saving the expense of an all-out war. This arrangement also made it easier for Augustus to invade the territory in the future if he felt that it was necessary.

A network of roads, bridges, and tunnels built by soldiers connected these far-flung frontiers. It allowed the army to march swiftly across great distances and quickly crush trouble wherever it arose. The roads helped the army keep order, but they also benefited everyone in the empire. The official mail service used the roads to keep information flowing across the empire. Rest areas and inns for overnight stays were built at regular intervals. Everyone in the empire could travel farther, faster, more easily, and more safely than ever before.

A BOOMING ECONOMY

These excellent roads also stimulated the economy by making it easy to transport and sell goods throughout the empire—basic goods as well as luxuries. Even citizens with limited incomes could afford African olive oil and Spanish salted fish. This flow of goods around the empire created a thriving economy as well as a sense of community. Roman merchants gained great benefits from all of this trade.

Rome's craftspeople produced beautiful objects that archaeologists have found as far away as Vietnam, but what flowed out of the empire most was money. The city of Rome itself was the main consumer of imports, or goods brought from other places. Rome especially needed food to feed its huge population. Agriculture, though still Rome's largest industry, was focused on luxuries such as fruit.

The most important Roman goods in terms of the quantity traded were wine, olive oil, and grain. Traders moved these bulky goods by ship before transferring them to slower ox-drawn carts. Adventurous traders looked far beyond the empire's borders. These merchants would sail east to India or travel the Silk Roads to China. There they sought to trade wool, gold, and silver for luxuries such as silks, spices, and gems.

The introduction of a standard currency, or money, throughout the empire made it easier to conduct trade as well as collect taxes and pay soldiers. The empire made coins called *denarii* (dih-NAIR-ee) out of silver and *sesterces* (SEHS-tuhrs) out of brass. Roman coins were accepted not only in the empire but also beyond. The expanded empire and the Pax Romana were certainly good for business.

ROMAN TRADE, c. A.D. 117

(map of Roman Empire showing trade routes)

Roman Empire at its height, c. A.D. 117
— Trade routes
— Slave trade

Goods traded
Gems | Spices
Grain | Textiles
Marble | Timber
Metals | Wild animals
Olive oil | Wine

0 300 600 Miles
0 300 600 Kilometers

REVIEW & ASSESS

1. **READING CHECK** What factors encouraged trade in the Roman Empire?

2. **INTERPRET MAPS** From which locations in the empire did Rome import grain to feed its citizens?

3. **ANALYZE CAUSE AND EFFECT** What were two positive effects of the flow of goods throughout the empire?

6.6.7 Cite the significance of the trans-Eurasian "silk roads" in the period of the Han Dynasty and Roman Empire and their locations; 6.7.3 Identify the location of and the political and geographic reasons for the growth of Roman territories and expansion of the empire, including how the empire fostered economic growth through the use of currency and trade routes; 7.1.2 Discuss the geographic borders of the empire at its height and the factors that

threatened its territorial cohesion; CST 3 Students use a variety of maps and documents to identify physical and cultural features of neighborhoods, cities, states, and countries and to explain the historical migration of people, expansion and disintegration of empires, and the growth of economic systems; HI 2 Students understand and distinguish cause, effect, sequence, and correlation in historical events, including the long- and short-term causal relations; HI 6 Students interpret basic indicators of economic performance and conduct cost-benefit analyses of economic and political issues. **329**

STANDARDS

HSS CONTENT STANDARDS:

6.6.7 Cite the significance of the trans-Eurasian "silk roads" in the period of the Han Dynasty and Roman Empire and their locations; **6.7.3** Identify the location of and the political and geographic reasons for the growth of Roman territories and expansion of the empire, including how the empire fostered economic growth through the use of currency and trade routes; **7.1.2** Discuss the geographic borders of the empire at its height and the factors that threatened its territorial cohesion.

HSS ANALYSIS SKILLS:

CST 3 Students use a variety of maps and documents to identify physical and cultural features of neighborhoods, cities, states, and countries and to explain the historical migration of people, expansion and disintegration of empires, and the growth of economic systems; **HI 2** Students understand and distinguish cause, effect, sequence, and correlation in historical events, including the long- and short-term causal relations; **HI 6** Students interpret basic indicators of economic performance and conduct cost-benefit analyses of economic and political issues.

PLAN

OBJECTIVE

Describe how trade contributed to Rome's strength and ability to endure over time.

ESSENTIAL QUESTION

What was the power and enduring legacy of the Roman Empire?

Rome controlled trade across the empire, making it easier for local and distant merchants to sell their goods. Lesson 1.2 discusses how Rome's efforts to improve trade led to a booming economy, which in turn made the empire more stable.

BACKGROUND FOR THE TEACHER

Trade was a very significant unifying influence in the early Roman Empire. While military campaigns brought new territories under Roman control, trade brought new goods into the empire. Equally as important, military expansion increased the cultural exchange between Rome proper and the frontiers. This financial and cultural interchange contributed to the empire's prosperity and stability over a huge geographic area. Stability allowed various communities and regions to begin specializing in the production of particular goods. Specialization, in turn, allowed for improved processes and products, and the development of new products altogether. Glassblowing, for example, developed during this period.

DIGITAL RESOURCES NGLSync.cengage.com

TEACHER RESOURCES & ASSESSMENT

 Reading and Note-Taking

 Vocabulary Practice

 Section 1 Quiz

STUDENT RESOURCES

 NG Chapter Gallery

INTRODUCE & ENGAGE

CONNECT TO MODERN LIFE

Ask students to consider what they know about trade in today's world: specifically, how do goods get to their home? Explain that modern transportation methods (planes, oceangoing ships, etc.) are the bedrock of international trade. However, in the Roman Empire, road building was the technology that allowed the empire to thrive. `0:10` minutes

TEACH

GUIDED DISCUSSION

1. **Explain** What was the relationship between the Roman army and trade? *(Possible answer: The Roman army built the roads as they conquered new regions. In effect, the army was opening new markets and providing access to those markets.)*

2. **Draw Conclusions** How do you think trade benefited smaller communities far from the empire's capital? *(Possible answer: Smaller communities located far from Rome itself would have benefited from trade in much the same way the capital did: access to a variety of goods was made possible by the security and speed of Roman roads. Additionally, communities located near desirable natural resources such as precious metals or good farmland, could afford to specialize in luxury commodities because they could get the staples needed to support the community through trade.)*

INTERPRET MAPS

Help students interpret the Roman Trade c. A.D. 117 map. Using the map scale, point out that the empire at this time covered tens of thousands of square miles. The ability to move quickly across such a large area was critical to the success of trade as well as the success of the empire itself. Also point out that the importance of trade by water is shown clearly on the map. `0:10` minutes

ACTIVE OPTIONS

On Your Feet: Fishbowl Have one half of the class sit in a close circle, facing inward. The other half of the class sits in a larger circle around them. Pose the question "What was the most important product that was imported to the city of Rome itself?" Students in the inner circle should discuss the question for 10 minutes while those in the outer circle listen to the discussion and evaluate the points made. Then have the groups reverse roles and continue the discussion. `0:20` minutes

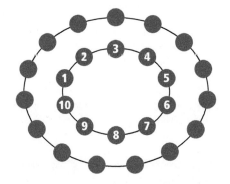

Critical Viewing: NG Chapter Gallery Ask students to choose one image from the Chapter Gallery and become an expert on it. They should do additional research to learn all about it. Then, students should share their findings with a partner, small group, or the class. `0:15` minutes

DIFFERENTIATE

STRIVING READERS

Summarize Read the lesson aloud while students follow along in their books. At the end of each paragraph, ask students to summarize what they read in a sentence. Allow them time to write the summary on their own paper.

INCLUSION

Describe Details in Maps Pair students who are visually impaired with students who are not. Ask the latter to describe the details in the Roman Trade map in detail for their partners. Then have the pairs of students work together to answer the map question in the Review & Assess.

Press **mt** in the Student eEdition for modified text.

See the Chapter Planner for more strategies for differentiation.

REVIEW & ASSESS

ANSWERS

1. Ease of transportation, security, and potential for profit were all factors that encouraged trade in the Roman Empire.

2. Rome imported grain from North Africa and Eastern Europe.

3. Two positive effects of the flow of goods in the Roman Empire were that goods became more affordable and trade fostered a sense of community across a large area.

Roman Engineering

Step outside your door and you'll see a road. Follow the road and you'll reach a city. In the city, you'll find large concrete buildings. Two thousand years ago, Roman engineers were perfecting the techniques that enabled the building of these "modern" constructions.

MAIN IDEA

The Romans were skilled engineers who helped transform how things were built.

ROMAN INVENTIONS

Arch
A curved structure over an opening

Vault
An extended series of arches

Dome
A rotated series of arches

ROADS

Before the Romans began building their network of roads, travel generally meant following dirt tracks. Rome's first great road was the Appian Way built in 312 B.C. It connected Rome with southern Italy. As the empire expanded, its armies built new roads back to the capital—which is where the saying "All roads lead to Rome" comes from.

The army used specialized tools and lots of human power to build roads. Soldiers marked the route, dug foundations, and built up the road with several layers of material. The center of the road was slightly higher than the edges, which helped rain run into drainage ditches.

Where possible, the soldiers built the road wide and straight, making marches shorter and easier. Engineers developed special techniques to overcome obstacles. Roads sometimes included bridges over rivers or tunnels through hills. Every mile a milestone marked the distance to major cities. By A.D. 300, the Romans had built about 53,000 miles of roads.

ARCHES AND AQUEDUCTS

Concrete is not usually very interesting, but at the time of Augustus it transformed construction. The Romans developed a new, stronger type of concrete and used it to build huge freestanding structures, like the Pantheon in Rome. This building, shown on the next page, was built in 27 B.C. as a temple to all the gods of ancient Rome.

Roman architecture was modeled on Greek architecture, but the use of arches, vaults, and domes created a distinctive Roman style. An **arch**, or curved structure over an opening, is strong and inexpensive to build. Lengthening an arch creates a vault, and joining a circle of arches at their highest point creates a dome.

Long stone channels called **aqueducts** (AK-wih-duhkts) carried clean water from hilltops into cities and towns. The engineers' precise calculations over long distances ensured a steady flow of water. Rome received 35 million cubic feet of water every day. While most of an aqueduct ran underground, sometimes huge arched bridges were built to carry the water across valleys. Many of these magnificent structures still stand as reminders of Roman engineering ability: building big and building to last.

+ **POSSIBLE RESPONSE**
Architects created an awe-inspiring mood, as if the opening provided a view to the heavens.

Critical Viewing This interior photo of the Pantheon shows the oculus—the opening in the center of the dome. What mood did Roman architects create using a tall dome with an opening at the top?

REVIEW & ASSESS

1. **READING CHECK** What techniques and constructions did Roman engineers develop?

2. **SUMMARIZE** What was the process Roman soldiers used to build roads?

3. **MAKE INFERENCES** How did aqueducts help unify the empire?

6.7.8 Discuss the legacies of Roman art and architecture, technology and science, literature, language, and law; 7.1.1 Study the early strengths and lasting contributions of Rome (e.g., significance of Roman citizenship; rights under Roman law; Roman art, architecture, engineering, and philosophy; preservation and transmission of Christianity) and its ultimate internal weaknesses (e.g., rise of autonomous military powers within the empire, undermining of citizenship by the growth of corruption and slavery, lack of education, and distribution of news).

331

HSS CONTENT STANDARDS:

6.7.8 Discuss the legacies of Roman art and architecture, technology and science, literature, language, and law; **7.1.1** Study the early strengths and lasting contributions of Rome (e.g., significance of Roman citizenship; rights under Roman law; Roman art, architecture, engineering, and philosophy; preservation and transmission of Christianity) and its ultimate internal weaknesses (e.g., rise of autonomous military powers within the empire, undermining of citizenship by the growth of corruption and slavery, lack of education, and distribution of news).

HSS ANALYSIS SKILLS:

HI 3 Students explain the sources of historical continuity and how the combination of ideas and events explains the emergence of new patterns.

PLAN

OBJECTIVE

Identify Roman contributions to structural engineering.

ESSENTIAL QUESTION

What was the power and enduring legacy of the Roman Empire?

Roman engineering was not just innovative; it solved practical problems with quality construction that was able to stand for thousands of years. Lesson 1.3 discusses Roman engineering techniques and ideas that are still used today.

BACKGROUND FOR THE TEACHER

The Pantheon is a remarkable building. That it is still standing is a testament to that fact. The dome was the largest in the world until the modern era. It is about 142 feet in diameter and about 77 feet tall. The oculus is 27 feet across and was the only means of lighting the interior. There are arches set on top of one another to support the dome inside the walls, which are 20 feet thick. The entrance has huge bronze double doors that are 24 feet tall—the earliest known examples of the style. Originally begun in 27 B.C., the structure was rebuilt between A.D. 118 and 128. However, the building has stood largely unchanged for well over 1,500 years. All of this gives the Pantheon a feeling of gravitas that can be felt as one gazes up at the beautiful light cascading down from the top of the dome.

DIGITAL RESOURCES NGLSync.cengage.com

TEACHER RESOURCES & ASSESSMENT

 Reading and Note-Taking

 Vocabulary Practice

 Section 1 Quiz

STUDENT RESOURCES

 NG Chapter Gallery

BRAINSTORM `STEM`

Ask students to think about what they already know about Roman architecture. Point out that it might be more than they think. As a class, brainstorm different buildings or architectural features they have seen that use Roman elements (e.g., stadiums, certain monuments, arched doorways, domes, vaults, etc.). Capture the ideas on the board and cross out those that don't apply. There should still be enough items to illustrate that Roman influence in architecture continues today. `0:05` minutes

TEACH

GUIDED DISCUSSION

1. **Make Inferences** Why would Roman ideas about architecture still be used today? *(Possible answer: Because they work—as is evidenced by the fact that buildings such as the Pantheon are still standing.)*

2. **Summarize** What are two examples of Roman engineering that we would consider public works today? *(Possible answer: Roads and aqueducts. Maintaining roads for transportation and delivering water to our homes are two Roman engineering feats that we use today and largely take for granted.)*

ANALYZE VISUALS

Review the Critical Viewing question for the image of the Pantheon with students. Explain to students that the oculus was intentional not only in function (to provide light), but in effect, too. The amount of light that comes in is limited and changes dramatically as the sun moves. This creates a dynamic environment inside the building and some architectural historians believe the Pantheon was one of the first ancient buildings that focused more on interior, rather than exterior, design. `0:10` minutes

ACTIVE OPTIONS

On Your Feet: Three Corners Post three signs in different parts of the room that read: *arch, vault,* and *dome.* Show students different examples of these architectural features and ask them to go to the sign matching the photo. `0:15` minutes

NG Learning Framework: Research and Compare `STEM`

ATTITUDE: **Responsible**
SKILL: **Observation**
KNOWLEDGE: **New Frontiers**

Have students do responsible online research to find photographs showing architectural features of ancient Roman buildings (e.g., arches, domes, vaults, etc.). Then they should find photographs of modern buildings where they observe the same type of feature. Have them present one of their comparisons to the class. `0:10` minutes

ENGLISH LANGUAGE LEARNERS `ELD`

Pose and Answer Questions Pair students at the **Emerging** level with English proficient students. Have students pose and answer questions that begin with the 5Ws. Remind them that *Who* refers to people, *What* to events, *Where* to places, *When* to dates or time, and *Why* to reasons. Invite students to share their questions and answers.

GIFTED & TALENTED `STEM`

Create Multimedia Presentations Instruct students to create a multimedia presentation about Roman engineering using photos, spoken words, and written text. The presentations should describe Roman buildings, roads, and bridges, and modern examples that show Roman influence. Invite students to share their presentations with the class.

Press **mt** *in the Student eEdition for modified text.*

See the Chapter Planner for more strategies for differentiation.

REVIEW & ASSESS

ANSWERS

1. Roman engineers developed roads, bridges, tunnels, arches, vaults, domes, and aqueducts.

2. Soldiers marked the route, dug foundations, and built up the road with several layers of material.

3. Aqueducts helped unify the empire by bringing water directly into major cities, which created a sense of familiarity and modernity across the empire.

The Colosseum

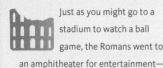

Just as you might go to a stadium to watch a ball game, the Romans went to an amphitheater for entertainment—but the "games" they watched were far more dangerous than the toughest sports we see today.

MAIN IDEA

The Colosseum was the stage for brutal games to entertain the Roman people.

A COLOSSAL STADIUM

The **Colosseum** in Rome was the world's largest amphitheater. The emperor Titus (TY-tuhs) opened it in A.D. 80. The building was designed to seat 50,000 spectators. An expertly engineered network of arches carried the structure's huge weight of stone.

Violent death was what Romans came to see at the Colosseum. In the morning, exotic animals hunted down defenseless criminals. After a break to clear the bodies, the main event began—the gladiators.

The **gladiators**, usually slaves or criminals, fought each other to the death. A successful gladiator might win fame, fortune, and his freedom.

The games, which could last 100 days, were usually paid for by the emperor. He hoped they would distract the poor from their problems.

Modern sports stadiums copied the Colosseum's design of tiered seating encircling a central stage.

1 DAY AND NIGHT
During the day, a huge canvas awning provided welcome shade, and a hanging light lit the action at night.

2 GOING UP
Underground elevators lifted the gladiators and animals into the arena.

3 BEHIND THE SCENES
Cages beneath the stage held the wild animals that would be featured in the games.

REVIEW & ASSESS

1. **READING CHECK** What were some of the games that took place at the Colosseum?

2. **MAKE CONNECTIONS** How did the Colosseum influence the design of modern sports stadiums?

3. **MAKE INFERENCES** Why do you think the emperor might have wanted to distract the poor from their problems?

6.7.8 Discuss the legacies of Roman art and architecture, technology and science, literature, language, and law; 7.1.1 Study the early strengths and lasting contributions of Rome (e.g., significance of Roman citizenship; rights under Roman law; Roman art, architecture, engineering, and philosophy; preservation and transmission of Christianity) and its ultimate internal weaknesses (e.g., rise of autonomous military powers within the empire, undermining of citizenship by the growth of corruption and slavery, lack of education, and distribution of news); HI 2 Students understand and distinguish cause, effect, sequence, and correlation in historical events, including the long- and short-term causal relations; HI 3 Students explain the sources of historical continuity and how the combination of ideas and events explains the emergence of new patterns.

PLAN

OBJECTIVE

Understand the role of the Colosseum in Rome and its lasting legacy.

ESSENTIAL QUESTION

What was the power and enduring legacy of the Roman Empire?

The Colosseum was a remarkable feat of engineering that was used for horrifically brutal entertainment. Lesson 1.4 shows the ingenuity—and endurance—of the building and describes some of the blood-sport distractions for which the Colosseum was used.

BACKGROUND FOR THE TEACHER

Also known as the Flavian Amphitheater, construction of the Colosseum was begun by the emperor Vespasian sometime between A.D. 70 and A.D. 72. The site chosen was on the palace grounds of former emperor Nero's estate. An extravagant artificial lake was drained and a theater for the public built in its place. The choice of construction site was symbolic—paving over the tyrannical ruler's home. However, the choice was also practical—nothing to tear down, just drain the lake and prepare the site for construction. The emperor Titus officially dedicated the Colosseum in A.D. 80, and Domitian completed final construction in A.D. 82.

INTRODUCE & ENGAGE

ANALYZE VISUALS

Have students review the Colosseum illustration and ask volunteers to point out interesting features of the structure. `0:05` **minutes**

TEACH

GUIDED DISCUSSION

1. **Identify** What was the main use of the Colosseum? *(to host a variety of violent sources of entertainment for the masses)*

2. **Draw Conclusions** What type of society do you think Rome had during this period? *(It would be easy to simply say that Romans were bloodthirsty and violent. Take the opportunity to remind students that judgments about any society based on a single aspect of that society are very likely to be inaccurate. While Roman citizens of the time did flock to see other humans torn apart by animals, this fact alone does not warrant any general statement about Romans.)*

MORE INFORMATION

Naval Battles It is sometimes said that the Colosseum floor could be flooded to hold mock naval battles along with other water-based shows. Archaeological evidence indicates that this may have been possible in the earlier years of the Colosseum's operation. However, later structural modifications to the building appear to have made flooding the amphitheater impossible. At the time, there were other venues in Rome that were built specifically to hold water for such shows. Thus, removing that ability from the Colosseum would have had less of an impact from an entertainment perspective.

ACTIVE OPTIONS

On Your Feet: Three-Step Interview Have student pairs interview each other about this topic: "Roman emperors used games in the Colosseum to distract citizens from other issues. Can you think of any other historical examples where governments or leaders have tried to distract their citizens?" Ask volunteers to report the results of their interview to the class. `0:20` **minutes**

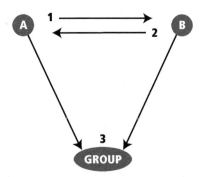

NG Learning Framework: Write a Brochure

ATTITUDE: Curiosity
SKILL: Communication

Have students select an element of the Colosseum that they are still curious about after exploring this lesson. Instruct them to write a short informational brochure about this element using information from additional source material. `0:20` **minutes**

DIFFERENTIATE

ENGLISH LANGUAGE LEARNERS ⬤ELD

Dictation Have students write a sentence summarizing the main idea of the lesson. Then have students get together in pairs and dictate their sentences to each other. Have them work together to check the sentences for accuracy and spelling. Provide the following sentence stem for students at the **Emerging** level: I think this lesson is about _____ .

GIFTED & TALENTED

Create Enhanced Illustrations Instruct students to use the book's Colosseum illustration as a foundation for their own, enhanced illustration. Based on reading and other research, have students add historically accurate elements to the illustration. Ask volunteers to present their work to the class.

Press (**mt**) *in the Student eEdition for modified text.*

See the Chapter Planner for more strategies for differentiation.

REVIEW & ASSESS

ANSWERS

1. Wild animals hunted criminals and gladiators fought each other to death in the Colosseum.

2. Modern sports stadiums copy the design of the Colosseum, including the concept of tiered seating surrounding a central stage.

3. Roman emperors might have wanted to keep the poor distracted so they would not cause trouble over issues the government should be handling, e.g., food shortages, public safety, or corruption.

1.5 Villas and Frescoes

Whether you rented rooms in a block of apartments or were rich enough to own a house, summer in the city of Rome was seriously hot for everyone. Summer also brought the risk of deadly diseases. There was no air conditioning to keep you cool and no antibiotics if you got sick. If you were really rich, you'd head for the fresh, clean air of your country home.

MAIN IDEA

Wealthy Romans lived in luxurious country houses called villas.

This detail of a Roman mosaic was uncovered at the ancient Roman town of Zeugma in modern Turkey. It is known as the "Gypsy Girl."

LIFE IN A ROMAN VILLA

Villas were large country houses designed to impress. Visitors entered through huge doors into a bright central courtyard. This was the main living room, where Romans would relax and entertain. They knew their guests would admire expensive features such as fountains, magnificent marble statues, and portraits of important ancestors. Many other rooms for working, eating, and sleeping stood beyond the courtyard.

Roman interior designers favored large rooms with high ceilings. Usually there were only a few pieces of very fine furniture, which were often beautifully carved or decorated. A very expensive design feature in Roman villas was mosaic (moh-ZAY-ihk) floors. A **mosaic** contains tiny colored stone cubes set in mortar to create a picture or design. A mosaic floor was a work of art, and keeping it clean was essential. Villas had many slaves who did all the work, from tending the fields to cleaning, cooking, and serving meals.

The Villa Adriana at Tivoli (TIH-vuh-lee) near Rome is a luxurious example of a country house that is still visible today. Built by the emperor Hadrian, it formed a vast group of 30 buildings, many copied and named after places Hadrian had admired on his travels. Covering an area equal to about 270 football fields, the villa included a theater, a stadium, baths, a library, and a palace.

FRESCOES

The Romans learned the art of painting frescoes from the ancient Greeks. A **fresco** is a picture painted directly onto the wall while the plaster is still wet. Rich Romans covered their walls with these paintings. Talented Greek artists were often employed to paint these frescoes.

Roman frescoes could show a variety of scenes such as landscapes, famous battles, and views of everyday life. Some pictures even included family members, posed to show off wealth and status. The Romans were great lovers of art, which they used to emphasize their position in society. To rich Romans, appearance was everything.

REVIEW & ASSESS

1. **READING CHECK** What kinds of luxurious features did the villas of wealthy Romans often have?

2. **MONITOR COMPREHENSION** For what purpose did wealthy Romans employ talented Greek artists?

3. **SYNTHESIZE** What was the relationship between art and status in Roman culture?

6.7.8 Discuss the legacies of Roman art and architecture, technology and science, literature, language, and law; 7.1.1 Study the early strengths and lasting contributions of Rome (e.g., significance of Roman citizenship; rights under Roman law; Roman art, architecture, engineering, and philosophy; preservation and transmission of Christianity) and its ultimate internal weaknesses (e.g., rise of autonomous military powers within the empire, undermining of citizenship by the growth of corruption and slavery, lack of education, and distribution of news).

HSS CONTENT STANDARDS:

6.7.8 Discuss the legacies of Roman art and architecture, technology and science, literature, language, and law; **7.1.1** Study the early strengths and lasting contributions of Rome (e.g., significance of Roman citizenship; rights under Roman law; Roman art, architecture, engineering, and philosophy; preservation and transmission of Christianity) and its ultimate internal weaknesses (e.g., rise of autonomous military powers within the empire, undermining of citizenship by the growth of corruption and slavery, lack of education, and distribution of news).

PLAN

OBJECTIVE

Recognize what can be learned about Romans through their art and architecture.

ESSENTIAL QUESTION

What was the power and enduring legacy of the Roman Empire?

Mosaics and frescoes from the Roman Empire draw us into the world of the Romans. Lesson 1.5 describes how the culture of wealthy Romans is kept alive today through their homes and artwork.

BACKGROUND FOR THE TEACHER

One school of thought holds that Roman homes were as much the owner's place of business as they were private residences. The home was a private, social, and commercial space. As a result, Romans decorated their homes as much to make a statement as they did to please their own eye. Mosaics, by their nature, are more abundant and accessible to modern researchers. Mosaics provide a wealth of material from which to study Roman living spaces and indeed Roman culture itself. How and where mosaics were placed in a particular floor plan can reveal much about the owner and the community.

DIGITAL RESOURCES NGLSync.cengage.com

TEACHER RESOURCES & ASSESSMENT

 Reading and Note-Taking

 Vocabulary Practice

 Section 1 Quiz

STUDENT RESOURCES

 NG Chapter Gallery

DISCUSS ART AS HISTORY

Ask students to think about what is hanging on their walls at home. Now ask them to consider what a stranger might learn about them simply by looking at their walls. This is part of what historians and archaeologists try to do. They examine what a person or culture has left behind, including their art, and try to figure out what can be learned about the people and the time in which they lived. **0:10** minutes

TEACH

GUIDED DISCUSSION

1. **Make Inferences** Why might there be more Roman mosaics than other types of Roman art? *(It may be that the way mosaics were created allowed them to hold up better over time than other types of art.)*

2. **Draw Conclusions** Why are mosaics and frescoes a valuable resource for studying ancient Rome? *(Roman mosaics and frescoes are valuable for studying the culture because they were created deliberately for a purpose. Using these artworks in conjunction with other clues can help researchers understand the purpose and meaning behind the art, which can lead to other insights about Roman culture.)*

ANALYZE VISUALS

Have students examine the mosaic called "The Gypsy Girl." Point out that the artist created an image by taking colored rocks and arranging them in a certain way—difficult and time consuming. Ask them to point to one detail they find particularly interesting.

(Possible answers: the color around the eyes possibly indicating makeup, or the single white stone in the iris that shows a reflection of light) **0:10** minutes

ACTIVE OPTIONS

On Your Feet: Build a Mosaic Challenge students to build a mosaic of their own. Bring colored pieces (stones, tile scraps, buttons, candy, pushpins, etc.) and have groups work together to create a mosaic. After they finish, ask students how difficult it was and how long it might take to cover an entire floor. **0:20** minutes

NG Learning Framework: Write a Travel Guide

ATTITUDE: Curiosity
SKILLS: Collaboration, Communication

Have students still curious about Roman villas form a group to research the Villa Adriana at Tivoli. Instruct them to collaborate on writing a travel guide about the site using information from the chapter and additional source material. They can present their work to the class. **0:20** minutes

ENGLISH LANGUAGE LEARNERS **ELD**

Read in Pairs Pair English language learners at all proficiency levels with native English speakers and have them read the lesson together. Instruct the native speakers to pause whenever they encounter a word or sentence construction that is confusing to their partners. Suggest that the native speakers point out context clues to help their partners understand the meanings of unfamiliar terms. Encourage English language learners to restate sentences in their own words.

PRE-AP

Write Dialogue Assign small groups to research and write a possible dialogue between a Roman homeowner and a friend that describes a particular choice of mosaic and its intended location in his home.

Press **(mt)** *in the Student eEdition for modified text.*

See the Chapter Planner for more strategies for differentiation.

REVIEW & ASSESS

ANSWERS

1. The villas of wealthy Romans often had fountains, magnificent marble statues, and portraits of important ancestors.

2. Wealthy Romans employed talented Greek artists to paint frescoes on the walls of their villas.

3. Art and status were closely linked. Art was used to illustrate and emphasize one's position in society.

1.6 Pompeii

As dawn broke on August 24, A.D. 79, the citizens of **Pompeii** (pahm-PAY) rolled out of bed and dressed for another day. Around noon, a dog was chained to a post, a crate of new pottery waited to be unpacked, and a kettle was filled with water. Then disaster struck. Within days, the whole city became a "living" history—entombed in ash for 1,900 years.

MAIN IDEA

The ruins and remains of Pompeii provide insight into everyday Roman life.

This man died fleeing the eruption of Mount Vesuvius, which rises in the background. Pompeians' final moments were preserved by the ash from the volcano and then revealed using plaster casts.

MODERN VESUVIUS

Mount Vesuvius is still an active volcano, and about 2.4 million people live in nearby Naples and its suburbs.

Vesuvius has erupted several times since the destruction of Pompeii. The last eruption was in 1944. Experts believe it is not a question of *if* the volcano will erupt again, but *when*.

DISASTER STRIKES

Pompeii was an average city resting in the shadow of Mount Vesuvius (vuh-SOO-vee-uhs), a volcano on Italy's western coast. The paved streets of the city followed an orderly pattern, and citizens there had all the civic comforts expected. Some 20,000 people worked, played, ate, slept, and lived within Pompeii's city walls until the afternoon of August 24, A.D. 79.

The Roman writer Pliny the Younger was near Pompeii that day. He had once described the city as "one of the loveliest places on Earth." After the events that occurred in Pompeii, he described a nightmare.

A violent explosion brought the city to a standstill. Pliny watched in horror as Mount Vesuvius erupted, shooting gas mixed with rock and ash high into the sky and creating an immense black cloud that blocked out the sun. Panic-stricken citizens fled as ash rained down.

As lava crept toward the city, fires raged and buildings collapsed. A vast volcanic ash cloud swept in to suffocate the city, burying its people and their possessions nearly 25 feet deep. A cloud of poisonous gas overtook and killed anyone who had not yet escaped. Over the next few days, lightning, earthquakes, and tidal waves followed. Finally after three days, Vesuvius went quiet—as silent as the deserted city of Pompeii.

A CITY PRESERVED

The volcanic ash that buried Pompeii also helped preserve its contents. The city's ruins were first discovered in the late 1500s. By 1861, archaeologists began carefully uncovering and working to protect their extraordinary find. Removing the ash, the scientists found houses, shops, and public buildings that contained mosaics, frescoes, and even graffiti. Many of the items had obviously been abandoned suddenly, in the first moments of the eruption. These artifacts offer a revealing glimpse into everyday Roman life. The ash preserved items such as leather shoes, wooden furniture, food, and a library of scrolls.

The ash also preserved some of its victims. It hardened around the bodies. Over time the bodies decayed and left behind an empty space. By pouring plaster into these spaces, archaeologists created exact casts of people, animals, and plants at their moment of death. All the discoveries are moving reminders of how suddenly death came to the city of Pompeii and froze it in time under a blanket of ash.

REVIEW & ASSESS

1. **READING CHECK** What items in Pompeii were preserved after the eruption?

2. **SEQUENCE EVENTS** What was the order of events that occurred in Pompeii on August 24, A.D. 79?

3. **ANALYZE CAUSE AND EFFECT** How were the ruins of Pompeii preserved?

CST 1 Students explain how major events are related to one another in time.

337

STANDARDS

HSS CONTENT STANDARDS:

6.7 Students analyze the geographic, poliitcal, economic, religious, and social structures during the development of Rome.

HSS ANALYSIS SKILLS:

CST 1 Students explain how major events are related to one another in time.

PLAN

OBJECTIVE

Analyze how the clues found at Pompeii can help us understand daily life in the Roman Empire.

ESSENTIAL QUESTION

What was the power and enduring legacy of the Roman Empire?

Pompeii is one of the most compelling stories of the ancient world: a city destroyed in a matter of days and hidden away for hundreds of years. Lesson 1.6 examines the end of Pompeii and the stories the city tells us about daily life in a Roman town.

BACKGROUND FOR THE TEACHER

Pompeii was a town long before the Romans gained control. Descendants of Neolithic peoples formed the first settlements in the region. Soon after, these settlements came under the influence of Greeks who had settled across the Bay of Naples. Influence in the region shifted to the Etruscans and back to the Greeks, and then the Samnite people conquered the region toward the end of the 5th century B.C. After this, a growing Roman presence increasingly came into conflict with the Samnites. Soon after 89 B.C., Rome conquered the Samnites, took control of the region, and established a colony of Roman veterans. The town was quickly Romanized, but was really only under Roman control less than 100 years before it was destroyed.

DIGITAL RESOURCES NGLSync.cengage.com

TEACHER RESOURCES & ASSESSMENT

 Reading and Note-Taking

 Vocabulary Practice

 Section 1 Quiz

STUDENT RESOURCES

 NG Chapter Gallery

INTRODUCE & ENGAGE

ACTIVATE PRIOR KNOWLEDGE

Ask volunteers to share what they already know about Pompeii. Ask leading questions such as, "What type of natural disaster destroyed the city?" "What types of photos of Pompeii have you seen?" Discuss as a class. `0:10` minutes

TEACH

GUIDED DISCUSSION

1. **Form Opinions** Millions of people still live near Vesuvius today. Why do people live in potential disaster areas? *(Answers to this question will vary widely and there is no right answer. However, people are usually aware of the natural dangers around where they live, but they have judged that they enjoy the area enough to risk facing a possible natural disaster.)*

2. **Make Inferences** Why is discovering a well-preserved city that is hundreds of years old so important for archaeologists and historians? *(Such a city allows researchers to examine not only the details of daily life, but also the daily life of people across a wide range of the socioeconomic spectrum.)*

ANALYZE VISUALS

Give groups of students a selected set of images of Pompeii's ruins. Ask them to look for identifiable features (e.g., streets, buildings, fountains, temples, etc.). Also present the groups with selected images of Pompeii's inscriptions and graffiti (with provided translations). Discuss how the inscriptions and graffiti provide evidence of Roman civic contributions and how they are similar to inscriptions and graffiti in the present day. `0:15` minutes

ACTIVE OPTIONS

On Your Feet: Card Responses Have half the class write 10 true-false questions based on the lesson. Have the other half create answer cards, writing "True" on one side and "False" on the other side. Students from the first group take turns asking their questions. Students from the second group hold up their cards, showing either "True" or "False." Have students keep track of their correct answers. `0:15` minutes

Critical Viewing: NG Chapter Gallery Have students examine the contents of the Chapter Gallery for this chapter. Then invite them to brainstorm additional images they believe would fit within the Chapter Gallery. Have them write a description of these additional images and provide an explanation of why they would fit within the Chapter Gallery. Then instruct them to do online research to find examples of actual images that fit their descriptions. `0:10` minutes

DIFFERENTIATE

STRIVING READERS

Use Your Own Words Have students work in pairs to explain in their own words the story of Pompeii and how it was preserved.

PRE-AP

Research Pompeian Culture Have students research some of the amazing discoveries made in Pompeii. Possible topics include graffiti, art, restaurants, and preserved everyday objects. Students should write a one-page essay with an introduction and a conclusion. Have them work with a partner to exchange and proofread each other's work.

Press **mt** *in the Student eEdition for modified text.*

See the Chapter Planner for more strategies for differentiation.

REVIEW & ASSESS

ANSWERS

1. Some of the items that were preserved include buildings, leather shoes, wooden furniture, food, and a library of scrolls.

2. There was an explosion that created a large black cloud. Ash began falling and eventually buried the city. Poison gas also moved through the city, killing anyone who was still alive. Lightning, earthquakes, and tidal waves occurred over the three days following the eruption, and then Vesuvius went quiet.

3. The ash buried everything in the city, protecting it from the weather and looters.

Origins
of Christianity

A man named Jesus who lived in Nazareth was a Jew whose beliefs became a threat to Jewish and Roman leaders. His teachings formed the foundation of a religion that has powerfully shaped the world for over 2,000 years.

MAIN IDEA

Christianity developed in Jewish communities and was based on the teachings of Jesus.

JEWISH ROOTS

As the empire expanded, the Romans were usually tolerant of the many different religions practiced throughout the empire. As long as people worshipped their emperor as a god, they could follow whatever faith they liked. This was not a problem for most religions. The exception was Judaism, the religion of the Jewish people.

As you've learned, the Romans captured the Jewish city of Jerusalem in 63 B.C. This brought the Jewish people under Roman control. At first the Romans allowed the Jews to worship one God. Over time, tensions grew. Rome began to enforce emperor worship, and the tensions exploded into conflict. In A.D. 70, Rome defeated the Jews, who then scattered to lands around the Mediterranean. This helped spread a new religion that was developing in the Jewish community: Christianity.

JESUS OF NAZARETH

Christianity is based on the teachings of **Jesus**, a man born into a poor family in Judea around 6 B.C. Most of what we know about Jesus' teachings comes from the four **Gospels**. These books were written after Jesus' death by four of his followers—Matthew, Mark, Luke, and John. The Gospels are part of the **New Testament**, which presents the history, teachings, and beliefs of Christianity. According to historical record, Jesus was a practicing Jew and worked as a carpenter. When he was about 30 years old, he began to teach ideas that differed from Jewish practices. Biblical accounts claim that Jesus could perform miracles, such as healing the sick.

In time, Jesus traveled around Judea preaching and gathering disciples, or followers. He chose his closest followers, known as the **Twelve Apostles**, to help spread his teachings. He often used **parables** (short stories about everyday life) to make his religious or moral points. In his Sermon on the Mount, Jesus declared that love for God and charity toward all people were more important than following Jewish law. He also promised that those who sought God's forgiveness for their sins would go to heaven after death. To his followers, Jesus became Christ, "the anointed one." They believed he was the promised Messiah—the one who would free them.

According to Christian writings, Jesus criticized Jewish practices while visiting Jerusalem during the Jewish observance of Passover. Jesus was arrested and turned over to Roman authorities. Pontius Pilate, the Roman governor of Judea, sentenced Jesus to death by crucifixion—being nailed to a cross and left to die. Jesus' body was buried, and then, according to the Gospel accounts, he was resurrected, or rose from the dead, and ascended into heaven. For Christians, the resurrection signals victory over sin and death. The man called Jesus was gone, but Christianity was just beginning.

The Last Supper, Leonardo da Vinci, 1498

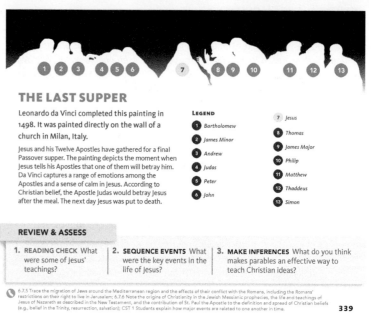

THE LAST SUPPER

Leonardo da Vinci completed this painting in 1498. It was painted directly on the wall of a church in Milan, Italy.

Jesus and his Twelve Apostles have gathered for a final Passover supper. The painting depicts the moment when Jesus tells his Apostles that one of them will betray him. Da Vinci captures a range of emotions among the Apostles and a sense of calm in Jesus. According to Christian belief, the Apostle Judas would betray Jesus after the meal. The next day Jesus was put to death.

LEGEND

1. Bartholomew
2. James Minor
3. Andrew
4. Judas
5. Peter
6. John
7. Jesus
8. Thomas
9. James Major
10. Philip
11. Matthew
12. Thaddeus
13. Simon

REVIEW & ASSESS

1. **READING CHECK** What were some of Jesus' teachings?

2. **SEQUENCE EVENTS** What were the key events in the life of Jesus?

3. **MAKE INFERENCES** What do you think makes parables an effective way to teach Christian ideas?

6.7.5 Trace the migration of Jews around the Mediterranean region and the effects of their conflict with the Romans, including the Romans' restrictions on their right to live in Jerusalem; 6.7.6 Note the origins of Christianity in the Jewish Messianic prophecies, the life and teachings of Jesus of Nazareth as described in the New Testament, and the contribution of St. Paul the Apostle to the definition and spread of Christian beliefs (e.g., belief in the Trinity, resurrection, salvation); CST 1 Students explain how major events are related to one another in time.

339

HSS CONTENT STANDARDS:

6.7.5 Trace the migration of Jews around the Mediterranean region and the effects of their conflict with the Romans, including the Romans' restrictions on their right to live in Jerusalem; **6.7.6** Note the origins of Christianity in the Jewish Messianic prophecies, the life and teachings of Jesus of Nazareth as described in the New Testament, and the contribution of St. Paul the Apostle to the definition and spread of Christian beliefs (e.g., belief in the Trinity, resurrection, salvation).

HSS ANALYSIS SKILLS:

CST 1 Students explain how major events are related to one another in time.

PLAN

OBJECTIVE

Describe the origins of Christianity and the history and teachings of Jesus.

ESSENTIAL QUESTION

What was the power and enduring legacy of the Roman Empire?

Christianity developed out of the Jewish community during the time of the Roman Empire. Lesson 2.1 discusses the origins of Christianity and the role of Jesus.

BACKGROUND FOR THE TEACHER

The Romans captured Jerusalem and destroyed the Second Temple in A.D. 70. This scattered Jews throughout the Empire, which also spread Christianity. For Jews today, however, this defeat holds one of the greatest sources of national pride. Zealots, a fierce and uncompromising Jewish sect, refused to surrender. They held the fortress of Masada, located on a mesa about 33 miles southeast of Jerusalem. The Romans laid siege to the fortress, but the nearly sheer sides of the mesa limited their efforts. For almost two years, 15,000 Roman soldiers battled a Jewish force of less than 1,000 people including women and children. Today, Masada is a popular attraction in Israel and is considered a source of Jewish national pride.

DIGITAL RESOURCES NGLSync.cengage.com

TEACHER RESOURCES & ASSESSMENT

 Reading and Note-Taking

 Vocabulary Practice

 Section 2 Quiz

STUDENT RESOURCES

 NG Chapter Gallery

INTRODUCE & ENGAGE

ACTIVATE PRIOR KNOWLEDGE

Ask students to think about any religious images they may have seen. Ask them what similarities and differences they have noticed among the images. Then ask why visual imagery might be important to a religion. *(Possible answer: Images can effectively convey ideas and themes. In other words, they can be an effective teaching tool.)* `0:10` **minutes**

TEACH

GUIDED DISCUSSION

1. **Explain** Why might the Romans have been fearful of a religion that refused to acknowledge the emperor as a god? *(Followers of a religion that refused to acknowledge the emperor as a god might be more likely to rebel whenever the will of the emperor conflicted with the tenets of the religion.)*

2. **Evaluate** How successful were the apostles at spreading Christianity? *(Given the number of Christians in the world today, the apostles were very successful.)*

ANALYZE VISUALS

Tell students that Leonardo da Vinci's *Last Supper* is considered a masterpiece and one of the most famous paintings in the world. Ask students if they find it compelling. Why or why not?

(Answers will vary. Considered a masterpiece of composition, da Vinci's painting captures the tension of a moment and focuses it through his simple composition and use of one-point perspective.) `0:15` **minutes**

ACTIVE OPTIONS

On Your Feet: Roundtable Have the class move their desks into a circle and guide a discussion about how and why a religion begins, spreads, and endures. `0:15` **minutes**

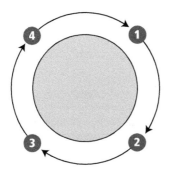

NG Learning Framework: Write a Biography

ATTITUDE: Curiosity
SKILL: Communication

Have students select one of the people they are still curious about after reviewing the painting of the Last Supper. Instruct them to write a short biography about this person using information from additional source material. `0:20` **minutes**

DIFFERENTIATE

STRIVING READERS

Summarize Have students work in pairs, and assign each pair one paragraph to read together. Encourage students to use a Main Idea and Details Chart to organize their ideas. Then have each pair summarize their paragraph in one or two sentences for the class.

ENGLISH LANGUAGE LEARNERS `ELD`

Make Vocabulary Cards Have students use flash cards to learn and practice unfamiliar words they encounter in this lesson. On one side of each card they should write the target word. On the other, they should write related words they are familiar with, draw or paste images that will help them recall the meaning of the target word, or write out other mnemonic devices. Encourage students to use their flash cards for review. Have students at the **Emerging** and **Expanding** levels work in pairs. Have students at the **Bridging** level work independently.

Press **(mt)** in the Student eEdition for modified text.

See the Chapter Planner for more strategies for differentiation.

REVIEW & ASSESS

ANSWERS

1. Jesus taught that believers should show love for God and charity toward all people. He also taught that those who sought God's forgiveness for their sins would go to heaven after they died.

2. Key events include the following: born in Judaea; worked as a carpenter; began preaching when he was about 30; arrested and executed in Jerusalem.

3. Parables are an effective way to teach Christian ideas because they apply larger moral concepts to relatable, everyday events. Parables make the teachings easy to access.

Christianity Spreads

Faith is very personal. We follow a particular religion (or no religion) for different reasons. Early Christians were the same way. Christianity had broad appeal and attracted a wide mix of people. They all believed that Jesus was the Messiah.

MAIN IDEA

Christianity attracted many followers and spread throughout the Roman Empire.

THE SPREAD OF CHRISTIANITY, c. A.D. 500

- Boundary of Roman Empire, c. A.D. 395
- Christian areas, c. A.D. 325
- Christian expansion, c. A.D. 500

APPEAL OF CHRISTIANITY

At first all Christians were practicing Jews who still met in synagogues, places for Jewish worship. However, soon Christianity placed less emphasis on the laws of Judaism and welcomed Gentiles (GEHN-tylz), or non-Jews. As a result of the split from Judaism, Christianity grew and developed its own identity.

Christianity appealed to a lot of people. The religion's main appeal was the promise of salvation made possible by the sacrifice of Jesus. Many followers were also attracted by Christianity's rejection of the Roman focus on wealth and image. They preferred Jesus' focus on living simply and peacefully, sharing property, and providing charity to help the less fortunate. The poor liked the way Christian communities shared their wealth and established hospitals, schools, and other public services to improve their lives. Women and slaves liked Christianity because it treated them more like equals than other religions and Roman society did. Finally, many people embraced the idea of a personal relationship with God.

SPREADING THE WORD

In spite of Christianity's broad appeal, the religion's survival was far from certain, and it could easily have faded away. Instead it thrived because Jesus' followers spread his teachings fast and far, including to Europe. Through the Roman road network, Christianity spread in Jewish communities across the empire. Another big break was that the Romans confused Christianity with Judaism and so ignored the new religion, which allowed it to grow.

Even so, life as a Christian wasn't easy. The Romans often persecuted, or punished, Christians for their beliefs. However, one of Christianity's fiercest persecutors, a man named **Paul**, eventually became its biggest champion.

Paul was most responsible for spreading early Christianity. He was a well-educated Jew and a Roman citizen. He converted to Christianity while traveling on the road to Damascus. According to Paul's own account, he had a vision in which Jesus was revealed to him as the Son of God. As a result, Paul became a **missionary**, a person who travels to another country to do religious work.

He began spreading Jesus' teachings. Paul was often arrested, but he always escaped to preach again. He wrote many letters, or **epistles** (ih-PIH-suhls), explaining Jesus' teachings by answering specific questions. According to tradition, Paul was killed in a Roman massacre of Christians in A.D. 64. By then, Roman leaders realized that Christianity was a separate religion from Judaism and a popular religion—too popular. Fearful that Christianity might threaten the stability of the empire, Roman rulers made the religion's practice illegal.

REVIEW & ASSESS

1. **READING CHECK** How did Christianity spread throughout the Roman Empire?

2. **INTERPRET MAPS** What natural features served as the northern border for Christian expansion by A.D. 500?

3. **MAKE INFERENCES** Why was Paul an effective spokesperson for spreading the teachings of Christianity?

6.7.6 Note the origins of Christianity in the Jewish Messianic prophecies, the life and teachings of Jesus of Nazareth as described in the New Testament, and the contribution of St. Paul the Apostle to the definition and spread of Christian beliefs (e.g., belief in the Trinity, resurrection, salvation); 6.7.7 Describe the circumstances that led to the spread of Christianity in Europe and other Roman territories; CST 3 Students use a variety of maps and documents to identify physical and cultural features of neighborhoods, cities, states, and countries and to explain the historical migration of people, expansion and disintegration of empires, and the growth of economic systems.

STANDARDS

HSS CONTENT STANDARDS:

6.7.6 Note the origins of Christianity in the Jewish Messianic prophecies, the life and teachings of Jesus of Nazareth as described in the New Testament, and the contribution of St. Paul the Apostle to the definition and spread of Christian beliefs (e.g., belief in the Trinity, resurrection, salvation); **6.7.7** Describe the circumstances that led to the spread of Christianity in Europe and other Roman territories.

HSS ANALYSIS SKILLS:

CST 3 Students use a variety of maps and documents to identify physical and cultural features of neighborhoods, cities, states, and countries and to explain the historical migration of people, expansion and disintegration of empires, and the growth of economic systems; **HI 2** Students understand and distinguish cause, effect, sequence, and correlation in historical events, including the long- and short-term causal relations.

PLAN

OBJECTIVE

Analyze how and why Christianity spread across the Roman world.

ESSENTIAL QUESTION

What was the power and enduring legacy of the Roman Empire?

The size and stability of the Roman Empire helped the spread of Christianity. Lesson 2.2 discusses how Christianity spread in the Roman Empire and why Christianity is one of the most powerful legacies of the Roman Empire.

BACKGROUND FOR THE TEACHER

Paul's conversion to Christianity on the road to Damascus came not only with a belief in Christ, but also with a belief that the Gospels should be conveyed to Gentiles without the need for Jewish conversion nor the inclusion of traditional Jewish ceremonies. This put him fundamentally at odds with the Jewish Christian community. Paul acknowledged that the Christian mission was for all people and necessitated a dramatic break from Jewish traditions. This universal, or catholic, belief heavily informed the development of the early Christian church.

DIGITAL RESOURCES NGLSync.cengage.com

TEACHER RESOURCES & ASSESSMENT

 Reading and Note-Taking

Vocabulary Practice

 Section 2 Quiz

STUDENT RESOURCES

 Biography

INTRODUCE & ENGAGE

PREVIEW

Call students' attention to the map showing the spread of Christianity. Review the map as a class. Call on volunteers to describe what they see. At the end of the lesson, ask students to describe the relationship between the map and the text. **0:10** minutes

TEACH

GUIDED DISCUSSION

1. **Analyze Cause and Effect** What was the effect of Rome's stability on the spread of Christianity? *(Rome's stability allowed people to travel across the empire in safety, which meant that individuals, such as Paul, who were trying to spread Christianity could move safely over great distances.)*

2. **Make Predictions** Have students consider the future of Christianity from this time period. **ASK:** Based on your knowledge and what you've read, what do you think happened next for Christianity and the Roman Empire? *(Answers will vary, but most students should recognize that Christianity would continue to spread, and they may guess that Christianity would become the official religion of the Roman Empire.)*

INTERPRET MAPS

Point out to students that many of the Christian areas c. A.D. 325 are along coastal areas or along rivers. **ASK:** Why might this be the case? *(Water was one of the most efficient means of travel at this time. As a result, it is not surprising that Christianity spread to coastal areas and along rivers first.)* **0:15** minutes

ACTIVE OPTIONS

On Your Feet: Numbered Heads Organize students into groups of four and give each student a number. Tell students to think about and discuss a response to this question: Why might Christianity have been so appealing? Then call a number and have the student from each group with that number report for the group. **0:15** minutes

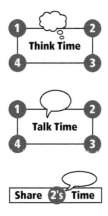

Think Time

Talk Time

Share 2's Time

Critical Viewing: NG Chapter Gallery Invite students to explore the Chapter Gallery to examine the images that relate to this chapter. Have them select one of the images and do additional research to learn more about it. Ask questions that will inspire additional inquiry about the chosen gallery image, such as: What is this? Where and when was this created? By whom? Why was it created? What is it made of? Why does it belong in this chapter? What else would you like to know about it? **0:15** minutes

DIFFERENTIATE

STRIVING READERS

Complete Sentence Starters Provide these sentence starters for students to complete after reading. You may also have students preview to set a purpose for reading.

- Gentiles are _____.
- The poor liked Christian communities because _____.
- The man who became Christianity's biggest champion was _____.

PRE-AP

Draw Conclusions Invite students to meet in small groups to draw conclusions about why Christianity was so appealing to so many people and why Roman leaders would outlaw its practice.

Press **mt** *in the Student eEdition for modified text.*

See the Chapter Planner for more strategies for differentiation.

REVIEW & ASSESS

ANSWERS

1. Christianity spread throughout the Roman Empire fast and far via Roman roads and the relative security of the empire.

2. The Rhine River and the Danube River served as the northern border for expansion.

3. Paul was well educated and a Jew. This gave him a credibility that other early missionaries may not have had.

DOCUMENT-BASED QUESTION

New Testament Literature

The Christian Bible is made up of two parts: the Old Testament (or Hebrew Bible) and the New Testament. The New Testament includes the Gospel of Luke and Paul's Epistles. At the core of the New Testament teaching is the death and resurrection of Jesus, giving the world a "new covenant" (new testament) that would enable all who repented of their sins to enter the kingdom of heaven.

This painting shows a moment from Jesus' parable of the Prodigal Son.

The Prodigal Son, Lucio Massari, c. 1614

DOCUMENT ONE

Primary Source: Sacred Text

The Parable of the Good Samaritan
This parable was recorded in the Gospel of Luke in the first century A.D. The Samaritans (suh-MEHR-uh-tuhns) were a community of people who were generally distrusted by the Jews, the audience of the parable. According to the Gospel of Luke, Jesus tells this parable to answer the question "Who is my neighbor?"

CONSTRUCTED RESPONSE How does the Samaritan's response to the beaten man differ from the responses of the priest and Levite?

Good Samaritan, Julius Schnorr von Carolsfeld, 1860

A man was going down from Jerusalem to Jericho, when he fell into the hands of robbers. They stripped him of his clothes, beat him, and went away, leaving him half dead. A priest happened to be going down the same road, and when he saw the man, he passed by on the other side. So too, a Levite [a Jew], when he came to the place and saw him, passed by on the other side. But a Samaritan, as he traveled, came where the man was; and when he saw him, he took pity on him. He went to him and bandaged his wounds, pouring on oil and wine. Then he put the man on his own donkey, took him to an inn, and took care of him. The next day he took out two silver coins and gave them to the innkeeper. "Look after him," he said, "and when I return, I will reimburse you for any extra expense you may have."

Luke 10:30—35

DOCUMENT TWO

Primary Source: Sacred Text

from Paul's Epistle to the Galatians
Paul wrote his letter to the Galatians (guh-LAY-shuhnz) in the first century A.D. The Roman province of Galatia contained a number of early Christian communities. In his letter, Paul stresses some important ideas of the Christian faith.

CONSTRUCTED RESPONSE What important Christian ideas is Paul stating in this epistle?

You all are sons of God through faith in Christ Jesus, for all of you who were baptized . . . have clothed yourselves with Christ. There is neither Jew nor Greek, slave nor free, male nor female, for you are all one in Christ Jesus.

Galatians 3:26—28

SYNTHESIZE & WRITE

1. **REVIEW** Review the ideas expressed in the parable of the Good Samaritan and Paul's Epistle to the Galatians.

2. **RECALL** On your own paper, write down the main idea expressed in each document.

3. **CONSTRUCT** Write a topic sentence that answers this question: What are some fundamental Christian ideas about how people should treat one another?

4. **WRITE** Using evidence from the documents and from the chapter, write a paragraph that supports your answer to the question in Step 3.

6.7.6 Note the origins of Christianity in the Jewish Messianic prophecies, the life and teachings of Jesus of Nazareth as described in the New Testament, and the contribution of St. Paul to the definition and spread of Christian beliefs (e.g., belief in the Trinity, resurrection, salvation); REP 4 Students assess the credibility of primary and secondary sources and draw sound conclusions from them.

343

STANDARDS

HSS CONTENT STANDARDS:

6.7.6 Note the origins of Christianity in the Jewish Messianic prophecies, the life and teachings of Jesus of Nazareth as described in the New Testament, and the contribution of St. Paul the Apostle to the definition and spread of Christian beliefs (e.g., belief in the Trinity, resurrection, salvation).

HSS ANALYSIS SKILLS:

REP 4 Students assess the credibility of primary and secondary sources and draw sound conclusions from them.

PLAN

OBJECTIVE

Synthesize information about New Testament Literature from primary source documents.

ESSENTIAL QUESTION

What was the power and enduring legacy of the Roman Empire?

The New Testament is the central element of modern Christianity's sacred text, the Bible. Lesson 2.3 provides a parable and an excerpt from one of Paul's letters as examples from Christianity's sacred text.

BACKGROUND FOR THE TEACHER

The New Testament is a collection of early Christian literature. The four Gospels deal with the life and the teachings of Jesus based on the memories of early Christians. The Book of Acts discusses the resurrection of Jesus to the death of Paul. The Letters, or Epistles, come from early Christian leaders, including Paul. The Epistles applied church teachings to issues facing early Christian communities. There was a large group of apocalyptic literature in early Christian writing. The only one included in the New Testament, however, was The Book of Revelation (the Apocalypse).

DIGITAL RESOURCES NGLSync.cengage.com

TEACHER RESOURCES & ASSESSMENT

 Reading and Note-Taking

 Vocabulary Practice

 Section 2 Quiz

STUDENT RESOURCES

 NG Chapter Gallery

INTRODUCE & ENGAGE

PREPARE FOR THE DOCUMENT-BASED QUESTION

Before students start on the activity, briefly preview the two documents. Remind students that a constructed response requires full explanations in complete sentences. Emphasize that students should use what they have learned in the chapter in addition to the information in the documents. `0:05` minutes

TEACH

GUIDED DISCUSSION

1. **Draw Conclusions** Why might the Parable of the Good Samaritan have used a Samaritan—a group that Jews distrusted—as the hero? *(to establish that good can be found everywhere and that global judgments are not always correct)*

2. **Make Inferences** Why would letters be included in a sacred text? *(Responses will vary. Possible responses: Paul's Epistles were written relatively close to the time of Jesus and are valuable sources of information about the beliefs of early Christians. Capturing these beliefs, particularly in the form of letters to real people with real questions, in a sacred text makes sense.)*

EVALUATE

After students have completed the "Synthesize & Write" activity, allow time for them to exchange paragraphs and read and comment on the work of their peers. Guidelines for comments should be established prior to this activity so that feedback is constructive and encouraging in nature. `0:15` minutes

ACTIVE OPTIONS

On Your Feet: Think, Pair, Share Give students a few minutes to think about this question: What is the most effective way to communicate important ideas? Then have students choose partners and talk about the question for five minutes. Finally, allow individual students to share their ideas with the class. `0:20` minutes

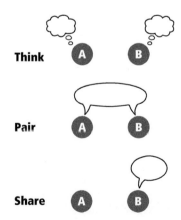

Think   A   B

Pair   A   B

Share   A   B

NG Learning Framework: Ask and Answer

ATTITUDE: **Curiosity**
SKILL: **Communication**

Have curious students find another primary source that fits in thematically with those included in the lesson. Have them write and answer a constructed response question of their own. Then have them rewrite their answer for item 4 under "Synthesize & Write," incorporating evidence from their new source. `0:30` minutes

DIFFERENTIATE

INCLUSION

Synthesize Help students minimize distractions by typing the two excerpts on one sheet of paper. Give photocopies of these to students along with highlighters. Tell students to highlight important words that appear in both documents. Then have them write a summary sentence using several of the words.

PRE-AP

Research the Prodigal Son Have students read the Parable of the Prodigal Son in the **Primary Source Handbook** and answer the questions that follow it. Encourage them to report on this parable and include it in their Synthesize & Write activity.

Press **mt** *in the Student eEdition for modified text.*

See the Chapter Planner for more strategies for differentiation.

CONSTRUCTED RESPONSE

ANSWERS
DOCUMENT 1
The Samaritan actually stopped to help the beaten man.

DOCUMENT 2
Paul is stating that all Christians are equal.

SYNTHESIZE & WRITE

ANSWERS

1. Help others; all Christians are equal.

2. Responses will vary.

3. Possible response: People should be kind to others and respect their differences.

4. Students' paragraphs should include their topic sentence from Step 3 and provide several details from the documents to support the sentence.

The **Early** **Christian** Church

Being different can make you a target for attacks. Early Christians were violently attacked, but their courage and determination ensured Christianity's survival.

MAIN IDEA

In time, Christianity became the official religion of the Roman Empire.

CONSTANTINE

Constantine was very generous to his supporters. Historians have suggested that he could afford to be so generous only because he robbed temples and used tax money for his own purposes. It is also clear that some of his supporters gained favor by faking conversions to Christianity.

THE CONVERSION OF CONSTANTINE

As you have learned, Christians were often persecuted by their Roman rulers. In A.D. 35, a Christian named Stephen became the first of thousands of Christian victims. He was killed for his religious beliefs. Roman leaders punished Christians for refusing to worship the emperors.

This persecution only got worse. In A.D. 64, the emperor Nero blamed Christians for a great fire that swept through Rome. He had thousands of Christians put to death. Just being a Christian became punishable by death. As a result, worshippers were forced to meet in secret. They buried their dead in hidden underground chambers called **catacombs** (KA-tuh-kohms).

In A.D. 312, Christian persecution had reached its highest point when an amazing change began. On the eve of a battle for control of the empire, a young Roman leader named **Constantine** prayed for help. He believed his prayers were answered with a vision of the Christian cross. The vision led him to paint a symbol on his soldiers' shields. Constantine went on to win the battle. As a result, he immediately put an end to Christian persecution.

Constantine made many other changes after he became emperor. He built churches in Roman lands and declared Sunday the Christian day of rest. He even had Christian symbols placed on coins. Constantine ruled for a long time. However, it was only after Constantine's rule that the emperor Theodosius officially closed all the temples to the Roman gods and made Christianity the official religion of Rome.

FORMATION OF THE EARLY CHURCH

With the legalization of Christianity, Christian communities could openly share their beliefs. Church leaders from across the empire held councils, or meetings, to discuss Christianity and the writings of religious scholars. Their discussions helped them define Christian beliefs and practices.

Christian practices were then communicated to Christian churches throughout the empire and beyond. Each church was led by a priest, and groups of churches were overseen by a bishop. The first bishop of Rome, according to Christian tradition, was the apostle Peter, who died for his beliefs in A.D. 64. Constantine had a church, St. Peter's Basilica, built over the apostle's tomb. The photo above shows the basilica, which was rebuilt in the 1600s. In time the bishop of Rome became the most important bishop, or **pope**. He was seen as the leader of the unified church, known as the **Roman Catholic Church**.

Church leaders standardized Christian beliefs into a common creed, or statement of beliefs. One such statement was the definition of God as a Holy Trinity: the union of Father, Son (Jesus), and Holy Spirit. Worship in the Christian church focused on some common sacraments, or religious ceremonies, such as baptism, an individual's acceptance by the church. As Christianity grew more structured and became more organized, it became a powerful religion.

REVIEW & ASSESS

1. **READING CHECK** How did Christianity become the official religion of the Roman Empire?

2. **DESCRIBE** How was the leadership of the early church organized?

3. **DRAW CONCLUSIONS** In what way did their persecution help unite the Christians?

6.7.6 Note the origins of Christianity in the Jewish Messianic prophecies, the life and teachings of Jesus of Nazareth as described in the New Testament, and the contribution of St. Paul the Apostle to the definition and spread of Christian beliefs (e.g., belief in the Trinity, resurrection, salvation); 7.1.1 Study the early strengths and lasting contributions of Rome (e.g., significance of Roman citizenship; rights under Roman law; Roman art, architecture, engineering, and philosophy; preservation and transmission of Christianity) and its ultimate internal weaknesses (e.g., rise of autonomous military powers within the empire, undermining of citizenship by the growth of corruption and slavery, lack of education, and distribution of news).

Catacombs

Catacombs are underground burial chambers. They often have tunnels with spaces cut into the walls for the bodies. Some catacombs also have large chambers where funeral feasts were held. There are about 40 early Christian catacombs around Rome, and they are the most extensive of any known catacomb system in the world. Shown below is the Catacomb of Priscilla in Rome, Italy.

‹ Saint Peter's Basilica, in present-day Vatican City

STANDARDS

6.7.6 Note the origins of Christianity in the Jewish Messianic prophecies, the life and teachings of Jesus of Nazareth as described in the New Testament, and the contribution of St. Paul the Apostle to the definition and spread of Christian beliefs (e.g., belief in the Trinity, resurrection, salvation); **6.7.7** Describe the circumstances that led to the spread of Christianity in Europe and other Roman territories; **7.1.1** Study the early strengths and lasting contributions of Rome (e.g., significance of Roman citizenship; rights under Roman law; Roman art, architecture, engineering, and philosophy; preservation and transmission of Christianity) and its ultimate internal weaknesses (e.g., rise of autonomous military powers within the empire, undermining of citizenship by the growth of corruption and slavery, lack of education, and distribution of news).

PLAN

OBJECTIVE

Understand the development and formation of the early Christian church.

ESSENTIAL QUESTION

What was the power and enduring legacy of the Roman Empire?

The conversion of Constantine began the process of making Christianity the official religion of the Empire. Lesson 2.4 discusses how Christianity became the religion of Rome and how the early church began to organize itself.

BACKGROUND FOR THE TEACHER

Soon after Constantine converted, he called and presided over the Council of Nicaea. This was a gathering of church leaders who were discussing church problems, specifically, the fact that Arius of Alexandria in the Eastern church had declared that Jesus was not divine, but a "created being." The council ultimately condemned Arius and wrote the Nicene Creed, which established church doctrine on the divinity of Christ. Constantine then exiled Arius—clearly demonstrating the ties between church and state. The council also issued decrees on the proper method of consecrating bishops, a condemnation of lending money at interest by clerics, and a refusal to allow bishops, priests, and deacons to move from one church to another.

DIGITAL RESOURCES NGLSync.cengage.com

TEACHER RESOURCES & ASSESSMENT

 Reading and Note-Taking

 Vocabulary Practice

 Section 2 Quiz

STUDENT RESOURCES

 NG Chapter Gallery

INTRODUCE & ENGAGE

PREVIEW

Remind students that the Christian church at this time was growing and still working out its leadership structure. Pose the question: *What challenges does any organization face as it expands?* `0:10` minutes

TEACH

GUIDED DISCUSSION

1. **Summarize** Summarize the events of Constantine's conversion and his actions afterwards. *(Constantine prayed for help on the eve of a battle and saw a vision of a Christian cross. He painted the symbol on his soldiers' shields and was victorious. He converted to Christianity, ended persecution of Christians, built churches, and even put Christian symbols on coins.)* As an extension, have students read the excerpt from the Edict of Milan in the **Primary Source Handbook** and answer the questions that follow it.

2. **Make Predictions** What might the long term effects be of Christianity becoming the official religion of the Roman Empire? *(Answers will vary, but most students should recognize that elements of Christian beliefs might start to guide political policy.)*

ANALYZE VISUALS

Point out St. Peter's in the photo. **ASK:** What about this building indicates that it's a church, and a Christian church in particular?

(The large, grand nature of the structure is often an indicator that the building is a church. Note for students that the church also looks like some government buildings. The cross at the top is an indicator that this is probably a Christian church.) `0:15` minutes

ACTIVE OPTIONS

On Your Feet: Research and Present Divide the class into groups of four and ask each group to do research about a specific aspect of Constantine's life. Have each group present their information to the class. `0:20` minutes

NG Learning Framework: Multimedia Presentation

ATTITUDE: **Responsibility**
SKILL: **Communication**
KNOWLEDGE: **Our Human Story**

Have students work in small collaborative groups to research more information about catacombs of early Christians in Rome. Tell students they should be respectful of the topic and of each other. Groups should present their findings to the class in a multimedia format. `0:30` minutes

DIFFERENTIATE

ENGLISH LANGUAGE LEARNERS `ELD`

Give a Thumbs Up or Thumbs Down Write a set of true-false statements about the lesson, such as "Constantine converted to Christianity." Read the lesson aloud while students follow along in their books. Then have them close the books and listen as you read the true-false statements. Students should give a thumbs up if a statement is true and a thumbs down if a statement is false. For the benefit of students at the **Emerging** level, you might read the lesson aloud in smaller sections, such as individual paragraphs or the text under each of the subheadings.

PRE-AP `STEM`

Research St. Peter's Have students research the history and construction of St. Peter's. Have students pick an aspect of the building's history and write a research paper about it. Encourage students to add visuals or possibly build physical models to illustrate elements of their report.

Press *in the Student eEdition for modified text.*

See the Chapter Planner for more strategies for differentiation.

REVIEW & ASSESS

ANSWERS

1. The emperor Constantine converted to Christianity and stopped the persecution of Christians. The emperor Theodosius made Christianity the official religion of Rome.

2. The leadership of the Roman Catholic Church was organized in a hierarchy, with priests, bishops, and the title of pope for the bishop of Rome.

3. Christian persecution ensured that Christians worked together to maintain their beliefs, which included the creation of secret underground burial areas known as catacombs.

3.1 The Third Century Crisis

Despite the occasional unbalanced emperor, the Roman Empire ran smoothly for 200 years. Then things began to fall apart. Disputes over who should be emperor caused the return of political violence and civil war. In some years, four or even six emperors were on the throne. By A.D. 235, the Roman world had plunged into a crisis.

MAIN IDEA

Military problems led to a crisis in the Roman Empire.

MILITARY PROBLEMS

So what went wrong? Arguably the empire had physically outgrown the emperor's ability to govern it. At its height, the Roman Empire stretched from Scotland to the Sahara, an area about half the size of the United States. This vast expanse, with huge geographic and cultural differences, was very difficult to govern effectively.

Defending such a large area also proved difficult. Rome faced attacks on two fronts at the same time, which drained money and resources all across the empire. In the east, Rome fought the powerful Parthian Empire from Persia, while Germanic tribes raided Rome's northern borders.

Meanwhile, warring groups within the empire once again fought to decide who would be emperor. Civil wars bled the empire of desperately needed food, money, and soldiers. As emperors fought expensive wars they could not win, enemies from outside the empire attacked. With so many Roman soldiers engaged in warfare, the invaders plundered, or stole riches from, the unguarded interior. It was a sure sign of trouble when cities, including Rome, rebuilt their long-neglected defensive walls. These military problems provoked further political and social problems.

POLITICAL, ECONOMIC, AND SOCIAL PROBLEMS

War was not only dangerous for soldiers; it was disruptive for everyone. Emperors were blamed for not protecting the empire, and they were regularly replaced or murdered. Fifty different emperors ruled between A.D. 235 and 285. People living in what would become Spain, France, and Britain preferred to trust local rulers. They broke from Rome to form a separate Gallic Empire. These events weakened imperial authority and prevented the strong, decisive, and long-term action needed to restore order.

This constant warfare also ruined the economy. Trade was interrupted, and the empire had to rely on its inadequate agricultural resources. The people suffered food shortages and higher taxes. Wars are expensive, and the emperors expected the people to pay for them. Even heavier taxes were enforced when the imperial currency lost value. This affected rich and poor but mostly the poor.

Ordinary people grew angry, criminal organizations grew, and outbursts of mob anger increased. It even became difficult to recruit local officials. Nobody wanted these jobs because people risked a beating for doing them. In these unstable times, good citizenship took second place to looking after oneself.

DECLINE OF THE ROMAN EMPIRE

Illustration of a parade honoring victories of Emperor Augustus

Military Reasons

- Fighting the Parthian Empire in the east
- Fighting Germanic tribes in the west
- Fighting civil wars at home

Stone relief showing a government bureaucrat at work

Political Reasons

- Difficult to govern huge empire
- Frequently changing emperors
- Power gained by local leaders

Relief depicting a tax payment

Economic Reasons

- Trade interrupted
- People heavily taxed
- Lower value of currency

Illustration of a Roman party with the poor waiting on the rich

Social Reasons

- Unrest from gap between rich and poor
- More criminal organizations
- Civic responsibility no longer important

REVIEW & ASSESS

1. **READING CHECK** Why did the size of the Roman Empire cause military problems?

2. **ANALYZE CAUSE AND EFFECT** What was the result of the emperors' expensive wars?

3. **DRAW CONCLUSIONS** How did Rome's military problems lead to political, social, and economic problems?

7.1.1 Study the early strengths and lasting contributions of Rome (e.g., significance of Roman citizenship; rights under Roman law; Roman art, architecture, engineering, and philosophy; preservation and transmission of Christianity) and its ultimate internal weaknesses (e.g., rise of autonomous military powers within the empire, undermining of citizenship by the growth of corruption and slavery, lack of education, and distribution of news); 7.1.2 Discuss the geographic borders of the empire at its height and the factors that threatened its territorial cohesion; HI 2 Students understand and distinguish cause, effect, sequence, and correlation in historical events, including the long- and short-term causal relations.

HSS CONTENT STANDARDS:

7.1.1 Study the early strengths and lasting contributions of Rome (e.g., significance of Roman citizenship; rights under Roman law; Roman art, architecture, engineering, and philosophy; preservation and transmission of Christianity) and its ultimate internal weaknesses (e.g., rise of autonomous military powers within the empire, undermining of citizenship by the growth of corruption and slavery, lack of education, and distribution of news); **7.1.2** Discuss the geograhic borders of the empire at its height and the factors that threatened its territorial cohesion.

HSS ANALYSIS SKILLS:

HI 2 Students understand and distinguish cause, effect, sequence, and correlation in historical events, including the long- and short-term causal relations.

PLAN

OBJECTIVE

Analyze the issues that led to a crisis for the Roman Empire in the third century.

ESSENTIAL QUESTION

What was the power and enduring legacy of the Roman Empire?

The power of Rome began to break down in the third century. Lesson 3.1 discusses the various factors that weakened the empire and would ultimately alter it forever.

BACKGROUND FOR THE TEACHER

Historians have debated for centuries the question of why Rome fell. The modern consensus is that there were multiple factors—of varying severity and duration—that converged to make the empire as it had been untenable. Military, political, economic, and social factors all contributed to what is considered the end of the Roman Empire. The truth is that these problems began long before the empire "fell." "The Third Century Crisis" is often identified as the point at which the empire began to unravel.

DIGITAL RESOURCES NGLSync.cengage.com

TEACHER RESOURCES & ASSESSMENT

 Reading and Note-Taking

 Vocabulary Practice

 Section 3 Quiz

STUDENT RESOURCES

 NG Chapter Gallery

INTRODUCE & ENGAGE

ANALYZE VISUALS

Review the feature on the decline of the Roman Empire as a class. Ask students to look for the bullet points in the text as they read. Point out that bullet points can be a good summary, but the text provides context. Specifically, the context in this lesson is that all of Rome's troubles were intertwined. `0:10` minutes

TEACH

GUIDED DISCUSSION

1. **Analyze Causes** Discuss as a group what sparked the various problems Rome faced in the third century. *(Possible answers: The military was weakened from internal civil wars and from being attacked on two fronts. Frequently changing emperors meant less political stability. War and political infighting inevitably hurt the empire economically. Arguably, the general unrest in other areas of society led to a social breakdown, which led to more crime and further distrust of those in power.)*

2. **Form and Support Opinions** If there were one thing that the Romans could have done differently to prevent the Empire's decline, what would it have been? Explain why. *(Answers will vary. Possible answers: They could have kept a bigger army to fight off their enemies. OR A strong leader could have stopped the political infighting and focused on stabilizing the empire.)*

MORE INFORMATION

Too Many Cooks in the Kitchen Below is a listing of emperors in 238—there were six. Ask students to imagine six different presidents in one year. That's a new president every two months!

Maximinus I A.D. 235–238
Gordian I A.D. 238
Gordian II A.D. 238
Balbinus A.D. 238
Pupienus A.D. 238
Gordian III A.D. 238–244

ACTIVE OPTIONS

On Your Feet: Four Corners Place signs around the room that list each of the four general reasons for the decline of the Roman Empire—military, political, economic, and social. Ask students to move to the sign for the reason that they feel was most responsible for Rome's decline. Have groups confer about their position and select a representative to present their position to the rest of the class. `0:20` minutes

NG Learning Framework: Support an Argument

SKILL: Collaboration
KNOWLEDGE: Our Human Story

Invite students to pair up and choose one of the four topics shown in the "Decline of the Roman Empire" feature that they believe was most responsible for Rome's decline—military, political, economic, or social. Have each pair research support for their choice. Have all the pairs for each topic get together to share their findings and then present the material to the class. `0:30` minutes

DIFFERENTIATE

ENGLISH LANGUAGE LEARNERS

Use Vocabulary Word Maps Pair students at the **Emerging** or **Expanding** level with students at the **Bridging** level. Have them use a Word Map for three words they are struggling with in the text. Have groups trade Word Maps and review.

GIFTED & TALENTED

Make a Poster Suggest that students use the text and online research to find reasons for the decline of the Roman Empire. Suggest to students that they visually represent those reasons on a poster. Have students display their final posters in class.

Press **mt** *in the Student eEdition for modified text.*

See the Chapter Planner for more strategies for differentiation.

REVIEW & ASSESS

ANSWERS

1. The vast borders of the Roman Empire meant that it could potentially take Roman soldiers a great deal of time to move from one location to another. This meant that invaders could potentially advance deep into Roman territory before encountering resistance.

2. Expensive wars ruined the economy. Trade was interrupted and emperors raised taxes to pay for the wars, which made life even harder for Roman citizens.

3. Rome's military problems caused hardships for the people and made it very difficult for a single emperor to stay in power for very long. People became increasingly disenchanted and the crime rate rose as people turned to taking what they needed. The constant war was expensive, and emperors used taxes to finance them. War also interrupted trade. So not only did people have less to spend, there were fewer available resources to buy, such as food.

3.2 Eastern and Western Roman Empires

The Roman Empire was too big for one person to manage. Unfortunately that didn't stop ambitious men from trying and failing. Then Rome's luck changed. In A.D. 284, the throne was seized by an emperor who had the sense and strength to make the big changes that could keep the empire alive.

MAIN IDEA

In A.D. 285, the Roman Empire was divided into the Western Roman Empire and the Eastern Roman Empire.

DIOCLETIAN DIVIDES THE EMPIRE

The new emperor was named **Diocletian** (dy-uh-KLEE-shuhn), and he had a lot on his plate. He faced endangered frontiers, overstretched armies, economic collapse, weak imperial authority, and widespread unrest. However, Diocletian had a radical plan: In A.D. 285, he divided the empire in two. Diocletian ruled the Eastern Roman Empire, and his trusted friend Maximian ruled the Western Roman Empire. Each man appointed a junior emperor to rule with him. This rule by four emperors, called a **tetrarchy** (TEH-trahr-kee), worked really well at first.

Each emperor focused on his specific region while cooperating to introduce reforms.

Together they increased the army to 400,000 men and reorganized and strengthened the frontier forces. They also created a mobile field army ready to tackle trouble wherever it broke out. On the political front, Diocletian and Maximian reformed government administration and divided the provinces into more manageable units. To promote unity, they enforced emperor worship and the Latin language everywhere. They encouraged economic recovery by reforming tax laws, controlling inflation, and stabilizing the currency. The empire was on the road to recovery, and after 20 years, Diocletian and Maximian retired, letting the junior emperors take over. However, this was as good as the tetrarchy got.

CONSTANTINE MOVES THE CAPITAL

You've learned that the emperor Constantine made the practice of Christianity legal in the empire. Before he did that, he had to fight to become emperor. Constantine's father was emperor of the Western Roman Empire. When Constantine's father died in A.D. 306, however, the tetrarchy refused his claim to be western emperor, sparking a civil war. Constantine won the war and became emperor of east and west. However, Constantine was more interested in the eastern half of his empire.

Rome's importance had long been decreasing. Emperors no longer lived in Rome, and Italy had lost its privileged status.

The differences between east and west were increasing. The east produced more people, more food, more taxes, and more soldiers, while the west just grew weaker. So Constantine moved the capital from Rome to the ancient Greek city of Byzantium, which he renamed Constantinople. (Today the city is called Istanbul.) He built his new capital on the strategically important Bosporus, a narrow stretch of water separating Europe and Asia.

Constantine also continued the reforms begun by earlier emperors, earning the title "the Great." However, his sons plunged the empire into another civil war. The emperor Theodosius later reunited the empire, but the division of east and west became permanent after his death in A.D. 395. From then on, the fortunes and futures of the two empires were very different.

ROMAN EMPIRE: EAST AND WEST, c. A.D. 395

NATURAL BORDERS The Rhine and Danube rivers on the northern border of the Roman Empire were difficult to cross, which made it easier for the Roman army to defend the empire.

CONSTANTINOPLE Constantine's new capital on the Bosporus provided easy access to many resources and allowed the empire to control trade.

ROME Diocletian's decision to rule the Eastern Roman Empire made it clear that Rome was no longer the center of political power.

- Western Roman Empire
- Eastern Roman Empire

REVIEW & ASSESS

1. **READING CHECK** Why did Diocletian divide the Roman Empire in two?

2. **INTERPRET MAPS** In what ways was Rome's location similar to that of Constantinople?

3. **IDENTIFY PROBLEMS AND SOLUTIONS** What was Diocletian's plan for ruling the vast empire more efficiently?

7.1.3 Describe the establishment by Constantine of the new capital in Constantinople and the development of the Byzantine Empire, with an emphasis on the consequences of the development of two distinct European civilizations, Eastern Orthodox and Roman Catholic, and their two distinct views on church-state relations; CST 3 Students use a variety of maps and documents to identify physical and cultural features of neighborhoods, cities, states, and countries and to explain the historical migration of people, expansion and disintegration of empires, and the growth of economic systems.

HSS CONTENT STANDARDS:

7.1.2 Discuss the geograhic borders of the empire at its height and the factors that threatened its territorial cohesion; **7.1.3** Describe the establishment by Constantine of the new capital in Constantinople and the development of the Byzantine Empire, with an emphasis on the consequences of the development of two distinct European civilizations, Eastern Orthodox and Roman Catholic, and their two distinct views on church-state relations.

HSS ANALYSIS SKILLS:

CST 3 Students use a variety of maps and documents to identify physical and cultural features of neighborhoods, cities, states, and countries and to explain the historical migration of people, expanion and disintegration of empires, and the growth of economic systems.

PLAN

OBJECTIVE

Explain how and why the Roman Empire was divided and administered.

ESSENTIAL QUESTION

What was the power and enduring legacy of the Roman Empire?

Diocletian divided the empire administratively so that it could be run more efficiently. Lesson 3.2 discusses Diocletian's division of the empire and Constantine's "reunification" of the empire and subsequent move of the capital to Byzantium, which he named Constantinople.

BACKGROUND FOR THE TEACHER

The division of the Roman Empire described in the first section of this lesson happened about 40 years before Constantine came to power. Diocletian did move his administrative capital to the East at Nicomedia—near Constantine's future capital of Byzantium. Maximian ruled the West, but from Milan, not Rome. Maximian chose to be in Milan because it was closer to the empire's border and he could more quickly respond to attempted Germanic invasions. Diocletian saw his rule as ordained, but by the Roman gods, not the Christian god of Constantine. Although Diocletian found a way to stabilize the empire, it was only a temporary fix that succeeding emperors could not emulate.

DIGITAL RESOURCES NGLSync.cengage.com

TEACHER RESOURCES & ASSESSMENT

 Reading and Note-Taking

 Vocabulary Practice

 Section 3 Quiz

STUDENT RESOURCES

 NG Chapter Gallery

REVIEW

Discuss how much area the Roman Empire covered. Review what students remember about the challenges of ruling such a large area. Ask students if they think ruling the empire might have been easier with some help. It seems obvious, and that's exactly what Diocletian did. `0:05` **minutes**

GUIDED DISCUSSION

1. **Compare and Contrast** Review the reforms of the tetrarchy and Constantine. What similarities and difference do you notice? *(Possible answers for similarities: tried to reform government, believed the power of the empire was in the East; Possible answers for differences: religious beliefs, tetrarchy versus sole emperor.)*

2. **Draw Conclusions** Tell students that the tetrarchy was very successful, but that soon after Diocletian and Maximian retired, the Roman Empire again fell into disarray. **ASK:** What conclusions can you draw about the tetrarchy? *(The success of the tetrarchy was largely due to the people in charge.)*

INTERPRET MAPS

Have students review the map and read the call-outs. Ask volunteers what they find interesting or what questions they have about the material shown on the map.

(Possible notes: rivers as borders in the north; cities next to water; the Roman Empire was on three continents) `0:10` **minutes**

ACTIVE OPTIONS

On Your Feet: Team Word Webbing Organize students into teams of four and have them record what they know about the division of the Roman Empire into East and West on a piece of paper. Encourage students to build on their teammates' entries as they rotate the paper from one member to the next. Then call on volunteers from each group to make statements about the division of the Roman Empire based on their webs. `0:15` **minutes**

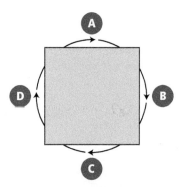

Critical Viewing: NG Chapter Gallery Have students explore the NG Chapter Gallery and choose two of the items to compare and contrast, either in written form or verbally with a partner. Ask questions that will inspire this process, such as: How are these images alike? How are they different? Why did you select these two items? How do they relate in history? `0:10` **minutes**

STRIVING READERS

Pose and Answer Questions Have students work in pairs to read the lesson. Instruct them to pause after each paragraph and ask one another *who, what, when, where,* or *why* questions about what they have just read. Advise students to read more slowly and focus on specific details if they have difficulty answering the questions, or to reread a paragraph to find the answers.

PRE-AP

Map Research Point out the discussion about the Rhine and Danube rivers being natural borders for the Roman Empire. Pair students up and have them research the other borders of the empire and what defined them.

Press (**mt**) *in the Student eEdition for modified text.*

See the Chapter Planner for more strategies for differentiation.

ANSWERS

1. Diocletian divided the empire so that it could be better managed and defended.

2. The location of Rome and Constantinople were similar in that they were both near water, and they were both near the center of the respective spheres of influence when they were established.

3. Diocletian split the empire in two with four rulers: an eastern and western emperor, each with a junior emperor. Diocletian and Maximian restructured the government and created more manageable territories.

Critical Viewing This painting shows Attila the Hun attacking a Roman city. In what ways has the artist made Attila seem very fierce?

+ POSSIBLE RESPONSE

The artist has used bright colors for Attila and more muted colors in the background, which makes Attila stand out. Attila also has wild-looking eyes and is looking straight out at the viewer, which makes him seem fierce.

350

End of the
Western
Roman Empire

If you lived in the Western Roman Empire in A.D. 375, you'd be unhappy with the way things were going. While the west struggled to rule itself, feed itself, pay its bills, and defend its borders, you would enviously watch the Eastern Roman Empire grow richer, stronger, and more stable. However bad things got, you could never imagine a world without the Roman Empire—but that reality was just 101 years away.

MAIN IDEA

Invaders attacked the Western Roman Empire and caused its downfall.

FOREIGN INVADERS

Diocletian and Constantine only delayed the end of the Western Roman Empire. The end came in the form of **barbarians**, a Greek word Romans used to describe all people outside of the empire. Three main tribes of barbarians would finally tear the Western Roman Empire apart. The Visigoths (VIH-zuh-gahths) and Vandals were Germanic tribes from northern Europe. Looking for better farmland, both groups migrated south toward the Roman frontier.

The Huns formed the third tribe of barbarians. Migrating from Asia, they were nomads, or wandering cattle herders. Their skill with horses and bows made them a ferocious fighting force. Beginning in A.D. 445, a man named **Attila** was their sole ruler.

THE WESTERN ROMAN EMPIRE FALLS

Attila and his army swept into Europe. Forced into the Western Roman Empire by the Huns, the Visigoths soon invaded Italy. Around the same time, the Vandals invaded Gaul and then Spain. By now the emperor, who had few Roman soldiers to call on, had to enlist barbarian fighters to defend the empire.

On August 24, 410, the Visigoths shocked the world by sacking, or destroying, Rome. They then conquered Gaul and Spain, driving the Vandals into North Africa. Then came Attila. The Huns attacked Gaul in A.D. 451, and the emperor relied on barbarian armies to fight them. Rome had lost control. In A.D. 476, the last emperor quietly left the throne.

The Western Roman Empire was broken up into many Germanic kingdoms, and the Eastern Roman Empire became known as the Byzantine Empire. The Roman Empire was over. Historians argue about why the Western Roman Empire fell. Did it end naturally because of internal failings? Was it brought down by external forces? Or was it simply transformed into something new?

REVIEW & ASSESS

1. **READING CHECK** What three barbarian tribes invaded Roman territory, leading to Rome's downfall?

2. **SEQUENCE EVENTS** What events led to the fall of the Western Roman Empire?

3. **DRAW CONCLUSIONS** Why were so many tribes able to invade the Western Roman Empire?

CST 1 Students explain how major events are related to one another in time; HI 2 Students understand and distinguish cause, effect, sequence, and correlation in historical events, including the long- and short-term causal relations.

351

HSS CONTENT STANDARDS:

7.1 Students analyze the causes and effects of the vast expansion and ultimate disintegration of the Roman Empire.

HSS ANALYSIS SKILLS:

CST 1 Students explain how major events are related to one another in time;
HI 2 Students understand and distinguish cause, effect, sequence, and correlation in historical events, including the long- and short-term causal relations.

PLAN

OBJECTIVE

Identify the forces that ultimately brought an end to the Western Roman Empire.

ESSENTIAL QUESTION

What was the power and enduring legacy of the Roman Empire?

Foreign invaders destroyed the Western Roman Empire. Lesson 3.3 discusses some of the groups involved in ending the Roman Empire.

BACKGROUND FOR THE TEACHER

The decline of the Western Roman Empire is complicated and multifaceted, but the deathblow is clear—the "barbarian" tribes rampaged across the Western Empire, sacking Rome several times. Regardless of the various factors that brought the Western Empire to its low point, once there, a Roman army that was increasingly in disarray could not check the military force of Germanic and Asian invaders. Desperate Roman generals would conscript defeated barbarian forces and move their people to less threatening areas. However, the Western Roman emperor had essentially lost control and the Eastern Roman Empire was not going to get mired in the fight.

DIGITAL RESOURCES NGLSync.cengage.com

TEACHER RESOURCES & ASSESSMENT

 Reading and Note-Taking

 Vocabulary Practice

 Section 3 Quiz

STUDENT RESOURCES

 Biography

ANALYZE VISUALS

Have students look at the painting of Attila in the lesson. Point out that it was painted in 1930—long after the fall of Rome—and that the artist was Italian. **ASK:** What does this painting tell you not only about Attila, but about the artist? `0:05` minutes

GUIDED DISCUSSION

1. **Explain** Why would multiple groups attacking the Western Roman Empire at the same time be more challenging to defend against? *(Multiple attackers would mean there was no single leadership with which to negotiate. Additionally, the various groups would have their own motivations for attacking and thus be harder to predict where their forces were headed.)*

2. **Make Inferences** Point out to students that the Eastern Roman Empire does not come to the aid of the Western Roman Empire during this period. Ask students why this might be the case. *(Answers will vary, but the Eastern Roman Empire was under attack as well. However, the East had better leadership and was able to keep invaders at bay through either military strength or negotiation.)*

MAKE PREDICTIONS

The Western Roman Empire was replaced by many smaller Germanic kingdoms. **ASK:** How do you think life in the former empire might have changed for the people who lived there? *(Answers will vary, but point out the loss of a large centralized bureaucracy being a significant change. Use this as an opportunity to foreshadow the Middle Ages.)* `0:10` minutes

ACTIVE OPTIONS

On Your Feet: Fishbowl Use a Fishbowl strategy to reinforce what students have learned. Have half the class sit in an inner circle and discuss the fall of Rome. Have the other half of the class sit in an outer circle, facing inward, and take notes on the discussion. On a signal, have the circles trade places. `0:15` minutes

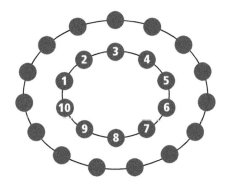

NG Learning Framework: Write a Speech

SKILLS: Collaboration, Communication
KNOWLEDGE: **Our Human Story**

Divide the class into groups—the Visigoths, Vandals, and Huns. Have each group collaborate to research and produce a speech describing their reasons for attacking Rome. Groups should choose a volunteer to read the speech. `0:15` minutes

STRIVING READERS

Create Sequence Chains Have students work in pairs to create a Sequence Chain that shows the events leading to the fall of Rome. Remind students to refer to the text to help them. Discuss their Sequence Chains as a group to assess their comprehension.

GIFTED & TALENTED

Create a Multimedia Presentation Ask students to create multimedia presentations about the fall of Rome using photos, text, and audio. Point out to students that their presentations should describe the events that led to the last emperor of Rome leaving the throne. Invite volunteers to share their presentations with the class.

Press (**mt**) *in the Student eEdition for modified text.*

See the Chapter Planner for more strategies for differentiation.

ANSWERS

1. The Visigoths, Vandals, and Huns invaded Roman territory.

2. The movement of the various tribes caused them to clash with the Romans at different times and places. In 410, the Visigoths destroyed Rome; in 445, Attila became sole leader of the Huns. In 451, the Huns attacked Gaul. In 476, the last emperor of Rome left the throne.

3. So many tribes were able to invade the Western Empire because weak leadership in Rome was unable to provide the support the army needed to fend off the attacks.

Latin and Literature

Students learning Latin have a rhyme: "Latin is a language as dead as dead can be. First it killed the Romans, and now it's killing me." But Latin is not dead. Latin is still used—especially by scientists and doctors. In fact, you use Latin words every day. It's part of Rome's legacy, or heritage.

MAIN IDEA

The Latin language spread across the empire and influences the way we speak and write today.

AN INFLUENTIAL LANGUAGE

As you've learned, the Roman Empire had dozens of languages, but the language spoken in Rome was **Latin**. Although Greek was also commonly used, Latin was established as the official language for international communication, government, law, and trade. It was used for official business from Britain to Egypt.

The Romans brought writing to northern Europe, and we still use the Latin alphabet today. However, back then the alphabet had only 22 letters. The letters *i* and *j* were interchangeable, as were *u* and *v*. The letters *w* and *y* did not exist at all.

After the Roman Empire fell, the Latin language lived on. Over time, new languages, called Romance languages, developed from Latin. These languages include French, Italian, Spanish, and Portuguese. Each language is distinctive but shares a common root in Latin, the "Roman" in *Romance*. The English language was greatly influenced by the Romance languages and uses many Latin words, including *campus, census, curriculum, index, item, sponsor,* and *stadium*.

ORATORY, POETRY, AND PHILOSOPHY

In addition to language, Rome left behind a legacy in literature, featuring speeches, poetry, and philosophical works. **Oratory**, or public speaking, was especially prized, and promising young men were trained in the art of argument and persuasion. As you learned previously, Cicero was one of Rome's greatest orators, and his speeches are still studied by serious students of public speaking.

The Romans also loved poetry, which was based on Greek traditions. The ultimate poem was the epic, a long story describing a hero's adventures. The most celebrated Roman epic was **Virgil's** *Aeneid* (uh-NEE-uhd), which fills 12 volumes. Written between 30 and 19 B.C., it tells the story of Aeneas, the legendary founder of Rome.

Roman philosophy was another extension of Greek ideas. Philosophy is the study of reality, knowledge, and beliefs. Ethical and religious arguments interested Romans more than theory and speculation. The Greek Stoic (STOH-ihk) philosophy was especially influential in Roman life. It stressed a practical approach to life in which people performed their civic duty and accepted their circumstances—good or bad.

The Roman Catholic Church became the keeper of Roman literature for centuries after the empire fell. It preserved works that could be used to educate young men in morality, government, and law. A 15th-century fascination with the ancient world revived the popularity of Roman literature and has ensured its widespread circulation ever since.

LATIN AND ENGLISH

Many English words have Latin roots, or origins. Examine the prefixes and suffixes listed. What words can you add?

-ty, -ity
FORMS NOUNS FROM ADJECTIVES
Similarity
Technicality

Sub-
UNDER
Submarine >
Subway

Re-
AGAIN
Rebuild
Remake

-ation
FORMS NOUNS FROM VERBS
Celebration
Formation

Pre-
BEFORE
Preview
Prepay

Dis-
NOT ANY
Disbelief
Disrespect

-ment
FORMS NOUNS FROM VERBS
Entertainment
Statement

-ible, -able
FORMS ADJECTIVES FROM VERBS
^ *Flexible*
Likable

Post-
AFTER
Postgame
Postwar

-fy, -ify
FORMS VERBS AND MEANS "TO MAKE"
< *Purify*
Humidify

LEGEND

● Prefix ● Prefix Definition ● Suffix ● Suffix Explanation ● Example Words

REVIEW & ASSESS

1. **READING CHECK** How has the English language been influenced by Latin?

2. **SEQUENCE EVENTS** What sequence of events helped keep Latin alive?

3. **MAKE INFERENCES** How did Roman ideas about philosophy support the ancient Roman approach to life?

6.7.8 Discuss the legacies of Roman art and architecture, technology and science, literature, language, and law; 7.1.1 Study the early strengths and lasting contributions of Rome (e.g., significance of Roman citizenship; rights under Roman law; Roman art, architecture, engineering, and philosophy; preservation and transmission of Christianity) and its ultimate internal weaknesses (e.g., rise of autonomous military powers within the empire, undermining of citizenship by the growth of corruption and slavery, lack of education, and distribution of news); CST 1 Students explain how major events are related to one another in time; HI 2 Students understand and distinguish cause, effect, sequence, and correlation in historical events, including the long- and short-term causal relations.

STANDARDS

HSS CONTENT STANDARDS:

6.7.8 Discuss the legacies of Roman art and architecture, technology and science, literature, language, and law; **7.1.1** Study the early strengths and lasting contributions of Rome (e.g., significance of Roman citizenship; rights under Roman law; Roman art, architecture, engineering, and philosophy; preservation and transmission of Christianity) and its ultimate internal weaknesses (e.g., rise of autonomous military powers within the empire, undermining of citizenship by the growth of corruption and slavery, lack of education, and distribution of news).

HSS ANALYSIS SKILLS:

CST 1 Students explain how major events are related to one another in time; **HI 2** Students understand and distinguish cause, effect, sequence, and correlation in historical events, including the long- and short-term causal relations.

PLAN

OBJECTIVE

Understand the lasting legacy of Rome in language and literature.

ESSENTIAL QUESTION

What was the power and enduring legacy of the Roman Empire?

Latin and literature are Roman legacies that have endured over 2,000 years. Lesson 4.1 discusses the written and spoken legacies of the Roman Empire.

BACKGROUND FOR THE TEACHER

The oldest existing example of written Latin is on a Greek cloak pin from around the 7th century B.C. Small communities along the Tiber River still spoke Latin as Rome began its rise. Latin became the language of Rome and then spread along with Rome's borders. Long after the Empire was gone, Latin was the language used in most major universities. The Roman Catholic Church required Latin to be used in religious services until the late 20th century.

DIGITAL RESOURCES NGLSync.cengage.com

TEACHER RESOURCES & ASSESSMENT

 Reading and Note-Taking

 Vocabulary Practice

 Section 4 Quiz

STUDENT RESOURCES

 Active History

ACTIVATE PRIOR KNOWLEDGE

Tell students that in this lesson, they will start to learn about some of the enduring legacies of Rome. Ask students to identify aspects of modern culture they know came from Rome. *(Possibilities: our alphabet; a variety of English words—either directly or derived; philosophy; the art of public speaking; art; architecture; law)* `0:05` **minutes**

TEACH

GUIDED DISCUSSION

1. **Summarize** Tell students that philosophy is a way of looking at the world. As mentioned in the text, Greek Stoic philosophy was influential in Roman culture. Have students summarize their understanding of stoicism and provide an example of what they believe would be a stoic approach to a situation. *(Answers will vary.)*

2. **Make Inferences** Why is language one of the most influential legacies a culture or civilization can leave behind? *(Possible answer: Language is not just an alphabet. Language is also the means by which ideas are passed from one person to another, from one culture to another. A language reflects a world view and if that language survives, carries a significant aspect of that culture into the future.)*

ANALYZE VISUALS

Have students review the prefix and suffix graphic. Walk through the chart as a class and discuss how a prefix or a suffix can change a word. `0:10` **minutes**

ACTIVE OPTIONS

Active History: Analyze the Roots of Modern Languages Extend the lesson by using either the PDF or Whiteboard version of the Analyze the Roots of Modern Languages Active History lesson. These activities take a deeper look at a topic from, or related to, the lesson. Explore the activities as a class, turn them into group assignments, or even assign them individually. `0:15` **minutes**

On Your Feet: Word Race Divide the class into two teams and line them up in front of two prepared writing areas. (blackboard, whiteboard, butcher paper, etc.) Write a prefix or a suffix above each team's writing area. On your count, the first student in each line will go up and write a word that uses their assigned prefix or suffix. When finished, they'll go to the back of the line and the next team member goes up, and so forth. Give each team 60 seconds to write as many words as they can. Each correct word scores a point. Add more rounds as desired. `0:20` **minutes**

STRIVING READERS

Strengthen Vocabulary Ask students to write the word *oratory* in a Word Square and then write its definition and characteristics. Have students provide examples and non-examples of it. After students complete the Word Square, ask them to create Word Squares for the other vocabulary words in the lesson.

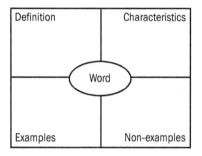

PRE-AP

Research the *Aeneid* Have students find an English translation of Virgil's *Aeneid*. Let them know that it was written in hexameters. Hexameter has not been a very widely-used style in English because the language does not easily lend itself to the format. Ask them to start scanning the text and find a passage that they like. Have them copy this passage and explain to the class what it means to them.

Press **mt** *in the Student eEdition for modified text.*

See the Chapter Planner for more strategies for differentiation.

ANSWERS

1. The English language contains many Latin words that we use everyday. Also, the Romance languages that developed from Latin influenced the English language.

2. Latin's continued use in education, literature, and in the Roman Catholic Church helped keep the language alive.

3. The Greek Stoic philosophy stressed a practical approach to life in which people performed their civic duty and accepted their circumstances—good or bad. This was very much in keeping with Roman society and government, which is why the Romans perpetuated this philosophy.

4.2 Art, Architecture, and Law

The Romans shaped the ancient world for a thousand years. But what have they ever done for us? Well, quite a lot actually. If you know what to look for, you can spot Rome's legacy in modern-day art, architecture, and law.

MAIN IDEA

The Romans developed many ideas that continue to influence our lives today.

This panel from a Roman sarcophagus is an example of bas-relief.

ART AND ARCHITECTURE

As with their philosophy, Romans preferred a realistic approach to art. The paintings and statues that decorated their homes showed people and things as they really looked. Like the Romans, people today often display realistic family portraits, although photos have generally replaced statues.

The Romans also made mosaics and frescoes popular on floors and walls around the world. Roman frescoes can be compared to modern murals and even some street art. The Roman **bas-relief** (bah-ruh-LEEF) is a realistic sculpture with figures raised against a flat background. These sculptures appear on monuments such as the National World War II Memorial in Washington, D.C. The photo on these pages is an example of a Roman bas-relief carved into the side of a sarcophagus, or stone coffin.

Rome's architectural influence is everywhere. Starting from the ground up, the Romans showed the world the benefit of an extensive, well-built, and well-maintained all-weather road network. European roads still follow Roman routes and sometimes cross original Roman bridges.

When a new Roman town was created, city planners took into account the city's climate and geography. The Romans always tried to establish a grid pattern for the streets. That means that the streets formed a network of intersecting horizontal and vertical lines. Many towns and cities use this pattern today.

Like the Romans, modern builders rely on concrete to build strong, tall, and unusual buildings. Roman architectural styles such as columns, arches, and domes can be seen in the U.S. Capitol and other buildings. Many modern stadiums follow the design perfected in the Colosseum.

LAW AND GOVERNMENT

Rome even influences the way people today live. Roman ideas of civic duty are encouraged in the United States and elsewhere. The structure of the U.S. government reflects elements of the Roman Republic, including representative assemblies and the system of checks and balances. Roman laws are the basis of law codes around the world, including that of the United States. The ideas of a fair judge, presumption of innocence, and equality under the law also come from the Romans.

The Latin language is still very much a part of modern law and other fields and professions. Legal documents, science papers, and memorial inscriptions are rich with Latin text. As you learned earlier, many everyday English words have their roots in Latin. Studying Latin can also make it easier to learn other modern languages that have Latin roots.

So don't just think about the legacy of Rome, search it out. It's in our language, laws, government, art, and architecture. The Romans are everywhere.

REVIEW & ASSESS

1. **READING CHECK** What Roman achievements in art and architecture influence our lives today?

2. **MAKE CONNECTIONS** How has the government of the Roman Republic influenced the structure of the U.S. government?

3. **COMPARE AND CONTRAST** How are the layouts of many towns and cities today similar to those in ancient Rome?

6.7.2 Describe the government of the Roman Republic and its significance (e.g., written constitution and tripartite government, checks and balances, civic duty); 6.7.8 Discuss the legacies of Roman art and architecture, technology and science, literature, language, and law; 7.1.1 Study the early strengths and lasting contributions of Rome

(e.g., significance of Roman citizenship; rights under Roman law; Roman art, architecture, engineering, and philosophy; preservation and transmission of Christianity) and its ultimate internal weaknesses (e.g., rise of autonomous military powers within the empire, undermining of citizenship by the growth of corruption and slavery, lack of education, and distribution of news); HI 2 Students understand and distinguish cause, effect, sequence, and correlation in historical events, including the long- and short-term causal relations; HI 3 Students explain the sources of historical continuity and how the combination of ideas and events explains the emergence of new patterns.

STANDARDS

HSS CONTENT STANDARDS:

6.7.2 Describe the government of the Roman Republic and its significance (e.g., written constitution and tripartite government, checks and balances, civic duty); **6.7.8** Discuss the legacies of Roman art and architecture, technology and science, literature, language, and law; **7.1.1** Study the early strengths and lasting contributions of Rome (e.g., significance of Roman citizenship; rights under Roman law; Roman art, architecture, engineering, and philosophy; preservation and transmission of Christianity) and its ultimate internal weaknesses (e.g., rise of autonomous military powers within the empire, undermining of citizenship by the growth of corruption and slavery, lack of education, and distribution of news).

HSS ANALYSIS SKILLS:

HI 2 Students understand and distinguish cause, effect, sequence, and correlation in historical events, including the long- and short-term causal relations; **HI 3** Students explain the sources of historical continuity and how the combination of ideas and events explains the emergence of new patterns.

PLAN

OBJECTIVE

Understand the lasting legacy of Rome in modern-day art, architecture, and law.

ESSENTIAL QUESTION

What was the power and enduring legacy of the Roman Empire?

Roman art, architecture, and law profoundly influenced the development of Western society. Lesson 4.2 discusses these aspects of the Roman Empire and how we can still see them all around us today.

BACKGROUND FOR THE TEACHER

City planning was a deliberate and thoughtful process in the Roman Empire. The preferred shape was a square. Wide avenues would run from the mid-point of each side directly across to the opposite side. Side streets were based off that grid. The forum was located near the center of Roman towns. Forums were open spaces where commerce was conducted and the business of politics took place. Purpose-driven structures often appeared on the perimeter of the forum, including shops, tax collectors, and temples. Large cities might have multiple forums dedicated to specific activities such as finance or administration. Timgad was a Roman city in the north of modern Algeria. It was abandoned in the 7th century and then largely covered by sand. Uncovered in 1881, Timgad is a well-preserved example of the Roman town layout.

DIGITAL RESOURCES NGLSync.cengage.com

TEACHER RESOURCES & ASSESSMENT

 Reading and Note-Taking

 Vocabulary Practice

 Section 4 Quiz

STUDENT RESOURCES

 NG Chapter Gallery

INTRODUCE & ENGAGE

BRAINSTORM: WHERE IS ROME?

Tell students that there are legacies of Roman culture that are clearly visible to us every day. As a class, brainstorm modern objects, ideas, art, etc., based on what students have learned so far. *(Select possibilities: language, legal theories, buildings, sculptures, civic duty)* `0:10` **minutes**

TEACH

GUIDED DISCUSSION

1. **Synthesize** Why are legal concepts such as a fair judge, a presumption of innocence, and equality under the law important? *(Possible answer: All of these concepts are designed to protect the innocent and to ensure that the law is applied the same way from trial to trial.)*

2. **Make Inferences** Why might something such as city planning be such a lasting legacy of the Roman Empire? *(Possible answer: The empire existed for a long time, and there was plenty of time to find out what worked and what didn't. So it makes sense that Romans found useful and efficient ways of doing certain things.)*

ANALYZE VISUALS

Have students review the bas-relief sculpture in the photo and remind them it is made out of stone. Ask them what they find interesting about it. *(Possible answers: the detail, the realism)* `0:05` **minutes**

ACTIVE OPTIONS

On Your Feet: Legacy Debate Divide the class into three teams: Art, Architecture, and Law. Give the teams some time to develop their reasons for why their Roman legacy is the most enduring aspect of Roman culture today. `0:20` **minutes**

NG Learning Framework: Compare Observations

SKILLS: Observation, Collaboration
KNOWLEDGE: Our Human Story, New Frontiers

Have students review the previous lessons, looking specifically for information about the legacy of Rome. They should work in pairs to create a list of observations about the Roman legacy and why elements of Roman culture have endured. Once they have completed their list of observations, each pair should exchange lists with another pair and discuss the new list. `0:15` **minutes**

DIFFERENTIATE

INCLUSION

Summarize by Matching Provide pairs of students with a set of index cards showing the following words and phrases in mixed order: *bas-relief, fresco, mosaic, column, arch, dome, representative assembly, checks and balances, equality.* Then have the students sort the cards into three groups: art, architecture, and government and law.

GIFTED & TALENTED

Describe Roman Art Have students use library resources or online sources to research Roman art. Instruct them to choose a way to describe Roman art. They might create a multimedia presentation with photos and descriptions; create their own sculpture, fresco, or mosaic; create a play or dialogue around Roman art; or write a traditional research paper. **ASK:** What makes Roman art worth preserving and emulating? *(Answers may vary but should include a comment about the enduring nature of art.)*

Press (**mt**) *in the Student eEdition for modified text.*

See the Chapter Planner for more strategies for differentiation.

REVIEW & ASSESS

ANSWERS

1. Some achievements include mosaics, frescoes, bas-relief, columns, arches, domes, and the use of concrete.

2. Representative assemblies and a checks-and-balances system have been used in the U.S. government.

3. They are based on a grid pattern.

A.D. 52

The system of aqueducts that supplied water to Rome and its empire was a major feat of engineering. In the capital city itself, 11 aqueducts carried fresh water from the area's surrounding rivers and lakes, some as far as 57 miles away. Not all of these structures were architectural masterpieces like the Claudian Aqueduct (shown here), which was completed in A.D. 52. Many consisted of simple underground pipes through which water flowed to various tanks throughout the city. The Roman aqueduct system fell apart after the breakdown of the empire, but the basic engineering principles behind its construction are still in use today.

6.7.8 Discuss the legacies of Roman art and architecture, technology and science, literature, language, and law; 7.1.1 Study the early strengths and lasting contributions of Rome (e.g., significance of Roman citizenship; rights under Roman law; Roman art, architecture, engineering, and philosophy; preservation and transmission of Christianity) and its ultimate internal weaknesses (e.g., rise of autonomous military powers within the empire, undermining of citizenship by the growth of corruption and slavery, lack of education, and distribution of news); HI 3 Students explain the sources of historical continuity and how the combination of ideas and events explains the emergence of new patterns.

357

HSS CONTENT STANDARDS:

6.7.8 Discuss the legacies of Roman art and architecture, technology and science, literature, language, and law; **7.1.1** Study the early strengths and lasting contributions of Rome (e.g., significance of Roman citizenship; rights under Roman law; Roman art, architecture, engineering, and philosophy; preservation and transmission of Christianity) and its ultimate internal weaknesses (e.g., rise of autonomous military powers within the empire, undermining of citizenship by the growth of corruption and slavery, lack of education, and distribution of news).

HSS ANALYSIS SKILLS:

HI 3 Students explain the sources of historical continuity and how the combination of ideas and events explains the emergence of new patterns.

PLAN

OBJECTIVE

Understand why aqueducts themselves were important, but also why they are powerful reminders of the once mighty Roman Empire.

ESSENTIAL QUESTION

What was the power and enduring legacy of the Roman Empire?

Sustaining and supporting a growing urban population was a constant effort in ancient Rome. Supplying water was a vital part of that effort. Lesson 4.3 shows a still-standing aqueduct that began bringing water to the city of Rome around A.D. 52.

BACKGROUND FOR THE TEACHER

Aqueducts are systems for providing water. Although the Roman aqueducts are the most famous water delivery system of the ancient world, they were not the first. Persia, India, and Egypt all had water supply systems in place hundreds of years before Rome. Still, the engineering mastery shown in the system of aqueducts that supplied the city of Rome with water was unmatched in the ancient world and would remain so until modern times.

INTRODUCE & ENGAGE

CONSIDER WATER SOURCES `STEM`

Have students consider the topography of their community—hills, valleys, etc.—and ask them to think about the nearest source of water. **ASK:** How would you move enough water for everyone in the community using only gravity? Explain that this was the challenge faced by Roman engineers across the empire. `0:10` minutes

TEACH

GUIDED DISCUSSION

1. **Analyze Visuals** Examine the photograph of the Claudian Aqueduct. What do you see? *(Responses will vary. Possible response: The structure dwarfs the people in the image. The structure looks old and battered, but still very solid.)*

2. **Make Inferences** What might be a disadvantage to having a water supply system such as this? *(Responses will vary. Possible response: An above-ground water system could be vulnerable to disruption by even minor earthquakes or deliberate attacks by enemy forces.)*

MORE INFORMATION `STEM`

Roman Engineering Across Europe Roman roads, walls, and aqueducts can be found throughout Europe. Among the things that the Roman army brought with them to conquered lands were ideas about civic improvement and defense. Hadrian's Wall in England; the aqueduct at Segovia, Spain; Roman roads in Portugal—all are examples of Roman engineering that are still visible today. Roman engineers built improvements wherever the empire spread, not with an eye toward a lasting legacy, but rather with the goal of bringing Rome to every part of the empire through stone and mortar.

ACTIVE OPTIONS

On Your Feet: True-False Write a series of true-false questions related to Roman engineering generally and aqueducts specifically. Establish one side of the room as "True" and another side as "False." Ask the questions and have students move to the side of the room that represents their answer. `0:15` minutes

Critical Viewing: NG Chapter Gallery Invite students to explore the entire NG Chapter Gallery and choose one image from the gallery they feel best represents their understanding of the chapter. Have students provide a written explanation of why they selected the image they chose. `0:10` minutes

DIFFERENTIATE

ENGLISH LANGUAGE LEARNERS `ELD`

Examine Related Words Students at all proficiency levels whose first language is Spanish might quickly understand the word *aqueduct*. The Spanish word for *aqueduct* is acueducto and comes from the same Latin roots. In both languages, the roots are from the Latin *aqua*, "water," and *ducere*, "to lead." Point to other vocabulary similarities between languages for terms in the lesson or that you can see on the page.

ENGLISH	LATIN	SPANISH
arch	arch	arco
pipe	pipe	pipa
cloud	nubes	nube

GIFTED & TALENTED

Build Models Have students research an ancient Roman aqueduct—there were 11. Have them use clay, papier-mâché, a drafting program, etc., to build a model of the aqueduct system. Have students display their models in the classroom.

Press *in the Student eEdition for modified text.*

See the Chapter Planner for more strategies for differentiation.

VOCABULARY

Match each word in the first column with its definition in the second column.

WORD	DEFINITION
1. aqueduct (HSS 6.7.8)	a. the practice and skill of public speaking
2. fresco (HSS 6.7.8)	b. thousands of tiny colored stone cubes set in plaster to create a picture or design
3. parable (HSS 6.7.6)	c. a painting done on plaster walls
4. barbarian (HSS 7.1.2)	d. a system of government in which there are four rulers
5. oratory (HSS 6.7.8)	e. a member of a tribe outside the empire
6. bas-relief (HSS 6.7.8)	f. a simple story told to make a moral point
7. tetrarchy (HSS 7.1.1)	g. a stone channel that carries water
8. mosaic (HSS 6.7.8)	h. a sculpture with figures raised against a flat background

READING STRATEGY

9. ORGANIZE IDEAS: SEQUENCE EVENTS If you haven't already, complete your time line of key people and events in the Roman Empire. Then answer the question.

People and Events in the Roman Empire

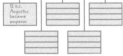

Which person or event do you think had the greatest impact on the Roman Empire? Why? (HSS CST 2)

MAIN IDEAS

Answer the following questions. Support your answers with evidence from the chapter.

10. What was accomplished during the Pax Romana? LESSON 1.1 (HSS HI 1)

11. What effect did safe seas and a network of excellent roads have on the Roman Empire's economy? LESSON 1.2 (HSS HI 6)

12. What role did Constantine play in the growth of Christianity? LESSON 2.4 (HSS 6.7.7)

13. Why did Diocletian divide the Roman Empire into the Eastern and Western Roman Empires? LESSON 3.2 (HSS 7.1.1)

14. How did Roman ideas about government and law influence the government of the United States? LESSON 4.2 (HSS 6.7.2)

CRITICAL THINKING

Answer the following questions. Support your answers with evidence from the chapter.

15. ESSENTIAL QUESTION What was the main reason the Roman Empire became so powerful and long lasting? (HSS REP 1)

16. SYNTHESIZE What steps did Augustus take to secure the support of the Roman people and bring peace to the Roman Empire? (HSS 6.7.4)

17. EVALUATE What role did technology play in Roman architecture? (HSS 6.7.8)

18. ANALYZE CAUSE AND EFFECT How did the Roman Empire's vast geographic expanse become a serious disadvantage in the third century? What was the effect of this disadvantage? (HSS 7.1.1)

19. MAKE CONNECTIONS How did the Latin language influence the Romance languages and English? (HSS 6.7.8)

20. YOU DECIDE Do you think Augustus was a great emperor or a clever politician? Support your opinion with evidence from the chapter. (HSS 6.7.4)

INTERPRET MAPS

ROAD NETWORK OF THE ROMAN EMPIRE, c. A.D. 117

21. Where is Rome located in relation to the rest of the Roman Empire? (HSS CST 3)

22. In A.D. 117 how far north and how far south did the Roman Empire extend? (HSS 7.1.2)

ANALYZE SOURCES

Read the following selection from Jesus' Sermon on the Mount. Then answer the question.

> Blessed are the poor in spirit, for theirs is the kingdom of heaven.
>
> Blessed are the meek, for they will inherit the Earth.
>
> Blessed are the merciful, for they will be shown mercy.
>
> Blessed are the pure in heart, for they will see God.
>
> —Matthew 5:3–8

23. SYNTHESIZE How might these teachings from Jesus have helped guide people to lead their lives during the Roman Empire? (HSS REP 4)

WRITE ABOUT HISTORY

24. EXPLANATORY Many social, political, and economic problems contributed to the decline and fall of the Roman Empire. Put yourself in the position of a senator at that time. Write a speech explaining three of these problems. (HSS 7.1.1)

TIPS

- Take notes as you review the portion of the chapter about the decline and fall of the Roman Empire.
- State your main idea and supporting details in a clear, well-organized way.
- Present evidence to support your explanation.
- Use vocabulary from the chapter to explain the problems.
- Make a concluding statement based on your explanation of and evidence about the decline and fall of the Roman Empire.

VOCABULARY ANSWERS

WORD	DEFINITION
1. aqueduct (HSS 6.7.8) g	**a.** the practice and skill of public speaking
2. fresco (HSS 6.7.8) c	**b.** thousands of tiny colored stone cubes set in plaster to create a picture or design
3. parable (HSS 6.7.6) f	**c.** a painting done on plaster walls
4. barbarian (HSS 7.1.2) e	**d.** a system of government in which there are four rulers
5. oratory (HSS 6.7.8) a	**e.** a member of a tribe outside the empire
6. bas-relief (HSS 6.7.8) h	**f.** a simple story told to make a moral point
7. tetrarchy (HSS 7.1.1) d	**g.** a stone channel that carries water
8. mosaic (HSS 6.7.8) b	**h.** a sculpture with figures raised against a flat background

STANDARDS

HSS CONTENT STANDARDS:

6.7.2 Describe the government of the Roman Republic and its significance (e.g., written constitution and tripartite government, checks and balances, civic duty); **6.7.4** Discuss the influence of Julius Caesar and Augustus in Rome's transition from republic to empire; **6.7.6** Note the origins of Christianity in the Jewish Messianic prophecies, the life and teachings of Jesus of Nazareth as described in the New Testament, and the contribution of St. Paul the Apostle to the definition and spread of Christian beliefs (e.g., belief in the Trinity, resurrection, salvation); **6.7.7** Describe the circumstances that led to the spread of Christianity in Europe and other Roman territories; **6.7.8** Discuss the legacies of Roman art and architecture, technology and science, literature, language, and law; **7.1.1** Study the early strengths and lasting contributions of Rome (e.g., significance of Roman citizenship; rights under Roman law; Roman art, architecture, engineering, and philosophy; preservation and transmission of Christianity) and its ultimate internal weaknesses (e.g., rise of autonomous military powers within the empire, undermining of citizenship by the growth of corruption and slavery, lack of education, and distribution of news); **7.1.2** Discuss the geographic borders of the empire at its height and the factors that threatened its territorial cohesion.

HSS ANALYSIS SKILLS:

CST 2 Students construct various time lines of key events, people, and periods of the historical era they are studying; **CST 3** Students use a variety of maps and documents to identify physical and cultural features of neighborhoods, cities, states, and countries and to explain the historical migration of people, expansion and disintegration of empires, and the growth of economic systems; **REP 1** Students frame questions that can be answered by historical study and research; **REP 4** Students assess the credibility of primary and secondary sources and draw sound conclusions from them; **HI 1** Students explain the central issues and problems from the past, placing people and events in a matrix of time and place; **HI 6** Students interpret basic indicators of economic performance and conduct cost-benefit analyses of economic and political issues.

READING STRATEGY ANSWER

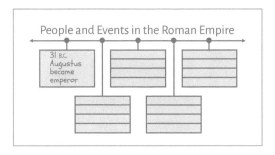

People and Events in the Roman Empire

31 B.C.
Augustus
became
emperor

9. Events and people listed on the time lines will vary, as will the explanations for which was most important and why. (HSS CST 2)

MAIN IDEAS ANSWERS

10. The Pax Romana was a 200-year period of peace that brought great prosperity to the Roman Empire—law and order began to return; art, literature, and education all improved; Rome was transformed into a magnificent capital. (HSS HI 1)

11. Safe seas and a network of excellent roads made it much easier to transport and sell goods throughout the Roman Empire, which greatly stimulated the economy. (HSS HI 6)

12. Constantine believed that the Christian god had helped him win an important battle. In gratitude, he converted to Christianity, stopped persecution of Christians, built churches, and dedicated the new capital of the Roman Empire to Christ. (HSS 6.7.7)

13. Diocletian divided the vast Roman Empire into the Eastern and Western Empires in order to make governing and defending the vast Roman Empire more efficient, and to restore order and stability. (HSS 7.1.1)

14. The United States government includes representative assemblies—both houses of Congress—and the constitution outlines the separation of powers among the different branches of government, all of which were important elements of the Roman Republic. (HSS 6.7.2)

CRITICAL THINKING ANSWERS

15. Answers will vary, but should include recognition of an aspect of Rome's power and endurance with support from the text. Possible aspects: military power; strong governance; advanced technology. (HSS REP 1)

16. Augustus worked within the law to create a hereditary monarchy that upheld ideals of the republic, but he had the supreme power as emperor. He secured people's support by guaranteeing the supply of grain, giving land and money to soldiers, encouraging the arts and education, and transforming Rome into an impressive capital with magnificent marble monuments—all worthy of a powerful empire. (HSS 6.7.4)

17. They used a new, stronger type of concrete and a combination of multiple arches, vaults, and domes to build huge, free-standing structures. (HSS 6.7.8)

18. In the third century, the Roman Empire covered such a vast geographic expanse that it became very difficult to govern and defend. Because of its size, the empire was attacked on two fronts along the eastern and western borders, which led to invasions in the empire's interior. The once mighty empire could no longer protect itself. (HSS 7.1.1)

19. Through local usage, the Latin language corrupted into new languages, including French, Italian, Spanish, and Portuguese, which are known collectively as the Romance languages. The English language has borrowed many Latin words and phrases that are used everyday, as well as written and read by scholars, scientists, doctors, and lawyers. (HSS 6.7.8)

20. Students' responses will vary. Students should clearly state their opinions regarding their view of Augustus and support that opinion with evidence from the chapter. (HSS 6.7.4)

INTERPRET MAPS ANSWERS

21. In relation to the rest of the Roman Empire, Rome is located at the center. (HSS CST 3)

22. In A.D. 117 the Roman Empire extended as far north as Britain and as far south as Egypt. (HSS 7.1.2)

ANALYZE SOURCES ANSWER

23. Students' responses will vary. Sample response: These selections from the Beatitudes offered hope and comfort to the poor and enslaved during the time of the Roman Empire, as well as a guide for how to live a more moral, meaningful life—something that humans continue to strive to do today. (HSS REP 4)

WRITE ABOUT HISTORY ANSWER

24. Students' paragraphs will vary, but they should construct a clear explanation and support that explanation with evidence from the chapter. For more in-depth instruction and practice with the writing form, assign the Social Studies Skills Writing Lesson on writing a speech. (HSS 7.1.1)

UNIT RESOURCES

On Location with National Geographic Grantee Steven Ellis
Intro and Video

 **Interactive Map Tool**

STORIES MAKING HISTORY **News & Updates**

Available at NGLSync.cengage.com

Unit Wrap-Up:
"Exploring Pompeii"
Feature and Video

"Roman Frontiers"
National Geographic Adapted Article
Student eEdition exclusive

"Rethinking Nero"
National Geographic Adapted Article

Unit 4 Inquiry:
Build an Empire

CHAPTER RESOURCES

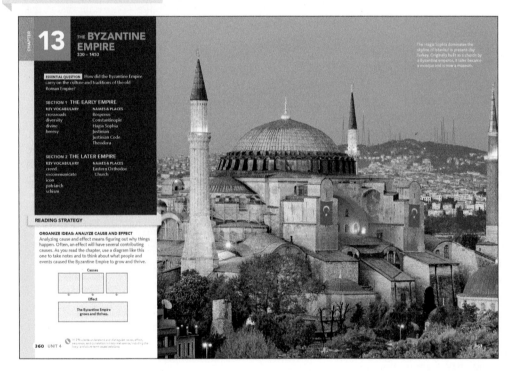

TEACHER RESOURCES & ASSESSMENT

Available at NGLSync.cengage.com

 Social Studies Skills Lessons
• Reading: Analyze Cause and Effect
• Writing: Write an Explanation

 Formal Assessment
• Chapter 13 Tests A (on-level) & B (below-level)

 Chapter 13 Answer Key

 ExamView®
One-time Download

STUDENT BACKPACK *Available at NGLSync.cengage.com*

• **eEdition** *(English)*   • **eEdition** *(Spanish)*   • **Handbooks**   • **Online Atlas**

Chapter 13 Spanish resources, Guided Writing prompts, and Financial Literacy lessons are available online.

SECTION 1 RESOURCES

THE EARLY EMPIRE

 Reading and Note-Taking

 Vocabulary Practice

 Section 1 Quiz

Available at NGLSync.cengage.com

LESSON 1.1 THE GEOGRAPHY OF THE BYZANTINE EMPIRE

• On Your Feet: Inside-Outside Circle

NG Learning Framework:
List Geographic Impacts

LESSON 1.2 JUSTINIAN AND THEODORA

 Biography
Theodora

Available at NGLSync.cengage.com

NG Learning Framework:
Write a Biography

• On Your Feet: Card Responses

MOMENTS IN HISTORY
LESSON 1.3 THE HAGIA SOPHIA

• On Your Feet: Descriptive Words
• Critical Viewing: NG Chapter Gallery

LESSON 1.4 LIFE IN CONSTANTINOPLE

• On Your Feet: Three-Step Interview
• Critical Viewing: NG Image Gallery

SECTION 2 RESOURCES

THE LATER EMPIRE

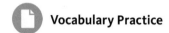 **Reading and Note-Taking**

 Vocabulary Practice

 **Section 2 Quiz**

Available at NGLSync.cengage.com

LESSON 2.1 THE CHURCH DIVIDES

 Active History: Interactive Whiteboard Activity
Compare Two Branches Of Christianity

 Active History
Compare Two Branches Of Christianity

Available at NGLSync.cengage.com

• On Your Feet: Thumbs Up/Thumbs Down

HISTORY THROUGH OBJECTS
LESSON 2.2 BYZANTINE MOSAICS

• On Your Feet: Four Corners
• Critical Viewing: NG Chapter Gallery

LESSON 2.3 THE END OF AN EMPIRE

• On Your Feet: Turn and Talk on Topic
• Critical Viewing: NG Image Gallery

CHAPTER 13 REVIEW

STRATEGY ❶
Record and Compare Facts

After reading a lesson, ask students to write two important facts they learned. Allow pairs of students to compare and check their facts and then combine their facts into one longer list. Ask a volunteer from each group to read the most important fact from the list.

Use with All Lessons

STRATEGY ❷
Preview and Predict

Before they read, have students preview the lesson. Ask them to locate and read the lesson title, the Main Idea statement, and any text in large blue type. Have students use that information to write a sentence that predicts what the lesson is about.

Use with All Lessons *For Lesson 1.2, tell students to use the lesson title and Main Idea to help them identify who ruled Byzantium during its golden age.*

STRATEGY ❸
Use Paired Reading

Pair students and assign each pair two passages in the lesson. Tell them that they will each take one passage, read it, take notes, become an expert on it, and share their expertise with their partner. After students have had time to prepare their passages, have them report on their reading to each other. Tell each listener to write two clarifying questions.

Use with All Lessons

Press **mt** *in the Student eEdition for modified text.*

STRATEGY ❶
Modify Main Idea Statements

Have each student work with a partner to preview the chapter by reading and copying each lesson's Main Idea statement onto a sheet of paper. Then have students look at the maps and other visuals in the text and add to each lesson's Main Idea. They can write complete sentences or notes on the page.

Use with Lessons 1.1–1.4 *For Lesson 1.4, have students use the illustration of the city of Constantinople to describe the city.*

STRATEGY ❷
Modify Vocabulary Lists

Limit the number of vocabulary words, terms, and names students will be required to master. Have students write each word from your modified list on a colored sticky note and put it on the page next to where it appears in context.

Use with Lessons 2.1–2.3

STRATEGY ❶
Use Visuals to Predict Content

Before reading, ask students at all proficiency levels to read the lesson title and look at any visuals. Then ask them to write a sentence that predicts how the visual is related to the lesson title. Repeat the exercise after reading and ask volunteers to read their sentences.

Use with Lessons 1.1–1.4 *Provide the following sentence stem for students at the **Emerging** level: I think this lesson is about _____. Ask students at the **Bridging** level to give reasons for their prediction.*

STRATEGY ❷
Use Pronunciation Keys

Preteach the meaning and pronunciation of vocabulary words before beginning each lesson. Give a brief definition or example for each word and then pronounce it slowly and clearly several times. Have students repeat after you. Then have students create a pronunciation key for each word.

After each lesson, have students write simple sentences using each word (for example, "A *creed* is a statement of belief"). Have students refer to their pronunciation keys to help them say the words correctly.

Use with All Lessons, All Levels *Encourage students at the **Bridging** level to develop more complex sentences for each word.*

STRATEGY ❸

Predict Vocabulary Meanings

Before reading, give students the following list of words and definitions and have them write the word next to the definition they predict is correct. Have students at the **Emerging** and **Expanding** levels work in pairs. Have students at the **Bridging** level work independently. After reading, have them check and correct any mistakes.

creed   icons   schism

excommunicated   patriarch

1. _____ images of Jesus and the saints

2. _____ leader of the Eastern Orthodox Church

3. _____ separation

4. _____ statement of belief

5. _____ no longer part of the church

Use with Lesson 2.1

GIFTED & TALENTED

STRATEGY ❶

Teach a Class

Before beginning the chapter, allow students to choose one of the two-page lessons listed below and prepare to teach the contents to the class. Give them a set amount of time in which to present their lesson. Suggest that students think about any visuals or activities they want to use when they teach.

Use with Lessons 1.1, 1.2, and 1.4

STRATEGY ❷

Create a Brochure

Tell students to imagine that they are living in the city of Constantinople and have been given the job of creating a brochure to encourage people to visit the city. Ask students to work with partners to design the brochure. Direct students to include factual information about the city, important sites, and places of interest. Students should use the information in the lesson as well as other resources to find the information. Have students share completed brochures with the class.

Use with Lesson 1.4

PRE-AP

STRATEGY ❶

Write a Feature Article

Have students use the Internet to research Byzantine art and architecture. Have them write a feature article describing what they have learned. Articles should focus on types of art, such as mosaics and frescoes, as well as descriptions of Byzantine architecture. Encourage students to include photos to accompany their articles.

Use with Lessons 1.3 and 2.2

STRATEGY ❷

Support an Opinion

Present a challenge to students to decide which achievement of Justinian made the greatest impact on the Byzantine Empire. Have them develop a thesis statement that explains their decision and write an essay that supports it. Ask students to share their essays with the class.

Use with Lessons 1.1 and 1.2

13

THE BYZANTINE EMPIRE
330 – 1453

The Hagia Sophia dominates the skyline of Istanbul in present-day Turkey. Originally built as a church by a Byzantine emperor, it later became a mosque and is now a museum.

ESSENTIAL QUESTION How did the Byzantine Empire carry on the culture and traditions of the old Roman Empire?

SECTION 1 THE EARLY EMPIRE

KEY VOCABULARY	NAMES & PLACES
crossroads	Bosporus
diversity	Constantinople
divine	Hagia Sophia
heresy	Justinian
	Justinian Code
	Theodora

SECTION 2 THE LATER EMPIRE

KEY VOCABULARY	NAMES & PLACES
creed	Eastern Orthodox
excommunicate	Church
icon	
patriarch	
schism	

READING STRATEGY

ORGANIZE IDEAS: ANALYZE CAUSE AND EFFECT
Analyzing cause and effect means figuring out why things happen. Often, an effect will have several contributing causes. As you read the chapter, use a diagram like this one to take notes and to think about what people and events caused the Byzantine Empire to grow and thrive.

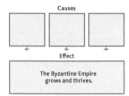

Causes

Effect

The Byzantine Empire grows and thrives.

HI 2 Students understand and distinguish cause, effect, sequence, and correlation in historical events, including the long- and short-term causal relations.

361

HSS ANALYSIS SKILLS:

HI 2 Students understand and distinguish cause, effect, sequence, and correlation in historical events, including the long- and short-term causal relations.

TEACHER BACKGROUND

INTRODUCE THE PHOTOGRAPH

Have students study the photograph of Istanbul and the Hagia Sophia. Explain that Istanbul was once called Constantinople and was an important city in the Byzantine Empire. Tell students that, in this chapter, they will learn about the factors that contributed to the growth of the Byzantine Empire and the importance of Constantinople to the empire.

ASK: *How would you describe the city of Istanbul? (Possible responses: Istanbul looks like an older city; it is densely populated.)*

SHARE BACKGROUND

Istanbul is the largest city and port in Turkey. The ancient city was known as Constantinople when it was the capital of the Byzantine Empire. Later, Constantinople became the capital city of the Ottoman Empire. The city became known as *Istanbul* off and on after it became the capital of the Ottoman Empire. After the creation of the Turkish Republic in 1923, however, *Istanbul* became the official name of the city. Although no longer its capital, Istanbul remains the cultural center of Turkey.

DIGITAL RESOURCES NGLSync.cengage.com

TEACHER RESOURCES & ASSESSMENT

 Social Studies Skills Lessons
- Reading: Analyze Cause and Effect
- Writing: Write an Explanation

 Formal Assessment
- Chapter 13 Tests A (on-level) & B (below-level)

 ExamView®
One-time Download

 **Chapter 13 Answer Key**

STUDENT BACKPACK
- **eEdition** (*English*)
- **eEdition** (*Spanish*)
- **Handbooks**
- **Online Atlas**

INTRODUCE THE ESSENTIAL QUESTION

HOW DID THE BYZANTINE EMPIRE CARRY ON THE CULTURE AND TRADITIONS OF THE OLD ROMAN EMPIRE?

Jigsaw Activity: Preview Content This activity will help students preview and make predictions about the topics covered in Chapter 13. Divide the class into seven groups. Assign one lesson from the chapter to each group. Have group members preview the lesson and consider the following questions:

Group 1 What effect might the geography of the Byzantine Empire have had on the empire?

Group 2 Who were Justinian and Theodora? How were they important to the Byzantine Empire?

Group 3 What is the Hagia Sophia? Why was it important to the Byzantine Empire?

Group 4 Where was Constantinople located? What was life like in Constantinople?

Group 5 What religion was important in the Byzantine Empire? What caused the church to divide?

Group 6 What are mosaics? Why are mosaics important in Byzantine art?

Group 7 What led to the decline of the Byzantine Empire? When did it end?

Regroup students so each new grouping has at least one member from each original group. Have students share their preview of their assigned lesson so that other students can learn what to expect from their reading in Chapter 13. `0:20` minutes

INTRODUCE THE READING STRATEGY

ORGANIZE IDEAS: ANALYZE CAUSE AND EFFECT

Remind students that cause and effect involves figuring out why things happen. A cause is an action or condition that makes something else happen. An effect is what happens as a result of the cause. An effect often has several causes. Model completing the diagram by reading the first paragraph under "Connecting East and West" in Lesson 1.1 and adding the phrase *location at crossroads of Europe and Asia* in one of the Cause boxes in the diagram. For more in-depth instruction and practice with the reading strategy, assign the Social Studies Skills Reading Lesson on analyzing cause and effect.

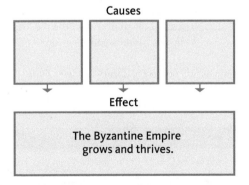

Causes

Effect

The Byzantine Empire grows and thrives.

INTRODUCE CHAPTER VOCABULARY

STUMP THE EXPERT

Have students play "Stump the Expert" with the Key Vocabulary words. Give each student a list of words or write the words on the board. Identify a student as the first expert. Have a stumper present a definition or clue. Give the expert a set time to name the word. If the response is correct, the next stumper offers a word challenge. Continue until the expert is stumped or until the expert answers three challenges. The student who stumps the expert becomes the new expert, and the procedure begins again.

KEY DATES	
A.D. **293**	Diocletian divides Roman Empire
A.D. **527**	Justinian becomes emperor of Byzantine Empire
A.D. **537**	Hagia Sophia is officially blessed
A.D. **711**	Arabs conquer parts of Byzantine Empire
A.D. **1054**	Church splits into Roman Catholic Church and Eastern Orthodox Church
A.D. **1204**	Christian Europeans conquer and occupy Constantinople
A.D. **1453**	Constantinople comes under Turkish control

1.1

The Geography of the **Byzantine** Empire

The Western Roman Empire fell in A.D. 476, but that's not the end of its story. For a thousand years after that date, the glory of Rome lived on in the Byzantine Empire.

MAIN IDEA

The Byzantine Empire was well located for trade but open to attack.

CONNECTING EAST AND WEST

From law to architecture, the Byzantine (BIHZ-uhn-teen) Empire's achievements were extraordinary. One reason for those achievements was the empire's location at the **crossroads** of Europe and Asia, the place where the trade routes from each continent met. As a result of the empire's geography, many influences came together to create the Byzantine civilization.

As you may recall from the previous chapter, the emperor Diocletian divided the Roman Empire in A.D. 293. The Eastern Roman Empire became known as the Byzantine Empire because its capital was built on the old Greek town of Byzantium (buh-ZAN-tee-uhm). In fact, the Byzantine Empire is often referred to as Byzantium. By A.D. 330, the emperor Constantine had transformed Byzantium into a grand "New Rome." He named the city **Constantinople**, or city of Constantine. Today it is called Istanbul.

While the Western Roman Empire was ripped apart by invading barbarians, the Byzantine Empire managed to survive similar attacks. A series of strong emperors fought off Byzantium's enemies and strengthened the empire. Thus, the Byzantine Empire continued the traditions of Roman civilization for another thousand years after the collapse of the Western Roman Empire. The people we now call Byzantines proudly called themselves Romans.

Constantinople occupied one of the ancient world's most important geographic locations. At the heart of the empire was the small but important land link between Asia and Europe that permitted trade between east and west. The empire itself reached into both continents. Its heartland was in what are now Greece and Turkey.

Constantinople was also located on the **Bosporus**, a strait that links the Black Sea with the Mediterranean. The city was a major trade center for goods traveling by land and sea from all over the world. Constantinople and the Byzantine Empire grew rich on this trade. The city also attracted people from many parts of the world. They came to trade goods from their homelands and wound up living in the bustling city. These immigrants gave Constantinople the cultural **diversity**, or variety, for which it was famous.

EXPANDING THE EMPIRE

The Byzantine Empire's location brought problems as well as advantages. Although Constantinople itself was well protected, the rest of the empire was surrounded by enemies. To the north and west were many barbarian kingdoms forcefully pressing on Byzantium's borders. To the east was an age-old enemy, the powerful and hostile Persian Empire.

The rich resources and great wealth of Byzantium made it a tempting target for raids and invasions. With no strong geographic barriers to prevent invasion by enemies, the empire was dangerously exposed. Its long borders were constantly under attack by invading neighbors.

The Byzantine Empire needed strong leadership to hold it together in the face of so many threats. Over a thousand years, its borders grew and shrank, depending on the ability of its rulers and the eagerness of its enemies to wage war. At its greatest extent, the empire completely encircled the Mediterranean Sea.

Probably the greatest Byzantine ruler was one of its earliest—**Justinian**, the emperor from A.D. 527 until his death in 565. He not only recaptured lost Byzantine lands but also reconquered large areas of the old Western Roman Empire. His armies defeated the Persians and reconquered North Africa, Italy, and parts of Spain. For a brief time, Justinian reunited the Eastern and Western Roman Empires. He built up the strength of the Byzantine Empire, even while Rome was being overrun by invaders. Justinian's legacy of leadership remained influential throughout the time of the Byzantine Empire and beyond.

THE BYZANTINE EMPIRE, A.D. 527–565

The Byzantine Empire before Justinian

Expansion under Justinian

REVIEW & ASSESS

1. **READING CHECK** Why was Constantinople's geographic location an advantage for trade?

2. **ANALYZE CAUSE AND EFFECT** What caused the Persian Empire and other enemies to attack and invade Byzantium?

3. **INTERPRET MAPS** How far west did the borders of the Byzantine Empire expand after Justinian's conquests?

7.1.3 Describe the establishment by Constantine of the new capital in Constantinople and the development of the Byzantine Empire, with an emphasis on the consequences of the development of two distinct European civilizations,

Eastern Orthodox and Roman Catholic, and their two distinct views on church-state relations; CST 3 Students use a variety of maps and documents to identify physical and cultural features of neighborhoods, cities, states, and countries and to explain the historical migration of people, expansion and disintegration of empires, and the growth of economic systems; HI 2 Students understand and distinguish cause, effect, sequence, and correlation in historical events, including the long- and short-term causal relations.

HSS CONTENT STANDARDS:

7.1.3 Describe the establishment by Constantine of the new capital in Constantinople and the development of the Byzantine Empire, with an emphasis on the consequences of the development of two distinct European civilizations, Eastern Orthodox and Roman Catholic, and their two distinct views on church-state relations.

HSS ANALYSIS SKILLS:

CST 3 Students use a variety of maps and documents to identify physical and cultural features of neighborhoods, cities, states, and countries and to explain the historical migration of people, expansion and disintegration of empires, and the growth of economic systems; **HI 2** Students understand and distinguish cause, effect, sequence, and correlation in historical events, including the long- and short-term causal relations.

PLAN

OBJECTIVE

Identify the geographic features of the Byzantine Empire.

ESSENTIAL QUESTION

How did the Byzantine Empire carry on the culture and traditions of the old Roman Empire?

When Diocletian divided the Roman Empire, the Eastern Roman Empire became the Byzantine Empire and continued hundreds of years after the end of the Western Roman Empire. Lesson 1.1 explains how the location of the Byzantine Empire made it well positioned for trade but open to attack.

BACKGROUND FOR THE TEACHER

The Bosporous connects the Sea of Marmara with the Black Sea. It also forms a dividing line between the European and Asian sections of the city of Istanbul. Lining the Bosporous are villages, ancient towers, and summer homes. In the 18th and 19th centuries, various European nations sought to control the strait. In 1923, the strait was internationalized; however, in 1936, the strait came under the control of Turkey. In 1973, a bridge across the Bosporous became the first southern link between Europe and Asia in almost 2,500 years.

DIGITAL RESOURCES NGLSync.cengage.com

TEACHER RESOURCES & ASSESSMENT

 Reading and Note-Taking

 Vocabulary Practice

 Section 1 Quiz

STUDENT RESOURCES

 NG Chapter Gallery

INTRODUCE & ENGAGE

ACTIVATE PRIOR KNOWLEDGE

Ask students to recall ancient civilizations they have learned about, such as those in Egypt and Mesopotamia. Ask them how the location of these civilizations helped make them become important civilizations. Students should indicate that both developed along rivers. Tell students that in Lesson 1.1, they will learn how geographic features contributed to the growth of the Byzantine Empire. `0:05` minutes

TEACH

GUIDED DISCUSSION

1. **Summarize** How did the location of Constantinople make it important for trade both on land and on water? *(Constantinople provided a land link between Asia and Europe, and its location on the Bosporus made Constantinople a major trade center for goods traveling by land and sea from all over the world.)*

2. **Draw Conclusions** Why was having a strong leader especially important for the Byzantine Empire? *(The Byzantine Empire was surrounded by enemies who sought the empire's resources and wealth and had no geographic barriers to prevent attacks and invasions. The empire needed strong leadership to be able to hold it together in the face of these threats.)*

INTERPRET MAPS

Draw students' attention to the map of the Byzantine Empire, focusing on the extent of the empire. Review how to use the distance scale. Ask students to determine the size of the Byzantine Empire at its height, from east to west. *(approximately 2,750 miles)* `0:15` minutes

ACTIVE OPTIONS

On Your Feet: Inside-Outside Circle Arrange students in concentric circles facing each other. Have each student in the outside circle ask a question about the geography of the Byzantine Empire. Then have each student in the inside circle answer his or her partner's question. On a signal, have students on the inside circle rotate counter-clockwise to meet a new partner and begin again. Have students trade roles so those on the inside ask the questions and those on the outside answer the questions. `0:10` minutes

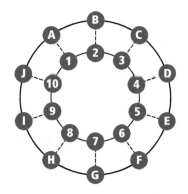

NG Learning Framework: List Geographic Impacts

SKILLS: Observation, Collaboration
KNOWLEDGE: Our Living Planet

Have students review Lesson 1.1 about the geography of the Byzantine Empire. They should work in pairs to create a list of observations about the empire's geographic features and how the Byzantine Empire was impacted by its environment. Once they have completed their list of observations, each pair should exchange lists with another pair and discuss the new list. `0:10` minutes

DIFFERENTIATE

STRIVING READERS

Summarize Read the lesson aloud while students follow along in their books. At the end of each paragraph, ask students to summarize what you read in a sentence. Allow them time to write the summary on their own paper.

ENGLISH LANGUAGE LEARNERS `ELD`

Use Sentence Strips Choose a paragraph from the lesson and make sentence strips out of it. Read the paragraph aloud, having students follow along in their books. Have students close their books and give them the set of sentence strips. Students should put the strips in order and read the paragraph aloud. Have students at the **Emerging** and **Expanding** levels work in pairs. Have students at the **Bridging** level work independently.

Press (**mt**) *in the Student eEdition for modified text.*

See the Chapter Planner for more strategies for differentiation.

REVIEW & ASSESS

ANSWERS

1. Constantinople's location on the Bosporus linked the Black Sea with the Mediterranean, making it ideal for trade between east and west. As a major trade center, Constantinople led to the growth and economic success of the Byzantine Empire.

2. Byzantium's rich natural resources and immense wealth caused the Persian Empire and other enemies to attack and invade.

3. After Justinian's conquests, the borders of the Byzantine Empire expanded as far west as North Africa and the southern tip of Spain.

Justinian and Theodora

There's a popular saying that two heads are better than one. This was certainly true of Justinian's reign. Justinian became Byzantium's greatest emperor thanks in part to the support and intelligence of his wife, Theodora.

MAIN IDEA

Justinian and Theodora ruled over a golden age for Byzantium.

A POWERFUL RULER

Justinian was born in A.D. 482 or 483 to a peasant farmer. It was a humble beginning, but Justinian's uncle rose to become a great general and then emperor. The uncle educated Justinian, gave him important jobs, and appointed him as his successor. It was a smart choice. Justinian was intelligent, talented, and ambitious. He modeled himself on the old Roman Caesars. After he became emperor in 527, Justinian worked to bring a golden age to Byzantium.

In many ways, Justinian proved to be a powerful and effective leader. As you have read, he greatly expanded the empire's borders. Within those borders, he made major improvements in the areas of government, construction, and law. He reformed Byzantine government to improve efficiency and get rid of corruption. Justinian also started an ambitious construction program. He ordered the building of the **Hagia Sophia** (HY-uh soh-FEE-uh), a church in Constantinople that today is considered a masterpiece of Byzantine architecture. He also sponsored many other civic projects in the city, including a magnificent new building for the Senate.

Justinian was a dedicated Christian actively involved in issues of faith. He punished those he found guilty of **heresy** (HAIR-uh-see)—beliefs contrary to church teachings—including Jews. For example, he prohibited Jews from building synagogues and reading the Bible in Hebrew.

Justinian also worked hard to settle the differences of opinion that divided the early church. For example, groups within the church had different beliefs about whether Jesus Christ was fully **divine** (having the nature of a god) and should be worshipped as an equal to God. This disagreement continued long after Justinian's death.

Justinian's reform of the law was far more successful. He reorganized and standardized confusing Roman laws and had the surviving laws written down clearly and logically in a single work called the **Justinian Code**. This remarkable work has formed the basis of European law until modern times.

A COURAGEOUS EMPRESS

Of all Justinian's advisors, the most influential was his wife, **Theodora**. An actress when she was young, Theodora was part of a lower social class, so Justinian had to have the law changed to marry her. Together, they formed an unstoppable team who shared power as nearly equal co-rulers.

Theodora was extremely bright and energetic. Justinian admired her intelligence and deeply respected her opinions. As a result, she had a huge influence on imperial policy. Theodora was probably behind the laws passed to protect women, children, and some Christian minority groups.

This sixth-century mosaic shows Justinian in the center with religious leaders on his right and government officials on his left.

Theodora even saved Justinian's crown. In 532, some of Justinian's opponents turned a riot between rival sports fans into a widespread rebellion against his policies. As Justinian prepared to flee the city, Theodora refused to leave. Her courageous determination to stay and fight the rebels inspired Justinian. He ordered the army to crush the rebellion, which led to the deaths of 30,000 protesters. Order was restored, along with the emperor's authority. Following these events, Justinian decided to rule more carefully in the future.

SPORTS, POLITICS, AND PASSIONS

The people of Byzantium passionately followed the sport of chariot racing. More than just entertainment, the races were a focus of life and politics in the city. The people were bitterly divided in their support of the two main chariot teams—the Blues and the Greens. Races were an emotional standoff between supporters who often became violent. Justinian and Theodora both supported the Blues.

REVIEW & ASSESS

1. **READING CHECK** In what areas did Justinian make major improvements during his reign?

2. **IDENTIFY MAIN IDEAS AND DETAILS** What evidence from the text shows that Justinian's law reforms were successful?

3. **ANALYZE VISUALS** What can you infer about Justinian's reign from the people portrayed in the mosaic?

7.1.3 Describe the establishment by Constantine of the new capital in Constantinople and the development of the Byzantine Empire, with an emphasis on the consequences of the development of two distinct European civilizations, Eastern Orthodox and Roman Catholic, and their two distinct views on church-state relations.

STANDARDS

HSS CONTENT STANDARDS:

7.1.3 Describe the establishment by Constantine of the new capital in Constantinople and the development of the Byzantine Empire, with an emphasis on the consequences of the development of two distinct European civilizations, Eastern Orthodox and Roman Catholic, and their two distinct views on church-state relations.

PLAN

OBJECTIVE

Identify key characteristics and events of the reign of Justinian and Theodora.

ESSENTIAL QUESTION

How did the Byzantine Empire carry on the culture and traditions of the old Roman Empire?

The emperor Justinian modeled himself after the old Roman Caesars. Lesson 1.2 discusses Justinian's rule over a golden age for Byzantium.

BACKGROUND FOR THE TEACHER

Theodora, the empress of the Byzantine Empire, was the most powerful woman in Byzantine history. She was born into a poor family, and at one point in her life she made a living as an actress and also as a wool spinner. Theodora's beauty and intelligence attracted Justinian, and they were married in 525. Theodora influenced many of the laws passed during Justinian's rule. She worked to pass laws that enhanced the rights of women, an issue that was not taken up by many governments at that time. She also skillfully handled political affairs, such as meeting with foreign rulers, which previously were actions carried out only by the emperor. Theodora died in 548.

DIGITAL RESOURCES NGLSync.cengage.com

TEACHER RESOURCES & ASSESSMENT

 Reading and Note-Taking

 Vocabulary Practice

 Section 1 Quiz

STUDENT RESOURCES

 Biography

INTRODUCE & ENGAGE

POSE AND ANSWER QUESTIONS

As a class, complete a K-W-L Chart exploring what students know and what they would like to learn about the Byzantine rulers Justinian and Theodora. Write students' ideas on the board in a chart like the one shown here. Give students the opportunity to return to the chart and review what they have learned after they have read the lesson. **0:15** minutes

K What Do I Know?	W What Do I Want To Learn?	L What Did I Learn?

TEACH

GUIDED DISCUSSION

1. **Synthesize** What achievements in government, construction, and law showed Justinian to be a powerful and effective leader? *(Students' responses will vary but should include that in government, Justinian reformed the government to improve efficiency and to get rid of corruption; Justinian started a construction program, ordering the building of the Hagia Sophia and other civic projects in the city; Justinian reorganized and standardized confusing Roman laws and had the remaining laws written down clearly and logically in the Justinian Code.)*

2. **Form and Support Opinions** How important do you think Theodora was to Justinian's success as a ruler? *(Students' responses will vary, but students should provide reasons for their opinions.)*

MORE INFORMATION

Mosaic of Justinian The mosaic of Justinian is located in the Basilica of San Vitale, a church in Ravenna, Italy. It is an important example of early Christian Byzantine art and architecture in Western Europe. In the mosaic, dated A.D. 547, Justinian is clad in a purple toga with a golden halo around his head and a crown on his head. In the mosaic, the military personnel and the government officials are on Justinian's right, and the clergymen are on Justinian's left. Every person in the mosaic is overlapped by someone else except the emperor, who overlaps everyone else, showing his importance and power.

ACTIVE OPTIONS

NG Learning Framework: Write a Biography

ATTITUDE: **Curiosity**
KNOWLEDGE: **Our Human Story**

Have students select one of the people they are still curious about after learning about the individual in this chapter. Instruct them to write a short biography about the person using information from the chapter and additional source material. **0:15** minutes

On Your Feet: Card Responses Have half the class write ten true-false or yes-no questions based on the lesson. Have the other half create answer cards, writing "True" or "Yes" on one side of the cards and "False" or "No" on the other side. Students from the question group should take turns asking their questions. Students from the answer group should hold up their cards, showing the correct answer. Have students keep track of their correct answers. **0:10** minutes

DIFFERENTIATE

INCLUSION

Use Supported Reading Have students work in pairs and assign each pair one paragraph to read aloud together. At the end of each paragraph, have them use the following sentence frames to identify what they do and do not understand:

This paragraph is about _____.

One fact that stood out to me is _____.

_____ is a word I had trouble understanding, so I figured it out by _____.

Be sure all students understand the content before moving on to the next paragraph.

PRE-AP

Extend Knowledge Have students conduct Internet research to find out more about Justinian or Theodora. Direct them to find out about the person's early life as well as more information about his or her accomplishments as a ruler. Encourage students to share their findings in an oral report to the class. As an extension, have students read the excerpt from the Justinian Code in the **Primary Source Handbook** and answer the questions that follow it.

Press **mt** *in the Student eEdition for modified text.*

See the Chapter Planner for more strategies for differentiation.

REVIEW & ASSESS

ANSWERS

1. Justinian expanded the empire by conquering former lands of the Roman Empire in Africa and the west. He undertook major building projects, including the Hagia Sophia in Constantinople. He also reformed Byzantine government to make it more efficient and clarified Roman laws in his Justinian Code.

2. The text states that the Justinian Code clarified and standardized confusing and contradictory Roman laws, organizing them logically in a single work that later formed the basis of European law.

3. Responses will vary. A possible response might be that the number and position of the people behind Justinian indicates that many people helped to run the government and were accountable to him, but that Justinian held all the power.

DECEMBER 27, 537

The newly completed Hagia Sophia, which means "Holy Wisdom," was officially blessed on this date. The church, which still stands, is considered a remarkable achievement in architecture. The centerpiece of the vast building is its extraordinary brick dome, which is 180 feet high and 100 feet across. After the fall of the Byzantine Empire, the Hagia Sophia was converted to a mosque—an Islamic place of worship. Today, it is a museum. In Justinian's time, the church symbolized Byzantine power and wealth.

366 CHAPTER 13

367

STANDARDS

HSS CONTENT STANDARDS:

7.1.3 Describe the establishment by Constantine of the new capital in Constantinople and the development of the Byzantine Empire, with an emphasis on the consequences of the development of two distinct European civilizations, Eastern Orthodox and Roman Catholic, and their two distinct views on church-state relations.

PLAN

OBJECTIVE

Identify the importance of the Hagia Sophia to the Byzantine Empire.

ESSENTIAL QUESTION

How did the Byzantine Empire carry on the culture and traditions of the old Roman Empire?

The emperor Justinian was known for his huge construction projects. The moment in history featured in Lesson 1.3 was the day that Justinian's major project, the Hagia Sophia, was dedicated.

BACKGROUND FOR THE TEACHER

The Hagia Sophia is actually the third structure constructed on its site. The current structure was built by two renowned architects of the time, ordered by the Emperor Justinian. The current structure was dedicated on December 27, 537. The Hagia Sophia drew on both Greek and Egyptian architectural styles. Its dome was designed by a mathematician and a physicist. The massive dome rests on multiple marble pillars. Earthquakes have damaged the structure, resulting in added reinforcements. The Hagia Sophia was chosen as a world heritage site by UNESCO in 1985, and it is an important site for tourism in Istanbul today.

INTRODUCE & ENGAGE

MAKE CONNECTIONS

Ask students about important and impressive buildings that they have seen or visited. Students might indicate buildings in their community or historical buildings like the U.S. Capitol. Discuss with students what makes these buildings impressive. Tell students that the photo in this lesson is of the Hagia Sophia, a significant and impressive building of the Byzantine Empire. `0:05` minutes

TEACH

GUIDED DISCUSSION

1. **Make Inferences** Why do you think December 27, 537, was a significant day for Emperor Justinian? *(Students might indicate that it was the dedication day for the Hagia Sophia, an ambitious building project completed under the orders of Justinian and a major accomplishment for him.)*

2. **Make Generalizations** Based on the photo of the dome of the Hagia Sophia, what generalization can you make about the condition of the structure today? *(Students' responses might indicate that though the Hagia Sophia is still beautiful and impressive, it is in need of repair and restoration.)*

ANALYZE VISUALS `STEM`

Have students examine the photo of the dome of the Hagia Sophia. Have them identify the various elements they see in the photo. List students' responses on the board. Discuss with students what the dome indicates about art and architecture in the Byzantine Empire. As an extension to the activity, have students read Paul the Silentiary's description of the Hagia Sophia in the **Primary Source Handbook** and answer the questions that follow it. `0:10` minutes

ACTIVE OPTIONS

On Your Feet: Descriptive Words Hand out two sticky notes to each student. Have students examine the details in the photograph of the dome in the Hagia Sophia. Then have them write a word or phrase on each sticky note that describes the dome and elements of the dome. Have students place their sticky notes on the board and discuss their descriptions. `0:10` minutes

Critical Viewing: NG Chapter Gallery Ask students to choose one image from the Chapter Gallery and become an expert on it. They should do additional research to learn all about it. Then, students should share their findings with a partner, a small group, or the class. `0:10` minutes

DIFFERENTIATE

INCLUSION

Describe Lesson Visuals Pair visually impaired students with students who are not visually challenged. Ask the latter to help their partners "see" the visual in this lesson by describing the elements in the photo and answering questions the visually impaired student might have.

GIFTED & TALENTED

Make a Poster Direct students to read the information about the Hagia Sophia in the lesson. Ask them to imagine that they are in Constantinople and have been tasked with constructing a poster advertising the event on December 27, 537. Have students work with a partner to create the poster, which should urge people to attend the event. Students' posters should include words that create interest in the building and excitement about the event. Display completed posters in the classroom.

Press (**mt**) *in the Student eEdition for modified text.*

See the Chapter Planner for more strategies for differentiation.

Constantinople was the vibrant center of the Byzantine Empire. Beginning with Constantine, the emperors adorned the city with numerous churches, monuments, and civic buildings. Every day, thousands of people from all around the ancient world thronged the streets, buying, selling, and socializing.

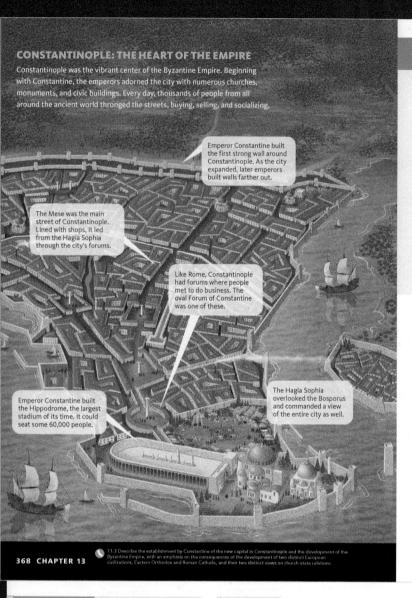

Emperor Constantine built the first strong wall around Constantinople. As the city expanded, later emperors built walls farther out.

The Mese was the main street of Constantinople. Lined with shops, it led from the Hagia Sophia through the city's forums.

Like Rome, Constantinople had forums where people met to do business. The oval Forum of Constantine was one of these.

Emperor Constantine built the Hippodrome, the largest stadium of its time. It could seat some 60,000 people.

The Hagia Sophia overlooked the Bosporus and commanded a view of the entire city as well.

7.1.3 Describe the establishment by Constantine of the new capital in Constantinople and the development of the Byzantine Empire, with an emphasis on the consequences of the development of two distinct European civilizations, Eastern Orthodox and Roman Catholic, and their two distinct views on church-state relations.

1.4 Life in Constantinople

You had to like people to enjoy living in Constantinople. It was the world's largest city, with its 500,000 inhabitants packed tightly together. The people of the city considered it the new Rome.

MAIN IDEA

Constantinople was a lively capital city modeled on ancient Rome.

THE CAPITAL CITY

Like Rome, Constantinople relied on resources from outside the city for its survival. The people consumed grain imported from Egypt and water piped in from more than 70 miles away.

Surrounded by the sea on three sides, Constantinople expanded to the west as it constantly attracted new people. Its strategic location on the Bosporus made it the richest and most influential city of its time. Merchants and traders from many parts of Europe and Asia brought in a constant flow of business and goods.

Like the residents of Rome, many of Constantinople's residents lived in poor conditions. They relied on government handouts of bread. Just a short walk away, though, spectacular public buildings and magnificent monuments inspired civic pride. As in Rome, a Senate house, public baths, triumphal arches, columns, and statues reflected the wealth and glory of the empire.

The city's people would frequently cram into the huge Hippodrome, a massive arena almost 1,500 feet long, to watch chariot races. The track was decorated with treasures from ancient Greece and Egypt. The emperor supervised the games from the imperial box, just as in Rome.

ROMAN CULTURAL INFLUENCE

Constantinople reflected everything that was glorious about ancient Rome. Its design, architecture, and monuments all reinforced the fact that the Byzantines considered themselves Roman. They saw themselves as the true inheritors of Roman cultural traditions—far more than Rome itself. Indeed, the Byzantine emperors brought many great monuments from Roman Italy, Africa, and Greece to adorn the capital.

Constantinople was also a center of cultural diversity because it was a center of trade. People who came from abroad to trade sometimes settled in the city. Greece was a strong influence as well. Greek, not Latin, was the people's language and the official language of the state. However, the Justinian Code, based on Roman law, continued as the basis for the Byzantine legal system. In this way, Byzantium helped preserve Greek and Roman learning for later generations.

REVIEW & ASSESS

1. **READING CHECK** What was one way in which Constantinople modeled itself on ancient Rome?

2. **MAKE INFERENCES** Why was trade with other regions necessary for Constantinople?

3. **INTERPRET VISUALS** What details in the drawing illustrate the idea that Constantinople was a busy, wealthy city?

STANDARDS

HSS CONTENT STANDARDS:

7.1.3 Describe the establishment by Constantine of the new capital in Constantinople and the development of the Byzantine Empire, with an emphasis on the consequences of the development of two distinct European civilizations, Eastern Orthodox and Roman Catholic, and their two distinct views on church-state relations.

PLAN

OBJECTIVE

Describe the ways in which Constantinople was modeled on ancient Rome.

ESSENTIAL QUESTION

How did the Byzantine Empire carry on the culture and traditions of the old Roman Empire?

Constantinople was the capital city of the Byzantine Empire. Lesson 1.4 describes how it was modeled on ancient Rome.

BACKGROUND FOR THE TEACHER

The Hippodrome was the center of Constantinople's social life. People bet huge amounts of money on the four teams that took part in chariot races. Each of the teams was sponsored by a different political party. Each chariot was powered by four horses, and up to eight chariots competed on the racing track. In addition to being sporting events, the races provided rare occasions for the emperor and citizens to come together in a single venue.

DIGITAL RESOURCES NGLSync.cengage.com

TEACHER RESOURCES & ASSESSMENT

 Reading and Note-Taking

 Vocabulary Practice

 Section 1 Quiz

STUDENT RESOURCES

 NG Image Gallery

INTRODUCE & ENGAGE

TEAM UP

Tell students to imagine they will be building a city in a prime location near a waterway. Have them brainstorm in groups. Tell them to use an Idea Web to list what they would build and the features they want their city to have. Tell students that in this lesson they will learn about the features the emperor Justinian included in the city of Constantinople. **0:15** minutes

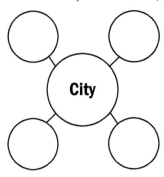

TEACH

GUIDED DISCUSSION

1. **Draw Conclusions** How did being the center of trade also make Constantinople a center of cultural diversity? *(Merchants and traders from many parts of Europe and Asia brought in business. Sometimes people who came from abroad to trade settled in the city, contributing to its diversity.)*

2. **Form Opinions** What factor do you think was most important in making Constantinople a great city? *(Answers will vary. Students should provide reasons for their opinions.)*

INTERPRET VISUALS

Focus students' attention on the drawing of Constantinople. Call on students to read the callouts. Ask students to use the information in the drawing to discuss what daily life might have been like for people living in Constantinople. **0:10** minutes

ACTIVE OPTIONS

On Your Feet: Three-Step Interview Have students choose a partner. One student should interview the other on the question, *In what ways was Constantinople modeled on ancient Rome?* Then they should reverse roles. Finally, each student should share the results of his or her interview with the class. **0:15** minutes

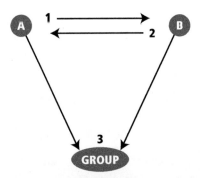

Critical Viewing: NG Image Gallery Invite students to explore the entire NG Image Gallery and create a Favorites List by choosing the images they find most interesting. If possible, have students copy the images into a document to form an actual list. Then encourage them to select the image they like best and do further research on it. **0:10** minutes

DIFFERENTIATE

STRIVING READERS

Outline and Take Notes Have students work in pairs, each pair numbering off from one through six. Assign each pair one paragraph to read together. Encourage student pairs to take notes on their assigned paragraphs. Then have students form larger groups made up of numbered pairs. Have them share their notes so that everyone in their group has notes for all paragraphs. Have pairs or groups work together to create an outline from their notes. Depending on the number of students involved, there may need to be two sets of six pairs.

GIFTED & TALENTED

Compare Architecture Have students use the Internet to conduct research and find examples of structures from the Roman and Byzantine empires. Tell them to download photos and organize them into a presentation that describes the architecture of the periods and compares similarities and differences of the architecture of the two empires.

Press **mt** in the Student eEdition for modified text.

See the Chapter Planner for more strategies for differentiation.

REVIEW & ASSESS

ANSWERS

1. Constantinople was modeled after ancient Rome, borrowing Rome's design, architecture, and monuments. Byzantines also continued Roman cultural traditions.

2. Trade was necessary because Constantinople relied on resources from outside the city for its survival.

3. The information about the Mese and the Forum of Constantine illustrate that Constantinople was a busy, wealthy city.

The **Church** Divides

It's Saturday afternoon in the Hagia Sophia. Just before the service, three men burst in, march up to the altar, slam down a piece of paper, shout in a foreign language, and storm out. You've just witnessed the Christian church being split in two—forever.

MAIN IDEA

Christianity in the East and the West developed differently, causing arguments and finally a split.

EAST VERSUS WEST

When the old Roman Empire divided, the cultures of its eastern and western empires developed very differently. Arguments arose over Christian religious practices. In the East, the emperor was seen as God's representative on Earth. The emperor had a great deal of influence over the church and its leader, the **patriarch**. The first patriarchs of Constantinople were bishops under the governance of the pope. Over time, however, they became more independent of Rome.

The West did not have an emperor after 476, when the Roman Empire fell. As you may recall, the pope in Rome grew extremely powerful and claimed absolute authority over all western Christians, even kings. He then claimed authority over the eastern Christians, which led to a long power struggle with the Byzantine emperors.

With different leaders and with very little contact, eastern and western Christians drifted apart in their beliefs and practices.

One key conflict was a disagreement about the Holy Trinity—the Father, the Son, and the Holy Spirit. The western church adopted a **creed**, or statement of belief, that claimed the Holy Spirit comes from the Father and the Son—God and Jesus. The eastern church maintained the belief that the Holy Spirit comes only from the Father.

Another major clash was over **icons**, images of Jesus and the saints. Many Christians had icons, and some began to pray to them. In the East, the emperor banned icons and ordered that they be destroyed. In the West, the pope rebuked the emperor and condemned the destruction of the icons. Religion was an extremely important topic to the Byzantine people. They believed their eternal salvation depended on proper understanding of God and the Bible. As a result, these religious disagreements brought about strong feelings.

THE EAST-WEST SCHISM

Growing disagreements created suspicion and hostility between eastern and western Christians. Finally, the pope's representatives in Constantinople announced that the Byzantine patriarch was **excommunicated**—no longer part of the church. They made this announcement by placing the letter of excommunication on the altar of the Hagia Sophia. The furious patriarch then excommunicated the pope. In 1054, the church split in what is called the East-West Schism (SKIH-zuhm) or the Schism of 1054. A **schism** is a separation. The Roman Catholic Church remained in the West, and the **Eastern Orthodox Church** developed in Byzantium.

Followers of each religion shared some important common ground. They both based their beliefs on Jesus and the Bible, and they both worshipped in churches with services led by priests and bishops. However, in

THE SCHISM OF 1054

Eastern Orthodox Church
Roman Catholic Church

the Roman Catholic Church, the pope had authority over all the clergy and even kings. Priests could not marry, and services were conducted in Latin. In the Eastern Orthodox Church, the emperor had spiritual authority over the clergy, priests could marry, and services were conducted in Greek.

ICONS

The word *icon* comes from the Greek word for "image." Many icons were painted on wood, but some were made from mosaic tiles, ivory, and other materials. Although Byzantine emperors banned icons more than once, people kept them in their homes and businesses and placed them in churches.

REVIEW & ASSESS

1. **READING CHECK** What was one principal difference between the eastern and western churches?

2. **DETERMINE WORD MEANINGS** How does knowing that *ortho* refers to "correct" and *dox* refers to "opinion" clarify the meaning of the word *orthodox*?

3. **INTERPRET MAPS** What does the map add to the text's description of the Schism of 1054?

7.1.3 Describe the establishment by Constantine of the new capital in Constantinople and the development of the Byzantine Empire, with an emphasis on the consequences of the development of two distinct European civilizations, Eastern Orthodox and Roman Catholic, and their two distinct views on church-state relations.

HSS CONTENT STANDARDS:

7.1.3 Describe the establishment by Constantine of the new capital in Constantinople and the development of the Byzantine Empire, with an emphasis on the consequences of the development of two distinct European civilizations, Eastern Orthodox and Roman Catholic, and their two distinct views on church-state relations.

PLAN

OBJECTIVE

Explain how differences in the development of Christianity in the East and the West led to a split in the church.

ESSENTIAL QUESTION

How did the Byzantine Empire carry on the culture and traditions of the old Roman Empire?

Cultures in the eastern and western parts of the old Roman Empire developed differently. Lesson 2.1 describes how differences in religious practices led to a split between Christians in the eastern and western parts.

BACKGROUND FOR THE TEACHER

The split between Christianity in the East and the West had its origin when the Roman Empire was divided into eastern and western parts. The Western Roman Empire was destroyed by the invasions of barbarian tribes, while the Eastern Roman Empire—the Byzantine Empire—thrived. Other differences also caused the two sides to drift apart. The main language in the West was Latin, while Greek was dominant in the East. After some time, few people spoke both languages, resulting in communication difficulties between the two sides and an increased split. The Church was also affected by the division between the East and the West, resulting in different rites and views of religious teachings and ultimately the East-West Schism.

DIGITAL RESOURCES NGLSync.cengage.com

TEACHER RESOURCES & ASSESSMENT

 Reading and Note-Taking

 Vocabulary Practice

 Section 2 Quiz

STUDENT RESOURCES

 Active History

ACTIVATE PRIOR KNOWLEDGE

Ask students to recall events in history when the United States experienced a split. Lead students to recall the Civil War and the split between the North and the South (or the Revolutionary War and the split between the colonies and Great Britain). Tell students that in this lesson they will learn about the split in Christianity that affected the Byzantine Empire. **0:05** minutes

TEACH

GUIDED DISCUSSION

1. **Analyze Cause and Effect** What was the effect of the excommunication of the Byzantine patriarch and then the excommunication of the pope by the patriarch? *(The effect was the split between the eastern and western churches in what is called the East-West Schism.)*

2. **Compare and Contrast** What are some ways in which the Roman Catholic Church and the Eastern Orthodox Church were alike and ways in which they were different in their beliefs? *(Both churches based their beliefs on Jesus and the Bible, and both worshipped in churches with services led by priests and bishops. They differed in that in the Roman Catholic Church, the pope had authority over all the clergy and even kings, priests could not marry, and services were conducted in Latin; whereas in the Eastern Orthodox Church, the emperor had spiritual authority over the clergy, priests could marry, and services were conducted in Greek.)*

INTERPRET MAPS

Have students examine the Schism of 1054 map. Help students interpret the map. Focus on the map legend. **ASK:** What do the colors used in the map represent? *(The gold color represents the places in which people followed the Roman Catholic religion, and the purple color represents the places in which people followed the Eastern Orthodox religion.)* What would be another way of showing the same information? *(Students might respond that a chart listing the places that followed each religion would be another way to show the information.)* Discuss with students why using a map such as this one is often a more efficient way of showing information. **0:10** minutes

ACTIVE OPTIONS

Active History: Compare Two Branches of Christianity Extend the lesson by using either the PDF or Whiteboard version of the Compare Two Branches of Christianity Active History activity. These activities take a deeper look at a topic from, or related to, the lesson. Explore the activities as a class, turn them into group assignments, or even assign them individually. **0:10** minutes

On Your Feet: Thumbs Up/Thumbs Down Divide the class into groups and have each group write six true-false statements about the lesson with the correct answers included. Collect the questions. Mix them up and read them aloud to the class, skipping any duplicates. Have students give a "thumbs up" for true statements and a "thumbs down" for false statements. Correct any misconceptions. **0:05** minutes

ENGLISH LANGUAGE LEARNERS

Match Words and Definitions Give students the following matching exercise. Have students at different proficiency levels work in pairs to match the words with their definitions and then write a sentence using each one.

1. patriarch   a. no longer part of the church
2. creed   b. images of Jesus and the saints
3. icons   c. separation
4. excommunicated   d. leader of the Eastern Orthodox Church
5. schism   e. statement of belief

PRE-AP

Write a Report Have students do Internet research in order to write a report about the beliefs and practices of the Eastern Orthodox and the Roman Catholic churches. Direct students to download photos of some of the practices in their reports. Encourage students to include a Venn diagram to illustrate the similarities and the differences between the two religions. Have students share their reports with the class.

Press **mt** *in the Student eEdition for modified text.*

See the Chapter Planner for more strategies for differentiation.

REVIEW & ASSESS

ANSWERS

1. There were principal differences between the eastern and the western churches. The western church claimed the Holy Spirit comes from the Father and the Son, while the eastern church maintained the belief that the Holy Spirit comes only from the Father. Icons were banned and destroyed in the East. In the East, the emperor had a great deal of influence over the church and the patriarch. The West did not have an emperor, and the pope grew very powerful.

2. The word means "having the right opinion."

3. The map indicates the extent of each of the churches and indicates the places that followed each one.

BYZANTINE MOSAICS

The Byzantine Empire developed an influential artistic culture. Its distinctive style is well represented by the remarkable mosaics found in churches such as the Hagia Sophia.

Covering entire walls and ceilings, Byzantine mosaics stood out for their exceptional quality and craftsmanship. Large expanses of gold-backed glass created a rich glow. Natural stone cubes helped create vibrant, detailed scenes. The breathtaking results still awe viewers today.

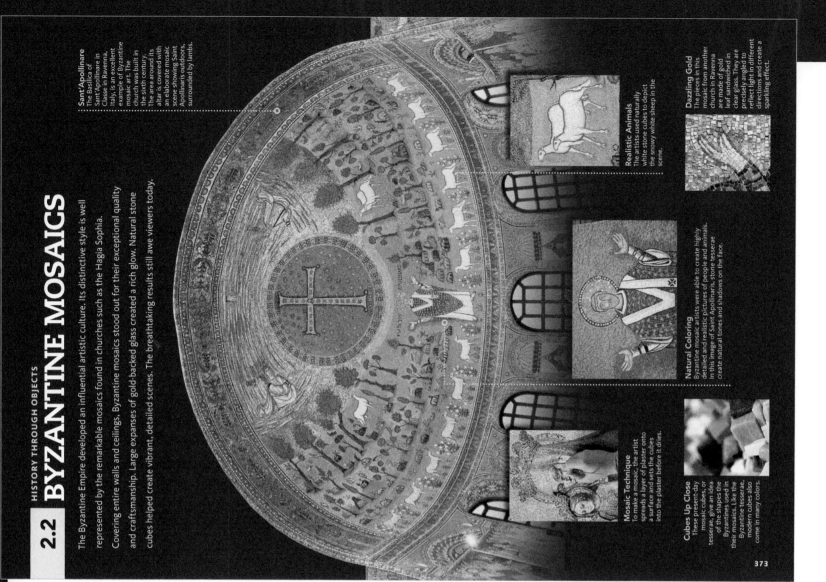

Sant'Apollinare The Basilica of Sant'Apollinare in Classe in Ravenna, Italy, is an excellent example of Byzantine mosaic art. The church was built in the sixth century. The area around its altar is covered with an elaborate mosaic scene showing Saint Apollinaris outdoors, surrounded by lambs.

Realistic Animals The artists used naturally white stone cubes to depict the snowy white sheep in the scene.

Dazzling Gold The pieces in this mosaic from another church in Ravenna are made of gold leaf sandwiched in clear glass. They are precisely angled to reflect light in different directions and create a sparkling effect.

Natural Coloring Byzantine mosaic artists were able to create highly detailed and realistic pictures of people and animals. In this image of Saint Apollinaris, stone tesserae create natural tones and shadows on the face.

Mosaic Technique To make a mosaic, the artist spreads a layer of plaster onto a surface and sets the cubes into the plaster before it dries.

Cubes Up Close These present-day mosaic cubes, or tesserae, give an idea of the shapes the Byzantines used in their mosaics. Like the Byzantine tesserae, modern cubes also come in many colors.

373

STANDARDS

HSS CONTENT STANDARDS:

7.1.3 Describe the establishment by Constantine of the new capital in Constantinople and the development of the Byzantine Empire, with an emphasis on the consequences of the development of two distinct European civilizations, Eastern Orthodox and Roman Catholic, and their two distinct views on church-state relations.

PLAN

OBJECTIVE

Describe the distinctive Byzantine style of mosaic art.

ESSENTIAL QUESTION

How did the Byzantine Empire carry on the culture and traditions of the old Roman Empire?

The Byzantine Empire's distinctive style of art is represented by the beautiful mosaics found in several churches throughout the empire. Lesson 2.2 describes some of the aspects of mosaic art.

BACKGROUND FOR THE TEACHER

The Basilica of Sant'Apollinare in Classe is located in Ravenna, Italy. Classe is the main port of Ravenna. Sant'Apollinare in Classe is a significant structure of Byzantine art. It is one of eight Ravenna sites listed on UNESCO's World Heritage List. The huge brick church was consecrated in 549 and dedicated to Saint Apollinaris, the first bishop of Ravenna and Classe.

DIGITAL RESOURCES NGLSync.cengage.com

TEACHER RESOURCES & ASSESSMENT

 Reading and Note-Taking

 Vocabulary Practice

 Section 2 Quiz

STUDENT RESOURCES

 NG Chapter Gallery

INTRODUCE & ENGAGE

MAKE CONNECTIONS

Discuss with students their experiences with putting together a jigsaw puzzle. Have them describe the kinds of puzzles they assembled and the number of pieces involved. Ask them how difficult assembling the pieces was and the reason for any difficulty. Tell students that in this lesson they will learn about the art of mosaics, a distinctive style of art of the Byzantine Empire. Tell them that creating a mosaic is similar in part to assembling a jigsaw puzzle in that small pieces form a montage to create a bigger picture. **0:05** minutes

TEACH

GUIDED DISCUSSION

1. **Describe** How do artists make a mosaic? *(They spread a layer of plaster onto a surface and set the cubes into the plaster before it dries.)*

2. **Make Generalizations** What generalization can you make about the characteristics of the people who created the mosaics pictured in the lesson? *(Responses will vary, but might include that the people were creative, artistic, attentive to detail, and imaginative.)*

ANALYZE VISUALS

Have students focus on the mosaic from the Basilica of Sant'Apollinare in Classe in Ravenna. Direct them to read the text and callouts. **ASK:** How were artists able to show different colors in the mosaic? *(They used stone cubes to create natural tones and shadows on faces and white cubes to depict the white sheep. To create a sparkling effect, artists angled cubes to reflect light.)* **0:15** minutes

ACTIVE OPTIONS

On Your Feet: Four Corners Ask students to examine the photos and callouts in the lesson. Post the four signs listed below and have students choose the word that best describes their opinion about and reaction to the Byzantine mosaics. Have group members discuss their opinions and reactions. Then ask one member from each group to report to the class. **0:15** minutes

| A. amazing | B. beautiful | C. unrealistic | D. not interesting |

Critical Viewing: NG Chapter Gallery Have students examine the contents of the Chapter Gallery for this chapter. Then invite them to brainstorm additional images they believe would fit within the Chapter Gallery. Have them write a description of these additional images and provide an explanation of why they would fit within the Chapter Gallery. Then instruct them to do online research to find examples of actual images they would like to add to the gallery. **0:10** minutes

DIFFERENTIATE

INCLUSION

Describe Details in a Photo Pair students who are visually impaired with students who are not. Ask the latter to be their partners' "eyes" and describe the details in the photos of Byzantine mosaics. Students should read the captions of the callouts to the visually impaired students before they describe the details in each one.

GIFTED & TALENTED

Make a Mosaic Have students use the information in the lesson and do additional Internet research to find out more about mosaic art and to find other examples of mosaics. Then have them create their own mosaics. Direct students to first draw an outline of a picture. They might draw a picture of an individual object, such as a flower, or they might draw an abstract design. Students might use small objects such as different-colored beads, sequins, or seeds to fill in their drawing. Display completed mosaics in the classroom.

Press **mt** *in the Student eEdition for modified text.*

See the Chapter Planner for more strategies for differentiation.

The End of an Empire

On May 29, 1453, the last Byzantine emperor died fighting as his enemies swarmed through his capital's shattered walls. That day, the Byzantine Empire ended. It was a heroic finale for an empire that had survived against the odds for a thousand years.

MAIN IDEA

After Justinian, the empire experienced invasions and another golden age before it finally collapsed.

GREEK FIRE

The Byzantine army had a secret weapon: Greek fire. It was liquid fire soldiers could propel at enemy troops. It burned with an incredible intensity, and not even water could extinguish it.

The formula for making Greek fire was a closely guarded secret that died with the empire.

DEBTS AND INVASIONS

After Justinian died in 565, the debts the emperor had taken out to pay for his many wars nearly bankrupted the empire. In addition, the plague, which had already attacked during Justinian's time, made a return. Rats arriving aboard grain ships from Egypt carried the deadly disease, and it spread quickly through the overcrowded city. At the height of the plague, perhaps 10,000 people died every day.

As if that weren't enough, Byzantium's old enemies, including the Persians, renewed their attacks on the empire's borders. And then, in 634, the Byzantine Empire confronted a new rival. The religion of

Islam had united Arab tribes, who formed a mighty Muslim army. This army conquered Egypt—a disaster for Constantinople's grain supply. By 711, the Arabs had conquered Syria, Egypt, parts of Southwest Asia, North Africa, and the Persian Empire.

NEW GOLDEN AGE AND FALL

Still, the Byzantine Empire was not yet down or out. By the early 1000s, the empire had entered a new golden age. Under the leadership of Basil II, Byzantium regained more control over trade, restored many of Constantinople's buildings and institutions, and spread Christianity among Slavic peoples to the north.

The empire's prosperity was short-lived, however. In 1096, an army of Christian Europeans launched a series of wars called the Crusades to fight the spread of Islam. The Crusaders soon came into conflict with Byzantine leaders. In 1204, they sacked Constantinople and occupied the city until 1261.

In time, the Byzantine Empire became a shadow of its former power—and then came the Turks, a people who had migrated into the region. By 1450, the Turks, who were Muslims, controlled all the lands around Constantinople. The city stood alone and surrounded.

In 1453, Mehmed II, the Turkish ruler, launched an army of 100,000 men against Constantinople's walls. The city's defenders, in contrast, numbered 7,000. On May 29, 1453, the Turks launched a final assault. They broke through the city's walls and killed the last Byzantine emperor, Constantine XI, as he charged into the invading army. By nightfall, Constantinople was under Turkish control.

+ POSSIBLE RESPONSE

The battle looks brutal and chaotic. The invading army looks well armed.

Critical Viewing This painting shows the invasion of Constantinople by the Crusaders. Based on this painting, how would you describe the battle?

REVIEW & ASSESS

1. **READING CHECK** What was one factor that led to the decline and collapse of the Byzantine Empire?

2. **ANALYZE CAUSE AND EFFECT** Why was the plague able to spread so quickly throughout Constantinople?

3. **SEQUENCE EVENTS** What events took place in Byzantium during the 1000s?

7.1.3 Describe the establishment by Constantine of the new capital in Constantinople and the development of the Byzantine Empire, with an emphasis on the consequences of the development of two distinct European civilizations, Eastern Orthodox and Roman Catholic, and their two distinct views on church-state relations; CST 1 Students explain how major events are related to one another in time; HI 2 Students understand and distinguish cause, effect, sequence, and correlation in historical events, including the long- and short-term causal relations.

HSS CONTENT STANDARDS:

7.1.3 Describe the establishment by Constantine of the new capital in Constantinople and the development of the Byzantine Empire, with an emphasis on the consequences of the development of two distinct European civilizations, Eastern Orthodox and Roman Catholic, and their two distinct views on church-state relations.

HSS ANALYSIS SKILLS:

CST 1 Students explain how major events are related to one another in time; **HI 2** Students understand and distinguish cause, effect, sequence, and correlation in historical events, including the long- and short-term causal relations.

PLAN

OBJECTIVE

Explain the factors that weakened the Byzantine Empire and ultimately destroyed it.

ESSENTIAL QUESTION

How did the Byzantine Empire carry on the culture and traditions of the old Roman Empire?

After the death of Emperor Justinian, the Byzantine Empire began to decline. Lesson 2.3 discusses the events that caused the decline and eventually led to the empire's collapse.

BACKGROUND FOR THE TEACHER

The bubonic plague contributed to the decline of the Byzantine Empire. The plague that hit the empire in the sixth century had a death rate from forty to seventy percent of its cases. The plague lasted four months, during which time daily life and work in the city of Constantinople stopped. The plague had a devastating impact on the empire's economy, which was primarily agricultural. One of the immediate effects was the loss of farmers. This in turn led to a shortage of food and famines after the plague ended. The diminished population resulted in a smaller tax base, which led to financial hardships for the empire.

DIGITAL RESOURCES NGLSync.cengage.com

TEACHER RESOURCES & ASSESSMENT

 Reading and Note-Taking

 Vocabulary Practice

 Section 2 Quiz

STUDENT RESOURCES

 NG Image Gallery

INTRODUCE & ENGAGE

UNDERSTAND MULTIMEANING WORDS

Ask students if they know what the word *decline* means. Write students' responses on the board. Explain that *decline* has more than one meaning, but in this lesson the term means "to grow weaker." Then direct students' attention to the lesson title. Ask students what they think the lesson, based on the title, will be about. **0:05** minutes

TEACH

GUIDED DISCUSSION

1. **Make Inferences** How was the geography of the Byzantine Empire a factor in the invasions that the empire experienced? *(Possible response: The empire's location with few physical barriers left it unprotected. This allowed invasions by Europeans from the north and west and Persians from the east.)*

2. **Analyze Cause and Effect** How do you think the plague contributed to the decline of the Byzantine Empire? *(Possible response might include that the plague killed tens of thousands of people in the Byzantine Empire. The deaths resulted in fewer people able to combat the oncoming invasions.)*

ANALYZE VISUALS

Show and discuss the painting of the invasion of Constantinople. Have students use the painting and the information in the lesson to answer the following questions:

- What does the painting show?
- What details do you see?
- Which two groups are represented in the painting?
- Which group appears to have the upper hand? What details in the painting lead you to think so?

0:15 minutes

ACTIVE OPTIONS

On Your Feet: Turn and Talk on Topic Have students form four lines. Give each group this topic sentence: *The Byzantine Empire grew weaker and shrank until it was finally destroyed.* Tell them to write a paragraph by having each student in the line add a sentence that supports the topic. **0:20** minutes

Critical Viewing: NG Image Gallery Invite students to explore the entire NG Image Gallery and choose one image from the gallery they feel best represents their understanding of each chapter or unit. Have students provide a written explanation of why they selected each of the images they chose. **0:10** minutes

DIFFERENTIATE

STRIVING READERS

Create a Time Line Display the events listed below and have students work in pairs to arrange them in the correct order on a time line.

- Christian Europeans conquer Constantinople. (1204)
- Justinian dies. (565)
- The Christian European occupation of Constantinople ends. (1261)
- Constantinople comes under Turkish control. (1453)
- Arabs conquer Syria, Egypt, Mesopotamia, Palestine, North Africa, and the Persian Empire. (711)

565   1453

ENGLISH LANGUAGE LEARNERS   ELD

Summarize Lesson 2.3 has six paragraphs. Have students at all proficiency levels work in pairs or small groups, and assign each pair or group one paragraph to read. Then each pair or group should summarize their paragraph in one or two sentences for the class.

Press **mt** *in the Student eEdition for modified text.*

See the Chapter Planner for more strategies for differentiation.

REVIEW & ASSESS

ANSWERS

1. The bubonic plague and enemy attacks and invasions led to the decline and collapse of the Byzantine Empire.

2. The deadly plague, carried by rats, was able to spread quickly because of the city's overcrowded conditions.

3. By the early 1000s, the Byzantine Empire had entered a new golden age. However, in 1096, an army of Christian Europeans launched a series of wars called the Crusades. These Europeans sacked Constantinople in 1204 and occupied the city until 1261. The Crusaders were followed by the Turks, who took control of the city in 1453.

VOCABULARY

Match each word in the first column with its meaning in the second column.

WORD	DEFINITION
1. divine (HSS 7.1.3)	a. an image of Jesus or another holy figure
2. patriarch (HSS 7.1.3)	b. a belief that goes against church teachings
3. heresy (HSS 7.1.3)	c. having the nature of a god
4. icon (HSS 7.1.3)	d. variety
5. diversity (HSS 7.1.3)	e. a leader of the Eastern Orthodox Church

READING SKILL

6. ORGANIZE IDEAS: ANALYZE CAUSE AND EFFECT If you haven't already, complete your diagram to identify the factors that caused the Byzantine Empire to grow and thrive. Then answer the question.

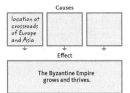

Causes

| location at crossroads of Europe and Asia | | |

↓

Effect

The Byzantine Empire grows and thrives.

What conditions made it possible for the Byzantine Empire to grow, thrive, and enter a golden age? (HSS HI 2)

MAIN IDEAS

Answer the following questions. Support your answers with evidence from the chapter.

7. In what ways was the location of Constantinople important to the growth of the Byzantine Empire? LESSON 1.1 (HSS 7.1.3)

8. In what ways did the Justinian Code improve on the Roman laws that it replaced? LESSON 1.2 (HSS HI 3)

9. What actions did Justinian take to bring a golden age to Byzantium? LESSON 1.2 (HSS 7.1.3)

10. Why did the Byzantines use ancient Rome as the model for their capital city, Constantinople? LESSON 1.4 (HSS HI 3)

11. How did the Byzantine emperor affect the religious life of the empire? LESSON 2.1 (HSS 7.1.3)

12. What effect did the plague have on the Byzantine Empire? LESSON 2.3 (HSS HI 2)

CRITICAL THINKING

Answer the following questions. Support your answers with evidence from the chapter.

13. ESSENTIAL QUESTION How did the Byzantine Empire carry on the culture and traditions of the old Roman Empire? (HSS HI 3)

14. DRAW CONCLUSIONS How do events that took place during the Byzantine Empire still affect the present-day world? (HSS HI 3)

15. ANALYZE CAUSE AND EFFECT Why was the Byzantine Empire a target for invaders throughout its long history? (HSS HI 2)

16. MAKE GENERALIZATIONS How does geographic location help determine whether a city will become wealthy and powerful? (HSS HI 2)

17. YOU DECIDE What was Justinian's greatest accomplishment? Support your opinion with evidence from the chapter. (HSS HI 1)

INTERPRET DIAGRAMS

Study the diagram below to compare and contrast the two branches of Christianity that developed after the East-West Schism. Then answer the questions that follow.

The East-West Schism

Roman Catholic Church
• Led by the pope
• Pope had authority over all Christians, including kings and emperors
• Priests could not marry
• Services conducted in Latin
• Worship and use of icons promoted by the pope

Similarities
• Faith based on belief in Jesus and the Bible
• Services held in churches led by priests and bishops

Eastern Orthodox Church
• Led by the patriarch
• Emperor had authority over all church officials
• Priests could marry
• Services conducted in Greek
• Some believed the worship of icons should be forbidden

18. In what way did the pope have greater influence in the West than patriarchs did in the East? (HSS 7.1.3)

19. How were the faiths of both branches of Christianity similar? (HSS 7.1.3)

ANALYZE SOURCES

The historian Procopius was present at and recorded the events of a rebellion in 532. Read his account of Theodora's speech to Justinian as the emperor prepared to flee Constantinople. Then answer the question that follows.

> I believe that flight, now more than ever, is not in our interest even if it should bring us to safety. . . . For one who has reigned it is intolerable to become a fugitive. May I *never* be parted from the purple [the imperial color]! May I *never* live to see the day when I will not be addressed as Mistress by all in my presence! Emperor, if you wish to save yourself, that is easily arranged. . . . But consider whether, after you have saved yourself, you would then gladly exchange safety for death.

20. What does this speech suggest about Theodora's character and influence? (HSS REP 4)

WRITE ABOUT HISTORY

21. INFORMATIVE Suppose you are in the court of the emperor Justinian. Write an explanation for your fellow citizens of how Theodora influences Justinian's rule of the Byzantine Empire. (HSS HI 1)

TIPS

• Take notes from the lessons about Justinian and Theodora.

• Write a topic sentence that clearly introduces your main idea about Theodora and Justinian.

• Choose relevant facts, concrete details, and examples for your explanation.

• Use vocabulary from the chapter where appropriate.

• Organize your details, facts, and examples clearly and logically.

• Provide a concluding statement that summarizes the information presented.

VOCABULARY ANSWERS

WORD	DEFINITION
1. divine (HSS 7.1.3) c.	a. an image of Jesus or another holy figure
2. patriarch (HSS 7.1.3) e.	b. a belief that goes against church teachings
3. heresy (HSS 7.1.3) b.	c. having the nature of a god
4. icon (HSS 7.1.3) a.	d. variety
5. diversity (HSS 7.1.3) d.	e. a leader of the Eastern Orthodox Church

READING STRATEGY ANSWER

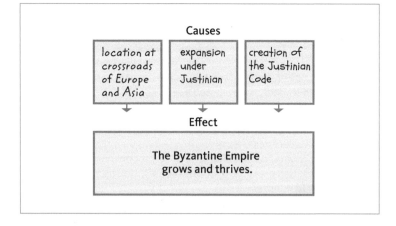

Causes

| location at crossroads of Europe and Asia | expansion under Justinian | creation of the Justinian Code |

↓

Effect

The Byzantine Empire grows and thrives.

STANDARDS

HSS CONTENT STANDARDS:

7.1.3 Describe the establishment by Constantine of the new capital in Constantinople and the development of the Byzantine Empire, with an emphasis on the consequences of the development of two distinct European civilizations, Eastern Orthodox and Roman Catholic, and their two distinct views on church-state relations.

HSS ANALYSIS SKILLS:

REP 4 Students assess the credibility of primary and secondary sources and draw sound conclusions from them; **HI 1** Students explain the central issues and problems from the past, placing people and events in a matrix of time and place; **HI 2** Students understand and distinguish cause, effect, sequence, and correlation in historical events, including the long- and short-term causal relations; **HI 3** Students explain the sources of historical continuity and how the combination of ideas and events explains the emergence of new patterns.

6. Many factors made it possible for the Byzantine Empire to grow, thrive, and enter a golden age. Constantinople's ideal geographic location, which made it a major trade center, resulted in great wealth and cultural diffusion. Another key factor in the creation of the empire's golden age was Justinian. As emperor, he was dedicated to restoring Byzantium's glory, and he took many steps to do so, including reforming government, undertaking massive building projects, and reforming Roman laws into the Justinian Code. (HSS HI 2)

MAIN IDEAS ANSWERS

7. Constantinople's geographic location on the Bosporus linked the Black Sea with the Mediterranean, making the capital city ideal as a major trade center between east and west. This brought great wealth to the Byzantine Empire. (HSS 7.1.3)

8. The Justinian Code clarified and standardized old Roman laws, making them more practical and easier to understand. (HSS HI 3)

9. Justinian expanded the empire's borders; made major improvements in the areas of government, construction, and law; reformed Byzantine government; started an ambitious construction program; ordered the building of the Hagia Sophia; and sponsored many other civic projects in Constantinople. (HSS 7.1.3)

10. The Byzantines used ancient Rome as the model for Constantinople because they considered themselves Roman and saw themselves as the true inheritors and keepers of Roman culture. (HSS HI 3)

11. The Byzantine emperor was seen as God's representative on Earth. The emperor had a great deal of influence over the church and the patriarch. The emperor had spiritual authority over the clergy. (HSS 7.1.3)

12. The plague had a disastrous effect on the Byzantine Empire. At the height of the plague, about 10,000 people died every day in the overcrowded city of Constantinople, weakening the empire. (HSS HI 2)

CRITICAL THINKING ANSWERS

13. The Byzantine Empire, like the Roman Empire, extended over a large area; the design, architecture, and monuments of Constantinople reflected those of Rome; the Justinian Code was based on Roman law. (HSS HI 3)

14. Possible response: The city of Constantinople is now Istanbul and still is an important location for trade; the Justinian Code has formed the basis of European law until modern times; the Roman Catholic Church and Eastern Orthodox Church continue today. (HSS HI 2)

15. The Byzantine Empire was surrounded by enemies and had no strong geographic barriers to prevent invasions; its rich resources and great wealth made the empire a target for raids and invasions. (HSS HI 2)

16. A city that is located on a major waterway or land link that is conducive to trade is more likely to become a center for trade and thereby more likely to become wealthy and powerful. (HSS HI 2)

17. Students' responses will vary. Students should clearly state their opinion regarding their view of Justinian's greatest accomplishment and support that opinion with evidence from the chapter. (HSS HI 1)

INTERPRET DIAGRAMS ANSWERS

18. The pope had greater influence in the west than the patriarch did in the east because the pope had authority over all Christians—including kings and emperors. (HSS 7.1.3)

19. Both branches of Christianity were based on the belief in Jesus and the Bible. (HSS 7.1.3)

ANALYZE SOURCES ANSWER

20. Students' responses will vary. Possible responses might include that Theodora was brave and loyal and exerted great influence over Justinian. (HSS REP 4)

WRITE ABOUT HISTORY ANSWER

21. Students' informative essays should

   - contain a topic sentence that introduces the main idea
   - support the topic sentence with facts, details, and examples from the chapter
   - include vocabulary words from the chapter
   - present the information in a clear, logical manner
   - contain a concluding statement

   For more in-depth instruction and practice with the writing form, assign the Social Studies Writing Lesson on writing an informative essay. (HSS HI 1)

ON LOCATION WITH Steven ELLIS

NATIONAL GEOGRAPHIC GRANTEE

▶ Check out more at NGLSync.Cengage.com

Archaeologist Steven Ellis surveys the ruins of Pompeii. His project focuses on the city's common people, which is a new approach to archaeological excavation.

NOT JUST DIGGERS

That's the misconception that annoys us the most! I dig up cities, yes, but it's what I learn from those cities that is important. Discovering artifacts is pretty cool, but piecing them together to tell a 2,000-year-old human story—that's what I find really exciting.

Pompeii is better preserved than any other Roman site, and because it's a city, you can relate to it more easily than, say, the pyramids. It's also got the drama of its sudden death, but we want to uncover its life. Pompeians lived in houses and went to shops and schools. I love that familiar urban element. They also had very different rules and did things differently. I think it's fascinating to try and recognize those similarities and differences.

Archaeologists like Steven Ellis spend long hours in the field, carefully uncovering signs of past civilizations.

TELLING THE HUMAN STORY

For 200 years we've mostly looked at what the rich were doing by unearthing the grandest buildings. I'm using archaeology to tell the story of ordinary people, the other 98 percent of the population. It's a fairly new approach. I was the youngest archaeological director at Pompeii, and I was also the new guy with new questions. I said, "I want to work in areas that you've ignored." So I'm looking at shops, bars, restaurants, and houses. They don't have fine art, but they do have bones, seeds, and pieces of pottery that tell us a story. Some of our discoveries are pretty obvious, like the fact that poor people lived in smaller houses and ate cheaper foods off cheaper plates. But they're expanding our understanding of Roman society beyond just the rich and revealing the complex layers of life in the middle and working classes.

Excavating in poorer communities is incredibly gratifying because you've got to work harder at it. The rich lived in the best houses, with the best decorations and the most stuff. This all survived better, so it's easier to uncover and study. I'm proud that we are excavating the stories of families whose histories would otherwise never be told.

WHY STUDY HISTORY ❓

❝ I study history because it's fascinating and *because I can*. In some countries, people are forbidden to study their own history, and that's a tragedy. I love finding out how similar or different people were from us. ❞ —Steven Ellis

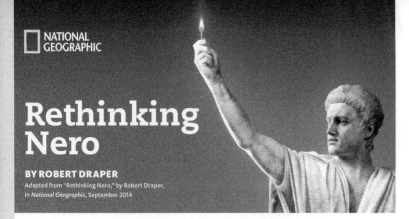

Rethinking Nero

BY ROBERT DRAPER

Adapted from "Rethinking Nero," by Robert Draper,
in *National Geographic*, September 2014

As the city of Rome burned in A.D. 64, the infamous emperor Nero allegedly sat around playing his violin. He also may have killed two of his wives, his mother, and his stepbrother. In the accounts of many historians, he is described as a murderer and a lunatic. But now some scholars are rethinking Nero's reputation.

In 2007, archaeologist Fedora Filippi discovered the base of a column while digging under a busy street in Rome. Burrowing further, she encountered a portico and the edge of a pool. After a year of analysis, she concluded that she had discovered the enormous public gymnasium built by Nero a few years before the Great Fire. At first her discovery garnered little attention. But it was an important find. "The gymnasium was part of a big change Nero brought about in Rome," Filippi says. "Before, such baths were only for the aristocrats. This changed social relations because it put everyone on the same level, from senators to the horsemen."

Nero's gymnasium and events early in his reign suggest that he was a reformer who desired the admiration of his people. He ended the secret trials of the previous emperor, issued pardons, and was reluctant to sign death warrants. He praised Greek culture, encouraging Greek-style contests of athletics and poetry. Instead of looting other countries to gain wealth, Nero taxed wealthy Romans to raise funds, a practice that made him unpopular with the most powerful members of society. These early accomplishments likely alienated him from the Roman senators. But his own outrageous behavior later in his reign is the reason why he went down in history as a madman.

"Nero was a fool obsessed with his own power, but a fool can also be charming and interesting," says Roman archaeologist Andrea Carandini. He became powerful by appealing to the popular desires and prejudices of his people. In turn, he cherished the masses who adored him.

Romans themselves were conflicted about their ruler. "He was a monster," says Roberto Gervaso, author of the biographical novel *Nerone*. "But that's not all he was."

For more from National Geographic
Check out "Roman Frontiers" at NGLSync.Cengage.com

UNIT INQUIRY: BUILD AN EMPIRE

In this unit, you learned about ancient Rome and its legacy. Based on your reading, what factors can help make an empire great? What factors can lead to its decline?

ASSIGNMENT Design an empire that you think would be successful today. The empire should have a geographic location, a government, an economy, a social structure, and its own culture. Be prepared to present your empire and explain it to the class.

Plan As you build your empire, think about ancient Rome—what made it successful and what made it grow weak. Make a list of these factors and try to incorporate or avoid them in your own empire. Use a graphic organizer like this one to help organize your thoughts. ▶

Produce Use your notes to produce detailed descriptions of the elements of your empire. Write them in outline or paragraph form.

Present Choose a creative way to present your empire to the class. Consider one of these options:

- Create a multimedia presentation using photos to represent different elements of your empire.

- Write an introduction to a travel guide that describes your empire.

- Draw a map of your empire to accompany the description of its overall structure.

```
Geography    Government    Economy
          \      |      /
           My Empire
          /          \
   Social Structure    Culture
```

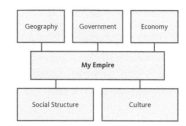

RAPID REVIEW UNIT 4

THE WORLD OF THE ROMANS TOP TEN

1. In the Roman Republic, power was shared between elected consuls and assemblies to prevent individuals from becoming too powerful.
2. After many civil wars, Rome became an empire ruled with absolute authority by a single emperor.
3. The wise rule of the emperor Augustus ushered in the Pax Romana, 200 years of peace and prosperity.
4. The Colosseum hosted spectacular and bloody games where gladiators fought to the death.
5. Romans spoke Latin, and we still use many Latin words today.

6-10. **NOW IT'S YOUR TURN** Complete the list with five more things to remember about the world of the Romans.

RAPID REVIEW

POSSIBLE RESPONSES

Possible responses for the remaining five things to remember include the following:

6. The ancient Romans were innovative architects and engineers who built roads, aqueducts, and spectacular buildings.

7. A massive volcanic eruption destroyed the city of Pompeii in A.D. 79.

8. The spread of Christianity threatened the Roman government, which made the practice of this new religion illegal.

9. The Roman Empire split into two empires, Eastern and Western, in A.D. 285.

10. Internal problems and invasions by barbarians contributed to the fall of the Western Roman Empire in A.D. 476.

UNIT INQUIRY PROJECT RUBRIC

ASSESS

Use the rubric to assess each student's participation and performance.

SCORE	ASSIGNMENT	PRODUCT	PRESENTATION
3 GREAT	• Student thoroughly understands the assignment. • Student participates fully in the project process. • Student works well with team members.	• Empire is well thought out. • Empire takes into account strengths and weaknesses of the Roman Empire. • Empire contains all of the key elements listed in the assignment.	• Presentation is clear, concise, and logical. • Presentation does a good job of creatively explaining the empire. • Presentation engages the audience.
2 GOOD	• Student mostly understands the assignment. • Student participates fairly well in the project process. • Student works fairly well with team members.	• Empire is fairly well thought out. • Empire somewhat takes into account strengths and weaknesses of the Roman Empire. • Empire contains some of the key elements listed in the assignment.	• Presentation is fairly clear, concise, and logical. • Presentation does an adequate job of creatively explaining the empire. • Presentation somewhat engages the audience.
1 NEEDS WORK	• Student does not understand the assignment. • Student minimally participates or does not participate in the project process. • Student does not work well with team members.	• Empire is not well thought out. • Empire does not take into account strengths and weaknesses of the Roman Empire. • Empire contains few or none of the key elements listed in the assignment.	• Presentation is not clear, concise, or logical. • Presentation does not creatively explain the empire. • Presentation does not engage the audience.

TURN AND TALK

One of the themes in this Why Study History? text is "global citizenship." Pair students and ask them to write about what this concept means to each of them. Then ask them to discuss their written responses. Finally, ask student pairs to discuss how trade affected and/or created global citizens throughout history.

WHY STUDY HISTORY **?**

TO UNDERSTAND THE SIMILARITIES AND DIFFERENCES AMONG CIVILIZATIONS

You just plowed through two units introducing civilizations with similar but different languages, cultures, and religions. As global citizens, our call to action is to understand that each civilization has its own unique identity. Recognizing the inherent worth and equality of all civilizations and cultures—and, in fact, of all people—is at the heart of global citizenship.

On the Framework of World History chart at the beginning of this text, the civilizations in Units 3 and 4 fall under "World Systems." The Greek, Roman and Byzantine civilizations continued to build on the foundations that early civilizations had established. All these civilizations established sophisticated cultures. Understanding the similarities and differences among them is one reason we study history.

Fred Hiebert
Watch the Why Study History video

These massive Roman aqueducts in Segovia, Spain, are evidence of ancient Roman technological advances in arch-building.

KEY TAKEAWAYS UNITS 3–4

PATTERNS IN HISTORY: SIMILAR DEVELOPMENTS ACROSS LOCATIONS

- Trade takes off on a global scale with the establishment of outposts around the Mediterranean and beyond, to South and East Asia.
- The cities of Alexandria and, later, Constantinople become centers of culture and trade.

GOVERNMENT

- Emphasis shifts to protecting ordinary people, with the development of democracy in ancient Greece and Rome.
- Elaborate systems of law are developed in Rome and standardized in the Justinian Code.

MOVEMENT OF PEOPLE AND IDEAS

- Hellenistic culture spreads through the empire-building of Alexander the Great.

- Roman culture spreads through colonization and trade.
- Christianity spreads throughout the Roman world and eventually becomes the empire's official religion.

ARTISTIC EXPRESSION

Artistic achievements include

- more realistic "selfies" in statues from ancient Greece
- frescoes in ancient Rome
- Byzantine mosaics

TECHNOLOGY & INNOVATION

Engineering and architectural developments include

- columns and temples from ancient Greece
- improved concrete and arches from ancient Rome

+ GUIDED DISCUSSION

In Units 1–4, students learned about different civilizations with their own cultures, languages, and religions.

1. **Time Out for a Definition!**
   The concept of "trade" is something students are likely familiar with, but one that should be examined in terms of its evolution and impact throughout history. Ask students to note examples of trade in the units they have completed. Consider the differences between local and global trade, the types of transportation required for each type, and how trade impacted the countries, regions, or cultures involved. Post examples of the types of trade students have read about on sheets of paper on a wall for discussion. As a class, sort the examples chronologically and according to similarities or differences.

2. **Compare and Contrast**
   As a class, use a chart to compare and contrast different civilizations from Units 1–4. Discuss how influences such as geography and technology affected these cultures differently.

IT'S ABOUT BEING A GLOBAL CITIZEN.

As a global citizen, you are empowered to act responsibly in the 21st century by showing empathy and respect for others, making informed decisions and finding your own voice, and actively participating in a rich and diverse environment. Go for it!

+ THINK BACK

Review the Why Study History? sections in the book, then pose this important question back to students: Why do YOU think it's important to study history? Ask students to verbally articulate an answer to this question or record an answer in their Field Journal and share it with the class.

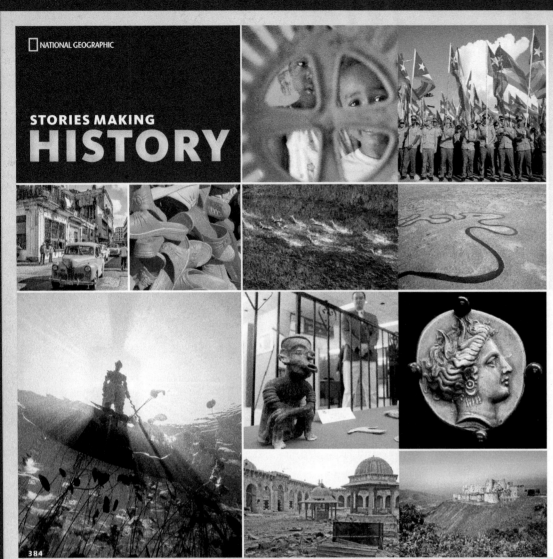

STORIES MAKING HISTORY

History is a living thing, and you are part of it.

You've just read about centuries and centuries of events that may seem like they have little connection to your life—but you might be surprised. Those long-gone people and dramatic occurrences have brought us to where we are today, and the things happening all over the world while you sit in class each day will shape your life for years to come. If you don't keep an eye on the issues that will someday become the history of your generation, who will?

As this *World History* book went to the printer, important new National Geographic stories were just hitting the news. So we narrowed them down to the five stories that follow. Remember: These are just a few of the many intriguing stories surfacing around the world, and they're still developing. As a global citizen, it's up to you to ask yourself: What happened next? How did this turn out? **Go find out!**

INTRODUCE STORIES MAKING HISTORY

As you know, part of studying the past is thinking about its implications for the future. Lots of people have repeated what has now become a little cliché: "Those who can't remember the past are condemned to repeat it." That comes from people as varied as Edmund Burke, George Santayana, and Kurt Vonnegut. Using current events in a World History class is a good way to make students aware of the connections among humans across time and place.

National Geographic is a great vehicle to use to bring contemporary stories to the classroom. In Stories Making History, we've offered brief articles on five stories in the headlines when this World History program went to press. Challenge students to follow these stories in online news sources and to identify other important stories that they think will affect their future.

Lead a discussion about the title "Stories Making History." Ask students to use their own words to explain what they think that means. Here are a few strategies to introduce Stories Making History to your class.

1. **Photo Preview** Preview the photos in the opening two pages of this section of the book. Have students identify what they think is shown in each photo and what, if anything, makes the photo particularly interesting or unusual. You might have them write a brief caption for each photo and share as a class.

2. **Read Aloud** Ask for a volunteer to read the two-paragraph introduction to Stories Making History aloud for the class. Ask students to explain in their own words what it means that "the things happening all over the world while [they] sit in class each day will shape [their lives] for years to come." **ASK:** What does that mean to you? Do you want to be part of those events? Discuss the idea of global citizenship (which by this point in the program should be familiar to them).

3. **News Sources** You might provide students with a variety of print news sources or direct them to online sources that they can explore as they read the Stories Making History in their text. **ASK:** What other stories are "making history" in the world today? Which of those stories affect the United States? What stories are important in their local communities? And what would they identify as the important "stories" in their school among their peers?

   Help students realize that understanding the events happening at a global level starts by understanding what's happening right around them in school, in their neighborhood, and in the larger community. Make the point that it's certainly a goal to understand events but it's also a goal to use their voices to affect change when it's needed.

4. **Jigsaw Activity** Break the class into three small groups and assign each group one of the articles in Stories Making History. Have students read the article and work together to create a simple presentation on the article to share with the class. Those same groups can do a little online research to track the status of their article today.

Have students discuss whether they agree with the statement "History is a living thing and you are part of it." Ask them to keep in mind the themes that have been echoing throughout this World History program:

- the enduring contributions of all civilizations
- the need for empathy and respect for the world's cultures
- the universal need to establish identity
- the role of global citizens
- the importance of preserving the human record
- being empowered to use their voices to speak up for themselves

As they read help them figure out which of these themes connects to each article. And remind them that the kinds of questions they ask—and their determination to keep a dialogue going about history, current events, politics, any issue in the news—will help shape the quality of their lives as adults.

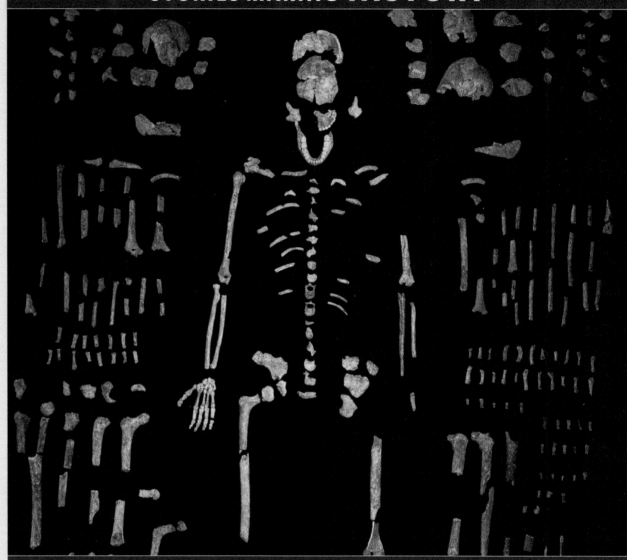

Rising Star: Redesigning the Human Family Tree

In September 2013, two recreational cavers were exploring Rising Star, a vast network of deep caves about 30 miles northwest of Johannesburg, South Africa. After navigating through narrow tunnels and over jagged walls of rock, they made a remarkable discovery—a chamber filled with hundreds of fossilized remains of early hominins, a group of two-footed primates that includes humans, their early ancestors, and other related species. Little did they know that their discovery may completely revolutionize our understanding of the origins of humankind.

˄ A complete skeleton of *H. naledi* is surrounded by hundreds of other specimens found at Rising Star.

Lee Berger holds the skull of an *A. sediba*, a new species of hominin discovered in 2008.

When paleoanthropologist and National Geographic Explorer-in-Residence Lee Berger received news of this remarkable find, he rushed to the site. Eager to bring the Rising Star fossils to the surface, he faced a big problem—excavating them. They were buried deep in the cave, and the only entrance was vertical chute less than eight inches wide. Using social media, Berger sent out a worldwide message to find skilled caver-scientists who were small enough to squeeze through the opening and skilled enough to handle one of the most rare archaeological finds in existence. Quickly but carefully, the Rising Star Expedition team was selected, funded by National Geographic, and led by Berger.

In November 2013, as the excavators, or "underground astronauts" as they were called, climbed carefully into the depths of the cave, dropping as much as 100 feet below ground level, Berger and his colleagues watched excitedly from the surface, viewing footage captured by the excavators' cameras. Over the next three weeks, the excavation team carefully removed dirt and debris from the fossils, placed them in containers, and raised them to the surface.

When the excavators finished, they had recovered nearly 1,500 fossils from at least 15 individuals. The fossils were also remarkably complete. Of the 206 bones in one body, the excavators found all but 20 of the bones. "If you're an anthropologist this is as good as it gets," says John Hawks, a professor of anthropology at the University of Wisconsin and a member of Berger's team of researchers.

Eager to share his discovery with the world, Berger put together a team of more than 50 scientists to analyze the specimens. The team was divided into smaller groups by body part. As the groups completed their analyses, one pattern became clear—some features appeared remarkably humanlike, while others appeared more primitive. Berger and his team agreed that these creatures belonged to the Homo genus but were unlike any other member. They had to name a new species, which they called *Homo naledi*.

"This fossil will be probably one of the best known hominin species discovered in the history of this science." –Lee Berger

This new species was revealed to the scientific community, and the world, on September 10, 2015. However, there are still many questions that remain. For instance, how did all those bones get into that cave? One extraordinary theory proposed by Berger is that the bodies of dead *H. naledi* were placed there by other *H. naledi* as a type of burial ritual. Since human beings are the only species known to bury their dead, this theory could mean that *H. naledi* is a direct predecessor of modern humans. We won't know for sure until the fossils are dated, which is not possible with current techniques.

Even if it turns out that *H. naledi* is a younger, more recent species, the repercussions are fascinating. It could mean that a separate species was evolving around the same time as our own. "No matter what the age," Berger says about his discovery, "it will have tremendous impact."

TURN AND TALK

Explain to students that Lee Berger's methods have been criticized by some in the scientific community as being controversial and unconventional. Berger argues that he is trying to break paleoanthropology out of its "lethargic pace of discovery." Lead the class in a discussion about whether it's better to try new, less proven methods and techniques to get information out to the public faster or to follow the traditionally slow proven methods that have been used by scientists for decades. What are the advantages and disadvantages of each?

Saving Cultural Heritage

Home to some of the oldest cultures on earth and six UNESCO World Heritage sites, modern-day Syria lies along the eastern coast of the Mediterranean Sea with Iraq to the east, Turkey to the north, and Jordan to the south—at the heart of the region referred to as the Middle East. Syria's modern borders were drawn in the 20th century, and crossed diverse cultures. This diversity makes it a place where people from all faiths gather, where cultural heritage is a part of people's identity, and greatly influences their way of life.

^
Destruction and looting have drastically altered the Umayyad Mosque in Aleppo, Syria, as seen in these before and after shots of its exterior and interior.

Salam Al Kuntar
2015 Emerging Explorer

Dr. Salam Al Kuntar, an archaeologist who grew up in Syria, can tell you all about what it's like to live in a place so rich in cultural heritage.

As a young girl picking olives, pistachios, and almonds in her family's orchard in Syria, Al Kuntar also collected pottery shards left behind by ancient cultures. At the time, she dreamed of becoming an astronaut. Today, she laughs as she admits that instead of taking her up into the sky, her career sends her digging below the ground!

Named a National Geographic Emerging Explorer in 2015, Al Kuntar's work has taken on an unexpected urgency. She and a team of experts are working to save ancient evidence of Syria's diverse heritage from the ravages of war. Since civil war erupted in Syria in 2011, violence has sent millions of Syrians fleeing from their homes to live in refugee camps. Years into the conflict, millions of Syrian children are unable to go to school. Instead of focusing on homework assignments, they think about their family's safety and whether or not they'll have enough to eat.

Syria's ancient monuments and museums, too, have been the victims of careless government airstrikes as well as bombing and shelling by various opposition groups.

In the city of Aleppo in April 2013, for example, the minaret, or tower, on the Umayyad Mosque dating from 1090 A.D. was completely destroyed. Other fragile archaeological sites have been damaged, and thieves have been looting antiquities—objects or works of art from the ancient past—and selling them illegally outside of Syria.

Syria's Ma'arra Mosaic Museum, southwest of Aleppo, was once a *caravanserai*, or inn. It holds a collection of Roman and Byzantine mosaics more impressive than any other in the Middle East. The museum was near collapse from damages sustained because of the war until preservationists and volunteers stepped in. Their efforts saved the collection.

The physical destruction of something tangible like Syria's historical monuments actually is intended to rob people of something intangible—their cultural heritage and identity. The impact is deeply felt when people can no longer visit a place or a monument that they have memories of visiting with their grandparents. The stories they've carried with them since childhood become harder to remember and share. Al Kuntar warns that the war "is killing the hope for the future."

But there is still hope even under these difficult circumstances. Salam Al Kuntar's team works closely with local activists to document the destruction of monuments. They map and identify damage, apply a harmless glue to keep the tesserae, or small cubes that make up the mosaics, intact, and use sandbags and wrapping materials to protect them. People sometimes try to escape from the war and seek refuge inside some of the remote ruins. Al Kuntar's team does emergency repairs to shore up crumbling stone so it doesn't crush these frightened and exhausted guests.

As an archaeologist, Al Kuntar knows something very important that keeps her going under dangerous and discouraging conditions: this effort to destroy Syria's cultural heritage ultimately is not going to work. The fact is that their cultural heritage is embedded in the hearts and minds of the Syrian people—in their memories of family and country—and it cannot be destroyed. Salam Al Kuntar describes Syria's diversity as "precious," and is determined to protect it for future generations.

→ TURN AND TALK

Talk with students about the assertion in the text that attempts to destroy Syria's cultural heritage aren't going to work because "their cultural heritage is embedded in the hearts and minds of the Syrian people." Ask students if they believe that's true in the United States too. What aspects of their own heritage can students identify as most important? Remind them that developing and practicing empathy and respect for all cultures is one reason they are studying world history.

GUIDED DISCUSSION

1. **The text says that the human record—the record of human history on Earth—is a nonrenewable resource. What does that mean? What happens to a cultural artifact when it is damaged or stolen? (Answer:** *When an artifact is damaged or stolen, it loses the historical context in which it was found and can't be used to support a research premise. Once an object loses its context, it is in effect lost to history and can never be replaced.***)**

2. **What happens when an object is repatriated? (Answer:** *It is returned to its country of origin.***)**

3. **Explain Fred Hiebert's efforts to fight looting and preserve cultural heritage. (Answer:** *Hiebert has developed a process, including conducting emergency inventories, for dealing with smuggled artifacts when they are discovered in suspicious shipments. He also trains customs agents in how to identify and safely handle artifacts, and works with local populations to help them become good stewards of their heritage.***)**

STORIES MAKING HISTORY

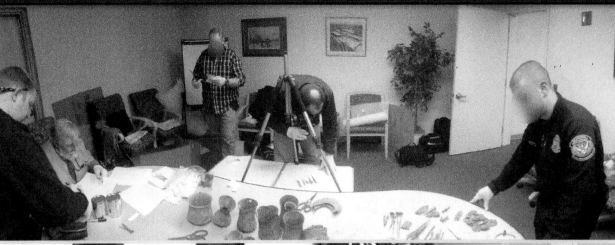

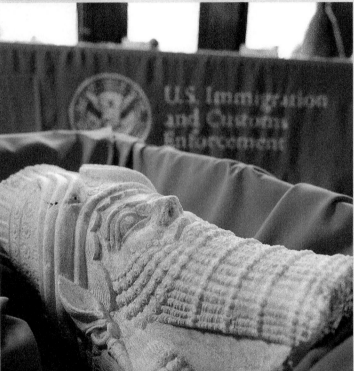

Our Shared History

Imagine if a symbol of the United States—for example, the Statue of Liberty—was stolen from New York Harbor and whisked away to another country. Most Americans would be angry that part of their history was lost to them. Across the world, this theft of the past happens regularly in areas that have been centers of civilization and are rich with archaeological sites and cultural artifacts. And it results in the same feeling of loss.

^
Top U.S. Customs agents at Dulles Airport in Washington, D.C., examine illegally shipped artifacts.

Bottom Left Head of a lamassu repatriated to Iraq

Bottom Right Paracas textile repatriated to Peru

Cultural artifacts are the little pieces of humanity left behind. They add to what we know of the human record, a non-renewable resource that we all share. When a cultural artifact is damaged or stolen, it is robbed of its identity and can never be replaced. The more conflict a region experiences, the less stable it becomes and the more vulnerable it is to looting, the illegal excavation and smuggling of cultural artifacts.

Some experts now work to help keep artifacts and identities where they belong. Dr. Fredrik Hiebert, National Geographic's Archaeology Fellow and an expert

Fred Hiebert

in documenting endangered collections around the world, calls these people "culture heroes" for their dedication to preserving the past. These historians, archaeologists, and anthropologists often support the goal of repatriation, the official returning of looted artifacts to their country of origin. National Geographic has helped bring about repatriations to Afghanistan, Egypt, and Peru.

Afghanistan 2009 Afghanistan was a gathering place for cultures that traded along the Silk Roads. Invasion by the Soviet Union in 1979 began more than three decades of violence that continues today. As a result, Afghanistan's archaeological sites and museums suffered rocket attacks that destroyed cultural artifacts. Such unintended damage is called collateral damage. Other damage is caused intentionally. In 2001, for example, the Taliban used explosives to blow up giant sandstone Buddha statues dating from the 6th century A.D. For years, looting was widespread. More than 1,500 objects spanning thousands of years were confiscated at Heathrow Airport in London and repatriated to Afghanistan in 2009.

Peru 2015 Sometimes what happens to an artifact isn't necessarily the result of violence or war. The 2,300-year-old textile shown on the opposite page has had numerous adventures on its journey home—yet is still in perfect condition. It was discovered as part of a necropolis, or ancient cemetery, in the 1920s and excavated by the founder of Peruvian archaeology, Julio Tello. The textile was stolen from the National Museum in Lima, Peru, not once, but twice. The second time, it found its way to Texas, where U.S. Customs agents recognized the illegal shipment and returned it to the Peruvian embassy. National Geographic helped return the textile in good condition to the museum in 2015.

Egypt 2010 and 2015 In 2008, U.S. Customs agents in Miami, Florida, became suspicious about a shipment with inconsistencies in the paperwork accompanying it. Two years later, the sarcophagus of a man named Imesy who lived during the 21st dynasty of Egypt was repatriated to the Grand Egyptian Museum in Cairo.

In April 2015, National Geographic hosted a ceremony for dozens more illegally shipped artifacts being repatriated from the United States back to Egypt, including a rare nesting sarcophagus from the 26th dynasty and even some mummy parts. Attended by both the U.S. Customs officers and archaeologists involved in solving the case, the ceremony was a moving recognition of an international effort to stop the looting of cultural artifacts and preserve them for future generations.

Fred Hiebert believes that every country is entitled to its own history. He is part of an effort to develop an "antiquities protocol," a process that can be deployed when smuggled artifacts are discovered in the world's ports. Hiebert conducts emergency inventories of looted artifacts, creating a "passport" or permanent record for these objects. But he claims that education is just as important: training customs agents to safely handle artifacts and teaching local residents to become better stewards for the objects that represent their heritage. "Who owns the past?" Fred Hiebert asks, and he has a ready answer: "All of us."

➡ TURN AND TALK

Lead the class in a discussion about what it means to be a "culture hero." Can they think of someone they would identify as a culture hero? It doesn't have to be someone in a position to physically save an artifact. Make sure they understand that there are other ways to contribute. A culture hero might be someone in the community who makes sure holidays like Diwali or Cinco de Mayo are celebrated along with more traditional American holidays. Challenge them to think of other ways to be a culture hero in one's community.

Think It Through

The articles in this section focus on history-making events and issues that have a profound effect on people and cultures across the globe. Consider and discuss the questions below to further your understanding of these important topics.

1 Choose one article that connects to your own life and experiences in some way and explain why. How does this article relate to your own personal history?

2 Which of the three articles would be most likely to motivate you to take action as a global citizen? How might you get involved?

3 Which topic are you most interested in finding out more about, and why? How might you seek additional information or updates?

Inquiry Project: Roundtable

Consider each of the newsworthy issues discussed in this section and select the one you feel is the most important or impactful within the world today. Why do you feel your chosen global issue is the most important one?

Assignment Become an expert on the issue you have chosen alongside others who have also chosen that issue. Participate in a roundtable discussion. Articulate why you feel your chosen issue is the most important one, and support your argument.

Plan Connect with other students in your class who share your opinion and discuss what you already know about this issue and what questions you still have. Develop a solid understanding of the topic by gathering information from multiple print and digital sources. Be sure to note your sources and summarize ideas in your own words.

Produce From your research, develop a list of reasons and arguments to support the notion that your chosen topic has the most impact on the world.

Present Participate in a classroom-wide roundtable discussion. Along with others who share your opinion about the topic you have chosen, work to explain why your topic has the most world impact. Use evidence from your research to support your argument. Listen respectfully as others present their viewpoints.

REP 1 Students frame questions that can be answered by historical study and research.

STANDARDS

HSS ANALYSIS SKILLS:
REP 1 Students frame questions that can be answered by historical study and research.

THINK IT THROUGH

Answers to all three questions will vary. Lead a discussion of student responses to each of the questions provided. You might also use one or more of the questions as a writing prompt, or for question 2, ask students to debate among themselves which article they found most motivating.

RUBRIC FOR INQUIRY PROJECT: ROUNDTABLE

Allow time in class for each group to conduct their roundtable for the class.

SCORE	ASSIGNMENT	PRODUCT	PRESENTATION
3 GREAT	• Student thoroughly understands the assignment. • Student participates fully in the project process. • Student works well with team members.	• Research is thorough and appropriate. • Reasons and arguments are well thought out and support the notion that student's topic has the greatest impact on the world. • Student's work meets all of the requirements listed in the assignment.	• Student's comments as he/she participates in roundtable discussion are clear, concise, and logical. • Student effectively communicates his or her views and evidence. • Presentation engages other participants and demonstrates student's ability to be an effective listener.
2 GOOD	• Student mostly understands the assignment. • Student participates adequately in the project process. • Student works well with team members most of the time.	• Research is fairly thorough and appropriate. • Most reasons and arguments are well thought out and support the notion that student's topic has the greatest impact on the world. • Student's work meets most of the requirements listed in the assignment.	• Student's comments as he/she participates in roundtable discussion are clear, concise, and logical most of the time. • Student is fairly effective in communicating his or her views and evidence. • Presentation engages some of the participants and demonstrates student's ability to be an effective listener most of the time.
1 NEEDS WORK	• Student does not understand most of the assignment. • Student does not fully participate in the project process. • Student struggles to work well with team members.	• Research lacks completeness and/or is inappropriate. • Reasons and arguments are not well thought out. They do not effectively support the notion that student's topic has the greatest impact on the world. • Student's work does not meet all of the requirements listed in the assignment.	• Student's comments as he/she participates in roundtable discussion are not typically clear, concise, or logical. • Student struggles to effectively communicate his or her views and evidence. • Presentation fails to engage other participants and does not demonstrate student's ability to be an effective listener.

STUDENT
REFERENCES

AVAILABLE ONLINE

Skills Handbook
Primary Source Handbook
Geography Handbook
World Religions Handbook
Economics and Government Handbook

GLOSSARY

A

acropolis *n.* the highest point in an ancient Greek city

agora *n.* an open space in an ancient Greek city that served as a marketplace and social center

agriculture *n.* the practice of growing plants and rearing animals for food

alliance *n.* an agreement between nations to fight each other's enemies; a partnership

anthropologist *n.* a scientist who studies the cultural development of humans

aqueduct *n.* a long stone channel that carries clean water

arch *n.* a curved structure over an opening

archaeologist *n.* a scientist who studies past human life by analyzing fossils and artifacts

aristocracy *n.* an upper class that is richer and more powerful than the rest of society

artifact *n.* an object made by humans from a past culture

artisan *n.* a person skilled at making things by hand

B

barbarian *n.* in this context, a person who lived outside the Roman Empire

barter *v.* to exchange goods

bas-relief *n.* a realistic sculpture with figures raised against a flat background

bureaucracy *n.* a system of government in which appointed officials in specialized departments run the various offices

C

cacao *n.* a bean used to make chocolate

caravan *n.* a group of people that travels together

caste system *n.* a rigid social hierarchy in India that divides people into hereditary classes

catacomb *n.* a hidden underground chamber where people are buried

catapult *n.* a weapon that hurls large stones

cataract *n.* a rock formation that creates churning rapids; also, a large waterfall

city *n.* a political, economic, and cultural center with a large population

city-state *n.* a self-governing unit made up of a city and its surrounding lands and settlements; a city that controls the surrounding villages and towns

civilization *n.* a society with a highly developed culture and technology

civil war *n.* a war between groups in the same country

clan *n.* a group of families that shares a common ancestor

codex *n.* a folded book made of tree bark paper

colony *n.* a group of people that settles in a new land but keeps ties to its native country

comedy *n.* a humorous form of Greek drama that often mocked famous people

consul *n.* one of two chief leaders elected yearly in ancient Rome

cosmopolitan *adj.* worldly

covenant *n.* a religious agreement

creation story *n.* an account that explains how the world began and how people came to exist

creed *n.* a statement of belief

crossroads *n.* the place where two roads meet

cultural diffusion *n.* the process by which cultures interact and ideas spread from one area to another

cultural hearth *n.* a place from which new ideas, practices, and technology spread

culture *n.* a group's way of life, including types of food, shelter, clothing, language, religion, behavior, and ideas

cuneiform *n.* the earliest form of writing, invented by the Sumerians

D

delta *n.* an area where a river fans out into various branches as it flows into a body of water

democracy *n.* a form of government in which citizens have a direct role in governing themselves or elect representatives to lead them

dharma *n.* the Buddha's teachings; divine law

dictator *n.* a person who rules with total authority

direct democracy *n.* a form of democracy in which citizens gather together to vote on laws and policies

diversity *n.* a range of different things; a variety

divine *adj.* having the nature of a god

domestication *n.* the raising of plants and animals to make them useful to humans

drought *n.* a long period of dry, hot weather

dynastic cycle *n.* the pattern of the rise and fall of dynasties in ancient and early China

dynasty *n.* a series of rulers from the same family

E

emperor *n.* the supreme ruler of an empire

empire *n.* a group of different lands and people governed by one ruler

enlightened despot *n.* an absolute ruler who applied Enlightenment principles to his or her reign

epic poem *n.* a long story in the form of a narrative poem

epistle *n.* a letter

excommunicate *v.* to officially exclude a member of a church from its rituals and membership

exile *n.* the forced removal from one's native country

F

famine *n.* an extreme lack of crops or food causing widespread hunger

fertile *adj.* encouraging the growth of crops and plants

filial piety *n.* the belief that children owe their parents and ancestors respect

fossil *n.* the remains of organisms that lived long ago

fresco *n.* a picture painted directly onto a wall

G

gladiator *n.* a man in ancient Rome who fought others for entertainment

glyph *n.* a symbolic picture used to represent a word, syllable, or sound

golden age *n.* a period of great cultural achievement

government *n.* an organization set up to make and enforce rules in a society

H

Hellenistic *adj.* relating to Greek history or culture

helot *n.* a state-owned slave who was part of the lowest class of ancient Greek society

heresy *n.* beliefs contrary to Church teachings; opposition to Church policy

hero *n.* a character who faces a challenge that demands courage, strength, and intelligence

hierarchy *n.* a system in which people belong to social classes of different ranks

hieroglyph *n.* a picture representing an object, sound, or idea that was part of the ancient Egyptian writing system

highland *n.* a type of land that is high above the sea

hunter-gatherer *n.* a human who hunts animals and gathers wild plants to eat

I

icon *n.* an image of Jesus or a saint

immortal *adj.* able to live forever

inoculation *n.* a vaccine containing a mild form of a disease to prevent the development of that disease

irrigation *n.* the supply of water to fields using human-made systems

isolate *v.* to cut off from the rest of the world

J

jury *n.* a group of people chosen to make a decision based on evidence presented in a trial

K

karma *n.* in Hinduism, a state of being influenced by a person's actions and conduct; determines the kind of life into which a person will be reborn

kosher *adj.* specially prepared according to Jewish dietary laws

L

labyrinth *n.* a maze

land bridge *n.* a strip of land connecting two landmasses

legacy *n.* the things, both cultural and technological, left to us from past cultures

legend *n.* a story from the past that is accepted as truth but cannot be proven

legionary *n.* a professional soldier in ancient Rome

lowland *n.* a type of land that is low and level

M

maize *n.* a type of corn first domesticated by early Mesoamericans

maritime *adj.* relating to the sea

matrilineal *adj.* relating to descendants traced through the mother

megafauna *n.* the large animals of a particular region, habitat, or geological period

metallurgy *n.* the science of obtaining metals in their natural form and preparing them for use

migration *n.* the movement from one place to another

missionary *n.* a person who goes to another country to do religious work; a person who tries to spread Christianity to others

monarchy *n.* a government ruled by a single person, such as a king

monotheism *n.* the worship of a single God

monsoon *n.* a strong seasonal wind in South and Southeast Asia

mosaic *n.* a grouping of tiny colored stone cubes set in mortar to create a picture or design

mother culture *n.* a civilization that greatly influences other civilizations

mummy *n.* the preserved body of a pharaoh or other powerful person in ancient Egypt

myth *n.* an old story told to explain an event or justify a belief or action

mythology *n.* a collection of stories that explains events, beliefs, or actions

N

nirvana *n.* in Buddhism, a state of bliss or the end of suffering caused by the cycle of rebirth

nomad *n.* a person who moves from place to place

O

oasis *n.* a fertile place with water in a desert

oligarchy *n.* a government ruled by a few powerful citizens

oracle bone *n.* an animal bone used to consult with the many gods worshipped by the Shang people

oral history *n.* an unwritten account of events, often passed down through the generations as stories or songs

oratory *n.* the art of public speaking

P

pantheon *n.* the gods of a group of people, a religion, or a civilization

papyrus *n.* a paperlike material made from reeds

parable *n.* in the Bible, a simple story to illustrate a moral or spiritual lesson

patriarch *n.* the leader of the Eastern Orthodox Church

patriarchy *n.* a society in which men hold all the power

patrician *n.* a wealthy landowner in ancient Rome

peasant *n.* a poor farmer

peninsula *n.* a piece of land surrounded by water on three sides

phalanx *n.* in ancient Greece and Rome, a battle formation in which soldiers stood close together to protect themselves from enemy attack

pharaoh *n.* an ancient Egyptian ruler

philosophy *n.* the study of the universe and our place in it

plague *n.* a disease that causes many deaths

planned city *n.* a city built with a specific layout in mind

plebeian *n.* a common person in ancient Rome

polis *n.* a Greek city-state

polytheism *n.* a belief in many gods

pope *n.* the leader of the Roman Catholic Church

primary source *n.* an artifact or piece of writing that was created by someone who witnessed or lived through a historical event

province *n.* an administrative district of a larger empire or country

pyramid *n.* a massive monumental tomb for a pharaoh

R

rabbi *n.* a Jewish spiritual leader

raw material *n.* a substance from which other things are made

record keeping *n.* the practice of organizing and storing information

reform *n.* a change to make a situation better

reincarnation *n.* in Hinduism, the rebirth of a person's soul into another body after death

religion *n.* the belief in and worship of one or more gods and goddesses

representative democracy *n.* a form of democracy in which people are elected to vote on the citizens' behalf

republic *n.* a type of government in which citizens vote for their leaders

ritual *n.* a formal series of acts always performed in the same way; a religious ceremony

S

satrap *n.* a governor of a province in the Persian Empire

schism *n.* a separation

GLOSSARY

scribe *n.* a professional writer who recorded official information

secondary source *n.* an artifact or writing created after an event by someone who did not see it or live during the time when it occurred

siege *n.* a military tactic in which troops surround a city with soldiers in an attempt to take control of it

silk *n.* a textile made from the cocoons of silkworms

silt *n.* an especially fine and fertile soil

slash-and-burn agriculture *n.* a method of clearing fields for planting

social class *n.* a category of people based on wealth or status in a society

specialized worker *n.* a person who performs a job other than farming, such as metalworking or toolmaking

staple *n.* a main crop produced in a specific place

subcontinent *n.* a large, distinct landmass that is part of a continent

surplus *adj.* more than is required or necessary; extra

synagogue *n.* a Jewish place of worship

T

technology *n.* the application of knowledge, tools, and inventions to meet people's needs

temple *n.* a place of worship

terrace *n.* a stepped platform built into a mountainside

terra cotta *n.* a fire-baked clay

tetrarchy *n.* a system of rule by four emperors

tolerance *n.* the sympathy for the beliefs and practices of others

trade *n.* the exchange of goods

tragedy *n.* a serious form of Greek drama in which characters endure suffering before an unhappy ending

tribe *n.* an extended family unit

tribune *n.* a representative who fought to protect the rights of ordinary citizens in ancient Rome

tribute *n.* a tax paid or goods and services rendered in return for protection

trireme *n.* an ancient Greek warship

truce *n.* an agreement to stop fighting

tyrant *n.* in ancient Greek city-states, a ruler who took power illegally

V

veto *v.* to reject a decision or proposal made by another government body

vizier *n.* a chief official in ancient Egypt who carried out much of the day-to-day work of governing

Y

yoga *n.* a series of postures and breathing exercises

Z

ziggurat *n.* a pyramid-shaped temple in Sumerian city-states

ACADEMIC VOCABULARY

A

absolute *adj.* complete (page 370)

accurate *adj.* without mistakes or errors (page 208)

advance *v.* to move forward (page 258)

appoint *v.* to give someone a particular job or duty (page 364)

C

capacity *n.* the ability to do something (page 15)

collide *v.* to crash together (page 145)

commerce *n.* the buying and selling of goods and services (page 302)

commit *v.* to promise to do something (page 326)

concentrate *v.* to focus on (page 74)

D

determination *n.* the quality that makes someone continue to try doing a difficult task (page 304)

distinctive *adj.* different in a noticeable way (page 41)

dominate *v.* to have power over someone or something (page 112)

E

emerge *v.* to rise or appear (page 36)

eternal *adj.* existing at all times; lasting forever (page 150)

F

flourish *v.* to be successful (page 290)

I

influence *v.* to affect or change someone or something indirectly (page 170)

interval *n.* the period of time between events (page 328)

P

policy *n.* a set of rules or ideas about how things should be done (page 127)

possession *n.* a personal article or possession (page 181)

predict *v.* to say that something will happen in the future (page 203)

privilege *n.* a right or benefit that only some people receive (page 114)

promote *v.* to encourage (page 154)

prosperous *adj.* successful, usually by making a lot of money (page 229)

R

reluctantly *adv.* with hesitation or doubt (page 265)

S

supervise *v.* to watch and oversee someone or something (page 69)

T

transform *v.* to dramatically change (page 26)

W

wage *n.* the amount of money a worker is paid (page 241)

A

acrópolis *s.* punto más alto en una ciudad griega de la antigüedad

acueducto *s.* canal largo de piedra que transporta agua limpia

ágora *s.* espacio abierto en una ciudad griega de la antigüedad que servía como mercado y centro social

agricultura *s.* práctica de cultivar plantas y criar animales para obtener alimento

agricultura de tala y quema *s.* método de limpiar los campos para sembrar cultivos

aislar *v.* apartar del resto del mundo

alianza *s.* acuerdo entre naciones para colaborar en la lucha contra los enemigos; asociación; pacto religioso

antropólogo *s.* científico que estudia el desarrollo cultural de los seres humanos

arco *s.* estructura curva colocada sobre una abertura

aristocracia *s.* clase alta que es más adinerada y más poderosa que el resto de la sociedad

arqueólogo *s.* científico que estudia el pasado de la vida humana mediante el análisis de fósiles y artefactos

artefacto *s.* objeto hecho por humanos pertenecientes a una cultura del pasado

artesano *s.* persona que se dedica a fabricar objetos de forma manual

B

bajorrelieve *s.* escultura realista que contiene figuras realzadas sobre un fondo plano

bárbaro *s.* en este contexto, una persona que vivía fuera del Imperio Romano

burocracia *s.* sistema de gobierno en que funcionarios designados en departamentos especializados están a cargo de distintas oficinas

C

cacao *s.* grano que se usa para hacer chocolate

campesino *s.* granjero pobre

caravana *s.* grupo de personas que viajan juntas

catacumba *s.* cámara escondida bajo la superficie en donde se entierra a los muertos

catapulta *s.* arma que lanza piedras enormes

catarata *s.* formación rocosa que crea rápidos agitados; además, una cascada grande

cazador-recolector *s.* ser humano que caza animales y que cosecha plantas silvestres para alimentarse

ciclo dinástico *s.* patrón del surgimiento y la caída de las dinastías de la China ancestral y antigua

cieno *s.* suelo especialmente fino y fértil

cisma *s.* separación

ciudad *s.* centro político, económico y cultural con una población grande

ciudad-estado *s.* unidad que se gobierna a sí misma, formada por una ciudad y sus territorios y asentamientos circundantes; ciudad que controla las aldeas y pueblos circundantes

ciudad planificada *s.* ciudad construida con un diseño específico en mente

civilización *s.* sociedad con una cultura y tecnología altamente desarrolladas

clan *s.* grupo de familias que comparten un ancestro en común

clase social *s.* categoría de personas basada en las riquezas o estatus en una sociedad

códice *s.* libro plegado hecho de papel de corteza de árbol

colonia *s.* grupo de personas que se asientan en un nuevo territorio, pero que mantienen sus lazos con su país nativo

comedia *s.* obra de teatro griega con un formato humorístico que solía burlarse de las personas famosas

comercio *s.* intercambio de productos; compra y venta de bienes

confederación *s.* grupo de aliados

cónsul *s.* uno de los dos jefes líderes elegidos cada año en la Antigua Roma

cosmopolita *adj.* internacional

credo *s.* declaración de creencia

crisol cultural *s.* lugar desde el cual se difunden nuevas ideas, prácticas y tecnología

cultivo básico *s.* cultivo principal producido en un lugar específico

cultura madre *s.* civilización que tiene una gran influencia sobre otras civilizaciones

cultura *s.* forma de vida de un grupo, que incluye tipos de alimento, vivienda, vestimenta, idioma, religión, comportamiento e ideas

cuneiforme *s.* primera forma de escritura conocida, inventada por los sumerios

D

delta *s.* área donde un río se divide en distintos brazos a medida que fluye hacia una masa de agua

democracia *s.* forma de gobierno en que los ciudadanos tienen un papel directo para gobernarse a sí mismos o para elegir a representantes que los gobiernen

democracia directa *s.* forma de democracia en que los ciudadanos se reúnen para votar sobre las leyes y las políticas

democracia representativa *s.* forma de democracia en que se eligen personas para que voten en representación de los ciudadanos

dharma *s.* enseñanzas de Buda; ley divina

dictador *s.* persona que gobierna con total autoridad

difusión cultural *s.* proceso mediante el cual las culturas interaccionan y las ideas se propagan de un área a otra

dinastía *s.* serie de gobernantes de la misma familia

diversidad *s.* rango de cosas diferentes; variedad

divino *adj.* tener la naturaleza de un dios

domesticación *s.* cultivo de plantas y animales de manera que fueran útiles para los humanos

E

edad de oro *s.* período de grandes logros culturales

emperador *s.* gobernante supremo de un imperio

epístola *s.* carta

escriba *s.* escritor profesional que anotaba información oficial

excedente *adj.* más de lo que se requiere o necesita; extra

excomulgar *s.* excluir oficialmente a un miembro de una iglesia de sus rituales y membresía

exilio *s.* expulsión forzada del propio país de origen

F

falange *s.* en la Antigua Grecia y Roma, formación de batalla en que los soldados se formaban juntos unos de otros para protegerse de los ataques de los enemigos

faraón *s.* gobernante egipcio de la antigüedad

fértil *adj.* que sustenta el crecimiento de cultivos y plantas

filosofía *s.* estudio del universo y de nuestro lugar en él

fósil *s.* restos de organismos que vivieron hace mucho tiempo atrás

fresco *s.* arte que se pinta directamente sobre una muralla

fuente primaria *s.* artefacto o texto escrito creado por alguien que presenció o vivió un acontecimiento histórico

fuente secundaria *s.* artefacto o texto escrito creado después de un acontecimiento por alguien que no lo vio o presenció durante el tiempo en que ocurrió

G

gladiador *s.* hombre de la Antigua Roma que luchaba contra otros como espectáculo de entretención

glifo *s.* dibujo simbólico usado para representar una palabra, sílaba o sonido

gobierno *s.* organización establecida para hacer y reforzar las reglas de una sociedad

guerra civil *s.* guerra entre grupos de un mismo país

H

hambruna *s.* escasez extrema de cultivos o de alimentos que causa hambre generalizada

helenístico *adj.* relacionado con la historia o cultura griega

herejía *s.* creencias contrarias a las enseñanzas de la iglesia; oposición a las políticas de la iglesia

héroe *s.* personaje que enfrenta un desafío que requiere valentía, fuerza e inteligencia

historia de la creación *s.* narración que explica cómo comenzó el mundo y cómo nacieron las personas

historia oral *s.* registro no escrito de acontecimientos, que a menudo se transmite de una generación a otra a través de historias o canciones

hueso oracular *s.* hueso de animal usado para consultar a los muchos dioses adorados por el pueblo Shang

I

ícono *s.* imagen de Jesús o de un santo

ilota *s.* esclavo que poseía el estado que era parte de la clase social más baja en la sociedad griega de la antigüedad

imperio *s.* conjunto de diferentes tierras y pueblos liderados por un gobernante

inmortal *adj.* que puede vivir para siempre

inoculación *s.* vacuna que contiene una forma leve de una enfermedad para prevenir el desarrollo de dicha enfermedad

intersección *s.* lugar en donde se juntan dos caminos

irrigación *s.* suministro de agua para los campos mediante el uso de sistemas hechos por el hombre

J

jerarquía *s.* sistema en que las personas pertenecen a distintas clases sociales que tienen distintos rangos en la sociedad

jeroglífico *s.* imagen que representa un objeto, sonido o idea y que era parte del antiguo sistema de escritura egipcio

jurado *s.* grupo de personas escogidas para tomar una decisión con base en la evidencia presentada en un juicio

K

karma *s.* en el hinduismo, estado de estar influenciado por las acciones y el comportamiento; determina el tipo de vida en que una persona volverá a nacer

kosher *adj.* preparado especialmente según las leyes dietéticas judías

L

laberinto *s.* lugar formado por encrucijadas, del cual es difícil salir

legado *s.* cosas, tanto culturales como tecnológicas, que nos quedan del pasado

legionario *s.* soldado profesional de la Antigua Roma

leyenda *s.* historia del pasado que se acepta como verdad, pero que no puede probarse

M

maíz *s.* tipo de elote que fue domesticado por los primeros mesoamericanos

marítimo *adj.* relacionado con el mar

materia prima *s.* sustancia a partir de la cual se fabrican otras cosas

matrilineal *adj.* relacionado con los descendientes que provienen de la madre

megafauna *s.* animales grandes de una región, hábitat o período geológico en particular

metalurgia *s.* ciencia que consiste en obtener materiales en su forma natural y prepararlos para el uso

migración *s.* mudarse de un lugar a otro

misionero *s.* persona que va a otro país para realizar labores religiosas; persona que trata de divulgar la cristiandad a otros

mito *s.* historia antigua contada para explicar un acontecimiento o justificar una creencia o acción

mitología *s.* colección de historias que explica acontecimientos, creencias o acciones

momia *s.* cuerpo preservado de un faraón u otra persona poderosa del Antiguo Egipto

monarquía *s.* gobierno liderado por una sola persona como, por ejemplo, un rey

monoteísmo *s.* alabanza a un solo Dios

monzón *s.* vientos estacionales fuertes en el Sudeste Asiático

mosaico *s.* agrupación de cubitos de piedra coloridos que se colocan sobre argamasa para crear un dibujo o diseño

N

nirvana *s.* en el budismo, un estado de dicha o del final del sufrimiento causado por el ciclo del renacer

nómada *s.* persona que se muda de un lugar a otro

O

oasis *s.* lugar fértil con agua en un desierto

oligarquía *s.* gobierno liderado por unos pocos ciudadanos

oratoria *s.* arte del discurso público

P

panteón *s.* dioses de un grupo de personas, una religión o una civilización

papa *s.* líder de la Iglesia Católica Romana

papiro *s.* material parecido al papel que se hace a partir de juncos

parábola *s.* en la Biblia, un relato sencillo que ilustra una moraleja o una lección espiritual

patriarca *s.* líder de la Iglesia Ortodoxa oriental

patriarcal *adj.* dicho de una sociedad en que los hombres tienen todo el poder

patricio *s.* terrateniente rico de la Antigua Roma

península *s.* porción de tierra rodeada por agua en tres de sus costados

permutar *v.* intercambiar productos

piedad filial *s.* creencia de que los niños le deben respeto a sus padres y ancestros

pirámide *s.* tumba masiva y monumental construida para un faraón

plaga *s.* enfermedad que causa muchas muertes

plebeyo *s.* persona común de la Antigua Roma

poema épico *s.* historia larga escrita como un poema narrativo

polis *s.* ciudad-estado griega

politeísmo *s.* creencia en muchos dioses

provincia *s.* distrito administrativo de un imperio grande o de un país

puente terrestre *s.* franja de territorio que conecta dos masas terrestres

R

rabino *s.* líder espiritual judío

reencarnación *s.* en el hinduismo, el renacer del alma de una persona en otro cuerpo después de la muerte

reforma *s.* cambio hecho para mejorar una situación

registros *s.* práctica que consiste en organizar y almacenar la información

religión *s.* creencia en y alabanza de uno o más dioses y diosas

república *s.* tipo de gobierno en que los ciudadanos votan por sus líderes

ritual *s.* serie de actos formales que siempre se realizan de la misma manera; ceremonia religiosa

S

sátrapa *s.* gobernante de una provincia en el Imperio Persa

seda *s.* textil hecho de los capullos de los gusanos de la seda

sequía *s.* período largo de estado del tiempo seco y caluroso

sinagoga *s.* lugar de reunión religiosa para los judíos

sistema de castas *s.* jerarquía social rígida en India que divide a las personas en clases sociales hereditarias

sitio *s.* táctica militar en que las tropas rodean una ciudad con soldados en un intento por controlarla

subcontinente *s.* gran masa de tierra que es parte de un continente

T

tecnología *s.* aplicación de conocimiento, herramientas e inventos para satisfacer las necesidades de las personas

templo *s.* lugar de alabanza

terracota *s.* arcilla cocida al fuego

terrazas *s.* plataformas de estepa construidas en la ladera de una montaña

tetrarquía *s.* sistema de gobierno de cuatro emperadores

tierras altas *s.* terrenos que están sobre el mar

tierras bajas *s.* tipo de terrenos nivelados de poca altura

tirano *s.* en las ciudades-estado de la Antigua Grecia, gobernante que obtenía el poder de forma ilegal

tolerancia *s.* respeto por las creencias y las prácticas de otros

trabajador especializado *s.* persona que realiza un trabajo que no está relacionado con la agricultura, como en la metalurgia o en la producción de herramientas

tragedia *s.* obra de teatro griega con un formato serio en que los personajes sufren antes de enfrentar un final triste

tregua *s.* acuerdo para detener un conflicto

tribu *s.* unidad familiar extendida

tribuno *s.* representante que luchó para proteger los derechos de los ciudadanos comunes en la Antigua Roma

tributo *s.* impuesto pagado o bienes y servicios proporcionados a cambio de protección

trirreme *s.* antigua nave de guerra griega

V

vetar *v.* rechazar una decisión o propuesta hecha por otro cuerpo gubernamental

visir *s.* oficial jefe en el Antiguo Egipto que realizaba la mayor parte del trabajo de gobernar cotidiano

Y

yoga *s.* serie de posturas y ejercicios de respiración

Z

zigurat *s.* templo con forma de pirámide en las ciudades-estado de Sumeria

SPANISH ACADEMIC VOCABULARY

A

absoluto *adj.* completo (pág. 370)

avanzar *v.* moverse hacia adelante (pág. 258)

C

capacidad *s.* habilidad de hacer algo (pág. 15)

colisionar *v.* chocar (pág. 145)

comercio *s.* compra y venta de bienes y servicios (pág. 302)

comprometerse *v.* prometer hacer algo (pág. 326)

concentrar *v.* enfocarse en algo (pág. 74)

D

designar *v.* dar a alguien un trabajo o responsabilidad determinado (pág. 364)

determinación *s.* cualidad que hace que alguien continúe intentando realizar una labor difícil (pág. 305)

dominar *v.* tener poder sobre alguien o algo (pág. 112)

E

eterno *adj.* que existe en todo momento; que dura para siempre (pág. 150)

F

florecer *v.* tener éxito (pág. 290)

I

influenciar *v.* afectar o cambiar alguien o algo de manera indirecta (pág. 170)

intervalo *s.* período de tiempo entre los acontecimientos (pág. 328)

P

peculiar *adj.* diferente de una manera perceptible (pág. 41)

política *s.* conjunto de reglas o ideas sobre cómo deben hacerse las cosas (pág. 127)

posesión *s.* artículo o propiedad personal (pág. 181)

precisión *adj.* sin faltas ni errores (pág. 208)

predecir *v.* decir qué sucederá en el futuro (pág. 203)

privilegio *s.* derecho o beneficio que sólo reciben algunas personas (pág. 114)

promover *v.* animar (pág. 154)

próspero *adj.* exitoso, usualmente por ganar mucho dinero (pág. 229)

R

reaciamente *adv.* con incertidumbre o dudas (pág. 265)

S

salario *s.* cantidad de dinero que recibe un trabajador (pág. 241)

supervisar *v.* vigilar y monitorear algo o alguien (pág. 69)

surgir *v.* emerger o aparecer (pág. 36)

T

transformar *v.* cambiar dramáticamente (pág. 26)

INDEX

SKILLS INDEX

ACKNOWLEDGMENTS

National Geographic Learning

National Geographic Learning gratefully acknowledges the contributions of the following National Geographic Explorers and affiliates to our program and to our planet:

Salam Al Kuntar, Archaeologist, National Geographic Emerging Explorer
Caroline Alexander, National Geographic Writer/Journalist
Nicole Boivin, Archaeologist, National Geographic Grantee
Steve Boyes, Conservation Biologist, National Geographic Emerging Explorer
Nina Burleigh, Journalist/Author
Michael Cosmopoulos, Archaeologist, National Geographic Grantee
Christopher DeCorse, Archaeologist, National Geographic Grantee
Steven Ellis, Archaeologist, National Geographic Grantee
Francisco Estrada-Belli, Archaeologist, National Geographic Grantee
Beverly Goodman, Geo-Archaeologist, National Geographic Emerging Explorer
Jeff Gusky, National Geographic Photographer
Fredrik Hiebert, Archaeologist, National Geographic Fellow
Patrick Hunt, Archaeologist, National Geographic Grantee
Louise Leakey, Paleontologist, National Geographic Explorer-in-Residence
Christine Lee, Bio-Archaeologist, National Geographic Emerging Explorer
Albert Lin, Research Scientist/Engineer, National Geographic Emerging Explorer
Jodi Magness, Archaeologist, National Geographic Grantee
Sarah Parcak, Archaeologist, National Geographic Fellow
Thomas Parker, Archaeologist, National Geographic Grantee
William Parkinson, Archaeologist, National Geographic Grantee
Matt Piscitelli, Archaeologist, National Geographic Grantee
Jeffrey Rose, Archaeologist, National Geographic Emerging Explorer
Max Salomon, National Geographic Producer
Aziz Abu Sarah, Cultural Educator, National Geographic Emerging Explorer
William Saturno, Archaeologist, National Geographic Grantee
Anna Secor, Political Geographer, National Geographic Grantee
Shah Selbe, Conservation Technologist, National Geographic Emerging Explorer
Maurizio Seracini, Cultural Heritage Engineer, National Geographic Fellow
Hayat Sindi, Science Entrepreneur, National Geographic Emerging Explorer
Christopher Thornton, Archaeologist, National Geographic Lead Program Officer of Research, Conservation, and Exploration
Soultana Maria Valamoti, Archaeologist, National Geographic Grantee
Juan José Valdés, National Geographic Geographer
Simon Worrall, National Geographic Writer
Xiaobai Angela Yao, Geographer, National Geographic Grantee
Dave Yoder, Photojournalist, National Geographic Grantee

Map Credits

Mapping Specialists, LTD., Madison, WI.
National Geographic Maps, National Geographic Society

Illustrator Credits

Unless otherwise indicated, all illustrations were created by Precision Graphics.

EMPATHY

OUR HUMAN STORY GLOBAL CITIZENSHIP

PRESERVING CULTURES

HISTORY WHY STUDY HISTORY?

THROUGH OBJECTS IDENTITY

CIVILIZATION

WHO OWNS THE PAST?

MOMENTS IN HISTORY

WHY STUDY HISTORY?

EMPATHY

CIVILIZATION

GLOBAL CITIZENSHIP

PRESERVING CULTURES

STORYTELLING

OUR HUMAN STORY

STORYTELLING

EMPOWERMENT

WHY STUDY HISTORY

PRESERVING CULTURES

CITIZENSHIP

EMPATHY

STORIES MAKING HISTORY

SAVING OUR PAST

CIVILIZATION

IDENTITY

EMPOWERMENT

EMPATHY

HISTORY

THROUGH OBJECTS

THE HUMAN EPIC

GLOBAL CITIZENSHIP

SAVING OUR PAST

THE HUMAN EPIC **GLOBAL CITIZENSHIP**

STORYTELLING

WHY STUDY HISTORY? EMPATHY

IDENTITY **CIVILIZATION**

STORIES MAKING HISTORY

EMPOWERMENT

SAVING OUR PAST

EMPATHY

EMPOWERMENT

PRESERVING CULTURES

SAVING OUR PAST

WHY STUDY HISTORY?

GLOBAL CITIZENSHIP

IDENTITY

THE HUMAN EPIC

STORYTELLING

OUR HUMAN STORY

HISTORY THROUGH OBJECTS

CIVILIZATION

PRESERVING CULTURES

GLOBAL CITIZENSHIP

PRESERVING CULTURES

EMPATHY

OUR HUMAN STORY

CIVILIZATION THE HUMAN EPIC

WHO OWNS THE PAST?

EMPOWERMENT

GLOBAL CITIZENSHIP SAVING OUR PAST

HISTORY

MOMENTS IN HISTORY SAVING OUR PAST

EMPOWERMENT

MOMENTS IDENTITY CITIZENSHIP EMPATHY